THE ACTS OF THE APOSTLES

VOLUME I

The
INTERNATIONAL CRITICAL COMMENTARY
on the Holy Scriptures of the Old and New Testaments

GENERAL EDITORS

J. A. EMERTON, F.B.A.

Fellow of St John's College
Regius Professor of Hebrew in the University of Cambridge
Honorary Canon of St George's Cathedral, Jerusalem

C. E. B. CRANFIELD, F.B.A.

Emeritus Professor of Theology in the University of Durahm

AND

G. N. STANTON

Professor of New Testament Studies,
King's College, University of London

FORMERLY UNDER THE EDITORSHIP OF

S. R. DRIVER
A. PLUMMER
C. A. BRIGGS

A CRITICAL AND EXEGETICAL COMMENTARY

ON

THE ACTS OF THE APOSTLES

BY

C. K. BARRETT
Emeritus Professor of Divinity in Durham University

IN TWO VOLUMES

VOLUME I

Preliminary Introduction and Commentary on Acts I–XIV

T&T CLARK
EDINBURGH

T&T CLARK LTD
59 GEORGE STREET
EDINBURGH EH2 2LQ
SCOTLAND

Copyright © T&T Clark Ltd, 1994

First published 1994

ISBN 0 567 09653 X

British Library Cataloguing-in-Publication Data
A catalogue record for this book is available from the British Library

Typeset by Trinity Typesetting, Edinburgh
Printed and bound in Great Britain by Page Brothers, Norwich

GENERAL EDITORS' PREFACE

Much scholarly work has been done on the Bible since the publication in 1951 of the latest volume in the International Critical Commentary (that of J. A. Montgomery and H. S. Gehman on the Books of Kings) — and the bulk of the series is, of course, much older. New linguistic, textual, historical, and archaeological evidence has become available, and there have been changes and developments in methods of study. In the last quarter of the twentieth century there will be as great a need as, and perhaps a greater need than, ever for the kind of commentary the International Critical Commentary seeks to supply. The series has long had a special place among works in English on the Bible, because it has sought to bring together all the relevant aids to exegesis, linguistic and textual no less than archaeological, historical, literary, and theological to help the reader to understand the meaning of the books of the Old and New Testaments. In the confidence that such a series meets a need, the publishers and the editors have planned both to commission commentaries on those books of the Bible which have never appeared in the series and to replace some of the older volumes. The work of preparing a commentary on such a scale cannot but be slow, and developments in the past quarter of a century have made the commentator's task yet more difficult than before, but it is hoped that the volumes will appear without too great intervals between them. No attempt has been made to secure a uniform theological or critical approach to the problems of the various books, and scholars have been selected for their scholarship and not for their adherence to any school of thought. It is hoped that the new volumes will attain the high standards set in the past, and that they will make a contribution to the understanding of the books of the Bible.

Cambridge and Durham,   J. A. E.
January, 1974   C. E. B. C.

PREFACE

To one who must approach New Testament Theology by way of New Testament History, the study of the Acts of the Apostles is essential, fascinating, and one may hope, fruitful. It is most likely to be fruitful if it is pursued in the light of the Pauline letters and of that other great quarry of theology, the Fourth Gospel. For this reason I do not regret too deeply the many years over which the writing of this commentary has extended, for the principal cause of delay has been work I could not avoid on Paul and John. The typescript of this first volume was finished at Christmas 1990. Some delay in production is the less to be regretted in that it means that work on Volume II is further advanced than I could have hoped.

Of course I cannot and do not claim that I have read everything that I should have liked to read. If a book on such a vast field as this is ever to be completed there comes a time when one must draw a line and put Pontius Pilate in reverse: What I have read, I have read. And there's an end of it. I may be able to include in Volume II a few backward glances at Chapters 1–14, seen in the new light that recent authors have thrown on them.

I have explained elsewhere (see pp. 1f.) why there is no conventional Introduction to this volume. Something of the kind will be found in Volume II. The rest of the book follows a fairly conventional form. Ever since I read, long ago, J. B. Lightfoot's great commentaries it has seemed to me unnecessary to burden a commentary with footnotes. A commentary ought to be straightforwardly readable, like a monograph, though the reader will of course expect, especially in a work that is not specifically aimed at beginners, to encounter references and quotations, not all of which will be expressed in his native tongue.

I am deeply grateful to my old friend and colleague Professor C. E. B. Cranfield who as General New Testament Editor for the International Critical Commentary looked at some early drafts; also to his successor Professor G. N. Stanton, who has made useful suggestions and drawn my attention to literature that I had missed.

The pleasing and generous award of a Forschungspreis by the Alexander von Humboldt-Stiftung encouraged me to spend longer in Tübingen and Münster than I otherwise should have done, and I am grateful to the Stiftung, to the Tübingen libraries and my New

Testament colleagues there (a number of younger scholars as well as those professors whose names are everywhere known), and to Professor K. and Professor B. Aland and their staff at the Stiftung zur Förderung der neutestamentlichen Textforschung in Münster.

C. K. BARRETT

CONTENTS OF VOLUME I

BIBLIOGRAPHIES AND ABBREVIATIONS

Commentaries referred to by the Author's Name only

Bauernfeind, O. *Kommentar und Studien zur Apostelgeschichte* (Wissenschaftliche Untersuchungen zum Neuen Testament 22. Herausgegeben von V. Metelmann), Tübingen, 1980.

Bengel, J. A. *Gnomon Novi Testamenti,* Editio Tertia, London, Edinburgh, Cambridge, and Oxford, 1862. Acts, pp. 388-489.

Beyer, H. W., *Die Apostelgeschichte* (Das Neue Testament Deutsch 5. 5. Auflage), Göttingen, 1949.

Blass, F. *Acta Apostolorum, sive Lucae ad Theophilum liber alter,* Editio philologica, Göttingen, 1895.

Braun, H., *Qumran und das Neue Testament,* two vols., Tübingen, 1966. The first volume is cited here in the form in which it originally appeared in *ThR* 28 (1962-3), 97-234; 29 (1963-4), 142-76; 30 (1964-5), 1-38, 89-137. Acts, 29. 147-76.

Bruce, F. F., *The Acts of the Apostles,* London, 1951 — cited as 'Bruce 1'.

Bruce, F. F., *The Book of the Acts* (New International Commentary on the New Testament), Grand Rapids, 1988 — cited as 'Bruce 2'.

Calvin, J., *The Acts of the Apostles,* translated by J. N. Fraser and W. J. C. McDonald, two vols., Edinburgh, London 1965, 1966.

Clark, A. C., *The Acts of the Apostles,* Oxford, 1933.

Conzelmann, H., *Die Apostelgeschichte* (Handbuch zum Neuen Testament 7), Tübingen, 1963.

Delebecque, É., *Les Actes des Apôtres,* Paris, 1982.

Field, F., *Otium Norvicense,* Pars Tertia, Oxford, 1881.

Haenchen, E., *Die Apostelgeschichte* (Kritisch-exegetischer Kommentar über das Neue Testament (Meyer) III), Göttingen, 1977.

Hanson, R. P. C., *The Acts* (New Clarendon Bible), Oxford, 1967.

Knowling, R. J., *The Acts of the Apostles* (The Expositor's Greek Testament II), London, 1900.

Loisy, A., *Les Actes des Apôtres,* Paris, 1920.

Lüdemann, G., *Das frühe Christentum nach den Traditionen der Apostelgeschichte: Ein Kommentar,* Göttingen, 1987.

Marshall, I. H., *The Acts of the Apostles* (Tyndale New Testament Commentaries), Leicester, 1980.

Metzger, B. M., *A Textual Commentary on the Greek New Testament,* Stuttgart, 1971.

Packer, J. W., *The Acts of the Apostles* (Cambridge Bible Commentaries), Cambridge, 1975.

Page, T. E., *The Acts of the Apostles,* London, 1918.

Pallis, A., *Notes on St Luke and the Acts,* Oxford, 1928.

Pesch, R., *Die Apostelgeschichte* (Evangelisch-Katholischer Kommentar zum Neuen Testament: V/1; V/2), Zürich and Neukirchen-Vluyn, 1986.

Preuschen, E., *Die Apostelgeschichte* (Handbuch Zuns Neuen Testament 4.1), Tübingen, 1912.

Rackham, R. B., *The Acts of the Apostles* (Westminster Commentaries), London, n.d.

Roloff, J., *Die Apostelgeschichte* (Das Neue Testament Deutsch 5), Göttingen, 1981.

Schille, G., *Die Apostelgeschichte des Lukas* (Theologischer Handkommentar zum Neuen Testament 5), Berlin, 1984.

Schmithals, W., *Die Apostelgeschichte des Lukas*. (Zürcher Bibelkommentare), Zürich, 1982.

Schneider, G., *Die Apostelgeschichte* (Herders Theologischer Kommentar zum Neuen Testament) V, two vols., Freiburg, Basel, Wien, 1980, 1982.

Stählin, G., *Die Apostelgeschichte* (Das Neue Testament Deutsch 5), Göttingen, 1962.

Strack, H. L. and Billerbeck, P., *Kommentar zum Neuen Testament aus Talmud und Midrasch*, six vols. in 7. Acts in 2.588-773. München, 1922-61.

Weiser, A., *Die Apostelgeschichte* (Oekumenischer Taschenbuch-Kommentar zum Neuen Testament 5/1; 5/2), Gütersloh, 1981, 1985.

Westcott, B. F. and Hort, F. J. A., *The New Testament in the Original Greek*, Volume II Introduction and Appendix. Notes on select readings, Appendix pp. 1-142 (Acts, 92-101). Cambridge and London, 1881 — cited as 'Hort, *Notes*'.

Wetstenius, J. J., *Novum Testamentum Graecum*, two vols. Acts in 2.455-657. Amsterdam, 1751, 1752. Cited as Wettstein.

Williams, C. S. C., *The Acts of the Apostles* (Black's New Testament Commentaries), London, 1957.

Note also: Jackson, F. J. F. and Lake, K. (eds.). *The Beginnings of Christianity*. Part I: The Acts of the Apostles. Vol. I, Prolegomenia; Vol. II, Prolegomena II, Criticism; Vol. III, The Text of Acts (by J. H. Ropes); Vol. IV, Translation and Commentary (by K. Lake and H. J. Cadbury); Vol. V, Additional Notes (ed. by Lake and Cadbury). London, 1920-33 — cited as *Begs.*

Monographs on (Luke-) Acts

Bovon: F. Bovon, *Luke the Theologian, Thirty-three years of Research (1950-1983)*, tr. K. McKinney, Allison Park, 1987.

Burchard: C. Burchard, *Der dreizehnte Zeuge*, Göttingen, 1970.

Cadbury, *Making*: H. J. Cadbury, *The Making of Luke-Acts*, London, 1958 (New York, 1927).

Dibelius: M. Dibelius, *Studies in the Acts of the Apostles*, ed. H. Greeven, tr. M. Ling and P. Schubert, London, 1956.

Dietrich, *Petrusbild*: W. Dietrich, *Das Petrusbild der lukanischen Schriften* (Beiträge zur Wissenschaft vom Alten und Neuen Testament 5.14 (94), Stuttgart, Berlin, Köln, Mainz, 1972.

Dupont, *Études*: J. Dupont, *Études sur les Actes des Apôtres* (Lectio Divina 45), Paris, 1967.

Dupont, *Nouvelles Études*: J. Dupont, *Nouvelles Études sur les Actes des Apôtres*, Paris, 1984.

Dupont, *Sources*: J. Dupont, *The Sources of Acts*, tr. K. Pond, London, 1964.

Epp, *Tendency*: E. J. Epp, *The Theological Tendency of Codex Bezae Cantabrigiensis in Acts* (Society for New Testament Studies Monograph Series 3), Cambridge, 1966.

Hemer: C. J. Hemer, *The Book of Acts in the Setting of Hellenistic History*, ed. C. H. Gempf (Wissenschaftliche Untersuchungen zum Neuen Testament 49), Tübingen, 1989.

Hengel: M. Hengel, *Acts and the History of Earliest Christianity*, tr. J. Bowden, London, 1979.

Knox, *Acts*: W. L. Knox, *The Acts of the Apostles*, Cambridge, 1948.

Kremer: J. Kremer, *Pfingstbericht und Pfingstgeschehen* (Stuttgarter Bibelstudien 63/64), Stuttgart, 1973.

Kremer, *Actes*: J. Kremer (Ed.), *Les Actes des Apôtres, Traditions, rédaction, théologie* (Bibliotheca Ephemeridum theologicarum Lovaniensium 48), Gembloux, Leuven, 1979.

Maddox: R. Maddox, *The Purpose of Luke-Acts*, Edinburgh, 1982.

Plümacher: E. Plümacher, *Lukas als hellenistischer Schriftsteller*, Göttingen, 1972.

Reicke, *Glaube*: Bo Reicke, *Glaube und Leben der Urgemeinde. Bemerkungen zu Apg. 1-7*, Zürich, 1957.

Torrey: C. C. Torrey, *The Composition and Date of Acts* (Harvard Theological Studies 1), Cambridge, Mass., 1916.

Wilckens, *Missionsreden*: U. Wilckens, *Die Missionsreden der Apostelgeschichte* (Wissenschaftliche Monographien zum Alten und Neuen Testament 5), Neukirchen-Vluyn, 1961.

Wilcox: M. Wilcox, *The Semitisms of Acts*, Oxford, 1965.

Wilson, *Gentiles*: S. G. Wilson, *The Gentiles and the Gentile Mission in Luke-Acts* (Society for New Testament Studies Monograph Series 23), Cambridge, 1973.

Wilson, *Law*: S. G. Wilson, *Luke and the Law* (Society for New Testament Studies Monograph Series 50), Cambridge, 1983.

Wilson, *Pastorals*: S. G. Wilson, *Luke and the Pastoral Epistles*, London, 1979.

Other works referred to by abbreviations

Abrahams, *Studies*: I. Abrahams, *Studies in Pharisaism and the Gospels*, first series, Cambridge, 1917; second series, Cambridge, 1924.

Aland, *Text*: K. Aland and B. Aland, *The Text of the New Testament*, tr. E. F. Rhodes. Grand Rapids/Leiden, ²1989.

Background: C. K. Barrett (ed.), *The New Testament Background: Selected Documents*, London, ²1987.

Barth, *CD*: K. Barth, *Church Dogmatics*, Eng. tr. thirteen vols. Edinburgh, 1936-69.

Bieler: L. Bieler, ΘΕΙΟΣ ANHP, Wien 1935, 1936 (Darmstadt, 1967).

Black, *AA:* M. Black, *An Aramaic Approach to the Gospels and Acts*, Oxford, ³1967.

Black, *Scrolls*: M. Black, *The Scrolls and Christian Origins*, London, Edinburgh, etc., 1961.

Bowker, *Targums*: J. Bowker, *The Targums and Rabbinic Literature*, Cambridge, 1969.

Brandon, *Fall*: S. G. F. Brandon, *The Fall of Jerusalem and the Christian Church*, London, 1951.

Brandon, *Trial*: S. G. F. Brandon, *The Trial of Jesus of Nazareth*, London, 1968.

Büchsel, *Theologie*: F. Büchsel, *Theologie des Neuen Testaments*, Gütersloh, ²1937.

Bultmann, *E&F*: R. Bultmann, *Existence and Faith*, tr. and ed. S. F. Ogden, London, 1961.

Bultmann, *Exegetica*: R. Bultmann, *Exegetica*, ed. E. Dinkler, Tübingen, 1967.

Bultmann, *Theologie*: R. Bultmann, *Theologie des Neuen Testaments*, Tübingen, ⁹1984 (ed. O. Merk).

Ch., M., S.: C. K. Barrett, *Church, Ministry, and Sacraments in the New Testament*, Exeter, 1985.

Clarke, *DH*: W. K. L. Clarke, *Divine Humanity*, London, 1936.

Conzelmann, *Geschichte*: H. Conzelmann, *Geschichte des Urchristentums* (Das Neue Testament Deutsch Ergänzungsreihe 5), Göttingen, 1969.

Conzelmann, *Theologie*: H. Conzelmann, *Theologie des Neuen Testaments*, München, 1967.

1 Corinthians: C. K. Barrett, *A Commentary on the First Epistle to the Corinthians*, London, 1992.

2 Corinthians: C. K. Barrett, *A Commentary on the Second Epistle to the Corinthians*, London, 1973.

Cullmann, *Christologie*: O. Cullmann, *Die Christologie des Neuen Testaments*, Tübingen, 1957.

Cullmann, *Petrus*: O. Cullmann, *Petrus, Jünger — Apostel — Märtyrer*. Zürich, Stuttgart, ²1952.

Cullmann, *V&A*: O. Cullmann, *Vorträge und Aufsätze, 1925-1962*, ed. K. Fröhlich, Tübingen, Zürich, 1966.

Cullmann, *Zeit*: O. Cullmann, *Christus und die Zeit*, Zürich, 1962.

Dalman, *SSW*: G. Dalman, *Sacred Sites and Ways*, tr. P. P. Levertoff, London, 1935.

Dalman, *Worte* (=*Words*): G. Dalman, *The Words of Jesus*, tr. D. M. Kay, Edinburgh, 1909.

Daube, *NTRJ*: D. Daube, *The New Testament and Rabbinic Judaism*, London, 1956.

Davies, *Land*: W. D. Davies, *The Gospel and the Land*, Berkley, Los Angeles, London, 1974.

Le Déaut, *Nuit Pascale*: R. Le Déaut, *La Nuit Pascale*, Rome, 1963.

Deissmann, *BS*: G. A. Deissmann, *Bible Studies*, tr. A. Grieve, Edinburgh, 1901.

Deissmann, *LAE*: A. Deissmann, *Light from the Ancient East*, tr. L. R. M. Strachan, New York, London, ²1911.

Delling, *Kreuzestod*: G. Delling, *Der Kreuzestod Jesu in der urchristlichen Verkündigung*, Berlin, 1971.

Delling, *Studien*: G. Delling, *Studien zum Neuen Testament und zum hellenistischen Judentum*, Gesammelte Aufsätze, ed. F. Hahn, T. Holtz, N. Walter, Göttingen, 1970.

Derrett, *Law*: J. D. M. Derrett, *Law in the New Testament*, London, 1970.

Dinkler, *Signum Crucis*: E. Dinkler, *Signum Crucis*, Tübingen, 1967.

Essays on John: C. K. Barrett, *Essays on John*, London, 1982.

Fitzmyer, *Essays*: J. A. Fitzmyer, *Essays on the Semitic Background of the New Testament*, London, 1971.

Flusser, *Entdeckungen*: D. Flusser, *Entdeckungen im Neuen Testament*, ed. M. Majer, Neukirchen-Vluyn, 1987.

Freedom & Obligation: C. K. Barrett, *Freedom and Obligation*. London, 1985.

Fuller, *Christology*: R. H. Fuller, *The Foundations of New Testament Christology*, New York, 1965.

Hahn, *Mission*: F. Hahn, *Mission in the New Testament* (Studies in Biblical Theology 47), tr. F. Clarke, London, 1965.

Hatch, *Essays*: E. Hatch, *Essays in Biblical Greek*, Oxford, 1889.

Jeremias, *Heiligengräber*: J. Jeremias, *Heiligengräber in Jesu Umwelt*, Göttingen, 1958.

Jeremias, *Jerusalem*: J. Jeremias, *Jerusalem in the Time of Jesus*, tr. F. H. and C. H. Cave, London, 1969.

Klausner, *Jesus*: J. Klausner, *Jesus of Nazareth*, tr. H. Danby, London, 1925.

Klein, *Apostel*: G. Klein, *Die zwölf Apostel*, Göttingen, 1961.

Knox, *Gentiles*: W. L. Knox, *St Paul and the Church of the Gentiles*, Cambridge, 1939.

Knox, *Hellenistic Elements*: W. L. Knox, *Some Hellenistic Elements in Primitive Christianity* (Schweich Lectures 1942), London, 1944.

Kosmala, *Hebräer*: H. Kosmala, *Hebräer — Essener — Christen*, (Studia Post-Biblica 1), Leiden, 1959.

Kümmel, *Einleitung*: W. G. Kümmel, *Einleitung im das Neue Testament*, Heidelberg, [19]1978.

Lindars, *Apologetic*: B. Lindars, *New Testament Apologetic*, London, 1973 (1961).

Lohse: E. Lohse, *Die Einheit des Neuen Testaments*, Göttingen, 1973.

Lohse, *Ordination*: E. Lohse, *Die Ordination im Spätjudentum und im Neuen Testament*, Göttingen, 1951.

Lohse, *Theologie*: E. Lohse, *Grundriss der neutestamentlichen Theologie*, Stuttgart, Berlin, Köln, Mainz, 1974.

Lohse, *Umwelt*: E. Lohse, *Umwelt des Neuen Testaments* (Das Neue Testament Deutsch Ergänzungsreihe 1), Göttingen, 1971.

Longenecker, *Christology*: R. N. Longenecker, *The Christology of Early Jewish Christianity*, (Studies in Biblical Theology 2.17), London, 1970.

Manson, *Studies*: T. W. Manson, *Studies in the Gospels and Epistles*, cd. M. Black, Manchester, 1962.

Marshall, *Luke*: I. H. Marshall, *The Gospel of Luke* (New International Greek Testament Commentary), Exeter, 1978.

Metzger, *Text*: B. M. Metzger, *The Text of the New Testament*, Oxford, 1964.

Metzger, *Versions*: B. M. Metzger, *The Early Versions of the New Testament*, Oxford, 1977.

Millar Burrows, *DSS*: Millar Burrows, *The Dead Sea Scrolls*, London, 1956.

Millar Burrows, *Light*: Millar Burrows, *More Light on the Dead Sea Scrolls*, London, 1958.

Moule, *Essays*: C. F. D. Moule, *Essays in New Testament Interpretation*, Cambridge, 1982.

Moule, *Origin*: C. F. D. Moule, *The Origin of Christology*, Cambridge, 1977.

Nestle-von Dobschütz: E. Nestle, *Einführung in das Griechische Neue Testament*, 4. Auflage völlig umgearbeitet von E. von Dobschütz, Göttingen, 1923.

NT Essays: C. K. Barrett, *New Testament Essays*, London, 1972.

Ramsay, *Church*: W. M. Ramsay, *The Church in the Roman Empire before A.D. 170*, London, New York, Toronto, 10th ed. n.d.

Ramsay, *Cities*: W. M. Ramsay, *The Cities of St Paul*, London, 1907.

Ramsay, *Paul the Traveller*: W. M. Ramsay, *St Paul the Traveller and Roman Citizen*, London, [10] 1908.

Reicke, *DF&Z*: Bo Reicke, *Diakonie, Festfreude und Zelos*, Uppsala, Wiesbaden, 1951.

Richardson, *Theology*: A. Richardson, *An Introduction to the Theology of the New Testament*, London, 1958.

Rohde, *Der gr. Rom.*: E. Rohde, *Der griechische Roman und Seine Vorläufer*, Darmstadt, [4]1960.

Romans: C. K. Barrett, *A Commentary on the Epistle to the Romans*, London, [2]1991.

Rowland, *Heaven*: C. Rowland, *The Open Heaven*, London, 1982.

Schlatter, *Th. der Ap.*: A. Schlatter, *Die Theologie der Apostel* (= revision of *Die Theologie des Neuen Testaments* II), Calw, Stuttgart, [4]1984.

Schlatter, *Theologie des NTs*: A. Schlatter, *Die Theologie des Neuen Testaments*, Vol. I, Calw, Stuttgart, 1909; Vol. II, Calw, Stuttgart, 1910.

Schlier, *Zeit*: H. Schlier, *Die Zeit der Kirche*, Freiburg, 1956.

Schweizer, *Beiträge*: E. Schweizer, *Beiträge zur Theologie des Neuen Testaments*, Zürich, 1970.

Schweizer, *CONT*: E. Schweizer, *Church Order in the New Testament* (Studies in Biblical Theology 32), tr. F. Clarke, London, 1961.

Sevenster, *Greek*: J. N. Sevenster, *Do you know Greek?* (SuppNovT 19), Leiden, 1968.

Signs: C. K. Barrett, *The Signs of an Apostle*, London, 1970.

Stauffer, *Theologie*: E. Stauffer, *Die Theologie des Neuen Testaments*, Stuttgart, 1945.

St John: C. K. Barrett, *The Gospel according to St John*, London, [2]1978.

Sukenik, *Synagogues*: E. L. Sukenik, *Ancient Synagogues in Palestine and Greece* (Schweich Lectures 1930), London, 1934.

Tcherikover: V. Tcherikover, *Hellenistic Civilization and the Jews*, Philadelphia, Jerusalem, 1959.

Tödt, *Menschensohn*: H. E. Tödt, *Der Menschensohn in der synoptischen Überlieferung*, Gütersloh, 1959.

Torrey, *Documents*: C. C. Torrey, *Documents of the Primitive Church*, New York, London, 1941.

Trajectories: J. M. Robinson and H. Koester, *Trajectories through Early Christianity*, Philadelphia, 1971.

van Unnik, *SpColl*: W. C. van Unnik, *Sparsa Collecta*, vols. I-III, Leiden, 1973-83.

De Vaux, *Institutions*: R. de Vaux, *Ancient Israel, Its Life and Institutions*, tr. J. McHugh, London, 1973 (1961).

Vielhauer, *Geschichte*: P. Vielhauer, *Geschichte der urchristlichen Literatur*, Berlin, New York, 1975.

Zahn, *Einleitung*: Th. Zahn, *Einleitung in das Neue Testament*, vol. I, Lepizig, 1897; vol. II, Leipzig, 1899.

The present Author's works referred to by abbreviations

Barrett, *Background*: C. K. Barrett (ed.), *The New Testament Background: Selected Documents*, London, [2]1987.

Barrett, *1 Corinthians*: C. K. Barrett, *A Commentary on the First Epistle to the Corinthians*, London, 1992.

Barrett, *2 Corinthians*: C. K. Barrett, *A Commentary on the Second Epistle to the Corinthians*, London, 1973.

Barrett, *Essays on John*: C. K. Barrett, *Essays on John*, London, 1982.

Barrett, *Freedom & Obligation*: C. K. Barrett, *Freedom and Obligation*, London, 1985.
Barrett, *NT Essays*: C. K. Barrett, *New Testament Essays*, London, 1972.
Barrett, *Romans*: C. K. Barrett, *A Commentary on the Epistle to the Romans*, London, ²1991.
Barrett, *Signs*: C. K. Barrett, *The Signs of an Apostle*, London, 1970.
Barrett, *St John*: C. K. Barrett, *The Gospel according to St John*, London, ²1978.

Festschrifts (FS) with abbreviated titles

Note: The letters *FS* have been used throughout although the word Festschrift is not used in every title, and some books initiated as Festschrifts unfortunately ended as memorial volumes.

Auer: *Mysterium der Gnade. FS für J. Auer*, Regensburg, 1975.
Bardtke: *Bibel und Qumran*, Berlin, 1968.
Black (1979): *Text and Interpretation. Studies in the New Testament presented to M. Black*, Cambridge, 1979.
Borgen: *Context. Festskrift til P. Borgen*, Trondheim, 1987.
Bruce (1970): *Apostolic History and the Gospel. Biblical and Historical Essays presented to F. F. Bruce*, Exeter, 1970.
Bultmann (1949): *Festschrift Rudolf Bultmann*. Stuttgart, Köln, 1949.
Bultmann (1954): *Neutestamentliche Studien für Rudolf Bultmann* (Beihefte zur ZNW 21), Berlin, 1954.
Bultmann (1984): *Rudolf Bultmanns Werk und Wirkung*, Darmstadt, 1984.
Caird: *The Glory of Christ in the New Testament: Studies in Christology in Memory of G. B. Caird*, Oxford, 1987.
Casey: *Biblical and Patristic Studies in Memory of R. P. Casey*, Freiburg, 1963.
Cullmann (1962): *Neotestamentica und Patristica. Eine Festgabe ... O. Cullmann ... überreicht* (SuppNovT 6), Leiden, 1962.
Cullmann (1972): *Neues Testament und Geschichte. O. Cullmann zum 70. Geburtstag*, Zürich, Tübingen, 1972.
Dahl: *God's Christ and His People. Studies in Honour of N. A. Dahl*, Oslo, Bergen, Tromsö, 1977.
Daube: *Donum Gentilicium, New Testament Studies in Honour of D. Daube*, Oxford, 1978.
Deissmann: *Festgabe für A. Deissmann*, Tübingen, 1927.
Dinkler: *Theologia Crucis — Signum Crucis. Festschrift für E. Dinkler*, Tübingen, 1979.
Dupont: `*A Cause de l'Évangile. Mélanges offerts à Dom J. Dupont*, Paris, 1985.
Dupont-Sommer: *Hommages à André Dupont-Sommer*, Paris, 1971.
Ellis: *Tradition and Interpretation in the New Testament. Essays in Honor of E. E. Ellis*, Grand Rapids, Tübingen, 1987.
Erfurt: *Dienst der Vermittlung. Festschrift zum 25jährigen Bestehen des Philosophisch-Theologischen Studiums im Priesterseminar Erfurt* (= Erfurter Theologische Studien 37), Leipzig, 1977.
Frings: *Die Kirche und ihre Ämter und Stände. Festschrift für J. Frings*, Köln, 1960.

George: *La Parole de Grâce. Études lucaniennes à la mémoire d' Augustin George*, Paris, 1981.

Gingrich: *Festschrift to Honor F. W. Gingrich*, Leiden, 1972.

Goguel: *Aux Sources de la Tradition Chrétienne. Mélanges offerts à M. Goguel*, Neuchâtel, Paris, 1950.

Goodenough: *Religions in Antiquity. Essays in Memory of E. R. Goodenough*, Leiden, 1968.

Grant: *The Joy of Study: Papers on New Testament and Related Subjects. Presented to F. C. Grant*, New York, 1951.

Greeven: *Studien zum Text und zur Ethik des Neuen Testaments. Festschrift ... H. Greeven*, Berlin, New York, 1986.

Haenchen: *Apophoreta. Festschrift E. Haenchen*, Berlin, 1964.

Hanson: *Scripture: Meaning and Method. Essays presented to A. T. Hanson*, Hull, 1987.

Harnack: *Harnack-Ehrung. Beiträge zur Kirchengeschichte*, Leipzig, 1921.

Harris: *Amicitiae Corolla. A Volume of Essays Presented to J. R. Harris*, London, 1933.

Heim: *Theologie des Glaubenswagnis. Festschrift für K. Heim*. Hamburg, 1954.

Holtz: *Kirche—Theologie—Frömmigkeit. Festschrift für G. Holtz*, Berlin, 1965.

Johnson: *Studies in Roman Economic and Social History in Honor of A. C. Johnson*, Princeton, 1951.

Jülicher: *Festgabe für Adolf Jülicher*, Tübingen, 1927.

Klijn: *Text and Testimony: Essays on New Testament and Apocryphal Literature in Honour of A. F. J. Kiljn*, Kampen, 1988.

Kümmel (1975): *Jesus und Paulus. Festschrift für W. G. Kümmel zum 70. Geburtstag*, Göttingen, 1975.

Kümmel (1985): *Glaube und Eschatologie. Festschrift für W. G. Kümmel zum 80. Geburtstag*, Tübingen, 1985.

Lake: *Quantulacumque*, London, 1937.

Lightfoot: *Studies in the Gospels. Essays in Memory of R. H. Lightfoot*, Oxford, 1955.

Lohse: *Wissenschaft und Kirche. Festschrift für E. Lohse*, Bielefeld, 1989.

Manson: *New Testament Essays. Studies in Memory of T. W. Manson*, Manchester, 1959.

Metzger: *New Testament Textual Criticism. Essays in Honour of B. M. Metzger*, Oxford, 1981.

Michel (1963): *Abraham unser Vater. Festschrift für O. Michel*, Leiden, Köln, 1963.

Michel (1974): *Josephus-Studien. Festschrift für O. Michel*, Göttingen, 1974.

Moule: *Christ and Spirit in the New Testament. Studies in Honour of C. F. D. Moule*, Cambridge, 1973.

Mussner: *Kontinuität und Einheit, für F. Mussner*, Wien, 1981.

Nida: *On Language, Culture, and Religion. In Honor of E. A. Nida*, Den Haag, Paris, 1974.

Piper: *Current Issues in New Testament Interpretation. Essays in Honor of O. A. Piper*, New York, 1962.

Reicke: *The New Testament Age. Essays in Honor of Bo Reicke*, two vols., Macon, 1984.

Rengstorf (1980): *Wort in der Zeit: Neutestamentliche Studien. Festgabe für K. H. Rengstorf*, Leiden, 1980.

Rigaux: *Mélanges Bibliques en hommage au R. P. Béda Rigaux*, Gembloux, 1970.

Sawyerr: *New Testament Christianity for Africa and the World. Essays in honour of Harry Sawyerr*, London, 1974.

Schillebeeckx: *Expérience de l'Esprit: Mélanges E. Schillebeeckx*, Paris, 1976.

Schreiner: *Dienst unter dem Wort. Festschrift für H. Schreiner*, Gütersloh, 1953.

Schubert: *Studies in Luke-Acts. Essays presented in honor of Paul Schubert*, London, 1968.

Schürmann: *Die Kirche des Anfangs. Festschrift für Heinz Schürmann*, Leipzig, [1977].

Stählin: *Verborum Veritas. Festschrift für Gustav Stählin*, Wuppertal, 1970.

Stamm: *Search the Scriptures*, Leiden, 1969.

Stendahl: *Christians among Jews and Gentiles: Essays in Honor of K. Stendahl*, Philadelphia, 1986.

Vögtle: *Jesus und der Menschensohn. Für Anton Vögtle*, Freiburg, Basel, Wien, 1975.

Vriezen: *Studia Biblica et Semitica, T. C. Vriezen dedicata*, Wageningen, 1966.

Works of reference

BA: W. Bauer, *Griechisch-Deutsches Wörterbuch zu den Schriften des Neuen Testaments und der frühchristlichen Literatur*, 6e ... Auflage herausgegeben von Kurt Aland und Barbara Aland, Berlin, New York, 1988.

BDR: F. Blass and A. Debrunner, *Grammatik des neutestamentlichen Griechisch*, bearbeitet von F. Rehkopf, Göttingen, 1979.

Beyer, *Syntax*: K. Beyer, *Semitische Syntax im Neuen Testament*, Band I, Satzlehre Teil 1 (Studien zur Umwelt des Neuen Testaments 1), Göttingen, 1962.

Black, *AA*: M. Black, *An Aramaic Approach to the Gospels and Acts*, Oxford, ³1967.

CAH: *Cambridge Ancient History*, ed. S. A. Cook, F. E. Adcock, M. P. Charlesworth, Vol. X (The Augustan Empire), Cambridge, 1952; Vol. XI (The Imperial Peace), Cambridge, 1936; Vol. XII (The Imperial Crisis and Recovery), ed. Cook, Adcock, Charlesworth, and N. H. Baynes, Cambridge, 1939.

Dalman, *Grammatik*: G. Dalman, *Grammatik des jüdisch-palästinischen Aramäisch*, Leipzig, 1894, ²1905.

EBib: *Encyclopaedia Biblica*, ed. T. K. Cheyne and J. S. Black, London, 1914.

Jastrow: M. Jastrow, *Dictionary of the Targumim, the Talmud Babli and Yerushalmi, and the Midrashic Literature*, New York, Berlin, London, 1926.

L.-B.: R. A. Lipsius and M. Bonnet, *Acta Apostolorum Apocrypha*, vols. I, II. 1 and II. 2, Darmstadt, 1959 (1891, 1898, 1903).

Lightfoot, *Apostolic Fathers*: J. B. Lightfoot, *The Apostolic Fathers*. Part I (S. Clement of Rome), Vols. I and II, London, 1890; Part II (S. Ignatius; S. Polycarp), Vols. I and II. 1, II. 2, London, 1885.

LS: *A Greek-English Lexicon*, compiled by H. G. Liddell and R. Scott, New edition by H. S. Jones and R. McKenzie, Oxford, [1940]; Supplement, ed. E. A. Barber; Oxford, 1968.

M.1: J. H. Moulton, *A Grammar of New Testament Greek*, vol. I Prolegomena, Edinburgh, 1908.

M.2: J. H. Moulton and W. F. Howard, *A Grammar of New Testament Greek*, Vol. II Accidence and Word-Formation, Edinburgh, 1929.

M.3: J. H. Moulton, *A Grammar of New Testament Greek*, Vol. III by N. Turner, Syntax, Edinburgh, 1963.

MAMA: *Monumenta Asiae Minoris Antiqua*, 6 vols., various editors, London, Manchester, 1928-39.

Mayser: E. Mayser, *Grammatik der griechischen Papyri aus der Ptolemäerzeit*, two vols. in six, Berlin, Leipzig, 1970.

MM: J. H. Moulton and G. Milligan, *The Vocabulary of the Greek Testament illustrated from the Papyri and other Non-literary Sources*, London, 1914-29.

Moule, *IB*: C. F. D. Moule, *An Idiom Book of New Testament Greek*, Cambridge, 1953.

Moulton, *Einleitung*: J. H. Moulton, *Einleitung in die Sprache des Neuen Testaments*, Heidelberg, 1911.

MPL: J. P. Migne, *Patrologia Latina*.

NA: *Novum Testamentum Graece*, ed. Eberhard and ER win Nestle, subsequently re-edited by K. Aland, M. Black, C. M. Martini, B. M. Metzger, A. Wikgren; further edited and provided with critical apparatus by K. Aland and B. Aland, Stuttgart, 1981.

ND 1, 2, 3, 4, 5: *New Documents illustrating Early Christianity*, by G. H. R. Horsley, vols. I-V, North Ryde, 1981-9.

NS: *The History of the Jewish People in the Age of Jesus Christ (175 B.C. — A.D. 135)*, by E. Schürer, Revised and edited by G. Vermes, F. Millar, P. Vermes, and M. Black, Vols. I-III.2, Edinburgh, 1973-87.

OCD: *The Oxford Classical Dictionary*, ed. N. G. L. Hammond and H. H. Scullard, Oxford, 1970.

PW: A. Pauly's *Real-Encyclopädie der classischen Altertums-wissenschaft* (new ed. by G. Wissowa; W. Kroll, K. Mittelhaus, K. Ziegler), Stuttgart, 1894-1978.

Radermacher: L. Radermacher, *Neutestamentliche Grammatik* (Handbuch zuns Neuen Testament 1.1), Tübingen, 1911.

Routh, *Rel. Sac.*: M. J. Routh (ed.), *Reliquiae Sacrae*, vols. I-IV, Oxford, 1846; vol. V, Oxford, 1848.

Schwyzer: E. Schwyzer, *Griechische Grammatik*, vol. I, München, 1939; vol. II (ed. A. Debrunner), München, 1950.

Singer: *The Authorised Daily Prayer Book of the United Hebrew Congregations*, tr. S. Singer (with annotations by I. Abrahams), London, 1912, 1914.

SVF: *Stoicorum Veterum Fragmenta*, ed. J. von Arnim. Stuttgart, 1964 (1924). Vols. I-IV.

Thackeray, *Grammar*: H. St. J. Thackeray, *A Grammar of the Old Testament in Greek according to the Septuagint*, vol. I, Introduction, Orthography and Accidence, Cambridge, 1909.

TWNT: *Theologisches Wörterbuch zum Neuen Testament*, ed. G. Kittel and G. Friedrich, Eleven vols. Stuttgart, Berlin, Köln, Mainz, 1933-78.

Veitch: W. Veitch, *Greek Verbs, Irregular and Defective*, Oxford, 1866.

WW: *Novum Testamentum Domini Nostri Iesu Christi secundum Editionem Sancti Hieronymi*, ed. J. Wordsworth, H. J. White, H. F. D. Sparks, and A. W. Adams, Pars Tertia (Actus Apostolorum, etc.), Oxford, 1954.

Zerwick: M. Zerwick, *Graecitas Biblica*, Rome, 1960.

Periodicals

ABR: Australian Biblical Review, Melbourne.
BASOR: Bulletin of the American Schools of Oriental Research, New Haven.
Bib: Biblica, Rome.
BJRL: Bulletin of the John Rylands Library, Manchester.
BZ: Biblische Zeitschrift, Paderborn.
CBQ: Catholic Biblical Quarterly, Washington.
EThL: Ephemerides Theological Lovanieuses, Leuven.
EvTh: Evangelische Theologie, Munich.
ExpT: Expository Times, Edinburgh.
HThR: Harvard Theological Review, Cambridge, Mass.
JBL: Journal of Biblical Literature, New Haven; Boston, Mass.; Philadelphia; Missoula.
JNES: Journal of Near Eastern Studies, Chicago.
JRS: Journal of Roman Studies, London.
JSNT: Journal for the Study of the New Testament, Sheffield.
JSS: Journal of Semitic Studies, Manchester.
JTS: Journal of Theological Studies, Oxford.
NovT: Novum Testamentum, Leiden.
NTS: New Testament Studies, Cambridge.
RB: Revue biblique, Paris; Jerusalem.
RHPhR: Revue d'histoire et de philosophie religieuses, Strasbourg.
RThPh: Revue de Théologie et de Philosophie, Lausanne.
SJTh: Scottish Journal of Theology, Edinburgh; Cambridge, Oxford.
SNTSB: Studiorum Novi Testamenti Socielas, Bulletin,
StEv: Studia Evangelica, Berlin.
StTh: Studia Theologica, Lund.
ThLZ: Theologische Literaturzeitung, Leipzig.
ThSt: Theologische Studien, Utrecht.
T&S: Texts and Studies, Cambridge.
TU: Texte und Untersuchungen zur Geschichte der altchristlichen Literatur, Berlin.
VetT: Vetus Testamentum, Leiden.
VigChr: Vigiliae Christianae,
ZNW: Zeitschrift für die neutestamentliche Wissenchaft, Giessen; Berlin.

NOTE The books of the Bible, and other ancient books, are referred to under the conventional and familiar abbreviated titles. The sigla of manuscripts and other sources of the text of the New Testament are those of the 26th edition of the Nestle-Aland Greek New Testament (Deutsche Bibelstiftung, Stuttgart, 1979, and subsequent prints).

PRELIMINARY INTRODUCTION

It is important that the reader should know what to expect, and what not to expect, in this part of the Commentary. Introductions to commentaries conventionally contain the commentator's opinion, founded on facts and supported by argument, on such matters as the date when and the place where the book in question was written, its author, the sources that he used, the intention with which and the persons for whom he wrote, the society of which he was a member, the accuracy of his narrative, and the theological views that he maintained and sought to communicate to his readers. These are all matters of great importance, by no means least in regard to the Acts of the Apostles, but they will not be treated in this Introduction. They all presuppose questions which, if they can be answered at all, can be answered only on the basis of considered and detailed exegesis of the whole work. The logical place for such an Introduction is not at the beginning but at the end of a commentary; and in this one it will appear in the second volume, where I hope to be able to give such conclusions as I have reached on the conventional, and possibly on some unconventional, topics. There are however certain facts which the student of Acts needs to have before him as he enters upon the detailed study of the text. Acts is contained in a large number of manuscripts, written in Greek and a number of other languages. They differ among themselves, sometimes quite strikingly. *A priori* judgments on the various forms of text must be avoided; every significant variant must be considered on its merits. But it is right that the student should know, and should know something about, the various authorities that bear witness to the text of Acts, and the families into which they fall; also that he should be aware of the most important questions that have been raised on the basis of these facts and the considerations that must be borne in mind as these questions are discussed. Manuscripts and quotations from ancient writers are themselves proof of the existence and use of Acts. It will be possible and useful to collect other evidence not only of the existence of Acts but also of what the ancient church thought about it — how, in what areas, and for what purposes, it was used, and perhaps where it was not used. The most important passages will be set out below. Ancient writers also held opinions about the author of Acts; again, the relevant passages can be collected.

This 'Introduction' is therefore an introduction in the strictest sense of the term. It introduces Acts to the reader by setting out the tradition by which the book has reached us, under the headings of Text, and Acts and its Author. This is followed by a short account of the sources and plan of Acts 1–14.

I. TEXT

The text of Acts is to be recovered from a large number of Greek MSS, written at many different periods of Christian history; from a number of ancient versions; and from quotations made by ancient writers. Here there is neither space nor need for detailed descriptions, which may be found in various standard works.[1] The attempt to reconstruct the original text, or perhaps one ought to say the original texts,[2] of Acts is perhaps the most difficult of all textual problems in the NT, and the most important of the witnesses must be mentioned here. The evidence they give, or some of it, will be heard and assessed in the course of the Commentary, and an attempt to sketch the history of the text will be made in Vol. II. At this point only the barest outline of the problem will be presented.

Materials

The Greek authorities fall into three classes: Papyri; vellum codices written in uncial characters; minuscules.[3]

Papyri.[4] Acts is contained in P^8 P^{29} P^{33} P^{38} P^{41} (which contains also a Coptic translation of Acts) P^{45} (contains also the gospels) P^{48} P^{50} P^{53} (contains also verses from Matthew) P^{56} P^{57} P^{74} (contains also the Catholic Epistles) P^{91}. Most of these are fragmentary and contain no more than a few verses.

P^{29} contains Acts 26.7, 8, 20. It was found at Oxyrhynchus;[5] its probable date is 3rd century, though some have placed it in the 4th. It is included here because notwithstanding its brevity it has been counted among the witnesses to the Western text;[6] it contains however no distinctively Western reading.

P^{38} contains 18.27–19.6, 12–16. It is not known where it was found; it is now at Ann Arbor, University of Michigan.[7] It has been dated

---

[1]For example, Ropes (*Begs.* 3); Metzger (*Text*; *Versions*); Aland (*Text*); also Introductions to the NT, e.g. Kümmel (*Einleitung* 454–78). Nestle-von Dobschütz (1923) is still useful.

[2]See below, p. 20–22.

[3]On lectionaries see below, p. 7.

[4]For details of discovery, publication, and discussion of these (up to P^{74}) see K. Aland, *Repertorium der griechischen christlichen Papyri I: Biblische Papyri*, Berlin and New York, 1976.

[5]First published in *P. Oxy.*13 (1919); no. 1597.

[6]On this term see below, pp. 21f.

[7]*P. Mich* 3(1936). 138; first published by H. A. Sanders, *HThR* 20 (1927), 1–9; see also *Begs.* 5.262–8.

as early as 200–250, as late as the 4th or 5th century; 300 or a little later is probably as safe an estimate as any. There is no doubt that this papyrus has a text related to that known in D 614 sy^hmg;[8] e.g. in 18.28 it inserts διαλεγόμενος, with D 614, and at 19.14, with some variation, shares the reading of D (w sy^hmg).

P[45] contained originally the four gospels and Acts; it is now fragmentary, but parts of all the gospels remain, and a considerable part of Acts (beginning at 4.27 and ending at 17.17). It was probably found at Aphroditopolis in the Fayyum; it is in the Chester Beatty collection.[9] There is wide agreement that it is to be dated in the 3rd century; AD 250 would not be far out. It is not easy to provide its text in Acts with a label. In Mk it is classed with the representatives (Θ, etc.) of the Caesarean text.[10] It may be right to think of a similar type in Acts; or it may be that the Caesarean is not so much an independent family text as a combination of Old Uncial[11] with Western readings. On the whole P[45] keeps fairly close to the great Alexandrian MSS to be mentioned below, but it also contains Western readings; thus at 5.34 it reads ἀνθρώπους, with ℵ A B al, against D E Ψ gig h sy mae al, and at 14.20 it has αὐτοῦ for αὐτόν, with D (E). It has been rightly pointed out that it agrees with minor rather than major Western variants; and not infrequently it goes its own way.

P[48] contains 23.11–17, 23–29. It was found at Oxyrhynchus and is now at Florence.[12] It belongs probably to the 3rd century, possibly to the 4th. It contains a Western type of text.[13] For example, at 23.14, after γεύσασθαι, it adds τὸ σύνολον, with gig h Lcf.[14]

P[74] is in the Bodmer collection at Geneva.[15] It contains parts of all seven Catholic Epistles and a considerable amount of Acts, between 1.2 and 28.31. It is not known where it was found; it was written in the 7th, or possible the 6th, century. It is in general agreement with ℵ A B, that is, the Old Uncial, or Alexandrian, text.[16]

---

[8]For these witnesses see below, pp.5f., 7, 12f. This text is undoubtedly of a broadly speaking Western kind; see further B. Aland, *EThL* 62 (1986), 12–36.
[9]*P. Chester Beatty* 1; one leaf is in Vienna, *P. VindobG* 31974; see H. Gerstinger, *Aegyptus* 13 (1933), 67–72.
[10]See B. H. Streeter, *The Four Gospels*, London, 1936 (1924), 77–102, and subsequent works on textual criticism.
[11]Or Alexandrian; see below, p. 21.
[12]In the Biblioteca Laurenziana, PSI 1165.
[13]See B. Aland, art. cit., 36–40.
[14]D as now extant has no overlap with P[48].
[15]*P. Bodmer* XVII.
[16]See P. Prigent, *RHPhR* 42 (1962), 169–74.

P[91] now exists in two parts, one in Sydney, Australia,[17] and one in Milan.[18] It contains Acts 2.30–37; 2.46–3.2. *P. Mil.* was published by C. Calazzi in *BASP* 19 (1982), 39–45; see now S. Pickering, *Zeitschrift für Papyrologie und Epigraphik* 65 (1986), 76–8. It may be dated 'metà del III sec., ovvero qualche anno appreso' (Galazzi, 40). 'Some "Western" readings are definitely excluded and none can be certainly admitted' (Pickering 76).

Uncials.[19] As a group these must be reckoned later than the papyri, but there are late papyri (e.g. P[74]) which are a good deal later than the earliest uncials.

ℵ, or S (01)[20], Codex Sinaiticus, is now in the British Library;[21] up to the middle of the 19th century it was in St Katherine's monastery on Mt Sinai. Its place of origin is not known, but its text is in general of the Alexandrian type, though with occasional Western readings.[22] It contained originally the whole Bible. Part of the OT has been lost, but the whole of the NT, including Acts, remains. The siglum ℵ[1] is used for corrections made in the 4th to 6th centuries. ℵ[2] for corrections from about the 7th century, ℵ[c] for corrections of the 12th century; see Aland (*Text* 108).

A (02), Codex Alexandrinus, is in the British Library.[23] It was written in the 5th century and reached England in 1627 as a gift from the Patriarch Cyril Lucar to King Charles I. Like ℵ, it was originally a complete Bible. Parts of the OT and of the NT have perished but the whole of Acts is present. The text of Acts (differing from that of the gospels) is close to that of ℵ and B and must be considered a good example of the Alexandrian type.

B (03) Codex Vaticanus, is in the Vatican Library,[24] where it has certainly been since at latest 1475. It was written in the 4th century and is the primary witness for the Alexandrian[25] or Old Uncial text. Originally a complete Bible it has lost its opening pages (part of Genesis) and the last (from Heb. 9.14, including 1, 2 Timothy, Titus, Philemon, Revelation). Acts remains.

---

[17]*P. Macquarie Inv.* 360.
[18]*P. Mil. Vogliano Inv.* 1224.
[19]See especially Ropes, *Begs.* 3.xxxi–lxxxviii; and n. 1.
[20]Gregory's numerical references serve the useful purpose of distinguishing between MSS that are denoted by the same letter.
[21]Add.43725.
[22]For the Egyptian origin of this MS see Ropes, *Begs.* 3.xlvi–xlviii.
[23]Royal I D VIII.
[24]Gr. 1209.
[25]For its origin in Alexandria see Ropes, *Begs.* 3.xxxiv–xxxviii.

C (04), Codex Ephraemi Rescriptus,[26] as a biblical MS was written in the 5th century; in the 12th it was re-used (as a palimpsest) to accommodate the writings of Ephraim. The text is of the Byzantine or Koine type, though it seems to have an Alexandrian base and contains some Western readings.[27] Since the break-up and re-use of the MS only parts of Acts remain.

D (05), Codex Bezae Cantabrigiensis, now in Cambridge University Library.[28] Originally it contained the four gospels, Acts, and the Catholic Epistles. Of the last only a fragment of 3 John remains, and Acts 8.29–10.14; 21.2–10, 16–18; 22.10–20; 22.29–28.31 are wanting. It is a bilingual MS, written with one column to a page, Greek on the left of the opening, Latin (its readings denoted by d) on the right. In both languages the text is written in corresponding sense lines (κῶλα). The fact that it is bilingual seems good evidence that it was written and used in an area where both languages were current, presumably somewhere in the Western part of the Empire (or of what had been the Empire), but various localities have been suggested. It was given to Cambridge University in 1581 by Theodore Beza, who said that it was found in the Monastery of St Irenaeus at Lyons during the unrest of 1562. It does not necessarily follow that the MS was written in Gaul; Southern Italy, Sicily, and the Roman province of Africa have been suggested.[29] The date of writing was probably 5th century, though both earlier and later dates have been maintained.

Beza is said to have given the MS to Cambridge because he thought its contents would be better concealed than published.[30] Undoubtedly it differs more sharply than any other Greek MS, and especially in Acts, from the familiar texts of the Koine revision[31] and the Alexandrian, or Old Uncial, text.[32] It is impossible here to anticipate the large number of variants that will be noted in the course of the Commentary; the following may be mentioned by way of example. Occasionally a completely fresh piece of information is added; the best example is at 12.10 where D (with a little support) adds that the angel and Peter κατέβησαν τοὺς ζ' βαθμούς. Sometimes a scene is differently pictured, as at 3.11 (where D evidently understands the relation of Solomon's Portico to the Temple differently from other Greek MSS). Sometimes a different turn is given to the same event, as at 8.24 where D's description of

---

[26]Paris, Bib. Nat. Gr. 9.
[27]Ropes, *Begs.* 3.lv.
[28]Nn. II 41.
[29]Ropes, *Begs.* 3.lxiii–lxviii; Nestle-von Dobschütz, 89.
[30]He wrote, 'asservandum potius quam publicandum'.
[31]See p. 21.
[32]See p. 21.

Simon's tears suggests more strongly genuine penitence on his part, and at 15.20, 29; 21.25, where D and its partners place a different emphasis on the terms of the Apostolic Decree.[33] Frequently D adds a detail, with the result of making the narrative livelier and more impressive; for example, D (with a little support) prefixes to 18.6 the words πολλοῦ δὲ λόγου γινομένου καὶ γραφῶν διερμηνευομένων, picturing the debates between Paul and the Jews. Frequently D shows a preference for pious but not very meaningful formulas, preferring for example 'the Lord Jesus Christ' to 'the Lord' or 'Jesus' or 'Jesus Christ'.[34] D is not the only but is the most important representative of the so-called Western text, for which see further pp. 21-6, and the discussion in Vol. II. D must not however be simply identified with the Western text.

E (08), like D, is a bilingual, Graeco-Latin, MS; the Latin text is denoted by e. It contains Acts only,[35] 26.29–28.26 being missing. Once in the possession of Archbishop Laud it is known as Codex Laudianus.[36] Much earlier it was used by Bede in his commentary on Acts; see below, p. 20. E shares many readings with D, but few of D's most characteristic readings, and is often in agreement with the late Byzantine, or Koine, text. It is however relatively early: 6th, or perhaps 7th, century.

H (014), Codex Mutinensis, contains Acts only.[37] The MS is of the 9th century, its text Byzantine.

L (020), Codex Angelicus;[38] a MS of the 9th century, text Byzantine. It contains in addition to Acts the Catholic and Pauline Epistles.

P (025), Codex Porphyrianus,[39] a palimpsest which contains (with many lacunae) in addition to Acts the Catholic and Pauline Epistles and Revelation. It is of the 9th century, and contains for the most part the Byzantine text, very occasionally (e.g. 15.25; 19.27) siding with D and its allies.

Ψ (044), Codex Athous Laurensis,[40] of the 8th or 9th century, contains, with some lacunae, the whole of the NT except Revelation.

[33]To say that the Old Uncial text gives a ceremonial, the Western text an ethical decree oversimplifies; see C. K. Barrett, *ABR* 35 (1987), 50–9.

[34]See Epp, *Tendency*, but also C. K. Barrett in *FS* Black (1979) 15–27.

[35]And must not be confused with E (07), of the gospels.

[36]In Oxford, at the Bodleian Library, Laud. Gr. 35.

[37]A considerable part of the text has been lost; the MS is in the Archducal Library at Modena, G 196.

[38]In the Biblioteca Angelica, 39, at Rome.

[39]In the Public Library, Leningrad, Gr. 225.

[40]Mount Athos, Laura B'52.

The text is Byzantine.

Parts (often small parts) of Acts are contained also in the following uncials: 048 049 057 066 076 077 093 095 096 097 0120 0140 0165 0166 0175 0189 0236 0244, and in a large number of minuscules. Of these it is unnecessary here to mention more than two.

614, a relatively late (13th century) MS, but of considerable importance especially in regard to Acts (it contains the epistles also), since it contains a number of early readings which distinguish it from the Byzantine text.[41] For their bearing on the problem of the Western text see below, p. 26. 614 is certainly to be found not infrequently in agreement with D and its other allies. For example, at 6.7 it joins D E Ψ it vg^cl sy^h in reading κυρίου (instead of θεοῦ): at 15.29 it joins D 1739 and other witnesses in adding the Golden Rule to the Apostolic Decree; at 19.5, after Ἰησοῦ, it adds Χριστοῦ εἰς ἄφεσιν ἁμαρτιῶν, with (P^38vid) D sy^h※※. It must be added that it sometimes sides with B against D; for example, at 5.3 D Ψ (and the majority of later MSS) add σε (after νοσφίσασθαι); 614, with P^8 P^74 ℵ A B E 1739 and others, does not.

1739, a 10th century MS from Mt Athos[42] which contains the epistles as well as Acts. In the Pauline epistles a colophon connects 1739 with a MS said, by the colophon, to contain a text used by Origen; and 1739 itself contains marginal notes taken from Irenaeus, Clement of Alexandria, Origen, Eusebius, and Basil the Great. No later writer is quoted, and it is reasonable to infer (though not absolutely certain) that (not 1739 itself but) an ancestor was written not long after the time of the latest author quoted. Basil died in 379. It is thus probable that 1739 gives us, no doubt with a number of copyists' errors, a text that goes back to c. 400. Not surprisingly, 1739 shows a good deal of independence in regard to the Byzantine text. For example, at 5.3, noted above, it agrees with 614 and the Alexandrian MSS and differs from both D Ψ and the majority, Byzantine, text.

A further source of information regarding the Greek text of the NT is provided by lectionaries. These await further exploration.[43] It is not surprising that, at least so far, little of importance for the study of Acts has appeared. This probably reflects the common use of Acts, which even when accepted as canonical was not regularly and continuously read in church services as the gospels and epistles were. See however pp. 9, 32.

---

[41]Milan, Biblioteca Ambrosiana, E 97 sup.
[42]Laura B'64.
[43]But see especially A. Wikgren, 'Chicago Studies in the Greek Lectionary Text of the NT', in *FS* Casey, 96–121.

Latin Versions.[44] Jerome's Vulgate was not the first Latin translation of the NT. Exactly when and where the earlier translations were made is disputed. It is probably true that many more or less independent versions were made by many translators in many places at more or less the same time.[45] Metzger (*Versions* 302–5) lists 22 Old Latin MSS of Acts. It must be understood that these MSS are not to be thought of as presenting a pure pre-Vulgate (see pp. 9f.) text. None of them was written before the publication of Jerome's text; all of them have been, to a greater or less extent, affected by it. In addition to those given below further details may be found in Metzger (loc. cit.). There is a convenient check-list in NA[26] 713f.

d (5)[46] is the Latin side of D; see above, pp. 5f. It is probable that the Greek text has affected the Latin and the Latin the Greek.[47]

e (50) is the Latin side of E; see above p. 6.

g, or gig (51), Codex Gigas, a 13th century MS in the Royal Library at Stockholm.[48] It contains the whole Bible, mostly in the Vulgate text, but Acts and Revelation are Old Latin. Its importance as a source for the Old Latin text of Acts lies in the fact that it frequently agrees with the quotations of Acts made by Lucifer of Cagliari (see below, p. 19). This means that the version in gig must go back to at least the middle of the 4th century.

h (55), Codex Floriacensis, formerly at Fleury, now in the Bibliothèque Nationale, Paris.[49] It is probably to be dated in the 5th century, though some have suggested the 6th or even the 7th. In addition to Acts (3.2–4.18; 5.23–7.2; 7.42–8.2; 9.4–24; 14.5–23; 17.34–18.19; 23.8–24; 26.20–27.13) it contains Revelation, 1 and 2 Peter, and 1 John. It has been reckoned that in h (Acts) there are only ten differences from the text of Acts contained in quotations in Cyprian, *Testimonia* (see below, pp. 18f.).[50] The MS must thus be considered a witness to a 3rd century text, probably current in Africa.

---

[44]See Metzger (*Versions* 285–93).
[45]Tot sunt (exemplaria) paene quot codices; Jerome, *Ep. to Damasus*, WW 1. p. 2 (with note).
[46]Here and below I give the traditional letter(s) followed in brackets by the number in the Beuron Old Latin list.
[47]Though which has been the more influential is disputed; see Metzger (*Versions* 317f.).
[48]Its name comes from its size; the page is 89.5 x 49 cm.
[49]Lat. 6400 G.
[50]Metzger (*Versions* 315), referring (n. 1) to H. von Soden, *Das lateinische NT in Afrika zur Zeit Cyprians* (TU 33; Berlin 1904), 221–42; 323–63; 550–67.

l (67), Codex Legionensis, a 7th century MS in the Cathedral Archive in León, is a palimpsest with Old Latin readings.

p (54), Codex Perpinianensis, a 13th century MS now in the Bibliothèque Nationale, Paris.[51] This contains on the whole the Vulgate NT, but for Acts 1.1–13.6; 28.16–31 an Old Latin text has been used, most closely related to the texts of Cyprian and Augustine, that is, to the African form of the Old Latin.

r, or scel, (57), Codex Schlettstadtensis, in the Bibliothèque Nationale, Sélestat (1093). 7th or 8th century; interesting because it is a lectionary containing 14 passages from Acts (see above, p. 7).

These Old Latin MSS of Acts,[52] though by no means in agreement among themselves, show in general a marked agreement with D, not least in some of its widest divergences from other texts. For example, at 3.11, D is supported by h: at 4.18, by gig and h; at 6.10, 11, by e h (and other Old Latin MSS); at 10.25 by gig; at 11.2, by p (also by w); at 11.25, 26, by gig p; and so on.[53] For the interpretation of this agreement in terms of textual history see Vol. II.

The Latin Vulgate was made by Jerome who in 382 was commissioned by Pope Damasus to revise the existing Latin versions with reference to the Greek original so as to produce a standard and trustworthy text.[54] The date at which he produced his revised version of Acts is not known.[55] Of the Vulgate as a whole there are many thousands of MSS;[56] for those used in the WW reconstruction of the original see WW 3.34. The recovery of the original Vulgate text (beyond which lie, of course, the further tasks of determining the Greek text that it represents and the place of this Greek text in the textual history of the Bible, and in particular of Acts) is thus a task of great difficulty.

[51]Lat. 321.

[52]For others see Metzger (*Versions*, not only 302–5, but the Addenda, 461f.); also NA[26], 713f.

[53]'On the whole the African form of the Old Latin presents the larger divergences from the generally received text, and the European the smaller. The diversity among the Old Latin witnesses is probably to be accounted for on the assumption that scribes, instead of transmitting the manuscripts mechanically, allowed themselves considerable freedom in incorporating their own and others' traditions. In other words, the Old Latin was a living creation, constantly growing' (Metzger, *Versions* 325).

[54]See Jerome's *Ep. to Damasus*; WW 1.1–4 (Novum opus facere me cogis ex veteri, ut post exemplaria scripturarum toto orbe dispersa quasi quidam arbiter sedeam et, quia inter se variant, quae sint illa quae cum Graeca consentiant veritate decernam).

[55]Or indeed whether it was Jerome himself who produced it; the question is disputed. See Metzger (*Versions* 356–9).

[56]See R. Loewe, *CHB* 2.102–154; B. Fischer, in K. Aland (Ed.), *Die alten Übersetzungen des NTs, die Kirchenväterzitate und Lektionare*, Berlin and New York, 1972, 1–92.

A revision of the text, which in more than a thousand years had suffered much corruption, was made by Pope Sixtus V and the result published in 1590. Sixtus's successor, Clement VIII, published a new revision in 1592, whose misprints were further eliminated in 1593 and in 1598. A modern critical edition of the Vulgate NT was begun by J. Wordsworth in 1877; he was assisted and succeeded by H. J. White, and other scholars joined in the project, which was completed by H. F. D. Sparks in 1954. Acts was published in 1905.[57]

A general view of the variants in Acts will probably be found to support the view that 'Jerome reacted against the predominance of the Western type of text, and deliberately sought to orientate the Latin more with the Alexandrian type of text' (Metzger, *Versions* 359). For example, the Vulgate supports none of the characteristically Western variants (at 3.11; 4.18; 6.10, 11; 10.25; 11.2; 11.25, 26) mentioned above on p. 9.

For secondary versions, made from Latin and not without value in reconstructing the history of the Latin text, see Ropes (*Begs.* 3.cxxxv–cxlii): Provençal, German, Bohemian, Italian); and cf. 'Minor Western Versions' (Anglo-Saxon, Old High German, Old Saxon (Old Low German)) in Metzger (*Versions* 443–60).

Syriac Versions. The earliest continuous Syriac version of the NT containing Acts known to us is the Peshitta (see below). It is certain that the Syriac-speaking church possessed a version of Acts before this; this is proved by quotations in the works of Ephraem Syrus, who died in 373. Long before his time the church possessed its own version of the gospels, the Diatessaron, made by Tatian in the 2nd century. Since this harmony of the four gospels naturally did not contain Acts it is unnecessary to consider the disputed questions of its precise date, place, and manner of composition, the language in which it was drawn up, and its subsequently highly diverse history. Subsequent to and correcting, or possibly existing unofficially (though the word *official* would perhaps in this context be misleading) alongside the Diatessaron was the so-called Old Syriac version, represented by two MSS only, the Curetonian, of the 5th century, and the Sinaitic, of the 4th, or early in the 5th. These MSS (now suffering from many lacunae) contained the gospels only.

The **Peshitta**, preserved in a considerable number of MSS, was long[58] ascribed either to the personal work or to the direction of Rabbula, bishop of Edessa, probably in the early years of his

---

[57]See also the important edition of the Vulgate by R. Weber, B. Fischer, J. Gribomont, H. F. D. Sparks, and W. Thiele, Stuttgart, 1969 (1975), which has been constantly consulted in this commentary.

[58]Since F. C. Burkitt, *S. Ephraim's Quotations from the Gospels* (T. & S.), Cambridge, 1901.

episcopate (411–435). This view was based on a claim made by Rabbula's biographer (writing in 450) and supported by the observation that before Rabbula's time Syriac literature showed no trace of the Peshitta, whereas subsequently no other version was used. More recently both arguments have been disputed.[59] The biographer may have meant a good deal less than he appears on the surface to have meant; and in the gospels Rabbula himself can be shown to have used frequently an Old Syriac text.

Most investigations of the Peshitta have been made on the basis of the gospels, for the good reason that it is here that we have available for comparison the texts of the Sinaitic and Curetonian MSS and (so far as it is known) that of the Diatessaron. For the Peshitta text of Acts see especially J. H. Ropes and W. H. P. Hatch, 'The Vulgate, Peshitto, Sahidic, and Bohairic Versions of Acts and the Greek Manuscripts', *HThR* 21 (1928), 69–95.[60] 'The simplest hypothesis ... would seem to be ... that the 'Western' readings [in the Peshitta] are due to the Old Syriac base, while the general Old Uncial character came from the Greek MS or MSS used in the revision' (op. cit., 82). 'The "Western" readings attested by the Peshitto are considerable in number and often noteworthy in character' (ibidem). There is no *a priori* reason why the revisers should not have used a Greek MS or Greek MSS containing the Antiochian text (see below, p. 21), but they do not seem to have done so. The determinative influence was rather that of the Old Uncials. No good reason has been adduced for dissenting from these judgments. Probably in the first third of the 5th century a progressive revision of current Syriac texts brought the Syriac-speaking church's text into line with that represented by the great Alexandrian uncials, but without destroying its earlier characteristics. It seems that the Nestorian and Jacobite groups, which separated in 431, both used the Peshitta.

Philoxenian. Philoxenus, bishop of Mabbug, is said[61] to have produced a revised Syriac version in 508, or rather to have had one made by his chorepiscopus Polycarp. The relation between this version and the Peshitta (also its relation to the Harclean; see below) is by no means clear. It may be that Philoxenus and Polycarp merely added translations of 2 Peter, 2 and 3 John, Jude, and Revelation, which are not contained in the Peshitta, but in the rest of the NT simply reissued the existing text. The text of the added parts of the NT may be studied

---

[59]See especially A. Vööbus, *Investigations into the Text of the NT used by Rabbula of Edessa* (Contributions of Baltic University, 59), Pinneberg, 1947; M. Black, 'Rabbula of Edessa and the Peshitta', *BJRL* 33 (1951) 203–10; also, with bibliographies, Metzger (*Versions* 48–63), and Aland (as in n. 56).

[60]The collation of the Peshitta, Sahidic, and Bohairic versions was made by Hatch; 69, n. 1.

[61]See Ropes (*Begs.* 3.cli).

but 'for the rest of the New Testament there is no means of reconstructing the lost Philoxenian version. It must have shown an affinity to the Peshitto at least as great as that to be observed in the choice of language found in the books not previously translated' (Ropes, *Begs.* 3.cliv).

Harclean. Thomas of Harkel (Heraclea), bishop of Mabbug, whence he had been expelled in 602, one of a group of refugee monophysite bishops resident in or near Alexandria, in 616 produced, probably at the request of Athanasius I, monophysite patriarch of Antioch, who had previously commissioned a revision of the OT, a new Syriac version of the NT. It is a painfully literal rendering of the Greek, or rather a Syriac revision (probably of the Philoxenian, since it seems to be unrelated to the Peshitta) in which the governing factor was the use of 'accurate and approved' Greek MSS which it is usually supposed that Thomas found at Alexandria.[62] So far the Harclean appears as a somewhat wooden representation in Syriac of an Antiochian Greek text. Some (not all) Harclean MSS however are provided with a critical apparatus, best described in Ropes' words. '(1) In the text itself many words, parts of words (such as pronominal suffixes), and phrases, with a few longer sentences, are marked with an asterisk (*) or with an obelus (⸓), the termination of the reference being exactly indicated by a metobelus (⸕) ... (2) In the margin, with points of attachment in the text marked by various characters, are found a great number of notes.'[63] The precise purpose of these signs and notes is not agreed; what is not in dispute is that they point to readings of a Western kind, and that they are particularly numerous and particularly clearly Western in Acts. This is not true of all; Ropes draws attention to some that offer variant translations, or explain Greek words and names. But there is close agreement with D, and, in a part of Acts where D is wanting, with P[48] (see above, p. 3). A complicated set of facts, which cannot be given in detail here, may be summed up in Ropes' words. 'The more common use of the Harclean asterisks ... is not to show the excess of the original over a standard translation, but to preserve on the page of the translation those readings of another (the "Western") type of text side by side with those of the (Antiochian) standard adopted by the editor' (clxx). 'The bulk of [the marginal readings] ... cannot be distinguished in character from the 95 asterisked phrases of the text' (clxxi). Dr B.

---

[62]B. Aland however writes (*EThL* 62 (1986), 60): 'Er benutzte aber keine alexandrinische Handschrift als Vorlage. Denn seine Übersetzung bietet keinen alexandrinischen Text. Dann bleibt nur als sehr wahrscheinlich übrig, dass er eine Handschrift aus seiner Heimat, aus Syrien, mitgebracht hatte, die er für "genau und zuverlässig" hielt.' This does not take into account the invasion of Alexandria by Antiochian readings which had certainly taken place before the 7th century.

[63]Ropes (*Begs.* 3.clxi f.); the whole description and discussion, pp. clviii–clxxx, is of great importance.

Aland takes this further: 'Sinn hatte das Verfahren nur, wenn [Thomas] Lesarten wählte, die in seiner syrischen Heimat bekannt und beliebt waren. Denn für seine syrischen Landsleute arbeitete er ja. Für sie wollte er einen revidierten, "genauen und zuverlässigen" Text des Neuen Testaments in Syrisch herstellen. An den Rand kamen *die Lesarten*, die aus dem kirchlichen Gebrauch bei den Syrern ausgemerzt werden sollten' (op. cit., 60). Or could he not bring himself to allow them to be forgotten?

The **Palestinian Lectionary** text is of no great textual importance in Acts.

Coptic Versions. For the various dialects of Coptic and the linguistic differences and relation between them see Metzger (*Versions* 127–32). Only the Sahidic, Middle Egyptian, and Bohairic need be considered here.

The **Sahidic** has been variously dated: 2nd century, 3rd, and 4th. Its text agrees on the whole with that of the Alexandrian Greek MSS, but it contains some Western readings. 'The Greek text presupposed by the Sahidic and the Bohairic (Fayyumic) belongs to the Alexandrian type represented by ℵ and B but contains many Western textual elements' (Metzger, *Versions* 134f.). This Ropes explains by the suggestion that 'the Greek from which the Sahidic of Acts was translated was a copy of a MS. in which a "Western" text had been almost completely corrected by a standard of the B-type' (*Begs.* 3.cxliii).[64] Any statement of this kind must turn upon the way in which the Western text is understood. If the Western text is thought of as originating at a specific time by a specific redactional operation Ropes' view can be maintained; it may however be better to think of the origin of the Western text as a process of continuous development in which one might see the Sahidic as marking a stage of that development. See below, pp. 27f., and Vol. II.

The **Bohairic**, formerly dated in the 7th century or as late as 700, is now, on the basis of papyrus discoveries, dated in the 4th century, possibly even earlier. Its text is much closer than the Sahidic to that of B and ℵ and has very few readings of the D-type (Metzger, *Versions* 138; also Ropes and Hatch, op. cit., 88–90).

Of great importance is the **Middle Egyptian** version, not known to Ropes (1926). In this Coptic dialect a MS containing Acts 1.1–15.3 has been known since 1961; it has not yet been published but readings based on microfilm are included in NA[26].[65] It has been

---

[64]See also Ropes and Hatch, op. cit. (p. 11 and n. 60), 86–8.
[65]It is Cop[G67] in the Glazier collection, in New York. See Metzger (*Versions* 118, n. 1). But see now H. M. Schenke, *Apostelgeschichte 1.1–15.3 im mittel-ägyptischen Dialekt des Koptischen (Codex Glazier)*. TU 137; Berlin, 1991.

variously dated, in the 4th, 5th, and 6th centuries. Its form is itself a problem, for it begins without any title and ends abruptly at 15.3, but not because pages have been lost. It ends on the recto of a folio; the corresponding verso has been left blank, and there follows an additional folio, on the recto of which is painted an ornamental device. The text is clearly of a Western kind. At 3.11 it joins D h in their different view of the Temple and Solomon's Portico; at 3.17 it joins D (E h) in reading ἄνδρες ἀδελφοί, ἐπιστάμεθα ὅτι ὑμεῖς μέν; at 6.3 it joins D h p in reading τί οὖν ἐστιν ἀδελφοί; ἐπισκέψασθε ἐξ ὑμῶν αὐτῶν ἄνδρας; at 9.8 it joins h (p w) in reading sed ait ad eos: Levate me de terra. Et cum levassent illum; at 11.25 it joins D⁽²⁾ (gig p syʰᵐᵍ) in reading ἀκούσας δὲ ὅτι Σαῦλος ἐστιν εἰς Θαρσὸν ἐξῆλθεν ἀναζητῶν αὐτόν, καὶ ὡς συντυχὼν παρεκάλεσεν αὐτὸν ἐλθεῖν.[66]

See Ropes, *Begs*. 3.cxlif. for the Ethiopic version, clxxxi–clxxxiv for the Armenian, Georgian, and Arabic; Metzger (*Versions* 153–268) for the Armenian, Georgian, Ethiopic, Arabic, and Nubian versions. None is of great importance in the study of Acts.

Patristic quotations are potentially of very great importance, for if we can ascribe to a known ecclesiastical writer a precisely worded quotation of a biblical text we know the form in which the text was current, or at least one form in which the text was current, at a particular time and place. They must however be used with great caution. (1) Writers (especially before concordances were made) were apt to quote from memory, and their memories were not infallible. (2) Where more than one form of a text was known the Fathers were apt to quote the form better suited to their argument. (3) The patristic texts themselves have to be initially reconstructed from MSS, and there were few points in which these were more likely to suffer corruption than in biblical quotations; a copyist would assume that the revered author must have quoted Scripture in what he, the copyist, believed to be the authentic text. For this reason it is always important to compare the text quoted with the surrounding argument, which on occasion will appear to presuppose a different reading from that given in the lemma.

---

[66]Other examples, taken from T. C. Petersen, *CBQ* 26 (1944), 225–41, in Metzger (*Versions* 140f.). Metzger also cites as examples of Western type readings not found elsewhere 2.25; 6.1; 7.31–4; 7.42; 7.48; 8.35; 8.39; 11.30; 12.8, 9. The freedom characteristic of the Western text still flourished in Egypt between 400 and 500. See also Epp, *Tendency* (see Index), and E. Haenchen and P. Weigandt, *NTS* 14 (1968), 469–81. It may be suggested that 15.3 is a good place for a 'Shorter Acts' to stop. We have had the commission of 1.8, the Pentecostal gift of the Spirit (2.1–4), the great Christological speeches, the martyrdom of Stephen, the conversion of Paul, the first mission to the Gentiles, and the recognition (15.3) that, notwithstanding objection, this was a ground for rejoicing.

Little more will be attempted here than a list of some of the most important patristic witnesses to the text of Acts, arranged in approximately chronological order.

Second century

Pre-Irenaean Witnesses. Of these there are virtually none. There may be (see below, pp. 34-45) some evidence here that Acts was known before the time of Irenaeus, but it is not such as to yield a precise text. Ropes (*Begs*. 3.clxxxv) thinks it 'likely' that Barnabas 5.8, 9 (. . . κηρύσσειν τὸ εὐαγγέλιον αὐτοῦ ἐξελέξατο . . .) shows knowledge of the Western text of Acts 1.2; possible, perhaps, rather than likely. He also (clxxxvi) thinks it 'not unlikely' that *Didache* 1.2 drew the form of the Golden Rule that it contains from the Western text of Acts 15.20, 29. But the Rule was too widely known for this to be plausible.

The most important question here arises over **Justin Martyr**, but it is one that concerns use rather than text; see below, pp. 41-44. Ropes (*Begs*. 3.clxxxvi) finds in some of Justin's quotations from the OT evidence that suggests knowledge of the way in which the OT passages are presented in the Western text of Acts. See however P. Prigent, *Justin et l'Ancien Testament* (1964), who shows that in his use of the OT Justin is independent. Zahn's argument[67] connecting Justin with the first chapter of Acts by the repetition of a four-stage process (resurrection appearances; visible ascent to heaven; receiving of the Spirit; preaching to all nations), shows at most a parallel tradition.

Irenaeus is the first Christian author extant to quote Acts explicitly. He does so frequently and at length. The evidence is complicated by the fact that it is drawn from the Latin translation, not the original Greek of Irenaeus; there is however reason to think that the Latin represents the Greek with some accuracy.[68] Ropes (loc. cit.) described the Acts text of Irenaeus as 'a thorough-going "Western" text, showing but few departures from the complete "Western" type.' This opinion has been widely accepted, but is challenged by Dr B. Aland,[69] with the conclusion (56), 'Der Actatext, den Irenäus benutzte, war eine frühe Handschrift vom paraphrasierenden Typ,' not in the proper sense a Western text. It is clear[70] that the question turns in part

---

[67]Th. Zahn, *Geschichte des neutestamentlichen Kanons* 1.2, Erlangen and Leipzig, 1889, 508f., 515f., 580.
[68]Ropes (*Begs*. 3.clxxxvii f.); A. Rousseau, *Sources Chrétiennes* 100, p. 110: 'Deux traits apparaissent d'emblée comme caractérisant cette version: souci d'une littéralité assez stricte, intelligence habituellement pénétrante de la pensée de l'original.'
[69]*EThL* art. cit., 43–56.
[70]See also below, pp. 27f. and Vol. II.

upon the definition of the terms used, especially of the term 'Western text', and correspondingly on the view taken of the origin of this text. There is no doubt that Irenaeus is often in agreement with readings found in D, in the Old Latin MSS, in the Harclean, or in combinations of these. A few examples must suffice.

2.17 ὁ θεός] κύριος D E latt Ir^lat (3.2.1) GrNy.
3.13 παρεδώκατε] + εἰς κρίσιν (E: κριτήριον) D (E) h p* sy^hmg mae Ir^lat 3.12.3 (in iudicium)
4.9 ἀνακρινόμεθα] + ἀφ'ὑμῶν D it sy mae Ir^lat 3.12.4 (a vobis) Cyp
5.31 δεξιᾷ] δόξῃ D* gig p sa Ir^lat 3.12.5(6) (gloria)
7.6 θεός + πρὸς αὐτόν D Ir^lat3.12.10(13) (ad eum)
8.36 βαπτισθῆναι+ 37 ... πιστεύω τὸν υἱὸν τοῦ θεοῦ εἶναι τὸν 'Ιησοῦν Χριστόν: so with variations E min pc (1739) it vg^clsy^h** mae Ir^lat3.12.8 (credo filium dei esse Iesum; in catena, πιστεύω τὸν υἱὸν τοῦ θεοῦ εἶναι 'Ιησοῦν Χριστόν
14.10 φωνῇ] + σοι λέγω ἐν τῷ ὀνόματι τοῦ κυρίου 'Ιησοῦ Χριστοῦ with variation C D E Ψ min (including 1739) h t sy^psy^hmgco Ir^lat3.12.9(12) (in nomine domini(nostri) Jesu Christi ambulare fecisset)
14.15 ὑμᾶς] ὑμᾶς ἵνα E it?: ὑμᾶς ἀποστῆναι P^45: ὑμῖν τὸν θεὸν ὅπως D it? mae Ir^lat3.12.9(12) (vobis deum uti)
14.15 τούτῳ] οὕτως D* gig sa Ir^lat3.12.14(17) (sic)
15.18 γνωστὰ ἀπ' αἰῶνος Ir^lat 3.12.14(17) cognitum a saeculo est deo opus eius. D agrees; there are similar but not identical variants in P^74 A E lat (sy)
15.20 καὶ τοῦ πνικτοῦ] om. D gig Ir^lat3.12.14(17)
αἵματος] +καὶ ὅσα ἂν μὴ θέλωσιν (ὁ. μ. - λουσιν D) αὐτοῖς (ἑαυ.D) γίνεσθαι ἑτέροις μὴ ποιεῖν (-εῖτε D) D min (including 1739) sa Ir^lat3.12.14(17) (et quaecumque nolunt sibi fieri, aliis ne faciant)
15.29 καὶ πνικτῶν] om. D l Tert Hier^mss Ir^lat3.12.14(17)
πορνείας] +καὶ ὅσα μὴ θέλετε ἑαυτοῖς γίνεσθαι, ἑτέρῳ (-ροις 1739 al) μὴ ποιεῖν (-εῖτε D² 614 pc) D min (including 614 1739) l p w sy^h** sa Cyp Ir^lat3.12.14(17) (et quaecumque non vultis fieri vobis, alii ne faciatis)
πράξετε] πράξατε, φερόμενοι ἐν τῷ ἁγίῳ πνεύματιD; cf. l; Ir^lat3.12.14(17) (agetis, ambulantes in spiritu sancto)
16.10 θεός] κύριος D 𝔐 gig sy sa Ir^lat3.14.1
17.26 ἐξ ἑνός] + αἵματος D E 𝔐 gig sy sa Ir^lat3.12.9(11) (sanguine)
κατὰ τὰς ὁροθεσίας] κατὰ ὁροθεσίαν D* Ir^lat3.12.9(11) (secundum determinationem)
17.27 ζητεῖν τὸν θεόν] ζ.τ. κύριον E 𝔇ℓ: μάλιστϲ ζητεῖν τὸ θεῖον ἐστιν D (probably by wrongful assimilation to d) (gig) Ir^lat3.12.9(11) (quaerere illud quod est divinum)
αὐτόν] αὐτό D* (gig) Ir^lat3.12.9(11) (illud)

17.31 ἐν ᾗ μέλλει] om. D Spec Ir^lat3.12.9(11)
ἀνδρί] +'Ιησοῦ D Ir^lat3.12.9(11)
20.28 θεοῦ] κυρίου P^74 A C* D E ψ min (including 1739) gig p sy^hmg co Lcf Ir^lat3.14.2 (domini)^71

To balance this set of readings another must be given. There are places where Irenaeus keeps other company.

2.23 ἔκδοτον] + λαβόντες D E ψ sy^h and others; not Irenaeus, who agrees with P^74 ℵ* A B C and others.
3.20 ἔλθωσιν] P^74 A C and many others; Ir^lat3.12.3 (veniant); D h Tert have ἐπέλθωσιν (supraviniant (sic); d has veniant)
7.38 ἡμῖν] A C D E ψ 𝔐 lat sy; ὑμῖν P^74 ℵ B min p co Ir^lat4.15.1; 4.26.1 (vobis)
7.43 ὑμῶν] P^74 ℵ C E ψ 𝔐 h vg sy^h mae bo Cyr; om. B D min gig sy^p sa Or Ir^lat 4.15.1; 4.26.1
10.37 ἀρξάμενος]+γάρ P^74 A D lat Ir^lat3.12.7(8); cf. 4.27.1 (enim)^72
10.39 καί^2] + ἐν P^74 ℵ A C E 𝔐 sy^h Ir^lat3.12.7(8); cf. 4.27.1; om. B D ψ min lat sy^p
15.7 ἐν ὑμῖν ἐξελέξατο ὁ θεός] P^74 ℵ A B C min bo Ir^lat3.12.14(17) (in vobis deus elegit); other readings in D E ψ 614 lat sy^psy^h sa
15.23 ἀδελφοί] P^33 P^74 ℵ* A B C D min pc lat Ir^lat3.12.14(17) (fratres); om. vg^ms sa Or^lat; καὶ οἱ ἀδ. ℵ^c E ψ 𝔐 sy bo^mss
16.8 κατέβησαν] κατήντησαν D; ἡμεῖς ἤλθομεν Ir^lat3.14.1 (nos venimus)^73

Irenaeus, then, often agrees with D and other representatives of the Western text. The agreements are often in small matters and not in themselves of great weight; this is probably in part because Irenaeus, who is concerned to set the teaching of the apostles over against that of the Gnostics, quotes the apostolic speeches more frequently than the narrative sections, where some of the most striking variants are to be found.^74 He does not by any means always agree with D and its associates, and it must be remembered that D, the various Old Latin witnesses (manuscript and patristic), and the Harclean apparatus

---

^71This 'improved' reading was evidently attractive; most MSS combine the two — τοῦ κυρίου καὶ (τοῦ) θεοῦ.
^72The witnesses for this reading are a mixed group. It is impossible to tell from the Latin (incipiens) whether Irenaeus read ἀρξάμενος or ἀρξάμενον.
^73This reading 'is subject to suspicion because it occurs in so free a summary; but [Irenaeus's] argument is scarcely sound unless he thought he had a Greek text with the first person' (Ropes, Begs. 3.152f.). But the first person in v. 10 may have led him to think that the narrative was continuous in this sense; how should Luke suddenly have appeared in Troas? And, as Ropes notes, there may have been confusion with 20.6, et venimus Troadem, quoted in the same paragraph.
^74So, rightly, B. Aland, art. cit. 44.

often differ among themselves.[75] The various possibilities that these data suggest — and allow — will be mentioned below (pp. 21–8) and further discussed in Vol. II.

Third Century

Clement of Alexandria, whose gospel text is on the whole Western, follows in Acts substantially the text of B ℵ, with occasional signs of Western influence, sufficient to show that in Acts also Western readings were not unknown in Alexandria. At 15.29 Clement has καὶ πνικτῶν, supporting the Old Uncial form of the Apostolic Decree. At 17.23 however he has instead of ἀναθεωρῶν, διιστορῶν (D has ἱστορῶν).[76]

Tertullian undoubtedly used a text of a Western kind. For example at 3.20 he joins D, as Irenaeus does not,[77] in reading ἐπέλθωσιν (superveniant: *Res. Carnis* 23); at 21.13, D* gig p in reading θορυβοῦντες (*Fug.* 6, conturbantes; but at *Scorp.* 15 he has contristatis). Of particular importance however is the material concerning the Apostolic Decree, which Tertullian cites more than once. In *Apol.* 9, written before Tertullian became a Montanist, the Decree appears in the Old Uncial form; in *Pudic.* 12, written in Tertullian's Montanist period, it appears in the Western form; in *Monogamia* 5 we have an intermediate form. This is pointed out by P. Corssen,[78] with the suggestion that the Western text may be of Montanist origin.

Origen. 'Origen's text of Acts was that of the Old Uncials (B ℵ A C 81)' (Ropes, *Begs.* 3.clxxxix). Ropes allows for a few trifling exceptions. The 'very few' agreements with the Western text are probably 'explicable as inaccuracies of quotation or the combination in memory of two parallel passages' (cxc). There seems to be no reason for disagreement with this judgment.

Cyprian's text is a primary witness to the African form of the Old Latin, and thus of great importance for the history of the Western text.[79] There is no need in this case to give many examples. At *Test.* 2.16 Cyprian quotes Acts 4.8–12 in full. In v. 8, after πρεσβύτεροι, he adds Israel, with D h p gig Irenaeus (others have τοῦ οἴκου

---

[75]See above, 5f., 13, and n. 53; and below, pp. 27f.
[76]See Ropes (*Begs.* 3.clxxxvii f.); and especially P. M. Barnard, *The Biblical Text of Clement of Alexandria in the Four Gospels and the Acts of the Apostles* (T. & S. 5), 1899.
[77]See above, p. 17.
[78]Review of F. Blass, *Acta Apostolorum*, 1895, in *Göttingische gelehrte Anzeigen* 158 (1896), 448f., supporting J. R. Harris, *Study of Codex Bezae*, 1891.
[79]See Hans von Soden as in n. 50, pp. 550–67.

Ἰσραήλ); in v. 9, he has ecce nos hodie interrogamur, alone; then a vobis, with D E it sy mae Irenaeus;[80] at the end of v. 10, instead of παρέστηκεν ἐνώπιον ὑμῶν ὑγιής, Cyprian, with E h sy^hmg (there are minor variations), has in conspectu vestro sanus adstat, in alio autem nullo; correspondingly in v. 12, he has non est enim nomen aliud sub caelo datum hominibus, in quo oportet salvari nos, with various measures of agreement in D, the Old Latin, and Irenaeus. Cyprian gives the Decree in the form (15.28f.), Visum est sancto spiritui et nobis nullam vobis imponere sarcinam quam ista, quae ex necessitate sunt: abstinere vos ab idololatriis et sanguine et fornicatione, et quaecumque vobis fieri non vultis, alii ne feceritis.

Fourth Century

Eusebius of Caesarea shows a mixture of Old Uncial and Western readings. It is possible that this should be described as a Caesarean text; see below, and see Ropes, *Begs*. 3. cxcviii, ccxciv.

Lucifer of Cagliari's text is akin to that of the Old Latin, and especially of gig (see above, p. 8). By way of example, in the narrative of 3.1–10 the following variants from the text of NA^26 may be noted. In verse

2:om. ὑπάρχων, D it Lcf
3:om. λαβεῖν, D 𝔐 it sy^h Lcf
6:ἔγειρε καί, read by A C E Ψ 𝔐 lat sy mae bo Ir^lat Cyp Eus Lcf, is om. by ℵ B D sa
7:αὐτόν, read by P^74vid ℵ A B C min *pc* lat sy Cyp Lcf, is om. by D E Ψ 𝔐
8:om. καί^4, P^74 A D h r mae Lcf
10: αὐτός, P^74 ℵ A C *pc* lat Lcf; οὗτος, B D E Ψ 𝔐.
An interesting group of readings occurs in ch. 16:
17: ἄνθρωποι] om D* gig Lcf
18: ἐξελθεῖν] ἵνα ἐξέλθῃς D e gig Lcf
26: παραχρῆμα] om. B gig Lcf

Athanasius of Alexandria 'uses for Acts, as elsewhere, the Old Uncial text, in clear distinction from the Antiochian and the "Western"' (Ropes, *Begs*. 3.cxcix).

Cyril of Jerusalem 'is said to show for Acts the use of a text of "Western" affinities'.[81]

---

[80]See above, p. 16.
[81]Ropes (*Begs*. 3.cxcviii), referring to Hermann von Soden, *Die Schriften des NTs* 1.3.1759: 'Die leider sehr spärlichen Citate bei diesen drei Kirchenvätern [Eusebius of Caesarea, Cyril of Jerusalem, Epiphanius] stimmen mit I überein.'

Fifth Century

Chrysostom is the first of the fathers mentioned here to have written a commentary, or rather, a series of homilies on Acts; he thus provides an almost continuous text. This is basically Antiochian, as might be expected, but shows from time to time awareness of Western variations.

Jerome. For Jerome's work on the Vulgate see above, pp. 9f. It would be easy and natural to take him as simply a witness to the Vulgate text; this would however be mistaken. In his own work he does not always use it. He 'folgt in seinen zahlreichen Werken oft einem davon abweichenden Text' (Nestle-von Dobschütz, 43). He thus agrees sometimes with the Old Latin.

Augustine, who lived at the time the Vulgate was produced (see pp. 9f.), not unnaturally presents a mixed text. He is, however, with Cyprian, an important witness to the African Old Latin text of Acts, agreeing frequently with p (see p. 9), though there are also indications that he was aware of the Vulgate revision.

Cyril of Alexandria. 'At Alexandria itself the Alexandrian tradition lives on through the fourth century, more or less disguised with foreign accretions, and then in the early part of the fifth century reappears comparatively pure in Cyril.'[82]

Speculum. The word appears in the list of patristic writers and writings in NA[26], p. 27*. It is cited in some editions of the NT among Old Latin texts, and is there denoted by the letter m. It is a collection of biblical texts, formerly attributed to Augustine, but now known not to have been written by him, though it goes back to his lifetime. It contains an Old Latin type of text. 'It appears to be a Spanish form of the African text, probably dating from the fifth century' (Ropes, *Begs.* 3.cxiv).

Bede wrote a commentary on Acts; in doing so he used the bilingual Codex Laudianus (E), which long afterwards came into the possession of Archbishop Laud.

Observations

1. The foregoing description of the various Greek MSS, versions, and patristic quotations which constitute for us the text of Acts has

---

[82]Hort, in B. F. Westcott and F. J. A. Hort, *The NT in the Original Greek, Introduction* 141, quoted by Ropes (*Begs.* 3.cxix.).

of necessity involved from time to time anticipation of the observation that these authorities fall into several clearly distinguishable groups. The fundamental analysis has been recognised since the time of Westcott and Hort.[83]

(a) The great mass of Greek MSS,[84] notwithstanding minor variations which permit the detection of sub-groups, have a common text which appears to go back to a recension to which Chrysostom already bears witness. It may well have been made by the martyr Lucian (who died in 311), but this is in no way essential to the observation. It is based on a conflationary method, and may in general be neglected in any attempt to establish the original text of the NT.

(b) The great uncials of Alexandria (ℵ A B C 81) bear witness to a second type of text, in which it is possible to distinguish between earlier and later, revised, forms.[85] In agreement with Ropes (especially *Begs.* 3.ccii) the term Old Uncial has been used here for this group as a whole. There is no doubt of its antiquity and importance. In Acts it is attested by Clement of Alexandria and also by the papyri (unknown to Westcott and Hort) P^{45} P^{74}. In Acts as throughout the NT this text in its early form was considered by Westcott and Hort to stand very close to the NT autographs. It should be added that recent editors do not differ widely from this view. For example, notwithstanding their disclaimer,[86] the editors of NA^{26} have on their own count (pp. 729–31) differed from the Westcott and Hort text in 191 places in Acts. When this number is reduced by 25 (placed within square brackets and meaning that Westcott and Hort placed the reading in their text but in square brackets) we find that a difference occurs in about one in six verses; and most of the differences are slight.

(c) D, with P^{38} P^{48}, the Old Latin, the Harclean apparatus, Irenaeus, Cyprian, and (in part) Augustine, bears witness to a different kind of text, usually (and in this commentary) called Western,[87] and differing frequently and sharply from the Alexandrian. Examples of differences have been given above (pp. 5f.; all from D); many more will be mentioned in the course of the commentary. Whether (to take one kind of difference only) places where the Western text is longer than the Old Uncial should be described as Western expansions or as

---

[83]*Introduction* (as in n. 82), 90–135; and indeed earlier: Bengel and Griesbach made similar analyses of the evidence.

[84]In NA^{26}, 𝔐 (= Mehrheitstext); in earlier editions, 𝔎 (= Koine); other terms used are Syrian text, Byzantine text, Antiochian text.

[85]To Westcott and Hort, Neutral and Alexandrian respectively.

[86]NA^{26}, Einführung, 5*, 'Die vorliegende [Textgestaltung] ist alles andere als identisch mit der etwa von Westcott/Hort.'

[87]This must not be understood as a geographical term, though it first came into use because this kind of text was first recognised as existing in the (geographical) West; it is found not only in the Syriac-speaking church but also in Egypt.

Alexandrian contractions is a very difficult question; see below (e.g. pp. 23f.). The reconstruction of the Western text itself, if indeed there ever was a unitary, subsequently diverging, Western text, is a major problem.

(d) It may be that P[45] represents a Caesarean text, as it has been held to do in the gospels. There is however doubt about the supposed gospel Caesarean text, which may turn out to have been not an independent recension but the result of a mixing of Old Uncial and Western readings, and in Acts the question must at present be left open.

2. It is clear that if the Western text did not exist there would be no serious problem in reconstructing the text of Acts. On the basis of the familiar principle *difficilior lectio potior* it would be possible to purge the early papyrus and Old Uncial text of scholarly and ecclesiastical 'improvements' and on this basis to set out, with some confidence, not of course Luke's own text of Acts but a close approximation to it. The Western text, with its many substantial variants, makes this impossible, so that the primary question with which the textual critic, especially in Acts, is faced, is, What is the Western text and where did it arise? This question may not have a simple answer, for behind it lies another. Is the Western text the product of a definite recension or redaction of the text, so that, notwithstanding the diversity of the witnesses, it may be attached to a specific time and place, or is it a tendency, shared by many, to expand, to paraphrase, to modify — chiefly by brightening descriptions and heightening interest? If the latter alternative is chosen, texts of a Western type may have arisen independently in many places and developed over many years. If the former we have to ask whether the editor corrupted the original text, or rediscovered it, restoring it from the tamer, milder form that his predecessors had produced. Many different answers to these questions have been given, and a sketch of them will help to clarify (if not to solve) the problem and to prepare the reader for the study of Acts.

3. (a) In *Acta Apostolorum sive Lucae ad Theophilum liber alter editio philogica*, (Göttingen, 1895), F. Blass gave full expression to his theory that two editions of Acts were produced by Luke himself. The first, written in Rome, was a sketch, containing many marks of unpolished style, unnecessary details, and ill-formed sentences; later Luke travelled east to Antioch, where he gained a more accurate notion of some matters and also had the opportunity to improve the style of his book. The first draft, originating in the West, gives us the Western text, the second, polished, draft, originating in the East, gives us the Oriental, or Old Uncial, text. The differences between the two texts were thus due to Luke himself, so that we have to think neither of a loose paraphrast nor of a pedantic emendator. This theory was taken up by Theodor Zahn, notably in *Die Urausgabe der*

Apostelgeschichte des Lukas, Leipzig, 1916,[88] but it won scarcely any other adherents. A review by P. Corssen[89] already made it difficult to hold Blass's view, and Ropes,[90] while giving due weight to the points in favour of it, argues that it obliges us to suppose that Luke reduced 'to a lower degree the serious and religious tone which at first he had adopted' (ccxxix) and came to hold a different mental picture of what took place. It seemed (but see below) that Blass's theory would not stand.

(b) In the discussion just cited Ropes made clear his own view. 'The purpose of the 'Western' reviser, as shown by his work, was literary improvement and elaboration in accordance with his own taste, which was somewhat different from that of the author' (ccxxxi). 'This effort after smoothness, fulness, and emphasis in his expansion has usually resulted in a weaker style, sometimes showing a sort of naive superabundance in expressly stating what every reader could have understood without the reviser's diluting supplement . . . In his language he uses a vocabulary notably the same as that of the original author, but with a certain number of new words — about fifty' (ccxxxii). Thus there was a '"Western" reviser' (see above) and a specific Western revision. It must have been made in Greek (not Latin or Syriac) or it could not have been so wide spread. It shows no special viewpoint; it is not for example Montanistic.

So far the Western text appears in Ropes' view to be secondary, but he allows the possibility that, since it was made on the basis of an early copy, it may occasionally present us with a reading superior to that of the Old Uncial text. His conclusion is 'that the "Western" text was made before, and perhaps long before, the year 150, by a Greek-speaking Christian who knew something of Hebrew, in the East, perhaps in Syria or Palestine. The introduction of "we" in the "Western" text of xi.27 possibly gives some colour to the guess that the place was Antioch. The reviser's aim was to improve the text, not to restore it, and he lived not far from the time when the New Testament canon in its nucleus was first definitely assembled. It is tempting to suggest . . . that the "Western" text was the original "canonical" text (if the anachronism can be pardoned) which was later supplanted by a "pre-canonical" text of superior age and merit' (ccxliv f.).

(c) In 1933 A. C. Clark published *The Acts of the Apostles*, Oxford,[91] which was an attempt to work back from D and the other

---

[88]Both Blass and Zahn collected a great deal of material relevant to the Western text, so that their work retains great value irrespective of the correctness of their textual theory.

[89]See n. 78; the whole review occupies pp. 425–48.

[90]*Begs*. 3. ccxxvii–ccxxix.

[91]See also Clark's *The Primitive Text of the Gospels and Acts*, Oxford, 1914, which proceeds on different lines.

witnesses to the primitive Western text and a vindication of this reconstituted text as a witness to the original text of Acts. Clark builds much upon the fact that D and d are written in στίχοι (sense-lines; though Clark rightly points out that this rendering is an over-simplification), arguing that "Γ [his term for the Old Uncial text] represents the work of an abbreviator who, having before him a MS written in στίχοι similar to those found in *D*, frequently (not, of course, always) adopted the rough and ready method of striking out lines in his model, botching from time to time to produce a construction' (p. viii). It must be added that whether this fundamental thesis is right or wrong Clark's book contains invaluable information on and discussion of the history of the Western text.

(d) In the same year that Clark's book was published (1933) appeared the commentary volumes (4 and 5) of *Begs.*, the work of K. Lake and H. J. Cadbury (with some collaborators in Vol. 5). They were not uncritical of their colleague J. H. Ropes, though it goes without saying that they admired his work on the text in Vol. 3,[92] and took up what is now usually described as the method of eclectic criticism. Every variant must be examined on its merits; none may be adopted or rejected on the ground that it occurs in a particular MS or family of MSS.

The same emphasis was expressed at about the same time by M. J. Lagrange in *Critique Textuelle II: La Critique rationelle*, Paris, 1935. On the method see Metzger, *Text*, 175–9.

(e) In the work just referred to, Lagrange, founder of the École biblique et archéologique in Jerusalem, wrote, 'L'hypothèse des deux éditions de Luc aura probablement disparu avec Zahn' (387). From the École itself there has now appeared what is virtually a resuscitation — and elaboration — of Blass's theory: M. E. Boismard and A. Lamouille, *Texte Occidental des Actes des Apôtres*, two volumes, Paris, 1984. The intention of the book is expressed in the opening sentence of the Avant-Propos: 'Le but premier de ces deux volumes est de réhabiliter le texte Occidental des Actes des apôtres en démontrant qu'il n' a pu être écrit que par Luc lui-même' (p. IX). To this end it is necessary to establish the original form of the Western text, and then to compile a list of stylistic and other characteristics of the undoubtedly Lucan part of Acts and to show that these are characteristic also of the Western 'additions', that is,

---

[92] 'Professor Ropes thinks that the Neutral text is the primitive text of the books of the New Testament, before they were formed into a Canon of Scripture. His main reason — which will call for much investigation — is that the Neutral text is intrinsically better than the Western, and therefore right. Is it?' (K. Lake, *The Text of the NT*, 6th edition revised by S. New, London, 1933, p. 86.

more accurately, of those passages where the Western text is found to be in excess of the non-Western text.[93] It is unnecessary here to summarise the account of the witnesses to the Western text, though it contains excellent observations. The vital argument is 'que le TO [texte occidental] abonde en caractéristiques stylistiques lucaniennes, que ce soit dans les sections qu'il a en propre ou dans les passages où il est parallèle au TA [texte alexandrin]' (97). There can be no doubt that substantial parallels exist.[94] More problematical is the assertion that TO (the original Western text) was a short text; that the original Western text suffered corruption is however no doubt true, though whether this can be so neatly expressed in terms of a TO and a TO^2 is another question. It may be that what we have in the tradition must be described as TO^1, TO^2, . . . TO^n.

In their second volume Boismard and Lamouille give first an explanatory apparatus criticus for every verse in Acts; then a list of about 1,000 'charactéristiques stylistiques', given first in alphabetical order, then in order of frequency, finally as they appear in Acts — a list which will certainly be of value to all students of Acts.

This theory is closer to that of Ropes than appears at first sight, for Ropes believed that the Western text as we have it derived ultimately from a very early and good source.[95] It is also however sharply distinguished from it, in that Boismard and Lamouille believe (a) that they are able to reconstruct the original TO from which was derived the TO^2 that we read in variously corrupt papyri, vellum codices, versions, and patristic quotations, and (b) that this TO can be proved, by many stylistic characteristics, to be the work of Luke himself, who also wrote TA. 'Luc aurait écrit une première rédaction des Actes dont nous trouvons un echo dans le texte Occidental; il aurait, un certain nombre d'années plus tard, profondément remanié son oeuvre primitive, non seulement du point de vue stylistique, comme le voulait Blass, mais encore du point de vue du contenu' (9).

(f) Finally, also not unrelated to though in some respects critical of the findings of Ropes, must be noted a paper by B. Aland.[96] Like Ropes, Dr Aland believes that the Western text (known to us in various corrupt forms), was the product of a *Hauptredaktion* made at a specific time by a *Hauptredaktor*, and like him she believes that this work of redaction should probably be located in Syria. She

---

[93]Cf. M. Wilcox in Kremer, *Actes*, 'Luke and the Bezan Text of Acts', 447–55; also E. Delebeque, *Les Actes des Apôtres. Texte traduit et annoté*, Paris, 1982 (and other works).

[94]As Ropes had pointed out; see above, p. 23.

[95]See above, p. 23.

[96]*EThL* 62 (1986), 5–65: 'Entstehung, Charakter und Herkunft des sog. westlichen Textes untersucht an der Apostelgeschichte'.

differs from him however in regard to its date. We have seen (above, p. 23) that in Ropes' view the origin of the Western text is to be placed very early, before 150. She thinks that it cannot be earlier than the first half of the 3rd century. A terminus ante quem is given by the two papyri P³⁸ P⁴⁸ (whose text she investigates in detail), which belong to the 3rd and 3rd or 4th centuries. Cyprian provides some confirmation. It is impossible to date the redaction earlier than this for it was made on the basis of a text of the type of 614 and its allies (which are shown to resemble the two papyri) and this cannot have been disseminated before the 2nd century. The question that arises immediately, in view of the account of Ropes' argument (above, p. 23), is the place of Irenaeus. Did he not already, in 180, use a Western text? No, answers Dr Aland. Irenaeus does not use a true Western text but represents a free, paraphrasing kind of text, related to 614, and the basis on which the Western text was eventually constructed. It is impossible here to reproduce or even to summarise Dr Aland's discussion of the text of Irenaeus,[97] but a decision regarding its validity will eventually be necessary. 'Der Actatext, den Irenaeus benutzte, war eine frühe Handschrift vom paraphrasierenden Typ' (op. cit. 56). This does not mean 'Verwilderung' of the tradition; the paraphrasts rather thought of themselves as conducting a διόρθωσις, a correction of the text they received. Irenaeus may be thought of as a forerunner but not as a representative of the Western text.

From this account of Dr Aland's study it is natural to proceed finally to some of the facts that must be studied and the questions that must be answered in any attempt to give a satisfactory account of the text of Acts.

Questions

1. There is no disputing the fact that we appear to have two different editions of Acts. 'Editions', indeed, may prove to be the wrong word (see above, p. 21 and below, pp. 27f.); 'types' of text is safer and may prove to be more accurate. The basic fact stands out with unmistakable clarity in Ropes' volume (*Begs.* 3.1–255), where the texts of B and D are set out on opposite pages. The first task of any student of the text of Acts must be to go through these pages underlining identities and marking differences between the two MSS. Broadly speaking, of course, and in innumerable details, they tell the same story; but nowhere else in the textual history of the NT can such divergence be found.[98]

---

[97]But see above, pp. 15–18
[98]Except of course in the case of other Alexandrian and Western witnesses for Acts.

It is equally clear that both types of text appeared very early. For the Alexandrian text this is proved by P[45] (which even if Caesarean rather than Alexandrian presuppoes the Old Uncial text), B, ℵ, and readings in Clement of Alexandria and Origen. For the Western text it is proved by P[38] P[48,] Tertullian, Cyprian, Old Latin MSS, and probably by the Syriac tradition and parts of the Coptic. We cannot expect to be able, after 1700 years, to be able to say which emerged before the other.[99]

2. The Old Uncial text appears primarily in Egypt, though there also there are traces of the Western text. This is not to say that it existed only in Egypt. It was used in the construction of the Antiochian (and of the Caesarean?) text, and the MS used by Jerome to revise the Old Latin was apparently of this kind. It is to be remembered that it is only in Egypt that climatic conditions favour the preservation of papyrus. Nevertheless, the observation is valid that, especially in the early period, the Old Uncial text seems to be focused in Alexandria. The Western text, on the other hand, appears in various localities: in Greek MSS (some probably written in the west, but not the papyri), in Latin versions and Latin fathers, in the Syriac-speaking church, and in Egypt (where there is both Greek and Coptic evidence). Whatever the Western text is, and wherever and whenever it arose, it was very popular. It need not be said that this does not prove it to be a 'good' text.

3. In view of Dr Aland's work[100] Irenaeus must be mentioned on his own, and allowed to raise a question of fundamental importance. If Irenaeus bears witness to the Western text, this text was in use in Gaul in 180, and no doubt for some years before, since it was important to Irenaeus to quote an established biblical text in his opposition to the Gnostics. He may even have brought his biblical text with him when he came to Gaul from Asia Minor.[101] If Irenaeus does not bear witness to the Western text we lose an important terminus ad quem,[102] and are also faced with the question what we mean by the Western text.

This question must in any case be raised. Witnesses to the Western text (as commonly understood) differ among themselves. D is not identical with the African Old Latin, the African Old Latin is not identical with the Harclean apparatus, the Harclean apparatus is not identical with the Middle Egyptian. Most students of the subject have nevertheless concluded that behind these diverse witnesses there stands a basic Western edition of the text of Acts, to some

[99]I leave the question of Irenaeus for the moment.
[100]See above, p. 26.
[101]Eusebius, *HE* 5.20.5f.
[102]See p. 26.

extent recoverable, and possibly capable of being dated and located. This should not be assumed. There would no doubt be a tendency to standardisation in various localities (Gaul, Africa, Syria) and this can to some extent be observed, but this is a different matter. At least the question should not be regarded as closed, and it may be asked how much difference there is between the two views, (a) that Irenaeus used the Western text, which was subsequently corrected and debased so as to produce for example the text of D, and (b) that Irenaeus used a free type of text which subsequently formed the basis of the *Hauptredaktion* that produced the Western text proper. Is it possible that the Western text should be thought of as a process in which a number of points of discontinuity can be observed?

4. Notwithstanding its early date the Western text often has a secondary, paraphrastic appearance. This has been shown beyond dispute by Ropes, and by other students of the matter. The paraphrases, however, as Ropes showed and others have subsequently emphasised,[103] are Lucan in style and outlook.[104] Here the old questions of Blass and Zahn, and their new formulation by Boismard and Lamouille, must be raised. It must however also be asked whether it would not be natural for an editor or copyist, working with a text with which he had long been respectfully familiar and introducing occasional additions or paraphrases, to do so in the style of the author whose work he believed that he was restoring to its proper form. If the answer to this question is yes, a good deal of the ground is cut away from under Boismard and Lamouille.

5. The problem of the Western text is not confined to Acts, but appears, though less acutely, throughout the NT. This fact suggests a double question. On the one hand, Why is there a universal Western problem? An editor's task in the gospels and in the epistles is different from an editor's task in Acts. On the other hand, given a universal Western problem, why is it so much more acute in Acts? Can it be simply that the Western text is not a redaction but a tendency to paraphrase and to enhance, and that in Acts copyists felt a greater freedom especially in the narrative portions (where the variants are more frequent and divergent) than they did in regard to the life and teaching of Jesus and the letters of the apostles?

6. Acts is a second book attached to the Third Gospel, which early appears, detached from its pendant, as part of the Four Gospel canon. If it was detached from Acts, Acts was detached from it, and it cannot

---

[103]See pp. 23, 24.
[104]Against P. H. Menoud, 'The Western Text and the Theology of Acts', *SNTS Bulletin* II (1951), and Epp, *Tendency*, who argue for special theological interests in D and the Western text, see C. K. Barrett, as in n. 34, and cf. B. Aland, art. cit. p. 21, n. 37.

be assumed that its place in the canon of the NT necessarily corresponded with that of the gospel. Detachment may have meant a different textual history. Ropes (see pp. 23f.) thought that the Western text might have been the first canonical form of Acts; it may have been otherwise. The freedom with which Acts was used may have been due to the fact that it was not yet regarded as canonical, as sacred Scripture.

This possibility suggests the next main section of this preliminary Introduction.

II. ACTS AND ITS AUTHOR

It was pointed out above (p. 1) that the question, or questions, implied by this heading, which include the identification of the author, the date at which and the place in which he wrote, the use made of his book, and the status accorded to it, can be satisfactorily dealt with only on the basis of an examination and assessment of all the evidence, external and internal, that bears upon them; such an assessment cannot be attempted until writer and reader have before them considered exegesis of the whole work and a discussion of what it affirms, in both history and theology, in the light of parallel, or possibly parallel, or perhaps contradictory, statements in other parts of the NT, in early Christian literature, and in more or less contemporary sources, literary, occasional, and archaeological. The proper place for this discussion will be the second volume of this commentary. What will be presented here[1] will be the essential parts of the basic information regarding the acceptance and use of Acts in the early church and the beliefs that were current about its author, together with some indication of where the problems lie and of the questions that will have to be raised.[2]

From about AD 200 the tradition presents (until it is confronted with internal evidence) no problem. Most ecclesiastical writers were agreed, and few were disposed to dispute with them, that the Third Gospel and Acts were written by the same author, who was Luke, the companion of Paul.[3] Luke's hand was held to appear in those passages[4] that are written in the first person plural; these meant that Luke himself was present on the occasions in question.

A representative statement of opinion as it was solidifying early in the fourth century is given by **Eusebius**, who has no hesitation in

---

[1]Cf. the section on the Text of Acts, pp.2-29
[2]The reader should not fail to consult the admirable statement and provisional discussion of 'The Tradition' by H. J. Cadbury in *Begs*. 2.209–64, where full Greek and Latin texts, together with translations, will be found. In some respects Cadbury's treatment is fuller than that offered here, but it does not go behind Irenaeus and thus misses evidence useful for dating Acts and illustrating the problematical use of it in the second century.
[3]Col. 4.14 — 'the beloved physician'; 2 Tim. 4.11. It should be noted that the former reference is in an epistle of doubtful authenticity, the latter in one almost certainly pseudonymous.
[4]16.10–17; 20.5–15; 21.1-8; 27.1–28.16; on 11.28 see the Commentary.

placing Acts among the 'acknowledged' books (ὁμολογούμενα) of the NT.[5]

H.E. 3.4.1

That, indeed, in preaching to the Gentiles Paul had laid the foundation of the churches from Jerusalem and round about even unto Illyricum, is an evident conclusion from his own words[6] and from what Luke has recorded in the Acts (ὁ Λουκᾶς ἐν ταῖς Πράξεσιν ἱστόρησεν). . .6 Now Luke, who was by race an Antiochene and by profession a physician (τὸ μὲν γένος ὢν τῶν ἀπ' Ἀντιοχείας, τὴν ἐπιστήμην δὲ ἰατρός[7]), was very frequently in the company of Paul, and had no merely casual acquaintance with the rest of the apostles.[8] So he has left us examples of that art of healing souls which he acquired from them, in two inspired books. These are, namely, the Gospel, which also he testified that he penned in accordance with what they delivered unto him, which from the beginning were eye-witnesses and ministers of the word, all of whom, he also goes on to say, he had followed closely from the first; and the Acts of the Apostles (ταῖς τῶν ἀποστόλων Πράξεσιν), which he composed, no longer from the evidence of hearing but of his own eyes[9] . . .10 In addition to these[10] there is also that Areopagite named Dionysius, the first to believe after Paul's speech to the Athenians in Areopagus, according to the record of Luke in the Acts (ἐν Πράξεσι).[11]

H.E. 3.25.1

But now that we have reached this point, it is reasonable to sum up the writings of the NT already mentioned. Well then, we must set in the first place the holy quaternion of the Gospels, which are followed by the book of the Acts of the Apostles (οἷς ἕπεται ἡ τῶν Πράξεων τῶν ἀποστόλων γραφή).

Acts thus takes the place it still occupies, following (ἕπεται) the gospels and thus linking the story of Jesus with that of the post-resurrection church. This has resulted in its separation from the

---

[5]The translation of Eusebius is taken from H. J. Lawlor and J. E. L. Oulton, *Eusebius, The Ecclesiastical History and The Martyrs of Palestine*, two volumes, London, 1927, 1928.
[6]Rom. 15.19.
[7]Cf. Col. 4.14.
[8]This, as the next lines show, was Eusebius's inference from Lk. 1.3, where he took πᾶσιν to be masculine.
[9]At least in the We-passages.
[10]Crescens, Linus, Clement.
[11]Acts 17.34.

gospel which, according to Eusebius (and others) was written by the same man. It is distinguished sharply (*H.E.* 3.25.4) from the (apocryphal) Acts of Paul. It is clear that Eusebius himself knows Acts as a book which he can use as a historical source (*H.E.* 2.22.1, 6, 7, 8).

Somewhat later, **Jerome** (c. 342–420), in whose Latin Bible Acts was of course included, summed up current belief about the book and its author in *De Viris Illustribus* 7.

Luke, a doctor of Antioch, was, as his writings show, not ignorant of the Greek language. The follower of the apostle Paul, and his companion in all his journeying (omnis eius perigrinationis comes),[12] he wrote the gospel, of which the same Paul says, 'We have sent with him the brother whose praise is in the Gospel through all the churches' and to the Colossians, 'Luke, the beloved doctor, greets you', and to Timothy, 'Only Luke is with me'.[13] He published also another excellent volume which is entitled 'Apostolic Acts';[14] its story extends as far as the two-year period of Paul's residence in Rome, that is, as far as the fourth year of Nero. From this we learn that the book was composed in that city.[15] We therefore consider that 'The travels (Περιόδους) of Paul and Thecla', and the whole tale about the baptized lion, belong among the apocryphal writings ... Some suppose that whenever Paul in his epistles says, 'according to my Gospel' he is referring to Luke's book, and that Luke had learned the Gospel not only from the apostle Paul, who had not been with the Lord in the flesh, but also from the other apostles. This he also himself declares, saying at the beginning of his book, 'As they who from the beginning themselves saw and were ministers of the word handed down to us.' The gospel therefore he wrote as he had heard; but the Acts of the Apostles he composed as he had himself seen. He is buried at Constantinople, to which city his bones, with the remains of the apostle Andrew, were translated in the twentieth year of Constantius.[16]

Approximately of this period, and a little later, are the well known lists of the canonical books of the NT.[17] The following will suffice

---

[12]Hardly so, even if he was responsible for all the We-passages.

[13]2 Cor. 8.18; Col. 4.14; 2 Tim. 4.11.

[14]Apostolicorum Πράξεων; Jerome retains the Greek word, though he treats it as if it were masculine or neuter — perhaps thinking of Acta?

[15]Jerome presumably means that Luke brought his work up to date, writing in Rome and, we must infer, in the fourth year of Nero (57–58).

[16]343–344.

[17]For other lists, and for details of the provenance of those given here, see B. F. Westcott, *A General Survey of the History of the Canon of the NT*, London, [7]1896; A. Souter, *The Text and Canon of the NT*, London, 1912; B. M. Metzger, *The Canon of the NT*, Oxford, 1987.

to illustrate the acceptance in the fourth century of a NT identical, or almost identical, with that current today, and of course including Acts. It is not unimportant that its relative position in the lists varies. This probably reflects lingering uncertainty about its purpose if not its place in the Canon.

The Cheltenham (or Mommsenian) List (*c* AD 360).

Four Gospels	Matthew,	2,700 lines (versus)
	Mark,	1,700 lines
	John,	1,800 lines
	Luke,	3,300 lines

All the lines make 10,000 lines[18]
Epistles of Paul, in number 13[19]

The Acts of the Apostles	3,600 lines
The Apocalypse	1,800 lines
Epistles of John, 3 one only (una sola)[20]	350 lines
Epistles of Peter, 2 one only (una sola)[21]	300 lines

In this list the order of the gospels is to be noted. Luke comes last; this may bear witness to a time when the two books, Luke and Acts, were not separated. In this list however Acts does not serve as a visible bridge between the gospels and the apostolic epistles. Compare the Chester Beatty Papyrus, P[45], which contains the gospels in the familiar order and Acts.

Athanasius. The earliest list with contents identical with those of the current NT is contained in the 39th Festal Letter of Athanasius (AD 367). After an introduction, in which he plays on the words of the Preface to Luke (Lk. 1.1–4), and a list of OT books, Athanasius continues:

It is not burdensome to name the books of the NT. There are four gospels, according to Matthew, according to Mark, according to Luke, according to John.[22] Then after these the Acts of the Apostles, the so-called Catholic Epistles of the apostles, seven in number, as follows... . In addition to these there are 14 epistles of Paul the apostle[23] ... And again, John's Apocalypse.

---

[18]The arithmetic is bad, unless the list allows for spaces between the gospels.
[19]Hebrews presumably is omitted.
[20]2 and 3 John were not universally accepted.
[21]2 Peter was not universally accepted; James is missing from this list.
[22]The familiar order, as for example in P[45]; Acts is now separated from Luke.
[23]Hebrews is now included.

Carthage. The same books were approved by the Third Synod of Carthage in AD 397 (Canon 39); it seems that the synod took up a list produced at Hippo Regius in 393.

It was decided that nothing should be read in church under the title of divine Scripture in addition to the canonical Scriptures. These canonical Scriptures are:[24]

Of the NT:
Of the gospels, four books
Of the Acts of the Apostles, one book
Of Paul the apostle, 13 letters
Of the same, to the Hebrews, one[25]
Of the apostle Peter, two
Of John, three
Of James, one
Of Jude, one
Of the Apocalypse of John, one book.

Here Acts precedes the Pauline letters, whereas in Athanasius's list it is adjacent to the letters of James, Peter, John and Jude.

It is unnecessary to go further; those who wish to do so will find in *Begs.* 2.234–245 additional quotations from Jerome and one from Adamantius, also the so-called Monarchian Prologue to Luke, which probably arose from the Priscillianist school, if not from Priscillian himself (d. AD 385). Of these it may be worth while to quote the short passage from Jerome, *Epist.* 53.9: 'The Acts of the Apostles seem, indeed, to express bare history (nudam historiam) and to narrate (texere) the infancy of the newborn church, but if we recognise that the author of Acts is Luke, a doctor, "whose praise is in the Gospel" (2 Cor. 8.18) we perceive that all his words are equally medicines for the sick soul.' Here some attempt is made to assess the purpose and use of the book. It has the appearance of history but has a deeper, religious use.

It will be well now to begin at the other end, starting with the earliest writers, with a view to learning when Acts first came into use and how it was understood by those who used it. Two passages in the NT itself must be considered.

2 Tim. 3.11 refers to persecutions experienced by Paul in Antioch, Iconium, and Lystra. Persecutions in these parts are described in Acts 13; 14. No details are given in 2 Timothy and it is quite possible that the information reached the author by tradition independent of Acts as a written work.

---

[24]An OT list stands first.
[25]Doubt about the authorship of Hebrews lingers and is here clearly implied.

Mk 16.15 records a commission given to his disciples by the risen Jesus; they are to preach to all creation; cf. Acts 1.8. It is foretold in 16.17 that they will speak with new tongues (γλώσσαις καιναῖς); cf. Acts 2.4 (ἑτέραις γλώσσαις); in 16.18 that they will pick up snakes without being harmed; cf. Acts 28.3–6; in 16.19 it is said that Jesus was taken up into heaven (ἀνελήμφθη εἰς τὸν οὐρανόν) and sat down at the right hand of God; cf. Acts 1.9–11 (ὁ ἀναλημφθεὶς ἀφ'ὑμῶν εἰς τὸν οὐρανόν); 2.33. Mk 16.9–20 (the 'long ending') is not an original part of the gospel; it was probably added in the second century, having already been in existence for some time.[26] It cannot be said to do more than prove the existence of traditions similar and parallel to those of Acts.

1 Clement. None of the passages alleged points unambiguously to knowledge of Acts; they reflect rather common use of more or less stereotyped language. The most important are the following.
2.1   Giving more gladly than receiving. Cf. Acts 20.35, where Paul claims to be quoting a saying of Jesus. An independent tradition of such a saying, whether genuine or not, could have reached Clement independently of Acts. There are also Greek parallels to the saying, which increase the possibility of complete independence. Here and elsewhere the possibility of parallel but independent traditions must always be borne in mind.
5.4   To his appointed place (εἰς τὸν ὀφειλόμενον τόπον); 5.7, to the holy place (εἰς τὸν ἅγιον τόπον). Cf. Acts 1.25 — though one may suppose that Judas did not go to the same place as Peter and Paul. Cf. Ignatius, *Magnesians* 5.1; Polycarp 9.2; Hermas, *Similitude* 9.27.3. The phrase was evidently in common use.
18.1   I have found a man after my own heart (κατὰ τὴν καρδίαν μου), David the son of Jesse, I anointed him with everlasting mercy. Ps. 89.21 and 1 Sam. 13.14 are combined, as at Acts 13.22. The composite quotation could be drawn from Acts, or possibly from a Testimony Book. It is against dependence on Acts that the passage in 1 Clement continues quite differently.
59.2   From darkness into light. Cf. Acts 26.18, but also 1 Peter 2.9; the image is too obvious to prove anything.
Other passages that have been cited include 2.2; 6.3; 12.2; 14.1 (see 2 Clement 4.4); 17.1. That Acts was known to Clement is not impossible, but is by no means proved.

Didache. Again, there is enough to hint at some shared traditions; no more.

---

[26]See for example C. E. B. Cranfield, *The Gospel according to St Mark*, Cambridge, ²1963, 472.

4.8   You shall have all things common (συγκοινωνήσεις) with your brother and you shall not say that things are your own. Cf. Acts 2.44; 4.32; but also Barnabas 19.8 (in Barnabas's version of the Two Ways). Many churches may have observed this practice.
9.2; 10.2 Jesus is described as *servant* (παῖς). The word is used at Acts 3.13, 26; 4.27, 30; 1 Clement 59.2–4.
More important than verbal parallels is the Didache's picture of travelling apostles and prophets (*Did.* 10.7; 11.3–12; 13.1–3).

Barnabas. There is no convincing evidence of literary connection.
7.2   Christ will judge the living and the dead (κρίνειν ζῶντας καὶ νεκρούς). Cf. Acts 10.42, but see also 2 Clem. 1.1 and Polycarp 2.1; the thought is a commonplace.
19.8   comes from the Two Ways and is parallel to *Did.* 4.8; see above. Compare also 5.9 (Acts 1.1 D); 16.2.

Ignatius. There is no convincing evidence of literary connection.
Magnesians 5.1   Each one shall go his own place (εἰς τὸν ἴδιον τόπον). Cf. 1 Clement 5.4 (see above).
Philadelphians 2.1f. Where the shepherd (ποιμήν) is, there do you follow as sheep. For many wolves ... Cf. Acts 20.28, 29; the imagery is too widespread to be significant.
Smyrnaeans 3.3.   After his resurrection he ate and drank with them (συνέφαγεν αὐτοῖς καὶ συνέπιεν). Cf. Acts 10.41 (also 1.4); also Lk. 24.30, 35, 42, 43; Jn 21.12, 13. Ignatius is probably not using the canonical NT; Jerome (*De Viris Illustribus* 2) notes that in 3.2 Ignatius has quoted 'evangelium quod appellatur secundum Hebraeos, et quod a me nuper in Graecum Latinumque sermonem translatum est, quo et Origenes saepe utitur'.

Polycarp. There is a somewhat stronger case here for knowledge of Acts; Polycarp can hardly be said to quote and certainly does not appeal to Acts as an authority, but his language may have been subconsciously affected by it. This may supply a terminus ante quem for Acts.
1.2   Whom God raised up, having loosed the pangs of Hades (λύσας τὰς ὠδῖνας τοῦ ᾅδου). Cf. Acts 2.24 (λύσας τὰς ὠδῖνας τοῦ θανάτου), quoting the same Psalm (17.6) and making the same mistranslation of חבלי. Where Acts has ἀνέστησεν, Polycarp has ἤγειρεν. It is possible that Acts and Polycarp may be dependent on the same Christian collection of OT texts.
2.1   Judge of the living and the dead. Cf. Acts 10.42, but cf. also Barnabas 7.2 (see above).
2.3   Cf. Acts 20.35.
3.2   recalls that Paul had visited Philippi; cf. Acts 16.12–40.
6.3   The prophets who proclaimed beforehand the coming of the

Lord (οἱ προκηρύξαντες τὴν ἔλευσιν τοῦ κυρίου). Cf. Acts 7.52 (τοὺς προκαταγγείλαντας περὶ τῆς ἐλεύσεως τοῦ κυρίου). The wording is not identical and the thought is commonplace, but recollection is not impossible.

12.2 May he give you a lot and share among his saints (det vobis sortem et partem inter sanctos suos), and to us with you, and to all who are under heaven (sub caelo). Cf. Acts 26.18 (κλῆρον ἐν τοῖς ἡγιασμένοις); 8.21 (οὐκ ἐστίν σοι μερὶς οὐδὲ κλῆρος); 2.5 (ἀπὸ παντὸς ἔθνους τῶν ὑπὸ τὸν οὐρανόν). The collocation of *sors*, *pars*, and *sancti* is suggestive, though not conclusive.

All the passages cited fall within what may be regarded as probably the later of the two epistles contained in the so-called Epistle of Polycarp,[27] to be dated *c*. AD 135.

2 Clement. A few passages may be regarded as possible, but quite uncertain, allusions.

1.1 Cf. Acts 10.42; also Barnabas 7.2. The phrase is too obvious to be convincing as an allusion to Acts.

4.4 We ought not to fear men but rather God. This is somewhat closer to Acts 4.19; 5.29 than is 1 Clement 14.1; but the wording differs and the thought is relatively commonplace.

20.5 To him who sent to us the Saviour and Prince of incorruption (τὸν σωτῆρα καὶ ἀρχηγὸν τῆς ἀφθαρσίας). Cf. Acts 3.15; 5.31. But Heb. 2.10 is enough to show that ἀρχηγός was a word used in more than one line of Christological development.

It would be in no way surprising that many Christians in the middle of the second century should have so much in common.

Hermas. There is no convincing evidence of literary connection. *Vision* 4.2.4; ... by no other can you be saved but through the great and glorious name. Cf. Acts 4.12.

Mandate 4.3.4 The Lord is a searcher of hearts (καρδιογνώστης). Cf. Acts 1.24; 15.8. καρδιογνώστης is a rare word, but evidently was coming into use among Christians.

Similitude 9.27.3 Cf. 1 Clement 5.4, etc.

Similitude 9.28.2 Those who suffered for the name (οἱ παθόντες ὑπὲρ τοῦ ὀνόματος) of the Son of God. Cf. Acts 5.41.

Papias. There is no evidence that Papias knew Acts (or the Third Gospel). His account of the fate of Judas Iscariot[28] is independent of that in Acts 1.18, 19.

---

[27]See P. N. Harrison, *Polycarp's Two Epistles to the Philippians*, Cambridge, 1936; Altaner (51). L. W. Barnard (*Studies in the Apostolic Fathers and their Background*, Oxford, 1966, 31–9), however, places the later letter *c*. 120.
[28]M. J. Routh, *Reliquiae Sacrae*, Vol. I, Oxford, ²1846, p. 9.

The Epistle to Diognetus contains a sentence (3.4) reminiscent of Acts 17.24f.: He that made heaven and earth and all the things that are in them and supplies to us all the things we need, would not himself be in need (προσδέοιτο) of those things which he himself provides for those who suppose that they give them [to him]. The argument is commonplace and cannot be used to prove that the writer was drawing on the Areopagus speech, though the thought certainly is parallel. See below on Justin (in whose works the epistle was formerly reckoned).

Epistula Apostolorum is of approximately the same date as the *Epistle to Diognetus*.[29] On the whole it seems probable that the author knew Acts, though in every passage that can be adduced there are differences from Acts, some of them substantial, so that one must infer either considerable editorial freedom or the use of different (though related) traditions. The evidence is as follows.[30]

3 ... our Lord and Redeemer Jesus Christ is God the Son of God, who was sent of God the Lord of the whole world, the maker and creator *of it,* ... that sitteth ... at the right hand of the throne of the Father . . . Cf. Acts 2.33; 5.31. But in this paragraph there is more that recalls John than Acts; '... the Son ... sent ... the word become flesh ... not of the will (lust) of the flesh, but by the will of God'.

15   Now when the Passover (Easter, pascha) cometh, one of you shall be cast into prison for my name's sake; and he will be in grief and sorrow, because ye keep the Easter while he is in prison and separated from you, for he will be sorrowful because he keepeth not Easter with you. And I will send my power in the form of mine angel Gabriel, and the doors of the prison shall open. And he shall come forth and come unto you and keep the night-watch with you until the cock crow. And when ye have accomplished the memorial which is made of me, and the Agape (love-feast), he shall again be cast into prison for a testimony, until he shall come out thence and preach that which I have delivered unto you.

This recalls the narrative of Acts 12, in that it relates that at Passover time an apostle is imprisoned, and released by an angel. It differs in that the apostle is not named, is said to be sad because he is not keeping Easter with his colleagues, who are observing the eucharist or agape, and returns to prison after his release. Is the

---

[29]Altaner's date, 'um 170?' (p. 125), seems as late as anyone is willing to go; H. Lietzmann, *The Founding of the Church Universal*, London, 1938, p. 120, says *c.* 140 or *c.* 170; most approximate at the middle of the second century, but R. M. Grant, *Greek Apologists of the Second Century* 1988, 178, suggests 'the late second century or the early third'.

[30]The translation of the *Epistula Apostolorum* is taken from M. R. James, *The Apocryphal NT*, Oxford, 1924.

author elaborating what he has read in Acts or using a different account? No confident answer can be given to this question.

16   I shall come upon earth to judge the quick and the dead. Cf. Barnabas 7.2, above.

18   ... ye shall see me, how I go up unto my Father which is in heaven. But behold, now, I give unto you a new commandment: Love one another and obey one another, that peace may rule alway among you. Love your enemies, and what ye would not that man do unto you, that do unto no man.

That the apostles are to witness the ascension (see 51, below) recalls Acts 1.9–11; in other respects this passage is more reminiscent of John. The negative form of the Golden Rule recalls the Western text of Acts 15.20, 29, but the Rule was too widely used for this to be important.

31   And behold a man shall meet you, whose name is Saul, which being interpreted is Paul: he is a Jew, circumcised according to the law, and he shall receive my voice from heaven with fear and terror and trembling. And his eyes shall be blinded, and by your hands by the sign of the cross shall they be protected (healed: *other Eth. MSS.* with spittle by your hands shall his eyes, etc.). Do ye unto him all that I have done unto you. Deliver it (? the word of God) unto the other. And at the same time that man shall open his eyes and praise the Lord, even my Father which is in heaven. He shall obtain power among the people and shall preach and instruct; and many that hear him shall obtain glory and be redeemed. But thereafter shall men be wroth with him and deliver him into the hands of his enemies, and he shall bear witness before kings that are mortal, and his end shall be that he shall turn unto me, whereas he persecuted me *at the first.* He shall preach and teach and abide with the elect, as a chosen vessel and a wall that shall not be overthrown, *yea,* the last of the last shall become a preacher unto the Gentiles, made perfect by the will of my Father. Like as ye have learned from the Scripture that your fathers the prophets spake of me, and in me it is indeed fulfilled.

And he said unto us: Be ye also therefore guides unto them; and all things that I said unto you, and ye write concerning me (tell ye them), that I am the word of the Father and that the Father is in me. Such also shall ye be unto that man, as becometh you. Instruct him and bring to his mind that which is spoken of me in the Scripture and is fulfilled, and thereafter shall he become the salvation of the Gentiles.

This is the crucial passage. The parallels with Acts are evident, but there is a great deal which the author has, at the least, re-expressed in his own words. It is probably correct to say that the passage is not so close to Acts as to *require* dependence, but that it is quite close enough to be consistent with dependence.

33   When shall we meet with that man, and when wilt thou depart unto thy Father and our God and Lord? He answered and said unto us: That man will come out of the land of Cilicia unto Damascus of Syria, to root up the church which ye must found there. It is I that speak through you; and he shall come quickly: and he shall become strong in the faith, that the word of the prophet may be fulfilled, which saith: Behold, out of Syria will I begin to call together a new Jerusalem, and Sion will I subdue unto me, and it shall be taken, and the place which is childless shall be called the son and daughter of my Father, and my bride. For so hath it pleased him that sent me. But the man will I turn back, that he accomplish not his evil desire, and the praise of my Father shall be perfected in him, and after that I am gone home and abide with my Father, I will speak unto him from heaven, and all things shall be accomplished which I have told you before concerning him.

In Acts Paul travels to Damascus to persecute the church not from Cilicia (Tarsus) but from Jerusalem. The author may have drawn a thoughtless and unwarranted inference from 'Saul of Tarsus'; or he may have had another source of information.

44   Whoso shall abide outside the sheepfold, him will the wolves devour.

Cf. Acts 20.29; but again the *Epistle* is at least as near to John as to Acts.

51   As he so spake, there was thunder and lightning and an earthquake, and the heavens parted asunder, and there appeared a light (bright) cloud which bore him up. And *there came* voices of many angels, rejoicing and singing praises and saying: Gather us, O Priest, unto the light of the majesty. And when they drew nigh unto the firmament, we heard his voice *saying unto us*: Depart hence in peace.

Cf. Acts 1.9–11, with which the central statement agrees. The additional details may point to the use of other sources, or may be free elaboration in accordance with the author's taste.

Polycrates of Ephesus wrote to Victor of Rome in AD 191. The letter is quoted in Eusebius, *HE* 5.2.4. The first of the following quotations shows local tradition which has not been assimilated to Acts. It is impossible to build on the second a case for knowledge of Acts.

5.24.2 ... Philip, one of the twelve apostles, who sleeps in Hierapolis, and his two daughters who grew old as virgins. And his other daughter having lived in the Holy Spirit rests in Ephesus.
The statement recalls Acts 21.8f., but differs in almost every detail.
5.24.7 For greater men than I have said, We must obey God rather than men (πειθαρχεῖν δεῖ θεῷ μᾶλλον ἢ ἀνθρώποις).
The wording agrees exactly with Acts 5.29, but the substance of the saying is much older than Acts.

Justin, who died a martyr in *c.* AD 165, is a key figure in the second century story of Acts. Did he know and use Acts? If he knew it, what did he think of it? It is well known that he took little or no notice of Paul and his writings, and that though he may well have known the Fourth Gospel he does not build upon it.[31] The evidence in regard to Acts must be set out.

1 *Apology*
39.3 From Jerusalem there went out into the world men, twelve in number, and they uninstructed (ἰδιῶται), unable to speak, but by the power of God they indicated (ἐμήνυσαν) to the whole human race that they had been sent by Christ to teach all men the word of God.

The word ἰδιῶται immediately suggests Acts 4.13; the clause that follows, λαλεῖν μὴ δυνάμενοι, may perhaps represent ἀγράμματοι. If it does, however, it would mean that Justin was not setting out to quote, but was recollecting the sense of what he had read, or perhaps heard from some other source. Acts does not say that the twelve apostles went out into the world; in 8.1 they alone stay in Jerusalem, and in ch. 15 they are still there. They are however bidden in 1.8 to act as witnesses up to the end of the earth.[32]

40.6, 11 The prophetic Spirit signifies (μηνύει) the alliance that took place between Herod the king of the Jews, the Jews themselves, and Pilate your [the Romans'] governor over them, together with his soldiers, against the Christ ... Why did the heathen rage, etc. (Ps. 2.1–12).

---

[31] *St John*, pp. 64f., 111.
[32] E. F. Osborn, *Justin Martyr* Tübingen, 1973, p. 167, stresses the importance of Isa. 2.3, but though this OT prophecy may have been important for Justin it is not used in Acts.

Acts 4.25, 26 quotes the same Psalm, or rather the first two verses of it, and sees it fulfilled in the joint action of Herod and Pontius Pilate, σὺν ἔθνεσιν καὶ λαοῖς Ἰσραήλ (4.27). Justin does not refer to Acts, though it may be that he borrowed the quotation; Christians however were busily engaged in scouring the OT for texts which they could claim had been fulfilled in the gospel story, and Luke may not have been the only one to find this one.

49.5 Those who came from the Gentiles, though they had never heard a thing about the Christ until his apostles who went out from Jerusalem signified the things concerning him and handed on the prophecies, were filled with joy and faith, said goodbye to their idols, and committed themselves to the ingenerate God.

There is here a distant resemblance to Paul's Areopagus speech (Acts 17.22–31), but that speech does not use the title Christ, saying only that God has raised from the dead one who will act as judge; it contains nothing about the prophecies, and does not seem to have led to much joy and faith. The passage does not disprove that Justin had read Acts; neither does it prove it. Paul was not one of the apostles who went out from Jerusalem.

50.12 So after he had been crucified even all his friends deserted him, but subsequently, when he had risen from the dead and appeared to them and had taught them to give attention to the prophecies, in which it had been foretold that all these things would happen, and when they had seen him ascending into heaven and had believed and had received the power sent thence from him to them, and had gone to the whole human race, they taught these things and were called apostles.

The only part of this passage that suggests a particular connection with Acts is the statement that men called apostles saw Jesus ascend into heaven. In Justin's time the ascension was well on the way to becoming an established part of the baptismal creed, which every Christian must have known, and it could hardly be asserted that it happened without the implication that some had seen it happen; and if not the apostles, who?

2 Apology
10.6 He encouraged them to recognise God, a God to them unknown (τοῦ ἀγνώστου αὐτοῖς).

The word ἄγνωστος recalls Acts 17.23, but it is placed on the lips of Socrates, and is insufficient to prove use of Acts.

Trypho

20.3f. This passage is too long to quote, and its wording is not related to Acts. It shows however that Justin was aware of a problem about foods. There are food regulations in the OT which Christians do not observe. Why do they disobey God's command? Justin claims that the commands were given to the Jews as a punishment for their sin in making the golden calf. Why, if he knew Acts and regarded it as authoritative, did he make no use of 10.14 or 15.29?

60.1 Trypho and Justin speak of the story of Moses and the burning bush. According to Trypho, it was an angel who appeared in a flame of fire (ὁ ὀφθεὶς ἐν φλογὶ πυρός), but God who spoke with Moses, so that both an angel and God, the two together (δύο ὁμοῦ ὄντας), were involved in the vision at that time.

It is unlikely that this is dependent on Acts 7.30, though there is some parallelism of language: ὤφθη αὐτῷ ... ἄγγελος ἐν φλογὶ πυρὸς βάτου. The OT itself refers to an angel (Exod. 3.2).

68.5 Ps. 131 (132).11; 2 Kdms 7.12–16; 1 Kdms 2.8 are combined more or less as at Acts 2.30.

80.3 I choose rather not to follow men or human teachings, but God and the teachings that come from him.

Cf. Acts 4.19; 5.29; but Justin is speaking of teachings, doctrines, the apostles of commands.

108.2 They deceive men, saying that he has risen from the dead and ascended into heaven (εἰς οὐρανὸν ἀνεληλυθέναι).

Cf. Acts 1.9–11; (Lk. 24.51). Reference to Acts is possible but not necessary.

118.1 This Christ is the judge of all the living and the dead. Cf. Barnabas 7.2 (above).

131.3 recalls Acts 13.17, but both are dependent on the OT.

This evidence is not easy to assess. Much has been made of Justin's emphasis on the role of the twelve apostles as missionaries sent out from Jerusalem into all the world, and the correspondence of this with Acts 1.8. There is force in this observation, but there would be a great deal more if Acts had described a world-wide mission on the part of the twelve; in fact, Peter travels as far as Caesarea, and nothing is said of any missionary work on the part of any other apostle. It is hard to see how anyone so deeply interested in the church's universal mission could, if he knew and valued Acts, have completely ignored the work of Paul. The use in this connection of the word ἰδιῶται is striking, and so is the statement that the apostles saw Christ ascend into heaven. But ἰδιώτηs (see LS 819, s.v. III) is widely used for men untrained or unskilled, and by Justin's time a bodily (and therefore visible) ascension was becoming an article of faith.

To prove the negative assertion, that Justin was totally unfamiliar with Acts, is impossible; but if he knew it he made little use of it, and made some statements that cannot easily be harmonised with it.[32a]

After Justin's time Acts moves steadily into the recognition that we have noticed in Eusebius and later writers.

Muratorian Canon is explicit. It is at least a generation later than Justin; c. 180–200. In the following lines a text occasionally restored by conjecture is translated.

2–8 The third book of the gospel, according to Luke, Luke the Physician[33] composed in his own name on the basis of respect[34] after the ascension of Christ, when Paul had taken him with him as a travelling companion.[35] Neither did he himself see the Lord in the flesh,[36] and so wrote as he could find out (what happened). And so he began to write from the birth of John.

34–39 The Acts of all the apostles were written in one book. Luke compiled for 'Most Excellent Theophilo'[37] the several things that were done in his presence, as he plainly shows by the omission of the passion of Peter and the departure of Paul from the city[38] when he set out for Spain.

Notwithstanding his special association with Paul, Luke is said to have written the Acts of *all* the apostles. This is certainly not a correct description of the book, and probably indicates a special

---

[32a]See further, O. Skarsaune, *The Proof from Prophecy* (Supp NovT 56; 1987), 104f.

[33]Cf. Col. 4.14.

[34]So Cadbury, *Begs.* 2.211; Latin, ex opinione.

[35]Reading socium itineris, for the MS iuris studiosum; the emendation has the advantage of agreement with the We-passages in Acts.

[36]Neither, Latin nec; the MS, which lacks the opening lines, probably made the same statement about Mark.

[37]Optimo Theophilo; the adjective is used in the gospel (Lk. 1.3) but not in Acts.

[38]Rome is clearly intended; this is probably an indication that the list was drawn up in Rome.

motivation on the part of the author. The book shows, or is alleged to show, the unity of the whole apostolic company.

The Martyrs of Lyons and Vienne. The contemporary account of the martyrdoms, written at the same time as, or perhaps a little earlier than, the Muratorian Canon, is contained in Eusebius, *H.E.* 5.1 and 2, and shows unmistakable knowledge of Acts. The use made of the language of Acts shows that the suffering church was able to recognise its own experiences in the story of events that happened more than 100 years previously.

1.15   They were cut to the heart (διεπρίοντο) against us. Cf. Acts 5.37; 7.54.

1.26   How should such people eat children, for whom it is not allowed to eat even the blood of irrational creatures? Cf. Acts 15.29.

1.49   All the remainder were added (προσετέθησαν) to the church. Cf. Acts 2.41, 47; 11.24.

1.60   They gnashed their teeth (ἔβρυχον τοὺς ὀδόντας) against them. Cf. Acts 7.54.

2.3   ... Prince of the life of God (... ἀρχηγῷ τῆς ζωῆς τοῦ θεοῦ). Cf. Acts 3.15; 5.31.
    ... that earnest prayers (ἐκτενεῖς εὐχαί) might be made. Cf. Acts 12.5.

2.5   They prayed for those who were treating them cruelly, as did Stephen, the perfect martyr (*or* witness, μάρτυς), Lord, do not let this sin stand against them (Κύριε, μὴ στήσῃς αὐτοῖς τὴν ἁμαρτίαν ταύτην). Cf. Acts 7.60. This passage proves beyond question knowledge of Acts, and confirms the impression made by the others.

Irenaeus (*c.* 130–200) is by far the most important witness in this period. He frequently refers to Acts and quotes the book at length. Only a selection of the evidence can be given here.

Adversus Haereses

1.6.3   [Heretics] eat articles of food sacrificed to idols (idolothyta), thinking that they will in no way be defiled by them. Cf. Acts 15.29; 21.25.

1.23.1, 2   Irenaeus tells the story of Simon Magus, drawing freely on the narrative of Acts 8 and in fact quoting 8.9, 10, 11, 20, 21, 23.

1.26.3   The Nicolaitans have as their teacher Nicolas, one of the seven first ordained to the diaconate by the apostles. Cf. Acts 6.1–6.

2.32.3 Magicians prove themselves to be 'not like Jesus our Lord, but like Simon Magus'. Knowledge of Acts 8 is assumed. The same paragraph goes on to say that the Lord was received up into heaven in the sight of his disciples; cf. Acts 1.9–11.

3.1.1 [The apostles] were endued with power from on high when the Holy Spirit came upon them; they were filled with all things (i.e., all spiritual gifts) and had perfect knowledge; they went out into the ends of the earth.

This can hardly not be based on Acts 1.7, 8. Irenaeus goes on to say that the apostles all proclaim one God and one Christ.

Luke, the follower of Paul (sectator Pauli), set down in a book the Gospel proclaimed by him.

Here Irenaeus treats the Third Gospel separately from Acts.

3.12.1 Irenaeus at this point begins to introduce material which is undoubtedly drawn from Acts, though he does not specify his source. The chapter begins

The apostle Peter, wishing, after the Lord's resurrection and his taking up into heaven, to make up the number of the twelve apostles and to elect by lot another chosen by God, said to those who were present . . .

Here and in what follows use is made of Acts 1.16, 17; 2.4, 13, 15–17, 22–27, 29, 30–36, 37, 38; 3.2, 6–8, 12–26; 4.8–12, 22, 24–28.

3.12.5 For then neither Valentinus nor Marcion was present, nor the rest of these subverters [of truth], nor those who agree with them. Therefore God the Maker of all things heard them [that is, heard the apostles in their prayer]. References to Acts 4.31, 33; 5.30–32, 42 follow.

In the rest of 3.12 there are references to the following chapters in Acts 7; 8; 9; 10; 14; 15; 17.

3.13.3 If then, on the basis of the Acts of the Apostles, anyone carefully studies the time concerning which it is written that he [Paul] went up to Jerusalem on account of the question mentioned above,[39] he will find those years previously mentioned by Paul to be in agreement. Thus Paul's statement is in agreement and as it were

[39]Irenaeus has spoken of the meeting described in Gal. 2.

identical with Luke's testimony concerning the apostles.

Irenaeus is here using a particular historical example to illustrate the unity that existed between Paul and the other apostles — an important point in his argument against heretics.

3.14.1 But that this Luke was inseparable from Paul and his fellow-worker in the Gospel, he himself makes clear, not boasting about it but moved by the truth itself.

Irenaeus is arguing, and continues to argue, on two fronts: first, that Paul is not the sole source of apostolic truth (as Marcionites maintained), and, secondly, that he was in agreement with the other apostles (and was not to be rejected, as by the Ebionites). Acts was an important support of both contentions.

3.15.1 Irenaeus here argues at some length that Ebionites have no right to accept material from Luke's gospel if they are unwilling to accept from Acts Luke's account of Paul's divine vocation and authorisation. He adds that the teaching of the apostles is clear and firm and holds nothing back, since they did not teach one set of truths in private (in abscondito) and another in public.

4.23.2 Irenaeus gives a full account of Philip and the Ethiopian Eunuch (Acts 8).

It is clear that Irenaeus found Acts useful in his reply to the heretics against whom he wrote. The only question that remains to be raised (but not at this point fully discussed) is the relation between Acts and Marcion, which is of prime importance for the understanding of the origin of Acts and its progress through the second century into the canon of the NT. The position has at least the outward appearance of paradox. The only gospel that Marcion used was a mutilated version[40] of Luke; but he did not use Acts, which was in fact used against him by Irenaeus and Tertullian.[41] For Marcion, Paul was the one true apostle and source of Christian doctrine; Acts contains a long and laudatory account of the work of Paul; but Marcion did not use Acts. It is indeed arguable[42] that Marcion replaced Acts by his *Antitheses*.

---

[40]J. Knox, *Marcion and the NT*, Chicago, 1942, holds that Marcion's form of Luke was the primitive one, which was subsequently expanded in an Anti-Marcionite sense.

[41]Tertullian refers to Acts much less frequently than might be expected in an Anti-Marcionite writer.

[42]C. K. Barrett in *FS Borgen*, 31f.

Early second century evidence for the existence of Acts is scanty and uncertain, but it should not be inferred that the book was not written before the middle of that century. There is evidence enough to prove that it was known by then, and not as a recently produced work. At this point it is relevant to recall those passages in Acts which show familiarity with the Roman provinces as they were in the first century and not as they became in the second.[43] Acts was known; but it is doubtful whether the church in the first half of the second century knew what to do with it.

---

[43]The evidence is to be found mainly in the later chapters of Acts; see the second volume of this commentary.

III. ACTS 1–14: SOURCES AND PLAN

The part of Acts dealt with in this volume begins in Jerusalem; it ends (14.28) in Antioch, where Paul and Barnabas report to the local Christians, themselves a mixed group of Jews and Gentiles, the success of their missionary tour among the partly Gentile communities of Asia Minor. God had opened a door of faith to the Gentiles. There can be little doubt (and this is confirmed in various ways by chs. 15–28) that it was Luke's intention in these opening chapters to describe a decisive step by which the faith of a group of Jews, and the Gospel that had been committed to them, were communicated to men who were of a different religious and racial background. This fact, sufficiently evident in itself, is made explicit in 1.8, where Jesus sends his witnesses from Jerusalem to Judaea, Samaria, and to the end of the earth. A quick reading of the text confirms the picture of progressive expansion. The Gospel is preached in Jerusalem; by 5.16 it has become known in the surrounding cities (that is, the cities of Judaea); in 8.5 it has reached the (or, a) city of Samaria. In the latter part of ch. 8 a devout Ethiopian, in ch. 10 a devout Roman, are converted. The former event passes without comment, though it is made clear that it is the direct consequence of the direction of the Holy Spirit; the latter leads to the conclusion on the part of the Christians of Jerusalem, Why then, to the Gentiles also God has granted the repentance that leads to life (11.18). Almost immediately (11.20) we hear of the evangelisation in Antioch of Greeks — non-Jews, a proceeding which receives the approval and participation of Barnabas, the representative of the mother church in Jerusalem.

The question of the relation of Gentiles to the Gospel, and through the Gospel to the Jewish people, is discussed in ch. 15, and thereafter the Gentile mission continues without hindrance, though the Decree that emanates from the Council in 15.29 is repeated in 21.25. This Decree is of fundamental importance for an understanding of Luke's view of the Gospel and the church, but it is not to be discussed here. It suffices to observe that in chs. 1–14 Luke has established the Gentile mission as a fact; it is not without problems and calls for regulation, but it is never called in question except by those whose opinion can be virtually ignored, and after deliberation by the apostles and elders it is energetically pursued and in the end reaches Rome itself.

It is when the first fourteen chapters are read with greater care that problems and difficulties appear. These are noted in the Commentary;

some of the most important may be mentioned here. Who were the Hellenists (6.1; cf. 9.29; 11.20)? Does the use of this term in 6.1 imply that the Gospel had already been preached to Gentiles? What of the Ethiopian? He was not a Jew; he was not a proselyte; if he could be converted and baptised what becomes of the importance of Cornelius? In the Cornelius story, what is the meaning of Peter's vision? Does it refer to food, or to people? If it does refer to food, does it not contradict the Decree, since it sets no limits to permitted food? If it refers to people, how far does it go? Does it permit preaching to Gentiles (who, if converted, must subsequently obey certain rules), or unrestricted intercourse with them? If the conclusion of the discussion that follows (11.18) means what it says, does it not make the debate arising out of 15.1, 5 pointless?

And what of Paul, who is introduced in 9.15 as one who will bear Christ's name before the Gentiles, and, from ch. 13 onwards, will be described as the leading missionary to the Gentiles? No sooner is he introduced than he is supplanted by Peter, whom Luke evidently regards as the first if not the greatest missionary to the Gentiles (15.7).

These questions are raised here because they bear on both the plan and the sources of acts. Many attempts have been made to present literary and historical analyses of Acts, whose author may be supposed to have planned his book in terms either of artistic literary criteria or of historical development — or of a combination of both. All such attempts run into difficulty when confronted by the questions that have been mentioned, and others like them. The following facts must be borne in mind. (1) The author was not present at the events narrated in chs. 1–14. If he was Luke, the companion of Paul, he first, on his own showing, enters the story at 16.10, the first occurrence in narrative of the second person plural.[1] Reports of earlier events must have come to him second-hand (at best). If he was not one of Paul's travelling companions, he stands at an even greater distance from the earlier events. (2) The entry of Gentiles into the church was accompanied by severe problems and bitter controversy. This is clearly proved by the Pauline epistles, but there is little sign of it in Acts. (3) It is a priori improbable that the development of the Gentile mission proceeded everywhere at the same speed and through the same stages. It is equally improbable that anyone in Jerusalem, or in other Christian centres, was aware of what was happening in all the other Christian centres.

The question of Luke's plan and the question of Luke's sources must be considered in relation to each other. There is no doubt that one of his primary interests was the extension of the Gospel to the Gentiles. It is a hypothesis worth pursuing that he made it his

[1]On 'We' in 11.28 see the note.

business to collect stories of early contacts with Gentiles wherever he could find them. He had four main sources of supply.

(1) Whatever we make of the historical value of 21.8, the verse claims, on the author's part, some contact with Philip the Evangelist. Even if the contact was less direct than a surface reading of the verse suggests, the author had access to traditions about, perhaps emanating from, Philip — we may again add, so as not to claim too much, whatever their historical value. These provided him with the stories of the Samaritan city (8.4–8[2]) and of the Ethiopian (8.26–40). The Samaritans were at best not full Jews; the Ethiopian was no Jew at all.

(2) The reference to Philip in 21.8 is also a reference to Caesarea; and Caesarea, as a place where Philip is found, is mentioned also at 8.40.[3] The author so wrote as to claim contact with Caesarea; he had been there. It does not seem a wild guess that (even if his contact was something less than that of a travelling companion in Acts 21) he should have asked the Christians there how their church (certainly, at the time when he was in contact with it, a mixed Jewish and Gentile church) had come into being, and that they told him about Cornelius — perhaps a very much shorter and simpler story than that which he tells in ch. 10, but with enough of Peter in it to lead him to introduce the story of a vision of clean and unclean beasts, which he had picked up elsewhere.

(3) Ancient tradition made Luke a native of Antioch;[4] this may or may not be true; it is clear from his book that he was aware of Antioch as an important Christian centre, and in particular that it was one of the bases from which Paul conducted his missions. The whole of the tour described in chs. 13, 14 was carried out under the auspices of the church of Antioch, which both commissioned the missionaries and received their report (13.3; 14.27f.), and subsequently sent them to Jerusalem to discuss the position of Gentiles (15.2). It is certain that Luke received traditional material from Antioch, and that the account that the Antiochenes gave of the origin of their church included the claim that almost from the beginning the Gentiles had been included.

(4) The author of Acts either was a companion of Paul, or represented himself as one, or drew on the memories of one. It is even more certain that he was an admirer of Paul, and that his admiration included the belief that Paul was a notable missionary to the Gentile world. Whether his connection with Paul was close or remote, immediate or second- or third-hand, he clearly used what information

---

[2]Possibly also 8.9–25, but the story about Simon Magus may come from a different source.

[3]There are further references to Caesarea at 9.30; 10.1, 24; 11.11; 12.19; 18.22; 21.16; 23.23, 33; 25.1, 4, 6, 13. There is no doubt that Luke was interested in Caesarea.

[4]So e.g. Jerome, *de Viris Illustribus* 7; p.32 above.

he could get from Pauline sources; and, though he seems not to have used the epistles, we may conclude from them that Pauline information must have included material bearing on the inclusion of the Gentiles and perhaps on the problems that arose from this step.

These were sources of information,[5] and their use provided not only information but at the same time the broad outline of the first part of Acts. Luke's first task was to lay a foundation in Jerusalem,[6] showing as well as he could what the apostles had had to say to their fellow Jews, how the church was constituted, and how it fulfilled the Lord's precept of love. After this he proceeded to give various examples — possibly all the examples he knew — of ways in which the Gospel was taken to the heathen. It was natural to begin with the Samaritans, who stood closest to Judaism; and one story about Philip carried the other with it. Next, in view of 15.7, the story of Peter and Cornelius had to be placed. It was a pity that the Roman centurion had to be preceded by the Ethiopian chancellor, but not so great a pity as to lead Luke to separate the two Philip stories. After that came the story of Antioch, and, arising out of it, the story of the first Pauline mission. They were neither artistic nor chronological considerations that determined Luke's plan; he simply presents a handful of sallies into the pagan world.

This does not cover the whole of Luke's story. What of the conversion of Paul and the immediately following events (9.1–30)? It is clear that the conversion of Paul was to Luke, who narrates it three times, an event of very great importance. He places it where he does because he wishes to represent Paul as the successor of Stephen (cf. 22.20) and perhaps as the colleague of Philip, but he does not in ch. 9 give any serious account of missionary work conducted by Paul because he knows also the tradition (15.7) that it was Peter who began the mission outside Judaism, as well as other independent stories about Peter (9.32–43; 12.3-19).

There is also a connecting line that runs back from the founding of the church in Antioch (11.19f.) to the persecution over Stephen (8.1–3) and the appointment of the Seven (6.1). It is probable that this was part of Antiochene tradition. The earliest churches founded outside Jerusalem would wish to show that they had valid contacts with the original Jerusalem church. Samaria had Philip, but (it may be) thought it well to supplement that contact by the account of a visit from Peter and John. Caesarea could appeal to Peter himself, and so perhaps did Lydda and Joppa. Antioch made the most it could of a somewhat remote connection with the first martyr, adding Barnabas

---

[5]Not necessarily literary sources.
[6]I shall return to the question what sources Luke may have used for this purpose; see below, pp. 53f.

— and Saul too, though he may have fallen out of favour and been replaced by Peter (cf. Gal. 2.13).

It is probably better at this stage to think of traditions, without specifying their form, than of written or even oral sources, if oral sources are understood as verbally fixed. Two theories of written sources, one dealing entirely, the other mainly, with material in chs. 1–14, should however be briefly considered. Both were given classical formulation by Harnack,[7] though there have been many subsequent contributions to the debate.[8]

The first is based on observations made in chs. 2–5, which, it is maintained, contain doublets. It is possible to set out two series of incidents. Harnack's statement of them, somewhat shortened, is as follows.

A 1. Peter and John go to the Temple and there is an astonishing miracle (3.1–10)
   2. Peter takes the opportunity of preaching a great missionary sermon (3.11–26)
   3. Miracle and sermon result in the conversion of 5,000 souls (4.1–4)
   4. Peter and John appear before the Council; are threatened but undeterred; are dismissed because the Council fears the people (4.5–22)
   5. Peter and John return to their brethren; prayer and thanksgiving (4.23–30)
   6. Earthquake, outpouring of the Spirit, and sharing of goods (4.31–33)
   7. No one is in need; the awful example of Ananias and Sapphira (4.34–5.11)
   8. Signs and wonders (5.12–16)

B 1. Outpouring of the Spirit and speaking with tongues (2.1–13)
   2. Missionary sermon by Peter, which presupposes (unmentioned) portents (2.14–36)
   3. Miracle and sermon result in 3,000 conversions (2.37–41)
   4. Apostles are thrown into prison but delivered by an angel (5.17–21a)
   5. Jewish authorities re-arrest the apostles; they fear the people and Peter refuses to obey the charge not to preach; scourging and release (5.21b–41)
   6. The apostles continue their work (5.42)

---

[7]*The Acts of the Apostles*, ET London, 1909, 162–202.
[8]Especially J. Dupont, *The Sources of Acts*, ET London 1964; also Haenchen (92–9); Schneider (82–9); Bultmann, in *FS* T. W. Manson, 68–80.

Harnack comments (183), 'It is, in my opinion, so clear that we have here a second narrative of the same events, that one can only wonder that the knowledge that this is so has not long ago become common property.' He adds as the continuation of A, 8.5–40; 9.31–11.18; 12.1–23. This is the Jerusalem-Caesarean, or Petro-Philippine, source. B is a more supernatural (and to Harnack less trustworthy) parallel to A. Luke possessed the two sources and combined them. This hypothesis is now almost universally abandoned, though it has been to some extent revived by Reicke,[9] who draws out parallels between 2.42–4.31 and 4.32–5.42. The parallels are expressed in two themes, The Common Life (where the parallels are between 2.42–47 and 4.32–5.14) and Persecution by Sadducees (where the parallels are between 3.1–4.31 and 5.15–42). Harnack's hypothesis has seemed implausible on general grounds: it is unlikely that the church of the earliest days would keep written records,[10] and in view of the observation by Jeremias[11] that the two narratives of the arrest and release of apostles are not parallel but sequential. In Jewish practice a breach of the law might be punished only if the transgressor was aware that he was breaking the law and making himself liable to punishment. One who like Peter and John was ἰδιώτης and ἀγράμματος (4.13) could be punished only if after warning he repeated his offence. This, according to Jeremias, is what happens in Acts 4 and 5.[12] It is perhaps not quite as simple as this. In 4.21, for example, it is said that the Council were unable to punish Peter and John not because of a legal technicality but because of the popularity of the Christians with the people. There is however quite enough in Jeremias's examination of Harnack's theory to make it no longer tenable. He also makes the point that the speeches in chs. 2 and 3 are not the only parallel speeches in Acts. It is in fact probable that Luke drew on a source that gave an account, perhaps gave specimens, of early Christian preaching, and set the speeches in narrative frameworks constructed from stories that could be collected in Jerusalem. There are however occasional hints of written sources (e.g. 1.15b), and there is no reason why some of his information should not have reached him on paper.

Harnack's second hypothesis[13] is based not on parallelism and doublets but on persons, places, and continuity of narration. If we begin at 6.1 we read of a division between Hebrews and Hellenists and of the appointment of Stephen and his six colleagues. After the martyrdom of Stephen a general persecution arises. All (except the apostles) are scattered (διεσπάρησαν, 8.1). This statement is picked

---

[9]B. Reicke, *Glaube und Leben der Urgemeinde*, Zürich, 1957.
[10]Knox, 27.
[11]*ZNW* 36 (1937), 205–21.
[12]See especially 4.17 (ἀπειλησώμεθα), 21.
[13]Op. cit., 164–78.

up in 8.4 (οἱ μὲν οὖν διασπαρέντες), but then dropped; a long digression is inserted and the theme returns at 11.19 (οἱ μὲν οὖν διασπαρέντες, again). This introduces the work of evangelism in Antioch, and Antioch remains the centre of the narrative till 15.35. '6.1–8[14] and 11.19–15.35 (with the exception of 12.1–24) form one great homogeneous passage which stands in sharp contrast to the rest of the context: *It is an Antiochean tradition*, distinguished as such by the phrase Νικόλαος προσήλυτος ᾿Αντιοχεύς at the very beginning, characterised as such by the fact that the point is throughout directed towards Antioch, and proved to be such by the indissoluble connection of the earlier sections with the concluding sections, which are unquestionably Antiochean in character' (172). Harnack goes on to argue that the tradition was in written form. This hypothesis has fared better than the other. Haenchen (95f.) rejects it, but, with minor variations, it is supported by Jeremias[15] and Bultmann.[16] Jeremias attributes to the source 6.1–8.4; 9.1–30; 11.19–30; 12.25–14.28; 15.35–41. He thus includes the story of Paul's conversion. Bultmann finds the source in 6.1–8.4; 11.19–30; 12.25. This Antiochian source was, he thinks, linked with the itinerary (partly in the first person plural) which forms the basis of chs. 13; 14; 16–21; perhaps 28. Bultmann thus includes neither Paul's conversion nor the Council. Benoit,[17] starting from the problem of Paul's second visit to Jerusalem, in which he sees a problem of the combination of sources, works on the basis of the theories of Harnack and Jeremias outlined above. His primary suggestion is that chs. 13 and 14 should be regarded not as coming from an (the) Antiochian source but from a Pauline source. Unlike both Harnack and Jeremias he considers 15.1–5 to be composite; 15.1, 2 is redactional, used like 12.25 to join chs. 13 and 14 with the rest; 15.3–5, like 11.27–30, belongs to the Antiochian tradition. But chs. 13 and 14 have been inserted in the wrong place; they should stand between 11. 26 and 11.27.

Harnack, Jeremias, and Benoit, who may be taken as classical representatives of source-theory, and especially of Antiochian source-theory, for Acts, all think, or appear to think, of written sources. Whether such written sources as they presuppose were available to Luke is questionable, and is questioned, notably by Haenchen. It is questioned on general grounds. 'Die Generation, welche sich für die letzte hält, schreibt nicht für eine kommende' (Haenchen 95). Even the notion of a travel journal, or itinerary, seems to Haenchen[18] improbable. His criticism is justified and so is his picture of Luke's

---

[14]Sic; the context shows that he means 6.1–8.4.
[15]Art. cit.
[16]Art. cit.
[17]*Exegèse et Théologie III*, Paris, 1968, 285–99.
[18]See 96f., where he is discussing the work of E. Trocmé, *Le livre des Actes et l'histoire*, Paris, 1957.

ways of collecting material. There is however one point that calls for further development. Haenchen pictures Luke as perhaps himself visiting, in order to gain information, the great Pauline centres, such as Philippi and Corinth, also Antioch and Jerusalem; perhaps if he could not himself visit a place where information was to be sought asking a friend who was travelling in the right direction to make inquiries on his behalf. Haenchen mentions also (97) the possibility that Luke may have written to various places for information. 'Endlich konnte er an die betreffenden Gemeinden geschrieben und um Auskunft gebeten haben.' The possibility is worthy of more consideration than Haenchen gives it. A good deal of letter-writing went on in the first century; this is amply attested by the Pauline letters (not only those we have in the canon but those to whose existence the canonical letters allude). Written inquiries will have brought written replies. Other letters must have been written. If for example a church such as Antioch undertook, through appointed representatives, a mission to distant parts it must have kept in touch with the churches that were founded; not to do so, within the limits of what was possible, would have been the gravest irresponsibility. Something of such reports as that of 14.27 may well have found its way on to paper. To say this is not to claim that any such written source is now even conjecturally recoverable, only that (as Haenchen 99 allows, though he lays much greater stress elsewhere) Luke probably had before him some written as well as much oral material. Traces of this can be found with some probability in Acts.

Consideration of the later chapters of Acts, and especially of the so-called We-passages, must await the second volume of this Commentary. From ch. 13 onwards there is a continuous narrative thread given and determined by the career of Paul. It is in the earlier chapters that Luke was confronted by serious problems, both in the search for material and in the arranging of it when he had found it. There is little more to say than that his literary and historical work was controlled by two practical motives: he wished to paint a picture of the life and preaching of the earliest church that would provide instruction and inspiration for his contemporaries, and he wished to show how the Gospel had been taken beyond the Judaism in which it was cradled into the Gentile world. By the time he had reached the end of ch. 14 these goals were achieved; it remained only to show (in ch. 15) how the Gospel was consolidated in the Gentile world and to tell the story of his hero, Paul, the great evangelist, setting it in the context provided by 1.8 and thus concluding at the 'end of the world'. It is idle to seek (though many have done so) an elaborate, or a simple, literary or historical pattern in chs. 1–12. We are given a series of pictures, each one told as well as Luke can tell it (and that means that it is very well told), but the links between them are slight and there is little attention to chronology.

IV. ACTS 1–14: CONTENTS

If the observations made above (pp. 49, 50) are correct, it will be idle to attempt to draw up a neat, formal, balanced analysis of the contents of Acts 1–14. It was not Luke's intention to create a narrative in which every section should be in due proportion with the rest, delighting the reader's eye by its skilful arrangement and his mind by its chronological precision. To him it was important to show that the Christian movement originated in the life, death, and resurrection of Jesus of Nazareth, and therefore had its origin in the place, Jerusalem, where Jesus had been crucified and raised by God from death; and that after its establishment in Jerusalem it had spread to parts of the world other than Palestine, and to people other than Jews. The story of this expansion was known to him in terms of places — Samaria, Caesarea, Antioch, and beyond—, and in terms of outstanding men — Peter, Stephen, Philip, Paul. He set down, one after another, the traditions he had collected on this basis.

I. **NECESSARY PRELIMINARY STEPS:** THE RESURRECTION RE-AFFIRMED AND THE APOSTOLIC GROUP BROUGHT UP TO STRENGTH.
1. Introduction and Recapitulation (1.1–14)
2. Judas and Matthias (1.15–26)

II. **THE CHURCH IN JERUSALEM** ESTABLISHED BY THE GIFT OF THE SPIRIT, BY PREACHING, BY MIRACLE, IN FELLOWSHIP, IN MUTUAL LOVE AND CARE; ITS RELATION WITH JEWISH AUTHORITY.
3. The Pentecost Event (2.1–13)
4. Peter's Pentecost Sermon (2.14–40)
5. The Pentecost Community (2.41–47)
6. Temple Miracle (3.1–10)
7. Peter's Miracle Speech (3.11–26)
8. Arrest and Examination of Peter and John (4.1–22)
9. Return of Peter and John (4.23–31)
10. Sharing and Witnessing Community (4.32–35)
11. An Example: Barnabas (4.36, 37)
12. A negative Example: Ananias and Sapphira (5.1–11)
13. Miracle-working, supernatural Community (5.12–16)
14. Arrest and Examination of Apostles (5.17–40)
15. Rejoicing and Witnessing Community; final Summary (5.41, 42)

I

NECESSARY PRELIMINARY STEPS
(1.1–26)

1. INTRODUCTION AND RECAPITULATION 1.1–14

(1) I wrote my first book, Theophilus, about all the things that Jesus began both to do and to teach (2) up to the day when, having through the Holy Spirit given a charge to the apostles whom he had chosen, he was received up. (3) To them, after he had suffered, he also showed himself alive by many certain proofs, appearing to them from time to time during forty days and speaking of the things concerning the kingdom of God. (4) And as he was eating with them[1] he commanded them not to leave Jerusalem but to await that which the Father promised — 'that which,' he said, 'you heard from me. (5) For[2] John baptized with water, but you shall be baptized with Holy Spirit, not many days from now.' (6) They then, when they had assembled, asked him, saying, 'Lord, is it at this time that thou art restoring the kingdom to Israel?' (7) He said to them, 'It is not yours to know times and seasons which the Father has placed within[3] his own authority; (8) but you shall receive power when the Holy Spirit has come upon you, and you shall be my witnesses in Jerusalem and in all Judaea and Samaria and up to the end of the earth.'

(9) When he had said these things, while they were looking, he was lifted up, and a cloud took him up from their sight. (10) While they were gazing into heaven, as he was going, there came two men in white clothes, who stood beside them. (11) They said, 'Men of Galilee, why do you stand looking into heaven? This Jesus who has been received up from you into heaven will come in the same way that you have seen him going into heaven.'

(12) Then they returned to Jerusalem from the mountain called Olive Grove, which is near Jerusalem — a Sabbath day's journey off. (13) When they entered the city, they went up to the upstairs room where they were staying, Peter, John, James, and Andrew, Philip and Thomas, Bartholomew and Matthew, James (son of Alphaeus) and Simon the Zealot, and Judas (son of James). (14) All these, in union with one another,[4] were continuing in prayer, with their wives, and[5] Mary the mother of Jesus, and his brothers.

---

[1] *Begs.*, lodging with them.
[2] *Begs.*, that.
[3] RSV, *Begs.*, fixed by; NJB, decided by.
[4] NJB, with one heart.
[5] NEB, and with them a group of women, including; similar.ly NJB.

Bibliography

F. H. Agnew, *JBL* 105 (1986), 75–96.

P. Benoit, *Ex. et Th.* 1.363–411.

G. Bertram, *FS* Deissmann, 187–217.

E. Best, *NovT* 4 (1960), 26-43.

E. Best, *JTS* 35 (1984), 1–30.

G. Bouwmann, *FS* Klijn, 46–55.

H. Braun, *Ges. St.* 173–7.

H. von Campenhausen, *StTh.* 1 (1947), 96–130.

L. Cerfaux, *Rec.* 2.157–74.

L. Cerfaux, *Rec.* 3. 185–200.

J. M. Creed, *JTS* 35 (1934), 176–82.

J. Dupont, *NTS* 8 (1962), 154–7.

J. Dupont, *Études*, 401–4.

J. A. Emerton, *JSS* 13 (1968), 282–97.

E. J. Epp, *FS* Metzger, 131–45.

A. Feuillet, *NTS* 24 (1978), 163–74.

J. A. Fitzmyer, *ThSt* 45 (1984), 409–40.

E. Franklin, *SJTh* 23 (1970), 191–200.

E. Grässer, Kremer, *Actes* 99–127.

E. Grässer, *FS* Dupont, 707–25.

K. Haacker, *NovT* 30 (1988), 9–38.

F. Hahn, *Bib.* 55 (1974), 418–26.

P. W. van der Horst, *ZNW* 74 (1983), 17–26.

J. W. Hunkin, *JTS* 25 (1924), 389–402.

J. Jeremias, *ZNW* 65 (1974), 273–6.

W. G. Kümmel, *StTh* 7 (1954), 1–27.

I. H. Marshall, *FS* Bruce (1970), 92–107.

D. L. Mealand, *ZNW* 80 (1989), 134–5.

P. H. Menoud, *FS* Bultmann (1949), 148–56.

P. H. Menoud, *FS* Cullmann (1962), 148–56.

P. H. Menoud, *Jésus Christ et la Foi*, 91–100.

B. M. Metzger, *FS* Stamm, 118–28.

C. F. D. Moule, *Essays*, 54–63.

H. Nibley *VigCh*, 20 (1966), 1–24.

D. W. Palmer, *NTS* 33 (1987), 427–38.

P. Parker, *JBL* 84 (1965), 52–8.

A. M. Ramsey, *SNTSB* 2 (1951), 43–50.

H. Schlier, *Besinnung*, 2.227–41.

D. R. Schwartz, *JBL* 105 (1986), 669–76.

P. A. van Stempvoort, *NTS* 5 (1959), 30–42.

A. Strobel, *FS* Stählin, 133–46.

D. D. Sylva, *ZNW* 74 (1983), 207–21.

T. C. G. Thornton, *ExpT* 89 (1978), 374.

D. L. Tiede, *FS* Stendahl, 278–86.

W. C. van Unnik, *SpColl* 1.386–401.

A. Vögtle, *Das Ev. u. die Ev.* (1971), 31–42.

W. O. Walker, *JBL* 88 (1969), 157–65.

S. G. Wilson, *ZNW* 59 (1968), 269–81.

Commentary

The question where the Introduction to Acts ends and the book proper begins is one that has received different answers. Some (e.g. Marshall) consider that the Introduction ends at v. 5; after this new questions are raised and the programme of the book is set out in v. 8. Verse 8 however contains no more than an outline programme; it tells the reader what sort of action he may expect, but it does not describe the action even in general terms, still less in detail. There is therefore a case for supposing that the Introduction ends at v. 8; undoubtedly the Ascension (vv. 9–11(12)) is the first independent narrative in the book. It is however a narrative that has a parallel in the former of Luke's two volumes (Lk. 24.51 — the reference to Bethany confirms that this is a genuine Ascension tradition), and leads to a further piece of stage setting (vv. 12(13)–14) in preparation for further action. It is arguable that the Introduction continues further still and that vv. 15–26 should also be included, since it is necessary that we should know who the apostles are before their acts are recorded, or rather (since Acts of the Apostles is not Luke's own title) that we should know the make-up of the core of the church before we read of its expansion. This view can be supported by the argument that the true action of a book that has been called the Acts of the Holy Spirit (Bengel: Luke wrote 'non tam apostolorum, quam Spiritus sancti Acta describens') begins on the day of Pentecost (2.1). The decisive consideration however is that whereas the appointment of Matthias breaks fresh ground, having no parallel in Lk., the whole of vv. 1–14 is paralleled in the gospel and is best regarded as a résumé of what the reader may be supposed to have already read. The ministry of Jesus is summed up in v. 1 as 'all the things that Jesus began to do and to teach'; this is followed by a summary of resurrection appearances (vv. 3–6), in which no details are given, together with a reference to John the Baptist's prediction

(v. 5; Lk. 3.16) of baptism in the Holy Spirit (a necessary preliminary to ch. 2). In vv. 7, 8 the apostles are promised the power of the Holy Spirit and charged to act as witnesses. This corresponds to Lk. 24.47–49, with close affinity in the language used (for details see the notes). The Ascension of Jesus, described here with some circumstantial detail, is briefly mentioned at Lk. 24.51 (on the text of this verse see below, and Marshall, *Luke* 909), and the list of names given in vv. 13, 14 corresponds with only minor differences in order (and the necessary omission of Judas Iscariot) with that in Lk. 6.14–16.

It follows from these observations not only that vv. 1–14 were intended to serve as an Introduction to the second volume of Luke's work but also that Luke himself wrote the paragraph, and (with a possible exception to be noted below) did not use special source material, whether written or oral. What sources he may have used in Lk. 24 is a question not to be discussed here; most of what he says there, and all of what he repeats here, was in all probability common Christian knowledge and common Christian opinion. This makes it surprising that the opening verses are marked by a number of difficulties, notably the absence of a δέ clause (to balance τὸν μὲν πρῶτον, v. 1), the textual variants in v. 2, and the parenthetical first person singular (ἣν ἠκούσατέ μου) of v. 4. To account for these there have been theories of redaction, some of them connected with the acceptance of Acts into the NT canon. Thus it has been suggested (e.g. by Menoud, *FS* Bultmann (1954), 148–56) that Luke-Acts was originally a single undivided work. At first only the 'gospel' part was required to join Mt, Mk, and Jn in the gospel canon, since there was no precedent for the canonization of a post-resurrection history. At this time (it is held) the whole was cut in two at a suitable point and the end of Part I and the beginning of Part II were doctored so as to make each an independent book capable of standing on its own. Later Acts, which had now become an independent work, was itself thought suitable for inclusion in the canon. This explanation is not convincing. That it does not correspond with what is known of the formation of the canon has been well shown by Haenchen (153): the canon was not drawn up by a Church Literature Committee which edited the texts thought appropriate; texts which already had a traditional shape did or did not impose themselves as authoritative. It has been shown that μέν solitarium and abrupt changes between first and third person are not uncharacteristic of Luke's style (see below). The textual variations, though complicated and puzzling, can be explained (see the detailed notes below). Hemer 405 somewhat surprisingly suggests that Lk. 24 may be 'read as an *appended summary* of Acts 1.6–12 and its aftermath'.

The one place where pre-Lucan tradition may reasonably be traced is in the narrative of the Ascension (vv. 9–11). This undoubtedly shows marks of Lucan style (see the notes), and Maddox (74) regards it as Luke's own composition; it is moreover without parallel in the NT. It seems however that Luke is writing up in his own way a conviction that was gradually achieving narrative expression in the later NT period; Schille 73 is probably right in seeing here Luke's editing of tradition. Cf. Lüdemann (35: 'Hier liegt eine Tradition zugrunde, deren Form nicht mehr zu erkennen ist').

The Introduction (vv. 1–14) taken as a whole is in fact a carefully constructed piece ('ein kunstvolles, vielfältig verflochtenes Sprachgewebe' (Weiser, 47)), which achieves the following aims. (a) It refers the reader to the following volume and indicates the continuity between the two. (b) It draws attention to the work of the Holy Spirit as an essential and characteristic feature of the new volume, a feature which also, through the connection with John the Baptist, strengthens the connection with Lk. (c) It underlines the function of the apostles as witnesses; this is a theme that recurs frequently in the book as a whole. (d) It points out that the church and its witnessing activity are to extend throughout the world. (e) It emphasises that details of the eschatological future, though determined by God, are not made known to men, even the apostles. (f) It nevertheless lays down the eschatological framework within which the Christian story is to unfold: Jesus has been exalted to heaven, borne up thither on a cloud; he will return in the same way. It is between these points that the church lives, and its life is determined by them. (g) The church is a fellowship at whose heart are the named eleven apostles, chosen by Jesus himself; into this new family the earthly, physical family of Jesus is integrated.

In addition to these points should be noted the Christological significance of the Ascension, though Luke characteristically makes no effort to bring it out. As an event, capable of being reported along with others, the Ascension is found elsewhere in the NT only at Lk. 24.51 (cf. Mk 16.19). Its roots are twofold: (a) the theological conviction, often expressed in terms of Ps. 110.1, that Jesus, after his earthly life and death, is now the Lord who reigns at the right hand of God and is thus 'in heaven' until the time of his parousia; and (b) the physical problem of the disappearance of the physical body of the risen Jesus. (a) does not call for discussion at this point; see 2.34f., where the Psalm is quoted, and for the origin and meaning of the term κύριος as applied to Jesus the note on v. 6, and the general discussion in Vol. II. (b) is more difficult to handle. It is clear that the NT has no single, agreed explanation to offer. Mt ends with an impressive appearance of Jesus to the Eleven and the promise that he will be with them continuously to the end of the present age (Mt. 28.20; cf. 18.20). It is not explained how or in what sense Jesus will be with them. In the original text of Mk, so far as we have it, the question is not raised. The longer ending (16.19) states that Jesus was taken up (ἀνε-λήμφθη) into heaven and sat down at the right hand of God.

John speaks of a departing (ὑπάγειν) or going up (ἀναβαίνειν) of Jesus to the Father, but it is not clear at what point this is to be placed (if indeed it is to be thought of as a datable event): possibly it should be understood as happening after the close of the book, but some think that it is implied that Jesus ascended between 20.17 (Touch me not, for I have not yet ascended, οὔπω γὰρ ἀναβέβηκα) and 20.20 (He showed them his hands and his side) or 20.27 (where Thomas is invited to touch the body of Jesus). Eph. 4.8–10; 1 Pet. 3.22 are theological pronouncements which do not contribute to the problem; neither does Phil. 2.9–11. Lk. 24.51 (διέστη ἀπ' αὐτῶν καὶ ἀνεφέρετο εἰς τὸν οὐρανόν) corresponds with the fuller narrative in Acts, but it has been held (notably by Bertram in *FS* Deissmann 187–217) that Lk. 23.43 presupposes an ascension of Jesus from the cross at the moment of death. This would be a pre-Lucan tradition, abandoned by Luke in favour of a temporary stay (forty days according to v. 3) of Jesus, terminated by an ascent. The supposed pre-Lucan tradition would imply a descent for the purpose of each resurrection appearance; there is no trace of this in the Lucan stories, and it may be doubted whether it ever existed as an intermediate stage between the conviction that Jesus was, or had become, κύριος, with a corresponding metaphorical use of such verbs as ἀναβαίνειν, ὑπάγειν, πορεύεσθαι, and the belief that on a certain day Jesus went up to heaven, conceived as a place, carried thither by a cloud. Bruce (2.40) sensibly points out that after each traditional appearance Jesus must have 'vanished'; once for the last time.

There is a further consideration that may have given this 'last time' the form that it has in Acts. Luke's imagery owes much to the early conviction that Jesus, as Messiah or Son of man, would come with the clouds of heaven, a picture that goes back to Dan. 7.13. Theologically this means that salvation was initiated by the historical Jesus and will be consummated by him at the End. Historically it means for Luke that the story he is about to tell is the story of Jesus' saving activity. He, the Lord, rules in heaven; occasionally he himself will appear on earth to effect his intentions (e.g. 9.5, 10); more frequently he operates through the Spirit (e.g. 13.1–3; 16.6f.).

1. τὸν μὲν πρῶτον λόγον. λόγος may mean 'a historical work', or 'one section of such a work (like later βίβλος)' (LS 1058, s.v., V 3); also 'section, division of a dialogue or treatise' (VI 3d). That here it refers to the gospel of Luke is clear, and it is perhaps pointless to ask whether the author would have regarded his two-volume composition as a historical work, or as a dialogue or treatise. He himself describes the first volume as containing both action and teaching; so it does, and so also does the second volume, and it is likely that Luke would have claimed that both volumes contained both the basic events on which the Christian faith was founded and its fundamental doctrines.

The use of τὸν πρῶτον (rather than τὸν πρότερον, *the former*, or τὸν πρόσθεν, or τὸν παρελθόντα, *the foregoing*) does not necessarily imply that Luke intended to write more than two volumes. πρῶτος (strictly, the *first* of more than two) was probably misused as frequently as the corresponding English superlative; cf. 7.12f.; 12.10. So M.1.79; also BDR § 62, with several examples. There is no δέ corresponding to μέν; this however is not uncommon in Acts (3.13, 21; 21.39; 27.21; 28.22; together with 23 passages where μὲν οὖν is used) or in Greek generally (see LS, 1101f., s.v. μέν; also 'Very many Greek plays begin with a clause containing μέν, which is sometimes followed by δέ, sometimes by some other form of antithesis' (A. O. Prichard, commenting on Aeschylus, *Prometheus Vinctus* 1, χθονὸς μὲν ἐς τηλουρὸν ἥκομεν πέδον. Bauernfeind however reduces the Acts examples to 3.13, 21; 27.21, which he says are not truly parallel, and sees here reason for suspecting the disturbing hand of a redactor. It is however correct to say with Schneider 189, 'Doch musste ein Autor nicht auch den Inhalt des neuen Buches angeben', and it may reasonably be said that a contrasting clause is implied in the summary of the contents of Acts in v. 8 — though Haenchen 152 says rightly that this is much more than a table of contents; it is a promise.

ἐποιησάμην, middle. According to Zerwick § 227 this means not '"priorem librum *scripsi*" (quod est ἐποίησα), sed "priori libro *narravi*"'. But (though rarely) the middle does govern the accusative λόγον, a book (e.g. Isocrates, *Ep.* 2.2, where however the meaning *book* is uncertain).

It is natural that a second part should begin with a brief reference to the contents of its predecessor; cf. e.g. Philo, *Vit. Mos.* 2.1: ἡ μὲν προτέρα σύνταξίς ἐστι περὶ γενέσεως τῆς Μωυσέως καὶ τροφῆς . . . It is natural also that the patron of the work, or its most important, or representative, intended reader should be addressed — ὦ Θεόφιλε. Cf. Lk. 1. 3, where however the mode of address is κράτιστε Θεόφιλε. For the meaning of the adjective see commentaries on Lk and the note on Acts 23.26, where it is used in a normal way as a proper address to the governor Felix. It served as equivalent to *egregius*, also however to *clarissimus* (of a senator?), and to *optimus* (more generally). ὦ is common with the vocative in classical but not in hellenistic use. Elsewhere in the NT its use is to be noted as exceptional and as requiring comment; not so, however, in the more classical Acts (cf. 18.14) — so Zerwick § 35. There can be no question that the same person is intended in Acts as in Lk., if, that is, a particular person is intended. Were the name without religious significance the matter would not be in doubt; but though as a name it is common enough (e.g. Theophilus, the Athenian comic poet of the 4th century BC; a Theophilus in *Ep. Arist.* 49; the father of the High Priest Matthias and the High Priest who succeeded Jonathan,

Josephus, *Ant.* 17.78; 18.123), its meaning (*Dear to God* probably rather than *Loving God*) makes it a possible cypher intended to represent the Christian (or Christian inquirer). The suggestion however that Luke's Theophilus was an ideal or representative rather than a real person fits ill with the κράτιστε of Lk. 1.3. He may have been an inquirer, a catechumen, a Christian seeking further information about the origins of his faith and the early history of the church, or a Roman magistrate. For a consideration of these possibilities see the general discussion of authorship in Vol. II; it is quite impossible to reach a confident conclusion, and Luke would probably not have wished to contradict Bede: Theophilus interpretatur dei amator vel a deo amatus. Quicumque ergo dei amator est ad se scriptum credat ... It was not unusual to introduce a dedication into the opening sentence of a book; cf. e.g. Josephus, *Ap.* 1.1, ἱκανῶς μὲν ὑπολαμβάνω καὶ διὰ τῆς περὶ τὴν ἀρχαιολογίαν συγγραφῆς, κράτιστε ἀνδρῶν Ἐπαφρόδιτε ... (cf. 2.1).

In the passage just referred to Josephus considered that he had, in his earlier work, written sufficiently περὶ τοῦ γένους ἡμῶν τῶν Ἰουδαίων (at least in certain respects; he is going to reply to detractors). Luke has written περὶ πάντων ὧν ἤρξατο ὁ (the article is omitted by B D, an interesting combination, but should be read; it is legitimately anaphoric, though the reference runs back into the preceding book; cf. BDR § 260.1; this may have been missed by B D, or o may have been omitted after ἤρξατο by haplography) Ἰησοῦς ποιεῖν τε (τε is specially characteristic of Acts in the NT) καὶ διδάσκειν. ποιεῖν and διδάσκειν seem a very adequate summary both of the contents and of the interests of the Third Gospel (it could be argued, with some exaggeration indeed, that Matthew had a special interest in διδάσκειν, Mark in ποιεῖν). Calvin emphasises the importance of both doing and teaching — 'a holy knot, which may not be dissolved'; Bede, with a somewhat different interest, 'primo facere, postea docere, quia Iesus bonum doctorem instituens nulla nisi quae fecit docuit'. ἤρξατο may be taken as an equivalent of the Aramaic שרי (see Torrey 23–8; Wilcox 125–7), used virtually as an auxiliary with no strong meaning of its own: 'all that Jesus did and taught'. Conzelmann 20 compares 'unbetontes lateinisches coepi'. The suggestion is not convincing. (a) There is no sufficient ground for the view that Acts 1–15 (or any substantial part of this) was translated from an Aramaic source (see Vol. II). (b) שרי is anything but a simple and natural equivalent of ἄρχεσθαι; see Jastrow, s.v. Torrey refers to Dalman (*Worte* 21f. = *Words* 26–8). But Dalman recognises that the meaning of שרי may be *acquiescing in, assenting to*. (c) It makes good sense to give ἤρξατο its full natural force. Acts contains an account of the continuing work of Jesus (through the Holy Spirit, through the church); the earlier volume contains therefore only the beginning of his work. Of this interpretation Conzelmann says that it 'natürlich ist nicht gemeint'; it is not easy to see why Luke should not have intended it. See M.2.455f., also against Torrey, and referring to J. W. Hunkin, *JTS* 25 (1924), 390–402. Moule (*IB* 181f.) suggests a different sense: *all that Jesus did from the beginning until* . . . This introduction, though much briefer and less formal than that of the gospel (Lk. 1.1–4), nevertheless represents a modest step into publicity (Schille 67). In the features that have already been noted (a dedication and a reference to an earlier work) it follows a pattern common in ancient literature. Many parallels can be found in the commentaries. Among the best are Xenophon, *Anabasis* 2.1 (ὡς μὲν οὖν ἠθροίσθη Κύρῳ τὸ Ἑλληνικόν, . . . ἐν τῷ ἔμπροσθεν λόγῳ δεδήλωται; Philo, *Quod Omnis Probus Liber sit* 1 (ὁ μὲν πρότερος λόγος ἦν ἡμῖν, ὦ Θεόδοτε, περὶ τοῦ . . .); Artemidorus, *Oneirocr.* 2 (Proem) (ἐν μὲν τῇ πρὸ ταύτης βίβλῳ, Κάσσιε Μάξιμε . . . ἐποιησάμην τὸν λόγον . . . ἐν δὲ ταύτῃ τῇ βίβλῳ . . . ἀποδώσω . . .) (cited by Plümacher 9); see also Polybius, 2.1.1f.; Diodorus Siculus, 2.1; 3.1; Josephus, *Ant.* 8.1f.; 13.1f.; Dio Chrysostom, 4.6

2. The text of this verse is in considerable confusion; see the admirable discussion in Metzger, 273–77. It is clear that the Old Uncial text and the Western text differed sharply from each other, but the reconstruction of the original form (or forms) of the Western text is itself no easy task; see Clark 336f., and Ropes' detached note in *Begs.* 3.256–61.

The Old Uncial text runs:

ἄχρι ἧς ἡμέρας ἐντειλάμενος τοῖς ἀποστόλοις διὰ πνεύματος ἁγίου οὓς ἐξελέξατο ἀνελήμφθη

So B ℵ A C 81; also the Antiochian.

The text of D is:

ἄχρι ἧς ἡμέρας ἀνελήμφθη ἐντειλάμενος τοῖς ἀποστόλοις διὰ πνεύματος ἁγίου οὓς ἐξελέξατο καὶ ἐκέλευσε κηρύσσειν τὸ εὐαγγέλιον

d is nearly but not quite identical:

usque in eum diem quem susceptus est quo praecepit apostolis per spiritum sanctum quos elegit et praecepit praedicare euangelium.

The difference between B and D lies mainly in the position of ἀνελήμφθη, and in D's addition of the command to preach the Gospel (a point suitable to the contents of the book — Blass 41). Other Western authorities however differ further. Thus Augustine (*c. Felicem* 1.4; *c. Ep. Fundan.* 9; *de Cons. Evang.* 4.8 — these sources agree except where stated): in die quo (usque in diem quo, *Cons; Find* hasque) apostolos elegit per spiritum sanctum et praecepit (mandans iussit, *Cons.*) praedicare euangelium. Here there is no equivalent to ἀνελήμφθη (replaced perhaps by praedicare euangelium), and instead of 'until the day when' we have 'on the day when'; this text differs from that of B and its allies more sharply than does that of D, and it seems best to think of D as a conflate text standing (in this case) midway between the Western and Old Uncial texts; it has changed *on the day* to *up to the day*, and inserted a reference to the Ascension. The original Western text may have run:

ἐν ᾗ ἡμέρᾳ τοὺς ἀποστόλους ἐξελέξατο διὰ πνεύματος ἁγίου καὶ ἐκέλευσεν κηρύσσειν τὸ εὐαγγέλιον

So Clark. Ropes (*Begs.* 3.256) sees an almost identical Greek text behind Augustine's Latin (he writes ἐν ἡμέρᾳ ᾗ instead of ἐν ᾗ ἡμέρᾳ), but thinks that καὶ ἐκέλευσεν κηρύσσειν τὸ εὐαγγέλιον is the Western glossator's expansion of ἐντειλάμενος, so that an even earlier form, which he accepts as the original Lucan text, would be: ἐν ἡμέρᾳ ᾗ ἐντειλάμενος τοῖς ἀποστόλοις διὰ πνεύματος ἁγίου ἐξελέξατο.

It is not easy to see what sense can be got out of the Western text when it has been reconstructed. Luke is referring to the contents of the earlier volume. It gives an account, he says, of all that Jesus began to do and teach (or, did and taught) on the day when he chose and charged the apostles. The gospel however contains a good deal more than what Jesus did and taught on this day; and this day (Lk. 6.13; cf. 9.1) does not mark the beginning of either the teaching or the action of Jesus. Bede has evident difficulty with the interpretation of his text (Usque in diem qua praecipiens apostolis per spiritum sanctum quos elegit adsumptus est). It makes straightforward sense to take the first volume as going on *up to* a day, and in particular the day of the Ascension (ἀνεφέρετο, Lk. 24.51). The question is whether we should take this to be what Luke wrote and the Western text corrupted, or whether the more difficult text should be regarded as original. The Ascension plays such an important part at the end of the gospel and at the beginning of Acts that it seems probable that Luke would refer to it as the dividing line separating the first volume from the second. Even this argument however can be reversed, for it could be claimed that an editor, seeing the importance of the Ascension, introduced a reference to it where no such reference originally stood. It is probably better to suppose that the Western reading, which lacks ἀνελήμφθη (cf. Lk. 24.51, where *Western* authorities omit καὶ ἀνεφέρετο εἰς τὸν οὐρανόν), came into being because an editor or copyist (especially if he was using the Western text of Lk. 24.51) took note of the fact that the Ascension had not yet happened and that a reference to it therefore seemed out of place. The change, especially when interpreted as a command to preach the Gospel, could be justified by Lk. 24.47 and Acts 1.8. Delebecque argues that the occurrence of κηρύσσειν in 28.31 supports the Western reference to preaching the Gospel. This is hardly convincing.

In the Old Uncial text ἐντειλάμενος must be coordinated with ἀνελήμφθη: Having charged them, after giving them a charge, he was taken up. For the relation between the charge of Lk. 24.44–49 and its resumption in Acts 1.6–8 see below. For *the apostles* see 1.21f. and the general discussion in Vol. II.

διὰ πνεύματος ἁγίου is awkwardly placed; the fact that the Western text is in this respect easier should probably be taken as an argument against its originality. It is probably better to take the phrase with ἐντειλάμενος than with ἐξελέξατο, both on linguistic grounds (the relative clause is most naturally taken to begin with οὕς) and because, though there is no reference to the Holy Spirit in Luke's account of the choice of the Twelve, both the Lucan charges refer to the Spirit (Lk 24.49 . . . the promise of my Father . . . power from on high; and Acts 1.8). A number of scholars however (e.g. Haenchen 145, Schneider 192, Marshall 57) take the alternative view. The difficulty and ambiguous reference of διὰ πνεύματος ἁγίου led Dibelius (90), comparing this passage with 4.25, to conjecture that the reference to the Holy Spirit did not stand in the original text; reference to the Holy Spirit was introduced under theological influence.

ἐξελέξατο. For Jesus' choice of the Twelve see Lk 6.13 (ἐκλεξάμενος). Note (with a view to 15.7 — see the note) that ἐκλέγεσθαι is properly constructed (not with ἐν); so also at 1.14; 6.5; 13.17; 15.22, 25.

ἀνελήμφθη. See vv. 9–11; also Lk. 24.51 (and perhaps Lk. 9.51). For Luke's understanding of the Ascension see below. According to Schille (68) the word had become a technical term for *rapture* (Entrückung).

3. For the question whether this verse is to be regarded as a parenthesis or as part of vv. 3–11 taken as a whole see Wilson, *Gentiles* 101. If the view taken above is correct Luke is composing for himself the whole of the Introduction; here he is still recapitulating the closing sections of the gospel. There Jesus shows himself alive to his disciples at Lk. 24.31, 34, 36.

παρέστησεν will undoubtedly have its simple sense of placing something (in this case, oneself) beside, in the neighbourhood of, a person. But the word is also used in the sense of *prove*, and this sense is also present. Cf. Lysias, 12.51, ἀμφότερα ταῦτα ἐγὼ πολλοῖς τεκμηρίοις παραστήσω (note τεκμηρίοις, and see below). Jesus presented himself alive and thus proved that he was alive.

μετὰ τὸ παθεῖν αὐτόν. ζῶντα shows that the *suffering* is understood to include death; παθεῖν is the word used by the tradition (it is not, *pace* Haenchen 152 and Conzelmann 20, a specifically Lucan word; nor can it be held to derive from סבל in Isa. 53.4) to denote the passion as a whole (Delling, *Kreuzestod* 87; see e.g. Mk 8.31 as well as Lk. 24.26, 46; Acts 3.18).

δι' ἡμερῶν τεσσεράκοντα. D* has the simple genitive (without διά), the normal Greek construction for 'time within which'; there can be little doubt either that Luke wrote διά or that his construction has the same meaning. The classical use of διά with the genitive gives the meaning *after* (BDR § 223, 2a, with the note that it is implied that the appearances took place 'not continuously, but "now and then"'). On this however Moule (*IB* 56) comments that 'it has been pointed out that *at intervals* is derived not from the words but from independent knowledge of the traditions. In itself it simply means *during* or *in the course of*... So 16.9'. Wilson (*Gentiles* 102) may well be right in the view that the period of 40 days was deduced (as a suitable approximation) from the fiftieth day (2.1). The forty-day interval is next mentioned by Tertullian (*Apology* 21). Lk. 24.50–53; Barnabas 15.9 suggest an Ascension on Easter Day. Other periods were conjectured; gnostics cited in Irenaeus, *Heresies* 1.3.2; 1.30.14 speak of 18 months; Ascension of Isaiah 9.16 of 545 days; Apocryphon of James of 550 days.

ἐν πολλοῖς τεκμηρίοις. See Lysias 12.51, quoted above; Luke's ἐν (not in Lysias) is a mark of Hellenistic development in Greek. τεκμήριον is a *proof*; in Aristotle, *Rhetorica* 1.2.16f. τεκμήρια are *necessary* proofs, ἀναγκαῖα, leading to certain conclusions; cf. Quintilian 5.9: Dividuntur autem in has duas species: quod eorum alia sunt (ut dixi) quae necessaria sunt, quae Graeci vocant τεκμήρια; alia non necessaria, quae σημεῖα. Dodd (*More NT Studies* 123) refers to Aristotle, *Poetica* 16.1454b.21, but though this passage deals with proofs of recognition it does not use τεκμήριον. Dodd's reference to Aeschylus, *Choephorae* 205, shows τεκμήριον used in the sense of proof of recognition but does little to establish its force; Electra's δεύτερον τεκμήριον (of the presence of Orestes) does little credit to her capacity for logic.

ὀπτανόμενος, followed not by ὑπό and the genitive but by the dative, must be intransitive deponent, *appearing to them*; BDR § 313. The form ὀπτάνεσθαι is a late present derivative from the aorist ὀφθῆναι; ὀπτάζεσθαι is also used. Cf. ἐμφανῆ γενέσθαι, 10.40. For ὀπτανόμενος Hesychius gives ὁρώμενος, ἐμφανιζόμενος; cf. also 2 Chron. 5.9; 3 Kdms 8.8; Tobit 12.19.

Jesus appeared to the apostles, thereby proving that he was alive, and spoke of things concerning the kingdom of God; the risen Jesus teaches thus no new (gnostic) doctrine but that which had been taught during the ministry (Weiser 55). *Kingdom of God* is used several times in Acts as a general term covering the whole of the Christian proclamation (1.3; 8.12; 19.8; 20.25 (here without God); 28.23, 31). Possibly elsewhere but very probably at this point it is used in order to establish a link between the message of Jesus after the resurrection and that which he had proclaimed during his ministry; also to prepare for v. 6. From Acts alone it is impossible to derive a clear and comprehensive view of what the phrase means; seriously to discuss its use in the gospel is in this place equally impossible. It seems to bear, in Lk., a somewhat wider range of meaning than occurs in the other synoptic gospels; this prepares for the wider use of the phrase in Acts. It is a future good, for whose coming men may pray (e.g. Lk. 11.2), as they did in Judaism (Lk. 23.51). It is near at hand (Lk. 10.9, 11). In the presence of Jesus and his work (especially his attack on the kingdom of Satan) it may be said to have come already (Lk. 11.20). It is God's gift to his own, who manifest that they are his own (Lk. 6.20; 9.62; 12.32), and though they suffer now they will enjoy the gift when the appointed time comes (Lk. 13.28, 29; cf. Acts 14.22). It is impossible to answer the question when the kingdom will come (Lk. 17.20). It is an inward, spiritually possessed thing (Lk. 17.21 — a verse often differently interpreted; see Marshall ad loc.). In the present verse the phrase looks forward to the question asked by the apostles in v. 6. The word βασιλεία was always open to misinterpretation in terms of earthly sovereignty (cf. 17.7); the Ascension and the gift of the Spirit were, in Luke's view, necessary before even the chosen disciples could understand the true meaning of the kingdom. See further on v. 6. Schneider (193) goes too far in saying that Acts speaks not of the coming (Kommen) but of the nature (Wesen) of the kingdom; Luke assumes both, but does little to define either.

4. According to Schneider 195-211 the story of the Ascension begins here. Augustine connects this verse with v. 2 (*feci*), writing *et quomodo conversatus est* . . .

συναλιζόμενος. συναλίζειν (long α in the antepenult) means *to bring together, collect, assemble* (transitive); in the passive, *to come together, assemble* (intransitive). Calvin's *congregans eos* treats the verse as if it were active, and will not do. συνάλίζεσθαι (short α in the antepenult) means *to eat salt with, eat at the same table with* (LS 1694, s.vv.). The variant (in 1 69 *al*), συναυλιζόμενος, *lodging together with*, is too scantily attested, and too clearly *lectio facilior*, to have much probability; and the variant (of D), συναλισκόμενος, *taken prisoner together with*, with its correction by a later hand, συναλισγόμενος, *being sullied with*, yields an impossible sense. συνᾱλιζόμενος is a word one would not expect to find in the singular (all the passages cited s.v. in LS relate to plurals); it does not really mean *meeting with them*. Accordingly we should read συνᾱλιζόμενος and take it to mean *eating (salt) together with them*. This recalls the Lucan resurrection stories: Lk. 24.30, 31, 35, 41–43. These passages are given (a) as proof of the bodily reality of the risen Jesus and (b) as indicating a common meal as the context of his self-disclosure. In the present context no stress laid on (a), though the point is consistent with the use of τεκμήριον (v. 3); later in Acts we shall find references (2.42, 46; 20.7; 27.35) to the breaking of bread, which may suggest a special context of fellowship with Christ. For this see the notes on the passages mentioned and the general discussion in Vol. II. It remains surprising that Luke should write συναλιζόμενος rather than (say) συνεσθίων. It may be that the allusion to salt has been dropped altogether and that Luke is thinking simply of eating together. This is perhaps the most probable view. There are however passages that suggest a significant use of salt in the church's holy meal. The evidence is collected by Fitzmyer (*Essays* 474 = Stendahl, *Scrolls* 227f.), who cites *Clem. Hom.* 4.6; 11.34; 19.25 (ἅλων μεταλαβεῖν) and 14.8 (μετὰ τὴν ἅλων κοινωνίαν); Cf. *Ep. Clem.* 9.1. συναλίζεσθαι occurs at *Hom.* 13.4, and salt and bread are mentioned together at *Diamartyria* 4.3. It is worth while to note the conjecture (which goes back to Hemsterhuis) that for συναλιζόμενος should be read συναλιζομένοις. Cadbury (*Begs.* 4.4f. ad loc. and *JBL* 45 (1926), 310–12) took συναλιζόμενος to be an orthographical variant of συναυλιζόμενος. Moule (*NTS* 4 (1958), 60) suggests that συναλιζόμενος be read and taken to refer to *festival lodging*. 'Once more the Galileans are on the verge of a feast, this time Pentecost; once more they are in temporary lodging in the environs of Jerusalem; and again the Lord is with them.' The text is discussed by Wilcox (106–9), who rejects Torrey's explanation in terms of the Aramaic מתמלח, *to eat salt in company with*, on the good ground that the root מלח does not occur with this meaning (though there may be a Syriacism here), and draws attention to the possible influence of a rare Hebrew root לחם. There seems to be no reason for invoking this; Luke's Greek though unusual is not difficult enough to warrant conjecture.

The Eleven are instructed ἀπὸ Ἱεροσολύμων (Luke uses sometimes Ἱεροσόλυμα, sometimes Ἱερουσαλήμ; attempts have been made to give reasons for the variation but none is successful) μὴ χωρίζεσθαι. Luke (cf. Lk. 24.6) may be correcting a tradition (in Mt., Mk, Jn 21) of Galilean resurrection appearances. *Begs.* 4.6 notes that both Eusebius and Chrysostom understood μὴ χωρίζεσθαι in the sense of *return to*. Davies (*Land* 264) noting the present infinitive mentions the possibility that a movement of the disciples to Galilee was in progress, and should be stopped. He rejects this view, however, and is unwilling to press the distinction between χωρίζεσθαι and χωρισθῆναι. He rightly notes that the reason for remaining in Jerusalem is that it is there that the disciples are to await the gift of the Holy Spirit. Indeed, emphasis upon Jerusalem as the holy place, the scene of crucifixion, resurrection (and appearances), ascension, and the gift of the Spirit is characteristically Lucan (for Conzelmann 21, ad loc., 'Jerusalem represents the continuity between Israel and the church'). Davies may be right so far, at least about Luke's own concerns; one must ask also whether among the sacred events the parousia was

I. 1

defensible
Gramm.[2] 1
Aramaic d
a whole. B
that is, 'in
Gen. 16.3;
οὗτος is u
earlier Gre
Mk 16.17 .
reverses th
The def. ar
connection
already est
demonstrat
or understc
This says p
is clear en
author mig
Moule (IB
a Latinism
sense; and,
with a char
— the only
deliberate;
τῆς πεντ
addition, as

6. On vv.
Klein (Apo
οἱ μὲν
phrase, and
so Weiser 5
signifies th
the close ap
is in fact an
assembled
asesemblea
in question
and though
Holy Spirit
they were
Thus it is tl
were those
ἠρώτων:
because the
given.

included (cf. 1.11, on which see the note; does the verse point to a parousia with clouds on the Mount of Olives?). A traditional saying behind the μὴ χωρίζεσθαι might have inhibited some of the original disciples from pursuing missionary work away from Jerusalem. Alternatively, a saying such as that in the text might have developed from the conviction that it was wrong to leave Jerusalem and evangelize the Gentiles. For the language cf. Demosthenes 21. 168 (569): τῶν τριηράρχων ἐχόντων παράγγελμα μὴ χωρίζεσθαι ἕως ἂν δεῦρο καταπλεύσωμεν.

The promise of the Father is the gift of the Holy Spirit; ἐπαγγελία is used in the sense of the thing promised; cf. Lk. 24.49; Acts 2.33 and perhaps 2.39. The promise referred to may be that quoted from Joel in 2.17–21; more probably the promise of the Father is that which the Father had spoken through Jesus. John the Baptist had hinted at the coming of the Holy Spirit (still a matter of promise) and Jesus made the promise explicit in the present context. For the fulfilment of the promise see 2.4 and the note. Bengel quotes the grammarian Ammonius: ὑπισχνεῖται ὁ τῷ αἰτήσαντι δώσειν ὁμολογήσας· ἐπαγγέλλεται δὲ ὁ ἀφ' ἑαυτοῦ δώσειν ὁμολογήσας, and adds, Quae verbi Graeci proprietas, ubi de divinis promissionibus agitur, exquisite observanda est.

With ἣν ἠκούσατέ μου the sentence switches abruptly from indirect to direct speech; for the reverse of this cf. 23.23f. (see also 25.4f. and Lk. 5.14). The change is not unusual even in classical writers: BDR § 470.2. The Western text (D* pc vg[cl]) has ἠκούσατε, φησίν, διὰ τοῦ στόματός μου — an evident 'improvement', not to be accepted on the ground that it introduces a Semitism (through my mouth). Such expressions were an easily imitable feature of Lucan style.

5. ὅτι is not recitativum; it means because, for. It is assumed that the reader of Acts has read Lk. and therefore does not need to be informed about John (Clark 337 gives statistics for the MS spelling of 'Ιωάνης and 'Ιωάννης). The verb ἐβάπτισεν shows immediately which John is meant; Theophilus will know that he is the one who went before Jesus in the spirit and power of Elijah (Lk. 1.17), that crowds gathered to him for baptism (3.7), that he foretold coming judgment (3.7, 9) and the coming of one mightier than himself (3.4–6, 16), that he inquired whether Jesus was the Coming One (7.19), and that Jesus himself declared that among those born of women there was none greater than John the Baptist, though the least in the kingdom of God is greater (7.28). John had also made the prediction (3.16), ἐγὼ μὲν ὕδατι βαπτίζω ὑμᾶς· ἔρχεται δὲ ὁ ἰσχυρότερός μου ... αὐτὸς ὑμᾶς βαπτίσει ἐν πνεύματι ἁγίῳ καὶ πυρί. It is probable that already in the gospel Luke envisaged the fulfilment of this prophecy in the gift of the Holy Spirit

on the day
meaning
Marshall
the referei
knew but
Ropes, wl
μὲν ἐβάτ
verb, acti
The Ho
say the ce
that bapti
the Christ
of a broɑ
surveying
attemptin
such as re
Spirit. Th
baptism v
do justice
with πνε
Holy Spi
It is sur
πνευματ
(the fluic
(instrume
following
perhaps
water sug
in which
proper to
(and he v
(to rid hi
of very l
It is n
Pentecos
Celsum
insofar ɑ
church v
and unde
find it na
in fact a
The pɪ
μετὰ πɩ
as a clea
dies (43
non pos

There is nothing in the word κύριε to show whether it is simply a respectful term used in addressing a person of some importance or has a specific theological content. The context shows that the speakers believe that the person addressed has the power at the appropriate time to restore government to Israel, that is, to put into effect (what is believed to be) the intention of God. He is the Messiah. For κύριος see further pp. 151f.

εἰ introduces a direct question. This use of the particle (which regularly introduces indirect questions) recurs at 7.1 but is not classical; it occurs elsewhere in the NT and also in the LXX, so that it is often explained as a Hebraism (BDR § 440; Zerwick § 401). The parallel with ὅτι, increasingly used to introduce direct as well as indirect statements, may have contributed to the development (cf. Zerwick § 402, n. 1). The question has been described as incredible after forty days of teaching about the kingdom of God. It may be that the reference to the Holy Spirit was taken to be a sign of the end; it is better to see here the way in which Luke provides an opportunity for a statement of great importance to be made.

χρόνος, normally an interval of time, must here denote a particular point in time: Is this the moment at which . . . ? It is thus indistinguishable from καιρός (cf. v. 7) — a warning that, in NT Greek, it is unwise to build much upon the distinction between the two words.

ἀποκαθιστάνεις, *are you restoring?* futuristic present. The verb form (instead of ἀποκαθίστημι) is an example of the tendency, begun already in Homer and virtually complete in Modern Greek (M.1.55), to replace –μι verbs with verbs in –ω. The question shows a Jewish interest (Klausner, *Jesus* 402), and has been held to prove the existence of a Zealot element among the disciples of Jesus (Davies, *Land* 338, mentions but does not hold this view). It is nearer to the truth to say that Luke uses the question to underline the non-nationalist character of the Christian movement; the disciples asked it (thus by their failure to perceive the truth eliciting the positive statement of v. 8) before the gift of the Spirit in ch. 2. Thereafter they would be in no doubt about God's eschatological plans, which Luke clearly understands to be universal rather than nationalist. See however on v. 8; the spread of the kingdom will happen through the witness of the apostles. With ἀποκαθιστάνεις, cf. ἀποκατάστασις in 3.22. Since Mal. 3.23 (LXX) the word had been an apocalyptic terminus technicus (Haenchen 149); according to Schneider 201 it represents קום (but not in Malachi) and there is an element of repetition (Wieder) in it — the restoration of what had formerly been. The latter point is correct here, but is given by the context rather than by the word itself. Bultmann (*Exegetica* 375) believes that at 3.22 (see the note) we may see the typological method operating on the principle *Mosezeit — Heilzeit*. Whether the present passage is to be understood in the same way is, he says, doubtful. We may however be confident that it should not be understood in this way, at least in Luke's intention. His concern here is not to bring out a parallel between the former Redeemer (Moses) and the latter Redeemer (the Messiah) but to point out a difference between a Jewish and the Christian understanding of the purpose of God. Restoration of the kingdom to Israel is regularly prayed for in the Eighteen Benedictions and in the Qaddish. In this verse the word βασιλεία stands by itself and probably means simply *sovereignty*; the apostles inquire whether Israel is once more to enjoy the wide dominion that it enjoyed in the time of David. According to Schille 71 it is necessary to supply with βασιλεία *of God*; this is correct only in the sense that when properly understood Israel's sovereignty is a way of expressing God's. It is, according to Luke, in the life of Christians that God's sovereignty is expressed.

D has ἀποκαταστάνεις εἰς τὴν βασιλείαν τοῦ Ἰσραήλ. Black (*AA* 115) suggests the possibility that here (and at Lk. 19.44, also D) we may have an Aramaism: εἰς could represent the Aramaic ל used as the sign of the direct object. His alternative explanation, however, that εἰς is a dittograph of the last syllable of ἀποκαταστάνεις, is more probable. Augustine (Ropes, ad loc.) several times has si in hoc tempore (re)praesentaberis, et quando regnum Israel. Bengel has the note, 'Apostoli, *re* praesupposita, quaerebant de *tempore*: et pariter se habet subsequens responsio.' This seems to be correct; that is, the apostles are not rebuked for asking an improper question; the question is a proper one, but no answer is to be given. See on the next verse.

7. The question of v. 6 receives no direct answer. Betz (98) compares the reply of Rhadamanthys to a similar question: ὁ δὲ ἔφασκεν ἀφίξεσθαι μὲν εἰς τὴν πατρίδα ... τὸν δὲ χρόνον οὐκ ἔτι τῆς ἐπανόδου προσθεῖναι ἠθέλησεν (Lucian, *Vera Historia* 2.27). There is however a good deal of difference between Acts and the *True Story*, and a more useful comparison is Mk 13.32, though in the Marcan context the parousia appears to be placed within the first generation of Christians (see however Cranfield, *Mark* 408). Luke is careful not to include the Son in his parallel to Mk 13.32 and to avoid any such approximation to the time of the end. *Begs.* 4.8 follows the Western text and translates, 'No one can know'. This reading is found only in Augustine (Nemo potest cognoscere) and may reflect no more than inaccurate quotation (possibly of Mk 13.32) from memory. It is not denied (see the quotation from Bengel on v. 6) that there will be a time when the kingdom is restored to Israel, though the book as a whole makes clear that Israel, the people of God, is receiving a new definition. This seems a better way of describing what is in mind than to say (Maddox 107) that the use of βασιλεία in Acts shows that Luke cannot mean that God will restore the kingdom of Israel. Bede with small variations quotes Jerome (MPL 26.181c): . . . ostendit quod et ipse sciat . . . sed non expedit nosse mortalibus; ut semper incerti de adventu iudicis sic cotidie vivant, quia die alia iudicandi sint; but Luke's intention is rather to emphasise a new development in God's dealings with the world than to threaten with the uncertainty of the future. Cf. Mekhilta Exodus 16.32 (59b): No one knows . . . when the kingdom of the house of David will be put back in its place, and when the evil kingdom will be wiped out.

It is hardly possible in this verse to make a clear distinction between χρόνος and καιρός, though one might think of καιροί (unspecified points of time) separated by χρόνοι (unspecified intervals). See however on v. 6, and on 3.20, 21 and cf. Dan. 2.21; Eccles. 3.1; Demosthenes 3.16(32) (τίνα γὰρ χρόνον ἢ τίνα καιρόν). Some Latin texts have only tempus, or tempora, possibly because of a lack of suitable synonyms (but cf. the Vulgate, tempora vel momenta). Somewhat similarly the Peshitto has zabna 'au zabne, time or times; Cyprian (*Testimonia* 3.89) has tempus aut tempora.

In Acts τίθημι is most commonly used of putting something in a place; it is therefore probable that οὓς ὁ πατὴρ ἔθετο ἐν τῇ ἰδίᾳ ἐξουσίᾳ means *placed within his own authority*, that is, *reserved for his own decision*, rather than *appointed by his own authority*. Cf. Mk 13.32: only the Father (not even the Son — still less anyone else) knows the time of the end. It is possible that this withholding of information reflects a time of disappointment over the delay of the parousia (Bultmann, *E&F* 295); certainly Luke has himself come to terms with the fact that there was to be a perceptible interval between the resurrection and the end. But the intention seems primarily to be to lay stress on the gift of the Spirit and the role of the apostles as witnesses, both mentioned in the next verse.

8. The verse looks forward to ch. 2 and receives a measure of interpretation from that chapter, in which the apostles, represented by Peter, act as witnesses, having received power through the gift of the Spirit. The connection with the preceding verse is important, and there is no doubt that a measure of contrast is intended. 'Not the kingdom for Israel (Acts 1.6), but the power of the Holy Spirit for the church' (Maddox 106; see the context). The verse raises the question, of fundamental importance for the understanding of Acts, of the relation between the gift of the Spirit and the end. 'Der Geist ist nicht mehr Potenz der Endzeit, sondern Ersatz für sie' (Conzelmann 22). It is nearer to the truth to say that the Spirit is an anticipation of the Endzeit in the present. The apostles as witnesses will be equipped for witnessing but must not expect victory without delay. 'They must fight before they can hope to triumph' (Calvin 31).

δύναμις is apparent in the physical accompaniments (fire, wind) of the Spirit, and in the ability to speak with tongues (see on 2.4).

δύναμις is used ten times in Acts. Three times (2.22; 8.13; 19.11) it means *miracles*; three times it is used of the power that effects miracles (3.12; 4.7; probably 10.38). Twice it refers to the power with which the apostles (4.33) and Stephen (6.8) do what they have to do — speaking and, probably, working miracles. At 8.10 Simon the Magus is said to be ἡ δύναμις τοῦ θεοῦ ἡ καλουμένη μεγάλη. This last reference contributes nothing, but the others may be added up to give the sense of δύναμις in 1.8. What is promised to the apostles is the power to fulfil their mission, that is, to speak, to bear oral testimony, and to perform miracles and in general act with authority. This power is given through the Spirit, and conversely the Spirit in Acts may be defined as the divine agency that gives this power. The Spirit is not defined here as the third of a Trinity of divine Persons, though it is associated with the Father and the Son (see especially 2.33; 5.3, 4; 10.38, and the notes). Cf. Mt. 28.20 for a different way of expressing the divine presence that aids believers. To say that in Acts the gift of the Spirit replaces an earlier conviction regarding the nearness of the parousia is an over-simplification of the evidence, but it is not wholly misleading.

With ἐπελθόντος . . . ἐφ᾽ ὑμᾶς cf. 2.3, ἐκάθισεν ἐφ᾽ ἕνα ἕκαστον αὐτῶν; also Lk. 1.35, πνεῦμα ἅγιον ἐπελεύσεται ἐπὶ σέ (and note in this verse the association with δύναμις). The use of ἐπί is probably not intended to convey anything more precise than a general notion of inspiration; note the parallel between ἐπί and εἰς (in composition) in Lucian, *Philopseudes* 16, (The demons) εἰσεληλύθασιν εἰς τὸ σῶμα . . . (the demon) ἐπῆλθεν ἐς τὸν ἄνθρωπον (Betz 156). It is worth noting that in this context the demon speaks ἑλληνίζων ἢ βαρβαρίζων, ἢ ὅθεν ἂν αὐτὸς ᾖ.

What follows may be regarded as in a sense the apodosis to vv. 1, 2; it expresses the content of Luke's second volume. The apostles are to be witnesses, μάρτυρες. Witnessing is a major theme in Acts and will be frequently discussed. The apostles are specifically witnesses to the fact of the resurrection (1.22), that is, to the divine vindication of Jesus, the proof that he was what he had claimed to be, what the apostles now claimed that he was. Witness to the resurrection thus includes witness to all the other propositions of the Christian proclamation; cf. 26.22 (the suffering and resurrection of Christ); 10.39 (the whole story of Jesus), 13.31; 26.16. Cf. Isa. 43.10. What takes place in the life of the church is the valid continuation and fruit of the work of the historical Jesus. It goes however too far to say, 'Die Geschichte der Kirche ist Heilsgeschichte' (Haenchen; but Haenchen says rightly, 'Die christliche Kirche, wie die Apg sie schildert, ist eine Missionskirche' (150), and that what the present verse contains is not a simple table of contents but a promise (152).

The work of bearing witness is to begin in Jerusalem; see chs. 2–7. It will continue in (ἐν is expressed in P⁷⁴ ℵ B C³ E Ψ 𝔐 lat, omitted by A C* D 81 323 *pc*) Judaea and Samaria; see chs. 8, 9. And it will go on ἕως ἐσχάτου τῆς γῆς. ἐσχάτου is to be taken not as masculine (*up to the last man on earth*), though there are parallels to this (see below), but as neuter. γῆ probably refers, as at 13.47, to the whole earth, not as is maintained by Trocmé to the land of Israel, though it is true that γῆ, like אֶרֶץ and אַרְעָא, is ambiguous in this respect. The phrase is a stock one; see Isa. 48.20; 49.6; Jer. 10.13; 1 Clem. 5.7 (τὸ τέρμα τῆς δύσεως, probably Spain); Horace, *Odes* 1.35.29f.: Serves iturum Caesarem in ultimos orbis Britannos; Sallust, *Catiline* 16.5: Cn. Pompeius in extremis terris bellum gerebat; Herodotus 3.25.1: ἐς τὰ ἔσχατα τῆς γῆς ἔμελλε στρατεύεσθαι. It has usually been supposed that in 'the end of the earth' there should be seen a reference to Rome (cf. Ps. Sol. 8.15: ἤγαγεν τὸν ἀπ' ἐσχάτου τῆς γῆς, him who came from the end of the earth — Pompey the Great; it is likely that the Psalmist thought of Pompey as coming from Rome, though geographically his route may have led him from Spain). Van Unnik (*NovT* 4 (1960), 39f.; see also *Begs.* 4.9) thought the reference a general one: the Gospel is to spread throughout the world. He claimed that 'the book nowhere shows a special interest for the capital of the Imperium Romanum' (39). This is hardly correct; see 19.21; 23.11, and the fact that the book does end in Rome. The truth probably is that the phrase does refer to Rome, but to Rome not as an end in itself but as representative of the whole world. It has been said that the reference cannot be to Rome because ch. 28 shows the mission to be still in progress; certainly Luke was aware of the existence of Spain and of other lands further west still untouched when Rome was evangelized, but an *a fortiori* argument would apply: if the Gospel can be preached and the church established in Rome there is no limit to their possible extension.

In the list of areas to be covered there is no reference to Galilee. Lohmeyer (*Galiläa und Jerusalem*, (1936), 52) notes that while Judaea alone would make a suitable connecting link between Jerusalem and the 'end of the earth', or Judaea and Galilee, or Judaea, Samaria, and Galilee, Judaea and Samaria (one unit for the Romans, as Luke notes at Lk. 3.1) is a combination not to be expected. He concludes that the omission of Galilee was intentional, and explains the omission on the ground that Galilee was already *terra Christiana*, where it was unnecessary for the apostles to go and to bear Christian testimony. Brandon (*Fall* 44) accepts the existence of a Galilean church as 'very probable'. W. D. Davies (*Land* 265) is probably nearer the truth when he observes that Luke 'pays no attention to any Christianity of any special significance in Galilee'. Luke has no stories to tell about Galilee and therefore does not include it in this programmatic verse. C. Burchardt (*ZNW* 61 (1970), 162) writes, 'Meines Erachtens ist in der Tat mit dem Ende der Apostelgeschichte

auch das in 1.8 angekündigte Zeugesein zu seinem Ende gekommen.'
This passage is thus to be distinguished from Mt. 28.18–20; it is not
a command and promise applicable to the whole world but comes to
an end with Acts 28.31. This however does not seem to be Luke's
point. Since the apostles are told that they will be witnesses up to the
end of the earth it is implied that the end of the world (age) will not
come till the end of the earth has been reached. The saying indicates
Luke's view of the future, though Dinkler (*Signum Crucis* 334) may
put the matter too strongly when he claims that the promise contains
'the hidden motivation of Luke's two works, namely that the
announcement of the message must go into all the world before the
parousia'. Luke had other motivations also, but if this is kept in mind
Dinkler's is a valid observation, though it may be that in this context
also the 'end of the earth' means Rome — or did so at some point in
the course of the tradition.

9. For vv. 9–11 see Wilson (*Gentiles* 96–107) in debate with
Menoud, Wikenhauser, Schille, and van Stempvoort, whose views
are reported. The question whether Luke is reproducing old tradition
or writing a fresh narrative is probably misleading; the verses
contain characteristic Lucan features (notably temporal ὡς, the use
of ἀτενίζειν, periphrastic tenses), but they stand on their own and
are not integrated into the flow of narrative. Luke is probably writing
up in his own way and to suit his own concerns a piece of traditional
material (though tradition that was neither old nor widespread, since
narratives of the Ascension are not to be found elsewhere in the NT).
The scene changes because (according to Preuschen) two narratives,
a farewell service and a rapture, are being combined; it may rather
be, however, that Luke saw specific significance in the Mount of
Olives (see below).

εἰπών . . . βλεπόντων. Ropes thinks that αὐτῶν βλεπόντων
overloads the sentence and should be omitted with D d sah (Aug).
The contrast between aorist and present participles is intentional and
significant. Jesus has now said all that he has to say to his disciples.
The promise of the Spirit and the commission to act as witnesses
complete his work on earth. The disciples however are still looking
at him, and are thus able to vouch for his ascent into heaven. For the
theological meaning of the Ascension and its place in Luke's
narrative see the introduction to this section and the general discussion
of Luke's theology in Vol. II. The use of βλέπειν places the
Ascension in the same category of events as any other happening in
the story of Jesus; at the same time features of the story recall
supernatural happenings — for the theme of flying in magic see Betz
(168), and for the cloud Betz (103), also below. C. M. Young (*JTS*
1 (1950), 156), quoting Dionysius of Halicarnassus, *Roman Antiquities*
1.77.2 (the god who has visited Ilia and told her that she is to become

(cf. v. 10, ἦσαν; also 5.25; 16.9). Very cautiously he offers as an equivalent in Aramaic: קמין אנתון חזין אנתון בשמיא . The conjecture is unnecessary; Luke is a descriptive writer, and he thinks of the apostles as they *stand* gazing into heaven. The question implies that this is a mistaken attitude; the apostles should proceed to the tasks that have been assigned to them. This is against Cullmann's argument (*Zeit* 140) that Luke believed that only a short time would intervene between Ascension and parousia; the interval would be at least long enough to make a nostalgic gazing after the disappearing figure of Jesus an unprofitable waste of time. The new period now begins in which the church must set to work. Haenchen takes this as a clear warning to Luke's readers that they must not look for a speedy return of Christ; Bauernfeind regards this as possible but improbable. Certainly there is more than Loisy's 'C'est temps perdu'.

Schille sees in οὗτος ὁ a liturgical, hymnic feature; see Wilson, *Gentiles* 103. There is little ground for this.

ὁ ἀναλημφθείς corresponds to the ὑπέλαβεν of v. 9: the cloud bore him up from beneath and he was received up (from above). Cf. 4 Kdms 2.11; Elijah ἀνελήμφθη; also 1 QH 3.20: העליתני לרום עולם. But Luke's account is in no way parallel to the rabbinic story of the four who entered into Paradise (Hagigah 14b). There may however be some relevance in the figure of Metatron who is in heaven with God to the belief that the ascended Christ is at the right hand of God (see on 2.33).

It may be that the second εἰς τὸν οὐρανόν should be omitted, with D gig Aug^pt, but it is more likely that these authorities wished to avoid repetition.

οὕτως ἐλεύσεται. For the construction cf. 27.25. He will come as he has gone ('so sicher, so real und so sichtbar' — Weiser 57 quoting Lohfink). According to Bede this means, 'in eadem forma carnis et substantia veniet iudicaturus in qua venerat iudicandus'. This however does not seem to be Luke's main intention. Clarke (*DH* 29f.) writes, '"So" will then refer to the cloud, and the implied wind and fire, and the Coming of the Holy Spirit at Pentecost with some of the accompaniments of a storm — rushing wind and celestial fire — will have been the fulfilment of the promise.' But wind and fire do not appear in the account of the Ascension, nor is there a cloud on the day of Pentecost; Luke does not describe the Pentecost event as a coming of Jesus. It is reasonable to say that Jesus will come, as he went, ἐπὶ τῶν νεφελῶν (Dan. 7.13). Luke has in mind the familiar picture of the parousia of the Son of man (though it is only at 7.56 that the term is used in Acts; cf. Lk. 17.24; 21.27). He predicts the coming of Jesus as Son of man with the clouds of heaven as an event that will in due course bring church history (which is just beginning) — and world history — to a close. He does not say when this may be expected to happen.

12. ὑπέστρεψαν, the proper response to the angels' (implied) rebuke. They obeyed the command of v. 4.

εἰς Ἰερουσαλήμ. For the spelling cf. vv. 4, 8. It is doubtful whether the variation has any significance; it may point to the use of different sources.

ἀπὸ ὄρους τοῦ καλουμένου Ἐλαιῶνος. The substantive is anarthrous, the attribute has the article. For such a construction see BDR § 270.2 (with reference to 7.35): the article and the attribute are added to the substantive 'um dieses nachträglich zu bestimmen'. Cf. M.3.218, a 'kind of afterthought' — but the naming of the place is hardly an afterthought here. To have written simply, 'They returned to Jerusalem from a mountain' would have been ridiculous. Ἐλαιῶνος is undoubtedly (as in Josephus, *Ant.* 7.202) the genitive singular of Ἐλαιών, an *olive grove, olive orchard*. In other passages it is disputed whether ελαιων is the nominative singular ἐλαιών or the genitive plural ἐλαιῶν, *of olives*. See the discussion in M.1.69, 235; M.2.152; also Deissmann, *LAE* (1927), 170f., where ἐλαιών is quoted from *BGU* 37 (a papyrus of 12 September 50); there is more detail in Deissmann, *BS* 208–12. The noun ἐλαιών is probably a form that came into being on the basis of the genitive ἐλαιῶν, which represents more literally the Hebrew הר־הזיתים (Zech. 14.4; LXX, τὸ ὄρος τῶν ἐλαιῶν). For the Mount of Olives see Dalman (*SSW* 261–8; more fully, *Jerusalem und sein Gelände* 21–55, with Plates 1–6, 31, 37); more recently, J. Murphy-O'Connor (*The Holy Land* 84–6).

The location of the Mount of Olives is given in 'heiliges Mass' (Bauernfeind); and the theological event of the Ascension is brought into relation with the theologically significant city (Schneider 205). This seems clear; not however that we have here (Schille) a Jewish regulation applied by Jewish Christians to a Christian festival (Wilson, *Gentiles* 103). Taking a Sabbath day's journey to be 2000 cubits (Mekhilta Exod. 16.29 (59a); Targum Yerushalmi 1 on Exod. 16.29; Erubin 51a; j. Berakoth 5.9a.40) and a cubit 56 cm., the distance given is 1120 metres; and this according to Dalman (*SSW* 267) is the distance from the city (presumably Dalman means from a central point in the city, but he does not specify one) to the summit of the mountain. 'Thus the traditional location somewhat north of the Bethany road, on the full height of the summit looking out towards Jerusalem, would suit all the data' (ibidem). It follows from this that Luke (or his source) was not following the stricter Qumran rule which forbade the observant to go out on the Sabbath further than 1,000 cubits (CD 10.21: אל יהלך איש לעירו על אלף באמה); only if pasturing a beast might he go 2,000 cubits (CD 11.5f.). Two Galilean inscriptions may show that the expression σαββάτου ὁδός, or something like it, was current in Greek. See Sevenster, *Greek* 121. Unfortunately one of the inscriptions is no longer extant, and of both Sevenster rightly comments that they 'could be of great significance if a certain interpretation of them could be established definitely and if it were known exactly when they were made.' The extant inscription is *CIJ* II, no. 992. According to Josephus, *Ant.* 20.169 the Mount of Olives is opposite the city and ἀπέχει στάδια πέντε; according to *War* 5.70 it was six stadia distant. The measurement given above falls between five and six stadia (taking the stadion as about 192 metres). The measurement of the distance in terms of what was permitted on the Sabbath might suggest that the Ascension took place on a Sabbath. This can hardly have been Luke's own view if he took strictly (and not as a 'biblical' approximation) the period of forty days referred to in v. 3. If the resurrection took place on the first day of the week a forty day interval does not bring us to the seventh. It is possible that the tradition on which Luke was dependent did place the Ascension on a Sabbath; possible that it did not distinguish, as Luke does, between resurrection and Ascension. The detail does however add (see above) to the Jewish atmosphere of the opening chapters of Acts; cf. 3.1 (Peter and John go to the Jewish Temple for Jewish prayers).

In stating the distance Luke uses ἔχειν where ἀπέχειν would be much more usual. The simple form however was used (though seldom) in this sense. Preuschen cites the *Periplus Mar. Erythr.* 37, Ὡραῖα... ἔχουσα ὁδὸν ἡμερῶν ἑπτὰ ἀπὸ θαλάσσηςἀπέχουσα.

13. εἰσῆλθον, into Jerusalem. In v. 12 Luke effected a transition from the narrative of the Ascension to the next stage in his story and now he gives a summary which prepares the way for the next event. Like his other summaries it contains little that could not have been generalised out of details supplied by narrative tradition. Luke's own hand is at work.

ὑπερῷον. In the NT this word occurs only in Acts (1.13; 9.37, 39; 20.8). In Lk. (22.12; also Mk 14.15) the room in which the Last Supper was eaten is described as an ἀνάγαιον (no parallel in Mt). It may be that Luke intended to distinguish the two rooms; certainly he does not go out of his way to identify them (though it is not impossible that the article τό should be regarded as anaphoric). It is more likely that in the gospel Luke was following Mk and that in Acts he had a different source, or perhaps wrote independently: ὑπερῷον (notwithstanding Moeris — 'διῆρες, 'Αττικῶς· ὑπερῷ-ον, κοινόν'; this distinction does not appear in Hesychius) has a better background in Greek. It is used by Homer (of the *'upper part of the house*, where the women resided' — LS 1871), but continued in use in Comedy. The Aramaic עילית is used similarly; there is evidence in both Greek (e.g. Aristophanes, *Knights* 1001) and in Aramaic (e.g. Baba Bathra 133b) for such an attic as a store room. Dalman (*SSW* 281) thinks of either an upper storey, or of a room erected on a flat roof. This is probable. The word is frequently used in this sense in the LXX; there are however a few passages (1 Chron. 28.11 (and 20, si v. l.); 2 Chron. 3.9; Jer. 20.2 — all with Hebrew עליה; Ezek. 41.7 — Hebrew עליון) where the word is used of a chamber in the Temple, and it has been suggested that the Christians were able to make use of such a room (cf. Lk. 24.53). There is no great probability in this; cf. 3.1, where Peter and John are going to the Temple. See however on 2.1f. StrB 2.594 give evidence of the use of upper rooms as meeting-places, as studies, and as places for prayer. To the last *Mart. Pol.* 7.1 corresponds. 'The mention of women would certainly indicate a private house rather than the Temple' (Knowling 61).

ἦσαν καταμένοντες. The periphrastic tense suggests continuity. We can hardly suppose that all the persons mentioned were *residing* in one room; the meaning must be that they habitually met there.

Repetition of the list of the names of the Eleven shows that the first Book (the third gospel) had been issued independently; it is not correct to think of Lk-Acts as originally one book that was at some point divided in two (see above). In content (apart from the dropping of Judas Iscariot) the list of names corresponds with that in Lk. 6.14–16. In the gospel the first name in the list is Simon, with the addition of the surname Peter. Simon's brother Andrew is neatly placed next in Lk.; in Acts (as in Mk 3.18) Andrew follows James and John. The order of James and John is reversed, and so is that of Thomas and Matthew. The last three names follow without alteration, except that in the gospel the second Simon is τὸν καλούμενον ζηλωτήν whereas in Acts he is simply ὁ ζηλωτής. Brandon (*Fall* 48) has suggested that James is made to follow John in order to diminish his importance and enhance that of James the Lord's brother (12.17; 15.13; 21.18); it is more likely that John's name was brought forward because of his prominence and association with Peter in the early chapters of Acts (3.1, 3, 4, 11; 4.13, 19; 8.14). The omission of the participle with the name of the second Simon does not seem to be significant, though (looking at the matter in reverse) its addition in Lk. might suggest that Zealot was only a name — he was called a Zealot but was not one. On the Zealots see W. R. Farmer, *Maccabees, Zealots and Josephus*, 1956; M. Hengel, *Die Zeloten*, 1976²; and *NS* 2.598–606, with the bibliography. They are often, and perhaps rightly, identified with Josephus's 'fourth sect' (*Ant.* 18.23); since Josephus does not in this passage use the word ζηλωτής the identification cannot be certain, and we cannot therefore (on the basis of *Ant.* 18.6, 9) say that the 'sect' came into being at the time of the first enrolment (Lk. 2.1f.; Acts 5.37). It can however be said that the activities of the Zealots described in Josephus, *War*, correspond with what is said of the 'fourth sect' in *Ant.* 18.23: 'This school agrees in all other respects with the Pharisees, except that they have a passion for liberty that is almost unconquerable, since they are convinced that God alone is their leader and master (ἡγεμόνα καὶ δεσπότην).

They think little of submitting to death in unusual forms and permitting vengeance to fall on kinsmen and friends if only they may avoid calling any man master.' What this passage leaves unsaid is the untold misery that the Zealots of *War* unhesitatingly inflicted not only on national foes but on fellow countrymen. The background of the word (which is not uncommon in non-biblical Greek) as used here may perhaps be quite different; cf. 1 Cor. 14.1; Titus 2.14; 1 Peter 3.13. But Mk 3.18 (Σίμωνα τὸν Καναναῖον), the parallel to Lk. 6.15, suggests that this disciple had been a Zealot in the political sense. Cullmann's paper 'Der zwölfte Apostel' (*V&A* 214–22), though it contains some interesting observations on the origin and meaning of *Iscariot*, fails to prove that the other Judas did not exist; he does not explain the origin of 'Ιακώβου. In addition to the lists in Mt, Mk, and Lk cf. that in *Acts of Thomas* 1 (L.-B. 2.2.99), which is almost identical with that in Acts. Hemer (221) notes that Halphai, Zebidah, and John all occur in an Aramaic inscription (*CIJ* 982) situated in Capernaum.

'Per hos paucos et contemtos homines, sine ullis praesidiis humanis, Christus mundum ad obedientiam fidei perduxit' (Bengel).

After the first four names (joined together with . . . τε . . . καὶ . . . καὶ . . . καὶ . . .) come two pairs formed by καί and standing in asyndeton (BDR § 444.4); then a group of three names also in asyndeton, joined with one another by two καί's. For such listing cf. 2.9–11 and other examples given by BDR loc. cit. But there is textual variation; D omits καί before the first James and the second Simon, probably because the names were arranged in two parallel columns.

It has been suggested that the names were arranged in order of call, as with those of the Essenes in Josephus, *War* 2.150. In 1 QS the order is regulated annually by a test taken by the members of the group.

14. ἦσαν προσκαρτεροῦντες, another periphrastic imperfect (cf. v. 13), emphasising continuity of action. This is implied by the verb itself, which is characteristic of the opening chapters of Acts (1.14; 2.42, 46; 6.4; 8.13; 10.7); elsewhere in the NT, Mt once, Romans twice, Colossians once. It is often connected with prayer (Acts 1.14; 2.42, 46; 12.12; Col. 4.2; also with other forms of Christian activity. It means resolute, sometimes obstinate, persistence; occasionally, but not by any means always, and not here, in face of some kind of resistance or opposition.

ὁμοθυμαδόν occurs frequently and characteristically in Acts. 'In the LXX (a) it is used to translate Hebrew words [יחד ;יחדו] which mean simply 'together', (b) it is interchanged with other Greek words or phrases e.g. ἅμα, ἐπὶ τὸ αὐτό, κατὰ τὸ αὐτό which mean simply 'together', (c) it occurs in contexts in which the strict etymological meaning [with one accord] is impossible' (Hatch, *Essays* 63). After listing the uses in the NT Hatch continues, 'In none of these passages is there any reason for assuming that the word has any other meaning than that which it has in the Greek versions of the OT, viz. "together"' (63f.). Reicke, who also notes the etymological meaning (einmütig) adds that the word 'in der Apg. nie die Einheit der Gefühle, sondern immer die Einheit der Individuen als einer korporativen Totalität bezeichnet, so dass es ungefähr *in corpore* bedeutet' (*DF&Z,* 27). This seems to be a fair observation.

τῇ προσευχῇ. The addition of καὶ τῇ δεήσει (C³𝔐) is probably due to assimilation to Phil. 4.6, but points to the correct meaning: they continued in prayer. It is true that προσευχή may mean *place of prayer* (cf. 16.13), but see 2.42, where the plural is used. It is unlikely that the article (*the* service of prayer) points to the synagogue service, still attended by the first Christians. The significance of this unceasing prayer is brought out by Origen, *c. Celsum* 8.22.

The most natural way to take σὺν γυναιξίν is, *with their wives*; so e.g. Calvin 37f., though on grounds of general probability, which would be disputed by those who argue (e.g. Schmithals 25) that the persons concerned are mentioned as witnesses, so that the women will be the women witnesses of Lk. 24.1, etc. *With certain women* (unspecified) would be σὺν γυναιξίν τισιν; *with the (well-known) women disciples* would be σὺν ταῖς γυναιξίν. The latter interpretation is supported by Delebecque (4), with the observation that the article is omitted with words denoting sex. Reference to the families of the Eleven is supported by the reading of D (σὺν ταῖς γυναιξίν καὶ τέκνοις; d, cum mulieribus et filiis); this reading is explained by Conzelmann as due to a failure to recognise that the list is a list of witnesses; it now however finds some support in the Acts capitula (in the MSS Monacensis Lat. 6230; Bambergensis A.1.7; Metensis 7 — in WW III 7), of which the second reads, 'De congregatione apostolorum et oratione quam cum altricibus suis mulieribus celebrarent.' See W. Thiele, in *ZNW* 53 (1962), 110f. (who, against WW, reads celebrabant). This Western interpretation may not give the original text but least shows how an early editor understood the original text.

Mary the mother of Jesus is referred to here only in Acts; see Lk. 1, 2 passim. The sources of Luke's infancy narratives are not to be discussed here; it is clear that Luke either has no information, or is not concerned to provide information, about Mary in the post-resurrection period. She has been represented (Lk. 1.38) as an ideal of trust and obedience: Behold the handmaid of the Lord; be it unto me according to thy word. 'The real import of Acts 1.14 is to remind the reader that she had not changed her mind' (R. E. Brown, K. P. Donfried, J. A. Fitzmyer, and J. Reumann, *Mary in the NT*, London, 1978, 177). The earthly family of Jesus is now taken up into his

spiritual family (cf. Mk 3.31–35). This is the point of the reference
to Mary and also of that to the brothers of Jesus which follows. These
are never again mentioned in Acts; even James (12.17; 15.13; 21.28)
is not described as the Lord's brother, though he is so described in
Galatians (1.19; cf. 2.9, 12). It is clearly impossible on the basis of
this verse alone to discuss the names, identity, and relation to Jesus
of those who are here described as his ἀδελφοί. For their names see
Mk 6.3. For a clear and critical account of the Helvidian view (that
the ἀδελφοί were sons of Mary and Joseph, born after the birth of
Jesus), the Epiphanian view (that they were sons of Joseph by an
earlier marriage, and thus older than Jesus), and the Hieronymian
view (that they were cousins of Jesus, children of Mary's sister), and
a new suggestion (that the ἀδελφοί were by descent cousins of Jesus
but on the side of Joseph, not Mary, and by up-bringing foster-
brothers of Jesus), see J. McHugh, *The Mother of Jesus in the NT*,
London, 1975, 200–254). The present verse contributes nothing to
the arguments for or against any of these theories, though it is fair
to add that the most natural meaning of ἀδελφός is blood-brother,
that foster-brother is not impossible, and that cousin is very improbable.
See J. B. Lightfoot, *Galatians* 252–91.

The repetition of σύν before τοῖς ἀδελφοῖς αὐτοῦ (by B C³ E
Ψ𝔐) distinguished the group of women, mentioned first, from the
group of men; it may have been intended to safeguard belief in the
perpetual virginity of Mary (Metzger). The omission of τοῦ before
Ἰησοῦ seems to be a simple error (so Ropes).

2. JUDAS AND MATTHIAS 1.15–26

(15) In these days Peter stood up in the midst of the brothers and said (the number of persons amounted in all to about 120), (16) 'Brothers, the Scripture had to be fulfilled which the Holy Spirit spoke in advance through the mouth of David, concerning Judas, who acted as guide to those who arrested Jesus; (17) for he had been counted among us and obtained the lot of this ministry. (18) With the reward of his unrighteous act he purchased a property. He fell flat on his face, burst in the middle, and all his intestines poured out. (19) This became known to all the residents of Jerusalem, so that the property was called in their language Aceldama, that is, Blood Field. (20) For it is written in the Book of Psalms, Let his steading be desolate, and let there be none who lives in it; and, Let someone else take his office.[1] (21) So then of those men who accompanied us in all the time the Lord Jesus went in and out among us, (22) beginning from the baptism of John until the day he was received up from us, one must become with us a witness to his resurrection.'

(23) They nominated two, Joseph called Barsabbas, who was surnamed Justus, and Matthias. (24) They prayed and said, 'Thou, Lord, who knowest the hearts of all men, show which of these two thou hast chosen (25) to receive the position of ministry and apostleship from which Judas fell away to go to his own place.' (26) They cast lots for them, and the lot fell on Matthias, and he was voted in along with the eleven apostles.

Bibliography

W. A. Beardslee, *NovT* 4 (1960), 245–52.

P. Benoit, *Ex. et Th.*, 1.340–59.

H. von Campenhausen, as in (1).

O. Cullmann, *RHPhR* (1962), 133–40.

J. D. M. Derrett, *JSNT* 8 (1980), 2–23.

J. D. M. Derrett, *ZNW* 72 (1981), 131–3.

J. Dupont, *Études*, 299f., 309–20.

J. Dupont, *FS* Reicke, 139–45.

J. Dupont, *Nouvelles Études*, 58–111, 133–50, 186–92.

J. A. Emerton, as in (1).

M. S. Enslin, *FS* Gingrich, 123–41.

[1] NEB, take over his charge; *Begs.* overseership.

R. H. Fuller, *StEv* 6 (1973;=*TU* 112), 140–6.

W. Horbury, *NTS* 32 (1986), 503–27.

P. W. van der Horst, as in (1).

A. Jaubert, *FS* Dupont-Sommer, 453–60.

A. Jaubert, *StEv* 6 (1973; = *TU* 112), 274–80.

J. A. Kirk, *NTS* 21 (1975), 249–61.

G. Lohfink, *BZ* 19 (1975), 247–9.

Ch. Masson, *RThPh* 3 (1955), 193–201.

P. H. Menoud, *RHPhR* 37 (1957), 71–80.

H. Mosbech, *StTh* 2 (1950), 166–200.

E. Nellessen, *BZ* 19 (1975), 205–18.

K. H. Rengstorf, *StTh* 15 (1962), 35–67.

J. Renié, *RB* 55 (1948), 43–53.

C. Roth, *HThR* 54 (1961), 91–7.

E. Schweizer, *ThZ* 14 (1958), 46.

L. S. Thornton, *JTS* 46 (1945), 51–9.

M. Wilcox, *NTS* 19 (1973), 438–52.

Commentary

There is a parallel but different account of the fate of Judas in Mt. 27.3–10; there is no NT parallel to the election of a replacement for him.

In Matthew Judas repents of his treachery after the condemnation but before the death of Jesus; he seeks to return the thirty pieces of silver that he has been paid, and in fact throws them into the shrine, goes off, and hangs himself. The chief priests take the money but decide that they cannot put it into the Temple treasury since it is the price of blood, τιμὴ αἵματος. Instead they buy the Potter's Field (τὸν Ἀγρὸν τοῦ Κεραμέως) as a burial place for foreigners; henceforth the field is known as Blood Field (Ἀγρὸς αἵματος). Matthew asserts that this happened in order to fulfil the prophecy of Jer. 32.6–9, but Zech. 11.12, 13 seem also to be in his mind. Luke tells us nothing of Judas's penitence; he himself used his pay (which apparently did not wound his conscience) to acquire a piece of land (χωρίον, not ἀγρός); he did not hang himself but fell headlong (perhaps from a height — from the roof of a house as Roloff (30) suggests, thus possibly after all by suicide) so that his body ruptured and his intestines came out; the field was called in Aramaic Aceldama, that is, Blood Field (Χωρίον αἵματος) — presumably not because it had been bought with bloodmoney but because of Judas's bloody end. Attempts, such as Knowling's, to harmonise the two traditions, are not convincing.

It is evident that Matthew and Luke report different traditions, which have in common only the belief that Judas died an unhappy death and knowledge of the existence in Jerusalem of a field called Blood Field, which had at some earlier stage come to be associated with Judas (for it is most unlikely that Matthew and Luke should both, independently, have made the association). Another, broadly similar story, of the fate of Judas is told by Papias, reported in a number of Catenae (for details see Routh, *Rel. Sac.* 1.9, and Routh's notes on pp. 25–8). According to this, Judas's body swelled to such an extent that he could not pass where a carriage could easily do so; in this condition he was crushed by a carriage with the result that his entrails were forced out. It may well be that nothing was precisely known of what became of Judas. There were two lines on which speculation could move; Matthew exploited the one, which brought out (for the admonition of possible traitors within the Christian community) the horror of remorse that would befall the faithless, Luke the other, which brought out (again, for the admonition of potential traitors) the terrors of divine judgment. There is no way in which more can be done to harmonise the two traditions. For the suggestion that ᾿Ακελδαμάχ could have been misunderstood and should really be taken to mean Field of Sleep (i.e., κοιμητήριον, cemetery), see below; it is unconvincing. The story as told by Matthew is supported by *Acts of Thomas* 84 (L.-B. 2.2.200), . . . κλοπῆς, ἥτις ᾿Ιούδαν ᾿Ισκαριώτην δελεάσασα εἰς ἀγχόνην ἤγαγεν.

Luke is interested in Judas as an example of divine judgment (cf. 5.1–11, the story of Ananias and Sapphira); also as one whose defection left a gap in the ranks of the Twelve. Of this, and of steps taken to replace Judas, no other NT writer seems to be aware; no other, of course, had occasion to write about the period at which the gap must have become apparent. Peter, who now for the first time in Acts takes the initiative and acts as leader of the disciples, takes it for granted that the gap must be filled, arguing from Scripture in general terms (v. 16) that Judas's defection was necessary because willed by God, and specifically from Ps. 69.25 and 109.8 that he should be replaced. These prooftexts were almost certainly thought of after the event; the assumption that led to them and to the action they were used to justify was that the number twelve was significant and must be maintained. K. H. Rengstorf (*StTh* 15 (1961), 35–67; more briefly in *FS* Piper, 178–92) plausibly suggested that the motive underlying this was that the Twelve represented the fullness (the twelve tribes) of Israel (cf. Mt. 19.28; Lk. 22.30). The defection of Judas and, still more, the crucifixion of Jesus, for which the Jews were held responsible, might have seemed to exclude them for ever from the good purposes of God: Jesus' summons and offer to Israel had been rejected and the mission to Israel was now at an end. But it was not so; and in order to make it clear that the followers of Jesus retained a responsibility for the ancient people of God they brought the number of their leaders once more up to twelve. There is much to be said for this view, though it was hardly Luke's own, since he does nothing to suggest it. Schmithals 26 goes beyond what can be proved from the texts in the assertion that for Luke Twelve means Israel and Seven means the Gentiles. Luke's own (or his source's) motivation is simply to show (a) that Judas's sin was foreknown and foretold — that is, it was not due to oversight or negligence on the part of Jesus, and (b) that it was unable to halt the progress of the Gospel.

One would be inclined to think that Luke had received from tradition the bare outline of Judas's death and the accession to the Twelve of a person called Matthias and had written up these bare data for himself, making his scriptural references, describing the use of the lot, and defining in his own way the qualifications of an apostle (cf. Lüdemann 39) were it not for the very awkward parenthesis in v. 15, which suggests the imperfect editing of a fuller body of traditional material. From this point onward, however, there seems to be no way of disentangling sources, whether oral or written; and (see the note) Bauernfeind may be right in minimizing the awkwardness of the inserted statistics. Attempts have been made to analyse the paragraph. Weiser (64–6) gives a clear account of various opinions, according to which Luke used one, two, or three traditions (he himself thinks of two). Bauernfeind 26 thinks that the careful structure of the paragraph must come from Luke himself, Schmithals 27 that vv. 21–6 are in Lucan style but a tradition may lie behind these verses. Haenchen (167) is certainly right in thinking that nothing in the speech can come from Peter himself. It is however probable that the lack of certain knowledge about Judas may have prompted the development of various rumours and legends that Luke used as the framework for a story that enshrines his understanding of the role of the apostles.

There is no further example in Acts (or in the rest of the NT) of the use of the lot by Christians to determine a matter. It may be that Luke wishes to show the difference made by the gift of the Holy Spirit: after the Day of Pentecost the church was led by the Spirit (e.g. 13.1–3; 16.6, 7) and had no need for such mechanical processes; it is certain that he wished to represent Matthias as being as truly chosen by Christ (ἀνάδειξον ὃν ἐξελέξω, v. 24) as his fellow apostles (1.2, ἐξελέξατο).

Pesch (92) argues that when two or more candidates for office, all equally suitable, appear there is something to be said for the lot as a means of deciding between them: a vote-catching campaign could lead equally to a chance decision and also introduce rivalry. In vv. 21–3 Luke shows how he understood apostleship. An apostle was not only one who could bear personal testimony to the resurrection of Christ (though this was his main task as μάρτυς τῆς ἀναστάσεως αὐτοῦ, v. 22); he must also be one who had been a companion of Jesus throughout his ministry (vv. 21, 22). The negative effect of this condition, strictly understood, was to exclude Paul from the ranks of the apostles, who had a ministry they could not hand on to others, but (Schmithals 27) Luke may be concerned not to attack Paul (in the light of the book as a whole this is inconceivable) but Paulinists who regarded him as the only apostle. The positive intention was to establish continuity between Jesus and the church.

15. ἐν ταῖς ἡμέραις ταύταις , between the Ascension (referred to in v. 22) and Pentecost (2.1). The dating is emphatic because Luke wishes to emphasize that the church was in a state of readiness for the gift of the Spirit, perhaps also to suggest (by the use of the lot) that until the gift was given it was not ready for its work. The expression is one of several Septuagintalisms in the verse, of which Haenchen (163) says, 'darum klang er für die Leser des Lukas selbst wie der Beginn einer biblischen Geschichte'.

For the first time Peter stands out (cf. *Martyrium Andreae Prius* 1 (L. -B. 2.1.46), ἀναστὰς ἐν μέσῳ αὐτῶν ὁ μακάριος Πέτρος εἶπεν ...) as spokesman and leader. His prominence continues until the beginning of Paul's first journey (ch. 13), is resumed in ch. 15, and is then dropped. Peter is also prominent in the gospels and in the tradition of the post-apostolic age (cf. 1 Clem. 5.4; Ignatius, *Romans* 4.3; *Smyrnaeans* 3.2). That he played a leading part in the early church is hardly to be doubted; see O. Cullmann, *Petrus*, and R. E. Brown, K. P. Donfried, J. Reumann, *Peter in the New Testament*, Minneapolis/New York, 1973. Peter stands up (ἀναστάς, probably another imitation of the LXX) in the midst of the *brothers* (for ἀδελφῶν, (C³) D E Ψ 𝔐 it sy mae Cyprian have μαθητῶν; P⁷⁴ has ἀποστόλων; both variants were probably intended to avoid confusion with ἀδελφοί in 1.14); probably the whole Christian group rather than the apostles only is intended, but note the σὺν ἡμῖν of v. 22. The word μαθητής is not used in Acts 1–5; ἀδελφός is used frequently throughout the book, sometimes of Jews, often of Christians. Christian usage reflects Jewish; believers are now all members of God's reconstituted family.

εἶπεν should introduce Peter's speech but is followed by a parenthetical clause (cf. Gen. 6.9, 10) giving the number of persons involved in the proceedings. It is difficult to think that any writer would willingly interrupt himself in this way, and it is therefore natural to suppose that at this point Luke was incorporating a statement from one source into another which he was in the main following. It is worth noting that τε is unusual in a parenthesis (δέ should be used; see BDR §§ 443, n. 4; 447.1(b)); possibly in Luke's source the clause was not parenthetical. There are however unexpected infelicities elsewhere in Acts, and it is possible that what we have in this verse is an unfortunate lapse which Luke omitted to remove from his work. Bauernfeind indeed (27) thinks the clause is not really awkward; it had to come at the beginning yet could not be part of the speech.

It is also unusual that ὄνομα should be used in the sense of *person*. This may be due to imitation of the Hebrew שמות (see e.g. Num. 1.18; 26.53, 55). *DBS* 196f. finds the same use in the papyri, but all his examples are in the singular: *BU* 113.11; 265.18; 531. ii. 9f.; 388. i. 16, cf. ii. 35: this is true also of *I.Eph.* II 555, l.1 (cited in *ND* 4.153). Of these the most satisfactory parallel is the first: ἑκάστῳ ὀνόματι παρα(γενομένῳ). Other examples in Greek literature have been found: Apollonius, *Epistle* 66, where λῷον ὄνομα seems to mean *a better person*, is the only one worth considering. Again, Luke is writing in the idiom of the LXX. ἐπὶ τὸ αὐτό (see the note on 2.47), *together, in all*, 'perpetually used in arithmetical statements' (M.1.107), and the approximation ὡσεί are both Lucan.

It has been noted that the number 120 = 10 x 12, and that there are Jewish parallels for a system of one leader for each of ten members; 1 QS 6.3f.; 1 QSa 2.22; CD 13.1f.; Sanhedrin 1.6; Aboth 3.6 are quoted but none of them quite proves the point. If the proportion is true, and is significant, and was significant for Luke, he has probably argued in reverse: Since there were twelve leaders there must have been 120 members. The argument is however unconvincing; the 120 of 1.14 included women, who would not have been counted in assessing the size of a Jewish community. It may be asked how the 120 are related to the 500 of 1 Cor. 15.6. It is possible, as Bruce suggests, that most of the latter group were in Galilee; but we are not dealing with a period in which precise numerical records were made and kept.

16. ἄνδρες ἀδελφοί. Cf. 4 Macc. 8.19; again, LXX style; see Plümacher (47). For the prefixed ἄνδρες see 1.11; for ἀδελφοί see on v. 15. It is used of fellow Christians (e.g. 6.3) and of fellow Jews (e.g. 2.29, 37), as well as of the brothers of Jesus (1.14). The next words convey Luke's belief about the OT as a whole. It was spoken by the Holy Spirit; the Holy Spirit spoke through notable persons, such as David; what was contained in the OT must needs (ἔδει; D* lat have δεῖ, which is proper in v. 22, which declares what we must now do, but incorrect in the present verse, which says what had to happen) be fulfilled since it is God's word. γραφή in the singular may refer to Scripture as a whole (as at 8.32; for this the plural αἱ γραφαί is more usual) or to a particular passage (as at 8.35). Here the reference must be to a passage in the Psalms (taken to be the work of David). What passage is in mind is disputed. Some think the reference is to those quoted in v. 20; perhaps more probable is Ps.

41.10. Luke can assume that his readers are familiar with his own or, less probably, some other account of Judas and his treachery. ὁδηγός does not occur in the Lucan narrative, but cf. Lk. 22.47, προήρχετο (and the variant, προῆγεν, D f¹ *al*).

17. ὅτι may introduce (Haenchen 164) the content of what the Holy Spirit said; more probably it explains why a vacancy had occurred: this was *because* he had been counted among us (κατηριθμημένος ἦν, periphrastic pluperfect — this was the position that he had now lost). For ὅτι, d vg have *qui*; this has been defended as an indication of underlying Aramaic, the particle ד, which may mean (among other things) both *because* and *who*, having been misunderstood. It is more likely that this is an internal Latin variation: in qui*a a*dnumeratus one *a* was omitted by haplography. So Wilcox (115f.).

καταριθμεῖν is used of the inclusion of someone in a list (e.g. Plutarch, *Solon* 12 (84): Epimenedes ὃν ἕβδομον ἐν τοῖς σοφοῖς καταριθμοῦσιν ἔνιοι).

κλῆρος is used in v. 26 in its primary sense of *lot*; here it means *that which is assigned by lot*, or at least might be thought of as having been so assigned; it is an allotment, often an allotment of land (as often גורל in the OT), here an allotment of a ministry (διακονία), given through a choice made by Jesus. The διακονία is the apostolic ministry, to be exercised by the eleven remaining apostles together with Matthias. This consists in bearing witness (1.8, 22); later it will be described as a διακονία τοῦ λόγου (6.4). Braun (148) and Stählin (25) among others are right in the view that κλῆρος here can hardly be rendered *office (Amt)*. This translation would not be justified by 1 QS 1.10; 1 QSa 1.13, 16; CD 13.12; 20.4 (where גורל and עבודה are used; for 1 QS 2.23 see on v. 25). What Judas once possessed was the privilege of service (cf. Josephus, *Ant.* 18.21, where διακονία is *help*). There is a striking parallel in Aeschines, *adv. Ctesiphontem* 13: ὅσα τις αἵρετος ὧν πράττει κατὰ ψήφισμα, οὐκ ἔστι ταῦτα ἀρχὴ ἀλλ'ἐπιμέλειά τις καὶ διακονία.

Wilcox (*NTS* 19 (1973) 447) points to a parallel in the wording of Gen. 44.18 in Targum D, and goes on to suggest (452) that vv. 17, 18, 19a (and perhaps 16a) contain traditional exegesis. If this is correct (but it may be judged possible rather than proved) it would follow, as Wilcox says, that vv. 17–19 cannot be regarded as an 'insertion'; they are the traditional material, and the more 'Lucan' verses are redactional.

This passage is reproduced in some detail by Irenaeus (*adv. Haer.* 3.12.1).

18. This verse and the next are an example of Luke's literary art

(Schneider 217f.); they contain no evidence of translation, only of a story with Aramaic roots (Wilcox 171). μὲν οὖν picks up the story (of the fate of Judas) after a small digression that looks back to what Judas had previously been; cf. 1.6. Peter appears to be telling his audience of an event in the fairly distant past; in fact it belonged to no more than a few weeks ago. The truth of course is that Luke is telling the story for the benefit of his readers; there was no need for Peter to tell it at all. Judas *purchased* (not simply *acquired*; see 8.20; 22.28; Aristophanes, *Birds* 598, 602) a piece of land (χωρίον); contrast Mt 27.7, where it is said that the *chief priests* bought an ἀγρός. χωρίον means an estate or farm (*Mart. Pol.* 7.1) rather than a field, but the difference between the two words is not great (cf. Xenophon, *History of Greece* 2.4.1: ἦγον δὲ ἐκ τῶν χωρίων ἵνα αὐτοὶ καὶ οἱ φίλοι τοὺς τούτων ἀγροὺς ἔχοιεν), and they are variant translations of לקח (used in the name Ἀκελδαμάχ, v. 19), which can mean both field and farm or estate. The use of χωρίον may have been suggested by Ps. 69.20. On the locality, see Benoit (*Ex. et Th.* 1.352–9); on the whole (340–59).

For ἐκ *by means of* cf. Lk. 16.9, ἐκ τοῦ μαμωνᾶ τῆς ἀδικίας. This parallel might suggest that in Acts also ἀδικίας is an adjectival genitive, but it is more probably objective; the reward he obtained for his unrighteous act (M. 2.440).

πρηνὴς γενόμενος means *having come to be prone*, that is, lying face downwards. The adjective is often used with a part of πίπτειν (e.g. Philo, *de Op. Mundi* 157, the snake ζῷον ἄπουν ἐστὶ καὶ πρηνὲς πεπτωκὸς ἐπὶ γαστέρα; also Josephus, *Life* 138; *War* 1.621; 6.64; *Ant.* 18.59; *Orac. Sib.* 4.110; all cited by BA 1404, s.v.), but γίνεσθαι is a tolerable alternative. There is thus no need for the conjecture (F. H. Chase, *JTS* 12 (1911), 278; Harnack, *ThLZ* 37.235) that it is equivalent to πρησθείς, still less for Pallis's (50) proposal that for πρηνής should be read περιτενής (distended, swollen) and that the Vulgate's *suspensus* (see below) is an error for *distensus*! The suggestion by Delebecque (5), that the reference is to a head bowed in hanging, is more serious, but not convincing.

ἐλάκησεν is to be derived from λακέω (or λακάω). There is a good parallel for this uncommon word in Aristophanes, *Clouds* 410, διαλακήσασα; cf. *Acts of Thomas* 33 (of a dragon). See LS 1025; BDR § 101, n. 45; M. 2.246.

ἐξεχύθη. Cf. the story given by Papias (Routh, *Rel. Sac.* 1.9), ὥστε τὰ ἔγκατα αὐτοῦ ἐκκενωθῆναι.

Cf. the death of Amasa in 2 Kdms 20.10 and that of Catullus in Josephus, *War* 7.453 (τῶν ἐντέρων αὐτῷ κατὰ διάβρωσιν ἐκπεσόντων). Luke no doubt understood Judas's death as Josephus (loc. cit.) understood that of Catullus (God τοῖς πονηροῖς δίκην ἐπιτίθησιν). There is however a textual tradition that accommodates the present narrative to Matthew's account (27.5) of Judas' suicide.

For the evidence see Metzger (286f.), and add Ropes' (*Begs.* 3.8) reference to Augustine, *c. Felicem* 1.4f. (et collum sibi alligavit et dejectus in faciem). Clark (338) thinks that this implies a στίχος lost in all existing MSS; after ἀδικίας (αὐτοῦ) should be added καὶ τὸν τράχηλον κατέδησεν αὐτοῦ. Bede read the Vulgate text and commented: Dignam sibi poenam traditor amens invenit, ut videlicet guttur quo vox proditionis exierat laquei nodus necaret.

It has also been suggested that Judas committed suicide by jumping (or possibly suffered an accident by falling) from a height; cf. Hullin 56b. See further Schneider (214). One may suspect that some interpreters, ancient and modern, have been moved by two motives: to remove from Scripture an apparent contradiction, and to make explicit details which may perhaps be better left in obscurity.

19. γνωστὸν (*notus* magis hellenisticum quam atticum — Blass 47) ἐγένετο. The sentence is turned into a relative clause by the addition of ὅ before καί (ℵ* D sy^p). This is Lucan in style and may be original. If the matter became known to all the inhabitants of Jerusalem it was not necessary for Peter to tell his hearers the story. Luke is of course telling it for his readers.

τῆ ἰδίᾳ (this word is omitted by ℵ B* D latt, but should be read; the pleonasm with αὐτῶν makes it lectio difficilior, and haplography with the next word may have contributed to the omission) διαλέκτῳ αὐτῶν. As the next word shows, this language was (not Hebrew but) Aramaic. Again we have Luke writing for the benefit of his Greek-speaking readers, not Peter speaking for his Aramaic-speaking hearers.

Ἀκελδαμάχ: so B 1175 *pc*. Several other forms are found: Αχελδαμαχ (P⁷⁴ ℵ A 81 *pc* lat); Ακελδαιμα (D); Ακελδαμα (CΨ𝔐 vg^cl); Ακελδαμακ (E). The spelling with χ as the second letter is lectio difficilior and may for that reason be preferred; κ is a better equivalent of Aramaic ‎ק‎ than χ — this may be a good enough reason for following P⁷⁴ ℵ rather than B. In any case we are dealing with a transliteration of the Aramaic חקל דמא, χωρίον αἵματος, field of blood. Dalman (*Gram.*¹ 161 n. 6 = *Gram.*² 202 n. 3) suggests that the final χ may have been added to make it clear that the word (in Greek) is indeclinable; he compares Ἰωσήχ in Lk. 3.26 for יוסי and Σειράχ in the LXX for סירא. This is very plausible, though M.2.153 mentions without specifically approving, and WS 63 n. 69 appears to prefer, alternative explanations, such as an aspirated pronunciation of א, or confusion of א with ה or ח. The suggestion that the last two syllables should be derived from דמכא, *sleep*, so that Aceldama means *field of sleep*, and of those who sleep (in death), i.e., cemetery (cf. Mt 27.7) is dismissed perhaps too readily by Dalman (loc. cit.), and by Wilcox (88); the verb דמך, דמוך, דמיך, can mean *to lie in the grave* (Jastrow, s.v.). It is however quite clear that this is not how Luke took the word.

He explains it as arising from the story of Judas; it is more probable that the story of Judas in the forms in which we have it arose at least in part from the field that bore this unusual name. For traditions concerning the locality and characteristics of Aceldama see Dalman (*SSW* 331–3).

20. Scripture (two passages, one referring to past events, the other to what is to be done in the future) was not merely aware of what was to take place (v. 16) but made provision for it. Ps. 69 (68).26 is taken to refer to Judas's deposition from his position (or office, but see on v. 16), or rather perhaps to his death. If it is taken strictly as referring to Judas's office it would mean that he should not be replaced. The wording is adapted from the LXX. In the first line αὐτῶν, in the Psalm (retained by assimilation in a few NT MSS) becomes αὐτοῦ (i.e., Judas's), and ἠρημωμένη becomes ἔρημος without change of meaning (though it may be that Luke had a different LXX text). In the second line there is variation in order and ἐν τοῖς σκηνώμασιν αὐτῶν becomes ἐν αὐτῇ (referring to ἔπαυλις). *Tents* seemed no doubt remote from the story of Judas; and ἔπαυλις (*homestead* — MM 230; see also *ND* 3.71) could be equivalent to χωρίον. The second quotation speaks not only of Judas's displacement but of his replacement, and is cited by Peter as the warrant (it is important that the believers are represented as acting in conformity with the instructions of the OT) for the step that is now to be taken. Acts follows the LXX of Ps. 109 (108). 8 precisely except that for λάβοι it substitutes λαβέτω, expressing an instruction rather than a wish (cf. BDR § 384 n.1). τὴν ἐπισκοπὴν αὐτοῦ of both Acts and LXX represents ו‌פקדתו. ἐπισκοπή is almost exclusively a biblical and Christian word (at Lucian, *Dial. Deorum* 20.6, sometimes cited, it means *visit*). Here, as a rendering of the Hebrew and as used by Luke, it means simply *office* and contains no more indication of the nature of the office than readers of Acts may have brought to the text. Bauernfeind (28) is not far wrong with a discussion that may be crudely summarised in the formula ἐπισκοπή + διακονία = ἀποστολή. It is clear that Matthias is to do what Judas would have done had he not defected, that is, he will, as one who had accompanied Jesus throughout his ministry, bear witness to his resurrection and thus establish the continuity between Jesus and the post-resurrection church. For the meaning of the corresponding *nomen agentis* ἐπίσκοπος as applied to Christian ministers see on 20.28.

It is important to note the authority ascribed here to OT scripture, and the way in which it is used. It cannot be said that any attention is given to the context, still less to the original meaning and reference, of the passages cited.

21. δεῖ οὖν, in obedience to Scripture (contrast ἔδει in v. 16), τῶν συνελθόντων ἡμῖν ἀνδρῶν is taken up by τούτων at the end of v. 22; the sentence runs somewhat out of control and in other respects does not represent Luke's best style. ἐν παντὶ χρόνῳ means *during the whole time* (not *on every occasion*; see Moule, *IB* 94f.), but with this the aorists εἰσῆλθεν, ἐξῆλθεν, seem inconsistent, for linear tenses are required (cf. 9.28). 'The rules appear to collapse with the "linear" aorists in Acts 1.21' (M.3.71). But Turner should not have included here the aorist participle συνελθόντων, which may properly be regarded as constative: their 'accompanying us' is something that can be thought of as a unit. The two verbs (which must point to more than the forty days of 1.3) can be regarded as a kind of zeugma, elliptical for εἰσῆλθεν ἐφ' ἡμᾶς καὶ ἐξῆλθεν παρ' ἡμῶν (BDR § 479.2 n. 5). On the credit side for Luke's style is the fact that the omission of the preposition ἐν before the relative ᾧ is classical: BDR § 293. 3 (e); cf. Demosthenes 9.25 (117).

Two negative points may be noted. Davies (*Land* 266) observes that there is no reference to Galilee as the scene of the ministry of Jesus, and raises the question whether the failure to refer to Galilee is deliberate. See the note on 1.8. In the present verse taken on its own there is really no point to make; for Peter's purpose it is important that Jesus exercised a public ministry and that certain people witnessed it. The scene of the ministry is not important. A weightier observation is that the qualifications laid down for appointment to the apostolic group are such as to exclude Paul. For this, and for the status accorded to Paul, see below. The role of the apostles is 'unersetzbar' (Schlatter, *Th. d. Ap.* 29).

22. The clause ἀρξάμενος . . . αὐτοῦ may be a Lucan addition (cf. 10.37; 11.4; Lk. 24.47): it helps to break the back of the sentence by separating δεῖ (v. 21) yet further from γενέσθαι and thus does much to create the awkwardness referred to in the note on v. 21. The construction of the ἀρξάμενος clause itself is not as difficult here as it is at 10.37, where see the note; also M.1.182, 240; 2.454; Moule (*IB* 31, 181). There is thus no need to suspect (with Torrey 25f.; see also J. W. Hunkin, *JTS* 25 (1924), 390–402) translation of the Aramaic מן שריא. Wilcox 148f. agrees that there is no need to presuppose an Aramaic original. ἀρξάμενος is naturally construed with ὁ Ἰησοῦς, though *Begs.* 4.14 prefers to regard it as a 'nominative absolute that has become adverbial' (cf. Dibelius 111, '"frozen" in the nominative'). τοῦ βαπτίσματος Ἰωάννου could be *his baptism by John* but more probably is the baptism John proclaimed and carried out (cf. 10.37; and the fact that all the gospels treat the ministry of John as the necessary beginning of their account of Jesus' ministry). Cf. Lk. 1.2, ἀπ' ἀρχῆς αὐτόπται. The relative ἧς is attracted in case, or possibly is to be taken as a genitive of time (Bauernfeind 29).

ἀνελήμφθη. See 1.9–11.

μάρτυρα. See 1.8; also, for Luke's understanding of the word, Maddox (75, with n. 37) and Klein (*Apostel* 204f.). The main theme of the apostolic testimony is, according to Luke, the resurrection, but it is important that the resurrection is the resurrection of the one who was baptized, conducted the ministry described in the gospel, and subsequently was killed. This passage brings out very clearly the meaning that Luke attached to the word μάρτυς. Nothing could make Joseph and Matthias more truly eye-witnesses than they already were; one of them was to assume the specific task of *bearing witness* to that which he had seen. μάρτυς, for Luke, is one who bears witness.

τούτων is added at the end of the verse to pick up the genitive plural συνελθόντων, now lost in the distance at the beginning of v. 21.

23. The community as a whole put forward (ἔστησαν) two candidates for the vacant position. For the procedure Bruce (2.51) compares the Athenian κλήρωσις ἐκ προκρίτων, in the constitution of Solon (described in Aristotle, *Ath. Pol.* 8). D* gig Augustine read the singular verb, ἔστησεν, of which the subject must be Peter. It is tempting but would be precarious to argue that the Western text was concerned to magnify the authority of Peter; cf. however 15.7 (v.1) and see Metzger (288) and Epp (*Tendency* 157f.). The corrector of D removed what he thought, perhaps rightly, to be a slip; Augustine probably quoted from memory. Luke himself ascribed the first stage in the process of selection, the establishing of a short list, to the whole body of disciples. The same procedure is adopted in ch. 6 (vv. 3, 6 — but see the variants here too).

It may be that Luke thought that Joseph and Matthias belonged to the group of 70 (72) whose appointment is mentioned in Lk. 10.1. This is claimed for Matthias in Eusebius, *H.E.* 1.12.3, but the same writer reports (3.29.4) the belief of Clement of Alexandria that he subsequently fell into heresy. If we know nothing of historical value about them they are in the same position as most of the Eleven, whom Matthias joined. The names Joseph and Matthias were common enough. Βαρσαββᾶς (cf. 15.22; D it have Βαρναβᾶς) probably means 'Son of (Aramaic בר) the Sabbath' that is, one born on the Sabbath; possibly, בר סבא, Son of the old man (one born in his father's old age), or simply Son of Saba. For the doubled β cf. Judges 4.4. The additional name Justus suggests some connection with the Roman world; conceivably like Saul (Paulus) he was a citizen. Hemer 221 cites from *CIJ* a Justus of Chalcis; cf. Josephus, *Life* 175. For an example of a double by-name see *ND* 1.91f. (*P. Vindob. Tandem* 11.20–22, 44–46). All such matters are guesswork; it is certainly true to say of the Twelve that the NT is much more interested in the fact *that* they existed than in *what* they did.

It is worth noting (as e.g. by Brandon, *Fall* 49) that James the Lord's brother was not considered as a candidate. If Luke's conditions are accepted, and if it is true that during his ministry 'his brothers did not believe in' Jesus (Jn 7.5), James, notwithstanding the appearance of 1 Cor. 15.7, did not qualify, as Paul, notwithstanding the appearance of 1 Cor. 15.8, did not qualify.

24. προσευξάμενοι εἶπαν. The tense of the participle is consistent with coincidence in time, as in προσηύξαντο καὶ εἶπαν. See BDR § 420.3 n. 4. 'Quis eas preces praeiverit non indicatur' (Blass 49): another reference to Peter might have been expected but does not occur.

καρδιογνῶστα. The word occurs elsewhere in the NT only at 15.8 (cf. Hermas, *Mandate* 4.3.4) and is not found in the LXX. The notion however that God is aware even of men's secret thoughts, intentions, and sins is biblical; see e.g. Ps. 17 (16).3; 44 (43).22; 94 (93).11; 139 (138).2. The Lord knows the thoughts of all men (it is surely impossible to take πάντων as neuter). Some (e.g. Conzelmann 25) take the *Lord* addressed to be God, but it is much more probable that Jesus is intended ('nam huius erat apostolum eligere', Bengel); he is asked to show (ἀνάδειξον, cf. Lk. 10.1) which of the two men he has chosen (ἐξελέξω; cf. 1.2; Lk. 8.13; also Prov. 16.33). That καρδιογνώστης appears to be applied in 15.8 to the Father is not against this (though see Clarke, *DH* 196f.). The choice is to be Jesus', not that of the Eleven; hence the use of the lot in v. 25. Cf. Josephus, *Ant.* 6.91, ἀπέδειξα τοῦτον ὃν αὐτὸς ἐπελέξατο.

25. Judas has left, and one of the two nominated is to fill, a τόπος. The word is used in much the same way as the English *place* or *position*. Cf. Epictetus 2.4.5: φίλου οὐ δύνασαι τόπον ἔχειν· δούλου δύνασαι; In Acts however the genitive that goes with τόπος is an office, not an official or character. Cf. the use of κλῆρος in v. 17; κλῆρος is perhaps not used here (it is read by ℵ C³ E 𝔐 sy) in order to avoid repetition. It is interesting to note the occurrence together of the two words at 1 QS 2.23 (מקום גורלו); but the terminology is also rabbinic — Jewish rather than specifically belonging to Qumran. According to Schille (85) τόπος 'weist in die Ordinationssprache'. He gives no references; 1 Clem. 40.5; Ignatius, *Smyrnaeans* 6.1 may be in mind but do not seem sufficient to prove the point: τόπος is a common word. Cf. also 1 Cor. 14.16.

Judas's position was one of διακονίας καὶ ἀποστολῆς; cf. v. 17. The parallel there lends support to the view (BDR § 442.9(b) n. 29) that we have here a case of hendiadys, though as a rendering 'apostolic ministry' would be hopelessly anachronistic: *service consisting of apostleship*, of being an apostle.

This place, lot, function, Judas left (παραβαίνειν, elsewhere *to transgress*; it means to cross the line, from right to wrong; here out of a kind of service), leaving one τόπος vacant and going to another, εἰς τὸν τόπον τὸν ἴδιον. There are two ways in which this phrase may be understood. At its earlier occurrence the word τόπος means a position, in the sense of a function. It may be said that Judas left his function as a serving apostle to take up his own function, the function peculiar to himself, of traitor. The phrase would then refer to the action of Judas in betraying Jesus. Alternatively it might refer to the consequence of his act; cf. 8.20, τὸ ἀργύριόν σου σὺν σοὶ εἴη εἰς ἀπώλειαν. On this view Judas's own place, his appropriate destination, would presumably be hell, perdition. On the whole this seems the more probable view. Cf. the Targum to Eccles. 6.6: On the day of his death his soul goes down to Gehinnom, the one place where all the guilty go (לאתר חד דכל חיבא אזלין תמן). Contrast 1 Clem. 5.4; Polycarp, *Philippians* 9.2. It is doubtful whether the occurrence of the words εἰς τὸν ἴδιον τόπον at Ignatius, *Magnesians* 5.1 shows knowledge of this passage.

26. The new apostle is selected by lot. This method of choice, for both religious and social purposes, was widespread among both Greeks and Romans. It is mentioned frequently in the OT, for example in the appointment of priests for service in the Temple (1 Chron. 25.8f.; 26.13f. cf. Tamid 1.2; 3.1) and for the designation on the Day of Atonement of the goat to be used as the sin-offering and of that which was 'for Azazel' (Lev. 16.8; cf. Yoma 3.9; 4.1). The lot is used also in the story of Jonah (Jonah 1.7). The religious use was continued and extended in post-biblical Judaism; e.g. Yoma 2.2 (. . . they ordained that they should not clear the Altar save by lot. There were four lots: and this was the first lot. The second lot was to determine who should slaughter . . .). Philo deprecated the use of the lot (e.g. *Quis Rer. div. Her.* 179, τεμνομένων (the goats) ἀδήλῳ καὶ ἀτεκμάρτῳ τομεῖ, κλήρῳ). For much more detail see PW s.v. Losung and *TWNT* s.v. κλῆρος, κτλ. 1 QS 5.3 shows the lot to have been in use at Qumran, but with reference to 1 QS 6.16, 18, 22 Braun (149) rightly says, 'Die Lospraxis entscheidet allgemein-jüdisch über priesterliche Funktionen; qumranisch über Aufnahme in die Qumran-gemeinde und über Rangplatze in ihr; hier in Acta 1.26 über die Zuwahl eines Apostels.' The use of the lot occurs nowhere else in Acts. 'Dum secum habebant apostoli Dominum, non usi sunt sorti: neque post adventum Paracleti ea sunt usi, c. 10.19; 16.6ss. sed in uno hoc intermedio tempore, et in uno hoc negotio usi sunt, convenientissime' (Bengel).

ἔδωκαν κλήρους: the verb commonly used is βάλλειν. Luke's διδόναι has been thought to be a Semitism; Lev. 16.8 has נתן but the LXX renders ἐπιθήσει. Luke's verb, with αὐτοῖς (D* E ΨΜ it syʰ have the easier αὐτῶν), has suggested that his meaning may be *gave* *(their) votes for them*, and this would harmonize with συγκατεψηφίσθη. But κλῆρος does not mean *vote* and ἔπεσεν ὁ κλῆρος seems clear, though it does not represent the usual method of casting lots, in which names were placed in a vessel and one was allowed to fall out (e.g. Josephus, *Ant.* 6.62, ὁ τῆς Βενιαμίτιδος κλῆρος ἐξέπεσε; cf. Livy 23.3.7). On the other hand, συγκαταψηφίζειν (from ψῆφος) does suggest a vote and according to Delebecque ὁ συν- indicates unanimity; it is probably however loosely used — cf. Plutarch, *Themistocles* 21.4(122). It was not a human decision but Christ's that enrolled Matthias with the Eleven Apostles (D has ιβ΄ - — *twelve*; thoughtlessly — or did the copyist take μετά to mean *among*?). For the significance of the number see pp. 93f.

'Non dicuntur manus novo apostolo impositae' (Bengel); contrast 6.6. Matthias simply takes his place, but equally with Joseph Justus is thereafter lost to sight.

Conzelmann (25) rightly judges that 1 QS 8.1 is not a valid parallel, and that nothing can be deduced from it regarding the constitution of the primitive church.

II
THE CHURCH IN JERUSALEM
(2.1–5.42)

3. THE PENTECOST EVENT 2.1–13

(1) When the Day of Pentecost had at length come,[1] they were all together in the same place, (2) and suddenly there came from heaven a sound as of a powerful rushing wind, and it filled the whole room [2] where they were sitting, (3) and there appeared to them tongues as if of fire, dividing up among them, and it rested upon each one of them, (4) and they were all filled with the Holy Spirit and began to speak with different tongues, as the Spirit granted them to give utterance.

(5) There were residing in Jerusalem Jews, pious men coming from every nation under heaven. (6) When this sound was heard the crowd assembled and were confounded, because each one of them heard them speaking in his own language. (7) They were astounded, and marvelled, saying, 'Why, are not all these men who are speaking Galileans? (8) So how is it that we, each one of us, hear them speaking in our own native languages? (9) Parthians, Medans, and Elamites, those who live in Mesopotamia, Judaea and Cappadocia, Pontus and Asia, (10) Phrygia and Pamphylia, Egypt and the parts of Libya adjacent to Cyrene, resident Romans, (11) Jews and proselytes, Cretans and Arabs, — we hear them speaking in our tongues the great deeds of God." (12) They were astounded and perplexed, saying to one another, 'What can this be?' (13) But others mocked and said, "They are drunk on sweet wine."

Bibliography

T. J. van Bavel, *FS* Schillebeeckx, 31–46.

F. W. Beare, *JBL* 83 (1964), 229–46.

O. Betz, *FS* Bardtke, 20–36.

J. A. Brinkman, *CBQ* 25 (1963), 418–27.

H. J. Cadbury, *JBL* 47 (1928), 237–56.

A. Causse, *RHPhR* 20 (1940), 120–41.

L. Cerfaux, *Rec.* 2.183–87.

---

[1] *Begs.*, Towards the completion of the "Weeks"; RSV, When the day of Pentecost had come; NEB, While the Day of Pentecost was running its course; NJB, When Pentecost day came round.

[2] *Begs.*, house; so RSV, NEB, NJB.

M. A. Chevallier, *FS* George, 301–13.

F. Cumont, *Klio* 9 (1909), 263–73.

N. A. Dahl, *FS* Sawyerr, 54–68.

J. G. Davies, *JTS* 3 (1952), 228–31.

J. D. G. Dunn, *NovT* 14 (1972), 81–92.

J. Dupont, *Études*, 481–502.

J. Dupont, *Nouvelles Études*, 193–8.

J. A. Emerton, as in (1).

J. A. Fitzmyer, as in (1).

C. H. Giblin, *StEv* 6 (= *TU* 112; 1973), 189–96.

S. M. Gilmour, *JBL* 80 (1961), 248–52; 81 (1962), 62–6.

M. Gourges, *RB* 83 (1976), 5–24.

E. Güting, *ZNW* 66 (1975), 149–69.

R. H. Gundry, *JTS* 17 (1966), 299–307.

K. Haacker, *FS* Stählin, 125–31.

R. A. Harrisville, *CBQ* 38 (1976), 35–48.

P. W. van der Horst, *JSNT* 25 (1985), 49–60.

G. D. Kilpatrick, *JTS* 26 (1975), 48f.

G. W. H. Lampe, *FS* Lightfoot, 159–200.

O. Linton, *FS* Sawyerr, 44–53.

E. Lohse, *EvTh* 13 (1953), 422–36.

I. H. Marshall, *SJTh* 30 (1977), 347–69.

P. H. Menoud, *RHPhR* 42 (1962), 141–7.

B. M. Metzger, *FS* Bruce (1970), 123–33.

R. Osler, *JBL* 101 (1982), 195–223.

V. C. Pfitzner, *FS* Rengstorf (1980), 210–35.

C. F. Sleeper, *JBL* 84 (1965), 389–99.

S. S. Smalley, *NovT* 15 (1973), 59–71.

K. Stendahl, *FS* Dahl, 122–31.

W. Stenger, *Kairos* 21 (1979), 206–14.

S. Weinstock, *JRS* 38 (1948), 43–6.

Commentary

Chapter 1 contains a number of hints that the work of Jesus will not be complete, and his followers will not be fully prepared for the work entrusted to them, until a notable activity of the Holy Spirit has taken place: see 1.5, 8, the expectant, preparatory atmosphere of 1.14, and the appointment of a replacement for Judas (1.15–26). The chapter of preparation is both dramatically and theologically effective; the reader's attention is directed to the new chapter and to the fundamental importance of the Spirit. He knows that the church, when it truly appears, will not be a merely human society but the vehicle of a divine agent. Bauernfeind (31) draws attention to a parallel in the gospel: Jesus first is baptized and the Holy Spirit descends upon him (Lk. 3.21, 22), then makes a programmatic proclamation of his message at Nazareth (4.16–30). The event duly takes place on the Day of Pentecost; for the — apparently untheological — significance of the date see below. The presence of the Spirit — the gift to the people of God in the eschatological age — is made known in visible and audible manifestations, particularly in the fact that when Peter and his colleagues speak they are understood by all the members of a large and diverse crowd assembled in Jerusalem, each member of which hears the apostles speaking in his own language. Luke devotes a considerable amount of space (vv. 9–11) to a list of the nations and territories represented, and evidently ascribes great importance to the miracle. Some of those who hear are impressed (though their conversion does not take place till after Peter's speech, 2.41), but others think the speakers to be drunk.

Luke appears to have two purposes in mind in this narrative. The first, as indicated above, is to demonstrate the fulfilment of Jesus' promise: his followers will receive supernatural power. The second amplifies the first. The church from the beginning, though at the beginning located only in Jerusalem, is in principle a universal society in which universal communication is possible. This appears to be Luke's twofold intention; it invites two comments.

(a) Neither the Pauline epistles (the earliest part of the NT), nor any other part, refers in this way to a special, 'founding' gift of the Holy Spirit. The closest parallel is Jn 20.22, but even this differs markedly. No one could lay more emphasis than Paul upon the importance of the Spirit (e.g. Rom. 8.9); but he describes no 'Pentecost'. It may be that he simply had no occasion to do so; he was not writing an account of the first weeks of Christianity. The fact remains that he supplies Luke's narrative with no confirmation. Moreover, Acts goes on from time to time to describe special interventions of the Spirit (2.38; 4.8; etc.), and one wonders what the gift of the Spirit at Pentecost meant if so soon afterwards Peter needed to be 'filled' with the Spirit. It is possible to make too much of this difficulty; the incidents in question can and probably should be understood in a simple, untheological, psychological way. Luke probably means only that whenever need arose Peter and other Christians received the promised help of the Spirit, which was manifest on such occasions as it could not be at other times; the fulfilment of Lk. 12.12 was important to him. It is however right also to bear in mind the existence of OT passages (notably Isa. 66.15–18 (LXX) which may have suggested to him such incidents as he describes here), parallels such as Test. Judah 25.3, and Philo, *De Decalogo* 46 which describe the phenomena accompanying the giving of the Law.

(b) Luke appears in this narrative to understand the gift of tongues (v. 4) to mean the ability to speak in a variety of foreign languages, intelligible to those with the appropriate linguistic background (vv. 6, 8). This seems to be a different view of glossolalia from that of Paul; see especially 1 Cor. 12; 14, where speaking with tongues is generally unintelligible unless there is an interpreter, and the qualification of the interpreter is not knowledge of languages but a special spiritual gift. Are we to conclude that Luke wrote so long after the Pauline period of ecstasy and enthusiasm that he no longer understood what speaking with tongues meant? Or were there two kinds of glossolalia? Should we in v. 4 emphasise the word ἑτέραις and take it to mean *foreign* (tongues)?

It is in the light of these facts that we must consider the question of the origin of Luke's story. He was not present in Jerusalem immediately after the resurrection, and it can hardly be supposed that it occurred to those who were that they should write down a carefully differentiated account of events. The experiences of the resurrection were not confined to a dozen witnesses; see both Acts 1.22 and 1 Cor. 15.6. There is no doubt that the crucifixion of Jesus was followed by events charged with profound religious and emotional power and conveying acute theological perception; it may well be doubted whether those who shared these experiences were always able to make a distinction and say, This was the presence of the risen Christ, and this the work of the Holy Spirit. Schneider (247) dismisses too easily the possibility that what we read in Acts 2 may be a variant version (edited by Luke in accordance with his own views, and perhaps on lines suggested by alternative traditions) of the appearance to more than five hundred mentioned by Paul (1 Cor. 15.6). Luke is about to use a speech which claimed, among other things, the fulfilment of Joel 2.28; how could this, for Luke, be manifested except by some kind of ecstasy? Cf. 10.48; 19.6, where speaking with tongues is taken as an unmistakable sign that the Holy Spirit is at work. But this supernatural phenomenon is crossed by Luke's desire, noted above, to show that the church was from the beginning universal, to provide 'a prototype of the mission to the world' (Dibelius 106). It is not hard to see how these convictions would help to give shape to such scanty traditions as are likely to have been preserved.

There have been many attempts to analyse the passage and to trace out sources or traditions, and to distinguish them from Luke's editorial work. There are excellent accounts of these in Schneider (243–7), and Roloff (37–40); see also Lüdemann 43-49. Conzelmann (27) speaks of three possibilities: (a) Two sources have been combined, one describing glossolalia (in the Pauline sense) and one a language miracle; (b) a mass experience of ecstasy was interpreted in the sense of a language miracle; (c) the language miracle itself was the substratum of tradition. This is correct if the assumption is valid that Luke was working upon sources that had already attained, whether in written or oral form, a measure of fixation. Many distinguish between vv. 1–4 and vv. 5–13; the latter passage cannot have been the original continuation of the former, according to Pesch (100); Kremer thinks that vv. 1–4 is not Lucan, whereas vv. 5–13 is Lucan. Weiser (78f.), however, seems to be correct in the opinion that the whole is marked by Lucan style, and the most probable view is that Luke himself composed the whole on the basis of the convictions outlined above and various traditions of outstanding events distantly recollected from the earliest days of the church. He used in addition a list of nations and countries (vv. 9–11): that this was taken over by Luke (so e.g. Rackham 22) is shown not only by the parallels but by the fact that it seems to be possible to isolate additions that he made to it (Schneider 243).

Weiser (79) makes the interesting observation that Passover and Pentecost are the only Jewish feasts taken over by Christians. This is probably because of the 'Christian' events associated with them, not because they were more adaptable than others. In the earliest period the name *Pentecost* was applied to the fifty days between Easter and the day of the Spirit, but Egeria describes a fourth century celebration in Jerusalem (*Peregrinatio* 43.1–3), which is somewhat surprisingly followed (43.4–6) by a commemoration of the Ascension.

1. ἐν τῷ συμπληροῦσθαι. M.3.145 takes ἐν τῷ with the infinitive to be 'causal, explaining why they were gathered together'. Turner also says on the same page, 'It is probably not quite true to say quite simply that *pres. infin. = while* and *aor. infin. = after. Aor.* is timeless while *pres.* is durative. The context must decide relative time.' Neither of these observations seem to give an adequate explanation of συμπληροῦσθαι τὴν ἡμέραν. The verb with its sense of completion is not necessary to explain the assembling of the Christians. For Luke this is already sufficiently explained by the fact that they shared the new faith; see 1.14; if any further explanation were needed it would have sufficed simply to say that the occasion was the feast of Pentecost. The natural meaning of συμπληροῦσθαι τὴν ἡμέραν, that the day was being completed, was drawing to its close, is inconsistent with 2.15: it was the third hour. 'While the Day of Pentecost was running its course' (NEB) is tempting, but does not really translate συμπληροῦσθαι. It seems probable that Luke had in mind the fifty-day interval between Passover and Pentecost and meant 'as this period approached completion,' that is, as the Day of Pentecost, the fiftieth day, began (though Luke evidently thinks of the day as beginning with dawn, not dusk). So *Begs.* 4.16 (citing Ropes, *HThR* 16 (1923), 168ff.); Haenchen (170) notes that the completion of a span implies a date. Cf. Jer. 25.12; Gen. 25.24; Lev. 8.33; Lk. 9.51; Acts 13.25. Kremer (94) puts the matter correctly. He notes first that, 'Der Ausdruck, der ursprünglich das Ausfüllen eines Zeitraums bedeutet, bezeichnet hier den Anbruch eines Termins.' He then asks why Luke chose this expression, answers that he wished to introduce the notion of the fulfilment of a promise, and adds, 'Eine Verheissung Jesu ist Apg 1.4–8 angeführt'. See further below. This view implies some loose writing on Luke's part, and loose attention to the Jewish reckoning of days; see however Lk. 24.1. Cf. Vg: Cum complerentur dies pentecostes.

τὴν ἡμέραν τῆς Πεντηκοστῆς. For the name of the feast cf. Tobit 2.1; Josephus, *War* 6.299 (. . . τὴν ἑορτὴν ἣ πεντηκοστὴ καλεῖται): in rabbinic literature it is שבועות (Weeks) or עצרת (that is, עצרת של פסח, the conclusion, or completion, of Passover). The Feast of Pentecost, that is, of the fiftieth day after Passover, was the OT Feast of Weeks; see Exod. 23.16; 34.22; Num. 28.26; and especially Lev. 23.15–21; Deut. 16.9–12. As these passages show, it was originally, and in the NT period continued to be, a Harvest Festival. Later, but not till the second century AD (StrB 2.601), it was connected with the giving of the Law: dies, quo data est lex (Wettstein 2.461, quoting Pesahim 68b, עצרת יום שניתנה בו תורה). It is tempting to use this connection in the interpretation of the Acts narrative. (a) The gift of Torah was an act of divine revelation in which the nature and will of God were made known on the basis of his gracious act of deliverance and with the result of a covenant between himself and his people; the Christian Pentecost is the new revelation through the Holy Spirit, based upon the new act of redemption and deliverance and issuing in the formation of a new, or renewed, people of God, based upon a new covenant. (b) According to Shabbath 88b, Every word that proceeded out of the mouth of the Almighty divided itself into seventy tongues (languages) — that is, though only Israel accepted the Torah and undertook to be obedient, it was heard by all nations in their own languages (for the notion that there were seventy nations and languages see Gen. 10, where, in MT but not in LXX, the nations listed amount to seventy; StrB 2.605f.). This interpretation is not however to be accepted. (a) The rabbinic material is too late to be relevant. Philo, *Spec. Leg.* 2.187, often cited, does not connect the feast with the Law. Jubilees 6.17, 18, reflecting an earlier period, connects the feast with the covenant made with Noah, not with that made with Moses (. . . the eternal covenant that there should not again be a flood . . . they should celebrate the feast of weeks . . . to renew the covenant). The annual renewal of the covenant at Qumran (see 1 QS 1.8–2.19) does not refer to Pentecost (Weeks): see Braun (149f.). (b) Nothing in Acts 2 directly suggests the giving of the Law on Sinai; see E. Lohse (*TWNT* 6.49–52). A more important OT passage is the account of the building of the Tower of Babel (Gen. 11.1–9) and the consequent dispersal of mankind by the confusion of languages; scattering and confusion are reversed by the miracle of tongues. Of this suggestion also, however, it must be said that Luke makes no attempt to call it to his reader's mind. It is probably best simply to observe that the Feast of Weeks was the next great pilgrim feast after Passover, the next occasion therefore after the crucifixion when Jerusalem would be filled with pilgrims from all over the world; so, essentially, Calvin 49. Luke's narratives are by no means always theologically motivated. He had a good deal of plain common sense.

On this occasion they were *all* (πάντες) together. A few MSS add οἱ ἀπόστολοι, inferring probably from 2.14 that only the twelve were concerned. The reading is certainly secondary, but the inference may be correct. It is however equally possible that the 120 of 1.15 are intended (so already Chrysostom, and e.g. Pesch 102f.); 2.17, 18 suggest that the gift of the Spirit was not narrowly confined. It was not (Schmithals 30) restricted to a group of πνευματικοί only — another blow aimed at the hyperpaulinists. Some believe that the disciples had met for common worship (so e.g. Schille 91, and with stress on ἐπὶ τὸ αὐτό, 94; also Pesch 102).

For ὁμοῦ, C³ E ΨᏆ have ὁμοθυμαδόν, probably by assimilation to Luke's customary use (ὁμοθυμαδόν occurs ten times in Acts; ὁμοῦ here only). The more common word as used in Acts (see on 1.14) suggests actual assembly rather than mere community, so that even if it were read it would hardly serve as a link with the story of Sinai (Le Déaut, *Nuit Pascale* 126, n. 164). ἐπὶ τὸ αὐτό (see on 2.47) is another phrase characteristic of Acts (four times in Acts 1–4), and adds little or nothing to ὁμοῦ; if they were all together they were all in the same place — it can hardly be translated "in their one community". A similar agglomeration of words has been noted in Terence, *Heautontimorumenos* 5.1.34, una mecum simul.

Bede: Hoc est in cenaculo quo superius ascendisse narrantur. Quicumque enim spiritu sancto adimpleri desiderant, carnis domicilium necesse est mentis contemplatione transcendant.

This verse is differently expressed, though without any significant change of meaning, in D: ἐγένετο ἐν ταῖς ἡμέραις ἐκείναις τοῦ συμπληροῦσθαι τὴν ἡμέραν τῆς πεντηκοστῆς ὄντων αὐτῶν πάντων ἐπὶ τὸ αὐτό. The use of ἐγένετο may suggest nearness to a Semitic (Hebrew) source; the genitive absolute does not. It is by no means clear why the text should have been re-written in this way (or, assuming the originality of D, in the reverse direction). On the reading see Ropes (art. cit., or better in *Begs.* 3.10). He translates: And it came to pass in those days of the arrival of the day of pentecost that while they were all together behold there came . . . This he says is correctly put into Latin by Augustine, and by t (except that this MS has in temporibus illis instead of in diebus illis) and resembles Ruth 1.1 (M): καὶ ἐγένετο ἐν ταῖς ἡμέραις τοῦ κρίνειν τοὺς κριτὰς καὶ ἐγένετο λιμός. If, he argues, the Western text is both Semitic and intelligible there is much to be said for it.

2. For the characteristic, and probably in some sense Semitic, use of καὶ ἐγένετο in Acts, see on 4.5. It is probably wrong to see any form of this use in the present verse. The subject of ἐγένετο is ἦχος, there came a sound. D enlivens the style by putting ἰδού between καί and ἐγένετο; this word in itself also suggests Semitism, though without clearly pointing to a Semitic original. It certainly does not suggest the Hebrew waw consecutive (וַיְהִי), where nothing can intervene between the conjunction and the verb.

ἄφνω. Cf. 16.26; 28.6; and see D. Daube, *The Sudden in the Scriptures*, Leiden, 1964, 34f. Daube is right in seeing in the word a suggestion of 'wondrous', 'awesome'; this is found in the LXX background and confirmed by the context. It is undoubtedly Luke's intention to describe a supernatural event.

ἦχος. The word occurs here only in Acts (Lk. 4.37; 21.25; Heb. 12.19 in the rest of the NT). Like the earlier form ἠχή it is used more often of inarticulate than of articulate sounds; so here. What is heard is like the noise of a rushing powerful wind. Cf. Gen. 1.2, πνεῦμα θεοῦ ἐπεφέρετο, especially if θεοῦ is to be regarded as serving as a substitute for a superlative (cf. 7.20, and see D. W. Thomas, *VetT* 3 (1953), 209–24). If however Luke had intended a straightforward literary allusion to Gen. 1.2 he would have written πνεῦμα rather than πνοή. The use of this word, with βίαιος (here only in the NT; cf. Arrian, *Alexander* 2.6.2, χειμὼν . . . καὶ ὕδωρ . . . καὶ πνεῦμα βίαιον), means that Luke is confining himself to a vivid natural analogy; when he intends to refer directly to the Spirit of God he will (v. 4) use πνεῦμα. There was a noise like that made by a powerful wind. πνοή can also mean breath (Betz 174, n. 6) but this meaning is not in mind here. Luke is accumulating features characteristic of theophanies; cf. 1 Kings 19.11; Isa. 66.15; 4 Ezra 13.10; and descriptions of the giving of the Law on Mount Sinai: Exod. 19.18f. and passages based on this, e.g. Philo, *De Decal.* 33, . . . πρὸς πῦρ φλογοειδὲς μεταβαλοῦσα καθάπερ πνεῦμα διὰ σάλπιγγος φωνὴν τοσαύτην ἔναρθρον ἐξήχησεν; 44).

ἐπλήρωσεν may grammatically have as its subject ἦχος or πνοή; since the latter word is simply part of the comparison the subject must be ἦχος. The sound was audible throughout the place where the believers were. Whether οἶκος should be rendered *room* or *house* (both meanings occur; see LS 1204f., s.v.) will depend on the meaning of καθήμενοι (C D have καθεζόμενοι). At every other occurrence in Acts (2.34; 3.10; 8.28; 14.8; 23.3) this word means *sit*, not *dwell* (the same ambiguous meaning applies to the usual Hebrew equivalent, ישב, of καθῆσθαι as used in the LXX). Probably it means here also *sit* (as in synagogue worship, not as in the Temple — Schille 95), and οἶκος will therefore mean *room*. The sound *echoed* (if one may play on ἦχος) throughout the room. We may think of the upper room of 1.13, of a room in a private house belonging to a Christian and used by the community, or of the Temple; in Josephus, *Ant.* 8.65 the word οἶκος is used both for the Temple itself and for chambers contained within it. ἦσαν καθήμενοι, periphrastic imperfect. Cf. 1.13.

3. In this verse γλῶσσα — surprisingly in view of v. 4 — can hardly mean *language*; in view of the adjectival genitive ὡσεί (characteristic of Acts; see 1.15) πυρός the word must mean *something shaped like the tongue* (LS 353, s.v. III). διαμεριζόμεναι (presumably middle, not passive) prepares for ἐκάθισεν ἐφ᾽ ἕνα ἕκαστον: each person present was touched with flame. εἰς emphasises the singularity of each one: in English, *each single one*, though this is probably more emphatic than Luke's intention. After γλῶσσαι the singular ἐκάθισεν is surprising (אֲ* D have ἐκάθισαν); Luke probably means that one tongue-like flame rested upon each person. Fire is sometimes said to rest on the heads of rabbis as they studied or disputed about the Torah; StrB 2.603, citing among other passages j Hagigah 2.77b.32, a story of Elisha b. Abujah about his father (וירדה אש מן השמים והקיפה אותם). Wilcox (101f.) cites an unpublished note in which Wensinck refers to the Fragment Targum on Num. 11.26, where the Aramaic verb שרי (*rest*, or *sit*) is used: the Holy Spirit sat, or rested, on them (ושרת עליהון רוח קודשא). Wilcox notes that the Hebrew שרה may be used in the same way. The thought of a divine presence resting on a person is not, however, distinctively Semitic in thought or in language.

The reference to fire plays so prominent a part in this account, immediately preceding the reference to filling with the Spirit, that it is very probable that Luke saw in it a fulfilment of the Baptist's prophecy (Lk. 3.16, βαπτίσει ἐν πνεύματι ἁγίῳ καὶ πυρί; Mt 3.11). Whether this was the original meaning of the words ascribed to the Baptist is another question. They may have referred (omitting ἁγίῳ) to the forthcoming judgment which would be carried out (like the cleansing of a threshing-floor) with wind and fire. See the discussion and references in Marshall on Luke 3.16. Fire is a phenomenon common in theophanies, biblical and other. See e.g. Exod. 3.2; 13.21f.; (1 Kings 9.12 — the Lord was, surprisingly, not in the fire). Wettstein has two columns on fire as Symbolum praesentiae divinae; e.g. Virgil, *Aeneid* 2.682–4 (Ecce levis summo de vertice visus Iuli fundere lumen apex, tactuque innoxia mollis lambere flamma comas et circum tempora pasci): Ovid, *Fasti* 6.635;

Homer, *Iliad* 18.214. See also Justin, *Trypho* 88 for the fire kindled in Jordan when Jesus was baptized (κατελθόντος τοῦ Ἰησοῦ ἐπὶ τὸ ὕδωρ καὶ πῦρ ἀνήφθη ἐν τῷ Ἰορδάνῃ).

4. There can be no doubt that Luke saw the event described here as the fulfilment of the promise of 1.5 (ἐν πνεύματι βαπτισθήσεσθε ἁγίῳ: cf. 1.8); it therefore appears that filling with the Holy Spirit and baptism with the Holy Spirit are synonymous. Luke's account of the Christian experience of the Holy Spirit is vivid, and central in his thought, but lacks consistency, thereby raising many questions. It is not easy to answer the question whether, for him, the Spirit, once given, is a permanent possession, or spasmodic. He says nothing that actually suggests that the Spirit was at any point taken away from those who had received it, yet at 4.8 Peter is *filled* with the Holy Spirit (πλησθείς, an aorist participle, suggesting that the filling took place there and then), and at 4.31 this is said of the whole group (ἐπλήσθησαν). It would be wrong to attempt to deduce from Acts a clear-cut and consistent doctrine of the Holy Spirit. Luke believes that the gift of the Spirit is constitutive of the Christian life (see 19.1–6; there is something wrong with a disciple who has not received the Holy Spirit): at the same time he has recorded and bears in mind the promise of Jesus (Lk. 12.12; cf. 21.15, a similar saying but without reference to the Holy Spirit) that the Spirit's aid will be given to those who must make defences in law courts. On the whole it is the latter understanding of the Spirit's work that predominates in Acts. It is elicited by exceptional circumstances such as the Day of Pentecost, or the appearance of an apostle before a Jewish court; inevitably therefore the manifest aid of the Spirit is thought of, or at least is described, as occasional rather than constant. Linguistically it is a coincidence that Luke's language appears in the comment on Num. 11.16 (the seventy elders) in Num. R. 13 (172a): כולם נתמלאו רוח הקודש. But the notion of empowerment by the Spirit of God at a specific time and for a specific purpose is common to both texts.

ἤρξαντο. For Luke's use of ἄρχεσθαι see on 1.1, and Wilcox (125–7). There is no reason to suspect Semitism here; Luke simply means that the disciples now did something they had not done before.

It is consistent with what has just been said that Luke should recognize special gifts of the Holy Spirit in phenomena such as speaking with tongues (cf. 10.46; 19.6). See above, p. 109; a problem arises when Luke's account of glossolalia is compared with Paul's (1 Cor. 12; 14). The next few verses claim that men drawn from various quarters of the earth hear Peter and his colleagues speaking in their (various) languages. Verse 13, however, suggests something more like Pauline glossolalia. Did Luke have in his own mind a clear picture of the Pentecostal events? Did he have first-hand — or even second-hand — experience of the gift of speaking with tongues? How widespread the Pauline gift of glossolalia was we do not know. It was highly prized at Corinth, but there is practically no evidence for it in any other Pauline church. On the other hand, Paul acknowledges that (though he made little or no use of the gift) he could speak with tongues more than any of the Corinthians (1 Cor. 14.8) — that is, to a very considerable extent. It is difficult therefore to believe that anyone in personal contact with the Pauline mission was unfamiliar with the phenomenon. If we are obliged to conclude that Luke was unfamiliar with it we shall probably have to infer that he was not a member of the Pauline circle. The problem is not completely solved by the occurrence of the word ἑτέραις, though Beyer (15) sees here the hint that Luke was combining two accounts and Weiser (81, 86) sees in the word the means by which Luke transformed a tradition of glossolalia into a foreign language miracle. It is doubtful whether ἑτέραις can bear the weight of this argument. It is used both alone and in composition in the quotation from Isa. 28.11 that Paul makes in 1 Cor. 14.21 (ἐν ἑτερογλώσσοις καὶ ἐν χείλεσιν ἑτέρων (v. l. ἑτέροις)). Kremer, (121) rightly notes Ecclus. Prol. 22, where εἰς ἑτέραν γλῶσσαν must refer to a different language; see also R. H. Gundry, *JTS* 17 (1966), 299–307 for the argument that both Paul and Acts are speaking not of unintelligible ecstasy but of foreign languages. It would however be a mistake to suppose that glossolalia was a single uniform phenomenon which wherever it occurred occurred in the same form. Those who are sufficiently out of control of their own functions to speak with tongues do not pause to consider whether they are doing so in the same way as others; and accounts of speaking with tongues as it occurs at the present time are not harmonious. Sometimes it is claimed that the tongues are actual languages used by divisions of the human race, sometimes they are held to be supernatural, completely unintelligible except to inspired interpreters. Luke's motives in writing his account of the Pentecostal event are discussed above (pp. 107-110); it was probably sufficient for him that he was aware of the phenomenon of inspired speech in which a speaker used a language which, whatever it may have been, was not his own. This would provide an adequate basis for him to build on. The old linguistically based divisions of mankind had now been overcome. 'Unitatem linguarum quam superbia Babylonis disperserat humilitas ecclesiae recolligit, spiritaliter autem varietas linguarum dona variarum significant gratiarum' (Bede).

ἀποφθέγγεσθαι: here and at 2.14; 26.25 only in the NT. In the present chapter, possibly but not certainly in ch. 26, Luke seems to use the word in the sense of inspired, though not necessarily ecstatic speech (Schille 96). It is not of human origin but the gift (ἐδίδου) of the Spirit. At Micah 5.11 ἀποφθεγγόμενοι translates מעוננים, so that some kind of supernatural knowledge is involved. Plutarch, *De Pyth.*

Orac. 23 (405E), uses the word of the Pythia's oracles; cf. Testament of Job 48.3; 50.1. Elsewhere the word with its cognates refers to brevity. Thus Plutarch's Ἀποφθέγματα Λακωνικά; the same author's *Brutus* 2 (985) (τὴν ἀποφθεγματικὴν καὶ Λακωνικὴν ἐπιτηδεύων βραχυλογίαν ἐν ταῖς ἐπιστολαῖς); also Philo, *De Vit. Mos.* 2.33 (οὐκ ἐπιτρέποντος μακρηγορεῖν τοῦ καιροῦ καθάπερ ἀποφθεγγόμενοι τὰ προταθέντα διελύοντο). All, πάντες, were filled with the Spirit and began to speak. See the note on πάντες in v. 1. In vv. 5–13 a number of speakers are implied; only to Peter (2.14–39) are specific words ascribed.

5. As Conzelmann (25) points out, the transition, from a private to a public event, remains unclear, at least as far as the location in the author's mind is concerned. There are textual variants in the first half of the verse which affect its meaning in important ways. The variation between εἰς and ἐν is not important. ἐν is contained in the majority of witnesses, εἰς only in ℵ* A 1175 *pc;* if, with NA²⁶, we read εἰς it must be understood in the sense of ἐν — a misuse (by classical standards) of the preposition which occurs not infrequently in Acts (see BDR § 205; in Modern Greek εἰς has taken over the meaning of ἐν; the tendency appears already in the Koine and is found in Mark, Luke, seldom in John, and frequently in Acts). More important are the following variations.

(a) ἦσαν δὲ εἰς/ἐν Ἰερουσαλὴμ κατοικοῦντες Ἰουδαῖοι ἄνδρες εὐλαβεῖς B A Ψ 𝔐

(b) ἦσαν δὲ εἰς/ἐν Ἰ. κατοικοῦντες ἄνδρες εὐλαβεῖς ℵ* vgᵐˢ syᵖ

(c) ἦσαν δὲ ἐν Ἰ. Ἰουδαῖοι κατοικοῦντες ἄνδρες εὐλαβεῖς E

(d) ἦσαν δὲ κατοικοῦντες ἐν Ἰ. ἄνδρες Ἰουδαῖοι εὐλαβεῖς C*

(e) ἐν Ἰ. ἦσαν κατοικοῦντες Ἰουδαῖοι εὐλαβεῖς ἄνδρες D

The reading of Augustine (*c. Felicem* 1.5f.; *c. Ep. Fund.* 9) is to be noted: Hierosolymis autem fuerunt habitatores [habitantes, *Fund.*] Iudaei homines . . . Ropes (*Begs.* 3.12f.) reconstructs the history of the text as follows. The original is to be found in ℵ: ἦσαν δὲ ἐν Ἰερουσαλὴμ κατοικοῦντες ἄνδρες εὐλαβεῖς. The Western text is to be found in Augustine: ἐν δὲ Ἰερουσαλὴμ ἦσαν κατοικοῦντες Ἰουδαῖοι ἄνδρες. The old uncials (other than ℵ) produced a conflate version, introducing Ἰουδαῖοι at different points and changing the relative position of κατοικοῦντες. D, conversely, while on the whole following the Western version, introduced the word εὐλαβεῖς though before rather than after ἄνδρες. If this reconstruction of the textual history is correct (and there is much to be said for it — it seems in general to be accepted by Metzger 290f.) two words in the verse are called in question, Ἰουδαῖοι (absent from ℵ and elsewhere occurring in different positions in the sentence) and εὐλαβεῖς (missing from the quotations in Augustine and Cyprian, elsewhere occurring in different positions in the sentence, but retained by Clark in his reconstruction of the Western text). Textually, Ἰουδαῖοι may have come in as a gloss on ἄνδρες εὐλαβεῖς while Clark (338f.) thinks that Ἰουδαῖοι was an ancient marginal note intended 'to show that the ἄνδρες εὐλαβεῖς in v. 5 were Jews by religion, though by race or residence they were Parthians, Medes, etc.' (see however Metzger). Alternatively, Ἰουδαῖοι may have been dropped as apparently inconsistent with the words that follow (ἀπὸ παντὸς ἔθνους), and with the words of the listeners in vv. 8, 11 (note ἐγεννήθημεν). It does not seem likely that Ἰουδαῖοι should mean simply Jews by religion; the word normally has a racial meaning in the NT and does so in v. 11. In the NT the adjective εὐλαβής occurs only in the Lucan writings: Lk. 2.25; Acts 2.5; 8.2; 22.12. εὐλάβεια occurs in Heb. 5.7; 12.28; εὐλαβεῖσθαι in Heb. 11.7. On the basis of this evidence the adjective can hardly be taken to denote a specific class of 'God-fearers' (see pp. 499-501); it is applied consistently to Jews (see Bultmann, *TWNT* 2.750; H. Kosmala, *Hebräer-Essener-Christen*, Leiden, 1959, 71, 297, 341). 'ἄνδρες εὐλαβεῖς bezeichnet hier nicht Halbproselyten . . . sondern, da es zu dem vorangehenden Ἰουδαῖοι gehört, fromme Diasporajuden, die aus aller Herren Ländern zu kommen pflegten, um die grossen Feste in Jerusalem mitzufeiern' (StrB 2.604). This view is modified by Hengel ('Zwischen Jesus und Paulus', 165–74), followed by Schneider (251), who thinks that the Jews were not pilgrims from the Diaspora but Diaspora Jews who had come to live (retire) in or near Jerusalem. Verse 5a alone could thus suggest that Luke was thinking of a great assembly of the best, most devout, most favourably disposed Jews, gathered in Jerusalem for the feast or for permanent residence. We are left however with the problem of ἀπὸ παντὸς ἔθνους and the languages referred to in vv. 8, 11, and these may suggest that Luke is here combining traditions or sources. What he himself wishes to suggest has already been pointed out (pp. 108-110): from the beginning the Christian church was an inspired community and a universal community. It therefore included both Jews and 'pious men' of every kind (cf. 10.34, 35, ἐν παντὶ ἔθνει). Inspiration was heavily underlined in vv. 1-4. In the following verses universality on a Jewish foundation is equally strongly but not so clearly stressed. It is not clear whether the crowds are festival pilgrims or not (Haenchen, 171); it is not clear whether all are born Jews or not (see v. 11, προσήλυτοι); it is not clear how Jews come to use from birth (v. 8) so many languages (see Knox, *Acts* 83): and the list of nations and countries may have been drawn from a list used originally for another purpose (see below on vv. 9–11). ἀπὸ παντὸς ἔθνους τῶν ὑπὸ τὸν οὐρανόν. Cf. Deut. 2.25; 4.19; 9.14; 29.19; Eccles. 1.3; 3.1; Bar. 5.3; 2 Macc. 2.18; Lk. 17.24; Acts 4.12; Col. 1.23; Eccles. 2.3 has *under the sun*, so also Demosthenes 18.270 (316) (ὑπὸ τοῦτον τὸν ἥλιον). The OT more often refers to all the nations *on earth*. If taken with *Jews* the phrase must mean, *from* (their residence among) *every nation under heaven*; if taken with *pious men* it could mean, *belonging to every nation under heaven*.

6. τῆς φωνῆς ταύτης may refer back to the ἦχος of v. 2 (so Preuschen; note ἐγένετο... γενομένης), or to the λαλεῖν (v. 4) of those on whom the Spirit rests. In view of v. 6b the latter is much more probable. That the voice should be the voice of the Spirit (mentioned by Haenchen as a third possibility) is very improbable; the Spirit speaks through those whom he inspires.

The great mass (πλῆθος — the word indicates a totality and is thus inconsistent with the analysis of vv. 9–11; so, unconvincingly, Schille 100) of people in Jerusalem were in the first instance attracted (συνῆλθεν) by the unusual event, then confounded (συνεχύθη); cf. Gen. 11.7 (συγχέωμεν ἐκεῖ αὐτῶν τὴν γλῶσσαν), 9 (ἐκλήθη τὸ ὄνομα αὐτῆς Σύγχυσις ὅτι ἐκεῖ συνέχεεν κύριος τὰ χείλη ...). The use of the word suggests an intended allusion to the story of Babel, but the word, or words (συγχεῖν, συγχύννειν), are not uncommon (in the NT Acts only: 2.6; 9.22; 19.32; 21.27, 31) and it would be unwise to press too strongly the thought of a reversal of the dispersion of mankind as a result of diversity of speech. Luke does not say that confusion (σύγχυσις) was ended; it was now caused by an unexpected ability to understand what was said.

Some MSS made the verb agree with the singular subject (ἤκουεν, or ἤκουσεν), but the noun of multitude, πλῆθος, naturally treated as a singular in συνῆλθεν and συνεχύθη, is equally naturally differentiated into individuals when the point is that *each one* (on εἷς ἕκαστος see on v. 3) heard in his own language. διάλεκτος is a local or national language (e.g. Diodorus Siculus, 5.6.5, διάλεκτον αὐτῶν ἔμαθον, the original inhabitants of Sicily learned the language of the Greek settlers); it thus corresponds with ἐν ἧ ἐγεννήθημεν (v. 8; this does not suggest Diaspora Jews). For τῆ ἰδίᾳ διαλέκτῳ λαλούντων D sy[p.hmg] Aug[pt] have λαλοῦντας ταῖς γλώσσαις, perhaps to emphasise that this was a miracle of speech, not of hearing. Cf. v. 8.

Those who thus come together represent not only Diaspora Judaism but the Gentiles whose languages they speak (Bauernfeind 40): the scene is programmatic (Stählin 37). But it is not drawn with clear lines.

7. ἐξίσταντο (some MSS add (ἅ)παντες, probably influenced by v. 12) and ἐθαύμαζον are virtually synonymous. If they are to be distinguished the former will emphasise that those concerned are almost out of their wits with astonishment, the latter that their attention is directed to a wonderful, marvellous object.

οὐχ ἰδού (οὐκ, P⁷⁴ A C Ψ 𝔐, and οὐχί, B, are probably both corrections of the unusual aspiration; but cf. Phil. 2.23 (ἀφίδω) and see BDR § 14.2 — possibly we should write οὐχ ἰδού) is often taken to be a Semitism (Torrey, CDA 28: 'οὐχὶ ἰδού reproduces לֹא הֵא. The Aramaic interjection is inserted very often for emphasis where הִגֵּה or הֻו would not be used in Hebrew'). A better explanation may be based upon Thackeray's discussion of irregular aspirates (*Grammar* 125f.). 'οὐχὶ ἰδού occurs in Acts 2.7 B, but not apparently in LXX. The origin of this rendering of הֲלֹא, *nonne*, is not clear, as there is no equivalent in the Hebrew for ἰδού. Only in 2 Chron. 25.26 do we find the combination הֲלֹא הֵם 'Behold are they not (written)?,' contrast 36.8 הִנָּם. The present writer would suggest that οὐχ ἰδού originated in a doublet. The interrogative הֲלֹא is only an alternative mode of expressing the positive הִנֵּה, and in Chron. הֲנֵּה sometimes replaces הֲלֹא in the parallel passages in Kings. הֲלֹא is principally rendered by (1) οὐχ ἰδού, (2) οὐκ or οὐχ, (3) ἰδού nine times e.g. Deut. 3.11. It is suggested that at least in the earlier books the oldest rendering was in all cases ἰδού , the translators preferring the positive statement to the rhetorical question. οὐχ(ί) was an alternative rendering, and out of the two arose the conflate ΟΥΧΙ ΔΟΥ This in time became the recognised equivalent for the classical ἆρ'οὐ;". On this view Luke (if he wrote οὐχ ἰδού) would be imitating the LXX rather than translating Aramaic, and imitating it not in a literal rendering of Hebrew but in an internal corruption. The phrase may well have seemed suitable to him as evocative of a biblical (rather than of a linguistically Semitic) idiom. Torrey's לֹא הֵא is not easy to find. He says that its use (*nonne*) occurs mainly in classical Syriac and cites Mt 24.2; surprisingly he does not point out that it occurs in the Peshitto of the present passage (*la ha g⁽ᵉ⁾lilaye*). Wilcox (150f.) sees no mistranslation of Aramaic here.

The speakers are Galileans. Blass (52) asks, Unde vero hi peregrini hoc sciunt? Stählin (34) says, perhaps by their clothes (*Tracht*)! It is of course Luke who knows that they are Galileans. Barth (*CD* 3.4.322) thinks that they are being contrasted with the εὐλαβεῖς; this is doubtful; Luke's interest here is not in relative piety but in language, possibly in the degree of education to be expected in Galileans, who would be unlikely to speak foreign languages. For popular opinions of Galileans see G. Vermes, *Jesus the Jew*, London, 1973, 42–57.

8. For καί as introducing a question sees LS 857, s.v.A II 2 (and cf. e.g. Euripides, *Phoenissae* 1348, καὶ πῶς γένοιτ' ἂν τῶνδε δυσποτμώτερα; Here, So how do we hear (is it that we hear) . . . ? πῶς introduces a surprised question, as at Mt. 16.11; Lk. 12.56; Jn 4.9; 7.15; Gal. 4.9 (Schneider 252). ἡμεῖς is expressed in order to point the contrast with the Galileans. For τῇ ἰδίᾳ διαλέκτῳ ἡμῶν, D* vg have τὴν διάλεκτον ἡμῶν, an improvement both in the case of διάλεκτος and in the avoidance of the reduplication of ἴδιος with ἡμῶν. On exhausted ἴδιος see the full discussion in M. 1.87–90; it is seen in literary Koine, but in the papyri ἴδιος still shows strong signs of life.

There is a formal parallel (see Delling, *Studien* 87) to Luke's words in Philo, *De Decalogo* 46 (τῆς φλογὸς εἰς διάλεκτον ἀρθρουμένης τὴν συνήθη τοῖς ἀκρωομένοις), but in Philo there is no suggestion either of a miracle of tongues or of a multilingual proclamation of Torah (see above, p. 111).

9–11. The list of names, including both countries and races, presents severe problems and has never been satisfactorily explained. Surprisingly (when its difficulty is considered) it shows little sign of textual corruption. In v. 9 there are a number of variants for ᾿Ιουδαίαν, which is supported by the great majority of witnesses but comes unexpectedly between Mesopotamia and Cappadocia and as a partner with the latter. It is probable that Jews (= ᾿Ιουδαῖοι) in syᵖ, Armeniam in Tert Augᵖᵗ, in Syria in Hier, and ᾿Ινδιαν in Chrys, are conjectural attempts to remove a difficulty. This is not to say that one of them may not be correct, if ᾿Ιουδαίαν is, as many believe, corrupt. This is argued by e.g. M. 3.170, on the ground that the word is strictly an adjective with γῆ understood and should therefore have the article. Since it is anarthrous it must be corrupt. Since however Turner on the same page cites Φρυγίαν καὶ Παμφυλίαν (which he himself notes as adjectives) in v. 10 the argument has little weight. BDR § 261.4 appear to share Turner's view. There are other reasons for considering the word corrupt; not only is its position surprising, it is odd to find it in the list at all: residents in Judaea were at home (it is still worth noting with Bengel, regarding the Judaeans, 'cujus dialectus differebat a Galilaea': and the name may be a relic of an older list, made from a different standpoint and perhaps for a different purpose, and inadequately revised by Luke). τε is omitted by D* it vgᶜˡ, probably in order to reduce the effect of pairing; there is no link between Judaea and Cappadocia. In v. 11, for ῎Αραβες, D* has ᾿Αραβοί — no more than a thoughtless error (according to Ropes a Latinism) in the form of the word (᾿Αράβιοι would have been satisfactory). Thus with the possible exception of the reference to Judaea we must be content to take the list as it stands.

Since the careful examination by B. M. Metzger (in *FS* Bruce (1970), 123–33) it has become impossible to hold the view that the list is based upon 'astrological geography'. The parallels in Paulus

Alexandrinus, *Rudiments of Astrology*, are by no means close enough to sustain it. See Metzger's article not only for discussion but also for bibliography. The nearest analogy to Luke's list appears to be the accounts of the distribution of Jews throughout the world. This is described in general terms by Josephus: *Apion* 2.282; *War* 2.398 (οὐ γάρ ἐστιν ἐπὶ τῆς οἰκουμένης δῆμος ὁ μὴ μοῖραν ἡμετέραν ἔχων); 7.43; *Ant.* 14.114–8 (quoting Strabo). Cf. Sib. Orac. 3.271 (πᾶσα δὲ γαῖα σέθεν πλήρης, καὶ πᾶσα θάλασσα). These passages recall v. 5 (ἀπὸ παντὸς ἔθνους), and 15.21. The distribution of Jews is described more particularly by Philo: *Flacc.* 45f. (on which see Box's notes, pp. 95–7): and especially *Leg. ad Gaium* 281f. (οὐ μιᾶς χώρας Ἰουδαίας ἀλλὰ καὶ . . . Αἴγυπτον, Φοινίκην, Συρίαν τήν τε ἄλλην καὶ τὴν Κοίλην προσαγορευομένην . . . Παμφυλίαν, Κιλικίαν, τὰ πολλὰ τῆς Ἀσίας ἄχρι Βιθυνίας καὶ τῶν τοῦ Πόντου μυχῶν . . . Εὐρώπην, Θετταλίαν, Βοιωτίαν, Μακεδονίαν, Αἰτωλίαν, τὴν Ἀττικήν, Ἄργος, Κόρινθον, τὰ πλεῖστα καὶ ἄριστα Πελοποννήσου . . . Εὔβοια, Κύπρος, Κρήτη . . . τὰς πέραν Εὐφράτου . . . Βαβυλὼν καὶ τῶν ἄλλων σατραπειῶν . . .). This list is by no means identical with that in Acts; there is no question of dependence, or, in the narrow sense, of a common source. The form however is similar, and it is probable that, unless we are to suppose that Luke made up his own list on the basis of his own knowledge of geography, he used the precedent of Jewish lists in order to construct a register of the potential people of God. For a somewhat similar conclusion ('Lukas nennt als die Adressaten der neuen durch die Ausgiessung des Geistes eingeleiteten Periode der Heilsgeschichte die ganze Menschheit') see E. Güting in *ZNW* 66 (1975), 149–69 (quotation from 169): but Güting thinks that Ἰουδαῖοι in v. 5 should be excised as a gloss and that in v. 9 Ἰουδαίαν should be emended to Λυκίαν (see below), whereas these words should perhaps be regarded as relics of the Jewish origin of the list.

For an account of Jewish settlements and communities in the areas listed see *Jewish Encyclopaedia* and the index of *NS* under the several names; also Hemer (222f.). It is impossible to give details here, nor would there be any point in doing so, since Luke's concern is only to assert that the various areas and peoples were represented in Jerusalem on the occasion in question. The list begins with the names of peoples rather than places; this is not against its having been originally a Jewish list; the peoples would define the areas in and the nations among which the Jews lived. *Parthians* (for Jews in Parthia see 1 Macc. 15.22 — Arsaces was king of Parthia), *Medes* (where the ten tribes had been deported: 2 Kings 17.6; 18.11), and *Elamites* are not mentioned elsewhere in the NT. In the OT Persians (= Parthians) and Medes are mentioned together at Esther 1.19; Dan. 5.28; 6.8, 12, 15; at Jer. 25.25 the kings of Elam and the kings of

Media are mentioned together. For Jews in Media see Josephus, *Ant.* 11.131. The three peoples (by no means wholly distinct from one another) represented the territory to the far east of Palestine, lying (as Luke would probably be aware) outside the Roman Empire, but not beyond the Jewish dispersion. The list moves westward to deal with the *inhabitants of Mesopotamia* (who had included Jews from the time of the Exile; note the existence of a synagogue in Dura-Europos (M. I. Rostovtzeff, *Dura-Europos and its Art*, Oxford, 1938), and cf. Josephus, *Ant.* 15.39, οὐ γὰρ ὀλίγαι μυριάδες τοῦδε τοῦ λαοῦ περὶ τὴν Βαβυλωνίαν ἀπῳκίσθησαν). At this point begins a sequence of pairs, linked by (τε) καὶ; cf. 1.13 and see the reference to BDR there. For Ἰουδαίαν see above. In addition to the ancient conjectures the following alternatives have been suggested: Idumaea, Lydia, India, Bithynia, Gordyaea, Cilicia, and Lycia (see *Begs.* 3.14; also Metzger 293f. and Güting, art. cit.). None of these is convincing; nor does *Judaea* seem to make good sense. It is probably best to conclude that 'Lk hier einen *schon vorhandenen*, aber aus anderem Zusammenhang stammenden *Völkerkatalog verwendet* hat' (Bauernfeind 35). With *Cappadocia* the list resumes its westward direction in eastern Asia Minor before turning northward to *Pontus* (for this and for the rest see Philo, *Leg. ad Gaium* 36), then westward again to (the province of) *Asia*. *Phrygia* (where Antiochus III settled 2,000 Jews — Josephus, *Ant.* 12.149) and *Pamphylia* fill up gaps in Asia Minor but do not furnish a complete account of that area — note the absence especially of Galatia, Bithynia, and Cilicia. Inscriptions as well as literary evidence prove the presence of Jews in these districts (see e.g. Tcherikover 288–90). Failure to mention these districts is against the suggestion that Phrygia and Pamphylia were introduced because of connections with Paul. From Asia Minor the list moves to Africa, mentioning *Egypt* and the parts of *Libya* adjacent to *Cyrene* (cf. Josephus, *Ant.* 16.160, ἡ πρὸς Κυρήνῃ Λιβύη; also Dio Cassius 53.12). Cyrene itself could well have been included if the intention had been to list all places with a Jewish population (see 1 Macc. 15.23; 2 Macc. 2.23; Josephus, *Ant.* 14.115, quoting Strabo; *Apion* 2.44f.; there was a synagogue at Berenice; see also Acts 6.9; 11.20). For the large and often turbulent Jewish population in Egypt see conveniently H. I. Bell, *Egypt*, Oxford, 1948; N. Lewis, *Life in Egypt under Roman Rule*, Oxford, 1983. οἱ ἐπιδημοῦντες Ῥωμαῖοι means probably not *visitors from Rome* but *Roman citizens* (so Ῥωμαῖος is used at 16.21, 37, 38; 22.25, 26, 27, 29; 23.27; not inhabitants of the city of Rome) *temporarily resident in Jerusalem*: ἐπιδημεῖν is to be distinguished from κατοικεῖν. It makes good sense to take the next clause, Ἰουδαῖοί τε καὶ προσήλυτοι as in apposition with that which precedes it. Why should Roman citizens have taken up residence in Jerusalem if they were not either Jews or proselytes? This might mean that Luke was making an addition to a previously existing list — if we follow Bauernfeind (above) in thinking that he was using one. This would be quite intelligible. He wished to indicate in a rough, approximate, impressionistic way that the whole world was represented at Pentecost. Rome had to be included if only because it marked the climax of Luke's book itself and of the preliminary sketch of Christian expansion given in 1.8. Why *Cretans* and *Arabians* should be added as a further supplement is not clear. Κρῆτες καὶ Ἄραβες cannot be a further appositional phrase. Crete (see Josephus, *War* 2.103; *Ant.* 17.327; *Life* 76 — his second wife came from Crete) is mentioned as a stage on Paul's journey in 27.7, 12, 13, 21, and as a place where he left Titus to continue his work (Tit. 1.5). Cretans are mentioned only in the uncomplimentary remark of Tit. 1.12. Arabia is mentioned at Gal. 1.17, apparently as a Gentile mission field; but as well as Paul Aqiba travelled there (Rosh ha-shanah 26a), so presumably there was a Jewish colony; see also Gal. 4.25. Packer (28) suggests that the final pair might mean 'all, from the isles to the deserts', but it seems a strange way of expressing this. Perhaps however it is wrong to think of this final pair as a supplement, and we should regard οἱ ἐπιδημοῦντες Ῥωμαῖοι, Ἰουδαῖοί τε καὶ προσήλυτοι as an insertion, and move from the inhabitants of Libya to Cretans and Arabs. They are still a surprising couple and, as Marshall (71) remarks, the list is an odd list. Luke may have built upon an existing list and added other names that occurred to him on the basis of interests and connections of his own. For proselytes see p.315; and for a proselyte in Jerusalem an ossuary, *CIJ* 1385 (Hemer 223).

ἀκούομεν in v. 11 picks up the earlier ἀκούομεν of v. 8; the list stands in a sort of apposition to both (implied) pronouns: We hear — we Parthians, etc. — we hear them speaking. . . . The new sentence emphasises that the miracle was one of speech. It is not merely that We hear each one in his language, but We hear them speaking in our tongues. No difference is intended between τῇ ἰδίᾳ διαλέκτῳ and ταῖς ἡμετέραις γλώσσαις (though they might come from different sources). Contrast the meaning of γλῶσσαι in v. 3, but cf. v. 4. The speakers were telling forth the *great deeds of God.* μεγαλεῖα is a LXX word: Deut. 11.2 (= גדלו); Ps. 70.19 (=71.19 גדלות); 104.1 (א: = 105.1 עלילותיו); 105.21 (Aᶜ; = גדלות): also eight times in Sirach. The word points to God's mighty acts in delivering his people and is used in ascriptions of praise; cf. 1 QS1.21. It is in this sense that Luke takes up the word. The preachers are declaring with praise the new redemption that God has wrought for his people. Cf. Luke's use of μεγαλύνειν, 5.13; 10.46; 19.17.

12. ἐξίσταντο as at v. 7. διηπόρουν (the old uncials א B A have the usual and more 'correct' διηποροῦντο) in comparison with ἐθαύμαζον (v. 7) stresses bewilderment rather than admiration.

ἄλλος πρὸς ἄλλον is a Hellenistic development of a classical idiom; cf. Plato, *Symposium* 220c, ἄλλος ἄλλῳ ἔλεγεν, they said one to another. τί θέλει τοῦτο εἶναι is not easy to parallel in Greek. Preuschen (12) quotes Herodotus 1.78.2, καὶ μαθοῦσι πρὸς Τελμησσέων τὸ ἐθέλει σημαίνειν τὸ τέρας, but σημαίνειν is not εἶναι. Cf. 17.20; also Lk 15.26D. The sense of *meaning* should not be stressed; they wondered what was going on. Wettstein quotes Anacreon 44.6 (= *Anacreontea* 30.6), τί θέλει ὄναρ τόδ' εἶναι; and Aelian, *V.H.* 3.20, τι βούλεται τὸ πέμμα ἐκεῖνο εἶναι;

13. ἕτεροι is surprising after πάντες in v. 12 (Haenchen 174), but it is simply a matter of careless writing; there is no ground for conjecturing the use of a fresh source. That the speakers were drunk was a natural comment; cf. 1 Cor. 14.23 — Pauline glossolalia could give the impression of madness. This does not fit what Luke has earlier claimed, namely that every person present heard not a meaningless noise but words uttered in his own language. Luke however knows (as Paul did — e.g. ? Cor. 2.15, 16) that the Christian message can never expect to win unanimous acceptance; cf. 17.32, οἱ μὲν ἐχλεύαζον. Luke does not intend to distinguish between the simple verb used in ch. 17 and the compound here; Hellenistic Greek affected compounds. μεστοῦν can be used in a literal sense but is often metaphorical (e.g. Plato, *Laws* 1. 649b, παρρησίας μεστοῦσθαι καὶ ἐλευθερίας — which could have been a favourable description of Peter and his colleagues). Here they are alleged to have drunk their fill of wine and to be showing the effects of it (this may be the force of the periphrastic perfect: they are in a state of fullness). γλεῦκος is used sometimes with, sometimes without, οἶνος for sweet new wine, though here at least it is evidently intended to be a strong rather than a weak drink. *Begs.* 4.20 quotes Lucian, *Philopseudes* 39, οἱ τοῦ γλεύκους πιόντες, but the effect described is indigestion rather than drunkenness. The same author at *Ep. Sat.* 22 contrasts γλεῦκος with ἀνθοσμίας, wine with a fine bouquet. The mockery may include the thought that the Christians have been getting drunk as cheaply as possible. In *Begs.* the question is raised how new wine, still in process of fermentation, could be obtained at Pentecost, which came just before the vine harvest. The problem, say Luke and Cadbury, 'is solved by Columella . . . who gives a receipt for keeping γλεῦκος from going sour.' Bruce (1.87; 2.65) quotes Cato, *De Re Rustica* 120 for a method. The problem is in truth solved by the fact that Luke was not aware of it. His Pentecost narrative is his own construction and he did not notice that γλεῦκος in v. 13 did not fit with Πεντηκοστή in v. 1. He was aware of the criticism that Christians speaking with tongues sounded, to the unsympathetic hearer, like drunken men, and thought that the charge could be neatly used to introduce Peter's speech (2.15). Cf. Philo, *De Ebrietate* 146–8: χάριτος δ'ἥτις ἂν πληρωθῇ ψυχή · γέγηθεν εὐθὺς καὶ μειδιᾷ καὶ ἀνορχεῖται · βεβακχεύεται γάρ, ὡς πολλοῖς τῶν ἀνοργιάστων μεθύειν καὶ παρακινεῖν καὶ ἐξιστάναι ἂν δόξαι... For negative uses of the analogy cf. Betz (111) and *TWNT* (4.550–2).

4. PETER'S PENTECOST SERMON 2.14–40

(14) Peter stood up with the eleven, lifted up his voice, and addressed them, 'Fellow Jews, and all you who are residing in Jerusalem, let this be known to you; give ear to my words. (15) These men are not, as you suppose, drunk, for it is the third hour of the day. (16) On the contrary, this is what was said through the prophet. (17) In the last days, says God, I will pour out my Spirit[1] upon all flesh; your sons and your daughters shall prophesy, and your young men shall see visions and your old men shall dream dreams. (18) Yes, upon my men slaves and my women slaves I will in those days pour out my Spirit,[1] and they shall prophesy. (19) I will give portents in heaven above and signs upon the earth beneath, blood and fire and smoky vapour. (20) The sun shall be turned into darkness and the moon into blood before that great and manifest day of the Lord comes. (21) And every one who calls on the name of the Lord will be saved.

(22) 'Men of Israel, listen to these words. Jesus of Nazareth, a man marked out for you[2] by God with mighty works and portents and signs, which God did through him in your midst, as you yourselves know, (23) this Jesus,[3] handed over by God's determinate counsel and foreknowledge, you, making use of men outside the law, nailed up and killed. (24) But God, when he had loosed the pangs of death, raised him up, because it was not possible that he should be held by it. (25) For David says of him, I set the Lord always in my sight before me; for he stands at my right hand, so that I may not be moved.[4] (26) For this reason my heart rejoiced and my tongue exulted, yes, my flesh shall dwell in hope. (27) For thou wilt not leave my soul in Hades, nor wilt thou permit thy godly one to see corruption. (28) Thou didst make known to me ways of life, thou wilt fill me with gladness in thy presence. (29) Brothers, I may say to you with all freedom of the patriarch David both that he died and that he was buried; and his tomb is with us to this day. (30) So he was a prophet, and knowing that God had sworn to him an oath to set on his throne one of his descendants, (31) he foresaw what would happen and spoke of the resurrection of Christ, saying that neither was he left in Hades nor did his flesh see corruption. (32) This Jesus God raised up, and all of us are his witnesses. (33) So, having been exalted by the right hand of God, and having received from the Father the promise of the Holy Spirit, he has poured out this that you both see and hear. (34) For it was not David who ascended into heaven; he himself says, The Lord said to my lord, Sit at my right hand, (35) until I set your enemies as a footstool for your feet. (36) So

---

[1]NEB, a portion of my Spirit.
[2]*Begs.*, appointed to you; RSV, attested to you; NEB, singled out by God and made known to you; NJB, commended to you.
[3]The name Jesus is not repeated here in the Greek.
[4]RSV, NEB, shaken; cf. NJB.

let all the house of Israel know for certain that God has made him both Lord and Christ, this Jesus whom you crucified.'

(37) When they heard this they were pricked in their consciences,[5] so that they said to Peter and the other apostles, 'What are we to do, brothers?' (38) Peter said to them, 'Repent, and let each one of you be baptized in the name of Jesus Christ for the forgiveness of your sins, and you will receive the gift of the Holy Spirit. (39) For the promise belongs to you and to your children and to all who are far away, all those whom the Lord our God calls to himself.' (40) With many other words he testified to them and exhorted them, saying, 'Accept your salvation from this crooked generation.'

Bibliography

W. F. Albright, *JBL* 65 (1946), 397–401.

A. W. Argyle, *JTS* 4 (1953), 212f.

E. Best, *NovT* 4 (1960), 236–43.

M. Black, *FS* Nida, 119–30.

H. W. Boers, *ZNW* 60 (1969), 105–10.

J. W. Bowker, *NTS* 14 (1968), 96–111.

G. W. Buchanan, *JNES* 20 (1961), 188–93.

M. A. Chevallier, *FS* George, 301–13.

G. Delling, *NTS* 19 (1973), 373–89.

R. J. Dillon, *NTS* 32 (1986), 544–56.

J. Dupont, *FS* Moule, 219–28.

J. Dupont, *Études*, 41–50, 133–55, 245–307, 404–9.

J. Dupont, *Nouvelles Études*, 58–111, 210–95.

E. E. Ellis, *ZNW* 62 (1971), 94–104.

E. E. Ellis, *FS* Rigaux, 303–12.

J. A. Emerton, as in (1).

C. A. Evans, *ZNW* 74 (1983), 148–50.

C. F. Evans, *JTS* 7 (1956), 25–41.

C. F. Evans, *FS* Rigaux, 287–302.

J. A. Fitzmyer, *CBQ* 34 (1972), 332–9.

C. H. Giblin, as in (3).

O. Glombitza, *ZNW* 52 (1961), 115–18.

L. Hartmann, *StTh* 28 (1974), 21-48.

P. W. van der Horst, as in (3).

J. S. Kennard, *JBL* 66(1947) 79-81.

A. Kerigan, *Sacra Pagina* 2.295–313.

G. D. Kilpatrick, *JTS* 15 (1964), 63.

[5]RSV, NEB, NJB, heart.

I. H. Marshall, as in (3).

F. Mussner, *BZ* 5 (1961), 263–5.

R. F. O'Toole, *JBL* 102 (1983), 245–58.

P. Pokorny, *NTS* 27 (1981), 368–80.

P. R. Rodgers, *JTS* 38 (1987), 95–7.

H. P. Rüger, *ZNW* 72 (1981), 257–63.

P. Schubert, *JBL* 87 (1968), 1–16.

H. Thyen, *FS* Bultmann (1964), 97–125.

U. Wilckens, *Missionsreden*, 32–7, 56–9.

Commentary

The first public proclamation of the Gospel presented by Luke is directly attached to the Pentecost event. This, Peter argues, cannot be explained as due to drunkenness; rather it is the fulfilment of Joel 3.1–5, which is quoted with occasional variations from the LXX text, of which the most important occurs in v. 17, where instead of Joel's μετὰ ταῦτα Luke writes ἐν ταῖς ἐσχάταις ἡμέραις, thereby making it clear that though some expected events remain in the future the final stages of history have now been reached; the gift of the Spirit belongs to the last days. Since this is so salvation is offered to all who call upon God's name. At this point in the speech (v. 22) there is an abrupt change marked by a fresh address to the listeners. It seems clear that Luke, in the words he ascribes to Peter, is now following a different source; there is little connection between the two parts of the speech. From v. 22 Peter turns to the Christological proclamation which appears here in much the same form as elsewhere (notably in chs. 3; 10; 13). The historical record of Jesus is appealed to; the hearers cannot fail to recognize it, and they will surely acknowledge that the mighty works contained in the record can only be explained by the fact that God was with him and commending him to Israel by his deeds. Notwithstanding these, however, he had not been accepted by those who beheld them; his own people, in collaboration with the Romans, had killed him. But God had set right this great wrong by raising Jesus from the dead. This was the testimony of those who claimed to be eye-witnesses, and Peter supports it by reference to the OT. David in the Psalms speaks of resurrection; the prophecy cannot refer to David himself since David is known to have died and to have remained dead, as is shown by the continuous existence of his tomb. There can be only one explanation. David referred not to himself but to his greater descendant, Jesus. Jesus had been raised up and exalted by the direct action of God who had thus finally set the seal of his approval upon him. Of this, the historical, visible aspect was the ascension (1.9–11). The historical, visible consequence of it was the gift of the Spirit, which God had poured forth, manifesting it in the things that 'you see and hear' (v. 33). It is presumably the reminder, uttered in this context, that *you* crucified this Jesus, that pricks the conscience of the hearers. When they ask what they should now do, they are told to repent and be baptized. If they do this the result will be twofold. They will receive forgiveness and the gift of the Spirit.

This speech and those that resemble it were subjected by C. H. Dodd to an analysis, the results of which have been to some extent modified by subsequent study (almost every writer on Acts having produced his own variations) but remain a classical analysis of Luke's understanding of the Gospel. By what literary or other channels they reached the author, and whether they also represent the way in which Peter and his colleagues in the 30s understood the Gospel, are of course further questions. Dodd notes six points which, he says, form a pattern common to the speeches in Acts as a whole (*The Apostolic Preaching and its Developments*, London, 1944, 21–4).

(1) The age of fulfilment has dawned.

(2) This has taken place through the life, death, and resurrection of Jesus, of which a brief account is given.

(3) By virtue of the resurrection, Jesus has been exalted at the right hand of God, as messianic head of the new Israel.

(4) The Holy Spirit in the church is the sign of Christ's present power and glory.

(5) The messianic age will shortly reach its consummation in the return of Christ.

(6) The preaching always closes with an appeal for repentance, the offer of forgiveness and of the Holy Spirit, and the promise of salvation to those who enter the elect community.

This is a substantially fair summary, though it is an inclusive summary and the six points do not all appear with equal clarity and fullness in every speech. The present speech, the first, delivered on what Luke evidently regards as the fundamental Christian occasion, is probably the most comprehensive example. The theme of fulfilment appears explicitly in v. 16 (but this should perhaps not be regarded as part of the speech proper). It is implicit in v. 23, for the determinate counsel and foreknowledge of God are declared in the OT, and again becomes explicit in the citation and exposition of Ps. 15.8–11 and Ps. 109.1 in vv. 24–31 and 32–6 respectively. The fulfilment is in the person of Jesus, and his ministry is summed up with special reference to his miracles in v. 22; it is assumed that the hearers (from personal knowledge) — and equally the readers (from Luke's first volume?)

— can fill in the details for themselves (καθὼς αὐτοὶ οἴδατε). A good deal of space is given to the resurrection, not simply as a marvellous event but as one foretold by the OT; the consequence of it is that Jesus is now κύριος and Χριστός (v. 36). A consequence of a different (observable) kind is the gift of the Spirit; v. 33 is in some respects obscure, but it is at least clear that the Spirit is the Father's promise which has been realized by Jesus. A striking absence from the present speech is any allusion to the return of Jesus; this may be to some extent made up by the reference in v. 20 to the great and manifest day of the Lord — the day when the Lord comes in glory and every eye beholds him. This again, however, is not in the main body of the speech. The close of the address is given special force by the fact that it is presented as the answer to a question asked by the hearers: τί ποιήσωμεν; They are told to repent and be baptized, and are promised forgiveness of sins and the gift of the Holy Spirit (v. 38) and therewith salvation (vv. 39f.).

No one will maintain that this speech contains the very words used by Peter on a specific occasion in the life of the earliest church. Such speeches were not recorded. It is however proper to ask to what extent the material in Acts represents the kind of thing that was said at the period that Luke is describing. Is the theology contained in the speech that of the 30s or that of the 80s and 90s, when Luke wrote? The question may be approached from several angles.

(1) It has been maintained (especially by C. C. Torrey) that the language of this sermon (and of the others that resemble it) bears witness to the influence of Aramaic upon its vocabulary and syntax. If this view can be proved, or at least made to seem probable, it can be inferred that the substance of the speech goes back at least to the early Palestinian, Aramaic-speaking church. This is not a proposition about which generalizations have any value. Alleged Aramaisms are discussed in the notes. If the judgments taken there are correct Aramaic influence amounts to little. This does not prove that the material is late; Aramaic dating from an early period and expressing primitive theology may have been translated into correct and idiomatic Greek. But there is no linguistic proof that the speeches are old, and the use of the LXX text of the OT points to a Greek rather than a Semitic environment.

(2) It is a fair comment that the speech shows no developed theology, especially when it is compared with the Pauline epistles. No positive effect is ascribed to the death of Jesus; this is characteristic of Acts as a whole (there is an exception at 20.28). He was wickedly killed by a conspiracy of Jews and Gentiles, but God (who, as the OT shows, had foreseen both the conspiracy and his response to it) did not allow this to be the last word and appointed the apostles as witnesses of the fact that he had raised Jesus from the dead, thereby making him Lord and Christ (see above). There is no suggestion,

here or elsewhere in Acts, that Jesus Christ was the incarnation of the Son of God who shared equal divinity with his Father. There is no question that this speech and those that resemble it present an elementary, undeveloped, theology and Christology. So far the speeches might seem to be proved not necessarily Petrine (there is no value in comparisons with 1 Peter, which may in any case not have been written by Peter) but at least early. We must however go back to ask whether the question posed above was rightly framed. Was it right to put it in terms of a disjunction: the theology of the 30s or the theology of the 80s and 90s? We have no right to assume a difference between the two. There have in every generation been Christians incapable of anything more than elementary theological thought, and those capable of thought on Paul's level have been very few indeed. In a justly famous article (first published in *EvTh* 10 (1950–1), 1–15), P. Vielhauer argued that Acts is prepauline in Christology, postpauline in its attitude to the Law, to the Gentiles, and to natural theology. The form of this proposition is itself sufficient to show the meaninglessness (in this connection) of the temporal prefixes pre- and post-. Chronologically, Acts is postpauline in all respects; whatever it contains is post-pauline, and it is more consistent, whether or not it is correct, to maintain with Schmithals (35f.) that the Christology of Acts is postpauline and antipauline, a reaction against the apostle's theology. It would moreover be impossible to maintain that in regard to Law, the Gentiles, and natural theology Acts represents a more profound level of theology than Paul. It was both later and less profound. What we may say with some confidence is that our speech, and the others, represent what Luke himself believed. He was not the kind of critical historian who could say, 'This is what my research has shown that Peter said, or is likely to have said; I do not myself believe it (or, I think it old-fashioned and out-of-date), but I give it in the interests of historical accuracy.' Rather it was Luke's desire to believe and to speak as the apostles believed and spoke; indeed it seems to have been one of his purposes to provide preachers in his own time with the best, apostolic, models. The speech then contains *Lucan* theology, the *Lucan* way of preaching the Gospel (probably, that is, the theology of the church as it was known to Luke): the question remains whether it was also the theology of the 30s, and this we have so far no clear and objective method of judging.

(3) There remains also the method of source criticism. As noted above, the speech falls into two main parts. The former (vv. 14–21) is closely related to the Pentecost event (which it may have helped to form) and could hardly exist independently of it. V. 33, with its closing words, This, which you both see and hear, equally points to this event, and v. 39 appears to take up the Joel quotation of vv. 17–21. These additions, however, and the introductory paragraph,

which is little more than a proof text intended to bring out the eschatological significance of the event, are probably Luke's own work and go with his narrative of a creative event which makes possible, in several senses, the universal testimony which believers are to bear. The remainder of the paragraph does not show the same keen interest in manifestations of the Spirit or in universality (these reappear in vv. 33, 39, as already noted). It is possible that Luke himself composed the remainder of the speech also, and in the same way composed the later speeches, adapting them in different ways to the settings in which he has placed them. The speech contains nothing that lay outside Luke's interest and ability, for it is based on a simple summary of the life and death of Jesus and on two OT texts, the one quoted and expounded at some length in order to prove the speaker's witness to the resurrection, the other taking the vindication of Jesus with the claim that he now sits at the right hand of God. Several considerations however suggest that the speech is not Luke's own — at least is not entirely his own, for there can be little doubt that he has written up whatever material he may have received. (a) Apart from the words already noted as Lucan supplements (vv. 33, 39) the speech contains nothing to connect it with the occasion. (b) The surface meaning of v. 36 is inconsistent with Luke's own Christology, though the wording is such (see the note) that Luke could have interpreted it in his own way. (c) There is a special interest in David (almost a negative interest: David was not raised up, David did not ascend into heaven, v. 34), shared by 13.22, 23, 34, 36. (d) This speech shares (see above) a common pattern with others in the first half of Acts.

If we conclude, somewhat tentatively, that Luke in composing this speech (and others) made use of some traditional material, we have not answered the question of the date and origin of the information on which he drew, or of the channels by which it reached him, whether written or oral. It can fairly be said that nothing requires a postpauline or a Johannine date; but this in no way proves that Christians were not still preaching in this manner at the time when Acts was written. If it is correct that it was one of Luke's intentions to provide an apostolic handbook for preachers, as it is certainly true that he venerated the apostolic figures of the first Christian generation, it is probable that he would seek out the oldest traditional material he could find. It is at least equally probable that he did not assess it as a critical historian. This does not differ seriously from Wilckens' view that narrative and speech belong so closely together that we must suppose that Luke wrote the whole, though use of sources or traditions is not thereby excluded.

14. D sy^p mae begin the paragraph with τότε; this has been taken as a possible mark of Aramaism, but against this see Ropes (*Begs.*

3. not only 14 but also ccxxxii; ccxliv). A speaker in the synagogue would sit, but here the circumstances are different; Peter is addressing a large crowd. He did not however act alone, but stood up with the eleven (those mentioned in 1.13, with Matthias; D* reading, for ἕνδεκα, δέκα ἀποστόλοις, presumably does not count Matthias, but the copyist has no strict views — in 1.26 D has δώδεκα). If however the reading of D* is accepted, or if σὺν τοῖς ἕνδεκα is taken to mean 'himself the eleventh', it would have to be assumed that we are dealing with a tradition that knew nothing of the replacement of Judas by Matthias, or perhaps placed it at a later point. D* vg^mss mae emphasise the participation of others by adding πρῶτος (E has πρότερον) after ἐπῆρεν: Peter was the first but not the only speaker. The verbs throughout the verse, including the participle, are aorists: σταθεὶς ... ἐπῆρεν ... ἀπεφθέγξατο. These follow aptly on the imperfects of 2.13. Cf. Lk. 4.22f.; Jn. 11.36f. 'Auch Äusserungen einer unbestimmten Mehrheit werden durch das Impf. eingeleitet, worauf die Erwähnung des Abschlusses im Aor. erfolgen kann' (BDR § 329; cf. 9.21; 17.18). For ἀπεφθέγξατο, the Western text (D* it (sy)) surprisingly has εἶπεν, lowering rather than heightening the tone of the sentence; it is hard to see any reason for this change. It may be that the Western text is original here, ἀπεφθέγξατο having been brought in to provide an example of the ἀποφθέγγεσθαι of 2.4. For the word see the note on that verse. Luke is certainly thinking of inspired though hardly of ecstatic utterance. Haenchen (180), Plümacher (43) agreeing, describes the speech as *feierlich*. ἐπαίρειν τὴν φωνήν is a Septuagintalism, rendering קוֹל נשא; but it occurs also in Greek without a Semitic background, e.g. Demosthenes 18.291 (323); Philostratus, *Vita Apoll.* 5.33.

For ἄνδρες in address cf. 1.11, and in this paragraph vv. 22, 29; it is common in Acts but ἄνδρες Ἰουδαῖοι) occurs here only. For κατοικοῦντες see 2.5, and for the contrast with ἐπιδημοῦντες, 2.10. Does Peter here distinguish between Jews and other permanent residents in Jerusalem? At this point it may seem so; but at v. 22 only Israelites are addressed. Luke still has in mind the theme of universality, but the main body of the address is spoken to Jews, who made use of Gentiles to do away with Jesus (v. 23). To this audience the exhortation ἐνωτίσασθε corresponds, as another Septuagintalism. The word is quoted by LS 579 only from Scripture; it occurs fairly frequently in the LXX, usually as the equivalent of אזן (hiph.). For γνωστὸν ἔστω cf. 1.19. Wilcox (90f.) cites a number of parallels from biblical Aramaic (notably 2 Esdras 4.12, 13; 5.8; Dan. 3.18) and a Hebrew letter (. . . ש לך יהי שידע: *BASOR* 131 (1953). 21 = *Discoveries in the Judaean Desert*, Oxford, 1961, 155ff.) which suggest that the formula was 'probably part of the normal stock-phrasing of letters and speeches'.

15. The mocking charge of 2.13 is rebutted by the simple observation that it was too early in the day for men to be drunk. According to *Begs.* 4.21 the normal Jewish breakfast time was the fourth hour (approximately 10 a.m.), on Sabbath the sixth. The latter observation is supported by Josephus, *Life* 279, if ἀριστοποιεῖσθαι means *to have breakfast*; Thackeray however translates *to take our midday meal*, a translation which accords with many uses of ἀριστοποιεῖσθαι (and of ἄριστον) but is a little odd in the context, since *noon* (the sixth hour) seems so natural a time for a midday meal as to be scarcely worth specifying. Evidence for the fourth hour as the weekday time of breakfast appears to be no earlier than Rashi (StrB 2.615), and evidence for the third hour as the regular hour for the morning prayer is inconclusive. It seems therefore that Peter is not saying, At this hour men are praying, not drinking, but simply, It is too early to find men drunk. They may, one supposes, be still sleeping off the effects of the previous night's carouse, but the new day's potations have not yet begun. Cf. Cicero, *Philipp.* 2.41.104: at quam multos dies in ea villa es perbacchatus; ab hora tertia bibebatur, ludebatur, vomebatur. There are further references in Wettstein.

The final clause in the verse gives the ground for Peter's rebuttal, whether (with NA²⁶) we read ἔστιν γάρ or (with D* lat Irenaeus) the genitive absolute, οὔσης ὥρας . . .

16. The Pentecostal event is the fulfilment of prophecy. In the majority of MSS the prophet is named: Joel. In D Ir^lat Aug^pt the name is omitted. It is hard to see what reason could have led to omission. It is true that names of minor prophets are not given at 7.42f.; 13.40f.; 15.16f., but there is no reason to think this a matter of principle, to be always observed. It would on the contrary be natural for copyists who could identify the quotation to add the source. In this case the Western text may well be original.

That the events he describes were the fulfilment of Scripture is a central part of Luke's understanding of them. The Gospel is about to move into the world outside Judaism, and Luke has already hinted that this will be so; but Judaism, or at least the OT, is and will remain its indispensable foundation; as Schneider (267) puts it, τοῦτό ἐστιν in this verse corresponds to καὶ ἔσται in v. 17. In the following verses this is expressed in terms of the fulfilment of a specific prediction; elsewhere, notably in chs. 7 and 13, the Christian events appear as the consummation of a historical narrative in which God has been active throughout. The quotation from Joel, in the form in which Luke gives it (his Christian interpretation involves some changes in the text), is important for Luke's understanding of eschatology: God has begun, but not completed, the work of fulfilment; Christians are living in the last days, but the last day has not yet come. Accordingly Bultmann (*Exegetica* 376) is right to note that the

Pentecost event is not interpreted typologically in terms of Sinai; it is not a matter of repetition, but of the fulfilment of prophecy. Schmithals (34) sees here one of many attacks on the 'hyperpaulinists' — Christians who exaggerated Paul's teaching. Against them he asserts that the gift of the Spirit is not something entirely new but continues the history of Israel; and Peter (not Paul) is its first exponent. This seems to read more out of the text than it contains.

17. In this verse and those that follow there are several variants, most of which are intended either to make the quotation conform more closely to the text of the LXX or to make it fit more neatly into the circumstances of the Day of Pentecost. The most important is the first. Instead of ἐν ταῖς ἐσχάταις ἡμέραις, B 076 (C *pc*) sa^mss have, in agreement with Joel 3.1, μετὰ ταῦτα. These MSS miss an important point. μετὰ ταῦτα simply looks forward and declares that the events in question will happen at some time in the future. ἐν ταῖς ἐσχάταις ἡμέραις points to the last act of history and claims that they are part of God's final act of redemption. It goes too far to say with Stählin (42), 'die verheissene Endereignisse sind Gegenwart', but Roloff (53) rightly says that the words refer to 'die letzte Epoche vor der Aufrichtung des eschatologischen Reiches', and Maddox (137f.) rightly finds in them both fulfilment and expectation; he adds that the stress is on fulfilment. Bengel, somewhat enigmatically: Omnes dies NT sunt dies ultimi. More soberly, Wilson (*Pastorals* 16) points to the parallel in 2 Tim. 3.1 (cf. 1 Tim. 4.1); these are the days of the church.

λέγει ὁ θεός (λέγει κύριος, D E latt Ir^lat, GrNy) is an addition to the text of Joel (3.5 has καθότι εἶπεν κύριος). An ascription is no doubt desirable in Acts; in Joel, after 2.27 (ἐγὼ κύριος ὁ θεὸς ὑμῶν) it was not necessary. For πᾶσαν σάρκα, D* has πάσας σάρκας; if this is not an accidental error it will probably be an attempt to emphasise even more strongly the universal scope of salvation. This motivation almost certainly lies behind the substitution (by D gig r) of αὐτῶν in the first two occurrences of ὑμῶν and the omission (by D r) of the second two. Peter is addressing Jews, or at least a limited group in Jerusalem; it is not their sons and their daughters only, not their young men and old men only, who will be moved by the Spirit. These modifications show a somewhat wooden approach to the text.

ἐκχεῶ 'signifies great abundance' (Calvin, 57). ἀπὸ τοῦ πνεύματός μου is a surprising rendering of רוחי; the LXX appear to have introduced a material concept of Spirit where the Hebrew text did not require it. For the use of ἀπό instead of a partitive genitive see M.3.208f. *Some of my Spirit* is hardly consistent with a developed view of the personality of the Spirit, but goes naturally with the image of *pouring out*. Christian prophecy plays an important part in

Acts; see 11.27; 13.1; 15.32; 21.10 (προφήτης); 19.6; 21.9 (προφητεύειν). Sometimes but not always the prophets make predictions; they speak in a distinctive way that can be recognized as inspired; they function as servants of the church, comparable with teachers. According to Conzelmann (29), Luke identifies prophecy with glossolalia; this is doubtful; see e.g. 19.6. *Seeing visions* and *dreaming dreams* are in synonymous rather than antithetical parallelism: young and old (the order in Joel reversed) alike will receive supernatural revelations.

The prophecy of Joel was taken up in Judaism and understood to refer to an outpouring of the Spirit in the age to come, when prophecy would cease to be confined to a few. Thus Tanhuma קרח § 4 (96b): In this age prophecy has been for one in a thousand but in the age to come prophecy will be for every man; this appears to make prophecy universal, but it should perhaps be understood in the sense of Tanhuma בהעלתך § 28 (31a), where the new gift of prophecy is restricted to every Israelite (כל ישראל). Joel 3.1 is quoted in both these passages, but Num. 11.29 was no doubt also influential. Other passages are quoted by StrB 2.615f. and Wettstein.

18. As in v. 17 (sons and daughters) no distinction is made between men and women; cf. Gal. 3.28. D gig r omit ἐν ταῖς ἡμέραις ἐκείναις, perhaps rightly; the words could have been added to harmonize with Joel 3.2, which contains them. D p* omit καὶ προφητεύσουσιν, this time agreeing with the LXX. If, as is probable, Luke added the words they testify to the high value he set upon prophecy, and thus interpret the gift of the Spirit; see on v. 17.

γε often loses its force in Hellenistic Greek, but not so here, though the order should be καὶ ἐπί γε (BDR § 439.2).

19. Joel 3.3a (LXX) reads: καὶ δώσω τέρατα ἐν τῷ οὐρανῷ καὶ ἐπὶ τῆς γῆς. Luke has made out of this two parallel lines, but his motivation was probably not poetical; he wished to add to heavenly portents signs, miracles, worked by the apostles which provided further proof that the age to come was now dawning. For his use of σημεῖον see v. 22 (Jesus); 2.43 (apostles); also 4.30; 5.12; 6.8; 14.3; 15.12. Signs are being done on earth in these last days; but (except so far as they may be included in the wind and fire of the day) portents in heaven have not yet appeared. Joel lists them freely, and Luke as freely takes them over. It is clear that he wanted the words with which he concludes his quotation in v. 21, but he could if he wished have omitted the intervening clauses. The language is conventional but is not for that reason to be allegorized or otherwise explained away (as by Bede: Sanguinem dominici lateris, ignem spiritus sancti, vaporem compunctionis et fletuum). αἷμα καὶ πῦρ καὶ ἀτμίδα καπνοῦ is omitted by D it; they may be right, for the words are in Joel and may have been added in other MSS to complete the text; even if they are omitted plenty of heavenly portents remain (v. 20). Barth (*CD* 4.4.79) goes too far with the claim that the signs must be understood as signs of judgment, and stand here because baptism (v. 38) means subjection and surrender to judgment. Bauernfeind (45) is more nearly right in describing them as signs of salvation.

20. There is no textual variation in the first part of the verse. For apocalyptic changes in sun and moon cf. Mk 13.24; Rev. 6.12. After πρίν, B 076 𝔐 add ἤ. Before ἡμέραν, P⁷⁴ ℵᶜ A C E ψ𝔐 add τήν. If this is read we have (in τὴν ἡμέραν before anarthrous κυρίου) an apparent violation of Apollonius' Canon. The reason for this may be that κύριος approaches more nearly to a *name* than does θεός; so Moule, *IB* 115, citing J. F. Middleton. Cf. τὸ πνεῦμα κυρίου at 5.9 Conzelmann (29) notes that the Hebrew here has the Tetragrammaton, so that the messianic use of the passage can have arisen only out of the Greek. *The great day* of the Lord is the last day, of salvation for his people and destruction for his enemies; the day of judgment therefore. ἐπιφανῆ (in the LXX) misinterprets נורא as from ראה, instead of from ירא. καὶ ἐπιφανῆ is omitted by ℵ D gig r. This great day, which will be such (*splendid* in *Begs*. 4.22 is perhaps an over-translation) that no one will fail to recognize it (cf. Lk 17.24), marks the end of the eschatological process. Elsewhere in the NT it is the day of Christ, or of the Lord Jesus (1 Cor. 1.8; 2 Cor. 1.14; Phil. 1.6, 10; 2.16), and there is no doubt that this is how Luke understands the day of the Lord; that is, it is not the *whole* day of Christ, from incarnation to parousia (Calvin 60), but the day on which the Lord Jesus Christ comes from heaven (cf. 1.11) to consummate the story of the people of God. ἐπιφανής (see *ND* 4.148) is taken from Joel 3.4 (LXX), but it also recalls the NT use of ἐπιφάνεια (2 Thess. 2.8; 1 Tim. 6.14; 2 Tim. 1.10; 4.1, 8; Tit. 2.13) which refers to the manifestation of Christ at the last day and recalls descriptions of state arrivals of secular monarchs. The verse thus does much to make clear Luke's understanding of the divine plan. His story lies within the period limited on the one hand by the resurrection and ascension and on the other by the return of Christ (for possible qualification of the word *return* see on 3.20). From the outset it is marked by the gift of the Spirit which initiates Christian prophecy; there will also be signs, σημεῖα (v. 19), on earth, and of these Luke will give examples (2.43, etc.). These will be followed (*followed*, since Luke cannot yet include them in his narrative) by celestial portents (darkening of the sun, and so forth), which will form the immediate prelude to the coming of Christ. For the first part of this interim period, the time of signs on earth, see further on 3.20. This is a simple outline, but it holds the Christian story firmly to its origin in the historical mission of Jesus and allowed Luke to find, and expound to the church, the significance of its history which — perhaps unexpectedly — had taken the place of an immediate parousia. See further the general discussion of Lucan eschatology in Vol. II.

21. This verse reproduces precisely the LXX version of Joel 3.5a; there is an allusion to 3.5b in v. 39 (see the note). Cf. Lk. 3.6. Of the present verse Schille (108) says, 'Die Schlusswendung trägt den Ton'. He also says that the Joel quotation is more suited as a baptismal text, so that Pentecost is to be regarded as 'eine Art Aposteltaufe'. This is a more doubtful proposition. The prophet was thinking of salvation as the great climactic day, and this conception of salvation is retained in the NT (e.g. Rom. 13.11, and regularly in Paul). So here Bengel: '. . . *salvus fiet*, effugiet poenas; beatitudinem assequetur'. Luke would, we may suppose, though without clear evidence, not wish to deny this sense of the word, but for him salvation is an event that happens to the believer in the present time. See e.g. 2.47 (τοὺς σωζομένους); Wilson (*Pastorals* 21) points out that Luke shares this view with the Pastoral Epistles; it is also however true (and is not denied by Wilson) that other NT writers (including on occasion Paul) think of salvation as occurring in the present and the Pastorals are not without a future eschatological outlook. Marshall (in his commentaries and also in *Luke, Historian and Theologian*, Exeter, 1970) takes salvation to be the central theme in Luke's theology.

The occurrence here of the word *name* (of the Lord, that is, of Jesus) is important. The word occurs frequently in the early chapters of Acts (see 3.6, 16; 4.7, 10, 12, 17, 18, 30; 5.28, 40) in such a way as to have led to the view that it is used in a magical sense; the name itself is an active power which can be employed by those who know how to invoke it. The sense in which Luke uses the word is however best defined by the two occurrences in the present chapter (vv. 21, 38). In the present verse it is used in the sense of calling on the name of the Lord, that is, of invoking him in faith (cf. Rom. 10.14: invoking rests upon believing). For v. 38 see below.

Calvin (62) stresses the universality of πᾶς ὃς ἄν. 'God admits all men to Himself without exception . . . since no man is excluded from calling upon God the gate of salvation is set open to all.'

22. For ἄνδρες (repeated in order to show the end of the quotation and the beginning of Peter's own words, perhaps also marking the use of a fresh source; see p. 129) in address see on 1.16; for Ἰσραηλῖται, see 3.12; 5.35; 13.16; 21.28. Luke represents Peter as addressing the same audience as that described in v. 14 as Ἰουδαῖοι καὶ οἱ κατοικοῦντες Ἰερουσαλήμ. He claims their attention: ἀκούσατε τοὺς λόγους τούτους; cf. 7.2; 13.16; 15.13; 22.1.

The *name of the Lord* (v. 21) is Jesus of Nazareth; it is brought to the beginning of the sentence for emphasis, though this means that it has to be taken up again by a resumptive pronoun at the beginning of v. 23. After the initial explanation of the speaking with tongues, which asserts the fulfilment of the OT, Christian preaching begins with the name of Jesus. He is first identified as ὁ Ναζωραῖος. This is best explained as 'of (the place called) Nazareth'. Other interpretations however have been given, based on the observations that it is not easy to see how the ω in Ναζωραῖος could be derived from the α in the corresponding syllable of Ναζαρέθ (Ναζαρά) and that *naṣorayya* is one of the names applied to the Mandaeans. This name has been derived from the Hebrew נצר, *to guard, to observe*, and given the meaning of *the observants*, that is, those who observed with particular care their rites of baptism and purification. The name may have been given to Jesus and his followers as *the observants* (see Braun, *Radikalismus* 2.121): it may have arisen through their connection with John the Baptist and his disciples (see Black, *AA* 197–200). B. Gärtner, *Die rätselhaften Termini Nazoräer und Iskariot*, Uppsala, 1957, 5–36, connects it with the passive Qal participle of נצר: Jesus was the one who was guarded, preserved; that is, he represented the remnant, the servant of the Lord. The name however was discussed at great length by H. Schaeder in *TWNT* 4.880–4, and his conclusion is to be accepted (884): 'Die Auffassung von Ναζωραῖος als Wiedergabe von aram *nāṣrājā*, abgeleitet vom Namen der Stadt Nazaret aram *nāṣrat*, ist sprachlich und sachlich unangreifbar; weder die Selbstbezeichnung der Mandäer als *nāṣᵒrājē*. . . noch der Name einer angeblich vorchristlichen Sekte der Νασαραῖοι ist imstande, eine andere, ursprünglichere Bedeutung von Ναζωραῖος zu erweisen.' See also Dalman (*SSW* 57–60).

The first proposition made about Jesus of Nazareth is that he was a man, ἀνήρ. It is from this starting-point that the Christology of Acts proceeds, not from the notion of a divine being who by some kind of incarnation or kenosis accommodated himself to the human world. Luke never abandons his assertion of the manhood of Jesus but introduces various qualifications, of which the first appears immediately. He was ἀποδεδειγμένον (δεδοκιμασμένον, D* lat Ir^lat) ἀπὸ τοῦ θεοῦ. ἀποδεικνύναι with a personal object normally means *to appoint* and takes a second accusative, as e.g. in Xenophon, *Anabasis* 1.1.2 (στρατηγὸν αὐτὸν ἀπέδειξε), sometimes with an infinitive, as in Herodotus 5.25.1 ('Ότάνεα ἀποδέξας στρατηγὸν εἶναι). The passive should thus be provided with a nominative complement (as in *OGIS* 379.5, ὕπατος ἀποδεδειγμένος for Latin *consul designatus*). One would therefore expect in the present verse some such clause as ἄνδρα ἀποδεδειγμένον Χριστόν; but the complement is wanting. Either Luke takes it to be implied by the context or ἀποδεδειγμένος must have a less technical meaning, *a man marked out* (Calvin 63, *approved*; Haenchen 182, *legitimiert*; cf. 1 Macc. 14.23, ἐν τοῖς ἀποδεδειγμένοις τῷ δήμῳ βιβλίοις; other quotations in Wettstein). This would fit the view, suggested by v. 36, that it was at a time after his resurrection that Jesus was appointed Christ. Luke appears to mean that Jesus was brought to your attention by his mighty works; they did not constitute his appointment, or proof of his status, but made it clear that he was one who stood in a special relation with God, one through whom God was acting in a unique way. It might seem to have been more natural to write ὑπό than ἀπό τοῦ θεοῦ. ἀπό may be due to the influence of ἀπό in ἀποδεδειγμένον, or to the influence (possibly, but improbably, the mistranslation) of מן (Torrey 28), or it may point to the origin in God of the miracles performed by Jesus. Cf. Gal. 1.1. δυνάμεις is the word regularly used in the Synoptic Gospels, including Luke, for the miracles — mighty works — of Jesus. Τέρατα καὶ σημεῖα (usually in the reverse order) is a common LXX phrase, representing אתות ומפתים. These are not necessarily miraculous, but Luke is certainly referring to the miracles of Jesus (though the words may have been suggested by the Joel quotation in v. 19 — so e.g. Stählin, 44). See also 2 Cor. 12.12; 2 Thess. 2.9; Heb. 2.4. By these means God showed that Jesus was (or was to be, if ἀποδεικνύναι here means *to designate*) his special agent: God performed (ἐποίησεν) the signs through Jesus (δι᾽αὐτοῦ); and he did this for your benefit, εἰς ὑμᾶς, that you might know who Jesus was (or was to be). For ὑμᾶς, D* 6ˢ 1241 *pc* have ἡμᾶς: the manifestation was not to Israel as a whole but to the speakers, who had followed Jesus. The appeal, however, to the hearers' own knowledge (καθὼς αὐτοὶ οἴδατε) supports ὑμᾶς. 'Apg 2, 22 ist die Vorstellung von Jesus als dem θεῖος ἀνήρ formelhaft zusammengefasst; vgl. Apg 10, 38' (Conzelmann, *Theologie* 97; cf. Bultmann, *Theologie* 133). This seems to say both more and less than is warranted by Acts; see further the general discussion of Christology in Vol. II. On the one hand, Acts (not least in the passage at present under discussion) affirms that Jesus was a man (ἀνήρ, not θεῖος ἀνήρ) and that God (a distinct being, not a δύναμις possessed by Jesus himself) worked through him in order to effect the mighty works, portents, and signs that onlookers had observed. On the other hand, in due course God had made him (v. 36) κύριος and Χριστός: he occupied the preeminent executive role in God's predetermined plan of salvation. Luke's Christology cannot by any means be described as advanced or developed; it does not include the notion of the incarnation of a pre-existent divine being. But it contains an eschatological element to which the θεῖος ἀνήρ theory fails to do justice. 'Wir gelangen so zu dem Ergebnis, dass der Satz 2.22f. von Lukas formuliert ist' (Wilckens 126).

23. He who was marked out by God was killed by you, a fact set forth 'in einem erschreckenden Gegensatz' (Weiser 92). τοῦτον picks up the accusative of the preceding verse; the verb is still some way ahead and Luke feels that the reader needs a reminder of what its object will be. The outline of the sentence is, You fixed him to (the cross) and (thereby) slew him. Notwithstanding the crucifixions by Alexander Jannaeus (M. Hengel, *Crucifixion*, 1977, 84f.), crucifixion was not a Jewish punishment in the Roman period; yet with the main verb ἀνείλατε Luke fixes responsibility for the crucifixion of Jesus upon the Jews. Not however without qualification. The action took place διὰ χειρὸς (singular; by the agency of) ἀνόμων. For the distributive singular cf. 15.23, contrast 14.3. See also 3.18, 21: 7.45; 21.24. Latin and Greek normally use the plural; the singular is known to Hebrew (e.g. Gen. 30.35 — Hebrew and Greek) and preferred in Aramaic. So BDR § 140. M. 2.462 notes Torrey's view that the same Aramaic ביד is translated παραδίδοται εἰς τὰς χεῖρας τῶν ἁμαρτωλῶν at Mk 14.41, but thinks that Luke's Greek is based on ביד without being a literal translation. See MM 145f., where it is argued that the phrase 'is obviously modelled upon the vernacular phrase διὰ χειρός, of money paid "by hand", "directly", ubiquitous in commercial documents: e.g. *P.Oxy.* 2 (1899). 268⁷ (AD 58)ἀπεσχηκυῖαι [παρὰ τοῦ Ἀντ]ιφάνους διὰ χειρὸς [ἐ]ξ οἴκου ὃ καὶ ἐπε[ίσθη]σαν κεφαλαῖον.' The connection is perhaps less obvious than MM supposed. Delling (*Kreuzestod* 86) may be right in thinking that διὰ χειρὸς ἀνόμων was a traditional expression. διὰ χειρὸς ἀνόμων will go with προσπήξαντες, not with ἔκδοτον, leaving it uncertain whether this word refers to the betrayal of Jesus to the Jews by Judas or to the Jews' treachery to their fellow countryman in handing him over to the Romans. In meaning ἔκδοτος is practically equivalent to παράδοτος; so *Begs.* 4.23, appealing to Josephus, *Ant.* 6.316; 14.355; 18.369, but of these only the last is reasonably clear. After ἔκδοτον, P⁷⁴ and others add λαβόντες, rightly perceiving (Field) that the adjective cannot stand alone. λαβεῖν, δοῦναι, and παραδοῦναι are common with ἔκδοτος; so Diodorus Siculus 16.2; Dionysius Halicarn. *Ant.* 7.53. Luke may have written ἔκδοτον γενόμενον; cf. 7.32; 10.4; 12.23; 16.27; Herodotus 6.85.1; Euripides, *Ion* 1251 (ἔκδοτος δὲ γίγνομαι). ἄνομοι does not mean that the Romans were in any way specially wicked, only that they lacked the privilege of the law.

The most important qualification of ἀνείλατε, however, is contained in the words τῇ ὡρισμένῃ βουλῇ (cf. Lk. 22.22, κατὰ τὸ ὡρισμένον)καὶ προγνώσει τοῦ θεοῦ. What appeared to be a free concerted action by Jews and Gentiles was in fact done because God foreknew it, decided it, and planned it. Cf. 4.27, 28. Why he did this, and how the predetermined event was applied in the work of salvation, requires explanation, but this passage should be noted, along with 20.28, as providing a theological framework for the otherwise uninterpreted affirmation, 'You killed him, but God raised him from the dead' (e.g. 3.15). What Luke (it seems) did not know,

God knew, and knew in advance (πρόγνωσις); perhaps a not unsatisfactory distribution. See further the general discussion in Vol. II. It is perhaps right to see in these words the Christological focus of the eternal decree (Barth, *CD* 2.1.521), but it would be wrong to suppose that Luke was aware of this. It is nearer to the truth that Luke was rebutting the charge that Jesus was but a poor creature, since he had not foreseen and avoided the consequence of his actions. Not at all, Luke replies; God himself foresaw and planned the whole.

24. The sentence takes an awkward turn: Jesus of Nazareth . . . you killed, whom God raised up. It is not ungrammatical but '. . . but God raised him up' would be neater. Cf. however 3.15 (ὃν ὁ θεὸς ἤγειρεν); the construction with the relative may be drawn from an early formulation of belief (cf. Phil. 2.6; Col. 1.15; 1 Tim. 3.16), possibly based, or modelled on the story of Joseph (Gen. 50.20, You meant evil against me, but God meant it for good). With reference to the resurrection of Jesus Luke most commonly uses transitive tenses of ἀνιστάναι (2.24, 32; (3.26); 13.(32), 34; 17.31): cf. the use of ἐγείρειν (3.15; 4.10; (5.30); 10.40; 13.30, 37; cf. 26.8). Intransitive ἀνιστάναι occurs at 10.41; 17.3. It is clear that Luke's main emphasis is on the fact that in this event, as in the miracles (v. 22), the prime actor was God; Jesus indeed rose, but he rose because he was raised. The point of this, a point developed by Paul rather than by Luke, is that the resurrection of Jesus was not an isolated and individual event but an anticipated part of the resurrection at the last day, brought forward in such a way that the rest of men might share in it by faith.

God raised Jesus up by *loosing the pangs of death*, a strange expression (since pangs are not normally said to be loosed), borrowed from Ps. 17.6 (LXX: ὠδῖνες ᾅδου περιεκύκλωσάν με, προέφθασέν με παγίδες θανάτου) or Ps. 114.3 (LXX: περιέσχον με ὠδῖνες θανάτου, κίνδυνοι ᾅδου εὕροσάν με). In each case the Hebrew seems to have intended not חֶבֶל, *pang*, but חֶבֶל, *cord* (Ps. 18.6,   מות מוקשי . . . חבלי שאול . . .; but there an emendation is probable; Ps. 116.3, חבלי מות ומצרי שאול. The LXX retain words suitable for *cords* (περιεκύκλωσαν, περιέσχον), and this connection will explain Luke's λύσας; it is not necessary to assume that he was himself translating, or mistranslating, Hebrew. Plümacher (42) thinks that the word came to Luke along a liturgical channel. For θανάτου, D latt sy^p mae bo have ᾅδου, possibly remembering Ps. 17 (18).6 rather than Ps. 114 (116).3, or thinking of the victory of Christ over the powers of the underworld (cf. Mt. 16.18), or affected by vv. 27, 31.

A different interpretation of Luke's words is possible. Field made the suggestion that they imply a picture of Death (personified) as in labour; God *put an end* (a possible meaning of λύειν) to death's travail pains; Death was to bring forth no more children, have no more effect. Stählin (44) accepts a similar interpretation, and Wilcox (46–8) finds support in 1 QH 3.28, where the language of Ps. 18.4 is taken up with the meaning 'the pangs of death will compass (people) about'. The context is eschatological and recalls the use of ὠδῖνες in the NT for the messianic woes. The meaning would be that in raising Jesus from death God was bringing to an end the messianic woes; he was therefore about to bring in the age to come. This is interesting and attractive, but use of the LXX is a simpler and better explanation of the text of Acts.

It may be that Polycarp, *Phil.* 1.2 (ὃν ἤγειρεν ὁ θεός, λύσας τὰς ὠδῖνας τοῦ ᾅδου) shows knowledge of this passage; if so it may well be the earliest known reference to Acts. See p. 36.

καθότι (cf. Joel 3.5) is used by Luke only in the NT; most often (Lk. 19.9; Acts 2.45; 4.35; 17.31) it means *according as* but at Lk. 1.7 it seems to mean *because*, which suits the present sentence. For this meaning cf. Ignatius, *Trallians* 5.2; the English *as* is probably capable of covering all the senses in which Luke uses καθότι. The clause is rightly interpreted by Barth (*CD* 2.1.606): 'He is the One for whom it was impossible that the resurrection from the dead should not take place.' This safeguards the observation made above that Luke regards the resurrection as an act of God. Luke, however, has his own understanding of the way in which the impossibility is to be expressed. The resurrection was foretold in Scripture, which could not fail of fulfilment. It is the resurrection, rather than any interpretation of the death of Christ, that Luke supports with OT authority.

25. *David* is assumed to be the author of the Psalms (except of course of those to which Scripture itself assigns other authors). Ps. 15 (16).8–11 is quoted in vv. 25–8; the question remains how the Psalm is to be interpreted. This is dealt with in vv. 29–31. It will be argued that David is not speaking of himself but of the Messiah; and protection from death (the theme of the Psalm in its original use) becomes deliverance from death.

Verse 25 quotes Ps. 15.8 in exact agreement with the LXX. ℵ D 614 *pc* sy^p add μου after κύριον; they are probably influenced by the quotation in v. 34.

προορώμην (for the omission of the augment see M 2.190) is an unexpected rendering of שויתי, which means *I set*, or *placed*. Presumably the LXX understood the word to mean *I set within my sight*, though *I fixed my gaze upon* would be more natural. The LXX probably took the prefix προ- in a spatial sense: I saw the Lord before me, in my presence; Luke may well have taken it to be temporal, since he regards the Psalm as a prediction (*Begs.* 4.24). BDR § 333.1b.6 and Delebecque 10 think that the imperfect has the force of the present.

If Luke understands διὰ παντός to mean that God was always consciously present to the person in question (Jesus), even at the time of the crucifixion, it is easy to understand his omission of the cry 'My God, my God, why hast thou forsaken me?' (Mk 15.34), and the words of Lk. 24.43, 'Today shalt thou be with me in Paradise', are more appropriate than the doctrine of a descent into Hades. ἐκ δεξιῶν μου provides a link with Ps. 110.1, quoted in v. 34; Pesch (122) points out the *Stichwortverbindung*. ἵνα μὴ σαλευθῶ renders בל־אמוט, which really expresses not purpose but a strong negative, proclaiming confidence in God (cf. Ps. 10.6; 15.5; 21.8; 30.7; 62.3, 7; 112.6). Luke however will have understood ἵνα in its normal Greek sense and thus have taken the whole clause to mean, God stands at my right hand (as armed defender, or perhaps as advocate) in order that I may not be moved (by my enemies).

26. This verse agrees exactly with Ps. 15.9. In the first clause the LXX text agrees with MT; in the second however instead of *my tongue* the Hebrew has כבודי, *my glory*, itself possibly a variant for כבדי, *my liver*, used in parallel with *heart* as the seat of the emotions. The aorist ηὐφράνθη points to the explosion of lively feeling; so Delebecque 10. These two clauses, though apt in the Psalm, do not bear upon the argument in Acts; they are included because they are in the text quoted. Luke shows no knowledge of the interpretation (StrB 2.618) contained in Midrash Psalms 16 § 10 (62a): 'Therefore my heart rejoices', that is, over the words of Torah; 'and my glory exults', that is, over the King Messiah.

ἔτι, *besides, moreover*, introduces the clause which, though parallel to the preceding two (my heart, my tongue, my flesh), comes nearer to Luke's immediate concern. *My flesh*, that is, my physical body, will rest, after death, in hope, hope of resurrection. ἐπ' ἐλπίδι renders לבטח, which suggests objective security rather than subjective hope. *Hope* however is sufficient for Luke's purpose. Rest (in death) for the flesh means not extinction but hope. If Luke thinks of David as speaking in his own person he will be expressing hope for the resurrection of Jesus; if he is speaking in the person of Jesus he will be referring to the interval between Good Friday and Easter Day.

27. This verse agrees exactly with Ps. 15.10, where the LXX are in sufficient agreement with the Hebrew. δώσεις represents the idiomatic use of נתן for *to permit*; τὸν ὅσιόν σου is חסידך (Qere; the Kethibh has חסידיך, plural): thy godly, faithful, pious one. διαφθορά renders שחת, which here is used in parallel with שאול, ᾅδης, though elsewhere it appears to be a part, the least pleasant part, of the world of the dead. This second clause is quoted again at 13.35. It is clear (for Luke) that the Psalmist is here expressing, in the person of the Messiah, the confidence that God will not allow his destiny to be that of the inferior, unhappy, existence which was all that men looked forward to after death. The first person is used in v. 27a; one must suppose that τὸν ὅσιόν σου was to be interpreted in the same way — me, thy godly one. The reasons for applying this confident hope not to David but to Jesus will be given in vv. 29–31.

28. This verse agrees exactly with the first two clauses of Ps. 15.11; the last clause is omitted (τερπνότητες ἐν τῇ δεξιᾷ σου εἰς τέλος). The Hebrew has the singular, *way of life* (חיים ארח) and means the way that is well-pleasing to God and therefore leads to life; Luke thinks of the way out of death back to life. The Psalm continues, literally, Fullness of joys is with thy face (or with thy presence, את־פניך). μετὰ τοῦ προσώπου σου is an over-literal translation of the Hebrew idiom. V. 28a states the positive converse of v. 27; 28b not only speaks of the joy that naturally follows upon God's deliverance of his servant from the power of death but adds the truth that joy arises not simply out of not being dead but out of living in the presence, before the face, of God. This verse does not add substantially to the argument and does not appear when the Psalm is used in the *Acts of Philip* 78 (15) (L.-B. 2.2.31). Philip goes on to use the same exegetical argument as that of the next verses (whence it is probably borrowed): ὁ δὲ Δαυὶδ ἐτελεύτησε, καὶ τὸ μνῆμα αὐτοῦ οἴδαμεν. ταῦτα δὲ πάντα εἴρηται περὶ τοῦ Χριστοῦ καὶ τῆς ἐκ νεκρῶν αὐτοῦ ἀναστάσεως.

29. Ἄνδρες ἀδελφοί. Cf. 1.16, but now the hearers are *brothers* not because they are fellow Christians but because they are fellow Jews. Superficially the passage quoted appears to refer to David, its author, who speaks of *my heart, my tongue, my flesh, my soul*. If it does so, and if this is its only reference, it is irrelevant to Peter's claim that God has raised Jesus from the dead. But is this the meaning of the Psalm? Peter can discuss the matter with his hearers. David was a great man, a patriarch (πατριάρχης; elsewhere the word is used only of the immediate family of Abraham — 7.8, 9; Heb. 7.4) of his people, but indisputably he died (according to j Hagigah 2.78a.41; j Betzah 2.61c.9; at Pentecost, on a Sabbath), and that he remained dead is proved by the continuous existence of his tomb, and not contradicted by the tradition (Derek Eretz Zuta 1 (StrB 2.26)) that he was one of the seven fathers (the others were Abraham, Isaac, Jacob, Moses, Aaron, Amram) not touched by corruption. For David's tomb see J. Jeremias (*Heiligengräber*, 57) and J. Murphy-O'Connor (*Holy Land* 74); its location is not important for the exegesis of Acts, where the only matter of importance is that the tomb still existed. Probably some at least in Jerusalem would be aware of the attempts to rifle the tomb, by John Hyrcanus (Josephus, *Ant.* 7.392–4; 13.249; 16.179; *War* 1.61) and Herod (*Ant.* 7.394;

16.179–83) which produced cash but did not disturb the royal coffins; they would know that (so far at least as these proceedings were concerned) the king's body had remained where it was. Jeremias (op. cit. 129) speaks of Peter's 'vorsichtige Bitte um Nachsicht' because he commits what would be regarded as blasphemy in the suggestion that David's body was corruptible. It is not however clear that this is the meaning of ἐξὸν εἰπεῖν μετὰ παρρησίας, which seems rather to mean, I may boldly say without fear of contradiction. For παρρησία see W. C. van Unnik, *De semitische Achtergrund van παρρησία in het NT*, 1962, and *The Christian's Freedom of Speech in the NT*, 1962; here, *quite openly*. There is a similar transference of application in 4QpPs37, 3.15f., where Ps. 37 is applied to 'the priest, the teacher of righteousness'.

For ἐν ἡμῖν, D Ψ syᵖ prefer the more suitable preposition, παρ' ἡμῖν. So the Psalm cannot have referred to David, its author; the way is open to refer it to Christ. It would however be wrong to avoid the question whether it does indeed refer to him and what authority and persuasive force the quotation should be allowed to have. P. Benoit (*Ex. & Th.* 1.3–*1*) discusses the question in terms of the relation between the Hebrew and the Greek, which diverge at the point where the Hebrew שחת is rendered by the Greek διαφθορά. As Benoit shows, the Hebrew depicts a man who has been delivered from peril and thereby permitted to live a little longer in this world; the Greek contemplates deliverance from the corruption of death itself. Is the LXX to be regarded as itself inspired, and not merely as a translation of an inspired Hebrew original? Origen and Augustine so regarded it, but Benoit is content to expose the problem. It is a serious one, but even more serious is the question whether either the Hebrew or the Greek was intended to refer to the death and resurrection of David's distant descendant, Jesus. Has an unjustified interpretation been imposed upon the OT text? or are we to say that the Psalmist wrote better than he knew? Perhaps every assertion of the victory of God over evil eventually finds a place in relation to the death and resurrection of Christ.

30. Since in the Psalm David was not referring to himself he must have been speaking of another, and of whom should he have spoken but of the one who God had sworn should be descended from him and inherit his throne? The argument is clear, though some linguistic points in the verse call for clarification. David was a prophet and knew what was to come in the future; Luke refers to the promise made to him in 2 Sam. 7.12f. This is quoted in 4 Qflor 1.10, 11, and given an interpretation similar to that given in 4 QpPs.37 to Ps. 37 (see above on v. 25): This is the Sprout of David (הואה צמח דויד). It is interesting to note that the Florilegium goes on (1.12) to quote Amos 9.11; cf. Acts 15.16. See Fitzmyer (*CBQ* 34 (1972), 332–9).

ὅρκῳ ὤμοσεν is sometimes classed as a Semitism, equivalent to the use of the Hebrew infinitive absolute, which according to Dalman is very rare in pure Aramaic (though Torrey contradicts this). Cf. 4.17 (Ψ𝔐 syʰ); 5.28; 23.14; also the Joel quotation in 2.17. M 2.443 refers back to M 1.75f., 245, where Moulton perhaps protests too much against Semitism (of some order). M 2.443 adds 'the many parallels in the language of Attic tragedy and the Old Comedy, e.g. φόβῳ ταρβεῖν, φόβῳ δεδιέναι, φύσει πεφυκέναι, νόσῳ νοσεῖν.' It is the proliferation of the construction that gives the impression of Semitism.

ὀμνύναι is commonly followed by an infinitive; so here: God swore that he would *place, cause to sit* (καθίσαι). This infinitive however has no object accusative, and one must be taken from ἐκ καρποῦ, this prepositional phrase being regarded as equivalent to a partitive genitive (BDR § 164.2). This becomes difficult (a difficulty that gave rise to variants in D* and 𝔐) to translate partly because of the figurative expression and partly because καρπός is used in the singular. In English one can hardly avoid paraphrasing: God swore to set on his throne one of his descendants. The reference of course is to the Messiah, assumed to come from the house of David, D and others add (τὸ) κατὰ σάρκα. Cf. Rom. 1.3; the question is raised whether the Western editor was familiar with the Pauline epistles; see on the text of vv. 30–32 Black (*FS* Nida 121–3).

31. David, then, as a prophet foresaw (προϊδών; προειδώς in D² 104 945 1739 *al* sa Cyrᵖᵗ is not significantly different in meaning and is due to mechanical error) what was to happen and spoke of the resurrection of the Messiah. The content of his prophecy is given in the ὅτι clause, which, with the appropriate change of tense, reproduces the content of v. 27. The two clauses introduced and connected by οὔτε . . . οὔτε are in essentials synonymous, though the former refers to the destiny of the soul after death, the latter to the fate of the physical body. The essential person of Jesus lived on; his flesh did not suffer corruption. For ᾅδην (א B 81 323 945 1739ᶜ 2495 *al*: cf. v. 27), ᾅδου is read by A Cᵛⁱᵈ D E Ψ 𝔐; this is a correction in accordance with classical usage (εἰς ᾅδου = εἰς οἶκον (or the like) ᾅδου). Cf. *Acts of Thomas* 156 (L.-B. 2.2.265), ὁ κατελθὼν εἰς ᾅδου μετὰ πολλῆς δυνάμεως.

1 QH 3.21 has been adduced as a parallel to this verse, but Braun (150) has shown that it is not relevant.

32. τοῦτον τὸν Ἰησοῦν ἀνέστησεν ὁ θεός. Cf. v. 24.

οὗ πάντες ἡμεῖς ἐσμεν μάρτυρες. Cf. 1.8, and other passages referred to in the note on that verse. οὗ may refer to Jesus (we are his witnesses; cf. 1.8, μου μάρτυρες) or to the whole of the preceding clause (we are witnesses of the fact that God raised him from the dead; cf. 1.22, μάρτυρα τῆς ἀναστάσεως αὐτοῦ). Neither the wording nor the parallels enable us to decide confidently between the alternatives.

33. There is a useful survey of discussions of the verse by J. Dupont in *FS* Moule, 219–27. Dupont shows that though some writers deal with this verse (and the next) in redactional terms, supposing that Luke either adapted an existing formula or created a suitable formulation for himself, a majority see behind his words the use of Ps. 68 (67). Bede saw a link with the Psalm quoted in v. 25: . . . quia dixerat psalmus, quoniam a dextris est mihi ne commovear. Cf. also Ps. 118.16 (LXX, not MT), δεξιὰ κυρίου ὕψωσέν με.

τῇ δεξιᾷ τοῦ θεοῦ (cf. 5.31) is ambiguous. The dative may be that of the instrument (by the right hand of God) or that of place (to the right hand of God). BDR § 199 take the latter view; but the only examples of the dativus loci they can cite in the NT are the present verse and 5.31, which is equally ambiguous. Conzelmann (30) also gives the dative a local meaning and cites Odes of Solomon 8.21; Odes of Solomon 25.9 can however be quoted on the other side. See further Zerwick § 57. The agency of God in v. 32 (ἀνέστησεν ὁ θεός) seems decisive in favour of the instrumental sense here. Jesus then was ὑψωθείς (Luke is here referring to the ascension rather than the resurrection): this word is the first pointer to Ps. 68 (67). 19 (עלית למרום; ἀνέβης εἰς ὕψος), the verse quoted expressly in Eph. 4.8. It continues ἔλαβες δόματα, which recalls τήν τε ἐπαγγελίαν τοῦ πνεύματος τοῦ ἁγίου λαβών, the special gift of the Spirit being naturally mentioned in the context of Acts 2. A further contact appears in v. 34 where it is pointed out, οὐ γὰρ Δαυὶδ ἀνέβη εἰς τοὺς οὐρανούς. Just as David was not the person referred to in Ps. 16 as one who was not left in Hades and whose flesh did not see corruption, so it was not he who, according to Ps. 68, went up into heaven. The latter point is made explicitly in v. 34 in the quotation of Ps. 110. Lindars (*Apologetic* 39, 42) thinks that there is a further connection with the last line of Ps. 16 (15).11, omitted from the quotation in vv. 25–8 (but quoted in the note on v. 28); and Knox (*Gentiles* 195) sees a reference to the Targum of Ps. 68. 34, He with his word (*memra*) gave with his voice the Spirit of prophecy to the prophets. Eph. 4.8 is sufficient to show that Ps. 68 was in use in the early church, and it is probably correct to hear echoes of it in vv. 33, 34; these must however be distinguished from the use that is made of Pss. 16; 110. These are quoted explicitly, the former at considerable length, and it is maintained that as prophecies they have been fulfilled in the life, death, resurrection, and glorification of Jesus. How far the echoes of Ps. 68 (67) would have been picked up by Luke's readers, how far he intended them to be picked up, how far he was himself aware of them, are questions which it is difficult to answer. Overtones of a familiar passage of Scripture may have come out unconsciously. They may however affect one exegetical question in the verse. Jesus received the promise (consisting) of the Spirit. Does this refer to his baptism (Lk. 3.22 — himself endowed with the Spirit he was able to confer the same gift on others) or to a receiving with a view not to his personal life but to transmission after the resurrection, that is, a receiving as part of his exaltation? The former view would be paralleled by 10.38, but the context established by allusion to the Psalm is decisive for the latter. It was part of the exaltation that he received gifts (cf. Phil. 2.9, ὁ θεὸς . . . ἐχαρίσατο αὐτῷ τὸ ὄνομα . . .); among these was the Spirit, a gift he received in order to give it away (the thought is on the way to that of Eph. 4.8, where ἔλαβες δόματα ἐν ἀνθρώποις has become ἔδωκεν δόματα τοῖς ἀνθρώποις). Here ἐξέχεεν (rather than, say, ἔδωκεν) is used in view of v. 17 (Joel 3.1). The promise is that given through Joel, though other OT passages speak of a gift of the Spirit in the last days. The concluding words, τοῦτο ὅ (according to Torrey the relative is a mistranslation of Aramaic יד, which should have been rendered as) ὑμεῖς καὶ βλέπετε καὶ ἀκούετε, clearly refer back to the context in which the speech is set; it may be that the whole verse was originally linked with the promise quoted from Joel in vv. 17–21.

Bede quotes Augustine (*De Trinitate* 15.26), accepit quippe ut homo et effudit ut deus. As Roloff (59) says, the words παρὰ τοῦ πατρός imply that Jesus is the Son of God; it cannot however be denied that Luke understands sonship in a mildly subordinationist sense. As Son Jesus remains 'das Werkzeug Gottes' (Schille 113). The theme of subordination is brought out also by Weiser, 94; but the instrument is a unique instrument, and the subordination is that of a Son.

34, 35. The position of οὐ suggests that the meaning is not simply, David did not ascend, but, It was not David who ascended. This recalls the proof in vv. 29–31 that Ps. 16 (15).8–11 did not refer to David but to Jesus, and (see above) takes up the ἀνέβης of Ps. 68 (67).19: that Psalm also must refer to Christ in his exaltation, but this is further developed by the quotation of Ps. 110(109).1, which is given in exact agreement with the LXX (unless we follow B* ℵ* D in omitting ὁ; the point is not important). If it was not David who ascended some other must be found who did so and thus fulfilled the Psalm; it was natural to find this other in the κύριος to whom David refers in Ps. 110(109), which is used not only here but in Mk 12.36 (and parallels) and alluded to in Mk 14.62 (and parallels). It is quoted also in 1 Cor. 15.25; Heb. 1.3, 13 and alluded to in a number of other passages. It evidently played an important part in early Christian thought, in which it was used (a) to associate Jesus with and at the

same time to distinguish him from David, and thus to affirm his
Messiahship; (b) to support the view that his apparent defeat was in
fact a stage on the way to glory; his disappearance from earth meant
that he had been received into heaven; (c) to set out the new two-
stage eschatology that Christians were obliged to adopt; they lived
between the exaltation of Jesus and the final submission of all his
enemies; (d) to show that the ascended Jesus was not only greater
than great David (who addresses him as κύριος) but was related to
God, at whose right hand he sits. This does not amount to the formal
claim that Jesus was God incarnate, but it places the early Christians
along with those Jews who were prepared to accept the notion of a
second power in heaven. On this, and on the Christology of Acts in
general, see the discussion in Vol. II; see also v. 36 (for the use of
κύριος and Χριστός).

36. οὖν: this verse sums up and states the conclusion of the speech
so far; Jesus' life, marked by miracles, his resurrection, and his
exaltation, means that Israel (only Israelites are being addressed)
may know for certain (for ἀσφαλῶς cf. e.g. Sophocles, *Oedipus
Tyrannus* 613, ἐν χρόνῳ γνώσει τάδ᾽ ἀσφαλῶς; also *P. Oxy.*
3312, 1. 6, γράψον μοι ἀσπαλῶς (Be sure you write to me; cited
in *ND* 3.7)) that God has made Jesus both Lord and Christ. *All the
house of Israel* is an OT phrase (e.g. 1 Kdms 7.2). It occurs also in
the Qaddish prayer (Singer, p. 37: בחיי די־כל־בית ישראל). *To appoint*,
or *to cause actually to become*, the holder of an official position is
an old use of ποιεῖν (e.g. Homer, *Odyssey* 1.386f., μὴ σέ γ᾽ἐν
ἀμφιάλῳ Ἰθάκῃ βασιλῆα Κρονίων ποιήσειεν). It is thus implied
that there was once a time when the crucified Jesus was not κύριος
and Χριστός, and the questions arise when he was appointed to these
positions, and exactly what positions the terms denote. The reference
to the crucifixion which follows (ὃν ὑμεῖς ἐσταυρώσατε) and that
to resurrection and exaltation which precedes (vv. 32–4) strongly
suggest that the appointment took place when God raised up and
thereby vindicated Jesus. It is true (and in this way Luke could have
accepted a source that did not share his own views on the matter —
see above, p. 133) that one could take the verse to mean, 'Resurrection
and ascension prove that God had, before his public ministry,
appointed Jesus to these offices', but this is not the most natural way
of taking the words used. 'Ebenso zeigen Rm. 1, 4 . . . und Act 2, 36,
dass man in der ältesten Gemeinde die Messianität Jesu von seiner
Auferstehung ab datiert hat' (Bultmann, *Theologie* 28). 'Hier ist
deutlich gesagt, dass die Kyrioswürde Jesus nach seiner Auferstehung
mit der Messiaswürde verliehen worden ist' (Cullmann, *Christologie*
222f.). This is, incidentally, clear proof that Luke is at this point
using a source; he would not have chosen to express himself in this
way. Schneider (266, cf. 276) takes a different view. 'Der Vers [36]

ist "lukanische" Zusammenfassung des Beweisganges [vv. 22–36] und repräsentiert keine altertümliche Adoptions-Christologie.' It does however seem that we have here that primitive kind of adoptionism that Paul was obliged to correct (Rom. 1.4; Phil. 2.6–11); it is a witness to the impact made by the resurrection. It seems clear that Jesus did not publicly claim Messiahship in the course of his ministry; almost equally clear that it was impossible to exclude messianic categories from the discussion of his work. For those who accepted it, his resurrection proved that nothing less could be the truth; and at the same time, returning from death, he appeared as Messiah in the role of a supernatural κύριος. This title certainly was in use in Aramaic (1 Cor. 16.22) and at an early date. Cullmann (op. cit.) thinks that κύριος must be understood as the LXX equivalent of the OT name of God, and cannot understand ('ich verstehe nicht') how others can question this. The reason for questioning it in the present context is to be found in v. 34, where κύριος is used in two senses, first as the name of God, then as the title of another person whom God invites to sit at his right hand. The remark quoted by Bede from Jerome (on Ps. 80.10–16: Prius nomen domini apud Hebraeos τετραγράμματον est, quod proprie in deo ponitur, secundum quod commune mortalibus quo et reges et ceteri homines appellantur . . .) is not wholly satisfactory as a comment at this point. The use of *dominus* noted by Jerome and Bede could be applied to David himself, but the Psalm (as understood here) applies κύριος to a person who is greater than David (since David speaks of him as *his* lord) but is distinguished from the God of the OT. We are dealing here with an unreflecting Christology (it is better to say unreflecting than primitive, or early), not yet submitted to such theological criticism as Paul was able to provide. He who shares the throne of God shares his deity; and he who is God is what he is from and to eternity — otherwise he is not God. This truth, evident as it is, was not immediately perceived; the staggering fact of the resurrection (which, however it may seem proper to describe or explain it, convinced the witnesses that a truly dead man was truly alive) both marked a contrast with the earthly life of Jesus and set his disciples in search of some terminology that might not seem wholly inadequate. Knox points out that 'the thought of a man attaining to divinity and immortality as a result of his good deeds was familiar to Gentile readers' (*Acts* 75, with many references, to be added to those Knox had already given in *Hellenistic Elements* 39f.). The silence of the gospels, especially Mark, about the Messiahship of Jesus remains an important matter; for this, and for the Christology of Acts in general, see the discussion in Vol. II. Wilckens (36) observes that this verse connects with v. 23 and is the theological summary of the speech.

The crucifixion of one who shares the throne of God is a sin against God; hence the force of the appeal for repentance which follows.

37. The speech breaks off as the hearers interpose a question. 'Die Unterbrechung ist literarisches Kunstmittel'; so rightly, Conzelmann (30). Cf. 10.44. The tension is heightened. The opening words are characteristically sharpened in the Western text: τότε πάντες οἱ συνελθόντες καὶ ἀκούσαντες. It must be made clear that the consciences of all present were touched. κατανύσσειν is, it seems, a mainly septuagintal word. It is used in the same sense at Gen. 34.7 (κατενύχθησαν οἱ ἄνδρες); cf. Ps. 109 (108).16 (κατανενυγμένον τῇ καρδίᾳ). This is the Psalm quoted at 1.20, and Wilcox (61) thinks that this may have suggested the use of the word here. καρδία is used for inward feelings; here, *conscience*. Cf. Eupolis, *Demoi* 6 (94.7), on Pericles' oratory: τὸ κέντρον ἐγκατέλιπε τοῖς ἀκροωμένοις. It is presumably their responsibility for the crucifixion (ὃν ὑμεῖς ἐσταυρώσατε, v. 36) that leads the hearers to question the speakers. τε binds clauses together and 'zeigt damit — im Vergleich zu καί — eine engere Zusammengehörigkeit an' (BDR § 443.2) — *and so they said*. This connection is lost in the variants: εἶπον δέ, Ψ 81 *pc*; καὶ εἶπον, E; καί τινες ἐξ αὐτῶν εἶπον, D* mae (note the variant at the beginning of the verse — *all* were pricked . . . *some* of them said); εἰπόντες, ℵ (Dᶜ) 614 *pc* syʰ. They addressed their question to Peter but also to the other (λοιπούς is omitted by D *pc* gig r boᵐˢˢ Aug — probably rightly (so Ropes); to suppose that the reader might find in the short text a hint that Peter was not an apostle was a piece of pedantry) apostles, who also had been speaking, presumably on the same lines (2.4). Again, the Western text adds colour to Luke's wording, adding, after τί, οὖν (D gig Irˡᵃᵗ), and, after ἀδελφοί, ὑποδείξατε ἡμῖν (D E it syʰᵐᵍ). These additions make no difference to the sense, and the force of Peter's words in vv. 38, 39 has already been heightened by the fact that they are presented as the answer to an interjected question. The people of God have put themselves in an impossible situation by rejecting God's own messenger; what is to be done? The question is reminiscent of Lk. 3.10, but the answer is different from that given by the Baptist. For ἄνδρες ἀδελφοί see on 1.16.

38. There are several variations in the opening words but P⁴⁶ᵛⁱᵈ ℵ A C 81 945 1739 1891 *pc* vg are probably correct with Πέτρος δὲ πρὸς αὐτούς· μετανοήσατε, φησίν. It may however be right to follow B *pc* Augᵖᵗ in omitting φησίν. So Metzger (300f.); but φησίν could have been omitted on the grounds that it interrupts the sequence μετανοήσατε καὶ βαπτισθήτω.

The answer to the question τί ποιήσωμεν; is in two parts: μετανοήσατε, which, in the plural, is presumably addressed to the whole house of Israel (v. 35), and βαπτισθήτω ἕκαστος ὑμῶν, which is specifically directed to the individual members of the crowd. Baptism may thus be thought of as an individualizing of the response that Israel as a whole should make. Repentance (as with John the Baptist, Lk. 3.3) is an element of baptism. The hearers' responsibility for the crucifixion has been so heavily emphasised that penitence for this supreme sin must be specially though of course not exclusively in mind, both in μετανοήσατε and in the particularization later in the verse in the phrase εἰς ἄφεσιν τῶν ἁμαρτιῶν ὑμῶν (D E Ψ 𝔐 it sy Ir^lat Cyp omit τῶν and ὑμῶν so as to produce the familiar baptismal formula — surely wrongly). μετανοεῖν is a fairly common word in Acts (2.38; 3.19; 8.22; 17.30; 26.20; μετάνοια, 5.31; 11.18; 13.24; 19.4; 20.21; 26.20) and occurs mostly in the context of conversion. It is usually connected with sin, and means sorrow for and turning away from a life. or an act, of disobedience, but it includes also the positive aspect of a turn to God (cf. 3.19, μετανοήσατε καὶ ἐπιστρέψατε; 'conversion of the mind', Calvin 78). Both these aspects are involved in baptism, which is described as being for, that is, as issuing in, forgiveness, but also as being ἐπὶ τῷ ὀνόματι Ἰησοῦ Χριστοῦ. For ἐπί, ἐν is read by B D 945 1739 1891 pc Did. Acts is not consistent in its use of prepositions with the name in baptism. At 8.16 Luke uses εἰς; at 10.48, ἐν; at 19.5, εἰς. We should probably be right in thinking that for Luke the preposition was relatively unimportant; what mattered was the name (which is used also in other contexts, notably the working of miracles (e.g. 3.6)). The varying relation in Acts of baptism to the gift of the Holy Spirit (here, baptism appears to precede; at 8.16 the two are not connected; at 10.44 the gift of the Spirit precedes baptism; at 18.26 baptism in the name of Jesus appears to be unnecessary; at 19.5f. baptism accompanied by the laying on of hands confers the gift of the Spirit) means that the name is anything but a magical formula. For further discussion of Luke's use of ὄνομα see the note on 3.16; when used in baptism it indicates that the person baptized becomes the property of, is assigned to the company of, Jesus (hence the correspondence of baptism to both aspects of μετάνοια). So most commentators; e.g. Haenchen (186), 'Damit tritt der Getaufte unter die Macht Jesu.' Cf. Stählin (53); Lohse (*Theologie* 66). Schmithals differs; Jesus is named as the great preacher of repentance (37). Through their loyalty to Jesus, Lord and Messiah (v. 36) the baptized belong to the renewed people of God in the last days. The eschatological reference of baptism is affirmed by the treatment of the gift of the Spirit in vv. 17–21. It is what God has promised for the *last days* (v. 17); it is (according to v. 38) those who are baptized who receive it; thus it is through baptism that they enter into the newly realized eschatological conditions.

καὶ λήμψεσθε: καί is probably something more than a simple additive conjunction; on καί consecutivum see BDR § 442.2. Do this, and in consequence you will receive . . . Pesch (125) goes a little too far in treating this as a conditional use of the imperative (If you are baptized you will receive . . .): Peter is truly issuing a command, or instruction (in answer to, What are we to do?). The genitive τοῦ ἁγίου πνεύματος is epexegetic: the gift consisting of. . . .

39. BDR § 189.2 explain the dative ὑμῖν as derived from the use of the verb cognate with the noun ἐπαγγελία, ἐπαγγέλλεσθαί τινι, but this hardly seems necessary; cf. Polybius 1.72.6, ἐπαγγελίας ποιεῖσθαί τινι. The variants ἡμῖν, ἡμῶν (D (p) mae Aug) align the speaker with his hearers as a fellow Jew. The promise here is in the first instance the promise of the Holy Spirit (v. 33 as well as v. 38). It would probably however be mistaken to confine it to this sense, or to the promise of the sending of a Messiah. It covers the covenant into which God entered with his people, to which he continues to be faithful (this, it may be added, gives a further significance to baptism, v. 38; cf. Stauffer, *Theologie* 139f.). Notwithstanding the crucifixion of Jesus God has not cast off his people (cf. Rom. 11.1, 2); the promise remains open — for those represented by the crowd surrounding Peter (cf. Rom. 11.28f.), and for their children, and for those far off. The scope of the promise is thus extended in time and space. J. Jeremias (*Infant Baptism in the First Four Centuries*. ET 1960, 40f.) argues that the reference to children constituted evidence for the baptism of infants probably in the earliest years of the church, certainly at the time when Acts was written, and (op. cit. 72) that the variants ἡμῖν, ἡμῶν (see above) showed that the Western editor took for granted the baptism of the children of Christian parents. This conclusion is rightly rejected by G. Delling (*Studien* 273): Jeremias' view 'geht jedoch von einer Vertauschung zweier Verwendungsweisen des Wortes "Kind" aus, der sich der neutestamentliche Sprachverbrauch widersetzt.' That is, τέκνον does not mean a little child, but any person, possibly quite adult, viewed in relation to his parents; offspring, or issue. Jeremias is right to question whether this extension of time would be in the minds of the first Christians in the earliest days of the church, but Luke has already made room for it in his treatment of the Joel quotation. εἰς μακράν is not, as is sometimes claimed, a Semitism; see the many parallels given in Wettstein, and in LS 1074. Most of the classical parallels have μακράν in the sense of distant time, and this might suggest that Peter's meaning is 'your immediate offspring and more distant generations'; but τέκνα is itself capable of covering more than one generation, and distance in space introduces into the speech a further thought which Luke (see above) was anxious to include. Potentially, from its beginning the church was a universal society and its message was addressed not to Jews only but to distant races. There is no need (with Roloff 63) to restrict the reference to

Diaspora Jews. Cf. Isa. 57.19, which is probably distantly in mind: εἰρήνην ἐπ'εἰρήνην τοῖς μακρὰν καὶ τοῖς ἐγγὺς οὖσιν. Cf. also Ps. Sol. 8.33, ἡμῖν καὶ τοῖς τέκνοις ἡμῶν ἡ εὐδοκία. Finally the speech takes up again the quotation from Joel 3.1–5 which was left incomplete in vv. 17–21. Joel 3.5 concludes: ὅτι ἐν τῷ ὄρει Σιὼν καὶ ἐν ᾽Ιερουσαλὴμ ἔσται ἀνασωζόμενος, καθότι εἶπεν κύριος, καὶ εὐαγγελιζόμενοι, οὓς κύριος προσκέκληται. It is easy to see that Luke could not include this verse as it stood. For one thing, it was (at least in parts) scarcely intelligible; for another, it seemed to locate salvation in Jerusalem, and this was contrary to one of the points Luke wished to make: the Gospel was worldwide in its scope. Nor could Luke be content with the perfect προσκέκληται, for it was his intention to describe the way in which God called men to himself through the expanding missionary work of the church. The relative is generalized (ὅσους ἄν for οὓς) and the verb is put in the aorist subjunctive. For God's call (expressed by the verb προσκαλεῖν) cf. 13.2; 16.10; Luke has other ways of expressing the same thought. For the combination of κύριος and θεός cf. 3.22, and a Yale papyrus, quoted in *ND* 2.32, which refers to Hadrian as ὁ κύριος ἡμῶν καὶ θεὸς ἐνφανέστατος.

40. Luke is aware of the improbability that Peter should have spoken for no more than about three minutes, but he has used the material available. πλείοσιν is probably not to be taken as a simple comparative but in a pregnant sense: *many more.* But more is already implied by ἑτέροις. Luke is here employing a reporter's stock device. So Dibelius (178), referring to Xenophon, *Hellenica* 2.4.42 (εἰπὼν δὲ ταῦτα καὶ ἄλλα τοιαῦτα). Polybius 3.111.11; 21.14.4; Appian, *Samn.* 10.6 (=10.2); *Bell. Civ.* 3.63 (257). For the connection by means of τε see on v. 37.

διαμαρτύρεσθαι (nine times) and παρακαλεῖν (eight times in the sense of Christian preaching; παράκλησις three or four times in this sense) are important words in Acts. They are not to be wholly distinguished, but the former stresses the objective statement of Christian fact and truth, the latter the persuasion added by the speaker.

σωθῆτε, aorist passive imperative, takes up the σωθήσεται of v. 21. It is often supposed that the verb is used here in a reflexive sense: Save yourselves. That the passive of σώζειν can be used in this way is clear, as e.g. when Crito urges Socrates, ἔτι καὶ νῦν ἐμοὶ πειθοῦ καὶ σώθητι, Take my advice and make your escape (Plato, *Crito* 44b). Here however there is no possibility that men will save themselves except in the sense that they call upon him who has already called them: thus, *Accept your salvation.* 'Gott will an euch handeln — lasst ihn an euch handeln!' So Stählin (55), drawing the interesting corollary that Christian baptism can never be self-administered. Here, and at 2.47; 11.14; 13.26, 46f.; 16.31; 28.28, salvation is a present event; so Maddox, 116f., but Luke does not abandon a future element in salvation. Salvation is from this crooked generation, so that one no longer shares its ways or its destiny. σκολιός is *crooked* in the literal sense, but in Greek as in English there is no need of change in order to express moral obliquity. γενεά may be generation or race; here it is probably both and refers primarily to the (unrepentant) Jewish contemporaries of Peter's hearers.

διαμαρτύρεσθαι, παρακαλεῖν and σκολιός are all words common in the LXX.

5. THE PENTECOST COMMUNITY 2.41–47

(41) So those who accepted Peter's[1] word were baptized, and in that day there were added about 3,000 souls. (42) They persisted steadily in the teaching of the apostles and in the fellowship, in the breaking of bread and in the prayers. (43) Fear lay upon every soul, and many portents and signs were done by the apostles. (44) All the members of the believing community[2] held all their belongings in common, (45) and they would sell their property and possessions and distribute them to all, as anyone from time to time had need. (46) Daily they continued together in the Temple, and breaking bread at home they took food with rejoicing and in simplicity of heart, (47) praising God and enjoying favour with all the people. And daily the Lord added the saved to the community.[3]

Bibliography

P. Benoit, *Ex. et Th.*, 2.181–92.

F. C. Burkitt, *JBL* 37 (1918), 234.

J. Y. Campbell, *JBL* 51 (1932), 352–80.

H. von Campenhausen, as in (1).

L. Cerfaux, *Rec.* 2.125–56.

E. J. Christiansen, *StTh* 40 (1986), 55–79.

J. Daniélou, *RHPhR* 35 (1955), 104–15.

G. Delling, *KuD* 16 (1970), 259–81.

B. W. Dombrowski, *HThR* 59 (1966), 294–307.

W. A. Dowd, *CBQ* 1 (1939), 358–62.

J. Dupont, *Études*, 503–19.

J. Dupont, *Nouvelles Études*, 296–318.

J. A. Emerton, as in (1).

J. A. Fitzmyer, *Essays*, 271–303.

F. C. Grant, *AThR* 27 (1945), 253–63.

L. Hartmann, *FS* Dupont, 727–38.

[1] Greek, his.
[2] *Begs.*, All those who believed together; RSV, all who believed were together; NEB, All whose faith had drawn them together; NJB, All who shared the faith.
[3] *Begs.*, together; RSV, NEB, to their number.

G. Haufe, *ThLZ* 101 (1976), 561–6.

P. W. van der Horst, as in (3).

K. Kertelge, *FS* Mussner, 327–39.

S. Lyonnet, *35th CongEuch*, 511–58.

D. M. Mackinnon, *FS* Lightfoot, 201–7.

D. L. Mealand, *ThZ* 31 (1975), 129–39.

D. L. Mealand, *JTS* 28 (1977), 96–9.

P. H. Menoud, *RHPhR* 33 (1953), 21–36.

I. Mircea, *Studii teologice* 7 (1955), 64–92.

F. Mussner, *GesSt*, 212–22.

P. Pokorný, *NTS* 27 (1981), 368–80.

D. Seccombe, *JTS* 29 (1978), 140–3.

B. E. Thiering, *NTS* 27 (1981), 615–31.

A. Vööbus, *ZNW* 61 (1970), 102–10.

Commentary

The new paragraph should probably be taken to begin at v. 41 rather than (as in e.g. NA^{26}) at v. 42. This is shown by Luke's use in v. 41 of μὲν οὖν (so e.g. *Begs.* 4.27), his usual method of resuming a narrative as he turns from a source he has been following either to a new one or to a piece of his own composition. The speech which ends (after interruption) at v. 40 was probably drawn (and edited with supplements) from a source; the origin of the new paragraph will be discussed below. It moves from an account of the response to Peter's speech to a summarizing description of life in the earliest Christian fellowship.

The speech is represented as extremely effective. Three thousand people accepted Peter's statement of the Gospel and were baptized — how so many could be dealt with by 120 Christians (1.15), some of whom were women whose participation might have raised awkward questions, Luke does not explain. The number may be traditional; there is no reason why a considerable number should not have accepted — in addition to a foundation in Jewish religion which may be assumed — the Messiahship of Jesus, and done so to the accompaniment of a good deal of religious excitement. It would be a mistake to think of 3,000 cases of an individual process of conviction which led from irreligion, or false religion, to a totally new faith expressed in a radical change of moral life. It would also be a mistake to think of formal liturgically executed baptisms. Mass baptisms would have been easy at a river (as in the descriptions of John the Baptist's use of the Jordan), but there were no natural large-scale supplies of water in the city (see e.g. G. Dalman, *Jerusalem und sein Gelände*, 1930, 266–84). The reference to baptism may arise out of Luke's familiarity with the practice of his own day. Baptized, the new believers entered upon the common life of Christians, of which four staple constituents are mentioned: the teaching of the apostles, fellowship, common meals, and prayer (see the notes on v. 42). Religious awe abounded and miracles happened (v. 43). Christians shared their goods as well as their faith (vv. 44f.). They were still Jews, and frequented the Temple as well as pursuing their own practices (v. 46), but they were Jews with a new joy (vv. 46f.), and their numbers continued to grow.

The activities described here (apart from those necessarily confined to Jews who had added acceptance of Jesus as the Messiah to their ancestral faith) have been familiar to Christians in all periods, and were no doubt familiar to Luke in the life of the Christian circles in which he himself moved. This means that he probably needed no historical source to inform him of what happened in Jerusalem some decades before he wrote; he simply transferred customs from his own time and place, and had only to add attendance at the Temple. To say this is not in itself to accuse him of error; rather (if the word accusation is proper) of common place. He tells us only what we should naturally suppose. Nor should we necessarily conclude that Luke had no special source material; this is a question that must be examined.

There are similar summary descriptions elsewhere in Acts, especially 4.32–5; 5.12–16 (others are too brief to fall into the same category; see Benoit *Ex. et Th.* 2.181), and the first question to ask is the purpose they serve in Luke's book. It is undoubtedly part of the truth to say, with Knox (*Acts* 57), that they were intended not to inform but to edify. Luke wished his readers to see what the life of Christians was like in the apostolic period in order that they might imitate it. It is also true (Schmithals 37) that summaries are necessary in consequence of Luke's 'Episodenstil' (the word is frequently used by Plümacher) method of writing history — episodes like pearls must be attached to a string; and that they serve to indicate the passage of time (Pesch 132) — it must not be assumed that the healing of 3.1–10 happened on the day after Pentecost. These observations go far towards explaining Luke's motivation. In addition, the summaries confirm his central theme of the triumph, the irresistible progress, of the word of God. The Gospel is accepted by more and more people and the quality of Christian life is maintained and developed in depth and intensity. They also enable him to make the point that his story is not simply a series of biographical sketches of the famous (which, without them, it might appear to be) but the story of a community, of the people of God.

An admirable summary of attempts to determine the sources of the summaries, especially of the present one, is provided by Haenchen

(194–7). Among more recent writers, Roloff (65f.) makes an analysis as convincing as any. He sees vv. 42f. as a piece of tradition bringing out the essentials of Christian life as the teaching of the apostles, the fellowship, the breaking of bread, prayer, and the miracles performed by the apostles. These are next expanded. In vv. 44f. Luke expounds fellowship in terms of the sharing of goods; in v. 46 he deals with the Christian meal, in v. 47 with prayer. Similarly 4.32, 34f. deal with fellowship, 4.33 with the teaching of the apostles. 5.12–16 concentrates on the apostolic miracles, with a brief reference in 5.12b to the apostolic doctrine. This analysis may correctly show how the paragraphs were built up in Luke's mind; it is however doubtful whether it is necessary to posit even Roloff's modest Traditionsstück as a foundation. Luke's own hand is visible throughout, as the following analysis of the vocabulary of the present paragraph shows: ἀγαλλίασις (Lk. twice; Acts once; rest of NT twice); ἀποδέχεσθαι (Lk. 2; Acts 5; rest of NT 0);ἀφελότης (Lk. 0; Acts 1; rest of NT 0);καθότι (Lk. 2; Acts 4; rest of NT 0); κοινός (Lk. 2; Acts 5; rest of NT 7); κτῆμα (Lk. 0; Acts 2; rest of NT 2); μεταλαμβάνειν (Lk. 0; Acts 4; rest of NT 3); ὁμοθυμαδόν (Lk. 0; Acts 10; rest of NT 1); προσκαρτερεῖν (Lk. 0; Acts 6; rest of NT 4); προστιθέναι (Lk. 7; Acts 6; rest of NT 5); τέρας (Lk. 0; Acts 9; rest of NT 7); τροφή (Lk. 1; Acts 7; rest of NT 8); ὕπαρξις (Lk. 0; Acts 1; rest of NT 1);ὡσεί (Lk. 9; Acts 6; rest of NT 6). The list could be extended; it is certainly worth while to note the occurrence of ἐπὶ τὸ αὐτό five times in Acts 1–4.

The paragraph could (see above) be constructed, or reconstructed, by anyone on the basis of general knowledge of the Christian life and Christian institutions, and in addition Haenchen convincingly shows how Luke may have generalized his summaries out of particular events that were known to him. The only feature that cannot be readily explained in this way is the breaking of bread (but see 1.4; 20.7–12; 27.33–8). If however it is correct that both at the time Luke wrote and at the time he wrote about the sacramental meal was not separated, and perhaps was not fully distinguished, from the ordinary common meal, it would naturally escape *narrative* attention; many stories (e.g. of preaching and healing) could be told without reference to a meal.

41. μὲν οὖν is Luke's common resumptive formula; see on 1.6. The addition of ἀσμενῶς before ἀποδεξάμενοι (E Ψ 𝔐 syᵖ·ʰ) is a conventional way of emphasising the effect of Peter's speech (cf. Josephus, *Ant.* 4.131, αἱ δ'ἀσμενῶς δεξάμεναι τοὺς λόγους). πιστεύσαντες (D (p r)) for ἀποδεξάμενοι puts the effect more precisely and theologically. ἀποδέχεσθαι is not used elsewhere in Acts of receiving the word; see however 8.14; 11.1; 17.11 for the simple δέχεσθαι in this sense. δέχεσθαι is similarly used by Lucian, *Nigr.* 4; *de Syr. Dea* 11, 15, 22 (Betz 132). οἱ . . .ἀποδεξάμενοι . . .

ἐβαπτίσθησαν is ambiguous. It may mean, 'They ... having received ... were baptized' or 'Those who received ... were baptized'. The latter alternative is more probable; Luke does not mean to suggest a unanimous conversion of all present (cf. the Western text of 2.37). Those then who accepted Peter's word were baptized. Who baptized these 3,000, and where, is not stated. There is no reason to doubt that considerable numbers adopted the Christian position, convinced at least that something out of the ordinary had occurred and willing to accept the latest messianic claimant. Stählin (55) raises the question whether these 3,000 should be identified with the 500 of 1 Cor. 15.6, but decides that the appearance to 500 took place in Galilee. For ψυχή נפש in the sense of *person* see *TWNT* 9.616f., 638 (Jacob, Schweizer): according to *Begs.* 4.27 the only pre-Christian examples of this are in the LXX. Luke likes to put ὡσεί (or ὡς) with numbers; see 1.15. For προστιθέναι cf. v. 47, and cf. also the use of יסף in e.g. 1 QS 6.14; 8.19; CD 13.11. This is not the use of προστιθέναι— יסף found in the OT.

No doubt it is intended to be understood that the 3,000 received the Holy Spirit (see 2.38) but Luke does not say so. Roloff (64) makes the interesting point that Luke does not use the concept *church*; at least, he does not use the word.

42. It is not agreed whether in this verse Luke is describing the meetings of the Jerusalem Christians or their way of life in general. This seems to be an unreal alternative. In an ideal community (and Luke is undoubtedly setting forth the primitive church in ideal terms) the church meeting constitutes a particular focus of the whole of the community's life, so that each consists of the same elements, though these will be expressed in different ways and perhaps in different proportions. προσκαρτερεῖν is an important word in Acts; see on 1.14 and cf. v. 46; 6.4; 8.13; 10.7. The meanings given in LS 1515, mutatis mutandis, fit well with these occurrences of the word: '*persist obstinately in ... adhere firmly to* a man, *be faithful to* him ... *remain in* one's *service ... remain in attendance* at a law-court ... *devote oneself to* an office or occupation'. Here the verb will apply to the four nouns in the dative case.

It is probable (but the matter will be mentioned below) that Luke lists four matters, arranged in two pairs. That they were all familiar features of Christian life in Luke's own time need not be questioned, nor that they had by then become to some extent institutionalized (Schille 115); they have been features of Christian life in all ages, and (whether Luke possessed direct evidence of this or not) it was probably so at the beginning. The precise meaning attached to each of the four nouns has of course varied and it is necessary to ask what each may have meant to Luke, and how far his understanding of them corresponds to their meaning in the earliest days.

The first noun, διδαχή, provides a good example of what was said above about the two wrongly opposed interpretations of this verse. The steady persistence in the apostles' teaching means (a) that the Christians listened to the apostles whenever they taught and (b) that they assiduously practised what they heard. The διδαχή of the apostles cannot be sharply or consistently distinguished from their preaching. In addition to the present passage the word occurs at 5.28, where it undoubtedly refers to public proclamation; 13.12, to the Christian message spoken by Paul and Barnabas at Paphos; 17.19, to Paul's preaching at Athens. That, in the company of their fellow Christians, apostles and others did more to draw out the practical consequences of the message they publicly proclaimed is no doubt true, but one can hardly infer a technical vocabulary and procedure of instruction. There is no indication how far the teaching of the apostles may have consisted in handing on the teaching of Jesus. From the reference to the apostles Schille (116) infers that in Luke's day there were no more charismatic prophets and teachers; a precarious inference — there are such people in 1 John and the *Didache*. For Luke's use of the word *apostle* see on 1.2.

According to *Begs.* 4.27 there are four ways in which the word κοινωνία may be taken: (1) it may refer to fellowship with the apostles; (2) it may mean the 'communism' of verse 44; (3) it may be equivalent to the breaking of bread; (4) it may be almost equivalent to almsgiving. By E. Lohse (*Theologie* 64), who thinks that this verse describes a gathering for worship, it is taken to mean 'Kollekte, Gaben für die Mahlfeier'. The word does not occur elsewhere in Acts (but cf. κοινός in 2.44; 4.32); it is however used by Paul (Rom. 15.26; 2. Cor. 8.4; 9.13) of his collection for the poor saints, and this, together with vv. 44f.; 4.32, 34–7; 5.1–11, lends some support to Lohse's view so far as it concerns the charitable motivation of the κοινωνία; it does not support its connection with the Christian meal. The sense of *generosity* is found in *Corpus Hermeticum* 13.9 (. . . τὴν κατὰ τῆς πλεονεξίας, κοινωνίαν), but in Greek usage generally the word often has the sense of *association, fellowship*, being used for example in parallel with φιλία (Thucydides 3.10.1, οὔτε φιλίαν ἰδιώταις . . .οὔτε κοινωνίαν πόλεσιν; Plato, *Gorgias* 507e, ὅτῳ δὲ μὴ ἔνι κοινωνία, φιλία οὐκ ἂν εἴη — see the whole context). This meaning for κοινωνία probably finds some support in the use at Qumran of יחד, though this is not a unanimous conclusion. Braun, for example, thinks 'dass יחד und κοινωνία die Gütergemeinschaft bezeichnen' (2.152; cf. 1.151). See however the discussion by Fitzmyer (*Essays* 283f.). With a preposition, יחד is used adverbially: הרבים ישקודו ביחד (1 QS 6.7, The Many shall watch together). Fitzmyer (284) quotes 1 QS 5.1: 'This is the rule for the men of the Community (לאנשי היחד) who devote themselves to turning from all evil and to adhering to all that he has commanded according to his good pleasure: to separate from the congregation of the men of iniquity, to form a communal spirit with respect to the Law and to wealth (להיות ליחד בתורה ובהון).' It will be seen that Fitzmyer gives different translations to יחד in the two places in which it occurs: *Community* (his capital C) and *a communal spirit*. This is perhaps doubtful; it might be better to drop the capital C in the first occurrence and retain community in the second; or possibly to have *fellowship* in each place. In the first the meaning of אנשי היחד is clear — 'the men of the community (fellowship)', and of course in the context of the Rule we know very well what community or fellowship is intended. In the second, the same persons are said to form a community (fellowship) 'in the sphere of Torah and property', that is, the purpose of their association is the proper fulfilment of Torah and the joint (not individual) management of their property. If for Torah we substitute the 'teaching of the apostles' this is very close to what we have in Acts (and 'turning from all evil' will recall the μετανοήσατε of 2.38). There exists a fellowship or community; its nature is determined by and is expressed in the apostolic message, and one of the forms taken by this is the common management of wealth. The dative τῇ κοινωνίᾳ looks back to the participle προσκαρτεροῦντες, and the meaning is that they continued in faithful adherence to the newly formed community of those who had accepted the Messiahship of Jesus and the belief that God's salvation of his people was being put into effect through him. The fellowship, thus based upon common acceptance of the apostolic message, came into action in charitable use of its material resources. That charity was not regarded by Luke as the sole meaning of κοινωνία is shown by the fact that it is not till v. 44 that he speaks of it explicitly. Calvin (85) is not far wrong with 'Mutual association, alms, and other duties of brotherly fellowship'.

Before τῇ κλάσει, א^c E Ψ 𝔐 sy insert καί. The effect of this is to make it clear that κοινωνίᾳ and κλάσει refer to different things. This is in any case probable; Luke gives (see above) a list of four things grouped in two pairs: A and B, C and D. It is less likely that (omitting καί, with א* A B C D 81 *pc* lat) we should take the meaning to be '. . . the fellowship which consisted in the breaking of bread . . .' (though vg (pesh sah boh) have *communicatione fractionis*, making the point clear). J. Jeremias (*Jesus als Weltvollender*, ?1929, 78; *Jerusalem* 131), who says that in Jewish usage *the breaking of bread* cannot designate a whole meal but only the rite with which it begins, takes the phrase to be a deliberately obscure reference to the eucharist designed to conceal it from outsiders; so also Lohse, loc. cit. With the noun κλάσις compare the use of the verb κλᾶν in v. 46; 20.7, 11; 27.35. The last of these passages (not to mention the account of the Last Supper in Luke's gospel) makes the theory of secrecy a very doubtful one. The gathering at Troas however in ch. 20 shows that the expression had become, or was on the way to becoming, a technical term for a specifically Christian meal. Benoit (*Ex. et Th.* 1. 221f.) is right to infer from v. 46 (μετελάμβανον τροφῆς) that the meal was a real and not merely a symbolic meal. Some (Stählin 56; Schneider 286) think that the passage refers to daily common meals; others see a specific reference to the eucharist (so Schille 116; Bauernfeind 54 — the latter adding, with some exaggeration, 'Die Gemeinschaft war ihrem Wesen nach Abendmahlsgemeinschaft'). Weiser (104) and Pesch (130) are right in seeing that the one description covers both a common meal and the Lord's Supper. Cullmann (*V. & A.* 509f.) emphasizes this. 'Das eucharistische Mahl der ersten Christen war ursprünglich eine ganz gewöhnliche Mahlzeit. Die Wendung 'das Brotbrechen' bezeichnete ganz allgemein das Einnehmen einer Mahlzeit. Zum Brot ass und trank man, was man wollte, denn die Art der Nahrung hatte noch keine spezielle Bedeutung. Der Gedanke, irgendeine Beziehung zwischen dieser Mahlzeit und den Worten Jesu über Brot und Wein herzustellen, fehlte völlig' (510). Here Cullmann is taking up the discussion by H. Lietzmann in *Messe und Herrenmahl*, 1926. Noting the expression κλάσις τοῦ ἄρτου Lietzmann writes (239), 'dass dies nicht eine Benennung a parte potiore ist, sondern dass wirklich nur Brot dabei gebrochen, nicht auch Wein getrunken wurde, ersehen wir aus 20.11 (vgl. 27.35) und vor allem der Schilderung des Brotbrechens Jesu vor den Jüngern in Emmaus (Luc. 24.30 vgl. 35).' This is part of the evidence Lietzmann adduces for two primitive eucharists, one with bread only, prolonging the fellowship meals that Jesus was accustomed to take with his disciples, and one which included also wine, which represented the sacrificial blood of Christ and was based upon the words of institution in the Last Supper narratives. Since the 'breaking of bread' was not a Jewish term for a meal its use in this sense must have been a Christian development, and it must be added that Luke himself was undoubtedly aware of a eucharist in which both bread and wine were used and that this was already traditional when he wrote (though it was probably still combined with a 'real' meal). For this speaks not only the Pauline evidence (1 Cor. 10.16; 11.23–6) but also the Lucan Last Supper narrative, in which historical and liturgical traditions appear to be combined (*Ch., M., & S.*, 71f.). I have argued (op. cit. 67f.) that it was Paul who brought together the church's fellowship meal with the tradition of the Last Supper; ἡ κλάσις τοῦ ἄρτου is probably an old traditional Christian term, antedating the Pauline development and retained by Luke, perhaps in order to give to his narrative the impression of antiquity.

There are some additional insights, well worth preserving, in Bengel's comment: '. . . *fractione panis*, id est, victu frugali, communi inter ipsos . . . Christianismus omnium et singulorum non modo ex cultu sacro, sed etiam ex victu quotidiano aestimatur.'

The converts were assiduous also in *the prayers*; cf. 1.14, where the singular, τῇ προσευχῇ, is used. The plural, with the article, implies that they not merely continued to pray, but continued to use certain specific prayers. The teaching of the apostles was, by definition, Christian teaching; the fellowship was the Christian fellowship; the breaking of bread was, it seems, a Christian meal; does it follow that there were also specific Christian prayers? Could there be an allusion to the use of the Lord's Prayer? Luke gives no hint elsewhere of a Christian set of prayers, and it is likely that (unless the plural is an intensive — they prayed more than others were accustomed to do) *the prayers* were familiar Jewish prayers; cf. 3.1; 10.9, and the notes on these verses. Stählin (57) thinks of the Psalter; the Eighteen Benedictions; the Lord's Prayer; new Christian psalms and hymns; all plausible guesses, no more.

In this verse Luke gives an idealized picture of the earliest church — idealized but not for that reason necessarily misleading. That it is not misleading appears at once if negatives are inserted: they ignored the teaching of the apostles, neglected the fellowship, never met to take a meal together, and did not say their prayers. This would be nonsense. The idealizing is in the participle προσκαρτεροῦντες, and that Luke did not intend it to be understood as unmarked by exceptions is shown by his story of Ananias and Sapphira (5.1–11). There is no ground for doubting the outline of Luke's account; if he had not given it we should doubtless have conjectured something of the kind. The question at whose answer we can only guess is the relation between the things the Christians *did* and that which constituted their existence as Christians. This is, in a word, the question of Frühkatholizismus, the relation of the form of the church to the faith of the church. It cannot be answered on the evidence of this verse alone. See further in Volume II.

43. φόβος is not simply reverence for God; this is an adequate rendering for 9.31 (see the note for the OT background), but here (and at v. 43b if the variant is accepted) and at 5.5, 11; 19.17 there is some genuine fear of further supernatural events. This kind of fear affected all who witnessed the miracle of tongues and listened to Peter's speech. πάσῃ ψυχῇ is a Septuagintalism; it renders כל־נפשׁ (e.g. Exod. 12.16) but also the simple נפשׁ, used in a collective sense (e.g. Gen. 12.5). The phrase cannot be dismissed as wholly un-Greek. It is given in a quotation from Plato by both Epictetus (1.28.4, πᾶσα γὰρ ψυχὴ ἄκουσα στέρεται τῆς ἀληθείας, ὡς λέγει Πλάτων) and, apparently, Marcus Aurelius (7.63, πᾶσα ψυχή, φησίν, ἄκουσα στέρεται ἀληθείας). The reference is presumably to *Sophist* 228c (ἀλλὰ μὴν ψυχήν γε ἴσμεν ἄκουσαν πᾶσαν πᾶν ἀγνοοῦσαν). ἐγίνετο (imperfect) describes a state; not *fear came upon* (as at 5.5, 11, ἐγένετο) but *fear lay upon*, as a continuous condition. Cf. Gen. 35.5; Ps. 104 (105).38; also 1 QH 4.26. For τέρατα καὶ σημεῖα see on 2.22. Jesus had performed such miracles; so did the apostles. The absence of the word δύναμις is not significant. Imperfect ἐγίνετο occurs again; Luke is summarizing a lasting state (possibly drawing his summary from such events as those described in 5.5, 11, changing the tense of the verb in the process).

It may have occurred to some editors and copyists that the word *fear* was misplaced; it would follow more naturally upon *portents and signs* than upon the description of the religious life of the Christians (v. 42); hence perhaps the addition after the second ἐγίνετο of ἐν ' Ιερουσαλήμ, φόβος τε ἦν μέγας ἐπὶ πάντας (+αὐτούς, Ψ *pc*). καί. This is contained in P⁷⁴ ℵ (A C) Ψ (326) 1175 (2495) *pc* lat mae bo. The shorter text, which is to be preferred, is in B D 𝔐 it syʰ sa. Ropes (*Begs.* 3.24) notes that the addition is not Western; not a Western paraphrase and therefore probably original. But if it was, why was it omitted? Perhaps because it seemed repetitious, but this does not seem a very good reason.

It is already clear that the apostles are thought of not only as leading but also as miracle-working persons; the way is prepared for the miracle of ch. 3.

44. οἱ πιστεύοντες (or πιστεύσαντες, read here, perhaps rightly, by ℵ B 36 104 2495 *pc* co) occurs elsewhere in Acts as a term for Christians; cf. 4.32, 5.14, (11.21); (13.39), and πιστεύειν, especially in the aorist, describes conversion. Here the present participle must be rendered, *the believers*; the aorist may be taken in the same sense but could be rendered, *those who had become believers*. For ἐπὶ τὸ αὐτό see on 1.15; 2.1; also on v. 47. If ἦσαν ἐπὶ τὸ αὐτὸ καί is, with most authorities, read, we must render *were together and*; B (2495) (it; Spec.) omit ἦσαν and καί, leaving a difficult clause in which ἐπὶ τὸ αὐτό must be constructed with πιστεύοντες (πιστεύσαντες). The difficult reading is almost certainly correct (though Metzger 303 surprisingly regards it as a 'stylistic improvement'), and in fact casts some light on Luke's understanding of the phrase ἐπὶ τὸ αὐτό, suggesting that those who believed believed themselves, as it were, into a society. One recalls the use of יחד in the Qumran scrolls (see on κοινωνία, v. 42; and cf. Wilcox, 93–5, 97–9). Conversely, all were members of the believing society.

Reminiscent of κοινωνία in a different way is the statement that the believers εἶχον ἅπαντα κοινά. We are reminded of those who would bring all their knowledge and strength and possessions into God's community at Qumran (1 QS 1.11f.: יביאו כול דעתם וכוחם והונם ביחד אל), that they might form a community in Torah and in possessions (1 QS 5.2: ליהות ליחד בתורה ובהון); see above, pp. 163f. The Essenes described by Josephus are also said to practise community of goods. 'Riches they despise, and their community of goods is truly admirable (θαυμάσιον παρ' αὐτοῖς τὸ κοινωνικόν); ...They have a law (νόμος) that new members on admission shall confiscate their property to the order, with the result that you will nowhere see either abject poverty or inordinate wealth; the individual's possessions (τῶν δ'ἐκάστου κτημάτων; cf. Acts 2.45) join the common stock and all, like brothers, enjoy a single patrimony' (War 2.122). Nothing is said in Acts about a law requiring converts to the Christian church to hand over their property (see 5.4), and other differences (see especially Braun, 151–7) distinguish the church as described in Acts from the Essenes and from the Qumran sect. It is however undoubtedly true and important that at the time of Christian origins various forms of communal rather than private ownership of wealth were being practised, and it is quite reasonable to conclude that the Christians followed a similar plan. Why they did so cannot be inferred from the text. Their practice may have been the result of their eschatological beliefs: if the world was to end shortly an immediate pooling and common charitable use of all resources might well seem prudent. There was no need to take thought for the morrow since there would not be one. Luke himself did not hold this view of the future and this may account for the absence from his text of this reason for a practice of which he retains an account. The Christians may have known and obeyed commands of Jesus such as Mt. 6.19–21, practising a 'communism out of love' (cited by Dibelius, 128, from Troeltsch). They may have been under pressure from Jews who did not accept the Christian position and have found a common life the only viable one; perhaps their poor members were excluded from Jewish charities which they had previously enjoyed. Luke tells us none of these things. He may have generalized too far from such stories as those of Barnabas (4.36f.) and of Ananias and Sapphira (5.1–11). Knowing of Jewish practices (see on 6.1) and of later Christian works of charity (11.27–30; cf. Gal. 2.10), he may have read them back into earlier times — and may have been quite correct in doing so. He was as usual making use of traditions regarding the early churches to admonish and instruct the church of his own day. He may also (on the basis of traditional hints) have thought it likely that the Christians would adopt one of the most admired practices of antiquity, and have observed it more fully and on a wider scale than their gentile contemporaries and predecessors. That friends share all things is one of the most widely quoted maxims in ancient literature. It is impossible to cite all the passages available; see Wettstein and other commentaries. Plato, Laws 5.739bc refers to τὸ πάλαι λεγόμενον ... ὡς ὄντως ἐστὶ κοινὰ τὰ φίλων. Aristotle, Eth. Nic. 9.8 (1168b) quotes παροιμίαι including μία ψυχή (cf. Acts 4.32) and κοινὰ τὰ φίλων. The poets are aware of the principle:

Euripides, *Andromache* 376f.: . . . φίλων γὰρ οὐδὲν ἴδιον, οἵτινες φίλοι ὀρθῶς πεφύκασ', ἀλλὰ κοινὰ χρήματα. Cicero, *De Officiis* 1.16.51, knows the Greek proverb: . . . ut in Graecorum proverbio est: Amicorum esse omnia communia. Philo gives a characteristic turn to the παροιμία, which he quotes (*de Abrahamo* 235) in the form, κοινὰ τὰ φίλων, noting that this is still more true with regard to the property τῶν ἀγαθῶν, οἷς ἐν τέλος εὐαρεστεῖν θεῷ. See further D. L. Mealand, *JTS* 28 (1977), 96–9.

45. Holding all things in common meant that owners sold their property. As in v. 44 (ἦσαν, εἶχον), the verbs are in the imperfect (ἐπίπρασκον, διεμέριζον, εἶχεν); Luke is describing a state which persisted for some time. κτῆμα is used in the same connection at 5.1; cf. the use of κτᾶσθαι at 1.18; 8.20; 22.28. ὕπαρξις is not used elsewhere in Acts (in the NT only at Heb. 10.34), but cf. the use of τὰ ὑπάρχοντα at 4.32. If κτήματα and ὑπάρξεις are to be distinguished it will probably be in the sense that the former represents land, the latter personal possessions. αὐτά is loosely used; it does not refer to the κτήματα (or to the ὑπάρξεις!) but to the money obtained by the sale; this was shared out to the needy *as anyone from time to time had need*. The old iterative force of ἄν survives in the NT only here and at 4.35, and at 1 Cor. 12.2 (so M l. 167) — but the classical use of it with the optative has been dropped (Zerwick § 358, who compares Mk 6.56b; 3.11; 6.56a; 11.19; 15.6 (D)). If Luke's words are taken strictly what is intended differs from the *daily* administration of charity in 6.1. In the present passage it is not clear whether the charitable distribution was confined to Christians or not; 6.1 suggests that it was.

D (sy^p) have ὅσοι κτήματα εἶχον ἢ ὑπάρξεις ἐπίπρασκον, with the implication that not all Christians were owners of property.

Bultmann (*Theologie* 65) is right in his opinion, 'Was man auf Grund von Act 2, 45; 4, 34ff. manchmal als die Gütergemeinschaft der Urgemeinde bezeichnet, ist in Wahrheit die lebendige Liebesgemeinschaft.' Taking the narrative in Acts at face value it would be correct to add that the stress should lie on the adjective *lebendige*. The ancient world, with its association of κοινωνία and φιλία, accepted the principle; the Christians put it into effect. But Luke shows no more interest in the Greek proverb (see on v. 44) than he does in either the pressure of eschatology or the recollected sayings of Jesus. There is no evidence that such sharing of property as Luke seems to describe was ever widely practised in primitive Christianity. Tertullian, for example, seems to speak of it in *Apology* 39 (Itaque quia animo animaque miscemur, nihil de rei communicatione dubitamus. omnia indiscreta sunt apud nos, praeter uxores), but in the same chapter he gives a more realistic account of the financial affairs of the church (modicam unusquisque stipem menstrua die, vel quum velit, et si modo velit et si modo possit, apponit; nam nemo compellitur, sed sponte confert).

46. καθ' ἡμέραν: so that the meals referred to later in the verse were not weekly celebrations of the Lord's resurrection but, much more probably, the necessary daily meals, which the believers took in common. προσκαρτεροῦντες: see on 1.14. ὁμοθυμαδόν, they met *together*; see on 1.14. ἐν τῷ ἱερῷ: v. 42 seems to mean, or to include the meaning, that the believers observed the Jewish hours of prayer, as in the Temple; cf. 3.1. 'Die Christen waren vorbildliche Juden!' (Schille, 122). κλῶντές τε κατ' οἶκον ἄρτον: cf. v. 42, ἡ κλάσις τοῦ ἄρτου. Cf. also the οἶκος of 2.2. According to Jeremias (*Jerusalem* 131, note 20) 'κατ' οἶκον is contrasted with "in the Temple," in the sense of "at home," as in Philemon 2. The sense is not "in their own houses," as it is (sic) shown by the presence of all the apostles. See also Acts 12.12; 2.1–2; 1.15, where we find the whole community foregathered.' This is not wholly correct; it is not said that all the apostles are present, nor is the whole church present at 12.12. The inference, therefore, that the church had at this stage its own meeting-house is anything but secure. It is quite possible to take κατ' οἶκον in a distributive sense — *in their various houses*; D has in fact κατ' οἴκους. In the first half of the verse (for καθ'ἡμέραν . . . κατ' οἶκον), D* has πάντες τε προσεκαρτέρουν ἐν τῷ ἱερῷ καὶ κατοικοῦσαν ἐπὶ τὸ αὐτὸ κλῶντές τε . . . κατοικοῦσαν should probably be regarded as a mere lapsus calami; if it is taken seriously it must be described as an imperfect lacking the augment and ending in the third person plural in -σαν. For this form see M. 2.194f.; BDR § 84.3 note the imperfect in -σαν but do not cite this example. Delebecque (13) thinks it possible to distinguish between οἰκία, as the material structure and οἶκος as all, family and servants, connected with the structure.

Benoit (*Ex.&Th.* 1.221f.) sees — rightly — in μετελάμβανον τροφῆς an indication that what is in mind here is a real, not a merely symbolic, meal, though one that is accompanied by spiritual joy. Cf. 27.36 (προσελάβοντο τροφῆς, v. l. μετελάμβανον). Reicke (*DFZ* 203) notes that it is proper to rejoice at Pentecost, the Feast of Weeks: Deut. 16.10–12 (. . . εὐφρανθήσῃ . . .); but Luke does not use the language of Deuteronomy or make any allusion to the feast; it is unlikely that the thought is in his mind. Bultmann (*Theologie* 43) is more nearly correct when he writes 'damit (ἀγαλλίασις) dürfte die Stimmung eschatologischer Freude gemeint sein' (cf. *TWNT* 1.20): salvation was now at hand. Cullman (*V. & A.* 507f.; *Heil* 292; *Christologie* 214) thinks it impossible that a meal characterized by ἀγαλλίασις should look back to and find its foundation in the Last Supper or in the meals Jesus shared with his disciples during his life: 'Diese Erinnerungen waren viel eher geeignet, wehmütige Gefühle wachzurufen.' This seems highly implausible; the disciples would have found it impossible to look back to the bread and wine of the Last Supper as if the resurrection had not happened. Cullmann also thinks that even the parousia hope would have been insufficient to drive away the sense of sorrow; only the Easter event could do this. The fact surely is that crucifixion, resurrection, and parousia were so closely bound up with one another as to be inseparable; each was interpreted by the others. Fuller (*Christology* 157) thinks of a 'present anticipation' of the future coming, and sees in it 'the basis for the later Hellenistic Jewish Christian development of the idea of the present Lordship of Christ'. Delling (*Studien* 326) sees in the ἀγαλλίασις of the early meal a factor that may have contributed to the development of the abuses at Corinth (1 Cor. 11.17–22). Most of these observations must be described as guesses resting upon a minimum of fact. Luke is probably describing the Christian meals of his own day, idealizing them, and setting them back in his description of the first days of Christianity. Even so he gives no details, and Fitzmyer (*Essays* 298), comparing Acts with the Qumran documents (especially 1 QS 6.4–5; 1 QSa 2.11–22), says correctly, 'The brief notice of the Christian meal in Acts . . . contains so little detail that one cannot really make a valid comparison.'

The meal was marked not only by exultant joy but also by ἀφελότητι καρδίας. ἀφελότης occurs nowhere else in the NT, is not in the LXX, and is rare elsewhere. Reicke (*DFZ*, 204) argues on the basis of Vettius Valens 153.30; 240.15 that it is equivalent to ἁπλότης, and this is confirmed by the Vg (*simplicitas*) and, for the cognate adjective, by Cicero (*Ad Atticum* 1.18.1, abest enim frater ἀφελέστατος et amantissimus). Reicke continues with the point that the present verse may be linked with 2.13f.; the Christians are not drunk; their rejoicing is of a harmless kind. Cf. Tertullian, *Apology* 39 (The gifts spoken of in the passage quoted above are not 'spent on feasts, and drinking-bouts, and eating-houses', non epulis, nec potaculis, nec ingratis voratrinis); also Pliny's discovery that the food eaten by Christians was promiscuum et innoxium (*Epist.* 10.96. 7) — no doubt they pointed this out to him. Preuschen (17) notes the use of ἀφελής for simple meals in Athenaeus, *Deipnosophistae* 10.419d (2.412.16, Kaibel), ἐστιαθεὶς ἀφελῶς καὶ μουσικῶς (opposite to τὰ πολυτελῆ δεῖπνα).

47. αἰνοῦντες τὸν θεόν gives a specific direction to the ἀγαλλίασις of v. 46, and ἔχοντες χάριν πρὸς ὅλον τὸν λαόν underlines the innocence claimed in that verse by the word ἀφελότης: the people recognized them as a pious group. It is suggested in *Begs.* 4.30 that this clause might mean 'giving (God) thanks before all the people', but this seems less probable. For λαόν D has κόσμον, emphasizing the point so strongly as to make it seem somewhat ridiculous. Cf. however Jn 12.19; כל עולם is used in the sense of the French tout-le-monde as κόσμος is not used in Greek. There is a stronger (but not convincing) case for Semitism here than in many much discussed passages. Black (*AA* 13) thinks that behind the D text there may lie confusion between the Aramaic עמא (people) and עלמא (world).

Meanwhile the Lord added (for προστιθέναι see on v. 41) to their numbers. The church's 'continued existence . . . implies the constant "adding" of men to it . . . Seen from below, this means that in obedience to the Word of God and under the compulsion of the Holy Spirit they wish to enter into and belong to it in recognition of the change in the times and in their own lives.' But also the church 'has no reason for existence apart from the kingdom of God, the call and Word of the Lord and the power of the Holy Ghost' (Barth, *CD* 3.4.491). For God's initiative in adding to the church cf. e.g. 16.14.

The grammatical structure of this sentence has been disputed. C. C. Torrey (10–14) regarded it as an 'exceedingly forcible' argument in support of his belief that Acts 1–15 was translated from an Aramaic source. ἐπὶ τὸ αὐτό he took to be a mistranslation of לחדא, which in Palestinian Syriac means *together*. 'But in the Judaean dialects of Aramaic the usual meaning of לחדא is "greatly, exceedingly", and this is precisely what is needed in the place of ἐπὶ τὸ αὐτό in Acts 2.47' (12f.). A second point is found in the ambiguous use of the Aramaic particle ל, which is used to mark not only the indirect, but also the direct object (being used for this purpose like the Hebrew את). Thus if the hypothetical Aramaic were correctly translated we should have instead of ἐπὶ τὸ αὐτό, σφόδρα, and instead of τοὺς σωζομένους, τοῖς σωζομένοις, which leads to the English, 'And day by day the Lord added greatly to the saved'. This suggestion has met with a mixed reception. J. de Zwaan (*Begs.* 2.55) accepted it. F. C. Burkitt (*JTS* 20 (1919) 321ff.) rejected it. M.2.173 notes the arithmetical connection of ἐπὶ τὸ αὐτό as relevant here, and at 2.473 Torrey's view is discussed. The principal objections to it are (a) Such a blunder is unlikely from one who could give the right rendering at 6.7; (b) a comparison of 1 Cor. 11.18 and 11.20 shows that ἐπὶ τὸ αὐτό was understood to be virtually equivalent to ἐν ἐκκλησίᾳ. Black (*AA* 10) questions Torrey's use of the Syriac versions, rejects his view, and refers to Wilcox (93–100), where attention is drawn to the Qumran use of יחד (see above). Black (loc. cit.) notes at 1 QS 5.7 the expression בהאספם ליחד, *to join the congregation*, which, he says, is precisely equivalent to προστιθέναι ἐπὶ τὸ αὐτό, and Wilcox adds 1 QS 8.19, לכול הנוסף ליחד, *for everyone who joins the Community*: cf. also 1 QS 10.17. If these parallels are pushed as far as they will go we reach a new Semitism in place of Torrey's. This however would be mistaken. The first Christians, like the Qumran sect, formed a dissident body within

Judaism, and it is not surprising that there should be formal parallels between the two groups, but this constitutes no ground for supposing that the Christians used and ultimately translated Qumran Hebrew. A. A. Vazakis (*JBL* 37 (1918), 106ff.) was right when, in 1918, long before the discoveries at Qumran, he claimed that ἐπὶ τὸ αὐτό was an ordinary Greek expression, very common in the LXX; in the NT (Acts 1.15; 2.1, 47; 1 Cor. 11.18, 20; 14.23) and in the Apostolic Fathers (Barnabas 4.10; Ignatius, *Ephesians* 13.1; *Magnesians* 7.1; *Philadelphians* 6.2; 10.1; 1 Clement 34.7) it is technical and signifies the union of the Christian body. It can be rendered by some such phrase as *in church* and there is no need for the conjecture that a number has fallen out.

It is probable that somewhat later editors and copyists either themselves failed to understand this use of ἐπὶ τὸ αὐτό or thought that it might be strange to their readers. Many MSS add (ἐν) τῇ ἐκκλησίᾳ, mending the original text in various ways. We have in place of ἐπὶ τὸ αὐτό:

(a) τῇ ἐκκλησίᾳ. Ἐπὶ τὸ αὐτὸ δὲ Πέτρος ... E Ψ 𝔐 sy
(b) τῇ ἐκκλησίᾳ ἐπὶ τὸ αὐτό. Πέτρος δέ ... 945 1739 (2495)*pc*
(c) ἐπὶ τὸ αὐτὸ ἐν τῇ ἐκκλησίᾳ. Ἐν δὲ ταῖς ἡμέραις ταύταις Πέτρος ... D (p) mae

None of these variants is to be preferred to the short text of P⁷⁴ᵛⁱᵈ ℵ A B C 095 81 1175 *pc* lat sa bo.

οἱ σωζόμενοι are those whom God calls into membership of the redeemed community of the last days. For Luke's understanding of salvation see on 4.12.

6. TEMPLE MIRACLE 3.1–10

(1) Peter and John were going up to the Temple at the hour of prayer, the ninth hour. (2) And a certain man, who had been lame from his mother's womb, was carried[1] and placed[2] every day by the Temple gate called Beautiful, to ask alms of those who were going into the Temple. (3) He saw Peter and John as they were about to enter the Temple, and asked to receive alms. (4) Peter fixed his gaze upon him (John too), and said, 'Look at us.' (5) The man paid attention to them, expecting to receive something from them. (6) But Peter said, 'Silver and gold I do not possess, but what I have I give you. In the name of Jesus Christ of Nazareth, walk!' (7) He took him by the right hand and raised him up, and immediately his feet and ankles were made sound. (8) He leapt up and stood and began to walk, and he went into the Temple with them, walking and leaping and praising God. (9) And all the people saw him walking and praising God. (10) And they recognized that he was the man who used to sit for alms at the Beautiful Gate of the Temple; and they were filled with wonder and astonishment at what had happened to him.

Bibliography

D. Hamm, *Bib* 67 (1986), 335–42.

O. Holtzmann, *ZNW* 9 (1908), 71–4.

O. Holtzmann, *ZNW* 12 (1911), 90–107.

P. W. van der Horst, *JSNT* 35 (1989), 37–46.

J. Jeremias, *FS* T.W. Manson, 136–43.

E. Stauffer, *ZNW* 44 (1953), 44–66.

Commentary

The story begins abruptly (less so in the Western text than in the Old Uncial; see on 2.47 as well as 3.1); there is no evident connection with either the Pentecost event or the description of the primitive community in 2.42–7, except that it presents a specific illustration of the τέρατα καὶ σημεῖα of 2.43 (cf. 2.19). Luke presumably

---

[1]*Begs.*, RSV, was being carried; NJB, was being carried along.
[2]NEB, laid. The Greek verb is active, literally, whom people used to place. *Begs.*, whom they used to set.

intends the reader to take it as an example of healings that happened frequently (cf. 4.30; 5.12, 15, 16). The paragraph shows few traces of characteristically Lucan style (see however vv. 2, 10; and see especially Weiser (108), and Wilcox (172) rightly says that 'there is little to suggest employment of sources in Aramaic'. It is more probable that Luke drew his material from a written source (editing it here and there) than that he composed it himself on the basis of oral tradition. Cf. 9.32–43; he probably knew a collection of miracles ascribed to Peter. Cf. 14.8–10.

The present paragraph leads directly to a speech set on the lips of Peter; see below, pp. 187-191. Though drawn from another source or line of tradition the speech in Luke's mind forms a unit with the introductory narrative, and this unit is continued into ch. 4 (see pp. 216-8, 241-2). As Haenchen 201 points out, Luke's handling of the narrative prepares for and makes possible the proclamation of 4.12. Schneider 295 thinks that the unit goes on to 4.31, 4.32–5 serving to introduce the next section; it is probable (see Weiser 107) that Luke, though he introduces the special material of 4.36f. and 5.1–11, sees no real break before 5.42.

As a miracle story the paragraph shows most of the features that are familiar in both biblical and non-biblical parallels. The stage is set (at the Beautiful gate of the Temple — important perhaps rather from a religious than a topographical point of view; Peter and John can be seen on their way to the Temple) and there is some stress on the severity of the disease: the man has been lame from birth, he must be carried, he can do nothing but beg. Confrontation between the sick man and the healers is emphasised; a word of command is given and is accompanied by an action involving physical contact between them. The suddenness (παραχρῆμα, v. 7) and completeness (ἐξαλλόμενος, ἔστη, περιεπάτει, περιπατῶν, vv. 8, 9) of the cure are underlined, and the effect on the onlookers (θάμβος, ἔκστασις, v. 10) is described.

The story has taken the traditional form, as such stories inevitably do. An unusual feature is that John is associated with Peter. This is probably Luke's work; here, as in ch. 4, John plays no active individual part (cf. 3.11, 12; 4.8; also 8.14, 15, 20), and the formulation of v. 4 (ἀτενίσας δὲ Πέτρος εἰς αὐτὸν σὺν τῷ 'Ιωάννῃ εἶπεν; cf. 4.13, θεωροῦντες δὲ τὴν τοῦ Πέτρου παρρησίαν καὶ 'Ιωάννου) suggests that his name is an addition to a narrative that did not originally contain it. Why should John be introduced? There is no hint (here, or in chs. 4 and 8) of an interest in the two as representative church leaders or ministers, as in Jn 21 (see *St John* 586f.; *Essays on John* 165–7); probably Luke wished to make it clear that from the beginning the church, represented by the Twelve, acted as a fellowship (ch. 5 expands the two into twelve), and of the names mentioned in 1.13 (with Matthias, 1.26) only Peter and John were known outside Palestine. This seems more probable than that Luke was showing that the requirement (Deut. 19.15) of two or three witnesses had been complied with. He refers frequently to witnesses (1.8; etc.), but never with the number two or three or an allusion to Deuteronomy.

Peter and John are represented as devout Jews who frequent the Temple (cf. 2.46, and perhaps also 2.42, ταῖς προσευχαῖς. They have no money, perhaps because members of the church have no private property (2.44, 45; it seems that the common fund was used to help members of the community, not casual beggars), or because lack of money emphasises what they do have (v. 6). Peter's Βλέψον εἰς ἡμᾶς (v. 4) may have helped to give rise to the notion (3.12) that it was some property of their own that enabled Peter and John to cure the lame man, but in v. 6 the reference to the name of Jesus Christ of Nazareth is emphatic and distinctive, and is characteristic of Acts; see e.g. 3.16; 4.7, 10, 12, 30 in the present story; also 5.28, 40, 41. Luke was as well aware as Calvin (95) of the Satanic temptation, 'Do you not see that this is a divine man? Then you owe him divine honour.' For the sense in which Luke uses ὄνομα the two earliest references, 2.21, 38, are of decisive importance, and, in their bearing on the interpretation of *the name*, of great significance for the understanding of Luke's theology in general. See the notes on 2.21, 38. 2.21 is an OT quotation which means that all who invoke the Lord by name, that is, all who know him for what he is and, knowing this, invoke his aid in faith, will be saved. 2.38 is a reference to baptism, and baptism into, or in, the name of Jesus means a rite in which the person concerned becomes the property of Jesus. He (and no doubt the person baptizing also) will call upon him by name, trusting him alone for salvation (4.12), and the baptized person in doing so surrenders himself into the hands of the one whom he invokes, so as to become his. Other passages are in agreement. The apostles (though forbidden to do so) speak freely in the name of Jesus; they do so because (4.12) in no other name is salvation to be found — this takes up 2.21. Miracles are done, as this one is (4.7, 10 as well as 3.6, 16) in the name of Jesus (so generally 4.30). Luke can, however, describe both the teaching and preaching activities of the apostles (e.g. 4.2, 29, 33; 5.20, 30–32, 42) and their miracle-working (e.g. 5.12, 15, 16) without the use of the word ὄνομα. This word in fact represents one way, but only one way, in which the supernatural power of Jesus is brought into operation; or rather, it is one way in which the believing and obedient invocation of the power of Jesus is described.

It is true that names are used in magic, and superficially Luke's use of ὄνομα does not seem far removed from this. It may be that the source from which he drew 3.1–10 took the event as a cure worked by magical means; it appears in 3.12, 16 that Luke is sensitive to, and deliberately rebuts, the view that the apostles accomplished miracles in this way. Some early Christians probably did think on these lines. It is however clear, not only from 3.16 (on which see the note) but also from passages such as 8.9–24; 13.6–12, that Luke himself strongly disapproved of magical practices, so that it is in the highest degree improbable that he would consciously ascribe them to the apostles. Did he do so unintentionally by unguarded use of the word ὄνομα? Not if the word may be taken to be sufficiently defined by the OT and Christian baptismal context supplied in 2.21, 38. Yet a reader concentrating on 3.1–10 (and a few other verses in chs. 4 and 5) might be excused if he ranked Luke's apostles among contemporary thaumaturges. He should however be careful to read the speech that Luke has provided to accompany and to interpret the miracle; here it is made clear that the apostles do not act in virtue of some power that they have in their own possession (3.12), and that *the name* implies the invocation of the name and that the invocation of the name implies faith (3.16). These two verses must be regarded as Luke's own addition to a traditional piece of preaching material; this makes them all the more important as indications of his own mind and of the way in which he understood the miracle. The curiously repeated descriptions of the healed man's *leaping* (v. 8) with their allusion to the OT (Isa. 35.6) provide an unusual and unexpected underlining of Luke's theological understanding of the incident and so far support Schmithals' observation that illness and cure are both signs pointing to faith in Jesus 'im eigentlichen Sinn' — though Luke would not have agreed that miracle-working faith was anything but authentic.

Whether Luke received it in oral or in written form, the story was a traditional one; it can therefore tell us nothing about Luke's knowledge of the topography of Jerusalem. In any case our own knowledge regarding the Beautiful Gate of the Temple is too uncertain to enable us to pass any judgment.

1. For the text of the opening words of this verse see the note on 2.47. That ἐπὶ τὸ αὐτό belongs to that verse and not to 3.1 is clear; it was not necessary to say that Peter and John, who speak and act in concert throughout, were going up to the Temple *together*. The new incident is abruptly introduced (Πέτρος δέ), though its opening may be taken to provide an instance of the regular use of the Temple mentioned in 2.46. Peter and John were on their way up to the Temple; ἀνέβαινον, imperfect, gives the circumstances in which the incident about to be described took place; the verb is suitable for ascent to the Temple mount. It is part of Luke's overall scheme to portray the first Christians as devout and observant Jews, maintaining Jewish practices and frequenting synagogue and Temple till forced out of them. Temple prayers may be intended by ταῖς προσευχαῖς in 2.46; here Peter and John are about to engage in public, not private, prayer. According to Pesch (137) the Temple is for Luke a place of prayer only, no longer of sacrifice; this however overlooks 21.26. The hours of prayer are discussed in detail in StrB 2.696–702; see for example T. Berakoth 3.6; Berakoth 26 ab; for Christian borrowing of the three hours of prayer see *Didache* 8.3; Tertullian, *Prayer* 25. There can be no doubt that prayer at the ninth hour, referred to in the present passage, was that which took its name from the offering of the afternoon Tamid sacrifice (see Josephus, *Ant.* 14.65 for the hour of the sacrifice; Dan. 9.21; Judith 9.1 for transference to prayer), or Minhah. The corresponding morning offering provided another recognized time at which the people gathered in the Temple for prayer; the time of the third (see further Ps. 55.18; Sirach 50.13ff.) is not clear.

The article is unusual with an ordinal (τὴν ἐνάτην), especially when the substantive is ὥρα. Its presence here may be explained by the intervening τῆς προσευχῆς; ἐνάτην was felt to need a link to connect it with ὥραν: so M. 3.179. After ἱερόν, D adds τὸ δειλινόν, *in the afternoon*. The addition seems unnecessary, unless the intention was to make clear the connection with the afternoon sacrifice; see Exod. 29.39, 41; Lev. 6.20 (MT 13); 3 Kdms 18.29; 2 Chron. 31.3; 1 Esd. 5.20; 8.72.

Here for the first time John is associated with Peter; see also vv. 4, 11; 4.13, 19; 8.14. He plays no independent part in the action but appears as little more than the shadow and echo of Peter. The story could be told without him and some sentences would be better if his name were omitted. It was probably added by Luke to a traditional narrative; for his motives in making the addition see above, pp. 175f.

2. The scene for the ensuing miracle is set immediately. After the opening καί, D* syᵖ mae add ἰδού. Ropes thinks this may be original because it is more Semitic than the shorter text. More probably the Western text is, as usual, adding more force (and a biblical atmosphere) to the text. There is a lame man (τις preceding a noun is characteristic of Luke in Acts; see especially 5.34; 9.10; 14.8; 17.34; but also 9.36, 43; 10.6; 15.36; 17.6; 18.2, 7; 19.1, 14; 20.9; 21.10; 25.16, 19), and his plight is serious. He has been lame from birth; χωλός often means no more than *limping*, but this man cannot move himself and is carried (ἐβαστάζετο; Bengel says of this, 'Medium' (i.e., middle voice); can he understand it to mean *had himself carried*?) and placed (ἐτίθουν, impersonal third person plural). He has no means of subsistence but can only beg from those who frequent the Temple. This writing up of the circumstances in which a miracle is performed is common in the NT and elsewhere. There is very similar language in 14.8 (χωλὸς ἐκ κοιλίας μητρὸς αὐτοῦ, cf. Lk. 1.15; also Judges 16.17); it is probably Luke's own. For the LXX background see Wilcox 61f. There is no need to think it liturgical, or to follow Bede in seeing the hint that the house of Israel had been rebellious from the earliest times. ὑπάρχειν too is a Lucan word (Lk. 15 times; Acts 25 times; rest of NT 20 times). If it is more than a mannerism, which is doubtful, it will stress the long unbroken continuance of the man's disability; this is certainly brought out by the two imperfects, ἐβαστάζετο and ἐτίθουν: the man was habitually carried and placed at the Temple gate. If this is the right way to take the verbs, Haenchen's argument (198) that the note of time in v. 1 cannot be original because the man would not be brought out to beg in the afternoon will not stand. The active ἐτίθουν where a passive might have been expected suggests Semitic idiom; see M. 2.447; Black (AA 127); Wilcox (127f.). There is however no good reason to suppose that the story as a whole was taken directly from Aramaic, so that if there is any weight in the point at all we should think of a writer sufficiently familiar with Hebrew or Aramaic (or with Greek translated from a Semitic language, such as that of the LXX) to use naturally, but occasionally, an idiom Semitic rather than Greek. It may have come from the source, written or oral, that Luke was using.

The man was laid πρὸς (justified by the preceding verb, τιθέναι, which implies motion) τὴν θύραν . . . τὴν λεγομένην Ὡραίαν. Of the Temple gates Josephus writes that 'nine completely overlaid with gold and silver, as were also their door-posts; but one, that outside the sanctuary, was of Corinthian bronze, and far exceeded in value those plated with silver and set in gold' (War 5.201). This gate is usually identified with the Nicanor Gate; see Middoth 2.3: 'All the gates that were there had been changed [and overlaid] with gold, save only the doors of the Nicanor Gate, for with them a miracle (נס) had happened; and some say, because their bronze shone like gold (נחשתן מצהיב)'. Cf. Yoma 38a. For the miracle see T. Yoma 2.4 (it happened when the gates were being brought from Alexandria). For the location of the Nicanor (Corinthian) Gate, see Josephus, War 5.204, 205. This passage unfortunately is by no means clear; the gate in question may be 'the gate between the court of the Gentiles and the court of the women, or between the court of the women and the court of the men' (Lake, Begs. 5.483). Lake (loc. cit.) prefers the former. But is the Nicanor, or Corinthian, Gate that which Luke means by the Beautiful Gate? The description given by both Josephus and the Rabbis seems to warrant the identification, but it is not explicit; and it is well to remember that ὡραῖος does not normally mean beautiful (see LS 2036 s.v.; only biblical passages are cited for this meaning). A traditional view is that Luke's gate is to be identified with the Shushan Gate (so called because on it was portrayed the palace of Shushan; Middoth 1.3; Kelim 17.9), situated like the Nicanor Gate on the eastern side of the Temple. It will appear below (see on vv. 3, 8, 11) that it is in some respects more consistent with the narrative, but the tradition is open to serious criticism; see *Begs.* 5.480. The tradition is not ancient, and the Shushan Gate was no place for a beggar to sit, since it would be used only by those entering the Temple from the Mount of Olives or from villages on the eastern side of the city and not by those who approached from the city itself. The fact is that no ancient source mentions the Beautiful Gate (even if ὡραῖα is a corruption of *aurea*, golden, we can do no better), and we do not know where it was located. The Nicanor Gate is probably the best guess; but see further on vv. 3, 8, 11. See also Dalman (*SSW* 299); Jeremias (*Jerusalem* 23, with the reference to E. Stauffer in *ZNW* 44 (1952/3), 44–66); *Begs.* 5.479–86. There are many quotations, not all relevant, in Wettstein 472–4. For an ossuary (*CIJ* 1256 = *OGIS* 599) containing the bones of the maker of the Nicanor Gate see Hemer (223).

τοῦ αἰτεῖν. The genitive of the articular infinitive is used to express purpose. This construction is quite common in Luke's work (e.g. 5.31) but too frequent elsewhere to be regarded as characteristic of his style.

For παρὰ τῶν εἰσπορευομένων, D has παρ'αὐτῶν εἰσπορευομένων αὐτῶν. The first αὐτῶν in this reading has been thought to be a Semitism, a representation in Greek of the idiomatic Aramaic use of the proleptic pronoun (M. 3.41). More probably it is a scribal error (Black, *AA* 97); this is supported by the fact that the error does not appear in d (ab his qui ingrediebantur). Ropes (*Begs.* 3.26) says that the scribe's blunder 'made necessary the insertion of the second αὐτῶν'. Presumably he meant, '. . . from them, as they were going in . . .'.

On lame beggars in the Temple see Jeremias (*Jerusalem* 117), with the argument that on legal grounds the man would not have been permitted to enter but obliged to sit at the entrance. 'Cripples who could get about with a stump were obviously allowed [Shabbath 6.8] in that part of the Temple that was forbidden to Gentiles, but for those who were altogether lame or legless and had to be carried around on a padded seat, this was forbidden.' But Dalman (*SSW* 291f.) plausibly points out that it is 'more probable that the real cause of the sitting at the Sanctuary gate was the good opportunity it afforded for begging' (292). The argument that this feature of the story (and thus its whole *mise en scène*) is unhistorical because those who entered the Temple would have no money with them is not well founded. It is true that Berakoth 9.5 says: 'He may not enter into the Temple Mount with his staff or his sandal or his wallet (אפנדתו, presumably from the Latin *funda*, with prosthetic aleph)', but T Berakoth 7.19 explains, it seems, that all that was necessary was to carry one's money unostentatiously (בפנדתו חגורה לו מבחוץ), with one's wallet not exposed to view. Cf. Berakoth 62b. It was of course necessary to have money in one's possession if gifts were to be offered.

3. The Western text (D h mae) begins the sentence, οὖτος (but the use of the relative is characteristic of Acts; see BDR § 293.2c, n. 12) ἀτενίσας τοῖς ὀφθαλμοῖς αὐτοῦ καὶ ἰδών . . . This adds a little to the vividness of the narrative but does not affect its substance: a characteristic Western development. ἀτενίζειν may have been borrowed from v. 4 (where D has ἐμβλέψας); ἀτενίζειν (a word characteristic of Acts) and (ἐμ)βλέπειν seem to be mixed up in the two texts.

μέλλοντας εἰσιέναι (this word occurs three times in Acts, once in Hebrews, nowhere else in the NT; it is not common in less literary Koine). Presumably Peter and John are still outside; this suggests that the Beautiful Gate was an outer gate of the Temple (like the Shushan but not the Nicanor). This conclusion however is not certain because of the ambiguity of ἱερόν, which is often used for the whole Temple area, including its outer courtyards, but could be intended to denote only the central sanctuary.

ἠρώτα, the purpose of the man's position at the gate. The imperfect presumably implies reiterated requests. In classical use ἐρωτᾶν means *to ask a question* rather than *to make a request*, but in later Greek (papyri as well as LXX and NT) it came to be equivalent to αἰτεῖν (without losing its original meaning). At the end of the verse λαβεῖν is omitted by D 𝔐 it syʰ; the Western text does not omit as a rule and Ropes thinks that here its shorter text is right. λαβεῖν could have been borrowed from v. 5. It may however have been original and omitted because it constitutes a somewhat unusual construction (but cf. 7.46; 28.20); ἵνα or ὅπως would have been more usual. There is however a close parallel in Aristophanes, *Plutus* 240, αἰτῶν λαβεῖν τι μικρὸν ἀργυρίδιον. Cf. also 1 Macc. 11.66; there are more parallels in Wettstein (473).

4. For ἀτενίσας (cf. 1.10), D has ἐμβλέψας (d h, intuitus); for βλέψον, D has ἀτένισον (d h, a(d)spice). There seems to be no reason for this interchange; see on vv. 3, 5. Peter returns the lame man's gaze and underlines for the reader the significant role that he and John (very awkwardly attached; the result of Luke's editing) are to play. Their part has first to be emphasised (βλέψον εἰς ἡμᾶς) and then freed from possible misunderstanding (3.12, 16).

5. The lame man does as he is told, quite naturally expecting an ostentatiously made gift of money. ἐπεῖχεν answers to βλέψον (v. 4): D has the participle ἀτενίσας, which corresponds even more closely with the same MS's ἀτένισον in v. 4 but leaves the sentence without a finite verb. It may be that the Western editor understood with ἐπεῖχεν not (as is more usual) νοῦν, *he paid attention*, but ὀφθαλμόν (cf. Lucian, *Dialogi Marini* 1.2, μόνη ἐμοὶ ἐπειχεν τὸν ὀφθαλμόν) *he directed his gaze*, and paraphrased this; but the variant was a copyist's slip rather than Western editing; d has adtendebat eos, h has contemplatus est eos. This verse carries the story forward, preparing the way for the dramatic effectiveness of the next verse.

6. The lame man's hope — to receive money — is to be disappointed; Peter and John have none to give. This is expressed by the use of the characteristically Lucan word ὑπάρχειν; the verb is used as here with the dative at Lk. 8.3; 12.15; Acts 4.32, 37; 28.7; with the genitive at Lk. 11.21; 12.33, 44; 14.33; 16.1; 19.8 — an interesting variation in use. *Silver and gold* will refer to minted metal, i.e. money; so Philo, *Quod Deus* 169; *Omnis Probus* 76; Josephus, *Ant.* 15.5. Lack of money is probably not (see on v. 2) to be explained as due to the fact that they were not allowed to carry money into the Temple; Luke presents the apostles as poor men. Cf. 2.44f.; 4.32, 34f.; the Christians shared their goods and did not consider that money belonged to them personally. But the apostles had it in their power to give a better gift than money. Cf. Herodotus 3.140.5: Ἐμοὶ μήτε χρυσόν, ὦ βασιλεῦ, μήτε ἄργυρον δίδου, ἀλλὰ ἀνασωσάμενός μοι [δὸς] τὴν πατρίδα Σάμον...

A word of command addressed by the healer to the sick person is found in many miracle stories; in miracles performed by Christians there is a natural invocation of the name of Jesus. Cf. e.g. *Acta Petri et Andreae* 18 (L.-B. 2.1.125), ἐν τῷ ὀνόματι τοῦ κυρίου ἡμῶν Ἰησοῦ Χριστοῦ τοῦ ἐσταυρωμένου κελεύω σοι κάμηλε ἵνα εἰσέλθῃς διὰ τῆς ῥαφίδος ταύτης. This is the first of a number of references in chs. 3 and 4 to the *name* of Jesus (3.6, 16; 4.10, 12, 17, 18, 30; cf. 4.7). The significance of the use of this word must be viewed in the light of all the references; here it must suffice to note in a preliminary way that the evidence does not support the view that *name* is used in Acts as a magical formula (see Additional Note XI by Silva New in *Begs.* 5.121–40). So still, however, Schille, 125: 'Die Meinung ist magisch-volkstümlich.' This view does not do justice to Luke's position. H. Bietenhard, after mentioning the present miracle and the exorcism of 16.18 refers to 9.34 and concludes, 'Von dieser Stelle aus gesehen, wird ὄνομα Ἰησοῦ geradezu als *praesentia Christi* gefasst werden müssen' (*TWNT* 5.277). H. D. Betz (155) questions this conclusion, but acknowledges that 19.13ff., where mere invocation of the name has an effect very different from that which its users hope for, shows a belief that Jesus is exalted above all magical compulsion. In fact Acts 3 and 19 are both among Luke's great anti-magical passages. To say this is not to say that no early Christians ever understood the name of Jesus to have magical significance and power; it is very probable that some did so understand it. Luke however did not share their view, and in Acts 3 and 4, as well as elsewhere, he does his best to combat it. So rightly Weiser (109):

'Damit ist weder eine magische Wirksamkeit noch eine Art Namenszauber gemeint ... Die Namensformel drückt aus, dass Jesus Christus es ist, der heilt.' The point was rightly seen by Calvin (94): '... *name* is taken for authority and power. We must not dream that there is any magic virtue in the sound of the word.' Cf. however Justin, *Trypho* 85: κατὰ γὰρ τοῦ ὀνόματος αὐτοῦ ... πᾶν δαιμόνιον ἐξορκιζόμενον νικᾶται καὶ ὑποτάσσεται. For the form Ναζωραῖος see on 2.22. It does not appear that Luke distinguished between ὁ ἀπὸ Ναζαρέθ, Ναζαρηνός, and Ναζωραῖος. All mean Jesus 'of (that is, who comes from) Nazareth'. It is however undoubtedly true that in other contexts Ναζωραῖος may mean something other than this.

The word of command is περιπάτει. This is the reading of B ℵ D sa, and is almost certainly correct. All other authorities fill it out to produce the common ἔγειρε καὶ περιπάτει.

7. The miracle follows immediately upon the command, supplemented by the usual action. πιάζειν is a Johannine word (eight times); in Acts it occurs only here and at 12.4 (in a different setting). Luke constructs correctly, with the accusative of the person and the genitive of the part grasped. Cf. Euripides, *Hecuba* 523, λαβὼν ... Πολυξένην χερός (cited by BDR § 170.2, n.4). Physical contact between the healer and the healed is a common feature of miracle stories; cf. 9.17, 41; 28.8; Lk. 5.13; etc. It would inevitably add some weight to the magical interpretation of the event.

αὐτόν should be omitted, with D E Ψ 𝔐; it may have been added in order to prevent even a moment's doubt whether ἤγειρε was to be taken as transitive or intransitive.

παραχρῆμα is a Lucan word (Lk. ten times; Acts six times; rest of NT twice); immediacy of healing is a common feature of miracle stories. See Betz (157), who quotes a number of examples from Lucian, and from Acts; in addition to this passage, 5.10; 12.23; 13.11; 16.26. After παραχρῆμα, the Western text (D h mae) adds ἐστάθη καί, filling out the details. In the context, ἐστερεώθησαν means 'brought into a strong and healthy condition'. Elsewhere the word is used in non-miraculous settings. Good stabling makes the hooves (τοὺς πόδας) of horses strong and firm (Xenophon, *de re equestri* 4.3, τὰ γὰρ τοιαῦτα σταθμὰ καὶ ἐφεστηκότων ἅμα στερεοῖ τοὺς πόδας); by exercise men's bodies are made fit and healthy (Xenophon, *Cyropaed.* 8.8.8, διὰ πόνων καὶ ἱδρῶτος τὰ σώματα στερεοῦσθαι). Nowhere else in the NT is βάσις used for *foot*. There is an admirable lexical note on this word and on σφυδρά in *Begs.* 4.33f. βάσις has a partly poetical background (but see e.g. Wisdom 13.18; Plato, *Timaeus* 92a; Josephus, *Ant.* 7.303), and seems often to retain something of the sense of motion (from βαίνειν) as well as that of a part of the body (the man had been paralysed; he could not *go*). σφυδρά means the ankles, sometimes specifically the ankle bones. For the spelling of the word see M.2.112 and BDR § 34.6. σφυδρά, B* ℵ* A C^vid *pc*, is probably what Luke wrote, though σφυρά is a more correct spelling. Schille 125 claims that both βάσις and σφυδρόν are medical technical terms, but though used by doctors they are not confined to medical books. Bauernfeind (61) is right in saying that we have here not 'Luke the doctor' but Luke the narrator of sacred history.

8. This verse gives Conzelmann (33) the impression of being overloaded, and he thinks that 8b shows Lucan redaction; it is not easy however to understand why Luke (or any subsequent editor) should overload the sentence with synonymous and repetitious words. It is clear that Luke wishes to say that the lame man leapt to his feet and accompanied Peter and John into the Temple (εἰς τὸ ἱερόν); cf. v. 3, with the same implication regarding the location of the Beautiful Gate), showing as he did so complete freedom of movement and gratitude to God for his cure. But after ἐξαλλόμενος . . . περιεπάτει it was hardly necessary, or indeed desirable, to add περιπατῶν καὶ ἁλλόμενος. Isa. 35.6, ἁλεῖται, may account for ἁλλόμενος but not for περιπατῶν. The repetition probably accounts for some of the variants in the verse. D retains the opening words and after περιεπάτει continues χαιρόμενος (sic; see below; E has χαίρων) καὶ εἰσῆλθεν σὺν αὐτοῖς εἰς τὸ ἱερὸν αἰνῶν τὸν θεόν; d is in agreement. h (et ambulabat g[audens] et exultans. introivit autem cum eis in tem[plum lau]dans deum) is even shorter, and Irenaeus (*Adv. Haer.* 3.12.3) is shorter still (et ambulabat et introivit cum ipsis in templum, ambulans et saliens et glorificans deum). Ropes (*Begs.* 3.26) says that 'the superfluous καὶ ἐξαλλόμενος ἔστη in D (om h Iren) is due to conflation with the B-text'. He thus presupposes the existence of a pre-D Western Text, open to conflation; it seems better to think of a variety of related attempts to improve a clumsy original. How Luke came to write such a clumsy sentence is another question to which no answer seems satisfactory; it is perhaps best to leave the sentence as one of a number of indications that Acts did not receive a final stylistic revision. D's χαιρόμενος evidently corresponds to gaudens in d h, but the middle or passive voice is not justified by the reference to Aristophanes, *Pax* 291, ὡς ἥδομαι καὶ χαίρομαι κεὐφραίνομαι (cited by M.1.161), since this is an intentional barbarism put into the mouth of Trygaeus. LS 1969, however, quote two other sources, and Pallis and BDR § 307 observe that χαίρομαι is used in Modern Greek. Ropes (referred to by Metzger) notes the possibility that the strange form could have been derived by mechanical error from the text of h, thus, χαίρω<ν καὶ ἀγαλλιώ>μενος.

The verse conveys the fact that the man was fully cured, conveys it (partly) in OT language (see Isa. 35.6), and adds that he praised God for his newly found health and accepted the company of his benefactors. This hardly proves him to have become a Christian, though in view of v. 6 ('in the name of Jesus Christ'; cf. 4.12) Luke would no doubt think it probable that he would do so. Cf. 4.14.

9. The result of the cure was seen by πᾶς ὁ λαός. For the use of λαός in Acts (where sometimes at least it means specifically the Jewish people) see on 4.25. Here Luke means no more than that among the (very largely but not necessarily or exclusively) Jewish inhabitants of Jerusalem the event was very widely known. That is, the λαός is the Jerusalem crowd, especially those visiting the Temple at the time. Peter can address them (3.12) as ἄνδρες Ἰσραηλῖται. This may support Schille (125) and Weiser (110) who think that the use of πᾶς ὁ λαός implies that those present were taken to represent Israel as a whole. αἰνοῦντα τὸν θεόν may have been added by Luke to prepare for and underline the theological meaning of the miracle.

Wilcox (113f.) notes that E P 462 g h p have αὐτόν immediately after εἶδεν, a position less natural and more Semitic, and suggests that this reading may therefore be preferred.

10. The crowd recognized the man; that is, they understood that he was the one who had been in the habit of sitting for alms, with a view to (πρός) receiving alms. Authorities are fairly evenly divided between οὗτος (B D E Ψ𝔐) and αὐτός (P⁷⁴ ℵ A C 36 81 pc lat Lcf). There is little difference in meaning between the two, though M. 3.41 sees the probability of some emphasis in αὐτός; cf. BDR § 277.3. The imperfect ἦν denotes time before the time of perceiving (BDR § 330). In sense therefore it goes with καθήμενος: they recognized that he was the one who had been in the habit of sitting . . .

For the Beautiful Gate see on v. 2.

As often in miracle stories the astonishment of the onlookers is underlined. θάμβος is here taken to be neuter third declension (genitive θάμβους; but C has θάμβου); on the gender of this word see M. 2.126. θάμβος (Lk. twice; Acts once; rest of the NT — not used) and ἔκστασις (Lk. once; Acts four times; rest of the NT twice) may both be described as Lucan words (but θαμβεῖσθαι and ἐκθαμβεῖσθαι are Marcan): so may συμβαίνειν (Mt. 0, Mk 1, Jn 0; Lk. 1; Acts 3). For this, γεγενημένῳ is given by D syᴾ; συμβεβηκότι is so much better Greek that the other may be right — so *Begs.* 4.34. Cf. τὸ συμβεβηκὸς . . . τῇ ἀδελφῇ αὐτοῦ in a 4th century papyrus (B. R. Rees, *BJRL* 51 (1968), 164–183, ll. 10, 11 = *ND* 1.63). Luke is here writing up his story in conventional style, and is almost ready to introduce the speech for the which he is preparing.

7. PETER'S MIRACLE SPEECH 3.11–26

(11) While he was holding on to Peter and John all the people ran together to them at the portico called Solomon's Portico, full of amazement. (12) When Peter saw what was happening he addressed the crowd, 'Men of Israel, why are you astonished at this, and why do you gaze at us, as if by our own power or piety we had made him walk? (13) The God of Abraham, of Isaac, and of Jacob, the God of our fathers, has glorified his Servant Jesus, whom you handed over and denied in the presence of Pilate, when he had given judgment to release him. (14) You — of all people — denied the holy and righteous one, and asked that a man who was a murderer should be granted you as a favour. (15) You killed the author of life,[1] whom God raised from the dead; we are his witnesses.[2] (16) By faith in his name, his name made strong[3] this man whom you see and know; the faith that comes through Jesus[4] gave him this perfect health in the presence of you all. (17) And now, brothers, I know that you did it in ignorance, as also did your rulers; (18) but God in this way fulfilled the things he had announced beforehand by the mouth of all the prophets, namely, that his Christ should suffer. (19) Repent therefore, and turn,[5] that your sins may be blotted out, (20) that there may come times of refreshment[6] from the presence of the Lord, and that he may send the Christ who has been appointed for you, namely Jesus, (21) whom heaven must receive and keep until the times when all things are restored[7] — times of which God spoke through the mouth of his holy prophets from the beginning. (22) Moses said, 'The Lord your God will raise up a prophet for you from among your brothers, as he raised up me; you shall listen to him in all the things he shall speak to you. (23) And anyone who does not listen to that prophet shall be cut off[8] from among the people.' (24) And all the prophets, from Samuel and those who followed him, all those who spoke, also announced these days. (25) You are the sons of the prophets, and of the covenant[9] which God made with your fathers when he said to Abraham, 'And in thy seed shall all the families of the earth be blessed'. (26) God raised up his Servant and sent him to you first, to bless you in turning each one of you[10] from his wicked ways.'

---

[1]*Begs.* Originator of life; *NEB* him who has led the way to life; *NJB* prince of life.
[2]*Or*, of which fact we are witnesses; so *RSV, NEB, NJB, Begs.*
[3]*NEB* the name of Jesus, by awakening faith, has strengthened.
[4]Greek, through him.
[5]*NEB* turn to God.
[6]*Begs.*times of revival; *NEB* a time of recovery; *NJB* the time of comfort.
[7]*RSV* the time for establishing all that God spoke; similarly *Begs.*: *NJB* till the time of universal restoration comes.
[8]*Begs.* and *RSV* destroyed; *NEB* extirpated.
[9]*NEB* you are within the covenant.
[10]*Begs.* in the turning of each; *NJB* as every one of you turns.

Bibliography

A. Barbi, *Il Cristo celeste presente nella Chiesa*, AnBib 64 (1979).

C. K. Barrett, *FS* Kümmel (1985), 1–17.

O. Bauernfeind, *FS* Michel (1963), 13–23.

K. Berger, *NTS* 17 (1971), 391–425.

N. A. Dahl, *FS* Schubert, 139–58.

R. J. Dillon, as in (4).

J. Dupont, as in (2) and in (4) (*Nouvelles*).

E. E. Ellis, as in (4) (*FS* Rigaux).

J. A. Emerton, as in (1).

E. J. Epp, *HThR* 55 (1962), 51–62.

C. F. Evans, as in (4) (*JTS* 7).

F. Hahn, Kremer *Actes*, 129–54.

A. von Harnack, *SPAW* 28 (1926), 212–38.

M. Hengel, *FS* Cullmann (1972), 43–67

P. W. van der Horst, as in (6).

G. Johnston, *NTS* 27 (1981), 381–5.

G. D. Kilpatrick, *NovT* 21 (1979), 289–92.

G. Lohfink, *BZ* 13 (1969), 223–41.

C. M. Martini, *Bib* 49 (1968), 1-14.

J. E. Ménard, *CBQ* 19(1957), 83-92.

D. P. Moessner, NovT 28 (1986), 220-56.

C. F. D. Moule, *FS* Schubert, 159–85.

F. Mussner, *GesSt*, 223–34.

J. A. T. Robinson, *JTS* 7 (1956), 177–89.

J. A. T. Robinson, *NTS* 4 (1958), 263-81.

C. H. H. Scobie, *NTS* 25 (1979), 399-421.

U. Wilckens, *Missionsreden* 37–44, 60f.

Commentary

Verse 11 is Luke's own editorial link connecting the sermon that follows with the miracle that precedes. It reduplicates the close (3.10) of the story, adding only a reference to Solomon's Portico, which Luke knew from tradition to have been a place frequented by Christians (5.12). Haenchen (210) thinks that v. 11 was constructed by Luke with a care that shows him to have had no basis on which to work, but to have been composing rather than handing on traditional material throughout the paragraph. The verse is indeed Luke's work, but neither the observation nor the inference is convincing. The

Portico was (if we follow the Old Uncial text) within the Temple (that is, within the Beautiful Gate, 3.2, 8, 10). It forms a suitable setting and the people's astonishment provides an occasion for an address, which Luke has linked to the miracle, it seems, by a few small additions, which also serve the purpose of preventing misunderstanding of the miracle itself. Weiser (115) thinks that Luke added to the tradition material drawn from the LXX, from apocalyptic, from primitive Christian liturgy, and from preaching; Schmithals (43) believes that Luke's concern can be seen in a desire to show that it was impossible, with the false teachers, to confess Jesus and at the same time to reject the OT. Luke's editorial procedures are discussed in detail in the notes on the verses concerned. Here the results of these discussions will be presented as briefly as possible.

At the beginning of the Pentecost speech (2.12) a misunderstanding is corrected. Similarly v. 12, which shows several marks of Lucan style, was intended to show that the cure was not self-explanatory in the sense that it could be ascribed to Peter and John themselves as holy men who by their own piety were able to force miraculous action out of God. This is an important Lucan theme. The apostles as described by him are undoubtedly centres of such outstanding supernatural power that onlookers, or readers, might be disposed to think of them as θεῖοι ἄνδρες, divine men. This however would be a radical error; the supernatural power that can be seen to be at work does not reside in them though it flows through them. The point is more naturally made in ch. 14 (14.15, We are men who have like passions with you), for no one in Jerusalem would be likely to think human beings divine, but there was a Jewish mistake corresponding to the heathen mistake, and Luke adapts his language so as to define and exclude it. V. 12 carries with it a partial reinterpretation of the opening words of the sermon proper in v. 13. The primary sense of this verse is that God had glorified his Servant by raising him from the dead, but Luke would probably not have wished to exclude the overtones which suggest that God has glorified his Servant by causing a miracle to be performed in his name. The last words of this verse, which emphasise Pilate's wish to release Jesus, may come from Luke's own hand. Verses 14, 15 are linked together structurally and are probably traditional, but v. 16 in its confused wording shows clear signs either of rewriting or of Lucan creation. To understand Luke's editing, it must be remembered that 3.1–10 forms only the beginning of a story that runs at least as far as the end of ch. 4. In this story the *name* of Jesus is frequently referred to and (following on 3.6) may well have been used to sum up the first act: Not we, but the name of Jesus effected this cure. This was a proposition that Luke could neither contradict nor simply omit; instead he stressed the role of faith in the miracle, to the linguistic detriment of his sentence. The verse is however the more important for this and controls the use of ὄνομα throughout chs. 3 and 4.

The only other part of the speech that can with any confidence be assigned to Luke is the phrase παθεῖν τὸν Χριστὸν αὐτοῦ in v. 18. The same words (without αὐτοῦ) occur in Lk. 24. 26, 46; cf. Acts 26.23. The characteristic form of prediction in the Synoptic Gospels is that the *Son of man* must suffer. For whatever reason, however, the phrase *Son of man* was dropped outside the gospel tradition (except at Acts 7.56); and the notion of a suffering *Messiah* appeared very early in Christian thought (e.g. 1 Cor. 1.23).

The rest of the speech is not characteristically Lucan (indeed it displays a number of unique features and unusual words), and for this reason, and because of the awkward (v. 16 as well as v. 12) attachment to the miracle, it must be taken to be an independent piece of tradition which Luke inserted at this point as he continues to combine event with interpretative discourse. Broadly speaking it shares the same outline as the Pentecost sermon (though, as Roloff 71 remarks, the proportions of Christology and call to repentance are reversed) and those of chs. 10 and 13: Jesus has been wrongfully killed by the collusion of Jewish and Gentile authorities; God has raised him from the dead, and thus offers forgiveness and blessing to those who repent of their sins; all this has happened as the fulfilment of OT Scripture; further acts of fulfilment bring about the consummation of the process of salvation which has now been initiated. This outline need not be further discussed at this point.

The special features of this speech are as follows.

(1) Jesus is described as God's servant (παῖς). This word occurs in Acts only at 3.13, 26; 4.27, 30; also at 4.25 of David (the occurrence at 20.12 has no Christological significance). This fact, with the other distinctive features, suggests strongly that the speech material in chs. 3 and 4 reached Luke by a special line of tradition. Verse 13 suggests a link with Isa. 52.13, but 4.25 makes it clear that παῖς is not connected in any exclusive way with the Servant Songs of Deutero-Isaiah. The word is in common use in the OT for those whom God employs in his service. Jesus is thus one whom God calls and uses; as such, he need not be more than a prophet. Other passages, notably 4.25, 27, suggest that he was the new and greater David, that is, the Messiah. Deut. 18 (in vv. 22, 23) claims that he was a new and greater Moses (see (8) below).

(2) Also in v. 13 it is stated that Pilate had decided to release Jesus. This is supported more clearly by the Lucan Passion Narrative than by Matthew and Mark. Pilate is here more completely exonerated than in Acts 2.23; 4.27; 10.39.

(3) In v. 14 Jesus is described as ὁ ἅγιος καὶ δίκαιος. These may be messianic titles; the latter occurs at 7.52; 22.14, the former nowhere else in Acts.

(4) In v. 15, Jesus is ὁ ἀρχηγὸς τῆς ζωῆς. The word ἀρχηγός occurs elsewhere in Acts only at 5.31. Cf. Heb. 2.10; 12.2.

(5) Verse 17 emphasizes the ignorance of the Jews as at least a partial excuse for their rejection of Jesus; there is a contrast here with 2.22, though the two verses can be brought together if 3.17 means that the Jews were ignorant of the true meaning of the events that they had witnessed. Haenchen (210) remarks that this makes possible the development of the thought of guilt and forgiveness; but it cannot be said that Luke develops it far.

(6) The expressions καιροὶ ἀναψύξεως (v. 20) and χρόνοι ἀποκαταστάσεως (v. 21) are without parallel in Acts. They lead to an emphasis on the parousia (though not an immediate parousia) which is not found in ch. 2.

(7) προχειρίζειν (v. 20) is not used elsewhere of the appointment of Jesus as Christ.

(8) Deut. 18.15, 16 (v. 23) is quoted elsewhere in Acts only at 7.37.

(9) The threat of extirpation for any who will not listen to the promised prophet (Deut. 18.19; Lev. 23.29) occurs only at v. 23.

(10) The promise in terms of the seed of Abraham (v. 25) occurs nowhere else in Acts, and though it is used also at Gal. 3.16 the line of argument there is different.

(11) In addition to these particular points there are distinctive features that are worth noting: the possibly liturgical background of παῖς (see p. 194): hints of a Joseph typology (a figure rejected but vindicated in the end; see p. 347); the possibility of Baptist traditions (see pp. 202–207, but note also the complete absence of any reference to baptism (contrast 2.38, 41)).

In the speech as it stands these special features add a little variety to the common pattern and give it a distinctive place in the series. It has also been maintained (see J. A. T. Robinson, *JTS* 7 (1956), 177–89; *NTS* 4 (1958), 276f.; Fuller, *Christology*, 158ff.) that the speech bears witness to a very early stage of Christian belief in which Jesus was not held to have been Messiah during his ministry nor to have become Messiah at his resurrection (as 2.36 may suggest). He had been the prophetic forerunner of the Messiah, a forerunner who would in the end turn out to be the Messiah himself. Grounds for this view are as follows. (For details see the notes.)

(1) Jesus is described as the Servant of God (vv. 13, 26), and Servant is not to be identified with Messiah; the word rather suggests a prophet.

(2) He is said to be the promised prophet 'like Moses'.

(3) The χρόνοι ἀποκαταστάσεως πάντων suggest the work of Elijah the prophetic forerunner (Mal. 3.23; cf. Sirach 48.10).

(4) τὸν προκεχειρισμένον Χριστόν means (according to some) that Jesus has been designated Messiah but has not yet taken up office.

These matters are discussed below. Here on the other side may be noted

(1) that the speech takes for granted the fulfilment of the OT as a whole; that is, not only the promise of a forerunner but the promise of the Messiah himself is taken to be fulfilled.

(2) There is a radical treatment of sin and evil; forgiveness is offered now, not at some time in the future.

(3) Those addressed are heirs of the covenanted salvation.

(4) Jesus is the unique 'seed of Abraham' (v. 25).

See the full discussion of the Christology of Acts in Vol. II. The speech makes an important contribution to Luke's eschatology, for it makes clear that in the interim period between ascension and parousia there are times of refreshment, occasions of partial fulfilment of the eschatological promise which make possible the life of Christians.

11. According to the Old Uncial text, the healed man clung to his benefactors, Peter and John; κρατεῖν with the accusative means *holding*, not *taking hold of*. Cf. 27.13, and Sophocles, *Oedipus Col.* 1380 (with accusative), 1385 (with genitive) — Page (99). As he did so all the people (πᾶς ὁ λαός, as at 3.9; see the note) ran together to (ἐπί) the Portico (στοά) called Solomon's Portico. In view of εἰσῆλθεν σὺν αὐτοῖς εἰς τὸ ἱερόν (3.8) this must mean that Solomon's Portico was inside the Beautiful Gate. The word στοά (in the NT, here, at 5.12, and at Jn. 5.2; 10.23) 'is applied to various types of building with a roof supported by columns, but principally to a long open colonnade . . . It was employed especially in shrines and in the agora . . . The stoa was the general purpose building of the Greeks. It offered shelter from sun, wind, and rain. It could be used as council-chamber or court-house, market-hall or class-room; and also for informal conversation as in several Socratic dialogues' (R. E. Wycherley, in *OCD* 1016). The location of Solomon's Stoa is uncertain. See Dalman (*SSW* 295f.) which is not clear, perhaps because clarity is not to be had. 'According to Josephus (*War* 5.184f.; *Ant.* 15.396–401; 20.220f.) it was on the Eastern side of the Temple. It is not mentioned in the Mishnah tractate Middoth, and certainty regarding its location cannot be achieved. See *Begs.* 5.483–6' (*St John* 379f.). The Western text gives a different topography, placing Solomon's Portico outside the Beautiful Gate. In D (to some extent supported by the Old Latin) the verse runs: ἐκπορευομένου δὲ τοῦ Πέτρου καὶ Ἰωάννου συνεξεπορεύετο κρατῶν αὐτούς, οἱ δὲ θαμβηθέντες ἔστησαν ἐν τῇ στοᾷ ἡ καλουμένη (sic; the copyist may have begun to write ἡ καλεῖται) Σολομῶνος. Unfortunately we do not know which of these texts is more correct topographically — and if we did, the knowledge would not answer the textual and historical question whether Luke conceived the relation of Gate to Portico correctly and his correct view was corrupted in one or other group of textual witnesses, or got it wrong, and was corrected by one or other text. On the whole, the probability seems to be that the Portico was inside the Gate and that Luke wrote, correctly, what we have in the Old Uncial text. Why however a Western editor should have spoiled a correct picture we do not know; for possible knowledge of Jerusalem displayed in the Western text see on 12.10. See further Duplacy, *Rev. ét. Aug.* 2 (1956), 231–42.

Σολομῶντος: D has Σολομῶνος; at 5.12 both B and D have Σολομῶνος. For the form and declension of the name see M.2.146f.; BDR §§ 53.1; 55.2. The Portico bore this name because it was 'angeblich von Salomo erbaut' (StrB 2.625, but without evidence).

ἔκθαμβοι, plural *ad sensum* with collective λαός. Cf. θάμβους (3.10).

12. ἰδών (this word does not appear in the Western text, which has ἀποκριθεὶς δὲ ὁ Πέτρος εἶπεν πρὸς αὐτούς — so D (gig mae)) has no expressed object. Luke means that Peter saw the gathering crowd, concluded that an explanation of the miracle was called for, and decided to turn this into an opportunity for preaching the Gospel.

ἀπεκρίνατο. In the LXX ἀποκρίνεσθαι often renders ענה, which does not necessarily mean *to answer* but simply *to intervene in speech*: here however it can be said that Peter is answering the question implied by the crowd's amazement and mistaken supposition regarding the cause of the cure. In Acts, the verb is never used in any tense but the aorist; here only is the middle voice used.

ἄνδρες Ἰσραηλῖται as at 2.22.

It is because the people do not think that God is personally at work that they marvel at what they have seen (taking τούτῳ as neuter; Haenchen 203 takes it as masculine and to refer to the lame man, mentioned just before and afterwards) and gaze (ἀτενίζειν, a Lucan word; see on 1.10; 3.4) at Peter and John as if the two men were themselves responsible for what had happened. To set aside this error is Peter's first concern; cf. 14.11–18; also *Clementine Recog.* 10.70. Whatever others in their ignorance may have thought, to Luke the apostles were not θεῖοι ἄνδρες; the powers they possessed they had as a gift from God. There is of course no suggestion here in Jerusalem (as there was in Lystra) that the apostles were actually divine; it is emphasized that no power or piety of their own was the cause of the cure. *To cause* is a not uncommon meaning of ποιεῖν, but the word is normally followed by an (accusative and) infinitive. Pleonastic τοῦ with the infinitive, as here, is characteristic of Luke (Zerwick § 386; cf. Lysias, *Epitaphios* 15, παραταξάμενοι δὴ ἰδίᾳ δυνάμει τὴν ἐξ ἁπάσης Πελοποννήσου στρατιὰν ἐλθοῦσαν ἐνίκων μαχόμενοι (Wettstein)). εὐσέβεια (not a specifically Jewish or Christian word) occurs ten times in the Pastorals, four times in 2 Peter, in the rest of the NT only here. Cf. however 10.2, 7 (εὐσεβής); 17.23 (εὐσεβεῖν). The use of the words ἰδίᾳ δυνάμει καὶ εὐσεβείᾳ (cf. *Ass. Mos.* 127) shows Luke's rejection of the θεῖος ἀνήρ account of the apostles taking on (in comparison with ch. 14) a Jewish colour (so also Bauernfeind 63). According to Weiser (115; similarly Bauernfeind 63 and perhaps Haenchen 203) Jews would not have ascribed a healing to *men*; it could however be said that it was precisely on the basis of their own δύναμιςand εὐσέβεια that the 'Jewish charismatics' (the expression is taken from G. Vermes, *Jesus the Jew,* 1973, 69–78) performed miracles. Honi the Circle-Maker and Hanina b. Dosa, the two examples discussed by Vermes, were undoubtedly men of piety, and, at least in some respects, seemed to have power that could virtually compel God to do what they wished. Simeon b. Shetah said to Honi, 'What shall I do to thee? thou importunest God and he performeth thy will, like a son that importuneth his father and he performeth his will; and of thee Scripture saith,' Prov. 23.25 (Taanith 3.8). Peter's rhetorical question implies that it is not his (and John's) miracle-working piety (or, one may add, though Peter does not, their filial relation with God) but Jesus' that has been effective.

As in ch. 2 Peter's speech begins with a reference to and explanation of the supernatural events of the Day of Pentecost (2.16–21), so here his second speech begins with a reference to the supernatural cure that has just taken place. The verse contains the Lucan form of address, ἄνδρες Ἰσραηλῖται, the Lucan ἀτενίζειν and redundant τοῦ, the Lucan theme that apostles are but men, and the late Christian word εὐσέβεια; it is almost certainly a Lucan construction uniting a speech derived from a different source (and containing few Lucanisms) to the miracle story, which Luke found elsewhere. There is a further reference to the miracle in v. 16; see the note there, and the introduction to this section, p. 188. D, with some Latin support, almost completely rewrites this sentence. For the opening clause, see above. The last clause is turned into a genitive absolute: ὡς ἡμῶν τῇ ἰδίᾳ δυνάμι (sic) ἢ εὐσεβίᾳ τοῦτο πεποιηκότων, τοῦ περιπατεῖν αὐτόν. The last three words are epexegetic of τοῦτο. There is no difference in meaning between the two forms of text. According to *Begs.* 4.35 the Western text has 'more vigorous but less conventional Greek', so that the Old Uncial text may be regarded as an Alexandrian correction.

13. *The God of Abraham, of Isaac, and of Jacob* (P⁷⁴ ℵ A C D 36 104 1175 *pc* lat sa^{ms} mae bo Ir^{lat} repeat ὁ θεός before the second and third names, A D omitting the article) has an OT ring, as has *the God of our Fathers*, but the words occur nowhere in the OT in precisely this form; see however Exod. 3.6, 15. Cf. also Acts 7.32; and the first of the Eighteen Benedictions (Blessed art thou, O Lord our God and God of our fathers, God of Abraham, God of Isaac, and God of Jacob). See also Wilcox (29f., 34) for a possible Samaritan connection. Peter begins by claiming that the new message which he is about to proclaim concerns no new deity but the God of the OT. He 'is bringing in no new religion such as would draw the people away from the Law and the Prophets. For God had forbidden them to listen to anyone who tried to do this (Deut. 13.3)' (Calvin 98). The OT reference becomes more precise with the words ἐδόξασεν τὸν παῖδα αὐτοῦ, which recall Isa. 52.13: συνήσει ὁ παῖς μου καὶ ὑψωθήσεται καὶ δοξασθήσεται σφόδρα. This passage, the fourth 'Servant Song', goes on to describe the humiliation and suffering, followed by the vindication and glorification (here anticipated) of one described in Isa. 53.11 as עבדי, my (God's) servant (the word παῖς does not occur in the LXX of Isa. 53). The extent to which the figure of the Suffering Servant appears in the NT and contributed to its Christology is disputed; there can be no question that the figure is to be seen here, and the context makes it clear that he is thought of not only as exalted but also as suffering. It is God's act of vindication after suffering that gives significance to the Servant. It would be mistaken to take the song of Isa. 52.13–53.12 as the only factor determining Luke's understanding of the word παῖς. The word (which in Acts occurs only in chs. 3 and 4) is also used of David (4.25), so that it must be taken as a royal title (see Büchsel, *Theologie* 91); and it is applied to many OT figures, such as Abraham and the prophets. This is brought out by E. Lohse (*Theologie* 55f.; they are servants of God, 'die er zu seinem Dienst berufen hat'), who adds, 'Das griechische Wort παῖς bedeutet jedoch nicht nur 'Knecht', sondern auch 'Sohn' und wurde als christologischer Titel in der hellenistischen Gemeinde in diesem Sinn verstanden'. This overtone, however, is scarcely to be heard in Acts 3 and 4. The association of Jesus with the Servant is placed here on the lips of Peter (also at 3.26; cf. 4.27, 30) and there are allusions to Isa. 53 in 1 Peter (2.22, 24, 25); Cullmann (*Petrus* 74f.; *Christologie* 72f.) thinks the use of Isa. 53 characteristically Petrine. It is more probably a late first century development in Christian thought. Haenchen (204) thinks that it derives from Jewish prayers; it certainly found an early place in Christian liturgy (*Didache* 9.2f.; 10.2f.; 1 Clement 59.2–4; *Mart. Poly.* 14.1; 20.2; Barnabas 6.1; 9.2).

The exaltation of Jesus the Servant followed upon his rejection by the Jews. For παρεδώκατε καὶ ἠρνήσασθε cf. 2.23; 4.10; 5.30. παραδιδόναι may suggest the betrayal by Judas but probably (and certainly if we accept the Western text's εἰς κρίσιν) refers rather to the fact that the Jewish authorities handed Jesus over to Pilate (Lk. 24.7, 30). At 7.35 it is said by Stephen that the Jews ἠρνήσαντο Moses. For the use of ἀρνεῖσθαι cf. the account of Peter's denial (Lk. 22.57, cf. 61 (ἀπαρν.)). The Jews before Pilate deny that they are in any way connected with Jesus (though in truth he is their Messiah).

κατὰ πρόσωπον 'used adverbially, as in Acts 25.16; 2 Cor. 10.1;

Gal. 2.11, is certainly not Semitic, but its prepositional use in Lk. 2.31; Acts 3.13, though not uncommon in Greek (cf. Xenophon, *Cyropaedia* 6.3.35, τὴν κατὰ πρόσωπον τῆς ἀντίας φάλαγγος τάξιν, "the post immediately in front of the enemy's phalanx") is suggested by the OT idiom [לִפְנֵי]' (M. 2.466).

κρίναντος ἐκείνου ἀπολύειν. More strongly than Matthew or Mark, Luke emphasises Pilate's reluctance to condemn and execute Jesus; see Lk. 23.4, 14, 15, 20, 22. Pontius Pilate was Roman prefect of Judaea, AD 26–36. The report in the gospel and the present statement are scarcely consistent with 4.27.

The glorification of Jesus may consist in his resurrection, or in the fact that through him God has performed the marvellous work of curing the lame man. The former alternative is suggested by the fact that the resurrection is explicitly mentioned in v. 15, by the association of the Servant with suffering and death (which are most naturally reversed by resurrection), and by the fact that the miracle is dealt with in v. 16; if it were alluded to also in v. 13 there would be a clumsy repetition. The latter alternative is suggested by the fact that the reference to glorification follows immediately upon the repudiation of v. 12: It is not we who performed the miracle; what has happened is that God has brought glory to his Servant by using his name in this way. The case for the former alternative is stronger, though it would be reasonable to claim that if Luke was drawing on some kind of 'speech source' he chose this speech for this occasion because its opening verse was able to hint at both the general truth, that the crucified Jesus had been raised from the dead, and the particular truth, that it was the name of Jesus that had raised up a lame man. The reference may be, in Bengel's words, 'ad utrumque conjunctim'. Weiser (116) somewhat similarly points out that the miracle presupposes the exaltation of Jesus.

ὑμεῖς is emphatic: You, of all men, handed over your own king. It is underlined by the following μέν (omitted, wrongly, by D 6 *pc*). This is not answered by the δέ at the beginning of v. 14 but (without δέ) by the contrasting clause κρίναντος ἐκείνου ἀπολύειν. You, Jews, wanted your Messiah condemned; Pilate, the Roman governor, had judged that he should be released.

It may be right to see in this verse signs of a 'Joseph typology'; see p. 347, and on the implications for Christology the discussion in Vol. II.

14. Who was it that you (again emphatic: You!) denied (v. 13)? τὸν ἅγιον καὶ δίκαιον. The use of only one article binds together the two substantival adjectives, and makes it less likely that we should look for two distinct lines of Christological thought; indeed there is much to be said for the view that the adjectives are simply descriptive: the one who was holy and righteous. This is reinforced by the

contrast, in the next clause, with ἄνδρα φονέα, a man who was a
murderer (Barabbas, Lk. 23.18, 19). For this use of ἀνήρ Knowling
111 finds parallels in Sophocles, *Oedipus Rex* 842; *Oedipus Col.*
944, but they are not close. That in the case of Jesus there is no
corresponding noun may reflect unease at describing Jesus simply as
a man; but cf. 2.22. According to Haenchen (205), however, both
ἅγιος and δίκαιος are 'messianische Prädikate'. For this use of
ἅγιος he cites only Mk 1.24; Lk. 4.34; Jn 6.69; we may add 1 Jn 2.20;
Rev. 3.7. It is important that this adjective is applied to παῖς and
used of Jesus in 4.27, 30; at 4.27 the addition of ὃν ἔχρισας suggests
that the 'holy Servant' was not as such Messiah; he was anointed by
God and so became Messiah. *Holy* is not a designation of the Servant
in Deutero-Isaiah (whereas ὁ ἅγιος τοῦ Ἰσραήλ is a common term
for God in Isaiah). *The holy one* is probably a term of Christian
origin, resting upon the moral character of Jesus and the conviction
that he was the one set apart by God to act as his Servant, to
accomplish his will. For ὁ   δίκαιος see 7.52; 22.14. These are
perhaps sufficient to show that for Luke (there is little evidence
elsewhere; Haenchen cites 1 Enoch 38.2; 53.6; cf. 47.1, 4) the term
is messianic. But in the present context it is more important that the
Servant of Isa. 53 is δίκαιος (53.11; παῖς is not used and the Greek
is obscure); cf. Cullmann, *Christologie* 72. It is surprising that
Longenecker (*Christology* 46f.) does not mention this; he does not
make a strong case for δίκαιος as a messianic title. James 5.6; 1
Peter 3.18; I Jn 2.1 are not relevant. It is perhaps safe to say that the
adjectives were chosen as conveying some hint of messianic status
but mainly because of their moral content in contrast with φονεύς.

For ἠρνήσασθε, D Ir^lat have ἐβαρύνατε (adgravastis). According
to Ropes (*Begs.* 3.28; see also WW ad loc.) Augustine has inhonorastis
et negastis; the text (Migne) has onerastis et negastis, a closer
parallel to the Greek of D and to Irenaeus. βαρύνειν is an unexpected
word and no good parallel to its use here has been adduced. Clark
(339) cites Plutarch, *Theseus* 32 (15); Dio Chrysostom 40.1; *P. Oxy.*
2(1899).298, 25-7; Dittenberger *OGIS* 2.669.3; also for aggravor,
Sirach 25.3, but none of these can be regarded as satisfactory. The
word is sometimes rendered *oppress*, but hardly in the sense of
sending someone to his death. It may have arisen through mistranslation
of Aramaic. ἠρνήσασθε could represent כפרתון or כבדתון and the root
כפר could have been confused with כבר or כדב with כבד. See Torrey
(*Documents* 145); Black (*AA* 13f.); and for a very full discussion
Wilcox (139–141). Both Black and Wilcox look with some cautious
favour on the suggestion, but a single mistake of this kind is very
hard to support. It presupposes a complete Aramaic text for the
speech (for we cannot think of a single Aramaic word standing in a
Greek source), and for this we have no supporting evidence. Nor do
we know that Western editors had access to Semitic versions of the

sources used by Luke himself in Greek. There may be some possibility of influence on D by early Syriac versions (F. H. Chase, *The Old Syriac Element in the Text of Codex Bezae*, 1893, 38). Bauernfeind (63) may not be wrong with the suggestion that the Western editor thought he would like a change of verb. According to Hemer (213, n. 100) βαρύνειν, for which the NT usually has βαρεῖν, is Atticistic, and must therefore be regarded as secondary.

Before ἡτήσασθε (cf. Lk. 23.25, ἡτοῦντο), E adds μᾶλλον. After φονέα, E h add ζῆν καί. For χαρισθῆναι cf. *P. Flor.* 1.61.59–61 (a papyrus of AD 85): ἄξιος μ[ὲ]ν ἧς μαστιγωθῆναι χαρίζομαι δέ σε τοῖς ὄχλοις, 'thou art worthy to be scourged but I give you freely to the multitude' (MM, 684).

15. This verse forms with the preceding one a rhetorical unit marked by a series of contrasting clauses:

a: You denied the holy and righteous one
a′:   You asked for a murderer to be granted to you
b: You asked for a murderer to be granted to you
b′:   You killed the author of life
c: You killed . . .
c′:   . . . the author of life
d: You killed the author of life
d′:   God raised him from the dead

These contrasts are partially explained by the content of the material about which Luke was writing, for it involved good and bad, life and death; but they are only partially explained in this way, and suggest careful and skilful composition. In this they contrast sharply with the clumsiness of v. 16.

Jesus is described as τὸν ἀρχηγὸν τῆς ζωῆς. Cf. 5.31; also Heb. 2.10; 12.2; 2 Clem. 20.5. On ἀρχηγός see not only G. Delling in *TWNT* 1.485f. but also Knox (*Hellenistic Elements* 26f.). There is a good list of interpretations that have been given for this word in Weiser (114). The word is used in the LXX and elsewhere of military and political leaders (e.g. Judges 9.44 (B), 'Αβιμέλεχ καὶ οἱ ἀρχηγοὶ οἱ μετ' αὐτοῦ; Aeschylus, *Agamemnon* 259; Thucydides 1.132.2, Ἑλλήνων ἀρχηγός (Pausanias)). Its primary adjectival sense is *beginning, originating* (e.g. Euripides, *Hippolytus* 881, κακῶν ἀρχηγὸν ἐκφαίνεις λόγον). From this come the meanings (a) Hero, founder and protector of a city (e.g. Plato, *Timaeus* 21e, τῆς πόλεως θεὸς ἀρχηγός τίς ἐστι, Αἰγυπτιστὶ μὲν ... Νηίθ, Ἑλληνιστὶ δὲ . . . 'Αθηνᾶ): (b) first cause (e.g. Heracleides Ponticus, *Hom. Alleg.* 34.7, Heracles as ἀρχηγὸς πάσης σοφίας). Knox (op. cit. 27) notes that Philo uses the closely related ἀρχηγέτης 'of God (*De Ebr.* 42), of Adam in his perfection (*De Op. Mundi* 142), and of Noah (*De Abr.* 46) as the τέλος of an old race and the ἀρχή of the new'. In Acts 5.31 (see the note) the sense of founder and protector (σωτήρ) is probably best, and this also fits the contrasting structure of the present verse: him who was bringing life into the world, and thereby establishing a new age, or reign, you put to death. If the word is taken to mean *leader*, τῆς ζωῆς must be taken as a genitive of direction, not of object; he was not a leader *of life* but one who led the way *to life*. Whether we are justified in speaking, with Knox, of an 'ἀρχηγός Christology' is doubtful. Origen uses the word in *c. Celsum* 5.33, but he probably picks it up as a biblical word which he can use as he takes up Celsus' description of Jesus as the Christians' διδάσκαλος and χοροστατής; he says nothing that suggests that he associated the word with a special development of Christology. Later in Acts 3 we are to hear of Jesus as the prophet like Moses (v. 22): Moses could have been spoken of as an ἀρχηγός, indeed as an ἀρχηγὸς τῆς ζωῆς, as one who leads into the good life of a new land. On the Christology of this speech see above, pp. 189f.; on the Christology of Acts in general, the discussion in Vol. II.

The relative clauses (ὅν . . ., οὗ . . .) recall the form of primitive creeds (in the NT, e.g. Phil. 2.6; Col. 1.15; 1 Tim. 3.16), but such clauses are common enough in Acts (e.g. 2.24; see the note), and we cannot infer the remains of a primitive creed every time they occur. As at 2.32, οὗ is ambiguous. If it is masculine (cf. 1.8) its antecedent is τὸν ἀρχηγόν (i.e. Jesus, v. 13): We are his witnesses. If it is neuter (cf. 10.38) its antecedent is the preceding clause: Of which fact (that God raised him from the dead) we are witnesses. It is impossible to decide between these possibilities, and unnecessary, for each implies the other. If we are witnesses of him, we are witnesses of him as the Risen One; if we are witnesses of the resurrection, we are witnesses of him who was raised. The statement of God's overruling of human sin and error may be intended to recall the story of Joseph; cf. p. 190.

16. Bauernfeind (64) observes that this verse (16) connects with v. 13a, and concludes that what intervenes is an insertion (Einschub). His observation is valid, and to it may be added the fact that v. 16 breaks the connection between v. 15 and v. 17. The correct inference appears to be that vv. 13a (and perhaps b) and 16 are the insertion. See p. 188.

The Greek of this verse is intolerably clumsy (though not, like that of some verses in Acts, untranslatable). Its clumsiness was explained by Torrey (14–16) as due to the mistranslation of Aramaic. His suggestion is as follows. ἐστερέωσεν τὸ ὄνομα αὐτοῦ may be put back into Aramaic as שְׁמֵהּ תַּקֵּף. So Luke presumably read the unpointed text of his Aramaic source. It should however have been pointed תַּקֵּף שְׁמֵהּ, which should be rendered ὑγιῆ ἐποίησεν (or κατέστησεν) αὐτόν. This hypothesis found a measure of agreement, but more recent comment has been more doubtful. רפא is not a natural word for ὑγιής; the verb might stand for ἐστερέωσεν, but this word is probably drawn from, or at least connected with, v. 7 (ἐστερεώθησαν αἱ βάσεις αὐτοῦ). Moreover, Torrey's new sentence, though an improvement on the old, is not free from clumsiness: And by the faith of his name this man, whom you behold and know, he (God) has made him well (Torrey's own English to some extent smooths out the difficulties). More of the clumsiness was removed by F. C. Burkitt (*JTS* 20 (1919), 325), who, accepting the reading of א* B 0236^vid 81 1175 *pc*, which omit ἐπί, connects the opening words of v. 16 with v. 15: Of whom (or which) we are witnesses, and to the faith in his name. But it is very hard to connect μάρτυρες with both a genitive and a dative. See M. 2.473f. Mere lack of adequate literary revision may provide a sufficient explanation of this awkward verse. Wilcox concludes his discussion (144–6) with the verdict, 'The claim for Aramaism does not seem to have an adequate basis,' and there are other passages in Acts that suggest lack of revision. The meaning of the verse as it stands is well enough summarized by Stählin (64): the miracle may be explained in two ways, each in itself correct — 'geheilt hat der Name, geheilt hat der Glaube'. Schille (128) understands the verse similarly and sees no redactional additions or combinations. He may be right; but the obscure expression of a straightforward belief seems to call for some kind of literary explanation. Lüdemann 57 says rightly, 'Die überladene Formulierung zeigt noch nur Lukas' Schwierigkeiten, der Überlieferung seine Theologie aufzuprägen.'

When taken in the context of the book as a whole the verse must be seen not as an example of a quasi-magical belief in the power of the invoked name (as e.g. by W. Heitmüller, *Im Namen Jesu*, 1903, 232, and many since) but of Luke's criticism and correction of such a belief. So e.g. Cullmann (*V. & A.* 619), according to whom Christ himself is present when his name is invoked; 'dieser Satz will nicht magisch verstanden sein; . . . Darum fügt Petrus hinzu: 'Der durch ihn gewirkte Glaube hat ihm vor euer aller Augen diese volle Gesundheit gegeben.' This however is not entirely satisfactory theologically (the name seems — magically? — to effect the presence of Jesus, thus simply throwing the magic back one step), and does nothing for the literary problem of the verse. It is probable that Luke is correcting a proposition, or implication, of which he did not approve. Schneider (321), who takes a similar view, denies that the verse is 'überladen und unklar' — a very surprising judgment in view of his own analysis of the verse as a chiastic structure of which both parts have been expanded by additions which introduce the theme of faith. The verse is overloaded, and it is precisely this fact that points to the view that Luke has introduced corrective material into it. There is a literary problem here, but it is not Schneider's. It has been argued above that Luke drew the story and the speech from different sources. It is intelligible that the story should have contained references to the miracle-working name of Jesus, which Luke might have wished to correct, but it would have been an extraordinary coincidence if the independent speech should have contained a similar reference, equally inviting correction. Luke fashioned the contact between miracle and speech; it seems to follow that he must have contributed the whole of the present verse. Why then should he have made such an unsatisfactory job of it? This is the literary problem. It is important to remember that the narrative unit, into which the speech of 3.12–26 was inserted, runs from 3.1 to at least 4.31; probably further — see pp. 241f. In this whole passage ὄνομα occurs frequently: 3.6, 16; 4.7, 10, 12, 17, 18, 30. Indeed it is very common in the whole of the first ten chapters of Acts; in addition to the above there are 2.21, 38; 5.28, 40, 41; 8.12, 16; 9.14, 15, 16, 21, 27, 28. Luke's own understanding of it has already been brought out at 2.21, 38; in the present passage he felt the need of a renewed caution against misuse. After Peter's words in 3.6 he could hardly object to the proposition,τοῦτον ἐστερέωσεν τὸ ὄνομα αὐτοῦ; hence his first addition, (ἐπὶ) τῇ πίστει τοῦ ὀνόματος αὐτοῦ. Even this however was not sufficient, and v. 16b was added to make it clear that it was not the name but the faith accompanying — evoked by and directed towards the name — that saved. ἡ πίστις ἡ δι' αὐτοῦ is 'of uncertain meaning' (M. 3.267): *faith which is caused by him* (author) or *faith in him* (circumstantial). 'Per Christum fides nostra ex DEO est et in DEUM tendit' (Bengel).

In v. 12, Peter rejects the notion that he and his colleagues are divine men or Jewish miracle-working charismatics. Here he rejects the notion that the mere naming of the name of Jesus carries with it a magical power. It is worth noting that Honi the Circle-Maker, whose power as a rain-maker was referred to in the comment on v. 12, in his prayer for rain said to God, I swear by thy great name that I will not stir hence until thou have pity on thy children (Taanith 3.8).

Blass (67) follows Lachmann in punctuating after ἐστερέωσεν, of which the subject is ὁ θεός (from v. 15). He does not comment on the singular verb ἔδωκεν with the double subject (His name and the faith that is through him). The faith in question is that of the apostles; the sick man was expecting money, not exercising faith.ὁλοκληρία is used nowhere else in the NT. It is used here in the sense of ὁλοκληρία τοῦ σώματος as in Plutarch, *De Stoic. repugn.* 30 (1047E), quoting Chrysippus (see *S.V.F.* 3.33), along with ὑγίεια. ὁλόκληρος occurs in 1 Thess. 5.23; James 1.4. The words are not technical medical terms; see e.g. Plato, *Timaeus* 44c (ὁλόκληρος ὑγίης τε παντελῶς) for use by a layman. See also MM 446, s. vv. and *ND* 1.132; 4.161. ἀπέναντι is used in a different sense at 17.7.

17. καὶ νῦν recalls the Hebrew וְעַתָּה, which it translates in the LXX. See BDR § 442.8(d), with the reference to Jeremias (*ZNW* 38 (1939), 119f.). In Acts cf. 10.5; 22.16; 7.34; 13.11, 20; 22.25. The speaker takes up his main point: Now then! He is leading up to v. 19: Repent! For οἶδα, D E it^{h p} mae have ἐπιστάμεθα, (agreeing in number with v. 15).

Peter's Jewish hearers may be to some extent excused: You did not know that you were killing the holy and innocent originator of life; he had been represented to you in a quite different light. This is not simply an excuse; 'Lukas will die Tat der Juden nicht verharmlosen, sondern erklären' (Schmithals 45). At this point Peter speaks as if addressing the common Jewish people who are distinguished from their ἄρχοντες (cf. 4.1, where these come on the scene). But the ἄρχοντες too were ignorant; they did not know what in truth they were doing (cf. Lk. 23.34, the application of which is uncertain; the present passage may suggest that Luke himself took it to apply to all who were concerned in the crucifixion). 1 Cor. 2.6, 8 is not parallel; the ἄρχοντες τοῦ αἰῶνος τούτου are probably spiritual powers, cf. Ignatius, *Ephesians* 19.1. The substance of 1 Tim. 1.13 (ἀγνοῶν ἐποίησα) is similar (ignorance can be taken as an excuse) but the construction is different. Luke prefers to use not a participle but a prepositional phrase (this is characteristic of Koine Greek, according to M. 3.154). For both substance and form cf. *Acta Thomae* 38 (L.-B. 2.2.156): Οὐ καταψηφίζεται ὑμῶν οὐδὲ λογίζεται ὑμῖν τὰς ἁμαρτίας ἃς ἐν πλάνῃ ὄντες διεπράξασθε, ἀλλὰ παραβλέπει ὑμῶν τὰ παραπτώματα ἃ κατὰ ἀγνωσίαν ἦτε πεποιηκότες. For ignorance as a partial excuse in Acts see 13.27 (ἀγνοήσαντες) and 17.30 (χρόνους τῆς ἀγνοίας); in the OT, Lev. 22.14 (κατὰ ἀγνοίαν). Cf. also Euripides, *Hippolytus* 1334f.: τὴν δὲ σὴν ἁμαρτίαν τὸ μὴ εἰδέναι μὲν πρῶτον ἐκλύει κακῆς.

18. God not only reversed your ignorant wickedness in putting Jesus to death by raising him from the dead, he actually used your folly as the means of fulfilling his own purpose, which he had previously declared through all the prophets. This was not difficult, since his purpose was that his Christ should suffer. παθεῖν is used to include the suffering of death. This is a Lucan form of expression; it is also Lucan to predicate the suffering of the Messiah (not of the Son of Man): see Lk. 24.26, 46 (in both of which the words παθεῖν τὸν Χριστόν occur); also Acts 26.23 (εἰ παθητὸς ὁ Χριστός). According to Fuller (*Christology* 179) this use of παθεῖν is not primitive but came into Christian use between Paul and Mark. It might be safer simply to observe that it is not distinctively Pauline (Mt. 3 times; Mk 3; Lk. 6; Jn 0; Acts, 5; Pauline homologoumena, 5; 2 Thess., 1; 2 Tim., 1; Heb., 4, 1 Peter, 11; Rev., 1). It is reasonable however to suppose that Luke's hand may be seen in the formulation of this verse (it must not be forgotten that Χριστὸς ἐσταυρωμένος is a sufficiently Pauline theme too); this does not mean that Luke was covering up (intentionally or otherwise) a primitive text which did not speak of the suffering of the Messiah because it came from a period when it was not yet believed that Jesus had been the Messiah during his earthly life. The whole context speaks of the fulfilment of prophecy, and this points in the direction of Messiahship. Crucifixion (the punishment of a rebel) must have suggested the theme of Messiahship as soon as it happened, even if messianic ideas had not already been current (as it seems that they were) during the ministry. Robinson (see above, p. 190) is obliged to remove Messiahship from this verse in order to establish his thesis, and it is doubtful whether this can be done.

Luke asserts that God foretold through all the prophets (διὰ στόματος is a LXX expression; e.g. 3 Kdms 17.1) that the Christ should suffer. He gives no references; even though in v. 13 Jesus has been described as God's παῖς, with a probable reference to Isa. 52.13, there is no allusion to Isa. 53 and the Suffering Servant. The conviction that the prophets must have foretold what was known to have happened was doubtless older than the collection of suitable testimonies. The saying attributed to R. Ḥiyya bar Abba in Berakoth 34b is sometimes quoted in this connection: All the prophets, all of them, prophesied only in regard to the days of the Messiah (לא נתנבאו אלא לימות המשיח). The parallel should be accepted with reserve and with the observation that it is preceded by a parallel saying to the effect that all the prophets prophesied only about him who marries his daughter to a *talmid ḥakam* and him who does business with a *talmid ḥakam*, and him who favours a *talmid ḥakam* with his possessions, and another according to which all the prophets prophesied only about those who repent. It was of course intended that the hyperbole involved in these sayings should be recognized. It is however worth noting (in view of vv. 20, 21, below) the contrast in the saying quoted between the Days of the Messiah and the Age to come, to which R. Ḥiyya applies Isa. 64.3 (. . . the Days of the Messiah, but (אבל) as for the Age to Come — Eye hath not seen, O God, beside thee). This work of the prophets is 'Trost und ernste Ermahnung zugleich' (Bauernfeind 65).

19. Verses 19–21 contain pre-Lucan tradition originating in Baptist circles; so Wilson (*Pastorals* 79) and Plümacher (72).

οὖν: you should repent because you have sinned, you may repent because you sinned in ignorance and now, knowing the truth as just disclosed by Peter (that the death of Jesus was the fulfilment of God's intention), may be expected to have come to a better mind. If there is a distinction between μετανοεῖν and ἐπιστρέφειν it will be that the former signifies a turning away from evil and the latter a turning towards good, or rather, in biblical usage, towards God. But the doubling of the verb (which is against the translation of a Semitic source since each Greek verb translates שוב) is probably no more than a means of emphasis.

Repentance has two purposes, expressed in two clauses introduced respectively by πρός (so B א; P⁷⁴ A C D E Ψ 𝔐 have εἰς, with no difference in meaning) τό with the infinitive and by ὅπως ἄν with the subjunctive (in v. 20). It is not possible on grammatical grounds to distinguish between a nearer and a more remote purpose, but it seems clear on the grounds of sense and word order that πρός τό introduces the immediate personal consequence of repentance and ὅπως ἄν the wider cosmic-historical consequence. In v. 19b (as in 19a) the plural is used (ὑμῶν τὰς ἁμαρτίας) but the meaning no doubt is that the sins of each penitent will be blotted out, though it is hoped that all Israel will repent and that therefore the corporate sin of murdering the Messiah will be blotted out.

ἐξαλειφθῆναι is nowhere else used in the NT for the blotting out of sin. The nearest parallel is Col. 2.14. In the LXX the word is used most frequently for blotting out people (or their names, or memory); see however Ps. 50 (51).1, ἐξάλειψον τὸ ἀνόμημά μου, 9; 108 (109).14; Isa. 43.25; Jer. 18.23; 2 Macc. 12.42. In non-biblical Greek see Lysias, *Against Andocides* 39, ... ὅπως ἐξαλειφθείη αὐτῷ τὰ ἁμαρτήματα; Demosthenes, 25.70 (791).

Forgiveness and the future salvation of the people of God (see vv. 20, 21) are thus dependent on repentance. As Weiser points out, it is not so much that repentance will hasten the parousia; it is necessary if the time of salvation is to come at all. The connection of thought is not unfamiliar in Judaism. The best known passage is Sanhedrin 97b–98a (see further StrB 1.162–5; also Bousset *RJ* 248, 390). Here R. Eliezer ben Hyrcanus argues that if Israel repent (אם ישראל עושין תשובה) they are redeemed (נגאלין); if they do not repent they are not redeemed. This opinion is not unopposed, and is debated on the basis of a number of Scriptural passages. That final messianic, redemption is in mind is shown by a saying ascribed in the same context to Rab: All the predicted terms of redemption are ended and the matter depends only on repentance and good works (בתשובה ומעשים טובים). תשובה summarizes admirably the two Greek words μετανοεῖν and ἐπιστρέφειν. Repentance has personal and corporate aspects and is called for in the present; the blotting out of sins similarly is both personal and corporate, and in its personal aspect belongs to the present; the coming of the Messiah means corporate redemption in the future. These observations are necessary for the correct understanding of vv. 20, 21.

20. According to v. 19 repentance is to lead to the blotting out of sins; it is the sins of those who repent that are blotted out, not the sins of others, though it is clear from the context that the chief sin in mind is the supreme one of rejecting and crucifying Jesus; this was a corporate sin and Peter presumably hopes for corporate repentance leading to corporate forgiveness. This broadened, less individual outlook appears in v. 20, at least in the second clause, ὅπως ἄν . . . ἀποστείλῃ . . . It will be well to consider this first and then return to the interpretation of καιροί ἀναψύξεως. The interpretation of v. 20b turns upon the meaning of the perfect participle προκεχειρισμένον (Calvin (102) surprisingly refers to the reading προκεκηρυγμένον, but it can hardly be taken seriously). This has been taken to mean that Jesus has not, even after the resurrection (contrast 2.36), become the Messiah; he is predestined to become the Messiah when in the future he is sent as such. So for example J. A. T. Robinson (art. cit.) and Fuller (*Christology* 166: 'In the Palestinian formulae [Fuller has referred to Acts 3.20] Jesus is not *adopted* at the resurrection to a new status or function, but *pre-destined* to be the eschatological judge at the parousia'). In the NT the word προχειρίζειν is used only in Acts, in addition to this passage at 22.14; 26.16, where the tense is aorist and the word refers simply to God's having appointed Paul to his office; he is of course appointed to it before he exercises it. The verb in general usage means (see LS 1541) *to make* πρόχειρος, that is, *ready to act* in a particular way determined by the context. See e.g. Lucian, *Toxaris* 62, ἀπὸ πολλῶν πέντε τούτους προχειρισάμενος; Demosthenes 25.13 (773), ἐγὼ . . . ὁρῶν ὑμᾶς . . . προχειριζομένους ἐπὶ τὴν τούτου κατηγορίαν; *P. Oxy*. 3275, 7–8: προκεχειρισμένων ὑπὸ τῶν συνιερέων ('selected by their fellow priests', *ND* 3.82). This meaning fits the passages already noted (with reference to Paul) and also the present one. Jesus (in א B D E 1241 *pm* p the name stands in apposition with Χριστόν — God will send a Messiah, namely Jesus; in P⁷⁴ A C Ψ 33 81 323 614 945 1739 2495 *pm* Ir^lat the order is reversed) has been put in a state of readiness to act as Messiah. The perfect tense suggests — it hardly proves — that he is now ready so to act, and does not say at what moment he became ready, that is, became Messiah, except that this must have been at a time before that at which Peter is speaking. This could have been at the resurrection, at his baptism, or at the time of his birth. It is of course clear that Luke believed that Jesus had been Messiah from birth (Lk. 2.11: ἐτέχθη ὑμῖν σήμερον σωτήρ, ὅς ἐστιν Χριστὸς κύριος); v. 18 shows that it was as Christ that he suffered. It has been said that ἀποστέλλειν is normally used to mean *send*, rather than *send back, send a second time*; but it would be absurd to claim that the word could not be used of a second sending. See Longenecker (*Christology* 48). Luke may well have understood the prefix προ- in a temporal sense; that this would have been against strict etymology is unlikely to have worried him (Haenchen 207).

Thus v. 20b refers to the sending as Messiah of Jesus, who is

Messiah now; Luke believes that he was Messiah during his ministry, but we cannot be certain that his source (if he was using one) shared this view. Many (e.g. Conzelmann 34; Stählin 67) suppose that the coming (ἔλθωσιν; D h Tert have ἐπέλθωσιν without difference in meaning) of καιροὶ ἀναψύξεως in v. 20a is synonymous with the sending of Jesus as Messiah at the End in v. 20b. Calvin, 101, by consistently treating καιροί as if it were singular, the *time* of refreshing, makes this interpretation almost necessary. It is accepted by Oepke in *TWNT* 1.390: 'καιροὶ ἀναψύξεως und χρόνων ἀποκαταστάσεως v. 21 stehen in Korrespondenz und erklären sich gegenseitig, bilden aber keine Tautologie. Sinnvoll markiert καιροί das Eintreten des Umschwungs, während χρόνων an den daurernden Zustand der erneuerten Welt denken lässt. Bezeichnet ἀναψύξεως die subjektive, so ἀποκαταστάσεως die objektive Seite der Sache.' Schweizer (*TWNT* 9.665) agrees. This is however improbable. It does not do justice to the plural καιροί (a number of specific points of time) or to the meaning of ἀνάψυξις, which suggests temporary relief rather than finality. See e.g. Exod. 8.11; Philo, *De Abrahamo* 152; Plato, *Symposium* 176a (for the cognate ἀναψυχή); 2 Tim. 1.16 (for the cognate ἀναψύχειν — note πολλάκις, and cf. Exod. 23.12). *Begs.* 4.37 points out that Galen, *San. tuend.* 3.7, distinguishes between ἀνάψυξις and ἀνάπαυσις. Luke does not see the period that must intervene (δεῖ, v. 21) between the resurrection and the parousia as one of unrelieved gloom. There are repeated conversions, as one after another is won to the new faith; there are moments of collective inspiration, such as 2.1–4; 4.31. These are brought about as men are penitent and turn to God, receiving the forgiveness of their sins and the gift of the Holy Spirit. It is characteristic of Luke that he does not abandon the notion of a futurist collective eschatology but believes this to be anticipated in a series of individual realizations. Miracles provide further examples of such moments of refreshment. For a full discussion of this point see *FS* Kümmel (1985), 10–13, and cf. Bauernfeind (66, 68); Rackham (53): 'The apostle has already learnt to distinguish between a present realization and a final and glorious establishment of the kingdom.'

21. Standing as it does in Acts the verse refers back to the ascension. This was when Jesus was received (δέξασθαι; in 1.11, ἀναλημφθείς) into heaven. δέξασθαι carries with it the notion of *remaining* where one is received; for this see LS 382 s.v. II 1, e.g. Plato, *Laws* 747e: τόποι . . . τοὺς ἀεὶ κατοικιζομένους ἵλεῳ δεχόμενοι. ἄχρι makes this meaning certain here. Naturally it is possible to conceive of a source, modified by Luke, which spoke only of the Messiah, or the predestined Messiah, as being in heaven until the time of the End; for Luke himself the heavenly session has a specific beginning. For receiving into heaven cf. 7.59; also *ND* 3.50 (an emended inscription). Jesus will remain where he is ἄχρι χρόνων ἀποκαταστάσεως πάντων. ἀποκατάστασις means *return to an appointed state, restoration* (see LS 201, s.v.); and this is its meaning here. The use of the word implies a creation that has diverged from the condition in which it was intended to be; it is perverted and must be put right. Black (*Scrolls* 135) refers to 1 QS 4.23, אדם כבוד כול להם, which he translates, 'To them belongs all the glory of Adam'. This, the notion of the glory of the first man now restored to God's elect, may be in mind here, but ἀποκατάστασις recalls in particular the prophecy of Mal. 3.22f., where God promises that he will send (ἀποστέλλω; שלח) Elijah, who will restore (ὃς ἀποκαταστήσει: והשיב) the heart of father to son and the heart of a man to his neighbour. Luke's πάντων is echoed in Mk 9.12, where the same prophecy is taken up in the words Ἡλίας μὲν ἐλθὼν πρῶτον ἀποκαθιστάνει πάντα. It would be unwise to base on this allusion an argument that Luke was presenting, or had in his source, an 'Elijah-Christology', according to which Jesus was thought of as the forerunner of God. Luke is careful never to use the noun ἀποκατάστασις (or the verb ἀποκαθιστάνειν, or any cognate) of Elijah; even when he clearly refers to Mal. 2.23 at Lk. 1.17 he rejects the LXX verb and uses instead ἐπιστρέψαι. Jesus as the coming Messiah will restore God's perverted world. It has however been held (e.g. by Bruce, *FS* Morris 67) that ἀποκατάστασις cannot here have its normal meaning since it is followed by πάντων and πάντων by the relative clause ὧν ἐλάλησεν ὁ θεός. It does not make sense to speak of the restoration of all the things that God spoke through the prophets. In this place therefore the word must mean *establishment* in the sense of *fulfilment*. The difficulty is that this use of the word cannot be supported. It is not borne out by references given by Bruce and in *Begs.* 4.38. The simplest explanation is that ἀποκατάστασις has its normal meaning, that ἀποκατάστασις πάντων means the restoration of all things (but on the gender of πάντων see below), and that the antecedent of ὧν is not πάντων but χρόνων. The antecedent of a relative is most often the nearest noun with which the relative agrees in gender and number, but it is not always so. And that all the prophets spoke of the Messiah has just been affirmed at v. 18.

One aspect of the restoration of all things is given in 1.6 (and in 1.7 χρόνοι and καιροί are brought together, as here) is the restoration (ἀποκαθιστάνεις) of sovereignty to Israel, but though Luke may not have thought as definitely as Black (see above) suggests about the restoration of creation to the sinless and blissful state of Adam in Eden it is clear that he did not think in nationalist terms. It was the little flock of Christian disciples to whom the Father had chosen to give the kingdom (Lk. 12.32). See Le Déaut (254). Luke is not developing a philosophy of history; there is no trace here of a cyclic view of time, as Dinkler (*Signum Crucis* 327) suggests. But Dinkler (259) is right when he compares Rom. 11.32, for Luke is looking to a final triumphant achievement of the purpose of God, and in speaking (334) of a tendency to universalism. There is indeed no reason why πάντων should not be taken as masculine rather than, or perhaps as well as, neuter. *All men*, the whole human race, will be restored. This would be in line with Mal. 3.23.

Roloff (72: 'Die prophetisch verheissene Restituierung des heilvollen Zustands der verlorenen Urzeit') takes the verse in substantially the way adopted here. Stählin (67) thinks it refers possibly to the fulfilment of all prophecies but more probably to the restoration of all things. Haenchen (207: 'Der [Terminus] der "Herstellung", der Verwirklichung aller prophetischen Verheissungen, die zugleich eine Wiederherstellung der schöpfungmässigen Ordnung ist') seems to want the best of both worlds. Preuschen (21) thinks the reference may be to Welterneuerung (he refers to Philo, *Quis Rer. Div. Her.* 293; Origen, *In Joh.* 1.16.91); or, better, to the conversion of the Jews (he refers to Heracleon in Origen, *In John* 13.46.29).

The text of the last phrase of the verse is in some confusion. διὰ στόματος corresponds to the Hebrew בפי, or על־פי, but it is not ungreek and there is no reason to suppose that Luke is translating (though he may be imitating the LXX; cf. e.g. Deut. 8.3; 3 Kdms 17.1; 2 Chron. 35.22; 36.21, 22; Ps. 49 (50). 16, though ἐν στόματι is more frequent). For ἀπ' αἰῶνος (omitted — perhaps rightly (*Begs.* 4.38) — by D (*pc*) it Tert) cf. Lk. 1.70 (Gen. 6.4; 1 Chron. 16.36; 29.10; Tobit 4.12). πάντων is added by many but not the oldest authorities; cf. vv. 18, 24. Wilcox (74–6) thinks that the language here may have a liturgical background. Wilckens (43) writes: '3.20f. macht so terminologisch und inhaltlich-sachlich den Eindruck eines Einschubs.'

22. For the form Μωυσῆς (better than Μωϋσῆς) and for its declension see M. 2.146; BDR §§ 38; 55.

According to Bultmann (*Exegetica* 375) this verse presents an example of typology in that the 'eschatologische Heilszeit' is regarded as a 'Wiederholung der Mosezeit'. This view is based upon the 'wie mich' of v. 22, but involves taking καιροὶ ἀναψύξεως as meaning the eschatologische Heilszeit and ἀποκατάστασις as a technical term with the meaning Wiederherstellung. Of these the former is improbable (see on v. 20); the latter is correct but it is to be understood in a prophetic rather than a typological way. The prophecy of Deut. 18.15 is used again at 7.37 and Dodd (*AS* 53–7) is much more probably correct in treating it as a primitive testimonium, probably the origin of Jn 6.14. It is indeed likely that the 'prophet like Moses' played a considerable part in Johannine thought; see especially

T. F. Glasson, *Moses in the Fourth Gospel*, 1963, and W. A. Meeks, *The Prophet-King*, 1967; all that need be noted of this here is that we have a parallel (of sorts) between John and Acts (see 1.8). All the theological subtlety is on John's side; Luke presents an OT text which he claims has been fulfilled in Jesus. 'Deut. 18.15, 18 wird in der rabbinischen Literatur äusserst selten erwähnt' (StrB 2.626). Deut. 18.18, 19 is however quoted fully in 4Q test 5–8, and may lie behind 1 QS 9.11 (עד בוא נביא). This passage seems to treat the prophet like Moses as a messianic figure, though not as *the* Messiah (Braun 158). Philo goes even less far (*De Spec. Leg.* 1.65). Moses recognized men's longing to know the future, and in forbidding them to use haruspicy and other forms of divination promised the coming of a prophet: ἀλλά τις ἐπιφανεὶς ἐξαπιναίως προφήτης θεοφόρητος θεσπιεῖ καὶ προφητεύσει. At *Clem. Recog.* 1.43 it is assumed that Jews give a messianic interpretation to the passage in Deuteronomy. This is justified only in respect of the Qumran passages quoted above, and then only in the broadest terms. The 'prophet like Moses' was a Jewish *Christian* theologumenon, except that the Samaritans also seem to have known it. 'Die Verwendung dieser Stelle mit Bezug auf den Messias ist aus den rabbinischen Schriften nicht zu belegen. Dafür ist Deut. 18.18 die Grundlage für die samaritanische Messias- oder Ta'eb-Erwartung' (J. Bowman, *Samaritanische Probleme*, 1967, 56, cf. 40). There is a probable allusion (which may in part or whole be Christian) to a Moses-like Messiah in *Sib Orac.* 5.256–9:

Εἷς δέ τις ἔσσεται αὖθις ἀπ' αἰθέρος ἔξοχος ἀνήρ,
Οὗ παλάμας ἥπλωσεν ἐπὶ ξύλον πολύκαρπον
Ἑβραίων ὁ ἄριστος, ὃς ἠέλιόν ποτε στήσεν,
Φωνήσας ῥήσει τι καλῆ καὶ χείλεσιν ἀγνοῖς.

Probably Luke is simply following here what had in his time become an accepted Christian testimonium. Jesus fulfilled all the messianic promises. The theological significance of the fact that Jesus fulfilled the law as well as the prophets (cf. Rom. 3.21) was not lost on some of Luke's contemporaries; whether Luke himself perceived it is not so clear (see ch. 15). Cullmann (*Christologie* 15f.) suggests that the returning Moses is the Servant of Isa. 53. This would help to tie up some loose ends in Peter's speech, but a prophet 'like Moses,' 'raised up in the same way as Moses,' is not exactly a returning Moses, and the background of Isa. 53 is probably more complicated ('Der Ebed Jahwe ist Deuterojesaja und Israel, der neue Mose ('Messias') und die Gemeinde, für die er zum Tode bereit ist, in einer Person' (Aa. Bentzen, *Messias Moses redivivus Menschensohn*, 1948, 66f.). Calvin recognizes that the passage in Deuteronomy refers to a series of prophets, and goes to great lengths (104f.) to justify Peter's application of it to the one person, Christ; somewhat similarly Wettstein (475).

The opening words of the verse are given in several forms. The shortest and simplest, Μωυσῆς μὲν εἶπεν (P[74] ℵ A B C 36 81 1175 pc vg bo), is probably best; it has been filled out with references to the (or our, or your) fathers, to whom Moses spoke. After ὁ θεός, ℵ[c] A D 36 81 323 945 1175 1739 pm lat Ir[lat] have ὑμῶν; ℵ* CE Ψ 33 614 1241 2495 pm sy[h] have ἡμῶν; B h p Tert Eus have no pronoun. ὑμῶν and ἡμῶν were pronounced alike, and confusion was easy. Peter might have thought himself to be addressing fellow Jews and used ἡμῶν; Luke might have thought of the Jews as not (like himself) Christians and written ὑμῶν. The likeliest supposition is that Luke used no pronoun and that copyists and editors supplied what they thought fit. The LXX has σου. There are several other small points in which the LXX diverges from Acts. The LXX of Deut. 18.15f. runs: προφήτην ἐκ τῶν ἀδελφῶν σου ὡς ἐμὲ ἀναστήσει σοι κύριος ὁ θεός σου, αὐτοῦ ἀκούσεσθε κατὰ πάντα . . . The last words of v. 22, ὅσα ἐὰν λαλήσῃ πρὸς ὑμᾶς, recall Deut. 18.19, ὅσα ἐὰν λαλήσῃ, though these belong to the thought of v. 23. Luke probably quotes the LXX from memory (his, or that of his source), but Wilcox (33, 39) considers the possibility that Luke may be using a non-LXX text, and the relation of his text to the Hexapla. For κύριος and θεός cf. 2.39.

23. It is often asserted that Luke in this verse completes his quotation from Deut. 18 with the addition of Lev. 23.29. Verse 23 is not unlike Deut. 18.19 but is not identical with it. The Hebrew may be translated with the RV:

Deut. 18.19: And it shall come to pass, that whosoever will not hearken unto my words which he shall speak in my name, I will require it of him.

Lev. 23.29: For whatsoever soul it be that shall not be afflicted in that same day, he shall be cut off from his people.

Two reasons are given for supposing that Luke has deserted Deut. 18: (a) he includes τοῦ προφήτου, which is not in Deuteronomy, and (b) it is Leviticus, not Deuteronomy, that speaks of the cutting off of the offending person. The latter is a valid reason; in ἐξολεθρευθήσεται ἐκ τοῦ λαοῦ Luke is using the language of Lev. 23.29. The former reason is less convincing; see Fitzmyer (*Essays* 88f.). *The Prophet* is indeed missing from MT but it occurs in the LXX of Deut. 18.19 (ὃς ἐὰν μὴ ἀκούσῃ ὅσα ἐὰν λαλήσῃ ὁ προφήτης) and in 4 Q test 7 (אשר לוא ישמע אל דברי אשר ידבר הנביא). It may be that Luke (or his source), the LXX, and Qumran shared a text of Deut. 18.19 which differed from MT in that it contained the word *prophet*. This however would not explain Luke's use of ἐξολεθρευθήσεται, which points fairly clearly to Lev. 23.29. The probability is that the two texts have been combined. This may have been because Luke was quoting from memory; it may have been because he was using a collection of *testimonia* in which the OT passages had already been combined — Fitzmyer (loc. cit.) considers that the data add some weight to the hypothesis of Hebrew collections of OT passages among the Jews before the time of Christ. The OT is certainly more important than the (late) use of the word in curses illustrated in *ND* 3.83.

The verse supports the command of v. 22 (αὐτοῦ ἀκούσεσθε) with a severe threat, the meaning of which will turn upon the meaning of λαός. If this refers (as it often but not always does in Acts) to Israel as the people of God, the threat, taken *au pied de la lettre* will mean that Jews who do not accept the messianic authority of Jesus not merely fail to become Christians but also cease to be what they hitherto have been, members of the people of God. The Jew who does not accept the Messiah ceases to be a member of Israel (Roloff 78). He cannot be cut off from the *new* people, to which he has never belonged; he is cut off from the *old* people, which still exists, though only in order that it may become the new people. Whether Luke meant so much is doubtful. He probably thought the verse a powerful means of expressing in negative terms what is positively stated in 4.12; salvation is to be had only in the name of Jesus Christ. 'That man severs himself from the Body, who refuses to be subject to the Head' (Calvin 106).

For πᾶσα ψυχή, see 2.43. In Kerithoth 1.1 the thirty six transgressions for which a soul may be cut off from Israel (כרת) are listed. This cutting off was understood as a punishment carried out by God himself, and thus distinct from all punishments inflicted by the community. It might take the form of premature or sudden death. We may think of the fate of Ananias and Sapphira (5.1–11); but Luke probably has in mind what might be called excommunication.

24. This verse takes up v. 21. All the prophets spoke of the times when the messianic restoration would take place. In particular, Moses (vv. 22, 23) foretold the coming of one, raised up by God as he himself had been. Moses being thus dealt with, the next great prophet, Samuel, is invoked as representative of all those who followed; he and all the rest foretold the messianic days, which have now begun and are moving towards their consummation. There is no doubt that this is the general sense of the verse, but a number of questions of detail remain.

καὶ πάντες δέ emphasizes the link with Moses: *and all the prophets too* . . . (BDR § 447.1(d)). Cf. 2.44, where however καί is weakly attested and must be omitted.

Samuel is probably mentioned by name as the next prophet after Moses, but the choice of Samuel was not only a matter of chronology.

In a saying attributed to R. Judah the Prince (j Hagigah 2.77a.27) it is said שמואל רבן של נביאים: he was the greatest of them all.
καθεξῆς is an adverb meaning *in a row, one after another*; οἱ καθεξῆς will therefore mean *the successors* (of Samuel), that is, as prophets. What is not clear is why this term should be in the genitive, τῶν καθεξῆς. One would have expected Luke to write either, All the prophets, Samuel and his successors; or, All the prophets, from Samuel onwards. He appears to have mixed the two constructions (so e.g. Conzelmann 35); this is probably to be taken as another mark of inadequate literary revision.

The connection between ἐλάλησαν and κατήγγειλαν is not clear. It is natural to suppose that they are simply linked by καί — *who spoke and announced* — but to take them in this way leaves the verse without a main verb. One may be taken from vv. 21, 22: God spoke through the prophets . . . Moses said . . . and *so did* all the prophets from Samuel onwards who spoke and prophesied. Alternatively the καί may be *also*: The prophets who spoke (about various matters) also prophesied . . . So Pallis (53), '. . . not only spoke but also announced . . .;' cf. Job 23.13; Demosthenes 1.11.(12)). Neither of these ways of construing the sentence is entirely satisfactory; again Luke seems to be convicted of some literary negligence. Torrey (29f.) explains the difficulty by retranslating into Aramaic. Haenchen (208) thinks that Luke is writing in a ceremonious style; he is not content with 'the prophets' but writes 'the prophets who spoke'. Ropes (*Begs.* 3.32) thinks that the Greek ὅσοι ἐλάλησαν was translated into Latin as *quotquot* (d h have *quodquod*) and that mistranslation of this produced the reading of D, ὃ ἐλάλησαν. If this is true we have an important fact about the origin of Greek D; it is secondary to the Latin d.

These days are the times just spoken of, the last days, of which the events of resurrection, ascension, and the gift of the Spirit mark the first.

25. All the prophets (cf. v. 18) — an understandable exaggeration — announced the coming days of salvation. And you are the sons of the prophets. This is meant both literally, for the persons addressed are of the same Hebrew stock as the prophets, and in the sense that they are the heirs of the prophets, potentially the recipients of what the prophets foretold. Cf. 2.39, ὑμῖν γάρ ἐστιν ἡ ἐπαγγελία. So Chrysostom (τί ἐστιν υἱοί . . .; κληρονόμοι, διάδοχοι; cf. a saying attributed to Hillel, The Israelites are sons of prophets (j Shabbath 19.17a 4; Pesahim 66a). It is implied that if others (non-Jews) are to be admitted to these blessings it will be subsequently and secondarily, by special arrangement, perhaps by the ordinary process of proselytization to Judaism. It is clear both that the question of a Gentile mission is not yet being raised (either because the speech is derived from a very early period or because Luke is carefully planning the development of his story) and that when it is raised it will provoke serious questions. See however the latter part of the verse, and v. 26. The hearers are also υἱοὶ τῆς διαθήκης. Cf. Jer. 11.10; Ps. Sol. 17.15 (17). The expression occurs at Ezek. 30.5 (πάντες οἱ ἐπίμικτοι καὶ τῶν υἱῶν τῆς διαθήκης μου μαχαίρᾳ πεσοῦνται). This omits a word of the Hebrew (הברית בני ארץ, sons of *the land of* the covenant) and apparently read ברית, *my covenant*; this may have been a corruption of ארץ כרתי, the land of the Kerethites. There is nothing helpful here; nor indeed is help of this kind needed. *Sons of the covenant* means 'those who have inherited a place in the covenant' which God made with Abraham (v. 25b makes it clear that it is this covenant that it is in mind). It is now renewed (so explicitly Lk. 22.20, ἡ καινὴ διαθήκη — *si v.l.*), and as Jews they are invited to take their place in the New Covenant. In virtue of their ancestry they have a right to the invitation (cf. Rom. 11.29); it is clear that they do not have a right to the Covenant itself irrespective of their reaction to Jesus. Calvin (106) is systematizing a looser kind of thought when he distinguishes between common election (not effective in all) and special election. For the use of διατίθεσθαι (*to make* a διαθήκη) cf. Lk. 22.29. For ὑμῶν (P[74] אᶜ A B E 81 945 1739 al vg^st sa^ms bo^mss), א* C^vid D Ψ 0165 𝔐 it vg^cl sy co have ἡμῶν; cf. v. 22. The expression *sons of the covenant* (בני ברית) occurs in Baba Qamma 1.2, meaning those who belong to the covenant of circumcision; for similar references see StrB 2.627f.

Verse 25b is a conflation of
Gen. 12.3: ἐνευλογηθήσονται ἐν σοὶ πᾶσαι αἱ φυλαὶ τῆς γῆς
18.18: ἐνευλογηθήσονται ἐν αὐτῷ πάντα τὰ ἔθνη τῆς γῆς
22.18: ἐνευλογηθήσονται ἐν τῷ σπέρματί σου πάντα τὰ ἔθνη τῆς γῆς

There is a somewhat similar conflation in Gal. 3.8 which led Dodd (*AS* 43f.) to think that the passages were already well known and included in a testimony collection, so that it was unnecessary to look them up severally in a copy of the OT. Peculiar to Acts is the use of πατριαί. This is probably a rendering of משפחות in Gen. 12.3. It translates this word twenty-four times in the LXX. Hanson (75f.) thinks that Luke takes σπέρμα to refer to Christ; either both Luke and Paul (see Gal. 3.16) were drawing on old tradition, or this must be regarded as a Paulinism in Acts. *Begs.* 4.39 and Roloff (78) also think that the word refers to Christ. Luke's thought however seems rather to be that Israel occupies a special place in God's purpose and receives the word of salvation before other nations. For the bearing of this verse and the next on the Gentile mission see Wilson (*Gentiles* 219–22, 228–31).

The promise to Abraham is certainly taken to contain a promise that the blessing offered in the first instance to him and his family would be extended to the non-Jewish people. The Christians were not the first to take the passages in this way; the LXX's passive verb ἐνευλογηθήσονται can hardly mean anything else. Whether this rightly represents the Hebrew ונברכו (Gen. 12.3; 18.18), והתברכו (22.18), is another question; probably it does not. For a discussion not only of the linguistic equivalents but of the implications for the inspiration, authority, and role of the LXX see Benoit (*Ex. et Th.* 1.10, and the whole essay.

26. πρῶτον implies that the offer of messianic salvation made to the Jews as heirs of the prophets and inheritors of the covenant (see above, v. 25) will be followed by another — to the Gentiles. Other ways of taking it, such as that Jesus was the first to be raised from the dead (cf. 1 Cor. 15.20), or that he was raised before the parousia took place, have little to commend them. The precise sense of this mission will be determined by the way in which πρῶτον is construed in the sentence. If the meaning is that God sent his servant to you (Jews) first, it is implied that there will be a subsequent sending of the servant to the Gentiles. This however is not how Luke understands the Gentile mission. The second sending of the Messiah will be at the End (v. 20); what happens before then is expressed in other terms. πρῶτον then must be taken closely with ὑμῖν: It was initially but not exclusively for your benefit that God sent his Servant; that is, the first sending will turn out not in the first instance but eventually to be of benefit not only to Jews but to Gentiles also: to the Jew first and also to the Greek (Rom. 1.16). Praevium indicium de vocatione gentium (Bengel). The relation between Judaism and the Christian church is a question that is frequently raised in Acts and one that cannot be adequately considered on the basis of one passage. The present passage does however suggest that for Luke the question was not a difficult one. It is God's intention to have a newly constituted people of which both the original heirs of the covenant and Gentiles, newly called through the Gospel, may be members. For both there is only one way into the inheritance: Jesus the Messiah.

Similar considerations to those applied in regard to πρῶτον will determine also the way in which ἀναστήσας is to be taken. In itself the word could refer to the resurrection of Jesus (cf. 13.33); here, however, as a raising up that precedes the (one) sending of Jesus as God's Servant, it must mean that God brought him on to the stage of history; so also e.g. Haenchen (208). Cf. Deut. 18.15, 18 (above, vv. 22f.); also Judges 2.16 (ἤγειρεν); and see Delling (*Studien* 358, n. 33).

For the use of παῖς in Acts 3 and 4 see on v. 13. According to Cullmann (*Christologie* 72), here (and at 4.23, 30) the word is a title, whereas at v. 13 it is a specific reference to Isa. 52.13. As a title, it grows out of wide-spreading roots. In the OT many are spoken of as God's servant: kings, priests, prophets, and others (e.g. Abraham). God sent his Servant (D with some Old Latin support improves the style by omitting αὐτόν) εὐλογοῦντα ὑμᾶς. It might be possible to take the present participle (which takes up ἐνευλογηθήσονται, v. 25) as descriptive of Jesus the Servant in the course of his ministry were the blessing not closely attached to 'turning from evils'; this (as far as Peter's hearers, and all who were subsequently to read Luke's book and hear the Christian message, were concerned) did not take place during the ministry of Jesus. The blotting out of sins (v. 19) remained as a purpose (εἰς τὸ . . .) and this determines the way in which εὐλογοῦντα must be taken. It is the future participle that is normally used as a means (alternative to ἵνα and other final particles) of expressing purpose, but occasionally the present participle is used (as e.g. at 15.27, ἀπαγγέλλοντας, to which there is a close parallel in Thucydides 7.25.7, ἀγγέλλοντας). It will be so here: the Servant of God was sent to bless you.

A further clause expresses the content of the blessing. ἐν τῷ introduces an adverbial determination of the process of blessing: he blesses you *in that* . . . (BDR § 404.2 n. 6, with a number of interesting parallels). What follows is ambiguous. ἀποστρέφειν may be active transitive, in which case the meaning is: In that he (the Servant) turns each one of you from . . . Alternatively, it may be intransitive: In that each one of you turns from . . . BDR § 308 n. 3 take it to be intransitive; in this case it will be parallel to the μετανοεῖν and ἐπιστρέφειν of v. 19. In Greek usage generally however (as BDR recognize) the intransitive sense seems to be most often expressed by the passive or middle, and the notion of blessing is more consistent with that of divine than human action. It is not impossible that the blessing should consist in the provision of an opportunity to turn away from evil, but it makes better sense if it is God's act in turning men from evil. *Begs.* 4.39 retains the ambiguity: 'in the turning of each of you from . . .'.

τῶν πονηριῶν will be much the same as ὑμῶν τὰς ἁμαρτίας (v. 19); in both the NT and the LXX πονηρία is much less common than ἁμαρτία. ὑμῶν is omitted by B, probably by accident; possibly because the plural pronoun seemed unsuitable after ἕκαστον, though Haenchen (208) probably rightly, takes the two words together — each one of you.

The speech ends abruptly; the offer of salvation is implicit; there is no reference to the Holy Spirit or to baptism. This is not to say (notwithstanding the present participle with which 4.1 begins) that the speech is unfinished.

8. ARREST AND EXAMINATION OF PETER AND JOHN 4.1–22

(1) While they were speaking to the people, the priests[1] and the Captain of the Temple and the Sadducees came upon them, (2) vexed because they were teaching the people and proclaiming in Jesus the resurrection from the dead. (3) They laid hands upon them and put them under guard until the next day; for it was already evening. (4) But many of those who heard the word believed, and the number of the men rose to about 5000.

(5) On the next day their rulers and the elders and the scribes were gathered together in Jerusalem, (6) with Annas the High Priest and Caiaphas and John and Alexander and those who belonged to the highpriestly clan. (7) They set them in the midst and inquired, 'By what power, or in what name, have you[2] done this?' (8) Then Peter, filled with the Holy Spirit, said to them, 'Rulers of the people and elders, (9) if today we are being cross-examined about a good deed done to a sick man, if you want to find out[3] by what means he has been cured, (10) then let it be known to all of you, and to all the people of Israel, that it is in the name of Jesus Christ of Nazareth, whom you crucified, whom God raised from the dead, that it is in this name[4] that this man stands before you fit and well. (11) He is the stone, despised by you builders, who has become head of the corner. (12) And in no other is there salvation, for there is no other name under heaven and given to men[5] by which we are to be saved.'

(13) As they observed the boldness of Peter and John, and took note of the fact that they were unlettered laymen, they were astonished, and they recognized them as former companions of Jesus; (14) and as they looked at the man who had been cured standing with them they could find no reply. (15) They commanded them to go out of the Council and discussed the matter with one another. (16) They said, 'What are we to do with these men? For that a manifest sign has been done by them is evident to all who live in Jerusalem, and we cannot deny it. (17) But that it may spread no further among [6] the people, let us threaten[7] them not to speak in this name to a single person.' (18) They summoned them and ordered them not to speak at all or teach in the name of Jesus. (19) Peter and John answered and said to them, 'Whether it is right in the sight of God to listen to you rather than to God, make up your own minds; (20) for we, for our part, cannot but speak the

---

[1.] NEB, chief priests.

[2.] NEB, men such as you.

[3.] These words, not in the Greek, are necessary in the English sentence. Cf. NEB, we are asked; NJB, asking us.

[4.] The Greek could equally mean, by him (so RSV).

[5.] Begs., RSV, among men.

[6.] Begs., to.

[7.] RSV, warn; NEB, caution.

things that we have seen and heard.' (21) They repeated their threats[8] and dismissed them because they could find no way in which they might punish them, for they were all glorifying God at what had happened; (22) for the man on whom this sign of healing had been done was more than forty years old.

Bibliography

D. Barag and D. Flusser, *IEJ* 36 (1986), 39–44.

F. Bovon, 239–89.

J. Dupont, *Nouvelles Études*. 58–111.

J. A. Emerton, as in (1).

A. George, *NTS* 23 (1977), 308–20.

P. W. van der Horst, as in (6).

M. Silva, *ZNW* 69 (1978), 253–7.

E. M. Smallwood, *JTS* 13 (1962), 14–34.

B. H. Throckmorton, *StEv* 6 (=*TU* 112, 1973), 515–26.

U. Wilckens, *Missionsreden*, 44f., 61f.

Commentary

Chapter 3 began with a miracle story to which Luke attached a specimen of Christian preaching, making a few narrative connections which at the same time served to make the important points that the apostles were not in themselves sources of divine authority and that the Christian use of the name of Jesus Christ had nothing to do with magic. In the present paragraph Luke returns to his narrative source which continues up to 4.31 and possibly into ch. 5. The opening verses of ch. 4 link the narrative material with the speech (1) by the opening words, λαλούντων δὲ αὐτῶν, (2) by the reference to Peter's proclamation of the resurrection, and (3) by the statement that of those who heard the word many believed. It is clear from v. 7 that in the story it is the act rather than the speech of Peter and John that provokes the authorities to arrest them. We thus find confirmation of the view (see pp. 175, 187f.; also below) that Luke is putting together narrative and discourse material. The narrative continues to be marked by the use of the word *name* (vv. 7, 10, 12, 17, 18; cf. 4.30). After 3.16 Luke can allow the word to stand; it does not need qualification every time it is used. A further link with the narrative in ch. 3 is the fact that the lame man is not merely mentioned (v. 9)

___
[8.] NEB, caution.

but is actually present (v. 14; cf. vv. 21, 22). A few Lucan expressions will be noted, but for the most part Luke appears simply to have continued with his narrative source; whether it was written or oral it is hardly possible to determine. Weiser's view (123f.) however that if redactional pieces are taken out no story is left is unconvincing, unless redaction is understood as including small verbal modifications of an underlying text.

It is however only when read superficially that the story gives the impression of harmonious development. There are 'Unebenheiten' (Roloff 80), of which the most notable are (a) the fact that Peter and John are arrested because they are preaching resurrection, whereas when they are brought before the Council it is not their preaching but their healing of the lame man that is inquired into, and (b) the recognition in v. 13 that Peter and John had been disciples of Jesus, whereas their association with him was already noted in v. 2. In addition, v. 4 may be said to interrupt the flow of the narrative. These are valid observations, but they do not quite justify the opinion of Conzelmann (41) that we have in this section a 'redaktionelle Überarbeitung einer Nachricht . . ., deren ursprüngliche Fassung nicht mehr zu rekonstruieren ist' (Schneider 342 agrees), unless this means only that a verbally exact reconstruction is impossible. The suggestion made above, that Luke is combining a traditional story with traditional preaching material, seems to account for the facts. The sermon was a Christian sermon, so that it had to be said that it was in Jesus that the apostles preached resurrection; but it was the miracle story that led originally to their appearance before the Sanhedrin. It was natural for Luke to add v. 4 to show the effect of the sermon.

Peter's reply to the Council's question (vv. 8–12) contains in effect what is a brief version of the proclamation of Jesus as this appears in chs. 2, 3, 10, and 13. It is possible that it was attached to the narrative source Luke used and retained by him though it is now overshadowed by the longer speech in ch. 3. Luke does not mean to miss an opportunity of proclaiming salvation in Jesus (Haenchen 221). Wilcox (172f.) can find no evidence for a Semitic source; in fact, he thinks — rightly — that Luke has written up the material so thoroughly that nothing can be said about sources. The speech makes the main points that are common to the early sermons. It points to Jesus, 'whom you crucified, whom God raised from the dead'. The language of Scripture is used in v. 11, and it is thus implicitly claimed that Jesus, crucified and risen, is the fulfilment of prophecy. The offer of salvation (as in ch. 3, without reference to baptism) is made in v. 12, with the warning that is implied in the assertion that salvation is to be had nowhere else. In the text as it stands this small speech provides the ground for the reference in v. 13 to the boldness of Peter and John, though this could have been prepared for by vv.

8b, 9, 10 alone, without vv. 11, 12. The climax of the paragraph, however, and this will be confirmed by observations to be made below about 4.23–31, is to be found in vv. 19, 20. Not only is the boldness of Peter and John most marked in their firm reply to the Council, it is made clear that official Judaism, so far from being the mouthpiece of God, has to be set over against him, so that men have to choose whether they will be obedient to the one or the other. Whatever some other parts of the book may suggest (and it will be important to read them in the light of the present paragraph), Luke makes it clear that Christianity is not Judaism: at least it is not the Judaism of those who officially represent Judaism. At the end (v. 21) three groups are clearly distinguished: the apostles and their company; the Jewish authorities; and the common people. This development is more important to Luke than his presentation of the personal courage of two Christian witnesses; rather, perhaps, we should say that it is characteristic of Luke to use the sort of story of outstanding Christians that he loves to tell as his means of presenting theological (and perhaps we should add, sociological) truth. See further on 4.23–31, which continues the present story.

1. λαλούντων δὲ αὐτῶν (D E *pc* it sy^{p.hmg} add, unnecessarily, τὰ ῥήματα ταῦτα). Luke has not said that both apostles were speaking; cf. 3.12, ὁ Πέτρος ἀπεκρίνατο. It is easy to complete the picture with the surmise that at the end of Peter's discourse John joined him in conversation with the crowd, but in fact throughout Peter is the real actor and John is simply added in; cf. 3.1 and especially 3.4. Notwithstanding the present participle Peter has finished his speech (so e.g. Schneider, 343). Stählin (70) notes that it is a characteristic Lucan device to represent a speech as unfinished; cf. 7.54; 10.44; 17.32; 22.22; 26.24. The interest of the narrative is thereby increased. It is probably right (see above, pp. 175, 187f.) to think of the speech as having a different source from that of the narrative; Luke now picks up the narrative thread. It is also possible that the miracle narrative and the trial narrative were originally distinct, but more probable that a single story thread runs through the whole of chs. 3 and 4 (and probably ch. 5 too): see above, p.216. The speech was made to the people in Solomon's Portico (3.11): hence the arrival of οἱ ἱερεῖς (B C have ἀρχιερεῖς), responsible for the conduct of the Temple and its ritual. For the conversion of many of them see 6.7; at this stage Luke can present them as opposed to the Gospel. The στρατηγὸς τοῦ ἱεροῦ (strangely omitted by D) was the סְגַן הכוהנים: for many details of his office, with many references to Mishnaic and Talmudic material, see Jeremias (*Jerusalem* 161, 163); also *NS* 2.237–308; and StrB 2.628–30, who think it possible, but less probable, that the reference is to the אִישׁ הר הבית, subordinate to the סגן and in charge of the police on the Temple Hill, or to the אִישׁ הבירה,

in charge of the inner area. 'The captain of the Temple had the permanent oversight of the cultus and, as the name *s^egan ha-koh^anim* indicates, over the whole body of officiating priests . . . In addition to the oversight of the cultus the captain of the Temple was the chief of police in the Temple area and as such had power to arrest' (Jeremias, op. cit. 163). At *Ant.* 20.131 Josephus mentions the στρατηγός Ananus (son of the High Priest Ananias); he uses the word στρατηγός at *War* 6.294, but possibly here it refers to one of the subordinate officers; so *Begs.* 4.40, with the suggestion that it is to this officer that Luke refers.

οἱ Σαδδουκαῖοι: See R. Leszynsky (*Die Sadduzäer*, 1912); Jeremias (*Jerusalem*, 228–32); J. le Moyne (*Les Sadducéens*, 1972); and most recently and with bibliography *NS* 2.404–14. Jeremias is correct in finding their chief strength in the lay nobility, but precisely by this means they were related to the leading priestly families; we must suppose that the priests just mentioned shared the Sadducean viewpoint; many but not all priests did so. As Roloff (80) remarks, the Sadducees *as a party* had no authority in the Temple.

ἐφιστάναι is a Lucan word (Lk, 7 times; Acts, 11; rest of the NT, 3). It is not always used in an aggressive sense, but cf. 6.12.

2. διαπονούμενοι. The participle expresses the reason for the action (ἐπέστησαν, v. 1). διαπονεῖσθαι occurs at Mk 14.4 (D Θ) and Acts 16.18; see also Eccles. 10.9; 2 Macc. 2.28; also in Aquila Gen. 6.6; 1 Kdms 20.30. It is more often used in the active (*to work laboriously*); here it must mean something like *worn out, brought to the end of one's tether, unable to put up with any more.* Cf. *P Oxy* 743.22 (BC 2), ἐγὼ ὅλος διαπον[ο]ῦμαι, 'I am quite upset' (Edd., perhaps a little weakly).

There is no ground for drawing a sharp distinction between διδάσκειν and καταγγέλλειν (D Ψ, ἀναγγ.). The authorities were vexed because (διά) Peter and John were teaching the people and in their teaching proclaiming . . .

The construction of καταγγέλλειν ἐν τῷ 'Ιησοῦ τὴν ἀνάστασιν τὴν ἐκ νεκρῶν is far from clear. If the words ἐν τῷ 'Ιησοῦ were omitted the sense would be that Peter and John were proclaiming, as any good Pharisee would (cf. 23.8) that at the time of the end there would be a rising from the world of the dead; not necessarily a rising up of all the dead, but at least of some of them. From Dan. 12.2 onwards this became a standard part of the apocalyptic hope: Many of them that sleep in the dust of the earth shall arise. Views of the fate of the wicked varied; see D. S. Russell (*The Method and Message of Jewish Apocalyptic*, 1964, 369–74). To proclaim a universal resurrection would require the omission of ἐκ, and would be clarified by the addition of πάντων (or of δικαίων τε καὶ ἀδίκων, as at 24.15). It would be understandable that the Sadducees (cf. v. 1 and 23.8) should be vexed by such a proclamation, though they would be used to hearing it from the Pharisees. As Maddox (40) remarks, Luke distinguished between the Pharisaic attitude to Torah (which he thinks wrong) and the Pharisaic attitude to eschatology (which he thinks right). But what of ἐν τῷ 'Ιησοῦ? Conzelmann's view that these words are simply placed first for emphasis is hardly adequate to explain the construction. The simplest and probably the best way of understanding this is to take ἐν as instrumental: They were proclaiming *by means of* (the story of) Jesus the resurrection . . . Quorum [Sadducaeorum] error unico exemplo . . . refutabatur penitus (Bengel). This is not very (but a little) different from the suggestion of Moule (*Origin* 67; cf. Delebecque, 17) that ἐν τῷ 'Ιησοῦ means 'in the case of Jesus'. If this is taken further to mean that '. . . in the case of Jesus the (ultimate) resurrection had taken place' the difference is somewhat greater. That the resurrection of Jesus was the firstfruits of the final resurrection is a NT thought, but it is not clear that Luke entertained it. Turner (*Insights* 153f.) goes further still with the rendering, They proclaimed that 'in Christ shall all be made alive' (1 Cor. 15.22). This can hardly be justified. Luke's language loses clarity because he tries to say several things in one sentence. These may be set out separately as follows.

1. The basic thought is that the Sadducees, who according to Luke (Acts 23.8) did not believe in the resurrection on any terms, were annoyed because the apostles were affirming what they denied.
2. The apostles themselves, whatever their previous convictions may have been, now associated belief in the resurrection with Jesus, whom they knew to have been dead and now believed to be alive. οὕτως ἰσχυρὰ ἐγένετο ἡ ἀνάστασις, ὡς καὶ ἑτέροις αἴτιον γίνεσθαι ἀναστάσεως (Chrysostom).
3. The resurrection of Jesus set the seal on his unique relation with God, and may therefore have carried implications (which Luke had certainly not thought out as Paul did) if not for the rest of mankind at least for his adherents.

D has ἀναγγέλλειν τὸν 'Ιησοῦν ἐν τῇ ἀναστάσει τῶν νεκρῶν — neatly avoiding the difficulty.

Whatever the construction of Luke's sentence may be, the complaint made by the Jewish authorities involves reference to Jesus; yet in v. 13 they seem for the first time to associate the apostles with him. This may be a mark of the editing of more than one source.

3. For ἐπιβάλλειν χεῖρας cf. 5.18; 12.1; 21.27. The expression is not exclusively biblical; see e.g. Polybius 3.2.8. D has ἐπ(ε)ιβαλόντες . . . καὶ ἔθεντο, which suggests a familiar Aramaic construction, and

is not Greek; see Black (*AA* 69). Cf. also h: et injectis manibus et tenuerunt . . . For similar examples see 5.21; 7.4; 8.2; 10.27; 12.16; 13.7; 14.6, 14; 20.10. It would be unwise to conclude that the Western text (and perhaps even the original form of Acts) was based on a Semitic text. Haenchen (68f.) thinks that the construction is to be explained by the influence of the Latin versions (since Latin has no equivalent to an aorist participle active), and mentions 5.23; 7.4; 12.16; 13.29; 14.6, 14; 16.17; 19.19; 20.10 as passages that can be explained in this way; see the note on 7.4. Haenchen does not mention 4.3, but in his note on this verse (213) says that the copyist of D has overlooked the fact that after changing the finite verb into a participle he ought to have dropped the καί. It may be that he was affected by the previous participle, διαπονούμενοι.

BDR § 316.1 n. 2 claim that ἔθεντο (middle instead of active) has classical parallels, and cite Demosthenes 56.4(1284), καταθησόμενος εἰς τὸ οἴκημα. It is not certain how τήρησις should be taken. The context suggests the meaning *put them in prison*, but, as its form implies, τήρησις is usually a *nomen actionis*, and *took them into custody* might be better. Thucydides 7.86.1 (quoted by LS 1789) is not a certain parallel: κατεβίβασαν ἐς τὰς λιθοτομίας, ἀσφαλεστάτην εἶναι νομίσαντες τήρησιν may mean 'thinking this the safest prison', but it could equally mean 'thinking this the safest way of keeping them, the securest custody'. Luke may well mean, 'put them under guard'. Conzelmann (35) quotes Josephus, *Ant.* 18.235 for the same ambiguity, but τήρησις there seems to mean *custody*.

ἑσπέρα: Peter and John were going up to the Temple at the ninth hour, 3 p.m. (3.1). Luke, who has recounted a miracle, a progress into the Temple, the assembling of a crowd, a sermon, the spread of the report to the authorities, and their action, could well suppose that several hours had elapsed. It hardly seems necessary to accuse the narrative of inconsistency at this point.

4. Postponement of the trial till the following day makes it possible for Luke to insert a comment on the further growth of the believing community. For *hearing the word* cf. 2.37 (also 2.41, ἀποδέχεσθαι). In the present verse *hearing* is not in itself the hearing of faith, since *many* (not *all*) of those who (physically) heard *believed*, that is, became believers. Cf. 2.44; at 2.41 the same response is expressed by ἐβαπτίσθησαν; there is no reference to baptism in chs. 3 and 4. Luke had previously reported the number of believers at 2.41; there is now an increase of 2,000.

M.2.173 notes that γίνεται is usual in expressing the result of an arithmetical process; also that 'χίλιοι with numerical adverbs is supplanted after 5,000 by χιλιάδες with cardinal: in Acts 4.4 we have this for 5,000 as well'. In Modern Greek all the thousands are expressed by means of cardinals with χιλιάδες. It is hard to know whether Luke here prefixes to the number ὡς (B D 0165 33 *pc*) as he often does, ὡσεί (E ΨἨ) as he somewhat less frequently does, or omits the qualification altogether (P⁷⁴ ℵ A 81 1175 *pc* vg). The third reading may well be right; copyists made up in different ways what seemed to be lacking.

Only in chs. 2 and 4 are large specific numbers of converts recorded. It is of course highly unlikely that in the first hours and weeks of the church's life anything like precise statistics were kept; it is however fair to note that only here (in ground covered by Acts) is it likely that such large accessions of believers took place, for only in Jerusalem (Galilee is in Acts surprisingly neglected) would there be found considerable numbers of people who had some idea of, and sympathy with, what Jesus had stood for, and needed only such impetus as the events of Pentecost and a supernatural healing could give to bring them over the boundary into the company of believers; and whatever judgment is reached regarding the historicity of these events there can be no doubt that the time was marked by a good deal of religious excitement. Hanson (76f.) defends the number 5,000 as credible, arguing that Jeremias's estimate of the population of Jerusalem (25,000–30,000) is much too small. He refers to Diodorus Siculus 40.3.8; Josephus, *Apion* 1.194, 197; *War* 6.422–5.

ἀνδρῶν if taken strictly would mean that the adult males added up to 5,000, with the possible addition *extra numerum* of women (and perhaps children); cf. Mt. 14.21; 15.38. It is possible that Luke here uses ἄνδρες in the sense of human beings (Bauernfeind 74 translates *Menschen*), but there is in fact no reason to suppose that he gives the word anything but its proper sense. There is no passage in Acts where ἄνδρες can be shown to include women and several times it is coupled with γυναῖκες (5.14; 8.3, 12; 9.2; 17.12; 22.4).

Weiser (126) notes the importance of expansion as a theme running throughout Acts, referring to 2.47; 5.14; 6.1, 7; 8.6, 12; 9.31, 35, 42; 11.21, 24; 12.24; 13.48, 49; 14.1, 21; 16.5, (14f.); 17.4, 11f., 34; 18.8, 10; 19.10, 20; 21.20.

5. Ἐγένετο δὲ ἐπὶ τὴν αὔριον συναχθῆναι recalls the Hebrew construction ...ו...ויהי and attempts by the LXX to render, or to imitate, it. ἐγένετο with the accusative and infinitive occurs frequently in Acts (9.3, 32, 37; 14.1; 19.1; 21.1, 5; 27.44; 28.8, 17); see the full discussions in M. 1.16f.; 2.425–8. D, continuing not with the infinitive but with συνήχθησαν (accompanied by nominatives), may be a conflation of the Old Uncial text with the Western, if the latter is represented by the reading of h (and syᵖ): postero die collecti sunt magistratus, etc. The infinitive leads to a grammatically difficult text (see on v. 6) and is in accord with Lucan style; it should be retained. After τὴν αὔριον, D adds ἡμέραν. This has been held by Chase to derive from Syriac, by Harris from Latin (see Metzger, 317, who compares 20.26; Rom. 11.8; 2 Cor. 3.14).

αὐτῶν (omitted by D, whose copyist may have seen the difficulty) should refer to those just mentioned, the new converts. Since these were Jews those who now assembled could be described as *their* rulers, etc., but this is hardly Luke's meaning. *Their* means *of the Jews*: but this is carelessly expressed. For other examples of an apparent lack of literary revision in Acts see e.g. 3.16; 4.25.

ἄρχοντες: see 3.17. Here they appear with the πρεσβύτεροι and γραμματεῖς as members of the Sanhedrin. The three groups represent correctly what appears to have been the constitution of the Sanhedrin in the Roman period (see *NS* 2.210–18; also E. Lohse in *TWNT* 7.861f.). The Mishnah (see Sanhedrin 4.4) reflects conditions after the end of political independence (or semi-independence) in AD 70; then the Sanhedrin consisted entirely of rabbinic scholars (γραμματεῖς). Πρεσβύτεροι was 'a general designation applicable to both priests and laymen' (*NS* 2.213); cf. 4.23, where γραμματεῖς is omitted, and in place of ἄρχοντες we have ἀρχιερεῖς (which is read instead of ἱερεῖς at 4.1 by B C). This alteration corresponds to the fact that Josephus sometimes has ἄρχοντες, sometimes ἀρχιερεῖς, but never the two together. That they do occur together at Lk. 23.13; 24.20 is probably due to lack of precise knowledge of Jewish institutions on Luke's part; in Acts 4 he is probably guided by his source. It may be taken that the two words have, in this setting, substantially the same meaning. ἀρχιερεῖς (see further on 4.23, and cf. v. 6) has been understood to mean *members of highpriestly families*, i.e., the High Priest together with previous High Priests and members of the noble families from whom the High Priests were drawn. A different view (Jeremias, *Jerusalem* 175–81) is that ἀρχιερεῖς refers to leading priests, especially that group of priests who were more or less permanently on the Temple staff. *NS* 2.236 points out that there may not in practice have been much difference between these two views. Even apart from the nepotism for which there is some evidence it would naturally happen that many Temple appointments would fall into the hands of leading and established families resident in Jerusalem. Undoubtedly Luke is thinking of a meeting of the Sanhedrin, which he describes correctly in the period in which rabbinic (Pharisaic) scholars were finding their way into what had previously been a predominantly Sadducean assembly. Haenchen (214) may be right in the view that Luke does not here mention Pharisees because he is at this stage minimizing controversy about the Law.

συναχθῆναι — in the לשכת הגזית described in Yoma 25a as like a great basilica (כמין בסלקי גדולה). This seems to be the place referred to by Josephus (*War* 5.144, where ξυστός will correspond to גזית; cf. 2.344; 6.354) and by Sanhedrin 11.2; Middoth 5.4; cf. Pea 2.6; Eduyoth 7.4. There is a tradition (Shabbath 15a; Rosh haShanah 31a; Sanhedrin 41a; Abodah Zarah 8b) that forty years before the fall of

Jerusalem (and thus about the time of the crucifixion) the meetings of the Sanhedrin were transferred from the לשכת הגזית to the חנות or חנויות, *shop* or *shops* (*bazaar*). This is accepted by Dalman (*SSW* 294f., 331) but rejected by *NS* 2.224f. on the ground that it 'lacks historical reliability'. No reason is given for this adverse judgment, which may nevertheless be correct.

There seems little point in the addition of ἐν 'Ιερουσαλήμ (hence perhaps its omission by 1838 h syᵖ); where else should the meeting have been held? εἰς 'Ιερουσαλήμ (ℵ 614 945 1241 2495 *pm*), in which εἰς is used for ἐν (see on 2.5), is no different, but may be original; so Ropes (*Begs.* 3.34). It may be that Luke wished to underline the fact that the Gospel was at work, and courageous and effective witness to it was being borne, in the heart of the old religion. The theological significance of Jerusalem at this point is emphasized by Roloff (81).

6. Luke lists the prominent members of the Sanhedrin, abruptly changing the construction of his sentence as he does so; he has forgotten the accusative and infinitive of v. 5 and uses the nominative case. This solecism was almost certainly responsible for the textual variant in v. 5; see above. Up to the destruction of Jerusalem the President of the Sanhedrin was always the High Priest. This is the evidence of Josephus and of the NT as a whole; rabbinic tradition identified the heads of the Pharisaic party with the President of the Sanhedrin, but this is an error (see *NS* 2.215f.). Here however the first name mentioned is that of Annas (in Hebrew, *Ḥanan*; to Josephus, 'Aνάνος), who was not (as Luke claims) High Priest. Cf. Lk. 3.2; Caiaphas had become High Priest in AD 18; according to Jn 18.13 he was Annas's son-in-law. It may be that Luke was simply confused; it may also be that his placing of Annas before Caiaphas and describing him as High Priest reflects a Jewish opinion that Annas, though deposed by the Romans, was still the rightful High Priest. Caiaphas might carry out the functions but could not (in strict Jewish opinion) replace his father-in-law. 'Annas had been High Priest from AD 6–15 (Josephus, *Ant.* 18.26–35) and was succeeded not only by his son-in-law Caiaphas but also by five sons (*Ant.* 20.198), so that Luke and John are doubtless correct in suggesting that he retained great influence, especially since his deposition by the Roman procurator Gratus could have no validity in Jewish opinion' (*St John* 524). According to *Begs.* 4.42, however, there is no evidence that anyone thought like this about a deposed High Priest; the attitude has been invented to account for Luke's mistake. It remains by no means improbable. 'Caiaphas was appointed by the Roman procurator Gratus, probably in or near AD 18; Vitellius, proconsul of Syria, removed from office both Pilate and Caiaphas in AD 36' (*St John* 406). See Josephus, *Ant.* 18.35, 95. Calvin (114) makes the surprising suggestion that the events of ch. 4 happened after Caiaphas had ceased to High Priest; Jonathan was High Priest and bore also the name of his father Annas.

For Ἰωάννης, D and some Old Latin MSS have Jonathan. If this reading is accepted (as by Jeremias, *Jerusalem* 197), the man in question (Josephus, *Ant.* 18. 95, 123) was the son of Annas, who succeeded his brother-in-law as High Priest in AD 37. Jeremias thinks it likely that he was at this time στρατηγὸς τοῦ ἱεροῦ (v. 1), but this may build too much on j. Yoma iii.8.41a.5 (the High priest was not nominated to the office unless he had first been Captain of the Temple). Neither John, if this be the true reading (all other authorities, including some Old Latin MSS, contain it), nor Alexander can be identified.

For the last clause, ὅσοι ἦσαν ἐκ γένους ἀρχιερατικοῦ, see the note on ἄρχοντες (v. 5). Jeremias is probably right in seeing in each verse an equivalent of the ἀρχιερεῖς so frequently mentioned in the NT. After the High Priest and certain named individuals come (as members of the Sanhedrin) the leading priests. 'The captain of the Temple . . . the leader of the weekly course of priests, whichever course was on duty, and the leaders of the four to nine daily courses of this week . . . the seven permanent Temple overseers, to which belonged the four chief Levites . . . three permanent Temple treasurers and their colleagues. The chief priests permanently employed at the Temple formed a definite body who had jurisdiction over the priesthood and whose members had seats and votes on the council' (Jeremias, *Jerusalem* 180). The reference to the γένος ἀρχιερατικόν (cf. Josephus, *Ant.* 15.40, ἦν Ἀνάνηλος ἀρχιερατικοῦ γένους; also 12.387 and *CIG* 4363) testifies to the nepotism practised in the Temple hierarchy. For this see Jeremias (*Jerusalem* 193–7): 'Of the twenty-five illegitimate [i.e., not Zadokite] High Priests of the Herodian-Roman epoch no fewer than twenty-two belonged to these four families: eight from the family of Boethus, eight of Hannas, three of Phiabi and three of Kamith' (194). 'The new hierarchy filled all the chief influential positions in the Temple with their own relations as a matter of course' (197).

7. ἐν τῷ μέσῳ may be used quite generally; but the Sanhedrin 'was arranged like the half of a round threshing-floor so that they all might see one another' (Sanhedrin 4.3). In this setting ἐν τῷ μέσῳ would have a precise sense. The theme of resurrection is now forgotten (Schmithals 49); it may have been Luke's contribution to the narrative. The Sanhedrin is primarily interested in the miracle and its consequences.

ἐν ποίᾳ δυνάμει ἢ ἐν ποίῳ ὀνόματι: ἐν here must be instrumental. ποῖος is used in substantially the same sense as τίς. The meaning 'What kind of?' cannot be stressed. Cf. 23.34; see BDR

§ 298.2. For δύναμις see on 1.8; 3.12; for the use of ὄνομα on 3.6, 16. Here δύναμις is the more general term, denoting supernatural force, capable of overthrowing disease; ὄνομα has the effect of linking this force with a particular person, whose name is invoked in order to set in motion the δύναμις required. The answer is given in v. 10 (cf. 3.6); the invocation of the name of Jesus liberates a δύναμις which is able to cure the diseased. This at least is the view represented by Luke's source; Luke qualifies it in 3.16, and now uses it to lead to the proclamation of the saving name of Jesus (v. 12). It does not seem that the Sanhedrin wish to accuse the apostles of black magic (Bauernfeind 74).

The juxtaposition of the pronouns τοῦτο and ὑμεῖς (lost in the variant of ℵ E, which reverses the order of ἐποιήσατε τοῦτο) is intentional and stresses both (BDR § 277.1). Luke is preparing for vv. 13 (ἀγράμματοι καὶ ἰδιῶται), 14, 22.

8. Πέτρος. For the present John drops out of the story (see v. 13 for his return). It seems that the author has introduced him into a narrative which originally dealt with Peter only. See on 3.1. πλησθεὶς πνεύματος ἁγίου: similar expressions occur at 4.31; 9.17; 13.9. Peter, along with others, was filled with the Holy Spirit on the Day of Pentecost (2.4), and the reader of Acts asks what Luke meant by the subsequent fillings that he mentions. The question may be answered in part in terms of sources. The present incident was probably drawn from a different source from that used in ch. 2; the author of the present source noted here that Peter was filled with the Holy Spirit and was involved in no clash with any earlier incident. Luke may not have noticed the clash (if such it is): it is certain that he did not believe that Peter had been in some way deserted by the Spirit between 2.4 and 4.8; he must have believed that Peter was directed by the Spirit when he uttered the speech of 3.12–26. It is probable that he had in mind (Bauernfeind 75 thinks that it was his chief interest) the promise of Lk. 12.12 (cf. Lk. 21.15, where a similar promise is expressed without reference to the Spirit). In times of special necessity a special endowment of the Spirit was given which enabled the speaker to say the right thing and to say it effectively. Luke had no occasion to theologize about the relation between the Third Person of the Trinity and the Christian life, and probably had no interest in doing so. Bruce (2.99) may be right in distinguishing between πλησθεὶς (a special moment of inspiration) and πλήρης (e.g. 6.5) describing abiding character; but this may make Luke more systematic than he was. Peter's speech here is, according to Luke, inspired, but there is nothing to suggest that it was in any way ecstatic.

ἄρχοντες τοῦ λαοῦ takes up v. 5 (and 3.17), though the combination does not occur elsewhere in the NT. Cf. however *P Eg.*

2, line 6 (ἄ[ρ]χοντες τοῦ λαοῦ). There is no reason to see any literary dependence of either document on the other. Cf. also Acts 23.5 (for the singular, quoting Exod. 22.27). λαός here refers to the Jewish people.

πρεσβύτεροι also takes up v. 5. By adding τοῦ Ἰσραήλ, D E Ψ 𝔐 it sy⁽ᵖ⁾ mae Irˡᵃᵗ Cyp produce a balanced phrase,

Rulers of the people,
Elders of Israel;

but textually this elegance is almost certainly secondary.

Stählin (72) notes the respectful form of address, which suggests that the Christians still feel themselves to be part of the Jewish community.

9. εἰ ἡμεῖς σήμερον, 'cum vi quadam indignationis' (Blass 73). ἀνακρινόμεθα. The word conveys a strong suggestion of legal proceedings; not only *to examine* but *to cross-examine*. This is of course appropriate to the narrative. In the NT cf. 1 Cor. 9.3 (with ἀπολογία, another forensic term, in reply)· cf. also Isaeus 5.32, ἀνακρίναντες δὲ ἡμᾶς πολλάκις καὶ πυθόμενοι τὰ πραχθέντα οἱ διαιτηταί … The word is used (see LS 109: also Schille 134 and *Begs.* 4.43) of magistrates preparing rather than trying a case, and this is suitable to the present context. Having made their investigation the judges see no way of proceeding except by a warning (vv. 16, 17). The addition of ἀφ᾽ ὑμῶν by D E it sy mae Irˡᵃᵗ Cyp is another example of what may be a Semitism in the Western text.

εὐεργεσίᾳ (on the word see A. D. Nock in FS Grant, 127–48; it occurs in an Isis aretalogy (2nd or 1st Century BC) — *ND* 1.10), ἀνθρώπου ἀσθενοῦς. For the genitive cf. Plato, *Laws* 850b, εὐεργεσίαν τῆς πόλεως, service rendered *to* the state. It is of course clear that the genitive cannot be subjective. At 10.38 Luke uses εὐεργετεῖν and ἰᾶσθαι of Jesus.

ἐν τίνι οὗτος σέσωται is epexegetic of ἀνακρινόμεθα: if you are examining us with a view to finding out … ἐν can hardly be taken otherwise than as instrumental. For its use with σῴζειν cf. Euripides, *Heraclidae* 498, ἐν τῷδε κἀχόμεσθα σωθῆναι λόγῳ. This might suggest that τίνι must be neuter and refer to ὄνομα. This it probably does, but for ἐν with a person cf. Sophocles, *Ajax* 519, ἐν σοὶ πᾶσ᾽ ἔγωγε σῴζομαι; Herodotus 8.60α, ἐν σοὶ νῦν ἐστι σῶσαι τὴν Ἑλλάδα. σέσωται is read by P⁷⁴ ℵ A Cyr, σέσωσται by B D E Ψ 0165 𝔐. According to Photius, οἱ παλαιοὶ ἄνευ τοῦ ς; LS 1748 say that σέσωται is according to Photius the Attic form; Veitch (531f.), 'We think it likely that both forms were in use.' Correction would probably go in the direction of what grammarians (rightly or wrongly) alleged to be Attic, and we may therefore prefer as Luke's own text σέσωσται (against NA²⁶, but apparently with BDR § 26 n.)

4; M. 2.260 notes the occurrence of both forms but does not choose between them). σῴζειν is used by Luke in both religious and secular senses, though the two come close together, especially in the present passage (see v. 12), and the secular sense helps to establish the meaning of the word when used in religious contexts. After three 'religious' uses in ch. 2 (2.21, 40, 47) it is employed here for the first time in a 'secular' way. It could be translated *cured*, but there can be no doubt that Luke already has in mind the way in which he will use the word in v. 12. *Salvation* (see I. H. Marshall, *Luke: Historian and Theologian*, 1970, 94–102) is in part a spiritual equivalent to the healing of a lame man. Man, who is spiritually lame and unable to act as it was intended that he should, is so restored as to be able to move and act freely.

10. If you wish to know, then here are the facts. Peter wishes them to be known (γνωστός is characteristic of Acts; see on 2.14) to the whole court (πᾶσιν ὑμῖν) and to the whole people (παντὶ τῷ λαῷ: for the use of λαός see on 2.47; 3.9). Naturally the answer takes the form of the question asked in v. 7. The δύναμις which has undeniably (v. 16) been at work is released by the invocation of the name (see on 3.6, 16) of Jesus, who as at 3.6 is given the full title, Jesus Christ of Nazareth (for Ναζωραῖος see on 2.22).

ὃν ὑμεῖς ἐσταυρώσατε, ὃν ὁ θεὸς ἤγειρεν ἐκ νεκρῶν. That Jesus was crucified by the Jews (or Romans, or both) and raised from the dead by God, is a standard formula in Acts; cf. 2.23f., 36; 3.13–15; 4.27f.; 10.39f.; 13.27–37. It is nowhere expressed so clearly and so briefly as here, where the formula is used not so much for theological purposes as to pin guilt upon the Jews (Schmithals 50): the two relative clauses suggest creed-like formulation (Haenchen 215). According to Stauffer (*Theologie* 222f., 323–5) this 'Petrusformel' was based upon existing OT and Jewish comments on the story of Joseph: see especially as their foundation Gen. 50.20: ὑμεῖς ἐβουλεύσασθε κατ' ἐμοῦ εἰς πονηρά, ὁ δὲ θεὸς ἐβουλεύσατο περὶ ἐμοῦ εἰς ἀγαθά. The contrast ὑμεῖς—ὁδὲ θεός is important; there are, as Stauffer shows, a number of parallels, but it is doubtful whether they are significant. Joseph was an evident example of the power of God to turn the evil machinations of men to his own purposes; he is taken up by Stephen (7.9–16) in this way. But perhaps surprisingly, Stephen makes in this context no more reference to Jesus than Peter does to Joseph, though the story of Jesus could not but focus upon the outstanding reversal of fortune in the resurrection. It is fair to observe (1) that neither Peter nor Stephen points out the analogy, and (2) that if the story of Joseph was in the mind of the early preachers, and indeed in any case, we are presented with the story of Jesus in the form of a tale with a happy ending: Joseph suffered at the hands of his brothers and in the Egyptian prison, but it all came right in the end; Jesus was crucified, but God overcame even this disaster. There is little or nothing to suggest that crucifixion was itself a victory, or that the resurrection meant the eternal presence of the Crucified, or that the death of Jesus was for our sins. This is a correct observation of Luke's simple (but not necessarily primitive, in a chronological sense) theology, but it is not quite the whole truth. On Luke's *theologia crucis* see *FS* Dinkler, 73–84, and the discussion of the theology of Acts in Vol. II.

ἐν τούτῳ: *in this name* or *in this person*? The slightly nearer antecedent is 'Ιησοῦς, but ἐν has been used with ὄνομα (to which τίνι in v. 9 may refer), and this probably determines the meaning. οὗτος of course refers to the lame man.

In vv. 10 and 12 the Western text is in some confusion. The original form of the Western text of v. 10 is probably given by E (ἐνώπιον ὑμῶν σήμερον ὑγιῆς καὶ ἐν ἄλλῳ οὐδενί . . .). Cyprian and h have sanus adstat in alio autem nullo . . . The Harclean margin has a similar reading, and these authorities make a corresponding omission in v. 12. The text of D is conflate. For more detail see Clark (340).

11. οὗτος (cf. v. 10) now refers not to the lame man but to Jesus, though this is the more remote antecedent; of this Zerwick (§ 214) rightly says, "'propinquitas' et "distantia" non grammaticaliter sed psychologice sumenda sit'.

Peter assumes that his hearers (Luke assumes that his readers) will detect the allusion to the OT in what follows.

Ps. 118.22: אבן מאסו הבונים היתה לראש פנה

117.22 (LXX): λίθον, ὃν ἀπεδοκίμασαν οἱ οἰκοδομοῦντες, οὗτος ἐγενήθη εἰς κεφαλὴν γωνίας.
The sentence is adapted to the flow of Peter's argument; in addition, it is cast in the second, not the third person plural, the noun οἰκόδομος is used instead of the participle, and ἐξουθενεῖν (in the passive) replaces ἀποδοκιμάζειν (in the active). Wilcox (51) considers the possibility that Luke used a non-LXX Greek version, Haenchen (215) that he used a testimony book. The passage was familiar in early Christian argument and debate (Mt. 21.42; Mk 12.10, 11; Lk. 20.17; 1 Pet. 2.7; Barnabas 6.4) and Luke could be confident that its significance would not escape his readers; it is surprising however that he does not draw attention to the fact that he is claiming the fulfilment of Scripture. The substance of the couplet reproduces the plain statement of v. 10: Whom you crucified, whom God raised from the dead. The use of OT language shows that what happened did so in fulfilment of God's eternal purpose and the prophetic disclosure of it, and thus provides the basis for theological interpretation. '. . . Alles aus dem Schöpferwillen Gottes stammt' (Schlatter, *Theologie der Apostel* 16), so that there is no room for dualism.

The choice of ἐξουθενεῖν (against the LXX's ἀποδοκιμάζειν) is surprising. Wherever else in the NT there is an allusion to Ps. 118.22 the LXX's word is used (in addition to the passages cited above see Mk 8.31; Lk. 9.22; 17.25; 1 Pet. 2.4), and ἐξουθενεῖν can hardly be called a Lucan word (Mk 9.12 (ἐξουθενοῦν or ἐξουδενεῖν): Lk. 18.9; 23.11; Paul, 8 times). Preuschen's observation that in 1 Kdms אסם is regularly translated by ἐξουθενεῖν does not seem important. The rewording of the Psalm is not Luke's own; it presumably came to him by tradition, and the tradition was not simply that Ps. 118.22 was a 'Christian' text, for if it had been so its text would have been given in the form used in the gospel; the tradition therefore was in all probability a tradition of a speech, or at least was contained in a preaching context. This conclusion is supported, though not very forcibly, by the use of οἰκόδομος rather than the participle of οἰκοδομεῖν. ἐξουθενεῖν shows that a measure of interpretation has been given to the quotation. A stone may be rejected (ἀποδοκιμασθῆναι) by builders as unsuitable for their purpose; it is unlikely to be despised (ἐξουθενηθῆναι). This is a word that suggests the identification of the *stone* with a person.

Roloff (82) draws attention to StrB 1.876, where passages are quoted in which rabbinic scholars are described as builders; this metaphor may have added a little to the force of the image, but the passages quoted are rather late.

On κεφαλὴ γωνίας see Jeremias (*TWNT* 1.793). It appears that the meaning is a *coping-stone*. Cf. Test. Sol. 22.7ff.; Tertullian, *adv. Marcionem* 3.7. The precise sense of the phrase is not important: the despised *stone* has come to occupy the position of greatest prominence and honour — 'whom you crucified, whom God raised from the dead'. It is not likely that we should see here any reference to the building of the church (Eph. 2.20; 1 Pet. 2.4).

12. ἐν ἄλλῳ οὐδενί, *in no other person*. It would be possible to supply ὀνόματι, which would suit the preceding verses, but the clause that follows, introduced by γάρ, deals with *the name*, and the logic of the argument runs: In no other person is there salvation, because there is no other name than that of Jesus by which . . . There is a close verbal parallel in Josephus, *Ant.* 3.23: ἐν αὐτῷ γὰρ εἶναι τὴν σωτηρίαν αὐτοῦ καὶ οὐκ ἐν ἄλλῳ. This suggests that there is little point in an attempt to distinguish between ἄλλος and ἕτερος. There is a parallel in a different setting in Aristophanes, *Lysistrata* 29f., ὅλης τῆς Ἑλλάδος ἐν ταῖς γυναιξίν ἐστιν ἡ σωτηρία, and another in Herodotus 8.118.3, ἐν ὑμῖν γὰρ οἶκε εἶναι ἐμοὶ ἡ σωτηρίη.

The Western text, represented by h Ir^lat Cyp, omits the first clause, καὶ οὐκ . . . σωτηρία, the greater part of it having been used in v. 10 (see the note). D p* omit only ἡ σωτηρία.

In Jesus, then, is salvation. The word σωτηρία occurs six times in

Acts (4.12; 7.25; 13.26, 47; 16.17; 27.34). σῴζειν occurs thirteen times (see on 2.21), σωτήρ twice (5.31; 13.23), σωτήριον once (28.28). Marshall (*Luke* 9) is undoubtedly right in claiming that a (he says *the*) 'key concept in the theology of Luke is "salvation"'. In the present context (and the same could be said elsewhere) the word must be interpreted in the light of secular use. In v. 9 the word σῴζειν undoubtedly means *to cure, to give physical health* (though it will have overtones when thus used by a Christian writer). The noun σωτηρία has a secular sense at 7.25; 27.34, the verb at 4.9; 14.9; 27.20, 31; possibly at 16.30. Such senses are common in Greek; see LS. 1748, 1751 s.vv. The theological sense of the word group can thus be understood only by asking from what theological distress or disability or danger, corresponding to lameness, or the danger of drowning at sea, man needs to be delivered. The basic meaning is provided by 2.40; those who are saved are saved from this perverse generation; that is, they are saved from belonging to this perverse generation and from sharing its fate; they are no longer perverse, and they will not experience the punishment of perversity. A corresponding positive side of σωτηρία consists in attachment to the people of God; see 2.47, the saved, οἱ σῳζόμενοι, are added, as it were, into a common stock, ἐπὶ τὸ αὐτό, and share a common life. Thus the primary meaning of salvation is detachment from the world of the unbelieving and disobedient and attachment to the true people of God of the last days, the ἐκκλησία, the community which is constituted on the one hand by its loyalty to Jesus, and on the other by his gift of the Spirit, which makes possible a new life conformed to the new loyalty and in other ways too (Luke is e.g. interested in the phenomena of inspired speech) manifests its supernatural origin.

This salvation is *in* Jesus. The preposition is not used in the same way as in the Pauline *in Christ*; it is essentially instrumental. Jesus is the agent of salvation, the σωτήρ (5.31; 13.23). Luke however does not explain what Jesus has done in order to effect salvation. He has indeed just spoken (v. 10) of Jesus' crucifixion and resurrection, and would doubtless have agreed that these acts were closely connected with the achieving of salvation, but he nowhere (except possibly at 20.28) attempts to explain how they were connected with it. His emphasis lies rather on the human appropriation of salvation, and this is regularly connected with Jesus (e.g. 2.21, Everyone who calls on the name of the Lord will be saved; calling implies believing, 16.31 (cf. Rom. 10.14) — with Jesus rather than with e.g. circumcision (15.1, 11) as the ground of appeal).

Believing is sometimes connected with baptism (8.12, 13; 11.16, 17; 16.15, 31–3; 18.8; 19.4, 5; cf. 2.38, 41; 22.16), and Bultmann (*Theologie* 136) sees such a connection here. 'Dass die Taufe die unerlässliche Bedingung für den Eintritt in die Gemeinde und die Teilhabe an Heil ist, versteht sich von selbst und ist Act 4.12

wenigstens indirekt ausgesprochen.' *No other name*, it is said, implies *the name of the Lord Jesus Christ*, pronounced in baptism. It must however be borne in mind that there are in the NT, and in Acts, passages where salvation is referred to without any allusion to baptism; that this is one of them; and that in this context the name of Jesus has been specifically related to the cure of a lame man. That is, the name of Jesus constitutes a means by which the saving power of Jesus is invoked and applied. That baptism is a special case of this invocation and application is certainly true, but it is not the only context in which men call on Jesus for salvation. Too narrow a baptismal interpretation of this verse (Roloff 83, e.g., thinks it derived from the Taufgottesdienst) leads to the notion that the name itself, once invoked, is in some way automatically effective; and Luke is at pains to show that this is not so (3.16; 19.13–16; cf. 8.14–17; 18.24–8).

No other name under heaven has such power. Calvin (118), thinking as a theologian, writes that Luke so expresses himself because 'men cannot ascend to heaven to attain to God', and refers to Rom. 10.6. Luke was probably not thinking theologically but uses ὑπὸ τὸν οὐρανόν (as Plato does, *Timaeus* 23c; *Epistle* 7. 326c) as in English one says 'under the sun'. There is no other saving name anywhere. This proposition is complicated by the addition of τὸ δεδομένον, described by Moule (*IB* 103, 106) as 'very odd'. Its oddness is attested by the fact that in a passage probably reflecting this one the *Acts of Philip* (9 (4); L.-B. 2.2.5) assert οὐκ ἔστιν ἕτερον ὄνομα ὀνομασθὲν ἐξ οὐρανοῦ εἰ μὴ τοῦτο. There is no difficulty in ὀνομασθέν, and this brings out the difficulty in δεδομένον. Moule (103) speaks of the possibility of a 'Semitic background ... possibly a misunderstanding of a Semitic participle', but he does not expand the suggestion. Robertson (778 and 1107) notes the presence of the article with the participle but not with the substantive and adds parallels, but offers neither explanation nor translation. Moule suggests *such as is given* and refers to Ps. 113.24 (LXX: = MT 115.16), τὴν δὲ γῆν ἔδωκεν τοῖς υἱοῖς τῶν ἀνθρώπων. BDR § 412.4 think that the articular participle is simply a substitute for the relative clause that would have been used in Classical Greek. This is probably correct. *Given* perhaps means *provided*, as an instrument of salvation. This leads in turn to the question why Luke should write ἐν ἀνθρώποις, *among men*, instead of simply ἀνθρώποις, *to* or *for men*, if the name is given as an instrument of salvation. Schneider (348) may be right in thinking that the prepositional phrase stands 'für den blossen Dativ'. Perhaps ὄνομα is moving in the direction of *person*, a meaning it has at 1.15. Jesus was not simply a useful commodity given to men (as Prometheus gave them fire) but a person who lived among them as the agent of God's salvation. The general meaning of the clause is clear: Jesus

Christ is the only source and ground of salvation available for mankind; but the mode of expression contains obscurities that cannot be cleared up with certainty. Torrey (30) supplies the Aramaic יהיב בבני אנשא, which gives little help; Wilcox's discussion (91f.) is inconclusive.

δεῖ σωθῆναι, again, is not happily expressed. If we are to be saved at all, it must be in this way, for there is no other. This is the meaning, but the protasis is not expressed.

In addition to the variants mentioned above, D has ὃ δεδομένον, which is to be explained by the Old Latin quod datum est. D lat Ir^{lat} omit ἐν before ἀνθρώποις and thus avoid the problem discussed above. For ἡμᾶς, B 1704 pc have ὑμᾶς (the speaker is saved already); sy^p omits.

13. Θεωροῦντες δὲ τὴν τοῦ Πέτρου παρρησίαν καὶ Ἰωάννου. Again (see 3.1) the reference to John has the appearance of having been inserted into a story that did not originally contain it. The behaviour of the two apostles is marked by παρρησίᾳ; on this word see W. C. van Unnik, *De semitische achtergrond van* παρρησία *in het NT*, 1962, and *The Christian's Freedom of Speech in the NT*, 1962, with useful bibliographical references. It originated in the sphere of Greek political life with the fundamental meaning of declaring the whole truth, and the implication of doing so without fear or favour. It was natural that friends should exercise παρρησία towards one another; in different circumstances the cost of practising it might be high. With the cognate παρρησιάζεσθαι it plays a considerable part in Acts: 2.29; 4.13, 29, 31; 28.31 (παρρησία); 9.27, 28; 13.46; 14.3; 18.26; 19.8; 26.26 (παρρησιάζεσθαι), used always (as van Unnik points out) in more or less close relation to preaching the Gospel to Jews, a fact the more striking in the light of the Greek origin of the word. Here of course it refers to the bold openness with which Peter and John address the Council. The Council, observing (present participle) their boldness took note (καταλαβόμενοι, aorist participle) of the fact that they were ἀγράμματοι and ἰδιῶται. In ordinary Greek use, ἀγράμματος means *illiterate*. Xenophon, *Memorabilia* 4.2.20, cited by LS 14, provides a good example: οὐκοῦν ὁ μὲν ἑκὼν μὴ ὀρθῶς γράφων γραμματικὸς ἂν εἴη ἄκων ἀγράμματος; Cf. Plutarch, *Apophth. Reg.* 186A, the man who voted for the ostracism of Aristides was ἄνθρωπος ἀγράμματος καὶ ἄγροικος. The opposite of ἀγράμματος is (in classical usage) γραμματικός. ἰδιώτης is in the first instance *the private man* who as such stands over against the state (the res *publica*); hence *the plebeian*; hence *the unskilled person* who stands over against the expert in any art, *the layman* (over against, e.g., the doctor). Cf. e.g. Thucydides 2.48.2; Plato, *Laws* 830a, where it is clear that the ἰδιώτης is not in a general sense an ignorant person but one who in a particular field is not a professional. It needs further development to reach *the ignoramus*. None of the meanings cited is entirely suitable to the present context. Bengel's "Ἀγράμματος est rudis, ἰδιώτης rudior' is neat but not satisfactory. For ἀγράμματος, the opposite word would be not the γραμματικός but (in NT usage) the γραμματεύς: hence, a man without scribal training in the law. The ἰδιώτης would not be greatly different: one who did not practise in the court — to lawyers, a layman. The pair of words suggest composition in Greek. The word ἰδιώτης was borrowed into Hebrew as הדיוט. It means an unskilled workman; see e.g. Sanhedrin 10.2; Moed Katan 1.8 (He that is not skilled (the הדיוט) may sew after his usual fashion, but the craftsman may make only irregular stitches). Dodd (*The Interpretation of the Fourth Gospel*, 1953, p. 82) renders the whole phrase in Hebrew as בור והדיוט, but בור ('uncultivated, an uncultured person, mannerless, ruffian', Jastrow 148b) is not really an equivalent of ἀγράμματος. See e.g. Aboth 2.6. Peter and John were laymen, conducting their own defence. Plümacher (22) notes a contrast between this verse and 4.19; 5.29, which recall Socrates; but Socrates in his defence hardly represented himself as a professional lawyer. Peter and John were laymen, yet they spoke with παρρησία (as, we may note, Socrates had done). And the lawyers were surprised, ἐθαύμαζον. They also *recognized* them; this is probably the meaning of ἐπεγίνωσκον (it is attested from the time of Homer — LS 627). If this is so the construction is not properly described as prolepsis, for the accusative αὐτούς is a genuine object to the verb and is not simply the subject of the ὅτι clause anticipated: Luke is saying two things, which he runs into each other. If separated, they are: They recognized them; they recognized that they had been companions of Jesus. Recognition at this point is surprising in view of v. 2, which suggests that it had been known from the beginning that Peter and John had been connected with Jesus, in whom they were now proclaiming the resurrection of the dead. V. 13 probably belongs to Luke's narrative source, according to which it was the miracle, not the preaching, that provoked the authorities. For the wording cf. Lk. 22.56.

καὶ ἰδιῶται is omitted by D, for no apparent reason — conceivably out of respect for the apostles, but ἀγράμματοι remains. MSS are divided between δέ and τε after ἐπεγίνωσκον. δέ is preferable as serving to introduce a parenthesis, but τε is a specially common word in Acts and may well be original. See BDR §§ 443.2. n. 4; 447.1b.

Justin, *1 Apol.* 39 may show knowledge of this verse, saying of the twelve men who went out from Jerusalem into the world that they were ἰδιῶται, λαλεῖν μὴ δυνάμενοι). Cf. also Origen, *c. Celsum* 1.62; *Clem. Recogn.* 1.62.

14. It is promised in Lk. 21.15 that disciples on trial will be given such wisdom that their adversaries will be unable *to gainsay* it (ἀντειπεῖν). The use of the same verb in the present verse is an allusion to the promise and a claim that it has been fulfilled. Both ἀντειπεῖν and the use of ἔχειν with the meaning *to be able* are well illustrated by Aeschylus, *Prometheus Vinctus* 51, οὐδὲν ἀντειπεῖν ἔχω; also Aristophanes, *Plutus* 485f., ἢ τί γὰρ ἔχοι τις ἂν δίκαιον ἀντειπεῖν ἔτι; Delebecque (19) has 'réellement guéri' to bring out the force of the perfect participle τεθεραπευμένον.

Before ἀντειπεῖν, D h add ποιῆσαι ἤ — possibly noting the fact that though the court does say something (v. 18) it is unable to do anything (v. 21).

15. συμβάλλειν is a Lucan word (Lk. three times; Acts 4.15; 17.18; 18.27; 20.14; nowhere else in the NT). It may therefore hint at Lucan rewriting of the story, but the exclusion of the apostles from the Court's private discussion of the case is a natural part of the narrative. The word when it means *to hold a discussion* often has λόγους or some other word as object (e.g Euripides, *Phoenissae* 693, θέλω πρὸς αὐιὸν συμβαλεῖν βουλεύματα.

16. This verse states the Sanhedrin's problem. There is no denying that a supernatural act of healing has taken place, and public opinion will not stand persecution of the agents. By their rejection of Jesus the authorities feel themselves committed to rejection of his followers, but the miracle has put them in an impossible position. For γνωστός see on v. 10; it is very characteristic of Acts. The word here is often translated *notable*, but Pallis (53) is right in pointing out that this is not its meaning. There is however no need to conjecture σωστός (which is virtually unknown in ancient Greek; though cf. σῶς). It is a *publicly known* sign; no one is in any doubt about that. κατοικεῖν is also characteristic of Acts (Acts, 20 times; Rev., 13 times; rest of the NT, 11 times).

For φανερόν, D has φανερώτερόν ἐστιν, 'comparative for elative superlative... *extremely obvious*' (M. 3.30; so also M. 1.236, adding 10.28 D). This mitigates the repetitiveness of γνωστόν ... φανερόν.

17. The Sanhedrin can do nothing about the past but it will do its best to prevent further damage in the future. At the beginning of the verse ἀλλά corresponds to μέν in v. 16 (Schneider 350). ἐπὶ πλεῖον is taken by Conzelmann (37) in a temporal rather than a spatial sense, but the verb διανέμειν (cf. 2 Tim. 2.17, νομὴν ἕξει) suggests dividing up and distributing, quite possibly of or over a territory. Of course, both space and time are in mind: the Christian movement is to spread no farther, gain no more members, and thus come to an end. 'The Christian movement' conjectures a subject for διανεμηθῇ;

publicity for the sign, or the message about Jesus, are possible alternatives.

In order to put an end to their work the authors of the disturbance must be *threatened* with the consequences of further action on their part. ἀπειλησώμεθα is read by P⁷⁴ᵛⁱᵈ ℵ A B D 33 323 614 945 1739 *pc* lat; to this ἀπειλῇ is prefixed by E Ψ 𝔐 (it) syʰ. It is hard to accept this addition (against the combination of ℵ B D), yet not easy to know why late copyists should introduce what is at least a secondary Semitism. See M. 1.75f., 245; 2.443; BDR § 198.6. There are Greek parallels, but they are not numerous, and on the whole it seems likely that NT occurrences bear witness if not to Hebrew originals at least to imitation of the LXX. It is more likely that a Western reviser saw fit to introduce a characteristic emphasis in a 'biblical' manner than that he was in touch with a Semitic source.

18. It is clear that the Western text began by stating the conclusion of the Sanhedrin's discussion: συνκατατιθεμένων δὲ αὐτῶν τῇ γνώμῃ (D), consentientibus autem ad sententiam (d h). After this D presents what can only be regarded as a corruption: παρηγγειλαντοκατατομη ... NA²⁶ give the first word as παρηγγείλαντο, but this verb is not used in the middle (no example is quoted in LS 1306), and it is better to suppose that the scribe of D agreed with all other witnesses in writing παρήγγειλαν, and then through oversight and inattention wrote the meaningless τοκατατο in place of τὸ καθόλου. These two words appear in P⁷⁴ ℵ¹ A E Ψ 𝔐; καθόλου alone in B ℵ*. If τό is read it should according to M. 3.142 be taken with the infinitive φθέγγεσθαι, according to BDR § 399.3.n.5 (cf. § 160.2.n.3) with καθόλου. In fact the article should be taken both with the adverbial accusative and with μή and the infinitive after a verb of preventing (BDR § 399 quote Plato, *Phaedo* 117c, οἵ οἱ τε ἦσαν κατέχειν τὸ μὴ δακρύειν). For τὸ καθόλου cf. Ezek. 13.3; Dan. 3.50 (Theodotion); Test. Gad 5.5.

The apostles are summoned (for καλέσαντες, D has φωνήσαντες; hardly an improvement) and ordered not φθέγγεσθαι or διδάσκειν in the name of Jesus. The infinitives are present; they are ordered to stop what they are now doing. φθέγγεσθαι occurs nowhere else in Acts (elsewhere in the NT only 2 Peter 2.16, 18); in the NT ἀποφθέγγεσθαι occurs only at Acts 2.4, 14; 26.25. The compound verb as used in Acts suggests inspired utterance not only in the Pentecost narrative of ch. 2 but also in ch. 26; Festus alleges that Paul is mad but Paul replies that though he may seem to speak in an 'inspired', enthusiastic, way he is nevertheless speaking words marked by truth and reason. The simple verb means essentially *to utter sounds*. Here it must mean more than that; the question to be asked is whether it is a synonym of διδάσκειν or adds a different thought. It seems on the whole likely that the Council is seeking to forbid both public proclamation, such as we have seen exemplified in chs. 2 and 3, and the private teaching of individuals and small groups. Both are attached to the name of Jesus, and there is nothing to suggest that they have different contents as well as different settings.

ἐπί with ὄνομα, as in v. 17.

19. D, retaining the plural finite verb εἶπον, uses a singular participle: ἀποκριθεὶς δὲ Πέτρος καὶ 'Ιωάννης. This invited grammatical correction, but is in line with the way in which Peter and John have been presented earlier in chs. 3 and 4; it may well be original and therefore need not mean that D wished to exalt Peter (as Metzger 320 thinks). There is an interesting parallel in 14.14 (see the note).

The reply made by Peter and John is that the command they have been given is one that cannot be observed; members of the Council may judge for themselves. If the disjunction (μᾶλλον ἤ) is accepted the Council must of course accept the conclusion that it is God who must be obeyed. Of the construction Black (AA 117) writes, 'Especially and idiomatically Semitic is the use of παρά or ἤ = *min* in an exclusive sense, e.g. Acts 4.19; 5.29 ("one must obey God, *not* (ἤ) man").' Black adds references to Rom. 1.25; Lk. 18.14; Gen. 38.26 (LXX). It is however hard to accept that there is a Semitism here in view of the parallel with the famous saying of Socrates, reported in Plato, *Apology* 29d, as πείσομαι δὲ μᾶλλον τῷ θεῷ ἤ ὑμῖν. The wording is closer to Acts 5.29 than to the present verse but the grammatical construction is the same in each place. ἀκούειν is used in a sense that is more Hebrew than Greek (for שמע often means *to hear and obey, to hear so as to obey*). Luke, who includes reminiscences of Socrates in his account of Paul's visit to Athens (ch. 17), was probably aware of the famous words of Socrates, which had indeed become a commonplace. See e.g. Plutarch, *Convivium VII Sapientum* 7(152C), τίς δ'ἄν, ἔφη, σοὶ τοῦτο πεισθείη ἤ τῷ θεῷ; Epictetus 1.30.1, ἐκείνῳ σε δεῖ μᾶλλον ἀρέσκειν ἤ τούτῳ; Livy. 39.37, vos ... timemus, sed plus et veneremur et timemus deos immortales. See also Sophocles, *Antigone* 450–460. Cf. Plümacher (19). Josephus, *Ant.* 17.159; 18.268 show that the thought was taken up also in Hellenistic Judaism; here however it must be borne in mind that the principle is to be found also in the OT. Obedience to God's command is of overriding importance; see e.g. 1 Sam. 15.22f.; Jer. 7.22f.; 2 Macc. 7.2; 4 Macc. 5.16–21. The reply from the Sanhedrin's side would be to question the disjunction made by Peter and John; how should God issue commands to a Jew if not through the highest authority in Israel? Surely the Jewish layman will obey God by obeying the council, as it interprets Torah. This in turn invites reply.

20. Peter and John appeal to what they have seen and heard. They refer presumably to the crucifixion and resurrection (of which they are appointed witnesses) and to the teaching of Jesus, rather than to the miracle. To them, these constitute the word and commandment of God, and if the Council disagrees, so much the worse for the Council. The pronoun ἡμεῖς makes the sentence emphatic: Whatever you may think of the matter, this is where *we* stand. The double negative οὐ δυνάμεθα ... μὴ λαλεῖν represents a strong affirmative: We must at all costs speak. Curiously, μή is omitted by D*. Probably this is merely an accidental error, but the same mistake occurs in d. As in v. 18, the present infinitive is used: We cannot stop speaking. Cf. Amos 3.8. Delebecque (20) notes that the construction should be μὴ οὐ λαλεῖν, but that οὐ is sometimes omitted, as at Thucydides 3.41.

21. There was nothing to do but repeat the threats of v. 18 (understood in the light of v. 17, ἀπειλησώμεθα); προσ- in composition signifies (among other things) addition: they added to the threats they had already uttered. They threaten and do no more; Bauernfeind 72 refers to the 'überraschende Friedfertigkeit des Synedriums'.

μηδέν is an accusative of respect: the Council let Peter and John go because (causal participle) they found no way in which ... (μὴ εὑρίσκοντες αἰτίαν, D p syᵖ mae bo, is the same in construction and sense). τὸ πῶς: the indirect question is substantivized by the article, a classical construction used in the NT only by Luke and Paul (so BDR § 267.2). The verb follows in the subjunctive, κολάσωνται; the middle (B has κολάσωσιν, active) suggests *have them punished* (see LS 971 s.v. 2). Punishment was impossible διὰ τὸν λαόν, because of the crowd (for λαός see on 4.25): they were glorifying God because of the event and would not have accepted punishment for those who were responsible for it. This means that it is impossible to infer from μηδὲν εὑρίσκοντες that the Council had decided that the Christian preaching was legitimate. Jeremias (*ZNW* 36, (1937), 208–13) explains differently the inability of the Council to take stronger action. Peter and John were recognized as uneducated men (v. 13), who therefore could not be expected to know in advance the consequences of their actions; they could be punished only if, after warning and explanation of what must ensue, they repeated their offence. No doubt it is possible that both reasons may have played a part in the Sanhedrin's discussion of the matter, but the legal consideration is not brought out as it probably would have been if Luke had been aware of it. 'Luke has not taken much trouble to penetrate the mysteries of rabbinical jurisprudence, or to help his readers to penetrate them. Thus it is true to say that Luke's presentation does not perfectly correspond to the way in which Jeremias reconstructs the events from the text' (Dupont, *Sources* 45).

22. According to Roloff (84) this verse may be taken as supplying the original close of the narrative of 3.1–10. ἐτῶν γὰρ ἦν πλειόνων τεσσεράκοντα. The man was of more years (genitive of definition) than forty (genitive of comparison — τεσσεράκοντα is indeclinable, so that there is no need to quote Aristophanes' πλεῖν ἑξακοσίους (*Birds* 1251) by way of comparison). See M. 3.216; Moule (*IB* 38, 42). On the tense of γεγόνει (ℵ A E Ψ 𝔐 have the correct pluperfect form, ἐγεγόνει) see BDR § 347.1. The sense is that of the aorist, but there is also an element of lasting result; the effect of the cure remained. The aorist is, as it were, combined with an imperfect.

The age of the cripple makes his cure particularly striking, but Luke can hardly have intended to suggest (as his words, especially γάρ, do) that the people might not have been glorifying God had he been only twenty — another example of inadequately revised language, though not this time of grammatical carelessness.

In τὸ σημεῖον τοῦτο τῆς ἰάσεως, τοῦτο is omitted by D gig p Ir^lat; this may well be original; so Ropes, *Begs.* 3.40.

9. RETURN OF PETER AND JOHN 4.23–31

(23) When they had been released they came to their own people[1] and reported what the chief priests and elders had said to them. (24) They, when they heard it, together lifted up their voice to God and said, 'Master, thou who didst make heaven and earth and sea, and all the things that are in them, (25) who, by the mouth of our father David, thy servant, through the Holy Spirit, didst say,[2] Why did the Gentiles behave insolently and the peoples make vain plans? (26) The kings of the earth stood there[3] and the rulers were gathered together against the Lord and against his Christ. (27) For of a truth in this city Herod and Pontius Pilate, with the Gentiles and peoples of Israel, were gathered together against thy holy Servant Jesus, whom thou didst anoint, (28) to do the things which thy hand and thy counsel foreordained should happen. (29) And now, Lord, look upon their threats, and grant thy servants to speak thy word with all boldness, (30) as thou stretchest out thy hand for healing and signs and portents happen through the name of thy holy Servant Jesus.' (31) And when they had made their prayer, the place in which they were assembled was shaken, and they were all filled with the Holy Spirit and continued to speak the word of God with boldness.

Bibliography

M. Dibelius, *ZNW* 16 (1915), 113–26.

F. G. Downing, *NTS* 28 (1982), 546–59.

J. Dupont, *Études*, 521f.

J. A. Emerton, as in (1).

D. Flusser, *Entdeckungen*, 32–9.

P. W. van der Horst, as in (6).

J. E. Ménard, as in (7).

C. F. D Moule, as in (7).

R. Rimaud, *MD* 51 (1957), 99–115.

[1]*Begs.*, their friends; NJB, the community.
[2]We may suppose that this is what Luke intended; it is not an exact rendering of the Greek, which is virtually untranslatable.
[3]*Begs.*, stood by; RSV, set themselves in array; NJB, take up position.

Commentary

Even though the story continues in ch. 5 this paragraph marks the climax of the narrative that began at 3.1 and we may look to it for a summary of what Luke intended the whole to convey. Peter and John may have seemed to be acting on their own; in truth however they are acting in relation to and on behalf of their own people (οἱ ἴδιοι, v. 23) who support them and must be informed of what has happened, and what has thereby appeared concerning the relation between the new community (represented by Peter and John) and the Jewish authorities (the chief priests and elders). When this is done, the whole group (if this means only the Twelve, the Twelve represent the whole Christian body) engage in prayer in such a way as to restate their (Luke's) view of the matter. Their God is the God of Judaism and of the OT, who inspired David to say what he said in the Psalms. Their God is the Creator (v. 24) and also the Lord of history (vv. 25b, 26, quoting Ps. 2.1, 2; vv. 27, 28, applying the Psalm); in comparison with him, Herod and Pontius Pilate, with their Gentile and Jewish supporters, are mere puppets who do only what they are allowed, or indeed are compelled, to do. They have collaborated in action against Jesus (v. 27), but the fact that these rulers were able to do no more than God permitted, and that the disciples prayed that more signs and portents might be done in the name of Jesus (v. 30), clearly implied that the crucified Jesus was now alive. Finally, to the accompaniment of supernatural portents (v. 31), the Spirit is given, with the usual result of inspired speech. Thus Luke makes it clear, not for the last time, that attacks upon the church and its message result only in further Christian expansion.

That the outline of this concluding paragraph comes from the same source or sources, or line of tradition, as that which precedes, is shown by the narrative connection and by the repetition of the word παῖς (v. 27, an important indication of the fact that Luke does not take the word in itself to mean the Messiah), though the word is used of David (v. 25) as well as of Jesus, so that it cannot be held to contain an exclusive reference to Isa. 53 and the Song of the Suffering Servant. παῖς has the effect of linking the prayer with the speech of 3.12-26, which we have seen not to have been originally connected with the miracle of 3.1–11. Luke inserted the speech into a narrative sequence, adapting it and making clear that in the miracle itself and in what followed ὄνομα was not to be understood in a magical sense. The question that remains is whether Luke himself wrote the prayer or derived it from old liturgical tradition. It is likely that the narrative source gave him a cue by saying that when Peter and John returned, after their release, the whole company offered prayer. A relatively late origin for the prayer as it stands is suggested by its appeal to God as creator and the use of Scripture to minimize the authority of earthly rulers; we may probably add its use of παῖς, for though this is often regarded as an early Christological term it does not appear in the Pauline letters or in the synoptic tradition (except at Mt. 12.8 in the quotation of Isa. 42.1). Luke probably used liturgical models (the use of παῖς may suggest eucharistic prayers) current in his own time (see especially the great prayer in 1 Clement, referred to below), adapting them to suit his own purpose. This view is held, for example, by Wilcox (69–72) and by Roloff (85f.); there is much to be said for the view of Schneider (355) that what Luke drew on was essentially Christological material; it may not yet have been given liturgical form. We have then a narrative sequence, which Luke may have had in written form, describing a miracle performed by Peter and John (perhaps originally by Peter only) which resulted in the appearance of the miracle workers before the Jewish court and their subsequent release. Into this Luke has inserted material from the preaching tradition that he possessed, and a prayer, probably based on current use but adapted to the circumstances. His final note (v. 31) is intended to show God's approval of what his people are doing. There are supernatural portents, a renewed gift of the Holy Spirit, and, notwithstanding threats, the disciples continue their witness with that boldness (παρρησία) that had already impressed the Jewish Council (4.13). Thus it is affirmed that Peter and John did well to heal a sick man; that their proclamation of God's word was as valid as it was effective; and that the work of the church will go forward with God's blessing.

An interest in Christian origins was probably combined with a desire to comfort, exhort, and (by the example of the past) to advise the church of Luke's own day.

23. The story continues as ἀπολυθέντες takes up ἀπέλυσαν (v. 21). Peter and John have been acting not on their own but as representatives of a group to which they now report. οἱ ἴδιοι often (e.g. Sirach 11.34) refers to the members of one's family, one's own people; it expands in meaning to include the members of one's nation (e.g. Philo, *Mos.* 1.177), in particular, fellow soldiers in an army (e.g. Josephus, *War* 1.42). Jn. 13.1 is not a parallel to the present passage; there the expression refers to the disciples but as the property, that is, the followers, of Jesus. They are his men (cf. *Corpus Hermeticum* 1.31, where οἱ ἴδιοι are God's elect). Here the reference is to Peter and John's fellow disciples, their own people in the sense of the Christian family. Cf. 12.12: 24.23. It is not made explicit whether we are to think of the remaining ten apostles, of the group of 120 (1.15), or of the 5,000 (4.4). Some commentators think that only the apostles are intended, but probably a majority view is that the Christian community as a whole is in mind; this is in agreement with Irenaeus 3.12.5 (Peter and John 'returned to the rest of their fellow-apostles and disciples of the Lord, that is, to the church . . . The whole church . . . lifted up their voice to God . . .'). The community 'as a whole', but not necessarily the whole of it; it is probably true that Luke thought of a church gathering such as he himself knew, of a size that could meet in a private house (Schille 138; Weiser 133; Haenchen 223). Verses 29, 30, however, taken with 4.33; 5.12 suggest that the apostles, as leaders in speech and action, are primarily in mind, though this is not to say that other members of the church did not pray for and with them.

The chief priests and elders constitute the Council (somewhat differently described in 4.5, 6). What they had said (the aorist, εἶπαν, as not infrequently, is equivalent to an English pluperfect) is the threat (4.17) and order (4.18) that Peter and John should cease to speak and teach in the name of Jesus. It is clear that the apostles had no thought of obedience to the Council.

24. Two characteristic Western additions (after ἀκούσαντες, D mae add καὶ ἐπιγνόντες τὴν τοῦ θεοῦ ἐνέργειαν; after σύ, D E Ψ 𝔐 gig p sy sa mae Ir^{lat} Lcf add ὁ θεός) fill out the text without adding to its substance.

ὁμοθυμαδόν: see on 1.14. φωνὴν αἴρειν, as at 2.14, but here in prayer, a biblical use. Schille (139) notes that vv. 24b–28 have nothing to do with the situation, which first comes to notice in v. 29, and concludes that Luke is using a traditional prayer text. This is probably correct; note the parallels given below.

δέσποτα. The same address to God is used at Lk. 2.29; at Rev. 6.10 the nominative is used for the vocative. The word is used of God or Christ at 2 Tim. 2.21; 2 Peter 2.1; Jude 4. It occurs not very frequently in the LXX (mostly as the equivalent of אֲדֹנָי, אֲדוֹנַי, most characteristically (except in Proverbs) of God, and in address to God (e.g. Tobit 8.17; Wisd. 11.26; Jer. 4.10; Dan. 9.8, 15, 16, 17 (bis), 19; it does not occur in the Psalms). Not used by Paul, it seems to have been introduced into Christian liturgical use towards the end of the first century (e.g. *Didache* 10.3; 1 Clement 59.4; 60.3; 61.1, 2), and the prayer that follows probably belongs to that setting, not in the sense that it is simply borrowed from an existing liturgy (how fixed liturgies were at this time is unknown; see R. Knopf on the prayers in 1 Clement 59–61, in *HNT* Ergänzungsband 1.137), but in that Luke used the kind of words and phrases that were familiar to him from the church's worship. There must have been many occasions when it seemed that earthly rulers were conspiring against the Christians, and words such as those of vv. 24–8 would seem appropriate; it was easy to add (vv. 29, 30) clauses that would bring them into specific relation with the particular circumstances of Acts 3 and 4.

God, addressed as δέσποτα, is defined (for σὺ ὁ Bauernfeind refers to Norden, *Agnostos Theos*, 1913, 201ff.; it is a liturgical form) as creator — a comforting thought for those persecuted by earthly rulers. The words recall many OT passages (in addition to the creation narratives). The closest (because of the participial construction) is Ps. 146 (145).6: τὸν ποιήσαντα τὸν οὐρανὸν καὶ τὴν γῆν, τὴν θάλασσαν καὶ πάντα τὰ ἐν αὐτοῖς. See also Isa. 37.16; 2 Esdras 19.6; 3 Macc. 2.2; Rev. 10.6; 14.7; Josephus, *Ant.* 4.40 (and cf. *War* 3.402, where he uses very similar language about Vespasian). The theme of creation plays an important part in early Christian prayer; so e.g. Did. 10.3; 1 Clement 59.2; Justin, *Trypho* 41; 1 *Apology* 65. Cf. Delling (*Studien* 404, 413).

25. In the majority of MSS the opening words of the verse run ὁ διὰ στόματος Δαυὶδ (τοῦ) παιδός σου εἰπών; there is no difficulty here, or in the same words with the addition after ὁ of πνεύματι ἁγίῳ, or in what appears to have been the Western text, ὃς διὰ πνεύματος ἁγίου διὰ τοῦ στόματος ἐλάλησας Δαυεὶδ παιδός σου. This appears in D, except that D, probably by accidental error, has λαλήσας (d has locutus est); Irenaeus (*Haer.* 3.12.5) has substantially the same reading. These words introduce the quotation from Ps. 2, claiming that the Psalm was written by David who was inspired by the Holy Spirit. This is no doubt also the meaning of the text of P⁷⁴ ℵ A B E Ψ 33 323 (945) 1739 *al*; but it is impossible to make a satisfactory analysis of the sentence as contained in these MSS. Torrey (17) suggests a simple misreading of Aramaic היא as הוא, היא די אבונא, '*that which* our father . . .', being taken as הוא די אבונא, ὁ τοῦ πατρὸς ἡμῶν. Torrey reconstructs the Aramaic text as הוא די אבונא לפום רוחא די קודשא דוד עבדכא אמר, That which our father, thy servant David, said by (or, by the command of) the Holy Spirit. It will be noted that Torrey's English translation alters the order of the words in his conjectured Aramaic and also paraphrases the unusual 'mouth of the Holy Spirit', for which 1 Chron. 12.23 (which he quotes) is an inadequate parallel (as is Theocritus 7.37, where στόμα appears to mean *mouthpiece*). M. 2.474 cites Torrey's proposal but passes no judgment on it. It is discussed by Wilcox (146f.), who concludes that Torrey's case has not been made out. His most important observations are (a) that the quotations in the prayer are in agreement with the LXX, which suggests use of a Greek rather than an Aramaic source; (b) that the idiom היא די would be more natural in Syriac than in Aramaic, where one would expect either ד alone or מד; (c) that Torrey's solution would destroy the parallelism of ὁ ποιήσας (v. 24) and ὁ . . .εἰπών. Wilcox notes that Torrey gives practically no consideration to the complicated textual evidence (see above) and is inclined to suggest textual corruption — as did Hort, who observed that 'if τοῦ πατρός is taken as a corruption of τοῖς πατράσιν, the order of words in text presents no difficulty, David (or the mouth of David) being represented as the mouth of the

Holy Spirit' (*Notes* 92). Clark (340f.) sees two 'roving variants', διὰ πνεύματος ἁγίου and τοῦ πατρὸς ἡμῶν. It is hard to doubt that the difficult text of the Old Uncials takes us as near to the original text as we can get (the alternatives being alleviations of the difficulty), but it is equally hard to believe that it is what Luke intended, even if it is what he wrote. H. W. Moule (*ExpT* 51 (1939–40), 396) suggested that the difficult text is a combination of three alternative ways of introducing the quotation: (1) ὁ διὰ πνεύματος ἁγίου εἰπών; (2) ὁ διὰ στόματος Δαυειδ [τοῦ] παιδός σου εἰπών (this is suggested by Preuschen as the original text); (3) ὁ διὰ στόματος τοῦ πατρὸς ἡμῶν Δαυειδ εἰπών. This leaves us asking why Luke left his copyists the task of sorting out or combining his intentions, but may well be on the right lines. Dibelius (90; cf. Schille 140) notes that the text is improved by the omission of the Holy Spirit, and suggests the conclusion that the original text 'may have been influenced by a view which might be called a theology of the Holy Spirit'.

We should note that David is described as God's παῖς, just as (in Acts 3 and 4) Jesus is. The word is therefore not an exclusively Christological designation. David is occasionally referred to in the OT as God's παῖς; e.g. 1 Chron. 17.4. If we take the text in its full form we note that God in Scripture spoke both by the mouth of a man, David, and through the Holy Spirit.

The prayer, which in several respects recalls the prayer of Hezekiah in Isa. 37.16–20, opens with the quotation of Ps. 2; in v. 25b, v. 1 is quoted, in v. 26 the second verse follows. Each is quoted in exact agreement with the LXX. The Rabbis seem to have understood the Psalm to refer to Gog and Magog; e.g. at Berakoth 10a it is referred to as the פרשה of Gog and Magog. The same two verses are quoted at the end of the first column of 4Qflor in a way probably closer to the use made of them here; unfortunately only fragments at the beginning of column 2 are preserved, but it is clear from 1.19 that the Qumran text understood the Psalm to refer to the true members of Israel and the attacks upon them made by the nations (עם ... is almost certainly the end of גוים). Those attacked are the Elect Ones of Israel; the construct plural בחירי is one of the words fully preserved. It is possible that they were also described as God's anointed ones, for in the quotation of 'against his Anointed (singular, the Messiah)' the noun falls in a lacuna, and (in view of the interpretation) it is possible that the MS read not משיחו but משיחיו. For the collective interpretation see Delling, *Kreuzestod* 157, n. 505. Delling may be right in the view that 'Lukas hat wohl zumindest die Verwendung von Ps. 2.1f. aus dem palästinischen Christentum übernommen, vermutlich auch die Deutung;' we should however remember the connection with his gospel that appears in v. 27, and the use of the LXX (though Luke's use of the available translation does not in itself mean that the use of the Psalm was redactional, as Lüdemann, 63, thinks).

ἐφρύαξαν translates רגשׁו, the meaning of which is disputed (*conspire*, or *behave tumultuously*). The meaning of the Greek verb, which as a rule is used in the middle, is clear. It suggests a haughty, insolent, abusive attitude. It is used in the plural because the neuter plural ἔθνη means people, indeed (v. 27) two particular people. These are Gentiles, and it is therefore natural to suppose that in the second line λαοί (לאמים, usually foreign peoples) refers to Israel, as it clearly must in v. 27. Since Luke (as that verse shows) has Israel in mind, the plural must have been an embarrassment to him. There is no parallel to it in Acts, nor is there much to support the view that in v. 27 λαοὶ Ἰσραήλ means the tribes of Israel. Calvin (126) thinks of the 'diversity of countries from which the Jews came together to the feast', but this is unconvincing. The plural must mean that Luke (or possibly a source) was using the LXX (not a Semitic document) and did not wish to alter it, even in v. 27, though he was giving the Psalm a meaning it did not have in the Hebrew. Elsewhere he was not under this constraint and used the singular for Israel.

ἐμελέτησαν κενά (א A D spell καινά, but this is only an orthographical variant) translates יהגו־ריק which perhaps means *to mutter empty threats*; the Greek suggests rather *to contemplate*, or *make, vain plans*. The main point is clear: neither Gentiles nor rebellious Israel will be able to thwart the plans of God.

26. By 'the kings of the earth' the Psalm generalizes; for Luke they are Herod and Pontius Pilate. παρέστησαν is a surprising rendering of יתיצבו; here it must mean not that *they stood beside* but that *they stood up against* (κατὰ τοῦ κυρίου). οἱ ἄρχοντες recalls, and was no doubt intended to recall 4.5, as well as Lk. 23.13, 35; 24.20. ἐπὶ τὸ αὐτό is a Lucan expression (see e.g. 2.47) but it cannot here be described as a Lucanism; it is drawn from the Psalm (where it translates יחד).

In this verse ὁ κύριος (the Lord God) is clearly distinguished from ὁ Χριστὸς αὐτοῦ (his, the Lord's, Messiah). It is wrong to suppose that whenever ὁ κύριος is used as a title of Christ it must identify him with the God of the OT.

27. Luke picks up the word συνήχθησαν as the most suitable for introducing his interpretation of the Psalm. Neither Herod (Antipas) nor Pilate was a king, but each was a ruler. Pilate undoubtedly represented the Gentiles; Herod might have wished to be regarded as a Jew, but Luke probably thought of him as a Gentile ruler. One of the few sons of Herod the Great to survive him, Herod Antipas ruled as tetrarch over Galilee; see Lk. 3.1; also H. W. Hoehner (*Herod Antipas*, SNTSMS 17, 1972) and *NS* 1.340–53.

ἐπ' ἀληθείας is a Lucan expression (seven times in the NT; three in Lk., two in Acts — here and at 10.34; also Isa. 37.18, in Hezekiah's prayer): one cannot infer that Luke alone was responsible for the prayer in view of the use of παῖς, which is peculiar to chs. 3 and 4, and therefore peculiar not to Luke but to a source or stratum of his work. For Jesus as παῖς see on 3.13; v. 25 suggests a connection with David ('. . . cujus typus David, nam hic eodem nomine appellatur', Bengel). It is not however a simple equivalent to Christ (Messiah), since God anointed (ἔχρισας; cf. Isa. 61.1) the παῖς and thus made him Χριστός, which presumably he had not previously been. Cf. 2.36 and especially 10.38, ἔχρισεν αὐτὸν ὁ θεὸς πνεύματι ἁγίῳ καὶ δυνάμει; here also Luke probably thinks of this kind of anointing, though he may well place it at the baptism (Lk. 3.21f.). For Pontius Pilate see on 3.13. There is no profound doctrine of the atonement here, but Schmithals (52) exaggerates in the view that Luke's exemplary doctrine of the cross is a counterblow against a 'hyperpaulinische Kreuzestheologie'.

These two came together, along with Gentiles (who carried out the crucifixion — ἄνομοι, 2.23) and with the peoples of Israel (λαοῖς; on this see v. 25; there is some Western support for λαός) in order to crucify Jesus. For the wording cf. Vergil, *Aeneid* 6.706, innumerae gentes populique. It is Luke only (Lk. 23.12) who describes the reconciliation of Herod and Pilate at the time of the crucifixion; there must be some connection between Luke's account of the reconciliation and his use here of Ps. 2.1f. It is not however easy to say what the connection is. Did Luke know of the reconciliation, and invoke Ps. 2 to show that it had been determined by God? Did he know the Psalm as a Messianic prophecy and invent the incident to show that it had been fulfilled? The incident in the gospel is not there brought into connection with the Psalm and it would be unwise therefore to say that Luke invented it in order to demonstrate a fulfilment which he does not trouble to mention. On the other hand there is no other evidence for a quarrel and its resolution. Luke shows some hints of access to the Herod family (Lk. 8.3; Acts 13.1), and it may be that he had heard a story about Herod and Pilate which reflection finally led him to connect with Ps. 2.

28. Luke neatly underlines that though Herod and Pilate no doubt came together in order to do what they thought fit they were in fact tools in the hand of God who used them to carry out his own purposes. Cf. 3.18: God fulfilled the purposes he had previously disclosed through the prophets by means of the ignorance of his people; here he does so by means of Gentile political manoeuvrings.

ἡ χείρ σου: the use of God's *hand* as a means of expressing his instrumentality occurs here and at 4.30; 11.21; 13.11; it may perhaps be regarded as a Lucanism, though there are other examples in the

New Testament and the image is not exclusively biblical; see Pindar, *Nemeans* 8.12, 13, where χείρ and βουλή are combined: βασιλεὺς χειρὶ καὶ βουλαῖς ἄριστος. βουλή (σου after this word is textually doubtful; the evidence is equally divided; fortunately the matter is not important) is undoubtedly a Lucan characteristic (Lk. twice; Acts 8 (7); rest of the NT 3; βούλεσθαι occurs 16(14) times in Lk.-Acts; 21 in the rest of the NT). On the other hand προορίζειν occurs here only in Acts, but it is the word that was needed and is not inconsistent with the view that Luke has edited if he did not write the prayer and its framework as a suitable conclusion for the narrative that begins with the healing of the lame man in ch. 3. Cf. 2.23 (τῇ ὡρισμένῃ βουλῇ; also 17.23, 31); Luke is thinking not of a general determinism but of the special disclosures of God's purpose in the story of Jesus (cf. Barth, *CD* 2.1.521).

29. τὰ νῦν is peculiar to Acts (4.29; 5.38; 17.30; 20.32; (24.25, τό); 27.22) in the NT. Its frequency makes it unlikely that it carries any special emphasis. Here it marks, in the prayer, a turning from the biblical quotation and its fulfilment in the story of Jesus to the recurrence of similar circumstances in the present, which are now brought before God with the petition that he will look upon them and act appropriately on behalf of his people. Such a turning is characteristic of Jewish prayers; see Delling (*Studien* 41). But the expression is common in Greek; Wettstein (480) quotes four occurrences in Sophocles, *Electra* (423, 460, 564, 587), and many others. The break in the prayer does not mean that Luke has up to this point been using a traditional prayer and now continues on his own; he has used traditional Christology (and, we may add, perhaps liturgical tradition) to construct his own prayer throughout (Schneider 355).

ἔπιδε: cf. Lk. 1.25, the only other occurrence of ἐπεῖδον in the NT. The verb is used especially of the gods; e.g. Homer, *Odyssey* 17.487, θεοὶ ... ἀνθρώπων ὕβριν τε καὶ εὐνομίην ἐφορῶντες. When the God of the Bible looks upon a human situation he acts; cf. Exod. 3.7 (quoted at Acts 7.34). For τὰς ἀπειλάς see 4.17, 21. For the use of διδόναι cf. e.g. Lucian, *Deorum Concilium* 2, ἀξιῶ δέ, ὦ Ζεῦ, μετὰ παρρησίας μοι δοῦναι εἰπεῖν. For παρρησία (and παρρησιάζεσθαι) see on 2.29; they are very frequent in Acts. The word (λόγος) of God (or of the Lord) is in Acts a very common term for the Gospel proclaimed by Christian preachers: 4.29, 31; 6.2, 7; 8.14, 25; 11.1; 12.24; 13.5, 7, 44, 46, 48, 49; 15.35, 36; 16.32; 17.13; 18.11; 19.10, 20; there are other passages where λόγος is used with the same meaning but without the genitive of a divine name or corresponding pronoun (e.g. 2.41). δοῦλος (which, as at Lk. 2.29, goes appropriately with δεσπότης) on the other hand is used only here, at 2.18 (in an OT quotation) and at 16.17 (on the lips of the possessed and prophesying girl). It may be that Luke uses δοῦλος here to distinguish Christians from Christ himself, who is God's παῖς (and from OT figures such as David). Preaching is to be continued, if God will make it possible, and is to be uninhibited.

30. Not only is the preaching (cf. 3.12–36) to be continued (4.20), miracle working (as in 3.1–11) is to be continued too. For the metaphorical use of χείρ, God's hand, see on v. 28. For the use of ἐν τῷ cf. 3.26; it seems here to be explanatory of δός in v. 29. God will make possible the bold proclamation of his word by the two actions described by the two infinitives of the ἐν τῷ clause, ἐκτείνειν σε and σημεῖα καὶ τέρατα γίνεσθαι, he is to stretch out his hand, signs and portents are to happen. The two are connected simply by καί but in fact they are related to each other as cause and effect: God stretches out his hand for healing (εἰς ἴασιν) and this means that signs and portents happen. For σημεῖα καὶ τέρατα see 2.22; here healings are primarily intended. These are to be done through the name of Jesus, who is God's servant (see 3. 13), God's holy servant, since he is the one whom God has set apart for his own use. Schmithals (51) points out that the occurrence of *name* in a prayer means that the church has no (magical) control over it and its effectiveness.

The words τὴν χεῖρά σου ἐκτείνειν σε are clear enough, but also, especially with the two pronouns, awkward enough to have given rise to a number of variants. They are given as above by ℵ* 36 104 614 2495 *al.* σου is omitted by B (τὴν χεῖρα ἐκτείνειν σε) and by P⁷⁴ A 1175 *pc* (τὴν χεῖρά σε ἐκτείνειν). σε is omitted by ℵᶜ D E Ψ 𝔐 (τὴν χεῖρά σου ἐκτείνειν) and by P⁴⁵ (ἐκτείνειν τὴν χεῖρά σου). The long text should be read. Hcl.mg. has a note that *name* does not occur in some copies, but no such copies are known.

31. This verse brings to an end the first part of a major section, beginning at 2.1, that Luke has composed with care. It narrows Luke's intention to say (Bauernfeind 81) that its purpose was to comfort persecuted Christians; this may have been in Luke's mind, but as an intention subordinate to that of painting an impressive picture of Christian beginnings. It is intentional that the section ends as it began with the gift of the Spirit, whose presence is shown by physical portents. The fire, noise and wind of 2.2, 3 are matched by the shaking (ἐσαλεύθη) of this verse. The verb is a 'Lieblingswort der LXX' (Haenchen 225, quoting Ps. 114.7; Isa. 2.19, 21), but there are many parallels elsewhere; see Betz (165, quoting e.g. Lucian, *Menippus* 10, ἅπαντα ἐκεῖνα ἐσαλεύετο); also Ovid, *Metamorphoses* 9.782ff.; 15.669-79; Vergil, *Aeneid* 3.89f., Da, pater, augurium atque animis inlabere nostri. Vix ea fatus eram: tremere omnia visa repente . . . Acts 16.26 is somewhat different in that the main interest in the earthquake is its effect in opening the prison doors. As at the beginning of ch. 2 all (see v. 23; it is still not clear whether ἅπαντες means all the twelve apostles or a larger group; Schmithals takes the latter view and thinks that Luke opposes the belief that the Spirit is confined to a special small group) are filled with the Holy Spirit. Luke does not mean to suggest that somehow the Spirit had been lost since 2.4; special 'fillings' took place (e.g. 4.8) on special occasions for special purposes. The result is the fulfilment of the prayer of v. 29. See on that verse for the meaning of παρρησία; it would go too far to take it as implying prophecy or speaking with tongues, but it is not far from this. There is however no ground for the view (Bultmann, *Theologie* 44) that Luke's source ended, καὶ ἐπλήσ-θησαν ἅπαντες τοῦ ἁγίου πνεύματος καὶ ἐλάλουν γλώσσαις.

ἐλάλουν, imperfect; they went on speaking. According to Bauernfeind 80 this refers not to preaching in public but to speech within their own (Christian) circle. This opinion is rightly rejected by Haenchen (225) and Schneider (361). Private instruction would call for no courage and would constitute an anticlimax.

At the end of the verse D E r vg^ms mae Ir add παντὶ τῷ θέλοντι πιστεύειν, a not too intelligent Western addition; they spoke the word to all, and the consequence showed who were and who were not willing to believe. For an ingenious but not convincing explanation of the addition see J. R. Harris, *Four Lectures on the Western Text*, 1894, 89f.

E. Schweizer (*Beiträge* 252f.; *CONT* 24a) distinguishes between this verse and 4.33. All members of the Christian community were filled with the Spirit and spoke the word; the apostles alone proclaimed the resurrection of which they were appointed witnesses. This may be Luke's view (see 13.31, 32, and the general discussion of the apostles in Vol. II); here however we must think of one source that ends at 4.31; in 4.32 Luke makes a new beginning.

10. SHARING AND WITNESSING COMMUNITY 4.32–35

(32) The whole company of those who had become believers had one heart and one soul, and not even one of them would say that any of the things that belonged to him was his own, but they held all things in common. (33) And with great power the apostles bore testimony to the resurrection of the Lord Jesus, and great grace was upon them all.[1] (34) Nor was anyone in want among them, for those who were owners of lands or houses would sell them[2] and bring the price of the things that had been sold (35) and they would lay them at the apostles' feet, and distribution was made to each one, as anyone from time to time had need.

Bibliography

P. Benoit, as in (5).

J. Dupont, as in (5) (*Nouvelles*).

B. Gerhardsson, *StTh* 24 (1970), 142–9.

P. W. van der Horst, as in (6).

S. J. Noorda, Kremer *Actes*, 475–83.

Commentary

Luke marks a second stage in the development of his story by a second summary passage. Cf. 2.41–7; the new summary makes substantially the same points with emphasis on the sharing of goods and ministry to the poor (possibly preparing for 6.1) and omission of any reference to the common meals observed by the Christians. Instead there is specific mention of the testimony borne by the apostles to the resurrection of Jesus.

That the picture of the church drawn in vv. 32, 34 is a generalization, and an idealized generalization, is immediately proved by the story of Ananias and Sapphira (5.1–11). That story does however bear negative witness (see below, pp. 261-4) to what Luke evidently thought was a common if not strictly universal practice. It is clear that he had some ground (possibly in traditional stories told about

---

[1]NEB, they were all held in high esteem; NJB, they were all accorded great respect.
[2]No object is expressed in the Greek.

Barnabas and Ananias and Sapphira) for thinking that members of the church disposed of their property in the common interest, and he uses this information as part of his picture of the church when the church was at its best. It is undoubtedly part of his intention to use example to show his contemporaries not only how to preach (see pp. 132f.) but also how the church should conduct its common life; though he never suggests, or hints, that church members ought at all times to dispose of their capital assets, and it is clear from the rest of the book that they did not do so. In this respect Luke's account differs widely from the rule of Qumran.

Notwithstanding the idealizing element in Luke's account and its edificatory intention, it is probable that some kind of sharing was practised in Jerusalem. It was probably not highly organized. 'Das Moment ungeplanter Spontaneität is unüberhörbar' (Roloff 89); but Roloff (91; also Stählin 80) speaks of factors that may have fostered the practice: the teaching and example of Jesus, the problems of Galileans living in Jerusalem, the example of the Pharisees and of Qumran, eschatological expectation. There were precedents outside Judaism: Strabo 7.3.9; Seneca, *Epistle* 90.3f.; Plato, *Laws* 5. 739c.

The wording of the paragraph is substantially Lucan (see the notes, and especially the clause καθότι ἄν τις χρείαν εἶχεν (v. 35), which is repeated word for word from 2.45. It is Luke's own composition, but not entirely free composition. Verse 33 intervenes between two statements of business arrangements (v. 32; vv. 34f.), and v. 32 and vv. 34f. do not give exactly the same picture of the way the Christians bestowed their goods. Weiser 135 finds it impossible to distinguish precisely between Lucan and pre-Lucan material; but this very fact is a pointer to the use of traditional information.

In addition to providing an edifying picture for the imitation of later Christians Luke helps to prepare for the conclusion in ch. 5 of the first stage in the working out of the relation between Christianity and Judaism. Schmithals (53) sees the paragraph as evidence that Luke's community was threatened by division and false teachers.

32. πλῆθος is an important Lucan word (Lk. eight times, Acts sixteen, out of a NT total of thirty-one) used here for the first time of the Christian community. Its precise sense will have to be discussed from time to time (see especially on 6.2, with the reference to Braun and to Qumran parallels), but there can be no doubt that here it means the whole company of Christians. In this it reflects Jewish use; see e.g. *CIJ* 2.804 (εἰρήνη καὶ ἔλεος ἐπὶ πᾶν τὸ ἡγιασμένον πλῆθος). The Christians are here described as οἱ πιστεύσαντες, those who had adopted the new faith. This is another Lucanism (see e.g. 2.44, in the first of the summaries); so far there is much to suggest that Luke's own hand is at work. καρδία and ψυχή also are common words in Luke and Acts (καρδία: Lk. twenty-two times, Acts twenty; ψυχή: Lk. thirteen times, Acts fifteen) but there is no parallel to their use with μία to describe the unity of a group. There are however OT parallels, notably Jer. 32.39, I will give them one heart and one way (so Hebrew; LXX 39.39, δώσω αὐτοῖς ὁδὸν ἑτέραν καὶ καρδίαν ἑτέραν — אחר presumably being read instead of אחד); 1 Chron. 12.38; 2 Chron. 30.12. The expression is not exclusively biblical; see Cicero, *De Amicitia* 92, . . . amicitiae vis sit in eo, ut unus quasi animus fiat ex pluribus; Aristotle, cited by Diogenes Laertius 5.1.20, (φίλος ἐστὶ) μία ψυχὴ δύο σώμασιν ἐνοικοῦσα.

At this point the Western text emphasized the unity of believers by a negative comment: καὶ οὐκ ἦν διάκρισις ἐν αὐτοῖς οὐδεμία (D Cyp), or καὶ οὐκ ἦν χωρισμὸς ἐν αὐτοῖς τις (E r); these additions, which add nothing to the claim that the whole company had but one heart and one soul, correspond more or less to the ὁμοθυμαδόν of 2.44; 5.12. Ropes (*Begs.* 3.44) thinks that Tertullian, *Apology* 39 may be a reminiscence of the Western text: itaque qui animo animaque miscemur, rei communicatione dubitamus. omnia indiscreta sunt apud nos praeter uxores.

The second half of the verse similarly corresponds with 2.44, 45; for the community and for the sharing of goods see on those verses. It is to be noted that v. 32b does not go as far as v. 34, according to which all those who owned properties sold them; here it is said only that property of all kinds was held in common. The two statements are separated by v. 33, which deals with an entirely different matter; they may come from different sources. καὶ οὐδὲ εἷς (stronger than οὐδείς) should mean not even one; that is to say, communal ownership was practised with complete unanimity. This is hardly in agreement with 5.4. The believers' property is described as τὰ ὑπάρχοντα; cf. the use of ὕπαρξις in 2.45 (with κτήματα; cf. κτήτορες, v. 35) and ὑπάρχειν in 4.37. With the dative, cf. Lk. 8.3; 12.15; also *P.Oxy.* 44 (1976). 3203, 12f. (*ND* 1.127).

ἦν αὐτοῖς ἅπαντα (so א A E Ψ 𝔐; P⁸ B D *pc*, πάντα) κοινά; cf. 2.44, εἶχον ἅπαντα κοινά. See the note on that verse. Against the view that in v. 32 Luke combines an OT description (one heart and one soul) with a Hellenistic proverbial ideal (κοινὰ τὰ φίλων) see B. Gerhardsson in *StTh* 24. 142–9, who argues that both parts are Jewish and that the underlying text 'ist kein geringer als der Schemaᵉ' (p. 145). In Deut. 6.5 man is bidden to love God with the whole heart, soul, and strength. *Heart* and *soul* appear in the first half of the verse: the community is thus united in its love for God. *Strength* was interpreted as mammon, that is, as property, wealth; the people of God as thus represented as united in heart and soul and in the use of their property. It must be allowed that there is nothing un-Jewish in this use of wealth for the good of all, but the repeated formula πάντα κοινά must owe something to the non-

Jewish element in Luke's environment; in ch. 2 we lack the reference to καρδία and ψυχή. Aristotle (cited by Preuschen) unites the 'one soul' and 'all things common' themes: αἱ παροιμίαι . . . 'μία ψυχή' καὶ 'κοινὰ τὰ φίλων' . . . (*Ethica Nicomachea* 9.8 (1168b).

33. The general sense of the verse is clear. The apostles bear witness, especially to the resurrection of Jesus; this is what they were appointed and charged to do (1.8, 22; *al.*). They were promised *power*, δύναμις, for their work (1.8); this could be manifested in miracles (2.22; 3.12; 4.7), but here is expressed in powerful, convincing speech — or perhaps in both (Schneider 365). The testimony is here *given*, ἀπεδίδουν; the verb is not used elsewhere in Acts in this sense (see 5.8; 7.9; 19.40); the compound verb perhaps means *duly rendered*. In the middle of the verse B (alone) has τοῦ κυρίου Ἰησοῦ τῆς ἀναστάσεως (which could be rendered, The apostles of the Lord Jesus bore testimony to (his) resurrection); all other MSS avoid this possibility by writing τῆς ἀναστάσεως τοῦ κυρίου Ἰησοῦ, or something similar. They probably give the sense Luke intended; the word order of B is unexpected, but BDR § 473.2 n. 4 comment, 'Mitunter ist die regelmässige Wortstellung verlassen, weil sie zu schleppend und ungefällig wäre'. Haenchen (227) notes that Luke never has the apostles with a genitive. Roloff (88) says that the common life described in vv. 32, 34, 35 is a sign of the power at work; Luke does not seem concerned to make this point.

It is not clear whether χάρις is here used as it is at 2.47, of the favour with the populace enjoyed by the apostles, or denotes the active favour of God, who approves of what the apostles are doing and encourages and helps their work. Schmithals (53f.) takes the former view; the verse supports Luke's belief that Christianity is true Judaism. Weiser thinks that both meanings are intended; this seems unlikely. The parallel in Luke 2.40 (Schneider 366) and the absolute use of χάρις (Page 109) lend greater probability to the latter view. It is χάρις μεγάλη; divine aid is bestowed in unusual measure. God's favour rests upon them all: all the apostles (mentioned in the preceding clause), or all the Christians? In view of v. 32, and of what follows in v. 34 (ἐν αὐτοῖς cannot refer to the apostles only), probably the latter; though if in v. 33 Luke was following a source, that may have referred only to the apostles.

34. ἐνδεής occurs nowhere else in the NT; it may be inferred that the clause is intended as a fulfilment of Deut. 15.4 (οὐκ ἔσται ἐν σοὶ ἐνδεής; but cf. Deut. 15.11). Weiser (137) remarks that this verse combined with v. 32 combines the OT with a Hellenistic philosophical ideal. 6.1 indicates some breakdown in the arrangements;

5.1–11 another kind of breakdown. In the present verse Luke is painting an ideal picture. This persists in the second part of the verse, where it is claimed that all property owners (ὅσοι κτήτορες ... ὑπῆρχον) sold what they owned and contributed the prices to the common fund (v. 35). κτήτωρ occurs here only in the NT, but of seven uses of κτᾶσθαι Lk. has two, Acts 3; of four uses of κτῆμα, Acts has two. The verbal statistics fit with Luke's often observed interest in property and poverty. The word κτήτωρ is not uncommon; see *ND* 2.89. For the wording of the verse cf. Isocrates, *Areopagiticus* 83 τότε μὲν οὐδεὶς ἦν τῶν πολιτῶν ἐνδεὴς τῶν ἀναγκαίων; Thucydides 7.82.2, . . . μὴ ἀποθανεῖν μηδένα μήτε βιαίως μήτε δεσμοῖς μήτε ἀναγκαιοτάτης ἐνδείᾳ διαίτης.

D with some other witnesses prefers ὑπῆρχεν to ἦν in the first part of the verse, ἦσαν to ὑπῆρχον in the second. If this is anything other than pointless variation it may be intended to say: There did not *exist* a single poor man . . . those who happened to be owners . . . πωλοῦντες has no expressed object. It is natural to think of the χωρία (another word characteristic of Acts: 1.18, 19 (bis); 5.3, 8, 28.7; elsewhere in the NT only three times) and οἰκίαι just mentioned, and of all of them. This however Luke does not explicitly say; it would be possible to take his words to mean that the owners sold some of the properties they possessed and brought the prices of what they sold to the apostles. Luke is not compiling statistics; he means to describe a great movement of generosity which could be spoilt only by the meanness and deceit of 5.1–11.

35. The imperfect ἔφερον of v. 34 is continued in the imperfects ἐτίθουν and διεδίδετο (the reading of ℵ B* A D E; for the form see M. 2.206 and cf. παρεδίδετο at 1 Cor. 11.23 (ℵ B* A C D E F G K 33)). The choice of tense describes a regular practice. Money was brought to the apostles who continued to be the administrators of charity until the new appointments of 6.2–6. Placing things at a person's feet (παρὰ τοὺς πόδας)) seems to be a Lucanism, mainly in the present context (4.37; 5.2; 7.58); other passages referred to by Haenchen, and Ps. 8.7 (Preuschen), do not apply. There are non-biblical parallels. Cicero, *Pro Flacco* 68, ante pedes praetoris in foro expensum est auri pondo; Lucian, *Philopseudes* 20, . . . ἔκειντο ὀβολοὶ πρὸς τοῖν ποδοῖν αὐτοῦ . . . ; *Dialogi Meretricii* 14, are valid parallels. CD 14.13 (על יד המבקר) and 1 QS 6.19–20 אל יד המבקר), cited by Fitzmyer (*Essays* 294) illustrate the sense but not the wording. Luke emphasises the authority of the apostles, but Stählin (79) is over-literal with the view that the apostles have 'erhöhte Sitzen', Peter for example speaking from such a cathedra at 5.3ff. Schmithals (55) sensibly observes that common property is safer in a time of persecution, but Luke does not seem to be thinking of this.

possible that Luke is using a source that repeated itself or that he is using the same source twice; it is more probable that the phrase is his own (or taken by him from current use) and that he is punctuating his narrative from time to time with summaries that he himself constructed. See pp. 160f.

11. AN EXAMPLE: BARNABAS 4.36, 37

(36) Joseph, who was named by the apostles Barnabas (which is translated 'Son of Exhortation'[1]), a Levite, a Cypriote by birth, (37) since he owned a piece of land, sold it, and brought the money and laid it at the apostles' feet.

Bibliography

S. Brock, *JTS* 25 (1974), 93–8.

J. D. Burger, *MH* 3 (1946), 180–93.

H. J. Cadbury, *FS* Harris, 45–56.

L. Cerfaux, *Rec.* 2.176–82.

A. Deissmann, *ZNW* 7 (1906), 91f.

P. W. van der Horst, as in (6).

S. J. Noorda, as in (10).

R. O. P. Taylor, *CQR* 136 (1943), 59–79.

Commentary

The practice of selling one's property and devoting the proceeds to the common good is illustrated by the story of Barnabas, a person who is mentioned elsewhere as, for a time, a companion of Paul's (9.27; 11.22, 30; 12.25; 13; 14; 15.12, 22, 30, 35). The relation between them comes to an end in 15.36–41. The separation from Paul appears again (but with different motivation) in Gal. 2.13, but 1 Cor. 9.6 probably means that it was not permanent. If therefore Luke, or the author of a source used by him, belonged to the Pauline group he may have had sufficient contact with Barnabas to have learned what is here described. The contact need not have been direct; it suffices that Barnabas had a place in Pauline and Deuteropauline traditions. Luke's information may have come by way of Antiochene tradition (Wilcox 179). Roloff (92) takes this view, and thinks that Barnabas has been confused with Manaen (13.1). In Acts as it stands the story of Barnabas illustrates the general statements of 4.32–5 (cf.

[1]RSV, NJB, encouragement.

2.44, 45): in fact Luke probably constructed his summaries on the basis of traditions such as this one about Barnabas (see above, pp. 251f.).

This paragraph, especially when taken with 5.1–11, shows that the sale of property and the sharing of the proceeds was not (as 4.34f. suggest) a universal practice; if it had been done by all there would have been no point in singling out Barnabas for special commendation. Wholesale community of goods must be regarded as Luke's idealizing generalization of what was done by some; so e.g. Plümacher (15; cf. 109f).; cf. Lüdemann (68). The example of Barnabas was no doubt held up as one that property owners of Luke's own day should follow (cf. Weiser 138).

Some (e.g. Weiser 138; Schneider 368) take Barnabas to be a Diaspora Jew, a Hellenist (cf. 6.1); others (Hengel 101; cf. Schmithals 54, who however thinks Luke's account of Barnabas to be in error — he was in truth a Hellenistic Jew) think that in terms of 6.1 he was a Hebrew. The latter view is correct. Luke represents him as an early member of the Jerusalem church who makes an outstanding contribution to its funds; though not one of the Twelve he is trusted by them so that they are prepared to accept Paul on his recommendation (9.27) and use him as an accredited inspector in Antioch (11.22).

36. The majority of MSS put the name Joseph into the Greek form Ἰωσῆς; a few have Barsabbas (cf. 1.23) instead of Barnabas. The man in question plays an important part later in Acts (see 9.27; 11.22, 30; 12.25; and chs. 13, 14, 15 passim) but is always referred to under the name given by the apostles. For double names see on 1.23. According to Luke, this name, which is evidently Semitic (*Bar* is Aramaic, *son of*), is to be translated υἱὸς παρακλήσεως. παράκλησις occurs again at 13.45, where a λόγος παρακλήσεως is such a discourse as might be given in a synagogue service: a word of exhortation, or perhaps of encouragement; a sermon. At 15.31 its meaning is less clear (see the notes); it could mean comfort — the Antiochenes were comforted by the thought that they were not being required to be circumcised; it could refer to the general exhortation contained in the Jerusalem letter (15.23–9); it could refer to the exhortation with which Paul and Barnabas accompanied the reading of the letter (cf. 15.32). At 9.31 the meaning is not clear and it would be unwise to build on this verse (see the notes). The cognate verb παρακαλεῖν occurs twenty-two times (twenty-three if it is read in 18.27) in Acts. It often means *to ask*, or more strongly, *to entreat* (e.g. 8.31; 9.38; 13.42; 19.31) but it also means *to exhort*, in a specifically Christian sense (e.g. 2.40; 11.23; 14.22). It may mean *to comfort*, but this is more doubtful (16.40 and especially 20.12). It seems certain that υἱὸς παρακλήσεως must mean *son of exhortation*, that is, *preacher*; and it corresponds with this that Barnabas is represented in Acts as an outstanding evangelist and (until their separation) partner of Paul's (cf. 1 Cor. 9.6; Gal. 2.1, 9, 13). It is not however clear how this meaning is to be derived from the name Barnabas. The simplest suggestion is that 'ναβας' is derived from נביא (son of *a prophet*) or from נביאתא (or נביאותא), son of *prophecy, inspiration*. This may well have been in Luke's mind, or perhaps in the mind of the apostles, if Luke's report is correct. It is however a piece of popular rather than scientific etymology; this makes it no less probable as a popular opinion. The name is familiar in Palmyrene inscriptions (see H. J. Cadbury, in *FS* Harris, 47f., and on the whole question S. Brock in *JTS* 25 (1974) 93–8, with a wealth of philological detail), and there seems to be little doubt that there it was originally Bar neʿbo, Son of Nebo (the Babylonian god). One may be confident that the apostles did not rename Joseph in this sense, and Brock (art. cit. 96f.) suggests that 'Luke analysed Βαρναβᾶς as *br + nby' (nbayya)* meaning, "Son of comfort". On the basis of classical Syriac this form could be taken as either 3 m.s. or 1 pl. of the imperfect, but, to judge by the earliest Syriac inscriptions, the 3 m.s. imperfect prefix *n-* did not replace *y-* until about the end of the third century AD, and so, if there is anything in the suggestion, Luke must have analysed the verbal form as 1 pl. imperfect, for which, as we have seen, there are parallels in the later onomastica. His loose and unscientific rendering of this by υἱὸς παρακλήσεως is simply characteristic of a large number of popular etymologies of this sort.' It is in favour of this view that the Peshitto renders υἱὸς παρακλήσεως by *bera debuya'a*. It is against it that (though Brock can cite parallels) the juxtaposition of *son of* with a finite verb is very awkward, and that for παράκλησις *exhortation* is a more probable rendering than *comfort*. There is still much to be said for derivation from *n-b-y-'*. A further suggestion with little to commend it is that 'ναβας' may be derived from נחמא, consolation; it is not clear that this word exists in Aramaic (it is not to be found in the dictionaries of Jastrow and of Dalman), or how, if it does, it could give rise to the Greek letters in question. A more important observation is that Son of consolation, or comfort, could well be the meaning of the name Manaen (13.1) which is derived from the Hebrew name Menahem (מנחם). Manaen shares with Barnabas a connection with Antioch; is it possible that there has been confusion between the two men? This is not impossible but can be nothing but a guess.

Whatever the name meant, it was given to Joseph ἀπὸ τῶν ἀποστόλων. Not surprisingly a number of MSS have ὑπό. Cf. 2.22; see BDR § 210.2 n. 2; there are occasional classical parallels. The naming (ἐπικληθείς) originated with, came from, the apostles (on whom see pp. 94f). It is unlikely that we should translate, Barnabas, (one) of the apostles, but see 14.4, 14.

Barnabas was a Levite. On the Levites see Jeremias (*Jerusalem*

207–13); *NS* 2.250–6, 284–7. Several Levites are known to have been 'outstanding in wealth and education, among them the chief Levite Johanan b. Gudgeda and Joshua b. Ḥananiah' (Jeremias, op. cit. 105). Not all Levites (by descent) carried out Temple functions; Barnabas, as a native of Cyprus, may not have done so. Κύπριος τῷ γένει denotes his place of birth; cf. 18.2 (Ποντικός), 24 ('Αλεξανδρεύς); see also Josephus, *Ant.* 20.142. According to Num. 18.20; Deut. 10.9 a Levite should not have owned an estate. But see Jer. 1.1; 32.7–9; Josephus, *Life* 76. Stählin (82) suggests that his parents or grandparents may have acquired the land, possibly as a burial place. For Cyprus see on 13.4; it would not be unreasonable to suggest that it was Barnabas' familiarity with the island that led to its choice as a field for evangelism.

37. The language of this verse is for the most part that of 4.34f. (ὑπάρχειν (but this word is differently used), πωλεῖν, φέρειν, τιθέναι) (aorist of these verbs, relating to one occasion), τοὺς πόδας τῶν ἀποστόλων). For the relation between the two passages see p. 258. In this verse we have instead of χωρίον or οἰκία, ἀγρός (nowhere else in Acts): instead of τιμή, χρῆμα (which here will mean *money*, *cash*: cf. 8.18, 20; 24.26; and see Herodotus 3.38.3f); instead of παρά (read here by P⁵⁷,⁷⁴ A B D Ψ 𝔐, assimilating), πρός (which sometimes, and certainly here, may bear the meaning of *beside*).

12. A NEGATIVE EXAMPLE: ANANIAS AND SAPPHIRA
5.1–11

(1) A man, Ananias by name, together with his wife Sapphira, sold a property (2) and kept back part of the price. His wife was privy to this. He brought part of the price and laid it at the apostles' feet. (3) Peter said, 'Ananias, why has Satan put it into your heart to deceive the Holy Spirit and keep back some of the price of the land? (4) While it remained did it not remain yours? And when it had been sold was it not under your authority? Why did you plan this act? You lied not to men but to God.' (5) When Ananias heard these words he fell down and expired, and great fear came upon all those who heard of it. (6) The young men rose up, prepared his body for burial, carried him out, and buried him. (7) There was an interval of about three hours; then his wife came in, not knowing what had happened. (8) Peter said to her, 'Tell me, did you sell the land for so much?' 'Yes,' she said, 'for so much.' (9) Peter said to her, 'Why did you agree to tempt the Spirit of the Lord? Behold, the feet of those who buried your husband are at the door, and they will carry you out.' (10) Immediately she fell at his feet and expired. The young men came in and found her dead. They carried her out and buried her beside her husband. (11) Great fear came upon the whole church and upon all those who heard these things.

Bibliography

H. J. Cadbury, *FS* Schubert, 87–102.

B. J. Capper, *JSNT* 19 (1983), 117–31.

J. D. M. Derrett, *Downside Review* 89 (1971), 225–32.

P. H. Menoud, *FS* Goguel, 146–53.

F. Scheidweiler, *ZNW* 49 (1958), 136f.

Commentary

At first sight, this paragraph forms a pair with the preceding one (4.36, 37), in which Barnabas sells his property and lays the proceeds at the feet of the apostles. Members of the church were making provision for the poor; Barnabas played his part, Ananias and Sapphira did not play theirs. Luke indeed probably intended his story to be taken in this way: first the carrot of a good example will be set before the donkey, and then the stick of a warning example will be applied behind. It is not however as simple as that, as analysis of the story shows. Ananias and Sapphira did make provision for the poor. They sold their property and presented the proceeds to the apostles. True, since they kept back part of the price they could have given more, could have been more, and more sacrificially, generous. But it is not avarice for which they are blamed but deceit. Jeremias (see p. 266) takes a different view, but Calvin is right: 'Luke condemns Ananias for only one crime, his wishing to deceive God and the Church with a false offering' (132). Ananias has deceived the Holy Spirit (v. 3); he has lied to God (v. 4). Sapphira has tempted the Spirit of the Lord (v. 9), presumably by lying to him, as her husband had done. If the story were abstracted from its context we should probably say that it was intended to teach (1) the wickedness and danger of attempting to deceive God ('Gott hat den Betrug furchtbar gerächt', Haenchen 237); and (2) the supernatural power, insight, and authority of Peter. The story in fact does not fit neatly into the context in which Luke has placed it. It assumes that Ananias was free to do what he liked with his own property, before and after sale (v. 4); this contradicts 4.34b, the plain meaning of which is that all who owned land sold it and brought the proceeds — the whole proceeds — to the apostles. And though it may have encouraged some to sell up for the benefit of the poor this is not a logical implication of the narrative. It is likely that the story was traditionally told for the two purposes mentioned; Luke saw a superficial appropriateness in setting it alongside the Barnabas story and used it as a foil. It is unlikely that it needed much modification; there are few signs of specifically Lucan writing.

What was the origin of the story? Did Peter in fact strike dead two unsatisfactory church members? Judas (1.18) and Herod (12.23) died unhappy deaths; Paul struck blind Elymas, the magus of the proconsul Sergius Paulus (13.11); and there is nothing more miraculous in striking dead than in raising the dead (e.g. 9.32–43). There are OT parallels, notably Lev. 10.1–5. The difference and the difficulty are moral as well as rational, but are mitigated by the fact that Peter is not actually said to have caused, or even to have willed, the two deaths. 'Petrus tötet sie [Sapphira]', writes Haenchen (235); in fact he foretells her death, but foretelling is not willing, and with Ananias he did not go even so far. It is however undoubtedly true that Luke meant to teach that it was very dangerous to trifle with the apostles (cf. 5.13). Whether he intended to represent Peter as the chief of the apostles and as leader of the church is another question. In the early chapters of Acts Peter is undoubtedly the outstanding figure (see the general discussion in Vol. II); Cullmann (*Petrus* 258) sees in the present story an example of the power to bind and loose conferred on Peter in Matt. 16.19 (but cf. Matt. 18.18 where the same power is conferred on disciples generally). It is only in the earliest days that Peter exercised leadership over the whole church (that is, when the church was confined, or almost confined, to Jerusalem); so Cullman, loc. cit.

It has been suggested (by Menoud, *FS Goguel*, 146–54) that the story originated with the deaths of two church members, who died at a very early date when it was expected that all Christians would survive till the parousia. The deaths of Ananias and Sapphira seemed inexplicable, and it was thought that they must have been guilty of some particularly grievous sin for which they were punished by death and consequent exclusion from the kingdom of God. S. E. Johnson (Stendahl, *Scrolls* 131f.) draws a parallel with Qumran, noting that v. 4 does not demand the giving up of property by all. Perhaps only entrance into the inner circle involved the giving up of possessions. 'In this case, Ananias and Sapphira were free to use their property and go back to private ownership up to the moment of their final vows; but now they have taken the vow fraudulently.' The suggestion is developed by B. J. Capper, *JSNT* 19 (1983), 117–31. Cf. 1 QS 6.24f., where false statements about one's property lead to exclusion from the Purity of the Group (שהרת רבים) for a year and withdrawal of a quarter of the food ration. It can be said only that if these were features of the story in its original form they have now been completely removed.

The paragraph has given much difficulty to commentators, and divergent views about it are held. According to Schille (148) we have to do with a 'reinen Petrus-Tradition' in which Peter is represented as a θεῖος ἀνήρ. Roloff (92) says that it is not a Petrus-Legende, observing that Peter does not say 'You have lied to *me*', considering himself either as a divinity or as representing an institution. We see thus not a θεῖος ἀνήρ but 'die Fähigkeit des Charismatikers' (94). The paragraph differs from the supposed parallel in 1 QS 6 in that the sin rebuked is deceitfulness. Roloff adds (1) that there is a rigorism here that is inconsistent with the spirit of Jesus (or with 1 Cor. 5.3), and (2) there is no recognition of the fact that the church is a mixed body, a field in which wheat and tares must grow together. Pesch (197) speaks of the event as a 'Tat-Folge, die der Täter sich selbst zuzieht', and (202–4) tries to give it a morally and theologically acceptable interpretation. 'Die Unterscheidung von "Leben" und "Tod" in der Gemeinde dient der Ermutigung der Freiheit: Wähle das Leben!' (203). Like Pesch, Weiser (140) takes the incident to be a Normenwunder, defining the term with Theissen (114): 'Normenwunder wollen heilige Forderungen durchsetzen'. In all, he gives (138–48) the fullest and most satisfactory discussion of the incident and of the historical and theological problems that it raises. Such narratives have many parallels: from the OT he cites Lev. 10; Josh. 7; 1 Kings 14, and many more from rabbinic literature and from the Hellenistic environment (using both inscriptions and literary texts). An interesting addition can be found in *ND* 3.27. Weiser is ᵖᵣₒₒₐₚiy right in thinking that behind Luke's story lies the recollection in Jerusalem of the death of a member of the early church in circumstances which it is no longer possible to determine, though Weiser thinks the pre-Lucan form of the narrative may be represented by vv. 1, 2b, 8 (with Ananias as the subject of the verb), 3a, 4a, 5a, 6, 5b. Luke used the tradition for edification. We may add that he may not have perceived all the implications of his account.

1. Ananias (the name of Shadrach, Dan. 1.6; 3.13) is introduced in a way that has parallels in the OT, e.g. Job 1.1 Neither this, however, nor the dative ὀνόματι, can be said to be Semitic rather than Greek. In itself δέ may introduce a further item in a list or mark a contrast with what precedes (the story of Barnabas) (so *Begs.* 4.49); there can be little doubt that Luke intends the contrast. The name (H)ananias is Hebrew, חנניא, or חנניה (the Lord is gracious); it was the name (interchanging with חנינה) of several Tannaim and Amoraim. Alternatively, the Greek may represent ענניה (Neh. 3.23, the Lord hears). In Acts we encounter also an Ananias who appears in the narrative of Paul's conversion (9.10–17; 22.12), and a high priest (23.2; 24.1). The Hananiah of this chapter cannot be identified. The earliest Hananiah among the Tannaim was סגן הכוהנים (see on 4.1) and thus lived before the destruction of the Temple but 'since he is given this title regularly, was probably the last to hold this office' (Strack, *Introduction* 109; for detailed references see Strack's note attached to this passage). The name of his wife, Sapphira, probably represents the feminine of the Hebrew adjective שפיר (שפירה), *beautiful.* Saphir appears as a man's name in Moed Qatan 11a. Ossuaries have been discovered in Jerusalem (*Suppl. Epigraph. Graecum*, ed. J. J. E. Hondius, VIII, 1937, 184, 201) bearing the name (in Aramaic) שפירא, one of them with the Greek Σαφεῖρα). It is uncertain whether the bones are those of a man or of a woman, but H. J. Cadbury (*FS Harris*, 1933) draws attention to one bearing the inscription Sapphira, wife of Simon (pp. 54f.). Klausner (*From Jesus to Paul* (n.d.), 289f.) thought one inscription referred to the Sapphira of Luke's narrative; the dating does not make this impossible, but it is of course impossible to prove and the numerical probability is obviously against it. The inscriptions at least demonstrate the use of the name in Jerusalem at about the right time. For the representation of פ by πφ (-φφ- D E; -μφ- ℵ) see BDR § 40 n. 4; for the dative ending in -ῃ (after ρ; see also v. 2) see BDR § 43.1 n.1.

ἐπώλησεν takes up the verb of 4.34, 37; the noun object κτῆμα looks back to 2.45 (but cf. κτήτωρ in 4.34). In older Greek (see LS 1002) the noun seems to have been used more frequently of personal than of real, landed, property, but later to have come into use in the singular for an estate, farm, or field. All we can say on the basis of this verse is that it does not mean cash, since it was sold for cash; a precise description of what was sold was of no particular interest to Luke. We may however note (Bauernfeind 85) that the word proves to be synonymous with χωρίον (vv. 3, 8). The ordering of the material is Luke's so that we cannot say that Ananias and Sapphira were motivated by a desire to share the good impression made by Barnabas (Roloff 93); the suggestion (Schmithals 56) that by claiming to have given all they had they would put themselves on the list for relief is farfetched.

2. ἐνοσφίσατο. On νοσφίζεσθαι (middle) see M. 2.408 and an excellent note in *Begs.* 4.50; an equivalent is ἰδιοποιεῖσθαι. The meaning is well summarized by Haenchen (232): the word means always '(a) ein geheimes Entwenden, (b) eines Teils von einer grösseren Summe, (c) die einer Gemeinschaft gehört.' The verb is derived from νόσφι, *apart, aside*, and means *to purloin*; see MM 430 s.v., also for the use of ἀπό (e.g. νενόσφισται ἀπὸ τῶν ἀμφιτάπων, PSI IV. 442⁴). 'This poetical word first appeared in prose in Xenophon, *Cyr.* 4.2.42, and is frequently found in Hellenistic authors' (M. 2 loc. cit.). See Josephus, *Ant.* 4.274 (μαρτυράμενος τὸν θεὸν μὴ νοσφίζεσθαι ἀλλότρια) and especially Joshua 7.1. The sense of the clause is brought out by its counterpart: He kept back for himself part of the price, and thus brought (ἐνέγκας; cf. 4.34, 37) not the whole but μέρος τι and laid it at (παρά as at 4.35; contrast πρός, 4.37) the apostles' feet. ἔθηκεν as at 4.37. M. 1.237 notes the unexpected middle, ἔθετο, in D, but beyond noting the similar variant (συγκαλεσάμενοι for συνεκάλεσαν) at 5.21 does not explain it. It could be that the copyist thought that a fundamentally selfish action was best expressed in the middle voice. Apart from the deceit involved the action of Ananias was not without merit; at Lev. R. 5 (108) Abban Judan is praised for selling half his land (Bauernfeind 85).

συνειδυίης καὶ τῆς γυναικός. Sapphira shared in her husband's plan. '*Share the knowledge of* something *with* somebody, *to be implicated* in or *privy to* it' (LS 1720f.) is a common meaning of συνειδέναι. For the unexpected η in the ending of συνειδυίης cf. Σαπφίρη in v. 1 and see the note.

3. διά τι ἐπλήρωσεν ὁ σατανᾶς τὴν καρδίαν σου. ὁ σατανᾶς is for Luke the supernatural power opposed to God, here to the Holy Spirit (Haenchen 232); cf. 26.18. For his action in leading men into wickedness cf. Lk. 22.3, which probably suggests the sense in which ἐπλήρωσεν is to be taken. The question is oddly put; does Peter really want to know why Satan acted as he did? We seem to have a combination of the question 'Why did you do it?' and the statement 'Satan has filled . . .'. So Haenchen and Conzelmann; it is not clear why Schneider (374) rejects this view. In itself the verb ἐπλήρωσεν could mean that Satan filled Ananias's heart *with something* — that is, with the evil intention to retain part of his money for his own use while giving the impression that he had contributed the whole. But as Satan *entered into* Judas Iscariot so probably the thought here is that he had entered into and filled Ananias's heart, thus taking control of his actions (his heart being the thinking, willing agent that directed them). Cf. 2.4 (ἐπλήσθησαν ... πνεύματος ἁγίου), etc.; 13.10 (πλήρης παντὸς δόλου ...). Metzger 327 rightly defends the reading ἐπλήρωσεν against ἐπήρωσεν (ℵ* *pc*) and ἐπείρασεν (P⁷⁴ vg), but the suggestion that the Greek means *to dare one to do something* is not convincing. For the connection between Satan and falsehood see Jn. 8.44. Schille (148) thinks of the baptismal renunciation of Satan and his works.

The infinitive ψεύσασθαι, though without ὥστε (see BDR § 391.4 n.8), expresses the result of Satan's filling Ananias's heart. With it is coordinated a second infinitive νοσφίσασθαι, so that Ananias appears to be accused of a twofold crime: he has deceived (or attempted to deceive) the Holy Spirit and he has kept back part of the price of his land (now χωρίον, settling the meaning of κτῆμα in v. 1). According to Jeremias (*Jerusalem* 130) the two offences were in fact the same. 'The sin of Ananias was not in fact his lie, but the withholding of something that had been dedicated to God; cf. v. 2, he 'kept back'; v. 3 ψεύδεσθαι + Acc., 'to cheat' ..., and in v. 4 the verb must have the same meaning' (see on v. 4). Cf. Blass's translation of ψεύσασθαι by *fallere*. This is not convincing. For the meaning of ψεύδεσθαι) Jeremias appeals to BDR § 187.3 n.3, with the rendering *betrügen*; see however MM 679 s.v. for the meaning *speak falsely, deceive by lies*; also LS 2021. 'ψεύδομαι cum accusativo ... aliquanto plus notat, quam cum dativo' (Bengel). Jeremias takes no account of v. 4, which seems to settle the matter in a different sense; see below. It was not (it seems) wrong to give up only part of the price; it was wrong to represent the part as the whole. The double clause (dependent on ἐπλήρωσεν) means '... to deceive the Holy Spirit by (deceitfully) keeping back ...'. The second infinitive supplies the content of the first. So Pesch 199: the καί is epexegetic, 'Er belog den Heiligen Geist, in dem er unterschlug'.

Barth (*CD* 1.1.526) argues from this verse and v. 4 (he does not note the two cases that follow ψεύδεσθαι in the two verses) for the deity of the Holy Spirit. Cf. Turner, (*Insights* 21), and Bede on v. 4: Supra dixerat eum mentitum esse spiritui sancto; patet ergo spiritum sanctum esse deum et errorem Macedonii damnatum fuisse priusquam natum. Even when the difference is taken into account the parallelism is striking. More central to the context however is the fact that Ananias's lie to Peter is taken as a lie spoken to the Holy Spirit. The Spirit so completely and radically dwells in the church as to be the one who experiences what is done to it. Cf. 9.4, τί με διώκεις;

4. The tenses, μένον ... ἔμενεν ... πραθέν ... ὑπῆρξεν, are worth noting and underline the point that is being made. As long as the land remained unsold it remained yours — your land; when it had been sold it (or more properly the price received for it) continued to be under your authority. It is impossible to evade the conclusion that (at least as far as this verse is concerned) the sale of property and distribution of the proceeds was voluntary; see above, p. 263. It must be deceit for which Ananias is blamed and this implies what is not stated in v. 2, namely, that when Ananias brought part of the price he had received he either directly or implicitly claimed that he was bringing the whole. Whether this gives a correct picture of what was taking place is another question (see pp. 262-4). According to Conzelmann (39) the statement is 'lukanische Erläuterung'. For Weiser's view see above, pp. 263f. Hanson (82) thinks it not impossible, though strained, to translate, Once it was sold, did it remain under your control? (expecting the answer No).

Only here and at v. 9 does τί ὅτι (BDR § 299.3 n. 3) occur in Acts (cf. Lk. 2.49). It is explained by the fuller form τί γέγονεν ὅ ι ι at Jn 14.22, but means simply Why? With ἔθου ἐν τῇ καρδίᾳ σου cf. Jn 13.2; the verb ποιῆσαι is supplied by P⁷⁴ D sa mae syᵖ.

ἐψεύσω ... τῷ θεῷ: here ψεύδεσθαι takes the dative; cf. v. 3, where the accusative is used. See the note. It is arguable that with the accusative ψεύδεσθαι means to cheat someone of something; that is, it is possible though (see above) unconvincing to argue that in v. 3 Ananias's crime is that of cheating the Holy Spirit of money, not that of deceiving him. Here it is difficult to translate otherwise than *lie to God*, though Jeremias (loc. cit.) argues that 'in v. 4 the verb must have the same meaning in spite of the dative, which is doubtless a Semitism here, cf. kiḥēš leʿ'. The only meanings however given by Jastrow for כחש ל are *to be false; to flatter*. A better guide is the Peshitta which in both verses uses *d-g-l bᵉ*. *To deceive* and *to lie to* have substantially the same meaning.

F. Scheidweiler alters the sense of this verse by conjecturing in place of οὐχί, οὐχ, ὅ). This is rendered: Keineswegs war, was unverkauft dir (ungeschmälert) blieb, auch nach dem Verkauf noch in diener Verfügungsgewalt. This makes better sense of the rest of the verse (*ZNW* 49(1958), 136f.). There seems to be no good ground for this alteration of the text, which could be adopted only on the assumption that there cannot have been a diversity of traditions behind what Luke has given us.

5. Ananias fell down and expired, ἐξέψυξεν. The word occurs in Hippocrates, *De Morbis* 1.5, but is not exclusively medical; it occurs in Herondas 4.29 and in Judges 4.21A; Ezek. 21.12. In the NT it is used only here, at v. 10 of Sapphira, and at 12.23 of Herod — always, that is, of the wicked who die a sudden or unpleasant death. This however is coincidence; in itself the word is no more unpleasant than ἐκπνεῖν, used of Jesus (Mk. 15.37, 39; Lk. 23.46). Stählin (83) recalls 3.23 and the use of the Hebrew כרת for the cutting off of a member of the people; Schneider 372 quotes Deut. 13.6 and other passages for the use of בער. It is not stated that Ananias died because Peter killed him, or wished him dead. Conzelmann 39 quotes Jerome, *Epistle* 130.14.5f., Apostolus Petrus nequaquam est imprecatus mortem, ut stultus Porphyrius calumniatur, sed Dei iudicium prophetico spiritu adnuntiat ut poena duorum hominum sit doctrina multorum. Cf. Schille (149). See also on vv. 9f., and pp. 262-4. In the next clause however Luke describes a reaction which implies the conclusion that, at least, supernatural and dangerous powers were at work; hence the fear that fell upon all who heard — not those who were present; they saw, not heard (Haenchen 233). Cf. v. 11. Had those who heard merely reflected, He has been so struck by his guilty conscience that natural forces have brought about his death, they would not have feared in this way; more is implied than the uneasiness that a sudden and unexpected death will often evoke among bystanders. The φόβος μέγας is fear of the supernatural.

D, accompanied by p, characteristically and unnecessarily underlines the impressiveness of the event by placing παραχρῆμα (cf. v. 10) before πεσών. It is however a Lucan word (Mt. twice; Lk. ten times; Acts six times (five of which concern supernatural events)). Cf. D. Daube, *The Sudden in the Scriptures*, Leiden 1964.

6. Immediate (E adds παραχρῆμα after ἀναστάντες δέ) action was taken by the νεώτεροι. This comparative form occurs at 1 Tim. 5.1; 1 Pet. 5.5 in contexts that refer also to πρεσβύτεροι. This word, however, in these contexts seems to refer primarily to older members of the congregations (though they probably exercise pastoral functions too) and there is nothing to suggest that the νεώτεροι constituted an ecclesiastical office as πρεσβύτεροι eventually did (and are beginning to do in 1 Timothy and 1 Peter). This is confirmed by the fact that in v. 10 those whom we may no doubt take to be the same persons are described as νεανίσκοι. The narrative assumes that such tasks will not be carried out by Peter himself or other senior members of the community; among the thousands involved (4.4) some would be active and eager enough to perform unpleasant duties. One is reminded of the 'young men', נערים, who formed the subordinate troops of the kings of Israel (e.g. 1 Sam. 14.1; 21.5), but here the LXX translates παιδάριον. *CIJ* II 755 (from Hypaepa, south of Sardes) speaks of 'Ιουδαί(ί)ων νεωτέρων.

ἀναστάντες has the ring of OT language, e.g. Gen. 22.3, ἀναστὰς ἐπορεύθη (וילך ויקם), but the LXX more often follows the Hebrew in using the finite verb (ἀνέστη καί . . .). συνέστειλαν could have one, or possibly both, of two senses. The word means *to draw together, to contract* (cf. 1 Cor. 7.29) and hence could be used for laying out a corpse (though περιστέλλειν is more usual for this purpose); it also means to cover with a shroud (e.g. Euripides, *Trojan Women* 377–9, οὐ δάμαρτος ἐν χεροῖν πέπλοις συνεστάλησαν, ἐν ξένῃ δὲ γῇ κεῖνται). Here it probably means that the body was (in a simple way) prepared for burial. ἐξενέγκαντες (Haenchen 233 surely misconceives the event and the period in the observation that the young men would not have bandaged the corpse in the room 'wo die Apostel thronen'; for the verb see the law quoted by Demosthenes 43.62 (1071), ἐκφέρειν δὲ τὸν ἀποθανόντα ...ὅταν ἐκφέρωνται ... ἐπειδὰν ἐξενεχθῇ ὁ νέκυς ...; the noun ἐκφορά was also used) ἔθαψαν (repeated in v. 10): it is enough to make it clear that Ananias was dead, unnecessary to specify the use of a bier or the kind of grave. The disgrace of unceremonious burial was not inflicted.

7. The simplest way of understanding the construction of this sentence is to take διάστημα with ἐγένετο: there was an interval of about three hours (ὡς, ὡσεί, *about*, is characteristic of Acts, c.g. 1.15). It is against this that ἐγένετο δὲ ...καὶ ...εἰσῆλθεν would correspond more or less to the OT Hebrew construction ויהי ותבוא. Luke however does not normally represent the Hebrew construction in this way, nor is there any reason to suppose that he is here translating a Hebrew text. There is therefore no need to take διάστημα as a nominative absolute (so *Begs.* 4.52) or to adopt any other expedient. See BDR § 144.2 n. 5. There is epigraphical evidence for διάστημα in *ND* 4.86. Cf. also *Passio Andreae* 14 (L.-B. 2.1.34), ἐπὶ ἡμιωρίου διαστήματος (dimidiae horae spatio).
For the kind of interrogation that follows, in which witnesses are examined separately, each in ignorance of what the other has said, cf. Susannah 44–62.

8. ἀπεκρίθη (recalling the Hebrew וַיַּעַן) is often used not in the sense of *answered* but simply *spoke, said*; though here Peter's words could not unreasonably be taken as a response to Sapphira's arrival. The Western text avoids the word (εἶπεν δὲ πρὸς αὐτὴν ὁ Πέτρος, D it vg^cl Lucifer). D also varies Peter's opening words: ἐπερωτήσω σε εἰ ἄρα ... The question elicits an answer that makes explicit the lie that was only implicit when Ananias brought to Peter a sum less than that which he had received for his property. Schneider (371) is perhaps not unfair in the judgment that Peter may be said to kill Sapphira in the sense that he provokes her lie. At least he does not help her to confess and repent. His words are usually printed with a question mark, but it would be not impossible to make the question an indirect one: Tell me (*or* I will ask you) whether you sold ... It is however more probable that εἰ is used here to introduce a direct question (as e.g. at 1.6; see the note): Tell me, did you sell . . .? For τοσοῦτος with reference to a specific but unspecified number cf. Lk. 15.29. The word occurs here only in Acts. The genitive is the genitive of price.

9. For τί ὅτι see on v. 4. That the construction occurs in Acts only in these two verses may point to the use of a special source. συνεφωνήθη ὑμῖν is paralleled in the papyri (cf. also Stobaeus, *Flor.* 39.32, συνεφώνησε τοῖς δήμοις and see BDR § 202.1 n.8, who also compare convenit inter vos); it seems to be more often followed by ὥστε and the infinitive than by the simple infinitive. *Why was it agreed by you?* The dative may be affected by the συν- in the compound verb.

For *tempting* (πειράσαι) God cf. 15.10; the notion and the word (rendering נסה) belong to the OT, cf. Exod. 17.2, τί πειράζετε κύριον; It means *to provoke*, by 'seeing how far you can go', in this case by deceit. τὸ πνεῦμα κυρίου is no doubt correct (cf. 8.39; it remains quite uncertain whether *Lord* refers to God or to Christ); τὸ πνεῦμα ἅγιον (P74 1838 *pc*) assimilates to v. 3.

Peter clearly predicts Sapphira's immediate death; whether he causes it is not expressly stated. See above, pp. 262-4. It is easy to rationalize in terms of the combined shock of the uncovering of her sin and the news of her husband's death, but this is not at all in the spirit of the narrative. For the burial of Ananias, and for the verb ἐκφέρειν, see v. 6.

For οἱ πόδες cf. Isa. 52.7; 59.7; Nahum 1.15; the biblical language is 'intended to increase the devotional sense of horror' (Dibelius 16).

10. For παραχρῆμα, which heightens the effect, cf. 3.7 and the note. The effect of Peter's words was instantaneous. For πρός, and the variant παρά (E Ψ 𝔐), see 4.35, 37; 5.2. For ἐξέψυξεν see v. 5. The rest of the verse is closely parallel to v. 5, though the νεώτεροι who carried out Ananias's burial are now νεανίσκοι (see on v. 5 for the significance of this). D (cf. syᵖ) makes the parallel closer by introducing the verb συνστέλλειν (συστείλαντες ἐξήνεγκαν καὶ ἔθαψαν)). For πρός in the sense of *beside* we may again compare 4.37.

11. In *Begs.* 4.52 this verse is taken as part of the summary (5.12–16) because it reduplicates v. 5, but just as v. 5 winds up the part of the story that deals with Ananias so this verse closes the story of Sapphira. The effect of the terrible and supernatural events just described, whether actually caused by Peter or not, is naturally to induce fear; in this verse φόβος must be more than reverence. It falls first upon the church, then upon all those, presumably on the edge of the Christian group, who heard what had happened (ταῦτα). This is the first occurrence in Acts of the word ἐκκλησία; it occurs fifteen times (omitting 7.38) in Acts 1–15; four times (omitting 19.32, 39, 40) in chs. 16–28. There is no doubt that here, with a look at the people of God in the OT, it refers to the whole company of Christians, though at this time the whole company of Christians is the local church of Jerusalem. Like the community of the new covenant at Qumran they claimed to be 'die neue Volksgemeinde Gottes' (Stählin 85). See further the notes on the relevant passages and the discussion in Vol. II. Hanson (83) mentions the use of ἐκκλησία by Josephus (e.g. *War* 1.550, 666; 4.159) 'to describe a kind of unofficial mass meeting called by some authority to sound public opinion on a certain point and to gain, if possible, a unanimous vote of approval', and thinks that 'this use contributed quite as much to the Christian use of the word *ecclesia* as' the use in the OT. This is doubtful, but there may at this point be something in the suggestion. Christian leaders may have thought it right that all should be aware of what had happened.

13. MIRACLE-WORKING OR SUPERNATURAL COMMUNITY 5.12–16

(12) Many signs and portents among the people were done at the hands of the apostles, and they were all together in Solomon's Portico, (13) and of the rest no one dared join them, but the people praised them. (14) Believers were added to the Lord in increasing numbers, crowds both of men and of women, (15) so that people carried out the sick even into the streets and laid them on mattresses and stretchers, in order that as Peter passed by at least his shadow might fall on one of them. (16) The crowd from the cities round about Jerusalem came together, bringing the sick and those who were afflicted by unclean spirits; all of them were healed.

Bibliography

P. Benoit, as in (5).

W. Bieder, *ThZ* 16 (1960), 407–9.

J. Dupont, as in (5).

P. W. van der Horst, *NTS* 23 (1977), 204–12.

Eb. Nestle, *ZNW* 8 (1907), 239f.

S. J. Noorda, as in (10).

D. R. Schwarz, *Bib* 64 (1983), 550–5.

Commentary

Notwithstanding a few difficulties, which will be mentioned below, the gist of this summary paragraph (note the imperfects, contrasting with 5.17 — Page 112; cf. 2.41–7; 4.32–5) is clear. It provides a link, in which miracles are emphasised (Bauernfeind 88; cf. above, p. 161) between the miracle of 3.1–10 and the legal proceedings that followed it on the one hand, and on the other the further events in ch. 5 (which may have been drawn from a different source). The thread of narrative was in danger of being lost in the story of Ananias and Sapphira. The material in the summary (miracle; the use of Solomon's Portico; the awed reaction of the crowds to recent events, presumably including the deaths of Ananias and Sapphira; Peter's outstanding activity as healer and exorcist) could easily have been derived from the surrounding traditional narratives; according to Weiser 149 the summary is a generalization on the basis of 5.11. These features are however put together in a surprising way. We hear first of miracles; then intervenes a remark about the place where the Christians were wont to assemble. They were marked out as a separate group (v. 13a), enjoying a high reputation (v. 13b). Next follows a statement superficially — though only superficially — in contradiction with what had been said about their separateness: No one dared to join them but many new believers did join them, the new converts including both men and women (v. 14). The consequence (ὥστε, v. 15) of this (of v. 12a, one would have thought, rather than of v. 14) was that people brought out their sick relatives and friends in the hope that Peter's shadow (evidently believed to have healing power) might fall on them. This movement extended beyond Jerusalem, and all the sick were healed. It is clear that there are bad joins between vv. 12a and 12b; 13a and 13b, 14; 14 and 15, 16. Otherwise put, miracle-working is the theme of vv. 12a, 15, 16; the relation of the Christians to the population of Jerusalem that of 13; the success of the apostles' preaching that of 14; and 12b stands on its own as a piece of information, interesting but adding nothing of substance. One would have thought that if Luke were simply composing a summary piece designed to lead his reader back to the main story-line, taken up again in 5.17, he would have ordered the material differently, putting like with like. From this observation suggestions naturally arise; thus Stählin 86f. places vv. 15, 16 between 12a and b; Pesch (205) thinks that the summary divides into two, vv. 12–14 and 15, 16, v. 14 being Luke's own expansion; similarly *Begs.* 4.53 suggests that vv. 12b–14 is editorial; Schneider (379) thinks the hypothesis (Benoit, *FS* Goguel 3f. (= *Ex. et Th.* 188); Zimmermann *BZ* 5 (1961) 78) that vv. 12b–14 are secondary unnecessary, but agrees that v. 15 links with 12a. It is undoubtedly true that the several sentences in the paragraph could be arranged in a more orderly fashion. It is however as difficult to suppose that Luke took up written or oral pieces and arranged them badly as that he himself wrote in a somewhat disjointed way. There is usually (see the notes) something that can be said to justify the connections that Luke makes, with the exception perhaps of v. 12b; as to this, Luke was interested in places and liked local colour. The most probable view therefore is that he himself composed the paragraph to introduce, or reintroduce, the traditional material written up in 5.17–42 (Cf. Haenchen 239; Lüdemann 72f.).

12. διὰ τῶν χειρῶν τῶν ἀποστόλων does not differ in meaning from διὰ τῶν ἀποστόλων (2.43) but has a Semitic appearance. It imitates the LXX, where however the singular, διὰ χειρός, is commonly used (as at Acts 7.25; 11.30; 15.23) in conformity with the Hebrew idiom. Stählin (86) however thinks that Luke's expression is to be understood literally: the sick were healed by the laying on of hands. For σημεῖα καὶ τέρατα also see 2.43. The signs and portents are publicly performed ἐν τῷ λαῷ. The λαός here must be the Jerusalem public, almost entirely Jewish. For Luke's use of λαός see on 4.25. At this point the theme of miracle working is dropped, to be taken up again in v. 15. It may be that in Luke's source there was direct connection between v. 12 and v. 15, but it is not easy to see why Luke should have disturbed it; vv. 12b, 13 could have opened the paragraph.

For Solomon's Portico see 3.11 (which may have suggested the introduction of the reference here). For ὁμοθυμαδόν see 1.14. Luke seems to regard the Portico as a regular meeting place for Christians. They probably had no meeting-house of their own. It is hard to agree that 'nun geht bereits an die Eroberung des Tempelplatzes!' (Schille 157). There is more to be said for Schmithals's view that the emphasis on the unitedness of Christians and their contact with the OT shows that Luke writes with Irrlehrer in mind.

13. τῶν δὲ λοιπῶν. For Pesch (206) οἱ λοιποί are the Christians other than the apostles; Haenchen (237), with greater probability, interprets them as οἱ ἔξω (Lk. 8.10, equivalent to Mk. 4.11). The verse suggests that the assembled Christians (ὁμοθυμαδόν, v. 12) formed a distinctive group on their own, separate from those who moved about in the Portico, and that to join the group was understood to be virtually equivalent to becoming a Christian, for in view of v. 14 Luke cannot mean that no one dared to become a Christian; many did so. Luke's narrative must be taken to mean that the deaths of Ananias and Sapphira contributed to the fear of the crowd, who feared 'zu nahe zu treten' (Roloff 97). Because v. 13a seemed to be in conflict with its context Torrey (31f.) suggested that κολλᾶσθαι must mistranslate an Aramaic root, which should have been rendered *to contend with*. One possible root is קרב: 'In Syriac, the *ethpaᶜal* might have either meaning.' Even more likely, according to Torrey, is לחם. 'The phrase would then have been להתלחמה עמהון, the infinitive being used exactly as is the same form in late Hebrew, התלחם, "contend". But in the northern (Syrian) dialect the words would have meant "to be united with them"; cf. the passage cited in Payne Smith: בחד עמא אתלחמו, "they were united into one people", and the root meaning (*ibid.*) of לחם, *consociavit.*' It is surprising that neither Black nor Wilcox mentions this suggestion, which is in itself linguistically one of Torrey's best. It is however unnecessary. Luke's meaning, though awkwardly expressed (Conzelmann) is clear enough: the only way to *join* (cf. κολλᾶσθαι in 8.29) the Christians as they gathered in Solomon's Portico was by committing oneself as a believer. This agrees with Burchard in *ZNW* 61 (1970) 159f.: 'Die Schwierigkeit löst sich einigermassen, wenn κολλᾶσθαι einfach "sich nähern" bedeutet: um die Gemeinde liegt ein unsichtbarer

Kordon, der Neugierige abhält . . . und den nur Übertrittswillige zu durchschreiten wagen.' Burchard refers to Bauernfeind (89: '. . . eine starke Exklusivität: wer nicht wirklich zu ihr gehörte, der getraute sich nicht, näheren Verkehr bei ihr zu suchen; entweder völliger Anschluss oder Hochachtung aus der Ferne'), Bruce, and Haenchen. Thus τῶν λοιπῶν will refer specifically to those who were not Christians; ὁ λαός, in this verse as in v. 12, will refer to the population at large. The Christians were (according to this verse) popular and left in peace, when not actually joined. This seems to make sense, but τῶν δὲ λοιπῶν has attracted a number of conjectures; see Metzger, ad loc. The most interesting is the suggestion by Torrey (*Documents* 96) that the Aramaic שביא was misread as שרויא, turning 'the elders' into 'the rest'.

From this verse Schmithals (58) infers that in Luke's time 'Gemeinde und Synagoge sind getrennt'. This observation fails to do justice to the double meaning of the verse; between church and synagogue the attitude was one of mingled attraction and repulsion.

μεγαλύνειν is a Lucan word (Mt. once, with τὰ κράσπεδα as object; Lk. twice; Acts three times; Paul twice). Most often the object is a divine being, but the verb is practically a synonym for *praise*.

14. As v. 13 connects with 5.11, so v. 14 connects with 5.26 (Schneider 381). μᾶλλον δέ is often used with the meaning '*much more* . . ., or *rather* . . ., to correct a statement already made' (LS 1076, s.v. μάλα II 3); this would be suitable after v. 13a but it is impossible after v. 13b, to which the new statement could not be adversative. The word however probably retains its comparative sense, δέ marking simple continuation (as in vv. 13 and 16: Page 112): even more were believers added to the Lord, that is, in increasing numbers (cf. 2.41; 4.4). For the use of προστίθεσθαι cf. 2.41, 47. ὁ κύριος is Jesus, thought of as the head of the new community, who gains more and more adherents. The sentence could be taken differently: Believers in the Lord were added (to the church). But it is natural to take the dative with προσετίθεντο. 'Formally, [the dative] is probably to be taken with πιστεύοντες, but in sense it may go with either or both' (Bruce 1.138).

πλῆθος is a Lucan word (Lk. eight times; Acts 17 (16); rest of the NT seven); see on 2.6; 4.32. The use of the plural here shows that no technical sense is in mind. Crowds of men and women: the concern for the role of women often noted in the gospel continues in Acts.

The language of this verse is reflected in *Acta Thomae* 27 (L.-B. 2.2.143), πολλοὶ δὲ καὶ ἕτεροι πιστεύοντες προσετίθεντο καὶ ἤρχοντο εἰς τὸ καταφύγιον τοῦ σωτῆρος. The author of the Acts of Thomas was certainly familiar with Acts.

15. The supernatural power at work in the community was manifested not only in the gathering of believers but in miraculous cures. Again, the connection is not good. The action of unnamed persons (not said and probably not thought to be Christians) in bringing out their sick friends would follow better upon v. 13b than upon v. 14. According to Bauernfeind (89), ὥστε looks back to the whole paragraph, especially v. 12a; Blass 83 takes v. 14 to be a parenthesis. It seems that Luke is combining statements about conversions with statements about cures. The general opinion of Christians was such that (ὥστε) . . . No subject is expressed for ἐκφέρειν; it is better to take one out of λαός (vv. 12, 13; non-Christian Jews in Jerusalem — Haenchen 238) than out of πλήθη (v. 14). ἐκφέρειν is now of course used in a sense different from that of 5.6, 9, 10. The sick were brought out καὶ εἰς τὰς πλατείας, *even into the streets* (but *even* relates to the whole clause including ἐκφέρειν), πλατεῖα, to be understood with ὁδός — main streets, perhaps, rather than narrow lanes. Their friends (presumably) laid the sick ἐπὶ κλιναρίων καὶ κραβάττων. κλινάριον is a diminutive of κλινή, κράβαττος the word for which Luke (Lk. 5.19) substitutes κλινίδιον when it is used at Mk. 2.4. It does not seem possible to distinguish between the two words (so *Begs.* 4.55). The sick were placed on small rough stretchers, so that Peter's shadow as he passed by might fall on them.

ἵνα . . . κἄν. Cf. Mk 6.56 (omitted by Luke). M. 3.100 rather vaguely: κἄν 'supplies a modifying or conditional element: *so that even if.*' Moule (*IB* 138) makes this clearer. 'An implied *conditional* clause may be detected lurking . . . *no more than the shadow*; so A.V. . . . *that at least the shadow.* But if a plain καί had been used, it is difficult to imagine that the ἄν would have been missed.' Best perhaps is Page (113): 'The sentence fully expressed would be, "that the shadow — *even if* only the shadow — of Peter . . .", = "that *at any rate* the shadow . . .".' Cf. vg, . . . saltim umbra illius obumbraret . . .'. See also BDR § 374 n. 6; *ND* 4.155, quoting *P.Köln* 2(1978). 111, 11 κἄν νῦν, 'at least' (the editor, however, translates 'auch jetzt').

That Peter's shadow had a healing effect is made explicit by the Western text, though D and E use almost completely different words, showing that it was felt in more quarters than one that the miracle needed to be brought out. No more astounding piece of miracle-working is described in the NT; Peter does not need to speak, to touch, or, it seems, to give any attention to the sick person. Daube (*NTRJ* 235) suggests that 'this manner of healing may well have been a modified imitation of what Elijah and Elisha had done: the former had 'measured himself' over a dead boy, the latter "lain and bent" over one. Peter was one of the apostles; according to the Rabbis Elijah and Elisha, when restoring the children, acted as שליחים delegates of God, literally, as "envoys", "apostles".' The parallel however is not close. Wettstein (484) refers to Cicero, *Tusc.* 3.12.26,

Nolite, hospites, ad me adire! illico istic Ne contagio mea bonis umbrave obsit. Tanta vis sceleris in corpore haeret. Cf. Pliny, *Hist. Nat.* 28.69: magi vetant eius causa contra solem lunamque nudari aut umbram cuiusquam ab ipso respergi. In magic, a man's shadow, hand, word, clothes have the effect of the man himself (so Schmithals 57). The verb ἐπισκιάζειν occurs, evidently with a reference to Septuagintal usage, at Lk. 1.35; 9.34; it has been claimed (e.g. by W. Dieterich, *Petrusbild* 238f.) that this points to the presence and power of God (cf. Ps. 91.1; 139.12), so that we should think here not of the effect of Peter's shadow but of the presence and power of God which Peter represented. This would cohere with the treatment of ὄνομα in ch. 3 (see pp. 176f.); also with the parallel in *Acta Thomae* 59 (56) (L.-B. 2.2.176), πάντες οἱ ἔχοντες νοσοῦντας ἢ ὀχλουμένους ὑπὸ πνευμάτων ἀκαθάρτων προσέφερον, οὓς δὲ καὶ ἐν τῇ ὁδῷ ἐτίθουν ἐν ᾗ ἔμελλεν διελθεῖν, καὶ πάντας ἐν τῇ δυνάμει κυρίου ἐθεράπευεν. It is true that the context mentions faith (πιστεύοντες, v. 14), but it cannot be maintained even that Luke himself thought that the crowd who came from neighbouring cities (v. 16) were all believers. Cf. also 19.12, where a similar miracle-working power is ascribed not only to Paul but to material objects connected with him (on the question whether Peter and Paul are being deliberately equated with each other in supernatural power see p. 610). It must be recognized that Luke believed (see explicitly v. 12) that supernatural powers accompanied the great apostles whose story he tells; it must also be recognized that he states explicitly that this power was separable from the apostles who did not possess it in their own right and, when questioned, ascribed it exclusively to one other than themselves. It would be wrong to build much on Luke's κἄν — *at least*, which hardly suggests a desire for closer contact than overshadowing. But Schnider (226), quoted by Schneider (382), is right with, 'Nach antiker Vorstellung spielt es keine Rolle, ob das Wunder durch den *Schatten*, die Hände oder durch ein Wort der Wundertäter geschieht. Der eigentlich Handelnde beim Wunder ist Gott.' It is accordingly a serious over-simplification to say, 'Dass damit das paulinische Verständnis des Apostolats . . . durch das frühkatholische abgelöst wird, lässt sich nicht gut bestreiten' (Haenchen 241). Bede sees here a picture of the church's work in the world: . . . quia Petrus typus ecclesiae est, pulchre ipse quidem rectus incedit, sed umbra cernitante iacentes erigit; quia ecclesia, mente et amore caelestibus intendens, quasi umbratice transcurrit in terra et hic sacramentis temporalibus figurisque caelestium renovat quos illic remunerat donis.

16. Not surprisingly, news of what was happening in Jerusalem spread beyond the city, and a crowd (πλῆθος as in v. 14) came together from τῶν πέριξ πόλεων Ἰερουσαλήμ. D E Ψ 𝔐 vg^mss ease the construction by inserting εἰς before Ἰερουσαλήμ, but this word is in fact governed by the preposition πέριξ. On the separation of the preposition from its case see BDR § 474.8 n. 15. The thought is first expressed as 'the surrounding cities' and then the more precise description 'cities surrounding Jerusalem" is added. Cf. Xenophon, *Anabasis* 7.8.12, τὰ μὲν πέριξ ὄντα ἀνδράποδα τῆς τύρσιος; Herodotus 7.124, τὰς μεταξὺ πόλιας τούτων.

The rest of the verse repeats v. 15 with the addition of ὀχλουμένους κτλ.; for this cf. Tobit 6.8 (οὐκέτι οὐ μὴ ὀχληθῇ, by an evil spirit); also Lk. 6.18. The verb occurs in medical writers but not exclusively there so that it cannot be reckoned a technical medical term.

All were cured (D it syᵖ Lucifer vary the language, not the sense: καὶ ἰῶντο πάντες). The short summary paragraph, which began with a reference to many signs and portents (v. 12) could not end more impressively.

14. ARREST AND EXAMINATION OF APOSTLES 5.17–40

(17) The High Priest, and those who were with him, the local party of the Sadducees, rose up. They were filled with envy, (18) and laid their hands on the apostles and put them in prison publicly.[1] (19) But an angel of the Lord opened the doors of the prison by night, led them out, and said, (20) 'Go, stand and speak in the Temple to the people all the words of this Life.' (21) When they heard this they entered the Temple at dawn and began to teach. When the High Priest and those who were with him arrived they summoned the Sanhedrin and all the Senate[2] of the children of Israel and sent to the gaol that they might be brought. (22) But the agents when they arrived did not find them in the prison. They returned and brought their report, (23) saying, 'We found the gaol closed in all security and the guards standing at the doors, but when we opened them we found no one inside.' (24) When the Captain of the Temple and the chief priests heard these words they were at a loss concerning them to know what this might mean.[3] (25) Then some one came and reported to them, 'See, the men whom you put in prison are standing in the Temple and teaching the people.' (26) Then the Captain of the Temple went off with the agents and brought them, not however with violence, for they feared the people, lest they should be stoned.

(27) When they had brought them they set them in the Sanhedrin, and the High Priest asked them,[4] (28) saying, 'We strictly ordered you[5] not to teach in this name. And now you have filled Jerusalem with your teaching, and you wish to bring this man's blood upon us.' (29) Peter and the apostles answered and said, 'We must obey God rather than men. (30) The God of our fathers raised up Jesus, whom you killed by hanging him on a tree. (31) This man did God exalt by his right hand to be a ruler and saviour, to give repentance to Israel, and the forgiveness of sins. (32) And we are witnesses of these things, and so is the Holy Spirit, whom God has given to those who obey him.'

(33) When they heard this they were incensed, and wished to kill them. (34) But there rose up one of the Sanhedrin, a Pharisee called Gamaliel, a teacher of the Law held in honour by all the people; he urged that the men be put outside for a little while, (35) and said to the members of the Sanhedrin,[6] 'Men of Israel, take heed to yourselves with regard to these men

---

[1]RSV, in the common prison; NEB, in official custody; NJB, in the public gaol.
[2]NEB, that is, the full Senate; NJB, this was the full Senate.
[3]RSV, what this might come to.
[4]NEB, began his examination.
[5]Or (with other MSS), Did we not strictly order you . . .?
[6]Greek, to them.

and consider[7] what you are about to do. (36) For some time ago Theudas rose up saying that he was somebody, and a number of men, about 400, adhered to him; he was killed, and all those who followed his lead were dispersed and came to nothing. (37) After him, Judas the Galilean rose up in the days of the census and drew a company after himself. He too perished, and all those who followed his lead were scattered. (38) And now, I tell you, steer clear of these men and let them alone, for if this plan or this deed comes from men it will be destroyed; (39) but if it is of God you will not be able to destroy them, and you may find yourselves[8] fighting against God.' They took his advice, (40) summoned the apostles, beat them, commanded them not to go on speaking in the name of Jesus, and dismissed them.

Bibliography

P. W. Barnett, *NTS* 27 (1981), 679–97.

J. W. B. Barns, *TU* 63. 6–9.

G. Baumbach, *ThLZ* 90 (1965), 727–40.

M. Black, *FS* Michel (1974), 45–54.

L. Campeau, *Sciences Ecclésiastiques* 5 (1953), 235–45.

J. Dupont, as in (2) (*Nouvelles*).

M. Hengel, *FS* Michel (1974), 175–96.

R. A. Horsley, *JSNT* 26 (1986), 3–27.

G. Johnston, as in (7).

F. E. Meyer, *NTS* 14 (1968), 545–51.

W. Nauck, *ZNW* 46 (1955), 68–80.

Eb. Nestle, as in (13).

A. A. Trites, *NovT* 16 (1974), 278–84.

A. Vögeli, *ThZ* 9 (1953), 415–38.

U. Wilckens, *Missionsreden*, 45, 62.

M. Wilcox, *JBL* 96 (1977), 85–99.

P. Winter, *EvTh* 17 (1957), 398–406.

Commentary

The Jewish authorities, jealous of the success and popularity of the Christians, arrest the apostles and put them in prison. They are delivered from prison by an angel and return to the work of preaching. The Council meets to consider the case of the Christians only to

---

[7]And consider is not in the Greek.
[8]*Begs.*, lest you be found to be.

discover that they are back in the Temple, continuing their evangelistic work. Their popularity makes the Council circumspect in dealing with them. Peter replies in terms similar to those of 4.19 and adds (vv. 30–32) a very short statement of the usual preaching about Jesus: he was crucified, he is risen, the apostles are his witnesses. The Council, though angry, is at a loss how to deal with the apostles until advised by Gamaliel to wait; time will tell whether the new movement is or is not from God. The apostles are beaten, ordered not to speak in the name of Jesus, and released.

At first sight this paragraph seems almost a doublet of 4.1–22 (cf. Schmithals 59; Weiser 154); the similarities between the two narratives lend some weight to Harnack's hypothesis of two parallel sources (2.1–47; 5.17–42 and 3.1–5.16; see pp. 53f.; also Vol. II, on Sources). See also Reicke (*Glaube* 108–10). There are few who now maintain this hypothesis (see Jeremias, *ZNW* 36 (1937) 205–21; and especially Haenchen 249–52, with criticism also of Jeremias and Reicke). There are significant differences between the two chapters. (1) Luke makes it clear that the incident marks a fresh stage in the proceedings: the apostles have been warned (4.18, 21; 5.28); they are therefore liable now to punishment as they were not before (so Jeremias, op. cit., especially 208–13; but see Haenchen 249; Stählin (95f.) rightly speaks of a 'Steigerung' of the original event). (2) The apostles are attacked on the ground of their teaching (though perhaps rather on the ground *that* they have taught than because of *what* they have taught) (v. 28); the miracle of ch. 3 and the use of the 'name' (but see v. 41) are now left behind. (3) The word παῖς, so strikingly used in chs. 3 and 4, does not appear in ch. 5. (4) The new chapter contains a miraculous rescue by an angel. (5) It also contains punishment: the apostles are beaten (v. 40). (6) Ch. 5 also contains the intervention by Gamaliel. (7) It refers not to two apostles only but to the whole group; all are exposed to suffering (Weiser 157).

These differences bring out the points that Luke wishes to make in the chapter. (1) He wishes to show that the apostles, as representative Christians, *all* the apostles as representative of *all* Christians, are exposed to public disgrace and suffering, yet are nevertheless under divine protection. (2) He wishes to show that Christianity is independent of Judaism, but also (3) that the Christian message relates to 'the God of our fathers' (v. 30) and is the fulfilment of his purpose and promise. (4) He paints a favourable picture of a 'good' Pharisee, representative no doubt of others, who is prepared to wait and see. The Pharisees are more favourable to Christianity than the Sadducees (4.1; 5.17). (5) The angelic release shows in advance the uselessness of fighting against God (Pesch 211).

The paragraph as a whole may be regarded as a piece of Luke's own composition (so explicitly Roloff 100; cf. Lüdemann 75: 'Der Abschnitt [vv. 21b–40] ist in toto lukanisch'), designed to conclude (only 5.41, 42, a final summary, remain) the first section of his book (Schmithals 59). It takes the form which Daube has shown (*NTRJ* 170–75) to be that of a number of passages in the gospels, 'Revolutionary action — Protest — Silencing of the remonstrants'. It was perhaps inevitable that such a form should exist. Daube writes, 'The tripartite form as a whole may owe something to the forensic scheme: action — charge — defence, or successful defence. After all, this scheme, which might be used by any author, must have appeared particularly appropriate to those who recounted Jesus's deeds after his death. They were resuming the trial, they were appealing against the original decision' (175). We may add that the resumption of the trial was not only a figure of speech. We have Paul's own word for the practice of persecution at an early date (before his own conversion to Christianity: 1 Cor. 15.9; Gal. 1.13, 23), and the present paragraph, though as it stands Luke's work, is probably correct in representing a trial of Christians. Luke, as we have seen, could base most of what he wrote in ch. 5 on general knowledge and on what he had written in ch. 4 (e.g. Bauernfeind 90). For the angelic rescue he had a parallel in 12.7–12, not to mention other similar stories. Gamaliel's speech is Luke's own composition, and an unhappy one in that he makes Gamaliel mention an event that had not taken place at the time of speaking (see the notes on vv. 36, 37). He may possibly show dependence on Josephus here. He does however ascribe to Gamaliel an attitude that is quite intelligible and credible within Judaism, and may have been aware of a vein of Pharisaic thought persisting in the church. If he was, or if one of his sources or informants was, personally related to Paul he had (or at least believed that he had — 22.3) a good reason for sympathy with and some knowledge of Gamaliel.

17. Ἀναστάς, a Septuagintalism (cf. 5.6), often introduces fresh action in Acts (e.g. 1.15; 5.34). The variant *Annas* (p mae) is in view of 4.6 a natural misreading (which is nevertheless thought by Dibelius (91) 'worth mentioning' and is accepted by Delebecque 24); καὶ ταῦτα βλέπων ἀναστάς (E) is an attempt to improve the connection with what precedes. No doubt Luke thought that the High Priest was Annas; see on 4.6. *All who were with him* is explained by the reference to the Sadducees (see on 4.1); there is a rough correspondence with ὅσοι ἦσαν ἐκ γένους ἀρχιερατικοῦ, but the different phraseology does not suggest the use of a continuous source in chs. 4 and 5. Blass notes Josephus *Ant.* 20.199, where Annas as High Priest is said to have followed the αἵρεσις of the Sadducees.

ἡ οὖσα αἵρεσις: 'The redundant use of ὤν is ... characteristic of Ac and the Ptol. papyri: Ac 5.17 ..., 13.1 ..., 14.13 D ..., Ro 13.1 ..., Eph 1.1 P⁴⁶ D ..., P. Tebt. 309 (ii/AD) ἀπὸ τοῦ ὄντος ἐν κώμη [τοῦ ἱεροῦ] θεοῦ)..., P. Lille 29, 11 (iii/BC) τοὺς νόμους περὶ τῶν οἰκετῶν ὄντας. It is conclusive from the papyri that the ὤν is redundant and means little more than *current* or *existent*. Translate *the local Zeus* (14.13D), *the local church* (13.1), *the local school of the Sadducees* (5.17)' (M. 3.152). Turner refers to *Begs*. 4.56, Schwyzer II 409, Mayser II 1, 347f. (a 'verbal flourish'), Moulton, *Einleitung* 360 (presumably rather than M. 1.228). If ὤν (οὖσα) means what Turner says it means it is hard to see why it should be described as redundant. The Sadducees (see *NS* 2.404–14) form a αἵρεσις; so also the Pharisees (15.5; 26.5), and the Christians (24.5, 14; 28.22), though in these passages Luke is quoting the opinion of others. For him, of course, the Christians represent the true way (ὁδός, 9.2, *al*.) for Judaism, from which others diverge in different directions. On the word αἵρεσις and its application to Christians, see *FS* Lohse, 96–110.

The success of the Christian preaching (5.14) filled the Sadducees, whom Luke thinks of as now less influential than the Christians, with envy (though it is possible — Stählin 89 — to give the word ζῆλος a better sense, *heiliger Eifer*, a holy zeal for the truth as they believed it to be). ζῆλος is neuter (genitive ζήλους) here in B* (also at 2 Cor. 9.2 ℵ B 33 and at Phil. 3.6 ℵ* A B D* F G). It is masculine in seven places (eight if we count Gal. 5.20, ℵ C Dᶜ 𝔐). The neuter is used in Modern Greek and was probably popular in Hellenistic times. So M. 2.126.

18. For ἐπιβάλλειν χεῖρας see 4.3. This time the apostles as a group, not Peter and John only (4.1, 3, 13), are attacked. For ἔθεντο εἰς τήρησιν (4.3) we this time have ἔθεντο ἐν τηρήσει, without difference in meaning, but with the possible suggestion of a different source (though a desire for variety could equally explain the difference of case and preposition). δημοσίᾳ could be an adjective agreeing with τηρήσει (so Schneider 389), but in view of 16.37; 18.28; 20.20 (here only in the NT) it is better taken as an adverb. Bauernfeind (92) writes: 'Die τήρησις δημοσία ist gewiss eine schwerere Form der Haft, als die einfache τήρησις', but gives no evidence for this. If δημοσία is to be regarded as an adjective it would recall the Latin *custodia publica*, which is quite common, e.g. Cicero, *de Divinatione* 1.25 (52) . . . Socrates, cum esset in custodia publica; *In Verrem* 3.26 (66) . . . alios in publico custodiri. δημόσιον (e.g. Thucydides 5.18.6,7) was taken into rabbinic Hebrew as דמוסין but more often for a public bath than a public prison.

At the end of the verse D mae add καὶ ἐπορεύθη εἰς ἕκαστος εἰς τὰ ἴδια, presumably in order to make it clear that a night intervene before the Jewish authorities reappear in the story.

19. In the course of the night the apostles were delivered from prison by an angel. Cf. 12.4–10, where Peter is delivered in the same way, and 16.25–34 where Paul and Silas are released by an earthquake. ἄγγελος κυρίου is an OT expression (e.g. Gen. 16.7); often the article is used: *the* angel of the Lord — here Stählin (89) thinks that even without the article this may be the intended meaning. Whether by κύριος Luke understood the OT Lord or Jesus it is impossible to determine; probably he would find it unnecessary to make up his mind on the question, if indeed it occurred to him. The MSS are fairly evenly divided between ἀνοίξας (P⁷⁴ ℵ A 36 453 1175 *pc*) and ἤνοιξεν (B (D) E Ψ 0189 𝔐). Since the apostles are immediately rearrested, Blass (84) asks 'Quis ergo usus angeli?' He answers, rightly, that the angel increases the confidence of the apostles and the wrath of their opponents.

διὰ νυκτός. M. 3.179 notes the omission of the article in such prepositional designations of time as classical; a number of MSS add it here — during the night in question. Schille (160) however rightly notes that νυκτός alone would be classical. θύραι is sometimes used for a single door, but here (cf. v. 23) there is no reason why all the prison doors, or all necessary, inner and outer, doors, should not be intended.

20. The apostles have been released in order to continue their work. They are to *stand* (as Peter did on the Day of Pentecost, 2.14) in the Temple and speak to the people. The Temple is the centre of the old religion and the place where they are sure to find a large concourse of people; Luke might have Solomon's Portico in mind (3.11; 5.12). He may also have a theological point: the Temple now belongs to the Gospel (Stählin 89); this proclamation is the purpose for which God intended the Temple (Roloff 102). This is more doubtful. The Gospel message which the apostles are to proclaim is described as τὰ ῥήματα τῆς ζωῆς ταύτης; cf. Jn 6.68. The apostles are to speak them all, πάντα, holding nothing back (out of fear, or tact?). ἡ ζωὴ αὕτη may mean this *way* of life; more probably it is the new life offered by Jesus as the ἀρχηγὸς τῆς ζωῆς (3.15). For this use of ζωή to express the content of the Gospel (much more common in John and Paul) cf. also 11.18; 13.46, 48. It is interesting to note that the Temple was sometimes described as בית חיינו, house of our life, or our house of life, but unlikely that Luke or his readers would be aware of any allusion. It is however conceivable that this expression might explain ταύτης (for which Pallis proposes to read ταῦτα).

21. The apostles did as they were told (for ἀκούσαντες δέ, E has ἐξελθόντες δὲ ἐκ τῆς φυλακῆς) and with the dawn (ὑπό with accusative of time is uncommon in the NT) entered the Temple. The gates were closed at night (Shekalim 5.1; Josephus, *Apion* 2.119) but must have been opened in time for the sacrifice at daybreak (Exod. 29.39; Num. 28.4, in the morning; Yoma 3.1, 2 (Eduyoth 6.1 is an exceptional opinion); Philo, *Spec. Leg.* 1.169, ἅμα τῆ ἔῳ). ἐδίδασκον is not distinguished from proclamation.

παραγενόμενος (a common and characteristic word in Acts) suggests (cf. vv. 22, 25; 9.26; and many other passages) that the High Priest arrived at the place where the apostles were teaching. This in the context it plainly cannot mean. Presumably therefore it means that he and his entourage (οἱ σὺν αὐτῷ) arrived at the place where the Sanhedrin was to meet (see on 4.5) and then summoned (συνεκάλεσαν) the other members. Unless Luke was ill-informed καί (after συνέδριον) must be understood *in sensu explicativo* (Zerwick § 455): the Sanhedrin was the γερουσία, or Council of Elders. Hesychius defines γερουσία as πρεσβυτέριον, πλῆθος γερόντων. The equivalence of the terms is supported by Dionysius Hal., *Ant.* 2.12, τοῦτο τὸ συνέδριον ἑλληνιστὶ ἑρμηνευόμενον Γερουσίαν . . ., and an inscription (*CIG* 2.3417) in which the same body is referred to as γερουσία and συνέδριον τῶν πρεσβυτέρων. It should however be added that Schneider (390) follows Preuschen 31 in distinguishing the two terms, regarding the γερουσία as a sort of Senate; so also Weiser (156). For the body in question see on 4.15. Pesch (222) sees significance in the words 'council of the children of Israel', in that they recall the deliverance of Israel from bondage. It is doubtful whether this was in Luke's mind.

For συνεκάλεσαν D mae have ἐγερθέντες τῷ πρωὶ καὶ συνκαλεσάμενοι. Here it is to be noted (a) that the middle voice is used and (b) that the participle is followed by καί and a finite verb (καὶ ἀπέστειλαν). (a) is dismissed by BDR § 316.2 in the words 'Bei einigen Verben wechseln Medium und Aktiv willkürlich'. (b) Black (*AA* 69) thinks to be a sign of the antiquity of the Western text and possibly a sign of Aramaic influence; he rejects the explanations of Haenchen and Lagrange who think the intrusive καί to be the result of the influence of D's Latin column on the Greek.

The authorities sent to the prison (δεσμωτήριον; as at Mt. 11.2; Acts 5.23; 16.26; nowhere else in the NT; not the word of v. 18) that the apostles might be brought to the Council. ἀπέστειλαν . . . . ἀχθῆναι αὐτούς. M. 3.138 observes that the passive after verba iubendi is Latin, but not classical Greek; so also BDR§ 392.4 n. 14 (quoting *P Tebt* II 331.16: ἀξιῶ ἀχθῆναι αὐτούς, and other papyri) and § 390.1 n. 3. But ἀποστέλλειν is not truly a verb of commanding. The construction in fact is too compressed, but the sense is clear: the High Priest sent men to the prison that the prisoners might be brought.

22. There is a further awkwardness in the word order οἱ δὲ παραγενόμενοι ὑπηρέται (P⁷⁴ ℵ A B 36 945 1175 1739 *al*); οἱ δὲ ὑπ. παρ. (D E Ψ 𝔐) is easier but secondary. The ὑπηρέται, sent on their unsuccessful mission to the prison, were the Temple guard who acted under the orders of the סגן הכוהנים (cf. 4.1). Their 'usual function was to watch the Temple at night (Middoth 1.2). Their arms and methods are recalled in a "street-ballad" (Klausner, *Jesus* 337):

> Woe is me, for the house of Boethus! woe is me for their club!
> Woe is me, for the house of Annas! woe is me, for their whisperings!
> Woe is me, for the house of Kathros (Kantheros): woe is me, for their pen!
> Woe is me, for the house of Ishmael (ben Phiabi): woe is me, for their fist!
> For they are the high priests, and their sons the treasurers: their sons-in-law are Temple-officers, and their servants beat the people with their staves. (Pesahim 57a; T. Menahoth 13.21 (533).' (*St John* 519).

A third word, φυλακή, is now used for *prison* (τήρησις, v. 18; δεσμωτήριον, v. 21). The last clause is rewritten by D lat (sy^h**) mae: καὶ ἀνοίξαντες τὴν φυλακὴν οὐχ εὗρον αὐτοὺς ἔσω. This gives only a very slightly more circumstantial picture of the event, and is evidently based on v. 23 (end).

23. The report is straightforward and clear. The word δεσμωτήριον (v. 21) returns, possibly because φυλακή could have caused confusion with φύλακας later in the verse. For θυρῶν (plural) see on v. 19. Outwardly everything was in order; but inside they found no one (οὐδένα: it would be wrong however to press Luke's words to mean that the apostles were the only occupants of the prison). Some (including Schneider 391) take ἔσω with ἀνοίξαντες: opening up within, we found no one. This is possible but does not seem to make as good sense as the usual way of connecting the words.

ἐν πάσῃ ἀσφαλείᾳ for ἀσφαλέστατα; ἐν of manner BDR § 219.4 n. 4). Cf. 17.31; and cf. J. W. B. Barns, *TU* 63. 3–9, a papyrus of AD 343, l. 22, ἐν ἀσφαλίᾳ ἀξιῶν ἀχθῆναι αὐτούς. But if this is to be regarded as a parallel (*ND* 3.154) it must not be translated *in custody*.

24. The perplexity of the στρατηγός (see 4.1) and of the ἀρχιερεῖς (also 4.1), though expressed by the active rather than the more usual middle deponent of ἀπορεῖν (cf. 10.17; possibly 2.12), is understandable. γένοιτο is potential optative in an indirect question (cf. 10.17); in the NT this literary construction is characteristic of Luke. Page (114) rightly observes that the corresponding direct question would be τί γενήσεται τοῦτο; which he translates, 'What will be the end, or result, of this?'

25. More information arrives. παραγενόμενος: see on v. 21. In view of the 2nd person ἔθεσθε, ὅτι must be recitative. ἰδού adds a touch of Semitic atmosphere (cf. e.g. הנה). *The men whom you put in prison*: v. 18. φυλακή as at v. 22. For standing and teaching see vv. 20, 21. The members of the Council are surprised; the reader is not. M. 3.88f. seems disposed to consider that εἰσὶν . . . ἐστῶτες may be a Semitism, though Turner does not express himself unambiguously, and notes that 'the periphrastic perfect persisted in the mainstream of the language and is in regular use at the present day.' He contrasts 25.10, where the idiom is very emphatic (see the note). Wilcox (125) finds the Semitism in the use of קאם as more or less equivalent to *to be*. Probably in this passage the periphrastic tense and ἐστῶτες mean primarily, and emphatically, 'Where are they? They are — doing precisely what they were told to do.'

26. ἀπελθών: the στρατηγός and the ὑπηρέται were officers of the Council and undertook practical tasks, such as arresting criminals. ἦγεν (P⁷⁴ᵛⁱᵈ B ℵ Dᶜ) is no doubt correct; the aorist (ἤγαγεν A E Ψ 𝔐; ἤγαγον D*2495 *pc* syᵖ) fails to make the point that the action persisted up to the point at which the apostles were brought into court (ἀγαγόντες, aorist, v. 27); see BDR § 327. n. 1; M. 3.66.

The apostles were popular figures (5.13) so that the authorities had to tread carefully. They proceeded οὐ (om. D*!) μετὰ βίας (classical usage would be οὐ βίᾳ, or οὐ πρὸς βίαν: BDR § 198.4 n. 5; cf. 24.7, si v.l.; also v. 18, δημοσίᾳ; v. 23, ἐν πάσῃ ἀσφαλείᾳ). They feared lest they should be stoned. Such a stoning could not be a formal legal penalty, since the only authority that could inflict such a penalty was the Council itself. This means that by λιθάζειν Luke understood a popular move by which a crowd threw stones at unpopular people. Stählin (90), however, thinks that the crowd are virtually accusing the Council of blasphemy, and wish to impose the appropriate penalty. At 7.58, 59 Luke uses a different word (λιθοβολεῖν); whether in that passage he means the same kind of stoning or not is a difficult question; see the notes. Knowling (152) suggests that ἐφοβοῦντο γὰρ τὸν λαόν may be a parenthesis, with λιθασθῶσιν dependent on οὐ μετὰ βίας; Delebecque (26) however describes ἐφοβοῦντο τὸν λαόν as a 'prolepse très classique'.

27. Judicial proceedings begin. For the arrangement of the Sanhedrin see on 4.7. The arraigned apostles would presumably be within the semicircle. The High Priest as president questioned them. It is interesting that he makes no reference to their surprising disappearance from the prison; this incident may have been an addition to a story which originally did not contain it.

28. ἐπηρώτησεν in v. 27 suggests that v. 28 will contain a question. This is given by the text οὐ παραγγελίᾳ παρηγγείλαμεν, *Did we not . . . ?*, a question implying an affirmative answer. οὐ is omitted by P⁷⁴ ℵ* A B 1175 *pc* lat boh Lucifer Cyril, but read by ℵᶜ D E (Ψ)𝔐 h p w sy sa mae. The former group thus has not a question but a statement: *We did . . .* The sense is the same and it is a nice question whether the lectio difficilior should be accepted or Luke given the credit for providing a proper link between the two verses. Metzger (331) thinks οὐ a 'scribal addition' — probably rightly.

παραγγελίᾳ παρηγγείλαμεν suggests a Semitic construction, either a translation or an imitation of a Hebrew infinitive absolute. M. 2.443 raises the question but hardly answers it; see on 2.30. BDR § 198.6 n. 9 is almost certainly right in describing the phrase as an imitation of the OT idiom. The construction occurs frequently in the LXX, and there are partial parallels in classical usage (e.g. γάμῳ γαμεῖν, φυγῇ φεύγειν). The High Priest is referring to 4.17, 18: . . . παρήγγειλαν . . . μὴ φθέγγεσθαι μηδὲ διδάσκειν ἐπὶ τῷ ὀνόματι τοῦ 'Ιησοῦ. So far from obeying this order they have filled (perfect, πεπληρώκατε; P⁷⁴ ℵ A 36 1175 *pc* have the aorist ἐπληρώσατε) Jerusalem with the forbidden teaching. Coupled with objection to what is evidently regarded as erroneous and undesirable teaching goes sensitivity to what was taken as a personal accusation: the Sanhedrin feels that it is being accused of responsibility for the death of Jesus. This has already been claimed, in general and qualified terms. 2.23 blames the Jewish people in general, as does 3.13; 3.17 mentions in particular οἱ ἄρχοντες ὑμῶν, but allows that all acted in ignorance; cf. 4.11, 27; 10.39. 13.27 also mentions οἱ ἄρχοντες ὑμῶν. For ἐφ' ἡμᾶς τὸ αἷμα cf. 1 Sam. 1.15; Mt. 23.35; 27.25 (which last, Bede says, the High Priest must have forgotten). Plümacher (71) notes that occasionally Luke makes not only the apostles but also their opponents use biblical language; cf. 4.16–18; 5.35–39. Haenchen (245) thinks that the Sanhedrin feared that the apostles were invoking divine vengeance; cf. Judges 9.24. This may well be what Luke thought that they thought; if the words have a historical basis it is more likely that the Sanhedrin would fear a popular uprising.

τοῦ ἀνθρώπου τούτου: 'fugit appellare Jesum' (Bengel). More probably the expression is disparaging.

29. Again Peter takes the lead among the apostles (according to D (h syᵖ) Peter alone speaks: ὁ δὲ Πέτρος εἶπεν πρὸς αὐτούς), using words so similar to those of 4.19 (see the note) that they suggest that the two 'trial scenes' are duplicates. The construction μᾶλλον ἤ is repeated; see Black (*AA* 117) quoted on 4.19. Cf. 2 Clement 4.4. Barth (*CD* 3.4.250), arguing that Peter's words do not preclude obedience to men, would presumably question the grammatical point, taking the verse to mean that if a choice has to be made God must have the preference rather than men. If the background is Socratic rather than Semitic (see on 4.19) this is not unreasonable. πειθαρχεῖν recurs at 4. 32; 27.21; elsewhere in the NT only at Titus 3.1. The principle — of the supreme authority of God — is one highly characteristic of Judaism itself, in which it had been established at a high cost in suffering. Peter's application of it, in its context, is new and shocking because it sets over against each other God and those men who were best qualified to expound God's command as expressed in his law. For the dative with πειθαρχεῖν see evidence in *ND* 2.105. Ropes (*Begs*. 3.50; cf. Clark 341) thinks that the Western text of this verse is given by h and Augustine (cf. Jerome): respondens autem Petrus et apostoli dixerunt, utrum oportet obaudire, deo an hominibus? at ille dixit, deo. et Petrus ait ad illos . . . This interrogative form may have been shortened, or the shorter form made livelier. The latter seems more probable; see the Introduction to this volume, pp. 21-9 and Vol. II.

30. The new verse begins without a connecting participle (P^{74} ℵ A supply δέ) and introduces a brief (vv. 30, 31, 32) statement of the Christian proclamation which shows no sign of special adaptation to the occasion. In writing up the incident Luke judges that a statement of the Christian position was called for, and inserted one; cf. 4.8–12. If he was composing the paragraph himself the contents of these verses could easily have been made up from material in chs. 2, 3 and 4.

ὁ θεὸς τῶν πατέρων ἡμῶν. As at 3.13 Peter begins by emphasizing that he is introducing no new God but is speaking of the God of the Fathers. The Christian faith is the fulfilment, not the contradiction, of Judaism, if Judaism is rightly understood. ἤγειρεν is ambiguous. It may refer to God's act in raising Jesus from the dead (as e.g. at 3.15), but it may mean that God brought Jesus on the human scene (cf. 13.37, of David; cf. ἀνιστάναι at 3.22, 26; 7.37; 13.32). Decision on this question probably turns on the interpretation of ὕψωσεν in v. 31. If this includes resurrection, ἤγειρεν probably bears the latter meaning; if ὕψωσεν refers to the post-resurrection exaltation of Jesus, ἤγειρεν will supply the otherwise missing reference. This is the preferable view, and is supported by the near parallel in 3.15. διαχειρίζεσθαι (middle deponent) occurs in biblical Greek only here and at 26.21. Peter shows no sign of retreating from the position complained of in v. 28.

κρεμάσαντες ἐπὶ ξύλου (cf. 10.39) recalls Deut. 21.22, 23 (ἐὰν . . .κρεμάσητε αὐτὸν ἐπὶ ξύλου . . . κεκατηραμένος ὑπὸ θεοῦ πᾶς κρεμάμενος ἐπὶ ξύλου), a passage of which important theological use is made by Paul (Gal. 3.13). No such use is made in Acts, and Delling (*Kreuzestod* 85) may be right in the view that Luke was not aware of the OT allusion but took the expression out of the familiar language of Christian proclamation. The word however does not seem to have been in common use for the hanging of persons in execution, and Luke may well have used an OT word without working out an interpretation. For the transformation of the 'cursed tree' into the 'tree of life', in both theology and Christian art, see Dinkler (*Signum Crucis* 73). The participle κρεμάσαντες denotes action coincident with the finite verb.

31. τοῦτον ὁ θεὸς ἀρχηγὸν καὶ σωτῆρα ὕψωσεν. The anarthrous accusatives are predicative: exalted him to be . . . (Schneider 396). The verse ('Eine traditionelle Erhöhungsaussage', Plümacher 72) forms an admirable summary of Lucan theology. As the object of divine action (ὕψωσεν) Jesus becomes its subject (ἀρχηγὸς καὶ σωτήρ) (Barth, *CD*3.3.439). For ἀρχηγός see 3.15 and the note. Without the genitive τῆς ζωῆς the word probably here stands nearer (so Bruce) to the simple meaning *leader* or *prince*; that is, it would not differ widely from κύριος (cf. 2.36). 1 QSb 5.20, נשיא העדה, prince of the community, who as Davidic Messiah saves Israel (4 Q Flor 1.13), is not a close parallel; Jesus is not described as prince of the community; and at Qumran salvation is political (Braun 1.159). σωτήρ is a word characteristic of the later NT writings (Eph. 5.23; Phil. 3.20; Pastorals ten times; 2 Peter five times), though σώζειν is frequent throughout. Notwithstanding its (not very frequent) use in the LXX (especially Psalms and Isaiah; except at Judges 3.9, 15, always of God — Stählin 91) it probably had pagan connections that were too strong to allow it to be easily taken into Christian use. It is hardly correct (as Bousset, in a classical discussion, *Kyrios Christos*, 1913, 293–9, argued) that the title was taken from its pagan use, primarily in the Ruler cults, into the Christian vocabulary. The thought of salvation through Christ must always have been pressing the word into Christian use; when eventually Christian thought seemed sufficiently firm to assimilate the word, however, it did in fact, and inevitably, bring with it something of its non-Christian background. This however is scarcely to be seen in the present verse, where the work of the Saviour is said to issue in repentance and the forgiveness of sins (according to Cullmann, *Christologie* 250, a characteristically Jewish Christian feature). God offers not vengeance but forgiveness; see on v. 28. For the combination of the two words σωτήρ and ἀρχηγός see 2 Clement 20.5, τῷ ἐξαποστείλαντι ἡμῖν τὸν σωτῆρα καὶ ἀρχηγὸν τῆς ἀφθαρσίας. The connection here (in 2 Clement's concluding ascription of praise) is liturgical; it is more likely that it is drawn from common Christian use than that it is based on Acts. Fuller (*Christology* 48) thinks that both terms (and ἀρχηγός at 3.15) are drawn from a Moses-prophet-servant context.

ὕψωσεν. See on v. 30. It is closely associated with resurrection (Delling, *Studien* 358), but is distinguished from it. τῇ δεξιᾷ αὐτοῦ is ambiguous, as at 2.33. The ambiguity should probably be resolved in the same was as there; that is, the dative should be taken as instrumental (Schneider 396 takes it as local).

τοῦ before the infinitive is characteristic of Luke-Acts and imitates the LXX; its occurrence here however may be due to dittography. μετάνοια occurs here for the first time in Acts, but see 2.38; 3.19 for μετανοεῖν in similar contexts. It is not enough that God should grant forgiveness to those who repent; he first makes repentance possible; cf. 11.18. See also Wisdom 12.19, and for the giving of opportunity or time for repentance, Josephus, *War* 3.127; 6.339. For the forgiveness of sins see 2.38. Stauffer (*Theologie* 119) sees here a picture of Christ as 'unser Hoherpriester, der im himmlischen Heiligtum steht und vor Gottes Angesicht für uns eintritt.' If Luke thought in these terms he does not say so.

For δεξιᾷ, D* gig p sa Irenaeus (Latin) have δόξῃ, presumably a mechanical slip; at the end of the verse, somewhat unnecessarily, D* h p sa mae add ἐν αὐτῷ.

32. For the apostles as witnesses (of these matters — that is, primarily of the resurrection; cf. 10.37) see 1.8, and many other passages. Cf. Isa. 43.10. The Holy Spirit also is a witness; where he is manifestly at work (in e.g. speaking with tongues; cf. 10.46) it is plain that there is divine action. For the combined testimony of apostles and Spirit cf. Jn 15.26f. In itself, this parallel, striking as it is, is not sufficient to establish literary dependence. The thought that Christians, and especially apostles, are witnesses is not uncommon (e.g. Mk 3.14), and the Holy Spirit bears witness (though in a somewhat different sense) in Rom. 8.16. For a different kind of testimony to the being and action of God see 14.17. The Holy Spirit was given by God to those who obey him: for the word πειθαρχεῖν see on v. 29. The aorist ἔδωκεν may suggest the gift of the Spirit at Pentecost (2.4), but Luke refers frequently to bestowals of the Spirit and it is unlikely that he wished to relate the gift exclusively to this event. Every manifestation of the Spirit bears witness to the Gospel. Schmithals (61) sees here a reference to 'Spirit-filled heretics'; Luke implies and insists that the mark of the Spirit is agreement with the apostles.

The structure of the sentence but not its sense is improved by the omission (possibly accidental) of ὅ (B *pc* Cyril).

33. For the reaction διεπρίοντο cf. 2.37, κατενύγησαν, which introduces a favourable response; but especially 7.54, where διεπρίοντο recurs with the same unfavourable response as here. In itself the word (literally *to saw through, to saw asunder*) denotes strong emotion of any kind. Chrysostom explains it as κακῶς παθεῖν. It is often used of the grinding of teeth, cf. Aristophanes, *Frogs* 926f., σιώπα . . . μὴ πρῖε τοὺς ὀδόντας. Cf. Hesychius: διεπρίοντο, ἐθυμοῦντο, ἔτριζον τοὺς ὀδόντας.

ἐβούλοντο, *they wished*, is read by A B E Ψ 36 104 614 *pc* co; ἐβουλεύοντο, *they planned*, by ℵ D (1175 1241) 𝔐. The words are different, but both come to much the same thing. If they seriously wished to kill they would at least begin (note the imperfect tense) to make plans to achieve their wish; if they made plans to kill it would be because they wished to kill. Conzelmann prefers (42; probably rightly)ἐβούλοντο, but notes a parallel in Achilles Tatius 7.1.1, ἤχθετο, ὠργίζετο, ἐβουλεύετο.

34. Planning however did not get beyond a beginning; it was interrupted by the intervention (ἀναστάς; see on v. 17) of Gamaliel, described by Luke as a Pharisee and a νομοδιδάσκαλος. On the Pharisees see *NS* 2.381–403. By Luke they are regularly taken to be more favourable (or less unfavourable?) to the Christians than the Sadducees (see v. 17), partly because they believed in resurrection as the Sadducees did not (23.8). It was their understanding of Judaism that survived the war of 66–70, and Schmithals (61) is no doubt right in pointing out that it was politic for Luke to represent them as at least tolerant of the church; but Luke may also have been right in this. νομοδιδάσκαλος is used at Lk. 5.17 (elsewhere in the NT only at 1 Tim. 1.7); Luke often prefers νομικός to the γραμματεύς of Mt. and Mk, less interested, perhaps in rendering סופר than in indicating the base of Jewish study and life. For Gamaliel see StrB 2.636–9 and *NS* 2.367–8. The reference must be to Rabban Gamaliel I, a Tanna of the first generation, according to 22.3 the teacher of Paul. Luke's statement that he was τίμιος παντὶ τῷ λαῷ agrees almost verbally with Josephus (*War* 5.527, Βοηθοῦ παῖς ἦν οὗτος . . . τῷ δήμῳ πιστὸς καὶ τίμιος) and corresponds with the opinion of the Mishnah (Sotah 9.15: When Rabban Gamaliel the Elder died, the glory of the Law ceased and purity and abstinence died). The statement (Sotah 49b; Baba Kamma 83a) that Gamaliel had 1,000 students learning the wisdom of the Jews and 1,000 learning the wisdom of the Greeks relates (so far as it is true) not to Gamaliel I but to his grandson, Gamaliel II, who lived towards the end of the first century. It is not correct that Gamaliel is here (wrongly) represented as presiding over the Sanhedrin; he is described as τις ἐν τῷ συνεδρίῳ, one who belonged to the Sanhedrin and exercised his right to express an opinion. Haenchen (246) appears to doubt whether Gamaliel was a Pharisee; it is not clear why. On Pharisees in the Sanhedrin see E. Lohse in *TWNT* 7.859–64. Bede refers to *Clem. Recog.* 1.65 for the belief that Gamaliel was a believer, but 'eorum consilio permanens apud Iudaeos ut eorum in tali turbine potuisset sedare furorem'. Luke gives no ground for thinking that Gamaliel ever became a Christian. παντὶ τῷ λαῷ, ethic dative, *in the opinion of* (cf. Euripides, *Hecuba* 309, ἡμῖν δ'Ἀχιλλεὺς ἄξιος τιμῆς).

τις ἐν τῷ συνεδρίῳ. ἐν with the dative here encroaches on the partitive genitive, though for this there are classical precedents and 'die lokale Bed. "in", "unter" ist in den meisten Fällen noch deutlich spürbar' (BDR § 164.1 n. 4). D E h p (sy^p) bo have ἐκ τοῦ συνεδρίου.

Gamaliel prefers to put his point of view in the absence of the apostles; the Sanhedrin can speak more freely and they will avoid giving the apostles the impression that they may perhaps be right.

35. ἄνδρες Ἰσραηλῖται. Cf. 2.22. προσέχειν, short for προσέχειν τὸν νοῦν, with a dative, is *attend to*, in an appropriate context, *beware of* (Lk. 12.1), *take heed to yourselves in relation to* (ἐπί) *these men*, or, taking ἐπὶ τοῖς ἀνθρώποις as a prolepsis (Delebecque 27), *take heed over what you are about to do to these men.* The sentence is expressed as an indirect question with τί (not ὅ) because Gamaliel assumes that no decision has yet been reached, the question is open. There are, he says, precedents which it will be useful to consider.

Gamaliel too speaks in biblical style (Plümacher 46). For his speech see Dibelius (186f.).

36. πρὸ τούτων τῶν ἡμερῶν; that is, before the time of speaking, and, one would think if the words stood alone, not in the immediate past.

Θευδᾶς, is usually thought to be equivalent to Θεόδωρος or Θεόδοτος, but see *ND* 4.183–5. A man of this name is mentioned by Josephus, *Ant.* 20.97, 98: During the period when Fadus was procurator of Judaea, a certain impostor (γόης) named Theudas persuaded the majority of the masses to take up their possessions and to follow him to the Jordan River. He stated that he was a prophet and that at his command the river would be parted and would provide them an easy passage. With this talk he deceived many. Fadus, however, did not permit them to reap the fruit of their folly, but sent against them a squadron of cavalry. These fell upon them unexpectedly, slew many of them and took many prisoners. Theudas himself was captured, whereupon they cut off his head and brought it to Jerusalem. This corresponds closely enough with what is said in the present verse about Theudas, though Luke's figure for his adherents (400) is smaller than Josephus's narrative suggests. The difficulty lies in the date. Fadus was procurator in 44, years after Gamaliel is said to have intervened in the Sanhedrin's discussion. This difficulty is compounded in the next verse; see below.

For λέγων εἶναί τινα ἑαυτόν cf. Gal. 6.3. D E 36 614 2495 *pc* gig h sy^p mae make the expression more wooden by adding μέγαν;

cf. 8.9. In fact this use of τις (or τι), without adjective, is common in Greek; e.g. Euripides, *Electra* 939, ηὔχεις τις εἶναι (the nominative is better than Luke's accusative). At the end of the verse εἰς οὐδέν has been held to be a Semitism (predicative ל). M. 2.462 refers back to M. 1.71f., which (not mentioning this passage) discounts Hebraism. BDR § 157.5 say that predicative εἰς shows unmistakable Semitic influence (notwithstanding the Greek parallels to which Moulton draws attention) but they do not cite this passage. Rightly, for here εἰς is not strictly predicative (Schneider 401: the expression is 'singulär'). Luke means that Theudas's revolt had no positive result, as in the English *came to nothing*.

For ἀνῃρέθη, D⁽ᶜ⁾ (p) have διελύθη αὐτὸς δι' ἑαυτοῦ) and omit διελύθησαν. This appears to mean that Theudas committed suicide, whereas Josephus (see above) says that he was beheaded. Could this be a hint that there were two men called Theudas? See further below.

διελύθησαν, they were scattered. Cf. Thucydides 2.23.2, διελύθησαν κατὰ πόλεις ἕκαστοι).

Daube (*NTRJ* 112) thinks that Theudas in his claim to be able to divide the Jordan represented himself as the prophet like Moses (Deut. 18.15; cf. Acts 3.22; 7.37). Knox (*Hellenistic Elements* 26) thinks that Theudas may have 'claimed to be Jesus-Jeshua returning to fulfil the prophecies of the end (cf. Mk. 13.6), hoping to enlist Christian support'. An interesting speculation.

37. μετὰ τοῦτον, after (the time of) Theudas — though Calvin (153), with his eye on the problems below, suggests that in post hunc surrexit Judas Galilaeus, *post* means 'over and above' or 'besides'. Judas the Galilaean is a well-known figure whose resistance at the time of the ἀπογραφή, *registration* or *census* conducted in AD 6 by Quirinius (Lk. 2.2) is described by Josephus (*Ant.* 18.4–10, 23; *War* 2. (56), 118) in an account which agrees substantially with the words attributed to Gamaliel. 'The populace, when they heard their (Judas and his colleague Saddok) appeals, responded gladly' (*Ant.* 18.6); but Josephus does not mention the end of Judas, either in the *Antiquities* or in the *War*. He was certainly unsuccessful in preventing the census, and Luke may well be substantially correct in saying that Judas himself ἀπώλετο and his followers διεσκορπίσθησαν, *were scattered* — at least for a time. According to Josephus (*War* 2.118; *Ant.* 18.9) they became the foundation of the so-called 'fourth philosophy', the Zealot movement.

The problem in vv. 36, 37 is that if the identifications of Judas and Theudas that have been given are correct, Judas did not rise up *after* Theudas, but nearly forty years before him; indeed, that Theudas did not initiate his revolt until about ten years after the time at which Gamaliel must be supposed to have been speaking. The identification and date of Judas are not in doubt; the simplest explanation of Luke's text, and the only one that does not involve him in some kind of error, is the view that there was another Theudas, otherwise unknown, who did take up arms at some point before Judas. This is of course possible; it does not seem probable — though it is worth noting Knowling's observation (158) that Josephus mentions four Simons in forty years and three Judas's within ten, all instigators of rebellion. Another solution turns on *Ant.* 20.102, where, just after his account of Theudas quoted above, Josephus writes, 'Besides this James and Simon, the sons of Judas the Galilean, were brought up for trial, and at the order of Alexander [the successor of Fadus as procurator], were crucified. This was the Judas who, as I have explained above, had aroused the people to revolt against the Romans while Quirinius was taking the census in Judaea.' Thus Josephus mentions Judas and his revolt *after* mentioning Theudas; it is suggested that Luke misread this passage (or perhaps the source on which it is based) and so made the mistake that we have observed. Again, this may be true, though Josephus's account is clear and there is no excuse for misreading. It is worth nothing that if Luke had read the *Antiquities* he was writing after 93, when Josephus's book was published (unless we complicate the hypothesis yet further by supposing, with B. H. Streeter, *The Four Gospels*, London 1936, 557f., that he had heard a pre-publication reading by Josephus). The matter may be more complex. In v. 36 the great majority of MSS describe the fate of Judas and his followers in the words ὃς ἀνῃρέθη, καὶ πάντες ὅσοι ἐπείθοντο αὐτῷ διελύθησαν . . . Instead of this D has ὃς διελύθη αὐτὸς δι' αὐτοῦ καὶ πάντες ὅσοι ἐπίθοντο αὐτῷ . . . D has little support but Eusebius (*HE* 2.11.1) has ὃς κατελύθη, καὶ πάντες ὅσοι ἐπείθοντο αὐτῷ διελύθησαν. If διελύθη αὐτὸς δι'αὐτοῦ means 'he committed suicide' it is plainly incompatible with Josephus's account of Theudas quoted above; it might be true about Judas — at least we have no evidence to the contrary. On this basis Clark, believing the Western text to be the original and to have been written in sense lines (as D is), suggested that there had been a transposition of στίχοι and that the original text ran

1. πρὸ γὰρ τούτων τῶν ἡμερῶν
2. ἀνέστη Ἰούδας· ὁ Γαλιλαίος
3. ἐν ταῖς ἡμέραις τῆς ἀπογραφῆς
4. ᾧ προσεκλίθη ἀριθμὸς ἀνδρῶν
5. ὡς τετρακοσίων,
6. ὃς κατελύθη αὐτὸς δι' αὐτοῦ
7. καὶ πάντες ὅσοι ἐπείθοντο αὐτῷ
8. διελύθησαν
9. καὶ ἐγένοντο εἰς οὐδέν.
10. μετὰ τοῦτον ἀνέστη Θευδᾶς, λέγων
11. εἶναί τινα μέγαν ἑαυτόν,

12. καὶ ἀπέστησεν λαὸν πολὺν ὀπίσω αὐτοῦ·
13. κἀκεῖνος ἀπώλετο καὶ ὅσοι ἐπείθοντο αὐτῷ
14. διεσκορπίσθησαν.

If now lines 2 and 3 are exchanged with lines 10 (apart from μετὰ τοῦτον) and 11, the Western text as we know it is produced (except that the copyist of D has in error dropped διελύθησαν and changed κατελύθη into διελύθη. See Clark (liv f., 33, 342f.). This is a very ingenious proposal; what is not explained is how the lines came to be interchanged. On the whole question see Black (*FS* Michel (1974), 45–54). We may go for the simple solution that Luke, writing Gamaliel's speech (for the Christians can hardly have had inside information of what was said in the Sanhedrin after v. 34 — unless Gamaliel's pupil, Saul of Tarsus, was present!), made a mistake, either unaware of the true date of Theudas or confusing him with some other rebel. An author who could misread a plain passage in Josephus could mistake any other source of information, so that we can draw no inference concerning the date of Acts. Hemer (162f., 224f.) adds little to the discussion.

Bede refers to the passages in Josephus concerning Judas and Theudas without observing that they constitute a problem.

38. Gamaliel draws the inference from his examples. τὰ νῦν, as at 4.29; here B* E omit τά. Wrong-doing brings its own reward; the Council therefore will be well advised to steer clear (ἀπόστητε) of these men. God will see to it that they get such reward or punishment as they deserve. Let them alone: ἄφετε αὐτούς. D E 0140 𝔐, without noticeable difference in meaning, have ἐάσατε αὐτούς, but add μὴ μιάναντες τὰς χεῖρας (E, μολύνοντες). On this reading see *FS* Black (1979), 26; Gamaliel is defending the apostles at least to the extent of seeking their release unharmed and his words must therefore mean something like, Do not defile yourselves with their blood. Cf. Isa. 59.3: αἱ γὰρ χεῖρες ὑμῶν μεμολυμμέναι αἵματι; Aeschylus, *Agamemnon* 209f.: μιαίνων παρθενοσφάγοισι ῥείθροις πατρῴους χέρας. If this plan (βουλή) or this work (ἔργον), the thing as conceived, the thing as executed, comes from a merely human origin it will be destroyed (καταλυθήσεται, which may have given rise to the reading with καταλύειν in v. 36). In this conditional sentence the protasis is expressed by ἐάν and the subjunctive; the corresponding conditional sentence in v. 39 has εἰ and the indicative. Moule (*IB* 150, cf. Schweizer, *Beiträge* 75; *CONT* 287) sees a real difference here, which indicates Gamaliel's own view (i.e., Luke's representation of it; Gamaliel would not speak Greek in the Sanhedrin): *If it should be . . .; but if in fact . . .* Zerwick § 307, however, believes that from the construction we can conclude nothing about Gamaliel's own mind; BDR § 372.1 agree:

Gamaliel is merely stating what he sees to be a logical consequence. Delebecque (27) translates v. 39: Mais si elle vient réellement de Dieu . . . It is interesting that Radermacher (144) sees the contrast between the two clauses as an example of fine style (Luke is expressing a distinction that is in his mind, though not in Gamaliel's), but also sees the transition without particle or conjunction from λέγω ὑμῖν to ἀπόστητε as a mark of non-literary colloqualism. Luke was capable of both.

39. On εἰ . . . ἐστιν, and καταλῦσαι, see on v. 38. The object of καταλῦσαι is, according to most of the oldest MSS, αὐτούς, but C*vid 𝔐 vg^cl sy^p sa^mss bo^ms have αὐτό, probably with ἔργον (v. 38) in mind rather than out of the conviction that καταλύειν should not have a personal object. A personal object is indeed unusual, and Blass's assertion (91) that it is Attic is not proved by Plato, *Laws* 4. 714c, which he cites, where the verb is passive and has an impersonal subject. The passive however does sometimes have a personal subject, and Preuschen correctly adduces Xenophon, *Cyropaedeia* 8.5.24.

As we have seen, the words of vv. 36, 37 can hardly have been spoken by Gamaliel. His conclusion however is one that he might well have reached. R. Johanan the Sandalmaker c. 140–165 said: Any assembling together that is for the sake of Heaven shall in the end be established, but any that is not for the sake of Heaven shall not in the end be established (Aboth 4.11; cf. 5.17). It is probably true that some Jews, including some influential Jews, took this line with regard to the Christians, and it may be correct to infer that their tolerant attitude made possible the emergence of Christianity (and of the Qumran group) and that it may have been only the developments which Luke is about to record that evoked resistance of a serious kind.

Western editors apparently thought that the sentence needed to be strengthened. After αὐτούς, E gig add οὔτε ὑμεῖς οὔτε οἱ ἄρχοντες ὑμῶν; 614 *pc*, with the intention of introducing the μήποτε clause, add ἀπόσχεσθε οὖν ἀπὸ τῶν ἀνδρῶν τούτων; D h sy^h** mae combine the additions, οὔτε ὑμεῖς οὔτε βασιλεῖς οὔτε τύραννοι. ἀπέχεσθε οὖν ἀπὸ τῶν ἀνθρώπων τούτων. Wisd. 12.14 is probably in mind: οὔτε βασιλεὺς ἤ τύραννος ἀντοφθαλμῆσαι δυνήσεταί σοι περὶ ὧν ἀπώλεσας.

If these longer readings are not accepted μήποτε must either be taken with ἀπόστητε (v. 38): *Steer clear of these men . . . lest . . .*, or understood in the sense of *perhaps: Perhaps you will be found. . . .* For θεομάχοι see Hatch (*Essays* 25f.). His references show that though the word is used in the LXX it is not used here in a LXX sense but in that given by its etymology, to resist a movement intended and supported by God. A similar observation had already been made by

Bengel: 'Hoc verbum Symmachus non semel pro Hebr. רפאים posuit'. Foerster (*Pal. Jud.* 163) points out that Gamaliel shows a characteristically Pharisaic fear of sin. But the thought is more widely expressed. Page (116) quotes Homer, *Iliad* 6.129, οὐκ ἄν ἔγωγε θεοῖσιν ἐπουρανίοισι μαχοίμην. Cf. Herodotus 9.16.4, ὅ τι δεῖ γενέσθαι ἐκ τοῦ θεοῦ ἀμήχανον ἀποτρέψαι ἀνθρώπῳ. Dibelius (190) considers whether here and elsewhere we have evidence that Luke had read Euripides *Bacchae*. For θεομάχοι cf. 45, ὃς θεομαχεῖ τὰ κατ' ἐμέ; 325, κοὐ θεομαχήσω, σῶν λόγων πεισθεὶς ὕπο; 1255f., ἀλλὰ θεομαχεῖν μόνον οἷός τ' ἐκεῖνος. But Stählin (94) rightly emphasizes that the thought is 'gut jüdisch', and in any case too popular to prove literary dependence. It reappears in Christian use: *Acta Philippi* 17 (12) (L. -B. 2.2.9) κατάστειλον· ἄνθρωποι γὰρ ὄντες θεῷ μάχεσθαι οὐ δυνάμεθα.

ἐπείσθησαν δὲ αὐτῷ. Gamaliel's argument prevails. Schille (164) is probably right in saying that we may see here one of Luke's major concerns (whether it should be called apologetic is another matter): 'Wo immer sich das Judentum treu bleibt, muss es den Kampf gegen die Christenheit unterlassen, sagt Lukas.'

40. δείραντες παρήγγειλαν μὴ λαλεῖν ἐπὶ τῷ ὀνόματι τοῦ Ἰησοῦ. The apostles had disobeyed the injunction of 4.18, but the Council could not do more than repeat the warning and enforce it with a beating (cf. 22.19). Schille (161) remarks that the beating is inconsistent with the treatment of the apostles in v. 26, but 'Geisselung zum Zweck der Abschreckung und Warnung war vielfach üblich (vgl. Sanhedrin 8.4c)' (Roloff 105).

D E Ψ 𝔐 lat sy Lucifer make the end of the paragraph neater by adding αὐτούς; τοὺς ἀποστόλους, the antecedent, is distant. V. 41, treated here as the beginning of a very short summary paragraph, is also a continuation of v. 40.

15. REJOICING AND WITNESSING COMMUNITY: 'FINAL' SUMMARY 5.41, 42

(41) So they went from the presence of the Council, rejoicing that they had been counted worthy to be treated with ignominy for the sake of the Name, (42) and every day in the Temple and at home they did not stop teaching and telling the good news that the Christ was Jesus.

Commentary

With these two verses Luke brings to an end the first stage of his work. As Stählin (95) and Bauernfeind (97) point out, there is a parallel with the end of the whole, 28.30f. He has demonstrated the truth of the resurrection of Jesus by many clear proofs (1.3). He has indicated that his story fills the gap between the departure of Jesus and his return (1.11), that the interval will be occupied by the bearing of witness to Jesus by disciples led and inspired by the Holy Spirit, and that this witness will extend throughout the world. He has brought up to full strength the apostolic group (1.15–26) and narrated the fulfilment of Jesus' promise that the Spirit would be given (2.1–4). He has given two long and two short accounts of the apostolic testimony to Jesus (2.22–40; 3.12–26; 4.8–12; 5.30–32). He has described a community that has increased in number to 5,000 members (4.4) and shown it at prayer, practising charity, and performing miracles. Its leaders are exposed to attack but enjoy divine protection. The concluding small paragraph shows the apostles rejoicing not least that they have the privilege of suffering for Christ, and continuing the work of teaching and evangelizing. On this foundation the story can develop. It has two bases: the apostles continue to use the Temple, that is, they think of themselves as Jews; and they bear witness to Jesus as Christ, that is, as the fulfilment of Judaism. We are now ready to take the next step, which will lead us out of Jerusalem. The question will also be raised: What will happen to Judaism now that it has been fulfilled? The answer to this will lead us out of the existing framework of Judaism, though Luke never ceases to treat this as a matter of fulfilment, not of simple negation.

There can be little doubt that Luke composed this short summary, which is in his style, is based on the stories he has already told, and serves a literary purpose.

41. This verse completes the narrative of the preceding paragraph but μὲν οὖν shows (cf. 1.6; 2.41) that Luke is now looking at the event from a different point of view; he is not only describing the last phase (the departure of the apostles from the court) but summing up the position now reached. The occasion is one for rejoicing (cf. 4.23–31), as Jesus had foretold (Lk. 6.22f.).

ἐπορεύοντο χαίροντες. BDR § 327.1 n. 1 note the difference between this construction (imperfect with present particle) and that of 5.26f. (imperfect with aorist participle, the participle marking the end of the process). Here, they say, it was not necessary to mark the end; it might be better to say that for Luke there was no end to mark; rejoicing continued. It is characteristic of Luke's two books (Schmithals 62), and fundamental to his understanding of the Gospel: 'Ohne Freude, kein Evangelium' (Bauernfeind 97).

ἀπὸ προσώπου (cf. 3.20; 7.45) suggests the Hebrew מלפני (e.g. Gen. 4.16); Luke however is not translating a Semitic source but writing in the style of the LXX (e.g. Num. 20.6, ἀπὸ προσώπου τῆς συναγωγῆς).

κατηξιώθησαν . . . ἀτιμασθῆναι is an intended oxymoron — 'Eximium oxymoron' (Bengel); cf. Phil. 1.29; 1 Pet. 2.19. To be disgracefully treated for Christ's sake is an honour. It marks one out as unmistakably his. The thought (that there are circumstances in which to be disparagingly treated is a cause for pride, not shame) however is not exclusively Christian; see e.g. Epictetus 1.29.49; 2.1.38f. (Wettstein 490).

ὑπὲρ τοῦ ὀνόματος (P⁷⁴ ℵ A B C D 323 1739 2495 pc Lucifer) is undoubtedly the correct reading; other authorities supply a genitive (αὐτοῦ or Ἰησοῦ or τοῦ κυρίου Ἰησοῦ). That Luke means 'for the sake of Jesus' is clear, but parallels such as 9.16; 15.26; 21.13 (given by Conzelmann 43 and Haenchen 248) are not valid since in these ὄνομα is followed by a genitive. Begs. 4.62f. asks, 'Can this be Jewish Aramaic? The Rabbis say "Le-Shem-Shamayim" = ὑπὲρ τοῦ θεοῦ (using "heaven" as a periphrasis for "God"). But they could scarcely say "Le Shem ha-Shem". The use of τὸ ὄνομα without qualification (cf. 3 John 7) seems to be Christian Greek rather than translated Aramaic. It is common in the Apostolic Fathers.' Schille (164) agrees and the last sentence is filled out by Haenchen with references to Barnabas 16.8; Ignatius, *Ephesians* 3.1; *Philadelphians* 10.1; and Lake and Cadbury may well be right. But לשם השם occurs at Zebahim 4.6. Le Déaut (*Nuit Pascale* 165 n. 87) writes, 'Le mot šem (nom) est un substitut ancien du nom divin, comme on peut le voir par Lev 24.11, 16.' Such occurrences of שם, however, may be a scribal substitute for the personal name *YHWH* which in any case שם represents, and though, as Le Déaut claims, the word שם could as well be used for God as מקום (place), it does not appear that it was so used; see the list of substitutes for God in StrB 2.308–311. Perhaps the best parallel to ὑπὲρ τοῦ ὀνόματος is the rabbinic לשמה, used especially for obedience to the law *for its own sake*, that is, without ulterior motive. It was for the sake of Christ only that the apostles suffered. The use of ὄνομα in chs. 3 and 4 must also be borne in mind. The name of Jesus involved trust in him and devotion to him; these were apparent in suffering. It is a little too neat to argue (with Stählin 95): The Jews used שם to avoid saying *God*; the Christians took this up for Jesus; therefore they thought of Jesus as God.

42. πᾶσάν τε ἡμέραν, all day; cf. Herodotus 7.203.1. Regardless of official reaction the apostles continued their mission. They also continued, as Jews, to use the Temple. κατ' οἶκον may mean *at home* (in private houses) or *in their* specifically Christian *meeting-house*. Cf. 2.46 (κατ' οἶκον) and 2.2 for an οἶκος where Christians met.

οὐκ ἐπαύοντο is stronger than the imperfects of διδάσκειν and εὐαγγελίζεσθαι would have been. At Lk. 1.19; 2.10; 3.18; 4.43; 8.1 and frequently in Acts, but not often elsewhere, εὐαγγελίζεσθαι takes an accusative direct object, of a person or theme (e.g. the kingdom of God), or of a person, group, or area evangelized. The wording is Luke's. Here, unless we are to translate 'the anointed Jesus', τὸν χριστόν will be an implied subject: they proclaimed the good news that the Christ was Jesus — that is, the promises were fulfilled; God was already active in saving his people. The preachers were thus disobedient to the Council, and were asking for trouble, which might well have come apart from the developments Luke is about to describe. Schille (165) rightly observes that Luke makes no distinction between διδάσκειν and εὐαγγελίζεσθαι.

III
PROBLEMS AND PERSECUTION
LEAD TO THE BEGINNING OF EXPANSION
(6.1 – 8.3)

16. APPOINTMENT OF THE SEVEN AND FURTHER
PROSPERITY 6.1–7

(1) In these days, as the number of the disciples was increasing, there arose a complaint on the part of the Hellenists against the Hebrews, to the effect that their widows were being overlooked in the daily ministration of charity. (2) The Twelve summoned the whole company of the disciples and said, 'It is not acceptable that we should forsake the word of God and serve at table. (3) But, brothers, look out from among you seven men of good repute, full of the Spirit and wisdom, whom we will[1] appoint over this business. (4) For our part, we will continue in prayer and in the ministry of the word. (5) This proposal pleased the whole company, and they chose Stephen, a man full of faith and of the Holy Spirit, Philip, Prochorus, Nicanor, Timon, Parmenas, and Nicolas, a proselyte from Antioch. (6) They set these men before the apostles, and when they had prayed laid their hands on them.[2]

(7) And the word of God grew and the number of disciples in Jerusalem increased greatly. A large number of the priests gave their obedience to the faith.

Bibliography

L. W. Barnard, *NTS* 7 (1961), 31–45.

J. Coppens, Kremer *Actes*, 405–38.

O. Cullmann, *FS* Kümmel (1975), 44–56.

D. Daube, *ANRW* 2.25.3 (1985), 2346–56.

J. Dupont, *Nouvelles Études*, 151–7.

E. Ferguson, *JTS* 26 (1975), 1–12.

W. Foerster, *FS* Schreiner, 9–30.

J. G. Gager, *FS* Stendahl, 91–9.

P. Geoltrain, *ThZ* 15 (1959), 241–54.

---

[1]RSV, may.
[2]NEB, who prayed and laid their hands on them.

A. George, *Études*, 368–94.

O. Glombitza, *ZNW* 53 (1962), 238–44.

W. Grundmann, *ZNW* 38 (1939), 45–73.

F. Hahn, *FS* Bultmann (1984), 316–31.

M. Hengel, as in (7).

M. Hengel, *NTS* 18 (1972), 15–38.

L. E. Keck, *ZNW* 56 (1965), 100—29.

L. E. Keck, *ZNW* 57 (1966), 54–78.

J. Kodell, *Bib* 55 (1974), 505–19.

E. Larsson, *NTS* 33 (1987), 205–25.

M. Lienhard, *CBQ* 37 (1975), 228–36.

C. F. D. Moule, *ExpT* 70 (1959), 100–2.

R. Scroggs, *FS* Goodenough, 176–206.

D. Seccombe, *JTS* 29 (1978), 140–3.

D. Sperber, *JSJ* 6 (1975), 86–95.

G. N. Stanton, *StBib* (=*JSNTSupp* 3, 1978), 345–60.

A. Strobel, *ZNW* 63 (1972), 271–6.

N. Walker, *NTS* 29 (1983), 370–93.

H. Zimmermann, *FS* Frings, 364–78.

Some of the works listed for paragraphs 17, 18, 19, 20 are relevant here too.

Commentary

It is important to take this paragraph on its own. The story of Stephen does of course arise out of it; so, rather less closely, does that of Philip; part of it is probably connected as Antiochene tradition with the founding of the mixed Jewish-Gentile church in Antioch, the mission to Pamphylia and Lycaonia described in chs. 13, 14, and the beginning of the dispute in ch. 15. It is however separated from all these by one of Luke's summary pieces (6.7; Pesch (227) is surely mistaken in describing this verse as 'vorlukanisch'). This describes the immediate outcome of the appointment of 'The Seven' (the expression is used at 21.8), which serves in Luke's mind as a further example, additional to those of chs. 3–5, of the way in which evil is overcome by good and the solution of a problem leads to the expansion of the church. This is what Luke intends to communicate to his reader: a minor deficiency in administration is immediately set right; it leads to the emergence of a new group of devoted Christians, and the consequence is a great increase in the number of believers, who now include many who had formerly been among the chief enemies of the new faith. The student of Acts, however, cannot forget that he has read the second part of ch. 6, and chs. 7 and 8, nor can he fail to put his ear to the ground and attempt to hear things other than those that Luke has chosen to amplify. Dibelius 181 is right in the view that Luke uses 'the choice of the seven as an introduction to the martyrdom of Stephen', but this is by no means Luke's only interest.

It is easy, and correct, to say that it was not Luke's intention here to describe the origin of the order of deacons (first suggested by Irenaeus, *Adv. Haer.* 1.26.3; 3.12.10; 4.15.1 — so Pesch 232). It is true that the words διακονεῖν and διακονία occur, but διάκονος does not, and even though the Seven are appointed to do what would later be thought of as work appropriate for deacons it is impossible that anyone should set out to give an account of the origin of the diaconate without calling its first holders deacons. A similar observation will apply even more powerfully against the suggestion, made on the ground that it was to the Jerusalem elders (presbyters) that Barnabas and Saul delivered the assistance sent from Antioch, that the paragraph recounts the appointment of the first presbyters. According to Chrysostom, the Seven were neither presbyters nor deacons (see below). It is however probably true that the story embodies the method of appointing ministers that was familiar to Luke himself: popular choice, approval by those already ministers, and the laying on of hands. He would think this a good pattern to follow — the pattern that must have been followed in the past. He may have intended to suggest to his readers what they knew as the order of deacons (Roloff 109f.; Bauernfeind 99 believes that Luke was thinking of deacons but did not feel that he could go so far as to introduce the word διάκονος into a source that did not contain it). He can however go further than this. He gives the Greek names of six born Jews and of one proselyte (see on v. 5) and describes collectively those whose interests they are to protect as Ἑλληνισταί. For the meaning of this word, and of its counterpart Ἑβραῖοι, see the note on v. 1. That it refers to Jews who spoke Greek and had some familiarity with the Greek world seems certain; what must remain uncertain (so far as the word itself goes) is the extent to which these men had adopted along with Greek speech Greek ways of thinking and living. The answer is probably, only to a limited extent. One of them was a proselyte; that is, he cared enough for what was distinctively Jewish to have been circumcised, and by this rite, repugnant to Greeks, and by a host of other customs, to have cut himself off from family and friends. He must have valued Judaism more highly than Hellenism, and his Jewish associates will not have thought meanly of their Jewishness. In addition to this inference, we have the accusations against Stephen (represented by Luke as false) in 6.11, 13, 14, with Stephen's speech (7.2–53), and with the fact of Stephen's death and the subsequent persecution (7.54–8.3; 8.4; 11.19). The stories about Philip in ch. 8 tell us little, except that Philip was prepared to have dealings with Samaritans and Gentiles. These matters will be dealt with in detail in due course; we return to consider the traditions at Luke's disposal.

Luke knows, and tells us repeatedly, that the first Christians practised charitable relief on such a scale that among them there was no one who was in need (4.34). He knows the names of seven notable early Christian leaders, not to be identified with the Twelve, and that these proved to be obnoxious to the authorities; and he can translate back into the past an appropriate method of appointing officials. In addition, he held certain convictions. One was that the early years of the church were exemplary. Evil had not yet entered, or, if it did (in Ananias and Sapphira), it was swiftly excluded by supernatural means. Christians of his own day should find in his pages an example to follow. Another conviction was that the unity of the ideal church was rooted in the (twelve) apostles, who were not only its leaders but its link with Jesus himself (1.21f.). Whatever was rightly done, therefore, was done under their authority. A third conviction was that the various developments of the church's life contributed to its extension, numerically, socially, and geographically. With these observations it is possible to understand Luke's handling of the material available to him.

That Luke begins at 6.1 to follow a fresh tradition (some would say, a fresh written source — see pp. 52, 54f. and the discussion of sources in Vol. II) is agreed by almost all students of Acts; note not only the fresh subject-matter (leading eventually from Jerusalem to Antioch) but the first use of μαθητής for Christians and the only use of οἱ δώδεκα (v. 2). He did not invent the fact that in the early years in Jerusalem there were Greek-speaking Jews who became Christians and had at their head a group of seven men, about two of whom he could hand on biographical details. It is worth noting that he was in the same position with regard to the Twelve, among whom he knew the story of the death of James (12.1 — but he has no detailed martyrdom story about James as he has about Stephen) and stories about the life and work of Peter (we cannot count the allusions to John in Peter's company), greater in extent than the stories about Philip. The Seven were somehow different from the Twelve, but the difference could be adequately stated in the fact that the one group was made up of Hellenists, the other of Hebrews (v. 1). This was Luke's theory; the word Ἑβραῖος was traditional (see further pp. 307-9) and Ἑλληνιστής (Luke's use of this word is arbitrary; see p. 309) served as a useful partner. What the difference between them really was cannot be properly discussed until all the relevant material has been looked at in detail. It may be that the Seven were in some way traditionally connected with the church's charitable activity; if not, we must suppose that Luke considered that such a connection would provide a suitable context in which they might emerge, but it is more likely that the connection is original, for if Luke invented it he told his story badly by first inventing a setting and then immediately leaving it — the poor widows are soon abandoned. It is quite understandable that men who were in fact connected with the distribution of alms should grow into preachers and controversialists but it would be bad writing first of all to make up a job for them and then represent them as neglecting it for another. Care for the poor may not, however, have been the only activity of the Seven. Schille (166) says that they were *Evangelisten*, not *Armenpfleger*; perhaps we should say, *Evangelisten* and *Armenpfleger*. It is clear that, in Luke's narrative, the apostles were both (4.35, 37; 5.2). Indeed, 21.8 suggests that the original designation of Philip and his colleagues may have been not Hellenists but Evangelists. Philip is 'the evangelist, one of the seven'. The reader asks, 'The seven — what?' It is natural to answer, 'The seven evangelists'. See Eph. 4.11; 2 Tim. 4.5; and cf. Stählin 99.

Luke's own contribution was to isolate the theme of charity and to link it specifically with widows, which was natural enough (since widows were a particularly vulnerable group in ancient society), and to represent it as immediately overcome by the intervention of the Twelve, who of course were able to carry the community as a whole with them. The Seven, in his finished picture, henceforth take an official position to which they are appointed with the approval of the Twelve if not actually by ordination at their hands (see on v. 6). The result of this (and it is to be noted that this is stated before Luke begins to use any of his special material about Stephen and Philip) is a further great expansion of the community of disciples, who are now augmented by a large number of priests (v. 7).

It would not be proper at this point to attempt to dig much further into the history of which Luke has given a simple and edifying version — a version which is not necessarily incorrect in the little that it affirms because there seems to be a good deal beneath the surface which Luke does not explicitly mention. Nor should it be assumed that what is not explicitly mentioned has been suppressed by him with the intention of falsifying the picture of the primitive church. Much of what is missing has in all probability simply dropped away with the passage of time as new circumstances arose in which old problems were no longer understood or were thought to be irrelevant. Luke's intention is not to supply the curious with all the information they would like to have about the church of the first fathers, but to edify the church of his own day. The modern reader of Acts will however be unable to dismiss certain questions from his mind. These will include: What were the distinctive views of the Seven? of the Twelve? How were these two groups, and those whom they represented, related to each other, and to official Judaism? Did the one provoke the authorities in a way the other did not? If so, why? Were the Seven related, in doctrine, in practice, in person, with the Samaritans? with the Jews of Qumran? How was Saul (7.58; 8.1) related to them? in the beginning? subsequently? What role did they play in the extension of the Gospel to the Gentiles? How did they preach? What conditions for membership of the church did they lay down? Can any traces of them be found in later Christian literature?

These are questions that inevitably lead — and often have led — to speculation. Speculation may be profitable but it is most profitable when it is based on the largest number of ascertainable facts; it will therefore be deferred until study of further passages has made more facts available. See below; also the general discussion in Vol. II. It is for the present sobering to reflect that whereas Cullmann sees a relation between Qumran and the Hellenists (*V. & A.* 276–9; in Stendahl, *Scrolls* 25f.; cf. Fitzmyer, *Essays* 277f.; against Cullmann, Haenchen 254f.), Black finds a connection with the Hebrews (*Scrolls* 76–80). In one paragraph, Bultmann (*Theologie* 59f.) says most of what can be said with confidence. It is however worth while to add, with Schlatter (*Theologie des NTs* 2.548): the narrative 'zeigt deutlich, dass das Amt als Dienst verstanden wird, nicht als Herrschaft, weshalb es so gestaltet wird, wie es dem Zweck der Gemeinde entspricht. Von einem göttlichen Recht oder einem Gebot Jesu, das das Amt so und nicht anders ordnete, sprechen bei Lukas die Apostel nicht; sie handeln in der Überzeugung, dass die Gemeinde die Vollmacht und die Pflicht habe, ihre Verhältnisse so zu ordnen, wie es für die Erfüllung ihrer Aufgabe dienlich sei.'

1. Ἐν δὲ ταῖς ἡμέραις ταύταις does not attempt precise chronology. Luke means, rightly or wrongly, at the time when the church was still confined to Jerusalem; before the earliest expansion. In Jerusalem, however, disciples (μαθηταί; the word, not found in the Pauline or Deuteropauline letters and occurring here for the first time in Acts, is usually taken as a mark of a new source or tradition) were multiplying, as we have already several times heard, most recently at 5.14. πληθύνειν has not previously been used but reappears at v. 7; 9.31; 12.24; cf. 7.7, of the Israelites in Egypt; cf. also the use of πλῆθος for the company of disciples (4.32, etc.).

The prosperity of the church was disturbed by a γογγυσμός, a *complaining*; cf. Jn 7.12; Phil. 2.14; 1 Pet. 4.9, the only other occurrences of the word in the NT; the cognate verb γογγύζειν occurs seven times. Both are used in the LXX, though not frequently and mainly of the murmuring of the Israelites in the wilderness (e.g. Num. 11.1). Phrynichus 336 prefers τονθρυσμός, τονθρύζειν; γογγυσμός, γογγύζειν, though not ἀδόκιμα, are Ionic. The complaint was made by the Hellenists against the Hebrews. The two terms are best discussed in relation to each other, since as used here they appear to be mutually exclusive and together to describe the whole of the Jerusalem church.' Ἑλληνιστής occurs also at 9.29 (but A 104 424 pc for Ἑλληνιστάς have Ἕλληνας) and at 11.20 (but P⁷⁴ ℵᶜ A D* have Ἕλληνας, ℵ* has εὐαγγελιστάς). On the text of these two passages see further the notes ad loc. Ἑβραῖος does not occur again in Acts but is found at 2 Cor. 11.22; Phil. 3.5. Neither word occurs in the Greek OT. Ἑβραῖος is used occasionally by the few Greek authors who have occasion to refer to Hebrews (Jews); apart from Acts and passages dependent on it Ἑλληνιστής is not used till much later. 'So-called Hellenists like Philo of Alexandria, Paul of Tarsus, and Josephus do not use it' (Cadbury, Begs. 5.60). As a noun in -ιστής it is derived from the verb ἑλληνίζειν, which for the most part has a linguistic connotation. It is used for speaking Greek, correct Greek, with βαρβαρίζειν as its opposite; so e.g. Lucian, Philopseudes 16: ὁ δαίμων δὲ ἀποκρίνεται ἑλληνίζων, ἢ βαρβαρίζων, ἢ ὅθεν ἂν αὐτὸς ᾖ; Sextus Empiricus, adv. Mathematicos 1.246. It is also used for speaking Hellenistic Greek over against Attic Greek (Posidippus 28: σὺ μὲν ἀττικίζεις ... οἱ δ' Ἕλληνες ἑλληνίζομεν). As a transitive verb ἑλληνίζειν can be used for making Greek, that is, civilizing (τὴν βάρβαρον (γῆν)), for translating another language into Greek (Dio Cassius 55.3.5). Ἑλληνιστί is used at 21.37 (and Jn. 19.20) also with a linguistic meaning. There is thus a virtual certainty that the Ἑλληνισταί spoke Greek (so e.g. Chrysostom: Ἑλληνιστὰς δὲ οἶμαι καλεῖν τοὺς Ἑλληνιστὶ φθεγγομένους), and probably no one would dispute this; the only difficulty is that the word Ἑβραῖος does not have a primarily linguistic connotation. Paul uses it of himself (2 Cor. 11.22; Phil. 3.5) though he was undoubtedly capable of using Greek. He must also have been able to use Hebrew and Aramaic if Acts 22.3 is correct in claiming that he had studied with Gamaliel (not to mention such direct statements as 21.40). Eusebius (HE 2.4.2) calls Philo a Ἑβραῖος; Philo himself however at de Conf. Linguarum 129 appears to contrast himself with Ἑβραῖοι, and it is sometimes argued that Philo's impossible etymologies of Hebrew words and names prove that he cannot have known Hebrew. The argument is invalid; Philo's etymologies are governed by homiletic not scientific principles, and the passage in de Conf. Ling. means no more than that Philo is writing Greek at the time. Ἑβραιστί (like Ἑλληνιστί) is used in a linguistic sense, but the adjective (and adjective used as substantive) are almost inevitably ambiguous, denoting both a race and the language used by that race (though so far as the word means Aramaic rather than Hebrew it was not peculiar to though it was characteristic of Jews). The question that is left open is the extent to which Ἑλληνισταί had adopted with the Greek language also Greek ways of thinking and habits of life. According to Weiser (165) they were 'weltoffener als die Juden und Judenchristen Palästinas und hatten wohl auch etwas von griechischem Geist und hellenistischer Kultur in sich aufgenommen'. A more prudent answer to the question would be that there was probably a very great variety. This is intrinsically probable and can be confirmed by observation of Diaspora Jews. Some were able to assimilate themselves almost entirely to their heathen environment; others (e.g. Paul's family) seem to have preserved the exclusiveness of their faith if not of their language. A wide variety of strains of Hellenistic Judaism is attested by Philo: Philo's own middle-of-the-road Judaism, which practised the letter of the law but was prepared to use allegory to elicit from it a spiritual (and often decidedly Greek) sense, and on either hand the extremists who abandoned either the spirit or the letter (E. Bréhier, *Les Idées philosophiques et religieuses de Philon d'Alexandrie*, 1950, 61–5). The word Ἑλληνιστής does not help us to determine the place in this variety occupied by those whom it describes; it is possible only to note what is said about them and on this basis to reconstruct as far as possible their contribution to the early history of Christianity. It is particularly important to note that Luke uses the word in three different senses (see my discussion in *FS* Borgen, 20, 21). This means that Luke had no precise understanding of a party of 'Hellenists' in the primitive church. See further the Introduction to this section (pp. 303–7) and the discussion in Vol. II. On the languages used in Palestine see *ND* 5.19–26.

It should be added that Cadbury (*Begs.* 5.59–74) took the word Ἑλληνιστής to mean *Greek*, that is, *Gentile*. The two strongest arguments in support of this view are (a) that its counterpart Ἑβραῖος is used with the meaning *Jew* (Cadbury cites effectively the synagogue inscription found at Corinth — συναγωγὴ Ἑβραίων), so that its partner, Ἑλληνιστής, may be expected to mean, *One who is not a Jew*; (b) at 11.19f. those copyists who, rightly or wrongly, wrote Ἑλληνιστάς must, if they gave any thought to what they wrote, have understood the word to mean Gentiles. The use of the word at 9.29 is not decisive. Against it are the strong linguistic, and less strong cultural, suggestions of ἑλληνίζειν κτλ., and the development of the narrative in Acts. If from 6.1 (or from the Day of Pentecost — see above, pp. 118, 122) there had been Jewish and Gentile elements in the Jerusalem church, or if Luke had believed that it was so, could he have made so much of Peter's preaching to Cornelius, of the founding of a mixed church in Antioch, of Paul's break with the synagogue at Pisidian Antioch, and of the Council of ch. 15?

παρεθεωροῦντο. In Classical Greek (which would probably have used παρορᾶν — Blass) the use of the indicative would have meant that the Hellenist widows here were in truth being overlooked; a mere unproven allegation would have been expressed in the optative. In Luke's Hellenistic Greek this inference cannot be drawn with confidence. At least, the assertion was made.

Haenchen (256) remarks that Luke is not interested in the question, Who is to blame? but only in, What did the apostles do to put things right? Pesch (228) observes that Luke puts tension between service of the Word and service at table (suggesting a community divided into service groups) in place of the tension between *Gemeindegruppen*, spoken of in his source.

3. ἐπισκέψασθε δέ. The Western text characteristically enlivens the opening, substituting for the first six words of the NA²⁶ text, τί οὖν ἐστιν, ἀδελφοί; ἐπισκέψασθε ἐξ ὑμῶν αὐτῶν ἄνδρας (D h p mae). There is no difference in meaning. For δέ, C E Ψ 𝔐 lat sy have the smoother οὖν; 1175 has δὲ οὖν; A has δή; P⁷⁴ has no particle, perhaps rightly, δέ (B ℵ) and οὖν being editorial improvements.

ἐπισκέπτεσθαι is a Lucan word (Lk. three times; Acts four; rest of the NT four), but is used in different senses: at 15.14 (cf. Lk. 1.68, 78) of God's visiting his people to redeem them, at 15.36 of looking up (someone), here of looking out, that is, seeking with a view to appointment. A similar range of meanings is more frequently expressed by the cognate ἐπισκοπεῖν. In the LXX cf. Num. 27.1, 16ff. and especially Exod. 18.21 (see on v. 2).

Seven men are to be found. Cf. Josephus, *Ant.* 4.214, where Josephus, reproducing Deut. 16.18, introduces the number seven (cf. 4.287; also *War* 2.571, where Josephus says that he appointed seven judges in every city in Galilee). Megillah 26a refers to the 'seven best men in a city' (שבעי טובי העיר); see also j. Megillah 3.74a.16. The evidence is slight, but may reflect a Jewish custom of appointing seven to carry out some task; cf. the Roman Septemviri epulones (Tacitus, *Annals* 3.64). Those who administered the care of the poor acted in pairs (Peah 8.7; T. Peah 4.15 (24); Baba Bathra 8b), which suggests though it does not require an even number of administrators. On the number seven, Bede, reflecting later developments, writes: Hinc iam decreverunt apostoli vel successores apostolorum per omnes ecclesias septem diaconos, qui sublimiori gradu essent ceteris et proximi circa aram quasi columnae altaris adsisterent et non sine aliquo septemarii numeri mysterio.

The chosen seven must be men of good repute. μαρτυρεῖσθαι is used absolutely only here in Acts; the sense is given by 16.2 (given a good report by the brothers); 22.12 (given a good report by the local Jews); cf. 10.33; 1 Tim. 3.7; Heb. 11.2, 4, 5, 39; 3 Jn 12; also Josephus, *Ant.* 3.59 (μαρτυρούμενον . . . ὑπὸ παντὸς τοῦ στρατοῦ); Ditt. *Syll.*² 366.28 (ἀρχιτέκτονας μαρτυρηθέντας ὑπὸ τῆς σεμνοτάτης <βουλῆς>). They must also be πλήρεις πνεύματος καὶ σοφίας. Here (and at v. 5) Moulton (M. 1.50; 2. 162) is evidently unhappy with indeclinable πλήρης (read here by A E H P *al*); BDR § 137.1 (noticing v. 5 but not the present verse) describe it as 'vulgär-hellenistisch'. For 'full of the Spirit', showing all the marks of the work of the Holy Spirit, see 2.4; 4.8, 31. σοφία is mentioned again as an attribute of Stephen at 6.10; thereafter in Acts only in regard to Moses (7.10, 22). For Luke it is not a theological term: the men appointed had to excel in spiritual and in natural gifts.

You, the πλῆθος, are to search out the right men (having done so you will have confidence in them); we, the Twelve, will then appoint them over this χρεία, that is, to deal with it. The word means 'need, want, . . poverty', but also 'business, employment, function' (LS 2002f.). Both senses are applicable here and it would be wrong to exclude either: there was a need, and meeting it constituted a piece of business, a service. Haenchen (256) says that in Hellenistic Greek χρεία is *Amt*, not *Bedürfnis*; the translation in *Begs*. 4.65 is *duty*. Page (117) insists on the translation, '. . . whom we may appoint', the second action being contingent on the first; but the wording (καταστήσομεν, future indicative) seems to mean that the apostles undertake to appoint the seven whom the people choose. Cf. Josephus, *War* 2.123, 565; Philo, *De Vita Contemplativa* 71 (ἐλεύθεροι δὲ ὑπηρετοῦσι, τὰς διακονικὰς χρείας ἐπιτελοῦντες).

Schille (170) notes how much *Ordinationssprache* there is at this point. There is however nothing surprising in the fact that at all times it has proved desirable that candidates for Christian office should be of good character and possess natural and spiritual gifts.

4. Between the Twelve and the Seven there was to be a complete division of labour. While the latter attended to the work of charity the former would continue (cf. 1.14) τῇ προσευχῇ (cf. 2.42; it is of course not implied that the others did not pray) and τῇ διακονίᾳ τοῦ λόγου. It is unlikely that προσευχή refers to a place of prayer in which the apostles were constantly to be found. It is usually supposed that διακονία τοῦ λόγου refers to the work of preaching, and this is supported by the use in Acts of λόγος (see on v. 2). B. Gerhardsson however (*Memory and Manuscript*, 1961, 245) believes that we should think not of proclamation but of teaching (διδαχή). 'There is no doubt that their work on the logos is to a large extent a matter of "doctrinal discussion", based on the reading of a text of Scripture and perhaps the reciting of the tradition of Christ as well, or on concrete problems which have been posed and discussed during the process of "taking stock" of that which is given in the scriptures and the tradition of Christ, and that which was "revealed" in the as yet unfinished miraculous course of salvation.' He thinks the Council of Acts 15 to be an example of such a session. It is unfortunate for this view that the Council is not described as διακονία τοῦ λόγου; as we have seen, λόγος points in a different direction. This is recognized by StrB 2.647: 'διακονία τοῦ λόγου entspricht formell dem Ausdruck שמושה של תורה = "Dienst der Tora"; inhaltlich sind beide Wendungen verschieden: während mit διακονία τ. λ. die Verkündigung des Evangeliums gemeint ist, bezeichnet שמושה של תורה das praktische Erlernen der Halakha aus dem Umgang mit den Gelehrten, so dass es schliesslich gleichbedeutend ist mit dem "Bedienen der Gelehrten" שמוש חכמים.' For the simple future προσκαρτερήσομεν, D (lat) have ἐσόμεθα ... προσκαρτεροῦντες. On this see Wilcox (123); cf. 10.6 (614); 14.4 (D). The variant is not in itself a Semitism though the frequency of periphrastic constructions in the early chapters of Acts may suggest a Semitic environment (BDR § 353). Here, however, against BDR, there may be an intention to emphasise the continuousness of the operation.

5. What the apostles said pleased the whole πλῆθος (see on v. 2; D h mae add τῶν μαθητῶν — somewhat unnecessarily making it clear that the reference was not to the whole population of the city!). ἤρεσεν ἐνώπιον is not conventional Greek (cf. e.g. Thucydides 1.129.3, τοῖς λόγοις τοῖς ἀπὸ σοῦ ἀρέσκομαι); BDR § 4.3 n. 8 however are almost certainly right to see here an example of spoken 'Jewish Greek' rather than a mark of translation. This is practically the same as Haenchen's (257) opinion that we have here not a formal *placet* but LXX style; cf. Gen. 34.18; 41.37; 3 Kdms 3.10. The people were pleased by the proposal because they recognized that it was in agreement with God's will (cf. v. 2), not simply because it came with the authority of the apostles (Stählin 98). For ἐκλέγεσθαι cf. 1.2, 24; here it corresponds to ἐπισκέπτεσθαι in v. 3.

Seven names follow. Bultmann (*Exegetica* 418) is of the opinion that such lists would not be found in oral tradition (similarly at 13.1; 20.4) — a written source is implied; probably, but not certainly correct. Only two of the names were given to Luke by further detailed stories (Stephen, Philip), and it should not be assumed that the list and the stories reached Luke along the same channels. We should perhaps conclude that if Luke did not see the names on paper they must have belonged to a very well known and influential group. Such the Seven may have been, though we can do little more than conjecture what their importance was and where their influence lay. All the seven bear Greek names; this does not prove that all were Hellenists (v. 1) since Greek names are found among the Twelve (Andrew, Philip, Bartholomew; 1.13) and were current, as was the Greek language, in Palestine, but it is at least consistent with this possibility. Lüdemann 83 thinks that the list of seven names (also v. 1b) was traditional.

Stephen: a reasonably common Greek name (e.g. Josephus, *War* 2.228, a slave of Caesar; Preuschen 36 gives references in *IG*). His story is told in 6.8–8.2; see also 11.19; 22.20. He was full (here indeclinable πλήρης must be read, with P⁷⁴ ℵ A C D E 33 614 1175 1241 *pm;* see on v. 3) of faith and of the Holy Spirit. Full of Spirit, as at v. 3; full of faith means of very strong faith; a firmly convinced believer. See v. 10.

Philip: another common name, borne by a several kings of Macedon, including the father of Alexander the Great, also by a son of Herod the Great (e.g. Lk. 3.1) and by one of the Twelve (Acts 1.13). The story of Philip (called at 21.8 the Evangelist) is told in Acts 8.

Prochorus: not a common name. Nothing further is known of this man; the Acts of John that bear his name were certainly not written by him.

Nicanor: it is surprising that this name should have been given to a Jew since it was that of a hated enemy (1 Macc. 7.26). The name however was a common one; Preuschen 36 gives references to *IG*.

Timon: a not uncommon name. Preuschen (36) gives references to *IG*. Nothing more is known of this man.

Parmenas is a shortened form of Παρμενίδης, Παρμένων, or some similar name. Preuschen (36) gives references to *IG*. Nothing more is known of this man.

Nicolas is a common Greek name. Preuschen (36) gives references to *IG*. The name occurs nowhere else in the NT, but cf. Rev. 2.6, 15, which refer with disapproval to the teaching of the Nicolaitans. As early as Irenaeus (*Adv. Haer.* 1.26.3) and Eusebius (*HE* 3.29.1–3) this sect was said to have been founded by the Nicolas of Acts 6; Clement of Alexandria (*Stromateis* 2.20.118) minimizes the connection. There is nothing to support Irenaeus's view, though it may be that a gnostic sect claimed descent from a (semi-) apostolic figure in order to add to their authority. Only of Nicolas is further information given in the present verse. He was a proselyte (a full convert to Judaism, admitted by circumcision, baptism, and the offering of sacrifice; cf. 2.10), and came from Antioch (presumably Syrian Antioch; see on 11.19). This description of Nicolas almost certainly implies that his six colleagues were born Jews (though some — improbably — take the word to mean that all were proselytes), and may mean that they were of Palestinian origin. Luke's use of the word Hellenist (see on v. 1) must not be taken to mean that they were necessarily Diaspora Jews.

6. The main company of disciples had been bidden (v. 3) to seek out seven men suitable for the purpose in question in order that the Twelve might appoint (καταστήσομεν) them. This is now done. The subject of ἔστησαν is τὸ πλῆθος (v. 5; as a noun of multitude this word has already taken the 3 p. pl. verb ἐξελέξαντο). The word πλῆθος must still be the subject of προσευξάμενοι ἐπέθηκαν, that is, the whole company of believers, not the apostles alone, laid their hands on the seven men. There is no question that this is the grammatical meaning of Luke's words (see e.g. Daube, *NTRJ* 237f.); if he meant something different he failed to express what he meant.

This was recognized by Western editors who accordingly rewrote the text in a form they thought appropriate: for οὕς ἔστησαν, D p syᵖ have οὗτοι ἐστάθησαν; for καί, D has οἵτινες. The reading of p syᵖ is sufficient to change the picture; after 'they stood before the apostles' the subject of ἐπέθηκαν must be the apostles; the reading of D makes assurance double sure. The Western reading is so much more in accord with later practice that it must be judged secondary; at the same time it shows that the Old Uncial reading was understood to mean something that had become objectionable. It is true (a) that in v. 3 the apostles said καταστήσομεν, and it is doubtful whether Daube is justified in claiming that 'we will appoint' means 'we, the Christian community as a whole, will appoint,' since the verse implies a contrast: ἐπισκέψασθε . . . ἐξ ὑμῶν . . . καταστήσομεν; and (b) that it is difficult to think of several thousand disciples (4.4) all laying their hands on seven men. But (a) presentation to the apostles (ἐνώπιον) implies their approval, that is, appointment by them, and (b) we must not think of the ordered dignity of a modern ordination. Weiser 167 notes that the narrative has the character of ordination; this is correct, but this does not mean that the Acts account should necessarily be interpreted in terms of post-biblical ideas of ordination; rather than the latter should, where necessary, be corrected by the former.

For the meaning of the imposition of hands see Daube (*NTRJ* 237–44); Schweizer (*CONT* 5m; 25c); E. Lohse (*Die Ordination im Spätjudentum und im NT*, 1951, 74–9); Jewish material in StrB 2.648f. Schweizer is right in arguing that the distinction made by Daube, between the *laying* on of hands (שׂים or שׂית) and the *leaning* on of hands (סמך), important in its own context, cannot be used in the study of the NT, including Acts, since only one Greek verb, ἐπιτιθέναι, is used. The act (cf. 13.1–3) signifies the blessing which accompanies the committing and the undertaking of a new kind of service. The seven do not become deacons (for the word διάκονος is not used, nor was anything like it associated with the work of charity in Judaism, where the collectors of alms were גבאי צדקה and the distributors מחלקי צדקה; see *Ch., M., and S.* 49f.); they occupy no specific office. This is in part because their position is to some extent the artificial product of Luke's rationalization of old traditions.

7. ὁ λόγος τοῦ θεοῦ (κυρίου, D E Ψ 614 *pc* it vg^cl sy^h) ηὔξανεν is an odd expression, though Luke evidently liked it (12.24; 19.20); it brings out the truth that the church is *creatura verbi* (Roloff 110). The meaning is clear: the word of God as the apostles continued to preach it (vv. 2, 4) had continually increasing influence and effect. It was responsible for the increasing number (ἐπληθύνετο ὁ ἀριθμός) of disciples, though these were so far confined to Jerusalem. They now included πολὺς ὄχλος τῶν ἱερέων ('Ἰουδαίων, read by

ℵ* *pc* syᵖ, either originated in a copyist's slip or arose out of the belief that priests, hitherto inimical to the new faith, were unlikely to accept it). Many, though not all, priests were Sadducees, and they have already (4.1, 6; 5.17) been noted as taking the lead in opposition to Christians. Fitzmyer (*Essays* 279) says correctly, 'Possibly some Essenes were included among the priests of 6: 7, but one could never restrict this notice to them alone.' It is unfortunate that on p. 296 this becomes, 'As we have already remarked, there were undoubtedly some Essenes among the priests converted to Christianity (Acts 6: 7)'! S. E. Johnson (in Stendahl, *Scrolls* 158) is more cautious. Theories of influence on the primitive church from Qumran, or of Hellenistic influence, cannot be built on this verse.

The priests ὑπήκουον (perhaps an inceptive use of the imperfect, *began to be obedient*; Knowling 172, *kept joining*) τῇ (D, αὐτῇ; probably a simple mistake rather than (Black *AA* 99) a rendering of an Aramaic proleptic pronoun) πίστει. The expression recalls Pauline usage (e.g. Rom. 10.16, ὑπήκουσαν τῷ εὐαγγελίῳ; cf. 1.5, ὑπακοὴ πίστεως). πίστις here must be *fides quae*, the content of Christian belief and life. Delebecque 29 translates 'répondait à l'appel de la foi,' adducing Homer, *Odyssey* 4.423; Aristophanes, *Acharnians* 405; Xenophon, *Symposium* 1.11; *Cyropaedia* 8.3.21.

17. ATTACK ON STEPHEN 6.8–15

(8) Stephen, full of grace and power, began to work great portents and signs among the people, (9) but there rose up some of those who belonged to the synagogue called the Synagogue of the Libertines, both Cyrenians and Alexandrians, and of those who came from Cilicia and from Asia,[1] disputing with Stephen, (10) and they were unable to withstand the wisdom and the Spirit with which he spoke. (11) Then they suborned men who said, 'We have heard him speak blasphemous words against Moses and God.' (12) And they stirred up the people and the elders and the scribes, and they came suddenly upon Stephen, seized him and carried him away, and brought him to the Sanhedrin. (13) They set up false witnesses, who said, 'This man never stops speaking words against the Holy Place and the Law; (14) for we have heard him say that this Jesus of Nazareth will destroy this place and change the customary rules which Moses handed down to us.' (15) And all who were sitting in the Sanhedrin fixed their eyes on him and saw his face as if it had been the face of an angel.

Bibliography

S. Arai, *NTS* 34 (1988), 397–410.

M. E. Boismard, *FS* George, 181–94.

O. Cullmann, as in (16).

O. Glombitza, as in (16).

H. Lietzmann, *ZNW* 20 (1921), 171–3.

C. F. D. Moule, *JTS* 1 (1950), 29–41.

F. Mussner, *FS* Vögtle, 283–99.

G. N. Stanton, as in (16).

Some of the works listed for paragraphs 16, 18, 19, 20 are relevant here too.

Commentary

Of the men named in 6.5 Luke is able to tell stories about only two. Of these two we hear nothing about Philip till 8.5. Luke however

---

[1]RSV, the synagogue of the Freedmen (as it was called), and of the Cyrenians, and of the Alexandrians, and of those from Cilicia and Asia; NEB, the Synagogue of the Freedmen, comprising Cyrenians and Alexandrians and people from Cilicia and Asia.

immediately takes up the story that he has to tell about Stephen and carries it through to its conclusion in 8.1 and its consequences in 8.1–4 (cf. 11.19). It is important at this point to consider first the links between the different components with which we have to deal in the whole passage, 6.1–8.4: (a) the story of the Hebrew and Hellenist widows; (b) the list of names in 6.5 and the appointment of seven men to special service; (c) the story of the arrest and stoning of Stephen; (d) the speech attributed to Stephen; (e) Stephen's martyrdom and its consequences in a general persecution and the eventual spread of the Gospel to Antioch. It must not be assumed that these constituent parts originally belonged together; indeed, it is by no means certain that any of them, except (d), is a single piece of material; see below.

We have seen above (pp. 303–7) that 6.1–7 is to be explained on the basis of a traditional list of the names of seven men who probably had originally some connection with the charitable work of the Jerusalem church but developed their Christian action beyond this so as to become a group of leaders not necessarily in opposition to but at least distinct from the Twelve, and that tradition connected them with the foundation of a mixed Jewish and Gentile church at Antioch; indeed, this may have constituted part of a (written or oral) Antioch source. This might account for paragraphs (c) and (e) of the above list (but see the more detailed examination below). (a) is probably Luke's writing up of the Antiochene tradition in such a way as to relate it to the Twelve; (d) probably has a separate origin (see pp. 334–40).

The present paragraph, 6.8–15, has its sequel in 7.53–8.1. It is an important fact that both paragraphs show signs of compilation. For the latter, see below, pp. 380–2. In 6.8–15 the charge against Stephen is given twice, in similar but not identical terms. In each case it is said that his opponents engineered false testimony against Stephen. In v. 11 they suborned (ὑπέβαλον) men, making the (false) accusation that Stephen had blasphemed against Moses and God. In vv. 13, 14 they set up (ἔστησαν) false witnesses with a charge that is put twice: He speaks against the Holy Place and the Law; We have heard him say that Jesus will destroy this Place and change the customs (laws) delivered by Moses. It is of course true that v. 11 relates to what was being publicly said, vv. 13, 14 to the charge brought before the Sanhedrin; there is a parallel to such repetition in 15.1, 5. It is however possible that here (and in ch. 15) Luke is putting together two sources, each of which contained its own formulation of the complaint brought formally or informally against Stephen. In the present passage this is confirmed by the related phenomenon in 7.54–8.1 (see pp. 380f.).

There is nothing in the preceding narrative (6.1–7) to suggest the charges brought against Stephen, unless the very word Hellenist is taken to imply one who has so far assimilated Greek culture as to abandon the principles of Judaism. They are (according to 6.9) members of a Hellenistic Jewish synagogue (or of Hellenistic Jewish synagogues) who dispute with Stephen, and it is possible to conclude that they were Jews who had maintained a more conservative position, and that not all Diaspora Jews sat loose enough to the Law to move easily over into the new Christian version of Judaism; and this we know to be true. Philo, for all his Hellenism, was essentially faithful not only to the thought but also to the practices of Judaism and censures those who abandon them (see above on 6.1) thereby incidentally proving the existence of these renegades. Stephen's speech also is proof of their existence (see pp. 338–40). But, as closer reading shows, it was not Stephen's Hellenism but Stephen's Christianity that (in Luke's view) provoked opposition. This has been well pointed out by Schille (177): 'So speziell er sich auf die Urchristenheit bezieht, trifft der Vorwurf wieder kein spezifisches Hellenistentum des Stephanus. Lukas sieht Stephanus nicht um irgendeiner Sondermeinung willen sterben. Dieser Mann ist angeklagt für Dinge, die jeder Christ bejaht, er stirbt stellvertretend für die ganze Christenheit.' Luke has in fact created the setting in which opposition to Stephen arose (he creates a similar setting for Paul, whom he seems to have viewed as Stephen's successor, in 9.29), though in doing so he was able to draw, as the parallels show, upon a double strand of tradition.

In his disputes with his fellow Hellenists Stephen presumably argued for the Messiahship of Jesus and the fulfilment in him of the promised salvation. This would be blasphemy against Moses only if he drew the conclusion that the Law was not the word of God and need no longer be observed. It would (on Jewish terms) be blasphemy against God only if Jesus were alleged to be a second God, sharing the throne of God and thus diminishing the honour paid to the one true God. That Stephen spoke against the Holy Place, the Temple, is attested by his speech (see 7.46–50), and it is important to note v. 14, with its allusion to the teaching of Jesus; for details see on this verse. Did Jesus say that he would destroy the Temple? He said (according to Lk. 21.6, 24) that it would be destroyed, but this is not quite the same. He did say (according to the gospel tradition) that the customs delivered by Moses were to be changed; Luke has omitted the cleansing of all foods (Mk 7.19), but he retains a good deal of Sabbath material. There is no other place in Acts where gospel teaching is alluded to in this way; 2.28; 10.38 are allusive but in general rather than specific terms. It seems probable that the trial and death of Stephen have been written up with the story of Jesus in mind; so for example Stählin (101) and Schneider (433), who gives a list of correspondences between Acts and the Lucan and Marcan Passion Narratives. This is in favour of Haenchen's view (265f.) that Luke was not adding, through his account of a trial, an element of legality to a 'lynching' source, or introducing violence into a 'trial' source, or combining two sources, of which one narrated a trial the other a lynching, but rather was making his own composition on the basis of traditions he had received and accommodated to the story of Jesus. This however does not account for the duplication of material: in the present paragraph the two charges against Stephen, similar but not identical, and in the account of the martyrdom the two occurrences of λιθοβολεῖν (7.58, 59) and other parallels noted below (pp. 380f.).

There is probably truth in both views — the view that Luke was freely writing up tradition and the view that he made use of sources that had already achieved a definite form. It would be mistaken to suggest that Luke has combined sources in the manner of a jig-saw puzzle so that they may be disentangled and rearranged so as to produce two distinct stories. Luke has written with greater freedom than this; yet his freedom has been to some extent inhibited by the existence of formulated material which he did not feel at liberty to jettison altogether even when it resulted in some repetition and inconsistency. Verses 10, 11 may be taken to lead on to the lynching story contained in 7.54–8.1, vv. 12, 13 (with their references to elders, scribes, and the Sanhedrin) to the trial and judicial execution narrative, and v. 15 to the heavenly vision of 7.55 (so for example Dibelius 110, 168, 207 and Roloff 111). To this v. 14 is probably Luke's own addition (note the repetition of ἀκηκόαμεν), intended to add fresh substance to the charge and, more important, to link the story of Stephen with that of Jesus. After this addition the trial narrative can continue. Haenchen 266 argues that the long speech of ch. 7 requires the setting of a trial; it could not have been delivered in the presence of a howling mob, and for this reason Luke was glad to find a tradition that included a trial. This is hardly convincing; Paul's speech in 22.1–21 is not so long as Stephen's but it is delivered in equally threatening circumstances, and one cannot think that Luke would have hesitated to put Stephen's speech outside a courtroom setting if his sources, or his own picturing of the situation, had required him to do so. This is not to say that the speech itself was part of the same piece of tradition; see e.g. p. 340. But it remains probable that vv. 12–13 (14) led to some sort of trial narrative with a formal sentence and execution.

Estimates and analyses of the paragraph have differed. Conzelmann (45) considers vv. 8, 9, 10, 11a, 12 traditional and painted over by Luke in such a way that the court appears to behave like a mob. Vielhauer (*Geschichte* 386f.) thought that the martyrdom was found by Luke already in writing; if the references to Saul are removed a smooth connected narrative is left. Weiser (171) takes v. 8 to be Lucan, v. 9 mainly pre-Lucan, v. 10 Lucan, taken from Lk. 21.15, and in vv. 11–15 everything that suggests a formal trial to be Lucan. Somewhat similarly Schille (177) writes, 'ab Vers 12b ist ohnehin nur noch Lukas am Werk gewesen'. It seems best to understand vv. 8, 9 as Luke's means of linking his account of the appointment of the Seven (which he had constructed) to the Stephen (Antiochene) tradition on which he now embarks. Verse 8 is probably his own introduction, in which he uses language that puts Stephen on the same level as the Twelve (cf. e.g. 5.12); v. 9 (cf. 9.29) may be based upon Jerusalem memory of a Hellenistic synagogue divided between those who did and those who did not accept the Messiahship of Jesus. Verse 15 links the story about Stephen to the speech which is attributed to him but was probably drawn from a different source.

8. Having introduced Stephen as one of the Seven, associating him with a group he describes as Hellenists, Luke proceeds with the traditions he has received about Stephen as an individual. After the list of names in 6.5 one might have expected the anaphoric article: ὁ Στέφανος, the above-mentioned Stephen. But nothing can be built on this, or on the absence of a participle with πλήρης, noted by M. 3.159, but noted as insignificant (except of the fact that Luke is not atticizing) since the same lack of a participle appears at Mk 1.23; Lk. 4.1; Acts 19.37; Heb. 7.2f. — and in Strabo, Appian, and Philostratus.

In 6.3 all the Seven are to be full of Spirit and wisdom; at 6.5 Stephen is full of faith and Holy Spirit; here he is (according to what is almost certainly the best text — that of P[8vid. 45 vid. 74] ℵ A B D 0175 33 323 614 945 1175 1739 2495 *al* lat sy[p] co) πλήρης χάριτος καὶ δυνάμεως. Other readings (πίστεως καὶ δ., 𝔐 sy[h]; χάριτος κ. π. κ. δ., E; πίστ. χάρ. πνεύ. κ. δ., Ψ) are due to assimilation. The new description is not proof of the use of a new source; Luke is ringing the changes and does not mean anything substantially different from what has been said before. χάρις (cf. 4.33) is a general term, the favour of God expressed in an abundance of gifts; δύναμις is the result of the work of the Holy Spirit (cf. 1.8) and corresponds to πίστις in v. 5; both terms relate to miracles which are immediately mentioned. Stephen worked *signs and portents*, as the Twelve had done (2.43; 4.30; 5.12); in this respect at least he is not inferior to them. This is the point that Luke means to emphasise, not that Stephen is the 'Vorbild des christlichen Pneumatikertums' (Roloff 112; cf. e.g. Pesch 236; Weiser 171). The signs and portents were done ἐν τῷ λαῷ; again cf. 5.12. There was at this stage and in this respect no difference between the Jerusalem crowd and the ancient people of God. The Western text makes one of its characteristically pious additions: διὰ τοῦ ὀνόματος (ἐν τῷ ὀνόματι, E) (τοῦ) κυρίου 'Ιησοῦ Χριστοῦ, D (E) (33 614) *al* it (sy[h**]) sa mae. The miracles are important but they are not represented as provoking opposition to Stephen; it is his teaching that meets resistance (Bauernfeind 109).

It will be noted that it is not said that Stephen gave any attention to the proper distribution of alms and the care of the Hellenist widows. The connection between him and the charitable arrangements is secondary, except to the extent that the Seven may have first come to prominence as agents of charity.

9. ἀνέστησαν recalls court scenes (e.g. Lk. 11.32), but is not used with that sense here; the word is of wide and general meaning, and the court is not reached till v. 11.

In the description of those who moved against Stephen the repeated article (τῶν . . . τῶν) suggests a division into two groups: some of those who belonged to a certain synagogue . . . some of those who came from . . . This division however cannot be regarded as certain. For some reason, though he had written *Cyrenians* and *Alexandrians* Luke did not intend to write *Cilicians* and *Asians* but to use ἀπό with the names of the provinces in question, and may have felt that the preposition should be preceded by the article. Some if not all of the persons concerned are associated with a synagogue. For this important Jewish institution see *NS* 2.423–54; also *Background*, 53–5, 204–6, 211. Its primary use was for the reading and exposition of Scripture, for prayer, and for instruction, but it served also as a meeting place for Jews and might have residential accommodation attached to it (see below). It is not clear, and is not agreed, how many synagogues are referred to here. Some think that five were intended, one for each of the groups mentioned, others that there were two, a second occurrence of συναγωγή being understood before the second τῶν, others, with perhaps greatest probability, that the one occurrence of the word means that Luke had only one synagogue in mind, and that all the groups shared in it.

In addition to the names of provinces, or of their inhabitants, stands the word λιβερτῖνος, a transliteration of the Latin *libertinus*, a freedman, understood especially with reference to his status in society (*libertus* describing him in relation to his manumitter); the word might also mean the son of a *libertus* (Suetonius, *Claudius* 24.1). Many Jews, originally enslaved as captives in war and transferred to other parts of the Roman world, came to enjoy the status of freedmen. Philo, *Leg. ad Gaium* 155, refers to Jews who had become Roman citizens, emancipated by their owners and able to live without giving up any of their native institutions, and Tacitus, *Annals* 2.85, to *libertini* who had become proselytes (*ea superstitione infecta*). The word λιβερτῖνος clearly does not belong to the same category as the other four descriptive terms; hence the conjecture Λιβυστίνων, which goes back to Beza. Dibelius 91 suggested Λιβύων. *Libyans* go neatly with the other African nations, Cyrenians and Alexandrians, but the reading is not thereby proved correct, and it is better to see if sense can be made of the text contained in the

MSS. 'Those of the Synagogue called that of the Libertines and Cyrenians and Alexandrians' retains to the full the anomaly of a social term on all fours with two geographical or racial terms. Better would be, 'Those of the Synagogue called that of the Libertines, both Cyrenians and Alexandrians'. The second τῶν can then be taken like the first in connection with τινες: 'and some of those who came from Cilicia and Asia'. These last, thus taken, are not said to belong to the same synagogue, though there is nothing to contradict this. There were synagogues in Jerusalem; one, known from an inscription (*CIJ* II, no. 1404, p. 333), has been held to be the Synagogue of the Libertines referred to here (see *NS* 2.425; Jeremias, *Jerusalem* 60, 66; *Background* 54f.; Hemer 176). It was founded by Theodotus, son of Vettenus, and provided with residential accommodation for the benefit of Jews coming from abroad. The name Vettenus suggests the Roman *gens Vettena*, and the suggestion is ready to hand that the father, or possibly an earlier ancestor, of Theodotus had been a slave of and received his freedom from one of the Vetteni (see Sevenster, *Do you know Greek?* 1968, 132, who accepts the connection; and Sukenik, *Synagogues* 70, who thinks it no more than possible). It may be the same synagogue that is referred to in rabbinic writings (T. Megillah 3.6 (224); j. Megillah 3.1, 73d.35; Megillah 26a). In the first two passages it is described as the Synagogue of the Alexandrians, in the third as that of the Tarsians (though some take the word to mean not Tarsians but *artisans*; see Jeremias, *Jerusalem* 66). It is attractive to infer that it was used by both Alexandrians and Tarsians (the latter coming of course from Cilicia); and then to conjecture that Cyrenians and Asians used it too; the Theodotus inscription refers simply to those who came ἀπὸ τῆς ξένης, from abroad. Whether or not the identification can be maintained, it appears that Stephen (according to Luke) may have found himself opposed by his own sort — Diaspora Jews who had not become Christians.

For Cyrenians cf. 11.20; 13.1 — Cyrenian Jews who had become Christians found their way to Antioch. See also Lk. 23.26 and parallels (Simon of Cyrene); and cf. Acts 2.10. From the time of Augustus Cyrenaica, a fertile region of North Africa, had been a senatorial province. There was a substantial Jewish population (see Tcherikover, 290f.; *NS* 3.60–62). For ossuaries which show a Jewish family from Cyrene resident in Jerusalem see Jeremias (*Jerusalem* 71); more sceptically, Sevenster (op. cit. 145–9). For Alexandrians cf. 18.24 (Apollos). It is well known that the great city of Alexandria contained a numerous and varied population of Jews, who caused their Egyptian fellows and the Roman administrators much trouble. See Tcherikover 284–5, 320–8, 410–15; *NS* 3.42–4, and many other passages. For Cilicia cf. 15.23, 41; also Gal. 1.21; but the most famous of Cilicians was Saul (Acts 21.39; 22.3; 23.34). For the bad reputation of Cilicia see passages in Wettstein 492; for Jews in

Cilicia *NS* 3.33f. For Asia (omitted here probably through homeoteleuton by A D*) cf. 2.9; 16.6; 19.10; and especially 21.27. For Jews in Asia see Tcherikover 287–99; *NS* 3.17–36. It is perhaps not unnatural that Hellenistic Jews who remained Jews and did not become Christians should be particularly incensed with those of their number who, in their view, betrayed the ancestral faith, and should initiate action against them. If in 9.29 Ἑλληνιστάς is read it is not used in exactly the same sense as at 6.1 (see on each verse) but Luke presumably means that Saul, whom he takes to belong to the same group as Stephen, suffered in the same way from the same (or similar) Diaspora Jews. These disputed, συζητοῦντες, with Stephen. Bornkamm (4.26) refers to the word as denoting Lehrgespräche. It is used of Saul in relation to the Hellenists (9.29) and the cognate συζήτησις occurs at 28.29 (si v. l.). The verb is Lucan (Lk. 2; Acts 2) and Marcan (Mk, 6).

10. The members of the synagogue argued with Stephen in vain. Cf. 4.14. The promise of Lk. 21.15 (δώσω ὑμῖν στόμα καὶ σοφίαν ᾗ οὐ δυνήσονται ἀντιστῆναι . . .) was fulfilled. The coincidence in language can hardly be accidental. For σοφία (D E h mae add τῇ οὔσῃ ἐν αὐτῷ) and for πνεῦμα (D E *al* add τῷ ἁγίῳ) see 6.3. Calvin (166) rightly interprets the two words in relation to each other: 'the wisdom with which the Spirit of God supplied him'; and Bede notes the appropriateness of the fulfilment of Jesus' promise in the work of the first martyr.

At the end of the verse the Western text has a long addition after ᾧ ἐλάλει. It appears in two forms. In D h t w (sy^hmg mae) it runs: διὰ τὸ ἐλέγχεσθαι αὐτοὺς ἐπ'αὐτοῦ μετὰ πάσης παρρησίας· μὴ δυνάμενοι οὖν ἀντοφθαλμεῖν τῇ ἀληθείᾳ (v. 11 follows). E has indicatives instead of the infinitive and participle and avoids ἀντοφθαλμεῖν: . . . διότι ἠλέγχοντο ὑπ' αὐτοῦ . . . ἐπειδὴ οὐκ ἠδύναντο ἀντιλέγειν. This is a characteristic 'brightening' of the narrative. There is no need to ascribe it to Montanist influence. For ἀντοφθαλμεῖν cf. 27.15, where the sense is literal, not metaphorical. For a metaphorical use cf. Wisd. 12.14. ἰσχύειν, *to be able*, with infinitive, is hardly a Semitism; see the passages cited by BA 778 s.v., including *P.Oxy.* 10(1914).1345, οὐκ ἴσχυσα ἐλθεῖν σήμερον.

11. Since argument failed Stephen's opponents had recourse to other methods. ὑποβάλλειν (here only in the NT) is more often used (when not in a literal sense) with the meaning *to hint, to suggest*, usually secretly, perhaps in a whisper. The best parallel is in *Mart. Pol.* 17.2, ὑπέβαλεν (the Evil One; v. l.,ὑπέβαλόν τινες) γοῦν Νικήτην . . . ἐντυχεῖν τῷ ἄρχοντι . . . The variant in Theodotion's version of Dan. 3.9 is worth little as a parallel and Test. Sym. 3.3

refers to inward suggestion rather than plotting and prompting; to infer from this passage that the motivation of Stephen's enemies was envy (Pesch 237) is quite unwarranted, though the conclusion may be correct. Most of the passages cited from Josephus do little to illustrate Luke's use of the word, but cf. *War* 5.439, τὸ δ' ἑτοιμότατον ἦν μηνυτής τις ὑπόβλητος ὡς αὐτομολεῖν διεγνωκότων ('the readiest expedient was to suborn an informer to state that they had decided to desert' — Thackeray). See also Appian, *Civil War* 1.74, ὑπεβλήθησαν κατήγοροι. It is clear that Luke considers it slanderous to assert that Stephen had spoken against Moses and God; cf. v. 13, μάρτυρας ψευδεῖς. ἀκηκόαμεν suggests but does not prove that Stephen had been preaching. Schille (175) rightly observes that Luke says nothing to suggest any difference between Stephen's preaching and that of the apostles. There is nothing to indicate that he attacked the Law. Allegations that he did so are described as false.

ῥήματα βλάσφημα: א* D 614 lat have ῥ. βλασφημίας, the qualitative use of the genitive, as in Hebrew; but the reading may have arisen through confusion and metathesis of letters with the next word — βλασφημα (ε) ις. εἰς itself, used with the same meaning as the more natural Greek κατά in v. 13, may be an Aramaism (Black, *AA* 195; Wilcox 134), but εἰς (ἐς) is used in Greek to mean *against* (e.g. Aeschylus, *Prometheus Bound* 945, τὸν ἐξαμαρτόντ' ἐς θεούς; Sophocles, *Philoctetes* 522f., εἰς ἐμὲ τοὔνειδος ἕξεις ἐνδίκως ὀνειδίσαι). For the question whether Stephen did speak against Moses see pp. 337f.; in the speech attributed to him in ch. 7 he speaks very highly of Moses (e.g. 7.20, 35). He blasphemed God only if Jesus, whom he accepted as Messiah, could be held to have done so. The accusation recalls that against James (Josephus, *Ant.* 20.200, ὡς παρανομησάντων); in Luke's time it had probably become customary. For blasphemy against Moses cf. Josephus, *War* 2.145 (σέβας δὲ μέγα παρ' αὐτοῖς μετὰ τὸν θεὸν τοὔνομα τοῦ νομοθέτου, κἂν βλασφημήσῃ τις εἰς τοῦτον, κολάζεται θανάτῳ). Cf. *Ant.* 3.307; *Apion* 1.279.

12. συνεκίνησαν. The subject is presumably the synagogue members of v. 9. Over against ὑπέβαλον (v. 11; and ἔστησαν, v. 13) this is a large-scale, rabble-rousing activity. τὸν λαόν, as elsewhere, is both the Jerusalem populace and the people of Israel. Conzelmann 45 thinks that Luke must here be following a source since in 5.26 the people look on the Christians with favour; he may be right about the source, but the point of συνεκίνησαν is that the disaffected Diaspora Jews found a means of persuading the crowds to change their attitude. For the elders and scribes see 4.5. ἐπιστάντες, intransitive, *they set upon him*; perhaps *came upon him suddenly, took him by surprise* (cf. 1 Thess. 5.3; Thucydides 8.69.3, ἐπέστησαν τοῖς . . . βουλευταῖς; Lucian, *Dialogi Deorum* 17.1, ἐφίσταται δὲ αὐτοῖς ὁ "Ηφαιστος). συναρπάζειν, to seize and carry away; in the NT only Lk 8.29; Acts 6.12; 19.29; 27.15. Schille (176, similarly Haenchen 264) thinks this 'merkwürdig, weil der Mob noch keine Polizeigewalt besitzt'; it is not hard to think of occasions in 18th century England when a mob carried off a dissenting preacher to the magistrate. For συνέδριον see 4.15.

Stephen is now brought into court, and the proceedings that follow must, in Luke's understanding, be understood to be of a more formal kind.

13. ἔστησαν is in itself a colourless word (caused to take their place in the witness box), but in the context, preceded by ὑπέβαλον (v. 11) and followed by ψευδεῖς, suggests a rigged trial: set up (which also could be innocent but hints at something more). ψευδεῖς (though in the NT the word occurs only here and at Rev. 2.2; 21.8; cf. Plutarch, Quomodo adulator ab amico internoscatur 24 (65A), ὁ δὲ ψευδὴς καὶ νόθος καὶ ὑπόχαλκος . . .) suggests accounts of the trial of Jesus, where compound words are used (ψευδομάρτυς, Mt. 26.60; ψευδομαρτυρεῖν, Mk 14.56, 57; ψευδομαρτυρία, Mt. 26.59). The story of Stephen shows further parallels with the story of Jesus; these will be noted. See also the charge of blasphemy in v. 11. The theme of false witness brought against the righteous and godly is an OT one; see Ps. 27.12; 35.11; Prov. 14.5; 24.28.

ὁ ἄνθρωπος οὗτος gives a derogatory tone to the reference. παύεται λαλῶν is a classical construction; cf. e.g. Aristophanes, Plutus 360, παῦσαι φλυαρῶν; Birds 859; Xenophon, Cyropaedia 1.4.2; also Josephus, Ant. 9.255.

λαλῶν ῥήματα κατά is reminiscent of Aramaic (see StrB 2.665; Black, AA 195; Wilcox 134), but speaking against (κατά) is not strange in Greek (e.g. Xenophon, History of Greece 1.5.2, κατά τε τοῦ Τισσαφέρνους ἔλεγον). The charge is similar to that of v. 11 but not identical with it; Knox (Acts 25) thinks there is no need to regard them as doublets. To speak against Moses and to speak against the Law are however, as near as may be, synonymous. Just as, in ch. 7, Stephen speaks highly of Moses so he speaks highly also of the Law; Moses received from God to transmit to his people living oracles (7.38).

τοῦ τόπου τοῦ ἁγίου τούτου, the Temple. τούτου is omitted, probably rightly, by P⁷⁴ ℵ A D E Ψ 0175 𝔐 lat. See Metzger (341). It is more likely that the word 'crept into the text from the next verse' than that P⁷⁴ etc. sought to remove the possible interpretation of the phrase as referring to the Sanhedrin's meeting place. There could in any case be no doubt what holy place was intended. מקום, אתרא, and τόπος were indeed used to denote synagogues (Sukenik, Synagogues 71; Manson, Studies 208f.), so that τόπος here could refer to the synagogue of the Libertines (v. 9), but the next verse is decisive for the Temple (so e.g. Schneider 437). For the Temple as τόπος, מקום, cf. Jer. 7.14; Neh. 4.7; 2 Macc. 5.19; Mt. 24.15; Jn 4.20; 11.48; Acts 21.28. The last passage mentioned (the accusation against Paul) is closely parallel to the present one, but adds κατὰ τοῦ λαοῦ. See further the next verse; and, for Qumran and the Temple, B. Gärtner, *The Temple and the Community in Qumran and the NT*, SNTSMS 1, Cambridge 1965. Stählin (103) suggests that originally מקום may have referred, as it often does in rabbinic use, not to the Temple but to God; cf. v. 11.

14. The false witnesses allege that they heard Stephen adduce sayings of Jesus in support of his attack on the Temple and the Law. For Ναζωραῖος see on 2.22. οὗτος is contemptuous, as in v. 13. This was already noticed by Calvin (169), 'They speak of Christ with contempt in this way'. It is not clear whether the falsehood of the witnesses lies in their alleging that they had heard Stephen say that Jesus would destroy the Temple, in the content of what they claimed to have heard, in the interpretation they put upon his words, or in some combination of these. The question is complicated by the fact that there is material in the sayings of Jesus (as recorded by Luke) that comes close to justifying what the 'false' witnesses claimed. At Lk. 21.6 Jesus declares that days will come when οὐκ ἀφεθήσεται λίθος ἐπὶ λίθῳ ὃς οὐ καταλυθήσεται; at 21.24 that Jerusalem ἔσται πατουμένη ὑπὸ ἐθνῶν. Cf. also Mt. 24.2; 26.61 (δύναμαι καταλῦσαι); 27.40; Mk 13.2; 14.58 (ἐγὼ καταλύσω); 15.29. See also Gosp. Thomas 71: Jesus said: I shall de[stroy this] house and no one will be able to build it [again]. In Jn 2.19 is the similar λύσατε τὸν ναὸν τοῦτον. It will be noted that Luke does not quote Jesus as saying, *I will destroy*; a prediction that the Temple will be destroyed is not the same as the threat *I will destroy it*. Bauernfeind 110 refers to Eisler's suggestion that the original saying of Jesus was in fact *irdischtempelstürmerisch* and that it was subsequently given by Christians a theological interpretation. Luke at least does not seem concerned to develop such an interpretation. Nothing is said about rebuilding or replacing the destroyed Temple. Stephen (as represented by Luke) thus differs from 1 Enoch 90.29 (The Lord of the sheep brought a new house, larger and higher than that first one, and he set it up on the site of the first one . . . (Knibb)); 1 QH 6.25–7, and the gospels, though it is possible to say that his (lying) accusers deliberately left out the positive part of what he had said.

τὰ ἔθη ἃ παρέδωκεν (the word will cover both written and oral tradition) ἡμῖν Μωυσῆς are laws; it is impossible to turn them into mere customs with no legal authority since what Moses handed down was *law*; cf. 15.1; 16.21; 21.21; 26.3; 28.17. For ἔθος as (Jewish) law cf. Josephus, *War* 7.424 (τοῖς πατρίοις ἔθεσι); *Ant.* 15.288 (τῶν κοινῶν ἐθῶν, which all must either preserve or die for). See also Wilson, *Law* 4–11. In the light of this evidence we must not make too much of Plato's ἔθος ἐστὶ νόμος ἀγραφος (*Laws* 7. 793a); there is little ground for Schneider's (439) 'Lukas bezieht die ἔθη wohl primär auf die kultische Gesetzgebung'. Jesus' most trenchant change in Mosaic regulations occurs at Mk 7.15, 19 (καθαρίζων πάντα τὰ βρώματα; Mt. 15.15–20); this does not occur in Luke. Luke on the other hand contains more references than Mark to Jesus' new attitude to the Sabbath (see Lk. 6.1–11; 13.10–17; 14.1–6). Whether or not Stephen said so, it seems that a strong case can be made for the belief that Jesus did foretell the destruction of the Temple, even if he did not say that he would himself destroy it, and that he did change Mosaic regulations, even if he regarded his changes as fulfilment rather than destruction. See Mt. 5.17; and cf. Pesch (238, Jesus did not change the Law but relativised it) and Roloff (114, Jesus did not do away with the Law but changed it, that is, he claimed to be the Messianic interpreter of Torah). See further Wilson (*Gentiles* 145f., and *Law* 61–3.).

The passage before us gives an interesting and important insight into Luke's understanding of Christianity. He recognizes that the new faith may appear (and Stephen's speech in ch. 7 confirms this) to disrupt the old, but to maintain this is a falsehood, misrepresenting both Jesus and those who preach his Gospel. This is not the way in which Paul expresses the dialectic of Law and grace; it is a historian's way rather than a theologian's. Weiser (173) draws from this passage the conclusion that the Hellenists preached a law-free Gospel, though they did not draw the theological consequences of this as Paul later did. This gives too great precision to the term Hellenists and probably misrepresents the position of those whom Weiser has in mind in using it; see below on ch. 15.

15. ἀτενίσαντες: a Lucan word (Lk., 2; Acts, 10; 2 Cor., 2), which is followed sometimes by εἰς and the accusative, as here (but D* has αὐτῷ; also, instead of the co-ordinated participle, ἠτένιζον . . . καί), sometimes by the dative. καθέζεσθαι is used in Acts only here and at 20.9; more frequently καθίζειν (-εσθαι). The occurrence together of a Lucan and an unusual word makes it difficult to draw any conclusion with regard to sources. Cf. Schneider (440): 'V. 15 ist von εἶδον an wahrscheinlich vorlukanisch'.

Looking at Stephen (defensionem expectantes — Blass) the members of the Sanhedrin saw his face ὡσεὶ (a Lucan word: Lk.-Acts, 16 (12); rest of the NT, 6) πρόσωπον ἀγγέλου (D h t mae add,ἐστῶτος ἐν μέσῳ αὐτῶν). StrB 1.752; 2.665f. quote a number of parallels; e.g. Targum Song of Songs 1.5: When the house of Israel prepared the (golden) calf, their face was dark, like that of the sons of Cush, who live in the tents of Kedar. But when they turned in penitence and were forgiven, then was the splendour of the glory of their face as great as that of the angels. Better perhaps is Deut. R. 11 (207d): When Sammael [the angel of death] saw Moses sitting, as he wrote the expressed name [YHWH], and as his face resembled the sun and he himself the angel of the Lord of Hosts, he fell back before Moses in fear. Cf. Joseph and Aseneth 14.9. Best of all are the biblical passages: Gen. 33.10; 1 Sam. 29.9; 2 Sam. 14.17; Esther 5.2, and especially Exod. 34.29–35. As the passage stands, the description of Stephen prepares the way for his speech, which is to be thought of as an inspired utterance; it may originally have been connected with 7.55, Stephen's vision of the glory of God, a glory which is communicated to him (Dibelius 110, 168, 207). Cf. *Acts of Paul and Thecla* 3: ποτὲ μὲν γὰρ ἐφαίνετο ὡς ἄνθρωπος, ποτὲ δὲ ἀγγέλου πρόσωπον εἶχεν. Cf. also *Martyrdom of Polycarp* 12.1: τὸ πρόσωπον αὐτοῦ χάριτος ἐπληροῦτο (when Polycarp declared himself a Christian and thus brought martyrdom upon himself). It is surprising that no reaction on the part of the beholders is described. They are neither impressed, as by the beauty and dignity of a heavenly being, nor frightened by the threat that such a being might constitute for those who opposed him.

18. STEPHEN'S SPEECH 7.1–53

(1) The High Priest said, 'Are these things so?' (2) He said, 'Brothers and Fathers, listen. The God of glory appeared to our father Abraham while he was in Mesopotamia, before he came to live in Haran, (3) and said to him, Leave your land and your family, and go into the land that I will show you. (4) Then he left the land of Chaldea and settled in Haran. And there, after the death of his father, God[1] transferred him into this land in which you now live, (5) and he gave him no inheritance in it, not even space to plant his foot,[2] and he promised to give it in possession to him and to his seed after him, although he then had no child. (6) God spoke thus, that his seed should be sojourners in a foreign land and that the native inhabitants[3] would enslave them and ill-use them 400 years. (7) And the nation they serve as slaves I will judge, said God, and afterwards they will come out and worship me in this place. (8) And he gave him the covenant of circumcision; so he begot Isaac and circumcised him on the eighth day, and Isaac begot and circumcised Jacob, and Jacob begot and circumcised the twelve patriarchs.

(9) The patriarchs were jealous of Joseph and sold him into Egypt, but God was with him (10) and rescued him out of all his afflictions and gave him grace and wisdom in the eyes of Pharaoh king of Egypt, and he[4] appointed him ruler over Egypt and over all his household. (11) But famine came upon the whole of Egypt and upon Canaan, and great affliction, and our fathers found no food.[5] (12) When Jacob heard that there was corn in Egypt he sent our fathers,[6] on the first occasion. (13) And on the second Joseph was made known[7] to his brothers and Joseph's race[8] became known[7] to Pharaoh. (14) Joseph sent and summoned Jacob his father, and all the family, in all seventy-five souls. (15) And Jacob went down into Egypt, and died, he himself and our fathers too, (16) and their bodies[9] were transferred to Sychem[10] and laid in the tomb that Abraham bought for a sum of money from the sons of Emmor in Sychem.[10]

(17) 'Now as the time for the fulfilment of the promise that God made to Abraham draw near the people grew and multiplied in Egypt, (18) until there arose a different king over Egypt, who did not know Joseph. (19) He

---

[1]Greek, he.
[2]Literally, a foot's length (so RSV); *Begs.*, a pace's length.
[3]Greek, they.
[4]The pronoun may refer to Pharaoh or to God.
[5]The Greek word usually refers to food for cattle.
[6]Or, . . . that there was corn (there), he sent our fathers into Egypt.
[7]Different words in Greek.
[8]*Begs.*, family.
[9]Greek, they.
[10]OT, Shechem.

tricked[11] our race and ill-treated our fathers, causing them to expose their infants, that they might not be preserved alive. (20) At this time Moses was born, and was a splendid child.[12] For three months he was cared for in his father's house, (21) and when he was exposed Pharaoh's daughter took him up and cared for him as a son. (22) Moses was trained in all the wisdom of the Egyptians, and was powerful in his words and deeds. (23) But when he had completed the span of forty years it came into his mind that he should visit his brothers, the sons of Israel, (24) and when he saw one of them being unjustly treated he defended him, and avenged him who was being wronged by smiting the Egyptian. (25) He supposed that his brothers understood that God was giving them deliverance by his hand, but they did not understand. (26) On the next day he appeared to them as they were fighting and tried to reconcile them and make peace. He said, Men, you are brothers; why are you wronging one another? (27) He who was injuring his neighbour thrust him aside, saying, Who appointed you a ruler and judge over us? (28) Do you wish to kill me, as yesterday you killed the Egyptian? (29) At this word Moses fled and became a sojourner in the land of Midian, where he begot two sons.

(30) 'When forty years were up an angel appeared to him in the wilderness of Mount Sinai in a fiery flame in a bush. (31) When Moses saw it he marvelled at the sight. As he approached so as to look closely the voice of the Lord was heard: (32) I am the God of your fathers, the God of Abraham, Isaac, and Jacob. Moses trembled with fright and did not dare to look closely. (33) The Lord said to him, Take off the shoes you are wearing,[13] for the place on which you are standing is holy ground. (34) I have indeed seen the ill-treatment of my people who are in Egypt and I have heard their groaning, and I have come down to rescue them. And now come, let me send you to Egypt. (35) This Moses, whom they disowned when they said, Who appointed you a ruler and judge? — this man God sent as ruler and redeemer, with the aid[14] of the angel who appeared to him in the bush. (36) This man brought them out; for forty years he did portents and signs in the land of Egypt, at the Red Sea, and in the wilderness. (37) It is this Moses who said to the children of Israel, God will raise up a prophet for you, from the midst of your brothers, as he raised up me. (38) This is he who was in the assembly of God's people in the wilderness, with the angel who spoke to him on Mount Sinai and with our fathers, who received living oracles to give to us. (39) Our fathers would not be obedient to him but thrust him aside and, in their hearts, returned to Egypt, (40) and said to Aaron, Make us gods to go before us; for this Moses, who brought us out of the land of Egypt, we do not know what has happened to him. (41) And in those days they made a calf, offered sacrifice to the idol, and made merry[15] over the works of their hands. (42) God turned and handed them over to worship the host of heaven, as it is written in the Book of the Prophets: Did you bring me sacrifices and

---

[11]*Begs.*, exploited; RSV, dealt craftily; NEB, made a crafty attack; NJB, took precautions.
[12]*Begs.*, RSV, beautiful before God; NEB, a fine child, and pleasing to God; NJB, a fine child before God.
[13]Greek, the shoes of your feet.
[14]Greek, hand.
[15]*Begs.*, rejoiced in; NEB, held a feast.

offerings forty years in the wilderness, O house of Israel? (43) You took up the tent of Moloch, and the star of your god Raiphan, the images which you made for worship, and I will transport you beyond Babylon. (44) Our fathers had the tent of testimony in the wilderness, as he who spoke to Moses charged them to make it, according to the pattern that he had seen. (45) Our fathers, with Joshua, entered into the succession and brought in the tent when they dispossessed the Gentiles, whom God drove out before the face of our fathers, up to the time of David. (46) He found favour with God and asked that he might provide a sacred dwelling-place for the house[16] of Jacob. (47) But Solomon built God[17] a house. (48) Yet the Most High does not dwell in things made by human hands, as the prophet says, (49) Heaven is my throne, earth is the footstool of my feet. What sort of house will you build me, says the Lord, or what is the place where I will rest? (50) Did not my hand make all these things?

(51) 'Stiff-necked and uncircumcised of heart and ears that you are! You are always contradicting[18] the Holy Spirit; as your fathers did, so also do you. (52) Which of the prophets did not your fathers persecute? They killed those who announced beforehand the coming of the Righteous One, of whom you have now become betrayers and murderers, (53) you who received the Law at the ordinance of angels, yet did not keep it.'

Bibliography

B. H. Amaru, *HUCA* 54 (1983), 153–80.

C. K. Barrett, *FS* Greeven, 57–69.

J. Bihler, as in (17).

M. E. Boismard, as in (17).

F. F. Bruce, *FS* A. T. Hanson, 37–50.

H. von Campenhausen, *FS* Vogt, 189–212.

R. J. Coggins, *NTS* 28 (1982), 423–34.

O. Cullmann, *NTS* 5 (1959), 157–73.

N. A. Dahl, *FS* Schubert, 139–58.

J. Daniélou, *VigCh* 11 (1957), 121–38.

W. D. Davies, *HThR* 47 (1954), 135–40.

R. le Déaut, *RechScR*, 52 (1964), 85–90.

T. L. Donaldson, *JSNT* 12 (1981), 27–52.

F. G. Downing, *NTS* 27 (1981), 544–63.

J. Dupont, *Bib* 66 (1985), 153–67.

J. A. Emerton, as in (1).

---

[16]RSV, NEB, God.
[17]Greek, him.
[18]NJB, resisting; similarly *Begs.*, RSV.

F. J. Foakes-Jackson, *JBL* 49 (1930), 283–6.

O. Glombitza, as in (16).

T. Holtz, *FS* G. Holtz, 102–14.

P. Katz, *ZNW* 46 (1955), 133–8.

G. D. Kilpatrick, *JTS* 46 (1945), 136–45.

A. F. J. Klijn, *NTS* 4 (1958), 25–31.

W. H. Mare, *WestminsterThJ* 34 (1972), 1–21.

C. F. D. Moule, as in (17).

W. Mundle, *ZNW* 20 (1921), 133–47.

F. Mussner, as in (17).

R. Pummer, *NTS* 22 (1976), 441–3.

E. Richard, *CBQ* 39 (1977) 190–208.

E. Richard, *JBL* 98 (1979), 255–67.

E. Richard, *NovT* 24 (1982), 37–53.

C. H. H. Scobie, *NTS* 19 (1973), 390–414.

C. H. H. Scobie, as in (7).

M. Simon, *FS* Goguel, 247–57.

M. Simon, *JEH* 2 (1951), 127–42.

G. N. Stanton, as in (16).

D. D. Sylva, *JBL* 106 (1987), 261–75.

T. C. G. Thornton, *JTS* 25 (1974), 432–4.

Unité de Recherche Arrivée, *FS* Dupont, 739–55.

F. M. Young, *NTS* 19 (1973), 325–38.

Some of the works listed for paragraphs 16, 17, 19, 20 are relevant here too.

Commentary

If there is any direct relation between length and importance, this is the most important speech in Acts. Such a conclusion would be an over-simplification, yet it is unthinkable that Luke should give at such length a speech that he did not regard as important in itself and significant in the development of the primitive church. It must be considered first in the setting in which Luke has placed it. In ch. 6 he sets over against — or alongside — each other two groups of Christians to whom he gives the names Hebrews and Hellenists; whether in fact they bore those titles is a question considered above (pp. 305–9) and not needing to be discussed here. The group designated Hellenists are in Luke's narrative represented by, and must have stood in close relation to, a company of seven men, all bearing Greek names (6.5). The first to take the lead among these is

Stephen, whom Luke clearly thinks of as a representative of his Hellenistic group. Stephen is arrested on the charge of blaspheming against God and attacking Moses (as giver of the Law) and the Temple. These, it must be noted, are new charges which have not been brought against the Twelve. Brought before the Sanhedrin, Stephen is questioned by the High Priest, whose question (7.1) must mean, Is the charge against you true? Do you admit it? Stephen replies at length, but his martyrdom, and wider persecution, follow. In this sequence of events the speech must be regarded not necessarily as a defence, for in accounts of martyrdoms the martyrs commonly glory in the fact that the charge is true: *Christianus sum* (e.g. Cyprian; *Acta Proconsularia* 1), but at least as a reply: Yes, it is, or, No, it is not true that Jesus will destroy the Temple and change the Mosaic precepts. Or, since questions cannot always be answered with a simple affirmative or negative, the answer might be: I must explain; the answer is Yes (or No), but not in the sense that you have in mind. What we have before us comes nearer to this qualified kind of answer, but even that would not describe it precisely. It contains some material that could be used in answering the High Priest, but such material is not immediately evident and there is no reference to the charges. That the issue of the 'defence' was martyrdom of course does not prove that Stephen did not use the words attributed to him; that much of his speech seems somewhat beside the point is a more serious consideration. According to Lüdemann (95), 'Eine einheitliche Konzeption hat die Stephanusrede nicht.' This is perhaps too sweeping.

That Luke had direct, or for that matter indirect, access to the proceedings of the Sanhedrin is out of the question; whence then did he derive the speech? Weiser 181 mentions three possibilities: (1) The speech was taken directly from Hellenistic Judaism; (2) it originated in Hellenistic Judaism but had already been modified in a 'deuteronomistic' sense by Hellenistic Jewish Christians before Luke used it; (3) it had its roots in Samaritan traditions. To these should be added, (4) that the speech 'von Anfang bis zu Ende von Lukas selbst gestaltet ist' (Stählin 112). Weiser himself prefers the second of his possibilities, but it is very difficult to distinguish between modifications made by unknown Hellenistic Jewish Christians and modifications made by Luke. Roloff (117) argues that the speech differs too much from Luke's own theology (e.g. with regard to the Temple) to be simply his composition; he must therefore have used some source material. This is a strong argument — stronger than the assertion Roloff goes on to make, that the criticism of the Temple comes not from a Hellenistic 'Enlightenment' but from Jesus. It is also true that if Luke had been simply composing on his own without reference to already existing material the plainly relevant Christian references would have appeared much earlier than v. 52. Conzelmann writes: 'Die polemischen Partien (v. 35, 37, 39–42, 48–53, fraglich

25, 27) lassen sich herauslösen. Dann zeigt sich, dass unter der jetzigen polemischen Oberfläche ein andersartiges Substrat liegt, eine erbauliche, heilsgeschichtliche Betrachtung, deren Sinn im Nachzeichnen der Geschichte als solchem liegt. Dahinter steht eine lange Tradition; vgl. das Dt; Josua 24 Ez 20 Neh 9 Ps. 105 (104); Jos Bell 5.357ff.; Pseud-Clem. Rec. 1.22ff. Strecker 221ff.)' (50f.). Other writers have added other similar comparative passages; Maddox (52) for example, adds Ps. 106.6–46; Judith 5.5–21; 1 Enoch 84–90; Acts 13.16–41. The parallels are not all of equal value. Ps. 105 does indeed review the early history of Israel, but in such a way as to summon the people to thanksgiving: O give thanks to the Lord (v. 1); So he led forth his people with joy . . . he gave them the lands of the nations . . . to the end that they should keep his statutes . . . Praise the Lord! (vv. 43–5). Neh. 9 also contains a review and notes the disobedience of the Fathers, but with penitence and with the intention henceforth to keep the covenant: Because of all this we make a firm covenant and write it, and our princes, our Levites, and our priests set their seal to it (9.38; Hebrew 10.1). Josh. 24 reaches a similar conclusion but includes the warning threat, You cannot serve the Lord; for he is a holy God; he is a jealous God; he will not forgive your transgressions or your sins (v. 19). Ezkl. 20 is much closer to Acts 7, in that it represents the generation addressed by the prophet as repeating or even exceeding the sins of their ancestors: Will you defile yourselves after the manner of your fathers and go astray after their detestable things? When you offer your gifts and sacrifice your sons by fire, you defile yourselves with all your idols to this day. And shall I be inquired of by you, O house of Israel? As I live, says the Lord God, I will not be inquired of by you (vv. 30, 31; Ezekiel continues with the hope of renewal when God acts for the sake of his holy name — a theme noticeably absent from Acts 7). Josephus (the correct reference for his speech urging surrender to the Roman besiegers is *War* 5.376–419) is akin to Stephen in that he uses his review of history to make a point with reference to the present: whenever the Israelites took up arms they were defeated; when they put their trust in God alone they were delivered. Peter's long speech in *Clem. Rec.* 1.22–74 begins with a sketch of OT history but continues (as Stephen does not) with a fuller account of Jesus and the apostles.

It will be seen that some of these reviews of OT history are not so much edificatory as critical not only of the past but also of the present. This means that it is not necessary to eliminate (as Conzelmann does) the polemical verses in order to arrive at an original form of the speech. This process in any case implies a rather odd procedure on Luke's part; if polemic was his aim, why should he embed his polemic in so much unpolemical material? It is to be noted also (see the commentary on the verses in question) that in some of Conzelmann's polemical sections there is material that cried aloud for Christian elaboration but did not receive it. Thus the rejection of Moses in vv. 25, 27 could have been used to point directly to the story of Jesus, by whose hand God gave deliverance (σωτηρία is a conveniently ambiguous word which can mean salvation of more kinds than one) to his people, who nevertheless rejected him as ruler and judge; not only was Moses vindicated by God as ruler and redeemer (v. 35 — what Christian could fail to see here a type of the risen Jesus?), he prophesied the coming of a prophet like himself (v. 37; the same prophecy was used at 3.22). We must conclude that this polemical material, unlike v. 52, which is there to provide the one Christian application that is explicitly present in the speech, could have been and probably was in the source Luke used. By no means all the polemical material is polemical in a specifically Christian sense. Israel's rejection of the living word of God in favour of its religious institutions is one of the commonest of prophetic themes.

To say this is not to say that the speech is irrelevant. (1) It teaches that God is constantly at work in the history of his people, and that his activity follows a recurring pattern in which good is brought out of evil. This recurring action is the working out of a covenant made between God and Abraham. (2) The pattern of divine action appears specifically in the story of individual persons, notably Joseph and Moses, who are rejected, made to suffer, and finally vindicated. (3) God is represented as active in historical events in which he calls for obedience, and as uninterested in sacrifices and unwilling to be provided with a settled home to live in. The relevance of these points to the story of Stephen, and to the story of Jesus, is too clear to call for elaboration. Luke has given the final illustration of Stephen's power to confute his enemies (6.10; 'Stephen geht mit wehenden Fahnen, nicht als gebrochener Mann unter,' Schille 180). He also gives 'an insight into the meaning of the historical moment concerned, but one which goes beyond the facts of history' (Dibelius 140), bringing out the meaning of the new Christian movement and especially of its relation with Israel, 'Israel, das Volk der Patriarchen, des Mose und der Propheten, und Israel, das immer zum Götzendienst bereite und prophetenmörderische Volk' (Haenchen 281). Stephen still holds fast to the God of the Fathers (Calvin 171); the new faith is the fulfilment of all that the old, represented by Abraham and Moses, rightly stood for, but it is a fulfilment so radical that it finally disintegrates the institutionalism that had for so long been the people's temptation. It is however only at the end that Luke makes the point that the whole record is crystallized in the recent event of the crucifixion of Jesus (there is no suggestion of his resurrection).

It is important to note that though the speech attacks the Temple (and so far proves rather than disproves the charge brought against Stephen) it does not oppose the Law (so far as this is separable from the Temple). The treatment of this theme is not Pauline (see Knox, *Acts* 24). Christ is not the end of the Law but the interpreter of the Law (Roloff 119). The covenant God made with Abraham was a διαθήκη περιτομῆς (v. 8); the promise to Abraham was fulfilled in the time of Moses (v. 17); Moses gave σωτηρία to his people (v. 25); God made Moses an ἄρχων καὶ λυτρωτής (v. 35); Moses received λόγια ζῶντα to give to us (v. 38 — *us*, not *you*, but for the text see the note on this verse); the Law was given εἰς διαταγὰς ἀγγέλων — so much greater the sin of not observing it (v. 53). Luke has no doubt subjected his source material to stylistic revision, but the only verse (in addition to v. 52) that stands out as a Lucan insertion is v. 37, the quotation of Deut. 18.15, which Luke had already used at 3.22; here it points to the coming of a new Moses, the Righteous One of v. 52.

We have thus a speech in which (a) the history of Israel is reviewed; (b) the patriarchs, especially Abraham and Joseph, are honoured, but (c) Moses is accorded a dignity that is more than human; (d) correspondingly, the Law, including the requirement of circumcision, is spoken of with great respect and with no suggestion that it should or could be abandoned or modified; but (e) the Temple is treated with no respect at all. The most probable explanation of this is that Luke gives us, in outline, a 'Hellenist' sermon; the sort of sermon that might be preached in a 'Hellenist', Diaspora, synagogue, and could easily be taken over and used when Hellenist Jews became Hellenist Jewish Christians. It may be that similar sermons can be traced in Acts 14 and 17. Diaspora respect for the Law can easily be paralleled; without it Jews would have faded (as some of them did fade) into their Gentile environment. Magnification of the figure of Moses, so that he becomes something like a cult figure (surrounded by the patriarchs) can also be paralleled. It is sufficient to refer to Philo, *De Vita Mosis*; to Ezekiel's *Exagoge*; and to the paintings in the synagogue of Dura-Europos. Disrespect for the Temple is harder to parallel. The Qumran sect did not in principle reject the Temple and its sacrifices (see Braun 2.157); they considered the priests who controlled it to be in error and unclean and therefore avoided it until it should be restored to its proper integrity. This in itself is not the same as Stephen's attitude, but it does manifest a readiness to criticize the operation of the Temple. The existence in Jerusalem itself of synagogues (see 6.9, and the note) is sufficient to show that the Temple was not thought to be sufficient for men's needs. Many Diaspora Jews travelled up to Jerusalem for the Pilgrim Feasts when and if they could, but those who could not, and some who did not make the attempt, must have decided, or discovered, as all Jews did after AD 70, that they could practise their religion without the Temple, which therefore, to say the least, could hardly be regarded as indispensable. 'Philo at one point inserts an unqualified condemnation of all sacrifices except "the fireless altars round which the virtues dance in chorus". No doubt the passage was taken over by a synagogue preacher from an exponent of the common view which appears in the Hermetic literature, that God needs nothing and therefore the only offering we can make to him is that of thanks and praise [Philo, *De Plantatione* 25; Asclepius III, 41a]. It was convenient for the exponent of this view that sacrifice might be offered only in Jerusalem, which was a long way off. Generally, however, we have a very high estimate of the value of the cultus of Jerusalem. No doubt this reflects the impression which the sanctuary made on the exile whose religion in theory was centred on the Temple which he hoped to visit one day as a pilgrim; distance saved him from coming into contact with the sordid politicians of the house of Annas' (W. L. Knox, in *Judaism and Christianity* II, 1937, ed. H. Loewe, 81). Perhaps the speech attributed to Stephen reflects the result of such contact. For the religion of the Therapeutae, which evidently needed no Temple, see Philo, *De Vita Contemplativa* (e.g., 25: ἐν ἑκάστῃ [οἰκίᾳ] δέ ἐστιν οἴκημα ἱερόν, ὃ καλεῖται σεμνεῖον καὶ μοναστήριον, ἐν ᾧ μονούμενοι τὰ τοῦ σεμνοῦ βίου μυστήρια τελοῦνται).

As between Qumran and the Hellenistic world as background to Stephen's speech, Braun (2.267) sums up correctly. 'Hier spricht — anders als Cullmann und Spicq meinen — eine *hellenistische* Kritik am Tempel, weil der Tempel mit Händen gemacht ist; nicht eine qumranische Tempelreserve, weil der Tempelkult zu unrein und an unrechten Festterminen gehandhabt wird ... Ich vermag deswegen der Stephanusrede keine spezielle Qumrannähe zuzuschreiben.' Contacts have also been found, with little more ground, between the speech and the beliefs of the Samaritans; see especially C. H. H. Scobie (*NTS* 19 (1973), 390–414), with a reply by R. Pummer (*NTS* 22 (1976), 441–3). After detailed discussion Schneider (452) concludes, 'Im ganzen wird erkennbar, dass eine Abhängigkeit von samaritischen Texten oder Theologoumena nicht zu erweisen ist.' For detailed discussion see the notes, and C. K. Barrett in FS Greeven, 57–69.

The speech of Acts 7, which can hardly have been spoken by Stephen in the circumstances described, recovers great historical value as a document of that sector of Judaism from which Stephen and his colleagues are said to have come. It is a valuable source for our knowledge of first-century Judaism and in addition gives us a glimpse of a non-Pauline line along which Christianity moved into the Gentile world, and thus does more than manifest 'Luke's ... attitude to a Christianity too narrowly and rigidly bound to Judaism ... and to the land' (Davies, *Land* 272; see the whole discussion, 267–75). Jewish Christians, represented by Stephen, had already blazed the trail by presenting the biblical faith as a religion of salvation for all, though, it seems, on the basis of the Law. It was the Law, and not least the law of circumcision, that remained to be questioned.

We can thus add another item to the collection of material that Luke had put together in compiling this part of his book. The corporate memory (possibly written in outline) of the mixed Jewish and Gentile church of Antioch provided the framework. This may have suggested to Luke, and local tradition may have confirmed, the division in Jerusalem between those whom he called Hebrews and Hellenists. The list of seven Greek names was traditional and so was an account, possibly two accounts, of the attack upon the first of the Seven, Stephen, and of his death. To these we proceed in the next verses (7.54–8.1a); there will follow the mission to Antioch (11.19–26) and the mission from Antioch (13; 14). Into this body of material Luke inserts his 'Hellenist' sermon, adapted to its context by the addition of a verse or two. It does not really fit the courtroom scene in which Luke places it, but it serves a more important purpose in that it demonstrates Luke's view of the relation between Christianity and Judaism. They share a common origin in the call of Abraham, in God's promise to him, and in the fulfilment of the promise in the living oracles given to Moses; but Christianity belongs to that critical prophetic strand of Judaism which refused to substitute institutions for the word of God, and claims that the final conflict between the two came to a head in the story of Jesus. This may account for the relation between this speech and Hebrews asserted by W. Manson, *The Epistle to the Hebrews*, 1951, 25–46 (briefly anticipated by Rackham, 92f.).

1. It is probably but not certainly correct (Weiser 182) that the unannounced appearance of the High Priest indicates that Luke is rewriting the story of a lynching. After ἀρχιερεύς the Western text (D E it mae) adds, unnecessarily, τῷ Στεφάνῳ.

εἰ introduces a direct question; see on 1.6. *P. Oxy.* 294.11 contains identically the same words (Pesch 247), but they are not a direct question. The idiomatic construction of ἔχειν with an adverb is fairly frequent in Acts (7.1; 12.15; 15.36; 17.11; 21.13; 24.9, 25 — four times with οὕτως, once with πῶς; four times in the whole of the fourteen-letter Pauline corpus). The question means in effect, Are the facts stated in the accusation true? Do you admit the charge? not simply, Did Jesus indeed say this? If this was a formal trial (as 6.15 suggests) the High Priest should not have asked a direct question that invited the accused person to convict himself. For this disputed proposition see the admirable discussion by I. Abrahams (*Studies* 2.132f.) It is a striking fact that the Mishnah tractate Sanhedrin, which contains a good deal on the interrogation of witnesses, never mentions the interrogation of the accused.

2. Stephen begins what at least appears to be a reply; but Bengel speaks too strongly: Nullo modo assentiri Erasmo aliisque debemus, quibus multa in hac oratione non ita multum pertinere videntur ad id, quod instituerit Stephanus.

The address ἄνδρες ἀδελφοί is frequently used in Acts; see on 1.16. Only here and at 22.1 is πατέρες added. '"Vater" ist ein allgemein Ehrentitel' (Schrenk, πατήρ κτλ., in *TWNT* 5.977). The word does not however seem to have been in regular use in the plural for the members of the Sanhedrin collectively. According to Haenchen the wording is Greek. This is probably correct, though it is easier to illustrate it in Latin (*patres conscripti*; . . . *principes, qui appellati sunt propter caritatem patres*, Cicero, *De Re Publica* 2.8.14; cf. Livy 1.8) than in Greek.

ὁ θεὸς τῆς δόξης. The expression occurs at Ps. 28.3 (LXX; Hebrew 29.3, אל־הכבוד). It is unlikely that there is an allusion to the Psalm; Stephen gives to his speech an impressive opening which would at the same time mark him out as a Jew concerned for the honour of the national religion. God ὤφθη τῷ πατρὶ ἡμῶν. πατήρ now means *ancestor*, and Abraham is *our* ancestor; again it is emphasised that the speaker is a Jew. The wording is similar to that of the *Genesis Apocryphon* 22.27: After these things, God appeared to Abram in a vision and said to him . . . This passage represents Gen. 15.1; there is no reason to suppose that Stephen (Luke) had it in mind. ὤφθη could be drawn from Gen. 12.7: Stephen does not repeat it with God as subject (cf. v. 30, ὤφθη . . . ἄγγελος).

The appearance to Abraham took place ὄντι ἐν τῇ Μεσοποταμίᾳ πρὶν ἢ κατοικῆσαι αὐτὸν ἐν Χαρράν). According to Gen. 12.1 God addressed the words that follow to Abraham after the move to Haran (Gen. 11.31: ἦλθεν ἕως Χαρρὰν καὶ κατῴκησεν ἐκεῖ). The temporal clause (πρὶν ἢ κατοικῆσαι — Luke seems to have no preference between πρίν (2.20), which is Attic, and πρὶν ἤ (7.2; 25.26), which is Ionic) seems to serve no purpose except to contradict the OT narrative; the use of the OT word κατοικεῖν is particularly notable. Philo, *De Abrahamo* 62; 71; *De Migratione Abr.* 32, is not interested in Haran as he is in Chaldea and what Chaldea stands for (astrology, polytheism). Josephus, having said that Abraham and his companions were living in Haran (μετοικίζονται πάντες εἰς Χαρράν, *Ant.* 1.152), goes on (154) to speak of the divine command which led Abraham to abandon Chaldea (καταλείπει τὴν Χαλδαίαν), Haran being now, it seems, forgotten, since Abraham is bidden to go (presumably from Chaldea directly) to Canaan (τοῦ θεοῦ κελεύσαντος εἰς τὴν Χαναναίαν μετελθεῖν). Cf. Pseudo-Philo 8.1. The omission of Haran by Luke may be due to the words of v. 3: ἔξελθε ἐκ τῆς γῆς σου. Chaldea was Abraham's γῆ, the place where his family and ancestors had lived, not Haran. There is no need to see behind Luke's statements a *Schultradition* — so rightly, Haenchen (269). Haran is Carrae, the site of the battle of 63 BC; see Plutarch,

Crassus 25; 28; 29 (558–562); Lucan, *Bellum Civile* 1.103–6.

3. Luke follows closely the LXX text of Gen. 12.1. The differences are:

LXX has ἐκ before τῆς συγγενείας; so have all MSS of Acts (and NA[26]) except B D.

LXX adds after συγγενείας σου, καὶ ἐκ τοῦ οἴκου τοῦ πατρός σου.

LXX does not have δεῦρο.

The text of the LXX, together with that of Acts and those given, or implied, by Philo (*De Migr. Abr.* 1; 16; 19; 20; 21; *Quis rer. div. her.* 56) and by Clement of Rome (1 Clement 10), is given by Hatch, *Essays* 154. In Acts the omission of *from thy father's house* was probably due simply to natural abbreviation; the thought was more or less implied by συγγένεια. δεῦρο has no equivalent either in the LXX or in the MT. According to Hatch it is an 'early and graphic gloss'. It is found however in the Pseudo-Jonathan Targum to Gen. 12.1 (לך; Wilcox 26f.; 159) and should perhaps be regarded as a variant reading. The only other occurrence of δεῦρο in Acts is at 7.34; there however it comes from Exod. 3.10. The word normally has the meaning *(Come) here!* It could therefore suggest that God was to be found in, or was specially associated with, Canaan (or Haran; vv. 1, 4), but in the context rather means that God is to be found by Abraham when he leaves his old associations to live on pilgrimage with no inheritance of his own (v. 5). See Davies (*Land* 268–72).

4. After the quotation Stephen resumes his narrative, ἐξελθών picking up ἔξελθε in v. 3. It is now, not at the earlier point given by Gen. 11.31 (MT and LXX), that Abraham settles in Haran. Here Abraham's father (Terah, but he is not named in Acts) dies; cf. Gen. 11.32, according to which Terah dies in Haran but before Abraham's call. This discrepancy must be noticed because it has been used to demonstrate dependence on the Samaritan Pentateuch and thus a connection between Stephen (and his colleagues) and the Samaritans. According to Gen. 11.26 Terah was seventy when Abraham was born, and according to Gen. 12.4 Abraham was seventy-five when he left Haran for Canaan. Terah was thus 145. He lived altogether 205 years (Gen. 11.32), and thus had a further sixty years to live after Abraham moved into the promised land. In these figures the LXX agrees with the Hebrew. The Samaritan Pentateuch however cuts sixty years off Terah's life, giving in Gen. 11.32 not 205 but 145 years, and so representing him as dying at the time when Abraham left for Canaan. See Wilcox 28f. It is not impossible that Luke (Stephen) derived his information from the Samaritan text, but this conclusion is by no means necessary. Anyone reading Genesis with less than full attention notes the statement in 11.32 that Terah died in Haran; in 12.1 that God called Abraham to leave his home; and in 12.4 that Abraham obediently departed from Haran. If the reader does not carefully follow the calculations given above he is likely to assume that the events happened in the order in which they are mentioned. Philo makes the same mistake: Abraham migrated from Chaldea and dwelt in Haran, and τελευτήσαντος αὐτῷ τοῦ πατρὸς ἐκεῖθι he removed from that country also (De Migr. Abr. 177).

D has ἐξελθών . . .καὶ κατῴκησεν, a participle followed by καί and a finite verb. This may be an Aramaism; see Black (AA 68f.), and cf. 4.3; 5.21; 8.2; 10.27; 12.16; 13.7; 14.6, 14; 20.10. Here and elsewhere however it may be due to careless assimilation to the Latin, which turns the participle into a finite verb and uses and (d: exibit (sic) . . . et habitavit).

μετῴκισεν αὐτόν lays great stress on the action of God in the story of Abraham. Abraham did not choose his, and his descendants', place of residence; God put him in it. The verb μετοικίζειν is suitably chosen; it means to lead settlers to another abode (LS 1121).

εἰς τὴν γῆν ταύτην εἰς ἥν . . . The repeated preposition with the relative can in classical use be dispensed with (as at 1.21; 13.2, 38; Hermas, Similitude 9.7.3). 'Bei stärkerer Abtrennung des Rel.-Satzes wird die Präp. wiederholt' (here; 20.18; Jn 4.53). So BDR § 293. 3, n. 14. This however does not explain the use of an inappropriate preposition: εἰς τὴν γῆν ἐν ᾗ (or simply ἥν) κατοικεῖτε would be expected: You go into the land, you live in it. But εἰς and the accusative, ἐν and the dative, were often in Hellenistic Greek loosely interchanged; see e.g. 2.5.

ὑμεῖς κατοικεῖτε appears to make a distinction between the speaker and his hearers; this would be suitable if the speaker were a Hellenist Jew normally resident in the Diaspora, but Stephen appears to have been resident in Jerusalem. A Western addition (καὶ οἱ πατέρες ἡμῶν οἱ πρὸ ἡμῶν, D) mitigates the distinction: the speaker, whatever his background, is a Jew and looks back to the same ancestors as his hearers. Some MSS, however, have this or a similar addition with pronouns of the second person, not the first.

5. The language of this verse recalls several OT passages. βῆμα ποδός is distinctive and occurs in the LXX only at Deut. 2.5:οὐ γὰρ μὴ δῶ ὑμῖν ἀπὸ τῆς γῆς οὐδὲ βῆμα ποδός (כף רגל). This has nothing to do with Abraham, or with 'the land which you now inhabit'. The language was recalled, subconsciously perhaps, and used because it was suitable to the intention of stressing the fact that for Abraham everything depended on God's promise. There are non-biblical parallels of no great importance (e.g. Libanius, Oratio 10.

312D, . . . μηδ'ὅσον δοῦναι χώραν ποδί; Cicero, *ad Atticum* 13.2, pedem ubi ponat in suo non habet). The clause at the end of the verse, οὐκ (negativing the participle as a statement of fact; BDR § 430. 2, n. 14) ὄντος αὐτῷ τέκνου, also emphasises that the inheritance depended on God's promise. κληρονομία here must mean not something inherited but simply possession. The word is not represented in either the MT or the LXX; it is however in the Samaritan of Deut. 2.5 (Wilcox 27). On the word see Derrett, *Law* 305, n. 2.

God gave Abraham not the land in actual possession but the promise that he would give it (αὐτήν) to him as a possession, εἰς κατάσχεσιν. The order of the words, δοῦναι . . . αὐτήν, is 'impossible' (*Begs.* 4.71), and the use of κατάσχεσις in the sense of *possession* seems to be almost entirely confined to the LXX, where it is a common translation of אחזה (see Acts 13.33 D). God would give it to him and his descendants; that is, the promise concerned not only the land but also the as yet unborn son, Isaac. It is repeated several times in Genesis:

12.7: τῷ σπέρματί σου δώσω τὴν γῆν ταύτην.

13.15: πᾶσαν τὴν γῆν, ἣν σὺ ὁρᾷς, σοὶ δώσω αὐτὴν καὶ τῷ σπέρματί σου ἕως τοῦ αἰῶνος.

17.8: δώσω σοι καὶ τῷ σπέρματί σου μετὰ σὲ τὴν γῆν, ἣν παροικεῖς, πᾶσαν τὴν γῆν Χανάαν, εἰς κατάσχεσιν αἰώνιον.

48.4: δώσω σοι τὴν γῆν ταύτην καὶ τῷ σπέρματί σου μετὰ σὲ εἰς κατάσχεσιν αἰώνιον.

It is hardly possible to say which of these passages Stephen (Luke) had in mind; probably his words are intended to give the general sense of all, but the occurrence in the last two of μετὰ σέ and εἰς κατάσχεσιν is to be noted. Notwithstanding the stress in this verse on God's promise, the theme of faith, so important in Paul's treatment of Abraham, is only hinted at (Stählin 107).

6, 7. The promise, which included not only possession of the land but also deliverance from Egypt and the opportunity to worship God, was not to be fulfilled immediately. Abraham's descendants were to live as temporary and unassimilated aliens in a land that was not theirs — Egypt. Again it seems that echoes of more than one OT passage are in mind. Most important is

Gen. 15.13f.·πάροικον ἔσται τὸ σπέρμα σου ἐν γῇ οὐκ ἰδίᾳ, καὶ δουλώσουσιν αὐτοὺς καὶ κακώσουσιν αὐτοὺς καὶ ταπεινώσουσιν αὐτοὺς τετρακόσια ἔτη. τὸ δὲ ἔθνος, ᾧ ἐάν δουλεύσωσιν, κρινῶ ἐγώ· μετὰ δὲ ταῦτα ἐξελεύσονται ὧδε μετὰ ἀποσκευῆς.

But see also

Exod. 2.22: πάροικός εἰμι ἐν γῇ ἀλλοτρίᾳ.

Exod. 12.40:   . . . ἔτη τετρακόσια τριάκοντα.

Exod. 3.12: ἐν τῷ ἐξαγαγεῖν σε τὸν λαὸν μου ἐξ Αἰγύπτου καὶ λατρεύσετε τῷ θεῷ ἐν τῷ ὄρει τούτῳ.

For the rabbinic interpretation of these texts see StrB 2. 668–71. The substance of what Stephen has to say is taken from Gen. 15.13f. ἐν γῇ οὐκ ἰδίᾳ (בארץ לא להם) becomes less clumsily ἐν γῇ ἀλλοτρίᾳ; Exod. 2.22 may have been subconsciously remembered (בארץ נכריה). The LXX's αὐτούς (read here by D lat) is rather woodenly replaced by αὐτό (agreeing with σπέρμα, though as a collective this is quite properly represented by the masculine plural pronoun). A more interesting change is the substitution of τόπῳ for ὄρει (in Exod. 3.12). In the OT context the promise concentrates upon the land of Israel; this is the place where God's people will worship him. But in the context in Acts (see 6.13, 14) τόπος must be taken to refer if not to the Temple itself at least to the Temple site. As Le Déaut (*Nuit Pascale* 162, n. 77) says, 'Étienne substitue aussi Sion (= le Temple) au Sinai.' In this note Le Déaut points to occasional confusion and to some deliberate assimilation of Sinai and Sion and sees the origin of this in Exod. 15.17: 'le but de l'Exode est Jérusalem, mais plus immédiatement le Sinai (3.12).' But was it (in view of what is to follow) really Stephen's intention to argue that the purpose of the Exodus was to establish (Temple) worship in Jerusalem? According to Schille (181) 'this place' stands for Canaan. Davies (*Land* 268–70) and Dahl (*FS* Schubert 143–6) discuss this question, connecting it with the expulsion of the Hellenists from Jerusalem (8.1); just as important, perhaps, is the fact that the original base of the Hellenists (if they were Diaspora Jews) was outside Jerusalem and the Land. See further on vv. 45 (ἕως τῶν ἡμερῶν Δαυίδ), 49 (ἡ δὲ γῆ . . . τίς τόπος . . .;); and note Stephen's emphasis on the apostasy of Israel at the time of the Exodus (vv. 39–43). Cf. Gal. 3.17, where the interval between the promise to Abraham and the giving of the Law is given as 430 years (no doubt in dependence on Exod. 12.40).

In v. 6 the subject of the verbs δουλώσουσιν, κακώσουσιν, though unexpressed, must be the inhabitants of the foreign land. For κακοῦν cf. e.g. Thucydides 1.33.3 (κακῶσαι ἡμᾶς); many other examples are given by Wettstein. In v. 7 the majority of MSS (including P³³ א B) have δουλεύσωσιν, subjunctive, rather than the future indicative of NA²⁶. For the use of the future indicative with the relative and ἐάν (in popular and LXX use for ἄν) see BDR § 380.3 n.5; M. 3.110. Cf. Lk. 12.8; 17.33. 'Except in the passive, in fact, the future was mainly a specialized form of the aorist subjunctive' (M. 1.149; cf. 184f., 240). See also BDR § § 318; 363.

Bede observes here an example of hyperbaton; the meaning is 'peregrinum erit semen eius annis quadrigentis, in cuius parte temporis etiam servitus accidit'. 'Redemption was therefore at a time prior to the temple and the worship of the Law' (Calvin 178).

8. In addition to the promise Abraham was given a covenant, an agreement that assured the promise. This consisted of circumcision. Again Stephen is dependent on the OT but does not quote it exactly.

Gen. 17.10–13: αὕτη ἡ διαθήκη, ἣν διαμαρτυρήσεις, ἀνὰ μέσον ἐμοῦ καὶ ὑμῶν καὶ ἀνὰ μέσον τοῦ σπέρματός σου μετὰ σὲ εἰς τὰς γενεὰς αὐτῶν· περιτμηθήσεται ὑμῶν πᾶν ἀρσενικόν . . . καὶ ἔσται ἐν σημείῳ διαθήκης . . . καὶ ἔσται ἡ διαθήκη που ἐπὶ τῆς σαρκὸς ὑμῶν εἰς διαθήκην αἰώνιον.

Gen. 21.4: περιέτεμεν δὲ 'Αβραὰμ τὸν 'Ισαὰκ τῇ ὀγδόῃ ἡμέρᾳ.

Luke's διαθήκην περιτομῆς sums up the content of the first of these passages: a covenant consisting of circumcision, a covenant which meant, on man's side, that every father must in every generation circumcise his male children. Without this action the covenant would lapse. Le Déaut writes (*Nuit Pascale* 209): 'On notera dans ce passage des *Actes* l'importance donnée à la circoncision dans l'histoire du salut: elle suit immédiatement l'allusion à Gen. 15 et au futur esclavage d'Israël en Égypte.' This seems to overstate the matter; this is the only verse in Stephen's speech in which circumcision is mentioned. It is however true (see above, pp. 337f.) that this speech, highly critical of the Temple, is not in the same way critical of the Law where the Law does not deal with the Temple cultus, true also that Judaism insisted on the inseparability of covenant and circumcision. 'Blood of the covenant' (the words of Exod. 24.8) came to mean the blood shed in circumcision; cf. the use of ברית מילה, ברית בשר (e.g. Menahoth 53b). Aboth 3.12 (11) (המפר בריתו של אברהם אבינו) was understood to refer to the undoing of circumcision (משך ערלה). See also Pseudo-Philo 9.15 (When she [Pharaoh's daughter] saw the child [Moses] and looked upon the covenant, that is, the testament in his flesh, she said: He is of the children of the Hebrews).

The rest of the verse emphasises the fulfilment of the promise (when it was made Abraham had no child (v. 5); in due course — οὕτως implies, the covenant having been made — he begot Isaac) and the obedience of Abraham and his immediate descendants. Cf.

Gen. 21.4 (quoted above) and for the next generations *Clem. Recog.*
1.34 (and for translation of and comments on *Clem. Recog.* 1.32–34
see H. J. Schoeps, *Aus frühchristlicher Zeit* (1950), 24–9).

9. This verse summarizes the OT story in words that recall

Gen. 37.11: ἐζήλωσαν δὲ αὐτὸν οἱ ἀδελφοὶ αὐτοῦ.

Gen. 37.28: ἀπέδοντο τὸν Ἰωσὴφ τοῖς Ἰσμαηλίταις
εἴκοσι χρυσῶν, καὶ κατήγαγον τὸν Ἰωσὴφ εἰς Αἴγυπτον.

Gen. 39.2: ἦν κύριος μετὰ Ἰωσήφ.

For ζηλώσαντες cf. Test. Symeon 2.6 (ἐζήλωσα), 7 (τὸ πνεῦμα
τοῦ ζήλου). The essential points in a familiar story are briefly and
effectively made. It is possible that Luke has in mind the fact that
Jesus was sold into the hands of his enemies (and that by one of his
'brothers'), but (adversative καί) that even in these circumstances
God was with him (cf. 10.38); that is, it is possible that Luke was
thinking typologically. Joseph was a prototype of the 'suffering
righteous' (Pesch 250). This question will arise again later (see pp.
349, 363); it is certainly true that at this point Luke gives no
indication that he is doing anything other than telling a plain story.

10. Again, a story told at length in Genesis is briefly summarized.
The first clause is Luke's own, the second is reminiscent of

Gen. 39.21: καὶ ἦν κύριος μετὰ Ἰωσὴφ καὶ κατέχεεν αὐτοῦ
ἔλεος καὶ ἔδωκεν αὐτῷ χάριν ἐναντίον τοῦ ἀρχιδεσμοφύλακος.

Luke has added *wisdom* (cf. 6.3, and for χάρις 6.8), evidently as a
summary of Joseph's skill in the interpretation of dreams, and —
cutting a long story short — has put in place of the chief gaoler
Φαραὼ βασιλέως Αἰγύπτου. In this phrase one would expect the
proper noun (Φαραώ) to be anarthrous (as it is) and the appositional
substantive (βασιλέως) to have the article (as it has not); so M.
3.206. There may be some doubt whether Φαραώ is a proper noun;
but if it is not it should have the article. The absence of the article
with βασιλέως may be due to the anarthrous genitive Αἰγύπτου that
follows. The third clause in the verse summarizes Gen. 41.38–45,
but is closer verbally to Ps. 104 (105).21: κατέστησεν αὐτὸν
κύριον τοῦ οἴκου αὐτοῦ καὶ ἄρχοντα πάσης τῆς κτήσεως
αὐτοῦ. There are however considerable variations. In the Psalm τῆς
κτήσεως αὐτοῦ (קִנְיָנוֹ) is used as a collective with the meaning of
κτήματα (see LS 1002, *s.v.* 2): *possession, property*, and thus, with
οἶκος, summarizes more adequately than Acts the contents of the
passage in Genesis. In Acts ἡγούμενον replaces both κύριον and

ἄρχοντα (of the Psalm); it is used especially in the papyri of various kinds of ruler. The most relevant use is in ἡγούμενος ἔθνους, which serves as an equivalent of *praeses provinciae*. Wilcox 27f. notes that Targum Pseudo-Jonathan (the same is true of Targum Yerushalmi) inserts the equivalent סרכן in Gen. 41. The subject of κατέστησεν is not Pharaoh but God; *Begs.* 4.72 rightly refers to Gen. 45.8. It is God who determines the course of history; cf. 4.28. This seems to be Luke's intention, though a more natural rendering of the last five words would be, 'He (Pharaoh) appointed him over all his (Pharaoh's) house.

11. Once more, Luke sums up a long narrative in a few words, some of which recall the OT though there is no quotation.

ἦλθεν: ἔρχεσθαι is never used with λιμός as subject in the LXX (it is used with the *years of famine* as subject; and cf. 2 Chron. 20.9 (ἐπέρχεσθαι) and Isa. 8.21 (ἥξει)). We may however note

Gen. 41.54: ἐγένετο λιμὸς ἐν πάσῃ τῇ γῇ (this means the whole earth with the exception of Egypt).

Gen. 42.5: ἦν γὰρ ὁ λιμὸς ἐν γῇ Χανάαν.

And many other passages. θλῖψις μεγάλη is Luke's own summarizing phrase. In the relevant context in Genesis θλῖψις occurs only at 42.21, and does not refer to the famine.

The majority of MSS read ἐφ' ὅλην τὴν γῆν Αἰγύπτου, a Hebraism (see BDR § 261. 7 n. 8). P⁴⁵ P⁷⁴ ℵ B A C Ψ 1175 *pc* have ἐφ' ὅλην τὴν Αἴγυπτον (D, ἐφ' ὅλης τῆς Αἰγύπτου); the article follows upon ὅλος.

οὐχ ηὕρισκον (the imperfect with the negative implies *could not find; Begs.* 4.73) χορτάσματα is an odd way of describing the shortage of food experienced by the patriarchs. The noun means *fodder, forage* — food for animals. The present verse is the only evidence cited by LS 2000 for the meaning *provender, food for men*. All occurrences in the LXX refer to animal fodder (translating מספוא, except at Deut. 11.15, where the Greek renders עשב). Gen. 42.27; 43.24 cannot have led Luke to use the word here, unless he meant that the patriarchs had no fodder for their cattle — which is indeed not impossible, since the patriarchs were graziers. Preuschen 39 finds an explanation in Ps. 36.19 (ἐν ἡμέραις λιμοῦ χορτασθήσονται; MT 37.19, ובימי רעבון ישבעו). If however the verb suffices as an explanation it is not necessary to go further than Lk. 9.17, ἐχορτάσθησαν πάντες.

12. The first clause gives the sense of Gen. 42.2, but in wording differs from it almost completely. Gen. 42.2 has ἰδὼν (not ἀκούσας) δὲ 'Ιακὼβ ὅτι ἔστιν (not ὄντα) πρᾶσις (not σιτία) ἐν Αἰγύπτῳ (not εἰς Αἴγυπτον, as in P⁷⁴ ℵ A B C E 453 1175 pc; D Ψ 𝔐 have ἐν Αἰγύπτῳ). ἰδών is a more literal, ἀκούσας a more idiomatic rendering of ויַרְא. σιτία (P⁷⁴ ℵ A B C D E 945 1175 1739 al) and σῖτα Ψ 𝔐 are both better renderings of שֶׁבֶר than πρᾶσις. Both words in the singular usually refer to grain, in the plural to food (especially food made of grain). σῖτα is the heteroclitic plural of σῖτος; σιτίον is a diminutive (but without diminutive sense). 'In the general sense of *food*, Prose writers prefer the dim. form σιτία, τά' (LS 1602, s.v. σῖτος, I 4). See M. 2.122; BDR § 49. 3. Field notes that the LXX use σῖτα for אֹכֶל or לֶחֶם, never for בַּר, דָּגָן, or חִטָּה. εἰς with the accusative is less correct here than ἐν with the dative, but the interchange of εἰς and ἐν is common; see M. 3.254, and cf. e.g. v. 4. *ND* 2.82 adds to MM's (222) examples of ἐξαποστέλλειν, but the meaning is in any case obvious.

πρῶτον (cf. ἐν τῷ δευτέρῳ, v. 13) is a somewhat unclear way of saying that Jacob's sons were sent twice — which is itself a simplification of the story in Genesis. With this use of πρῶτον (instead of πρότερον) cf. 1.1. According to Ramsay (quoted by Bruce 1.165, who however does not agree) the use of πρῶτον must refer to three visits, the third when the whole family went down (v. 14).

13. ἐν (D has ἐπί, without significant difference in meaning) τῷ δευτέρῳ: *on the second occasion, second visit*; the article may be called anaphoric with reference to πρῶτον in v. 12, and perhaps in the sense that the reader is expected to know the OT story. The use of a preposition is Hellenistic; classical use would be content with the dative case. For the story see Gen. 45. It has been suggested (*Begs.* 4.73) that the careful distinction between first and second visits is intended to point to the first and second comings of Jesus. This is unlikely; even if Luke is making typological use of the figure of Joseph (see p. 347) he can hardly use the movements of Joseph's brothers in this way.

ἀνεγνωρίσθη (so NA²⁶) is the reading of the majority of MSS, but B A p vg are probably right with ἐγνωρίσθη; the compound verb is assimilated to Gen. 45.1. Both readings however improve on the LXX's tense (ἀνεγνωρίζετο). With ἀνεγνωρίσθη the dative that follows is, or is very close to, a dative of the agent: *was recognized by*. With ἐγνωρίσθη it will be like τῷ Φαραώ in the second part of the verse, *was made known to, became known to*. Cf. Ruth 3.3; Ezkl. 20.5; and for the active verb Acts 2.28. See BDR § 191. 2 n. 5, and cf. Aristotle, *Poetics* 11.1452b. 6: ἡ μὲν 'Ιφιγένεια τῷ 'Ορέστῃ ἀνεγνωρίσθη.

The second half of the verse sums up and reflects, not very clearly, the language of Gen. 45.2, 16 (ἀκουστὸν ἐγένετο εἰς τὸν οἶκον Φαραώ ... διεβοήθη ἡ φωνὴ εἰς τὸν οἶκον Φαραώ). τὸ γένος is ambiguous. It may refer to Joseph's own racial background and origin; that is, it became known to Pharaoh that Joseph was a Hebrew. This use of the word is common, for example in the conventional question addressed to a stranger, ποδαπὸς τῷ γένει δ'εἶ; (cited here from Aristophanes, *Peace* 186). The word may however refer to *race*, or more narrowly *family*, in a collective sense: Joseph's brothers and eventually his father became personally known to Pharaoh. In view of the use of τὸ γένος in v. 19 this must be considered more likely. Anarthrous 'Ιωσήφ (P³³ B C *pc*) is probably correct; P⁷⁴ ℵ A E vg have αὐτοῦ; P⁴⁵ D Ψ 𝔐 have τοῦ 'Ιωσήφ.

14. This verse sums up the narrative of Gen. 45.9–11 and 46.

ἐν in this verse 'eludes classification' (M. 3.265), but probably is used, as in the papyri (see MM 209f., s.v.) in the sense of *amounting to* (see M. 1.103). BDR § 198. 1 classes this use with the classical dative for 'die begleitende Heeresmacht'. The added preposition may be in part due to the Hebrew use of ב for this purpose. Cf. Deut. 10.22. For the number cf. in addition to the material in Genesis Deut. 10.22, where however the number given is not 75 but 70 (ἐν ἑβδομήκοντα ψυχαῖς κατέβησαν οἱ πατέρες σου), and Exod. 1.5 (ἦσαν δὲ πᾶσαι ψυχαὶ ἐξ 'Ιακὼβ πέντε καὶ ἑβδομήκοντα); in the latter passage however the MT has 70 (though a Qumran MS, 4QExod.⁴, has 75; see Fitzmyer, *Essays* 87, n. 75). The number 70 given in Gen. 46.27 is explained in Bereshith R. 94.9: Gen. 46.26 gives 66; add the two sons of Joseph (46.27), Joseph himself, and Jochebed, conceived in Canaan but born 'at the gates of Egypt' (see Bowker, *Targums* 270). Philo, *De Migr. Abra.* 199–201 notes the number 75 in Exod. 1.5 (LXX) and 70 in Deut. 10.22. He offers no historical explanation but allegorizes. Cf. also Jubilees 44.33: *All the souls of Jacob which went into Egypt were seventy souls. These are his children and his children's children; but five died in Egypt before Joseph, and had no children.* Part of the question was seen by Bede: *Addito ipso Iacob et Ioseph cum duobus filiis qui erant in Aegypto septuaginta solummodo animos invenies.*

15, 16. Again Stephen summarizes, using language for the most part different from that of the LXX. εἰς Αἴγυπτον is omitted, possibly rightly, though by B only; it may have been inserted by assimilation to Gen. 46.6 (εἰσῆλθεν εἰς Αἴγυπτον, 'Ιακὼβ καὶ πᾶν τὸ σπέρμα αὐτοῦ). Jacob's death is mentioned in Genesis, but the word ἐτελεύτησεν is probably drawn from Exod. 1.6 (ἐτελεύτησεν δὲ 'Ιωσὴφ καὶ πάντες οἱ ἀδελφοὶ αὐτοῦ καὶ πᾶσα ἡ γενεὰ ἐκείνη). τιμῆς ἀργυρίου summarizes; there was no point in mentioning the exact price. The genitive is a genitive of price (BDR § 179. 1). At the end of v. 16 ἐν Συχέμ (ℵ* B C 36 323 945 1175 1739 *al*) is the reading to be preferred. τοῦ ἐν Συχέμ (ℵᶜ

A E *pc*) locates Emmor in Sychem, which does not change the sense greatly; τοῦ Συχέμ (P⁷⁴ D Ψ 𝔐 vg), which must mean *the father of Sychem*, is 'nur inhaltlich richtig, nicht aber sprachich möglich', since 'die Bezeichnung des Vaters nach dem Sohn ist unmöglich (BDR § 162. 3. n. 5).

In these verses, as in v. 4, the question of Samaritan influence arises; see Jeremias, *Heiligengräber* 37f. (a) The end of v. 16 contains a simple error. Abraham is mentioned instead of Jacob. It was Jacob who bought (Gen. 33.19) from the sons of Hamor, Shechem's father, for 100 pieces of silver, the piece of land on which he had pitched his tent. This passage has been confused with Gen. 23.3–20, where Abraham bought for 400 shekels of silver the cave of the field of Machpelah (that is, Hebron), where in due course he buried Sarah. (b) A natural reading of vv. 15, 16 would take the subject of the verbs μετετέθησαν and ἐτέθησαν to be αὐτὸς ('Ιακὼβ) καὶ οἱ πατέρες ἡμῶν; but according to Gen. 49.30; 50.13 Jacob was buried at Hebron, so that (unless Stephen is guilty of further confusion and error) the subject must be limited to οἱ πατέρες ἡμῶν, that is, the patriarchs other than Jacob. Of these, the OT gives the information (Joshua 13.32) that Joseph was buried at Hebron, but does not say where Jacob's other sons, Joseph's brothers, were buried. Some Jewish sources maintain that they were buried at Hebron, in the piece of land that Jacob had bought: so Jubilees 46.9; Test. Ruben 7.2; Josephus, *War* 4.532; *Ant.* 2.199. This tradition however is by no means unanimous. Hebron was originally Kirjath Arba, קרית ארבע, the City of Four. From this name it was deduced that four men (with their wives) were buried there. Of these, three were undoubtedly Abraham, Isaac, and Jacob; the most popular candidate for the fourth place was Adam. The sons of Jacob were thus excluded. (c) This, according to Jeremias, leaves the question whether Stephen is expanding the statement of Joshua 24.32 to cover Joseph's brothers or is dependent on local Shechemite tradition. Jeremias chooses the latter alternative, adding that the Shechemite tradition will be Samaritan. He supports this choice by reference to Jerome, *Epistles* 57.10; 108.13 (both passages are referred to by Bede in his comment) and to Georgius Syncellus, *Ekloge Chronographias* 284 (Dindorf). The conclusion is less conclusive than the exposition of the problem. It is doubtful whether Samaritan tradition was ever strong enough to inhibit the rise and spread of the alternative Hebron tradition. The most probable view is that the statement of Joshua 24.32 was simply generalized to cover all the brothers. Bauernfeind (115) however asks, 'Woher dieser seltsame Irrtum? Stehen wir hier vielleicht doch vor dem Rest eines vollauf authentischen Berichtes?' No, answers Schille 182, rejecting also the theory of a Samaritan tradition. But Wilcox (31, 160) considers the possibility of the use of a version of Joshua 24.32 nearer than the LXX to the Hebrew.

17. καθώς, a post-classical word (Phrynichus 397) must here have a temporal sense (Bauernfeind 116); it is so used here only in the NT; cf. 2 Macc. 1.31; Aristeas 310. These passages hardly prove but are consistent with the view that this use of καθώς was current in Hellenistic Jewish circles. כאשר has a similar double use (*according as, when*). According to Page (122) however, the sense is not temporal; he translates, *As* the time drew near, *so* the people . . . But χρόνος seems to demand a temporal meaning.

ὁ χρόνος (here used of a point not extent of time) τῆς ἐπαγγελίας is the time to which the promise referred, the time for the fulfilment of the promise. The promise itself is that of vv. 6, 7. Fulfilment had waited long but the time was at length drawing near. The promise made by God to Abraham was thus to be fulfilled at the Exodus; this was a Jewish not a Christian view. Contrast Gal. 3.16, 19.

ὁμολογεῖν seldom means *to make* (a promise); Josephus, *Ant.* 6.40, cited as a parallel by BA 1151, s.v., is hardly valid (Samuel *agreed*, ὡμολόγησεν, rather than *promised*, to appoint a king; Thackeray and Marcus translate *consented*). That this use of the word is unusual accounts for the variants ἐπηγγείλατο (P⁴⁵ D E p vgᵐˢˢ mae) and ὤμοσεν (Ψ 𝔐 gig sy⁽ᵖ⁾ bo). For the growth of the people of God see Exod. 1.7 (οἱ δὲ υἱοὶ Ἰσραὴλ ηὐξήθησαν καὶ ἐπληθύνθησαν καὶ χυδαῖοι ἐγένοντο καὶ κατίσχυον σφόδρα σφόδρα). Luke abbreviates, and substitutes ὁ λαός (for his use of this word see on 4.5) for οἱ υἱοὶ Ἰσραήλ.

18. This verse is connected with the preceding one by ἄχρι οὗ; apart from this it reproduces Exod. 1.8. The Western text, which differs in two respects (omitting ἐπ᾽ Αἴγυπτον, P⁴⁵ᵛⁱᵈ D E 𝔐 gig p syʰ, and substituting ἐμνήσθη τοῦ, D E gig p, for ᾔδει τόν) may be original here; there would be a tendency to assimilate to the LXX. For the identification of the Pharaoh concerned see commentaries on Exodus ad loc.; also Noth (119, Ramses II) and Bright (113, Sethos I; Ramesses II).

19. The first part of the verse summarizes Exod. 1.9–14, using some of its words (τὸ γένος τῶν υἱῶν Ἰσραήλ . . . κατασοφισώμεθα αὐτούς . . . ἵνα κακώσωσιν αὐτούς . . .). This paragraph in Exodus relates only to the conditions under which the Israelites were obliged to work; the attack on the children is described in 1.15–22.

κατασοφίζεσθαι, *to trick, to dupe*; a late word, with Exod. 1.10 (see also Judith 5.11; 10.19; Plutarch and Lucian) one of the earliest occurrences. According to Pallis (57), since σοφός is used for πανοῦργος, κατασοφισάμενος will be equivalent to καταπανουργησάμενος and we may compare Ps. 82.4 (LXX); he translates *having acted villainously towards*.

τοῦ ποιεῖν gives the content of ἐκάκωσεν; the ill treatment

consists in the exposure of Hebrew infants (in Exod. 1.16, 22 of the male infants only). The construction is loose. Zerwick (§ 392) says that the infinitive may be rendered by a gerundive or participle, and compares 15.10. BDR § 400.8 notes that here the consecutive force often found in τοῦ with the infinitive is very weak, and that the meaning is that of an epexegetic infinitive ("'so dass", "indem er machte" = ποιῶν oder καὶ ἐποίει'). Cf. also 9.15; 18.10; and especially 3 Kdms 17.20 (σὺ κεκάκωκας τοῦ θανατῶσαι τὸν υἱὸν αὐτῆς). It is easy to see that Stephen has taken the word ζωογονεῖν (more often to propagate or engender living creatures than to preserve alive; see below) from his source (Exod. 1.22: πᾶν ἄρσεν . . . εἰς τὸν πόταμον ῥίψατε · καὶ πᾶν θῆλυ, ζωογονεῖτε αὐτό); his use of ἔκθετα ποιεῖν is however unexpected. The adjective is rare in this sense though the cognate verb ἐκτιθέναι is common (neither is used in the Exodus narrative). εἰς τό indicates the purpose of the action. At the end of the verse τὰ ἄρρενα is added by E gig, the copyists thereby attempting to bring the text into line with the LXX.

Calvin (184) renders μὴ ζωογονεῖσθαι 'So that they may not be increased', thus taking ζωογονεῖσθαι in its usual and proper sense (against Erasmus, and most modern writers — e.g. Begs. 4.74, 'The force of the γονεῖν seems to have been weakened'). He adds, 'The life of a people always persists and survives in their offspring.' This is true enough, but the sense of the word in Exodus seems clear and this was probably understood and taken over by Luke.

20. ἐν ᾧ καιρῷ (cf. the use of χρόνος in v. 17; it is impossible to find in Acts a consistent distinction between the two terms), as the affliction was reaching its height, Moses was born, to be the deliverer and law-giver for his people. Stählin (108) notes the parallel with Joseph; see also Plümacher (20). Stephen (Luke) evidently holds a very high view of Moses, and goes on to describe his career in some detail. He was ἀστεῖος; the word comes from Exod. 2.2 (LXX). It is not easy to see why the LXX chose at this point to render טוב in this way. LS 260 take it to apply in this case to outward appearance and suggest the meanings pretty, graceful; the latter seems particularly unsuitable for a new-born infant. The word has various meanings. According to Aristotle, Nic. Ethics 4.7 (1123b) τὸ κάλλος ἐν μεγάλῳ σώματι, οἱ μικροὶ δ'ἀστεῖοι καὶ σύμμετροι, καλοὶ δ'οὔ. At Judges 3.17 Eglon king of Moab is ἀνὴρ ἀστεῖος σφόδρα, a very handsome man (according to LS), but here the Hebrew is בריא, and the context shows that the meaning is, as the Hebrew word requires, fat. Luke probably means that Moses was an entirely satisfactory child, without physical or mental handicap. Cf. Plutarch, Themistocles 5.4(114). The adjective is derived from ἄστυ, town, city, and its primary meaning is of the town, hence town-bred, polite;

witty. But these meanings are evidently unsuitable here. Philo, using of course the same LXX source, says that Moses was εὐγενῆ καὶ ἀστεῖον ὀφθῆναι (*De Vit. Mos.* 1.18). Luke is following the LXX text and the choice of the word there must be explained by students of the LXX. Josephus from the same text draws the idea of beauty but avoids the word: *Ant.* 2.224 (μεγέθους τε ἕνεκα καὶ κάλλους), 232 (μορφῇ τε θεῖον καὶ φρονήματι γενναῖον). Targum Yerushalmi 1 takes טוב differently: Moses was born at six months; his mother saw that the premature infant was capable of living, and kept him for the next three months. Exodus R. 1 (66d) is different again: Tob (Tobiah) was his name. Light shone at the time of his birth; God saw the light that it was good (טוב; Gen. 1.4).

Conzelmann (47) notes that 'Schönheit ist eine Eigenschaft des θεῖος ἀνήρ, Lucian, *Alex.* 3, Bieler 1.51ff., Betz 104f.'. The theme of Moses as divine man will recur frequently in the notes on the following verses.

τῷ θεῷ is described in M. 1.104 as 'dative of the person judging'; cf. 1 Cor. 14.11, τῷ λαλοῦντι. M. 2.443 adds that the use is a Hebraism, corresponding to לאלהים; cf. Jonah 3.3 and perhaps 2 Cor. 10.4. M. 3.239 judges similarly, referring also to D. W. Thomas in *VetT* 3 (1953), 15ff. BDR § 192 adds Barnabas 8.4; 4.11; *Protev. James* 10.1; the dative is an ethic dative, but its use in this way, as a sort of superlative (Pallis: ἀστειότατος), must be regarded as a Hebraism. Aeschylus, *Agamemnon* 345 has been cited as a parallel but is none. The construction does not appear at this point in the LXX and must therefore be the work of the author of the speech. It seems unlikely that it should be the work of Luke.

There is a further verbal variation from the LXX. Exod. 2.2 agrees that Moses was kept in his parental home for three months but expresses this in the words ἐσκέπασαν (the plural subject must be the parents, unless the third person plural is used impersonally and is equivalent to a passive) αὐτὸ μῆνας τρεῖς. Luke's verb, ἀνατρέφειν, is used both of bodily and of mental and spiritual nourishment; in the former sense in the present verse, in the latter sense in the next. Clearly no more than physical feeding can be meant when the word is used of a baby up to the age of three months. σκεπάζειν, the LXX word, refers rather to shelter and protection.

21. ἐκτεθέντος. See on ἔκθετα, v. 19. D w sy^{h**} mae add παρὰ τὸν ποταμόν, filling out the story from the LXX. E has εἰς τὸν ποταμόν; with this cf. Ezekiel (Tragicus) 13 (τάρσενικὰ ῥίπτειν ποταμὸν εἰς βαθύροον), but also 17 (παρ' ἄκρα ποταμοῦ). For the language cf. Exod. 2.5 (ἡ θυγάτηρ Φαραώ ... ἐπὶ τὸν ποταμόν ... ἀνείλατο [τὴν θῖβιν] ... ἐκ τοῦ ὕδατος ἀνειλόμην). αὐτοῦ: the pronoun is unnecessarily repeated (... αὐτόν ... αὐτόν); see BDR § 278; cf. 22.17 and contrast 16.15, 19. ἀνείλατο may be taken literally: she lifted up the baby, but the word is also used in the Koine for acknowledging one's child or adopting a child. See Plutarch, *Antony* 36.3 (932); Epictetus 1.23.7; for papyrus usage, MM 33f. s.v., including P.Oxy. 1.37.6, ἀνεῖλεν ἀπὸ κοπρίας ἀρρενικὸν σωμάτιον. 'Both the LXX and the NT passages reflect the terminology of these nursing contracts from Egypt' (*ND* 2.9).

ἀνεθρέψατο: see on v. 20. The addition of ἑαυτῆ makes the clause doubly reflexive (BDR § 310. 2. n. 4); better, perhaps, it is a sign that the full force of the reflexive middle was no longer felt (Radermacher 121).

εἰς υἱόν, according to M. 2.462, is a Hebraism, εἰς representing the Hebrew predicative ל. Moulton himself did not think so. At M. 1.71f. (citing not this passage but 8.23; 13.22) he writes, 'The vernacular shows a similar extension of the old use of εἰς expressing destination: so for example KP 46 (ii/A.D.), ἔσχον παρ' ὑμῶν εἰς δά(νειον) σπέρματα, a recurrent formula' (72). The same conclusion is reached by Radermacher (16f., 100), who gives further examples. The expression is used at Exod. 2.10, ἐγενήθη αὐτῆ εἰς υἱόν.

The exposure (ἐκτιθέναι; other words also are used) of infants was not uncommon (though not among Jews); more often female infants would be exposed, boys preserved (ἐὰν ἦν ἄρσενον ἄφες, ἐὰν ἦν θήλεα ἔκβαλε, *P Oxy*. 4(1904).744, 9f.).

22. ἐπαιδεύθη, Moses was *trained, educated* (cf. Xenophon, *Cyropaedia* 1.1, ποίᾳ τινὶ παιδείᾳ παιδευθείς). The dative πάσῃ σοφίᾳ Αἰγυπτίων specifies the field in which he was trained; cf. Plato, *Republic* 430a, ἐπαιδεύομεν (τοὺς στρατιώτας) μουσικῆ καὶ γυμναστικῆ. At *Crito* 50d however Plato uses ἐν: ἐν μουσικῆ καὶ γυμναστικῆ παιςεύειν. The two constructions correspond to the two readings πάσῃ σοφίᾳ (B Ψ 𝔐 d vg) and ἐν πάσῃ σοφίᾳ (P⁷⁴ᵛⁱᵈ ℵ A C E gig p). D⁽ᶜ⁾ has πᾶσαν τὴν σοφίαν, which also is not without precedent.

For the 'Moses legend' see J. Jeremias in *TWNT* 4.869f.; for the difference between Hellenistic and Palestinian forms, 860. It is however an over-simplification to suggest that Hellenistic Judaism looked upon Moses as a θεῖος ἀνήρ while Palestinian Judaism thought of him primarily as a saviour. The fullest account of the education received by Moses in Egypt is given by Philo, *De Vit. Mos.* 1.21–4 (διδάσκαλοι . . . παρῆσαν, οἱ μὲν ἀπὸ . . . τῶν κατ' Αἴγυπτον νόμων . . . ἀριθμοὺς μὲν οὖν καὶ γεωμετρίαν τήν τε ῥυθμικὴν καὶ ἁρμονικὴν καὶ μετρικὴν θεωρίαν καὶ μουσικήν . . . Αἰγυπτίων οἱ λόγοι τὴν τῶν οὐρανίων Χαλδαϊκὴν ἐπιστήμην . . .). In all this Philo is no doubt simply describing and enlarging his own Graeco-Egyptian education. The Jewish poet Ezekiel claims only that Moses was brought up in τροφαῖσι βασιλικαῖσι καὶ παιδεύμασιν (37; cf. Luke's use of παιδεύειν), but Origen (c. Celsum 3.46) says that Stephen was 'no doubt basing his statement on ancient documents which have not come to the notice of the multitude'. This may mean that they had come to Origen's notice; did Origen suppose that Stephen knew what Philo or Ezekiel had written? According to Jubilees (47.9) Moses's education was Jewish: 'Amram thy father taught thee writing.' The Egyptians were notable for their wisdom (Herodotus 2.160.1: τοὺς σοφωτάτους ἀνθρώπων Αἰγυπτίους) but the rabbis thought of it as consisting primarily of magic and astrology (StrB 2.678f.). It is clear that even if Stephen might have approved of these pursuits Luke certainly would not have done so (he does not approve of magicians: 8.20–23; 13.10). The source, whatever it may have been, was concerned simply to glorify Moses, as the whole Jewish tradition did; cf. Josephus, Ant. 2.205, 210, 216, 224, 229–31, 236.

Moses was δυνατὸς ἐν λόγοις καὶ ἔργοις αὐτοῦ. Cf. Sirach 45.3. His powerful works, granted him by God, are described in detail in Exodus; they include the ten plagues which finally induced the Pharaoh to let the Israelites go. That he was also powerful in speech is in contradiction with Exod. 4.10–16 (ἰσχνόφωνος καὶ βραδύγλωσσος ἐγώ εἰμι). This is not to be dismissed as mock modesty on Moses's part or as a way of excusing himself from a difficult and dangerous task, since in the end God agrees that Aaron shall speak for Moses. It is sometimes claimed that there is a parallel in Josephus, Ant. 2.271, 272, but in fact in this passage God promises to supply Moses's deficiency. Philo has every reason to magnify the figure of Moses but at no point in De Vit. Mos. 1.21–30 does he claim that Moses was a good speaker. Ezekiel, Exagoge 113–119, paraphrases the OT at length. Stephen's words are a Lucan expression; cf. Lk. 24.19,δυνατὸς ἐν ἔργῳ καὶ λόγῳ. Stephen (Luke) undoubtedly wishes to give Moses an exalted position, perhaps to make Moses parallel with Jesus (Stählin 108), and the Lucanism slips in inadvertently, as Luke edits his source. The difficulty is avoided if we may take the λόγοι in question to be written words. Good speech is another mark of the θεῖος ἀνήρ; see Betz (135), with numerous references.

23. ἐπληροῦτο. For Luke's use of (συμ)πληροῦν of periods of time cf. v. 30; 2.1. When he was fully forty years old; but the expression also reflects the divisions of Moses's life into periods of forty years. See Deut. 34.7 (he lived to the age of 120). On this the comment in Sifre (§ 357; 150a) is, Moses was in Egypt forty years, in Midian forty years, and for forty years he led Israel. There are many parallels. Cf. Pseudo-Philo 9.3 (Amram . . . said . . ., Since the word was passed which God spoke to Abraham, there are 350 years). Add the first eighty years of Moses's life and the figure 430 (Exod. 12.40) is reached. Cf. Jubilees 14.13 (with Charles's note) and see Le Déaut, Nuit Pascale 149, n. 45.

Ἀναβαίνειν ἐπὶ τὴν καρδίαν (or ἐν τῇ καρδίᾳ), Lk. 24.38; 1 Cor. 2.9; Acts 7.23 may be good Greek, but looks like a literal translation of (לבב) עלה על לב (so LXX, e.g. 4 Reg. 12.5; Jer. 3.16; 28 (Heb. 51). 50' (Moule, *IB* 183). The expression may be described as a Lucan septuagintalism (Wilcox 63 thinks it due to the influence of Isa. 65; 66 in particular), but here it could well have been drawn from the (equally septuagintalizing) source that Luke was using. For ἐπισκέπτεσθαι see 6.3; 15.14, 36. Here it is clear that the meaning includes more than the conventional sense of *visit*; Moses intends to come out of his royal environment not only to see but to assist his fellow Israelites. Cf. Lk. 1.68; 7.16; but Moses was not God, had not yet been commissioned by God to act on his behalf, and his attempt failed.

24. The sentence is not clearly expressed though it is not hard to fill in the gaps that Luke has left. The person being injured (or unjustly treated) must be an Israelite, though this is not stated (except by D E gig sy^{ph**} mae, which add ἐκ τοῦ γένους (αὐτοῦ)). The person committing the injury must be an Egyptian, though this is not stated till the end of the verse. The story is told in simpler language in Exod. 2.11: ὁρᾷ ἄνθρωπον Αἰγύπτιον τύπτοντά τινα Ἑβραῖον.

The verb ἀμύνειν is used in the middle without a direct object (and without an indirect object unless τῷ καταπονουμένῳ is taken with ἡμύνετο as well as with ἐποίησεν ἐκδίκησιν). In this voice the verb is used to mean *to defend oneself*, with accusative of the person or thing defended against and genitive of 'that from which danger is warded off' (LS 87, s.v.). It is used absolutely to mean to '*defend oneself, act in self-defence*'. It is clear that Moses was not acting in self-defence and it must be supposed that Luke has used the middle where the active would be more appropriate. This means *to ward off*, with accusative of the thing or person defended against. This is inappropriate here and we must take A 1.b from the LS article, *defend, aid, succour* (cf. Haenchen 272), though this would normally require a dative (perhaps to be found in τῷ καταπονουμένῳ). ποιεῖν ἐκδίκησιν will mean *to effect vengeance for*, that is, *to avenge*. Cf. Lk. 18.7, 8, though here the persons avenged are expressed in the genitive.

καταπονεῖν is not used in the relevant passage in Exodus, but πατάξας τὸν Αἰγύπτιον is in Exod. 2.12 (as also is ἔκρυψεν αὐτὸν ἐν τῇ ἄμμῳ, added here by D w). The present participle means that the Israelite was *on the point of* being overthrown.

25. συνιέναι is a present infinitive so that we must translate, He supposed that his brothers understood (not, . . . that they would understand). Now for the second time (cf. vv. 9, 10) Stephen (Luke) introduces the theme of the divinely chosen ruler whose role is misunderstood by those who should gratefully look to him as their leader; there is a similar but not identical reversal of fortune in the story of Abraham (vv. 4, 5). The case of Moses is developed at greater length and is treated in such detail as to suggest that the speaker thinks of him as a type of Jesus; this point however is never made in the speech; see p. 363. The use of the word σωτηρία in particular suggests this connection, but it can of course be properly used quite simply of rescue from any unfortunate circumstances, such as slavery. There is much weight in Delebecque's observation (33) on this verse: 'Les mots οὐ συνῆκαν sont la clé du discours. Luc les tire de son évangile, 2.50 . . .'

For διὰ χειρός, and the question whether it should be regarded as a Semitism, see on 2.23.

26. τῇ τε ἐπιούσῃ ἡμέρᾳ is an improvement on τῇ ἡμέρᾳ τῇ δευτέρᾳ (Exod. 2.13). ὤφθη however is a surprising variant for the LXX's ὁρᾷ; the Hebrew is הנה. This aorist passive is unusually frequent in Acts (2.3; 7.2, 26, 30, 35; 9.17; 13.31; 16.9; 22.16) but in no other passage does it occur where the active might have seemed more natural. Stephen (Luke) may be dependent on a version otherwise unknown; or the word may have seemed appropriate for the appearance of a figure of more than usual, perhaps of more than human, dignity. Again, αὐτοῖς μαχομένοις is surprisingly vague: *to them as they were fighting.* The LXX's description makes the incident much clearer: δύο ἄνδρας Ἑβραίους διαπληκτιζομένους. On the use of Exod. 2.13f. in vv. 26–28 see Hatch, *Essays* 169f. ('the narrative portion of the text differs from that of Exodus, but the dialogue nearly agrees and is probably a quotation', 169). After μαχομένοις, D* diverges further by adding καὶ εἶδεν αὐτοὺς ἀδικοῦντας (picking up the verb used in v. 24).

For συνήλλασσεν, A E Ψ 𝔐 have συνήλασεν, changing the verb (to συνελαύνειν) and also missing the conative force of the imperfect. See BDR § 326; also M. 1.129, for an interesting note on the AV (*would have set them at one again*) which seems to have got the right sense by translating the wrong verb. συναλλάσσειν occurs nowhere else in the NT (Paul's word for *reconcile* is regularly καταλλάσσειν) but is not uncommon in prose. εἰς εἰρήνην is an unnecessary addition, but has the effect of emphasis. Reconciliation is a work of the θεῖος ἀνήρ; Conzelmann refers to Bieler 1.101f.; Lucian, *Demonax* 9; Philostratus, *Apollonius* 1.15; 6.38.

Moses's words as given in Acts correspond to the sense but not the wording of the LXX (διὰ τί σὺ τύπτεις τὸν πλησίον), which is a straightforward rendering of the Hebrew (למה תכה רעך). D, as often, makes the language somewhat more forceful, replacing the first three words with τί ποιεῖτε, ἄνδρες ἀδελφοί; ἀδικεῖτε no doubt deliberately echoes ἀδικοῦντι in v. 24. 'Suivant l'usage attique, la suppression de l'interjection ὦ a quelque chose de brutal' (Delebecque 34).

27. ὁ δὲ ἀδικῶν (vv. 24, 26) τὸν πλησίον (this word may show knowledge of the LXX of Exod. 2.13, quoted above). ἀπωθεῖσθαι is picked up in v. 39 and used again at 13.46; elsewhere in the NT only at Rom. 11.1, 2 (in an OT allusion) and 1 Tim. 1.19. With the man's words the text of the LXX is taken up and followed precisely. καθίστημι had been used with reference to the appointment of Stephen himself (6.3). ἄρχων (שׂר) is a general term for one in authority (cf. e.g. 3.17); δικαστής(שׁפט) occurs only here and at v. 35 in the NT, but is used from Herodotus onwards for a judge, distinguishing under the law right from wrong. The question is rhetorical, but Stählin rightly points out that Luke's answer is — God.

28. The words follow exactly the LXX of Exod. 2.14; the LXX corresponds to the Hebrew. Moses who seeks to rescue and reconcile his people is dismissed as a mere bully, prepared to deal violently with anyone, Egyptian or Hebrew.

29. Such complete failure to understand his intentions (οἱ δὲ οὐ συνῆκαν, v. 25) was too much for Moses, who *fled* (ἔφυγεν). The picture is sharpened by the Western text (D* (E gig p mae)) with οὕτως καὶ ἐφυγάδευσεν (the verb is used intransitively, in the aorist, with the meaning *to go into banishment*). It was what his fellow Israelites said that caused Moses's flight: he fled ἐν τῷ λόγῳ τούτῳ. M. 2.463 describes this as a causal use of ἐν, probably influenced by the Hebrew ב; Zerwick § 119 translates, quia ei dictum erat, Quis te . . .? BDR § 219. 2 are in essential agreement, classifying the use of ἐν as instrumental but defining it as giving the reason. Cf. 24.17. The construction is practically the same as the English 'at this word he fled'. There is also a temporal element: because the word caused his flight it also gave the time of his flight. The OT narrative diverges in that there Moses flees from Pharaoh; the death of the Egyptian could not be concealed and Pharaoh ἐζήτει ἀνελεῖν Μωυσῆν (Exod. 2.15).

ἐγένετο πάροικος introduces a thought not contained in the LXX's ᾤκησεν. (Hebrew, וישׁב); it suggests (cf. v. 6) that in Midian Moses was no more than a temporary resident alien (cf. the more or less synonymous μέτοικος; cf. Exod. 2.22). Moses was not to remain permanently in Midian, a territory occupying the east coast of the Gulf of Aqaba, thus to the south of Edom. Stephen (Luke) omits the account of Moses's marriage but mentions the birth of two sons. One, Gershom, is mentioned in Exod. 2.22; 18.3; Eliezer is added in 18.4. 'The reference to these sons is irrelevant' (*Begs.*

4.76). Or was the intention to emphasise that but for the divine call Moses would have good reason to remain in Midian?

30. Another period of forty years elapses (cf. v. 23) and the next stage of the story of Moses is reached. Again the verb πληροῦν is used (D[(c)] has μετὰ ταῦτα πλησθέντων αὐτῷ ἔτη τεσσεράκοντα). The rest of the verse sums up briefly what is said in more circumstantial detail in Exod. 3.1, 2. Acts omits as irrelevant that Moses was pasturing the sheep of his father-in-law and that the burning bush was not consumed. More important is the fact that the OT (both Hebrew and Greek) refers at this point to the holy mountain not as Sinai but as Horeb. Stephen speaks, or Luke writes, from memory, and Sinai was the name that came to mind. Sinai lay on the other side of the Gulf of Aqaba; Moses and the flock were some distance from Midianite territory.

An angel of the Lord (so the OT) appeared (ὤφθη; cf. v. 26 and the note) to Moses ἐν φλογὶ πυρός. So ℵ B D Ψ 𝔐 gig p sy[h], but P[74] A C E 36 323 945 1739 *al* vg sy[p] have ἐν πυρὶ φλογός. It is hard to see any difference between the two — a fiery flame or a flaming fire. If the MSS of the LXX were not themselves divided one would probably choose the NT reading that differed from that of the OT, ascribing the other to assimilation, but this argument is not available. The genitive βάτου is loosely attached. The LXX's ἐκ τοῦ βάτου (MT, הסנה מתוך) is better.

Angels appear in God's service and for the benefit of his people in vv. 30,35, 38, 53; cf. 1 QS 3.24f. (The angel of his truth helps all the sons of light). This passage however is dualistic in tone, as Acts is not. It is an angel who appears, but God who speaks; it is doubtful whether Luke intends in this way to emphasise the transcendence of God (Schmithals 71). Calvin (190) takes the angel to be Christ, through whom God communicates with men; it is very doubtful whether Luke had this identification in mind.

31. Again a somewhat more circumstantial narrative is abbreviated. Moses marvelled (durative imperfect, ἐθαύμαζεν, though A B C Ψ 326 1175 *pc* have the aorist) at the sight and approached so as to have a good look at it. The compound verb κατανοῆσαι should have perfective force; it 'should describe the *completion* of a mental process. In some passages, as Lk. 20.23 ('he *detected* their craftiness'), or Acts 7.31 ('to *master* the mystery'), this will do very well; but the durative action is most certainly represented in the present κατανοεῖν, except in Acts 27.39 (? 'noticed one after another')' (M. 1.117). For the last three words of the verse D (sy[p]) have ὁ κύριος εἶπεν αὐτῷ λέγων. Neither text has been assimilated to the LXX, and it is hard to see any particular motivation at work in either.

32. The words are those of Exod. 3.6 except that in Exodus (a) ἐγώ is followed by εἰμι, (b) *fathers* (πατέρων) is used in the singular (πατρός), (c) θεός is repeated before Ἰσαάκ and Ἰακώβ. In Exod. 3.15, 16 however the only difference is (c). These differences would suggest no more than inexact quotation from memory were it not that at Exod. 3.6 the Samaritan Pentateuch, differing from Hebrew, LXX, Vulgate, and Peshitto, has *the God of thy fathers* (plural). Some have seen here evidence of a connection between Stephen (or the Hellenists in general) and the Samaritans, or at least a connection between this passage and the Samaritan Pentateuch (Wilcox 29f.). The evidence is in fact worthless. In 3.15f. the plural *fathers* occurs in the Hebrew and all versions, and assimilation no doubt occurred. For a similar quotation see Justin, *1 Apology* 63.7. The saying of this verse constitutes a vital part of narrative and argument. The same God was at work through the whole of the OT tradition, notwithstanding the patriarchs' treatment of Joseph and the Israelites' rejection of Moses. Luke will extend this thought; the Christians (notwithstanding the rejection of Jesus) also worship the same God.

ἔντρομος may perhaps be called a Lucan word: here and 16.29; elsewhere in the NT only Heb. 12.21. It is not in the LXX at this point (ἀπέστρεψεν . . . τὸ πρόσωπον αὐτοῦ· εὐλαβεῖτο κατεμβλέψαι ἐνώπιον τοῦ θεοῦ, which bowdlerizes the Hebrew — Moses was afraid to look at God, אל־האלהים. We may infer that Luke uses the word in an abbreviation that he (or the kindred writer of a source) has made. Trembling with fear, Moses did not dare to look (for κατανοῆσαι, see v. 31).

In this verse, and indeed in vv. 31–4, mae makes an extensive addition, based on the OT narrative. For details see Metzger (348) and T. C. Petersen (*CBQ* 26 (1964), 234f.).

33. Here the copyist of D uses the phrase ἐγένετο φωνή which he avoided in v. 31: καὶ ἐγένετο φωνὴ πρὸς αὐτόν. Stephen (Luke) here alters the order of the OT, where this warning precedes God's self-disclosure. The words are similar to but not identical with those of Exod. 3.5. Acts has λῦσον (active) for λῦσαι (middle); this is anything but an improvement (BDR § 310. 1 n. 1). Acts has simply τῶν ποδῶν σου, *the shoes* (or *shodding*) *of your feet*, instead of . . . *from your feet* (though Delebecque 34 says that τῶν ποδῶν depends on λῦσον, not on ὑπόδημα); again the LXX is preferable. Acts has ἐφ' ᾧ for ἐν ᾧ (see Wilcox 41f. for the suggestion that this may be due to use of the Hebrew, or of Aquila), a slight improvement, and drops the unnecessary σύ before ἕστηκας. These differences could all arise from defective memory, and it is not necessary to infer a court room scene (or the use of a version other than the LXX) to account for them. Cf. J. A. Emerton, *JSS* 13 (1968), 289f.

The removal of shoes (probably as bearing uncleanness which it would be very difficult to remove) on approaching a holy place was (and is) a common religious rite. See Berakoth 9.5 (He may not enter into the Temple Mount with his staff or his sandal or his wallet, or with the dust upon his feet . . .), and cf. Juvenal 6.159 (observant ubi festa mero pede sabbata reges).

34. In this verse we have a combination of Exod. 3.7, 8, 10. The first ten words are taken exactly from Exod. 3.7. Next, for τοῦ στεναγμοῦ αὐτῶν (B D have αὐτοῦ, in agreement with λαός) ἤκουσα, LXX has τῆς κραυγῆς αὐτῶν ἀκήκοα ἀπὸ τῶν ἐργοδιωκτῶν. Luke's στεναγμός may be an alternative translation (of נאקתם), but more probably comes from Exod. 2.24; 6.5. The tense of the verb is not significant, and may owe something to the same verses (εἰσήκουσεν, εἰσήκουσα). Reference to the taskmasters would have added nothing to Stephen's argument. κατέβην ἐξελέσθαι αὐτούς is taken exactly from Exod. 3.8; there was no need to reproduce the rest of the verse; all that mattered was that God (who has now taken the place of the angel of 7.30; Exod. 3.2) has personally come to rescue his people. The last seven words are taken from Exod. 3.10, except that for εἰς Αἴγυπτον the LXX has πρὸς Φαραὼ βασιλέα Αἰγύπτου (Hebrew, אל־פרעה).

καὶ νῦν represents ועתה, Come now; cf. 10.5; 22.16; 3.17; see further however BDR § 442. 8d n. 26. It is not only in Hebrew that *now* can on occasion have a weak consequential as well as a temporal sense. The subjunctive ἀποστείλω was changed by Ψ 𝔐 into the future ἀποστελῶ (see Moule, *IB* 22). The LXX has ἀποστείλω. This should not be regarded simply as a mis-spelling; 'it is a matter of syntax, not orthography' (M. 2.70). According to M. 1.185 the primitive futuristic use of the aorist subjunctive 'reappears in the κοινή, where in the later papyri the subjunctive may be seen for the simple future.' Moulton adds, 'So Acts 7.34 (LXX).' The interchangeability (though not in the present case) is illustrated by Thackeray's claim (*Grammar* 91) that 'the Pentateuch translators were fond of using a fut. ind. in the first clause of a sentence, followed by a deliberative conjunctive in the later clauses: Gen. 22.5 . . ., 43.4 . . ., 44.16 . . ., Exod. 8.8, ἐξαποστελῶ . . . καὶ θύσωσιν' (Exod. 8.4 in other editions). BDR § 364. 1 n. 1 relates the subjunctive to the preceding δεῦρο (cf. ἄφες with ἐκβάλω in Mt. 7.4 = Lk. 6.42); cf. Rev. 17.1; 21.9; Euripides, *Bacchae* 341, δεῦρό σου στέψω κάρα; *Clem. Hom.* 13.3 (v. 1), ἐάσατέ με προαγάγω ὑμᾶς. The meaning is no doubt somewhere between, Come, I will send you, and Come, let me send you; in translation the latter should be chosen because the former would have been perfectly expressed by ἀποστελῶ.

.

35. At this point there begins (according to Stählin 109) a sort of Moses hymn, related to the Christ hymn of Col. 1.13–20. (1) The man rejected by the people becomes ruler and lord; (2) he becomes deliverer through signs and wonders given by God; (3) he is both prophet and prototype of the Coming One; (4) he is mediator between God and people; (5) he is the receiver and giver of words of life; (6) his people reject him. That this and the following verses give high honour to Moses, finding him a central place in the purposes of God, there is no doubt. Questions however arise, first in regard to the form of the supposed hymn. Sections (1) and (6) seem virtually the same. They fit the story of Moses but do not fit so well into the praise of Moses. A second question is: If this is a hymn, where did it originate, among Jews or among Christians? The latter is not an impossible supposition; cf. 1 Cor. 10.2, where it is probable that the notion of baptism into Moses arose by analogy with the existing practice of baptism into Christ. If on the other hand this is originally Hellenistic Jewish material we have a further example of a post-biblical development in Jewish thought about Moses as the founder of a religion.

Moses had been rejected by his fellow countrymen, but God thought otherwise and overruled their reaction for their own good. The object of ἀπέσταλκεν is brought to the beginning of the sentence for emphasis: τοῦτον τὸν Μωυσῆν, this very man. For ἠρνήσαντο cf. 3.13; the parallel is significant. Moses had been treated by Israel as Jesus was to be. For the construction of ἠρνήσαντο εἰπόντες see BDR § 420. 3 n. 4. The aorist participle does not here (as it most often does) refer to action before that of the main verb (the saying and the denying were the same thing and coincident in time); the tense is justified because it is the participle that introduces the fact of speaking. Cf. Jn 11.28; Lk. 22.8; Acts 21.14.

τίς σε κατέστησεν . . .; See v. 27. Here, by assimilation, ἐφ'ἡμῶν is added by ℵ C D Ψ 36 81 453 1175 pc co, ἐφ' ἡμᾶς by E 33 945 1739 pm. τοῦτον resumes the object of the verb and the subject now appears: ὁ θεός. It is God's intention for Moses that determines what Moses is. The word ἄρχων is retained; δικαστής is dropped (Moses, great though he is, is not judge) and in its place Moses is said to be the λυτρωτής of his people. The word occurs here only in the NT; cf. however λύτρον (Mt. 20.28 = Mk 10.45), λυτροῦσθαι (Lk. 24.21; Tit. 2.14; 1 Pet. 1.18), and λύτρωσις (Lk. 1.68; 2.38; Heb. 9.12). This group of words is characteristic of the Deutero-pauline and post-pauline writings; Paul himself prefers ἀπολύτρωσις (Lk. 1; Paul, 3; Ephesians and Colossians, 4; Hebrews, 2 times). LS 1067 quote only biblical passages for λυτρωτής, and BA 980 say 'nicht b. Profanen', but λυτροῦσθαι is widely used for *release by payment of a ransom*. In the LXX the word is used only twice, each time of God (Ps. 18 (19).14; 77 (78).35). The verb is much more frequent, representing most often גאל and פדה. It can bear the meaning given above (e.g. Exod. 34.20), but its most characteristic meaning is that of release without payment, release effected by means of a rescue operation. The most important passage to quote, because it probably lies behind the use of the noun here, is Exod. 6.6: ῥύσομαι (the speaker is God) ὑμᾶς ἐκ τῆς δουλείας καὶ λυτρώσομαι ὑμᾶς ἐν βραχίονι ὑψηλῷ. Moses can be described as λυτρωτής because he is the agent of the redeeming God; clearly redemption here means deliverance and no price is paid. The process is described in v. 36.

ἀπέσταλκεν is taken by BDR § 343. 1 n. 2 as an example of the narrative (aoristic) use of the perfect. Moulton is more hesitant. 'In Acts 7.35, ἀπέσταλκεν, with the forest of aorists all round, is more plausibly conformed to them [than the perfect in James 1.24], and it happens that this word is alleged to have aoristic force elsewhere. But, after all, the abiding results of Moses' mission formed a thought never absent from a Jew's mind' (M. 1.144). If we have here a pre-Christian Jewish sermon (see pp. 338f.) the thought may be that Moses continues to be a ruler and redeemer for his people. For the significance of Moses cf. 3.22 and see further below. To speak of him in this way rebuts the accusation of 6.11, 14 (Bauernfeind 110).

Moses was not sent without supernatural authority and assistance. σὺν χειρί is unusual. It may be an equivalent of ἐν χειρί, διὰ χειρός, and an alternative rendering of דיב, meaning simply *through, by the agency of* (though it is hard to understand why ב should be rendered σύν), or mean that Moses would be accompanied by the angel, or the angel's power. Cf. v. 38. τοῦ ὀφθέντος stands after the anarthrous ἀγγέλου to determine it in the way in which a relative clause would determine it: *an angel, namely the one who . . . ἐν τῇ βατῷ*: βάτος is taken as feminine. This seems to be correct, though opinion is divided on the question whether Hellenistic usage, over against Attic, makes the word masculine or feminine. See BDR § 49. 1 n. 1, with the references. Thackeray (*Grammar* 146) finds ὁ βάτος in Aristophanes and Theophrastus. Here and in v. 30 Stephen refrains from saying that God appeared to Moses, though God spoke to him. Knox (*Hellenistic Elements* 70) compares the repeated οὗτος in vv. 35–38 with the ἐγώ εἰμι of John and so with Hellenistic aretalogies.

36. οὗτος, emphatic (see v. 35), *this man* Moses brought them out. Discussion of the question whether ποιήσας is an aorist participle of subsequent action (cf. v. 27) is probably beside the point (though M. 1.133's 'the constative ἐξήγαγεν describes the Exodus as a whole' is a good explanation). If the sentence ended at ἐν γῇ Αἰγύπτῳ there would be no problem: Having performed portents and signs (with his staff and hand, and in the plagues; for τέρας and σημεῖον see 2.22) he led them out. This is probably as far as Luke had thought when he wrote ποιήσας; having got so far he recalled

and added the portents at the Red Sea and in the wilderness —
forgetting the construction.

γῇ Αἰγύπτῳ (ℵ A E 𝔐) is a Hebraism (BDR § 261. 7 n. 8). ἐν
τῇ Αἰγύπτῳ is read by B C 36 453 *pc* d, ἐν γῇ Αἰγύπτου by P⁷⁴
D Ψ 614 945 1739 *al* lat. ἐρυθρὰ θάλασσα means the Red Sea; in
the LXX the words translate ים־סוף, properly Sea of Reeds, by which
term was understood arms of what is now known as the Red Sea,
most often (and so in Exod. 10.19) the Gulf of Suez, sometimes the
Gulf of Aqaba.

For the verse as a whole cf. the description of Moses in Ass. Mos.
3.11: ... qui multa passus est in Aegypto et in mari rubro et in
heremo annis quadraginta.

37. οὗτος, again emphatic; see on v. 35. Moses was not only
himself a ruler and redeemer; he was a prophet, and foretold the
coming of another prophet like himself. For the use of Deut. 18.15
see on 3.22, where it is quoted by Peter. The quotation in the present
verse agrees closely but not exactly with the wording of 3.22. The
differences are: (a) Here God is ὁ θεός only, in 3.22 he is κύριος
ὁ θεὸς ὑμῶν (some MSS omit the pronoun, others have ἡμῶν)); (b)
3.22 continues with the exhortation to listen to the prophet; this is
omitted here, though C D⁽ᵗ⁾ 33 36 323 614 945 (1175) 1241 1739 *al*
gig sy mae bo add αὐτοῦ ἀκούσεσθε. Both passages agree substantially
with Deut. 18.15a. Neither in this verse nor in the speech as a whole
(until v. 52) is it claimed or implied that the prophecy was fulfilled
in Jesus.

38. οὗτος, again emphatic. Moses was in, in the midst of, with the
ἐκκλησία. For this word see on 5.11, and the general discussion in
Vol. II. It occurs at Deut. 23.1(2), the first occurrence at which it
means a body of people, the Lord's people (ἐκκλησία κυρίου).
There are earlier occurrences in Deuteronomy (4.10; 9.10; 18.16)
where it is used in the formula (ἡ) ἡμέρα (τῆς) ἐκκλησίας, with
reference to the day of gathering together, assembling, at Mount
Sinai, when — it might be said — the Israelites became the people
of the Lord, constituted as such by the Law. This was the people *in
the wilderness*, the wilderness of Sinai. So much is clear, but it is
very doubtful whether Luke wrote, or any early Christian read, this
verse without thinking of the Christian ἐκκλησία, of which he would
see a foreshadowing in the ancient people of God. Here however as
in v. 37 Stephen (Luke) gives no indication that his words may point
forward to the Christian development of the ἐκκλησία

μετὰ τοῦ ἀγγέλου; cf. v. 35, σὺν χειρὶ ἀγγέλου. It has been
suggested (*Begs.* 4.78) that in this verse μετά ... καί represents the
Hebrew ובין ... בין , *between ... and*, so that Moses stood between
the angel and the fathers, and so was the mediator (μεσίτης, Gal.

3.19) who mediated the Law from its angelic origins to the people. There is no reason to accept this. μετά . . . καί does not mean *between*, and in v. 53 (cf. Gal. 3.19; Heb. 2.2) it is angels (plural) who give the Law. The connection with v. 35 is not close. Whatever σὺν χειρί means it is not the same as μετά, and the angels are different, in v. 35 the angel seen in the burning bush and here the angel who spoke on Sinai. It is noteworthy that whereas in the Pentateuch God himself speaks to Moses and gives him the Law, here the speaking is done by an angel. Reverence puts God at a further remove from earthly affairs.

λόγιον occurs only four times in the NT, infrequently in the OT (more frequently in Ps. 118 (119) than in the rest of the OT put together). The expression λόγια ζῶντα does not occur, but cf. Ps. 118 (119).50, τὸ λόγιόν σου ἔζησέ με (A S² R). There is no need to restrict the reference to the Ten Commandments; the whole of Torah was lifegiving; see Deut. 30.15–20; 32.47; Mt. 19.17; Aboth 2.7 (The more study of the Law the more life . . . if he has gained for himself words of the Law he has gained for himself life in the world to come). There is in this speech no sign of disparagement of the Law except in so far as it related to the Temple. Calvin (199) shows himself aware of the theological problem raised by this positive treatment of the Law. 'The Law offers life; but because of our corruption we ourselves can receive nothing but death from it. It is therefore death-bearing only with regard to men.'

By ἡμῖν at the end of the verse Stephen associates himself with his Jewish hearers. This is the text of A C D E Ψ 𝔐 lat sy; but P⁷⁴ ℵ B 36 453 2495 *al* p co have ὑμῖν. There would probably be a tendency on the part of copyists to differentiate Stephen from Jews and ἡμῖν should probably be accepted, though the evidence against it is strong.

39. Notwithstanding his supernatural support Moses was unable to win the obedience of his people. ᾧ takes up the οὗτος that has begun the previous verses; use of the relative to continue a narrative is characteristic of Luke's style. For ᾧ D has ὅτι; the reading seems impossible but could have arisen as an error in an Aramaic stage of the tradition; see Black (*AA* 74). This is not probable. In place of ἡμῶν there is support for the second person pronoun but it is much less strong (only Ψ 81 *pc* saᵐˢ mae) than in v. 38. In view of v. 27 it is probable that Moses should be taken as the intended but unexpressed object of ἀπώσαντο, though the *living oracles* are a possible alternative (Schneider 464). The fathers turned (ἐστράφησαν; D *pc* have ἀπεστράφησαν, by assimilation to Num. 14.3) in their hearts to Egypt — a not very clear way of expressing their desire to return there. Slavery in Egypt was better than freedom coupled with the service of God and the rigours of life in the desert.

40. εἰπόντες. Cf. v. 36. Here the aorist participle expresses coincident action. The desire to return to Egypt and the proposal to Aaron belong together. The request is expressed in the words of Exod. 32.1, 23 with a few slight changes, of which the most significant is the omission of ὁ ἄνθρωπος, which makes ὁ Μωυσῆς οὗτος even more contemptuous. ἐγένετο replaces the LXX's γέγονεν (but D E Ψ 𝔐 have γέγονεν). Stephen's ἐκ γῆς Αἰγύπτου is closer to the Hebrew מצרים מארץ than is the LXX. M. 1.69 draws attention to the *nominativus pendens* (ὁ Μωυσῆς . . . αὐτῷ), 'as much at home in English as in Greek'. BDR § 466. 1 explains it as due to the necessity of having an antecedent for the relative clause. Moule (*IB* 176) rightly (since this is a translation of the Hebrew OT) speaks of the 'Semitic way of handling pronouns, as it were retrospectively'. Betz (129 n. 8) refers to passages where ποιεῖν is used for making (images of) gods; here of course ποίησον is simply a translation of עשה.

41. The complete apostasy of the people is described in the OT story, though here for the most part Stephen (Luke) uses his own words.

ἐμοσχοποίησαν must mean what μόσχον ἐποίησεν (singular; Exod. 32.4) means, but why the compound verb was used is not clear. It is formed in the same way as εἰδωλοποιεῖν, which (as BA 1070 observes) is used from the time of Plato. It does not however mean *to make an idol* but *to form a (mental) image* (e.g. Plato, *Republic* 605c), but could have suggested to a Jewish or Christian reader the making of an idol and thus have constituted an analogy on the basis of which a suitable new word could have been formed. And, though we lack the evidence, it is not impossible that Plato's word was popularly used in a different sense.

ἐν ταῖς ἡμέραις ἐκείναις, at the time of the Exodus, but with no attempt at precision.

ἀνάγειν is occasionally used in the LXX for the offering (= עלה, hiph'il) of sacrifice, but not at Exod. 32.6, in the story of the golden calf (ἀνεβίβασεν ὁλοκαυτώματα καὶ προσήνεγκεν θυσίαν σωτηρίου). Luke or his source is writing freely, though not uninfluenced by LXX usage. The same is true of εὐφραίνοντο, in the passive *to make merry, enjoy oneself* (LS 737), which presumably represents ἐκάθισεν ὁ λαὸς φαγεῖν καὶ πεῖν καὶ ἀνέστησαν παίζειν (Exod. 32.6). ἐν τοῖς ἔργοις τῶν χειρῶν αὐτῶν refers to the calf as a man–made and thus idolatrous object. Never had a people been so privileged or so completely negated their vocation.

42a. ἔστρεψεν: the active of στρέφειν is more commonly transitive than intransitive, so that the verb here may take αὐτούς as object (sharing it with παρέδωκεν): God turned them over and gave them up. So the Old Latin h: pervertit illos deus. Cf. 3 Kdms 18.37. But στρέφειν is also occasionally intransitive (e.g. Xenophon, *Agesilaus* 2.3, στρέψαντες βαδὴν ἀπεχώρουν), and it is probably better to take it so here: God turned (changed his attitude to the Israelites). In the LXX this sense is conveyed by the compound ἐπιστρέφειν (active), e.g. Ps. 6.4, ἐπίστρεψον, κύριε, ῥῦσαι τὴν ψυχήν μου. For παρέδωκεν λατρεύειν cf. Rom. 1.24, 26, 28 (with the consequence expressed in v. 25, ἐλάτρευσαν τῇ κτίσει παρὰ τὸν κτίσαντα).

λατρεύειν and cognates are used of any kind of service, sometimes specifically of the service of divine beings; so e.g. Plato, *Apology* 23c (τὴν τοῦ θεοῦ λατρείαν). In the LXX the verb regularly translates עבד (e.g. Exod. 20.5, οὐ προσκυνήσεις αὐτοῖς οὐδὲ μὴ λατρεύσῃς αὐτοῖς — idols). The word itself is not used in the LXX with ἡ στρατιὰ τοῦ οὐρανοῦ (or τῶν -ῶν), but προσκυνεῖν (and similar words, such as θυμιᾶν) are so used (e.g. 2 Chron. 33.3; Jer. 19.13). *The host of heaven* (צבא השמים) are the heavenly bodies, worshipped as deities.

42b, 43. Stephen elaborates and supports his charge of idolatry by quoting Amos 5.25–27. His words are on the whole in agreement with the LXX, though there are a few differences, which will be noticed as they arise. It is doubtful whether they justify the view that Stephen (Luke) was following a non-LXX text. Amos 5.26 is quoted in CD 7.14f., where it is combined with Amos 9.11 (quoted in Acts 15.16) and Num. 24.17 (which may be referred to in Mt. 2.2; Rev. 22.16). The quotation of Amos 5.25–27 (from *the Book of the* (Twelve Minor) *Prophets*) does not exactly correspond to the charge that the Israelites worshipped the *host of heaven*, unless Moloch and the star of Raiphan point in this direction.

The first line of the quotation (μὴ σφάγια καὶ θυσίας προσηνέγκατέ μοι) is cited in exact agreement with the LXX; this in turn agrees with MT except in one particular, מנחה (singular) becomes the plural θυσίας. There is little difference, for the Hebrew word may be understood collectively — *the giving* (of offerings). The interpretation of the line will depend on where the stress is laid. It may lie upon the action of the verb; in English, *Did* you bring me sacrifices . . .? with an implied negative answer, No, at that time we did not (cf. Jer. 7.22). Or it may lie upon μοι: Was it *to me* that you brought . . .? with the implied answer, No, it was to false gods that sacrifices were offered. These two emphases lead to different inferences, the former to the inference, Then sacrifices such as are offered in the Temple are no necessary, or even desirable, part of the true worship of God; they were not used in the ideal period of Israel's life. It is against this that the context does not represent the Exodus as an ideal period but rather as one of apostasy. The latter emphasis reinforces what is said before and after: No, you did not bring your offerings to the true God; you brought them to the golden calf, to Moloch, and to Raiphan. Alternatively, μοι may be an ethic dative, and we should translate, Did you offer sacrifices in the desert, I should like to know? No; and you were quite right not to do so; your sacrificial cult now is nothing but sacrifice to pagan gods. According to Hanson (100) this is what Amos meant, but Stephen took his words to mean that the Israelites had sacrificed to pagan gods at the time of the Exodus. Bruce (2.154) makes a similar distinction. The question expects the answer No, but for Amos it was, No; we then brought true heart-worship and righteousness, whereas for Stephen it was, No; we then offered sacrifices to other gods. There is fairly general agreement with the assessment of Stephen's meaning in *Begs.* 4.79: 'They were idolaters all the time that they were in the desert.'

The second line of the quotation agrees with the LXX except in order: the LXX has ἐν τῇ ἐρήμῳ τεσσεράκοντα ἔτη, agreeing with the MT. For the forty year period see Deut. 2.7, et al.

The third line agrees exactly with the LXX. The MT is different: ונשאתם את סכות מלככם, in which סכות must be a proper name: You have taken up Sikkuth your king. The verb is perhaps rightly interpreted by Page (126). You have taken it up 'after each halt, to carry it with you instead of the tabernacle of Jehovah'. CD 7.14 agrees with MT except in the verb, which is והגליתי, And I will banish. This word occurs in Amos 5.27 with *you* as object (אתכם והגליתי; cf. v. 43d). When however in CD the passage is interpreted, it appears that the Qumran writer has, like the LXX, pointed the first noun as *sukkath, the tent of: the books of the Law* ספרי התורה , *they are the tent* (or *booth*) *of the king.* Targ. Jonathan differs again in the noun, giving פתכומרכון (with the variant פתריכון); each of these words means *your painted things,* that is, *your idols.* It is not our task to elucidate the very complicated tradition that lies behind these versions, still less to identify the Sikkuth of MT (though Sakkut, the Assyrian god of war, seems a likely candidate). What is important is (a) that Stephen is made to quote the LXX rather than the Hebrew (or the Targum, though he is nearer to this than to the MT), and (b) that in Hebrew, Greek, and Aramaic, and for Stephen and Qumran, the words accuse Israel of idolatry. See further below.

The fourth line agrees with the LXX, except that ὑμῶν (contained in the LXX) is omitted by B D 36 453 *pc* gig sy^p sa (followed by Ropes), and that the name Ῥαιφάν (P^74 א^c A 453 1175 *pc* sy; C E Ψ 33 36 *pm* have Ῥεφάν) appears in various forms: Ῥομφά (א*: -φάν)) B Or; Ῥεμφάν (D: -άμ) 323 945 1739 (1241 2495: -φφάν) *pm* lat Ir^lat; Ῥεφά (81: -μφά) 104 *pc*. Before the Hebrew can be taken into account it is necessary to look at the fifth line of Greek, in which Stephen differs slightly from the LXX, which adds αὐτῶν after τύπους, and has ἑαυτοῖς where Stephen has προσκυνεῖν αὐτοῖς. The MT differs widely: And Kiyyun (presumably a proper name;

Kewan, another Assyrian god, is a reasonable guess) your images, the star of your god(s) which you made for yourselves. CD 7.15 after the passage quoted above continues, and Kiyyun your images. It proceeds: מאהלי דמשק, the whole being dependent on the initial verb (see above) והגליתי (borrowed from Amos 5.27). We may translate: I will banish Sikkuth your king and Kiyyun your images from the tents of Damascus. Vermes (104) however, translates *from my tents to Damascus*; Millar Burrows (*Light* 355) translates as here; Lohse (81) translates, *fort über die Zelte von Damaskus hinaus*. Targum Jonathan agrees with MT, reverentially substituting טעוחכון, *your idols* (*errors*) for your gods. In this line Stephen's variations from the LXX call for little comment. He drops αὐτῶν (possibly thinking that *your* images would be better and not seeing that *their* images could mean the images of *Moloch and Raiphan*), and προσκυνεῖν αὐτοῖς was a very natural addition and doubtless correct in sense — for what other purpose would the Israelites have made the images?

Indeed, from Stephen's point of view his changes of the LXX text are trifling and his variations from MT are in effect no more significant. What does it matter whether a false god is called Sikkuth or Moloch, Kiyyun or Raiphan? They are all false gods, to worship them is idolatry, and it will be punished. It is true that the MT of Amos puts both offence and punishment in the future (ונשאתם and והגליתי) whereas the LXX and Acts put the offence in the past (perhaps at the time of the Exodus). This is the only important difference and it is necessary to Stephen's argument, for he is concerned to point out the constant disobedience that Israel has manifested throughout its history (vv. 51–53). Even so, Stephen cites the passage 'as an example of what happened to Israel because of her idolatry. He thus uses the text in a way which is far more faithful to the original context than does the author of CD' (Fitzmyer, *Essays* 41). For CD 7.16–19 continues: The king is the community (הקהל) . . . and the kiyyun of the images are the books of the prophets whose words Israel despised and the star is the student (דורש) of the Torah. Nevertheless, it is important that, as Lohse (285) points out, the Qumran writer, with the aid of Amos 9.11 and Num. 24.17, achieves the following interpretation. 'Damaskus = Land des Nordens = Exil der Gemeinde; Sikkut = Hütte des Königs = Bücher des Gesetzes. Gott hat verheissen, die zerfallene Hütte Davids wieder aufzurichten, das heisst: in der Gemeinde des Bundes wird das Gesetz wieder aufgerichtet. Beweis: David = König = Gemeinde. In ihr stehen neben dem Gesetz die Bücher der Propheten, die Israel verachtet, in Gültigkeit.' The last point here recalls v. 52, but Stephen's allegation that Israel has constantly rejected and persecuted the prophets is not based on the citation of Amos 5.26, 27.

The last line of the quotation is identical with the LXX except for the last word. Where the LXX has Δαμασκοῦ, Stephen (Luke) has

Βαβυλῶνος. The reading of D* gig (e p), who put ἐπὶ τὰ μέρη in place of ἐπέκεινα, brings the meaning though not the wording of the text into closer agreement with the LXX, for *the district of Babylon is beyond Damascus*. This was a Western editor's way of solving a problem, for it is by no means clear why Luke should have substituted Babylon for Damascus (which the author of CD can relate to the history of the sect). Knox (*Hellenistic Elements* 14f.) explained the change in terms of rhetorical practice. 'The effect of this alteration is that this section of the speech is made to end not, as Amos does in the LXX, with the worst possible rhetorical ending, the end of a hexameter (ἐπέκεινα Δαμάσκου)), but with the best possible; for ἐπέκεινα Βαβυλῶνος gives a cretic with the second long syllable resolved and a trochee.' But was the author of (for example) 3.16 so concerned about rhetorical niceties? He may have thought to give a more accurate statement of the deportation to Assyria (which was beyond Babylon; StrB 2.682). He may have thought of the deportation (later than the time of Amos) to Babylon; or he may simply have been guilty of a lapse of memory.

44. A summary of OT material, mostly in LXX language though without direct quotation. ἡ σκηνὴ τοῦ μαρτυρίου (opposed to the σκηνή of Moloch, v. 43) is a regular LXX term for the Tabernacle, equivalent to both אהל עדות and אהל מועד. See Exod. 27.21 (the first reference) and many other passages. It is clear that Stephen thinks the Tabernacle preferable to the Temple; see below and cf. Heb. 8.1–5.

τοῖς πατράσιν ἡμῶν (ἡμῶν is omitted by P⁷⁴ 33 326 *pc*) are those of the Exodus. For διετάξατο cf. διαταγή in v. 53; the verb is not used in the LXX for this charge to Moses, but see Exod. 25.1 (ἐλάλησεν κύριος πρὸς Μωυσῆν), 9 (ποιήσεις μοι κατὰ πάντα, ὅσα ἐγώ σοι δεικνύω ἐν τῷ ὄρει, τὸ παράδειγμα τῆς σκηνῆς ... οὕτω ποιήσεις), 40 (ὅρα ποιήσεις κατὰ τὸν τύπον τὸν δεδειγμένον σοι ἐν τῷ ὄρει). *He who spoke to Moses* is of course God. *A model to be imitated* is not the commonest meaning of τύπος (cf. v. 43), but see Plato, *Republic* 398b. There is a clear positive command to Moses to make a tent; an οἶκος (vv. 47, 49) is different.

45. οἱ πατέρες ἡμῶν are now the next generation of Israelite ancestors, those subsequent to Moses and contemporary with Joshua. κατάσχεσις occurs at v. 5: what Abraham was not allowed to receive was given to the Israelite settlers after the Exodus. διαδέχεσθαι means *to succeed to the possession of something* but here may have a weaker sense. 'I think διαδεξάμενοι, *simpliciter dictum*, may be taken adverbially for ἐκ διαδοχῆς, "in their turn". Cf. Herodotus 8.142.1: ὡς δὲ ἐπαύσατο λέγων Ἀλέξανδρος, διαδεξάμενοι ἔλεγον οἱ ἀπὸ Σπάρτης ἄγγελοι ...' (Field, ad loc.).

κατάσχεσις means *possession*, but ἐν τῇ κατασχέσει τῶν ἐθνῶν is obscure — at least, it is clear enough that Luke means that the Israelites took possession of that which formerly had been the property of the Gentiles, but it is not clear how his words can be given this sense. Again it is difficult to see how ἕως τῶν ἡμερῶν τοῦ Δαυίδ can be taken with ἔξωσεν (א* E 33 *pc* give this word the syllabic augment, ἐξέωσεν). It is no doubt true that the non-Israelite inhabitants of Canaan were not completely driven out till the time of David (if indeed the process was complete then). In view of vv. 46, 47 the meaning must be that the Tabernacle remained in use until the time of David. Thus the several parts of the verse become clear: Joshua's generation succeeded to that of Moses in the use of the Tabernacle; they also drove out the Gentile inhabitants of the land and thus took possession of what had been promised to Abraham; their use of the Tabernacle persisted to the time of David. This prepares for the next verses; but the sentence is by no means clearly written.

46. In the OT it is not said in so many words that David found favour before God (but cf. 2 Kdms 15.25, ἐὰν εὕρω χάριν ἐν ὀφθαλμοῖς κυρίου); passages such as 1 Kdms 16.12 (ἀγαθὸς ὁράσει κυρίῳ) are however equivalent.

ἠτήσατο εὑρεῖν. For the construction cf. 3.3 (ἠρώτα . . . λαβεῖν). The middle should be given its full force: *he asked for himself that he might find* (might have the privilege of finding). There is an allusion to Ps. 131 (132).5: ἕως οὗ εὕρω τόπον τῷ κυρίῳ, σκήνωμα τῷ θεῷ 'Ιακώβ. In the Psalm σκήνωμα renders משכנות; in the OT context we must think that it means *house* rather than *tent*. It is followed in the Psalm in Hebrew by the words לאביר יעקב, for the Strong One (i.e., God) of Jacob. This is followed by א^c A C E Ψ 𝔐 lat sy co, which read τῷ θεῷ 'Ιακώβ; this however is the easier reading, and that (τῷ οἴκῳ 'Ιακώβ) which is contained in P^74 א* B D H 049 *pc* sa^ms should probably be preferred — though Preuschen declares it to be Unsinn, and Weiser (187) prefers θεῷ. The difference between the two readings is not as great as is sometimes thought: a dwelling for the God of Jacob is undoubtedly a temple for him to dwell in, and a dwelling for the house of Jacob is a place that the house of Jacob may use as a temple, that is, it means a dwelling (for God) to be used as such by the house of Jacob. Cf. *Begs.* 4.81, also the long discussion in Metzger 351–353, and the references given there.

David's desire to build a house (οἶκος, בית) is expressed in 2 Sam. 7.2, cf. 7.5. His plan is at first approved by the Prophet Nathan (7.3), but later, on God's instructions, Nathan withdraws permission, adding however that David's son would build a house for God's name (αὐτὸς οἰκοδομήσει μοι οἶκον τῷ ὀνόματί μου; הוא יבנה־בית לשמי, 7.13; 7.4–17). In the course of Nathan's speech it is made clear (7.7) that God had never previously asked for or desired a permanent dwelling. This material is reproduced in 1 Chron. 17.1–15.

47. See on v. 46. So far we have a plain statement of fact: David asked leave to build a dwelling-place; Solomon actually built a house. This is in agreement with the OT account; neither praise nor blame for Solomon's act is expressed. Blame may be already implied. Bruce (2.158) observes that the early Christians would take David's son, who was to build the house (2 Sam. 7.12), to be not Solomon but the Messiah. In providing an abode for God Solomon wrongfully anticipated the work of Christ; the οἶκος he provided was in contravention of the prophetic principle stated in v. 48.

'Templo antiquior est lex; lege, promissio' (Bengel, who evidently considers priority in time to be coincident with priority in importance).

οἰκοδόμησεν. This first aorist indicative has no augment. The unaugmented form occurs in Ionic (Herodotus); In Attic only when οι is is followed by a vowel. For these statements, and for other examples of unaugmented verbs beginning with οι, see M. 2.191 and BDR § 67. 1 n. 1; these writers also suggest an explanation in terms of the pronunciation of οι and ω.

48. οὐχ ὁ ὕψιστος. The position of the negative 'may be altered to achieve emphasis, and in Acts 7.48 the position of οὐχ puts *the Most High* in relief' (M. 3.287); similarly BDR § 433.1 n. 1, with the provision, 'es ist doch wohl nicht gemeint, dass jemand anders darin wohnt.' *Begs.* 4.81, however, thinks it possible that Zahn may be right in thinking that it is implied that the gods of the heathen did dwell in temples. There was an obvious logical problem for anyone who wished to assert both that the heathen gods were so confined and that in fact they did not exist. The emphasis and the associated problem are lost in the reading ὁ δὲ ὕψιστος οὐ κατοικεῖ (D (syᵖ)).

In the LXX ὁ ὕψιστος, rendering עליון, is a common name, or description, of God (e.g. Gen. 14.18). The word is also used of Zeus (see LS 1910 s.v. 2), and was sometimes thought by the heathen a suitable term for the solitary Jewish deity; it may also have been used in syncretistic Jewish cults (see C. Roberts, T. C. Skeat, and A. D. Nock, 'The Gild of Zeus Hypsistos', *HThR* 29 (1936), 39–88; now also *ND* 1.25–9). In the present passage, of course, there is no question that the one supreme God of the OT is intended.

He does not dwell ἐν χειροποιήτοις. This word (rendering אליל) has in the LXX a uniformly bad sense and is connected with idolatry. Cf. also such passages as Isa. 2.8; Ps. 115.4 (113.12) (ἔργα χειρῶν ἀνθρώπων). To associate such language with the Temple must have been highly offensive in Jewish ears. It is possible that Stephen's word was not intended to carry this connotation, but it is in any case affirmed that God does not dwell in houses of human construction. To this belief there are Hellenistic parallels; see Betz (61). Preuschen quotes (Pseudo)Euripides, Frag. 1130 (Frag. 104, p. 989, ed. Dindorf): Ποῖος δ'ἀν οἶκος, τεκτόνων πλασθεὶς ὕπο, δέμας τὸ θεῖον περιβάλοι τοίχων πτυχαῖς; also among Christian writers Barnabas 4.11; 6.15f.; 16; Ignatius, *Philadelphians* 8.1; Justin, *Trypho* 22. The precise force of Stephen's words depends on the meaning assigned to the OT quotation with which it is supported (καθὼς ὁ προφήτης — Isaiah —λέγει), and on the meaning of ἀλλά with which the statement is introduced. This word must have some adversative force; the question is whether this is slight, so that v. 48 is little more than an expansion of v. 47 (Solomon built a house for God, but we must not think that God is confined to it), or strong, so that v. 48 contradicts v. 47 (Solomon built a house for God, but this was a complete misunderstanding of the nature of God and should not have been done). The latter is more probable. ἀλλά is most often used in correlation with a preceding negation, giving its positive counterpart (so BDR § 448.1); when, as here, negative and positive clauses are reversed in order the sense is often the same (so BDR § 448.2, giving Mt. 24.6; 1 Cor. 3.6; 6.11; 10.5, 23 as examples). We may say, Though Solomon built a house God does not dwell in such structures; there must be some correlation between οἶκος and χειροποίητα.

This verse states only what the OT (1 Kings 8.27) already knows; so Schneider (467). This is true; it is however significant that Stephen (Luke) here picks out not the many OT passages that glorify the Temple but some of the few that criticise it and gives a sharp summary of their content. As Conzelmann (50) observes, Jews could criticise the Temple (he cites Philo, *De Cherub.* 99ff., Josephus, *Ant.* 8. 107ff.; 2 Macc. 14.35), but usually in the end offer some defence of it, as in turn does Calvin (209). So far as the present passage is concerned Weiser (187, 'Bei Lukas ist die Kritik radikal und grundsätzlich gemeint . . . Gott nicht mehr im Tempel wohnt, sondern nur dort, wo der erhöhte Christus ist') and Pesch (257, 'Das Handgemachte ist dem Menschen verfügbar, Gott aber nicht. In der vorluk. noch nicht christianisierten Tradition war damit vielleicht vom Diasporajudentum die Möglichkeit der wahren Gottesverehrung (aufgrund der Tora) ohne den Tempel beansprucht') see a radical rejection of the Temple. But do they do justice to passages in Acts 1–5 where it appears that Christians continued to use the Temple, and to Paul's readiness (according to Acts — see 21.26) to do so? There must in fact have been in the first few decades a swing away from the Temple, and the Diaspora Judaism which seems to be represented in the speech attributed to Stephen may well have contributed to it. Delebecque (36) sums up Stephen's meaning: 'Donc Dieu n' habite pas le Temple.'

49, 50. The quotation is from Isa. 66.1, 2 and is given in very close agreement with the LXX. The first line is in precise agreement (unless we follow P⁷⁴ D* in reading μου instead of μοι). Cf. Ps. 11.4: that God reigns in glory in heaven is a common OT thought; it does not imply that he is inactive on earth, rather the contrary — he is so great a king that he can do whatever he pleases. Thus the second line (also identical with the LXX unless we follow B h in reading καὶ ἡ instead of ἡ δέ) establishes the connection between heaven and earth. Earth may in comparison with heaven serve a humbler purpose, but it is where God puts his feet. In the third line ποῖον οἶκον οἰκοδομήσετέ μοι is taken directly from Isaiah; the words λέγει κύριος occur not at this point but at the beginning of Isa. 66.1 and again half way through 66.2. The fourth line again is identical with the LXX except that for τίς the LXX has ποῖος (which is read here by D h). In place of the rhetorical question of the fifth line the LXX has the equivalent statement πάντα γὰρ ταῦτα ἐποίησεν ἡ χείρ μου. P⁷⁴ A C D E *pm* h have the LXX order, πάντα ταῦτα. There is no significant difference in the Hebrew. Most OT scholars are now agreed that the prophecy did not originally constitute an attack on the Temple; see however De Vaux (*Institutions* 330): 'The question asked in 1 Kings 8.27 here receives a different answer from the one in Deuteronomy: Yahweh has no need of any Temple.' It seems probable that this is how Stephen (Luke) understood Isaiah (cf. Acts 17.24f.). It is not adequate to say, with Schneider (468), that Stephen attacks not the Temple but a misunderstanding of the Temple.

T. C. G. Thornton (*JTS* 25 (1974), 432–4) has drawn attention to an Aramaic midrash contained in two MSS of the Targum of Jonathan on Isaiah (see also Stenning 226f.). In this passage Isaiah threatens the people that if they are proud before God because of the house built by Solomon and put their trust in it God will send Nebuchadrezzar to destroy it. Manasseh is filled with anger; Isaiah runs away and a carob tree opens its mouth to swallow him; Manasseh cuts down the tree and Isaiah's blood flows like water. Thornton points out that if this interpretation was current in the first century it would facilitate the transition of thought to v. 52 (the persecution and killing of prophets) and would illuminate the charge against Stephen, who has (it is claimed) threatened the destruction of the Temple. Unfortunately it is impossible to establish the date of the midrash; the MSS that contain it date from the 12th and 13th centuries, though the midrash itself may of course be very much older. At more periods of their history than one the Jews have been obliged to learn to do without a Temple, and for many, perhaps most, of the Jews of the Diaspora this was the condition of their whole life. Stephen appears to have denied, as Jeremiah (7.21–26) had done before him, that God required the sacrificial worship that was the Temple's *raison d'être*, and he (or Luke) may have thought it inconsistent with the majesty of God. Bede comments: Non aureus utique vel marmoreus terrestris habitaculi locus, sed ille quem propheta subnectit: super quem autem requiescit spiritus meus nisi super humilem et quietum et trementem sermones meos?

51. Stephen's apostrophe of Israel is expressed in OT language, but it is not a quotation of any OT passage. For σκληροτράχηλος see e.g. Exod. 33.3; for ἀπερίτμητοι καρδίαις see e.g. Lev. 26.41; for ἀπερίτμητοι τοῖς ὠσίν see Jer. 6.10. *Begs.* 4.82 quotes Deut. 10.16, περιτεμεῖσθε τὴν σκληροκαρδίαν ὑμῶν καὶ τὸν τράχηλον ὑμῶν οὐ σκληρυνεῖτε. Cf. Jer. 4.4; also Jubilees 1.7 (I know their rebellion and their stiff neck), 23 (I shall circumcise the foreskin of their heart . . . and I shall create in them a holy spirit); 1QS 5.5 (They shall circumcise the foreskin of the inclination (יצר)); 1QpHab 11.13 (He did not circumcise the foreskin of his heart). Stephen claims that his hearers are, as their ancestors have been, stubborn and disobedient, as good as (uncircumcised) heathen, not in their flesh but in readiness to hear and accept God's word. He is less concerned here to bring out the positive significance of Moses and of Jesus than to accuse the Jews (Schmithals 72).

It is surprising to read καρδίαις (anarthrous) immediately before τοῖς ὠσίν. This probably accounts for the variants: ταῖς καρδίαις ὑμῶν, ℵ (Ψ) 945 (1175) 1739 1891 *pc*; καρδίας, B; τῇ καρδίᾳ, E 𝔐 it vg^mss sy^p Lcf GrNy. Moule (*IB* 114) notes but does not explain this. Knox (*Hellenistic Elements* 15) notes the harsh consonants in vv. 51–56 as expressing Stephen's anger and emotion. But Stephen will not have spoken Greek in the Council, so that the consonants, if they show anything, show how well Luke entered into the occasion.

τῷ πνεύματι τῷ ἁγίῳ ἀντιπίπτετε. Cf. Isa. 63.10 (ἠπείθησαν καὶ παρώξυναν (מרו ועצבו) τὸ πνεῦμα τὸ ἅγιον αὐτοῦ. The verb is not common; see Num. 27.14. Used by Plutarch, *Theseus* 28 (13) it seems to mean *contradict*. Braun (1.165) observes that nothing in the present text corresponds to the (dualistic) Qumran notion of two spirits.

ὡς οἱ πατέρες ὑμῶν: evidence has been given in the speech and is repeated and amplified in v. 52ab. καὶ ὑμεῖς: this is implied in the prosecution of Stephen but is given its chief point in v. 52c. According to Stephen, the history of Israel consists of messages (*living oracles*, v. 38) addressed by God to his people, and of his people's disobedience and recalcitrance.

52. Stephen's words can only be described as an exaggeration, pardonable in the circumstances in which he is said to be speaking. The OT does not provide evidence of the (implied) persecution of all the prophets, or their killing. *Begs.* 4.82 gives an interesting note on the development of apocryphal legends provoked by this verse and designed to support it. The reference given here to T. Schermann's edition of the *Prophetarum vitae fabulosae* (Bibl. Teubneriana, 1907) and his 'Propheten- und Apostellegenden' in *TU* 31.3 (1907) is developed by G. D. Kilpatrick (*JTS* 46 (1945) 136–45), who suggests that 'the original of the phrase [containing the word ἔλευσις] is to be found in the Greek form of the cycle of Jewish pseudepigrapha ascribed to the prophets' (142). He thinks that the word ἔλευσις was used for the coming of the Messiah, παρουσία for the coming of God; Paul used the latter word for the coming of the Messiah Jesus who was thus put on a level with God. On this however see J. Dupont, Σὺν Χριστῷ (1952), 55–9.

τοὺς προκαταγγείλαντας. D prefixes αὐτούς; for the possibility that this proleptic pronoun may be a Semitism see Black (*AA* 71), Wilcox (128, 130).

τοῦ δικαίου. For this description of Jesus, and the question whether it is a title — the Righteous One — see on 3.14. Here at least it is hard to avoid the conclusion that it is a title.

'νῦν, *nunc*) *Nunc* respondet voculae *prae* in *praenunciantes*' (Bengel).

προδότης occurs in the NT only here and at Lk. 6.16 (of Judas); 2 Tim. 3.4. προδιδόναι is a normal Greek word for *to betray* but occurs only at Rom. 11.35, in a different sense; the NT uses παραδιδόναι for this purpose (but does not have παραδότης). See 3.13: the Jews handed Jesus over to Pilate; such an action towards their fellow countryman could be described as betrayal. In this sense they were also his murderers, φονεῖς. Cf. 2.23, ἀνείλατε.

53. Those who thus proved to be betrayers and murderers were the more culpable in that they had received the highest privileges. They had received the Law εἰς διαταγὰς ἀγγέλων. Cf. v. 38 (the angel who spoke to Moses on Mount Sinai); Gal. 3.19; Heb. 2.2. In these passages the Pauline statement in Gal. 3.19 stands alone in that there the participation of angels in the giving of the Law serves as a relative disparagement. It is questionable whether Beyer (*Syntax* 1.269) is justified in describing the sentence as an example of conditional parataxis.

In this verse οἵτινες is not simply equivalent to οἵ but is correctly used in a qualitative sense: . . . *people who* . . . (BDR § 293. 2b). εἰς is equivalent to the instrumental use of ἐν (= ἐν διαταγαῖς). So BDR § 206. 1; also Zerwick § 101 (mandantibus angelis). Torrey (33) regards εἰς as a rendering of ל which sometimes means *according to, by*: he cites Ps. 119.91 (למשפטיך, according to thy ordinances) and translates Luke's Greek into the Aramaic לפוקדני מלאכין, by the ordering of angels). M. 2.463 notes this without comment, but the hypothesis of translation is quite unnecessary.

For διαταγή Deissmann (*DLAE* 86 (89f.)) quotes Ruphus of Ephesus (physician, c. AD 100) in *Collectanea Medicinalia* of

Oribasius (ed. Bussemaker and Darenberg I. 544.6f.): μόνον δὲ χρὴ τῇ ἐφεξῆς διαταγῇ τὸ σῶμα ἀνακομίζειν εἰς τὴν ἰδίαν τάξιν (it is only necessary by a subsequent *ordered way of living* to bring back the body into proper order), and Vettius Valens, *Catalogus Codicum Astrologorum Graecorum* V. 2. p. 51.16: κατὰ τὴν τοῦ κελεύοντος διαταγήν. These passages (which certainly do not prove that the author of Acts was a medical man) add little or nothing to the basic sense of *command, ordinance*. For the word in the sense of imperial authorization see *I.Eph.* 7.2.3511 (=*ND* 4.129).

The participation of angels in the giving of the Law was believed in Judaism. It is already expressed in Deut. 33.2 (ἐκ δεξιῶν αὐτοῦ ἄγγελοι μετ' αὐτοῦ; the Hebrew is different. Many details are given in StrB 3.554–6; it suffices to quote Pesiq R 21 (103b): Why did they (the angels) descend (at the giving of the Law)? R. Ḥiyya b. Rabba said, In honour of the Torah; R. Ḥiyya b. Jose said, In honour of Israel. There can be no doubt that most Jews would have accepted both explanations, and that they would have seen in them added obligation to observe the Law obediently. For Qumran, see CD 5.18 (ביד שר האורים); but Braun, 1.166, rightly points out that other Jewish material is closer to Stephen than this, 'denn der "Lichterfürst" von CD 5.18 gehört in einen Dualismus, der den einfachen "Engeln" der Acta-Stelle und der üblichen jüdischen Texte fernliegt'. The ἄγγελοι of Josephus, *Ant.* 15.136 may be human messengers.

For φυλάσσειν in the sense of observing obediently cf. Lk. 11.28; 18.21; Acts 16.4; 21.24. Elsewhere its meaning is different. The failure of Israel to observe the Law has been documented in the speech and forms its main content; it has reached its climax in the killing of Jesus. Luke does not indicate whether Stephen had finished his speech or was interrupted. It seems probable (see pp. 334–40) that the reference to Jesus was added as a new climax for a Hellenistic Jewish sermon intended to expose the errors of the people and summon them to repentance.

19. STEPHEN'S MARTYRDOM 7.54–8.1a

(54) As they listened to these things they were cut to the quick and gnashed their teeth against him. (55) But he, full of the Holy Spirit, gazed into heaven and saw the glory of God, and Jesus standing at God's right hand. (56) He said, 'Look, I see the heavens opened, and the Son of man standing at God's right hand.' (57) They shouted with a loud voice, stopped their ears, and together rushed at him. (58) They threw him out of the city and stoned him; and the witnesses laid down their clothes at the feet of a young man called Saul. (59) And they stoned Stephen, as he called upon the Lord,[1] and said, 'Lord Jesus, receive my spirit.' (60) He knelt down and cried with a loud voice, 'Lord, do not let this sin stand against them.' And when he had said this he fell asleep.

(1) Saul was in full agreement with his killing.

Bibliography

R. E. Bailey, *ZNW* 55 (1964), 161–7.

C. K. Barrett, *FS* Haenchen, 32–8.

J. Bihler, as in (17).

M. E. Boismard, as in (17).

P. Doble, *NTS* 31 (1985), 68–84.

S. Dockx, *Bib* 55 (1974), 65–73.

W. Foerster, as in (16).

O. Glombitza, as in (16).

G. D. Kilpatrick, *ThZ* 21 (1965), 209.

G. D. Kilpatrick, *ThZ* 34 (1978), 232.

F. Lentzen-Deis, *Bib* 50 (1969), 301–27.

O. Michel, *ZNW* 35 (1936), 285–90.

F. Mussner, as in (17).

H. P. Owen, *NTS* 1 (1955), 224–6.

R. Pesch, *Bibel u. Leben* (1965), 92–107, 170–83.

M. Sabbe, Kremer *Actes*, 241–79.

G. N. Stanton, as in (16).

Some of the works listed for paragraphs 16, 17, 18, 20 are relevant here too.

---

[1]The Lord is implied but not contained in the Greek.

Commentary

It was pointed out above (pp. 319–22) that there was some reason for thinking that in the paragraph 6.8–15 two sources had been combined, and that a similar phenomenon was to be found in the paragraph which (the speech intervening) went on to describe Stephen's death. The simplest form of this view is that 6.9–11; 7.54–58a constitute a 'lynching' source (which represented Stephen as the victim of a popular move), 6.12–14; 7.58b–60 a 'trial' source (in which his death was the outcome of judicial procedure). It is important to note that just as in ch. 6 the verb ἀκηκόαμεν is repeated (vv. 11, 14; cf. also ὑπέβαλον in v. 11, ἔστησαν in v. 13) so ἐλιθοβόλουν is repeated in ch. 7 (vv. 58a, 59). The first attack is marked by a mad rush upon Stephen (ὥρμησαν, v. 57), the second by the presence of witnesses (v. 58b), who had presumably taken part in the trial. This separation of two sources is fundamentally sound, but the process by which the paragraph reached its present form is more complicated than the simple juxtaposition of two pieces. This is borne out by the variety of the attempts that have been made to analyse it. A full account of these is given by Pesch (261). Schneider (471) thinks that the editor added only parallels with the story of Jesus and the references to Saul. Weiser (190f.) on the other hand takes almost the whole to be redactional. 'Vers 58a dürfte zusammen mit 8.2 den vorluk Lynchbericht ausmachen und mit 6.9, 11, 12 überliefert worden sein.' *Begs.* 4.85 thinks that Luke intends to make the point that Stephen was not legally condemned but lynched. Conzelmann (52f., cf. Lüdemann 97f.) takes an opposite view, finding only one source, which 'berichtete von Person und Tätigkeit des Stephanus (6.8–10), einem Tumult (6.11a, 12), der Steinigung, (einem letzten Wort?), der Bestattung . . . Lk. übermalte, indem er als Rahmen eine Verhandlung vor dem Synhedrion entwurf, das Bild des Märtyrers ins Typische erhob, Saulus einführte und die Geschichte im Zusammenhang eines umfassenden Geschichtsablaufes zum Wendepunkt im Verhältnis der Kirche zum Judentum machte.' This might do, were it not for the repeated words noted above, but it is certainly correct to see Luke's hand in the paragraph as it stands, in a number of characteristic expressions (see the notes) as well as in some major features of the story. If, as seems probable, Luke possessed two accounts of Stephen (Stählin 115 compares the two accounts of the death of James, in Josephus, *Ant.* 20.200 and in Eusebius, *H.E.* 2.23.11–18 (Hegesippus)), he has not been content to put pieces of them side by side. He has introduced Saul (7.58; 8.1), and in so doing shows his ignorance of the proper procedure by which stoning as a legally imposed punishment (as distinct from stone-throwing by a mob) was carried out (see the note on 7.58; it may be that the source misled him by referring to witnesses, and perhaps also to the removing of clothes). He has also introduced allusions which bind the story of dying Stephen to the story of the trial and crucifixion of Jesus. Stephen's vision of the Son of man standing at the right hand of God recalls Lk. 22.69; his prayer, Receive my spirit, recalls 23.46; his intercession for his murderers, 23.34 (if the long text is read). The inclusion of references to Saul may show the effect if not of Acts 22.20 (note συνευδοκῶν) at least of the tradition on which Luke based that verse.

That there should have been two accounts of the attack on Stephen and of his death bears witness to the impression made by the event on the church's memory. This is the more readily understandable if it did indeed make a deep impression on Saul. Acts 22.20 suggests this, but it is not confirmed by any reference in the epistles, even in those passages (1 Cor. 15.9; Gal. 1.15) in which Paul speaks of himself as having persecuted the church. It must be recalled that the present paragraph is part of Luke's account of the contribution of the group led by Stephen to the extension of the Gospel into the Gentile world. In part at least (see pp. 54f.) this is based upon Antiochene tradition, into which Luke was concerned to integrate the story of Saul (Paul). He was concerned also (see p. 305) to show that this evangelistic move was rooted in original Jerusalem Christianity, though his narrative shows signs of disagreement, which, if he does not cover them up, he does nothing to develop. But just as Stephen's speech shows an at least partially negative attitude to Judaism, so his martyrdom represents the No of Judaism to the Gospel. Perhaps this was a No that had to be spoken before the Gospel could be taken outside the limits within which it was born (cf. not only 13.46; 18.6; 28.28 but also Rom. 9–11), and was (after the resurrection of Jesus, and indeed as part of this) the supreme example of the power of God, already attested in Stephen's account of Joseph and Moses, to bring good out of evil. Pesch 266 rightly points out that this passage forms (even arithmetically) the mid-point of Acts 1–12, the first part of the book, which opens the way to the wider mission recounted in chs. 13–28. Stephen's resistance to the authorities and his intercession for Israel 'bestimmen aber die ganze Denkweise des Buchs. Daher ist es für Lukas völlig ausgeschlossen, dass er die Religion Israels angreifen oder herabsetzen könnte' (Schlatter, *Theologie der Apostel*, 452).

The question of the historicity of the event, and the question, assuming its historicity, of its date, may be raised in the light of Jn 18.31, according to which the Jewish court had under the Roman administration no authority to pass, or at least to execute, sentence of death. The correctness of John's statement is disputed (*St John* 533–5); if it is correct the court cannot have ordered and carried out the stoning of Stephen. One answer that has been given to the question that arises is that the event may have taken place in the interregnum between the recall of Pilate and the arrival of his successor. See *NS* 1.382f. and cf. Josephus, *Ant.* 18. 89f., 237. The matter is not clear; it is not even clear whether Pilate was succeeded by Marcellus, as no more than acting procurator until the arrival of Marullus, or whether these two names denote the same person. E. M. Smallwood (*JJS* 5 (1954), 12–21) is probably right in the view that Pilate left Judaea at the very end of 36 or early in 37. Marullus was appointed by the emperor Gaius, it seems (Josephus, *Ant.* 18.237) shortly after the death of Tiberius (16 March 37). The interregnum was thus very short. The proceedings against Stephen could have been pushed through quickly, but it does not seem probable that they should be explained in this way. (a) They make the conversion of Saul (9.1–18) impossibly late (unless, with S. Dockx, *Bib.* 55(1974), 65–73, we are prepared to take the improbable view that he was converted before the death of Stephen). (b) If Stephen died at the hands not of justice but of a mob no such explanation is called for.

The bare fact of the martyrdom is, it seems, doubly attested, but the two accounts are not harmonious, and some at least of the details are due to Luke.

54. Listening to Stephen's speech provoked the hearers to greater rage. διαπρίεσθαι occurs in the NT only here and at 5.33, where there is nothing corresponding to ταῖς καρδίαις, though it is clear that the same metaphorical sense, denoting extreme anger, is intended. Metaphorical use of the verb (literally, *to saw through*) is not common. Strangely, in view of the present context, the verb is used, in the active, with τοὺς ὀδόντας as object (Lucian, *Calumniae* 24); again, the meaning is anger. Contrast 2.37, where κατενύγησαν is used to describe a completely different reaction. The inward reaction (ταῖς καρδίαις) is expressed outwardly, ἔβρυχον (the Attic spelling is with κ, not χ) τοὺς ὀδόντας. βρύχ(κ)ειν alone means *to eat greedily, to gobble*; with *teeth* as object it presumably means to make a gobbling noise, but without food. Cf. Ps. 35 (34).16 (ἔβρυξαν ἐπ'ἐμὲ τοὺς ὀδόντας αὐτῶν); 37 (36).12. Cf. however Plutarch, *Pericles* 33 (170), quoting Hermippus.

Both verbs, διεπρίοντο and ἔβρυχον, are imperfects, presumably inceptive: as they listened they began to feel (increasingly) angry and to gnash their teeth against Stephen.

55. Stephen was chosen as one of the Seven because he was *full of Spirit and wisdom* (6.3, 5), and as preacher and controversialist *he spoke in the Spirit* (6.10). Luke knows however that Christians are given special help by the Holy Spirit in times of special need (see e.g. 4.8, and the note). It is the Spirit that enables Stephen to see a vision of heaven and to face death. The vision may be linked with Stephen's angelic appearance (6.15; see Dibelius 168). Visions are characteristic of martyrdoms (Schille 188), but Weiser (192) rightly says that the point of both the vision and the bestowal of the Spirit is to show that 'Gott ist auf seiten des Stephanus, nicht seiner Gegner'. For ἀτενίσας εἰς τὸν οὐρανόν cf. 1.10. The expression is Lucan, and may arise from Luke's casting into narrative form what he deduced from a saying ascribed in tradition to Stephen and contained in v. 56. *Jesus* would then be Luke's clarification of *the Son of man* (see Rowland, *Heaven* 369; also Schneider 473). Haenchen (286) thinks that the explanation reflects the separate use of the Third Gospel and Acts; readers of Acts would not have read the earlier book and therefore would not know that the Son of man was Jesus. Le Déaut (*Nuit Pascale* 140f.) notes that Stephen's vision is similar to that ascribed to Isaac at the time of the Aqedah (cf. also Ascension of Isaiah 5.7; Assumption of Moses 10.3). Targum Pseudo-Jonathan on Gen. 27.1 (Isaac's eyes were dim so that he could not see) explains, 'When his father bound him he saw the throne of glory, and from that moment his eyes began to become dim'. Bereshith R. on Gen. 27.1 (65; 138a) contains the same tradition (הבים בשכינה). Kosmala (275 n. 11; cf. Wilson, *Gentiles* 136) suggests that the sharp reaction of the orthodox Sanhedrin to Stephen was caused, or at least augmented, by his claim to have seen the glory of God (practically equivalent to God himself). Rowland (369) replies that it is Stephen's speech, ending at 7.53, that inflames the hearers. It does however seem impossible altogether to separate this passage from the question, which gave rise to much dispute in Judaism, and between Jews and Christians, whether there is anyone who may share the throne of God. Cf. 1QS 11.6f. (My eyes have gazed on that which is eternal, on wisdom concealed from men, on knowledge and wise design (hidden) from the sons of men; on a fountain of righteousness and on a storehouse of power, on a spring of glory (hidden) from the assembly of flesh — Vermes). Luke however does not say that Jesus (or in v. 56 the Son of man) shares the throne of glory (of God). Stephen saw the glory of God; Jesus (the Son of man) was standing at the right hand of God — standing, not sitting on a throne. For the significance of this see on v. 56; and cf. 3 Enoch 16.3–5 (Aḥer (Elisha b. Abuya) saw Metatron sitting on a great throne and said, There are indeed two powers in heaven. Then, at the command of the Holy One, the Prince struck Metatron with sixty lashes of fire and *made him stand to his feet*). Jesus is already standing. For *the right hand of God* cf. 2.34 (= Ps. 110.1), and see the note on v. 56. See R. Pesch, *Bibel und Leben*, 1965, 92–107, 170–83.

It would be mistaken to lay too much stress on the Christological significance of the vision; its effect is to confirm what Stephen has already said (see Ellis, quoted by Maddox 103).

In this verse οὐρανός is used in the singular, in v. 56 in the plural. Schneider 474 explains the difference by the fact that v. 55 simply points out the direction of Stephen's gaze, whereas v. 56 envisages different parts of heaven.

56. In this verse also the language is Lucan (θεωρεῖν: cf. especially Lk. 10.18; 24.37; Acts 9.7; 10.11; διανοίγειν, Lk.-Acts, seven times, rest of NT, once), so that if Luke is drawing on tradition he may well have rewritten it. Weiser (193) however, thinks that the verse is based on Lk. 22.69. Cf. *IG* 3816 (=*ND* 4.70) l.2,οὐρανὸν ἀνθρώποις εἶδον ἀνοιγόμενον.

Here only outside the gospels does ὁ υἱὸς τοῦ ἀνθρώπου (with the articles) occur in the NT. It is true that instead of ἀνθρώπου, θεοῦ is read by P⁷⁴ᵛⁱᵈ 614 boᵐˢˢ, and that this reading is defended by G. D. Kilpatrick (*ThZ* 21 (1965), 209; 34 (1978), 232), but it seems impossible to accept it. Here only, and in v. 55, is Jesus, the Son of man (Messiah) said to stand, rather than sit, at the right hand of God; most NT passages are affected by Ps. 110.1. Luke was certainly not unfamiliar with the term *Son of man*; it occurs 26 (25) times in the gospel, and it is there that its meaning must be evaluated. Here, as in 1 Enoch, the Son of man appears as a heavenly being, ready to perform eschatological functions; and here he is identified with the risen and ascended Jesus (as in 1 Enoch he is identified with the ascended Enoch). The fact that he is standing has been variously interpreted. (1) C. Colpe (in *TWNT* 8.466f.) suggests that a Samaritan predicate (קים) not of the Messiah but of God is here applied to the Son of man. There is little to be said for this suggestion. (2) A. Richardson (*Theology* 200) thinks that the Son of man is standing to minister as priest in the heavenly Temple. (3) Marshall (149) takes the significance of the Son of man to be that he is one who has suffered and been vindicated; he rises to plead Stephen's cause and to welcome him; cf. (5) and (7) below. (4) Lowther Clarke (*DH* 30) says that the Son of man is rising to help Stephen; so also Page (129), quoting Gregory the Great, 'Stephanus stantem vidit quem adiutorem habuit'. (5) Stauffer (*Theologie* n. 446) believes that the Son of man is standing in order to intercede for Stephen; so also Pesch (264), and Schneider (475; referring to the promise that those who confess Jesus before men will be acknowledged by the Son of man). (6) Cullmann (*Christologie* 160, 188f.) thinks that the Son of man is standing not as himself the judge but as witness in the judgment, appearing for Stephen and against his accusers and murderers; he ascribes this use of Son of man not to Luke but to the Hellenist group which Stephen represents. A somewhat similar view is taken by C. F. D. Moule (*Origin*, 17; *Phenomenon*, 60, 90f.), with the added point that the significance of the title Son of man lies in the martyrdom context in which it is used. (7) According to Weiser (194) the Son of man has risen in response to Stephen's accusation of the people; but Stephen is in fact seeking forgiveness for his opponents

(v. 60). (8) Tödt (*Menschensohn* 274–6) thinks that the Son of man stands as do the angels in the heavenly court. (9) According to Stählin 113 the Son of man is standing in order to welcome Stephen into heaven; *Begs.* 4.84 takes a similar view and works out its implications at greater length. Stephen is proceeding to heaven immediately on his death; cf. Lk. 23.43, Today shalt thou be with me in Paradise. (10) Somewhat similarly Bauernfeind (120) thinks that the Son of man welcomes Stephen, but this means that Stephen is now experiencing what others will experience only at the end, at the day of the Lord. (11) Again somewhat similarly Kümmel inclines to the view that the Son of man is standing because he is about to come — to the martyr at the time of his death as at the end he will come to all men. If this is correct (and, in Kümmel's view, in any case) we should have in this verse not a piece of early community tradition but Luke's own writing. Similarly Barrett (*FS Haenchen* 32–8); Wilson (*Gentiles* 77f.) agrees.

Bede asks why the term Son of man is used rather than Son of God, and answers, It will encourage the martyr that 'deus homo crucifixus apparet coronatus in caelo'. Again however it would be a mistake to make too much of the Christological implications of the verse. The main point is that Stephen in his dispute with the Jewish authorities is proved right by God himself.

57. The council had been angered by the speech; now (whether or not they saw in Stephen's vision a threat to the unity of God) they would hear no more. But can the subject (οἱ κράξαντες . . .συνέσχον . . . ὥρμησαν) be the members of the council? Not according to h (tunc populus exclamavit voce magna et continuerunt aures suas, et inruerunt pariter omnes in eum), which may (*Begs.* 4.84) represent the original form of the Western text. Certainly the proceedings are not those of a reputable court. For the suggestion that Luke is here moving from a source that described a trial followed by a legally conducted execution to a source that described a spontaneous popular lynching see pp. 380–2. συνέσχον τὰ ὦτα αὐτῶν could follow immediately upon 7.53; it would be wrong to suppose that it must have done so. For ὁρμᾶν see 19.29 (and cf. 14.5,ὁρμή). ὁμοθυμαδόν is a Lucan word: ten times in Acts, in the rest of the NT only Rom. 15.6. φωνὴ μεγάλη occurs frequently in the NT; its frequency probably owes something to the OT גָּדוֹל קוֹל, but is not un-Greek (cf.μεγαλοφωνία).

58. ἐλιθοβόλουν. The same part of the same verb is used in v. 59; the same verb is used at 14.5. It occurs also at Lk. 13.34 (=Mt. 23.37); Mt. 21.35; Heb. 12.20. The verb λιθάζειν is used at Acts 5.26; 14.19; and at Jn 8.5; 10.31, 32, 33; 11.8; 2 Cor. 11.25; Heb. 11.37. It does not seem possible to establish any difference between the two words, or in the word, not used in the NT, (κατα)λεύειν. In any case only one word is used in the present paragraph, so that for the purpose of analysis it would be futile to argue that one means *to pelt with stones*, the other to carry out the judicial method of execution by stoning. This is described in some detail in Sanhedrin 6.1–4. The place of stoning was far from the court. The person to be stoned was stripped and thrown down from a height at least twice that of man. This might suffice. If he still lived a witness took a stone and dropped it on his heart. If he still lived he was stoned by all Israel. Nothing in Luke's account, except the ἐκβαλόντες ἔξω τῆς πόλεως, corresponds to this description. For example, in this verse the witnesses take off their clothes (ἀπέθεντο τὰ ἱμάτια αὐτῶν). In Sanhedrin it is the victim who is stripped; the witnesses do not have the strenuous task of throwing a large number of stones and have no need to remove their clothes. See the introduction to this paragraph (pp. 380–2). So far as lynching rather than execution is in mind Stählin's argument (114) that stoning proves that the charge against Stephen was blasphemy, arising not out of the speech but v. 56, loses force.

The introduction in the last words of this verse of a young man called Saul is a fine touch of Luke's dramatic instinct. It need not be said that much more will be heard of this young man; it would be wrong to anticipate here information that Luke will supply later. He is described as a νεανίας. In Philo, *De Cherubin* 114, the νεανίας falls between the πρωτογένειος (the youth with the first beard) and the τέλειος ἀνήρ. It does not occur frequently in the LXX but renders most often נַעַר, sometimes בָּחוּר. The former is too widely used to be helpful; the latter is most often a young man not yet married. These facts tell us little about Saul's age. Schmithals (74) thinks that Luke represents Saul as a young man in order to minimize his guilt. This is improbable in view of the fact that in 9.1f. he goes out of his way to underline it.

It is interesting to compare the two parts of the verse in respect of pronouns. In the first part Luke is content, as it were, to borrow αὐτόν from the preceding verse; no object is expressed for ἐκβαλόντες . . . ἐλιθοβόλουν. This is classical. In the second part there is an unnecessary pronoun αὐτῶν (B *pc*, ἑαυτῶν) with ἱμάτια (similarly in v. 57, τὰ ὦτα αὐτῶν). It would however be wrong to use this observation as more than slightly supportive of the belief that more than one source is being used, though it may confirm the view that v. 58b is an editorial insertion — designed according to Weiser 191 to give Saul a 'walking-on' role (Statistenrolle).

59. ἐλιθοβόλουν. See v. 58. Dibelius (207) notes the repetition of the word as an indication that v. 58b is an insertion.

ἐπικαλεῖν is a word characteristic of Acts (twenty times; rest of the NT, ten times). Elsewhere however it is used in the passive with a name (1.23; 4.36; 10.5, 18, 32; 11.13; 12.12, 25; (15.17)) or in the middle with an object (a divine person or name, or, in a legal context, the Emperor: 2.21; 9.14, 21; (15.17); 22.16; 25.11, 12, 25; 26.32; 28.19), except at 25.21, which is similar to the latter group. It is clear from what immediately follows that Stephen is invoking the Lord Jesus (though Page 129 recalls Bentley's conjecture that ΘΝ (θεόν) had fallen out after ON, at the end of Στέφανον), but the absolute use is not easy to parallel. Rom. 10.14 can scarcely be cited since there an object is implied in the relative; Ps. 4.2 is better, but here also the sentence comes near to providing an object (ἐν τῷ ἐπικαλεῖσθαί με εἰσήκουσεν . . . ὁ θεός).

For the use of κύριος with Jesus see on 2.36. Betz (122 n. 4) compares Lucian, *Peregrinus* 36, δαίμονες μητρῷοι καὶ πατρῷοι δέξασθέ με εὐμενεῖς) (at the moment of self-immolation). Cf. also Seneca, *Hercules Oetaeus* 1703f. (spiritum admitte hunc precor in astra), 1725f. Schille (190) is probably right in thinking that such Hellenistic prayers are not genuine analogies. The use of δέχεσθαι (as in Lucian) is to be noted, but Luke (or the tradition used) is closer to Lk. 23.46, though there the verb is different (παρατίθεμαι; variants παρατίθημι (D *al*),παραθήσομαι (L 𝔐)). It is apparently presupposed that the person has a πνεῦμα which survives the death of the body so that it may be entrusted to the divine protector. Whereas Jesus invokes the Father, Stephen invokes Jesus, whom he has seen at the right hand of God. Maddox 104 observes that Lk. 23.43, 46; Acts 7.59 demonstrate 'a small element of "individual eschatology" in Luke-Acts'. Cf. 3.21, with the reference to *ND* 3.50.

60. Stephen continues his prayer, of which presumably the first part was offered standing. Now he kneels. τιθέναι τὰ γόνατα is a Latinism (cf. e.g. Ovid, *Fasti* 2.438), genua ponere. It occurs also at 9.40; 20.36; 21.5; (Mk 15.19; Lk. 22.41). Other Latinisms in Acts noted by Moule (*IB* 192) are 17.9 (cum satis accepissent); 19.38 (fora (*or* coventus) aguntur).

φωνῇ μεγάλῃ. Cf. v. 57, but here especially Lk. 23.46.

κύριε presumably refers to Jesus, as in v. 59, though Bauernfeind (120) thinks that here it probably refers to God. Transitive tenses of ἵστημι are sometimes used in financial contexts (e.g. ὁ σταθεὶς τόκος, P. Grenf. 1.31.1), partly because the word (like the Hebrew שקל) also meant *to weigh*, and money was weighed. The Lord is thus asked not to allow *this sin* (of murder, whether by perverted justice or by lynching) to stand in the record, or balance sheet, against those who committed it. Alternatively (*Begs.* 4.86), ἵστημι may mean *to establish*, hence (when used positively and with sin as object) the opposite of *forgive* (as at 1 Macc. 13.38, 39; 15.5). However ἵστημι is taken the meaning is the same.

The closest parallel is the saying of Jesus recorded in Lk. 23.24, where however there is an important variant. The words πάτερ, ἄφες αὐτοῖς, οὐ γὰρ οἴδασιν τί ποιοῦσιν, are omitted by P⁷⁵ ℵᶜ B D* W Θ 0124 1241 *pc* a syˢ sa boᵖᵗ, a varied and formidable list. If the words did not originally stand in the gospel they may have been added on the basis of Acts 7.60. If they did, they may have been removed by those who thought the crucifixion an unforgivable sin. If they did not, the words attributed to Stephen were probably derived by Luke from tradition; if they did, Luke may have added their equivalent in Acts, basing his account of the first Christian martyr on the story of Jesus.

Calvin (221) notes that Stephen's prayer falls into two parts. 'In the first part, where he commends his spirit to Christ, he shows the firmness of his faith. In the second where he prays for his enemies he bears witness to his love for men. Since the complete perfection of our religion lies in these two directions we have, in the death of Stephen, a rare example of a man dying in a godly and holy way.'

ἐκοιμήθη. κοιμᾶσθαι (and κοίμησις) and καθεύδειν (but not in Acts) are used frequently in the NT as terms for death, mainly but not exclusively for the death of Christians; cf. 13.36 (David). The same image is used in the OT (e.g. 3 Kdms 2.10, also David) and in post-biblical Judaism, e.g. in the Villa Torlonia catacomb in Rome (*CIJ* I 55.340; conveniently in *ND* 1.115; see also Delling, *Studien* 41). For the theological significance of the words see Barth (*CD* 3.2.638f.). The usage is not exclusively biblical; see e.g. Homer, *Iliad* 11.241, κοιμήσατο χάλκεον ὕπνον — of death in battle.

1a. Saul: see v. 58. συνευδοκεῖν: cf. 22.20 (Lk. 11.48). Saul gave his approval — and continued to approve (up to 9.1, 2). So Haenchen (284) and Schneider (478), stressing perhaps somewhat too strongly the periphrastic imperfect used.

ἀναίρεσις (not death but *killing* — so already Field), here only in the NT, but ἀναιρεῖν is a Lucan word (Acts nineteen times; Lk. twice; rest of the NT three times). Like the reference to Saul in 7.58 this is probably Luke's own editorial work.

20. PERSECUTION 8.1b–3

(1) At that time[1] there arose a severe persecution against the church in Jerusalem, and all were dispersed through the districts of Judaea and Samaria, except the apostles. (2) Devout men buried Stephen, and made loud lamentation over him. (3) Saul violently attacked the church, and going into house after house and dragging off men and women handed them over to prison.

Bibliography

B. Dehandschutter, Kremer *Actes*, 541–6.

Commentary

Stählin (116) rightly observes that whereas in chs. 1–7 and again in 13-28 Luke follows a single thread of narrative, in 8–12 he combines four: the stories respectively of Paul, the unknown Hellenists, Philip, and Peter. This means that in the five chapters chronological sequence is obscure; also that this brief introductory passage lacks clarity. It is probably to be ascribed in its entirety to Luke's editorial work as he combines the various pieces of source and traditional material at his disposal. V. 2 is the conclusion of the story of Stephen. It could have been drawn from one of the sources Luke used, if so, probably from the lynching story (see pp. 380–2); but (as the word εὐλαβεῖς suggests) it was more probably contributed by Luke himself, who could not believe that Stephen's body was treated like that of a common criminal. It is however surprising that Luke should allow this verse to separate vv. 1b and 3, which must also be ascribed to him. One of his sources (see pp. 54–6) told him of the activities of οἱ διασπαρέντες (8.4; 11.19); it was necessary to prepare for this by saying that πάντες διεσπάρησαν. The addition that excepted the apostles from this dispersion was probably added in order to prepare for 9.27, perhaps also to guarantee 'die Kontinuität der Urgemeinde' (Haenchen 288). There were however not only apostles but disciples in Jerusalem (9.26): Luke's editorial work is not

---

[1]Literally, On that day.

watertight. It is not true that all were scattered; it will probably be correct to see here the scattering of a Hellenist group who were more obnoxious to the authorities than the Twelve. Saul's persecuting activity in v. 3 prepares the way for 9.1f. and for later references, 22.4, 19; 26.9–11.

To say that the three verses are all due to Luke's editing is not to deny them all historical value. We have Paul's own word (1 Cor. 15.9; Gal. 1.13, 23; Phil. 3.6; cf. 1 Tim. 1.13) for persecution at a very early period, and it is very probable that persecution led to the dispersion of the persecuted, and thereby to the propagation of the Gospel over a wider area. And 'der Übergang vom Martyriumsbericht zur Pauluslegende' (Haenchen 289) is a transition that undoubtedly happened, for so far as the *Pauluslegende* includes Paul's conversion and subsequent missionary activity it is undoubtedly in essence (though not in detail) correct. Roloff (129) points out that this short paragraph corresponds to the summary passages in the earlier chapters; like them it was composed by Luke, but based on traditional material.

1b. ἐν ἐκείνῃ τῇ ἡμέρᾳ, as at 2.41; Lk. 6.23; 10.12; 17.31. The plural is more common; the singular is no doubt intended to narrow down the period referred to (though not of course to twenty-four hours; cf. Gen. 15.18 and many other passages for the OT idiom). The specific time reference underlines the force of διωγμὸς μέγας; Luke means to imply that something now happened that had not happened previously (in chs. 4, 5); the apostles had had a brush or two with the authorities, but this was severe persecution, an attack ἐπὶ τὴν ἐκκλησίαν, upon the church. For the word ἐκκλησία see on 5.11; it occurs much less frequently in Acts than might be expected. So far as we know there was at this time no church except in Jerusalem; Luke may be emphasising this (the church — which of course was located in Jerusalem), or may possibly be writing out of his own chronological context (I mean the church in Jerusalem, not any of the others which we all know now exist).

Presumably as a result of the persecution, πάντες δὲ (variants πάντες, πάντες τε, καὶ πάντες are scantily supported, and δέ may have been omitted through haplography on account of its partial resemblance to the first syllable of the next word) διεσπάρησαν. The verb occurs only here and at the related verses 8.4; 11.19 (on which see the notes); the cognate noun occurs at Jn 7.35; James 1.1; 1 Pet. 1.1. διασπείρεσθαι is used of the dispersal of a group in Lucian, *Toxaris* 33; Josephus, *Ant.* 7.244; 12. 278. Persecution was one of the causes that had led to the Jewish Diaspora. The Christian dispersion was at this time limited to the districts of Judaea (immediately adjacent to Jerusalem) and Samaria (next to Judaea and under the same civil administration — see further on 1.8 and 8.5), and Dodd (*New Testament Studies*, 1953, 58) may be right in saying that at an early date Christians in these areas were regarded as non-resident members of ἡ ἐκκλησία, 'the church', i.e., the church in Jerusalem. χώρα is here taken to refer to political districts (regiones); so *Begs.* 4.87. BA 1773 gives the meaning *das flache Land*, but the use of the names seems to require the other sense.

Notwithstanding πάντες 'it is certain that they were not all scattered' (Calvin 225); so most interpreters, referring to 9.26f., 31; 11.22. Historically this is probably true; but see Wilson (*Gentiles* 137, and especially 142f.) who insists that Luke meant what he wrote. This is in fact underlined by the specific exception that Luke notes: πλὴν τῶν ἀποστόλων. Luke may be thinking of the fact that at 9.27 he is to say that Barnabas introduced Saul to the apostles in Jerusalem. In addition it is perhaps true that 'für den Verfasser ist es selbstverständlich, dass in Verfolgungszeiten der Gemeindeleiter seinen Posten nicht verlassen dürfe' (Preuschen 46). This had been said earlier in somewhat different terms: Calvin (225, they stayed because they were good pastors); Bengel (the apostles were in greater danger than others, 'neque tamen existimarunt, se debere prae ceteris securitati suae consulere. Pericula sustinere debent, qui majore gradu et mensura fidei sunt'). Cullman has several times drawn attention to this exception, drawing the conclusion that the apostles did not share the radical attitude, especially to the Temple, of the Hellenists (*V.u.A.* 238, 275; *Heil* 258; *Petrus* 37, 45; at *Petrus* 59 he deduces that it is unlikely that Peter founded the church at Antioch). All this may be true; Peter and others had made use of the Temple (2.46; 3.1, 11; 5.12, 21, 25, 42). In the NT πλήν is predominantly a Lucan word (Luke-Acts, nineteen times; Mt., five times; Mark, once; Paul, five times, Revelation, once). The figures favour but by no means prove the view that πλὴν τῶν ἀποστόλων is a Lucan addition; in fact (see above,) Luke is probably composing throughout this paragraph.

2. The verse interrupts the connection between vv. 1 and 3. The general sense of συνεκόμισαν is clear, but not the precise meaning: the body of Stephen was treated with proper respect. Mishnaic law prescribes limited funeral rites for executed criminals; see Sanhedrin 6.5, 6 (They used not to bury him in the burial-place of his fathers, but two burying-places were kept in readiness by the court, one for them that were beheaded or strangled, and one for them that were stoned or burnt. When the flesh had wasted away they gathered together the bones and buried them in their own place [the family tomb] . . . And they used not to make [open] lamentation but they went mourning, for mourning has place in the heart alone). That this procedure was not followed is in favour of the lynching rather than the trial story (see pp. 380–2). It is not certain however that the Mishnaic law was in force in the first half of the first century AD, nor if it was that Luke had it in mind. He may simply have believed that the martyr's body must have had decent burial.

κομίζειν seems to mean not actually *to bury* but *to carry out for burial*. In the compound verb συγκομίζειν the force of the compounded σύν may be (1) perfective; the burial (or cremation) is completed; (2) to suggest the collecting of more than one corpse; (3) to refer to those who jointly carry out the task (*to help in burying* or *cremating* — LS 1666). The last of these is not borne out by the passage cited by LS (Sophocles, *Ajax* 1048; see Campbell and Abbott's note ad loc.). (1) is supported by Plutarch, *Sulla* 38 (475), but not by the same writer's *Agesilaus* 19 (606), which suggests without clearly stating the collecting of bodies — whence it is evident that the word had more than one meaning, even in one author. Here (1) is as good as certain: the men in question completed the burial of Stephen — burial (rather than cremation), not because this is implied by the word but because it was the Jewish practice. If κοπετός (here only in the NT) means public lamentation (and with μέγας it must; cf. Abodah Zarah 18a, הספידוהו הספד גדול) in the manner described in Moed Katan 3.7–9 it was forbidden (see Sanhedrin 6.6, above) and must be regarded as a defiance of the authorities by Stephen's friends. Stählin (117) describes it as a protest. But the word (and the verse) may be Luke's insertion of what seemed a suitable close for his account of Stephen.

Wilcox (136f., 174) notes that ἐποίησαν κοπετόν is the 'lone Semitism' (Aramaism rather than Hebraism) in this small paragraph. It is however a Septuagintalism (e.g. Micah 1.8), though in the LXX κόπτεσθαι κοπετόν is more common.

Since the verse is probably to be regarded as Luke's own editorial work it is profitable to ask only what may have been in Luke's mind as he wrote ἄνδρες εὐλαβεῖς. The adjective occurs in the NT only at Lk. 2.25 (Simeon); Acts 2.5; 8.2; 22.12 (Ananias), the cognates εὐλάβεια and εὐλαβεῖσθαι only in Hebrews. Roloff (130) points out that Luke must be thinking of Jews, since he has just said that all the Christians (apart from the apostles) had left the city; Kosmala (296–8) adds that they cannot have been Pharisees because they were persecuted by the Pharisee Saul; v. 3 however does not say that Saul persecuted these men, and if he did persecute them it could have been because they were renegade Pharisees. The word seems to be one that Luke uses for 'good' Jews who if not already Christians are ready to be persuaded.

In this verse D has συγκομίσαντες . . . καὶ ἐποίησαν, un-Greek and resembling an Aramaic construction. Black (*AA* 69) thinks the reading primitive and evidence for Aramaic influence.

3. Luke completes the present reference to Saul, who is presumably the chief agent in the severe persecution of v. 1. Wettstein (504) gives very many references for λυμαίνεσθαι and there is an excellent note in *Begs.* 4.88. The word means *to ill-treat*, and can be used of both physical and mental ill-treatment; the context shows that the former is mainly in mind here. Philo uses it of the ill-treatment of Jews in *Leg. ad Gaium* 134 (statues of Gaius were set up in synagogues); see also P Lond. 1912.86 (the letter of Claudius to the Alexandrines: conveniently in H. I. Bell, *Jews and Christians in Egypt*, 1924, 25, 28, 36). It is to be noted that τὴν ἐκκλησίαν stands in close connection with the ἄνδρες εὐλαβεῖς of v. 2, but that there is no attempt to relate them to each other. κατά is used distributively, *from house to house*; but what were the οἶκοι? the private residences of Christians or their meeting-houses? The same question arises elsewhere: see 2.2, 46; 5.42; 20.20. The answer is that there is no difference. The Christian meeting-houses were the dwelling-houses of the wealthier Christians, to which others were invited.

σύρων: the word is used of violent personal constraint at 14.19; 17.6; elsewhere in the NT only at Jn 21.8; Rev. 12.4, in different senses. Cf. Epictetus 1.29.22 (σύρῃ εἰς τὸ δεσμωτήριον); at 4 Macc. 6.1 it is used of dragging a man off to torture. Cf. Plautus, *Poenulus* 788, obtorto collo ad praetorem trahor.

παραδιδόναι does not here suggest treachery, merely *handing over* from one to another. παραδιδόναι εἰς φυλακήν becomes in 22.19 φυλακίζων. Both men and women are dragged off to prison; they are equally members of the church, and equally offensive to the persecutor.

IV
THE GOSPEL REACHES SAMARIA
(8.4–40)

21. EVANGELIZATION OF SAMARIA: SIMON MAGUS 8.4–25

(4) So then those who had been dispersed went on their way, preaching the word as good news. (5) Philip went down to the[1] city of Samaria and proclaimed Christ to them. (6) With one accord the crowds paid attention to the things said by Philip as they listened and saw the signs that he performed. (7) For unclean spirits, crying with a loud voice, came out of many,[2] and many paralysed and lame people were cured; (8) and there was great joy in that city.

(9) A certain man, Simon by name, had for some time past been in the city practising as a magus and astounding the Samaritan nation, saying that he was someone great. (10) All of them, from the least to the greatest, paid attention to him, saying, 'This is the power of God called great.' (11) They paid attention to him because for a long time he had been astonishing them by his magical practices, (12) but when they believed Philip as he preached the good news about the kingdom of God and the name of Jesus Christ they were baptized, both men and women. (13) Simon himself also became a believer, and when he had been baptized he continued in Philip's company, and as he beheld the signs and mighty works that were done he was astonished.

(14) When the apostles in Jerusalem heard that Samaria had received the word of God they sent to them Peter and John, (15) who went down and prayed for them that they might receive the Holy Spirit, (16) for it had not yet fallen on any of them; they had only been baptized in the name of the Lord Jesus. (17) Then they laid their hands upon them and they received the Holy Spirit. (18) When Simon saw that the Spirit was given through the imposition of the apostles' hands he brought them money, (19) and said, 'Give me too this power, that anyone on whom I lay my hands may receive the Holy Spirit'. (20) So Peter said to him, 'May your money perish with you, because you thought to acquire God's gift by money. (21) You have no part or lot in this matter, for your heart is not straight in the sight of God. (22) Repent of this wickedness of yours, and beseech the Lord, if perhaps your intention may be forgiven, (23) for I see that you are full of bitter poison, bound by unrighteousness.' (24) Simon answered, 'Do you pray to the Lord on my behalf that none of the things you have spoken may happen to me.'

---

[1] Or, a; so *Begs., NEB, NJB*.
[2] This is not an exact translation of the Greek but seems to be what Luke intended.

(25) So they bore their testimony and spoke the word of the Lord and returned to Jerusalem; and they evangelized many villages of the Samaritans.

Bibliography

C. K. Barrett, Kremer *Actes*, 281–95.

R. Bergmeier, *ZNW* 77 (1986), 267–75.

K. Beyschlag, *ZThK* 68 (1971), 395–426.

T. L. Brodie, *Bib* 67 (1986), 41–67.

L. Cerfaux, *Rec.* 1.259–62.

R. J. Coggins, as in (18).

J. Coppens, as in (16).

J. D. M. Derrett, *ZNW* 73 (1982), 52–68.

M. Gourges, *RB* 93 (1986), 376–85.

W. Grundmann, *ZNW* 39 (1940), 110–37.

D. A. Koch, *ZNW* 77 (1986), 64–82.

G. Lüdemann, *NTS* 33 (1987), 420–6.

J. E. L. Oulton, *ExpT* 66 (1955), 236–40.

R. Pummer, *CBQ* 41 (1979), 98–117.

K. Rudolph, *ThR* 42 (1977), 279–359.

C. H. H. Scobie, as in (18) (*NTS* 19).

W. C. van Unnik, *ZNW* 58 (1967), 240–6.

H. Waitz, *ZNW* 5 (1904), 121–143; also 7 (1906), 340–55.

W. Wilkens, *ThZ* 23 (1967), 26–47.

R. McL. Wilson, Kremer, *Actes*, 485–91.

Commentary

This passage, though given in the form of a single connected story, nevertheless combines a number of themes that are important in Acts. Consideration of these may throw some — but not much — light on the sources and traditions used by Luke. Not much light, for Luke has not only imposed his own style on the material but has organized it into a straightforward narrative. This indeed is not a universal opinion; Weiser (199), for example, says, 'Der Aufbau stellt sich also recht kompliziert dar.' It is at least fairly clear that vv. 5–13, in which Philip is the central Christian character, and vv. 14–24, in which nothing is heard of him and the apostles Peter and John occupy the centre of the stage, must originally have been distinct.

Verse 4 is almost certainly Luke's own editorial link, based on and

pointing forward to 11.19 (so Weiser 199, against Bultmann). Philip
was one of the Seven, the leaders of those who appear to have been
dispersed from Jerusalem (8.1, διεσπάρησαν; see p. 390) so that the
story of Philip is naturally introduced by a reference to οἱ διασπαρέντες,
those who were dispersed and were later to take the Gospel as far as
Antioch. With v. 5 begins the account of Philip's preaching in the (or
a — see the note) city of Samaria. The textual variation here opens
the question whether we are to think of the evangelization of
Samaritans (who were not Jews but were by no means totally
different from or unrelated to them) or of Gentiles. The work of
evangelizing results in the conversion and baptism of many others
and of Simon the Magus (v. 13). This is preceded by an account of
Simon (vv. 9–12) which is sometimes described as a 'flashback'
(Rückblende) which disturbs the narrative. It is however difficult to
see how Luke could have proceeded without some description of
Simon before bringing him on the scene. It is at this point that Philip
disappears, mentioned no more till v. 26, when he sets off, at the
command of an angel, to Gaza. For the geography of his movements
see on 8.26; it is by no means easy to rationalize them on a map, and
this suggests, what later consideration may confirm, that it was
really Simon, said by some early Christian writers (see on v. 9) to
come from Gitta in Samaria, and not traditions about either Philip or
Peter, who determined the scene of the incident. After the disappearance
of Philip (which must mean the end of any 'Philip tradition' known
to Luke), Peter and John (for their work as a pair see on 3.1) arrive
on the scene (v. 14), and by prayer and the laying on of hands bring
about what previously had been wanting; the Holy Spirit falls upon
the new converts, and the context makes clear that the results were
manifest. Simon then makes his request to purchase for money the
right to confer the Holy Spirit — for he has seen the Spirit given
when Peter and John lay their hands on the baptized converts. He is
rebuked by Peter, and the whole paragraph closes with a missionary
tour by Peter and John on their way back to Jerusalem. There has
been no contact between them and Philip. Thus any implied relation
between the Seven (or Philip) and Twelve (or Peter and John) 'is
Luke's own product rather than tradition. In other words, Simon is
not a piece of cement holding Philip and Peter together — this in fact
is something he does not do; he is rather a piece of traditional
material existing in his own right, and providing Luke with three
objects that he can achieve in one paragraph. Luke notes an important
milestone in the expansion of Christianity; he emphasises afresh the
unity of the church in its ideal age; and he has something to say about
Simon himself' (Barrett, in Kremer, *Actes* 285). He also has something
to say about such matters as baptism and the Holy Spirit.

For the meaning of μάγος, μαγεύειν, μαγεία, see the note on
v. 9. Later Christian tradition (notably Irenaeus, *Adv. Haer.* 1.23)

made Simon the father of gnosticism, but of this there is no hint in Acts. The most that can be said has been said by E. Lohse (*Umwelt* 198f.): 'Hinter der Erzählung, wie sie die Apostelgeschichte bietet, wird eine frühe Auseinandersetzung sichtbar, die sich zwischen gnostischer Lehre und christlicher Verkündigung vollzogen hat. Denn die Behauptung, die grosse Kraft zu sein, kann nicht einfach als Meinungsäusserung eines Zauberers verstanden werden, sondern bedeutet vielmehr den Anspruch, Träger göttlicher Offenbarung zu sein. Die polemische Berichte, mit denen sich im zweiten Jahrhundert n. Chr. die Kirchenväter Justin, Irenäus und Tertullian gegen die simonianische Gnosis wenden, zeigen einerseits, dass von diesem Simon, der in Samaria auftrat, eine Bewegung ausgegangen ist, die nicht nur in Palästina, sondern alsbald auch in Rom Anhänger fand, und schildern andererseits den ausgesprochen gnostischen Charakter dieser Lehre.' Attempts to go further than this are unconvincing (e.g. Haenchen 297f.). And Lohse's main point, that no magician would call himself 'the Great Power', is unsatisfactory (see on v. 10). It is undoubtedly true that so-called Simonian gnosticism existed in the second century and that it was attacked by the anti-gnostic church fathers, who alleged that it had been originated by the Simon of Acts 8. It is by no means so certain that they were right in this belief, or, if they were, that Luke also was aware of the connection. If he was aware of it he did nothing to make it known. 'Man sollte hier sehr zurückhaltend urteilen' (Roloff 137, adding that Luke represents Simon as a 'divine man' but not as the giver of a secret doctrine of salvation). The view of himself that he makes Simon express is simply that he was 'someone great'; that he was the 'power of God called great' is ascribed to others, and is itself not specifically gnostic. Luke's magi (here and in ch. 13) are magicians, not proto-gnostics. Simon is blamed not for false doctrine (except in so far as it is erroneous to suppose that the Holy Spirit, or the right to bestow the Holy Spirit, can be bought for cash) but simply for Simony; and this blemish was removed (according to Luke) as soon as it showed itself. Luke is sensitive to money matters in general, and attempts to make profit out of the supernatural arouse his indignation.

This leads to the true understanding of the most disputed feature of the passage. Philip preaches to the Samaritans; they believe; they are baptized; and they do not receive the Spirit. Peter and John visit them; pray for them; lay hands on them; and they do receive the Spirit. Why did they not receive the Spirit at baptism (cf. e.g. 2.38)? Did Philip (not one of the Twelve) lack the necessary competence? Could only apostles confer the Spirit? Is confirmation by the imposition of hands a necessary complement of baptism? Is it true that the writer 'wanted to assert the apostolic right of confirmation' (Dibelius 17)? None of these questions can be answered in the affirmative on the basis of the evidence of Acts. Elsewhere in Acts the Spirit can be

given when the person baptizing is not an apostle (9.17f.), or even
when the convert has neither been baptized nor received the imposition
of hands (10.44–48). What Luke intends to teach is that the Spirit (by
which he means not basic Christian existence — as at Rom. 8.9 —
but something more like inspiration) is conferred ubi et quando
visum est Deo; man cannot control it, either by liturgical means (for
there is no reason to think that baptism carried out by Philip was
liturgically defective), or (as Simon was to discover) by money.
Always and everywhere the Spirit is Lord. 'The church possesses the
inestimable privilege of having the Spirit as its guide and defender,
but it has the privilege as a gift which it may depend on but cannot
control, and never possesses in its own right' (Barrett, in Kremer,
Actes 295). To this we may add, as we return to the literary analysis
of the paragraph, that Luke, whether by accident or design, avoids
saying that Simon received the Spirit.

According to Hahn (*Mission* 48f.; similarly most commentaries,
e.g. Weiser 200f.), the paragraph consists of several component
parts: vv. 5–8, Philip's work in the town of Samaria; 9–13, continuation
of Philip's work in the conversion of former followers of Simon
Magus and of Simon himself; 14–17, an editorial passage describing
the intervention of Peter and John; 18–24, Peter's rebuke to Simon;
25, an editorial conclusion. On the basis of this analysis he rightly
rejects Cullmann's view (see p. 410) that vv. 14–17 contain a
historical account of the taking over of a 'Hellenist' mission to
Samaria by representatives of the Twelve, a move which (according
to Cullman) has independent confirmation in Jn. 4.38. If one takes
into account Hahn's statement that 'in its present form everything
has certainly been worked in together by Luke' this literary analysis
may probably be accepted, but it leaves open a number of questions.

In the detailed comment attention is drawn to some verbal repetitions.
(a) The crowds paid attention (προσεῖχον) to what was said by
Philip (v. 6). Note ᾧ (Simon)προσεῖχον (v. 10); προσεῖχον αὐτῷ
(Simon, v. 11). (b) The crowds were impressed by Philip because of
his signs (v. 6). They were impressed by the μαγεῖαι practised by
Simon (v. 11). (c) In the past, Simon had astonished (ἐξιστάνων) the
local population (v. 9). He had astonished (ἐξεστακέναι) them by
his μαγεῖαι (v. 11). Simon was himself astonished (ἐξίστατο) by
Philip's signs and mighty works (v. 13). (d) Simon said that he was
someone great (μέγαν, v. 9). The people said that he was the power
of God called great (μεγάλη, v. 10). (e) The people believed and
were baptized (ἐπίστευσαν, ἐβαπτίσθησαν, v. 12). Simon believed
and was baptized (ἐπίστευσεν, βαπτισθείς, v. 13).

With this observation may be set another. If we follow Hahn's or
some similar analysis it may seem that Luke was in possession of two
distinct accounts of Simon, one of which described his conversion
and baptism, the other his attempt to purchase the right to confer the

Holy Spirit. This is not probable; or, to put the matter positively, it seems more likely that there should have been available to Luke a number of scraps of information about Simon than that there should have been two distinct and sharply contrasting stories, one describing his conversion and faithful attendance (προσκαρτερῶν, v. 13) upon Philip, the other his magical misapprehension of Christian truth and stern reprimand by Peter. It must not be forgotten that 21.8 suggests some measure of contact between the author of Acts and Philip, whatever conclusion may be reached regarding the so-called We-passages (see the discussion in Vol. II).

It is probably best to conclude that in this paragraph Luke has done his best to combine information that connected Philip with Simon and thus with Samaria with the tradition of Hellenist evangelization, and introduced Peter (and John, as in earlier chapters) to make it clear that the Hellenists were allies of the original disciples, who guaranteed the connection between the church and Jesus, and neither rivals nor subservient to them. The initiative was Philip's; Peter and John shared in it. Stählin (123) is right in saying that the Twelve carry out missions of inspection but are not pioneers, but not in claiming that from 6.1 the Seven are being subordinated to the Twelve.

The historical trustworthiness of this section has been assessed in relation to Luke's supposed convictions: anything that does not correspond with these must be old tradition which Luke has not fully assimilated. Thus (Weiser 199) Luke must have got Philip's Samaritan mission from tradition because it does not correspond to his own idea of an *apostolic* mission carried out by the Twelve. Verses 12, 13 must be an insertion because they do not correspond to Luke's understanding of the relation between baptism and the Holy Spirit. The fact however is that Luke appears to have no hard and fast views on the relation between baptism and the Holy Spirit (see above) and on the proper form and basis of missionary work: for him, the greatest of all missionaries was not, it seems, an apostle, certainly not one of the Twelve.

The mission to Samaria contrasts with the precept of Mt. 10.5. If Luke was aware of this saying ascribed in the Matthean tradition to Jesus he would probably have remarked that it concerned only the time before the crucifixion and resurrection. It would hardly however have stood in the gospel if there had not been some Christians who took it to be a command of perpetual obligation upon the church. It may be that the mission of Peter and John reflects controversy caused by the Samaritan mission. Was it or was it not a legitimate Christian development? We must send trustworthy men to find out. There seems to be no other sign of doubt, though it may be that the figure of Simon is held up as a warning of the sort of error that might arise in Samaria.

'Die traditionelle katholische Auslegung benutzte die Texte zur Begründung der Unterscheidung von Taufe und Firmung' (Pesch 283). The passage is explicitly used by Innocent I (AD 402–417) to justify the reservation of the sacrament of confirmation to bishops: 'Nam presbyteri, licet secundi sint sacerdotes, pontificatus tamen apicem non habent. Hoc autem pontificium solis deberi episcopis, ut vel consignent, vel Paracletum Spiritum tradant, non solum consuetudo ecclestiastica demonstrat, verum et illa lectio Actuum Apostolorum, quae asserit Petrum et Ioannem esse directos, qui iam baptizatis traderent Spiritum Sanctum. Nam presbyteris, sive extra episcopum, sive praesente episcopo cum baptizant, chrismate baptizatos ungere licet, sed quod ab episcopo fuerit consecratum; non tamen frontem ex eodem oleo signare, quod solis debetur episcopis, cum tradunt Spiritum Paracletum' (*Epist.* 25.3). Earlier the laying on of hands had been part of the baptismal rite (e.g. Tertullian, *Bapt.* 8; and see G. W. H. Lampe, *The Seal of the Spirit*, 1951. The matter is discussed by Luther (*De captitivitate Babylonica ecclesiae*, Weimar Edition 6.549f.) and by Calvin (*Institutes* 4.19.4–13). For Luther, 'Satis est, pro ritu quodam Ecclesiastico seu cerimonia sacramentali confirmationem habere . . . quia promissionem divinam non habent, sacramenta fidei dici non possunt.' For Calvin, the bestowal of the Holy Spirit in Acts 8 was a matter of visible and audible gifts (e.g. speaking with tongues) which (according to Calvin) are no longer given to the church. In the 25th of the Thirty-nine Articles of the Church of England confirmation is said not to be a sacrament because it has 'not any visible sign or ceremony ordained by God'. In the Order of Confirmation in the Book of Common Prayer the bishop's prayer includes a reference to the example of the Holy Apostles, which presumably alludes to Acts 8.

4. That the narrative here takes a fresh turn, though one that is related to the preceding material, is marked by the characteristic μὲν οὖν (1.6 (see the note), 18; 5.41; 8.25; 9.31; 11.19; 12.5; 13.4; 14.3; 15.3, 30; 16.5; 17.12, 17, 30; 19.32, 38; 23.18, 22, 31; 25.4, 11; 26.4, 9; 28.5). The subject, οἱ διασπαρέντες, resumes 8.1, πάντες διεσπάρησαν . . . πλὴν τῶν ἀποστόλων, and points forward to 11.19; indeed, Bultmann (*Exegetica* 422) holds that the present sentence is incomplete, since διῆλθον requires an expressed goal, which is furnished not here but in 11.19 (ἕως Φοινίκης . . .). This finds some support in Luke's use of διέρχεσθαι (8.40, ἕως τοῦ ἐλθεῖν . . .; 9.32, πρὸς τοὺς ἁγίους; 9.38, ἕως ἡμῶν; 11.19; 12.10, ἐπὶ τὴν πύλην; 13.6, ἄχρι Πάφου; 13.14, εἰς 'Αντιόχειαν; 14.24, εἰς τὴν Παμφυλίαν; 19.1, εἰς "Εφεσον; 19.21, εἰς 'Ιεροσόλυμα; 20.2, εἰς τὴν 'Ελλάδα), but not sufficient support; see also 15.3, 41; 16.6, and especially 10.38; 17.23; 20.25, where the verb neither has a goal nor takes an accusative expressing the ground covered in the journey, but refers to general and unspecified movement. It is however true (*Begs*. 4.108) that for Luke διέρχεσθαι usually refers to a missionary journey; this suits the context here. The dispersed believers, whom we may broadly identify with the Seven (6.5) and their followers (see p. 390), moved at large through the area specified in 8.1, τὰς χώρας τῆς ᾿Ιουδαίας καὶ Σαμαρείας, preaching as opportunity offered. It is quite possible that (as Bultmann suggested but hardly proved) the story of the foundation of the church at Antioch followed directly upon the account of the persecution, perhaps in an Antiochene source (see pp. 54–6); if so, Luke has interposed a group of stories which illustrate the διέρχεσθαι, the (partially unpremeditated) preaching tours he has in mind, in particular the stories about Philip. Once these were added, especially in the form of the present paragraph, it was natural to add stories about Peter, and it was necessary to add also the conversion of Saul in order to prepare for 11.25. Pallis (59), thinking the aorist διῆλθον unsuitable, conjectures διῆγον, with the meaning (see LS 392) *they continued evangelizing*. An alternative explanation of the aorist could be that it originally referred to a single journey from Jerusalem to Antioch.

When λόγος stands as the object of a verb meaning *to preach* it is often (e.g. 4.31) provided with a defining genitive; here τοῦ θεοῦ is added by E t w vg^cl sy^p bo^mss. The addition is textually secondary but correct as interpretation. It is the word communicated by God that the scattered Christians proclaimed as good news (εὐαγγελιζόμενοι; see 5.42 — the verb is characteristic of Luke, who in both volumes uses the cognate noun εὐαγγέλιον only twice). Cf. 2 Baruch 1.4 (I will scatter this people among the Gentiles, that they may do good to the Gentiles).

That μέν has no immediately answering δέ is sufficiently explained by Luke's customary use of μὲν οὖν (see above); it is therefore unnecessary to seek a δέ (J. Jeremias, *ZNW* 36 (1937), 216) in 9.1, ὁ δὲ Σαῦλος. It is true that this gives a neat sense: the victims of Saul's persecution, on the one hand, continued their missionary work; Saul himself, on the other, embarked on further persecution. But the reader cannot have been expected to keep μέν in his mind from 8.4 to 9.1. It is of course possible to imagine a source used by Luke in which this interval did not occur.

5. The δέ of this verse is not an answer to the μέν of v. 4, since Philip (not, in Luke's mind, the apostle, since the apostles remained in Jerusalem — 8.1) is not contrasted with οἱ διασπαρέντες but is one of their number. For his appointment as one of the Seven see 6.5; 8.40 brings him to Caesarea, where he is encountered again at 21.8. See the notes on these verses. κατέρχεσθαι is used, without reference to physical altitude, of movement from Jerusalem to other places. Samaria lends to the διῆλθον of v. 4 the precision of a specific example; in view of 1.8 it is for Luke a significant example. In accordance with the programme sketched there the Gospel had been preached in Jerusalem and in Judaea (5.16; 8.1); Samaria would mark the next stage in its progress towards the Gentile world. For the history of the Samaritans, and their varying relations with the Jews, see *NS* 2. 15–20; J. Jeremias in *TWNT* 7.88–94; Black (*Scrolls* 62–6); also *St John* 228–44. The NT regularly takes them as occupying a middle position, neither full Jews nor mere Gentiles. Luke's interest is to show Philip at work in this middle region; the precise location in which he worked is obscured by a textual variant. C D E Ψ 𝔐 read εἰς πόλιν τῆς Σαμαρείας, *to a city* (unspecified) *of Samaria*. Samaria is thus to be understood (as probably in 1.8) as a district, in which there are several cities; Luke does not know, or at least does not name, the city in question. This manner of writing is supported by v. 8 — there was great joy ἐν τῇ πόλει ἐκείνῃ. Again, the city is not named; all that matters is what happened in it. In the present verse however P⁷⁴ ℵ A B 1175 *pc* add the article, εἰς τὴν πόλιν τῆς Σαμαρείας. This reading means *either* that Luke supposed that the district of Samaria possessed only one city (cf. v. 25, πολλὰς κώμας), *or* that he was referring to the capital city, the Samaria of the OT. Against the latter alternative are the facts (a) that the city was known as Sebaste (Josephus, *Ant.* 15.392; *War* 1.403; Strabo 16.2.34 (760); see *NS* 2.160–164), and (b) that an appositional genitive with placenames is unusual, agreement in case being preferred, so that here the accusative would be expected. *Begs.* 4.89 makes this point but there are not a few exceptions, not only in epic poetry (e.g. Ἰλίου πόλιν (Homer, according to Robertson 498, giving no reference, but *Iliad* 5.643 will serve; cf. *Odyssey* 1.2) but also later (e.g. Aeschylus, *Agamemnon* 29; Herodotus 7.156.2, Καμαρίνης τὸ ἄστυ). The former possibility (that Luke believed that there was only one significant city in Samaria) is sometimes dismissed as unlikely, and of course much turns on the sense given to πόλις, but it may well be that Samaria (Sebaste) was regarded as the only city in the district. See Josephus, *War* 2.96f.: 'The ethnarchy of Archelaus comprised the whole of Idumaea and Judaea, besides the district of Samaria . . . The cities subjected to Archelaus were Strato's Tower [Caesarea], Sebaste, Joppa, and Jerusalem.' Joppa and Jerusalem were certainly in Judaea, and so it seems was Caesarea (see *NS* 2.116), leaving only Sebaste. Sebaste was a highly hellenized community, not so much Samaritan as Gentile. This may seem inconsistent with the narrative, and could have led to the omission of τήν. Luke, it may be, had in mind Sebaste, *the* city of the district of Samaria; copyists saw the difficulty in this and made the simplest possible change. It must not be assumed that the city name Samaria dropped immediately out of use (Hemer 225f.).

If however the reading without the article is accepted one may consider the interesting suggestion (*Begs.* 4.89) that the city in question was Gitta, according to Justin (1 *Apol.* 26) the hometown of Simon Magus; but the fact is that Luke has no interest in, and perhaps no knowledge of, precise geographical location; his concern is with the events that took place, and took place in a Samaritan environment. Another suggestion is that there has been confusion between the two meanings of the Hebrew hnydm (Aramaic anydm), which means sometimes *city*, sometimes *province*; cf. Lk. 1.39 (with both Marshall and Fitzmyer ad loc.). But there is no confirmatory evidence for a Semitic source at this point in Acts.

There is for Luke no difference between telling the good news of the word of God and proclaiming Christ; he is the good news. It is doubtful whether the article (τὸν Χριστόν) should be taken to mean that Philip preached Jesus as the (Samaritan) Messiah, though no doubt Samaritan converts will have accepted him as the fulfilment of their own form of the messianic hope. Probably Χριστός is little more than a name; cf. 8.35, εὐηγγελίσατο αὐτῷ τὸν Ἰησοῦν.

αὐτοῖς is a very natural expansion of πόλις: *the inhabitants of the city*. See BDR § 282. 1 n. 2 and cf. 16.10; 20.1f.

6. Philip's preaching made a great impression on the Samaritans. They *paid attention* (προσεῖχον, sc. τὸν νοῦν; the word occurs three times in this paragraph and may here have been borrowed from the account of Simon) to what he said *with one accord* (ὁμοθυμαδόν, a Lucan word; see on 1.14, but in the present passage it can have the full sense that Luke often gives it only in an incipient way — they began to be united with one another as they accepted the Christian message). *Begs.* 4.89 takes προσεῖχον to be equivalent to ἐπίστευσαν in v. 12; there seems to be no good reason for this; Luke describes a process in which attention precedes faith. The hearers were impressed as they listened to Philip's words (ἐν τῷ ἀκούειν αὐτούς) and also as they witnessed (καὶ [ἐν τῷ] βλέπειν) the signs that he performed. *Signs*, σημεῖα, in the sense of wonderful and significant acts, are mentioned, often in association with τέρατα, at 2.22, 43; 4.16, 22, 30; 5.12; 6.8; (7.36, of Moses); 8.6, 13; 14.3; 15.12. The use of the word at 2.19 (quoted from Joel 3.3) is different. It is not said that the Samaritans believed (v.12) because of the signs they saw, only that this encouraged them to pay attention to Philip's message. Luke, however, is interested in the evidential value of miracles (e.g. 15.12) and regarded them as providing part of the ground on which faith rests.

7. The signs referred to in v. 6 are illustrated; γάρ justifies the assertion that they beheld and were impressed by σημεῖα. So much is clear, but the construction of the sentence is not. It would be just possible to translate what is certainly the original text as Many of those who had unclean spirits, which cried with a loud voice, came out (that is, out of the city, to meet Philip). But this is not what Luke means. He begins as if he intended to say, Many of those who had unclean spirits were relieved of them, but ends as if he had said, Many unclean spirits came out (of those who had been possessed by them). The error is a natural enough example of the peril of 'swapping horses'. Like other confused sentences this one suggests that the book did not receive a final revision; so for example Metzger (357), agreeing with *Begs.* 4.90. It has been conjectured that ἅ may have dropped out after ἀκάθαρτα; the textual tradition contains a number of attempts to mend the sentence. For πολλοί D reads πολλοῖς, which is accepted, as an ethic dative, by Pallis (59). In D* something seems to have preceded πολλοῖς. This is given in the apparatus to NA²⁶ as ἀπό (with dative!); Scrivener read the letters as π[αρ]α, Blass as π[αμ]; see Ropes (*Begs.* 3.76), who does not venture beyond the initial π. d has *a multis*.

Luke adds further examples of cures. The language of the verse and the things it describes are common in the NT (and elsewhere). For πνεύματα ἀκάθαρτα see 5.16 (later in the book Luke has πνεῦμα πονηρόν, 19.12–16); Lk. 4.36, et al. For demons and spirits crying aloud see Lk. 4.41; Acts 16.17 (κράζειν). For ἐξέρχεσθαι in exorcism see Lk. 4.35; Acts 16.18f. (here only in Acts). For the paralysed see Lk. 5.18; Acts 9.33 (here only in Acts). 'παραλελυμένος zieht Lukas dem vulgären παραλυτικός (nicht: Paralytiker, sondern "gelähmt") vor' (Haenchen 292; cf. BA 1253 s.v.). For the lame (χωλοί) see Lk. 7.22; Acts 3.2; 14.8 (here only in Acts). The language is conventional and we may probably infer that Luke is writing up a tradition that told him, at most, that Philip had been connected with Samaria. It will hardly serve as evidence for the origin in apostolic days of the practice of baptismal exorcism! (Richardson, *Theology* 338).

8. Luke has not yet spoken explicitly of the conversion of the Samaritans (v. 12), and it is therefore probable that the joy in the city should be thought of as due to the cure of the sick and possessed. This verse could very naturally be followed by v. 12; they rejoiced in Philip's healing work, and, when they believed the Gospel that he preached, were baptized. Vv. 9–11 interrupt the sequence and were probably drawn from a different source; see p. 409. In view of the connection between Simon and Samaria (see on v. 9) it may be that this source, responsible for the introduction of Simon into the story, was responsible also for locating the incident in Samaria, though Luke will have been glad to find a means of introducing Samaria into his account of the expansion of the church and the spread of the Gospel.

For [τὴν] πόλιν see v. 5; here for τῇ πόλει, 614 has τῇ χώρᾳ.

See above on the ambiguity of מדינא, מדינה.

9. Vv. 9–24 are described by Plümacher as an example of Luke's *Episodenstil* — the use of traditional narratives to help the reader to keep his attention on the over-all picture. The new source (if the suggestion made in the note on v. 8 is accepted; see also Schille 202) introduces a figure referred to nowhere else in the NT but mentioned in other early Christian sources. According to Justin (1 *Apol.* 26; cf. 56; *Trypho* 120.6) Simon was a Samaritan who came from Gitta. This is often identified with Kuryet Jit, six miles west of Nablus, Justin's own home, so that one might expect Justin to be well informed on the matter. Justin represents him as empowered by demons to perform magical acts, and as honoured in Rome as a god. Justin however is undoubtedly mistaken in claiming that a statue in Rome bore the inscription *Simoni Deo Sancto*; this must be a misreading of an inscription discovered in 1574, which runs *Semoni Sanco Deo Fidio* (*CIL* 6.567; see also Tertullian, *Apology* 13). It may be that the Simonian gnostics rather than Justin personally were responsible for the misreading. It is with Irenaeus that a major development in the picture of Simon takes place; in *Adv. Haer.* 1.23 Simon, identified by quotations from Acts 8, is described as the founder of the sect of the Simonians and as one 'from whom all sorts of [gnostic] heresies derived their origin'. His party 'both lead profligate lives and practise magical arts'. These statements are repeated and expanded by later Christian writers, e.g. Origen, *c. Celsum* 6.11; Eusebius, *H.E.* 2.13–15. In the Pseudo-Clementine literature Simon is sometimes used as a disguise for Paul, who is attacked (from the Jewish Christian side) under this name.

In Acts Simon is not described as a gnostic but as μαγεύων (v. 9) and practising μαγεῖαι (v. 11), that is, as a μάγος (the word is used in 13.6, 8). For the meaning of μάγος see A. D. Nock in *Begs.* 5.151–163 and G. Delling in *TWNT* 5.360–363; also Barrett (Kremer *Actes*, 286–90). There are useful references in Betz (108, n. 6). μάγος '"is a loanword in Greek, borrowed from Persian to describe the priestly Median tribe. Members of this tribe performed the daily worship of fire, and one of them had to be present at every sacrifice and sing a chant narrating the birth of the gods" (Nock 164). The word thus has a dignified origin. "It is therefore with some surprise that we find μάγος used in the fifth century BC to mean "quack"'" (Nock 165). Nock is able to show that both senses continued to be applied to the word in later Greek literature, though the latter became more common. There is no passage, perhaps, that puts the two meanings together more neatly than Philo's *Spec. Leg.* 3.100f.' (Barrett, Kremer, *Actes* 286). Philo writes: The true magic . . . is felt to be a fit object for reverence and ambition and is carefully studied not only by ordinary persons but by kings and the greatest kings . . . But there is a counterfeit of this . . . pursued by charlatan mendicants and parasites and the basest of the women and slave population . . .'. Simon is one of a class that Luke strongly dislikes; he has illicit dealings with the supernatural, and makes money out of them (see below; and cf. 13.6–11; 16.16–24; 19.13–20, 23–40). There is nothing in Luke's text to suggest the initiator of a gnostic doctrine (so e.g. Pesch 279). For Luke, magic is 'ein synkretistisches Pneumatikertum, in dem sich samaritanisch-jüdische Elemente mit hellenistisch-heidnischen vermischten' (Roloff 132). Weiser (202) argues convincingly against Haenchen's and Lüdemann's view that Simon really was a gnostic, downgraded into a magus by Luke for polemical reasons. It is incredible that Luke, who thought highly of Paul, intended him to be represented (as in the Clementines) by the magus and heretic Simon.

μαγεύων, ἐξιστάνων are supplementary (or perhaps adverbial) participles to προϋπῆρχεν, in which the compounded προ – must be intended to point to the time before Philip reached the Samaritan city; Simon was already there and in possession of the field. He was practising magic and astonishing the population by his achievements. This is virtually repeated in v. 11. He also claimed to be *someone great*, εἶναί τινα ἑαυτὸν μέγαν. It is true that the sentence would make sense without μέγαν (as in English one could say, Making himself out to be someone; cf. Gal. 6.3), but this is no reason for regarding μέγαν as an addition (mentioned in BDR § 301. 1 n. 3 as a possibility). The adjective reappears in the next verse. Stählin (120) draws attention to 5.36 and thinks the claim is messianic.

10. προσεῖχον: see on v. 6. Philip has now taken the place previously occupied by Simon. Luke in writing his account of Philip may well have taken up the word (used also in v. 11) from the tradition about Simon that he was using.

ἀπὸ μικροῦ ἕως μεγάλου, meaning *all, of whatever rank* (possibly, *young and old*: Pesch 274; cf. 22.6) does not seem to be a current Greek idiom; it is however Hebrew, מקטון ועד גדול, e.g. 1 Sam. 5.9 (translated in the LXX as here). There is little to support the suggestion (*Begs.* 4.90f.) that the words are out of place and belonged to the teaching of Simon, who according to Hippolytus, *Refutation* 4.51, used the Pythagorean phrase, τὸ μικρὸν μέγα ἔσται.

V. 9 contains what purports to be Simon's statement about himself; it is quite vague and unspecific — *someone great*. V. 10b purports to give popular opinion, but it is rightly pointed out (e.g. Bauernfeind 126) that οὗτός ἐστιν in the 3 p.s. corresponds to a 1 p.s. ἐγώ εἰμι, an expression not unfamiliar in aretalogical statements (*St John* 291f.) and reflected in other passages. The 'divine man' in Origen, *c. Celsum* 7.8f. declares ἐγώ ὁ θεός εἰμι ἢ θεοῦ παῖς ἢ πνεῦμα θεῖον, and according to Jerome (*in Matt.* 24) Simon himself said,

Ego sum sermo Dei, . . . ego omnipotens, ego omnia Dei. It is probable that popular opinion accepted what Simon claimed for himself: he was ἡ δύναμις τοῦ θεοῦ ἡ καλουμένη (L 614 pc have λεγομένη; Ψ 𝔐 syᵖ sa mae omit) μεγάλη. It is a fairly common view that in this claim τοῦ θεοῦ is a Lucan explanatory supplement, since δύναμις is used to mean God. Cf. Lk. 22.69, where τῆς δυνάμεως τοῦ θεοῦ is parallel to the τῆς δυνάμεως of Mk. 14.62. So for example *DBS* 336; *DWJ* 200–202; cf. more recently Haenchen (293); Schneider (489). The equation is supported by the use of גבורה for God (e.g. Shabbath 87a) and of חיל 'which stands for God in Samaritanism' (Black, *Scrolls* 64f.). Black adds a reference to the Gospel of Peter 19, but it is doubtful whether here δύναμις means God. See also Eusebius, *H.E.* 2.23.13. Conzelmann (53) rightly notes the alternative possibility, which is in fact preferable: that the text should be taken as it stands and does not mean that Simon claimed, or was believed, to be the supreme God. A distinction between the supreme Being and a μεγάλη δύναμις is supported by inscriptions. One from Lydia, dealing with the religion of Men, runs Εἷς θεὸς ἐν οὐρανοῖς, μέγας Μὴν Οὐράνιος, μεγάλη δύναμις τοῦ ἀθανάτου θεοῦ, and seems to distinguish between Men and the immortal God, and another (interestingly, from Samaria) runs Εἷς θεός, ὁ πάντων δεσπότης, μεγάλη κόρη ἡ ἀνείκητος. For some discussion of these inscriptions, and of the relation between Kore and Sol Invictus, see *ND* 1.105–7; for the former, see *ND* 3.32. Speculation regarding *powers* of God (understood in more biblical terms) had reached an advanced stage in Philo (see *NS* 3.881–85, also for bibliography). As a rule Philo distinguishes the δυνάμεις from the God whose powers they are; *Moses* 1.111, where he speaks of God himself as ἡ ἀνωτάτω καὶ μεγίστη δύναμις, is exceptional, but shows that the word was capable of being used in more senses than one. Important also are passages such as Sanhedrin 4.5 (. . . that the heretics should not say, 'There are many ruling powers (רשויות) in heaven)'; Hagigah 15a; 3 Enoch 16.3, which show that there was a (heretical) belief that there were two (or more) ruling powers in heaven. Simon was evidently no orthodox figure, and might have inculcated the belief that of all the Powers of God he was the great one. In fact it may well be that the view of Haenchen and Lüdemann (above) should be reversed. The historical Simon may have been not a speculative gnostic theologian downgraded by Luke but a very ordinary magician upgraded so as to appear as a divine man; by doing this Luke would find himself able to kill two objectionable birds with one stone. Josephus, *Ant.* 20.142 tells of a Cyprian Jew named (in some MSS) Atomus, who pretended to be a magus; a well attested variant names him Simon. It must be recalled that Philo (see above) is able to speak of God himself as ἡ ἀνωτάτω καὶ μεγίστη δύναμις. As a Greek word, μεγάλη makes excellent sense; it is mistaken to see behind it the participle מגלה (מגלא), meaning revealer.

11. This is a curiously repetitive verse. προσεῖχον repeats v. 10 (the same word); ἐξεστακέναι repeats v. 9 (ἐξιστάνων); ταῖς μαγείαις is at least very similar to μαγεύων (v. 9). Luke is probably gathering together the material about Simon in order to make a transition back to Philip, so that it is better not to put a full stop at the end of this verse: They gave heed to Simon . . ., but when they believed Philip . . .

ἱκανῷ χρόνῳ. One would expect the accusative. According to M. 3.243, 'Class. usage has accus.; Hell. Greek uses dat. (even Josephus) mainly with transitive verbs.' Turner suggests as a reason that some reticence may have been felt 'at placing a second accus. alongside a verb which already had an accus. of dir. object.' But here αὐτούς is fairly well out of the way. Zerwick § 54 notes a variant ἱκανὸν χρόνον (not in NA[26] or in *Begs.* 3; see Tischendorf and von Soden for the very slender attestation).

12. The correct reaction to the preached word is faith. In Acts πιστεύειν is often used absolutely, meaning *to be a believer* (e.g. 2.44); in the aorist, as here, *to become a believer*. Haenchen 294 rightly contrasts ἐπίστευσαν with the imperfect προσεῖχον. Attention continued and at a certain point became faith. πιστεύειν is used with the dative of a divine person (e.g. 16.34), or with ἐπί and the accusative of a divine person (e.g. 9.42). It is somewhat unusual to find the dative of the preacher, as here, but the use is quite understandable; the first step towards faith in a full theological sense is to recognize, What this preacher says is true. Philip was believed as he preached the Gospel (for εὐαγγελιζομένῳ cf. v. 4, εὐαγγελιζόμενοι). The content of the Gospel that he preached is defined in terms of *the kingdom of God* and *the name of Jesus Christ*. See on 1.3 and on 3.6, 16. It seems clear that for Luke in Acts *kingdom of God* can serve as a general summary of Christian belief and preaching (e.g. 28.23); it is not necessary to go back to the gospel tradition and inquire exactly what the expression meant in the teaching of Jesus. The other expression occurs more frequently. In addition to sixteen passages which use the words *name of (the Lord) Jesus (Christ)* sixteen more are to be noted where *the name of the Lord, his name*, or some such expression amounts to the same thing. The passages discussed and referred to at 3.6, 16 are decisive for its meaning. The *name* of Jesus is a term for the active power of Jesus, visibly at work in the healing of disease and in spiritual healing also. His name is invoked, men and women are baptized in his name; faith is thereby expressed and saving power is appropriated. Philip's Gospel is thus a statement of Christian truth, in which at least the terminology of eschatology is retained — God is at work establishing his rule, and making an offer of salvation.

Those who accepted this message were baptized; that is, they were baptized as believers. Calvin (232) notes this, but adds that 'they were admitted to baptism on this condition, that their families were consecrated to God at the same time,' so that 'the Anabaptists are being quite absurd'. There is in fact nothing in the text about this condition, and if the persons baptized did consecrate their families to God there is nothing to indicate that this was done by baptism. For baptism in Acts see on 2.38, and the general discussion in Vol. II. It is not said here (as e.g. at 2.38) that baptism is in (or into) the name of Jesus Christ; probably Luke thought that a further reference to the name would be superfluous after his summary of Philip's preaching. Just as men and women equally were exposed to persecution (8.3) so here they are offered equally the benefits of the Gospel.

13. There is nothing in this verse to suggest that Simon, in his believing (ἐπίστευσεν) and in his receiving baptism (βαπτισθείς), was less sincere or in any way a less satisfactory convert than the other Samaritans (ἐπίστευσαν, ἐβαπτίζοντο: v. 11). So also Pesch (275); but Stählin thinks otherwise ('sein "Glaube" war kein wahrer Glaube, seine Bekehrung keine echte Bekehrung; er bleibt der Magier'); Calvin (233) takes a middle position ('There is some middle position between faith and mere pretence . . . They are not making pretence to a non-existent faith in the eyes of men, but they think that they do believe'). προσκαρτερεῖν is a Lucan word (in Acts six times, all in chs. 1–10; in the rest of the NT, four times); θεωρεῖν is also common in Acts (fourteen times; apart from the gospels, four times; but it is a narrative word), and it is characteristic of Luke to take note of σημεῖα and δυνάμεις. These observations do not prove that v. 13 is an editorial note, but they are consistent with that view; perhaps better, with the view that Luke, provided with basic information about Philip's work as an evangelist (ὁ εὐαγγελιστής, 21.8) and Simon (who offered an opportunity for an attack on μαγεία), himself drew up the paragraph in the form in which we have it.

The *signs and mighty works* look back to vv. 6, 7. With ἐξίστατο cf. ἐξιστάνων (v. 9) and ἐξεστακέναι (v. 11). It was now Simon's turn to be astonished.

14. Luke's narrative takes a fresh turn. The apostles in Jerusalem (the phrase οἱ ἐν Ἱεροσολύμοις ἀπόστολοι could be taken to imply that there were also apostles elsewhere, but Luke is simply referring back to 8.1: when others left the apostles stayed in Jerusalem, and were still there) heard what had happened in Samaria (ἡ Σαμάρεια might refer to the city (now Sebaste) or to the district; see on v. 5).

This is described as accepting the word of God (cf. v. 4), which is equivalent to believing (v. 12; cf. 2.41, with ἀποδέχεσθαι instead of δέχεσθαι). The apostles thereupon sent two of their number to Samaria. For the association of Peter and John see on 3.1. In this passage both pray (v. 15) and lay their hands on the new believers (v. 17), but only Peter speaks — as in chs. 3, 4, 5. Cf. 11.22, where Barnabas is sent to Antioch. Luke gives no reason for the sending of Peter and John, and the reader can only conjecture what they were intended to do. Vv. 15f. suggest that they may have been sent in order to convey a gift that Philip had not been able to provide, v. 17 may mean that they were to carry out a rite (the laying on of hands) which only apostles (and therefore not Philip) were able to perform. They may have been sent to inspect, and so to approve or disapprove, a new development in the Christian mission; they may have been sent to share in what had already been recognized as a desirable step forward. Cullmann, who refers to the matter in several publications (e.g. *Heil* 258; *V. und A.* 238, 275; in Stendahl, *Scrolls* 27), sees a parallel in Jn 4.38, which he takes to mean that it was the Hellenists, not the Twelve, who began to evangelize the Samaritans; later the Twelve 'entered into their labours'. The parallel with 11.22 suggests but does not prove that the motive was inspection, and all that can be said with confidence is that here, as in ch. 6, Luke wished to show that the Seven and the Twelve, his 'Hellenists' and 'Hebrews', acted in harmony, but that new Christian developments needed, by association with the Twelve, to be integrated, and to be seen to be integrated, into the movement that flowed authentically from the work of Jesus (cf. 1.21f.).

How far this takes us towards a Lucan understanding of church and ministry is doubtful and disputed. A traditional view is expressed by Bede, who quotes the passage from Innocent I given above (p. 400): Notandum autem quod Philippus qui Samariae evangelizabat unus de Septem fuerit; si enim apostolus esset, ipse utique manum imponere potuisset ut acciperent Spiritum sanctum. 'Hoc enim solis pontificibus debetur. Nam presbyteris sive extra episcopum seu praesente episcopo cum baptizant chrismate baptizatos ungere licet, sed quod ab episcopo fuerit consecratum; non tamen frontem ex eodem oleo signare, quod solis debetur episcopis, cum tradunt Spiritum Paracletum'. This is reflected in Weiser (203), who thinks that vv. 14–17 come from Luke's own hand and show his hierarchical 'Amts- und Kirchenverständnis'. Calvin, on the other hand, thinks that the intention was 'that the Samaritans might learn to cultivate brotherly union with the first church conscientiously . . . secondly, He wished to honour with this privilege the apostles . . . so that they might all grow closer together into the one faith of the Gospel.' He notes the special applicability of this consideration to Jews and Samaritans (234f.). Bauernfeind (126) comments on the role of the apostles, 'Es fing nicht alles bei ihnen an, aber es bewegte sich alles zu ihnen hin'. Luke has in fact other interests (see above, pp. 397–9, and Barrett (Kremer, *Actes* 295)), more important to him than any theory of ministerial office. He perhaps sows seeds that would grow into Frühkatholizismus, but the development has not yet taken place. The mission to Samaria is part of the movement whose links with Jesus are affirmed by the apostles whom he chose. It is a part of a wider mission inspired by the Spirit, who is Lord over the process, not to be coerced whether by payment or by ritual processes.

15. οἵτινες is here equivalent to οἵ and does not have the full force found in e.g. 7.53. καταβαίνειν is regularly used for journeys from the capital, irrespective of the elevation of the destination. προσεύχεσθαι is sometimes followed by περί (in Acts, here only, but see Lk. 6.28), occasionally by ὅπως (in Acts cf. 8.24, δεήθητε . . .ὅπως; Mt. 9.38 = Lk. 10.2; James 5.16; cf. 2 Thess. 1. 12); here only by both prepositional phrase and purpose (or content) clause. But περὶ αὐτῶν is not exactly a prolepsis of the subject of the following clause (Delebecque 41). For receiving the Holy Spirit cf. 10.47; 19.2, and see the notes on 1.8; 2.38.

Calvin (236), who cannot believe that Philip's baptism failed to confer the Spirit, thinks that 'Luke is not speaking here about the general grace of the Spirit, by which God regenerates us to be His own sons, but about those special gifts, with which the Lord wished some to be endowed in the first days of the Gospel.' See further on v. 17.

16. ἐπιπίπτειν is a Lucan word (Lk. twice; Acts seven times; rest of the NT four (three) times), used exclusively in the first part of Acts of the gift of the Spirit, never so used in the second part. Luke never uses the simple πίπτειν of the Spirit. For the illapse of the Spirit see 10.44; 11.15, both referring to Cornelius and his companions. The Spirit had not fallen on the Samaritans; they had only been baptized εἰς τὸ ὄνομα τοῦ κυρίου Ἰησοῦ. This expression occurs here and at 19.5; elsewhere Luke uses ἐν or ἐπί (there are textual variants) τῷ ὀνόματι Ἰησοῦ Χριστοῦ (2.38; 10.48). The two expressions are sharply distinguished by M. Quesnel (*Baptisés dans l'Esprit* (1985), who takes εἰς τὸ ὄνομα to be of Gentile origin and to mean *so as to become the property of*. This conclusion (though not equally Quesnel's other views) may be accepted. See also Barth (*CD* 4.4.91–100), who does not make Quesnel's distinction. The *name* signifies (according to Barth) the Lord in all his characteristics. 'When the community baptises, and when its candidates are baptised, they are on the way into that strong tower [Prov. 18.10], on the way to the One who enters Jerusalem [Mk 11.9], the Lord, their Creator, Reconciler and Redeemer' (94). εἰς expresses destination; cf. Phil. 3.12 (95).

So much may be regarded as interpretation, possibly slight over-interpretation, of the sense of belonging which Greek commercial usage suggests for εἰς τὸ ὄνομα. See also BDR § 206. 2 n. 4.

Unusually, this verse contains two periphrastic pluperfects. ἦν ... ἐπιπεπτωκός is active intransitive, *had fallen*. In βεβαπτισμένοι ὑπῆρχον, ὑπῆρχον is virtually equivalent to ἦσαν (BDR § 354. 2), and the whole is a pluperfect passive, *had been baptized*.

17. Peter and John laid their hands on the baptized men and women and they received the Holy Spirit. For ἐπιτιθέναι χεῖρας in Acts see on 6.6. The action is employed in a variety of senses; in the context of baptism here and at 19.6 (perhaps at 9.12, 17; see the notes). Preuschen (50) observes that the laying on of hands in relation to baptism is not mentioned in the Didache or by Justin, but that Heb. 6.2 proves the antiquity of the custom. The narrative element in the verse is clear; less clear is Luke's purpose in including it. He does not mean that baptism as carried out by Philip was in any way defective; there is no suggestion in 8.38 that it needs any supplement. He does not mean that the gift of the Spirit is contingent upon the laying on of hands; in 10.44 the Spirit is given even before baptism, and there is no reference at all to the imposition of hands. He does not mean that baptism is complete and effective only in the presence of an apostle (one of the Twelve); witness once more 8.38, and 9.17f. Luke is describing a special case, in which the work of one of the Seven was combined with the work of two of the Twelve; to show their unity and cooperation was probably one of his motives. He is about to tell (v. 19) of Simon's request to purchase the power of conferring the spirit and needs a suitable context for Peter's response. There must have been something, done by Peter and John, for Simon to *see* (v. 18). Most important, perhaps, is his desire to show that, just as the Spirit cannot be bought for money, so the Spirit cannot be controlled by the performance of rites, even Christian rites performed by good Christians (see p. 398; also Barrett, Kremer, *Actes* 281–95). It is also to be noted that for Luke the mark of the Holy Spirit was regularly the utterance of inspired speech (e.g. 2.4; 10.46; 19.6). It is unlikely that he means that the baptized Samaritans were not Christians; they were Christians, but they did not manifest the charismatic phenomena of inspiration. This (it seemed to Luke — and quite possibly to Peter) was a deficiency that should be made up; Peter and John prayed that it should be made up and accompanied their prayer with the universal gesture of blessing; and it was made up, in such a way that Simon was able to perceive the signs of inspiration. There is some truth in Conzelmann's 'Das ist zunächst eine Konsequenz aus dem Kirchengedanken des Lukas, nach welchem Jerusalem der Vorort der Kirche ist. Es könnte aber eine Andeutung darin stecken, dass der Fortschritt der Mission von den Orthodoxen zu den Ketzern in Jerusalem Diskussionen auslöste, bis man ihn dann anerkannte' (*Geschichte* 49f.). But it is not the greater part of the truth. For the first time the Spirit is given outside the land of Israel; see Davies, *Land* 273f.

18. See on v. 17. The gift of the Spirit, as understood here, was not a purely inward spiritual experience but a perceptible phenomenon. This was already noticed by Chrysostom: οὐκ ἂν εἶδεν εἰ μή τι αἰσθητὸν ἐγένετο, ὥσπερ καὶ Παῦλος ἐποίησεν ὅτε ταῖς γλώσσαις ἐλάλουν; similarly Pesch (276): 'Lukas lässt . . . an ekstatische Phänomene wie Glossolalie und Prophetie denken.' There is nothing to suggest that Simon was omitted in the laying on of hands; yet his behaviour is not consistent with possession of the Spirit; this is noted by Haenchen (295), who infers a seam in the narrative. It is probably better to think of a logical oversight on Luke's part as he constructs his story.

προσήνεγκεν: elsewhere in Acts (7.42; 21.26) προσφέρειν is used of the offering of sacrifice; cf. however ἐνέγκας at 5.2. χρῆμα is used at 4.37 in the account of the free giving of property for distribution.

The story is filled out in *Actus Petri cum Simone* 23 (L.-B. 1.71): Rogo vos, accipite a me mercedem quantum vultis, ut possim manum imponere et tales virtutes facere . . . Putans [leg. putas] temptare nos pecuniam velle possidere? Cf. *Passio Apostolorum Petri et Pauli* 6 (L.-B. 1.227): Iste et ad nos [Peter and Paul!] venit et baptizatus voluit virtutem divinam pretio conparare.

19. At the beginning of the verse D gig p add παρακαλῶν καί — a characteristic Western intensifying of the narrative; cf. the Western reading in v. 24. κἀμοί, to me, so that I as well as you may have it; it is not implied that the apostles were to give, or had given, the power to anyone else.

Simon's readiness to pay for the right to confer the Spirit presumably implies that he would charge for the gift as he bestowed it (so Calvin 238). Luke, who is interested in wealth and poverty as well as in the Holy Spirit, has a marked dislike for those who make money out of their dealings with the supernatural — for magi, in the lower sense of the term (see on v. 9). See Barrett, (Kremer, *Actes* 287–91). Bauernfeind (127) observes that if one's only concern is for profit, 'denn sind Arznei und Gift, Sakrament und Magie allerdings kaum zu unterscheiden'. Peter and John are, in Luke's estimation, certainly not θεῖοι ἄνδρες; Simon represents his evaluation of such persons.

20. In Luke's story (and doubtless also in fact) Peter shares Luke's dislike of money made by magic. εἰς ἀπώλειαν: εἰς indicates direction and thus destiny. It is used with ἀπώλεια at Mt. 7.13; Rom. 9.22; 1 Tim. 6.9; Heb. 10.39; Rev. 17.8, 11. 'May your money perish along with you!' Similar words occur at Dan. 2.5 (Theodotion), εἰς ἀπώλειαν ἔσεσθε; 3.96 (Theodotion), εἰς ἀπώλειαν ἔσονται. There is however no literary connection. ἀπώλεια occurs in all parts of the OT, representing a variety of Hebrew words, and pointing as a rule to destruction brought upon men by God for their rebellion against him. As Plümacher (47) points out, when the apostles curse they do so in biblical style! Cf. 13.10f. 'Curse' however is scarcely the right word. οὐκ ἔστι ταῦτα ἀρωμένου ἀλλὰ παιδεύοντος, ὡς ἄν τις εἴποι· τὸ ἀργύριόν σου συναπόλοιτό σοι μετὰ τῆς προαιρέσεως (Chrysostom).

The use of spiritual (or intellectual) gifts for money-making is widely condemned in Greek literature. 'As to that class of monstrous natures who not only believe that there are no gods, or that they are negligent, or to be propitiated, but conjure the souls of the living and say that they can conjure the dead and promise to charm the gods with sacrifices and prayers, and will utterly overthrow whole houses and states for the sake of money (χρημάτων χάριν) — let him who is guilty of any of these things be condemned' (Plato, *Laws* 909ab); Sophocles, *Oedipus Rex* 387–9, the magus ὅστις ἐν τοῖς κέρδεσιν μόνον δέδορκε. In the NT cf. Mt. 10.8, δωρεὰν ἐλάβετε, δωρεὰν δότε.

τὴν δωρεάν τοῦ θεοῦ ought, in the argument, to refer to the power to bestow the Holy Spirit by the imposition of hands, but it is probable that, by a natural extension, it has here been assimilated to the use in 2.38; 10.45; 11.17 (the only other passages in Acts in which δωρεά is used) and refers to the gift of the Holy Spirit. κτᾶσθαι is a Lucan word (Lk., twice; Acts three times; rest of the NT, twice), but it means *to procure for oneself, get, acquire* (LS 1001) and was a natural word to use, so that no conclusions can be drawn about Lucan editing.

21. His request shows that Simon has no place within the Christian movement. μερίς (*part, portion*) and κλῆρος (*lot, allotment*) are in this context virtually synonymous. Cf. Neh. 2.20 (= 2 Esdras 12.20), ὑμῖν οὐκ ἔστιν μερὶς ... ἐν Ἱερουσαλήμ; Wisdom 2.9, αὕτη ἡ μερὶς ἡμῶν καὶ ὁ κλῆρος οὗτος. The two words are combined also in the statement about the Levite that οὐκ ἔστιν αὐτῷ μερὶς οὐδὲ κλῆρος μεθ' ὑμῶν (Deut. 12.12; 14.27, 29).

Simon has no rights, no share, ἐν τῷ λόγῳ τούτῳ. λόγος may be used here in the sense of *matter* (that is, the bestowal of the Spirit as the ground of Christian existence). λόγος is occasionally used in Acts in senses approaching this (see 6.5; 10.29; 11.22; 15.6; 19.38) but it is much more frequently used in the sense of speech, especially Christian speech, *the word of God*, or *of the Lord* (e.g. 4.31; 8.14,

25), and it is not impossible that this is its meaning here; Christian initiation is bound up with the proclamation of the word of God, and Simon's proposal shows that he has no understanding of this. Opinions differ on this question. Calvin (239), for example, preferred Erasmus's *in ratione hac* to the Vulgate's *in sermone isto*. Pesch (277) has 'an dieser Sache', Roloff (136), '... Wort (des Evangeliums)'. Haenchen (295) is probably right when he recognizes that λόγος is virtually equivalent to Christianity.

Ropes (*Begs.* 3.78) adds the observation, 'That the "Western" text read τη πιστει ταυτη for τω λογω τουτω is indicated by the agreement in that reading of perp gig pesh Aug Const. Ap. vi. 7.2'.

Simon's fault is stated in terms of his relation with God, in words that are close to Ps. 77.37 (ἡ δὲ καρδία αὐτῶν οὐκ εὐθεῖα μετ'αὐτοῦ; MT 78.37, עמו לא־נכון לבם). The adjective εὐθύς occurs in the NT in quotations of Isa. 40.3, 4, at 2 Peter 2.15, and in Acts. It is used at 9.11 as the name of a street, here and at 13.10 (also in the account of a magus) metaphorically. Used literally the word means *straight, direct*; as an ethical metaphor, *straightforward, frank, honest*. Simon is attempting to cheat God, to infringe the divine prerogative of bestowing the Spirit in accordance with his own will. ἔναντι, and the longer form ἐναντίον, occur in the NT only in the Lucan writings.

22. The only thing for Simon to do (οὖν) is to repent. μετανοεῖν and μετάνοια are fairly common in Lk. and Acts, for the most part used either in general terms or possibly with special reference to the Jewish sin of rejecting Jesus, here only with reference to a specific sin and here only with that sin introduced by ἀπό (cf. the use of ἐκ with μετανοεῖν at Rev. 2.22; 9.20, 21; 16.11). Noting this, with the parallels at Jer. 8.6 (here only with ἀπό in the LXX) and 1 Clem. 8.3, Wilcox 102–105 argues that the expression is a Semitism. It does indeed imply the equivalence of μετανοεῖν with שוב (literally *to turn* but with the derived meaning *to repent*), which is naturally followed by מן both in the OT and in post-biblical Hebrew (e.g. 1 QS 5.1, לשוב מכל רע; cf. CD 15.7). So convinced is Wilcox of the Semitic origin of Luke's Greek that he writes, 'We may probably conclude that it is to be traced to the "ipsissima verba Petri", and so, in this place, constitutes a token of the authenticity and antiquity of the traditions embodied by Luke in Acts 8.21ff.' This is a very optimistic conclusion. As soon as μετανοεῖν became established in the sense of a penitent turning the thought of *turning from* became inevitable. BA 1036 s.v. adds Justin, *Trypho* 109.1 (also ἀπὸ τῆς κακίας), and in the NT itself Heb. 6.1 (μετανοίας ἀπὸ νεκρῶν ἔργων), by demonstrating this development, severely weakens Wilcox's case.

εἰ is used in a manner related to its use in indirect questions (so BDR § 375). The measure of doubt involved in such a quasi-question is strengthened by the addition of ἄρα (Moule, *IB* 158, . . . *in the hope that perhaps* . . .). In 17.27 εἰ ἄρα γε is still stronger (Page 133). Zerwick § 403 adds that an element of *attempt* is also involved ('subintelligendum videtur verbum aliquod tentandi').

ἐπίνοια, *design, purpose*; cf. v. 21. The *heart* is evidently here regarded as the seat of thought where purposes are entertained and plans made. It is clear that Peter does not regard forgiveness as impossible, but it is dependent on penitence. 'Vis dubitandi cadit super poenitentiam et preces Simonis, non super remissionem doli, poenitenti sperandam' (Bengel). It can hardly be mere coincidence that Justin, writing (1 *Apol.* 26) of Simon as a father of heresy, says that Helena, who accompanied Simon, was called πρώτη ἔννοια and that Hippolytus (*Refutatio* 6.19) similarly speaks of her as ἐπίνοια. It does not follow that the historical Simon developed a gnostic system in which ἔννοια or ἐπίνοια played a part, or that this was personified by Helena, or for that matter that Simon had as a partner a woman called Helena. The process may have gone the other way: ἐπίνοια, met with in the text of Acts, was a good gnostic-sounding term, and Peter himself alleged that Simon had in his heart an ἐπίνοια; and the orthodox would be glad to find — or invent — an illicit relationship as a stick with which to beat the proto-gnostic.

23. The accusative and participle construction with a verb of perceiving (ὁρῶ σε ὄντα, *I see that you are*) is not common in the NT; cf. 17.16. For ὁρῶ, D E 614 *pc* have θεωρῶ.

εἰς may be used (as in v. 20) to express destination (Moule, *IB* 69, quotes J. B. Lightfoot's rendering (in *Apostolic Fathers* 2.2.24), *destined for, reserved for*, adding however, 'But is he right?'). If taken in this way the phrase will describe Simon's lot if he does not repent. Alternatively, εἰς may be used as almost equivalent to ἐν (read here, with datives replacing the accusatives, by D*); cf. M.1.71. A decision on this matter depends on the meaning of the nouns. The genitives are presumably qualitative, and suggest Hebrew idiom. The metaphorical use of χολή is found 'mostly in poets' (LS 1997), with the meaning *bitter anger, wrath*. πικρία intensifies this meaning. Cf. Prov. 5.4, ὕστερον μέντοι πικρότερον χολῆς εὑρήσεις; Deut. 29.18 (17), ἐν χολῇ καὶ πικρίᾳ. σύνδεσμον ἀδικίας occurs at Isa. 58.6 (cf. 9). Cf. also 4 Kdms 11.14, where it appears to mean *conspiracy* (קֶשֶׁר). In the present context χολὴν πικρίας taken alone, with εἰς in the sense of destination, would make good sense: 'You are destined for bitter anger, that is, to experience the wrath of God (on the assumption that you do not repent)'. It is however doubtful whether there is a way of taking σύνδεσμον ἀδικίας that corresponds with this; 'You are destined for the bondage (in hell) deserved by unrighteousness' is perhaps possible but not convincing. It makes better sense to say, 'In your present state of mind you are in bondage to unrighteousness.' If however we return to χολὴν πικρίας it seems impossible to accommodate this phrase to σύνδεσμον ἀδικίας: 'You are in a state of bitter anger' is sensible enough in itself but bitter anger was not Simon's sin, and to accuse him of it would be incompatible with the context. It must be remembered that the sentence is built on the words ὁρῶ σε ὄντα; if these are taken strictly they mean that Peter is describing what he is able to perceive in Simon's behaviour. Deut. 29.17 supplies the best hint. Simon is like the man described there as going after the gods of the nations. He is in effect going after false gods because his proposal manifests a false understanding of the God Peter proclaims. The notion of anger is thus not to be understood in χολή and the meaning becomes, 'You are full of bitter poison, bound by unrighteousness.' Cf. *Passio Sanctorum Apostolorum Petri et Pauli* 48 (L.-B. 1.160), Μηδέποτε εἴη σοι καλῶς, Σίμων μάγε καὶ πικρίας ἀνάμεστε. There is little room for penitence on Simon's part here; see the next verse.

24. Simon's words are preceded in D 614 *pc* gig r sy[h**] mae by παρακαλῶ; cf. the variant in v. 19. The Western text makes further verbal changes of no great importance (for ὑπέρ, D* *pc* have περί; for κύριον, D 33 614 2495 *pc* p vg[mss] sy[ph] mae have θεόν, but at the end of the verse, after ἐπέλθῃ, D* (sy[hmg]) mae have μοι τούτων τῶν κακῶν ὧν εἰρήκατέ μοι. ὃς πολλὰ κλαίων οὐ διελίμπανεν (for the participle see BDR § 414. 1), which suggests much more strongly than the Old Uncial text that Simon was truly penitent, though it may have been the Western editor's intention simply to magnify the effect on Simon of Peter's rebuke. Ropes (*Begs.* 3.80) agrees with J. R. Harris (*Four Lectures on the Western Text*, 1894, 94) that Chrysostom used the Western text of this verse. *Clem. Hom.* 20.21; *Recog.* 10.63 say that Simon shed tears of rage and disappointment.

ὑμεῖς is presumably emphatic: You have told me to pray (v. 22); *you* pray on my behalf (ὑπέρ — but this is probably synonymous with περί in v. 15). It is probably unfair to Simon to suggest that he is still moving in the sphere of magic, in that he believes that a prayer offered by Peter will have automatic effect. Cf. Terence, *Adelphi* 4.5.65–71: Abi domum, ac Deos comprecare . . . Abi, pater: tu potius Deos comprecare: nam tibi eos certe scio, Quo vir melior multo es quam ego, obtemperaturos magis. Schneider (495) says, says, 'Die Antwort des Simon ist "reumütig". Er wagt nicht, selbst zu bitten.' Pesch (277) disagrees.

In v. 22 δεήθητι was correctly followed by a genitive; here πρός is used with the accusative (see Radermacher 103).

ὧν εἰρήκατε might suggest that χολὴ πικρίας and σύνδεσμος ἀδικίας were punishments. This is not a necessary conclusion, however; Simon might be looking back to ἀπώλεια in v. 20. On the whole, Simon does appear to be penitent, though possibly motivated by a desire to escape the consequences of his sin rather than to amend his life. 'We are entitled to conjecture that he did repent . . . What we read about Simon elsewhere can rightly be regarded with suspicion for many reasons' (Calvin 242). The issue is not clear because Luke was not greatly interested in it; the personal fate of Simon was not his major concern. Equally, Luke was not attempting either to encourage or to discourage the return of gnostic sects to the church (Lüdemann 103); he has in mind no more than the relics of 'hellenistischer Vulgärreligiosität' (Weiser 205). Weiser goes on (206) to observe, rightly, that to attempt to control the Holy Spirit is a permanent danger of every Christian and of the church as a whole; Luke warns against this.

25. On Luke's use of μὲν οὖν see on 1.6. The words usually draw attention to a transition, here to the end of the paragraph that began at v. 4, but perhaps also (in accordance with Luke's usual practice) to the opening of the next section. If it points forward (so *Begs.* 4.95) it is probably right to infer that οἱ refers to Peter, John, and Philip (see 8. 26). But the aorist participles διαμαρτυράμενοι and λαλήσαντες point backward, and the verse is probably about Peter and John. After this point Peter disappears till 9.32, John completely (apart from the link that connects him with his brother James in 12.2).

διαμαρτύρεσθαι is a deuteropauline word (Lk. once; Acts nine times; Pastorals three times; in addition only 1 Thess. 4.6; Heb. 2.6). Its sense has already been given by 2.40; the apostles fulfilled the commission of 1.8. Speaking the word of the Lord (so ℵ B C D E 𝔐 lat sy^h sa mae; P^{74} A Ψ 326 *pc* t sy^p bo have θεοῦ) is virtually a repetition, as is εὐηγγελίζοντο, here a transitive verb with κώμας as its object (contrast v. 4, where the object is λόγον).

πολλὰς κώμας (accusative perhaps because of the general sense of instruction contained in εὐαγγελίζεσθαι — so Page 134) is intended to indicate only an extensive evangelistic tour among Samaritan villages; we cannot infer that there was only one place in Samaria worthy of the title πόλις; see on v. 5. For the contrast, or contradiction, between this passage and Mt. 10.5 see above, p. 399.

22. PHILIP AND THE ETHIOPIAN 8.26–40

(26) An angel of the Lord spoke to Philip, and said, 'Get up and travel at midday[1] on the road that goes down from Jerusalem to Gaza; this is deserted'.[2] (27) He got up, and went. And there was an Ethiopian man, a eunuch and minister of Candace, Queen of the Ethiopians, who was in charge of all her wealth. He had gone to worship in Jerusalem, (28) and was returning, sitting in his chariot and reading the prophet Isaiah. (29) The Spirit said to Philip, 'Go up to this chariot and join it.' (30) Philip ran up, heard him reading the prophet Isaiah, and said, 'Do you, I wonder, understand what you are reading?' (31) He said, 'How should I be able to, unless someone guides me?' And he asked Philip to get up and sit with him. (32) The passage of scripture that he was reading was this: As a sheep he was led to slaughter, as a lamb before the one who shears it is dumb, so he does not open his mouth. (33) In his humiliation his judgment was taken away. Who shall recount his generation? For his life is taken away from the earth. (34) The eunuch took up the conversation and said to Philip, 'Pray, about whom does the prophet say this? About himself or about someone else?' (35) Philip opened his mouth, and, taking this Scripture as his starting-point, proclaimed to him the good news of Jesus. (36) As they travelled along the road they came upon some water, and the eunuch said, 'Look, here is some water; what prevents me from being baptized?'[3] (38) He gave orders for the chariot to come to a halt and the two of them went down into the water, Philip and the eunuch, and Philip[4] baptized him. (39) When they came up out of the water the Spirit of the Lord caught away Philip and the eunuch saw him no more, for he simply continued on his way, rejoicing. (40) Philip arrived at Azotus; he continued on his way, evangelizing all the cities till he came to Caesarea.

Bibliography

E. Barnikol, *WZ* 6 (1957), 593–610.

E. F. F. Bishop, *AThR* 28 (1946), 154–9.

M. Black, as in (4).

T. L. Brodie, as in (21).

H. von Campenhausen, *VigCh* 25 (1971), 1–16.

E. Dinkler, *FS* Kümmel (1975), 85–95.

[1]Or, south; so *Begs.*, RSV, NEB.
[2]This may refer to the road (so RSV, NEB, NJB) or to the city.
[3]V. 37 is to be omitted on textual grounds.
[4]Greek, he.

A. Grassi, *CBQ* 26 (1964), 463–7.

C. H. Lindijer, *NovTSupp* 48.77–85.

S. Lörsch, *ThQ* 111 (1930), 477–519.

D. Minguez, *Bib* 57 (1976), 168–91.

R. F. O'Toole, *JSNT* 17 (1983), 25–34.

E. Ullendorf, *NTS* 2 (1956), 53–6.

W. C. van Unnik, *SpColl* 1.328–39.

H. Waitz, as in (21) (*ZNW* 7).

Commentary

At first sight this paragraph seems to pose few questions. It is told in a straightforward, though supernatural, style. Supernatural powers direct Philip and cause him to fall in with an Ethiopian eunuch who is a high official under the queen of his country. The traveller is reading the OT; Philip interprets it to him in Christological terms; the eunuch seeks and is given baptism; Philip is removed to Azotus by even more extraordinary means than those by which he was brought into action; and the eunuch proceeds on his way. A conversion has taken place, and the supernatural accompaniments make the point that all that was done was done by the will of God.

To describe it as a simple conversion story is not to dismiss it. Christianity grew by such conversions, and it may be that Luke's intention, and the intention of those from whom he obtained the story, was to illustrate the power of the Gospel and the oversight of the mission by God. It is however probable that Luke, who in 1.8 set out a pattern of expansion, would see how this story fitted into the pattern and would use it to show how the pattern was being followed. Here however a difficulty arises in that the story might seem to be out of order. The Ethiopian was not a Jew by birth (if he had come from a Jewish expatriate family living in the Sudan Luke could not have expressed himself as he does in v. 27 — see the note), nor as a eunuch could he have become a proselyte. He was thus a stage more remote from the people of God than Cornelius, whose story follows in ch. 10, and his conversion marked an even more radical stage in the rise of the gentile mission than Peter's visit to Caesarea. It has been suggested that originally the two stories represented rival claims to tell the story of the origin of the Christian mission beyond Judaism, that Luke chose the Cornelius story for the purpose, and subordinated to it the story of the Ethiopian by describing him as a pilgrim to Jerusalem and as reading the Bible, and by interpreting *eunuch* to mean *official* (finance minister). There is a measure of truth in this, and the twelve points made by Weiser (209–11) undoubtedly demonstrate Lucan interests in the story as we have it.

Not all the twelve points however are of equal weight. To some extent they draw attention to septuagintal features, which others no doubt shared with Luke, and interest in for example joy, Scripture, and place-names are not peculiar to Luke. The more however Lucan features are detected the more it becomes necessary to ask how Luke understood and how he edited the material that he used. It has been maintained that his concern was to show the fulfilment of Isa. 56.3–5 (Let not the eunuch say, Behold, I am a dry tree . . . To the eunuchs who . . . hold fast my covenant . . . I will give them an everlasting name which shall not be cut off) and Ps. 68.31 (32) (Let Ethiopia hasten to stretch out her hands to God); if this was a major part of his intention it is surprising that he did not quote the passages in question.

It is well to remember the reappearance of Philip in Caesarea at 21.8. There is no need to assume any particular theory of the origin of the We-passages (in one of which 21.8 occurs) to recognize a contact that must have been in some way a source of supply of material contained in Acts. Directly or indirectly Luke obtained information about the activities of Philip, one of the Seven. He had given one such story (8.5–13) and combined it with stories about Simon and Peter. It was natural to proceed to the second Philip story as soon as Simon Magus was out of the way and Peter and John had returned to Jerusalem, and it will be noted that both the work of Philip (8.40; 21.8) and that of Peter (9.32–10.1) converge on Caesarea, where there was at an early stage a mixed Jewish and Gentile church. The church of Caesarea did not tell the story of the eunuch as the foundation of mixed churches; it saw this event as taking place in Caesarea itself. It is probable that in fact mixed churches came into being in different places at more or less the same time. This issue however indicates the major difference between the Ethiopian and Cornelius, both of whom are described as neither born Jews nor proselytes but sympathetically interested in Judaism and its religion, and therefore as constituting the same problem to the Christian missionaries — the same problem, and, when accepted, the same achievement. The difference is that after his baptism the eunuch saw Philip no more but continued on his journey to his native Ethiopia, whereas Cornelius was baptized as one of a group who formed the kernel of a church which continued in existence and in relation with the church of Jerusalem. In this sense the story of Cornelius marks a definite advance on the story of the Ethiopian. It is thus nearly but not quite right to describe, with Plümacher (91), the story of the Ethiopian as an episode, not directly connected with the main thread of Luke's narrative. Luke is for the present clearing the Philip account and allowing it to rest until the return much later to Philip the Evangelist. But so far as his interests enter into the story-telling it is fair to say, with Haenchen (304), that the Ethiopian is left in the twilight lest Philip should usurp Peter's place.

It has so far been assumed that Philip is the man referred to in 6.5 and subsequently described not as the apostle but as the evangelist. Pesch (289f., 295f.) argues that the Philip of this story is the apostle (1.13). That the church at a later date confused the two is well known (Eusebius, *H.E.* 3.31.3, 5; 5.24.2f.) and the identity of names meant that such confusion was always possible. But it is not likely here. The Philip who evangelized Samaria is associated with those who were scattered from Jerusalem (8.1, 4, 5) and these did not (according to Luke) include the apostles. It is not said that the evangelist of vv. 26–40 started his journey from Jerusalem; we are not told where he joined the Jerusalem-Gaza road. There was some sort of contact (how direct we must not assume) between the author of Acts and Philip the evangelist.

There is no means of checking the historicity of the narrative unless it can be assumed that angels do not exist or that they do not order missionaries about or provide transport for them. There is no evidence of a first-century church in Ethiopia, though according to Irenaeus, *Adv. Haer.* 4.23.2, and Eusebius, *H.E.* 2.1.13, the eunuch was the first missionary there.

26. The story of Philip is resumed from 8.13, which itself was probably Luke's rounding off of the two traditions, of Philip's teaching and preaching mission, and the activity in Samaria of Simon. The new development in the narrative is ascribed to divine initiative by the reference to *an angel of the Lord* (cf. 5.19; 10.3, 7, 22; 11.13; 12.7–11, 23; 27.23). Later, instructions will be given by the Holy Spirit; in this chapter as in ch. 10 there is in this respect little or no difference between the two agencies (8.26, 29; 10.3, 19). The conversion of the Ethiopian was planned not by Philip but by God, who used his messenger to bring together the evangelist and the Gentile already interested in the Scriptures; for in ἄγγελος κυρίου the κύριος is not necessarily and perhaps not probably the Lord Jesus. ἄγγελος κυρίου is a very common OT expression (almost always for מלאך יהוה) and will probably have its OT sense here. The angel instructs Philip what he must do; cf. e.g. Gen. 16.9; εἶπεν δὲ αὐτῇ ὁ ἄγγελος κυρίου, Ἀποστράφητι . . . Philip must himself go where he is told; there is no supernatural transport, as in v. 39 (by the Spirit, or by an angel; see the note on the text). It is natural that the angel should speak in biblical style (Plümacher 48). For parallels with the Elijah stories see Rackham 121.

ἀνάστηθι (ἀναστάς, omitting καί, in P[50] D) is unnecessary; it is an example of Luke's biblical, septuagintalizing style; cf. e.g. Gen. 21.18, ἀνάστηθι λάβε (קומי שאי). Philip must travel κατὰ μεσημβρίαν. The expression is ambiguous. Etymologically μεσημβρία (cf. Zeph. 2.4, LXX) means *midday, noon*, and κατὰ μεσημβρίαν will accordingly denote the time at which Philip was to depart; but naturally (cf. French *midi*) the word came also to be used of the position of the sun at midday, *the south*, so that κατὰ μεσημβρίαν will denote the direction in which he must travel. Opinions on Luke's meaning differ. Chrysostom by using πρός for κατά indicates that he is thinking of direction; so also does e.g. Weiser (211), 'weil sie dem luk Missionskonzept entspricht'. It is not clear what missionary concept requires this meaning, but it may be allowed that it corresponds with the general geographical position, whether Philip is thought of as starting from (the city or district of) Samaria or from Jerusalem (see below). *Midday* however may be preferred precisely because noon was no time to travel over hot desert country. It was by ordering such unusual action that the angel (as God's agent) ensured that Philip should fall in with the Ethiopian; this new step in the progress of the Gospel was willed not only in general but in particular terms by God.

τὴν ὁδὸν τὴν καταβαίνουσαν. Just as one regularly goes *up* to Jerusalem (so that ἀναβαίνειν becomes a technical term for making a pilgrimage; see e.g. Lk. 2.42; Acts 15.2), so one goes *down* from Jerusalem; but the journey involved descent from a mountain city (2400–2500 feet) to the coast, so that καταβαίνειν is physically appropriate. It is not clear whether Philip 'and the Ethiopian were approaching Gaza on the direct Jerusalem road or on the coast road; if the former, Philip must have returned to Jerusalem (forgetting about the persecution) and then set out again in the direction opposite to that which he had taken in verse 5; if the latter, he must have travelled first north west almost as far as Caesarea before turning south, only to return again northwards to Caesarea (v. 40)' (Barrett, Kremer *Actes*, 284f.). There is no means of determining this problem, of which Luke was probably unaware. The student of Acts must use maps, but in doing so must remember that he will be better informed than Luke was. It is also unclear whether αὕτη refers to the road or to Gaza. The statement αὕτη ἐστὶν ἔρημος could apply to either. According to BDR § 290. 1 n. 2 it applies to the road; 'yet no possible route from Jerusalem to Gaza could be called desert' (G. A. Smith, *Hist. Geog.* 136), and the old town of Gaza, after it had been sacked by Alexander Jannaeus (96 BC), remained long in a state of desolation (πολὺν χρόνον ἐρήμους (Gaza and other cities before rebuilding), Josephus, *Ant.* 14.88; μένουσα ἔρημος, Strabo 16.2.30). There is evidence that when a new Gaza was built the old city was known as ἡ ἔρημος Γάζα (Smith, op. cit. 135 referring to an anonymous writer for whom and for many more details see *NS* 2.101f., n. 77). On this ambiguity also opinions differ. Luke's parenthetical clause could be more or less equivalent to 'I refer to the old deserted Gaza'; but why the Ethiopian should choose to travel on this route is not indicated. Schneider (501) and Weiser (211) think that Luke notes that the road was desert in order to make it clear that Philip and the eunuch were at leisure for undisturbed conversation; Bauernfeind 128 makes the better point that the action takes place on the road not in the town, which is of no significance in the story.

Gaza was one of the five cities of the Philistines. It was taken by Alexander the Great, destroyed by Alexander Jannaeus (see above), rebuilt in 56 BC by Gabinius (Josephus, *Ant.* 14.86). It was again destroyed (perhaps only partially) in AD 66 (Josephus, *War* 2.460).

27. Answering to God's plan is Philip's instant and complete obedience to the angel's command. This is equally part of Luke's theme. It results in his encounter with the Ethiopian. καὶ ἰδού is another (see on v. 26) example of Luke's OT style (cf. 1.10; והנה); it introduces an Ethiopian eunuch. Knox (*Hellenistic Elements* 16) notes that it was a 'commonplace of hellenistic literature that the Ethiopians, living at the back of beyond, were an exceptionally pious race'. He cites Diodorus Siculus 3.2.2ff.; Philostratus, *Apollonius* 6.2; Pausanias 1.33.5 (legd.4); Nicolas of Damascus, Fragment 142 (*Frag. Griech. Historiker* 2.385), and refers to Erman, *Die Religion der Ägypter* 355, and Rohde, *Die gr. Rom.*[2] 210ff., 470. This is a valid observation, at least to the extent that it is probably Luke's intention to bring out for the first time the contrast he will later underline between the Jews who reject the Gospel and the Gentiles who accept it. Schmithals (84) notes an interest in Ethiopia in Luke's time, arising probably in part out of Nero's expedition, sent in AD 61, ad investigandum caput Nili (Seneca, *Nat. Quaest.* 6.8.3, 4; cf. Pliny, *Nat. Hist.* 6.181ff.; 12.19; Dio Cassius 63.8.1). The Ethiopians were ἔσχατοι ἀνδρῶν (Homer, *Odyssey* 1.23; cf. Acts 1.8). More important among the early Christians than this general interest must have been OT passages. For Ethiopians see Ps. 68 (67).32, Αἰθιοπία προφθάσει χεῖρα αὐτῆς τῷ θεῷ (כוש תריץ ידיו לאלהים), a passage quoted on v. 26 by Bede; Zeph. 3.10 (ἐκ περάτων ποταμῶν Αἰθιοπίας οἴσουσιν θυσίας μοι); cf. 2.4, for Gaza and the word μεσημβρία. The Ethiopian kingdom was not the modern Ethiopia (Abyssinia) but the Sudan; its capital was Meroe.

Eunuchs were excluded from the Lord's assembly (קהל יהוה, ἐκκλησία κυρίου); so Deut. 23.1 (23.2, LXX) is usually interpreted, but Yebamoth 8 (cf. Niddah 5.9) suffices to bring out the difference between one impotent from birth and a man who has been subsequently mutilated. The question of interpretation is further complicated by the derivation and use of the Hebrew סריס. This word had originally nothing to do with sexual impotence, and the present verse may bear some witness to its original reference to persons of state (this man was a δυνάστης — see below). In late Hebrew however (see Jastrow s.v.; the סריס אדם, made so by man, and the סריס חמה, born so from when he (first) saw the sun, are equally important) the word seems to have acquired a purely physiological meaning, and this is confirmed at an earlier date by Isa. 56.3–5 (see above and below), where the eunuch says, I am a dry tree (עֵץ יָבֵשׁ), and is consoled for having no children. This passage is important because it holds out to the eunuch as to the non-Israelite the hope that they will eventually be accepted into God's people. Luke does not refer to it but (as with Ps. 68) many early Christians will have known it. *ND* 3.40–43 quotes an inscription (*AE* 828; *SEG* 28(1978). 1536) in which a woman is praised as εὐνοῦχον, which here presumably must mean *chaste*. This is scarcely relevant to the use of the word in Acts (which *ND* takes to mean *court chamberlain*).

The Ethiopian is at once εὐνοῦχος and δυνάστης. The combination of physical defect and high office is not unusual (see above on the ambiguity of the Hebrew סָרִים), and is not in itself a ground for suspecting editorial activity. ἐπιεικῶς γὰρ εἰώθεσαν εὐνούχους ἔχειν γαζοφύλακας (Plutarch, *Demetrius* 25.5 (900)). As a δυνάστης he was a leading man, a man of power, in his own country. The word has in itself no precise meaning, and translates a number of Hebrew words in the OT. He had power as an agent Κανδάκης βασιλίσσης ((τῆς β, Ψ 𝔐; β.(τινος, D* (t)) Αἰθιόπων. Luke seems to have taken Candace as a personal name; in fact it appears to transliterate the title that appears in Ethiopic inscriptions as k(e)ut(e)ky, and to be reduplicated by βασίλισσα (a later form replacing the classical βασίλεια; cf. Phrynichus 202, Βασίλισσα· οὐδεὶς τῶν ἀρχαίων εἶπεν, ἀλλὰ βασίλεια ἢ βασιλίς). Cf. Pliny, *Nat. Hist.* 6.186.(25), regnare feminam Candacen, quod nomen multis iam annis ad reginas transiit; see also Strabo 17.1.54 (820); Dio Cassius 54.5.4; Bion of Soli, *Aethiopica* 1. See further E. Dinkler in *FS* Kümmel (1975), 92–4. Precision is given to δυνάστης by the clause ὃς ἦν ἐπὶ πάσης τῆς γάζης αὐτῆς; he was the queen's chief finance officer. It is not impossible that Luke intends a pun between Γάζα, the place, and γάζα, *treasure*. γάζα is a word of Persian origin; according to Servius (Scholion on *Aeneid* 1.119), Gaza Persicus sermo est, et significat divitias; unde Gaza urbs in Palaestina dicitur, quod in ea Cambyses rex Persarum, cum Aegyptiis bellum inferret, divitiis suis condidit. But Calvin (244) long ago pointed out that עַזָּה (= Γάζα) existed long before Cambyses.

Luke thus describes a man of authority and position; and adds that ἐληλύθει προσκυνήσων (as at 24.11, future participle expressing purpose; BDR § 351) εἰς Ἰερουσαλήμ. In what sense had he worshipped in Jerusalem? He was not a born Jew but an Ethiopian, and therefore had no right based on race to take part in Temple worship, though he could have entered the Court of the Gentiles. As a eunuch he could not (see above) have become a proselyte. If it is right to speak of a special class of 'God-fearers' or 'half-proselytes', who accepted much of Jewish belief and practice without taking the decisive step of becoming proselytes by circumcision, baptism and sacrifice, the eunuch may have been one of such persons; certainly it is clear that he read the Jewish Scriptures and engaged, so far as he could, in the worship that was practised in Jerusalem, and this observation is, in the present context, more important than the general one (for which see on 10.2). One must ask whether a man could be found of whom all these predicates are true: he was an Ethiopian; he was a eunuch; he belonged to the ruling class of his people; he read the Bible; he went on pilgrimage to Jerusalem. He was certainly a rare bird. Would Luke have regarded him as standing on the same level as Cornelius, or does he represent a slightly different stage in the expansion of the church? Palestinian Jews, Hellenistic Jews, Samaritans, the Ethiopian, Cornelius, Gentiles? It may be that Luke believed him to belong to an earlier stage, nearer to the promises than Cornelius, because of the favourable prophecy of Isa. 56; but this is not quoted, and it is doubtful whether Luke had it, or even the Zephaniah passages in mind. In fact the Ethiopian was more remote from the people of God than Cornelius, for Cornelius could at any time have become a proselyte whereas the eunuch could never become one. Probably we must be content to take the story as a piece of tradition about Philip which Luke placed here not because it fitted into his scheme of Christian expansion but because this was the point at which he was dealing with Philip.

If the sentence is read with the word ὅς immediately before ἐληλύθει we must supply a part of the verb *to be*: Behold there was a man . . . who had gone to Jerusalem to worship. ὅς is read by P⁵⁰ ℵᶜ B C² Dᶜ E (Ψ) 𝔐 (it), but is omitted by P⁷⁴ᵛⁱᵈ ℵ* A C* D* p vg. If the word is omitted we must translate: Behold, a man . . . had gone to Jerusalem to worship. The variant makes no difference to the sense. ὅς was probably original and omitted because 'the full sentence-building virtue of ἰδού was not felt' (Ropes, *Begs.* 3.81).

28. The Ethiopian was now returning; he 'had *not* received the Spirit at Jerusalem' (Davies, *Land* 274, noting that 'geographical limits to "the Spirit" are transcended' by his conversion — though it cannot be said that Luke was concerned to point this out since, except in a secondary text, he does not say that the eunuch received the Spirit). He was sitting in his wagon (for the expression cf. Josephus, *Ant.* 8.386, τῷ ᾿Αχάβῳ ἐφ᾿ἅρματος καθεζομένῳ); perhaps we should say *on* (ἐπί with the genitive) *his wagon*, the vehicle being probably little more than a flat board on wheels. Little is known of the construction of travelling vehicles in antiquity, but the ἅρμα was certainly not the most luxurious kind of vehicle. That the word was used sometimes for a racing-chariot, sometimes for a war-chariot, does not suggest comfort in travelling; it is contrasted with the ἁρμάμαξα (a compound of ἅρμα with ἅμαξα), the (Persian) covered carriage by Herodotus (7.41.1; cf. Aristophanes, *Acharnians*

70). Blass (111f.) thinks that Luke uses ἅρμα for ἁρμάμαξα. At Gen. 41.42; 46.29 it translates מרכבה, a vehicle for travel, though the word has other meanings (and other Greek translations) elsewhere in the OT. All we can say is that Luke thought of a vehicle capable of holding two passengers. It cannot have moved very rapidly (it was probably ox-drawn) since Philip was able to run and join it (v. 30).

ἦν ὑποστρέφων is descriptive rather than a simple periphrastic tense: *he was on his way back*. The usual imperfect ἀνεγίνωσκεν describes the Ethiopian's occupation as he moved slowly along the road. He was fortunate to possess for himself a copy of a biblical book, and must have been enthusiastic in the practice of such features of the Jewish religion as were available to him. He was reading aloud, as was customary in antiquity; Haenchen (300) rightly disagrees with *Begs.* 4.97, where the usual interpretation of Augustine, *Confessions* 6.3 (Cum legebat [Ambrose], oculi ducebantur per paginas et cor intellectum rimabatur, vox autem et lingua quiescebant) is rejected. See also Betz (2 n. 6). Jews thought it desirable to read aloud because to do so helped the memory to retain what was read (StrB 2.687).

29. In v. 26 an angel spoke to Philip; now the Spirit does so. Luke has so much to say about the gift of the Spirit that it is hard to think that he put the Spirit and angels on the same level, but here both serve the same purpose of directing events in accordance with the will of God. Cf. 10.3, 19, etc. It may be that Philip would need specific instructions before approaching a person of (presumably) higher social standing.

On κολλᾶσθαι see C. Burchard (*ZNW* 61(1970), 159f.), referred to on 5.13 (cf. 9.26; 10.28; 17.34). It is not so easy in the present verse to accept Burchard's rendering *draw near to* because this would be tautologous with προσελθεῖν; the command would become *approach and draw near to this chariot*. The difficulty is not great. In 5.13 *drawing near to* the group of recognized Christians meant virtually joining them. So here. Philip is physically to approach the chariot (a necessary preliminary), and then attach himself to it, or rather to the man travelling in it. This he does by asking about the passage which he hears (see on v. 28) the Ethiopian reading.

30. προσδραμών makes sense: Philip quickened his pace. The variant προσελθών (P⁵⁰ *pc*) is a somewhat thoughtless assimilation to the word of command in v. 29. Again Philip is instantly obedient (cf. v. 27). He ran up and heard the Ethiopian reading (aloud; see on v. 28). The exchange that follows is a 'gem of Greek conversation' (Knox, *Hellenistic Elements* 16). Philip's question is introduced by ἆρά γε, the precise force of which is not easy to grasp, or at least to express. In itself, ἆρα implies neither a positive nor a negative answer (cf. however Xenophon, *Memorabilia* 1.5.4, where a definitely positive answer is expected). According to Moule, *IB* 158, γε 'perhaps adds a sense of doubt'; according to LS 340 it adds emphasis; according to BDR § 439.1 it is no more than an 'unbedeutenden Anhängsel'. Page (134) takes the particles to mean Dost thou really? implying that he does not. *Begs.* 4.96f. translates, Do you after all know what you are reading? We should perhaps emphasise the word *Do* in the question: *Do* you understand what you are reading?' 'γε ajoute de la vivacité à la question' (Delebecque 43).

The question contains a neat example of paronomasia, γινώσκεις ἃ ἀναγινώσκεις; the contrast between reading and understanding is familiar in Judaism; see Daube (*NTRJ* 434) and the whole context; and see on v. 35. It was right to use a journey for study; e.g. Erubin 54a; cf. Aboth 3.8.

31. The Ethiopian replies in Greek as stylish as Philip's (see Knox, *Hellenistic Elements* 16). The optative with ἄν (*How should I be able . . .?*) has been described as, in the NT age, old-fashioned (M. 3.123), or as a mark of education (Radermacher 128); certainly it is a sign of conscious style (cf. 17.18; 26.29; see BDR § 385. 1, 'in der Volksprache ganz abhanden gekommen'). γάρ adds a nice touch, implying a protasis. Bengel puts it neatly: 'elegans particula, hoc sensu: quid quaeris?' One may render, 'Of course I do not (fully) understand, *for* how should I be able to so so unless . . .?' Or, 'You need not ask, *for* how . . .?' After these niceties it is surprising to read, with ἐὰν μή, the future indicative ὁδηγήσει (so P⁵⁰ (B*) C E L 6 614 1175 al; P⁷⁴ A B² Ψ 𝔐 have ὁδηγήσῃ), but it may be that this should be regarded as no more than an orthographic variant of the aorist subjunctive; the two would be pronounced identically. Delebecque (43): πῶς γάρ adds weight to a negative reply; ὁδηγήσῃ must be read — Luke is writing in classical style as he describes for himself an everyday scene.

The OT is not self-explanatory; Schneider (503) and Roloff (140) among recent commentators both point out that, for Luke, the OT needs Christological interpretation, the former drawing the parallel with Lk. 24.13–35, the latter pointing out that the Ethiopian's failure to understand does not mean that he is deficient in intelligence. The OT bears witness (so Luke, like other NT writers, believed) to Jesus Christ, but the witness is intelligible only if one is able to begin with Jesus. This is the advantage that Philip has over the Ethiopian (v. 35, εὐηγγελίσατο αὐτῷ τὸν Ἰησοῦν). One cannot simply begin with the OT and extract Jesus from it. The traveller is seeking guidance and invites Philip's assistance. It is surely incorrect to translate (with M. 3.65) '*he made Philip come up* (not *invited*)'. The fact that παρεκάλεσεν is aorist cannot change the meaning of the verb to such an extent, though it may imply (as the narrative will shortly show) that the request was successful. BDR § 328. 2 n. 3 observe that where a request is not said to be granted the imperfect is usual; here however their comment is justified, 'Erfüllung also selbstverständlich nicht erwähnt.' But this is still not *made him come!*

32, 33. These verses indicate what the Ethiopian was reading in Isaiah, but there remains some lack of clarity. In ἡ περιοχὴ τῆς γραφῆς ἥν, the antecedent of ἥν may be περιοχή or γραφῆς. The phrase may thus mean (1) The passage of Scripture which (i.e., which passage) . . ., or (2) The content of the Scripture (i.e., Scripture passage) which (i.e., which Scripture) . . . περιοχή itself is ambiguous (as is the corresponding Hebrew, ענין; see StrB 2.687f.), and the meaning of γραφή (Scripture as a whole; unit of Scripture) can be adjusted to fit, though when Scripture as a whole is intended the plural γραφαί is more often used. The difference is slight, but may have some bearing on the question whether Luke intends the reader to think of the words quoted (ὡς πρόβατον . . . ἡ ζωὴ αὐτοῦ) as constituting all that was in mind or as representing a longer passage of which it could be regarded as a specimen. A common-sense view of the verses suggests that on a long slow journey the Ethiopian would be likely to cover more than six lines, and that these are quoted as a summary of a longer passage. This would carry two implications, of somewhat different import: (1) that we may take the whole of the fourth Servant Song (Isa. 52.13–53.12) to be under consideration, and (2) that Luke considered the words quoted, which, as has often been observed, contain no reference to the word παῖς or to vicarious suffering, as adequately summarizing the Song. Cf. Delling (*Kreuzestod* 90):

'Unmittelbar vor der Aussage über den Zusammenhang zwischen dem Leiden des Gottesknechts und den Sünden der anderen (V. 8d) bricht das Zitat ab, wie es auch erst nach den Sätzen über das stellvertretende Leiden des Knechtes (V. 4–6) einsetzte. Das Zitat in Apg. 8.32f. zeigt, was für Lukas an Jes. 53 entscheidend war. Es entspricht durchaus dem Schema, das in den Reden begegnet, bzw. das Schema deutet sich selbst in dem Ausschnitt des Zitates an: den ihr getötet habt (in Erfüllung des Ratschlusses Gottes, wie er im Alten Testament angezeigt ist), den hat Gott auferweckt. Der Kreuzestod Jesu bleibt seinem Sinn nach ein — in Gottes Willen eingeborgenes — Geheimnis.'

Elsewhere (e.g. 2.29–33; 4.27f.) Luke gives an interpretation of OT passages that he quotes; not so here (Roloff 141). Schmithals (85) finds here an example 'der konsequenten Eliminierung der paulinischen Kreuzestheologie durch Lukas in seiner Auseinandersetzung mit den Irrlehrern'. Bauernfeind (129) suggests that it may have been the missionary communities of the Seven who developed the use of Isa. 53.

The Isaiah passage (53.7, 8) is quoted in agreement with the LXX, with small variations that have affected the transmission of the text of Acts. κείραντος is probably original in Acts (P⁵⁰ᵛⁱᵈ P⁷⁴ ℵ C E L Ψ 36 104 323 614 1175 2495 *al*); κείροντος is read by B 𝔐; MSS of the LXX differ. In v. 33 the first αὐτοῦ is omitted by P⁷⁴ ℵ A B 1739 *pc* lat Irˡᵃᵗ; it is not in the LXX and may have been omitted by assimilation. After τήν, δέ is added by P⁷⁴ E (Ψ) 𝔐 it Irˡᵃᵗ; this is not in the LXX and the text that differs is probably right, though the omission of δέ is strongly supported (by ℵ A B C *pc* vg Eus). In two places the Hebrew differs from the LXX (and thus from Acts):

LXX: ἐν τῇ ταπεινώσει ἡ κρίσις αὐτοῦ ἤρθη
MT: מעוצר וממשפט לקח
From (as a result of) oppression (coercion) and judgment he was taken off
LXX: ὅτι αἴρεται ἀπὸ τῆς γῆς ἡ ζωὴ αὐτοῦ
MT: כי נגזר מארץ חיים
For he was cut off from the land of the living.

In the first passage the LXX presumably read משפטו לקח; in the second, חיים and נגזרו.

The meaning of v. 32 is reasonably clear; it speaks of one who suffered without complaint. The Ethiopian may well be excused for failing to understand v. 33, especially in the form in which we see it. Whom could the prophet be portraying?

34. ἀποκριθείς . . . εἶπεν. Cf. 4.19. The Ethiopian replies to the unexpressed question, Do you understand these few lines immediately before you? Up to a point their meaning is clear, but he cannot tell to whom they refer. For the interpretation and application that Luke ascribes to Philip see on v. 35.

For the interpretation of the Servant among Jews in the NT period see especially J. Jeremias in *TWNT* 5.676–98, though he is not to be followed in the view that there was at this time a strand of interpretation that identified the Servant with the Messiah; on this G. Dalman (*Der leidende und der sterbende Messias*, Berlin, 1888) is still convincing: the Servant was one or another of the great righteous men of Israel's past, or Israel as a whole. It has been held that the Suffering Servant motif was 'one of wide application among the Qumran Covenanters. It was applied to the community as a whole, to a special group of twelve or fifteen men who actually (or ideally) headed the society, to the Teacher of Righteousness, and probably also to the Messiahs of Aaron and Israel' (W. H. Brownlee, in Stendahl, *Scrolls* 50). This view has not won wide acceptance (see already Millar Burrows, *DSS*

266f.; *More Light* 316f.); the Qumran sect probably did not add further confusion to the Ethiopian's perplexity.

περὶ ἑαυτοῦ. Jeremias (op. cit. 5.684) notes that there is no parallel to the view that in Isa. 53.7f. the prophet was speaking of himself, though other Servant passages (e.g. 49.5; 50.4) are expressed in the first person singular and could thus give rise to this belief. Haenchen (302) refers to K. F. Euler, *Die Verkündung vom leidenden Gottesknecht aus Jes 53 in der griechischen Bibel*, 1934, whom however he does not find convincing.

35. ἀνοίγειν τὸ στόμα is another of Luke's biblical phrases (cf. 10.34; 18.14). It occurs frequently in the LXX as a rendering of פתח פי, which continued in use. 'In Rabbinic language, "to open one's mouth", *pathaḥ piw*, as a rule shortened into "to open", frequently denotes "to open a lecture on Scripture" or even "to lecture on Scripture"' (Daube, *NTRJ* 434). Daube refers to *Aboth de R. Nathan* 8, where 'R. Johanan ben Zaccai asked Eliezer ben Hyrcanus: "Open and expound", *pathaḥ udherosh*.' When Philip thus began to speak he εὐηγγελίσατο αὐτῷ τὸν Ἰησοῦν, that is, he represented Jesus as the one of whom the prophet spoke, and further claimed that the fulfilment of prophecy in Jesus constituted good news, εὐαγγέλιον. Page (135) — he 'described the life of Jesus, and pointed out its correspondence with the account of the Messiah given in Isaiah' — reads too much into εὐηγγελίσατο, even if the Christian syllogism 'Jesus is the Messiah; Jesus is the Servant; therefore the Servant is the Messiah' is assumed. For the various constructions of the verb εὐαγγελίζεσθαι see on 5.42.

The εὐαγγέλιον is clearer than the exegesis. Philip evidently claims that Jesus fulfils the OT; that God has acted in his death and resurrection; and that in consequence salvation is offered to those who will accept it in faith. V. 32 not only depicts Jesus as an uncomplaining sufferer but also suggests that his death was in some sense sacrificial, though the force of this is lowered by the parallel between the slaughtering and the shearing of a sheep. V. 33a may continue the theme of suffering: he was humiliated and in the process his (right to) fair trial (judgment) was taken away from him. Alternatively, Luke may have seen here the first reference to God's vindication of his Servant. In the very midst of his humiliation, and because he accepted it, the judgment against him was removed, cancelled. Cf. Phil. 2.6–11. It is hard to make sense of v. 33b unless one can assume that γενεά is used in a transferred sense of the disciples, followers of Jesus. Christians are becoming, or will become, so numerous that no one will be able to count them. This of course is part of the vindication of the sufferer. V. 33c is as ambiguous as v. 33a. It could refer to suffering: his life is taken away, that is, he is killed. It may however refer to his ascension (1.9–11); his earthly life is lifted up his earthly life is lifted up from earth to heaven. On all this however see *Begs.* 4.97: 'As Philip does not give us his explanation we do not know it.'

ἀρξάμενος recalls somewhat distantly Lk. 24.47; Acts 1.22 (see the note), more closely Lk. 24.27 (ἀρξάμενος ἀπὸ Μωυσέως καὶ ἀπὸ πάντων τῶν προφητῶν). Philip began his preaching (the word is justified by the use of εὐαγγελίζεσθαι though the congregation consists of one person) from the passage quoted, but may have introduced further OT material. The continuation of the narrative shows that the Ethiopian accepted the message delivered by Philip.

36. The Ethiopian and Philip continue their journey together (ἐπορεύοντο), conversing presumably as they travel κατὰ τὴν ὁδόν. There is no ground for regarding this phrase as a Semitism (see also v. 39); cf. Josephus, *Ant.* 8.404 (where by a curious coincidence one of the travellers is a eunuch) and Lucian, *Cataplus* 4, though these passages suggest *on the way* rather than *along the road*, and the phrase should perhaps be connected with ἦλθον rather than with ἐπορεύοντο. There is good winter rainfall on the coastal strip (cf. v. 26), and it is therefore not surprising that the two ἦλθον ἐπί τι ὕδωρ, (τὸ ὕδωρ, in P⁷⁴ 326 *pc*, does not make good sense and must have originated in a simple slip). Although water might well be found in this area Plümacher (91) is not wrong in finding in it a further example of the providentia specialissima that marks the story. Luke does not say whether the water was a stream or a pool; he does not share the concern of the Didache (7.1f.) that baptism should be if possible in running (living) water.

The eunuch proposes baptism in the question, τί κωλύει με βαπτισθῆναι; What hinders, prevents, me from being baptized? In similar baptismal contexts the verb κωλύειν occurs at 10.47; 11.17; Barth (*CD* 4.4.49) notes that all are related to the baptism of Gentiles, where it might have been expected that some objection would be made. This makes against Cullman's suggestion (*V. & A.* 524–531) that the term is a liturgical one, used to raise the question whether any impediment to baptism is alleged. This suggestion is accepted by Dinkler (*Signum Crucis* 116; cf. 111, where Dinkler observes in this story the order, word, faith, baptism, Spirit), but the evidence is slight, and κωλύειν is a common enough word, used for example in Acts in non-baptismal contexts at 16.6; 24.23; 27.43. Its use at Mk. 10.14 (and parallels) need not be connected with baptism at all, and certainly does not settle the question of infant baptism. τί (or τίς) κωλύει; seems to be a fairly common idiom whose meaning differs little from Why not? So for example Plato, *Euthyphro* 9d, τί γὰρ κωλύει, ὦ Σώκρατες; Josephus, *War* 2.395; it occurs also in Latin: Vergil, *Aeneid* 5.631, Quis prohibet muros iacere . . .? Petronius 104, Quis, inquit, prohibet navigium scrutari? 127, Quid prohibet et sororem adoptare? 'It is, of course, impossible to identify this water, but the Wadi el Hasi north of Gaza has found advocates' (*Begs.* 4.98).

In the majority of MSS the Ethiopian's question receives no answer in words; a few add v. 37, the authenticity of which is defended by Cullmann, loc. cit.

37. This verse is added as follows: εἶπεν δὲ αὐτῷ (+ ὁ Φίλιππος E)· εἰ (ἐὰν E) πιστεύεις ἐξ ὅλης τῆς καρδίας σου (om. 323 *pc*) ἔξεστιν (σωθήσει E). ἀποκριθεὶς δὲ εἶπεν· πιστεύω τὸν υἱὸν τοῦ θεοῦ εἶναι τὸν Ἰησοῦν Χριστόν (εἰς τὸν Χριστὸν τὸν υἱὸν τοῦ θεοῦ E) E 36 323 453 945 1739 1891 *pc* (it vg^cl sy^h** mae Ir Cyp). These MSS (it should be noted that D is not extant from 8.29 to 10.14) thus provide an answer to the question (v. 36), τί κωλύει and do so in the form of an elementary confession of faith. There is no racial qualification for baptism, but right belief is necessary. Most are agreed that this verse represents an accommodation of the text to later baptismal belief and practice; Cullmann (see above) is almost alone in defending it (but see also Rackham 123). If however the verse had been originally part of Luke's text it is hard to see what motive could have led to its omission; on the other hand, some copyists may have thought the shorter text dangerously inadequate. A further argument against the authenticity of the verse is that in the two clauses it seems to use the word πιστεύειν in different senses. In Philip's requirement that the Ethiopian should 'believe with his whole heart' the sense of the word is *fiducia*, whole-hearted confident trust in God (or Christ). This is Luke's own understanding of the word; see e.g. 2.44. In the reply the word denotes acceptance of a dogmatic proposition. The two senses are related, yet distinguishable. This is the first occasion in Acts on which Jesus is described as the Son of God (cf. 9.20, in Paul's preaching in Damascus; see the note). The author of the Third Gospel undoubtedly believed Jesus to be the Son of God (e.g. Lk. 1.32, 35), but metaphysical relations and pre-existence were not major concerns of his (or, it seems, of most of the earliest Christians). The words have been said (e.g. Weiser 214) to recall Rom. 10.9, but this is described by Paul as a summary of preaching rather than as a baptismal confession. They must however, even if not written by Luke, be regarded as one of the earliest witnesses to the second article in the baptismal creed (cf. e.g. Irenaeus, *Adv. Haer.* 1.2, . . . καὶ εἰς ἕνα Χριστὸν Ἰησοῦν τὸν υἱὸν τοῦ θεοῦ . . .).

38. The subject of ἐκέλευσεν will be the eunuch, both as subject of the preceding sentence (whether v. 37 is included in the text or not), and as in control of the wagon. It is implied that he had a driver.

κατέβησαν: the water, pool or stream, was naturally lower than the level of the road. The two men both went into the water, εἰς τὸ ὕδωρ; ἐβάπτισεν would naturally mean that Philip immersed his companion, but it must include also the words that gave meaning to the action — presumably (to judge from passages such as 2.38; 8.16) some such words as βαπτίζω σε ἐπὶ (or ἐν) τῷ ὀνόματι Ἰησοῦ Χριστοῦ (or εἰς τὸ ὄνομα τοῦ κυρίου Ἰησοῦ). Unless the long text of v. 39 (see the note) is accepted there is nothing in this passage to tell us how Luke understood baptism. Equally there is nothing to suggest that Philip was in any way unable completely to initiate a believer into the Christian faith; it is most improbable that Luke meant to suggest this when he introduced Peter and John at 8.14.

39. ἀνέβησαν corresponds to κατέβησαν in v. 38. 'Mutavit Aethiops pellem suam, id est corde peccatorum abluto, de lavacro Jesu dealbatus ascendit' (Bede).

πνεῦμα κυρίου. Cf. vv. 26, 29. God through his agents continues to control the whole event. The eunuch is now a baptized Christian; Philip's work for him is done. Anarthrous πνεῦμα (contrast 5.9, τὸ πνεῦμα κυρίου; 16.7, τὸ πνεῦμα Ἰησοῦ) may suggest a Semitic background (Knox, *Hellenistic Elements* 16). *The Spirit caught away Philip:* elsewhere in the NT ἁρπάζειν is used of the rapture of persons to heaven, or to God — 2 Cor. 12.2, 4 (Paul is caught up into the third heaven, Paradise); 1 Thess. 4.17 (believers living at the time of the parousia will be caught up to meet the returning Lord in the air); Rev. 12.5 (the child born to the woman will be rescued by being caught up to God). The word is regularly used however to mean *carry off to a different place* (in the NT cf. Jn 6.15), and there is no difficulty in the supernatural application given to it here. See Betz (168f.), with interesting though not completely satisfactory parallels from Lucian; none of them describes the simple transference of a human being from one place on earth to another. At *Dial. Deorum* 4.1, for example, Ganymede is taken from his shepherding by Zeus, but in order that Zeus may enjoy his company; so also at 5.1f., with Hera. There are better parallels in the OT; see 3 Kdms 18.12; 4 Kdms 2.16 though here the verb is different: πνεῦμα κυρίου ἀρεῖ σε εἰς γῆν, ἣν οὐκ οἶδα ... ἦρεν αὐτὸν πνεῦμα κυρίου). Cf. also Philostratus, *Apollonius* 8.10. Blass (113) surprisingly thinks that πνεῦμα should here be translated *wind*: 'ventus domini . . . nam de spiritu s. hic cogitare subabsurdum sit'. Not more absurd, note *Begs.* 4.98, than having Philip blown to Azotus.

The subject of ἐπορεύετο must be the eunuch, since Philip's whereabouts and next actions are reported in v. 40; as far as the eunuch is concerned, he vanishes. γάρ is at first surprising but is explained by an ellipse. The sense is: The eunuch saw no more of Philip, for he, unlike Philip, was not supernaturally removed but simply continued his journey. He did so rejoicing, having now become a Christian, understanding the OT in the light of its fulfilment, and, through baptism, receiving the forgiveness of his sins. It is not said (but see below) that he received the Holy Spirit. There is no need (with Lüdemann 109) to consider v. 39d a redactional addition. The accusative τὴν ὁδὸν αὐτοῦ has been said to be a Semitism (Wensinck, cited by Black, *AA* 303), but the NT parallels given (Lk. 9.57; Acts 8.36) are not parallel, and Moed Qatan 3.7 must be a mistaken reference. Gen. 4.7 in the Fragment Targum אזל חבל לארחה is parallel but on its own a scanty foundation. Wilcox (137f.) however agrees that this is a Semitism. Xenophon, *Cyropaedeia* 5.2.22 (cited by BA 1124 s.v. ὁδός), ὁ δὲ Κῦρος ... οὐ μόνον τῷ πορεύεσθαι τὴν ὁδὸν προσεῖχε τὸν νοῦν ..., is hardly good enough to establish the usage as Greek.

Another textual variant, comparable with v. 37 but supported by different witnesses (A 36 323 453 945 1739 1891 *pc* 1 p (w sy^h**) mae), though both may be of Western origin (it will be recalled that D is wanting at this point), brings the baptism story into line with conventional baptismal expectation by reporting that the Holy Spirit (πνεῦμα ἅγιον) fell (ἐπέπεσεν, cf. 8.16) on the eunuch. An angel of the Lord (cf. v. 26) is now brought in not merely to direct but to transport Philip: πνεῦμα ἅγιον ἐπέπεσεν ἐπὶ τὸν εὐνοῦχον· ἄγγελος δὲ κυρίου ἥρπασεν τὸν Φίλιππον. The long text is defended by Black, *FS* Nida, 123.

40. The Spirit brings Philip by supernatural means to Azotus, the OT Ashdod, modern Esdud, just over twenty miles up the coast from Gaza. For an excellent brief account see *NS* 2.108f. The town does not enter into the story of Acts, though it is probably correct to say (Bauernfeind 129), 'Asdod wird als zeitweiliger, Caesarea als endgültiger Wohnsitz des Philippus bekannt gewesen sein.'

εὑρέθη is a Semitism according to Wensinck (Black, *AA* 303), but again (cf. the notes on v. 39) the only satisfactory parallel cited is from the Fragment Targum (Gen. 28.10, ואשתכח בהרן). Some supposedly parallel passages (Deut. 20.11; 4 Kdms 14.14; 1 Esr. 1.19; 8.13; Bar. 1.7) refer to situation rather than arrival; better are Esther 1.5; Hermas, *Similitude* 9.13.2 (both with εἰς), cited by BDR § 313. 2; they translate 'kam nach A.', 'tauchte plötzlich in A. auf'. For a parallel in a sixth century papyrus see *ND* 2.69.

Philip continues his evangelistic journey. For διερχόμενος see on 8.4; here as there it is helped out by εὐαγγελίζεσθαι; see on 5.42. ἕως τοῦ with the infinitive is post-classical (BDR § 403. 5: Gen. 24.33; 28.15; 33.3; Polybius, Josephus, papyri). Caesarea is a further fifty-five miles or so up the coast, as the crow flies. Important cities on the way were Jamnia and Antipatris (23.31). Lydda (9.32–5) and Joppa (9.36–43; 10.5–23) lay east and west of the road respectively, but not far from it.

Eventually Philip reached Caesarea, the capital of Judaea. It was there rather than at Jerusalem that the Roman authorities had their seat (Tacitus, *Histories* 2.79, . . . Mucianus Antiochiam, Vespasianus Caesaream: illa Suriae, haec Judaeae caput est). Earlier called Strato's Tower, Caesarea was refounded and rebuilt with great magnificence by Herod the Great and named Caesarea in honour of Augustus. The population was chiefly Gentile (Josephus, *War* 3.409, . . . Καισάρειαν, μεγίστην τῆς τε Ἰουδαίας πόλιν καὶ τὸ πλέον ὑφ' Ἑλλήνων οἰκουμένην), and there were many conflicts between Jews and Greeks, resolved by Nero in AD 61 in favour of the Greeks (Josephus, *Ant.* 20.183f.). According to Josephus, *War* 2.457, the whole Jewish population (20,000) was massacred in AD 66. See further *NS* 2.115–118.

Philip reappears at Caesarea at 21.8, in a 'We-passage', and it is probably correct to think (Dibelius 15) of the present verse as a postscript to the story of the Ethiopian designed to make the connection and based on inference. Luke does not say when Philip reached Caesarea, though a natural reading of this verse suggests (not necessarily correctly) that he did so fairly soon after his arrival at Azotus. Discussion of the 'We-passages' must not be anticipated here (see Vol. II), but whatever their relation to the author of the book as a whole it is not unreasonable to consider the possibility that Philip provided a link at some point between the finished work and some of the stories of the first eight chapters.

V

SAUL THE GREAT EVANGELIST
PREPARED FOR MISSION (9.1–31)

23. SAUL'S CONVERSION 9.1–19a

(1) Saul, still breathing threatening and murder against the disciples of the Lord, approached the High Priest (2) and asked from him letters to Damascus, to the synagogues, so that if he found any, men or women, who belonged to the Way, he might bring them as prisoners to Jerusalem. (3) As he was on his way, he was drawing near to Damascus; suddenly a light from heaven shone round him. (4) He fell to the ground and heard a voice saying to him, 'Saul, Saul, why are you persecuting me?' (5) He said, 'Who art thou, Lord?' The other answered, 'I am Jesus, whom you are persecuting. (6) But get up and go into the city, and it will be told you what you must do.' (7) The men who were travelling with him stood still, struck dumb; they heard the voice but saw no one. (8) Saul got up from the ground, and when he opened his eyes he saw nothing; but they led him by the hand and brought him into Damascus. (9) For three days he saw nothing, and neither ate nor drank.

(10) In Damascus there was a disciple called Ananias. In a vision the Lord said to him, 'Ananias.' He said, 'Here I am, Lord.' (11) The Lord said to him, 'Get up and go to the street called Straight Street, and in the house of Judas seek for one called Saul, a Tarsiote, for behold he is praying, (12) and in a vision has seen a man, Ananias by name, come in and lay his hands on him, so that he may recover his sight.' (13) Ananias answered, 'Lord, I have heard about this man from many people — heard how much harm he has done to thy saints in Jerusalem; (14) and here he has authority from the chief priests to arrest all who call upon thy name.' (15) The Lord said to him, 'Go, for this man is a chosen vessel to me, to bear my name before nations[1] and kings and the sons of Israel; (16) for I will show him what he must suffer for my name's sake.' (17) Ananias went off, entered the house, laid his hands upon him, and said to him, 'Brother Saul, the Lord has sent me, Jesus, that is, who appeared to you on the road by which you came, that you may recover your sight and be filled with the Holy Spirit.' (18) And immediately something like scales fell from his eyes. He recovered his sight, got up, and was baptized. (19) And when he had taken food he grew stronger.

---

[1] Or, the Gentiles (so e.g. *Begs.*).

Bibliography

F. W. Beare, *JBL* 62 (1943), 295–306.

C. Burchard, *ThLZ* 100 (1975), 881–95.

B. Dehandschutter, as in (20).

E. von Dobschütz, *ZNW* 29 (1930), 144–7.

J. Doignon, *RScPhTh* 64 (1980), 477–89.

J. D. G. Dunn, *FS* Caird, 251–66.

J. Dupont, *FS* Bruce (1970), 176–94.

E. Fascher, *ThLZ* 80 (1955), 643–8.

P. Fredriksen, *JTS* 37 (1986), 3–34.

R. H. Fuller, Kremer *Actes*, 505–8.

J. G. Gager, *NTS* 27 (1981), 697–704.

D. Gill, *Bib* 55 (1974), 546–8.

K. Haacker, *ThBeiträge*, 6 (1975), 1–19.

C. W. Hedrick, *JBL* 100 (1981), 415–32.

E. Hirsch, *ZNW* 28 (1929), 305–12.

A. J. Haltgren, *JBL* 95 (1976), 97–111.

T. Holtz, *ThLZ* 91 (1966), 321–30.

P. W. van der Horst, *NovT* 12 (1970), 257–69.

J. Jervell, Kremer *Actes*, 297–306.

F. J. Leenhardt, *RHPhR* 53 (1973), 331–51.

J. L. Lilly, *CBQ* 6 (1944), 180–204.

G. Lohfink, *BZ* 9 (1965), 246–57; 10 (1966), 108–15.

S. Lundgren, *StTh* 25 (1971), 117–22.

S. Lyonnet, *FS* George, 149–161.

S. V. McCasland, *JBL* 77 (1958), 222–30.

P. H. Menoud, *FS* Haenchen, 178–86.

O. Michel, *FS* Daube, 40–50.

H. R. Moehring, *NovT* 3 (1959), 80–99.

J. Munck, *StTh* 1 (1947), 131–45.

J. Munck, *StTh* 3 (1951), 96–100.

J. Pathrapankal, Kremer *Actes*, 533–9.

D. M. Stanley, *CBQ* 15 (1953), 315–38.

O. H. Steck, *ZNW* 67 (1976), 20–28.

G. Steuernagel, *NTS* 35 (1989), 619–24.

G. P. Wetter, *FS* Jülicher, 80–92.

A. Wikenhauser, *Bib* 29 (1948), 100–11; 33 (1952), 313–23.

U. Wilckens, *ZThK* 56 (1959), 273–93.

H. Windisch, *ZNW* 31 (1932), 1–23.

G. Wingren, *StTh* 3 (1951), 111–23.
H. G. Wood, *NTS* 1 (1955), 276–82.

Commentary

That Luke narrates this event three times (22.6–16; 26.12–18) measures the importance that it had for him. He gives the fundamental proclamation of Jesus — baptized, ministering, crucified, risen — six times (2.22–36; 3.12–26; 4.8–12; 5.29–32; 10.34–43; 13.16–41). He says twice that Jesus ascended (Lk. 24.51; Acts 1.9–11). He tells the story of the conversion of Cornelius twice, and alludes to it again (10.1–48; 11.1–18; 15.7–9). These are all highly significant matters for Luke, and the conversion of Saul takes a prominent place among them; Paul himself is so prominent a figure that it could hardly be otherwise. The existence of the parallels in chs. 22, 26 justifies us in taking vv. 1–19a as a unit; otherwise there would be much to be said for including vv. 19b–22, which set the seal on the story of conversion by showing the new convert as actively engaged in Christian work in Damascus. The three accounts have much in common but are by no means identical. They may be set out as follows:

	Acts 9		*Acts 22*		*Acts 26*	
1.	Paul is travelling to Damascus	v.3	Paul is travelling to Damascus	v.6	Paul is travelling to Damascus	v.12
2.	A light shines about him	v.3	A light shines about him	v.6	A light shines about him	v.13
3.	He falls to the ground	v.4	He falls to the ground	v.7	All fall to the ground	v.14
4.	A voice addresses him	v.4	A voice addresses him	v.7	A voice addresses him in Hebrew	v.14
5.	Saul, Saul, why are you persecuting me?	v.4	Saul, Saul, why are you persecuting me?	v.7	Saul, Saul why are you persecuting me? It is hard for you to kick against the goad.	v.14
6.						
7.	Who art thou, Lord?	v.5	Who art thou, Lord?	v.8	Who art thou, Lord?	v.15
8.	I am Jesus, whom you are persecuting	v.5	I am Jesus the Nazarene, whom you are persecuting	v.8	I am Jesus, whom you are persecuting	v.15

9.   Paul is commissioned
                                         as missionary to
                                         Jews and
                                         Gentiles. v.16–18

10.   Companions see
                       light but do not
                       hear   v.9

11.   What shall I do? v.10

12. Paul is sent into   Paul is sent into
    Damascus for   Damascus for
    instructions v.6   instructions   v.10

13. Companions hear
    the voice but do
    not see   v.7

14. Paul gets up,   Paul is blind   v.11
    blind   v.8

15. Paul is led into   Paul is led into
    Damascus   v.8   Damascus   11

16. Paul, blind, eats
    and drinks
    nothing for
    three days   v.9

17. Ananias is intro-   Ananias is intro-v.12
    duced and told   duced
    of Paul's
    calling v. 10-16

18. Ananias heals   Ananias heals
    Paul   v. 17,18   Paul   v.13

19. Paul is   Paul is
    baptized   v.18   baptized   v.16

20. Paul eats   v.19

21.   Vision in the
                       Temple; Paul is
                       commissioned
                       as missionary
                       to Jews and
                       Gentiles   v.17–21

The agreements are much more important than the disagreements. Small variations in order are insignificant. For the apparent contradictions between (10) and (13) see the notes on the relevant verses. The question, What shall I do, Lord? (11), though without parallel, forms a natural introduction to the instructions and commissioning that Paul receives in each narrative, though in ch. 9 we learn of future tasks only through what is said to Ananias. In ch. 9 Ananias is described as a disciple (v. 10); in ch. 22 he is a devout observant of Torah, enjoying a good reputation with the local Jews. There is no reason why he should not have been both, and there is good reason for the stress on his Jewishness in ch. 22. The account in ch. 26 shows signs of compression, in the omission of Ananias and the Temple vision (which is in ch. 22 only — and again there is good reason for a reference to the Temple vision in this chapter) and the inclusion of the commission in the initial event outside Damascus; it is the more surprising that the words of Jesus should be expanded by the addition of a Greek proverb (see on 26.14).

The agreements are due in part to the appearance in all three accounts of common features of theophanies: the light, the prostration of the recipient of the vision, the supernatural voice, the authoritative commands, the commissioning. Reference has often been made to the story of Heliodorus in 2 Macc. 3, where most of these elements are found. After the heavenly vision, which checked his intended raid on the Temple treasury, Heliodorus 'suddenly fell to the ground and deep darkness came over him'; 'his men took him up and put him on a stretcher and carried him away' (2 Macc. 3.27, 28). 'He lay prostrate, speechless because of the divine intervention and deprived of any hope of recovery' (3.29). The High Priest Onias was asked 'to call upon the Most High and to grant life to one who was lying quite at his last breath' (3.31). 'Be very grateful to Onias the High Priest, since for his sake the Lord has granted you your life. And see that you, who have been scourged by heaven, report to all men the majestic power of God' (3.33, 34). These contacts are real, but relatively superficial. The main substance of Heliodorus' report to the king who sent him is that, if the king should be sending another messenger to obtain the Temple gold, he would do well to choose one of his worst enemies, since he would be sure to get a thorough drubbing. Another parallel to which attention is often drawn is the account of the conversion of Aseneth, in *Joseph and Aseneth*. Aseneth 'fell upon the ashes and wept with great and bitter weeping all night with sighing and screaming until daybreak' (10.15). 'The man called her a second time and said, "Aseneth, Aseneth". And she said, "Behold, here I am, Lord. Who are you, tell me." And the man said, "I am the chief of the house of the Lord and commander of the whole host of the Most High. Rise and stand on your feet, and I will tell you what I have to say".' (14.6–8). Again the resemblances are unmistakable, but superficial. In the story of Saul there is no parallel to Aseneth's long prayer of penitence, and though Aseneth is converted to Judaism and thus becomes an example to be followed the setting of her conversion, the marriage between her and Joseph which the conversion makes possible, is without parallel in Luke's account of Paul.

Of greater importance as parallels are the OT stories of the call of prophets, notably Isa. 6.1–13; Jer. 1.4–10; cf. Gal. 1.15. These parallels suggest the question, raised acutely by K. Stendahl (*Paul among Jews and Gentiles*, 1977, 7–23), whether the event should be described as a conversion or a call. The fact is that it is both: a conversion in the Christian sense is always at the same time a call. It is true that Paul did not find a new God to worship; he would always insist that the God he worshipped as a Christian was the same God he had worshipped as a Jew — the God of Abraham, Isaac, and Jacob. 'The Lord,' however, whom he addresses and who addresses him is Jesus, and it is Jesus who determines the thought of God that is involved. Whatever Judaism at large may have understood God to be, for Paul he had been one with whom one could amass a store of credits (Phil. 3.7); this was done by obedience to the Law. These credits Paul now regarded as debits, since they could only make it harder to do what clearly one now had to do, namely, to put one's whole trust not in one's own legal, moral, and religious achievements but solely in Jesus Christ. This was a radical change of religious direction, and it was accompanied by as radical a change of action: the active persecutor became an even more active preacher and evangelist. If such radical changes do not amount to conversion it is hard to know what would do so. This must not however lead us to eliminate or undervalue the element of vocation. This element, plainly present in Acts (9.6, 15; 22.15, 21; 26.17, 18, 20), is confirmed in Gal. 1.16 (ἵνα εὐαγγελίζωμαι αὐτὸν ἐν τοῖς ἔθνεσιν).

Conversion and vocation are thus necessary complements to each other; it is however a correct observation that the balance of the two elements differs in the various accounts of the event that we possess. It is not surprising that the balance should be most even in Paul's own account in Gal. 1, where the appearance of Christ (1.16), the communication of the Gospel (1.12), the radical change of life (1.23), and the call to missionary activity (1.16) all appear side by side. It is probably correct to observe in Acts an increasing emphasis on the element of vocation. Bauernfeind, for example, writes (131), 'Die Berufung des Paulus durch den Herrn tritt immer deutlicher, immer unvermittelter zutage.' This means for Luke, he adds, 'Ergänzung und nicht Widerspruch'. In Acts 9 the effect on Paul is vividly described, but we hear what the 'elect instrument' is subsequently to do only through what the Lord says to Ananias (9.15, 16). In ch. 22

Paul describes his return to Jerusalem and visit to the Temple, where the Lord sends him far off to the Gentiles (22.17–21). In ch. 26 the sending is brought into the Damascus event and expressed at greater length (26.16–18). These observations show Luke's own interests, and have a bearing on the question of the source or sources that he may have used (see below).

In essentials, the three Acts narratives agree with one another, and with the evidence of the epistles, contained in Gal. 1.15f.; Phil. 3.7–11; 1 Cor. 9.1; 15.8. Rom. 7 is not an account of Paul's conversion — see *Romans* (142–4); Cranfield (*Romans* 1.340–7). What happened to Paul was not the resolution of an inward conflict in an unhappy, divided, and unsatisfied man; it was the appearance of Christ to a self-satisfied and self-righteous man, an appearance that had the immediate effect both of providing a new basis for his personal life and of initiating the Gentile mission (Gal. 1.17, ἀπῆλθον εἰς Ἀραβίαν — which is missed in Acts; see *Freedom and Obligation*, 8).

A number of questions are left over by the three conversion narratives in Acts. Three in particular may be mentioned here.

(1) How and when was the substance of the Gospel communicated to Paul? Many have conjectured but Acts does not say that Paul was instructed by the Christians in Damascus, or perhaps, a little later, by the church in Jerusalem. Paul himself claims that his Gospel came to him by revelation (Gal. 1.12), and that he was not taught it. There is no reason why this should not be accepted. If it is correct (and we have Paul's own word for it as well as Luke's) that Paul had gone to great trouble to persecute the church we may reasonably assume that he had also gone to some trouble to inform himself concerning the erroneous teaching which he took it upon himself to stamp out. The appearance of Jesus proved at once that Jesus was alive and (since God had vindicated him) that he had been right and his opponents wrong, and that the new faith which was focused upon him was true. The rest followed, not indeed in detail and immediately but as the result of theological reflection. It is noteworthy that though Luke does represent Paul as immediately (9.19b) associating with the disciples in Damascus and as quickly making his way to Jerusalem (9.26) no more than Paul himself does he say that Paul was at any stage instructed what as a Christian preacher he must say.

(2) A notable difference between Acts and Paul's own accounts of his conversion is that Paul makes no reference to Ananias. Did Paul omit such reference in order to represent himself as more independent than he really was? Did Luke introduce Ananias in order to establish a connection between Paul and the church that Paul would have discountenanced? Formulated in this way these questions could lead to extreme positions. It is understandable that for Paul himself the appearance and presence of Christ were so commanding that secondary

actors in the story scarcely counted and did not have to be mentioned. For Luke it is important that (as is pointed out by Wilson, *Gentiles* 165) Ananias acts as the representative not of the church but of God, so that he does not invalidate Paul's claim to be an apostle not from men or through man (Gal. 1.1). It is most improbable that Ananias is a fictitious character, though Luke may not have known precisely who he was or what he did.

(3) In the epistles Paul claims that his vision of Christ was a resurrection appearance of the same kind as those granted to others; the last of the series, but genuinely belonging to it (1 Cor. 15.5–8). It made him an apostle (1 Cor. 9.1). In Acts it is separated from the resurrection appearances by the ascension, and is of a different order; correspondingly, Acts differentiates between Paul and the Twelve, and avoids calling him an apostle. On the two exceptions to this statement (Acts 14.4, 14) see the notes. It is also clear from the epistles that there were those who denied that Paul was an apostle (1 Cor. 9.2). What was Paul's position in the church and what was his relation to those who were apostles before him (Gal. 1.17)? A full discussion of the role that Luke assigned to Paul (and of the role that Paul assigned to himself) must wait for consideration of the story of Paul as told in later chapters of the book. At present it may suffice to quote Haenchen (318): 'Ihn als den dreizehnten Zeugen neben die Zwölf treten zu lassen, ist Lukas nicht in den Sinn gekommen. Statt dessen erfüllt er später den in 1.8 von Jesus gegebenen Auftrag'; and to add that it would not be theologically inappropriate that the Lord's plan should be fulfilled outside rather than within the framework of officialdom.

What then may be said about Luke's source or sources for the event that he describes? The view is now very generally abandoned that he used three distinct sources in chs. 9, 22, 26. The three accounts differ not because they reached Luke by different channels but in accordance with the contexts in which they are placed. 'Die Differenzen lassen sich als literarische Variation (und zT Unachtsamkeit) erklären; sie hängen mit der Anpassung an die jeweilige Situation zusammen' (Conzelmann 59; cf. Lüdemann 115). Luke probably thought that in ch. 9 he was supplying the basic facts in as striking a manner as possible. The account in ch. 22 is adapted to the Jewish audience to which it is addressed. The High Priest and the council of elders are invoked to testify to Paul's Jewish zeal (22.5); Jesus becomes Ἰησοῦς ὁ Ναζωραῖος (22.8); Ananias is described not as a disciple but as a devout observant of the Law, respected by all the local Jews (22.12), and he speaks not in the name of the Lord Jesus but in that of the God of our fathers (22.14); it is in the Temple that Paul in a vision receives his instructions (22.17); he takes the opportunity of giving his Jewish credentials as a persecutor (22.19, 20); only when he claims to have been sent by God to the Gentiles does he provoke dissent (22.21, 22). In ch. 26 (see above) there are clear signs that Luke is abbreviating his narrative: it was not necessary to tell the story in full detail a third time (compare the third reference to the Cornelius episode in ch. 15). Speaking in Greek to Festus and Agrippa Paul thinks it necessary to point out that the heavenly voice addressed him in the Hebrew (Aramaic) language (26.14); the commission is given at once, and in terms that should have been moderately intelligible to Gentiles (26.16–18).

That Paul was engaged in persecution, that he was in the neighbourhood of Damascus, that he was confronted by one whom he was obliged to recognize as Jesus crucified — nay rather, risen, that in this confrontation he was commissioned to act as ἐθνῶν ἀπόστολος: all this Luke will have received by fairly direct tradition from Paul himself; Paul had indeed written it all in various letters. How far such details as the light, the fall, the blindness, the conversation, and the role of Paul's companions and of Ananias can be traced back in the tradition, we have no means of knowing. Probably some of them at least originated as stock features of supernatural encounters, whether at the stage of writing or at some earlier point.

1. ὁ δέ is anaphoric and ἔτι helps to pick up the previous reference to Saul as a persecutor. If Luke is following a written source ἔτι could well be his insertion; more probably he is himself composing on the basis of tradition. In either case he means to indicate that Saul's fierce opposition to the new movement did not abate with time. ἐμπνέων is vivid: *breathing threatening and slaughter upon the disciples*. ἀπειλῆς and φόνου stand in the genitive, described in BDR § 174 as the genitive of 'smelling of'. ὄζειν is thus used with a genitive, and so is ἐμπνεῖν by Perictyone, quoted in Stobaeus, *Florilegium* 85.19 (Gaisford 3.160: οὐδ᾽ ἀλείψεται ᾿Αραβίης ὀδμῆς ἐμπνέοντα). Cf. also *Clem. Hom.* 13.16, μύρου δὲ πνέει, τῆς ἀγαθῆς φήμης; Joshua 10.40 is a less close parallel. In Classical Greek the accusative is used; so e.g. Euripides, *Bacchae* 620; Aristophanes, *Frogs* 1016 (= 1048). *ND* 4.147 quotes an intransitive use of ἐυπνείειν from *I GUR* 1379. ἀπειλὴ καὶ φόνος is often taken as a hendyadis: *threats of slaughter*. Haenchen rejects this weakening of the sense: 'Saul hat nach Lukas wirklich gemordet'. *Begs.* 4.99 also rejects the hendyadis but thinks that Luke means no more than that Saul threatened to slaughter the Christians. It is at least possible that what Luke intends is a heightening of the first term: He threatened them, and actually carried out his threats and killed.

For μαθητής as a description of Christians see 6.1; it is used frequently throughout this chapter.

τῷ ἀρχιερεῖ. Cf. 4.6. The High Priest is there named as Annas; Caiaphas is mentioned with him. The latter was the High Priest recognized by the Romans; according to Jn. 18.13 he was Annas' son-in-law.

2. ἠτήσατο . . . ἐπιστολάς. It is difficult to find any consistency in Luke's use of the active and middle forms of αἰτεῖν; active appears at 3.2; 16.29. Paul asked for letters addressed to synagogues that would enable him to exercise disciplinary measures. Such a letter was an אגרא דאקף; see StrB 2.689; also e.g. 2 Cor. 3.1. To issue such letters would presuppose authority on the part of the High Priest to require, or at least request, action by local Jewish communities in territory outside Palestine and under a different civil government. Whether such authority existed and, if it did, how it was exercised cannot be determined with certainty. 1 Macc. 15.16–21, a letter from the Roman Consul Lucius to Ptolemy of Egypt, seems to supply a precedent: it requires support for the Jews and adds 'if any pestilent men have fled to you from their country, παράδοτε αὐτοὺς Σιμωνὶ τῷ ἀρχιερεῖ, ὅπως ἐκδικήσῃ αὐτοὺς κατὰ τὸν νόμον αὐτῶν.' The same letter was sent, according to 1 Macc. 15.22, 23, to a variety of destinations. Josephus does not mention this letter, which, if written by the Consul Lucius Caecilius Metellus, must have been sent to Ptolemy VIII (= Euergetes II, 145–116 BC) and be dated in 142 BC, but does refer (*Ant.* 14.145) to a decree initiated by 'Lucius Valerius, son of Lucius, the praetor (στρατηγός; the Latin VS has *consul*)'. This refers to Numenius, an envoy of the Jews; a similar reference to 'Numenius and his party' in 1 Macc. 15.15 strongly suggests that though Josephus places his decree in the time of Hyrcanus (if Hyrcanus I, probably c. 139 BC, if Hyrcanus II, c. 47 BC; see *NS* 1.195–7) both passages refer to the same decree. This gives the decree double attestation, but also diminishes our confidence in its dating and in its content, for the decree given by Josephus contains no reference to the right of extradition. In any case the latest date to which the decree can be assigned (if it ever was enacted) is about eighty years before the time of Saul, and there can be no certainty that such an arrangement would remain in force for so long in very disturbed times. There is moreover a contradictory piece of evidence in Josephus, *War* 1.474 ('No other sovereign had been empowered by Caesar, as he [Herod] had, to reclaim a fugitive subject even from a state outside his jurisdiction'). Further, the evidence we have considered deals with relations between Jews and Romans. Any value it may possess will apply to the present case only if at the time in question Damascus was under Roman rule. This may have been so, but there is some ground for thinking that it was not; see on 9.23–25. It is however unnecessary to suppose that Paul's actions carried, or needed, any authority beyond the confines of Judaism. Given the good will of the synagogues in Damascus it would be quite possible for Jews known to be Christians to 'disappear' (our own age is familiar with the phenomenon, and the word) and subsequently to find themselves in unwelcome circumstances in Jerusalem. The important historical question is that of the relation between the High Priest and Sanhedrin and provincial synagogues. It is unfortunately a question to which no precise answer can be given. 'The extent to which Jews outside Judaea were willing to obey the orders of the Sanhedrin always depended on how far they were favourably disposed towards it. It was only within the limits of Judaea proper that it exercised direct power' (*NS* 2.218). Known compliance with the policy of the Sanhedrin may have been a reason contributory to the choice of Damascus as a place in which to pursue anti-Christian action.

Damascus is about 135 miles NNW of Jerusalem, a large and prosperous commercial city, a member of the Decapolis League (Pliny, *Nat. Hist.* 5.74). It had a large Jewish population: according to Josephus, *War* 2.561, the Gentile inhabitants massacred 10,500 Jews; the figure 18,000 in 7.368 seems to include women and children; according to 2.560 many of the wives of Gentile citizens had become proselytesses. See *NS* 2.127–130. If Paul left Jerusalem to persecute Christians in distant Damascus he must have been confident not only that he would be welcomed in the synagogues (see above) but also that he would find a considerable number of Christians. So far there has been no suggestion in Acts that the church had been planted so far afield. Christians had indeed been scattered throughout Judaea and Samaria (8.1), and some may have fled even further from danger, but not all Christians in Damascus were, on Luke's showing, refugees, since Ananias has only heard of Paul's persecuting activity (v. 13); he does not claim to have experienced it at first hand. That Paul's conversion was at the least connected with Damascus is proved by Gal. 1.17, πάλιν ὑπέστρεψα εἰς Δαμασκόν; that is, Paul had been in or near Damascus before he went away to Arabia. There were, therefore, Christians in Damascus: a valuable reminder of the fact that Acts provides us not with a full record of everything that happened in the early years of Christianity but with a few selected events. We do not know how or why Christians first came to Damascus. When Schechter first published the 'Zadokite Document' (Cambridge, 1910) with its account of the Covenanters of Damascus speculation connecting this group with the Christians of Damascus flourished. It is now clear that the two movements, of Christians and of Qumran sectaries (if in the latter case a geographical movement is to be thought of), were quite distinct. See Millar Burrows, (*More Light* 219–27). The suggestion that when Luke wrote Damascus he meant Qumran has nothing to commend it.

According to Acts, Saul went as a שליח of the Sanhedrin to look for Christians in Damascus. In the conditional clause within the purpose clause (cf. Thucydides 2.6.3, εὗρε τοὺς ἄνδρας διεφθαρμένους) the verb of cognition takes an accusative and participle; that the participle is so far separated from the object (τινας . . . ὄντας) may introduce a measure of uncertainty: *any who might be* . . . For Saul's indiscriminate readiness to arrest Christians of both sexes cf. 8.3 and the note.

There is nothing to indicate whether the Christians whom he hoped to find were native Damascenes or refugees from the persecution in Jerusalem. They are described as τῆς ὁδοῦ ὄντες. This use of ὁδός recurs at 19.9, 23; 22.4; 24.14, 22; cf. 16.17; 18.25, 26. Its background is disputed. The closest parallels are to be found in the Qumran literature, where not only expressions such as אל דרך (CD 20.18) occur but also the absolute use of The Way: בוחרי דרך (1 QS 9.17, 18), סוררי דרך (1 QS 10.21), סרי דרך (CD 1.13), סוררי דרך (CD 2.6). Cf. also 1 QS 11.13. The Way was understood as strict observance of the Mosaic Law; so, rightly, Fitzmyer (*Essays* 282), quoting 1 QS 8.12–15, where Isa. 40.3 is quoted with the interpretation היאה מדרש התורה [אשר] צוה ביד מושה. This is not how even the most conservative Jewish Christian groups understood their 'Way', but the two have in common the exact performance of what is understood to be the revealed will of God. There is moreover in the Qumran terminology a dualistic element which is not to be found in the use in Acts (Braun 1.167). For many more details, not all of them probable, see Kosmala (332–44). At 24.14 it appears that the Way was described as a αἵρεσις; it was thus (and with this 22.4 would agree) not only a term for a manner of behaviour but also for those who adopted the behaviour; to this there does not seem to be a Qumran parallel, though it is a not unnatural development. See 1 QS 9.17, 18, quoted above; 'those who choose the Way' may be said to constitute the Way. The development however does not seem to have taken place in the Jewish use of דרך, or of הלכה which also may be considered part of the background of ὁδός. For the predicate genitive see Robertson 497.

For ἀγάγῃ in the sense of *arrest and bring* to a place of trial or punishment cf. Aristophanes, *Birds* 1077f. Here it is helped out by δεδεμένους, *in custody*. The Christians are to be brought to Jerusalem, not punished locally (as Paul himself appears later to have been — 2 Cor. 11.24). A recently discovered example of the perfect participle of δέω in this sense (cf. 9.21; 22.5; 24.27) is given in *ND* 1.47–49: . . . δεδεμένον ἐπὶ τὴν ἐμὴν διάγνωσιν πεμψάτω (P. Coll. Youtie 1.30, pp. 261–74; AD 198–9).

3. For Luke's use of various constructions (here accusative and infinitive) with ἐγένετο, in more or less close imitation of the Hebrew . . . ויהי, see e.g. 5.7; 9.32, 37. He chooses here to write in biblical style because he is describing a theophany (Christophany) and an event comparable with the call of the prophets. ἐξαίφνης is perhaps his own word (Mk, once; Lk., twice; Acts, twice — here and at 22.6 in the second account of Paul's conversion). The suddenness emphasises the supernatural character of the event; see D. Daube, *The Sudden in the Scriptures*, 1964, 28–34. A sixth century source (Antoninus, *Itinerary* 46) places the event at the second milestone (from Damascus).

Light is a common feature of theophanies, e.g. Ps. 27.1; 78.14; Isa. 9.2; 42.16; 60.1, 20; Micah 7.8; also in non-biblical use, e.g. Xenophon, *Cyropaedeia* 4.2.15 (λέγεται φῶς τῷ Κύρῳ καὶ τῷ στρατεύματι ἐκ τοῦ οὐρανοῦ προφανὲς γενέσθαι). The word is also used of God himself, and light is inward illumination — salvation (e.g. *C.H.* 1.21, φῶς καὶ ζωή ἐστιν ὁ θεὸς καὶ πατήρ; 9.3, τῷ ὑπὸ τοῦ θεοῦ πεφωτισμένῳ; 13.18, φωτισθεὶς ἀπὸ σοῦ (gnosis)). Paul himself understood the event as revelation (Gal. 1.12, 15), but not in a gnostic sense. Nor does light mean for Luke illumination of a gnostic kind; it is a physical representation or accompaniment of the divine glory of Christ. At 22.6 the same word περιαστράπτειν is used, at 26.13 περιλάμπειν. 22.11 suggests physical blinding by a dazzling light. The light came ἐκ τοῦ οὐρανοῦ; it is pointless to ask whether Luke meant *from heaven* or *from the sky*. These were not distinguishable.

4. Paul fell to the ground; another feature of theophanies. Cf. Ezk. 1.28; Dan. 8.17; Rev. 1.17. For the parallels in 2 Macc. 3 and in *Joseph and Aseneth* see the introduction to this section. ἤκουσεν is followed by the accusative; for the use of ἀκούειν with the genitive see on v. 7. In the present verse it is clear that Paul both perceived a sound and distinguished the words that were spoken; according to Delebecque 45 the accusative means that Saul did not *see* the speaker. He is addressed by his Hebrew name, Σαούλ, שאול; cf. 26.14. Both here and in ch. 22 his companions are relegated to a subordinate position; they failed to perceive the significance of what was taking place.

τί με διώκεις; Saul was persecuting Christians. Traditional interpretation, from Augustine (passim) to Barth (*CD* 4.1.666; 4.2.658) has laid great stress upon the implied unity between Head and members of the body. This is not wrong, but it must not be supposed that Luke's thought is at this point profoundly theological. So Schneider (2.26), who compares the thought with Mt. 25.35–40, 42–45 (already referred to by Bede) rather than with Paul's doctrine of the body of Christ; Pesch (303) sees some relation between Luke and Paul here. In fact any leader is injured if his followers are attacked. Cf. Euripides, *Bacchae* 784–95. It is interesting to note that this parallel contains the proverb used in 26.14. By some MSS this proverb is added here, by others in v. 5; almost all students reject it as not part of the original text of ch. 9, but see Clark (345), who thinks that the two occurrences of διώκεις in vv. 4, 5 led to the dropping of a whole στίχος; Luke, he believes, would not have been so inartistic as not to use the proverb at his first telling of the conversion story. The question has the effect not only of initiating conversation but of throwing Paul's actions and life into question. Irenaeus, *Adv. Haer.* 3.12.9 makes the point neatly: τὸν ἴδιον δεσπότην ἐδίωκε διώκων τοὺς μαθητὰς αὐτοῦ.

5. τίς εἶ, κύριε; The question corresponds to the ἐγώ εἰμι that follows. Saul is aware that he is confronted by a superhuman being; the context (the light from heaven, the fall to the ground, the mysterious question) shows that though Saul has not yet identified his interlocutor κύριε is not simply a polite address to a fellow man (as in many contexts it could be). The question leads to identification: the superhuman stranger is Jesus, which implies the converse: Jesus, once dead, is now alive and more than man. The discovery that the crucified Jesus was in fact alive agrees with Paul's own accounts of the origin of his Christian life (Gal. 1.15, 16; 1 Cor. 9.1; 15.8; cf. Phil. 3.7–11), and was the root of the new understanding of the OT and the reinterpretation of Judaism that were the foundation of his theology. See *Romans* 7–9.

On Jesus' self-identification Bede commented: Non dixit, ego sum deus, ego sum dei filius, sed humilitatis, inquit, meae infirma suscipe et tuae superbiae squamas depone. The contrast with the conventional figure of the 'divine man' is striking. See also *Passio ss. ap. Petri et Pauli* 39 (L.-B. 1.152) and *Acta Petri et Pauli* 60 (L.-B. 1.205f.); in both Jesus is identified with ἡ ἀλήθεια, which Saul persecutes.

6. Paul is not to receive further instruction by the roadside but must continue his journey into Damascus, where he will be told what to do. Luke emphasises not so much the powerlessness of Saul as the power of Christ (Haenchen 311). 'Anders als Gal. 1.12f. erfährt Paulus nicht in der Erscheinung selbst das Evangelium. Er wird an die Kirche als Mittlerin der Lehre gewiesen' (Conzelmann 57). This is a somewhat misleading simplification of the story as Luke tells it, in which Saul is brought into contact with one disciple who is instructed in a vision comparable with Saul's own not to instruct Saul in Christian doctrine but to cure his blindness. The Lord points out to Ananias that Saul is a chosen instrument (v. 15) and that he himself will show him what the future holds for him (v. 16). It is probable but not certain that Ananias baptizes Saul (vv. 17, 18); Saul immediately, without any hint of instruction, preaches in the synagogues (9.20). Luke is indeed concerned to represent Paul as integrated into the life of the church as a whole (9.19, in Damascus; 9.27, 28, in Jerusalem) and does less than justice to the tensions that are manifest in the epistles. But he does not represent Paul as a derivative person acting under direction from 'the church'.

ἀλλά: according to M. 3.330 this is 'not so much adversative as connective, and is best translated as an interjection, *Well!*' Cf. Mk 16.7; Mt. 9.18; Mk 9.22; Acts 10.20; 26.16. This does not seem quite satisfactory in English. See LS 68, s.v. II 2, 'with imper. or subj., to remonstrate, encourage, persuade, etc., freq. in Hom.'. We might paraphrase: You have been persecuting me, but that is to end now. Up you get, go into the city . . . ἀλλά thus retains some adversative force. Cf. Plato, *Protagoras* 311a, ἀλλ' ἴωμεν, There is no reason why we should not go to him at once . . . let us start (So Jowett's translation; one might paraphrase, Let us not delay *but* go at once).

For ὅ τι, E Ψ 𝔐 have τί. BDR § 300. 1 observe that here only is ὅστις used in the NT in an indirect question. This use is very rare also in the papyri of the Ptolemaic period.

7. Luke does not say who Paul's travelling companions were; he was probably interested in them only in that their reaction brings out more forcibly the effect of the event on Paul and at the same time established its objectivity (see Roloff 150; Schneider 2.27). There is no reason to think that they were Paul's assistants in the work of persecution. In the interests of security travellers went in groups rather than singly (cf. Lk. 2.44, συνοδία). The fellow travellers (for συνοδεύειν cf. Herodian 4.7.6; Plutarch, *Antony* 13 (921)) stood, halted by the evident fact that something extraordinary was taking place, ἐνεοί. According to Hesychius the adjective means ὅς οὔτε ἀκούει οὔτε λαλεῖ, that is, *deaf and dumb*; the sense may be transferred (cf. Xenophon, *Anabasis* 4.5.33, barbarians, not knowing Greek, had to be treated ὥσπερ ἐνεοῖς). For Acts, LS 563 give the meaning *dumbfounded, astonished*. If this means that they were struck dumb it will probably do, but LS give no other authority for this sense.

ἀκούοντες μὲν τῆς φωνῆς. Cf. 22.9, τὴν δὲ φωνὴν οὐκ ἤκουσαν. M. 1.66 accepts the view that the apparent contradiction is to be explained by the difference between the genitive of the present verse and the accusative of 22.9: the men were aware of sound but could not distinguish the words used. Turner (M. 3.233) thinks that 'there may be something in' this explanation, but Moule (*IB* 36) thinks that NT usage of the cases with ἀκούειν defies classification and that it is impossible to find a satisfactory distinction between the genitive of this verse and the accusative of 22.9. In view of the accusative in v. 4 this opinion should probably be accepted. The same verse is against Bruce's view that the voice they heard was Paul's, as he spoke with the unseen Jesus. Luke, without too much concern for rigid consistency, wished in each narrative to express the thought that all recognized a supernatural event but only one understood its meaning. For hearing without seeing cf. Deut. 4.12 (φωνὴν ῥημάτων ὑμεῖς ἠκούσατε καὶ ὁμοίωμα οὐκ εἴδετε); Dan. 10.7; Sophocles, *Ajax* 15; Euripides, *Hippolytus* 86. The travellers saw no one; it is implied that Paul saw Jesus (as he claims to have done: 1 Cor. 9.1; 15.8). Cf. *Acts of Thomas* 27 (They heard his voice only but did not see his form, for they had not yet received the additional sealing of the seal (post-baptismal chrism)). This cannot serve as an explanation of the present passage; Saul himself was not yet baptized. Supernatural beings become visible when and to whom they choose; cf. especially Homer, *Odyssey* 16.154–163 (Athene is seen only by Odysseus and the dogs). Lüdemann 115 takes 22.9 to be a Lucan correction of this: only Saul receives the revelation.

8. Instead of the first six words of this verse h (p w) mae have, Sed ait ad eos: Levate me de terra. Et cum levassent illum . . . — a characteristic 'brightening' of the narrative by the Western text. Saul rose, opened his eyes, and found that he was blind (for οὐδὲν ἔβλεπεν, Aᶜ C E Ψ 𝔐 have οὐδένα ἔβλεπεν, meaning presumably that he no longer saw Jesus; cf. Mk 9.8). Saul's blindness is the result of his supernatural encounter; physically, one might say, he is blinded by the light of v. 3 (cf. 22.11). Betz (55) compares Lucian, *Dialogi Marini* 14.2, but the story of the Gorgon is not a very close parallel. For χειραγωγοῦντες cf. 13.11, ἐζήτει χειραγωγούς — a clear sign of blindness; Wettstein gives many parallels, but the point is too obvious to need illustration. Conzelmann (58) rightly points out that blindness is not a punishment but a mark of the powerlessness of the hitherto powerful persecutor. Led by the hand, and not at all as he intended, Saul enters Damascus; a dramatic touch by Luke. ἠγέρθη (passive) may mean that Paul could not raise himself (Delebecque 45).

9. The blindness lasted three days. BDR § 353.7 considers ἦν . . . μὴ βλέπων to be not strictly a periphrastic tense; the participle (with negative) is adjectival, equivalent to τυφλός. Cf. 13.11, ἔσῃ τυφλὸς μὴ βλέπων τὸν ἥλιον. h may be said to support this with the reading sic mansit per triduum neque . . .

At the same time Saul neither ate nor drank; his fast ends at v. 19. He was 'overcome by shock and probably by penitence' (Marshall 170). This is to some extent a rationalization of what Luke probably thought of as a supernatural effect; but it is justifiable rationalization and certainly a better suggestion than that we have here an anticipation of the prebaptismal fast enjoined or described in *Didache* 7.4; Justin *1 Apology* 61; Tertullian, *De Bapt.* 20, though this is maintained by Schille (221) and Schneider (2.28); Weiser (225) thinks it possible; Pesch (305) is against it.

At this point Luke leaves Saul and takes up the second actor in his story.

10. There is a close formal parallel between the present story and that which follows in ch. 10. In each story, each of two persons (Saul, Peter; Ananias, Cornelius) receives a vision and audition; these lead to a meeting of the two persons. Saul has now seen and heard Jesus; it is the turn of Ananias. For the introduction of Ananias cf. 16.1 (καὶ ἰδοὺ μαθητής τις ἦν ἐκεῖ ὀνόματι Τιμόθεος); also 5.1; 8.9. As at v. 1, μαθητής means *Christian*, presumably a local, Damascene, Christian, since he has heard (v. 13) of Saul's attack on the Christians in Jerusalem but does not claim to have experienced it himself; he is not a refugee. In 22.12 he is described as a devout man according to the Law; in ch. 26 he does not appear. For the name Ananias see on 5.1, though of course the Damascene Christian is a different man. The Lord spoke to him in a vision; that is, the Lord (evidently Jesus; see v. 17) was both seen and heard. He calls Ananias by name (as he had called Saul). Cf. Jn 10.3. Ananias replies in words that suggest the Hebrew הנני (Moule, *IB* 183); cf. e.g. 1 Kdms 3.4. By this word he indicates both his presence and his readiness to carry out the Lord's will.

11. The Lord gives specific directions, which appear to have the effect of diminishing Ananias's readiness to obey. ἀναστάς (B *pc* have ἀνάστα) is pleonastic, in the OT style that Luke likes to imitate; cf. e.g. Gen. 13.17. The content of the command begins with πορεύθητι.

In earlier Greek ῥύμη suggests *motion, force, swing, rush*; here, and in later Greek, a *street*. The street called Straight (τὴν καλουμένην means that Εὐθεῖαν is a name, not a mere description) is commonly identified with the main east-west axis of the city, which is still to be seen (known as Darb el-Mostakim), though its line has been slightly altered; formerly it ran somewhat to the south of the present street. Judas (the name is a common one) is quite unknown. He was presumably a Jew; Paul's residence with him may have been on a purely commercial basis, but he may possibly have been a local Christian. In *Begs.* 4.102 it is pointed out that if a vision of this kind is to be given at all it must be given with all the necessary detailed directions; they are required on both natural and supernatural grounds. It is inferred that the names of the street and of Paul's host are not to be taken as conveying old tradition. It is however fair to remark that v. 9 required a continuation; Paul could hardly be left lying by the roadside. The narrative makes a connected whole. Hemer (226) refers to addresses, or directions, in papyrus letters.

Saul is Saul of Tarsus; the city is mentioned here for the first time. There was no point in inventing it; here at least Luke is using traditional material. Schmithals (89) reinforces this by the argument that Luke wished to emphasize Paul's contact with Jerusalem; he would not gratuitously have introduced a Hellenistic city. Tarsus was an important place. Not only does Paul at 21.39 describe it as οὐκ ἄσημος πόλις; others speak similarly. See e.g. Xenophon, *Anabasis* 1.2 ... Ταρσούς, πόλιν τῆς Κιλικίας μεγάλην καὶ εὐδαίμονα ... διὰ μέσης δὲ τῆς πόλεως ῥεῖ ποταμός, Κύδνος ὄνομα, εὖρος δύο πλέθρων. Its prosperity was based on the linen industry; in the first century BC it became as important in philosophy as it had long been, and long continued to be, in government. For evidence of Jews in Tarsus see *NS* 3.33, 34. *ND* 4.173 gives three occurrences of Ταρσεύς.

Ananias may be assured that Paul is in need of help and that he may be safely approached because he is praying. This attestation of his piety is immediately confirmed by further details.

12. Saul has had a vision; this will stand, though ἐν ὁράματι has varying positions, and is omitted (rightly in Ropes's view — see *Begs.* 3.85) by ℵ A 81 perp gig vg sa bo. The vision is not described directly, only at second hand in the Lord's words to Ananias. He has seen Ananias doing what in fact he does in v. 17. The laying on of hands (ἐπιθέντα αὐτῷ τὰς χεῖρας — there is strong evidence for the omission of τάς, also for the singular χεῖρα, but the long text of ℵᶜB E is probably correct) is given a specific purpose: ὅπως ἀναβλέψῃ. See 6.6; if the view of Daube is to be maintained it must be supposed that here ἐπιτιθέναι represents שׂים or שׁית, in 6.6 סמך. There is nothing in the Greek text to suggest this. It is more probable that to Luke the laying on of hands was a gesture of blessing whose precise meaning was determined by the context in which it took place. For the laying on of hands in healing cf. 9.17; 28.8; Lk. 4.40; 13.13. Nothing in the present passage suggests that it was a part of or associated with baptism.

The whole of this verse is omitted by h; this is probably best explained as an accidental scribal mistake. There is no need to take the verse as a scribal gloss, otherwise universally adopted, though it is true that its contents could have been derived from the ensuing narrative, and Ananias's doubts expressed in v. 13 would follow better on a bare reference to Saul of Tarsus such as that in v. 11a. Clark, liii, 345f., thinks that the words καὶ εἶδεν ἄνδρα ... ἀναβλέψῃ should follow v. 9.

13. Ananias fears that Saul is still out to persecute, and, presumably, that the prayer and vision are a hoax (a hoax, we must add, that had apparently taken in the Lord). See above; Ananias has not experienced the persecution himself but has heard about it from others, indeed from many, who presumably had escaped from Jerusalem. They had reported ὅσα κακὰ τοῖς ἁγίοις σου ἐποίησεν. 'Attisch wäre im Sinne von "etwas mit jemand tun" der doppelte Akkusativ allein möglich' (Radermacher 99), as e.g. at Mt. 27.22.

It is the Lord's ἅγιοι who have been attacked. The word ἅγιος is common in Acts, and has already been applied frequently to the Spirit (1.2; etc.), to Christ (3.14; etc.), to the prophets (3.21), to the Temple (6.13), and to the ground near the burning bush (7.33); it has not however been applied to Christians. This application of the word is repeated in this chapter (9.32, 41), and thereafter only in 26.10, again with reference to the victims of Saul's persecution. In the Pauline epistles the word is one of the most common terms for Christians, though occasionally it is applied particularly to the Christians of Jerusalem (Rom. 15.26; 1 Cor. 16.1; 2 Cor. 8.4). For Luke also it may have this narrow sense here and at 26.10; it may be also that the Christians of 9.32, 41 are thought of, and by the word described, as Jewish Christians, even perhaps as 'country members' of the Jerusalem church. The general meaning of the word is clear: that is ἅγιος which is especially devoted to God. This theme however is nowhere developed theologically by Luke (see however 20.32; 26.18 for the use of the participle ἡγιασμένοι, which if taken strictly will imply that they are ἅγιοι not by nature, or birth, but because God has made them so). 'Holy ones' is a description of the people of God characteristic of 1 Enoch; in rabbinic use קדוש tends to be confined to an élite among them.

14. Ananias is well informed on what we have learned from vv. 1, 2. There are two differences. (1) In v. 1 Saul approached the High Priest (singular); here he is said to have authority from the high priests (plural). To Luke the plural seems to mean the High Priest together with his entourage, with whom he acts in concert; cf. 4.1, 6, 23; 5.17, 21, 24, 27. (2) Christians are not now those who belong to the Way (v. 2), but those who call upon (Jesus') name. This is a Pauline expression; cf. 1 Cor. 1.2. For ἐπικαλεῖσθαι cf. 2.21; 9.21; 22.16. The OT passage behind 2.21 (Joel 3.5) is interpreted as referring to Jesus. Cf. Rom. 10.12, 13. Ananias's continuing hesitation serves to emphasize the incredible wonder of this conversion.

15. Ananias's objection is overruled. The Lord knows what he is doing. πορεύου repeats the πορεύθητι of v. 11 — a warning not to take differences of tense too seriously even in the Lucan writings. The Lord gives reasons for his instructions, speaking in the biblical style that Luke considers suitable for such purposes; see Plümacher 48 (referred to on 8.26).

This man, Saul, is a σκεῦος ἐκλογῆς. A similar expression, in the plural, occurs at Rom. 9.23 (σκεύη ἐλέους; cf. Rom. 9.23, σκεύη ὀργῆς; also 2 Cor. 4.7; 2 Tim. 2.21). σκεῦος, properly *vessel* or *instrument*, is used *de homine* at Polybius 13.5.7, according to Blass (117), but this use is not common and here it reflects the use of the

Hebrew כֽלי in the OT. 1 Macc. 2.9 is not parallel. Like σκεῦος, ἐκλογή also is a Pauline word (Rom. 9.11; 11.5, 7, 28; 1 Thess. 1.4) and refers to God's gracious act (cf. ἔλεος in Rom. 9.23) in determining the salvation of those whom he calls. Assuming the metaphorical use of σκεῦος this could be the meaning here: Saul, notwithstanding his past, is nevertheless one whom I have called to be a Christian; he is one of the elect. It seems however probable that the defining genitive ἐκλογῆς is used here in a sense that Paul once gives to the adjective ἐκλεκτός (Rom. 16.13, Ῥοῦφον τὸν ἐκλεκτὸν ἐν κυρίῳ; cf. also *Mart. Poly.* 20.1, where ἐκλογή seems to be used in this sense). All those mentioned in Rom. 16 are Christians; Rufus is singled out as outstanding. Luke, probably with a deliberate attempt to use Pauline language, means that Saul is one whom the Lord has singled out for special service. This is specified in the clause beginning τοῦ βαστάσαι, the genitive of the articular infinitive being used here in consecutive sense (BDR § 400. 2).

The object of βαστάσαι is τὸ ὄνομά μου; this use of the verb is unusual. There is no parallel in Acts, where βαστάζειν is used literally of the carrying of a man (3.2; 21.35) and metaphorically of something that could not be borne (endured; 15.10), or in the rest of the NT. *P. Oxy.* 10 (1914). 1242, col. 1, 17f. (see H. A. Musurillo, *The Acts of the Pagan Martyrs*, 1954, 44) is only superficially parallel: ἕκαστοι βαστάζοντες τοὺς ἰδίους θεούς, each party bearing its own gods. The Alexandrians had a bust of Sarapis (3.51f.); what the Jews carried is not told (unless in part of the papyrus that has perished). Hermas, *Sim.* 8.10.3; 9.28.5 may give the right sense, of Christians who confess (or fail to confess) the name of Christ; the context in Acts however suggests rather that Paul will not merely confess that he is a Christian (though this is certainly intended, and is strongly emphasised by for example Roloff 151 and Weiser 226), but that he will bear the Christian message, regarded as summed up in *my name* (cf. e.g. 8.12), before the persons mentioned. He will take the name of Christ throughout the world that all may hear it.

ἐθνῶν (P⁷⁴ ℵ A C² E Ψ 𝔐) must be translated *nations*; if the article τῶν is read (with B C* *pc*) we must translate *the Gentiles* (as opposed to the Jews). This would fit the familiar picture of Paul as apostle of the Gentiles (cf. Rom. 11.13), but for that reason should probably be regarded as textually secondary. Paul will appear before nations and kings; then, almost as an after thought, attached by τε, of course the sons of Israel too. They are not excluded. Stählin (137) thinks that we have here a combination of two familiar pairs: Nations and kings, Gentiles and Jews.

16. ἐγὼ γὰρ ὑποδείξω. Sophocles, *Philoctetes* 1421f. is not a very close parallel. The pronoun is presumably emphatic and one is inclined to translate: You, Ananias, have now received your own commission, but I myself will ... This however translates γάρ as if it were δέ. Maddox (78f., cf. Burchard 100–3) explains γάρ in relation to the interpretation of *bearing the name* as suffering martyrdom: You, Ananias, may safely approach Paul, for I will tell him of his sufferings. Page (139) explains γάρ in a similar but not identical way: You, Ananias, may boldly do what I ask, for I will show Saul what *he* will have to suffer. In fact the emphatic ἐγώ alone is sufficient to justify γάρ: You, Ananias, need not hesitate to perform the task I am giving you, for I myself will be personally engaged in it.

ὑποδεικνύναι is *to show*, perhaps with an element of warning; cf. Xenophon, *Memorabilia* 4.3.13 (αὐτοὶ οἱ θεοὶ οὕτως ὑποδεικνύουσιν); Lk. 3.7. ὅσα could be exclamatory (as sometimes in classical use: How great ...!), but more probably is used for πάντα ἅ; so BDR § 304. 5.

Patitur Paulus quae fecerat Saulus. Paul's sufferings are described in the rest of Acts; the epistles, especially 2 Cor. 11.23–33, present a grimmer picture. Luke is caught between two motivations, on the one hand to show how much Paul was prepared to suffer for Christ, on the other to show the power of God to deliver him from suffering. For suffering ὑπὲρ τοῦ ὀνόματος cf. 5.41.

17. Ananias was convinced and carried out his instructions. See vv. 11, 12. He addresses Saul as ἀδελφέ, recognizing him as a fellow Christian (1.15), though he has not yet been baptized. He uses Paul's Hebrew name. The laying on of hands is certainly not a rite subsequent to baptism; as usual in Acts, it is a sign of blessing, to be interpreted as the occasion suggests. Here it is an act of healing. Ananias's words represent fairly enough what had been said to him. 'The Lord' of the previous verses is now clearly identified with Jesus. ('Ιησοῦς is omitted by 𝔐 sa^ms, but is undoubtedly part of Luke's text). ὅπως ἀναβλέψῃς takes up precisely the ὅπως ἀναβλέψῃ of v. 12, but πλησθῇς πνεύματος ἁγίου is now added. Illumination by the Spirit is parallel to the physical gift of sight (Stählin 138). It is perhaps better to say (with Roloff 152) that Luke's narrative swings between a miracle of healing and the imparting of the Holy Spirit. By the gift of the Spirit Paul is made to stand on the same level as the original apostles (2.4); but indeed this means no more than that he is a Christian (2.33, 38; etc.). Unlike the Twelve however he is outside the land of Israel. 'Paul himself was given the Spirit, not in the land, but in Damascus, a famous "haven for heretics"' (Davies, *Land* 274, cf. 167). It is to be noted that at this point no visible or audible phenomena mark the giving of the Spirit.

18. Perhaps as the intended result of Ananias's act in laying his hands on Saul, Saul's blindness was immediately (as often in miracle narratives; see 3.7) cured. The subject of ἀπέπεσαν is not expressed, unless we are to take ὡς λεπίδες in the sense of 'something like scales'. This is possible, and probably the best available translation, though ὡς would more naturally be taken as a conjunction, implying ὡς λεπίδες ἀποπίπτουσιν. The inexactness of expression confirms the view that Luke is not writing with the care of a professional medical man. It is true that the word λεπίς is used by medical writers; see especially Galen, in *CMG* V 4, 1, 1 p. 77, 3, οἷον λεπὶς ἀπέπιπτε. But the word has many meanings (see LS 1039): *egg-shell*; *cup* of a filbert; *coat* of an onion; *scales* of fish and of serpents; *flakes* that fly from copper in hammering. For the popular use cf. Tobit 11.12 (B A), ἐλεπίσθη ἀπὸ τῶν κανθῶν τῶν ὀφθαλμῶν αὐτοῦ τὰ λευκώματα. Cf. Tobit 3.17. For the supposed medical language of Acts see the general discussion in Vol. II.

ἀναστάς (as in v. 11) is superfluous, but gives a 'biblical' tone to the narrative. ἐβαπτίσθη, *he was baptized*; at 22.16 (in the second account of Saul's conversion) the middle, βάπτισαι, is used. Moule (*IB* 26) asks whether the difference is significant. Did a Christian 'baptize himself', 'get himself baptized', or 'submit to baptism?' The question is one that will call for discussion in the later narrative. Here the simple passive can only be taken to mean that Paul was baptized, almost certainly by Ananias. Weiser (222) thinks that the baptism may have been Luke's addition to his narrative source (or tradition). This is possible; he may have thought the narrative of a conversion incomplete without it. One can hardly go further.

19a. In this verse it is almost as important to observe what is not said as to note what is. This is put strongly, and correctly, by Weiser. 'Der Schlussteil lässt nochmals deutlich erkennen, dass es in der Erzählung nicht um die Berufung des Saulus zum Missionar, sondern um seine Berufung zum Christen geht' (226). 'Saulus wird auch nicht "an die Kirche als Mittlerin der Lehre" (Conzelmann 57) verwiesen und der kirchlichen Tradition subordiniert . . .; denn es erfolgt keine Übergabe des kirchlichen Verkündigungsinhaltes an Saulus, sondern nur die Taufe und die Geistmitteilung . . .' (227).

λαβὼν τροφήν. There is nothing here to suggest a reference to the eucharist. Paul had eaten nothing for three days (v. 9); it is not surprising that he felt better after taking food.

ἐνίσχυσεν is active intransitive; *he strengthened* would be unusual but not altogether impossible in English, with the meaning *he gained strength*. Blass 118 says that this intransitive use is in Aristotle and Diodorus, but gives no references. ἐνίσχυσεν is the reading of P⁷⁴ ℵ A C² E Ψ 𝔐, and should be accepted. B C* 323 945 1175 1739 *pc* have ἐνισχύθη, without any real difference in meaning. This reading is supported by P⁴⁵ which has ἐνισχύσθη, for which see BDR § 70. 3 n.4.

24. SAUL FROM DAMASCUS TO JERUSALEM 9.19b–30

(19) Saul[1] was some days with the disciples in Damascus (20) and immediately in the synagogues he proclaimed Jesus, affirming that he was the Son of God. (21) Those who heard him were astonished, and said, 'Is not this he who in Jerusalem made havoc of those who invoke this name, and had come here for this very purpose, to bring them bound before the chief priests?' (22) But Saul grew stronger and stronger and confounded the Jews who lived in Damascus, teaching that this man was the Christ.

(23) When many days were completed the Jews plotted to kill him, (24) but their plot became known to Saul. They were watching the gates day and night in order to kill him, (25) but his disciples took him by night and let him down by the wall, lowering him in a basket.

(26) When he reached Jerusalem he tried to join the disciples, and they were all afraid of him because they did not believe that he was a disciple. (27) But Barnabas took him in hand, brought him to the apostles, and told them how on the road he had seen the Lord and that the Lord had spoken to him, and how in Damascus he had spoken boldly in the name of Jesus. (28) And he was with them, going in and going out, at Jerusalem, speaking boldly in the name of the Lord. (29) He spoke and debated with the Hellenists, but they tried to kill him. (30) When the brothers learned this they brought him down to Caesarea and sent him off to Tarsus.

Bibliography

F. W. Beare, *JBL* 63 (1944), 407–9.

J. Cambier, *NTS* 8 (1962), 249–57.

J. Dupont, *Études*, 167–71.

St. Giet, *RechScR* 41 (1953), 321–47.

St. Giet, *RevScR* 31 (1957) 329–42.

M. Hengel, as in (7).

E. A. Knauf, *ZNW* 74 (1983), 145–7.

D. R. de Lacey, *NTS* 20 (1974), 82–6.

R. Liechtenhan, *FS* Harnack (1921), 51–67.

O. Linton, *StTh* 3 (1949), 79–95.

C. Masson, *ThZ* 18 (1962), 161–6.

P. H. Menoud, as in (23).

---

[1]Greek, he.

P. Parker, *JBL* 86 (1967), 175–82.

D. F. Robinson, *JBL* 63 (1944), 411f.

A. W. Wainwright, *StEv* 6 (= *TU* 112, 1973), 589–94.

Commentary

A striking feature of this passage is that it contains a number of contradictions with the epistles. (1) Paul is said to stay after his conversion in Damascus ἡμέρας τινάς (ἱκανάς, P⁴⁵). He preached in the synagogues and disputed with the Jews. According to Gal. 1.17 Paul at this time went away into Arabia, a journey of which Acts shows no knowledge; it must however be observed that after this journey according to Galatians he returned (πάλιν ὑπέστρεψα) to Damascus, thereby implying that he had previously spent some time, however short, in the city. (2) Eventually, according to Acts, Paul left Damascus, under considerable pressure. The Jews were plotting to kill him and to this end were watching the city gates; in order to escape them Paul was let down from a window in a basket. In 2 Cor. 11.32f. there is a very similar narrative, but there Paul is escaping from the Ethnarch of Aretas, king of the Nabataean Arabs. It is impossible to doubt that the same incident is in mind, and that Paul's version of it is more likely to be correct than any other. Luke probably blamed the Jews because he had no exact information and had come to think that whenever trouble arose it must have been caused by them (cf. e.g. 20.19). More important than this is the difference in atmosphere between the two stories. For Paul, as the context in 2 Corinthians shows (see *2 Corinthians* 303f.; *NT Essays* 95ff.), the event is a supreme danger and humiliation. For Luke it is an example of the apostle's daring and God's readiness to care for his own. (3) In Acts, after escaping from Damascus Paul makes straight for Jerusalem. After some initial difficulty and with the assistance of Barnabas he finds his way into the apostolic headquarters (*to the apostles*, v. 27), and engages in mission work until the Hellenists plot to kill him. According to Gal. 1.17 he did not immediately go up to Jerusalem but delayed his visit for three years, and then stayed only a fortnight and saw only Peter and James.

There are other features of the story in Acts that give rise not exactly to contradiction but to some difficulty, especially when the evidence of Galatians is taken into account. If three years (rather than a number of days) intervened between Saul's conversion and his visit to Jerusalem it is hard to understand why the apostles were suspicious of him. After so long a time it must have been recognized that he had genuinely become a Christian and a missionary, and was not an agent provocateur. Mediation by Barnabas would not then be necessary (Haenchen 323 — how was it that Barnabas knew the truth and the apostles did not?). It may be that what lay behind any difficulty the Jerusalem group may have had in accepting the new convert was no doubt of his sincerity but disagreement with his theological understanding of the Christian faith. If this was so, a role may after all be found for Barnabas, who was himself one of the earliest Jerusalem Christians (4.36), yet was prepared to work with Paul as a colleague (11.25; 13.2; etc.; Gal. 2.1).

Luke's interests (which were not the same as those that motivated Paul in the writing of Galatians) can be clearly seen in the distinctive features of his narrative. (1) He wishes to show Paul in close association with the church and represents him as a preacher of orthodox doctrine; he preaches that Jesus is the Son of God (v. 20 — the first time this designation is used in Acts) and the Christ (v. 22). He tries, at first unsuccessfully, to attach himself to the apostles, and finally is taken in hand by Barnabas (v. 27). He is then accepted, not as a fellow apostle (there is no word in Acts about such a possibility; see below and on 14,4, 14) but at least as an acceptable evangelist. It is important not to overstate Luke's position in this respect. He does not say that the apostles gave any sort of validation to Paul's ministry or that they imparted to him the contents of the Gospel. It is probably true that there were others who said what Luke does not say; they are vehemently repudiated in Gal. 1.12; 2.6. Haenchen (324) says as much as can properly be said on the basis of this passage. 'Er ist nun nicht nur von Christus berufen, sondern auch von den Aposteln anerkannt, und damit in jeder Hinsicht "rite vocatus".' This is true at least in a negative sense. The apostles could have said, This man is an impostor. They did not say it. They could have said, This man's understanding of Christian truth is false. They did not say it. Instead they recognized Paul as sharing in their ministry: at least, they did nothing to prevent his doing so, and took no steps to warn against error in his preaching. How far this is a historically correct and complete account of relations between Paul and the Jerusalem church cannot be discussed at this point.

(2) Luke characteristically depicts the victory of the word of God in the story of those who speak it. It is in vain that enemies, in Damascus and in Jerusalem, attack Paul; he is able to defeat them in argument, and when they attempt violence with the aid of his fellow Christians he is able to escape their clutches. Luke, who has already recounted the death of Stephen, knows that Christians do not always escape physical harm, but he sees in the escapes that with the Lord's help they are able to make signs of the truth that there is nothing that can stop the spread of the Gospel. (3) To this must be attached a positive point: attacks on the church are not only doomed to failure (see 9.31: the church was at peace and flourished), they provide a means by which the Gospel is more widely spread. Paul, threatened in Jerusalem, is sent to Caesarea and Tarsus.

That Paul was a great preacher was common knowledge, and even if Luke had no positive evidence that he preached in Damascus this was a natural inference, as were the effectiveness of the preaching and the surprise that it evoked. The story of the escape from Damascus was probably in general circulation among those who had any contact with Paul or with the Pauline circle. Luke's general picture (escape by the city wall in a basket) is correct though some of his details are mistaken. It must also have been widely known that Paul visited Jerusalem and had contacts with those who were apostles before him. Luke is correct in saying that Paul travelled from Damascus to Jerusalem, wrong in his dating of the event. He infers that Paul would preach in Jerusalem and in describing what took place is probably influenced by his view of Paul as the replacement for Stephen ('Paulus erscheint als der, welcher in die durch den Tod des Stephanus gerissene Lücke tritt' — Conzelmann 60, quoted with approval by Weiser 235). It is thus not difficult to see how the paragraph was built up on the basis of traditionally known events, helped out with inferences, some not wholly correct. Luke writes so as to make two points, which are not contradictory but stand in a certain degree of tension. Paul was a great independent evangelist and a formative influence in Christian theology; Paul cannot have been out of harmony with the original apostles who guaranteed the connection between Jesus and the post-resurrection church. Once more, Luke is not wrong in seeing and making these two points: Paul was independent, and he did go to considerable trouble to maintain relations with Jerusalem. Yet Luke is wrong in detail; and not only in detail. He misses the stormy atmosphere that often disturbed the relations he describes. All was happening at a greater depth than he allows us to see, especially at a point such as this, where both language and content point to the fact that Luke is not following closely a clearly defined source but making his own composition on the basis of a rather sketchy general acquaintance not so much with the events themselves as with their outcome.

In the setting of the book as a whole Luke has now brought Paul fully on the stage. Paul is a Christian, a noted Christian worker, and is accepted at Christian headquarters. Pesch (315) writes: 'Im Rahmen der Apostelgeschichte ist mit 9.1–31 die lukanische Paulusdarstellung exponiert; der lukanische Paulus kommt in 22.17 auf 9.26–30 zurück, in 26.20 auf die anfängliche Predigt in Damaskus (9.20, 22) und in Jerusalem (9.28).' It is a fair judgment that Luke has allowed us a glimpse of Paul as he wishes us to see him — no doubt as he himself saw him. The details must be filled in from the rest of the book, but already we see Paul as a converted Pharisee, exemplifying the truth that Luke commends in more ways than one, that Christianity is genuine, fulfilled Judaism. At the same time, as Stephen's successor, he is a Hellenist — a Hellenist Jew who has become a Christian and is not loved by Hellenist Jews who have not become Christians. He is prepared for a life of travel and hardship. He will take the Gospel to the Gentiles. For the present he may be safely left at Tarsus (v. 30) till he is summoned to Antioch (11.25f.). He is then ready to embark on the part of his career that Luke is able to describe with more confidence and in greater detail.

19b. It is reasonable (with most editions and most, but by no means all, commentaries) to begin a new paragraph at this point, though grammatically ἐγένετο δέ could follow upon ἐνίσχυσεν with no more than a comma, and no interval of time is implied. The subject of ἐγένετο is Saul, the subject of ἐνίσχυσεν; the sentence is not to be taken as an imitation of the Hebrew ויהי followed by *waw* consecutive: *Saul was with the disciples.* For Damascus see on 9.2; for μαθηταί as a designation of Christians on 6.1. οἱ ἐν Δαμασκῷ μαθηταί suggests without requiring a gathered group of disciples, not a number of isolated individuals; that disciples should form such a group is in any case likely.

ἡμέρας τινάς is a vague expression of time; cf. 10.48; 16.12; 24.24; 25.13. P45 has ἡμέρας ἱκανάς (h, plurimos); cf. v. 23. Luke seems to use both expressions when he has no precise length of time in mind, but ἱκαναί suggests a longer period.

20. εὐθέως: without waiting for further instruction or commission. The same word is used in Gal. 1.16, but there not to indicate that Saul began immediately to preach in the synagogues of Damascus but rather that, without waiting to make any contact with Christians in the city, set off for Arabia. For the synagogue as an institution see on 6.9; for synagogues in Damascus cf. 9.2.

κηρύσσειν is not used frequently in Acts: never of the early speeches by Peter (nor are κήρυγμα and κῆρυξ used anywhere in Acts), first of Philip in 8.5, where also the verb takes a direct object, as here. There it is τὸν Χριστόν, here τὸν Ἰησοῦν (cf. 19.13; also 15.21, where Moses is proclaimed; at 20.25; 28.31 the object is τὴν βασιλείαν). Where Χριστόν is object some content is immediately imported into the proclamation — it is claimed that the person to whom the proclamation relates is the Messiah; where the object is Ἰησοῦν, unless the context (as in ch. 19) supplies content, the expression lacks it; hence Luke's addition here, ὅτι οὗτός ἐστιν ὁ υἱὸς τοῦ θεοῦ. οὗτος of course takes up *Jesus*. Here for the first time in Acts Jesus is said to be the Son of God; elsewhere only at 13.33, in the quotation of Ps. 2.7, on which Haenchen (319) thinks the present passage is based. The term is somewhat more frequent in the Third Gospel, but in special Lucan material it occurs only at Lk. 1.32 (ὑψίστου), 35. It can hardly be claimed that it is one that was of special significance to Luke, or that he was making a special point of the claim that Paul was the first Christian to use so important a title. It was a traditional title, and one was needed to fill out the sense of κηρύσσειν. There is no indication in Acts of a belief in the essential identity of the Father and the Son. Luke is reporting only that Saul now came out clearly and positively on the Christian side. It is however true (Stählin 140) that the words look like a confessional formula.

21. Not surprisingly, those who heard Paul preach were astonished at the complete transformation of the persecutor. P⁴⁵ᵛⁱᵈ P⁷⁴ Ψ* *pc* omit οἱ ἀκούοντες. There was no reason for omitting these words, very little for adding them. It is possible that the omission was due to homoeoteleuton (πάντες . . . (ἀκούοντες).

οὐχ οὗτός ἐστιν . . .; the question summarizes what the reader already knows. πορθεῖν, used of the destruction of a city, is used at Gal. 1.13, 23; *Begs.* 4.105 describes this as perhaps 'the nearest approach that there is to verbal evidence of literary dependence of Acts on the Pauline Epistles', but rightly goes on to deny that it proves such dependence. For *those who invoke the name* of Christ as a description of Christians see 9.14; for the thought involved see 2.21; 22.16; cf. 15.17. εἰς is used for ἐν (which is read by B C E Ψ 𝔐): *at Jerusalem* (in contrast with ὧδε).

ἐληλύθει, pluperfect, indicates a state of things that has now ceased to be; the perfect would have meant that Saul was still looking for victims. 'Plusquamperfecto . . . inest indicatio voluntatis mutatae' (Blass 119). BDR § 347. 1 explain the pluperfect as '= Aor. + Impf.'. εἰς τοῦτο anticipates and is explained by the ἵνα clause that follows. For this cf. 9.2; εἰς 'Ιερουσαλήμ there is replaced here by ἐπὶ τοὺς ἀρχιερεῖς, before the chief priests (as constituting, or representing, the Sanhedrin). εἰς 'Ιερουσαλήμ has already been used in this sentence. For δεδεμένους see on 9.2.

22. They might be as surprised as they would; Saul simply grew stronger ((ἐν) τῷ λόγῳ is now added by (C) E *pc* h l p (mae), doubtless giving the main part of the intended sense). ἐνδυναμοῦν is a Pauline and especially Deuteropauline word (Rom. 4.20; Eph. 6.10; Phil. 4.13; 1 Tim. 1.11; 2 Tim. 2.1; 4.17 only in the NT). If ἐνεδυναμοῦτο is middle it will simply mean that Saul grew stronger; if it is passive it will mean that he was strengthened by God — which is in any case implied.

After a specific call to act as missionary to Gentiles it is perhaps surprising that Saul should begin by arguing with the Jews (Schmithals 98); Luke however is already following what he takes to have been Paul's regular plan of starting mission work in the synagogue. συνχύννειν is peculiar to Acts in the NT; this is the only place in which it is used in the active (cf. 2.6; 19.32; 21.31). The Jews who argued with Paul found themselves unable to establish their position; he tied them in knots. For the Jewish inhabitants of Damascus and their synagogues see 9.2. τοὺς 'Ιουδαίους τοὺς κατοικοῦντας is straightforward Greek; this supports the omission of the first article by א* B 36 453 1175 pc, since they give the harder reading.

συμβιβάζειν also is a word characteristic of Acts (16.10; 19.33; elsewhere in the NT only 1 Cor. 2.16). For the present passage LS 1675 (s.v. III 1) give the meanings, *elicit a logical consequence, infer*. Infer is not a satisfactory rendering since no grounds for inference are given. Paul was not drawing an inference but affirming something and alleging evidence to prove it. More suitable is LS III 2: *teach, instruct*, for Paul is pressing his own conclusion upon his hearers (cf. v. 20, ἐκήρυσσεν ὅτι . . .). For this meaning LS cite only biblical passages (Exod. 4.15; Deut. 4.9, συμβιβάσεις τοὺς υἱούς σου; Isa. 40.14), but for Luke these would be satisfactory support. In such a context as this there is little difference between *teach* and *prove*; the speaker would consider that he was offering proof, and his arguments were such that his hearers were too confused to reply. The arguments were no doubt Scriptural; so rightly Stählin (140), but it is not necessary to confine them to the Servant passages, Ps. 110.1 and Ps. 2.7. The content of Paul's teaching was that *this man* (Jesus) *was the Christ*. Luke probably takes this to be identical in meaning with v. 20; that is, in v. 20 (*Son of God* (see above) does not have a metaphysical sense, but is a correlate of Messiahship. An allusion to the baptism of Jesus is brought out by the Western (gig (h l p)) addition, *in quo Deus bene sensit*.

23. The use of πληροῦν (συμπληροῦν) of time is common in Acts. See 2.1. *Begs.* 4.105 suggests that here the use of the imperfect suggests the meaning 'As time went on'. For ἡμέραι ἱκαναί cf. ἡμέραι τινες in v. 20. For the Jews in Damascus see v. 22. They consulted together and prepared a plan — Luke would not have objected to the pejorative *plot* rather than *plan*. This was the first but not the last such plot (cf. 20.19, and see the use of ἐπιβουλή in v. 24). Their intention was to kill Paul. ἀναιρεῖν is a Lucan word: Mt., once; Lk., twice; Acts, eighteen times; 2 Thess., once; Heb., once. Such figures support the view that Luke is here writing up a story he knew in outline from tradition.

24. ἐγνώσθη τῷ Σαύλῳ: not *was known by Saul* (which would require ὑπό and the genitive), but *became known to Saul*; it came to his ears. The verb is passive with intransitive sense (BDR § 313). For ἐπιβουλή cf. 20.3, 19; 13.30 (the only occurrences in the NT). Wettstein (513) quotes Thucydides 8.92.2, where stealthy violence seems to be implied — premeditated assault.

At this point the narrative becomes strikingly parallel to but not identical with that of 2 Cor. 11.32, 33. In Acts, the Jews watched the gates (of the city) day and night in order to kill Paul. In 2 Corinthians 'the ethnarch of King Aretas guarded (ἐφρούρει) the city of the Damascenes in order to seize (πιάσαι) me'. It is surely correct to identify the two occasions; it is too much to suppose that Paul twice left Damascus in a basket. But was he threatened by Jews or by the agent of Aretas? We must suppose that Paul knew whom he had to fear; Luke probably did not know the source of the threat that led to Paul's escape and was only too ready to blame any bad feeling towards the Christians on the Jews. The reference to Aretas may however be used to date the event since Aretas died in AD 39. We do not know what sort of official the ἐθνάρχης was and can draw no safe conclusions about whether Romans or Arabs were in control of the city at the time, though the failure to find in the remains of Damascus any coins of the Emperor Gaius might suggest that from AD 37 to 39 Aretas was ruler of the city (see 2 *Corinthians* 303f.). It must be borne in mind that the ethnarch, who was keeping an eye on the *city*, may have been operating outside it. It is of course conceivable that there was collusion between Jews and Arabs, the former watching the gates within, the latter guarding the city without; but this does not seem likely. Pesch (315) suggests that the Jews may have accused Paul before the Ethnarch. See further Hemer (163f., 215).

25. Paul's way of escape was better adapted to avoiding foes who watched the gates within than one stationed outside with a clear view of the walls. Evidently however it did suffice to fool the Arabs.

Calvin (271) is at pains to justify Paul for infringing the sanctity of city walls (cf. Cicero, *de Oratore* 2.100 (24), Lex peregrinum vetat in murum adscendere). It was of course a spurious holiness, designed to add to the security of the inhabitants and it is unlikely that it ever hindered the escape of one whose life was threatened — or often hindered the entry of one intent on crime.

The most difficult question in this verse is prompted by the subject of the verb — οἱ μαθηταὶ αὐτοῦ (so NA[26]). It has already been noted (see on 6.1) that in Acts μαθηταί are almost always disciples of Jesus, that is, Christians; nowhere else do we hear of disciples of a Christian leader such as Paul. The text as quoted is read by P[74] ℵ A B C 81* *pc* vg[st]; οἱ μαθηταί is read by 36 453 *pc*; αὐτὸν οἱ μαθηταί is read by E Ψ (6 81[c] 1175) 𝔐 gig vg[cl] sy. It is in favour of αὐτοῦ that is unusual and difficult; it is however perhaps too difficult. Metzger (366) thinks that αὐτοῦ was due to 'scribal inadvertence' and that αὐτόν was original. Haenchen (320) similarly takes αὐτόν to be original but early corrupted to αὐτοῦ; this was then corrected back to αὐτόν. NEB, supported by Packer (74), accepts αὐτοῦ and translates 'his converts' (RSV has 'his disciples'), and it is possible that Luke meant to refer to Christians who owed their faith to Paul and stood particularly close to him. No solution of this problem is wholly convincing; if the reading with no pronoun were somewhat better attested one would be inclined to suppose that it was what Luke wrote, and that copyists thought that it could be improved by the addition of a pronoun. Knowling (240f.) quotes Alford who reads αὐτοῦ and takes it to be governed by λαβόντες; this is unusual, but he compares Lk. 8.54 and classical parallels.

The relevant words in the parallel in 2 Cor. 11.33 are διὰ θυρίδος ἐν σαργάνῃ ἐχαλάσθην διὰ τοῦ τείχους. Cf. Joshua 2.15. Paul's last three words appear identically in Acts; the aorist passive indicative is represented in Acts by the active participle χαλάσαντες; Acts uses a different word for basket (σπυρίς), adds καθῆκαν, and has no parallel to διὰ θυρίδος; it is of course obvious that Paul must have emerged either through a window or from the battlements of the city wall. The pictures given by the two accounts are as nearly identical as could be expected. A σπυρίς is a large basket; there is little to indicate what size may be expected in a σαργάνη but Paul no doubt knew that one could be big enough to hold him. χαλᾶν means in general *to slacken, to loosen*, but the reader of the NT recalls Mk. 2.4, the letting down of man and mattress through a roof. At the beginning of the verse Black (*AA* 125) follows Jeremias in taking λαβόντες to be an example of the Semitic use of *take* as an auxiliary which adds no meaning to the sentence (cf. 16.3; 27.35); so also Wilcox (125). This may be a correct judgment, but is not necessarily so. There is certainly nothing un-English in 'His disciples got hold of him and let him down . . .'

According to Schlatter (*Theologie des NTs* 2, 1910, 425) this is the only verbal contact between Acts and the Pauline letters (cf. the reference to *Begs.* 4 on v. 21); this is because Luke 'Paulus nicht als Denker auffasst und darstellt' — a remark to be pondered.

26. Read superficially the verse presents no problem. It was natural that Saul, now himself a Christian, should seek to join the disciples (for the use of μαθητής see on 6.1) in Jerusalem. It was equally natural for the disciples not to trust him; would he not prove to be a surreptitious infiltrator, perhaps an agent provocateur? It was impossible to believe that a man who recently was organizing the persecution of Christians was now himself a disciple. Read more closely the verse presents problems. Why should Saul, commanded to evangelize Gentiles, go to Jerusalem? What apostles did he see? And why should they have feared him? It is hardly what is suggested by Acts but we know from Gal. 1.18 that his first visit to Jerusalem did not take place till three years after his conversion; there had been plenty of time for Saul to prove its sincerity and for this to become known. Luke's answers to these questions turn on the disappearance of the visit to Arabia, mentioned in Gal. 1.17 but ignored in Acts. It seems that Luke did not think of a three year interval; after no more than a few days the Jerusalem Christians might well have distrusted Saul. It is also evident that Luke did not consider a vocation to conduct a mission to the Gentiles ground for leaving Jews untouched; nor for that matter did Saul himself, who might well have visited Jerusalem for this purpose as well as to visit Cephas (Gal. 1.18), itself an intention that could easily grow into a desire to join the Jerusalem disciples. Roloff (155) notes that rejection by Jews in Jerusalem followed by the Gentile mission would be a primary example of a pattern that recurs several times in Acts. Did Paul seek, and does Luke represent him as seeking, authorization and legitimation from the original apostles? According to Conzelmann (59), 'Der historische Paulus wahrt seine Selbständigkeit, der lukanische wird an Jerusalem gebunden und dadurch legitimiert.' There does not however seem to be any word in this passage that can justify *legitimiert*. The historical Paul in fact did his best to live in unity with the Twelve; he did however succeed in this less well than appears in Acts.

παραγενόμενος is Lucan (Lk., 8; Acts twenty times; rest of the NT, eight times (+ Jn 8.2)). For κολλᾶσθαι see on 5.13; the meaning here is not in doubt (Saul wished to throw in his lot with his fellow Christians) and probably determines the meaning in 5.13.

27. For Barnabas see on 4.36. He is rightly described by Hengel (101) as a Hebrew; cf. *FS* Borgen (23). This is a better description than Bauernfeind's 'Mittelstellung' — better, that is, for history, not necessarily for Luke's account. Later Barnabas will appear as Paul's colleague in Antioch (11.25, 26), his travelling companion on the mission of help to Jerusalem (11.27–30; 12.25), his fellow missionary (13; 14), and delegate along with him from Antioch to the Jerusalem Council. Later still he will separate from Paul (15.37–40; Gal. 2.13), though not it seems permanently. Why he should have acted as Paul's sponsor remains unknown; Luke gives no hint. Barnabas himself (though originally from Cyprus) was a Jerusalemite and enjoyed the confidence of the apostles. It may be that Luke thought that one known to have contacts with Jerusalem, and known to have worked with Paul, would make a suitable bridge-builder.

ἐπιλαμβάνεσθαι normally takes a genitive; there is no exception here since αὐτόν is the object of the main verb ἤγαγον; cf. 16.19; 18.17; see BDR § 170. 2 n. 2. Burchard (*ZNW* 61 (1970), 165) thinks that the word suggests no closer relation between Paul and Barnabas than that Barnabas accompanied Paul ('nahm ihn mit'); there is no Mittlertätigkeit. One is however left asking why Barnabas accompanied Paul, and whether the apostles would have received him if Barnabas had not vouched for him.

πρὸς τοὺς ἀποστόλους. Cf. Gal. 1.18f. Bengel laconically comments, 'Petrum et Jacobum. Gal. 1.18, 19.' So also Hengel (86). Stählin unconvincingly attempts a compromise with 'Besonders Petrus and Johannes' (141). Paul's account must be accepted. Luke was aware of a visit to Jerusalem but had no details and supposed that Paul would have seen all the apostles (as no doubt he would have done himself). He would think that 8.1 was still valid; the apostles were in Jerusalem.

Barnabas's introduction of Saul consisted of an account (διηγήσατο) of his conversion and subsequent work as a Christian witness. The subject of διηγήσατο is usually, and probably rightly taken to be Barnabas; Burchard (147f.) takes it to be Paul; on this view Barnabas's role is reduced to very small proportions. The verb is followed by πῶς, which occurs twice (*narrated how he had seen . . . and how he had spoken boldly*). Between these occurrences (in NA²⁶) stands a ὅτι clause, which presumably must be rendered: *and that he had spoken to him*. This variation (πῶς . . . ὅτι . . . πῶς) is not impossible, but it may be better (with Bruce 1.206) to read the relative ὅ τι (which occurs in 945 1704 *al*, and could be intended in many other MSS in which no spaces are left between words and letters). We should then render, How he appeared, what he had said, and how Paul had preached. The essence of the matter however is that on the road (cf. 9.17) Saul had seen the Lord (though the narratives do not actually say this (Knowling 242)), that words had passed between them, and that since that time Paul had acted as a Christian. This, Luke means, convinced the apostles. It is not clear whether Paul or Jesus is the subject of ἐλάλησεν and whether αὐτῷ refers to Jesus or Paul. The grammar of the sentence gives no indication of a change of subject, and this suggests that ἐλάλησεν has the same subject as εἶδεν and ἐπαρρησιάσατο — Saul. But Luke is not so rigidly bound by the rules of grammar as to invalidate the thought that ἐλάλησεν may indicate the initiative of Jesus, who in the conversion story opens the conversation (9.4).

Saul ἐπαρρησιάσατο. The word occurs here and at 9.28; 13.46; 14.3; 18.26; 19.8; 26.26 (elsewhere in the NT only at Eph. 6.20; 1 Thess. 2.2). It always denotes bold, open Christian proclamation. There is nothing to suggest that it implies ecstatic speech (glossolalia, or the like); it points rather to a blunt statement of the truth regardless of the consequences. To speak ἐν ὀνόματι Ἰησοῦ (so P⁷⁴ ℵ E 𝔐; κυρίου is read by A *pc*, τοῦ κυρίου Ἰησοῦ by (104) 326 1241 *al* p, τοῦ Ἰησοῦ Χριστοῦ by Ψ *pc*, the first two variants being probably due to assimilation to v. 22) probably means more than to speak about Jesus; it is to speak on his behalf, almost in his person. On the use of ὄνομα see pp. 182f.

28. It is clearly implied that Saul was accepted by the apostles;

Beyer (63) may be right in thinking that this (in Luke's mind) constituted a bridge between Hebrews and Hellenists (6.1), but since Luke has said nothing about a breach between them (even though we may think that we see such a breach behind ch. 6) it is impossible to speak confidently of a bridge. *Going in and going out* implies the regular conduct of life, whatever that may be, and (though according to Haenchen 321 ἦν with the participles expresses continuity of action) it is better to connect the verb with εἰς 'Ιερουσαλήμ, εἰς being understood in the sense of ἐν. This is a better explanation than that of BDR § 479. 2 n. 8, who take εἰς with the participles as a kind of zeugma. The wording suggests that Saul was not only with the apostles but shared their activities, and there is nothing to suggest that he did not do so on equal terms (cf. Hengel 86). At the same time, there is nothing to indicate on what basis, and with what measure of conviction and cordiality, Saul was accepted.

καὶ ἐκπορευόμενος is omitted by P⁷⁴ 𝔐, perhaps because it seemed to go badly with εἰς 'Ιερουσαλήμ.

παρρησιαζόμενος ἐν τῷ ὀνόματι. In Jerusalem Saul continued to do what he had already done in Damascus (v. 27).

29. That παρρησιάζεσθαι does not refer (or at least does not refer exclusively) to ecstatic speech is shown by ἐλάλει τε καὶ συνεζήτει. For συνζητεῖν cf. 6.9 (the only other occurrence in Acts); Lk. 22.23; 24.15. It means discussion, which may be friendly or the reverse.

The discussion is with τοὺς Ἑλληνιστάς (A 104 424 *pc* have Ἕλληνας, but neither external attestation nor inherent probability supports this reading). On the word Ἑλληνιστής see on 6.1 and the general discussion in Vol. II. Those with whom Stephen disputed (6.9: Cyrenians, Alexandrians, men from Cilicia and from Asia) were presumably Hellenist in the sense of Jews with roots in the Greek-speaking world, but Luke does not say so, though he probably wishes to suggest that Saul entered into the same conflict as Stephen. In the present passage he is probably following a different source, or, as is more likely, writing up his own account of Paul's brief stay in Jerusalem. It was part of his understanding of events that Paul should early in his career be associated with Jerusalem, equally part of it that he should not stay there long, and a Jewish plot was a natural way of bringing his visit to a close (as previously of his stay in Damascus, v. 23). In himself as in his opponents Paul was for Luke the new Stephen, a great Hellenist Christian leader. For ἐπιχειρεῖν cf. 19.13; Lk. 1.1. As its composition suggests it means simply to take some project in hand. For ἀνελεῖν cf. v. 23.

30. ἐπιγνόντες, inceptive aorist, *when they found out*. The subject is ἀδελφοί; for this as a term for Christians see on 1.15. It may be significant that Luke does not repeat the word ἀπόστολος from v. 27, but it would be rash to infer from the change of word any coolness between Paul and the apostles. Even if this existed Luke would not wish to use language that might suggest it and here he is probably writing freely rather than reproducing the language of a source. κατήγαγον is naturally used of a journey to the coast, especially from the capital as starting-point. On Caesarea see on 8.40. E (614 *pc*) it sy^p.h** sa mae add διὰ νυκτός — a characteristic example of the Western text's tendency to make the narrative more dramatic and circumstantial.

Saul was to be got well away from Jerusalem. ἐξαποστέλλειν is another characteristically Lucan word (Lk., four times; Acts, seven times; rest of the NT, twice), increasing the plausibility of the view that Luke is here composing his own narrative. *Begs.* 4.106f. shares the view of most writers that the most natural way to take Luke's words is with reference to a sea journey to Tarsus but rightly questions the opinion of many that the corresponding verse Gal. 1.21 implies a journey by land. We have already learned that Paul came from Tarsus (9.11); for the possible significance of this place of origin see on 9.11 and 22.3. We hear no more of Saul until Barnabas goes to Tarsus to bring him to Antioch (11.25f.). How he occupied the intervening period Acts does not tell us. Some (e.g. Bauernfeind 136) think of a period of preparation for later work; others (e.g. Stählin 142, referring to 22.21; 26.17ff.) of missionary work otherwise unrecorded. Paul himself records (Gal. 1.18) his short visit to Jerusalem, three years after his conversion, and that after this he went into Syria (in which Antioch was situated) and Cilicia (where Tarsus lay). After an interval of fourteen years (whether measured from his conversion or from his previous visit is uncertain) Paul again visited Jerusalem, accompanied by Barnabas and Titus (Gal. 2.1). In the meantime he remained personally unknown to the churches of Judaea (Gal. 1.22) — a fact which is difficult to reconcile with Acts 9.26–29 but harmonizes with Paul's own statement that he had spent no more than a fortnight in Jerusalem and had met only Cephas and James (Gal. 1.18, 19).

The second αὐτόν is omitted by P^74 A E 323 945 1739 *pm* latt. The sentence is better without it, but it probably stood there till copyists thought fit to leave it out.

25. THE CHURCH IN JUDAEA, GALILEE, AND SAMARIA: A SUMMARY 9.31

(31) So the church throughout Judaea, Galilee, and Samaria had peace; it was being built up and walked in the fear of the Lord under the influence of[1] the Holy Spirit, and it increased in numbers.

Bibliography

K. N. Giles, *NTS* 31 (1985), 135–42.

Commentary

This verse, standing on its own, can hardly be anything other than a summary editorial note, inserted by Luke. Compare the earlier summaries, 2.42–47; 4.32–35; 5.12–16; 6.7. μὲν οὖν is a formula with which Luke often begins a new section of his book (e.g. at 8.4), and it would not be improper to take the verse as the beginning of the new section that continues as far as 11.18, a section that first takes Peter to Joppa, where he waits for the summons that leads to the founding of a mixed church, including Gentiles, at Caesarea. The formula is, however, in itself backward-looking, and here means that new developments will rest on a sound foundation laid in Judaea, Galilee, and Samaria. Since the verse is related both to what precedes and to what follows it seems necessary to consider it on its own as a connecting link.

Nothing has hitherto been said about the founding of churches in Galilee; see the notes below. The occurrence of Galilee at this point probably signifies only that the church is now (according to Luke) settled and established in all Jewish areas, including the half-Jewish area of Samaria. Galilee could hardly be omitted. The church is at peace and flourishing, and is now ready for further expansion; the first steps in this direction Luke will proceed in the next sections to describe.

31. μὲν οὖν is a characteristic Acts construction; see on 1.6. BDR § 451. 1 n. 3 rightly comment, 'es wird hier teils angegeben, was

---

[1] *Begs.*, RSV, in the comfort of; NEB, upheld by; NJB, encouraged by.

weiter geschah, teils die Summe aus dem Vorhergehenden gezogen, um den Übergang zu etwas Neuem zu bilden.' The use is classical. For ἐκκλησία see on 5.11. Luke uses the word, normally in a local sense, to denote the community of Christians. It is impossible to learn from the word itself what Luke understood this community to be; this can be discovered only by reading what he says about it. The present verse describes it in its proper functioning, but makes no attempt to say by what means it may be built up and live in the fear of the Lord, except that such means depend upon the work of the Holy Spirit.

καθ' ὅλης . . . The use of κατά (*throughout*) is Hellenistic (see BDR § 225. 2, n. 3, quoting Polybius 3.19.7, κατὰ τῆς νήσου διεσπάρησαν). Cf. 9.42; 10.37 (also with ὅλος). For Judaea cf. 1.8; 2.9; 8.1; it is easy to suppose that what happened, and what was proclaimed, in Jerusalem spread through the surrounding area. For Samaria cf. 8.4–25. Galilee has not previously been mentioned (and is mentioned, but not as a mission field, only at 10.37; 13.31). This has been taken to mean (E. Lohmeyer, *Galiläa und Jerusalem*, 1936, 51f., referred to by Bauernfeind 138 and by Davies, *Land* 412) that Galilee was already *terra Christiana*; it was not evangelized from Jerusalem because it was already the seat of a Christian church (which itself had, perhaps, evangelized Damascus; see 9.1). This view is criticized by Davies (*Land* 421f.). Silence about Galilee in Acts may mean not that a church was already established there but that there were very few Christians in that region. 'One might even argue that Judaea, Galilee, and Samaria in Acts 9.31 serve only as a convenient formula to assert that the whole Jewish-Christian Church was at peace, without any implication that there was an organized community in Galilee or not' (*Land* 422). Cf. Hengel (76): 'Out-of-the-way, "backwoods" Galilee quickly lost its significance for the future history of earliest Christianity and could not regain it even after the destruction of Jerusalem in AD 70.' It seems more probable that there were few Christians in Galilee than that there were many and that the rest of Christendom engaged in a conspiracy of silence designed to conceal their existence. Christianity never became established in Galilee; for evidence up to AD 325 see A. Harnack, *The Mission and Expansion of Christianity in the First Three Centuries*, 1908, 2.97–120, 330. It is possible but not known that Christian missionaries had more success in the short period before AD 66.

εἶχεν εἰρήνην. εἰρήνη is not used in Acts in the theological sense of e.g. Rom. 5.1 except at 10.36. Schille (237) indeed thinks that here it does refer to 'Heilszustand' (he quotes the Hebrew שלום), but the context implies that Luke means simply that the Christians now lived an undisturbed life, which however made for Christian development. The church was *built up*; for οἰκοδομεῖν cf. 20.32. Calvin (275) rightly says that here the sense is both external (the number of church members increased) and internal (the members made progress in piety). The verb and the cognate noun are important for Paul, especially in the Corinthian letters. The church grew in strength and security. Moule (*IB* 185; cf. *Begs.* 4.107) suggests that πορευομένη may have been coloured by the Hebrew idiom in which a verb of motion gives progressive force to another verb. This would presumably mean translating *was built up more and more*; but for this the participles are in the wrong order, and τῷ φόβῳ is left unexplained. BDR § 198. 5 n. 6 note this as a striking use of the dative, since classical usage has the dative when the sense is literal (e.g. Thucydides 2.98.1, (ἐπορεύετο... τῇ ὁδῷ ἦν... αὐτὸς ἐποιήσατο) but the accusative when the sense is metaphorical (e.g. Thucydides 3.64.3, (ἄδικον ὁδὸν ἰόντων). But Hellenistic and biblical usage does not make this distinction, and the metaphorical use of πορεύεσθαι itself determines this context; cf. 14.16. *The fear of the Lord* (φόβος κυρίου, יִרְאַת יהוה) is a very common OT expression, and though it is not used in the OT with πορεύεσθαι (but cf. Targ. Onq. Gen. 5.22; 6.9) the OT use gives the sense here, except in so far as κύριος now refers to, or gains some definition from, the Lord Jesus. The meaning is well defined by Roloff (157) as 'Das Sich-Unterstellen unter die richtende Macht Gottes (1 Pet. 1.17; 3.2)'. It is probable that here Luke simply takes over the familiar expression: the church was built up and observed the due practices of piety.

τῇ παρακλήσει will be coordinated with τῷ φόβῳ but its meaning is uncertain. At 4.36 (see the note) it probably means (prophetic) *exhortation*; similarly at 13.15. At 15.31 however the word seems to mean *comfort*, though *encouragement* is not impossible. The cognate verb παρακαλεῖν occurs more frequently but seems for the most part to mean *to exhort*, sometimes weakened to *to ask*. Followed here by the subjective genitive τοῦ ἁγίου πνεύματος it is not wrong to allow it to refer to whatever it is that the Holy Spirit does, and this will include both the (messianic) consolation (cf. e.g. Lk. 2.25) and the stirring up and enabling of Christians to live as they should (cf. 1.8). Maddox (173) draws attention to the use of the cognate noun παράκλητος in Jn 14.16, 26; 15.26; 16.7; cf. 1 Jn 2.1. The resemblance is interesting, but insufficient to establish direct literary contact between Acts and the Fourth Gospel. πληθύνειν refers to growth in numbers, as at 6.1, 7; 7.17.

The sentence as a whole is changed into the plural number (αἱ ἐκκλησίαι... εἶχον... οἰκοδομούμεναι... πορευόμεναι... ἐπληθύνοντο) by (E Ψ) 𝔐 it syʰ boᵐˢˢ; the singular is read by P⁷⁴ ℵ

A B C (Ψ) 81 323 453 945 1175 1739 *pc* vg (sy^p) co. Preuschen (61) thinks the plural 'richtiger', pointing to the plural at 16.5; it should however be regarded as a Western alteration (the older MSS that contain it show Western influence), but it should not be taken to imply a different, congregational or independent, view of the church over against a catholic view; the singular may have been conformed to the plurals of 15.41; 16.5 (so Metzger 367). Except at 20.28 (on which see the note) Acts uses the word ἐκκλησία to denote a local church, and probably does so here. The area described is not so large that the Christians in it could not be regarded as constituting a unit, though no doubt they met in a number of different groups in different towns — 'the original Jerusalem church in dispersion' (Bruce 2.208). The Western editor probably wished to show how extensive the church had become and how widespread was its prosperity.

VI
THE FIRST PREACHER TO GENTILES AND
THE FIRST GENTILE CHURCH (9.32–11.18)

26. PETER'S MIRACLES ON THE WAY TO CAESAREA
9.32–43

(32) It happened that Peter passed through all these areas[1] and came down also to the saints who lived at Lydda. (33) There he found a man called Aeneas who for eight years had lain on his bed; he was paralysed. (34) Peter said to him, 'Aeneas, Jesus Christ has healed you;[2] get up and make your own bed.[3]' And immediately he got up. (35) And all those who lived in Lydda and in the Plain of Sharon saw him and turned to the Lord.

(36) In Joppa there was a woman disciple called Tabitha (which, translated, is Dorcas). She was constantly practising good works and giving alms. (37) In those days it happened that she fell sick and died. They washed her body and laid it in an upper room. (38) Since Lydda was near to Joppa the disciples, when they heard that Peter was there, sent two men to him, with the request, 'Please do not hesitate to come to us.[4]' (39) Peter got up and went with them. When he arrived they took him up to the upper room, and all the widows were present with him, weeping and displaying the tunics and cloaks that Dorcas made while she was with them. (40) Peter put everyone out, knelt down, and prayed. He turned to the body and said, 'Tabitha, get up.' She opened her eyes, and when she saw Peter she sat up. (41) He gave her his hand and raised her up. He called the saints and the widows and presented her to them alive. (42) This became known through the whole of Joppa, and many believed in the Lord. (43) Peter stayed on a number of days in Joppa, with a man called Simon, a tanner.

Bibliography

F. W. Beare, *JBL* 62 (1943), 295–306.

H. J. Cadbury, *JTS* 49 (1948), 57f.

J. Smit Sibinga, *FS* Klijn, 242–6.

---

[1]These areas is not in the Greek.
[2]*Begs.*, RSV, heals you; NEB, NJB, cures you.
[3]*Begs.*, lay the table for yourself.
[4]*Begs.*, Do not fail to come to us; NJB, Come to us without delay; similarly NEB.

Commentary

Peter, apparently engaged on a missionary tour or on an inspection of Christian centres comparable with that of 8.14, or perhaps simultaneously on both, came to Lydda, where there was already a group of Christians (ἅγιοι; for the meaning of the word, and the possibility that it may refer to others rather than Christians, such as members of the Qumran sect, see on v. 32). How there came to be Christians in Lydda is a matter on which Luke provides no information. If we wish we may guess that the churches were founded by Philip on his way from Azotus to Caesarea. In the locality was a sick man, Aeneas. We do not know whether he was a Jew or a Gentile, or whether he had become a Christian; the probability is that he was a Jewish Christian. He was healed by Jesus Christ (v. 34; there is no reference here to the *name* — contrast 3.6, 16; 4.7, 10, 30) and his healing led to many conversions, though we still do not know whether he was or became a Christian; it is however because it is not said that he became a Christian after his healing that one infers that he was a Christian at the beginning of the story. Many not only in Lydda but throughout the plain of Sharon turned to the Lord. In the nearby town of Joppa was a disciple (Luke almost certainly means a Christian disciple, though it is conceivable that his source intended one belonging to a different religious group) called Tabitha (in Greek, Dorcas), noted for her charitable works. On her death her fellow disciples sent to Lydda for Peter (which surely means that they were Christian disciples), who travelled to Joppa and raised Tabitha from death. This new miracle also led to many conversions, and for some days Peter stayed in Joppa; this provides a link with the next incident, the conversion of Cornelius (10.1–48). There are similarities between the two stories; the naming of the persons concerned (Aeneas, Tabitha), the word ἀνάστηθι, the use of ἅγιοι. Schneider (2.49) is probably right in concluding that they were combined before Luke used them.

The former of the two miracles is related in the simplest possible terms, but in a form common to miracle stories in general; it recalls some features of Mk. 2.1–12. It is hard to see any motive that Luke could have had in telling the story beyond the following: (1) It provided a further example (cf. 5.15, 16) of the power of Jesus working through Peter; (2) it was connected in tradition with Lydda and thus served to bring Peter on the way to Caesarea (ch. 10). Luke had to bring Peter to Caesarea but he had no need to supply stopping-places on the way, so that it may be accepted that Lydda (otherwise unnamed and insignificant in Luke's narrative) stood in the tradition in connection with the incident. It is probable that Luke has edited the piece at the beginning and the end.

The latter story, as a resurrection, is even more striking and is told more fully, but it seems to acquire no additional motivation and to have been intended to teach no further truth. We learn from it that there was in Joppa a Christian group with a fairly developed charitable organization. The Christian group includes, or is related to, a clientele of widows (cf. 6.1; 1 Tim. 5.9–16), who are supplied with clothing. They are not an order; they are not said to perform any service for the church; they are rather its beneficiaries. Their existence suggests a community not of recent origin. The story recalls Mk 5.36–43; 1 Kings 17.17–24; 2 Kings 4.18–37 (see Weiser's table, 238). Haenchen is probably right in seeing here the intention to show that the apostles did not come behind the prophets; whether we should think of the 'greater works' of Jn. 14.12 is more doubtful. The raising of Tabitha is hardly greater than that of Mk 5 or Jn 11 — or Lk. 7.

The fact (see above) that the Christian group at Joppa seems to have reached a relatively advanced stage of development reminds us that we have no means of dating this cycle of stories about Peter; it is attractive to suggest that 12.17 (Peter went εἰς ἕτερον τόπον) marks the chronological point at which Peter left Jerusalem for a wider mission field (see Roloff 159); but see on that verse.

The double story is a good example of Luke's Episodenstil (Plümacher 110) but it must be understood as part of the development of Luke's narrative as a whole. We know that the story of Cornelius was of great importance to him; he regarded it as the beginning of the Gentile mission (15.7). Here he is preparing for it. Saul has been called and we know that he is to be a missionary to the Gentiles but he is being held in reserve till 11.25. Philip has almost stepped outside the bounds of Judaism (8.4–13, 26–40). Peter (whose importance at this stage of the book is high) is on his way, but is still a missionary and pastor to Jews. At 8.40 Philip is said to reach Caesarea; there is no sign of him in ch. 10, but he could have passed through Lydda and Joppa on his way from Azotus. It seems probable (see below, p. 496) that the story of Cornelius the Centurion was Caesarea's own traditional account of the foundation there of a mixed Jewish and Gentile church. The two miracles may always have been attached to the Caesarea story — Caesarea's explanation of how Peter came to be in the vicinity (10.5): a general missionary or supervisory tour of Peter's, presumably confined to Jews, led him to the neighbourhood of Caesarea and thus prepared for his excursion outside the confines of Judaism. Alternatively, but perhaps less probably, we must suppose that Luke picked up a couple of pieces, or one double piece, of loose tradition which he himself chose to use as introductory to the story he found in Caesarea. Schmithals rightly points out that for Luke this means that Gentile Christianity is not a break with but a fulfilment of Judaism. According to Schille (237) the pair of stories presents a different picture of Peter from Luke's: they describe him as a travelling apostle, Luke thinks of him as a resident settled in Jerusalem. The fact seems rather to be that in Luke's view Peter was always an evangelist who gradually extended his range of operation till he covered the whole racial and religious scale, though not the whole geographical area, available.

32. ἐγένετο (see on 4.5) hints at the Hebrew construction with ויהי but, taking the accusative and infinitive, does not represent it closely. The same quasi-biblical expression occurs at v. 37. Luke's interest now returns to Peter, who has not been mentioned by name since 8.20, though his presence is implied at 9.27. Luke is now preparing for the story of Cornelius in ch. 10 which plays an important part in the development of his account of the spread of the Gospel. For διέρχεσθαι see on 8.4, 40; in these passages it certainly refers to a missionary journey since it is accompanied by εὐαγγελίζεσθαι. That verb is not used here but διέρχεσθαι may retain the same sense. This turns to some extent on the meaning of διὰ πάντων. Torrey (34) explains this by retroversion into Aramaic. 'Peter passed through "*the whole* (region)," διὰ πάντων, בכלא. כלא is often used thus absolutely, when the context makes the meaning evident. For a Judean writer, to whom Palestine was "*the* land" (cf. כל ארעא in 11.28 . . .), this was doubtless the usual expression in such a context.' If this view is correct we may compare 9.31 (καθ᾽ ὅλης τῆς 'Ιουδαίας . . .) and 1.8; it does not however explain the plural or tell us what noun should be understood with the plural pronoun. It is unlikely that this should anticipate τοὺς ἁγίους, though it has been suggested that we should render, Peter passed among all the saints (i.e. all the Christian communities) until he came to those at Lydda. It could refer to cities and villages, and thus connect with 8.25, only if Luke was writing loosely (since πόλις and κώμη are both feminine). The phrase remains obscure, and *Begs.* 4.108 may be right in the observation that if a new source begins at this point the context might originally have supplied the meaning. This observation offers some support to the view that Luke is here following a written source. Preuschen (61) thinks that the Peshitto's διὰ πόλεων may be original. p has transeuntem per omnes civitates et regiones. Haenchen takes the reference to be to all the areas mentioned in 9.31.

Also unexplained is the καί (before πρός) — *also to the saints.* In addition to whom? Possibly to the Christians in Judaea, Galilee, and Samaria (9.31), were it not that these would already have included any to be found between Jerusalem and Lydda. τοὺς ἁγίους are most naturally understood as Christians, though this designation of them, common in Paul's letters, is rare in Acts: see only 9.13; 26.10 (both connected with Paul) and in this paragraph vv. 32 and 41. According to Kosmala (*Hebräer* 53) they were not Christians; the same persons (οἱ κατοικοῦντες Λύδδα) are mentioned in v. 35 and it is at that point that they are converted to Christianity. They were not (according to Kosmala) Christians but members of the local Essene community. That there were such communities in addition to the main group at Qumran (if indeed these are rightly described as Essene) is undoubtedly true (Kosmala rightly quotes Philo, *Hypothetica* 11.1; *Quod Omnis* 76; Josephus, *War* 2.124); see further on vv. 38, 41. It seems however improbable that a Christian writer, who could on occasion use ἅγιος to mean Christian, would employ it in another sense, though it is arguable that Luke's source used the word to refer to Essenes and that Luke misunderstood it to mean Christians.

On Lydda (in the OT, Lod; later, Diospolis) see *NS* 2.190–8. It was situated on the road from Jerusalem to Joppa (v. 36), a day's journey from Jerusalem, a village (κώμη) 'in size not inferior to a city' (Josephus, *Ant.* 20.130; in this place Josephus writes Λύδδα as first declension singular, as do C E 𝔐 here; at *War* 2.515; 4.444 he has the neuter plural). Lydda was the head of a κληρουχία or τοπαρχία (Josephus, *War* 3.54, 55). See also 1 Macc. 11.34; Pliny, *Nat. Hist.* 5.70.

33. εὗρεν does not imply that Peter looked for the man; he *came across* him. The name Aeneas does not suggest but equally does not exclude Jewish origin; it occurs in Palestinian inscriptions (see BA 43 s.v.). In view of Luke's treatment in ch. 10 of Peter's encounter with Cornelius we may conclude that (rightly or wrongly) Luke did not think of Aeneas as anything other than a Jew; he could hardly have failed to mention the matter if he had thought that Peter was already having dealings with a Gentile. *Begs.* 4.109 thinks he was not a Christian, Weiser (242) thinks he was; Weiser is probably right, since if his cure had led to his conversion Luke would have remarked on this.

ἐξ ἐτῶν ὀκτώ, possibly *from the age of eight*, more probably, *for eight years*. κράβαττος: at Mk 2.4 the word evidently means something like a stretcher since it could be lowered through a hole in a roof; in the parallel it is avoided by Luke. Here it presumably means something more permanent since it has been Aeneas's resting-place for eight years; 'a "poor man's bed"' (*ND* 2.15). Like the man in Mk 2, Aeneas is paralysed; at Mk 2.3 he is described as παραλυτικός; in the Lucan parallel (Lk. 5.18) as here he is described in the words ὃς ἦν παραλελυμένος. It is not clear, nor does it make much difference, whether we take the verb as a periphrastic pluperfect (*who had been paralysed*) or as the imperfect of εἶναι with an adjectival participle (*who was paralysed*); each implies the other. Luke, in the customary style of the miracle narrative, makes clear that Aeneas was seriously ill and had been so for so long a time that recovery seemed impossible.

34. Peter addresses Aeneas; cf. 3.4, 6. Ropes (*Begs.* 3.91) notes that p sa have intendens autem in eum Petrus dixit ei, which he regards as the true Western text. The name of Jesus is not invoked (contrast 3.6), but Peter's words explain what the name of Jesus means when the phrase is used (Roloff 160): it is none other than Jesus (certainly not Peter) who is the agent of the cure: ἰᾶταί σε ᾽Ιησοῦς Χριστός. M. 1.119 follows Burton (*Moods and Tenses*, 1894, 9) in taking ἰᾶται as an aoristic present; cf. 16.18. So also BDR § 320, where the point is made that punctiliar (aorist) stems form no present tenses; there is therefore no alternative to using the present with an aoristic sense. Cf. 26.1. M. 3.64 accepts the punctiliar present (adding 8.23 in comparison), but M. 2.60 notes the possibility that the verb might be the perfect ἴαται. A strong case for this is made by H. J. Cadbury (*JTS* 49 (1948), 57f.) though he appears not to have noticed the reference in the second volume of Moulton. He notes the important parallel in the words ἡ πίστις σου σέσωκέν σε (Mt. 9.22; Mk 5.34; 10.52; Lk. 7.50; 8.48; 17.19; 18.42 — this perfect is evidently specially favoured by Luke; see also Acts 4.9, σέσωσται). Metzger 367 notes that B writes ειαται, as at Mk 5.29, where the perfect tense is certainly intended; this is not however proof that B intended the perfect here. ει for ι is a common itacism. Calvin (276) translates *Jesus Christ heal thee*, sanet, presumably understanding ἰᾶται as a subjunctive. The translation does not seem possible. 'Grata Lucae medico paronomasia' (Page 142, noting the words ἰᾶταί σε ᾽Ιησοῦς; cf. 4.30; 10.38). Jesus is the healer.

The command to the sick man to get up is familiar in healing stories; στρῶσον σεαυτῷ is without parallel in the NT; elsewhere the word is used only of the action of the crowds in spreading their clothes and foliage in Jesus' path as he enters Jerusalem (Mt. 21.8; Mk 11.8) and of the furnishing of the room in which the Last Supper was held (Mk 14.15; Lk. 22.12). The word is usually understood to mean that Aeneas is being told to make the bed for himself, that is, in this case, to pack it up since he will need it no longer. This is possible, though when used in this sense the word usually means to make a bed with a view to lying on it. *Begs.* 4.109 takes the command to be *lay a table for yourself* with a view to having a meal. This is supported by Pallis (60f.), according to whom in Modern Greek στρώνω (τὸ τραπέζι) is *to lay the tablecloth*, etc. Ezk. 23.31, however, though used to support the reference to a table, when read as a whole supports reference to a bed. στρωννύναι is frequently used for spreading bedclothes and it is best to take it so here. Miracles of healing are elsewhere accompanied by commands to the person cured to deal with his own bed instead of being carried on it; e.g. Mk 2.11.

The cure took place immediately, εὐθέως, another characteristic feature of miracle stories; cf. 3.7.

35. As often in miracle stories, the reaction of onlookers is noted. These are οἱ κατοικοῦντες Λύδδα, the words used at v. 32. Here C E 𝔐 are joined by P⁵³ P⁷⁴ in reading Λύδδαν. These were not originally Christians, since they now ('οἵτινες introduces a subsequent act', *Begs.* 4.109; cf. 8.15; 11.20) turned to the Lord (Jesus). They were Jews; converted Gentiles are said to turn to God (Weiser 243). With the inhabitants of Lydda are joined those of 'the Sharon', that is, the plain of Sharon, the coastal plain, at that time thickly populated and famous for its fruitfulness. There are several variants which probably reflect knowledge — and ignorance — of local usage. τὸν Σαρῶνα, which is probably correct, is read by P⁷⁴ (ℵᶜ A: Σαρρῶνα) B C E Ψ 6 2495 *al* gig. 𝔐 has τὸν Ἀσσαρῶνα; P⁵³ has Σαρῶνα, ℵ* Σαρρῶνα (without the article); P⁴⁵ 36 81 323 614 945 1175 1739 *al* have τὸν Σαρώναν. In the LXX ὁ Σαρών occurs only at Isa. 33.9. Elsewhere שרון is translated by τὸ πέδιον, ὁ δρυμός, or οἱ δρυμοί. For ἐπιστρέφειν as a conversion word cf. 3.15; 11.21; 14.15; 15.19; 26.18, 20; (28.27). It occurs frequently in this sense in the LXX.

36. Peter continued on the road leading towards the coast, which he would reach at Joppa. On this town see *NS* 2.110–14, where for the present passage the most important observation is, 'Despite its close association with Judaea, Joppa seems to have been a Greek city proper' (114); cf. Josephus, *War* 3.56. That is, when Peter reached Joppa he was well on his way into a Gentile environment (though this does not necessarily mean that he stirred far outside the synagogue community). It should be noted that Acts, like 1 Maccabees (10.74ff.; 12.33; 13.11) and the MSS of Josephus, uses the spelling Ἰόππη; most non-biblical sources have Ἰόπη. The coins show sometimes one form, sometimes the other.

In Joppa there were disciples (v. 38), including a woman, described as a μαθήτρια. The feminine form is not common, but occurs in a few pagan authors and in *Gospel of Peter* 50 (with reference to Mary Magdalene). The form μαθήτρια is not classical; Moeris for example has: μαθητρίς, Ἀττικῶς· μαθήτρια, Ἑλληνικῶς. For the use of μαθητής in Acts see on 6.1; 9.25; 19.1. Undoubtedly the word normally refers to Christians, disciples of Jesus Christ, and it must be assumed to do so here, unless strong reasons to the contrary can be adduced. Kosmala (*Hebräer* 54; see also on v. 32 and on v. 41) thinks that the disciples in question had heard of Jesus, but need not have accepted his Messiahship. This carries caution too far, at least as far as Luke's understanding of the matter is concerned. It is of course possible that Luke had heard of a Jewish sect of 'disciples' and wrongly supposed that it was Christian.

The woman was called Tabitha. See Wilcox (109f.). The name represents the feminine form of the Aramaic טביא, *deer, gazelle*. The corresponding Greek is δορκάς (LS 445: 'an animal of the deer kind (so called from its large bright eyes), in Greece, roe . . .; in Syria and Africa, gazelle'). There are several other forms (δόρξ, δόρκος, δόρκων, ζορκάς, ζόρξ, ἴορκος). The masculine form of the name, Tebi, was used; it was borne for example by a slave of Gamaliel's (Berakoth 2.7). The translation of the name is introduced in a relative clause beginning with ἥ; according to Begs. 4.110 the only occurrence in Acts of ἥ rather than ἥτις. διερμηνεύειν is used here only to mean translate (but cf. 1 Cor. 12.30; 14.5, 13, 27); for the translation of names cf. Jn 1.39, 43; 9.7; Heb. 7.2 (ἑρμηνεύειν). It is probable that in the mixed society of Joppa both names, the Aramaic and the Greek, would be in use; cf. Josephus, War 4.145. For inscriptions see Preuschen (62) and BA 411, 1601 s.vv. Further examples of the name are given in MM 169, 624 and ND 4.177f.; see also Hemer (226).

For the metaphorical use of πλήρης (abounding in) cf. the frequent expression 'full of the Holy Spirit' (6.3, 5; 7.55; 11.24; also the use of πληροῦσθαι); for the use with moral and religious qualities cf. 6.8; 13.10; 19.28. Tabitha was constantly at work doing good and giving alms. Good works are defined by Calvin (278) as 'voluntary acts of love', and Tabitha's good works are specified in v. 39.

37. The sentence begins with ἐγένετο followed by an accusative and infinitive, as at v. 32; see the note there. Here the infinitive has a qualifying participle: She fell sick (aorist participle, ἀσθενήσασαν) and died. In those days means at the time when Peter was in that region.

Tabitha's body was prepared for burial. The washing of a corpse was a very widespread practice; so Homer, Iliad 18.350 (λοῦσάν τε καὶ ἤλειψαν λίπ' ἐλαίῳ); Euripides, Phoenicians 1318f. (1328f.); Plato, Phaedo 115a; Vergil, Aeneid 6.219 (. . . corpusque lavant frigentis et unguunt); and equally among Jews; so Shabbath 23.5 (They may make ready on the Sabbath all that is needful for the dead, and anoint it and wash it . . .). As appears from these (and many other) passages it was customary also to anoint the body; this rite is not mentioned here. The body was placed (the pronoun αὐτήν in some MSS precedes, in others follows, ἔθηκαν, and is omitted, perhaps rightly, by B 36 453 614 pc) in an (or the: τῷ is read by P⁵³ P⁷⁴ A C E 36 323 945 1175 1739ᵐᵍ al, omitted by P⁴⁵ ℵ B Ψ 𝔐) upper room. For ὑπερῷον see 1.13; 20.8. Luke may be thinking of a regular place of Christian assembly; the Christian meeting room. Bauernfeind (140) draws attention to 1 Kings 17.19, which may have affected the telling of the story. Pesch (323) on the other hand claims that an upper room was the only possible place for exposing a corpse and that the OT parallel may be insignificant. Schille (239) again has a different view: 'Das Porträt der reichen Dame setzt sich fort'.

38. The distance between Lydda and Joppa is about ten miles. The disciples (cf. v. 36) must in Luke's view have been Christians; see however on that verse for the caution of Kosmala (*Hebräer* 54). They sent *two men* to Peter; δύο ἄνδρας is however omitted by 𝔐, and it is not easy to see why. On the other hand it is not likely that all the earlier MSS should simply have imported this feature, intentionally or absent-mindedly, from 10.7 (see also Lk. 7.19; 10.1; Acts 19.22; 23.23), and the long text may therefore be accepted even though the origin of the shorter must remain in doubt. On the sending of emissaries in pairs see J. Jeremias, 'Paarweise Sendung im NT', in *FS* T. W. Manson, 136–43.

μὴ ὀκνήσῃς is often taken as no more than a polite form of imperative, or rather request: Please come, Be so good as to come. It is doubtful whether the evidence adduced is sufficient to support this reduction of the formula to no more than a polite introduction to a request. The closest parallel is Num. 22.16, μὴ ὀκνήσῃς ἐλθεῖν πρός με (אל-נא תמנע מהלוך אלי); cf. Sirach 7.35, μὴ ὄκνει ἐπισκέπτεσθαι ἄρρωστον ἄνθρωπον. But even in these passages (still more in Josephus, *Life* 251; *c. Apionem* 1.15, and papyri cited by MM 444f.) there lingers the sense of hesitation or delay which is found in classical usage, where the word is used of reluctance, caused by shame, fear, pity, cowardice, or indolence (LS 1212); thus Sophocles, *Philoctetes* 93f., ὀκνῶ προδότης καλεῖσθαι, I shrink from being called a traitor. That the request is introduced in this way is not a pure formality; it hints at the fear that Peter might for some reason be unwilling to come. Why? Hardly because ten miles was too long a journey; Peter was engaged on a tour (v. 32) which had already brought him from Jerusalem to Lydda. Possibly because Joppa was a Greek city (v. 36); possibly even because the Christians in Joppa were not Jews, though this would throw Luke's chronological scheme into confusion, and is very improbable.

διέρχεσθαι in this verse cannot be used in the sense that it may have in v. 32; if Peter does not come without delay (and this may be part of the meaning of μὴ ὀκνήσῃς) Dorcas will be buried.

39. ἀναστάς is superfluous except as a mark of 'biblical' style; cf. 1.15. Peter complies at once with the request.

For the ὑπερῷον (now with the anaphoric article) see v. 37. πᾶσαι αἱ χῆραι: they are mentioned not as an order (as perhaps in 1 Tim. 5.9–16) but as poor. At a later period they helped to dispense the church's charity; here they are recipients of it. This may well mean that Acts is to be placed somewhat earlier than the Pastoral Epistles, and must cast some doubt on the belief that they were written by the same author. The widows were weeping; for κλαίειν as a reaction to death cf. e.g. Lk. 8.52. The picture has the effect of representing Peter as not only powerful but compassionate. Dorcas's beneficence to the needy had taken the form of providing clothing; the χιτών is an inner, the ἱμάτιον an outer garment. ἐπιδεικνύμεναι, middle: 'Medium quasi describit, quomodo ostenderint vestes quibus actu indutae erant' (Zerwick § 234). This may go somewhat too far; the middle of ἐπιδεικνύναι is more common than the active, and one of its meanings is that one shows what is one's own. The widows had the clothes but were not necessarily wearing them. Page (142) says that the middle means to show with pride, or satisfaction. He also says that ὅσα is not equivalent to ἅ but means *all which; Begs.* 4.111 and probably most recent writers do take the two forms of the relative as equivalent. Delebecque (48) however takes ἱμάτια ὅσα ἐποίει to be equivalent to ὅσα ἐποίει ἱμάτια, toutes les tuniques et tous les manteaux. He also takes μετ'αὐτῶν, avec elles, to mean that Dorcas had had an ouvroir, a workshop, with the widows.

40. Peter put out all who had gathered in the upper room; πάντας (masculine) can include the widows but must include men also. The same words (ἐκβαλὼν πάντας) are used at Mk 5.40, but are omitted by Luke at that point. A further possible contact between the story about Peter and Mark's story of Jesus will be mentioned below; next however is the reference to Peter's prayer, which has a parallel in 4 Kdms 4.33 (in the presence of the dead boy Elisha prayed) but none in the story of Jesus. This emphasises the fact that Peter did not effect cures in his own right but by appealing to divine power (cf. 3.12). For θεὶς τὰ γόνατα cf. 7.60.

Peter addresses Tabitha. The fact that he uses that name suggests that he was speaking Aramaic. His words, Ταβιθά, ἀνάστηθι, recall the words of Jesus to the daughter of Jairus, not so much as they are given in Lk. 8.54 (ἡ παῖς, ἔγειρε) but as they are given in Mk 5.41 in Aramaic, ταλιθά κούμ (where several variants show knowledge of and confusion with the name Tabitha). The resemblance between the two sayings, both addressed to the dead, has been variously assessed. To Stählin (145) it is 'nur zufällig'; to Roloff (160) it is 'kein Zufall'. Bauernfeind (139) thinks that the parallel cannot be 'zufällig oder . . . in der Sache begründet'. The case for pure coincidence is by far the stronger. ταλιθά is not a name; that it shares some letters with Tabitha means nothing. If Luke had been intending to evoke memories of words which in his gospel he does not use he would have done so more effectively.

After ἀνάστηθι some Western authorities add *in the name of our Lord Jesus Christ* — a characteristically pious addition, which Preuschen (63) believes must be original because a resurrection without the invocation of the name is unthinkable!

Further agreements with other narratives of the raising of dead people follow. Tabitha opened her eyes; cf. 4 Kdms 4.35, ἤνοιξεν τὸ παιδάριον τοὺς ὀφθαλμοὺς αὐτοῦ. When she saw Peter,

Tabitha sat up; cf. Lk. 7.15, ἀνεκάθισεν ὁ νεκρός. The story is told in the conventional form of a miracle story. This continues in the next verse.

41. ἀνέστησεν does not refer here to raising to life; Tabitha is already alive. She has been lying on a bier; she has come to a sitting position (v. 40); Peter helps her to her feet. The local religious community (by τοὺς ἁγίους Luke means Christians, but see on vv. 32, 38) and the widows (it would be wrong to infer that they are not also Christians) are summoned to receive Tabitha back.

42. Tabitha has been publicly known to be dead; she can now be seen to be alive. The news would spread rapidly. So marvellous an event encouraged faith. For faith as the appropriate response to the Christian message see on 2.44 (οἱ πιστεύοντες).γνωστὸν ἐγένετο is a Lucan phrase; cf. 1.19; 19.17.

43. For the construction with ἐγένετο cf. v. 37. Here, surprisingly, the infinitive has no expressed subject P⁷⁴ ℵᶜ A E 81 323 945 1175 1739 al have αὐτόν after δέ; C Ψ 𝔐 have αὐτόν after μεῖναι; P⁵³ ℵ* B 104 pc omit). It is of course clear that Peter is meant. ἡμέρας ἱκανάς is a common expression in Acts; cf. 9.23; 18.18; 27.7 (ἱκανὸς χρόνος is also used). The reader cannot know how long is intended since Luke himself did not know. He knows, however, that it was a definite ended time; hence the aorist μεῖναι. He is preparing for 10.5, 6 (Dibelius 12).

Peter stayed on in Joppa with Simon, a tanner. βυρσεύς is the Hellenistic word for tanner; Attic is βυρσοδέψης. The name must be traditional; pure invention would never have invited confusion by making Simon Peter stay with another Simon. This of course does not confirm the historicity of the event. One would think it likely that Peter would stay with a fellow Christian. If Simon the tanner was a Christian this makes some of the remarks that follow more pointed, but it remains quite uncertain. Lüdemann (129) thinks that the statements in this verse cannot go back to tradition.

That the second Simon was a tanner may however be significant. Tanners were despised in Judaism. Thus Ketuboth 7.10: These are they that are compelled to put away their wives: he that is afflicted with boils, or that has a polypus, or that collects [dogs excrements], or that is a coppersmith or a tanner; Pesahim 65a: Woe to him that is a tanner. Cf. Shabbath 1.2; Megillah 3.2; Beba Bathra 2.9; Kiddushin 82b. Tanners were suspected of immorality, and their work involved a bad smell. See Jeremias, *Jerusalem* 310; StrB 2.695. It may be significant that Peter was willing — or perhaps was obliged — to live in a low class area, and with one of very doubtful repute in Jewish eyes. 'Verum id [uncleanness] Petrus parum curabat, maiora mox non curaturus' (Blass 123). It was 'an indication of Peter's broadmindedness' (Hengel 93). Cornelius may have seemed to be a step up in religious society. But Plümacher is probably right in thinking that residence with the tanner is after all not important. 'Warum sollte Lk die Pointe der folgenden Vision des Petrus durch Vorwegnahme abschwächen?' Similarly Haenchen (329) and Weiser (245).

27. PETER AND CORNELIUS: CAESAREA 10.1–48

(1) A certain man in Caesarea, Cornelius by name, a centurion belonging to the Cohort called Italica, (2) pious and god-fearing with all his household, making many charitable gifts to the People and constantly at prayer to God, (3) saw plainly in a vision, at about the ninth hour of the day, an angel of God, who came in to him and said, 'Cornelius.' (4) He stared at him, and struck with fear said, 'What is it, Sir?' The angel[1] said to him, 'Your prayers and your charitable gifts have come up before God for his remembrance. (5) So now you must send men to Joppa, and send for one Simon who is surnamed Peter. (6) He is lodging with one Simon a tanner, who has a house by the sea.' (7) When the angel who spoke to him went away, Cornelius[2] sent two of his servants and a pious soldier from among those who attended him, (8) and when he had explained the whole matter to them he sent them to Joppa.

(9) On the next day, while they were on their way and drawing near to the city, Peter about the sixth hour went up on the roof to pray. (10) He felt hungry, and was wanting to eat. While they were preparing a meal a trance fell upon him (11) and he saw heaven standing open and a sort of vessel descending, like a great sheet let down on the earth by the four corners. (12) In it were all the quadrupeds and reptiles of the earth and birds of heaven. (13) There came a voice to him, 'Get up, Peter, slaughter and eat.' (14) But Peter said, 'Certainly not, Lord, for I have never eaten anything profane or unclean.' (15) Again, a second time, a voice came to him, 'Things that God has cleansed, do not you treat as profane.' (16) This happened three times, and immediately the vessel was taken up into heaven. (17) While Peter doubted in himself what the vision he had seen might mean, Behold, the men who had been sent by Cornelius, having asked after Simon's house, came and stood at the gate. (18) They called and asked, 'Does Simon who is surnamed Peter lodge here?' (19) While Peter was reflecting on the vision, the Spirit said to him, 'Here are some men looking for you.[3] (20) Get up and go down and go with them, with no hesitation, for I have sent them.' (21) Peter went down to the men and said, 'I am the man you are looking for; what is the reason on account of which you have come?' (22) They said, 'Centurion Cornelius, a righteous man and one who fears God, of good reputation with the whole nation of the Jews, was instructed by a holy angel to send for you to come to his house and to hear words from you.' (23) So he asked them in and put them up.

On the next day he arose and went with them, and some of the brothers from Joppa accompanied him. (24) On the next day he entered Caesarea. Cornelius was awaiting them, and had gathered his relatives and closest

---

[1]Greek, he.
[2]Greek, he.
[3]*Begs.*, two men are seeking you; RSV, three men are looking for you.

friends. (25) As Peter entered, Cornelius met him, fell at his feet, and did him reverence. (26) But Peter raised him up, saying, 'Get up; I too am myself a man.' (27) Conversing with him, he went in, and found many assembled. (28) He said to them, 'You know that it is unlawful for a man of Jewish race to attach himself to or approach a man of another race; but God has shown me that I should not call any human being profane or unclean. (29) For this reason, when I was sent for I came without gainsaying. So I ask you[4] for what reason you have sent for me.' (30) Cornelius said, 'Four days ago, at this very hour,[5] I was saying the ninth hour of prayer in my house when behold, a man stood before me in bright clothing, (31) and said, Cornelius, your prayer has been heard and your charitable gifts have been remembered before God. (32) So send to Joppa and summon one Simon who is surnamed Peter. He is lodging in the house of Simon a tanner, by the sea. (33) So I sent for you at once, and you were so kind as to come. Now therefore we are all in the presence of God to hear all that has been laid upon you by the Lord.'

(34) Peter opened his mouth and said, 'Of a truth I perceive that God has no favourites, (35) but that in every nation he who fears him and works righteousness is accepted by him. (36) The word which God sent[6] to the children of Israel, bringing the good news of peace through Jesus Christ (he is Lord of all) . . . (37) You know the event that happened throughout the whole of Judaea, beginning from Galilee after the baptism that John proclaimed, (38) Jesus of Nazareth, how God anointed him with the Holy Spirit and power, who went about doing good and healing all who were overpowered by the devil, for God was with him. (39) And we are witnesses of all that he did in the land of the Jews and in Jerusalem. They killed him by hanging him on a tree; (40) God raised him up on the third day and granted to him that he should be revealed, (41) not to all the People but to witnesses who had been appointed beforehand by God, namely to us, who ate and drank with him after he had risen from the dead. (42) And he charged us to proclaim to the People and to testify that he is the one who has been marked out by God as judge of the living and the dead. (43) All the prophets bear witness to this, that everyone who believes in him receives through his name the forgiveness of sins.'

(44) While Peter was still speaking these things the Holy Spirit fell upon all who were listening to his speech. (45) And the circumcised believers who had accompanied Peter were astonished that the gift of the Spirit had been poured out upon the Gentiles too — (46) for they heard them speaking with tongues and magnifying God. Then Peter spoke up: (47): 'Can anyone forbid the water so as to prevent from being baptized these men who have received the Holy Spirit, just as we did?' (48) And he gave orders for them to be baptized in the name of Jesus Christ. Then they asked him to stay on for some days.

---

[4]You is not in the Greek.
[5]NJB, At this time three days ago.
[6]*Begs.*, He sent the word; RSV, You know the word which he sent; NEB, He sent his word; NJB, God sent his word.

Bibliography

R. Barthes, *RechScR* 58 (1970), 17–37.

F. Bovon, *ThZ* 26 (1970), 22–45.

C. Burchard, *NovT* 27 (1985), 281–95.

J. M. Bussler, *Bib* 66 (1985), 546–52.

G. Delling, as in (4).

J. Dupont, *FS* Ellis, 229–36.

J. Dupont, *Études* 75–81, 321–36, 409–12.

J. Dupont, *Nouvelles Études*, 319–28.

J. Dupont, as in (2) (*Nouvelles*).

J. Dupont, as in (4).

E. E. Ellis, *StEv* 4 (=*TU* 102, 1968), 390–9.

E. E. Ellis, as in (4).

T. Finn, *CBQ* 47 (1985), 75–84.

C. F. Evans, as in (4) (*JTS* 7).

J. G. Gager, as in (16).

K. Haacker, *BZ* 24 (1980), 234–51.

E. Haulotte, *RechScR* 58 (1970), 63–100.

J. Jervell, *StTh* 19 (1965), 68–96.

A. T. Kraabel, *Numen* 28 (1981), 113–26.

A. T. Kraabel, *FS* Stendahl, 147–57.

K. Löning, *BZ* 18 (1974), 1–19.

R. S. Mackenzie, *JBL* 104 (1985), 637–50.

L. Marin, *RechScR* 58 (1970), 39–61.

F. Mussner, *FS* Auer, 92–102.

F. Neirynck, *EThL* 60 (1984), 109–17, 118–23.

J. A. Overman, *JSNT* 32 (1988), 17–26.

H. Riesenfeld, *FS* Black (1979), 191–4.

H. Schlier, *Die Zeit der Kirche*, 90–107.

R. Schnackenburg, as in (1).

A. F. Segal, *SBL Seminar Papers* 1988, 336–69.

J. B. Tyson, *NTS* 33 (1987), 619–31.

W. C. van Unnik, *SpColl* 1.213–58.

M. Völkel, *ZNW* 64 (1973), 222–32.

A. Weiser, *FS* Dupont, 757–67.

A. Wikenhauser, as in (23).

U. Wilckens, *ZNW* 49 (1958), 223–37.

U. Wilckens, *Missionsreden*, 46–50, 63–70.

M. Wilcox, *JBL* 96 (1977), 85–99.

M. Wilcox, *JSNT* 13 (1981), 102–22.

Commentary

Like his account of the conversion of Saul (9.1–19a) this is a narrative that Luke repeats, thereby pointing out the importance he assigned to it. It was unnecessary in the immediately following section (11.1–18) to repeat so many details; it would have sufficed to say at 11.4, 'At this Peter told them all things, exactly as they had happened,' and to proceed at once to 11.18 and the conclusion of the matter. Luke not only repeats the story at some length but further underlines the importance that he sees in the event by putting into Peter's mouth a significant reference to it in 15.7–9, where it is represented as the beginning, under God's decision and choice, of the evangelization of Gentiles. Divine participation and control are made clear in the elaborate construction of the story with its complementary visions carefully fitted together, angelic messengers, and finally the spontaneous gift of the Spirit. The importance of the story for Luke and for Luke's book is thus unmistakable. It marks the final critical stage in the extension of the Gospel and the expansion of the church. At first the Gospel is preached to and accepted by Jews; next it moves as far as Samaritans; then comes the devout Ethiopian, who is all but a proselyte, going on pilgrimage to Jerusalem and reading the Bible privately. Finally there is Cornelius, on whose conversion even Jerusalem Christians, who at first object to Peter's dealings with an uncircumcised man, are obliged to remark, Why then, to the Gentiles also God has granted repentance unto life (11.18). Such is Luke's scheme; but the observant reader will have noticed a number of difficulties, and there is a long history of critical discussion of the incident. Haenchen (343f.) gives a good account of the main developments from Zeller to Dibelius. See Dibelius (109–22, 161–4); also Wilson, (*Gentiles* 171–8). Haenchen himself (347) thinks Dibelius mistaken in that the early church, with its conviction that the end of all things was at hand, is not likely to have preserved, as Dibelius thought, a simple narrative of a conversion; the point of the story is to be found in two sets of repetitions: (1) 10.14, 28, 47; 11. 2, 8, 17 — the Christians were at first opposed to the inclusion of Gentiles in their number; (2) 10.3, 11–16, 22, 30; 11.5–10, 13 — God overruled their objection and himself brought the Gentiles in. Some other views of the origin and meaning of the story will be mentioned below; the discussion by Weiser (249–62) is particularly important, and his conclusion must be quoted:

Lukas empfing eine wohl schon schriftliche Überlieferung, die zum Inhalt hatte die Vision des römischen Hauptmanns Kornelius, die Vermittlung durch seine Boten und die Anweisung des Geistes an Petrus, die Geschehnisse im Haus des Kornelius: Begegnung zwischen Petrus und dem Hauptmann, Visionsbericht des Kornelius, Geistempfang und Taufe. Auf Lukas gehen vor allem zurück: die Einfügung der aus anderem Überlieferungsgut stammenden Petrusvision 10.9–16 und in Verbindung damit 10.28, 29a; 11.2f., die ganz redaktionell gestalteten Reden 10.34–43; 11.5–17 und die damit zusammenhangenden Aussagen 10.22, 24b, 33b; 11.4, die religiöse Charakterisierung des Kornelius 10.2, 4, 22, 31, die Erwähnung der Petrusbegleiter 10.23b, 45; 11.12b, die Überleitungs– und Abschlussverse 11.1; 10.48b; 11.18 und eine durchgehende Bearbeitung auch der aus der Tradition aufgenommenen Teile (262).

This is an important judgment, grounded in detailed discussion, not all parts of which, however, are equally convincing.

Samaritans and eunuchs were in special positions. For the (varying) attitudes of Jews to Samaritans see on 8.5; eunuchs were excluded from the assembly of the Lord by Deut. 23.1, but Isa. 56.4f. had given them hope (see on 8.27). Christianity had already spread to Damascus, Lydda, and Joppa (9.2, 32, 36, 43), though there is no reason to think that others than Jews had been converted — or that Luke's relative chronology is correct. That Christians, scattered from the persecution that arose on account of Stephen, whose homes were in Cyprus and Cyrene, began (11.20) to preach in Antioch to Gentiles as well as Jews also appears to be regarded as the beginning of the mission to Gentiles. This new development, it seems, had to be reviewed by the Jerusalem church, who sent Barnabas to inspect it (11.22). After 11.18 this might have seemed unnecessary; and after 11.1–18 the whole conference described in Acts 15.1–29 might have seemed unnecessary, at least so far as it was intended to deal, and did deal, with the matters raised in 15.1, 5. It is true that there are differences, emphasised by both Stählin (149) and Weiser (252), between the story of the Ethiopian and the story of Cornelius: the latter deals with a group of Gentiles, not with a single individual; the Christian agent is not Philip but the apostle Peter; the convert's new status is recognized in Jerusalem and in general terms (10.45; 11.18); the religious position of the eunuch had been left unclear. These differences to some extent mitigate the difficulties, but they do not remove them.

The questions so far considered arise before we look in detail at the contents of 10.1–48. Questions here do not relate to the mechanics of the story, its narrative framework. Difficulties may be found in regard to the number of messengers sent by Cornelius and the time they took on their journeys, and these are complicated by variant readings. These however are small matters, arising out of occasional ambiguity or obscurity of expression and possibly some negligence in handling details; see the notes on vv. 10, 15, 19, 30, 36. More serious are the following.

(1) The drift of the section as a whole, especially when it is viewed in the setting provided for it by Luke, is that the event marks a notable step in the extension of the Gospel to the world outside Judaism. This point has already been made above; 15.7–9 is particularly important here. Yet within the narrative, Luke goes out of his way to show how close Cornelius was to Judaism. True, he was not a Jew and he was not a proselyte; but he practised alms-giving and prayed constantly; he enjoyed a high reputation among the Jews. The conversions of persons such as those described in 1 Cor. 6.19, 20 might have been more impressive.

(2) Peter's vision gives rise to a group of problems. Peter is bidden to slaughter (for θύειν see on v. 13) and eat; he immediately assumes, without justification in the text as Luke sets it before us, that he is to slaughter and eat an unclean animal. Why should he not have chosen a permitted animal? That the command is quoted in Augustine, *C. Faustum* 31.3 in the form *Quicquid in vase vides, macta et manduca* (the words are ascribed to Faustus) does not remove the difficulty. Does Peter think that the Lord is setting out to trap him into doing what he ought not to do? The Lord cannot really intend him to do as he is told. This must be a temptation, and Peter is therefore bold enough to reply in the negative, Μηδαμῶς, κύριε (v. 14). This is in itself surprising; was it Jesus' habit to lay traps for the unwary? Even more surprising is the fact that Peter evidently does not contemplate the possibility that the Lord (Jesus) might have no objection to his killing and eating an animal unclean according to the Law. The historicity of Mk 7.15–19 cannot be discussed here, but unless Mark is completely misleading we may suppose that Peter had heard Jesus say something to the effect that no food entering a man from without could defile him, had heard him (in Mark's formulation of the matter) cleanse all foods. It is true that Luke has no parallel to Mk 7.1–23 (=Mt. 15.1–20); this may explain Luke's literary presentation of the matter and his ability to set this presentation out without self-contradiction, but on the historical question it does not help at all. In addition, we may note that Luke's own account of the Jerusalem Council (especially Acts 15.20, 29) suggests that the Jerusalem church (which, no doubt, would follow the lead of men such as Peter) did not give up the notion that some foods cause defilement. As Haenchen (349) points out, what appears to be said in the vision of ch. 10 agrees neither with Jerusalem, Peter, nor the Decree. The Decree (see the commentary and the general discussion in Vol. II) does not indeed distinguish between clean and unclean animals in the manner of Num. 11; Deut. 14; but it does imply that to eat food offered to idols causes defilement (note the different words in 15.20 and 15.29, ἀλισγήματα and εἰδωλόθυτα)

and that to eat blood or meat that has not been killed in accordance with the Law is equally defiling and therefore forbidden. Finally, there is the question of the application of Peter's vision. If the story of the vision were abstracted from its setting in the Cornelius episode the reader would certainly conclude that it referred to the question what foods Christians, including Christian Jews, were allowed to eat. Were they bound to observe the dietary regulations of Torah? As soon as there were non-Jewish Christians the question was of great importance; the vision, it seemed, answered it. But in 10.28 the vision is given a different interpretation: God has shown me that I must treat no human being (ἄνθρωπον, emphatic) as profane or unclean. It is true that these affirmations were not unrelated, since part (though only part) of the Gentile's uncleanness was due to the unclean foods that he ate. An important difference, however, remains, and it is at least sufficient to cause the reader to wonder whether Luke has given the vision a meaning different from that which it originally bore.

(3) Peter's visit to the household of Cornelius provokes objection in 11.2. He justifies himself by giving an account of what had happened and as a result those who had complained give glory to God with the conclusion, Why then, to the Gentiles also God has given repentance unto life. See the notes on this verse (11.18); unless we take the improbable view that ἔδωκεν refers to one special occasion only, from which it is impossible to infer that on other occasions also God will permit uncircumcised Gentiles to receive life (salvation) on the ground of repentance and faith only, this means that the admission of Gentiles to the church without the necessity of their first becoming proselytes had been granted. This event, it has been said, should be described as the first Council of Jerusalem; that described in ch. 15 is the second. Not only is this so; the first seems to make the second otiose; the question raised in 15.1, 5 (which *prima facie* Luke presents as the question under debate in the rest of ch. 15) has already been settled — and settled on more liberal terms than those of 15.20, 29, since no requirements of any kind are laid down for the Gentiles to fulfil. If 11.1–18 be taken as it stands, ch. 15 is superfluous, unless we take it to be dealing not with the admission of Gentiles but with the conditions of (table-) fellowship between Jewish and Gentile Christians — and there is (see the general discussion in Vol. II) something to be said for this view. The first question was, May they come in? The second question was, Now that they are in, how are they and we (Jewish Christians) related to each other? What Jewish rules, if any, must Gentiles now admitted to the church observe in order that the church may be one? That this was the purpose of the Council of Acts 15 does not accord with 15.1, 5, but may be inferred from some of the evidence. There is however other evidence which is inconsistent with this; see the notes on ch. 15 and the general discussion in Vol.

II. According to Lüdemann (136), 'Man darf auf der historischen Ebene also nicht fragen, warum die Ereignisse von Apg 15 nach denen von Apg 10f. möglich waren, und diese durch einen verstarkten Nomismus der Jerusalemer Gemeinde erklären ... Das ist eine voreilige Historisierung, die der Aussageabsicht des Lukas nicht gerecht wird.' It is correct that one should not approach the historical issue without first considering Luke's intention, but it must eventually be faced.

This proliferation and complication of problems means that the interpretation of Acts 10 is unlikely to be simple. One thing is clear: Luke intended his reader to understand that he was witnessing a decisive step, perhaps the decisive step, in the expansion of Christianity into the non-Jewish world. The theological interpretation of this step is hinted at in 10.47; 11.18, and given explicitly in 15.7–9. Its foundation is that there is no respect of persons with God (10.34); non-Jews are welcomed into the people of God, and the only sign of their initiation is baptism. They are not required to be circumcised and, it appears, Peter not only baptized but ate with them (11.3; cf. 10.48). That he did in fact eat with uncircumcised Gentile Christians is confirmed by Gal. 2.12 (he ate with them until threatened from without). We have however already seen that the true, complete, story was not so simple. What then has the author of Acts done? He may have manufactured a story so as to provide the starting-point he needs if he is to write the further history of the expansion of Christianity into the Gentile world. This seems unlikely; it would mean that his creative hand worked too freely, for apart from this one he has other stories of the 'beginning' of the Gentile mission. By inventing this one, if he did so, he produced for himself a number of unnecessary difficulties.

Pesch (330) holds the view that the story belongs to pre-Lucan tradition about Peter and to the same group of stories as 9.32–35, 36–43. The composition also is pre-Lucan (333), and Cornelius appears only as a subordinate figure. A sermon by Peter must have been included, though this was submitted to Lucan editing. Roloff (164f.) holds a similar view, and supports it negatively by four arguments against the view that the passage is primarily a conversion story in which Cornelius is the central figure. (1) The form of the story is determined by a pair of 'Korrespondenzvisionen', which have the effect of bringing together two parties. (2) The chief actor is Peter; it is his vision that evokes the resistance that has to be overcome in order that the conversion may take place. (3) Cornelius is a subordinate figure. All he seeks is full membership of the people of God. It is not he but Peter who is 'converted'. (4) Features of the story point to an origin in a Jewish Christian environment. From these arguments Roloff concludes: 'Die Erzählung war ursprünglich eine judenchristliche Missionslegende, die anhand einer fundamentalen Erfahrung des

Petrus für die Mission an den "Gottesfürchtigen" und ihre volle Integration in die Geminde ohne Beschneidung eintrat' (165).

Of the four arguments (1) is a valid observation; the story is about the bringing together of Jewish Christianity and a group of Gentiles; this was a matter of no small interest in Caesarea (see below). The weight of (2) depends on whether the biographical interest in Peter was in the earliest form of the tradition or was introduced by Luke. (3) is not convincing as stated by Roloff. (4) is covered by the fact that, however it originated, the church at Caesarea must have been founded by Jewish Christians and retained a Jewish Christian element.

Another view is that Luke found the story in existence but in less elaborate form and with less far-reaching significance attached to it. It was, Dibelius argues, a pious legend of a conversion, told for the religious edification of any who might take it up. It must be asked whether there was any motivation for the preservation of such stories, especially when told not about notable figures like Paul but about secondary and otherwise unknown characters. It is doubtful whether the motivation, 'He is a Roman official,' would suffice; in any case it would at once remove the material to a different level, for the Roman official would certainly not be a Jew, and this fact would draw in the whole question of a mission to Gentiles. See further Haenchen (347f.). The best suggestion is that in, or behind, the story of Acts 10 and 11 we have its own account of the founding in Caesarea of a church that included Gentiles, and of the final recognition in Jerusalem that this had been a proper step. This step was so unprecedented, and so full of (at the time only partially perceived) theological meaning, that it was probably recorded in more churches than one, even if only in their folk memory. Antioch (see 11.20) had a similar recollection, which was not attached (except in the second degree — see 11.22, 25) to any of the great names but only to certain men of Cyprus and Cyrene, acting as a result of, or in association with, the expulsion of Hellenist Christians from Jerusalem.

Luke has not simply taken over the Caesarean story. Two questions in particular suggest themselves. (1) The difficulties inherent in the story of Peter's vision have already (see pp. 493f.) been pointed out; can this have been an original part of the Caesarean narrative? (2) At 8.40 Philip came to Caesarea; at 21.8 he is still there. Did he, after preaching to and baptizing the Samaritans, conversing with and baptizing an Ethiopian eunuch, make no contribution to the founding of a church in Caesarea? The suggestion is attractive that Luke, aware of Peter's ultimate participation in Gentile evangelization (Gal. 2.11; 1 Cor. 1.12; 9.5) and desirous of giving the Twelve as well as the Seven a share in the founding of Gentile, or mixed, churches, detached a story originally relating to Philip and gave it to Peter, using the story of the vision to effect the transference. This however will not do. It builds too much on 8.40, and also assumes the chronological priority of the stories about Philip. It also fails to deal with the difficulties we have noted in the account of Peter's vision.

We must, it seems, conclude that there was current in the church at Caesarea a story of its founding by Peter, which included the assertion that it was from the beginning a church that included Gentiles, and that this was accepted by Christians in Jerusalem. For this view cf. Knox (*Acts* 33); Brandon (*Fall* 178); and see *NT Essays* 112–14. The outline of the story can be traced in 10.1–8, 17–24, 30–48; 11.2, 3, 18, though within these passages Luke himself is probably responsible not only for connecting links, such as 10.17a, 19a, but also for the contents of Peter's sermon, which follows the usual Acts sermon outline (see pp. 129–33). Schneider (2.60) argues that the sermon fits the situation, because it emphasizes the universality of salvation; it hardly does so more strongly, however, than 2.39. It may be that there was originally a 'sermon' in the source which Luke had conflated with his own material; this could account for the intolerable syntactical structure of 10.37, 38. Luke also received by tradition an account of a vision seen by Peter, preserved as an explanation of 'How Peter changed his mind' — perhaps not on the question, What may you eat? but With whom may you eat? (see Schneider 2.62). Luke decided that this was a suitable place at which to incorporate the vision, primarily because it enabled him to make doubly strong the assertion that the conversion of the Gentiles was the will and work of God: God directed Peter and Cornelius each toward the other. This probably meant reinterpretation of the vision, not only for the positive reason that Peter had to learn that all men (or at least, some men who were not Jews) were acceptable in God's eyes but also for the negative reason that the question of food would not arise; Cornelius (as the story affirms) stood so close to the Synagogue that he would not have contemplated offending a Jewish guest by setting pork on the table. Moreover, Luke's interpretation of the vision avoids contradiction with 15.20, 29.

It is impossible to date this event, though Caesarea was not far from Jerusalem and the traditional Caesarean story would be pointless if not attached to a fairly early date. Roloff (166) rightly speaks of the event as one of several steps into the Gentile world. It suggests a few other matters that may be briefly dealt with. Schmithals (102f.) sees here further marks of Luke's polemic against the hyper-Paulinists, who wished to cut Christianity off from its Jewish and OT origins; No, Luke argues, the Gentile church itself sprang from Jewish Christian roots. Luke insists once more (see p. 188) that apostles, great and miracle-working bearers of the word of God though they are, are human, not divine (vv. 25, 26). Calvin (288–90) sees a profound theological question which most commentators ignore. What is the meaning of the assertion in v. 34 that in every race he that fears God and works righteousness is acceptable to God? It must mean that Cornelius is already accepted by God. But if this is so, why preach the Gospel to him, why baptize him? According to Calvin, Cornelius's works were acceptable because they were preceded by faith. That he had faith is proved by the fact that he prayed, which no one does unless he believes. 'Moreover his fear of God and his piety clearly demonstrate that he was born again of the Spirit' (288). Further, it can be proved that Cornelius knew Christ, though he 'must be placed in the category of the fathers of old who hoped for salvation by a Redeemer not yet revealed' (290). It cannot be said that this (or *Institutes* 3.17.4) is very satisfactory. Calvin, a theologian noted for strictness in logical argument, was not well fitted to understand Luke, who, so far as he was a theologian, was a theologian apt to express his meaning in loose and popular terms. What Luke means is that God judges men fairly in accordance with their opportunities. Cornelius is not to be condemned for not believing a Gospel he had never heard; he is rather to be rewarded for having lived up to the opportunities he had had by being allowed to learn more and to believe more. God looks with favour upon those who so far as they know him fear him, and so far as they know what righteousness is practise it. Luke does not intend to deny the love of God for the sinful; he is dealing with one thing at a time without Paul's concern and ability to see and hold together both sides of a theological proposition. Calvin must be given credit for seeing and having the courage to deal with the questions raised by the text, even if his answers are not satisfactory. The question is also seen by Rackham (155f.), but his discussion of it is no more satisfactory.

1. For the introduction (ἀνὴρ δέ τις) of a new character and a new story cf. 8.9. For Caesarea see on 8.40; also Sevenster (*Greek* 103–7). There were many Jews in the city but Greek was the principal language, and Caesarea 'was the centre of Roman administration and the headquarters of the Roman army in the province, especially in the period when it was under Roman procurators' (Sevenster 104). Bauernfeind (143) suggests that Luke may have thought that Philip (8.40) had not yet reached Caesarea; it is more probable that Luke has simply run out of information about Philip and does not mean to be prevented from telling his story about the founding of the church in that city.

ἦν is placed between τις and ἐν by 𝔐 gig vg sy. If this is accepted the opening sentence stops at the end of v. 2: In Caesarea there was a man . . . If, with P⁵³ P⁷⁴ ℵ A B C E Ψ 33 81 945 1175 1241 1739 *al* p, ἦν is not read, the sentence runs on into v. 3: A certain man . . . saw . . . No difference is made to the sense.

Κορνήλιος: the name (for the absence of the *cognomen* see Hemer 177, 266f.) was that of a patrician family in Rome and was borne by many of the family and its dependants. In 82 BC L. Cornelius Sulla had freed 10,000 slaves, who entered his *gens* and used the name Cornelius (Appian, *Civil War*, 1.100). This man is mentioned nowhere else in the NT. He was a centurion (ἑκατοντάρχης; so Luke usually writes the word; see Lk. 7.2; Acts 22.25; (28.16) for ἑκατόνταρχος; Mark has κεντυρίων), the commander of a century (one hundred men); two centuries made a maniple, three maniples a cohort, ten cohorts a legion, of 6,000 men. These however were paper figures, by no means always rigidly adhered to. Centurions received considerably higher pay than common soldiers and, especially as they rose to seniority in the legion, became persons of some consequence. Cf. Lk. 7.8. A retired centurion was normally given equestrian rank.

Cornelius was a centurion (presumably one of six) in the Cohors Italica. For σπεῖρα as the equivalent of the Latin cohors see Polybius 11.23.1; for the form σπείρης (with η) see M. 2.118. For many details see T. R. S. Broughton in *Begs*. 5.441–443; also *NS* 1.363–5. From Dessau *ILS* 9168; *CIL* 6.3528; 11.6117 may be deduced the full name of the cohort (Cohors II Miliaria Italica Civium Romanorum Voluntariorum quae est in Syria) and that it was in Syria before (but how long before we cannot tell) AD 69. Cohorts of voluntarii, or freedmen, were enrolled only in periods of great need. *ILS* 9168 shows that it was a company of archers (sagitarii), and the title Italica suggests some connection with the west, but what this connection was is not known. It is sometimes observed that Roman troops would not be stationed in Caesarea during the rule of Agrippa I (AD 41–44), and conclusions drawn regarding the chronology of Acts (the events of ch. 10 must have happened before 41 or after 44) or its historical accuracy (Luke read into an earlier period circumstances he found to obtain at a later date). None of these conclusions is necessarily correct. As Broughton points out, Cornelius seems to be surrounded by family and friends and had perhaps retired and settled in Caesarea (though if this were so he would hardly be able to send a soldier with his servants — v. 7 — unless of course the soldier also had retired). Cornelius would be a Roman citizen.

2. εὐσεβής is used in Acts only in this context (v. 7). εὐσέβεια occurs at 3.12; εὐσεβεῖν at 17.23; elsewhere the word group occurs only in the Pastorals and in 2 Peter — i.e., in the latest parts of the NT. σέβεσθαι (elsewhere only at Mt. 15.9; Mk 7.7, both quoting Isa. 29.13) occurs at 13.43, 50; 16.14; 17.4, 17; 18.7, 13; 19.27. φοβεῖσθαι with God (or pronoun standing for God) as object occurs at 10.2, 22, 35; 13.16, 26. These passages are listed here in view of the long accepted but recently questioned belief that οἱ σεβόμενοι τὸν θεόν, and οἱ φοβούμενοι τὸν θεόν, were alternative designations of a specific class of persons, not Jews, and not proselytes, but

attached to the synagogue by their acceptance of Jewish religious
and ethical principles and general sympathy with the Jewish way of
life. These were the 'God-fearers'. StrB (2.715f.) clearly distinguish
(a) Ganzproselyten or Vollproselyten, in the NT προσήλυτοι (Acts
2.10; 6.5), in Rabbinic usage גרים or גרים צדיקים, proper proselytes,
גרי צדק, or in contrast with the next group, גרי אמת; (b) Proselyten des
Truges, גרי שקר, those who have become proselytes not out of
conviction but for some kind of unworthy motive; (c) Halbproselyten,
יראי שמים, Gottesfürchtige, God-fearers, in the NT οἱ σεβόμενοι, οἱ
φοβούμενοι; (d) the גר תושב or resident alien; this expression is
translated προσήλυτος in the LXX, but does not denote a proselyte
in the sense of a convert, or even a half-convert, to Judaism.
Criticism of Billerbeck's word Halbproselyt, often expressed, is not
very important. The word was perhaps not well chosen, since (as has
been rightly pointed out) one either is or is not a proselyte; a 'half-
proselyte' is an impossibility. But it is clear that by *Halbproselyt*
Billerbeck meant not half of one proselyte but one who was half-way
to being a proselyte, one who had taken several steps but not the final
decisive step towards becoming a proselyte; and this is a description
that makes sense. More important is the fact that in and around the
first century Jews, proselytes, and occasionally Gentiles might be
described as fearing, or reverencing, God; that is, the expressions
σεβόμενοι, or φοβούμενοι, τὸν θεόν, were not necessarily
technical terms but could be simply descriptive of the pious. Luke
himself does not use them consistently; see 13.16; and cf. the
inscription from the theatre at Miletus (*CIJ* 2.748), τόπος Εἰουδέων
(sic) τῶν καὶ θεοσεβίον (sic); born Jews could be said to fear God,
to be God-fearers. Luke however does tend to use the two expressions
for Gentiles who were attached and favourable to the synagogue.
Cornelius was such a man. Whether as such he was a member of a
recognized class is a question of considerable historical importance
though not of direct relevance to the present passage. Discussion of
it has taken various turns; the present stage is dominated by the
Aphrodisias inscription (J. Reynolds and R. Tannenbaum, *Jews and
Godfearers at Aphrodisias*, Cambridge Philological Society,
Supplementary Volume 12; also *NS* 3.25f., 166), which records the
foundation, and the founders, of what appears to be a building,
though its description as a πατέλλα (Latin, *patella*, usually *dish*) is
far from clear. The contributors are evidently a synagogue community,
and they include, after a list containing a number of Hebrew names,
and introduced by the heading καὶ ὅσοι θεοσεβῖς (and such as are
theosebeis, God-worshippers), a further list, which contains a number
of town-councillors but no Hebrew names. It seems clear that these
are Gentiles who were sufficiently attached to the synagogue to
contribute to its funds and projects and to be thought worthy of
monumental commemoration. The evidence cited above, however,

must not be forgotten. θεοσεβής and kindred terms were not so fully and universally technical in the description of Gentile adherents that they could not be used of Jews and full proselytes. This means (as would in any case be true) that the evidence of the new inscription applies to Aphrodisias but must not be assumed to apply universally; it seems, for example, that it did not apply at Miletus, and it is by no means certain that it applies to Acts. The use of a particular label is not important. What is important is (a) that some Gentiles were attracted to Jewish ethics, theology, and worship, but did not become proselytes; (b) that in some places (one!) they formed a recognized and valued element in the synagogue community, though the degree of their religious attachment to it is not specified and remains unknown; (c) that such Gentiles presented a great opportunity to Christian evangelists; (d) that Luke was aware of this. For the discussion of this important matter see further the articles listed above under the names of Finn, Gager, Kraabel, Overman, and Wilcox.

In his piety Cornelius carried his household (οἶκος) with him. In Acts, οἰκία seems always to be a building; so frequently is οἶκος, but this form of the word can also mean household and occasionally (e.g. 16.15) it becomes important to ask whether the οἶκος includes small children. Here the members of his οἶκος, who may include slaves (Delling, *Studien* 297–307, especially 302; see Josephus, *Apion* 2.210, 258, 282; Juvenal, *Sat.* 14.96–99), share Cornelius's attitude to religion, and it must be assumed that they were of an age to do so consciously. His piety was expressed in *almsgiving* and *prayer*; both are very characteristic features of Jewish religion. In Aramaic מצותא, literally (the fulfilling of a) *commandment* came to mean *charity*, a clear pointer to the fact that charity, almsgiving, was regarded as the greatest of all commandments; cf. the use of δικαιοσύνη in v. 35. Prayer in the sense of communion with God is evidently a central religious practice; it was connected with almsgiving and penitence in a frequently repeated exegesis of 2 Chron. 7.14 (Gen. R. 44 (27c); Tanh. B. Noah § 13 (19a); Mdr. Qoheleth 5.6 (25b); 7.14 (36a); j. Taanith 2.65b.3; j. Sanhedrin 10.28c.6; StrB 1.454).

πολλάς evidently goes with ἐλεημοσύνας; he made many charitable gifts, and he made them τῷ λαῷ, *to the* (Jewish) *people*. διὰ παντός (cf. Ps. 34(33).2) correspondingly goes with δεόμενος; χρόνου must be understood: he was constantly at prayer. Cf. 2.25; Heb. 13.15; 1 Thess. 5.17 (ἀδιαλείπτως προσεύχεσθε). Schille (242) does not exaggerate in the statement that Cornelius was 'ein für jüdische Ohren relativ unanstössiger Mann'.

3. εἶδεν: the subject is ἀνήρ (v. 1). In the NT ὅραμα is used once in Matthew, eleven times in Acts, always of some kind of supernatural *vision*, though in Greek use generally it refers to any object of sight.

φανερῶς, *openly, plainly, manifestly*; there was no possibility of mistake on Cornelius's part. Preuschen 64 takes ἐν ὁράματι and φανερῶς to be contradictory and would omit ἐν ὁράματι. This is mistaken; a vision may be perfectly clear. It is also mistaken to find φανερῶς confirmed by the note of time that follows: angels do not need daylight to make themselves visible.

ὡσεὶ περὶ (this word is omitted by 𝔐 latt) ὥραν ἐνάτην, so that the vision is not to be thought of as a nocturnal dream. M. 3.248 notes that the accusative of point of time is not unclassical (Demosthenes 54.10 (1260), ἐκείνην τὴν ἑσπέραν; cf. Gen. 43.16; Exod. 9.18; Justin, *1 Apol.* 67.8 (but the dative occurs at 67.3)). In the NT see Jn 4.52; Acts 10.30; 20.16; Rev. 3.3. Turner also cites M. 1.63 for Koine usage. Moulton there refers to *P. Oxy.* 3(1903). 477, 8, τὸ πέμπτον ἔτος, a recurrent phrase, but does not mention Acts 10.3 — possibly because he noticed περί (and Turner did not — unless he accepted its omission). According to BDR § 161. 3 the accusative of ὥρα is classical (Aeschylus, *Eumenides* 109; Euripides, *Bacchae* 723f.; Aristotle, *Pol. Ath.* 30.6; Demosthenes 54.4 (1257)); they do not refer to Acts 10.3 (presumably reading περί). For the *ninth hour* as a time of prayer see on 3.1.

Angels play a considerable role in Acts in promoting action in accordance with God's will. Cf. 5.19; 8.26; 12.7; 27.23. The various divine ministries in the present narrative are fitted together with some care, and have the effect of showing that Peter's visit to and conversion of Cornelius are due to God's initiative. The angel came into (εἰσελθόντα) the house, or room, where Cornelius was and addressed (εἰπόντα) him by name. Cf. 9.10, where the speaker is the Lord himself.

4. ἀτενίζειν is a Lucan word (Lk., twice; Acts, ten times; 2 Cor., twice), but one that is quite natural in the present context. The supernatural appearance draws Cornelius's gaze and evokes fear (ἔμφοβος also is Lucan: Lk., twice; Acts, twice; Rev., once). There is some ground for thinking that Luke is here writing up in his own words a story that has been told him. For Cornelius's question τί ἐστιν; cf. 21.22, τί οὖν ἐστίν; He addresses the angel as κύριε and is not rebuked; contrast v. 25.

Cornelius's prayers (no difference is intended between προσευχαί in this verse and δεόμενος in v. 2) and his charitable gifts ἀνέβησαν εἰς μνημόσυνον (cf. v. 31, ἐμνήσθησαν, with no difference in meaning). Cf. Mt. 26.13; Mk 14.9, λαληθήσεται εἰς μνημόσυνον, and, for ἀνέβησαν also, Targum Esther 6.1 (In that night there went up (or perhaps *in*, עַל) the memory (דכרן) of Abraham, Isaac, and Jacob before their Father who is in heaven, that there should be sent from on high an angel, Michael, chief of the army of Israel). The actions referred to will be brought into memory, be remembered;

here (and possibly in Mt. and Mk also), before, that is, by, God. In the OT such remembering is often the effect of a sacrifice (e.g. Lev. 6.8 (LXX), ὀσμὴ εὐωδίας, τὸ μνημόσυνον αὐτῆς τῷ κυρίῳ), but the thought is widened; cf. Ps. 141.2; Sirach 35.16f.; Tobit 12.12; Phil. 4.18; Heb. 13.15f. For the double sense of remembering (men remember with gratitude God's gracious acts; God remembers men in their need) see Le Déaut (*Nuit Pascale* 70f.). Here the latter sense is intended; God is about to take action on behalf of Cornelius by bringing him within reach of the Gospel. He does this, one might say, because Cornelius has shown by his devotion and his charity that he deserves it. This theme runs through the narrative; it is reasonable to ask whether it is consistent with, for example, Pauline theology.

5. The angel gives Cornelius orders which must be fulfilled if he is to take advantage of God's favourable attitude. For Joppa see on 9.36. In καὶ νῦν, καί strengthens the interjection νῦν: *Very well then* (BDR § 442. 8d, n. 26). Cornelius must send for one Simon (τινα is omitted by ℵ E Ψ 𝔐 it syʰ), who is called (ὃς ἐπικαλεῖται, P⁷⁴ᵛⁱᵈ ℵ A B C 36 81 945 1175 1939 *al*; τὸν ἐπικαλούμενον, E Ψ 𝔐) Peter. Luke uses the middle, μετάπεμψαι; cf. Moeris, 'μετέπεμψε, Thucydides; μετεπέμψατο, Demosthenes.' Also Hesychius: 'μεταπέμπεται, μετακαλεῖται, μεταστέλλεται.'

6. ξενίζειν is Lucan: Acts, seven times; rest of the NT, three. For the fact see 9.43. This verse adds that the tanner's house was παρὰ θάλασσαν; his unclean occupation called for supplies of water. The information is of course provided in order to help the messengers to find the house. See on 9.11 the reference to Hemer 226.

Black (*AA* 83) notes that three minuscules (68 137 614) begin the verse, καὶ αὐτός ἐστιν ξενιζόμενος πρὸς Σίμωνά τινα, and thinks that this, recalling in form a Semitic circumstantial clause, may perhaps be original. Wilcox (123) is, rightly, not prepared to lay much weight on this. M. 3.206 observes the exception to the normal rule that a substantival attribute with a proper noun takes the article; cf. 7.10; 13.1; 21.16. But the article would not give the meaning that Luke evidently desires — a certain Simon, who was a tanner. See WM 172f.

7. An οἰκέτης is a household slave, but especially in such a household as that of Cornelius there is no reason why a slave should not have been on fairly close terms with his master; these two were men to whom Cornelius could disclose his intimate concerns (v. 8). Like Cornelius the soldier too was εὐσεβής (v. 2). If the soldier was on active service Cornelius would not have retired (see above); it is quite possible that if Cornelius had retired he might have retained on a private basis the services of a soldier who was himself coming out

504 COMMENTARY ON ACTS

of the army. τῶν προσκαρτερούντων suggests retirement; cf.
Demosthenes 59.120 (1386), servants *who remained*
(προσκαρτερούσας) in employment.

8. ἐξηγησάμενος: another Lucan word (Lk. 24.35; Acts 10.8;
15.12, 14; 21.9; elsewhere only Jn 1.18. ἅπαντα: Cornelius told
them the full story of what had happened, and with this sent them to
Joppa. According to Blass the distance was 'XXX milia p. = XLV
milia metrorum nostrorum'. Conzelmann says c. 50 km, Bauernfeind
45–50 km. This would be about thirty (English) miles. See v. 9 for
the time taken on the journey. According to Schille 243 Peter was not
in Joppa but in Caesarea, and v. 24b connects immediately with v.
8. If Peter had been so far away Cornelius could not have estimated
his time of arrival and assembled his guests at the right moment. We
may probably say that Schille sees a difficulty in the story that did
not occur to Luke.

9. Luke now takes up the story of Peter as the three messengers are
drawing near to Joppa. For the coordinated revelation cf. Strabo
4.1.4 (*ND* 4.81). 'It appears all the clearer that the whole affair was
controlled by the wonderful plan of God' (Calvin 292). The messengers
can hardly have left before 5 p.m.; they had made good speed if they
had covered thirty miles and were arriving at noon on the next day.
Haenchen (334) thinks that they travelled through the night, Bruce
that they left on the morning after the vision and were mounted
(1.217). *Begs.* 4.114 suggests that they started on the morning after
the vision and that τῇ ἐπαύριον refers to the day after that. While
they were on their way (present participles, ὁδοιπορούντων, ἐγγιζόντων)
Peter went up (aorist, ἀνέβη) to the roof, where presumably he
would be able to pray undisturbed. Cf. Taanith 23b: Abba Hilkiah
said to his wife, Let us go up to the roof and pray for mercy (StrB
2.696). Cf. also 4 Kdms. 23.12; Jer. 19.13; Zeph. 1.5; Dan. 6.10;
Tobit 3.17.

The sixth hour (‭‮א‬‬ᶜ 36 *pc* have ἐνάτην, but this is probably due to
unconscious assimilation to v. 3) was the usual hour for prandium
(though this might be as early as the fifth if only two meals were
taken in the day), but not a normal time for the afternoon (מנחה)
prayer. It is probably pointless to attempt to fit the narrative into
Jewish, Greek, or Roman habits of eating and prayer. Prayer was a
fitting setting for Peter's vision, hunger a psychological framework
for the form that the vision took; Luke has no further interests. StrB
conclude (2.699), 'So kann man das Gebet des Petrus um die sechste
Stunde (= mittags 12 Uhr) als vorzeitiges Mincha gebet erklären';
see however on v. 10.

10. ἐγένετο πρόσπεινος suggests that it was only after he had gone up to the roof to pray that Peter felt hungry; this is inconsistent with the suggestion that his prayer was the afternoon prayer placed early in order to accommodate an earlier than usual meal. Probably we should be content with the thought that for Luke apostles were men who prayed more frequently than most. If (see on v. 9) one takes Luke's timing of meals and prayers seriously Peter was unwise to begin his prayer at midday. 'Every man eats at the fourth hour, workmen at the fifth, חכמים תלמידי (disciples of the sages = students of Torah) at the sixth' (Shabbath 10a; similarly Pesahim 12b). πρόσπεινος is a very rare word, cited only from a medical author (Demosthenes Ophthalmicus, apud Aetius 7.33 — LS 1522, s.v.) — a fact on which no conclusion regarding the authorship of Acts should be based.

γεύσασθαι here must mean *to eat, to have a meal*, though more usually it means *to taste* (the active means *to give a taste*). In the NT Lk 14.24 (γεύσεταί μου τοῦ δείπνου) comes near to the present meaning (though '. . . shall have even a taste of my dinner' gives the sense appropriately), though for it LS 346 quote only the medical writer Hipparchus and a fourth century papyrus (*P Lond med.* 2487). Tobit 2.4 (B A; the reading in ℵ gives the sense); Josephus, *Ant.* 6.199 do not support the meaning *to have* (as distinct from merely tasting) *a meal: Ant.* 6.338 (συνηνάγκασεν ἡ γυνὴ (the witch of Endor) γεύσασθαι) does. In Modern Greek γεύεσθαι and γευματίζειν mean *to dine*. We can only take note of a late and in the first century still rare development of the word. There is no point in the reference to Peter's desire for food and the preparation of the meal if it is not intended to prepare for the form in which Peter is instructed in the vision. He desires food; let him slaughter for himself.

παρασκευάζειν can mean *to prepare* almost anything; but cf. e.g. Herodotus 9.82.1f., Μαρδονίῳ δεῖπνον παρασκευάζειν . . . παρασκευάσαι Λακωνικὸν δεῖπνον). It is needless with Pallis (61) to conjecture αὐτῷ in place of αὐτῶν (though ei — unless it is a slip for eis — occurs in an Old Latin MS). We cannot identify the αὐτῶν; the pronoun is used impersonally, as an indefinite *they* is often used in English. Cf. 21.10, 31; Mt. 17.14; Herodotus 5.11.2; Thucydides 4.135.2. The plural can hardly be satisfied by Simon the tanner alone; possibly we should think of him and his servants, possibly of local Christians (9.38, 42). Just as an apostle is more pious than others (above), so many would be glad to serve him.

ἔκστασις (cf. 11.5; 22.17) is here stronger than in 3.10; *trance, ecstasy*. Cf. Gen. 15.12; Philo, *Quis rer. div. haeres* 264 (ἔκστασις καὶ ἡ ἔνθεος ἐπιπίπτει κατοκωχή τε καὶ μανία). ἐγένετο is almost certainly the original text (P⁷⁴ ℵ A B C 36 81 323 453 945 1175 1739 *pc* Or; P⁴⁵ has ἦλθεν, E Ψ 𝔐 latt sy *pc* Cl have (ἐπ)έπεσεν).

11. θεωρεῖν is used in Acts (and elsewhere) of both natural (e.g. 3.16) and supernatural (7.56) vision. For the opened heaven cf. Lk. 3.21; Acts 7.56 (διανοίγειν); it is a standard feature of apocalyptic and other visions. For the irregular forms of (ἀν)οίγειν see M. 2.189, 228; BDR § 101, n. 54.

From the opened heaven an object was descending. σκεῦος is used over so wide a range as to be scarcely more definite than the English *thing*. It refers however not infrequently to *containers* of one kind or another, and does so here — simply in the sense that it contained something. It was like ὀθόνη μεγάλη. ὀθόνη is *fine linen; a piece of fine linen cloth; a piece of cloth*, of any kind. The diminutive ὀθόνιον is used in the NT of cloths in which a corpse is wrapped (Lk. 24.12 (si v. 1.); Jn 19.40; 20.5, 6, 7). ὀθόνη itself came to be used of cloth employed for specific purposes: a woman's dress (in Homer), sails of a ship. It has been suggested that the image might have been suggested by the fact that Peter, before falling into his trance, was gazing out to sea from Joppa and had seen the ships' sails, secured by their corners. If we are to think of a historical, psychologizable, event, this seems not impossible. The ὀθόνη is a sheet of cloth, let down by the four corners. That ἀρχή is used of the *end* or *corner* of a bandage (e.g. Galen, *de Chirurg.* 2 (Wettstein 517)) as well as of other things tells us nothing about the authorship of Acts; Pallis (61), for example, can quote Euripides, *Hippolytus* 761f. (ἐκδήσαντο πλεκτὰς πεισμάτων ἀρχάς). That the object was being let down ἐπὶ τῆς γῆς may be slightly against the suggestion that behind the vision lay the appearance of ships' sails.

The text of the verse is in some confusion though hardly in doubt. It has been affected by the difficulty felt by copyists in imagining the vision, and by the parallel in 11.5. Ropes (*Begs.* 3.93) thinks that the agreement of d and *Apostolic Constitutions* 6.12.6 gives as the original Western text καὶ τέσσαρσιν ἀρχαῖς δεδεμένον σκεῦός τι ὡς ὀθόνην λαμπρὰν καὶ καθιέμενον ἐπὶ τῆς γῆς. Preuschen (65) follows the *Syriac Didascalia* 24 in omitting ὀθόνη and thinks that the σκεῦος was thought of as a box.

12. It is clear from the context that, whatever the text, Luke means that the sheet contained specimens of every variety of living creature. The enumeration recalls various OT passages such as Gen. 1.24 (τετράποδα καὶ ἑρπετὰ καὶ θηρία τῆς γῆς — birds have already been mentioned in 1.20). Recollection of such passages is probably responsible for the addition of θηρία and the variable position of τῆς γῆς in many MSS. The text of P[74] ℵ A B C[2vid] 81 (945) 1175 (1739) *pc* lat co Cl Or, τετ. καὶ ἑρπ. τῆς γῆς καὶ πετεινὰ τοῦ οὐρανοῦ, is probably correct. The OT (e.g. Lev. 20.25) distinguishes clearly between clean creatures, which might be eaten, and unclean, which might not.

13. ἐγένετο φωνή: the vision is accompanied by a divine (in v. 14 the speaker is addressed as κύριε) voice, a characteristic feature of calls and revelations; cf. Lk. 9.35, φωνὴ ἐγένετο; also Acts 9.4. This is not however an explanatory voice but one that prepares the way for revelation, and requires obedience. Explanation comes in v. 15.

ἀναστάς is superfluous; Peter would not be able to slaughter an animal without getting up. The idiom is common in Acts from 1.15 onwards; it is one of a number of Septuagintalisms in vv. 13–15. Wilcox (72–4) rightly suggests that they may have in part a liturgical background.

Πέτρε is omitted by P⁴⁵ gig Cl Ambr, possibly rightly. It is hard to see any reason that could have led copyists to think the text better without Πέτρε, whereas if Luke originally included no vocative it would be quite natural to think that the text would be clearer if it named the person addressed. Metzger (371) however thinks the omission 'probably accidental'.

Οὗσον may mean simply *slaughter*, but it retains from its primary meaning at least overtones of *sacrifice*. In the LXX it translates mainly זבח and שחט; StrB 2.703 take it to be equivalent to שחט (Hebrew and Aramaic). Peter is called upon to perform a religious act, which as such will be completed by eating.

14. μηδαμῶς (cf. Ezek. 4.14 for a similar reply) occurs nowhere else in the NT except at 11.8, the repetition of the present verse in Peter's report. In the LXX it represents (among other Hebrew words) חלילה, a strong negative, and in Greek the word is used 'in replies, as a strong negative' (LS 1125, s.v.): βραχύτερα . . . ἀποκρίνωμαι ἢ δεῖ; Μηδαμῶς, ἦν δ'ἐγώ (Plato, *Protagoras* 334d). See however Page (145), who comments, 'not οὐδαμῶς: a protest, not a refusal'. The use of μή rather than οὐ may be significant, but even so it is hard to deny that Peter refuses categorically to do as he is bidden. The verse is full of problems. Peter recognizes that the voice is divine, for he addresses the speaker as κύριε (so that it is difficult to agree with Roloff (169) that the command seemed to him 'eine teuflische Versuchung'). Why then does he disobey? The only rational explanation is that he supposes that the Lord is testing him, to see whether he will observe the law regarding food or not. Cf. 1 Kings 13.18 for a similar testing. This does not seem probable; it may therefore be better to say that Luke (or Peter, if the narrative does in fact go back to him) failed to see the logical implication of what was said. Moreover, could it be true that Peter, a Galilean (and, though the matter has sometimes been overstated, Galileans did not have the best of reputations for the observance of the Law), had never eaten anything κοινόν or ἀκάθαρτον? Again, Peter had been a disciple of Jesus; Mk 7.14–23 may or may not be historically correct, but it is certainly true that Jesus had not established a reputation for precise observance of the food laws.

Again, why should Peter, with all living creatures before him, take for granted that he was being told to slaughter and eat an unclean animal? Why should he not pick out a clean, permitted one? It is no answer to say that the command required indiscriminate slaughter. The command indeed did not discriminate but Peter was free to do so. A further problem will arise at v. 28; see the note.

The primary sense of κοινός is given by the fact that it serves as the opposite to ἴδιος and thus means what is not one's own but is common to a group or society (cf. 2.44; 4.32). The sacred is that which is proper to God; that which is common to human society is thus un-sacred, or profane. This meaning of the word however is not common in Greek. It occurs in the NT at Mk 7.2, 5; Rom. 14.14; Rev. 21.27; cf. Heb. 10. 29; it was probably coming into use in Hellenistic Judaism. The word itself is rare in the LXX and hardly ever occurs with a Hebrew equivalent; see however 1 Macc. 1.47 (Antiochus Epiphanes gave orders θύειν ὕεια καὶ κτήνη κοινά), 62 (many in Israel determined μὴ φαγεῖν κοινά); 4 Macc. 7.6 (Eleazar is praised because οὐδὲ . . . γαστέρα ἐκοίνωσας (v. 1., ἐκοινώνησας) μιαροφαγίᾳ). ἀκάθαρτος occurs frequently in the OT, most often as the equivalent of the root טמא; see for example Lev. 20.25, referred to above (. . . κτηνῶν . . . καθαρῶν . . . κτη. . . . ἀκαθάρτων . . . πετεινῶν . . . καθ. . . . πετ. . . . ἀκαθ.).

According to Zerwick § 446 (cf. Torrey 7) οὐδέποτε ἔφαγον πᾶν is expressed in terms of a Semitic idiom. לא . . . כל is certainly a Hebrew idiom, but (see M. 2.22, 433f.) attachment of οὐ to the 'wrong' word is not unusual in Greek. See e.g. Aristophanes, Wasps 1091, πάντα μὴ δεδοικέναι(= μηδὲν δεδοικέναι); Dionysius of Halicarnassus, Ep. ad Pompeium 756R, οὐκ ἀπὸ τοῦ βελτίστου πάντα περὶ αὐτῶν γράφων; P. Ryl. 2(1915). 113, 12f. 2.113.12 (AD 133), where one complains of unjust treatment from persons μὴ ἔχοντες πᾶν πρᾶγμα πρὸς ἐμέ. In view of these parallels it would be very hard to argue for a Semitic source here, though if we are to think of Peter as speaking Hebrew, לא אכלתי כל־פגול וטמא (Delitzsch) would express his thought nicely. It is also interesting to note that the somewhat surprising καὶ ἀκάθαρτον becomes in 11.8 ἢ ἀκάθαρτον.

15. The supernatural voice is heard again. BDR § 484 say that πάλιν ἐκ δευτέρου is not an example of pleonasm because ἐκ δευτέρου defines more precisely the sense of πάλιν, but since the voice had previously spoken only once it was hardly necessary to say that the next occasion was the second.

The words of the voice are given in balanced form, σύ being set against ὁ θεός. Peter is instructed, μὴ κοίνου. This word, as we have seen, occurs in 4 Macc. 7.6, where it undoubtedly means (as would be expected in a verb in -όω) to make κοινόν, to make profane. The meaning here is given by v. 28 (κοινὸν ἢ ἀκάθαρτον λέγειν). Peter must not call the animals in question profane or unclean. He cannot absolutely *make* things profane or sacred, but it may fairly be said that to treat a thing as profane in a sense makes it so; cf. Rom. 14.14 (τῷ λογιζομένῳ τι κοινὸν εἶναι, ἐκείνῳ κοινόν). Peter is objecting to the use for food of at any rate some of the animals before him, that is, he regards them as κοινά, and therefore they are κοινά in that he will not eat them. This he must not do with things which ὁ θεὸς ἐκαθάρισεν. The questions must now be asked (a) whether καθαρίζειν means *to declare clean* (so e.g. Haenchen 335; Schneider 2.69) or actually and objectively *to cleanse* (so far as these two are distinguishable — see above on κοινοῦν), and (b) when the changed treatment, or act of cleansing took place. Does the aorist ἐκαθάρισεν refer to a point in time? If so, what point? or is it constative? The first question, though it arises logically, is not really meaningful. The distinction between clean and unclean, sacred and profane, is one that exists, if it exists at all, in the mind and will of God. If God decides to treat a thing as clean, it is clean; that is, if he counts it clean and treats it as clean he has thereby made it clean. The second question is more important. Is it here being claimed that the OT distinction between clean and unclean represents a misunderstanding of the mind of God, a distinction that he did not intend? that God has always counted these creatures clean so that there has never been any reason why they should not be eaten? The alternative is to suppose that at some point in time God changed his attitude to food: previously he had regarded some foods as clean and usable, others as unclean and to be rejected; now he permitted all to be used. If this view is held it would be natural to associate it either with the present moment or with Mk 7.19, καθαρίζων πάντα τὰ βρώματα — when Jesus said that nothing entering a man from without could defile (κοινῶσαι) him he was actually making καθαρόν what had previously been κοινόν. This is an attractive view, but it must be borne mind that Luke has no parallel to Mk 7.19, and nowhere claims explicitly that the work of Jesus included the cleansing of foods. Moreover, the interpretation of the vision given in v. 28 does not relate it, directly at any rate, to food and food laws. This must again be related to vv. 34, 35, and to the cleansing spoken of in 15.9 (καθαρίσας). On the whole, the context of the chapter seems to require that what is being given in the vision is a revelation of what eternally is the mind of God, rather than a statement of a new order of things that God has now initiated, though it is arguable that God in the past willed to keep Jews and Gentiles separate in order later to unite them in the way that seemed to him good. Cf. Midrash Ps. 146 § 4 (268), All the animals which in this world are declared unclean, God will in the future [that is, in the days of the Messiah] declare clean (StrB 2.702).

16. τοῦτο must refer to the conversation; the vessel is lowered in v. 11 and is not said to be removed till v. 16b. ἐπὶ τρὶς is used for εἰς τρίς, which is more common in classical use. As soon as the conversation had taken place the third time (εὐθύς, in P⁷⁴ ℵ B C E 81 *pc* vg sy^hmg bo; D Ψ 𝔐 p sy^h sa^mss mae have πάλιν, and P⁴⁵ 36 453 1175 *pc* d sy^p sa^mss bo^mss omit — perhaps rightly) the vessel was withdrawn into heaven: ἀνελήμφθη, as at 1.11, of the ascension.

17. Luke is now ready to bring together the two strands of his story. By the addition of ἐγένετο after ἑαυτῷ, D p give a different turn to the sentence: When he came to himself (out of his trance, v. 10, and into himself), Peter . . . It is unlikely that this is the original text; ἐν ἑαυτῷ must be taken with διηπόρει: Peter doubted in himself . . . The imperfect suggests 'bleibende Ratlosigkeit' (Schneider 2.69). The verb is Lucan: Lk. 9.7; Acts 2.12; 5.24; 10.17; nowhere else in the NT. He wondered what the vision (ὅραμα, v. 3) might be, that is, might mean. εἴη, optative; most of the optatives in the NT are in the Lucan writings, a mark of literary style. ἄν adds a further element of doubt (Page 145: what it could be). Luke's reader is expected to understand that the vision is a mysterious communication (Weiser 265).

While (ὡς) Peter was wondering what the vision meant the next stage in the story was reached. ἰδού (still more καὶ ἰδού, read by C D E Ψ 𝔐 p sy^h; cf. 1.10) gives a Semitic, 'biblical', flavour to the narrative, but does not prove the use of a Semitic source. The men sent by (or *from*, if with A C D ἀπό is read) Cornelius (v. 8), *having asked* (having asked *earnestly*, or *constantly*, if weight is to be allowed to the compound διερωτᾶν) after the house of Simon (the tanner — it was not Simon Peter's house, though it was he the men were looking for), *came and stood* (aorist ἐπέστησαν) at the gate. If full weight is to be allowed to πυλών a large building with a gatehouse is implied. Haenchen (336) may be right in thinking that a tanner would not have such a house; in this case Luke would mean little more than a πύλη, which can be an ordinary house door. Cf. however 12.13.

18. Having arrived at the house the messengers made the natural inquiry. ἐπυνθάνοντο is better than the aorist ἐπύθοντο (B C); it was while they were inquiring that the Spirit spoke (εἶπεν, v. 19) to Peter. For the rest of the words in this verse see vv. 5, 6. 'The fact that εἰ can be used to introduce a *direct* question and that ἐνθάδε, *here*, is strictly incorrect for an *indirect* question, which requires ἐκεῖ, *there*, may point to this not being intended to be indirect at all, but a direct question: they were inquiring, *Does Simon . . . lodge here?* see *Beg.* [4.116] *in loc.*' (Moule, *IB* 154).

19. This verse picks up Peter's side of the story: *While Peter was reflecting on the vision* . . . An angel spoke to Cornelius (v. 3); a voice spoke to Peter (vv. 13, 15); now the Spirit speaks. Luke's theology is not so developed that we are encouraged to think of any different kind of authority. Dibelius (120) notes that this verse repeats v. 17 — perhaps a sign that the original story has been modified. Weiser (265) observes that the Spirit makes no reference to the vision, 'ein Indiz dafür, dass beide ursprünglich voneinander unabhängig waren'.

ἰδού again (cf. v. 17) is biblical style. For τρεῖς, B has δύο, a surprising reading in view of v. 7. The number is omitted altogether by D Ψ 𝔐 1 p* syʰ Spec. This may be the original text, many MSS filling in the number *three*, B (thinking of the soldier as a guard, not a messenger) preferring *two*. Alternatively, *two* may be original; copyists found this number difficult so that some omitted it and others changed it to *three*. If *three* was original it is hard to know why it should have been either changed or omitted. To the three (= 2 + 1) messengers there is a curious — and entirely coincidental — parallel in Homer, *Odyssey* 9.90; 10.102. For ζητοῦντες (P⁷⁴ ℵ B 81 *pc*), P⁴⁵ A C D E⁽*⁾ Ψ 𝔐 have ζητοῦσιν — better Greek, and therefore probably secondary.

20. ἀλλά: see the note on 9.6. A similar point may be made here. The word retains some adversative force: You might be inclined to object, *but* it is my will that you should go with them. ἀναστάς is hardly necessary; it is a mark of Luke's biblical style; cf. 1.15. Haenchen (336) remarks that ἀλλά is classical, ἀναστάς Septuagintal; a Lucan mixture.

μηδὲν διακρινόμενος, *having no doubts, without hesitation.* When this story is recalled at the Council of ch. 15, διακρίνειν is used in the active (15.9) with the meaning, *to make a distinction.* If διακρινόμενος is middle it could possibly have the same sense, or the same sense intensified (*making no distinctions in one's own mind*, or *in one's own practice*), but it is more probably used as at Rom. 14.23; James 1.6 — though the middle or passive is used again in a different sense at Acts 11.12. The words that follow (*for I have sent them*) could follow upon either *with no hesitation* or *making no distinction* (between Jew and Gentile), and therefore do not decide the matter. Page (146) distinguishes: here, 'Go, without letting the distinction between Jew and Gentile perplex your mind'; at 11.12, 'Go, without letting that distinction cause you to hesitate in action'.

In *I have sent them* the ἐγώ presumably refers to the speaker, the Spirit (v. 19), though it was the angel of v. 3 who commanded Cornelius to send messengers to Joppa. Luke would no doubt have been content to say that all these commands and messages bore the authority of God.

21. Peter obeys the Spirit's command, comes down from the roof, and greets the messengers. ἰδού is used as at v. 19.

D (sy^h) sharpen Peter's inquiry by prefixing τί θέλετε ἤ: a characteristic Western reading, adding liveliness but no substance. The rest of the sentence is a rather wordy way of inquiring what the visitors want. In the NT as a whole, and in Acts, αἰτία is used in both its fundamental senses: (a) '*responsibility*, mostly in bad sense, *guilt*, *blame*, or the imputation thereof, i.e. *accusation*' (LS 44); (b) *cause*. The use with διά is common in the NT (Lk. 8.47; Acts 10.21; 22.24; 28.20; Pastorals and Hebrews).

22. The description of Cornelius is taken up from v. 2; see the notes there. For μαρτυρεῖσθαι (*to be of good repute*) see 6.3; for the use with ὑπό (as at 16.2; 22.12) see Deissmann (*BS* 265) who gives papyrus examples. χρηματίζεσθαι (cf. Lk. 2.26) describes what is recorded in vv. 3–6; for μεταπέμψασθαι cf. v. 5. εἰς τὸν οἶκον αὐτοῦ is not merely circumstantial; to enter Cornelius's house is what a Jew might be expected to be unwilling to do; hence the stress that Cornelius is δίκαιος ('sensu Judaico, observans praecepta Dei' — Blass 127) and is a synagogue adherent (if this is the meaning of φοβούμενος τὸν θεόν). It is not said in the vision that Peter is to speak, but this is no doubt implied. 'To hear words' is indefinite, but it probably goes too far to say that this expression is used so as to make clear that everything, including the content of Peter's speech, is left open to divine prompting.

23. εἰσκαλεῖσθαι occurs here only in the NT and is infrequent in Greek generally; this may account for the variants προσκαλεσάμενος (E) and εἰσαγαγών (D p sy^p). There are other small variations however. Peter gives proof of his readiness to have dealings with Gentiles, and to enter a Gentile house, by inviting Gentiles into the house where he is staying. Presumably the tanner would not object, but Luke is not interested in the question.

τῇ ἐπαύριον: the day after Peter's vision and the arrival of the messengers. Unless we allow an extra day between vv. 8 and 9 (see above) this was on the day after Cornelius had received instructions from the angel, so that we are now at the third day of the narrative as a whole.

ἀναστάς: cf. v. 20. Peter was accompanied by some of the Joppa Christians; according to 11.12 there were six of them. For this use of ἀδελφός see 1.15. At 9.32, 41 the Christians in this area are called ἅγιοι; this might be an argument against the view that the two stories about Peter at the end of ch. 9 were drawn from the same source as the Cornelius episode. But it may be that Luke was simply introducing variety into his vocabulary. According to Conzelmann (63) the presence of the brothers turns the event into 'eine kirchliche Aktion';

he also however notes that they serve as witnesses (11.12). Cf. v. 24.

24. τῇ ἐπαύριον; cf. v. 23. Again the journey lasts into a second day. We reach the fourth day of the story.

εἰσῆλθεν (singular, concentrating the story upon Peter and reducing the force of Conzelmann's observation on v. 23) is read by B D Ψ 049 81 614 *pc* lat sy; the plural εἰσῆλθον, describing naturally the movements of the party as a whole, is read by P⁷⁴ ℵ A C E 𝔐 gig syʰᵐᵍ. Change in either direction could easily be understood and there is no strong ground for reaching a decision; it may be however that the plural is due to accommodation to αὐτούς. For Caesarea see on v. 1.

The next part of the verse is given in a somewhat different form by D (p* syᵐʰᵍ): . . . ἦν προσδεχόμενος αὐτοὺς καὶ συγκαλεσάμενος . . . φίλους περιέμεινεν. The variant makes little or no difference to the sense; Cornelius had gathered together a company to hear Peter; evidently he believed that the divine message was not for him alone. Luke does not tell us whether religious considerations entered into Cornelius's choice of guests, though it is natural to suppose that they did, and that all were relatively 'unobjectionable' Gentiles. Cornelius's *relatives* (συγγενεῖς) are present. For a soldier on service this must almost certainly mean (wife and) children. Also present are τοὺς ἀναγκαίους φίλους. ἀναγκαῖος used of persons may denote those who are related by necessary or natural ties, that is, by blood. This cannot be the meaning here, since *relatives* have already been mentioned, and if this had been intended φίλοι would hardly have been used. The meaning is probably friends so close as to be like blood relations (as with *necessarius* in Latin). Almost the same expression (συγγενῶν καὶ ἀναγκαίων ἀνθρώπων) occurs in Demosthenes 19.290 (434); cf. Euripides, *Andromache* 671 (τοὺς ἀναγκαίους φίλους); Josephus, *Ant.* 7.350.

25. Peter, who in v. 24 entered Caesarea, now enters Cornelius's house. Cornelius met him, and, evidently associating him with the supernatural experiences that he had had, fell at his feet, considering him to be more than man. That his action expressed more than the respect naturally accorded to an outstanding religious teacher (which itself would have been surprising enough in a Roman to a Jew — Weiser 265) is proved by Peter's reply (v. 26). If Cornelius had to any degree accepted Judaism he could not have thought of Peter as divine; presumably he took him to be an angel; cf. Rev. 19.10; 22.9. 'Kornelius will natürlich in Petrus Gott selbst ehren' (Schille 247); this does not seem to go far enough. In the NT προσκυνεῖν is directed towards God or Christ, but it may also be a gesture of great respect ('esp. of the Oriental fashion of *prostrating oneself before kings and superiors*' (LS 1518), but later of respectful greetings). The grammar of the opening words is not clear. If ὡς δὲ ἐγένετο

is taken to be a (secondary) Semitism (imitating the Hebrew ויהי),
the τοῦ is pleonastic; cf. 3.12. M. 2.427 compares *Acta Barn.* 7,
ὡς δὲ ἐγένετο τοῦ τελέσαι αὐτοὺς διδάσκοντας. Moule,
IB 129, takes τοῦ εἰσελθεῖν to be the subject of ἐγένετο (cf. 2.1
D), *When Peter's entry took place.* Cf. Lk. 17.1; Acts 27.1.
Possibly because the construction was harsh but more probably
in order to present the scene more vividly the Western text
rewrites the opening clause: προσεγγίζοντος δὲ τοῦ Πέτρου
εἰς τὴν Καισάρειαν προσδραμὼν εἷς τῶν δούλων
(according to Metzger, 374, one of the messengers; to Epp,
Tendency, 161, a look-out; to Hanson 123, a slave of Peter's)
διεσάφησεν παραγεγονέναι αὐτόν. ὁ δὲ Κορνήλιος
ἐκπηδήσας καὶ συναντήσας αὐτῷ. Clark (xxiii, 346) thinks
this the vivid original, the Old Uncial, a 'tame abbreviation'. Few
agree with him, but Delebecque 51 does, maintaining that D
avoids a piece of bad Greek and is Lucan in style and vocabulary.

26. This is not the way to treat an apostle, who, though entrusted
with a divine message, is in himself a human being and nothing
more. Even the angel of Rev. 19.10 will not accept honour due to God
alone; cf. Wisdom 7.1, where Solomon denies that he holds any
position higher than that of common humanity (εἰμὶ μὲν κἀγὼ
θνητὸς ἄνθρωπος ἴσος ἅπασιν). What is offered is (according
to Bauernfeind 147) not *Anbetung* but *Huldigung*; even so, Peter will
not have it. He raises the prostrate Cornelius (the use of ἀνιστάναι
is not to be compared with that at v. 20) and declares his common
humanity. Whatever Luke may think the apostles to be he does not
think of them as 'divine men'; see pp. 188, 192f. Cf. Aelian, *Varia
Historia* 8.15, where Philip gives an attendant the duty of reminding
him ὅτι ἄνθρωπός ἐστι.

Again the Western text heightens the narrative. For ἀνάστηθι, D
has τί ποιεῖς; p (w) sy^hmg add this to ἀνάστηθι. At the end of the
verse, D* E it mae bo^mss add ὡς καὶ σύ.

Conzelmann (63) takes vv. 27–29 to be an insertion by Luke into
his source because they refer to Peter's vision, itself, in his opinion,
an insertion. It is true that v. 26 could connect immediately with v.
30; this however does not in itself prove that the intervening verses
were not an original part of the narrative.

27. Peter, engaging in conversation (συνομιλῶν) with Cornelius,
enters the house, and there finds many gathered together; see v. 24. D
for no apparent reason omits συνομιλῶν, reading καὶ εἰσελθών τε
καὶ εὗρεν ... This is grammatically impossible (as Greek, but not as
Aramaic; see Black *AA* 69) but is probably (so Ropes, *Begs.* 3.96) part
of a general Western rewriting (see especially v. 25). συνομιλῶν
though not essential to the story provides a good cue for v. 28.

28. Private conversation with Cornelius is followed by words to the *many* who have assembled (πρὸς αὐτούς). All are sufficiently close to Judaism to notice that something unusual is happening: ὑμεῖς ἐπίστασθε. The visitors from Joppa are probably in mind also. D (cf. mae) has βέλτιον ἐφίστασθε (sic). βέλτιον is described by M. 1.78, 236 as an elative comparative, with 4.16 (D); 24.22; 25.10 for comparison (see also Jn 13.27; 2 Tim. 1.18). M. 3.30 concurs. This is another example of the way in which the Western editor sharpens the text; not *You know*, but *You know very well*.

What Peter assumes that his hearers know is a matter of Jewish law. See Wilson (*Law* 69). θέμις means what is *laid down*, established as lawful whether by decree or custom. ἀθέμιτος (D has the poetical form ἀθέμιστος) applied to a person means *lawless*; applied to things it means *unlawful*. In the LXX it occurs only at 2 Macc. 6.5; 7.1; 10.34; 3 Macc. 5.20. Its background use is Gentile rather than Jewish, and θεμιτόν is common; e.g. Herodotus 3. 37.3, . . . τὸ ἱρόν, ἐς τὸ οὐ θεμιτόν ἐστι εἰσιέναι ἄλλον γε ἢ τὸν ἱρέα; cf. 5.72.3. A Gentile would recognize that to a Jew many things were what he would call ἀθέμιτα and must therefore be avoided. Tacitus, writing of the Jews, says, separati epulis, discreti cubilibus (*Histories* 5.5). Here it is said that it is unlawful for a Jew (the repetitive ἀνδρὶ Ἰουδαίῳ has a Semitic, or at least OT, LXX, ring) κολλᾶσθαι (continuous tense: to keep company with) ἢ προσέρχεσθαι ἀλλοφύλῳ (P⁵⁰ D syᵖ have ἀνδρὶ ἀλλ., borrowing from the previous phrase). Similar verbs are combined by Plutarch, *de Amicorum Multitudine* 4 (94E), διὸ δεῖ μὴ ῥαδίως προσδέχεσθαι μηδὲ κολλᾶσθαι τοῖς ἐντυγχάνουσι. For κολλᾶσθαι see on 5.13; προσέρχεσθαι is more general, *to approach*. The meaning of the passage is correctly given in *NS* 2.83: 'The statement in Acts that a Jew may not associate with Gentiles . . . does not mean that such an association was forbidden, but that each such association was a cause of defilement; Gentile possessions needed to be purified before they were used by Jews.' This understanding of the relation between Jew and Gentile is old; see e.g. Jubilees 22.16: Keep yourself separate from the nations, and do not eat with them; and do not imitate their rites, nor associate yourself with them. See further StrB 4.374–8; Bousset (*RJ* 93f.).

Thus it would at any time have been open to Peter (or any observant Jew) to have dealings with Cornelius, though to do so would have meant the incurring of uncleanness, which would have had to be removed by the processes prescribed by law. Peter however has learnt that uncleanness is not involved. It is natural to suppose that in κἀμοί the καί must be taken to have at least some adversative force: You know that (it is generally reckoned that) it is unlawful . . . *but* God has shown me . . . Page (147) denies this, taking the emphasis to be on ἐμοί: Ye know that . . . and *to me* it was God who showed . . . In other words, I know the Law as well as you, and a divine revelation alone explains my conduct. This does not seem to remove the adversative sense completely. The language of v. 28b is so closely parallel to that of v. 14 that it is impossible to suppose that ἔδειξεν does not refer to the vision. There is however an important difference. In the vision Peter is bidden to kill and eat indiscriminately, that is, that his killing and eating may include unclean animals. When he objects he is told not to make, that is, to consider, anything κοινόν; that is, he may eat what is according to the Law κοινόν or ἀκάθαρτον. The two adjectives apply to food, animal food, that is, to animals. In the present verse these adjectives apply to human beings (μηδένα . . . ἄνθρωπον — the position of μηδένα is emphatic, *no single one*, and so is that of ἄνθρωπον, *no human being*). The question is immediately raised whether the conclusion of v. 28 and the vision really belong together. That the two propositions are closely related is undoubtedly true, since one major cause of the ceremonial uncleanness of the Gentiles was the unclean food that they ate. This however was not the only cause of the impurity of Gentiles and Gentile houses (see e.g. Oholoth 18.7); vision and conclusion do not speak in identical terms. The suggestion naturally arises that the vision and the interpretation in the present story do not belong together; see the introduction to this paragraph (pp. 493f., 497). Weiser (286) writes that Luke, concerned not with food but with the admission to the church of Gentiles uncircumcised, understands the vision allegorically. This is true; but is this how the vision was originally understood?

29. Peter had been sent for, μεταπεμφθείς; see vv. 5, 22; and he had come without gainsaying, ἀναντιρρήτως (= ἀναμφιβόλως, Hesychius); cf. 19.36, where however the corresponding adjective is used with passive sense. See Zerwick § 142.

The wordy form of interrogation (τίνι λόγῳ μετεπέμψασθέ με; there are parallels in Plato, *Gorgias* 512c; Euripides, *Iphigeneia in Tauris* 1358) recalls that of v. 21. The meaning is clear: For what reason have you sent for me? This is intended to give Cornelius his cue; the messengers have already told Peter that Cornelius wishes to hear words from him, and these can hardly have referred to anything but the Christian Gospel. Schneider (2.72) points out that though Peter is already prepared to speak to Cornelius there must be another divine intervention (vv. 44–46) before he is prepared to baptize.

30. Cornelius proceeds to recount what has happened. His opening words are not clear. ἀπὸ τετάρτης ἡμέρας μέχρι ταύτης τῆς ὥρας suggest the meaning, 'from a (the) fourth day (counting backwards) up to this hour,' i.e., I have been praying continuously starting from that point and continuing to the present. This however is certainly not what Cornelius means; he was praying at a particular time, the ninth hour, and at that time something about to be described happened. Moule (*IB* 73) describes ἀπὸ τετάρτης ἡμέρας as a 'peculiar idiom', and refers forward to his treatment of πρό. This seems to lead to the suggestion that ἀπό is here used as an adverb: *back in the past, to the extent* (genitive of quantity) *of four days*. But if this is intended it is not clear why the ordinal τετάρτης and not the cardinal numeral should be used. Common sense suggests that what Cornelius means to say is, 'On the fourth day back from now, at this hour of the day (the hour at which we now stand) I was praying . . .'. Can this be got out of the Greek? The answer seems to be no, and it is therefore important here to note Torrey's observation (*CDA* 35) that 'it is perfectly good Semitic, however: דא שעתא עד רביעיא יומא מן; that is," on the fourth day back, reckoning up to this same hour".' But the natural sense of מן and עד is the same as that of ἀπό and μέχρι. It has often been suggested (e.g. Haenchen 338) that μέχρι may have been suggested to a thoughtless writer by the occurrence of ἀπό, to which it often serves as correlate (*from . . . up to*). As for ἀπό one can only guess that the writer began to say 'From now, four days ago . . .' but changed his construction. This is a heavy charge to bring against an author, but the facts seem to warrant it. For other evidence that suggests a lack of adequate revision on Luke's part see Vol. II. For other conjectures see Metzger 376.

The words just discussed are altered by D but apparently in the interests of chronology rather than of grammar: ἀπὸ τῆς τρίτης ἡμέρας μέχρι τῆς ἄρτι ὥρας. It is important that ancient editors seem to have been less troubled than modern by the construction; there may be Greek idioms that have not yet come to light either in literary texts or the papyri. For the reckoning of time see above on vv. 23, 24. Metzger (375) suggests that the copyist of D counted the occurrences of ἐπαύριον (vv. 9, 23, 24).

After his first note of time Cornelius proceeds with his narrative. He was τὴν ἐνάτην προσευχόμενος. If this means that he was *praying at the ninth hour* the accusative (instead of the dative) is used to indicate a point of time. This may be so; cf. v. 3, if περί is omitted, and see M. 1.245; 3.248. In the latter passage however the suggestion is made that τὴν ἐνάτην should be taken as a cognate accusative with προσευχόμενος: I was praying the ninth hour prayers. For this see also Moule (*IB* 34). The Western text adds that Cornelius was also fasting, and E indicates the length of his prayer: νηστεύων καὶ τὴν ἐνάτην ὥραν προσευχόμενος, (P⁵⁰ Aᶜ) D⁽*⁾ Ψ 𝔐 it sy mae (P⁵⁰ Aᶜ *pc* omit ὥραν); νηστεύων καὶ προσευχόμενος ἀπὸ ἕκτης ὥρας ἕως ἐνάτης, E. Conzelmann (64) notes that this makes Cornelius accomplish the required three-day fast before baptism; probably the Western editor wished only to show how exceptionally pious Cornelius was.

The last clause in the verse takes up v. 3. The ἀνὴρ ἐν ἐσθῆτι λαμπρᾷ is clearly the angel of God. For the use of ἀνήρ cf. 1.10; for the clothing cf. Mt. 27.3; Mk 16.5; Lk. 24.4 (ἐν ἐσθῆτι ἀστραπτούσῃ); Jn 20.12; also Lk. 23.11.

31. paraphrases v. 4.

32. paraphrases vv. 5, 6. μετακάλεσαι replaces μετάπεμψαι without serious change of meaning. At the end of the verse the Western text (with some followers) unnecessarily fills out the narrative by adding ὃς παραγενόμενος λαλήσει σοι (C D E Ψ 𝔐 it sy (sa mae)).

33. Cornelius had immediately done as he was commanded; see vv. 7, 8. There is no verbal equivalent there for ἐξαυτῆς (characteristic of Acts: 10.33; 11.11; 21.32; 23.30; in the rest of the NT only twice) but the sense of it is implied. After πρὸς σέ the Western text adds, somewhat unnecessarily, παρακαλῶν ἐλθεῖν σὲ πρὸς ἡμᾶς (D⁽*⁾ p sy^{h**} mae).

σύ is in emphatic contrast, *I sent* and *you came*. καλῶς ποιεῖν (cf. Phil. 4.14; 2 Pet. 1.19; 3 Jn 6) with a participle is often used in requests (for *please*). MM 319 quote among other examples of colloquial use *P. Hib.* 1.82.17, καλῶς οὖν [π]οιήσεις συναν[τι]λ[α]μβανόμενος προθύμως περὶ τῶν εἰς ταῦτα συγκυρόντων, which the editors translate, 'Please therefore to give your zealous cooperation in all that concerns this.' A particularly good parallel (because in the past tense) is given by the 'very illiterate' third century AD *P. Oxy.* 7(1910) 1067, 3f., οὐ καλῶς ἔπραξας μὴ ἐλθεῖν, 'you did not do well in not coming'. Here the meaning is, *You did well to come, You were so kind as to come.* παραγενόμενος is an aorist participle of coincident or identical action (M. 1. 131, 228; cf. BDR § 414. 3). D's addition of ἐν τάχει before παραγενόμενος is again a brightening of the narrative.

In the second part of the verse Cornelius sets himself and his colleagues over against Peter (without ἡμεῖς, πάρεσμεν would naturally have been taken to refer to all, including Peter). Peter stands apart as the messenger to whom is committed a task, consisting in saying certain things (ἀκοῦσαι πάντα τὰ προστεταγμένα) laid upon him by the Lord. For ὑπό (ℵ* B Ψ 𝔐), P⁴⁵ P⁷⁴ ℵ A B D *pc* have ἀπό, E has παρά; and for κυρίου (P⁴⁵ ℵ A B C E Ψ 81* 323 614 945 1175 1739 *al* lat sy^h bo), P⁷⁴ D 𝔐 p sy^p sa mae bo^{ms} have θεοῦ. The angelic visitation has made it clear to Cornelius that a divine message is to be given him; it is a solemn occasion (ἐνώπιον τοῦ θεοῦ); he and his colleagues are ready to hear.

The Western text sharpens the narrative further. For οὖν, D¹ syᵖ (sa mae) have the more exclamatory (and biblical) ἰδού. For ἐνώπιον τοῦ θεοῦ, D* *pc* lat syᵖ sa mae have ἐνώπιον σοῦ. Ropes (*Begs.* 3.98) thinks that σοῦ may be preferable to the more religious τοῦ θεοῦ. For πάρεσμεν ἀκοῦσαι πάντα, D* (it syᵖ) have ἀκοῦσαι βουλόμενοι παρά σοῦ (to be linked presumably with ἰδού).

34. For ἀνοίξας τὸ στόμα cf. 8.35; it adds a solemn (and biblical, e.g. Job 3.1) touch to the proceedings. ἐπ᾽ ἀληθείας also is biblical, e.g. Dan. 2.8. καταλαμβάνομαι, as at 4.13; 25.25. 'Petrus non putabat antea, Deum esse *personarum acceptorem*. sed nunc primum experitur, ex quo luculentissime conspicitur, DEUM non esse *personarum acceptorem*' (Bengel).

προσωπολήμπτης (with its cognates, προσωπολημπτεῖν, προσωπολημψία, and πρόσωπον λαμβάνειν) is a biblical word based upon the Hebrew idiom נשא פנים, literally *to raise up the face* (of one who has prostrated himself?), hence *to show favour*. In the NT this is usually understood *in malam partem*, to show favour unfairly, perhaps because bribed or otherwise improperly persuaded to do so. The adjective does not occur elsewhere in the NT, but it is said at Rom. 2.11; Eph. 6.9; Col. 3.25 that there is no προσωπολημψία with God (James 2.1, 9 reprehends favouritism among men). It is not clear whether it is Peter's vision (cf. v. 28) or the evident fact that God, through his angel, has had dealings with Cornelius, that leads Peter to perceive that he is not προσωπολήμπτης; the narrator may well have both factors in mind. Although Peter shares the word-group with Paul (according to Bauernfeind (149) Paul took up the expression from the primitive church) their emphasis is different. Peter recognizes that a Gentile may be as good as an Israelite, and be treated by God with equal favour; Paul is compelled against his natural wish to recognize that Jews, like Gentiles, are sinners in God's eyes.

35. God does not practise favouritism. The words ἐν παντὶ ἔθνει are emphatic. Appropriately qualified persons are acceptable to God whether they are Jews or belong to some other race. 'Non *indifferentismus religionum*, sed *indifferentia nationum* hic asseritur' (Bengel). So much is clear; what is not clear is how men are qualified to be acceptable to God. Two requirements are laid down: that one should fear God and practise righteousness. It has already been said (v. 2) that Cornelius feared God; see the note. Here at least it seems that Luke is not employing a technical term ('God-fearer') but uses his word descriptively in a way that could be applied to a Jew, to a proselyte, or to the kind of Gentile who possessed the qualities and observed the practices that are commonly in mind when the term 'God-fearer' is used as a technicality. τί κύριος ὁ θεός σου αἰτεῖται παρὰ σοῦ ἀλλ' ἢ φοβεῖσθαι κύριον τὸν θεόν σου . . . (Deut. 10.12). God's first requirement is that men should reverence him, that is, should treat him as God (cf. Rom. 1.21). Deut. 10.12f. continues with the requirement that men should love and serve God and φυλάσσεσθαι τὰς ἐντολὰς κυρίου τοῦ θεοῦ σου καὶ τὰ δικαιώματα αὐτοῦ; this corresponds to Luke's ἐργαζόμενος δικαιοσύνην (for the expression cf. Ps. 14.2 (LXX); Heb. 11.33; James 1.20; and cf. for similar expressions Mt. 7.23; Rom. 2.10; 13.10; Gal. 6.10), but it remains to be asked whether Luke (or Peter, at this stage) understood the practice of righteousness in terms of observing all commandments and righteous ordinances. In this sense the phrase could describe only a Jew or a proselyte, and this Cornelius was not, for he had not been circumcised (11.3). Since Cornelius is certainly included something less (or other) than this must be in mind, possibly observance of the commandments of the sons of Noah (regarding judgments, blasphemy, idolatry, incest and adultery, murder, theft, and eating meat containing blood; see *NS* 3.1. 171, 172). It is unlikely that 'practising righteousness' would be understood as simply 'being good', if these words are taken in a vague, modern sense. Schille (248) is correct in the negative statement that δικαιοσύνη is not used here in its distinctively Pauline sense, and may be right in his positive definition of righteousness as meaning (as, according to Schille, in the Sermon on the Mount) 'das rechte Gesellschaftsverhalten gegenüber dem Partner Gott'. The meaning may be narrower. In a Baraita in Baba Bathra 10b Johanan ben Zakkai (who seems subsequently to have changed his mind) interprets Prov. 14.34 to mean, 'As the sin-offering makes atonement for Israel, so alms-giving (צדקה) makes atonement for idolaters'. It is certainly true that צדקה (cf. the Aramaic זכא), which in classical Hebrew would be translated *righteousness*, was often used with the meaning *alms-giving*, which Cornelius practised, and it may well be that the present verse simply repeats v. 3, though (perhaps deliberately) casting it in a form capable of a wider meaning. Wilson (*Law* 70), observes that what is described here is 'a "liberal" Jewish position', and goes on to refer to Philo, *Spec. Leg.* 2.62, 63 (. . . two main heads: one of duty to God as shewn by piety and holiness, one of duty to men as shewn by humanity and justice (δικαιοσύνη)). Calvin (319) finds himself in difficulty because he assumes that δικαιοσύνη must have its Pauline sense, or something like it. 'It is not their own worth that determines the value of works, but faith, which borrows from Christ what works lack.' True in itself, this statement does not match what is in mind in the present passage; see above.

A person, then, who reverenced God and observed the laws that were appropriate to him would be (not simply acceptable but actually) *accepted*, δεκτός, corresponding to the rabbinic מקבל.

Dibelius (47) notes a contrast between this passage, which claims that 'every righteous man is pleasing to God' and Paul's Areopagus speech in ch. 17, which claims that 'every man is related to God'. If Cornelius is indeed accepted by God it is hard to see why he should not be regarded as a member of the people of God (see the note on v. 29). Perceptible manifestations of the Holy Spirit will confirm the matter for Peter (vv. 44–48).

36. The language of this verse, of v. 37, and to some extent also of v. 38, is so difficult as to be untranslatable. The general sense indeed is reasonably clear. God sent to the children of Israel through Jesus Christ the good news of peace. What happened is well known: the story begins in Galilee with the work of John the Baptist; he was followed by Jesus of Nazareth, whose ministry led him to Judaea; God anointed him with the Holy Spirit and power, and was with him, so that he was able to heal the sick and undo the works of the devil. This summary of the work of Jesus (more like a gospel than a sermon — Wilckens 50; cf. 70, 102f.) is similar to that of 2.22 and like it leads up to the crucifixion and resurrection. The details however are not clear and are complicated by textual problems. It will be helpful to consider these first; they are bound up with the problems of construction and exegesis.

The addition of γάρ between τόν and λόγον by C* D 614 *pc* l p t sy$^{p.h**}$ is simply an attempt to introduce v. 36 and connect it with v. 35; it is almost certainly secondary. A much more serious problem is raised by ὅν after λόγον. This word like γάρ is regarded by Ropes (*Begs.* 3.98) as an attempt at amelioration of a difficult text, but the case is not so clear. ὅν (which may have arisen by accidental reduplication of the last two letters of λόγον, or have been omitted by haplography) is read by P^{74} ℵ* C D E Ψ 𝔐, omitted by ℵ^1 A B 81 614 1739 *pc* latt co. If it is omitted the verse will stand on its own with a straightforward construction: He (God) sent the word to the sons of Israel, proclaiming the good news of peace through Jesus Christ (he is Lord of all). At this point we may pause to note the meaning of the clause, since, whatever the text and construction, it undoubtedly represents at least part of what Luke intends to say. The subject of ἀπέστειλεν will be God, who is regularly in Acts the one who initiates the work of salvation. He sent a message (λόγος is not personified in Acts; cf. e.g. 2.41) in the first instance to the children of Israel (cf. 2.39; 3.25f.). It was a message proclaimed as good news by Jesus; its content was peace, in the first instance between men and God (cf. Lk. 2.14), but also, since Jesus is Lord of all (not of one race only), between Jews and Gentiles. This assertion follows aptly upon v. 35, which claims that men of every nation may be accepted by God.

What however if the relative ὅν is read? This word now becomes the object of ἀπέστειλεν, and the accusative τὸν λόγον is left in suspension. It is possible to take a verb to govern it out of v. 37 (ὑμεῖς οἴδατε, *you know* the word), but this is remote, and to use οἴδατε in this way aggravates the problem of v. 37. Torrey (35) translates into Aramaic, noting two points. (1) In Aramaic suspended clauses (such as, The word which he sent to the sons of Israel . . .) are more frequent and acceptable than in Greek; (2) οὗτός ἐστιν πάντων κύριος is translated into Aramaic as הוא מרא כלא הוא; הוא can be taken simply as a demonstrative, or article, and the phrase translated into English as 'this (the) Lord of all'. This phrase, referring to God, will serve as the subject of ἀπέστειλεν, and the verse as a whole introduces v. 37: As for the word which the Lord of all sent to the sons of Israel, preaching peace through Jesus Christ, you know . . . One is left with the question why Luke made everything so difficult by putting τὸν λόγον in the accusative. See further criticism in Wilcox 151f.

ὁ πάντων κύριος was a not unfamiliar phrase. Cf. Plutarch, *De Iside et Osiride* 12 (355E), ὡς ὁ πάντων κύριος εἰς φῶς πρόεισιν; Epictetus 4.1.12, ὁ πάντων κύριος Καῖσαρ. Cornelius, and Luke's readers, may well have met it in both religious and political settings. πάντων is to be understood as masculine (i.e., as personal) rather than neuter. Page (149) finds this clause the 'very gist and essence of Peter's argument'; οὗτος is emphatic: He, yes he, is Lord of all. But in fact the clause, though undoubtedly representing what Luke believed, seems to be parenthetical. See however Riesenfeld (*FS* Black (1979), 191–4), with the suggestion that τὸν λόγον ὅν resumes the ὅτι- clause of vv. 34, 35. See further F. Neirynck (*EThL* 60 (1984), 118–23).

It seems that we must either accept the short text without ὅν: God sent the Gospel word through Jesus Christ, the Lord of all, or suppose that Luke, after writing his parenthesis (this Jesus is Lord of All), forgot how the sentence was intended to run. This is better than using οἴδατε as the verb to govern τὸν λόγον.

37. In the first clause the omission of ῥῆμα by D does not affect the construction or the sense; some such word would have to be understood with τὸ γενόμενον if the participle stood alone. ῥῆμα does not necessarily mean *word*; it may be *thing*, and here for τὸ γενόμενον ῥῆμα *what happened* would suffice. The aorist participle is constative and looks at the ministry of Jesus taken as a whole: You know the affair that happened in (through) the whole of Judaea. It is not clear why Luke singles out Judaea, especially as he is about to say that the event he had in mind began in Galilee and his gospel records only the final scenes of the life of Jesus as located in Judaea. Peter appeals to his hearers' knowledge (ὑμεῖς οἴδατε) as he does in 2.22 (καθὼς αὐτοὶ οἴδατε). This is natural enough in Jerusalem, and the example in ch. 2 shows that we do not need to think of

Christian hearers (as Roloff 172 does), but it is much less easy to understand in Caesarea. A probable inference is that Luke is here putting in Peter's mouth a traditional piece of preaching material. If οἴδατε has been taken with v. 36 to govern λόγον, τὸ ῥῆμα must be understood as a second appositional object: You know the word which God sent . . ., I mean the event that happened . . .

It is not surprising that the masculine nominative participle ἀρξάμενος was changed by P⁴⁵ 𝔐 Did into the neuter (or masculine accusative) ἀρξάμενον. The masculine nominative singular has nothing in the sentence with which to agree. Torrey (27) compares it with 1.22, where however there is no serious grammatical problem; see the note. See also Lk. 23.5; 24.47. But simply to note that 'the verb, or participle, of "beginning" is one which is often used loosely in Palestinian Aramaic, even to the point of redundance' (Torrey 25f.) does not explain why a translator should fail to put it properly into Greek. 'Acts 10.37 is fairly hopeless as it stands' (M. 1.240). Moulton goes on to cite the view of Blass that ἀρξάμενος ἀπὸ τῆς Γαλιλαίας is interpolated from Lk. 23.5. He also notes, and this is a more hopeful step, the reading ἀρξάμενος γάρ (P⁷⁴ A D lat Ir^lat), and thinks that 'this may preserve the relics of a better text, in which a new sentence beginning there was combined with 'Ιησοῦς ὁ ἀπὸ Ναζαρέθ, ὃν (D) ἔχρισεν . . . οὗτος (D).' The outline of the sentence would be, 'For beginning from Galilee . . . Jesus . . . whom God anointed . . . went about . . .' Once more however we meet the question, if this is what Luke wrote, how did it come to be altered into the impossible sentence we now read? Primitive, accidental, corruption is possible, and we must assume either that this took place or that Luke wrote a sentence he ought not to have written and indeed did not intend to write, and never reread and corrected his first draft. The parallels to the pendent nominative ἀρξάμενος adduced by J. W. Hunkin (*JTS* 25 (1924), 391ff.) will hardly justify Luke's Greek. Clark (lii f.) wishes to rearrange the stichoi in which the MS D is written. These are as follows:

1 ὑμεῖς οἴδατε τὸ γενόμενον καθ' ὅλης 'Ιουδαίας
2 ἀρξάμενος γὰρ ἀπὸ τῆς Γαλιλαίας
3 μετὰ τὸ βάπτισμα ὃ ἐκήρυξεν 'Ιωάνης
4 τ̄η̄ν̄ τὸν ἀπὸ Ναζαρὲθ τ̄η̄ν̄ ὃν ἔχρισεν ὁ θ̄ς̄
5 ἁγίῳ πνεύματι καὶ δυνάμει
6 οὗτος διῆλθεν εὐεργετῶν

'Sense is restored by putting στ. 2–3 ἀρξάμενος . . . 'Ιωάννης after στ. 5. 'Ιησοῦν in στ. 4 comes naturally after οἴδατε τὸ γενόμενον κ.τ.λ. in στ. 1: also οὗτος in στ. 6 after ἀρξαμ.' (lii, liii).

Wilckens (107) writes: 'So wird man zu ἀρξάμενος Act 10.37 doch am besten 'Ιησοῦς als logisches Subjekt hinzugedacht auffassen, obwohl "Jesus" im folgenden dann im Akkusativ steht und erst 10.38 Subjekt wird.' This is reconstruction rather than explanation. Delebecque (53) is more elaborate. 'Luc emploie encore une expression très attique ἀρξάμενος ἀπό, dans laquelle la personne, ou la chose, dépendant de la préposition, est la première ou la plus importante par opposition à d'autres, ou à une totalité, ici ὀλῆς. De là l'emploi du nominatif absolu, et le sens "avant tout", "essentiellement", "principalement", "à commencer par".' He refers to Plato, 1 Alcibiades 118D; Symposium 173d; Republic 600e; Xenophon, Hell. 7.1.32; Cyrop. 1.6.8.

It remains probable that we have a piece of careless and uncorrected writing, and we may be thankful that the general meaning of vv. 36, 37 remains clear. There may be an allusion to Isa. 52.7 or Neh. 2.1 (or both); on God as the εὐαγγελιζόμενος see Barth (CD 4.2.196f.).

The work of Jesus is dated from the baptism proclaimed by John (as in Mark). For the significance of John the Baptist in Acts see 1.5, 22; 13.24, and the notes. It may be hinted here but is not expressly stated that it was at his baptism by John that God anointed Jesus with the Holy Spirit and power; see v. 38. It is suggested in Begs. 4.119 that 'the original text may have been μετὰ τὸ βάπτισμα ὃ ἐβάπτισεν Ἰωάννης τὸν Ἰησοῦν'. But is it likely that βαπτίζειν would take a double accusative in this way?

38. In Acts Jesus is described by the adjective Ναζωραῖος at 2.22; 3.6; 4.10; 6.14; 22.8; 24.5; 26.9; here only is he ὁ ἀπὸ Ναζαρέθ. For the suggestion that Luke originally had the name in the nominative, or an explicit reference to the baptism of Jesus, see above. ὃν ἔχρισεν (D* it sy mae) is neater than the majority text, but not for that reason original. It has been suggested that ὡς is a rendering of the Aramaic ד, which should have been rendered by the relative. Pallis 63 claims that ὡς . . . αὐτόν is equivalent to ὅν, ὡς (like ὅτι) being used as an indeclinable relative, like the Hebrew אשר. See Wilson (Gentiles 116–18); and cf. Isa. 61.1; Lk. 4.18.

There may well (see above) be a reference here to the baptism of Jesus. Spirit and power are elsewhere associated in Acts: 1.8; 6.5, 8, 10, and it is not wrong to see here a kind of hendiadys: the power of the Spirit. God bestowed the Spirit upon Jesus and as a result he was filled with power.

ἔχρισεν presumably means that God made him χριστός, Christ. When did this happen? The present passage suggests, at his baptism. But cf. 2.36; 3.20, with the notes; and cf. also Lk. 2.11, which suggests the answer, at his birth.

διῆλθεν (περιῆλθεν, P⁴⁵vid sin Ir^lat; Pallis (63) conjectures διῆγεν) is rightly described by M. 3.72 as a constative (complexive) aorist; the ministry is regarded as a unit (cf. γενόμενον in v. 37). Turner however does not note the present participles (εὐεργετῶν, ἰώμενος) that accompany the aorist indicative. BDR § 332. 1 do notice them, and their '"immerfort" (oder "immer wieder") bis zum Ausgang in Jerusalem v, 39' brings out the point; the ministry regarded as a whole was made up of a continuous series of acts of beneficence. εὐεργετεῖν (cf. Lk. 22.25) is the action of a public benefactor (there is a good example in *P.Stras.* 637, ll. 10, 11 (*ND* 1.61)), but here *doing good* is a strong enough rendering. Luke describes it in terms of healing, of the overthrow of the devil, and of the presence of God himself (on the combination of humanity and divinity see Barth, *CD* 3.2.210; Luke himself does not develop the point theologically). Those who were oppressed by the devil include not only cases of possession (by demons, the devil's agents) but also illness of any kind. The ascription of mental and physical disorder to the activity of the devil provides an important interpretative element: the work of Jesus constitutes God's decisive attack upon the (personally conceived) power of evil; cf. e.g. Mk 3.23–27, and parallels. The statement that 'God was with him' represents in itself a minimal Christology; it claims no more than that Jesus was a man whom God accompanied and aided as he might have been said, and was said, to have accompanied and aided e.g. Abraham, Moses, or David. Luke's Christology is never highly developed but it does on occasion go further than this; see the discussion in Vol. II. '*Deus erat cum illo*: id est, pater cum filio: melius enim sic intellegere quam divinitatem filii cum homine quem adsumpsit cohabitantem significare, ne Christi personam geminare et in Nestorii dogma cadere videamur' (Bede).

39. For disciples and especially the Twelve as witnesses see 1.8, 22; 2.32; 3.15; 5.32; 13.31; 22.15; 26.16, and the notes on these passages. The importance of this role is brought out by Bauernfeind (148). Instead of πάντων (witnesses of all the things that he did), D (syᵖ) have αὐτοῦ (his witnesses of the things that he did). The difference is not great; D recalls 13.31. At this point witnessing seems to be restricted to the events (especially the healings) of the ministry of Jesus; witness to the resurrection will be mentioned in v. 41. The ministry was confined to Jewish territory (see Davies, *Land* 274); Peter is now in Caesarea; the question whether God's action is extended beyond the Land is about to be decided.

ἐν before 'Ιερουσαλήμ is read by P⁷⁴ ℵ A C E 𝔐 syʰ Irˡᵃᵗ, omitted by B D Ψ 2495 *pc* lat syᵖ. It is difficult to make a decision, and for the general sense not important. The matter is however related to the position of τε, for which cf. 25.23 and see BDR § 444. 5, n. 6: 'Die Stellung des korrelativen τε ist in der Regel die nach dem ersten Wort der in Korrelation gestellten Glieder; Ausnahmen: hinter der vorausgehenden, den verbundenen Begriffen gemeinsamen Präposition.' This is also classical (K.-G. 2.245), and means that the text of B D etc. is grammatically more acceptable — and therefore secondary?

ὃν καὶ ἀνεῖλαν, whom they actually killed (so *Begs*. 4.121). For ἀνεῖλαν cf. 2.23; here no subject is expressed, but one may be taken out of Ἰουδαίων . . . Ἰερουσαλήμ. Peter refers to the Jews, or Jewish authorities. For κρεμάσαντες ἐπὶ ξύλου cf. 5.30 (also Gal. 3.13; Deut. 21.23). Whether or not the Jews carried out the crucifixion (as they certainly did not), Peter (or the traditional preaching material used by Luke) ascribes to them moral responsibility for it.

It is possible to see Joseph typology (see) here only if it is believed to occur wherever there is a reference to the death and resurrection of Jesus.

40. Upon the crucifixion follows resurrection. For τοῦτον (taking up the preceding clause as object of the verb) ὁ θεὸς ἤγειρεν cf. 3.15; 4.10; 5.30. In none of these passages is there a reference to *the third day*; see 1 Cor. 15.4; Lk. 9.22; (13.32); 18.33; 24.7, (21), 46; also Mt. in references to the resurrection; Mk has μετὰ τρεῖς ἡμέρας, and probably reflects Jesus' prophecy that after a short (but unspecified) time he would be vindicated by God. Reference to the third day probably arose when it was known that after crucifixion on Friday 'resurrection events' began to take place on the following Sunday. At this point Luke shows no interest in the chronology: it is important that God raised Jesus up, not important that he did so on one day rather than another. The majority of MSS (P⁷⁴ ℵ𝑐 A B D² E Ψ 𝔐 have τῇ τρίτῃ ἡμέρᾳ; only ℵ* C *pc* have ἐν. D* l t have the surprising μετὰ τὴν τρίτην ἡμέραν; it is not to be supposed that these MSS were consciously proposing a different date for the resurrection; probably a copyist, absentmindedly thinking of Mk, began to write μετὰ τρεῖς ἡμέρας and corrected himself after writing the preposition, not noticing the effect of the preposition on the chronology (though he noted its effect on the case of adjective and noun).

δοῦναι with accusative and infinitive is regarded by *Begs*. 4.121 as a Semitism (cf. 2.27 (=Ps. 16.10); 14.3) Wilcox (64f.) rightly prefers to describe it as a Septuagintalism.

Elsewhere in the NT ἐμφανής occurs only at Rom. 10.20 (quoting Isa. 65.1). It is appropriately used for the appearing of the risen Christ; cf. Aristophanes, *Wasps* 733–735, σοὶ δὲ νῦν τις θεῶν παρὼν ἐμφανὴς ξυλλαμβάνει . . . — a god makes himself present and manifest. The word occurs in legal use for producing 'a person or thing *in open court*' (LS 549; see Antipho 5.36); and in view of 1.3 it is interesting to note Euripides, *Electra* 1109, . . . φήμης φέροντες ἐμφανῆ τεκμήρια. The witnesses (again, a courtroom scene is suggested) supply legally acceptable proof of the living presence of Jesus, a supernatural figure. It is not to be claimed that all of this is actually contained in the word ἐμφανής, only that it was a word suitable for Luke's purpose. It was God who granted to Jesus that he should thus be revealed, in addition to actually raising (ἤγειρεν) him from death. *ND* 4.148 refers to *P.Oxy.* 7.1021.2 (Claudius is ἐμφανὴς θεός); 36.2754.4 (Trajan).

41. The manifestation was not to all the (Jewish) people (τῷ λαῷ) but to chosen witnesses, witnesses now not only of the earthly life of Jesus (v. 39) but of the resurrection. χειροτονεῖν (14.23, see the note; 2 Cor. 8.19) means *to appoint*; προχειρ. (here only in the NT) *to appoint beforehand* (cf. προχειρίζειν in 3.20). These witnesses, appointed as such in God's providence, are *we*, ἡμῖν; the following words show that Luke has in mind the apostles, the Twelve, men who (οἵτινες is correctly used, cf. v. 47) ate and drank with Jesus after the resurrection (see 1.3, 4, especially if συναλιζόμενος refers to meals shared by Jesus with the apostles). The primary significance of eating and drinking is given by Lk. 24.36–43: they prove the physical reality of the body of the risen Jesus. Cf. Tobit 12.19: Raphael, an angel, neither eats nor drinks. Possibly we should add Lk. 24.30, 31, 35: the presence of the Lord is disclosed at a meal.

The Western text emphasises the relation with ch. 1 and elaborates the narrative: after αὐτῷ, D(ᶜ) it syʰ mae add καὶ συνεστράφημεν, and after νεκρῶν, D E it sa mae add ἡμέρας μ' (cf. 1.3).

It is possible but not certain that knowledge of this verse may be shown by Ignatius, *Smyrnaeans* 3.3: μετὰ δὲ τὴν ἀνάστασιν συνέφαγεν αὐτοῖς καὶ συνέπιεν ὡς σαρκικός, καίπερ πνευματικῶς ἡνωμένος τῷ πατρί. Ignatius may well be drawing on common tradition.

42. The subject of παρήγγειλεν (D, ἐνετείλατο) is, it seems, God, though in 1.8 it is Jesus who commands the Twelve to act as his witnesses. κηρύξαι has no independent object noun or clause to give it content, so that it must probably be taken with διαμαρτύρασθαι (a Lucan word: Lk. once, Acts nine times, in the rest of the NT five times): they are to proclaim and testify to the (Jewish) people (τῷ λαῷ) that this person (Jesus) is the one who has been appointed, marked out, as judge. Elsewhere in Acts (13.20; 18.15; 24.10) κριτής is used only of human judges; only at 17.31 is the verb κρίνειν used of a future judgment which God will carry out by 'the man he appointed (ὥρισεν)', that is, Jesus. Judgment ζώντων καὶ νεκρῶν became a standard formula, especially in creeds; see many examples in A. Hahn, *Bibliothek der Symbole und Glaubensregeln der alten Kirche* (Breslau, ³1897), the first of them § 4, Bekenntnis der gegen Noetus in Smyrna (Ephesus) versammelten Presbyter. It became common in later Acts: *Acta Andreae et Matthiae* 14 (L.-B. 2.1.80); *Acta Joannis* 8 (L.-B. 2.1.156); *Acta Thomae* 28, 30 (L. -B. 2.2.145, 147).

The time at which the appointment of Jesus as judge was made cannot be determined by the tense of ὡρισμένος except that it was before the time of speaking; for the verb cf. Lk. 22.22; Acts 2.23; 11.29; 17.26, 31; cf. Rom. 1.4; Heb. 4.7. That Jesus will preside at the last judgment does not in itself claim that he is divine, though it does mean that he is entrusted with a divine function. Delling (*Kreuzestod* 91) thinks that the explicit reference to judgment may have been thought necessary in view of the Gentile audience: 'in 10.42 könnte Lukas bei seiner Einführung an die noch heidnischen Hörer denken, denen die jüdische Eschatologie weniger bekannt sein mag als der Monotheismus und die Ethik des Judentums.' It remains however a somewhat surprising conclusion for the speech, except in that it sums up and emphasises the assertion, It is Jesus with whom you have to do, and makes a suitable framework for the offer of forgiveness in the next verse. Cf. Rom. 2.16.

43. If the sentence ended with μαρτυροῦσιν, τούτῳ would certainly be taken as masculine: To him (this man) all the prophets bear witness. The sentence however continues, and though it may still be right to take τούτῳ as masculine (To him all the prophets bear witness that . . .) it is possible also to take τούτῳ as neuter (To this all the prophets bear witness, namely that . . .). The latter is the more probable way of taking the sentence, and it agrees with the fact that elsewhere in Acts the prophets are not said to bear witness to Christ but rather to certain facts about him (2.16, 30; 3.18, 21, 24; 13.27, 40; 15.15; 24.14; 26.22, 27; 28.23, 25). μαρτυρεῖν is followed by the accusative and infinitive (BDR § 397. 3, n. 7).

The prophetic testimony is that everyone who believes in Christ receives the forgiveness of sins through his name. For ἄφεσις ἁμαρτιῶν see 2.38 and the note; for the use of *name* see 3.16 and the note. It is by no means clear what prophetic passages (πάντες οἱ προφῆται!)) may be in mind. Isa. 33.24 (ἀφέθη γὰρ αὐτοῖς ἡ ἁμαρτία); 55.7 (ἀφήσει τὰς ἁμαρτίας ὑμῶν) specifically connect ἀφιέναι and ἁμαρτία, but Jer. 38 (LXX; 31, MT). 34 (ἵλεως ἔσομαι ταῖς ἀδικίαις αὐτῶν καὶ τῶν ἁμαρτιῶν αὐτῶν οὐ μὴ μνησθῶ ἔτι), in the new covenant prophecy, may be more important. Luke and his contemporaries were confident both that forgiveness of sins was to be had in Christ and that the age of salvation had been foretold. Cf. also Lk. 24.47.

The last words are significant: *everyone who believes in him*. The only qualification required is faith; it is not necessary to be, or to become, a Jew. Without saying so (and according to Luke's narrative without knowing that he has done so) Peter has prepared for what follows.

44. ἔτι λαλοῦντος. According to 11.15 the event took place as Peter began to speak. In fact he had completed the outline of preaching common to many occasions in Acts (see pp. 130f.). The work, death, and resurrection of Jesus have been recounted; prophetic testimony has been claimed; the offer of forgiveness has been made. There was nothing else for Peter to say. Luke is concerned to emphasise the spontaneity of the Spirit's action, and its unexpectedness. From first to last in this story it is God who takes the initiative. For the gift of the Holy Spirit in Acts see on 2.4. The verb ἐπιπίπτειν is used at 8.16; 11.15; the meaning is not different from that of ἐπέρχεσθαι (1.8) or πίμπλημι (2.4) or λαμβάνειν (2.38) or διδόναι (8.18) or βαπτίζεσθαι ἐν (1.5). The new access of divine life that Christians identified with the promised gift of the Holy Spirit was experienced by all who were listening to Peter's address (the word — of God, or of the Lord); Luke however is thinking primarily of the Gentiles present, who, on the basis of nothing but the proclamation of Jesus, had manifestly been brought within the scope of salvation.

45. Peter's companions were astonished. They are described as believers and as ἐκ περιτομῆς. The same expression (without πιστοί) is used at 11.2, nowhere else in Acts, but see Gal. 2.12; Titus 1.10; cf. Col. 4.11. On occasion οἱ ἐκ (τῆς) περιτομῆς describes a party, contending for the obligation to observe the Jewish Law including circumcision. Elsewhere the phrase means no more than Jews: those who came from the circumcision side of the great gulf. So here; and they are hardly to be blamed (and Luke does not blame them) for entertaining Jewish presuppositions. Notwithstanding their error concerning the Gentiles (attested by their surprise), they are still called believers (Calvin 318). They were astounded that the gift of (consisting of) the Holy Spirit had been poured out. ἐκκέχυται in the normal sequence of tenses (BDR § 345) refers to the time before that of ἐξέστησαν; that is, the perfect becomes in English a pluperfect. ἐκχύνεσθαι recalls the use of ἐκχεῖν at 2.17, 18, 33 (Joel 3.1, 2) and was no doubt intended to do so. The parallel between the gift of the Spirit to the original disciples and the new gift (outside the Land: Davies, *Land* 274) of the Spirit to the Gentiles is emphasised at v. 47; 11.15; 15.8. See Mekhilta Exod. 12.1 (1b): Before the land of Israel was chosen, all lands were proper for the word of God; after the land of Israel was chosen all the other lands were omitted . . . (see the rest of the quotation in StrB 2.705).

46. That the Spirit has been given is proved (as usual for Luke) by audible phenomena. The Gentiles speak with tongues, as the believers did on the day of Pentecost (2.4; see on this verse for glossolalia) and they magnify God. For μεγαλύνειν (with God, or similar term, as object) cf. Lk. 1.46; also Acts 19.17; Phil. 1.20. It is common in the LXX (e.g. Ps. 33 (34).3, μεγαλύνατε τὸν κύριον σὺν ἐμοί), but does occur elsewhere (e.g. Euripides, *Bacchae* 320, τὸ Πενθέως

28. PETER AND CORNELIUS DEBATED 11.1–18

(1) The apostles and the brothers who were in Judaea heard that the Gentiles also had received the word of God. (2) When Peter went up to Jerusalem those who represented circumcision[1] debated with him, (3) saying, 'You went[2] into the house of uncircumcised men and ate with them.' (4) Peter began to set things out for them in order, saying, (5) 'I was in the city of Joppa praying, and in a trance I saw a vision, a sort of vessel coming down like a great sheet let down from heaven by the four corners, and it came right up to me. (6) I peered in and considered it, and saw the quadrupeds of the earth, and wild beasts, and reptiles, and the birds of heaven. (7) And I heard a voice saying to me, Get up, Peter, slaughter and eat. (8) But I said, No indeed, Lord, for nothing profane or unclean has ever entered my mouth. (9) The voice answered a second time from heaven, Things that God has cleansed, do not you treat as profane. (10) This happened three times, and the whole was drawn up again into heaven. (11) And immediately there were three men standing by the house in which we were,[3] sent to me from Caesarea. (12) The Spirit told me to go with them, making no distinction;[4] there went with me also these six brothers and we went into the man's house. (13) And he reported to us how he had seen the angel in his house, who stood and said, Send to Joppa and summon Simon who is surnamed Peter. (14) He will speak to you words by which you will be saved, you and all your household. (15) As I began to speak the Holy Spirit fell upon them, as he had done upon us at the beginning, (16) and I remembered the word of the Lord, how he said, John baptized with water, but you shall be baptized in the Holy Spirit. (17) If then God gave to them when they believed in the Lord Jesus Christ the same gift as he gave to us, who was I to be able to stand in God's way?' (18) When they heard these things they fell silent and glorified God, saying, 'Why then, to the Gentiles also God has given that repentance that leads to life.'

Bibliography

F. Bovon, as in (27).
J. Dupont, as in (2) (*Nouvelles*).
E. E. Ellis, as in (27).
E. Haulotte, as in (27).
L. Marin, as in (27).

Many more of those listed for (27) are more or less relevant here also.

[1] Literally, those of the circumcision.
[2] *Begs.*, Why did you go . . .?
[3] *Begs.*, NEB, I was.
[4] *Begs.*, without any hesitation; NJB, to have no hesitation.

Commentary

The greater part of this paragraph is devoted to an abbreviated repetition of the story told in 10.1–48. It was noted above that this is an indication of the importance Luke attached to that story. The repetition was called for by the report of the Cornelius episode that came to the ears of the Jerusalem church (v. 1) and naturally evoked objection on the part of those who valued their Jewish as well as their Christian status (vv. 2, 3). The inevitable reply on Peter's part was simply to give his own account of what had happened; in response the objectors recognized that God had made it possible for the Gentiles to repent and thereby receive life. The repeated narrative contains a few unimportant differences from the original; these will be mentioned in the notes. Only the new material that constitutes the framework of the paragraph will be considered here.

The complaint that Peter had 'gone into and eaten with' uncircumcised men is not quite fair (unless based on information not given in the text of Acts). He had indeed gone into the place where Cornelius and his friends were assembled (10.25). This was probably Cornelius's house; it would certainly be Gentile property. This would have meant incurring uncleanness, though a measure of uncleanness to which Jews must have been fairly frequently exposed, especially in the Diaspora; there were means of removing it. It is not stated that Peter ate with Cornelius, though, religious considerations apart, it would be natural for Cornelius to offer his guest a meal; the apostles and brothers in Judaea may have drawn the inference, or Luke may have thought that they had positive information. Meals are certainly implied by the residence for 'some days' asked for in 10.48; this however was after Cornelius had (rightly or wrongly) been accepted as a Christian, so that at this point a new question will tend to supplant the original one (it might perhaps have been expected to precede it): No longer, May a Jew, even if a Christian and going about Christian duties, have domestic and table fellowship with a Gentile? but, May those who are not Jews become Christians, and, if they wish to do so, is it necessary that they should first be circumcised as Jews before being baptized as Christians? The interplay of these questions, which it must often have been very difficult to keep separate from each other, complicates the story of the Gentile mission as this is unfolded in Acts; the complication appears in the fact that at v. 18 the dispute, which began with the complaint that a Jew had had dealings with a Gentile, ends with the recognition that Gentiles are to be accepted as recipients of God's gift of life. In the present case it will be borne in mind (and must have been recognized at the time) that a Gentile in good standing with Jews, as Cornelius was, would not insult his guest with unclean food. Peter in fact does not deal at all with the question of domestic and dietary uncleanness but moves rapidly to the end of the story. Without waiting for baptism, still less for circumcision, the Holy Spirit had come upon Cornelius and his friends precisely as he had done upon Peter and his colleagues at the beginning. Peter had remembered the Lord's words, quoted previously at 1.5; he could not refuse the water of baptism (τὸ ὕδωρ κωλῦσαι, 10.47), or, as he now puts it, he could not prevent God from doing what God evidently intended to do (κωλῦσαι τὸν θεόν, v. 17). These Gentiles had believed (this is not stated in so many words but it is implied); they had received the gift of the Spirit. How could it be denied that they were now (whatever they may have been earlier) members of the people of God? True, they had not received the Christian sign of membership. This could be, and was, speedily added. The truth of Peter's argument was recognized, for v. 18 must mean, God has granted these men, while still uncircumcised, salvation (life); and this is expressed in a general proposition about 'the Gentiles'. 'Ab exemplo ad omnes concluditur' (Bengel). It cannot have been intended to add, 'Provided that they are now circumcised'. It needed no new revelation or argument to tell Jews that Gentiles might become, by circumcision, full proselytes and so share in the divine promise.

Something new, marking an advance on the earlier stages reached in Acts, has now been said, and it answers in advance the questions raised by the demands of 15.1, 5. Since this is so, why is a further discussion held in ch. 15? The problem is sharply stated by Preuschen (69: '... so ist v. 1–18 als Parallelerzählung zu 15.1–29 zu betrachten, durch deren Einschiebung an dieser Stelle der Verf. oder Redaktor c. 15 völlig unverständlich gemacht hat') and not fully resolved by Bauernfeind (152f.: 'Über den Gedanken, dass mit dem Ausgang der Corneliusgeschichte eigentlich schon das Apostelkonzil vorweggenommen sei, würde er [Lukas] sehr erstaunt gewesen sein'). The question is one to which we must return in dealing with ch. 15 (and in the general discussion of the matter in Vol. II). It is striking that whereas the dispute in ch. 11 begins with the legitimacy or otherwise of contacts between Jews and Gentiles and ends with the general question of salvation for the uncircumcised, that in ch. 15 moves in the opposite direction, beginning with the conditions of salvation and ending with what may appear to be rules designed to regulate table fellowship between (Christian) Jews and Gentiles. At present it will suffice to mention various possibilities: that the Lucan chronology is mistaken; that Jewish attitudes hardened between ch. 11 and ch. 15; that the questions were too complicated for Luke to set out in the space at his disposal — perhaps too complicated for him (writing at a later period) fully to understand. These suggestions may all prove to be true.

The possible over-simplification of a very complicated set of problems leads to the question of the literary source of the paragraph.

The view of ch. 10 taken above (see p. 496) is on the whole confirmed. The Caesarean church's story of its own origin probably concluded with the recognition by Jerusalem of its legitimacy. This Luke expanded by making and putting into the mouth of Peter his own summary of the detailed story he had given in the previous chapter. It is quite possible that behind the general proposition of v. 18 (which gives so much trouble when we attempt to combine it with ch. 15) there was a much more restricted approval of what had happened in Caesarea (cf. Schille 254), to which Luke gave a wider setting and a fuller meaning. A somewhat similar view is taken by Dibelius and Conzelmann (see the discussion in Wilson, *Gentiles* 173) but they see Luke as giving universal significance to a simple conversion story; it is more probable that what (if anything) Luke universalizes was a particular local arrangement that could have served, and did serve (15.7–9) as the basis of a general agreement. The insistence on the gift of the Spirit, with the reference to the saying of 1.5, probably means that Luke saw the event in Caesarea as a Gentile Pentecost and drew the conclusion, 'Nach dem "Pfingsten der Heiden" kann die Heidenmission beginnen, wie nach dem Pfingsten in Jerusalem die Judenmission begonnen hatte' (Pesch 347). The form of the story enabled him to make without waiting for the discussion in ch. 15 and its conclusion (15.29) the claim 'Das Evangelium gelangt nicht zu den Heiden, weil Israel oder seine Führenden es ablehnen, sondern weil es Gottes universalem Heilswillen und der Verheissung des Auferstandenen entspricht' (Weiser 271). It is possible that Luke failed to recognize that Peter's visit to Jerusalem from Caesarea and Paul's two visits from Antioch (11.30; 15.2) all belonged to the same occasion (= Gal. 2.1–10); see *Begs.* 4.125; 5.195–204. Discussion of this must be deferred until more evidence has been collected.

At this point one further historical question may be raised: that of the role and position of Peter implied by this story. It is clear that at the outset his actions were freely called in question by members of the church; his authority was not such as to carry automatic approval of his activities. It appears that 'die Amtsträger, selbst die Apostel, der Gemeinde, der sie vorstehen, verantwortlich sind und von ihr zur Rechenschaft gezogen werden können' (Stählin 158). In the end he carries the church with him, but, as Benoit (who sees Peter as exercising a universal leadership — though at this time 'universal' does not stretch very far) says (*Ex. et Th.* 2.289), at this stage 'l'autorité est encore exercée d'une façon très démocratique'. Benoit also notes that James is not mentioned in this narrative, either as leader in Jerusalem or as having jurisdiction over a wider area.

1. The events described in ch. 10 became known in Jerusalem. According to W. D. Davies (*Land* 276) ἤκουσαν implies official cognizance. This may be a valid inference from the context but it is not supported by the common use of ἀκούειν itself. In Acts however cf. 8.14; 11.22; 15.24.

οἱ ἀπόστολοι καὶ οἱ ἀδελφοί together make up the whole church: its leaders together with the rank and file. For *apostles* see 1.2, 15–26; for *brothers* as a term for Christians see on 1.15. The whole body undertakes the task of examining the behaviour of the apostle (cf. Schweizer, *CONT* 5m and n. 281). κατά means simply *in* (BDR § 224, n. 1; classical and in papyri; cf. 24.12). There were (according to Acts) Christians outside Judaea, notably in Samaria and in Damascus; Luke is concerned with Judaea partly because this is where the church's origin, and no doubt its headquarters, were to be found, and partly because elsewhere the question would not have arisen in the same way.

For receiving (δέχεσθαι) the word of God, that is, receiving and accepting it so as to become believers, cf. 8.14 (Samaria); 17.11.

The first clause in the verse appears in D (syᵖ) in a somewhat different form: ἀκουστὸν (this word is not used elsewhere in the NT) δὲ ἐγένετο τοῖς ἀποστόλοις καὶ τοῖς ἀδελφοῖς ἐν τῇ Ἰουδαίᾳ. There is no difference in sense; this is probably part of the rewriting of which more appears in v. 2.

2. In due course Peter returned from Caesarea to Jerusalem, which evidently was still his base. ἀναβαίνειν is a natural word to use for a journey from the coast to Jerusalem (2500–2600 feet), but it was also used as a 'pilgrimage' word. Cf. 15.2; and perhaps 18.22. Peter found his actions in Caesarea the subject of dispute. διακρίνεσθαι is here used in a sense different from that of 10.20 (and from that of the active in 11.12; 15.9). Here, with πρός, it will mean *disputed, debated* (cf. Ezek. 20.35, διακριθήσομαι πρὸς ὑμᾶς; Herodotus 9.58.2, πρὸς τοὺς ἀψευδέως ἀρίστους ἀνθρώπων μάχῃ διακριθῆναι), though this meaning is not common. It is however not easy to distinguish it from the meaning *to reach a decision*, said to be illustrated in the *Epistle of Philip* (in the works of Demosthenes 12.17 (163)), σκοπεῖσθε πότερον κάλλιόν ἐστιν ὅπλοις ἢ λόγοις διακρίνεσθαι. It may be said that οἱ ἐκ περιτομῆς were seeking to reach a conclusion with Peter — by words, we may hope, not arms. For οἱ ἐκ περιτομῆς cf. 10.45, where πιστοί is added. The same word must be understood here; they are among the apostles and brothers of v. 1. They must be Jews, but cannot be understood as men who insisted on circumcision for all (as apparently do οἱ ἐκ περιτομῆς in Gal. 2.12); Peter's companions in 10.45 are surprised but raise no objection, and Peter's story convinces those of 11.2; see v. 18. They cannot be God-fearers for if there were such persons in Jerusalem they had not at this stage been baptized (Bauernfeind 152). According to Conzelmann, for Luke they are the whole

Jerusalem church. Wilson (*Law* 73) raises the question whether they are the minority group of 15.5 (and thus not equivalent to the apostles and brothers) or the whole Jewish leadership; if they were the former, he says, v. 18 may be understood as on their part a tactical silence. There is a sense in which Hanson is right in saying that the term is an anachronism: at this time the whole church was a 'circumcision party', in that all its members were circumcised. But this does not mean that all equally were advocates of circumcision for all.

The verse appears in a longer form in D (p w mae): ὁ μὲν οὖν Πέτρος διὰ ἱκανοῦ χρόνου ἠθέλησε πορευθῆναι εἰς Ἱεροσόλυμα· καὶ προσφωνήσας τοὺς ἀδελφοὺς καὶ ἐπιστηρίξας αὐτούς, πολὺν λόγον ποιούμενος, διὰ τῶν χωρῶν διδάσκων αὐτούς· ὃς καὶ κατήντησεν αὐτοῖς καὶ ἀπήγγειλεν αὐτοῖς τὴν χάριν τοῦ θεοῦ. In this variant, μὲν οὖν is an expression very characteristic of Acts (see on 1.6); ἱκανός of time occurs eight times in Acts (twice in Luke, once in the rest of the NT); προσφωνεῖν occurs twice in Acts (four times in Luke, once in the rest of the NT); ἐπιστηρίζειν is in the NT peculiar to Acts; κατανταν occurs nine times in Acts, four times in the rest of the NT. Thus the language of the variant is Lucan; this however may mean no more than that it was written by an editor familiar with the vocabulary of Acts. It is hard to see any theological or ecclesiastical interest in it (it can hardly be said to make a serious defence of Peter); it is free storytelling by one who liked to embroider. Clark (xxiv, 347) thinks it may have been original and omitted by homoeoteleuton (τοῦ θεοῦ (v. 1) . . . τοῦ θεοῦ).

3. ὅτι may introduce direct speech (either, *You went in . . .* or *Did you go in . . .?*) or be used (instead of τί) for *Why? (Why did you go in . . .?).* This latter use of ὅτι with the meaning Why? occurs in Mk 2.16 (probably); 9.11, 28; possibly in Lk. 15.2; 19.7. It is, according to LS (1263b) 'rare and late'. The example of ὅτι = warum? given by BA (1192), Josephus, *Ant.* 12.213 seems to contain an indirect rather than a direct question and is therefore not a valid parallel. See also Athenagoras, 34.1 (ὅτι ἂν εἴποιμι τὰ ἀπόρρητα). There is a probable example in Jer. 2.36 (where Rahlfs reads τί κατέφρονησας . . ., against the MSS, which have ὅτι) and it is worthwhile to note 1 Chron. 17.6, where Rahlfs takes ὅτι as introducing a statement but the parallel in 2 Kdms 7.7 has τί ὅτι (Why?). LS (1263; s.v. ὅστις)have a somewhat doubtful quotation from Apollonius Dyscolus, *Adv.* 140.12. There is an excellent note in *Begs.* 4.124 (on which Moule, *IB* 132, 159, looks with some favour), but it concludes, 'Possibly this curious construction should be regarded as not strictly an interrogative, but the enunciation of a difficult or surprising statement followed by "what about it?"

understood,' and since the direct statement, which becomes a possibly aggressive assertion ('You went in . . .') makes good sense it is better to suppose that Luke (unlike Mark) avoided a use of ὅτι with no precedent in good Greek style.

εἰσῆλθες πρός appears to be a short form of saying, You went into their house (BDR § 239. 2, n. 2); this would have been unclean; and συνέφαγες would imply at least the risk of eating unclean food — possibly no more than the risk, since Cornelius as a Godfearing man, well thought of by Jews (10.2, 22), would hardly present a Jewish guest with what he knew to be objectionable food, but adversaries bent on making objections would press the possibility; with Gentiles you never know. The accusation is thus that Peter voluntarily and unnecessarily entered into an association that can hardly have failed to produce some measure of uncleanness. Preaching to a Gentile would not do this; and the uncleanness incurred could be removed. It is to be noted that the objectors do not raise the question of the admission of Gentiles to the Christian church (though this is what is accepted in v. 18). They speak as Jews to a Jew who has entered into social relations with a Gentile. They may have argued, 'Ein Dienst Jesu, der zu "verbotenen" (10.28) Handlungen führt, kann nicht wahrer Dienst Jesu sein!' (Bauernfeind 152). Bauernfeind adds that the followers of James (Gal. 2.12) probably said the same to Peter. The word ἀκροβυστία occurs here only in Acts, elsewhere in the NT only in the Pauline corpus. The expression ἀκροβυστίαν ἔχειν, for to be uncircumcised, occurs here only. The complaint is put in the third person (εἰσῆλθεν . . . συνέφαγεν) by P⁴⁵ B L 33 36 81 453 614 1175 al syᵖʰ. This reading is probably due to failure to see that ὅτι was introducing direct speech (or a direct question). The second person is read by P⁷⁴ᵛⁱᵈ ℵ A D E Ψ 𝔐 945 1739 pc latt syʰᵐᵍ co, and is probably correct.

4. Peter's answer was simply to relate what had happened; as the Lucan narrative unfolds it is this relation that takes the event out of the area of Judaism (Why did Peter eat with Gentiles on Gentile premises?) and into that of developing Christianity (May Gentiles become Christians, and if so on what terms?).

ἀρξάμενος . . . ἐξετίθετο can hardly be explained as an inversion ('Umkehrung') of the more usual finite mood of ἄρχεσθαι coupled with an infinitive (e.g. 1.1, ἤρξατο ποιεῖν), though BDR § 308. 2 seem to suggest this. It is better to classify the clause with such constructions as φθάσαντες δὲ οὗτοι τὸ ἱερὸν καταλαμβάνουσι (Josephus, Ant. 14.58: they anticipated and took, that is, they acted first and took). The construction is Hellenistic (see Radermacher 168f., quoting also Xenophon of Ephesus, 388, 31: ἐκεῖθεν ἀρξαμένη ἄλλοτε ἄλλως ὑπὸ τῆς συμφορᾶς κατέχομαι), a Lucanism rather than a Semitism (Wilcox 148f.). BDR § 419. 3, n. 3 point out that ἀρξάμενος is strictly pleonastic, but make the suggestion that it may be related to and affected by καθεξῆς (*in a row*, that is, *in order* — in place of the more usual ἐφέξης). Peter set out the relevant events in order, *beginning with* ... The order is mainly chronological but the intention is primarily logical.

The narrative that follows is closely related to and often verbally repeats that of ch. 10. On the whole, the notes here will be confined to noting differences between the two accounts, whose existence proves how important Luke considered the event to be.

5. See 9.43 (Joppa); 10.9, 10, 11. Peter omits the roof, the hour of prayer, his hunger, and the preparation of a meal. Here he is ἐν ἐκστάσει whereas in ch. 10 an ἔκστασις came upon him: no difference is intended. Here the word ὅραμα is borrowed from 10.17; reference to the opening of heaven is omitted, but the σκεῦος (p, splendidum magnum; sy^hmg, magnum) is let down *from heaven* rather than *upon the earth* (10.11). The present verse adds καὶ ἦλθεν ἄχρι ἐμοῦ.

6. εἰς ἥν ἀτενίσας gives a neat and Lucan connection; ἀτενίζειν is a Lucan word (Lk., twice; Acts ten times; 2 Cor. twice), and connections by means of a relative are frequent in Acts. Luke is probably here providing his own summary of a narrative he had earlier given in substantially traditional form. κατανοεῖν also is Lucan (Lk., four times; Acts, four times; rest of the NT, six times). Imperfect is followed by aorist: I was considering it and then I saw (Page 151). The contents of the vessel here include θηρία, not mentioned in 10.12, but the relation between the two verses is complicated by textual variants. See the note on 10.12; here the ἑρπετά are omitted by D*. This however is probably an accidental error due to homoeoteleuton (καὶ τά ... καὶ τά).

7. ἤκουσα) is introduced, so that φωνή now appears in the genitive (accusative in D). The command appears in the same words as in 10.13.

8. Peter's reply is in substance the same as in ch. 10 but the wording is different. The essential words, κοινόν, ἀκάθαρτον, are retained, but whereas in 10.14 Peter says that he has never eaten (ἔφαγον) such things, here he says that they have never entered his mouth. This expression (a Hebraism; cf. especially Ezek. 4.14, οὐδὲ εἰσελήλυθεν εἰς τὸ στόμα μου πᾶν κρέας ἕωλον) occurs nowhere else in Luke or Acts; it is interesting that it occurs in the discussion of clean and unclean foods in Mt. (15.11, 17; not Mk), a passage that has no parallel in Luke.

9. There is considerable textual variation in the opening words of the verse, probably given correctly by P⁴⁵ P⁷⁴ ℵ A 81 945 1739 *pc*: ἀπεκρίθη δὲ φωνὴ ἐκ δευτέρου ἐκ τοῦ οὐρανοῦ. Instead of ἀπεκρίθη, D has ἐγένετο (10.15 has no verb). E Ψ 𝔐 include μοι and D has πρός με. There are some variations in order. The words of the voice agree with 10.15.

10. This verse corresponds closely with 10.16. εὐθύς is omitted and πάλιν is added. For ἀνελήμφθη, ἀνεσπάσθη (the only other occurrence of this word in the NT is at Lk 14.5) is substituted. For τὸ σκεῦος, ἅπαντα (not only the vessel but the animals contained in it) is substituted.

11, 12a. These verses sum up 10.17–23a. Naturally Peter describes the event from his point of view, saying nothing, for example, about the messengers' inquiry for Simon the Tanner's house and their appearance at his door.

ἰδού is paralleled in 10.17, 19. ἐξαυτῆς is used at 10.33, but this is in a different context. τρεῖς ἄνδρες occurs (in reverse order) at 10.19. ἐπέστησαν occurs at 10.17, but with ἐπὶ τὸν πυλῶνα, not ἐπὶ τὴν οἰκίαν. ἐν ᾗ ἦμεν is a conveniently brief way of specifying the house, and it is not surprising that P⁴⁵ E Ψ 𝔐 lat sy co, interested in Peter to the exclusion of others, write ἤμην; P⁷⁴ ℵ A B D 6 *pc* are right with ἦμεν. Who *we* are is not clear; possibly Simon Peter and Simon the Tanner (and those who prepared the meal), but more probably Simon Peter and the colleagues mentioned at v. 12 and at 10.23, 45. ἀπεσταλμένοι ἀπὸ Καισαρείας πρός με sums up the story of the messengers. εἶπεν δὲ τὸ πνεῦνά μοι corresponds to εἶπεν αὐτῷ τὸ πνεῦμα (10.19). The Spirit's command is given in indirect speech, and συνελθεῖν αὐτοῖς replaces πορεύου σὺν αὐτοῖς (10.20). μηδὲν διακρίναντα replaces μηδὲν διακρινόμενος but may have a different meaning. The middle διακρινόμενος means (see on 10.20) *not doubting, not hesitating*. The active διακρίνας can hardly mean this; we must translate, *making no distinction* (between Jew and Gentile). This is the way in which Luke uses the word at 15.9; he is probably here rewriting the tradition that he follows in ch. 10. It is worth noting that 𝔐 has μηδὲν διακρινόμενον (as in 10.20), P⁷⁴ μηδὲν ἀνακρίναντα (*making no inquiry*; cf. 1 Cor. 10.25, 27); the two words are omitted by P⁴⁵ᵛⁱᵈ D l p* syʰ. The difficult text of ℵ ⁽*⁾ A B (E Ψ) 33 81 945 1175 1739 *al* should be followed.

12b. corresponds to 10.23b. *Some of the brothers from Joppa* have now become *these* (because present and ready to take part in the discussion) *six* (the number is added) *brothers*.

We (Peter and his six companions) *entered* (εἰσήλθομεν, cf. εἰσελθεῖν, 10.25) *into the man's house* (εἰς τὸν οἶκον τοῦ ἀνδρός). Peter thus admits the first part of the charge in v. 3 (εἰσῆλθες πρός); but he does not tell the story well, for so far he has not mentioned any *man*: we do not know whose house he entered, or what sort of man the owner was. Peter knew that he was a Gentile centurion (10.22); his hearers must have known it too — that or something of the kind is implied in their charge. But, as reported in ch. 11, Peter has given them no details. Should we conclude that Peter thought it unimportant that Cornelius was φοβούμενος τὸν θεόν?

13, 14. The unnamed ἀνήρ proceeds to tell his story. These verses abbreviate 10.30–33. With a minimum of detail Cornelius (still unnamed) tells of his angelic visitor. τὸν (omit P⁴⁵ D Ψ) ἄγγελον ought (like τοῦ ἀνδρός in v. 12) to be anaphoric, but there is no antecedent reference (except in ch. 10, which serves the reader well enough but not the Jerusalem audience) — a further mark (cf. v. 12) of carelessness on the writer's part. The angel *stood* (σταθέντα, corresponding to ἔυ ιη in 10.30) and *said* (εἰ ιιόν ι α, corresponding to φησίν in 10.31) . . . Cornelius, as reported, omits the complimentary reference to his prayers and almsgiving. ἀπόστειλον εἰς 'Ιόππην corresponds to πέμψον οὖν εἰς 'Ιόππην (10.32). μετάπεμψαι τὸν Σίμωνα τὸν ἐπικαλούμενον Πέτρον corresponds to μετακάλεσαι Σίμωνα ὃς ἐπικαλεῖται Πέτρος (10.32; μετακαλεῖσθαι occurs four times in Acts, μεταπέμπεσθαι eight times). Cf. 10.5. In ch. 10 the angel gives no hint about what Peter will say when he visits Cornelius. Cornelius expects him to speak (10.33, ἀκοῦσαι); here he expects a message (ῥήματα) of salvation. How Luke understands salvation (see also 4.12) becomes clear in what follows: Cornelius receives the Holy Spirit and is baptized into membership of the people of God.

Not only Cornelius himself but his *household* (οἶκος) will be saved. For the meaning of this term see on 10.2.

15. ἐν τῷ ἄρξασθαί με λαλεῖν, *as I began to speak* (BDR § 404. 1, n. 3), does not agree precisely with ἔτι λαλοῦντος τοῦ Πέτρου (10.44), even if ἄρχεσθαι is used in Semitic fashion as an auxiliary (e.g. Bruce 1.233), and neither statement agrees with the fact that Peter had already completed the usual content of the proclamation characteristic of the early chapters of Acts; see on 10.44. ἐπέπεσεν τὸ πνεῦμα τὸ ἅγιον ἐπ' αὐτούς agrees very closely with 10.44; see the notes on that verse, and for ὥσπερ καὶ ἐφ' ἡμᾶς see 10.47. Here ἐν ἀρχῇ is added to make the parallel with the event of Pentecost more emphatic. The divine initiative has placed Cornelius and his colleagues in the same position as the Christian leaders in ch. 2.

16. The conclusion drawn by Peter in 10.47 is that baptism with water may be immediately conferred. Since this cannot be intended as a means of conferring the Holy Spirit it is presumably thought of as the means of entry into the redeemed, forgiven, community — a privilege for which those who already have the Spirit are evidently qualified. If this is how baptism is thought of Schweizer's view is not necessarily correct: 'Vor allem wird in 11.16f., was wegen der Parallele 1.5 doch wohl lukanische Formulierung ist, die Taufe (10.47f.) nicht mehr erwähnt, ja eigentlich nach V. 16 logisch ausgeschlossen' (*Beiträge* 78). Schweizer is certainly correct in saying that baptism, though fairly frequently mentioned, is not central in Luke's thought, and it is fair comment that Luke has no consistent doctrine of baptism. His use of the Lord's saying, quoted also in 1.5 (see the note, including the reference to Braun) with only a slight variation in word order, leaves the reader in doubt whether Christian baptism called for the use of water (though 8.36; 10.47 make it quite clear that Luke was familiar with a Christian rite in which water was used as it was in John's). The difference between the simple dative ὕδατι and ἐν with the dative πνεύματι may be merely stylistic, as *Begs.* 4.126 suggests; Moule (*IB* 77) is disposed to question this (ἐν may be instrumental; cf. Eph. 5.18), but he does not develop the point. See further the general discussion in Vol. II.

The saying is introduced by the words ἐμνήσθην τοῦ ῥήματος: see the note on the remembering formula and the part it may have played in the collection of sayings of Jesus by Robinson in *Trajectories* 96f. Cf. 20.35; Lk. 22.61; Jn 15.20; 1 Clem. 13.1–2; 46.7–8; Polycarp, *Phil.* 2.3. The saying in question appears to go back to John the Baptist (Lk. 3.16); defective memory, and new applications of the material, may have led to misattribution of some sayings.

17. repeats the argument of 10.47 but in rather different terms. It is set in the form of a conditional sentence, in which the protasis restates the content of v. 15. *If God gave them the like gift as (he gave) to us*: the construction with ἴσος and ὡς is classical; see BDR § 453. 4, n. 7, referring to K.-G. I 413 11. πιστεύσασιν, dative plural, could be taken with αὐτοῖς or with the nearer ἡμῖν. If Luke was thinking logically the former is the better choice, but 'Both in grammar and sense πιστ. seems properly taken both with αὐτοῖς and ἡμῖν' (Page 151). *Belief* is not mentioned in ch. 10, but one may reasonably suppose that the reaction to Peter's address was belief in Jesus; Peter and his fellow apostles had believed in Jesus long before the day of Pentecost. It was when Cornelius and his friends believed that they received the gift of the Holy Spirit.

If this was so, the apodosis, expressed as a question, follows. τίς is here a predicate (BDR § 298. 5): *I was — who?* Cf. 4 Kdms. 8.13; Lucian, *Demonax* 12 (ἠρώτα τὸν Δημώνακτα, τίς ὢν χλευάζοι τὰ αὐτοῦ;). BDR § 131 give examples where the neuter τί is used in a similar way. κωλύειν with the accusative of a person is *to hinder, prevent*. It is not well used here. Peter could have forbidden the use of water, that is, the baptism of Cornelius (10.47); he could not prevent God from doing what he intended to do, still less could he prevent God from doing what he had already done (in giving the Spirit). The general sense however is clear: God had made plain his intention; who was I to act in a contrary fashion? A variant in D w (p sy^h** mae) underlines the bad logic by adding at the end of the verse, τοῦ μὴ δοῦναι αὐτοῖς πνεῦμα ἅγιον πιστεύσασιν ἐπ' αὐτῷ. Page 151 points out that the question is really a double one: (1) Who was I that I should . . .? and (2) Was I able to . . .?

18. ἀκούσαντες . . . ἡσύχασαν: the subject must be οἱ ἐκ περιτομῆς of v. 2, who brought the complaint of v. 3. Their objection was silenced by the spontaneous action of God who thereby showed that he approved of what Peter had done. There was no gainsaying this. On the contrary, they glorified God, that is, gave him thanks for what he had done (cf. 4.21; 21.20), though it may be that we should refer to Josh. 7.19 (δὸς δόξαν . . . τῷ κυρίῳ; שׂים־נא כבוד ליהוה where a similar expression is usually taken to mean, Admit the truth.

The complainants do not say, You were after all justified in going into a Gentile house and eating there (though this is implied); they make the much fuller statement, Why then (ἄρα, in later usage 'always with inferential force', but in drawing conclusions 'more subjective than οὖν' (LS 232)), to the Gentiles also God has given that repentance that leads to life (ζωή, that is, salvation; cf. 5.20; 13.46, 48). Delebecque (56) takes the verse as a question. 'Tiens? même aux païens, la conversion spirituelle en vue de la vie, Dieu la leur a donnée?' Taking the conclusion of the paragraph in this interrogative, or at least hesitant sense, might solve some problems in the interpretation of ch. 15. The article τοῖς makes it clear that the reference is not to Cornelius and his friends alone but to *the Gentiles*, as a class; and repentance and life have been given to them as they are. It would make nonsense of the verse if it were supposed that the speakers were saying that God has granted them repentance and salvation on the assumption that they will now be circumcised. God has accepted Gentiles as Gentiles, and there is no hint that they should be circumcised. This fact causes problems when ch. 15 is borne in mind; see the introduction to the present section and, in Vol. II, the introduction to ch. 15 and the general discussion. It might seem that the whole question of the Gentile mission had now been settled, at least in principle.

For the connection between repentance and life (salvation, the forgiveness of sins) cf. 2.38; 3.19; 26.20; 5.31 (τῷ Ἰσραήλ); 20.21.

There is no immediate connection with what follows, in which a new beginning of the Gentile mission is described.

VII
THE CHURCH FOUNDED AT ANTIOCH
AND APPROVED BY JERUSALEM (11.19–30)

29. FOUNDATION OF THE CHURCH AT ANTIOCH 11.19–26.

(19) Those who had been scattered by the persecution that arose on account of Stephen went on their way as far as Phoenicia, Cyprus, and Antioch, speaking the word to none but Jews only. (20) But there were some of them, men from Cyprus and Cyrene, who when they came to Antioch spoke also to the Hellenists, as they told the good news of the Lord Jesus. (21) The hand of the Lord was with them, and a large number who believed turned to the Lord. (22) The report about them came to the ears of the church that was in Jerusalem, and they sent out Barnabas to make his way to Antioch. (23) When he arrived and saw that the grace of God was at work[1] he rejoiced, and exhorted them all to continue with the Lord in the purpose of their hearts, (24) for he was a good man, and full of the Holy Spirit and of faith. And a considerable number was added to the church. (25) Barnabas[2] went off to Tarsus to seek out Saul, (26) and when he had found him brought him to Antioch. It now[3] happened that they met[4] in the church for as much as a whole year[5] and taught a considerable company, and that in Antioch for the first time the disciples came to bear the name of Christians.

Bibliography

E. J. Bickermann, *HThR* 42 (1949), 109–24.

C. Burchard, *ZNW* 69 (1978), 143–57.

W. Grundmann, *ZNW* 39 (1940), 110–37.

C. H. Kraeling, *JBL* 51 (1932), 130–60.

B. Lifshitz, *VigCh* 16 (1962), 65–70.

H. B. Mattingly, *JTS* 9 (1958), 26–37.

W. Michaelis, *ZNW* 30 (1931), 83–9.

[1]Literally, saw the grace of God.
[2]Greek, he.
[3]Now is not in the Greek.
[4]*Begs.*, were entertained.
[5]Greek, even a whole year.

P. Parker, *JBL* 83 (1964), 165-70.

E. Peterson, *Studi e Testi* 121 (1946), 355-72.

C. Spicq, *StTh* 15 (1961), 68-78.

Commentary

In 10.1-11.18 we have heard what appears to be the story (edited and expanded by Luke) of the beginning of the mission to Gentiles. This is located in Caesarea. In the new paragraph we have a second account of what may equally be taken to be the beginning of the mission to Gentiles. It is located in Antioch. It is in no way surprising that there should be two such stories. At some time, whether in the manner in which Luke describes it or not, a church arose in Caesarea, some of whose members were not Jews and did not become Jews (by circumcision). At some time, whether as Luke describes it or not, a similarly mixed Christian group came into being at Antioch (as is confirmed by Galatians). It cannot be doubted that these churches came into being: but even if Luke's accounts accurately describe exactly what happened (and this of course is open to inquiry) we cannot be certain which event happened first; there is no need to suppose that either church knew how or when — or even that — the other was founded. It may have recalled something of the manner of its own foundation without knowing the date.

The foundation at Antioch is ascribed to οἱ διασπαρέντες: the term looks back to 8.4 and 8.1, and refers to the Christians who were dispersed by the persecution that arose in consequence of Stephen's martyrdom. Those whom we may, in dependence on 6.1, call Hellenists (but see pp. 307-309) were Jews, and, as we have seen, faithful Jews, and they did not at first extend their mission to the Gentiles. Eventually they did so, with the (probably astonishing and disturbing) result that a large number turned to the Lord. It was important to Luke (and it may be that it was important also to the Jewish evangelists) that this development should not be and should not appear to be a new independent piece of religious enthusiasm. It must be, and be seen to be, a valid expression, result, and continuation of the work of Jesus. In historical terms this could be tested only by Jerusalem, which still housed the apostles who represented and maintained the link between the historical Jesus and the post-resurrection consequences of his work (1.21f.). Jerusalem saw the necessity for this and responded to it by sending Barnabas (4.36f.; 9.27) on a mission of inquiry. He was more than satisfied; took part in the work and went off to Tarsus to look for Saul (9.30). The two took up residence in Antioch and became leading members of an established and flourishing church.

The paragraph contains a number of Lucan expressions (see

especially vv. 19, 21, 24) and is by its opening words fitted into the Lucan narrative framework. It has been described as a Lucan summary (e.g. Schille 262; cf. *Begs.* 4.127), but it differs from the earlier summaries (2.42–47; 4.32–35; 5.12–16) in that it contains specific rather than merely generalized narrative. Its events are once-for-all events; even the year spent in Antioch by Paul and Barnabas is described by the aorist infinitive συναχθῆναι, which shows that Luke thought of it as a unit event in the story he is unfolding. Luke's hand may be seen at work, but he is not so much constructing a summary as editing a tradition (written or oral). It is unlikely that he made it up himself. The work of the scattered evangelists in Cyprus (v. 19) anticipates the work on the island of Paul and Barnabas (13.4–12); their approach to non-Jews is told without reference to the Cornelius story and would scarcely have been allowed by Luke writing freely to precede the arrival of Paul (vv. 20, 25f.). Luke would probably have had Barnabas sent by the apostles, whom he had been careful to leave in Jerusalem (8.1). Luke then has traditional material at his disposal and it is probable that he collected it in Antioch, or at least through Antiochene contacts.

Bauernfeind (154) correctly points out that argumenta e silentio ought not to be based on this passage; for example, it ought not to be inferred that, because they are not mentioned, the conversion of non-Jews provoked no discussions about the law, circumcision, table fellowship and the like; and he is almost certainly right in making one exception to his own proposition. The passage opens immediately, with no attempt to date the events it describes; this probably means that Luke did not intend to assert that they happened after the events in Caesarea recounted in 10.1–18. His Caesarean story raised the issues involved in the acceptance of Gentile converts and included a discussion of these issues in Jerusalem; the Antioch story did not. Luke wished however to include the latter because one of his major interests was the extension of the gospel to the Gentile world and he made it his business to collect as much information on the subject as he could find. Antioch provided him with the interesting record of men who 'ohne offizielle Sendung, ohne Organisation, ohne Programm' (Stählin 162) extended their preaching beyond its original Jewish audience. It was important to Luke (see above) to show that this new development (like that in Caesarea) was not an independent innovation but was based on the original Jerusalem Gospel and those who could guarantee its connection with Jesus. Since in the narrative as we have it this is done in two ways it is probable that the connection was already made in the Antiochene tradition on which Luke drew. On the one hand, the evangelists are said to be those who, originating in Jerusalem and bearing the stamp of the Twelve's approval (6.1–6), had been driven out on account of the persecution connected with the death of Stephen. On the other hand, once the innovation had been made, the Jerusalem church, hearing of it, sent an envoy, Barnabas, who first satisfied himself that the work was of God and then joined in it. Each of these assertions prompts a literary and a historical question.

The reference (v. 19) to *those who had been scattered* (οἱ διασπαρέντες) is clearly linked with 8.1, 4, and thus with the martyrdom of Stephen, the appointment of Stephen and his six colleagues, and the division and dispute between Hebrews and Hellenists in the Jerusalem church. These events have been held (see pp. 54f.) to form the components of an Antiochene source. In recent years this source theory has been severely criticised (see pp. 55f.) and it is hardly possible now to hold it in the form given to it by Harnack and later by Jeremias. The story, however, may well represent Luke's own edited version of a belief cherished in Antioch: We have our own direct link with the martyrs and confessors of the earliest church. The church of Antioch is proved by Galatians to have been one of very early foundation, and its belief that it was founded from Jerusalem is probably correct. The view that Antioch was evangelized from Galilee, and that the 'Hellenists' came not to but from Antioch is criticized by Wilson (*Gentiles* 147; see the whole discussion).

From the literary point of view, Barnabas, whose visit to Antioch bears a superficial resemblance to the visit of Peter and John to Samaria (8.14), may be Luke's own contribution. Luke believed, rightly (see Gal. 2.13), that Barnabas had connections with Antioch, and with Paul in Antioch, and knew that he had to bring the two together in preparation for 11.27–30; 12.24f.; 13.1–3. The introduction of Barnabas as given here may then simply be Luke's own construction, and it has been questioned whether the church in Jerusalem did carry out visits of inspection. But Luke at least had something to build on. Gal. 2.12 proves that at least one official or semi-official visitation of Antioch did take place, and there is good reason to think that Judaizers based on Jerusalem moved about the Pauline churches. To what extent these anti-pauline missions had official backing is a difficult question, not to be discussed at this point. Luke refers to another Jewish Christian visit to Antioch in 15.1, and may have confused accounts of different missions; see on ch. 15 and the general discussion in Vol. II. If Luke did conjecture a visit at this point he was writing within the bounds of probability. That there was in Antioch a mixed church which Paul had not himself founded seems clear, and that Luke used Antiochene traditions is very probable. But he has modified the traditional source, and he has shown his hand by a use of the word *Hellenist* that is inconsistent with the use of it in 6.1 and 9.29. In any reconstruction of sources and of history it must always be borne in mind that Antioch is solid reality, a real place with real people, 'the Hellenists' a speculative idea to which Luke and modern historians have both contributed. Antioch has an assured place in history; whether 'the Hellenists' have is another question.

Haenchen (357) has a different view of Barnabas. 'In Wirklichkeit aber haben wir damit zu rechnen (Bauernfeind hat es in seiner zurückhaltenden Art schon S. 155 angedeutet), dass Barnabas einer der διασπαρέντες war und zusammen mit Lucius von Cyrene und einigen andern Männern die antiochenische Heidenmission begann.' There is little evidence to support this view. In fact, though the witness of Acts is complicated by the fact that Luke seems to regard Paul and Barnabas as standing in succession from Stephen, Barnabas seems on the whole to belong to 'the Hebrews' rather than to 'the Hellenists'. Certainly Gal. 2.13 shows him falling in with the followers of James in opposition to Paul. See further on v. 22.

It is in this passage that Luke notes the earliest use of the term Christian (v. 26). If he is correct in his statement that this word was first used in Antioch the fact casts a little more light on the constitution of the Antiochene church, for the new designation was probably needed when it first became apparent that the believers, who had left their old Gentile way of life, were no more Jews than they were heathen — in fact, a third race, Christians. Haenchen (358) rightly points out that this was a development that caused both social and religious problems. If they were not Jews they could not claim the status of a religio licita; if they were not Jews, their relation with the OT, with the law and the prophets, was thrown into question. Throughout the rest of the book, as previously, the claim is repeatedly emphasised that Christianity is the true form of Judaism, the heir of the OT promises.

19. μὲν οὖν is one of Luke's ways of beginning a new paragraph; see on 1.6. For οἱ μὲν οὖν διασπαρέντες see 8.4; here as there Luke points back to 8.1, διεσπάρησαν; if these are Lucan editorial notes so will this verse be (Weiser 275). The reference is made explicit in the words that follow, ἀπὸ τῆς θλίψεως τῆς γενομένης ἐπὶ Στεφάνῳ. Here ἀπό has been claimed as a Semitism, reflecting the use of the Hebrew (and Aramaic) מן. But this causal use of ἀπό is both classical (e.g. Thucydides 1.24.2; 4.30.1) and vernacular (M. 2.461). The affliction, caused by persecution, arose on account of Stephen, ἐπὶ Στεφάνῳ. This is the reading of ℵ B 𝔐; the reading of D, ἀπὸ τοῦ Στεφάνου, will require the same translation, but that of P⁷⁴ A E Ψ 6 33ᵛⁱᵈ pc, ἐπὶ Στεφάνου, is at the time, on the occasion, of (the death of) Stephen (BDR §§ 234. 5; 235. 2). The reading of ℵ B is to be preferred.

διῆλθον looks at the journey as a whole; λαλοῦντες describes the way in which it was conducted: it was a preaching mission; cf. 8.4, διῆλθον εὐαγγελιζόμενοι τὸν λόγον. διέρχεσθαι without addition sometimes suggests such a journey; see e.g. 13.6.

Phoenicia was not an 'official', provincial name, but denoted the narrow coastal plain between the Lebanon and the Mediterranean. It is mentioned as early as Homer (*Odyssey* 4.83, Κύπρον Φοινίκην τε καὶ Αἰγυπτίους ἐπαληθείς . . .). It included Sidon (Josephus, *Ant.* 1.138), Tyre, and Byblos. The Phoenicians were well known as a trading people, and as founders of Carthage. See Acts 12.20; 21.3, 7; 27.3. *Cyprus* was visited by Paul, whose visit with Barnabas is described (13.4) as if it were the first by Christian missionaries; this leads Weiser 274 to conclude that the present reference must be a piece of pre-lucan tradition. This may be so, but the argument is not strong; the clash (if such it be) was one that could easily have escaped Luke's notice. See also 4.36; 15.39; 21.3, 16; 27.4. In the NT period, and for long afterwards, Cyprus was a minor senatorial province. It had passed under Roman rule in 58 BC when it was attached to the province of Cilicia. Julius Caesar gave it to Cleopatra; Augustus after Actium took it back. It lies in the north eastern corner of the Mediterranean and occupies about 3500 square miles. From Cyprus (if Luke is giving us a connected account of their movements — he does not say that he is doing so) the scattered Christians made their way back to the mainland and reached *Antioch*, undoubtedly one of the most important cities of antiquity (according to Josephus, *War* 3.29, the third city in the Roman world), though founded as late as 300 BC by Seleucus I and bearing a name based on that of many of the Seleucid house (Antiochus I was the son of Seleucus I). It lay about fifteen miles inland, on the left bank of the Orontes (Strabo, *Geogr.* 16.2.4; Pliny, *Nat. Hist.* 5.79). Nearby was Daphne, 'a park . . . dedicated by Seleucus I to the royal gods, especially Apollo' (A. H. M. Jones, in *OCD*, 313). Its moral reputation was bad; Juvenal in a famous line describes the evil influence of the east on the west in the image, 'Syrus in Tiberim defluxit Orontes' (*Sat.* 3.62). There were many Jews in Antioch, and they received many privileges from its founder (Josephus, *Ant.* 12.119, 120; *Apion* 2.39). A similar reference to royal patronage in *War* 7.43–45 has led some to speak of good relations between Jews and Greeks in the city; 7.46–53 gives a different impression. There is a lively account of Antioch in Mommsen, *Provinces* 2.126–135; see now W. A. Meeks and R. L. Wilken, *Jews and Christians in Antioch*, 1978; *NS* 3.13; G. Downey, *A History of Antioch in Syria*, 1961.

On their way to and at first in Antioch the dispersed Christians *spoke the word* (τὸν λόγον is evidently the Christian message — common Lucan usage) to Jews only. This restriction was not to continue. 'To the Jew first, and also to the Greek' was a principle not discovered for the first time by Paul.

20. ἐξ αὐτῶν, *of them*, of those who had been scattered from

Jerusalem. These cannot be thought of as simply the six who were left after the death of Stephen, and they were hardly (in spite of 8.1) all the Jerusalem Christians apart from the Twelve. We may say that they were the Hellenists provided that we recognize that the word in itself solves no problems and raises quite a number. See above. These persons (if, as we must, we connect them with 8.1) were normally resident in Jerusalem but some of them at least were not of Palestinian origin. Some were *men of Cyprus* (see above, p. 549), others *men of Cyrene*. Cyrene itself is mentioned at 2.10 and the adjective Κυρηναῖος is used at 6.9; 11.20; 13.1. See *NS* 3.60–62, noting that the passages in Acts may 'indicate the region of Cyrenaica rather than the city of Cyrene itself' (61) and that 'in *Cyrenaica*, which was settled by Greeks in the seventh century BC, and remained Greek-speaking, Jews were very strongly represented' (60). These Cypriotes and Cyrenaeans spoke not only to Jews but also to Gentiles. Weiser (274) is probably right in claiming that this must be pre-lucan tradition; after giving the Cornelius story Luke would not have invented it. At this point a formidable textual and linguistic problem arises. That the context demands a reference to non-Jews is certain: the contrast between εἰ μὴ μόνον . . . and καὶ πρός puts this beyond doubt. 'That contrast surely forces one to explain it [the word after πρὸς τούς] of Gentiles' (Calvin 328). In B Dᶜ E Ψ 𝔐 the persons evangelized are Ἑλληνιστάς; in P⁷⁴ ℵᶜ A D* they are Ἕλληνας. ℵ* has the certainly incorrect εὐαγγελιστάς — certainly incorrect, but it may point to an original Ἑλληνιστάς affected by the following word, εὐαγγελιζόμενοι. The Latin VSS have *ad Graecos*, as at 6.1 they have *Graecorum*; the evidence of the VSS is of no importance here. The textual question is bound up with the question of the meaning of the very unusual word Ἑλληνιστής. It appears to be used differently at 6.1 (where the Ἑλληνισταί are apparently Christian) and at 9.29 (where they are not Christian). It is thus by no means impossible that the word should have a third meaning here: at 6.1, Greek-speaking Jewish Christians; at 9.29, Greek-speaking Jews; at 11.20, Greek-speaking Gentiles (probably not natives of Greece, who would more naturally be Ἕλληνες). Luke undoubtedly drew on sources, written or oral, and the word may have been used in different ways in different sources. If this explanation is adopted an interesting consequence follows. 6.1 and 11.20 are not both drawn from the same Antiochene source. This conclusion may of course refer only to 6.1 (not to 6.2–6 and the appointment of the Seven); this verse may be Luke's own writing, and this would carry with it the conclusion that the Hellenists as a party are his invention. See on 6.1 and 9.29, and the general discussion in Vol. II.

Ἑλληνιστάς may thus refer to the non-Jewish, Greek-speaking inhabitants of Antioch, and it seems likely that this is what Luke wrote and meant, the copyists of P⁷⁴ D* and a few others changing this to "Ἕλληνας because they remembered the meaning of Ἑλληνισταί in 6.1 and 9.29 and could see from the context that in the present context Jews (even though they spoke Greek) could not be intended. Transcriptional probability is strongly on the side of Ἑλληνιστάς (similarly Metzger 388). Bauernfeind (153) and others argue that Luke cannot have written Ἑλληνιστάς because for him this word meant something that he did not in this context intend to say. The argument loses weight because Luke has already used the word in two senses, and it fails to meet the transcriptional argument.

εὐαγγελίζεσθαι may take the accusative of the (divine) person proclaimed (5.42; 8.35; 11.20; 17.18), the accusative of the message (8.4; 10.36 (εἰρήνην); 13.32 (ἐπαγγελίαν); 15.35; 17.18), the accusative of the persons to whom the Gospel is addressed (8.25 (κώμας), 40 (πόλεις); 13.32; 14.15, 21 (πόλιν); 16.10), the dative of the persons addressed (8.35), πρός and the accusative of the persons addressed (11.20), περί with the message (8.12), or no complement at all (14.7). The word was virtually a Christian invention and was still unstandardized. None of the uses found in Acts creates any difficulty.

At the end of the verse the Western text characteristically fills out the sacred name, adding Χριστόν (D 33ᵛⁱᵈ *pc* w mae).

21. That the new step was successful is expressed by Luke in one of his 'biblical' phrases. There are partial parallels at 4.28, 30; 13.11, but the only true parallel in the NT is at Lk 1.66 (χεὶρ κυρίου ἦν μετ'αὐτοῦ — John the Baptist). Cf. e.g. 3 Kdms 18.46 (χεὶρ κυρίου ἐπὶ τὸν Ἠλίου — in the OT *upon* is used rather than *with* — Luke is imitating rather than quoting or translating.

ἀριθμός as a noun of multitude is a Lucan expression, used here and at 4.4; 5.36; 6.7; 16.5. It is naturally followed by the singular participle and verb. The article ὁ is omitted by D E Ψ 𝔐, but should be read: *a large number who believed (became believers) turned*, not *a large number believed and turned*. For ἐπιστρέφειν cf. 3.19; 9.35; 14.15; 15.19; 26.18, 20; 28.27. At 9.35; 14.15; 15.19; 26.20 it is followed by ἐπί.

22. News of the conversion of the Hellenists reached Jerusalem. Cf. 11.1; but here a different expression is used. The passive of ἀκούειν occurs here only in Acts, and nowhere else with εἰς τὰ ὦτα (if ears are referred to, ἐν τοῖς ὠσίν is more usual). In the OT men speak in the ears of others, but the only close parallel seems to be Isa. 5.9 (ἠκούσθη γὰρ εἰς τὰ ὦτα κυρίου σαβαὼθ ταῦτα). Again Luke appears to be imitating rather than translating or quoting. On the Semitic background of the phrase see Black (*AA* 300). λόγος now means *report*, not (as in v. 19) the Gospel message.

οὔσης is unnecessary if Luke means no more than 'the church that was in Jerusalem'. It cannot however be taken as ἡ οὖσα in 5.17: 'the local church in Jerusalem' would hardly make sense. Delebecque overtranslates with 'la vivante Église'. We must be content to note that Luke has written one more word than necessary.

The word ἐκκλησία has not been used since 9.31; it will be used again at v. 26 and at 13.1; 14.23, 27. If there was a source that recounted the beginnings of Christianity in Antioch and its expansion from that base we may conclude that the Christians in Antioch described their community by this word.

ἐκκλησία as a noun of multitude takes the plural verb ἐξαπέστειλαν. The Christians in Jerusalem (apostles are not mentioned) sent Barnabas to Antioch. The use of ἕως as an improper preposition is Hellenistic (BDR § 216. 3, n. 10). Luke clearly understands Barnabas (chosen perhaps as a fellow Cypriote) to have been sent as an official inspector on behalf of Jerusalem, charged to see what was going on in Antioch and presumably if necessary to put an end to it. Both Bultmann (*Theologie* 65) and Hahn (*Mission* 62) think this mistaken. At 11.30; 12.25 Barnabas appears as a delegate from Antioch to Jerusalem, and 13.1 shows him as a leading member of the church in Antioch. He was (so Bultmann) one of the Hellenists who had been driven out of Jerusalem and helped to found the church in Antioch. It is not easy to see any substantial grounds for this conjecture; see above, p. 548. In 4.36, 37 Barnabas appears as a very early and very generous member of the Jerusalem church; he is not mentioned in ch. 6; in 9.27 he is able to introduce Paul to the apostles in Jerusalem. In the end (Gal. 2.13) Barnabas sided with the Judaizing separatists, but he appears as a Pauline colleague in 1 Cor. 9.6.

Barnabas was sent, according to the long text, διελθεῖν to Antioch. For the word, see on v. 19; it is possible that if it is to be read here it may have the meaning, *to pass through on a tour of investigation or inspection*; cf. 9.32. The word is omitted by P[74] ℵ A B 81 1739 *pc* vg sy[p] bo.

23. ὅς, as a relative, connects with Barnabas in the previous sentence, but in fact it is used virtually as if it were a demonstrative: He, when he arrived, . . .: a characteristic Lucan (Acts) expression. Barnabas saw what was going on, but it is described not in human terms but as the grace of God. It was this that caused the conversion of the Hellenists. τὴν χάριν τοῦ θεοῦ is the reading of P[74] D E Ψ 𝔐; τήν is inserted before τοῦ by ℵ A B *pc*. This addition may reflect only an itch for correctness; the adjectival phrase should be preceded by the article; it is however hard not to feel a certain predicative sense in the expression: he saw the gracious work that was going on and was obliged to recognize that it was of God.

χάριν . . . ἐχάρη, paronomasia, a probable sign of composition in

Greek (rather than translation of a Semitic original). For παρακαλεῖν (an allusion to Barnabas's name (4.36)?) see on 2.40. Here it must mean *exhort*. There is a similar use of προσμένειν at 13.43; in addition 18.18, together with Mt. 15.32 = Mk 8.2; 1 Tim. 1.3; 5.5, shows that the meaning is *stay on, continue*. The MSS that add ἐν before τῷ κυρίῳ (B Ψ *pc*) give the sense: they are to continue in their relation (of faith, v. 21) to the Lord; this indicates the objective direction of their continuance. Its subjective character is given by the other dative, τῇ προθέσει (cf. 2 Tim. 3.10) τῆς καρδίας, *in heart-felt purpose*. This has been described as a biblical expression (Schille 263), reference being made to Ps. 10.17 (Symmachus). This however appears to be the only biblical reference available, and one reference to Symmachus is scarcely enough. The suggestion *with determination* (*Begs.* 4.129) may say all that is needed.

Barnabas is here acting as an apostle of the Jerusalem church (*Begs.* 4.129, with reference to ἐξαπέστειλαν in v. 22). Haenchen objects to the use of the term apostle (352), but adds 'Barnabas wird als bevollmächtigter Beauftragter Jerusalems gedacht sein.' *Bevollmächtigter Beauftragter* seems to be an excellent rendering into German of the Hebrew שליח!

24. Barnabas so decided, acted, and spoke *because he was a good man and full of the Holy Spirit and faith*. To Luke it was so evident that Gentiles must be included in the Christian mission that he was convinced that any good and honest Christian must approve of the step taken in Antioch; those who, in Antioch and Jerusalem, took the view recorded in 15.1, 5 had small chance of a favourable comment from him. It would, however, be wrong to conclude that, even if mistaken, they were not sincere in their opinion. It is only to Barnabas that the adjective ἀγαθός is applied in Acts (cf. 9.36, πλήρης ἔργων ἀγαθῶν; 23.1, συνειδήσει ἀγαθῇ; cf. Lk. 23.50, where the adjective is applied to Joseph of Arimathaea); the word may well have been found in Luke's source. Cf. Josephus, *Ant.* 12.358; 18.117, ἀγαθὸν ἄνδρα (John the Baptist); also Thucydides 5.9.6. *Full of the Holy Spirit and of faith*, another Lucanism, has its closest parallel in the description of Stephen at 6.5, where the terms are reversed; this parallel may be not insignificant. Cf. also 6.3, 8. Luke also uses πλήρης in the opposite (bad) sense: 13.10; 19.28.

The result of the whole process — approach to the Gentiles and the visit of Barnabas — was (as is usual in Acts) an increase in the number of believers. For προσετέθη cf. 2.41, 47; 5.14 (with the notes); the word is characteristic of the first part of Acts. ἱκανός also is a characteristically Lucan word (Lk., nine times; Acts, eighteen times; rest of the NT, thirteen times). It is used again with ὄχλος at v. 26; 19.26.

25. ἐξῆλθεν δὲ εἰς Ταρσόν. At 9.30 Saul, whom the Hellenists were seeking to kill, was sent, presumably for his safety, to Tarsus, according to 22.3 his native place. See on 9.11. Previously Barnabas had convinced the apostles that Saul was a genuine Christian and no *agent provocateur*; he had done this because he knew and was able to report that Saul had seen and spoken with the Lord and in Damascus had spoken boldly in the name of Jesus (9.27). After this, Saul had continued in Jerusalem to speak boldly in the name of the Lord (9.28) and had engaged in disputation with the Hellenists (9.29). In the narrative as presented to us in Acts this provides the necessary link with the present passage: Barnabas knew Saul to be not only a bold evangelist but one who specialized in dealing with Hellenists. This would constitute good reason for Barnabas's visit to Tarsus to seek out (ἀναζητῆσαι; according to MM 32f. the word is used for searching for human beings, with an implication of difficulty (so Delebecque 57); here only in Acts; in the rest of the NT only Lk. 2.44, 45) Saul. There are however problems in this simple connection; they may be said to focus on the word Hellenist. This (see above) seems to be used in different senses in the two passages and one or both may be Luke's own creation; there is also 6.1 to bear in mind, and the fact that Luke (see the notes on ch. 15 in Vol. II) seems to hold the view that Paul and Barnabas at the Council represented the 'Hellenist' position (the position of Stephen). That there was a special relation between Paul and Barnabas, however, is not to be doubted; the evidence of Acts (which includes the account, unlikely to be invented though possibly modified, of a rift between the two, 15.36–41) is supplemented by that of the epistles; see 1 Cor. 9.6; Gal. 2.1, 9; cf. Col. 4.10. Gal. 2.13 is particularly important: *even* Barnabas was carried away. This verse also connects both men with Antioch. That the connection between Saul, Barnabas, and Antioch existed is certain; if it did not come about in the way described by Acts we do not know how it originated.

At this point there arises a serious problem in the dating of Paul's movements. It seems that only about a year intervened between Paul's arrival in Antioch and his visit to Jerusalem described in 11.30. If this is correct, and if this is the visit to Jerusalem mentioned in Gal. 2.1, Paul must have been in, or at least based on, Tarsus for ten years or more. The matter cannot be discussed until data have been collected from passages already considered and from 11.27–30; 12.24f.; 15; and from Galatians.

Verse 25 and the first words of v. 26 appear in a different form in the Western text: ἀκούσας ὅτι Σαῦλός ἐστιν εἰς Θαρσὸν ἐξῆλθεν ἀναζητῶν αὐτόν, καὶ ὡς συντυχὼν παρεκάλεσεν ἐλθεῖν εἰς Ἀντιόχειαν (D (gig p* sy^hmg) mae). This gives substantially the same sense as the Old Uncial text, though it suggests that information about Saul's whereabouts had been brought to Barnabas who did not go so much to look for him as to ask him to come with him to Antioch. Probably the Western editor thought that this made better sense than a speculative journey; he may have forgotten 9.30. He also makes Saul more of a free agent; in the Old Uncial text Barnabas brings him to Antioch, in the Western text he asks Saul to come.

26. See the previous note for the text of the first clause. The textual confusion continues. In D, supported to some extent by g p sy[hmg], the rest of the verse runs: οἵτινες παραγενόμενοι ἐνιαυτὸν ὅλον συνεχύθησαν ὄχλον ἱκανόν, καὶ τότε πρῶτον ἐχρημάτισαν ἐν ᾽Αντιοχείᾳ οἱ μαθηταὶ Χρειστιανοί. The construction differs somewhat; reference to the church (ἐν τῇ ἐκκλησίᾳ) disappears and (possibly a related change) συναχθῆναι is replaced by συνεχύθησαν. There is no serious difficulty in the Old Uncial text (ἐγένετο . . . ἱκανόν) though καί (omitted by 𝔐 before ἐνιαυτόν) is surprising: *even a whole year.* But that Paul and Barnabas stayed for a year in a place where there was so much to do, and that they taught (Stählin takes this to include their work as missionaries) many people (ὄχλον ἱκανόν) seems natural enough. The Western text is given by Metzger (390) as, '. . . When they had come, for a whole year a large company of people were stirred up . . .'. This is clearly not a translation; in order to obtain it we have to turn ὄχλον ἱκανόν into the nominative and take it as the (plural equivalent) subject of συνεχύθησαν. This however would leave οἵτινες παραγενόμενοι in the air, a difficulty with which Metzger does not deal. It can hardly be maintained that the Western text is original, but it may stand at least as near to the original as the Old Uncial does. Ropes (*Begs.* 3.108) thinks that συνεχύθησεν (-αν) may be the original for which συναχθῆναι has been substituted in other MSS.

The meaning of συναχθῆναι is disputed. Schille (264) says that it 'meint terminologisch den Gottesdienst'; cf. the word Synagogue. *Begs.* 4.130 suggests the meaning 'were entertained' — as guests; cf. Mt. 25.35ff.; Deut. 22.2. This translation Haenchen (363) describes as impossible; it is not easy to see why. The fact is that the church (so far as it is described in other NT documents) was a body both social and liturgical. Nothing is more natural than that Saul and Barnabas should be given board and lodging by their fellow Christians and should also join them in their meetings. They were 'hospitably received in the Ecclesia' (F. J. A. Hort, *The Christian Ecclesia*, 1914, 61). συναχθῆναι and διδάξαι must be taken as constative aorists, looking at the year's work as a single whole. See M. 3.72; BDR § 332. 2, n. 3 ('Auch wiederholte Handlungen stehen im Aorist, wenn die Wiederholung summiert und begrenzt ist'); Zerwick § 253.

χρηματίζειν. 'In later writers, from Polybius downwards, the active χρηματίζω takes some special senses: 1. *to take and bear a title* or *name, to be called* or *styled* so and so' (LS 2005, s.v. III). Many examples can be given. Schille 265 says that the passive shows that the title arose without rather than within the church; the verb is in fact active in form, but it may well be true (see below) that the title was not produced by the Christians themselves. πρώτως is used as an adverb from Aristotle; πρῶτον (and πρῶτα) are used as far back as Homer. πρῶτον is read here by P⁷⁴ (Dᶜ) E Ψ 𝔐. See M. 2.163; Rutherford, *Phrynichus* 366.

Χριστιανοί. Χρειστιανοί and Χρηστιανοί are simply spelling variants, the latter interesting in that it illustrates the possibility that *Chresto* in Suetonius, *Claudius* 25 may be an error for *Christo*. The origin of the term *Christian* is obscure. The suggestion (Richardson, *Theology* 357) that it arose because Christians were anointed with the Holy Spirit may safely be set aside. The ending *-ianus* is Latin, and could never be used to suggest *anointed*; the nearest to this that is conceivable is *adherents of the Anointed One*, which indeed it does mean, though in its formation *Christus* has almost certainly become a proper name. Analogies are such party names as *Caesariani, Galbiani, Pompeiani, Augustiani*. It is interesting also to note the *Herodians* of Mt. 22.16; Mk 3.6; 12.13, but too little is known of them; they may have been not partisans but the household, slaves and freedmen, of Herod. In an important article (*JTS* 9 (1958), 26–37), H. B. Mattingly pursues the connection with the Augustiani of Nero's time. These functioned as Nero's claque, who attended his athletic and histrionic performances and manifested (whether or not they felt) wild enthusiasm for the great — divine — man. Mattingly connects the giving of the name by the Antiochene populace with the visit to Antioch of Nero's general Corbulo in AD 60. 'From Antioch the name would soon pass to Rome and by AD 64 it was current among the common people' (Mattingly 32, quoting Tacitus, *Annals* 15.44, quos . . . vulgus Christianos appellabat). Rebutting the charge of incendiarism against himself, Nero charged the Christians with arson. 'Was this not a brutally ironic way of making these rivals of his *Augustiani* ministers to his artistic ambitions?' (Mattingly 35). All this could be true, though Hemer (177) is 'not persuaded'. Luke does not say that the name Χριστιανοί originated in Antioch at the time of the one-year ministry of Saul and Barnabas; and if he thought this (as the context suggests that he did) he may have been mistaken. It seems probable however that the name was used (possibly in an attack on Christians) in Pompeii between the earthquake of AD 62 and the destruction of the town in AD 79. It probably appears in a graffito published in *CIL* 4.679, and discussed in detail by E. Dinkler (*Signum Crucis* 138–41). This does not help us to determine the origin of the name or its original meaning. It is a not unreasonable suggestion that it reflects a situation in which Christians were becoming numerous and were clearly distinguishable from Jews. They might call themselves μαθηταί (as in this verse), or πιστεύοντες, or, in relation to one another, ἀδελφοί. These words were useless to outsiders unless it was made clear whose disciples they were, in whom they believed, in whose family they were brothers. *Christiani* was a clear and useful term which the *vulgus* (Tacitus, above) could easily take up, though (to judge from Tacitus, who may have written *Chrestianos;* see K. Weiss in *TWNT* 9.473, n. 11, with references) they mistakenly pronounced *e* whereas the better informed knew that the *auctor nominis eius* was *Christus.* The addition of a Latin termination to a Greek name would be no hindrance. The same was done with *-inus, -anus,* and *-enus* as with *-ianus.* See M. 2.359f.

There is a long note in Haenchen (363f.); see also BA 1768, and Grundmann in *TWNT* 9.529. The word recalls the party slogan of 1 Cor. 1.12; it is however unlikely that it arose internally, whether as a party designation or as a label for Christians in general. The earliest use of Χριστιανός as a Christian self-designation is by Ignatius (*Eph.* 11.2; *Rom.* 3.2; *Magn.* 10.3; *Pol.* 7.3). For other early occurrences see Pliny, *Epistles* 10.96; Suetonius, *Nero* 16.2; Lucian, *Alexander* 25; 38; *Peregrinus* 11, 12, 13, 16.

30. THE CHURCH AT ANTIOCH INDEPENDENT 11.27–30

(27) In these days prophets came down from Jerusalem to Antioch. (28) One of them, Agabus by name, stood up and declared through the Spirit that there was to be a great famine over the whole inhabited earth; this happened in the time of Claudius. (29) Each of the disciples, as he prospered, determined to send[1] to the brothers who lived in Judaea. (30) This in fact they did, in that they sent to the elders by the hand of Barnabas and Saul.

Bibliography

F. W. Beare, *JBL* 63 (1944), 407–9.

P. Benoit, *Ex. et Th.* 3.285–99.

J. Dupont, *Études*, 163–5.

J. Dupont, *Nouvelles Études*, 157–63.

E. E. Ellis, *FS* Bruce (1970), 55–67.

R. W. Funk, *JBL* 75 (1956), 130–6.

K. S. Gapp, *HThR* 28 (1935), 258–65.

St. Giet, *RevScR* 25 (1951), 265–69.

J. Jeremias, *ZNW* 27 (1928), 98–103.

H. Patch, *ThZ* 28 (1972), 228–32.

D. F. Robinson, *JBL* 63 (1944), 169–72, 411f.

G. Strecker, *ZNW* 53 (1962), 67–77.

A. Strobel, *ZNW* 49 (1958), 131–4.

C. H. Talbert, *NovT* 9 (1967), 26–40.

Commentary

This small paragraph marks in Luke's narrative an important stage in the development of the church of Antioch — a stage which was to lead to even more important developments (13.1–3). The church owed its foundation to Jerusalem in two senses: the original missionaries, who had taken the daring step of preaching the Gospel to Gentiles, had come from Jerusalem, dispersed by the persecution that arose

---

[1]That is, to send aid; RSV, NJB, to send relief.

over Stephen (11.19); and the Jerusalem church, represented by its envoy Barnabas, had approved of what had been done (11.22f.). It now as an adult child was able and willing to care for its mother in her need. This proved both its independence and a continuing relationship.

The core of this paragraph was probably drawn from Antiochene tradition: it was the sort of thing the church would be glad to remember. See below, p.560. The Antiochene memory may well have included the reference to Barnabas and Saul. That both were closely connected with Antioch is proved by Gal. 2.13, and Acts 15.1–5, whether it is regarded as an account of a separate event or as a doublet of this one, confirms the picture of a sending of the two from Antioch to Jerusalem. The narrative builds up towards the commissioning in 13.1–3. It seems, however, that at some stage (possibly under Luke's hand but perhaps previously) a prophecy of a famine in Judaea was developed into a world-wide famine, and it may be that Luke, who knew of Agabus (21.20), introduced him as a representative prophet; the later reference, however, is in a We-passage and it may be that Agabus himself supplied the information. It is unlikely that Luke noticed that he seemed to be introducing prophecy into Antioch and the presbyterate into Jerusalem. He was himself familiar with both prophets and elders and took them for granted. His reference to Claudius betrays the hand of one who was writing towards the close of the century and could look back to the 'time of Claudius' (fourteen years in fact) as a relatively small period. 'The mention of Claudius may be taken as an implication (*a*) that the prophecy was made before the time of Claudius, (*b*) that the author was writing after his reign' (*Begs.* 4.131). Luke also shows awareness of what Christian charity had become since the early days when Christians were prepared to sell off their assets. What he describes here is the method employed by Paul in his collection (cf. 1 Cor. 16.2, ὅ τι ἐὰν εὐοδῶται; 2 Cor. 9.7, καθὼς προῄρηται). It is thus incorrect to say (Schweizer, *Beiträge* 74) that Luke has substituted this voluntary relief work for Paul's collection because the latter resembled too closely the Jewish Temple tax. The virtual disappearance of Paul's collection from Acts is better explained by K. F. Nickle (*The Collection*, 1966, 148–51) as due to the fact that it might have seemed illegal.

A further visit of Paul and Barnabas to Jerusalem is described in Acts 15. That these two visits are in fact one visit may be accepted with confidence in the sense that ch. 15 corresponds with Gal. 2.1–10 and that Gal. 2.1–10 was only the second visit of the Christian Paul to Jerusalem. The relation between Acts 15 and Galatians 2 will be considered in the discussion (in Vol. II) of Acts 15, but it is inconceivable that Paul should have been so foolish (not to say so untruthful) as to omit in the controversial epistle to Galatia a visit of which his adversaries could have made good use. Whether the identity of 11.27–30 and ch. 15 is due to Luke's handling of a source or sources, as was believed by Harnack (*Acts* 196–200) and more recently by Jeremias (*ZNW* 36 (1937), 205–21), is another matter. It would be a neat solution — but perhaps too neat a solution — of the problem if Luke had two sources, one of which dwelt on the question of circumcision and conditions of table fellowship between Jewish and Gentile Christians, the other on the organization and discharge of charitable relief. The two themes both appear in Galatians 2, and, notwithstanding Haenchen (363), it is possible (though by no means certain) that Gal. 2.10 means that Paul had on that very occasion been actively engaged in bringing relief to the poor in Jerusalem (see e.g. Lightfoot, *Galatians* 110f.). If Luke saw, or heard, two accounts of a Jerusalem meeting, one of which dealt with one, the other with the other aspect of the conference business, he might have mistakenly supposed that the two accounts referred to two conferences not one. It is however against this suggestion that in Galatians 2 relief for the poor is mentioned if not as a stipulation at least as a very firm request made by the authorities in Jerusalem; in Acts it is a spontaneous gesture on the part of the Christians in Antioch, stimulated but hardly demanded by Agabus's prophecy. The true explanation may well be more complicated.

Analysis of ch. 15 must wait; there seems to be some probability in the view that 11.27–30 was put together by Luke (whose style appears at several points) on the basis of several strands of tradition. Weiser (275), for example, mentions three pieces of tradition which he thinks that Luke put together in his own editorial framework. (1) It was known that an early prophet called Agabus had foretold a great famine. (2) It was known that Saul (Paul) had been responsible for bringing to Jerusalem the proceeds of a collection. (3) It was known that the direction of the church in Jerusalem had passed into the hands of a body of elders (though Luke shows no awareness of how this came to be). Somewhat similar points are made by other writers (e.g. Haenchen 361–5; Roloff 181f.; Schneider 2.94; and see especially G. Strecker, *ZNW* 53 (1962), 67–77). These suggestions make a valuable contribution to the analysis of the paragraph. What they fail to recognize, in addition to the hand of Luke which can here and there with some probability be seen, is the Antiochian interest in the whole. That which gives unity to the two sections (29: 11.19–26 and 30: 11.27–30) is the story of Antioch as it originates in Jerusalem and returns to Jerusalem. The extension of the Gospel to the Gentiles, the problems this causes, and the resolution of these problems, are major Lucan interests, which Luke pursued wherever he could find them. There was material to be had in Antioch, though (unfortunately, Luke probably thought) it was not attached to such interesting persons and events as that which he found in Caesarea.

On the date of the 'famine visit', which Antioch, perhaps not too precisely, remembered, see pp. 563–5.

27. ἐν ταύταις δὲ ταῖς ἡμέραις is a vague note of time. It refers most naturally to the year spent in Antioch by Barnabas and Saul (11.26), but could be understood of a later time. We do not know when the disciples were first called Christians (11.26b); this may be a note referring to a different period. Black (*AA* 99; cf. Wilcox 129f.) observes that for ταύταις, D has αὐταῖς and thinks that this may be a genuine Semitism, αὐταῖς representing the Aramaic proleptic pronoun. Cf. the readings of D at 6.7; 7.52. This is possible; a decision depends on whether there is sufficient evidence to suggest that the Western text as a whole has a Semitic base.

κατῆλθον, the usual verb for leaving the capital city. προφῆται: the first reference in Acts to Christian prophets; see 13.1; 15.32; 21.10; cf. 2.17, 18; 19.6; 21.9. For wandering prophets at more or less the period at which Acts was written cf. *Didache* 11.7ff. For early Christian prophecy see E. E. Ellis (in *FS* Bruce (1970), 55–67); D. Hill, *NT Prophecy* (London, 1979); D. E. Aune, *Prophecy in Early Christianity and the Ancient Mediterranean World*, 1983; and among older books E. Fascher, ΠΡΟΦΗΤΗΣ (Giessen, 1927). In the present passage, and at 21.10, the prophets foretell the future. This role is not mentioned at 15.32, and in the Pauline epistles (1 Cor. 12.28, 29; 14.29, 32, 37) it seems that, inspired by the Spirit, the prophets speak the word of God to the congregations. There is of course no reason why this should not on occasion include revelation of the future. The prophets mentioned here are not native Antiochene Christians but have come from Jerusalem; contrast 13.1, though it is easy to imagine that a visit from Jerusalem had the effect of establishing prophecy as a local phenomenon. From his account of Pentecost onwards Luke has assumed that the Jerusalem church experienced spiritual activities, possibly because he supposed that the mother church of all Christendom must have manifested every kind of true Christian life. This may be why he introduced Jerusalem prophets here, but it seems an inadequate reason. They are probably to be linked with the fact that aid was sent from Antioch to Jerusalem. If the famine was in fact universal no church would have been in a position to send help to any other; it seems best therefore to suppose that in v. 28 (see the note) Luke has heightened the description of the famine by including the words ἐφ' ὅλην τὴν οἰκουμένην and that originally the Jerusalem prophets (including Agabus, who in 21.20 also comes from Judaea) foretold a famine in Jerusalem, or Judaea. This could well have led the relatively fortunate Antiochenes to send help southward. If the famine appeared imminent a reason immediately appears for a visit from Jerusalem to Antioch: the prophets were appealing for help. This may be the answer to Haenchen's question

(361), Why should the Jerusalem prophets visit the capital of Syria? It may not, however, be necessary to find logical reasons for the movements of migrant charismatics; moreover, if Antioch at this time was a *Sündenbabel* Christian evangelists might have taken this as good reason rather for paying a visit than for staying away.

28. Luke's own account is clear. The prophets (Schille 266 thinks that originally only Agabus was mentioned) have been prophesying, that is, edifying the community by their inspired speech, and one of them in particular rises up to make his inspired prediction. ἀναστάς is not quite superfluous, as it is in some other passages (e.g. 10.13, 20); in a seated company the prophet rises to speak. He speaks διὰ τοῦ πνεύματος; this differs little from saying that the Spirit speaks through him. What he says is occasioned by the Spirit and has the Spirit's authority. The prophet in question is *one of them*, that is, one of those who have come down from Jerusalem. He is a single member of a group; it does not seem necessary to see in the use of εἷς an Aramaism, where the Aramaic חד should have been rendered by τις (Black, *AA* 104–106). Agabus is mentioned, again as a predictive prophet, at 21.10; nothing else is known of him. The Greek ῎Αγαβος presumably represents a Semitic name but it is not certain what the Semitic form may have been. Ezra 2.45 refers to Hagabah (חגבה), 2.46 to Hagab (חגב), which appear in the LXX as Αγαβα, Αγαβ. The Hebrew חגב means *locust*. An alternative possibility is suggested by the occurrence in a Palmyrene inscription (*Répertoire d'épigraphie sémitique* II (1914), No. 1086) of the female name עגבה (in Syriac עגב is *to lame, to paralyse*). NA²⁶ (probably with Ezra 2.46 in mind) print the name with a rough breathing and some commentators write Hagabus, but it does not seem worth while to change the traditional Agabus (so the Vulgate; Syriac spells the name with alaph). Agabus comes from Jerusalem and is found visiting both Antioch and Caesarea; he thus recalls the itinerant prophets of *Didache* 11. Luke will have met the name in tradition if he did not meet the man in person.

Agabus' intervention is described not by the verb προφητεύειν (which would have followed clumsily upon the noun) but by ἐσήμανεν (so, aorist, in P⁷⁴ ℵ A E 𝔐 gig; B (Ψ) d vg have the imperfect ἐσήμαινεν, without much difference in meaning; D, to fit the variant given below, has the participle σημαίνων). The word recurs at 25.27 in a different setting; cf. Jn 12.33; 18.32; 21.19 (all in the expression σημαίνων ποίῳ θανάτῳ . . .); Rev. 1.1. The word is used of oracles. The famous saying of Heraclitus (93 (11): ὁ ἄναξ, οὗ τὸ μαντεῖόν ἐστι τὸ ἐν Δελφοῖς, οὔτε λέγει οὔτε κρύπτει ἀλλὰ σημαίνει) is not particularly apt since here there is no question of concealment or half-concealment. Schille (266) is surely wrong with 'σημαίνειν . . . hat hier . . . den Sinn einer rätselhaften

Orakelrede'. Reference to the future is paralleled in Thucydides 2.8.2 (...ἐδόκει ἐπὶ τοῖς μέλλουσι γενήσεσθαι σημῆναι), but here, as against Acts, the reference is to a portent (an earthquake). For the sense of prediction see also Josephus, *Ant.* 6.50; 8.409. In fact the word is often used to mean simply '*signify, indicate, declare*' (LS 1592f.), and it means little more here.

The reference to the future is expressed by μέλλειν (omitted by P⁴⁵ P⁷⁴ 36 323 453 614 945 1739 *pc*) and the future infinitive. This use of the future infinitive is common in Classical Greek, but in the NT the present infinitive is used eighty-four times, the future three times (all in Acts), the aorist five or six times (including 12.6 (v. l.)); so M. 1.114; 3.79. What is to come is λιμὸς μεγάλη; for this use of the adjective cf. 4 Kdms 6.25; Thucydides 4.2.2; 8.56.1. The coming famine will apply ἐφ' ὅλην τὴν οἰκουμένην. οἰκουμένη (with which γῆ is understood) means *the inhabited land*, and *land* means as little or as much as the writer chooses (a particular country, the Greek world (excluding barbarians), the whole world, the Roman world   see LS 1205 s.v.). Luke (cf. 17.6, 31, 19.27; 24.5) probably thought of the whole world, though he may (see on v. 27) have exaggerated an original reference to a more local famine, perhaps in Judaea (see below). There is no need to see here (with Torrey, 18ff.) a misrendering of the Aramaic ארעא, which may refer to the world or to the land of Israel. As is shown above there is sufficient ambiguity in the Greek word without calling in Aramaic. See M.2.474.

At the end of the verse 'we seem to expect ἥπερ ἐγένετο' (M. 1.92), that is, ἥπερ would be used in Attic Greek, but ὅσπερ (*the very man who, the very thing which* — LS 1262) is not used in the NT. For ἐπί and the genitive, *in the time of*, see on 11.19.

Claudius was emperor from AD 41 to 54. There are several references to famines in his time. One is mentioned in passing by Josephus, *Ant.* 3.320 (Κλαυδίου Ῥωμαίων ἄρχοντος Ἰσμαήλου δὲ παρ' ἡμῖν ἀρχιερέως ὄντος, καὶ λιμοῦ τὴν χώραν ἡμῶν λαβόντος — the reference to Ishmael is presumably in error since he appears not to have become high priest till after the death of Claudius; alternatively, Claudius may be an error for Nero). More detail is given in *Ant.* 20.51–53, where Queen Helena of Adiabene is said to have relieved the poor, and more still in 20.101 (τὸν μέγαν λιμὸν κατὰ τὴν Ἰουδαίαν συνέβη γενέσθαι); the famine took place in the time of Tiberius Alexander, procurator AD 46–48 (for the reading and the date see Jeremias, *Jerusalem* 142). We should probably be right to think of the famine in the year 47, aggravated by the Sabbatical year which fell in 47-48 (Sotah 7.8, for the previous Sabbatical year). Cf. Hemer (164f.); he prefers to date the mission of Barnabas and Saul in A.D. 45-56. It is mistaken to claim that Luke dates the famine wrongly because 11.27-30 precedes the death of

Herod Agrippa I (12.23); what happens in 11.27 is not the famine but a prophecy that there will be a famine. It is possible that this is why Luke completes the story in 12.24, 25. To say this is not to claim that Luke had a precise and accurate notion of when the famine took place. For more detailed discussion, and possible references to the famine under Claudius in Yebamoth 15b; T. Sukkah 2.3.193; T. Eduyoth 2.2.457, see Jeremias (*Jerusalem* 141–3). For other references to hardship in the time of Claudius see Tacitus, *Annals* 12.43; Eusebius, *Chronicon* 181 (Helm); Orosius, 7.6.17; Dio Cassius 60.11; Suetonius, *Claudius* 18 (assiduae sterilitates). Several commentators (e.g. Bauernfeind 157; Stählin 164; Haenchen 111) think that what was intended (if not by Luke by his source or informant) was a prediction that the Messianic woes, including a famine, were about to begin. This is possible; for famine as part of the woes see Mk 13.8; Rev. 6.5f. But there is nothing in the text to suggest it. We should note Luke's interest in integrating the events of Christian history into secular history; cf. Lüdemann (141).

In the Western text the opening words of the verse appear as follows: ἦν δὲ πολλὴ ἀγαλλίασις· συνεστραμμένων δὲ ἡμῶν ἔφη εἷς ... σημαίνων ... (D (p w mae)). ἀγαλλίασις occurs at Lk. 1.14, 44; Acts 2.46; also at Heb. 1.9 (quoting Ps. 45.8); Jude 24; ἀγαλλιᾶσθαι is somewhat more common, and the notion of rejoicing among Christians occurs frequently (e.g. 2.46). Of greater interest here is the occurrence of the first personal pronoun with συνεστραμμένων; this (if the Western text is adopted) is the first of the 'We-passages'; see on 16.10, and the general discussion in Vol. II. Bultmann (*Exegetica* 421f.) argues that the Western reading may well be original, 'denn die Einbringung des "Wir" scheint mir als spätere redaktionelle Arbeit nicht verständlich zu sein' (422). Conzelmann (68) counters this with 'Doch! Nämlich die spätere Identifizierung des Lukas mit Lucius 13.1'. So also Schneider (2.96), and others. But was the Western editor so subtle? and so interested in this identification? It is perhaps a sufficient explanation that he saw here a way of making history livelier and of giving it greater authority. Bultmann thinks that 11.27–30 and 12.25 belonged to the Antiochene source and that it was written in We-style (op. cit. 423). Harnack (see Metzger 391) thought that the original Western text was συνεστραμμένων δὲ αὐτῶν, and that αὐτῶν was changed to ἡμῶν in order to avoid confusion with the αὐτῶν that follows. Clark (348) thinks it perverse of Ropes to say that the Bezan reviser introduced 'we' because he knew the tradition that Luke came from Antioch. The tradition, found in Eusebius and Jerome, was based on the NT, and was probably based on this passage in the Western form. This may be true even if the Western text is not the original. Klijn, *Survey* (1949), 20 and note 74, believes that this is a different 'we'.

29. The title *Christians* (11.26) is now dropped, and *disciples* comes back into use; see 9.26 and the note. There is no longer any suggestion of pooling capital (as at 2.44f.; 4.32, 34–37; 5.1–11). The Christians were engaging in business and some at least were prospering (εὐπορεῖτο, *had plenty*). καθώς is used in the sense of measure: *in proportion as any prospered.* Earlier usage has εὐπορεῖν, later (as here) εὐπορεῖσθαι. D improves a rather clumsy construction: οἱ δὲ μαθηταὶ καθὼς εὐποροῦντο ...

ὥρισαν ἕκαστος αὐτῶν. As at 2.6, ἕκαστος (singular) takes a plural verb; the construction is helped out by the plural μαθητῶν but goes back as far as Homer (e.g. *Iliad* 1.606, οἱ μὲν κακκείοντες ἔβαν οἰκόνδε ἕκαστος, they went *each* to his own home (LS 499f., s.v.); see also M. 3.312). ὁρίζειν is Lucan (Lk., once; Acts, five times; rest of the NT, twice); cf. Gen. 30.28 (Symmachus). Here it seems that each disciple was free to decide what he should do with his profits. This was how Paul conducted his collection; see e.g. 2 Cor. 9.7 (ἕκαστος καθὼς προήρηται ... μὴ ... ἐξ ἀνάγκης). According to Field (ad loc.) ὥρισαν must be connected with εἰς διακονίαν. 'The disciples, as every man had to spare, set apart each of them for a ministration to send unto the brethren, which dwelt in Judaea.' This seems to take πέμψαι as explanatory of εἰς διακονίαν; so also *Begs.* 4.131. This is better than taking πέμψαι as directly connected with ὥρισαν. Schneider (2.96) thinks that we must either supply *something (etwas)* as an object for πέμψαι, or use καθὼς εὐπορεῖτό τις (*eine Abgabe je nach Vermögen*). English (like Luke's Greek) seems able to dispense with an object. διακονία too is a Lucan word (in Acts, 1.17, 25; 6.1, 4; 12.25; 20.24; 21.29) but also recalls Paul's collection (Rom. 15.31; 1 Cor. 16.15; 2 Cor. 8.4; 9.1, 12, 13). Here it is service directed towards the brothers (Christians) who lived in Judaea (whence the prophets had come — they had probably prophesied and begged with reference not to the whole world but to the land of Israel).

30. The antecedent of ὅ is the preceding clause. ἀποστείλαντες is an aorist participle of coincident action: *This they did, in that they sent* ... It is not said that they sent their aid immediately; and Haenchen (360) notes that no reader would suspect the interval of several years between v. 29 and v. 30. This is true, but Haenchen assumes more than we know of what happened at this time. If the prophets arrived within a year or so (11.26, 27) of the founding of the church in Antioch, and if the famine and the relief visit took place in about AD 47, then there was a considerable interval of which Luke gives no hint. It is probable that there was a major famine in or near AD 47, but the other propositions are much more doubtful. We do not have evidence on the basis of which a year by year account of Antioch and of Jerusalem, and of the contacts between them, can be constructed. There may have been more coming and going than we are aware of — perhaps than Luke was aware of. Cf. Hengel (111f.).

Here Christian elders (πρεσβύτεροι) are mentioned for the first time, apparently as the officials who deal with financial (and doubtless also other) matters. See later 14.23; 15.2, 4, 6, 22, 23; 16.4; 20.17; 21.18. For Jewish πρεσβύτεροι see 2.17; 4.5, 8, 23; 6.12; 23.14; 24.1; 25.15. 'The Essenes had such "elders" too. In the ranks of the Qumran community the priests take precedence over the elders, as they meet in full assembly (1 QS 6.8). They take their place along with the priests and the Levites in pronouncing blessings and curses after the defeat of the enemy in the eschatological war (1 QM 13.1). In general, respect for them is inculcated (CD 9.4). But there is nothing to indicate that the elders of the Christian community were in any way a derivative of the Essene institution. Both communities derived the institution rather from Old Testament tradition, as Acts 2.17 and *Damascus Document* 5.4 would suggest' (Fitzmyer, *Essays* 295). *Elder* (זקן), however, does not seem to have been a regular religious or civil so much as an academic office. Zebahim 1.3; Yadaim 3.5; 4.2 refer to decisions of seventy-two elders, but these are members not of the Jerusalem Sanhedrin but of the Academy of Yabneh, as the contexts show (*NS* 2.210). The term was also used for the leading members of local synagagues (*NS* 2.427–433), and it is probably these that served as the pattern for the Christian institution.

For διὰ χειρός cf. 2.23. For Barnabas and Saul see 11.25f.; 12.25; 13 and 14 passim; 15.36–41. Luke makes it clear that they were now leading members of the Antiochene church; having been entrusted with a material commission they were later to be given a spiritual one. Here as a pair they resembled the pairs in which Jewish שליחים entrusted with the carrying of money were sent. The verb ἀποστέλλειν is too common to suggest a necessary connection with the Hebrew and Aramaic root שלח but for the sending of two envoys cf. the Jewish evidence cited in J. Jeremias, 'Paarweise Sendung im NT' (*FS* T. W. Manson, 136–43).

VIII
RETURN TO JERUSALEM (12.1–25)

31. JAMES, PETER, AND HEROD 12.1–23

(1)At that time King Herod laid his hands on some of those who belonged to the church so as to harm them.[1] (2) He killed James, the brother of John, with the sword. (3) When he saw that this was pleasing to the Jews he went on to arrest Peter also. These were the days of Unleavened Bread. (4) He seized Peter and put him in prison, handing him over to four squads of four soldiers each to guard him, with the intention of bringing him up to the people after Passover. (5) So then Peter was being kept in the prison, and prayer was being earnestly offered to God by the church on his behalf.

(6) When Herod was about to bring him forward, that night Peter was asleep between two soldiers, bound with two chains, and guards posted before the doors were keeping the prison. (7) And behold, an angel of the Lord came and stood over Peter[2] and light shone in the prison cell. He struck Peter's side and awakened him, saying, 'Get up quickly.' His chains fell from his hands, (8) and the angel said to him, 'Fasten your belt and put on your sandals.' He did so. The angel[3] said to him, 'Put on your cloak, and come with me.' (9) He went out and followed, and did not know that what was being done by the angel was true, but supposed that he was seeing a vision. (10) When they had passed through the first watch and the second they came to the iron gate that led to the city; this opened to them of its own accord. They went out and traversed one street, and immediately the angel left him. (11) Then Peter came to his right mind, and said, 'Now indeed I know that the Lord has sent his angel and rescued me out of the hand of Herod and from all that the people of the Jews were expecting.' (12) When he had considered this he went to the house of Mary, the mother of John called Mark, where many were assembled and praying. (13) He knocked at the door in the gateway and a girl called Rhoda came forward to answer the knock. (14) When she recognized Peter's voice she did not open the door for joy, but ran in to report that Peter was standing at the gateway. (15) But they said to her, 'You are mad.' She however persisted that it was so. They said, 'It is his angel.' (16) Peter went on knocking; when they opened the gate they saw him and were astonished. (17) Peter motioned to them to be quiet, and recounted to them how the Lord had brought him out of the prison, and said,

---

[1]*Begs.*, attempted to ill-treat.
[2]In Greek the name is not expressed.
[3]Greek, he.

'Report these things to James and the brothers.' Then he went out, and went to another place.

(18) When day broke there was no small confusion among the soldiers as they wondered what had become of Peter. (19) When Herod looked for him and did not find him he examined the guards and ordered them to be led off for punishment. He went down from Judaea to Caesarea and stayed there.

(20) He was angry with the Tyrians and Sidonians. Together they presented themselves before him, and having got Blastus, the king's chamberlain, on their side, they asked for peace, because their country was supplied by that of the king. (21) On an appointed day, Herod put on royal robes, sat on the tribune, and addressed them. (22) The assembly called out, 'The voice of a god, not of a man!' (23) Immediately the angel of the Lord struck him down, because he did not give God the glory. He was eaten by worms and expired.

Bibliography

P. Benoit, *Ex. et Th.* 4. 311–46.

J. Blinzler, *NovT* 5 (1962), 191–206

A. Böhlig, *NovT* 5 (1962), 207–13.

O. Cullmann, *RechScR* 60 (1972), 55–68.

J. Dupont, *Études*, 217–41.

J. Dupont, *Nouvelles Études*, 157–63, 329–42.

M. Hengel, *FS* Kümmel (1985), 71–104.

B. T. Holmes, *JBL* 54 (1935), 63–72.

J. H. Moulton, *JTS* 3 (1902), 514–27.

Eb. Nestle, as in (13).

W. K. Prentice, *FS* Johnson, 144–51.

D. F. Robinson, *JBL* 64 (1945), 255–67.

A. Strobel, *NTS* 4 (1958), 210–15.

M. R. Strom, *NTS* 32 (1986), 289–92.

C. P. Thiede, *Bib* 67 (1986), 532–8.

A. Vögeli, as in (14).

E. Zuckschwerdt, *ZNW* 68 (1977), 276–87.

Commentary

This paragraph, not distinctively Lucan in style (a fact noted, and perhaps somewhat overstated, by Haenchen 376), is more easily detachable from the main thread of narrative in Acts than any other. Verse 25 could follow immediately upon 11.27–30. Plümacher, who makes much of Luke's Episodenstil, rightly describes vv. 1–19 as 'eine dramatische Episode' (110). It is therefore the more important first of all to ask what purpose it seemed to Luke to serve. The contents are (a) the death of James, as part of an attack on the church by Herod (vv. 1, 2); (b) the arrest and escape of Peter (vv. 3–19); (c) the fate of Herod (vv. 20–23).

It is hard to see how the progress of Luke's story is affected by (a). Apart from Peter (occasionally accompanied by his shadow, John), the twelve apostles do nothing but exist, so that — as far as Luke's narrative goes — the loss of one of them would hardly make any difference. It is perhaps significant that whereas the place of the defecting Judas had to be filled (1.15–26) we hear nothing of any attempt to fill the place of James, but if this is intended to make the point that there is a difference between treachery and martyrdom we can say only that Luke must have thought the point so obvious (as indeed it is) that he saw no need to make it explicit. He may have thought it time to bring out once more the theme of persecution; the progress of chs. 10 and 11 must not lead the reader to forget that there was a powerful and relentless opposition. Or Luke may have been looking forward. He may have felt the need of a counterpoise to the miraculous deliverance of Peter; he would not have the reader assume that such escapes happened every time. Suffering and death were a real part of the experience of the early church. This may be so; Luke has his own version of the theologia crucis (see 'Theologia Crucis — in Acts?' in *FS* Dinkler, 73–84). A different emphasis is given to this by Haenchen 374, who thinks that the story about James is intended to serve as a foil to that about Peter. It does indeed reflect the element of suffering that was part of early Christianity, but its purpose is to underline the deliverance of Peter. 'So hat er [Lukas] das Kreuz, das sich im Martyrium des Zebedaiden ankündigte, zwar nicht ganz verschwiegen. Aber das Licht fällt nicht darauf, sondern auf den greifbaren Erweis der Gottesmacht und Gotteshilfe.' If this image is to be used it would be better to say that in the story of James the Cross is plainly to be seen, but that Luke intends that it should be viewed in the light of deliverance — just as he insists that the cross of Jesus himself is always to be viewed in the light of the resurrection. It is possible that Luke saw some such meaning in the death of James and had this purpose in mind as he recounted it; it is however hardly likely that he invented the martyrdom in order to make his point. There is other — admittedly shaky — evidence for the martyrdom of James; see p. 575. It is probably best to conclude that (a) stands where it does simply because it was attached in tradition to (b). The story is expanded in a passage quoted by Eusebius (*HE* 2.9.2f.) from Clement of Alexandria. Weiser (289), and some others, think that Luke was abbreviating; he knew more about James than he told. It is hard to find any solid basis for this view.

(b) also is a persecution story. Interest is focused primarily on Peter, but also, secondarily, on Herod, who is a constant factor though the whole section, so that the question is raised whether (b) comes from a Peter tradition or a Herod tradition. Luke appears to have had contacts with the Herod family. At 13.1 he will refer to Manaen the σύντροφος of Herod the Tetrarch (uncle of the Herod of the present passage); cf. Lk. 8.3, Joanna the wife of Chuza, Herod's steward.

Herod, however, is peripheral to the story (as Luke tells it — it may have been different in a source used by him). The main purpose of Luke's narrative seems to be twofold. In the first place, it gives a particularly striking example of the power of God to watch over his word and to guard those who proclaim it. Just as Jews and Gentiles (cf. 4.27) combined in the attempt to eliminate Jesus, but found the attempt vain, so Jews and Herod (who at v. 3 seems to be differentiated from the Jews, though he was accustomed to make much of his Jewishness — see on this verse) both tried to extinguish the church, but tried in vain. They were no match for the supernatural resources that were allied to the apostles; cf. 5.19–21, a story briefer and less circumstantial than but in many ways similar to the present one. Secondly, it may contain a hint suggesting how James (the Lord's brother, though this is not stated) came to succeed Peter as head of the Jerusalem church. Peter went (v. 17) to another place. This means both that he got clean away from Herod and that he vacated the leadership in Jerusalem. His destination can be matter only for speculation. Luke however knew (as appears later in Acts) that James came to occupy a leading place in Jerusalem; and he may have been (as the modern reader must endeavour not to be) anachronistic not only in the date he ascribes to James's accession to power but also in his understanding of what at the time 'power' meant.

The second point is probably best thought of as Luke's addition to a traditional story about Peter whose primary interest was in the miraculous deliverance (a point stressed by both Bauernfeind and Haenchen). This is told (see especially Haenchen 375, contrasting the positive attitude of Paul and Silas in ch. 16) in such a way as to emphasise the fact that everything turns upon God's gracious initiative, exercised through an angel. Peter is fast asleep, and contributes nothing more than sheer incomprehension and incredulity. Verse 11 brings the first part of the story to an end; it is only with the departure of the angel that Peter perceives what has happened and that the Lord has delivered him from Herod and the Jews. The second part of the story is marked by the introduction of several names. Compare the references to Aeneas, Dorcas, and Simon in 9.32–43; the cycle of stories about Peter evidently contained a number of names, and we need not suppose that Mary, John Mark, and Rhoda were added by Luke. (John) Mark is connected with Peter elsewhere in early Christian tradition; see 1 Peter 5.13, and the story told by Papias and quoted by Eusebius (*HE* 3.39.15; cf. 5.8.3 for a quotation from

Clement of Alexandria). In the rest of Acts he is — temporarily at least — connected with Paul: 12.25; 13.13; 15.37. See also Col. 4.10; Phm. 24; 2 Tim. 4.11. For guesses related to his mother Mary and her house see on v. 12. The name Rhoda suggests no such connection; it must have stood in the tradition used by Luke. Her joy at hearing Peter's voice is understandable, but the unbelief of the rest of the company does little credit to their belief in the possible efficacy of the prayers they were said to be offering in his behalf (v. 5 as well as v. 12). They were evidently convinced that he was as good as dead, if not yet actually executed. This thought will not have occurred to Luke; his concern is to show the piety of the church and the gravity of the peril from which Peter was delivered. He may however have had in mind the thought that the Christians were praying not only for last minute deliverance but also for the continuing faithfulness of one who stood on the brink of death.

For Luke's further interests see on v. 17. There was no need to explain who was meant by James (it may be that the martyrdom of James the son of Zebedee was mentioned partly in order to exclude another possible identification); Luke knows, here as in chs. 15 and 21, that his readers will immediately identify James as the famous leader of the Jerusalem church. He is represented as, in a sense, the nominee of Peter; at least, as one to whose prominence Peter assents. It may however go too far to suggest that Peter's message amounts to, 'Tell James it is now time for him to take over.' In any case, before this could make sense we should have to ask precisely what James was to take over, and for how long. 'During my temporary absence'? For his part, Peter got safely away from Herod. It may be that Luke also thinks of him as set free to commence missionary operations elsewhere, though after this point Luke's only reference to Peter relates his presence at the Council of Jerusalem (15.7–11).

A few other points may be taken up here. It is often observed that the two parts of Acts contain parallel accounts of Peter and Paul; similar experiences befall each. For example, each is unexpectedly delivered from prison, Peter by an angel, Paul by an earthquake (16.25–34). This is true, but within the parallel Dibelius (132) points to a difference. In the story about Peter, all the emphasis falls upon the release of Peter; in that about Paul, the result is the conversion of the gaoler and his household. Roloff (187) considers that one motivation for the story was the desire to clear Peter of the suspicion of having run away: what happened was not of Peter's choice but the work of the angel of the Lord. Weiser (284) gives a remarkable list of stories of the supernatural release of prisoners. Some of these will be referred to below (pp. 580–2); they show beyond doubt that the theme was a very popular one in folk and in higher literature.

The third component of the paragraph, (c), calls for little explanation. It consists of popular, Jewish and Christian, report concerning the fate of Herod. The closely parallel story in Josephus (see the notes) shows how the event was popularly understood. That Herod died a very painful death may be assumed; the agreement of Luke and Josephus is probably good enough evidence that it was preceded by a public event at which Herod received public acclamation as a divine being — there was nothing new in the thought that a Hellenistic monarch was some sort of god. The contrast between this pinnacle of pride and the agony of death would strike both Jews and Christians in the same way: the man showed the supreme ὕβρις of claiming to be god, or of permitting the claim to be made on his behalf, and in consequence God struck him down. For Luke there is an added point of contrast. Peter, in humble obedience to God, was prepared to accept death as the price of faithfulness, and was delivered from death; Herod in his arrogance claimed the position of an immortal god, and was delivered to a gruesome death. Each side of the picture serves to emphasize the other by contrast. Luke does not, however, explicitly make this point, and does not represent Herod's death as the punishment of a persecutor. This does not prove that the story cannot be of Christian but must be of Jewish origin: like Jews, Christians would be horrified by the thought that Herod claimed to be divine. It belongs to the area in which Jews and Christians are one.

The paragraph taken as a whole — parts (a), (b), and (c) — is a unity, though this has been somewhat overstated by Schmithals (115, cf. Haenchen 373), who in the whole passage 11.27–12.25 detects a chiastic pattern:

a. 11.27–30: Barnabas and Saul travel from Antioch to Jerusalem
b. 12.2–(3)5: Acts of Herod
c. 12.(3)5–17: the legend about Peter
b. 12.18(20)–23: Death of Herod
a. 12.24, 25: Barnabas and Saul return from Jerusalem to Antioch

The concurrence of the first and fifth points has to do with chronology rather than with literary form, and 12.1–23 is a continuous narrative. Luke has however used his material with great skill to achieve a number of purposes. He winds up one part of his book and prepares the way for another. The age of the Twelve, founder members of the Jerusalem church, is now coming to an end. The Twelve themselves disappear (apart from Peter's share in the Council of Acts 15); their function as local leaders in Jerusalem is henceforth fulfilled by James (not an apostle). But the age of the Twelve ends gloriously. James the son of Zebedee receives the crown of martyrdom; Peter is willing to accept martyrdom but is marvellously delivered; the foe of the church is humbled and destroyed. The themes of the paragraph are themes that Luke loves to display: the bearing of witness at any cost; the Lord's readiness and ability to look after his own; the piety of a praying church; its victory over all opponents. It is quite possible to pick logical and theological holes in the way in which these themes are presented. Were the lives of the soldiers of no consequence? Why should Peter be rescued but not James? Did the church not pray for James? Did those who were praying for Peter not believe that their prayer could be effective? It is as clear here as anywhere in Acts that strict logical and theological consistency were not Luke's aim (or his forte); he has given, as he no doubt set out to do, a striking story which will make his points effectively to all but the sophisticated. His writing up of traditional material is minimal but effective. He lays great stress on the gracious miracle-working power of God. He sees Peter off the Jerusalem stage, and introduces James; he also introduces John Mark as a representative of an old Jerusalem Christian family; Mark will accompany Paul a little way, but not far, into the next stage of unrestricted missionary activity.

1. The introductory note of time is imprecise. Cf. 6.1; 19.23 (κατὰ τὸν καιρὸν ἐκεῖνον). For the date of Herod's death see the note on v. 20; for the relation between the 'famine visit' of Barnabas and Saul and the events of the present paragraph see on 12.25. Luke means that both events happened at the same early period of Christian history. The expression he uses does not itself mean the period during which Barnabas and Saul were in Jerusalem, though this may be implied by the resumption of 11.27–30 in 12.25. *Begs.* 4.132 suggests that the narrator indicates that he is picking up a thread; it is not clear however what thread Luke would have in mind.

Ἡρῴδης ὁ βασιλεύς. ℵ Ψ 81 614 1241 *pc* have ὁ βασιλεὺς Ἡρῴδης, a less usual order, but it is correct for the appositive to take the article when the proper name is shared by others and it is important to distinguish the person concerned from them; see BDR § 268. 1; cf. 25.13. The Herod in question is Herod Agrippa I, or rather Julius Agrippa I; he bears the family name Herod only in Acts. The Agrippa of 25.13–26.32 is his son, Agrippa II. Agrippa I was the son of Aristobulus and grandson of Herod the Great. He had a varied career (for details see *NS* 1.442–454). Born in 10 BC, he travelled to Rome, became a friend of Caligula's, was imprisoned by Tiberius, but, on Tiberius' death, released and honoured by Caligula, who gave him the tetrarchies that had been held by Philip and Lysanias (cf. Lk 3.1) and conferred on him the title of king. The accession of Claudius, which Agrippa did not a little to achieve, brought him further advancement; Judaea and Samaria were added to his kingdom, so that he ruled over as wide an area as his grandfather, Herod the Great. Especially when in Judaea, Agrippa, notwithstanding his Roman and Greek interests, lived and seems to have been recognized as a good Jew; see especially Sotah 7.8; Josephus, *Ant.* 19. 292–294, 331 (τὰ πάτρια καθαρῶς ἐτήρει; though the context speaks of his friendship for Greeks). Towards the end of his life his adventurous foreign policy in the East caused him to lose favour with Claudius; his death is described later in this paragraph. His actions in regard to James and Peter may be regarded as part of his role as the 'good Jew' who would naturally be concerned to put down a heretical sect. In addition to Agrippa II, his two daughters are mentioned in Acts, Drusilla in 24.24, Bernice in 25.13.

ἐπιβάλλειν τὰς χεῖρας is usually (in Acts see 4.3; 5.18; 21.27) followed by a dative or by ἐπί with the accusative, and means *to attack* someone; here only by an object infinitive (perhaps as if the author wished to avoid details? — so Bauernfeind 159). With an infinitive ἐκβάλλειν (or ἐκτείνειν, cf. Lk 22.53) would be more usual, suggesting the Hebrew שלח ידים and could be rendered *attempted to* or *set out to*. *Begs.* 4.133 points out that ἐπιβάλλειν χεῖρας occurs in Polybius and papyri, and therefore cannot be regarded as a Semitism. Here the infinitive κακῶσαι (cf. 18.10) must be taken as epexegetic of the main verb: He laid his hands (on them), so as to harm (them). Cf. 1 Ezra 9.20 (LXX). κακοῦν is a Lucan word (of physical injury at 7.6, 19; 12.1; 18.10; of causing disaffection at 14.2; elsewhere in the NT only at 1 Peter 3.13). Examples of Herod's attack follow in the stories of James and Peter; Herod (to judge from this account) thought it best to attack the Christian society through its leaders. This is reinforced by the use of τινας — not the whole church but some of its members. Alternatively Schille (268) suggests that Luke wrote τινας because he could quote only two examples.

ἀπὸ τῆς ἐκκλησίας will mean *of the church* (of those who belonged to the church). For Luke's use of ἐκκλησία see 5.11 and the discussion in Vol. II. Here D p w sy^{h**} mae add ἐν τῇ Ἰουδαίᾳ — a sensible though secondary addition; we have just heard of the church in Antioch, and the Western text makes clear that there is now to be a change of scene.

2. ἀναιρεῖν is used eighteen times in Acts (in the rest of the NT, once in Mt., twice in Lk., once in 2 Thess., once in Heb.), always in a destructive sense except at 7.21. For James the brother of John see 1.13, where James is not so described, and Mk 3.17, where the relationship is expressed in reverse. It is clear that this James must be distinguished from the James mentioned in v. 17 (and presumably in 15.13; 21.18); this second James is usually taken to be the Lord's brother, but Calvin (337) thinks of James the son of Alphaeus. See below.

James was killed μαχαίρῃ (for -ῃ where -ᾳ would be expected see BDR § 43. 1). According to Brandon (*Trial* 48), followed by Derrett (*Law* 340) the use of the sword rather than any other means of execution shows that the charge against James was political, that is, that Herod saw the Christian movement as a political threat to his regime. This rests upon Sanhedrin 7.3 (The ordinance of them that are to be beheaded is this: they used to cut off his head with a sword as the [Roman] government does. R. Judah says: This is shameful for him; but, rather, they lay his head on a block and cut it off with an axe). It is worth noting however that at 9.3 death by beheading is briefly described as by the sword (בסיף). Moreover, it is evident from the passage cited that the older custom was to behead with the sword. These considerations cast some doubt on the position maintained by Brandon and Derrett; on their side however it may be noted that though μάχαιρα is used for several kinds of swords and daggers (and for a carving-knife; see LS 1085 s.v.), in *Cat. Cod. Astr.* 8 (4).173 ἐπὶ μαχαίρᾳ τασσόμενοι means 'possessing powers of life and death *(jus gladii)*' (also LS). If something of this kind is to be inferred from Luke's word, matters have progressed from the stage described in chs. 4 and 5. The Christians are now more than a religious nuisance; they threaten the security of the state. Verse 3 suggests that Herod had at first acted on his own; it was only after the death of James that he found that the Jews were pleased. The remainder of Acts however represents action against the Christians, in Jerusalem as well as elsewhere, as arising from Jewish religious rather than from Roman or other civil authorities.

The martyrdom of James is referred to in an epitome of Philip of Side (*c.* AD 430; contained in Codex Baroccianus 142 (Oxford), published by C. de Boer, *TU* V. 2 (1888), 170), in the words, 'Papias in his second book says that John the Divine and James his brother were killed by Jews (ὑπὸ 'Ιουδαίων ἀνῃρέθησαν)'. The use of ἀναιρεῖν will be noted; the fact that in Acts the subject of the (active) verb is not the Jews but Herod is not necessarily inconsistent, since Luke points out (v. 3) that the death of James pleased the Jews. It would not stretch the evidence very far to suggest that Herod acted with the intention of pleasing the Jews, of doing what they would have done themselves had this been possible for them. For further evidence bearing on the supposed early martyrdom of the two brothers see *St John* 103f. It is not convincing. It will be noted that there is in Acts no reference to the death of James's brother John (though this has sometimes been introduced into the text by conjecture). Bauernfeind (160) counters the suggestion that Luke deliberately concealed the death of John by the observation that had he wished to do this he would have mentioned John in his account of the Council (ch. 15). See also Lüdemann (149).

3. Herod is here distinguished from *the Jews* (to whom his action was pleasing) though in general he liked to associate himself with them and so far as possible to regard himself as one of them. Luke probably thought of him as the first Gentile adversary of the church, whose miserable end might furnish an appropriate warning to others. After 'Ιουδαίοις, D p* sy^hmg (mae) add (as a subject for ἐστιν) ἡ ἐπιχείρησις ἐπὶ τοὺς πιστούς. This introduces a false concord (with ἀρεστόν); the neuter adjective would be allowable if the subject were a generalization (BDR § 131. 1). This makes the Western reading *lectio difficilior*, but it is probably to be taken as an unnecessary clarification; for the Western tendency to make unnecessary explanatory additions see pp. 6, 28.

προσέθετο συλλαβεῖν. This construction has been described as the only Hebraism in Josephus (see M. 1.233; 2.445; MM 551; with the references given in each place). It undoubtedly recalls the Hebrew הוסיף ל, with infinitive. According to Thackeray (*Grammar* 52f.) this is represented in three ways in the LXX: (a) προσέθετο (προσέθηκεν) λαβεῖν; (b) προσ. καὶ ἔλαβεν; (c)προσθεὶς (προσθέμενος) ἔλαβεν. Of these (c) is the only one 'for which approximate classical parallels could be quoted', and is the least common. (a) is by far the most common, and corresponds to the use in Acts. The same construction is found in Lk. 20.11, 12 (προσέθετο πέμψαι, parallel to Mk 12.4, πάλιν ἀπέστειλεν), and there are parallels in 1 Clem. 12.7 (προσέθεντο αὐτῇ δοῦναι σημεῖον) and Hermas, *Mandate* 4.3.1 (ἔτι . . .προσθήσω τοῦ ἐπερωτῆσαι). There can be little doubt that the construction must be described as a Hebraism, but it is probably due not to the translation of a Hebrew source but to Luke's imitation of the style of the LXX. Cf. BDR § 435. 4; also Thackeray, *JTS* 30 (1929), 361–70.

A parenthesis is awkwardly inserted (cf. 1.15), introduced by δέ (see BDR § 447. 1 (b), n. 4, with the reference to Thucydides 1.26.5, ἔστι δ'ἰσθμὸς τὸ χωρίον), with the intention of indicating the time in the year (but not the year). For the possible significance of this see on v. 4. For τὰ ἄζυμα cf. Mk 14.1: the festival of unleavened loaves. Passover was eaten with unleavened bread (Exod. 12.15) and it was followed by the seven-day feast of unleavened bread; not unnaturally the combined feast was sometimes known as τὸ πάσχα, sometimes as τὰ ἄζυμα. See Lk. 22.1, ἡ ἑορτὴ τῶν ἀζύμων ἡ λεγομένη πάσχα. In view of this *Begs.* 4.134 is hardly justified in saying that the present passage reads as though Unleavened Bread preceded Passover. For the neuter plural (where ἄζυμοι (sc. ἄρτοι) might have been expected) see BDR § 141. 3, and cf. the classical Διονύσια, Παναθήναια, and later 'Αρσινόεια. It is hard to decide whether, before ἡμέραι, αἱ should be read (with A D E Ψ 𝔐) or omitted (with P^45vid ℵ B L 0244 6 1175 1241 1739 *al*).

4. After the parenthesis the sentence is resumed by the use of the relative, as not infrequently in Acts (e.g. 2.24). Herod having seized Peter put (ἔθετο, middle, to express the fact that Herod was acting in accordance with his own intended purpose) him in prison.

παραδούς, aorist participle, seems to refer to action coincident with rather than prior to ἔθετο. The new clause is intended to emphasise the measure taken to secure the prisoner and thus serves to heighten the miracle that Luke is about to describe. τετράδιον means 'a company of four: it is an instance of the specialising force of the suffix -ιον (W. Petersen, *Greek Diminutives in -ιον (1910)*, p. 84ff., where τετράδιον is not mentioned)'. So M. 2.176. The word is not frequently but sufficiently attested; see Philo, *Flaccus* 111, στρατιώτην δέ τινα τῶν ἐν τοῖς τετραδίοις φυλάκων. The four detachments of four soldiers each were probably detailed to guard in turn during the four watches of the night. Thus *P. Oxy.* 2156.10 and Vegetius, *de re militari* 3.8 (Et quia impossibile videbatur in speculis vigilantes singulos permanere, ideo in quattuor partes ad clepsydram sunt divisae vigiliae ut non amplius quam tribus horis nocturnis necesse sit vigilare). Cf. also Philostratus, *Apollonius* 7.31 (Apollonius accompanied by four guards). Luke does not say where Peter was imprisoned; most archaeologists and commentators think of the Antonia (see Benoit *Ex. et Th.* 4.311–346), but Roloff (189) suggests Herod's Palace near the Jaffa Gate.

Herod's intention was to bring Peter up (from prison) to the people (τῷ λαῷ, the Jews; cf. v. 2) after Passover. ἀναγαγεῖν can hardly mean here *bring him up for a public trial* (Herod already knew what was to be done with Peter); it will mean for *public execution*. For τὸ πάσχα cf. the note on τὰ ἄζυμα (v. 3). It was at Passover time that Jesus died (cf. Lk. 22.1); it is at Passover time that the apostle is threatened with death. The symbolic parallelism however may be positive rather than negative; that is, it may relate rather to deliverance than death. See especially A. Strobel, 'Passa-Symbolik und Passa-Wunder in Act. xii.3ff.' (*NTS* 4 (1958), 210–15), taken up in Le Déaut (*Nuit Pascale*, 286, 292). Passover night was expected to be a night of messianic deliverance (see Le Déaut, 279–98), and this understanding was continued in the church in relation to the Christian Pasch (Easter) and to the eucharist. See e.g. *Epistula Apostolorum* 15: Now when the Passover (Easter, pascha) cometh, one of you shall be cast into prison for my name's sake; and he will be in grief and sorrow, because ye keep the Easter while he is in prison and separated from you, for he will be sorrowful because he keepeth not Easter with you. And I will send my power in the form of mine angel Gabriel, and the doors of the prison shall open. And he shall come forth and come unto you and keep the night-watch with you until the cock crow. And when ye have accomplished the memorial which is made of me, and the Agape (love-feast), he shall again be cast into prison for testimony, until he shall come out thence and preach that which I have delivered unto you. (ET from M. R. James, *Apocryphal NT*, 1924, 489, 490). Here is undoubtedly a second-century creation of a vaticinium ex eventu based on the narrative of Acts, or on a narrative like it (for here, among other differences, Peter returns to prison). This is not a complete explanation, partly because of the differences just noted and partly because the later verses in Acts contain possible allusions to significant OT acts of deliverance (see on vv. 6, 7, 8, 11 below). Apart from these allusions Luke himself does nothing to bring out the Paschal significance of his story, and may not have been aware of it; it may have been implicit in the tradition he was using. Marshall (208) correctly points out that the church was praying for Peter, not for the coming of Christ at that Passover. For the bearing of the reference to Passover on the date of the incident see on vv. 20–23.

5. μὲν οὖν indicates that Luke is summing up the position so far reached. The imperfects correspond with this: Peter *was being kept* (ἐτηρεῖτο) in the prison, and prayer *was being offered* (ἦν . . . γινομένη). The second proposition adds to what has been said in v. 4. It is of course natural that the Christians should pray for their leader, and natural that they should pray *earnestly*, ἐκτενῶς. The adverb occurs in the comparative degree at Lk. 22.44 (si v.l.) and at 1 Peter 1.22, the adjective at 1 Peter 4.8. The sentence is differently expressed in D (p): πολλὴ δὲ προσευχὴ ἦν ἐν ἐκτενείᾳ περὶ αὐτοῦ ἀπὸ τῆς ἐκκλησίας πρὸς τὸν θεὸν περὶ αὐτοῦ. ἐν ἐκτενείᾳ (the noun occurs at 26.7; cf. Judith 4.9; 1 Clem. 33.1; 37.1) replaces the adverb; in addition there is said to be *much* (πολλή) prayer; ὑπό is replaced by ἀπό (cf. 11.19 for the use of this preposition); περὶ αὐτοῦ is inadvertently repeated. This is almost certainly a secondary reading (it was an editor who failed to notice that he was introducing a repetition). In the majority reading ἐκτενῶς is replaced by ἐκτενής in Aᶜ E Ψ 𝔐. Phrynichus (285) advises, Ἐκτενῶς μή, ἀλλ' ἀντ' αὐτοῦ δαψιλῶς λέγε, but this (*pace* Metzger) will hardly explain the variation, since the adjective is no better than the adverb. Rutherford points out in his note on Phrynichus, 'Adjective, adverb, and substantive, ἐκτενής, ἐκτενῶς, and ἐκτένεια all occur with frequency in late writers, but are unknown in Attic Greek' (p. 365).

Another unusual variant occurs in the first clause: Peter was being kept in prison *a cohorte regis* (p* syʰ** (mae)). *Cohors* is probably used in its loose sense of any detachment of soldiers and refers back to the guard described in v. 4.

Brandon (*Fall* 135) correctly notes the contrast between the fervent prayer offered by the church on behalf of Peter, and the complete absence of reference to any such reaction when Paul is arrested and imprisoned (chs. 22–28). Whether this contrast is significant for the history itself, or for Luke's interests in recording it, it will be proper to discuss when the later chapters are reached.

6. Passover is presumably now past (v. 4, μετὰ τὸ πάσχα), and

Herod is about to (ἤμελλεν) bring Peter forward — no doubt for execution. For προαγαγεῖν (P⁷⁴ A 36 81 453 945 *al*), B 33 *pc* have προσαγαγεῖν, D E 𝔐 have προάγειν, ℵ Ψ 6 1241 2495 *pc* have προσάγειν. In Classical use μέλλειν usually takes the future infinitive; in the NT this occurs only in Acts (see on 11.28). In the NT the tense of the infinitive that occurs most frequently is the present; the present is the only passage in Acts where the aorist infinitive is used — a fact that strengthens the case for accepting either προ- or προσαγαγεῖν. Whichever of these is accepted the meaning is probably much the same as that of ἀναγαγεῖν (v. 4).

τῇ νυκτὶ ἐκείνῃ recalls the original Passover deliverance (Exod. 12.12, ἐν τῇ νυκτὶ ταύτῃ), but it is perhaps more probable that Luke is telling a vivid story than that he is working out a subtle typological scheme.

The continuous tenses of v. 5 (see the note) appear to be continued in the periphrastic imperfect ἦν ... κοιμώμενος, though it is possible that here the participle is adjectival, so that we should translate not *was sleeping* but *was asleep*. Luke's thought is not that the sleep was supernaturally induced but that it was remarkable — as his friend marvelled at the sound sleep of the condemned Socrates (Plato, *Crito* 43b, ἀλλὰ καὶ σοῦ πάλαι θαυμάζω αἰσθανόμενος ὡς ἡδέως καθεύδεις). δεδεμένος will certainly be adjectival: not *he had been bound* but *he was asleep ... bound*. The *two* (δυσίν is Hellenistic; cf. Phrynichus 185, Δυσὶ μὴ λέγε, ἀλλὰ δυοῖν) *chains* are, like the account of the military guard, a sign of the security with which Peter was held and thus of the magnitude of the miracle by which he was released. Finally, the reference to the guards, who stood before the door, is repeated. 'Luc est, avec Jacques 5.9, le seul auteur du NT à donner à πρό + genitif son sens local très classique: deux seuls autres exemples, Actes 12.14 et 14.13' (Delebecque 59). Again, the imperfect ἐτήρουν describes the state of things upon which the action of the angel supervened.

7. καὶ ἰδού. Cf. 1.10; not a translation but an imitation of the Hebrew הנה. ἄγγελος κυρίου also recalls the LXX (e.g. Gen. 16.7) but see 5.19. The whole of the present narrative recalls 5.19–25.

The imperfects of vv. 5, 6 are interrupted by the aorist ἐπέστη: the angel of the Lord *came and stood over* Peter (τῷ Πέτρῳ, a correct interpretation, is added by D p sy⁽ᵖ⁾ʰ** sa mae). ἐπέστη (and ἀπέστη in v. 10) both connote suddenness (so Page 157). The word is however to some extent formal in such a context; see e.g. *IG* 10.2.255, 11.3.4: ...ἔδοξε καθ' ὕπ‹ν›ον ἐπιστάντα [παρ' αὐ]τὸν Σάραπιν ἐπιτάξαι ὅπως ... (quoted in *ND* 1.29; further examples in 2.22f.). The appearance of the angel is accompanied by light; cf. Lk. 2.9. For light as an accompaniment of a supernatural manifestation see 9.3 (with the note); 22.6; 26.13. οἴκημα, for which

Begs. 4.135 has *building*, may be any place in which people live; here it is evidently Peter's *prison*, and for this meaning there is non-biblical precedent (though Thucydides 4.47.2 is not a good example, if *prison* is to be taken to mean a place habitually used for incarceration; Demosthenes, 32.29(890) will serve).

πατάξας suggests a rather violent blow (cf. ἐπάταξεν in v. 23; Homer, *Iliad* 10.157–159 is a somewhat distant parallel); hence no doubt the gentler νύξας (*nudged*) in D gig. ἤγειρεν here must be *roused, wakened*. Peter must still be told to get up.

With ἀνάστα ἐν τάχει Strobel (op. cit.) compares Exod 12.11, μετὰ σπουδῆς); the escape from Egypt had to be made with haste. Obedience is made possible by the falling off of the chains.

The parallel to the release of Peter provided by the 'release' of Dionysus in Euripides' *Bacchae* was already noticed by Origen in *C. Celsum* 2.34. Celsus had drawn attention to the contrast between Dionysus, who was able to free himself, and Jesus, who (apparently) was not. The servant arresting Dionysus says, αὐτόματα (cf. v. 10) δ' αὐταῖς δεσμὰ διελύθη ποδῶν, κλῇδές τ' ἀνῆκαν θύρετρ' ἄνευ θνητῆς χερός (*Bacchae* 447, 448). Dionysus himself declares, λύσει μ' ὁ δαίμων αὐτός, ὅταν ἐγὼ θέλω (498; Dionysus himself is the δαίμων — he will release himself). The theme is echoed by Horace, *Epistles* 1.16.76–78, who repeats the story adding his own interpretation. '"In manicis et compedibus saevo te sub custode tenebo." "Ipse deus, simul atque volam, me solvet."' Horace adds (78, 79), 'Opinor, hoc sentit, "moriar". mors ultima linea rerum est.' See also Ovid, *Metamorphoses* 3.699, 700. It is clear that the parallel is only superficial. The idea of self-liberation is taken up by the archetypal 'divine man', Apollonius of Tyana, who takes his leg out of his fetters (to prove that he can do it), and puts it back again (Philostratus, *Apollonius* 7.38; cf. 7.34; 8.30). The apostle has no such powers of self-preservation. For later Christian development see *Acts of Thomas* 122.

8. With ζῶσαι καὶ ὑπόδησαι τὰ σανδάλιά σου Strobel (op. cit.) compares Exod. 12.11, . . . περιεζωσμέναι καὶ τὰ ὑποδήματα ἐν τοῖς ποσίν . . .; the first paschal escape was made with haste by those who were prepared to move on the word of command. It must be noted that though these words may evoke echoes of the Exodus they also serve Luke's purpose of demonstrating that God himself was at work, directing operations; and of course they are also common-sense instructions — Peter will have to walk, and had better be clothed and shod. Contrast the hurried escape in Horace, *Sat.* 1.2.132, discincta tunica fugiendum est et pede nudo. M. 3.77 draws attention to the tenses of the last two verbs used by the angel: Put your cloak on (περιβαλοῦ, aorist, punctiliar) and keep behind me (ἀκολούθει, present, continuous).

9. ἐξελθών: probably, in view of what follows, out of the inner room in which Peter was chained. Peter obeys the angel's command, ἠκολούθει (cf. v. 8), but without understanding what is happening. He supposed he was seeing a vision. δέ here expresses a stronger antithesis than usual; ἀλλά might have been expected. The thing was not *true*, ἀληθές in the sense of *real*.

10. φυλακή must now have a different sense from that of vv. 4, 6 (prison). Here the word will mean *watch* or *guard*; it is possible that in each of the detachments guarding Peter two soldiers were chained to Peter himself, the third and fourth constituting the first and second watches respectively. But Luke does not say this. The absence of the article with πρώτην and δευτέραν is conventional; see BDR § 256. *The iron gate* (cf. Homer, *Iliad* 8.15, ἔνθα σιδήρειαί τε πύλαι καὶ χάλκεος οὐδός) unfortunately gives us no clue to the identity of the prison in which Peter had been confined. If τὴν φέρουσαν (cf. Xenophon, *Hell.* 7.2.7, αἱ εἰς τὴν πόλιν φέρουσαι πύλαι (BA 1706, with other examples)) εἰς τὴν πόλιν is a distinction rather than a simple description it may give a hint. The Antonia tower opened on one side upon the city, on the other upon the Temple. If, as many think, Peter was imprisoned in the Antonia we should have a statement that he went not towards the Temple but towards the city. At least, Luke's words are consistent with this location. After ἐξελθόντες D adds (κατέβησαν τοὺς ζ' βαθμοὺς καί); p has descenderunt grades; d has descenderunt septem grados et processerunt gradum (*not* vicum) unum. This variant might give us a clue to the location of the prison if anything more were known of the seven steps. The variant may rest on (but it does not prove) local knowledge on the part of the Western editor; it is hard to see what theological or other point could be served by the addition. Reference to Ezk. 40.22, 26 provides no explanation. Clark (348) thinks that the detail was brought by John Mark (vv. 12, 25) and given to the author in Antioch ('We' in 11.28).

The gate (ἥτις used for ἥ; cf. 8.14f.; BDR § 293. 2) opened *of its own accord*. Here as at Mk 4.28 αὐτόματος is an adjective of three terminations (M. 2.158; BDR § 59. 1). For its meaning (moved by itself) see BDR § 117.2. Here it takes the place of an adverb used in a similar passage in Josephus, *War* 6.293 (ἡ δ'ἀνατολικὴ πύλη τοῦ ἐνδοτέρω ναοῦ ... ὤφθη ... αὐτομάτως ἠνοιγμένη; cf. Tacitus, *Histories* 5.13, apertae repente delubri fores). In this case the omen was an evil one for the Jewish people. There are many other parallels; miraculous escapes were a popular theme in ancient imagination. Cf. Homer, *Iliad* 5.749 (= 8.393); Vergil, *Aeneid* 6.81f.; and the deliverance of Moses reported in a fragment of Artapanus preserved in Eusebius, *Praeparatio Evangelica* 9.27.23 (When the king learned this, he confined him in prison (φυλακήν). But when night came, all the doors of the prison opened of themselves (αὐτομάτως), and some of the guards died, while others were relaxed by sleep and their weapons were broken. Moses came out (ἐξελθόντα) and went to the royal chambers. He found the doors open and went in. There, since the guards were relaxed, he woke the king (ET by J. J. Collins in Charlesworth, *OT Pseudepigrapha* 2.901). Yoma 39b and j. Yoma 43c.61 contain references to the miraculous opening of gates of the Temple.

Having emerged through the door of the prison (and, if we follow the Western text, descended the seven steps), Peter and the angel προῆλθον ῥύμην μίαν: perhaps *they traversed one street*, but *Begs.* 4.136, rightly noting that in Hellenistic use ῥύμη means a narrow street, or lane (for evidence see BA 1476 s.v.), take the meaning to be that they went 'along the main street until its intersection by a ῥύμη'. In any case μίαν is probably to be regarded as a numeral, not as a substitute for τινα. Even however if it does serve as an indefinite article it need not be regarded as a Semitism (Black, *AA* 105); this use of εἷς was coming into Hellenistic Greek, though the few occurrences in the NT may have been aided by the general Semitic background (M. 1.97). The angel had done his work and departed (ἀπέστη; cf. ἐπέστη in v. 7); Peter was in a position to look after himself.

11. ἐν ἑαυτῷ γενόμενος, when he came to his right mind, is a not uncommon Greek expression; cf. e.g. Xenophon, *Anabasis* 1.1.5, ἀκούσας ταῦτα ὁ Κλέαρχος, ἐν ἑαυτῷ ἐγένετο; Herodotus 1.119.6, ἰδὼν δὲ οὔτε ἐξεπλάγη ἐντός τε ἑωυτοῦ γίνεται. Cf. also Lk. 15.17; the style of this verse is on the whole Lucan (Haenchen 376). Peter recognizes and declares the truth: I know truly, of a truth, that the Lord has sent his angel . . . Cf. v. 7. Cf. also another Passover act of deliverance, the deliverance of the three Hebrews from Nebuchadnezzar's furnace (see Strobel, op. cit. 210); at Dan. 3.95 Nebuchadnezzar declares that God ἀπέστειλεν τὸν ἄγγελον αὐτοῦ καὶ ἐξείλατο τοὺς παῖδας αὐτοῦ (Theodotion; LXX has ἔσωσε for ἐξείλατο). ἐκ χειρός should be regarded as a Septuagintalism (for מיד), though BDR § 217. 2, n. 5 quote Aeschines 3.256, ἐκ τῶν χειρῶν ἐξελέσθαι τῶν Φιλίππου. Delebecque 60 observes that Luke chooses Greek expressions which are also Hebrew.

πάσης τῆς προσδοκίας presumably means *the whole content of their expectation*, that is, all that they expected. See v. 3; the death of James had pleased the Jews, who knew that Herod had arrested Peter to please them further and could therefore expect that he too would be executed. For Luke, ὁ λαός is usually sufficient to denote the Jewish people; he adds τῶν 'Ιουδαίων   to emphasise the connection with v. 3. Peter, a representative Christian, is now separated from the Jewish people (Weiser 290).

12. συνιδών (Vg. *considerans*), as in the plural at 14.6, includes both perception and consideration (see Field, ad loc.). Metzger (395) notes the (unnecessary) conjectures of Hammond (σπεύδων) and of Pallis (συντείνων). Peter had now grasped the truth of the matter (v. 11) and could see that his next step must be to get in touch with his fellow Christians. Accordingly ἦλθεν ἐπὶ τὴν οἰκίαν τῆς Μαρίας τῆς μητρὸς 'Ιωάννου. τῆς before Μαρίας is read by P⁷⁴ ℵ A B D 81 *pc*, omitted by E Ψ 𝔐. For the rule in such cases see BDR § 268. 1 (referred to on v. 1). The proper name should not have the article and for this reason Turner (M. 3.206) thinks that, notwithstanding its strong attestation, the word should be omitted. The opposite conclusion should be drawn; Luke was not incapable of breaking the rules of grammar and style, and copyists would tend to correct him. For John Mark (the correct accentuation is Μᾶρκος since the a in the Latin Marcus is long; see BDR § 41. 3) see 12.25; 13.5, 13; 15.37, 39; also Col. 4.10 (where ἀνέψιος is shown by Lightfoot 302f., followed by e.g. E. Lohse, to mean *cousin*, though BA 131 have 'd. Verwandte, d. Neffe, d. Vetter', and in Modern Greek ἀνιψιός means (MM 42) *nephew*); 2 Tim. 4.11; Phm. 24; 1 Peter 5.13. Later tradition connected him with Peter and with the writing of the second gospel. The earliest evidence is that of Papias (in Eusebius, *HE* 3.39.15); for more detail and much speculation see *Acta Barnabae* (in L.-B. 2.2.292–302). Such guesses as that John Mark was the young man with a linen cloth (Mk 14.51f.) and that his mother's house was the place at which the Last Supper was eaten have no foundation and are of no value. For the patristic material see Zahn, *Einleitung* § 51 n. 7. It is striking that no man is mentioned as husband of Mary and father of Mark; somewhere behind Luke's narrative lies a tradition of a Christian family in Jerusalem where the father either was already dead or had not become a Christian. For the double name see *ND* 1.95.

We have already learned that earnest prayer was being made for Peter (v. 5). At least in part this was corporate prayer for which Christians assembled. Jeremias (*Jerusalem* 131) seems to think that the whole Jerusalem church was assembled; Luke does not say this, and it is quite impossible that the numbers he has mentioned (2.41, three thousand; 4.4, five thousand) should have met in any private house. He is thinking of a large (ἱκανοί, rather like the English *considerable*; the word is Lucan — Lk., ten (nine) times; Acts, eighteen times, Mt., three times; Mk, three times; Paul, six, (five) times; 2 Tim., once) gathering, large, that is, in relation to the size of the place in which it was held (see on v. 13).

In view of their incredulity at the report of Peter's presence (vv.

15, 16) it is reasonable to ask what the company were praying for; if for his escape they can hardly be said to have fulfilled the condition of Mk 11.24. It may be that they had decided that the situation was hopeless and that they were praying that Peter might be comforted in the time of distress and at the hour of death; but this explanation seems somewhat too sophisticated for a writer such as Luke, and there is no positive evidence to support it.

Schille (274f.) makes the following observations about the state of the church implied by this notice. (1) The church has a regular meeting place; Peter knows where to go. (2) The church observes Passover. (3) No other apostles are left in Jerusalem. (4) There are no high officials. (5) A gathering for prayer does not need a Peter or a James. These seem valid conclusions apart from (2). Luke does not say that the Christians had met to observe Passover but to pray for Peter.

13. Peter, having arrived at the house, knocked on τὴν θύραν τοῦ πυλῶνος. θύρα is a *door*, πυλών a *gateway* or *gate-house*; cf. 10.17. Presumably we are to think of a large house with a large gateway in which was set a wicket-door that would be used for ordinary purposes; see however v. 14. The knocking was answered by a παιδίσκη (cf. Jn 18.17), who might have been a young woman member of the family (or of the church) or a slave (the later meaning of the word); see Phrynichus 216, Rutherford (312f.). Mention of her name is perhaps slightly in favour of the former alternative. Nothing else is known of *Rhoda* (properly the word means a rose-bush). The name was a popular one for slaves, but it was the name of the lady who owned the slave Hermas (Hermas, *Vision* 1.1.1), and was in use among Jews (*CIL* 9.2619); other examples in Hemer 227. Peter *knocked* (κρούσαντος) and she *approached* (προσῆλθεν; but א B² pc lat have προῆλθεν, *she came forward*) to *answer* the knock (ὑπακοῦσαι). κρούειν and ὑπακούειν are both classical in this sense; see Xenophon, *Symposium* 1.11, κρούσας τὴν θύραν, εἶπε τῷ ὑπακούσαντι . . .; Plato, *Phaedo* 59e, ὁ θυρωρός, ὅσπερ εἰώθει ὑπακούειν). For ὑπακοῦσαι, P⁷⁴ has ὑπαντῆσαι. In D, after τὴν θύραν τοῦ, there is a rasura in which Blass thought he could read ἔ[ξ]ω. d has . . . januam foris . . .

14. It is clear that, notwithstanding the church's prayer, Rhoda did not expect the arrival of Peter. She recognized his voice and was so delighted (so that, if she was a slave, she was probably a Christian too) that she did not stop to admit him. She acted ἀπὸ τῆς χαρᾶς; this has been thought to be a Semitism, and the use of ἀπό does correspond to the causal use of מן; but 'this usage is classical' (M. 2. 461; cf. LS 192 s.v. III.6, 'of the cause, means, or occasion *from, by, or because of* which a thing is done'). Rhoda did not open τὸν πυλῶνα. Here πυλών seems to be more or less synonymous with θύρα; contrast v. 13. Luke might perhaps reply that to open the θύρα in the πυλών in fact had the effect of opening the πυλών. As the sentence continues δέ has the meaning *but on the contrary*; cf. v. 9, and see the note. Rhoda ran into the room where the Christians were praying and reported what had happened.

15. Rhoda was not believed; she must be out of her wits. Cf. 26.24. Initial disbelief emphasises the wonder of the deliverance. In the NT διισχυρίζεσθαι occurs elsewhere only at Lk. 22.59 (but cf. Acts 15.2 D); see *P. Mich.* (1977). 659, 14 (quoted in *ND* 2.81). Rhoda's strong affirmation brought the response that if anything had given her the impression that Peter was there it must have been his angel. 'Ita colligebant ex similitudine vocis' (Bengel); she had not seen him but only recognized his voice (v. 14). Judaism believed in protecting and guiding angels, and these were sometimes thought to resemble the human beings they protected. See StrB 1.781 783; 2.707; Dussct, (*RJ* 324), also Gen. 48.16, Tobit 3.4–6, 21; Mt. 18.10; Hermas, *Vision* 5.7 (with Dibelius's long note in *HNT* Ergänzungsband 494–496). The neatest illustration, though it is not early, is in GenR 78 (50a): R. Hama ben Hanina said, It was Esau's angelic prince with whom Jacob struggled: to this Gen. 33.10 refers, I have seen thy face as the appearance of the face of the angel; as the angel's face was, so is thy face. According to D, the opinion was expressed less confidently; for . . . ἔλεγον· ὁ ἄγγελος . . ., D sy^p have . . . ἔλεγον πρὸς αὐτήν, τυχὸν ὁ ἄγγελος . . . On guardian angels, see Barth (*CD* 3.3.518).

16. ἐπέμενεν κρούων. Certain Greek verbs are used in a finite tense with a complementary participle where (in some modern languages, including English) it seems natural to reverse the parts of the verb, translating the participle as a finite verb. The NT makes little use of this construction, but adds two fresh verbs to the list, τρέμειν (2 Peter 2.10) and ἐπιμένειν; so Radermacher (169), but here it is quite proper to render, Peter went on knocking. Eventually he succeeded in gaining access to the prayer meeting. The astonishment of those who saw him is understandable, though it must mean that they had had no hope of his release. The reading of D (ἐξανοίξαντες δὲ καὶ ἰδόντες αὐτὸν καὶ ἐξέστησαν) is not Greek and may reflect the Aramaic construction in which a participle can stand in paratactic connection with a finite verb. See Black (*AA* 69); even if the observation is correct it cannot be used as an argument for a special Semitic element in the Western text, for, as Black observes, there are cases where D has hypotaxis when other texts have parataxis. If it is significant (and not due to, e.g., an assimilation of the Greek to the Latin side of a bilingual MS) it will point to an underlying Semitic stratum in Acts, sporadically refined away in the textual tradition.

Haenchen (376) finds this a moment of 'höchster Spannung'. Peter stands at the door knocking. People in neighbouring houses will be wakened; they will see Peter in the street and inform the authorities; Peter will be rearrested and execution will undoubtedly follow. Will the Christians within open the door in time to take him into the house and out of sight? Rhoda's joy and the incredulity of the company defer the moment of safety and thus heighten the tension. This is a very modern reading of the situation and it is very unlikely that it ever occurred to Luke's mind or the mind of his readers. The angel had done his work and Peter was now safe. God would not bungle the rescue and leave the work half done.

17. In the NT κατασείειν occurs only in Acts (at 12.17; 13.16; 21.40 with the dative of χείρ, as is more usual; at 19.33 with the accusative); the word may refer to many different kinds of movement or shaking, is often used of a (manual) signal, and is not infrequently an orator's gesture. Cf. Josephus, *Ant.* 4.323 (Μωυσῆς τοὺς μὲν πόρρω τῇ χειρὶ κατασείων . . .); Lucan, *Bell. Civ.* 1.298 (dextraque silentia iussit); Tacitus, *Annals* 1.25 (stabat Drusus silentium manu poscens). It is supplemented by σιγᾶν — Peter needs silence in order to explain what has happened. For the infinitive, D has ἵνα σείγασιν (sic; lgd. σιγῶσιν or σιγάσωσιν), which may be taken as a step on the way to the replacement in Modern Greek of the infinitive by νά and the subjunctive (M. 1.240). D also adds εἰσῆλθεν καί — probably to be taken as an example of the Western editor's unwillingness to leave anything to the imagination.

For διηγεῖσθαι, *to relate an event*, cf. 9.27. The word is characteristic of Luke. The relation is given in the briefest and plainest terms (contrast the repetition of the story of Cornelius in ch. 10 and the repetition of the account of Paul's conversion in chs. 22 and 26). There is no reference to the angel, who acted on the orders and as the agent of the Lord. The report is to be passed on *to James and the brothers*. Luke apparently assumes that his readers will know, without any explanation, who James is (Brandon, *Fall* 27). James must therefore have been a person of considerable importance in the early years of the church; this is amply confirmed by Gal. 2 (not only 2.9 but especially 2.12, where Peter apparently accepts the authority of James). From Gal. 1.19 we infer that this James was one of the brothers of Jesus (for the meaning of *brother* in this context see on 1.14); cf. Mk 6.3. James (presumably this James) will reappear at 15.13; 21.18; on both these passages see the notes; see also the introduction to this paragraph (pp. 570f.) and the general treatment in Vol. II. He appears to have become the leader of the church in Jerusalem, with some sort of claim to wider if not universal authority. See A. Ehrhardt, *The Apostolic Succession*,

1953, 23 et passim. Calvin, rightly equating this James with one of the three pillars of Gal. 2.9, and believing that an apostle would not be passed over in comparison with a disciple, thinks that this James must have been the son of Alphaeus; few if any have followed him. *The brothers* are probably, as at 1.15, the Christians in general. All (not leaders only) are to be informed.

Peter then left the house (ἐξελθών) and went (ἐπορεύθη might be *travelled*, implying that Peter left Jerusalem, but the usage of πορεύεσθαι in the NT does not require a stronger translation than *went*)εἰς ἕτερον τόπον. For some account of the many conjectures concerning this unnamed τόπος see Cullmann (*Petrus* 40–5), with the conclusion that the meaning is that Peter now embarked on widespread missionary activity (cf. Dinkler, *Signum Crucis* 278, with the inference that the Council of Acts 15 at which Peter reappears must be set at the time of 11.27–30). That Peter did engage in missionary activity is the witness of the old tradition and of the NT itself (Acts 9.32–10.48; 1 Cor. 9.5; Gal. 2.11–15). It seems however probable that if Luke, for whom the mission to the Gentile world was one of the deepest interests, had meant this he would have been more explicit; perhaps he was running out of information about Peter; probably he meant only that Peter got clean away; the ἕτερος τόπος was a place where Herod was unlikely to lay hands on him. This may mean another town (Stählin 170 suggests Antioch), or, as Calvin (344) seems to imply, simply another house, not known as a Christian meeting-place. Dibelius (96) takes 'another place' to be a feature of legend; Bauernfeind (162) thinks that Luke could not express himself more precisely because Peter changed his residence frequently. There is nothing to suggest that Luke had in mind a journey to Rome. Whether Peter's departure meant that he was now stepping down from a position of authority is disputed. According to Cullmann (op. cit.) Peter now ceded the headship of the church to James; henceforth he was to be a missionary, as such deriving his authority from James. This is disputed by Benoit (*Ex. et Th.* 2.259, 289), according to whom Peter now informed James, the local authority, that in his (Peter's) absence, his (James's) responsibility would be greater than it had been. It is probably anachronistic to think in terms of such regional delimitations of authority, or indeed of the kind of authority that could be so delimited. It is speculative to suggest (with Bauernfeind 164) that James was related to the Twelve in the same way as Stephen and his companions; we have a (questionable) account of the relation of the Seven to the Twelve; we have no such account for James. The suggestion that the first stage of resistance to the Christian movement meant that the Seven were dispersed, the Twelve spared, the next that the Twelve were dispersed and only the strictest Jews (such as James) were spared, imposes too much system on Luke's narrative and (in all probability) on the events themselves.

18. In the morning there was naturally a good deal of *confusion, disorder* (τάραχος is synonymous with more common ταραχή) among the soldiers. Presumably during the night they had been asleep, their sleep being in Luke's mind supernaturally caused. They ask, What can (ἄρα) have become of Peter? τί serves as a direct predicate in a way not possible in English. Cf. Jn 21.21 and Josephus, *Life* 296, οἱ δ'εἴκοσι ... χρυσοῖ ... τί γεγόνασιν; What has become of the twenty gold pieces? See BDR § 299.2. For the characteristically Lucan litotes of οὐκ ὀλίγος cf. 14.28; 15.2; 17.4, 12; 19.23, 24; 27.20; and see Cadbury (*Making* 120f.). It is not unnatural that some of the versions should paraphrase: 36 453 1175 *pc* (sy^p) as mae bo^mss have μέγας (or the equivalent); more surprising is complete omission by D gig p Lcf.

19. καὶ μὴ εὑρών: the καί is concessive, *sought but did not find,* perhaps (so BDR § 442. 1a) in the sense of καὶ ὅμως, *sought and yet did not find.* The next step was naturally to cross-examine the soldiers (ἀνακρίνειν is most used in judicial contexts) who had allowed their prisoner to escape. Their fate was inevitable; ἀποκτανθῆναι in D* sy bo makes explicit the probable meaning of ἀπαχθῆναι (cf. Lk. 23.26): *led off to execution.* It is true that in Greek generally, including the papyri (see MM 51; BA 158), ἀπάγειν more frequently means *to arrest, to take to court,* or *to take to prison,* but the stronger sense is called for here. Cf. e.g. Demosthenes, 24.113 (736); Pliny, *Epistles* 10.96.3 (... interrogavi, supplicium minatus; perseverantes duci iussi). The death penalty might be expected. Blass (142) refers to the Codex Justinianus 9.4.4 (Instituto Romano custodes, si vinctus effugisset, pro eo pares poenas luebant). This rule would not automatically apply in Herod's kingdom, but it would be surprising if it did not. Cf. Petronius, *Satyricon* 112.

Herod left Jerusalem; this is what Luke means by Judaea, though he is not using the word in its official sense. Caesarea was the capital of Judaea, which therefore Herod did not leave. For κατέρχεσθαι (a Lucan word: Lk twice; Acts thirteen times; James, once) in the sense of leaving the capital cf. 8.5; 9.32; 11.27. Caesarea on Sea is meant; see on 10.1. This note of place leads immediately to the next part of the story, and may give its date. According to Josephus, *Ant.* 19.343 Herod visited Caesarea in order to celebrate spectacles in honour of Caesar; see below, on v. 23.

20. The word θυμομαχεῖν occurs here only in the NT (cf. Polybius 27.8.4). Sidon and Tyre were free cities on the Phoenician coast, Sidon some twenty miles north of Tyre, thus falling within the province of Syria. This means that it is impossible to take θυμομαχεῖν in the sense 'to be at war with'. Herod was very angry.

An account of the death of Herod (Agrippa I), in many respects closely parallel to that given here in Acts, is found in Josephus, *Ant.* 19. 343–353; see also the brief reference in *War* 2.219, and Eusebius, *HE* 2.10.3–9 (where the narrative of *Ant.* 19 is quoted). The most important parallels and differences between these accounts will be noted. The contrasts are discussed by Dibelius (19f.). In his opinion Acts contains a Jewish legend, older than the account given by Josephus.

The Tyrians and Sidonians (we must of course think of their representatives) presented themselves before Herod jointly (for ὁμοθυμαδόν, not merely *in agreement* but *together*, see on 1.14). The Western text underlines the fact of representation, and from both cities (οἱ δὲ ὁμοθυμαδὸν ἐξ ἀμφοτέρων τῶν πόλεων) (μέρων, 614) παρῆσαν πρὸς τὸν βασιλέα, D 614 (sy^{hmg}) mae). In this variant πρός with the accusative is retained, though παρά with the dative would correspond with classical usage. *Blastus* is not mentioned in the other accounts of Herod's death (so that Luke is independent of Josephus and uses a different source), and is otherwise unknown, though his office as ὁ ἐπὶ τοῦ κοιτῶνος is a familiar one (cf. cubiculo praepositus, Suetonius, *Domitian* 16) and the phrase became common in late Greek, κοιτών now replacing the Attic δωμάτιον (Phrynichus 227). Conzelmann (71) takes the intervention of Blastus as one of several points which, remaining unexplained, indicate that Luke is abbreviating a longer version. The point is explained if Pallis (64; also Rackham 181) is right in translating πείσαντες, *having paid* or *bribed*. He cites Xenophon, *Memorabilia* 3.11.1, but it is quite uncertain that in this passage persuasion means persuasion by payment, and it is better to leave Luke's meaning open: they persuaded Blastus to act on their behalf, but by what means they persuaded him we do not know.

The delegations ἠτοῦντο εἰρήνην. In itself this sounds like a petition for the end of hostilities, but (see above) it is unlikely that actual warfare had been taking place. More probably we should think of economic sanctions applied by Herod against Tyre and Sidon. The narrative in Josephus says nothing about this; the assembly had gathered (*Ant.* 19.343) because of spectacles celebrated by Herod in honour of Caesar. Tyre and Sidon needed good relations with Herod and Palestine because they were supplied (τρέφεσθαι, *nourished*, as of a child, but the word was widely applied) from the king's territory. They drew their food supplies from his kingdom. Again, the Western text makes it clear that Tyre and Sidon, though acting in concert, were distinct regions: D lat have τὰς χώρας αὐτῶν. For χώραν (χώρας), E 33 have πόλιν; see Wilcox 142 for the suggestion that behind this variant lies the ambiguous מדינה. That Tyre and Sidon were thus supplied must mean that 'Palestine had an exportable surplus of food' (Clarke, *NTP* 112). This fits ill with the necessity of sending supplies from Antioch to Jerusalem (11.27–30); but the famine which may be referred to there (see the note) is to be dated several years after the death of Herod.

21. τακτῇ δὲ ἡμέρᾳ, on an appointed, prescribed, day — appointed for the meeting with the Tyrian and Sidonian delegation, though it seems that others also were present (δῆμος, v. 22).

Herod put on royal robes, no doubt splendid ones; Josephus (*Ant.* 19.344) says that on the second day of the festival he put on στολὴν ἐξ ἀργύρου πεποιημένην πᾶσαν, ὡς θαυμάσιον ὑφὴν εἶναι The silver texture was caught by the rays of the morning sun. Thus attired Herod sat on the tribune (βῆμα, *'raised place* or *tribune* to speak from in a public assembly;, LS 314, s.v. II 2) and addressed them. δημηγορεῖν is *to make a public speech*, and not more than this may be intended, but the word is sometimes used in a pejorative sense; e.g. Demosthenes 3 (*Third Olynthiac*). 3(29), πρὸς χάριν δημηγορεῖν ('haranguing for popularity', tr. Pickard-Cambridge); cf. Plato, *Gorgias* 503ab (rhetoric is of two sorts, τὸ μὲν ἕτερόν που τούτου κολακεία ἂν εἴη καὶ αἰσχρὰ δημηγορία). It may well be that Luke had this overtone of the word in his mind. In Josephus's narrative Herod does not speak. It has been suggested (J. Morgenstern, *HUCA* 20 (1947), 90, 91) that Herod was intentionally representing himself as the sungod at an equinoctial or solstitial festival. Both Josephus and Luke however attribute the claim to divinity to the hearers rather than Herod, but Herod (according to both) was not unwilling to accept it, and may have intended to make a supernatural impression.

22. The Western text has not finished with the political circumstances, and adds at the beginning of the verse, καταλλαγέντος δὲ αὐτοῦ τοῖς Τυρίοις (D (p^c w sy^h**)). This means that Herod's graciousness in pardoning the Tyrians (but not the Sidonians?) contributed to if it did not constitute the ground on which he was acclaimed as divine. The attribution of divinity is said to come not from the delegations but from ὁ δῆμος, the popular assembly of the citizens (of Caesarea, we must suppose; v. 19). This fits Josephus's account better than that in Acts, where one would suppose that, in addition to Herod and his entourage, only the Tyrians and Sidonians would be present. According to Josephus the speakers were οἱ κόλακες, the flatterers; they shouted, ἀνεβόων. According to Luke the δῆμος *called out*, ἐπεφώνει, claiming that the voice (φωνή) they had heard came not from a man (ἄνθρωπος) but from a god (θεός); cf. *Ant.* 19.345, θεὸν προσαγορεύοντες. Josephus makes a wordy addition: May you be propitious (εὐμενής) to us; if we have hitherto feared you as a man, yet henceforth we agree that you are more than mortal in your being (κρείττονα θνητῆς φύσεως). Tacitus, *Annals* 14.15; 16.22; Suetonius, *Nero* 21 are somewhat distant parallels.

23. By putting himself, or allowing himself to be put, in the place of God Herod has committed the most fundamental of sins, and Luke describes immediate punishment. Cf. Ezk. 28.2, 6, and for Luke's language especially 9 (σὺ δὲ εἶ ἄνθρωπος καὶ οὐ θεός — spoken to the Prince of Tyre). παραχρῆμα is a Lucan word (see on 3.7). Because Herod accepted for himself the glory that he, and the people, should have given to God alone (cf. Rom. 1.21), an angel of the Lord (recalling the ἄγγελος κυρίου who delivered Peter (v. 7), but of course not necessarily to be identified with him) struck him down. For this use of πατάσσειν cf. 2 Kdms 19.35 (ἐξῆλθεν ἄγγελος κυρίου καὶ ἐπάταξεν; contrast πατάξας in v. 7). The word ἄγγελος occurs in the narrative of Josephus, though in a different setting, and the version of Eusebius differs again. According to Josephus (*Ant.* 19.346), after being hailed as divine Herod looked up and saw an owl perching on a rope over his head. This recalled an incident, described in 18.195, 200, in which the appearance of an owl was interpreted as a sign of approaching good fortune, but at the same time the prediction was made that the next time Herod saw an owl the sight would mean that evil was about to befall him. He now recognized the owl as ἄγγελος (messenger, harbinger) κακῶν as formerly ἄγγελος τῶν ἀγαθῶν. In Eusebius (*HE* 2.10.6) Herod saw τῆς ἑαυτοῦ κεφαλῆς ὑπερκαθεζόμενον ἄγγελον. This he understood to be now κακῶν αἴτιον, as formerly τῶν ἀγαθῶν. It is usually supposed that Eusebius edited out the superstitious owl, but Lawlor and Oulton (2.64) argue that the text may have been modified before it reached Eusebius.

Herod was eaten by worms (σκωληκόβρωτος; the word is used elsewhere of vegetable matter and is not used by physicians, though men are said to be eaten by σκώληκες) and died (ἐξέψυξεν; elsewhere in the NT the word is used only at 5.5, 10, of the deaths of Ananias and Sapphira).

The theme *de mortibus persecutorum* (Lactantius), the deaths of persecutors and other bad characters, is a very common one. Many can be collected from Wettstein and other commentators. Worms or the like are found in all the following. Judith 16.17 (the Lord's enemies in general); *Apocalypse of Peter* 27 (persecutors in general); 2 Macc. 9.5–12 (Antiochus Epiphanes, ending in v. 12 with δίκαιον ὑποτάσσεσθαι τῷ θεῷ καὶ μὴ θνητὸν ὄντα ἰσόθεα φρονεῖν); Plutarch, *Sulla* 36 (474) (Sulla; lice, not worms); Lucian, *Pseudomantis* 59 (Alexander the false prophet); Josephus, *Ant.* 17.168–190 (Herod the Great; 169 . . . σῆψις σκώληκας ἐμποιοῦσα); Eusebius, *HE* 8.16.4 (Galerius); Tertullian, *ad Scapulam* 3 (Claudius Lucius Herminianus). For the role of angels see e.g. 2 Kdms 24.16; 4 Kdms 19.35.

Herod is more explicitly a 'divine man' (θεῖος ἀνήρ) even than the magi of chs. 8 and 13. Luke doubtless deemed his fate appropriate to such a person. He is not likely to have thought of the apostles in these terms.

On ἀνθ' ὧν, Moule (*IB* 71) comparing this passage with Lk. 1.20; 19.44; 2 Thess. 2.10, all (but not Lk. 12.3) with reference to judgment upon wrong, thinks that the ὧν seems grammatically illogical and is probably due to Semitic influence, representing the Hebrew תחת אשר. See however BDR § 208. 1, where the construction is described as classical and is said to occur also in papyri. Of the classical examples given in LS 153 (s.v. ἀντί), Aeschylus, *Prometheus Vinctus* 31 is less effective than the others (Sophocles, *Oedipus Tyrannus* 264 and Thucydides 6.83.1), because in it it is possible to find a straightforward antecedent for ὧν. By ἔδωκεν τὴν δόξαν τῷ θεῷ Luke probably means exactly what he says. If there is a further meaning it will be that of Joshua 7.19 (confess the truth) rather than 'pray for forgiveness' (Pallis 64f.).

The death of Herod calls for one further note. Its date is discussed in great detail by Lake in *Begs.* 5. 446–52. The evidence is not unambiguous, but there is a high degree of probability that Herod died in AD 44, and a lower degree of probability that he died on March 5. This date assumes that the games described by Josephus fell on the foundation day of the city, March 5. But they could have been held on Augustus's birthday, August 1. See also *NS* 1.452f. If he died on March 5, and if the references to Unleavened Bread in v. 3 and to Passover in v. 4 are to be accepted, we must conclude that Luke has telescoped his narrative and that Peter's arrest and escape took place about Passover time in AD 43, since 5 March 44 will have been before Passover in that year. It may be however that Herod died later in the year; in this case the story of Peter will fall in the year 44. In either case, however, the death of Herod occurred before the probable date of the famine in 11.27–30. Luke's narrative is not to be taken as a chronologically ordered sequence of events.

32. A CONNECTING LINK 12.24, 25

(24) The word of God grew and multiplied. (25) Barnabas and Saul returned, having fulfilled their service in Jerusalem,[1] and having picked up as companion John who was called Mark.

[1]*Begs.*, returned to Jerusalem in completion of their mission; RSV, returned from Jerusalem when they had fulfilled their mission; NEB, their task fulfilled, returned from Jerusalem; NJB, completed their task at Jerusalem and came back.

Bibliography

V. Bartlett, *JTS* 4 (1903), 438–40.

M. Black, *FS* Nida, 119–30.

C. D. Chambers, *JTS* 24 (1923), 183–7.

J. Dupont, *Études*, 217–41.

W. F. Howard, *JTS* 24 (1923), 403–6.

J. Kodell, as in (16).

A. Nairne, *JTS* 11 (1910), 560–2.

P. Parker, as in (29).

A. T. Robertson, *JTS* 25 (1924), 286–9.

Commentary

It would be possible, and might be desirable, to treat these two verses as part of the preceding paragraph. Haenchen and some other commentators do so on the ground that they form a concluding counterpart to 11.27–30. But 11.27–30 is not directly linked with 12.1, and since 11.27–30 is not part of the complex contained in 12.1–23 it is better to treat its partner separately too. Moreover, though the material contained in 12.1–23 is on the whole traditional (with some Lucan editorial touches), vv. 24, 25 are transitional and undoubtedly provided by Luke himself. Verse 24 has a number of parallels. Whatever happenings have to be described, to Luke the outcome is the same. God so orders events that, though James the apostle and Herod the persecutor die, though Peter gives place to James, his word grows and multiplies.

In v. 25 Luke takes up the narrative of 11.27–30. Whatever be the solution of the textual puzzle in this verse, the mission of Barnabas and Saul on behalf of the church at Antioch is brought to a successful conclusion, and Luke is able to take up his Antioch material in ch. 13. This again, like some of the content of 12.1–23 (see above, p. 572) serves to mark a turning-point in the story. Antioch has established itself in relation to the old church of Jerusalem; it is now ready to move out into new fields and establish new churches dependent on itself.

Thus 12.24f. is both the conclusion of 12.1–23 and the introduction to chs. 13 and 14. For this reason, and because Luke is here writing on his own and providing an editorial link between passages in which he is using and handing on tradition, it is better to allow the verses to stand by themselves as a very short independent piece. Cf. 9.31.

C. Burchard (*ZNW* 61 (1970), 165f.) prefers to take these verses with 13.1–3, making a unit of 12.24 (25)–13.3 (which, he says, has a parallel in 1.12–14: 'In beiden Abschnitten folgt auf eine Rückkehr (1.12/12.25) eine Liste (1.13/13.1) und ein Hinweis auf Gottesdienst (1.14/13.2a)'). This does less than justice to the reference back to 11.27–30. Benoit (*Ex. et Th.* 3.292), who thinks that 11.27–30 is continued in 15.3, argues that 12.25 is 'une addition rédactionnelle', 'une simple suture' (294). With this we may agree (but on Benoit's reconstruction of Paul's visits to Jerusalem see the discussion of ch. 15 in Vol. II). With less probability Bultmann (*Exegetica* 421f.), who accepts the reading with ἡμῶν at 11.28 and thinks that in 13.2 Luke's source may have read λειτουργούντων δὲ ἡμῶν, ascribes v. 25 to the Antiochian source. None of these suggestions seems preferable to the view taken here, that Luke himself wrote both v. 24 and v. 25, as a conclusion to the story that occupies chs. 1–12, as a note on the successful conclusion of the mission undertaken in 11.27–30, and as setting the stage for the scene described in 13.1–3. That Luke wishes us to think (Roloff 192) that Barnabas and Saul were in Jerusalem during the persecution, and that 'gerade in der Stunde der Not die Gemeinden von Jerusalem und Antiochien trotz aller ihrer Verschiedenheit eng zusammenstanden' is a motivation of only secondary importance. Schille (277) is nearer the mark with 'Die kommende Heidenmission wächst organisch aus der alten Judenmission heraus'.

There is no doubt that a natural consecutive reading of Luke's text suggests that the 'famine visit' and the death of Herod happened at approximately the same time. In fact the famine took place at least three years later; the famine visit must of course have been later still. The natural point at which to place it is at the end of ch. 14 and the beginning of ch. 15 — if, that is, the missionary journey of chs. 13, 14 is correctly placed. On this see below.

24. Herod and the Jews had thought to put an end to the Christian movement by an attack on its leaders; Luke is happy to report that the outcome was precisely the reverse of their intention. For ὁ λόγος τοῦ θεοῦ see on 4.31; it is one of Luke's most frequent expressions for the Christian message (6.2; 8.14; 11.1; 13.5, 7, 46, 48; (16.32); 17.13; 18.11). It is the reading here of P⁷⁴ ℵ A D E Ψ 𝔐 gig p sy co; the alternative (ὁ λόγος τοῦ κυρίου, supported only by B vg bo^mss) has some claim to originality in that it is not Luke's usual phrase and might have been brought into conformity with the rest. On the other hand, Metzger (397) thinks that it may have been influenced by κυρίου in 12.23. There is similar variation at 16.32. The verb αὐξάνειν goes oddly with λόγος, but Luke uses it as at 6.7 (see the note) and 19.20. The same may be said of πληθύνειν, elsewhere used only of (the number of) Christian disciples, of the church, and of the people of Israel. Luke means of course that the word of God increased in effectiveness and in effect, so that the number of believers multiplied. It is clear that he is summing up the results of the narrative he has now completed before turning to the new material of the following chapters.

25. The reference to Barnabas and Saul looks back to 11.30, where they were last mentioned. To the name Saul some Western witnesses (614 p* sy^h** mae) add ὃς ἐπεκλήθη Παῦλος, anticipating the name from 13.9. Whatever is made of the textual problem discussed below, they had completed the mission that had been entrusted to them. They therefore returned; ὑποστρέφειν is a Lucan word. The next words vary in the MSS.

εἰς Ἰερουσαλήμ   ℵ B 𝔐 sa^ms
ἐξ Ἰερουσαλήμ   P⁷⁴ A 33 945 1739 al
ἀπὸ Ἰερουσαλήμ   D E Ψ 36 323 453 614 1175 al

Of the Latin VSS, WW (3.119) say, '**ab** apud nostros non fluctuat', noting that it might represent either ἐξ or ἀπό. εἰς Ἀντιόχειαν is read (in nearly every case added to ἐξ or ἀπό Ἰερουσαλήμ) by E 104 323 945 1175 1739 pc p w sy^p sa.

Of the first three readings the first, which appears to state that Barnabas and Saul returned to the place where they already were, is undoubtedly the most difficult; but if read in this way it is too difficult to be accepted. It does not make sense. But ἐξ and ἀπό are clearly corrections of the difficult εἰς (with the addition in many cases of εἰς Ἀντιόχειαν to help the connection, and perhaps to retain the εἰς), and cannot be accepted. The possibilities that remain are (a) to suppose that there was a primitive corruption of the text and to conjecture the original, and (b) to find an alternative way of taking the Greek that Luke appears to have written. If (a) is followed, the simplest course is to suppose that the words are out of order and to rewrite them as τὴν εἰς Ἰερουσαλὴμ πληρώσαντες διακονίαν (so Hort, *Notes* 2.94), and to translate them, 'having fulfilled their ministry to Jerusalem', or (recalling the virtual equivalence of εἰς and ἐν in Hellenistic Greek), 'having fulfilled their ministry in Jerusalem'. The latter translation however hardly requires a conjecture. Luke did not always adopt the 'correct' order of words, and his words as they stand can be rendered in the way suggested; (b) is probably the better choice. See the very full discussion, reaching this conclusion, by J. Dupont (*NovT* 1 (1956), 275–303=*Études* 217-41). He draws attention to the difficulty of explaining the reference to John Mark (see on 12.12) if the verse is translated *they returned to Jerusalem*. *Begs.* 4.141 thinks that, if εἰς is read, v. 25 may be an intended repetition of 11.30, made in order to show that the famine and famine visit took place after the death of Herod. Schmithals (119) thinks that Luke wrote ἐξ or ἀπό and that copyists changed this to εἰς, dating the arrival in Jerusalem of Barnabas and Saul at this time because it seemed incredible that they should have been in Jerusalem during the events of 12.1–23 and yet have taken no part in them. See further Black (*FS Nida* 123f.) and J. C. Hurd (*The Origin of 1 Corinthians*, 1965, 34f.).

Related to the question of text is Moulton's discussion (M. 1.133) of the tenses of the participles πληρώσαντες and συμπαραλαβόντες. Rackham (184) wished to translate 'they returned to Jerusalem and fulfilled their ministry and took with them John.' Moulton comments, 'Now "returned . . . in fulfilment . . ." is a good coincident aorist and quite admissible. But to take συνπαραλαβόντες in this way involves an unblushing aorist of *subsequent* action, and this I must maintain has not yet been paralleled either in the NT or outside.' Moulton prefers Hort's conjecture (above); in any case, grammar is best satisfied by 'They returned (that is, to Antioch, whence they had set out) . . . having fulfilled . . . and having picked up Mark (as a future associate in their work; cf. 2 Tim. 4.11, ἀναλαβών . . .'. See Metzger (398–400) for other conjectures. Williams (152) refers to C. D. Chambers (*JTS* 24 (1922), 183ff.) and W. F. Howard (op. cit., 403ff.) for the translation 'in order to fulfil', which, notwithstanding 25.13, is very improbable.

In view of ἐπικληθέντα we should perhaps not ascribe to Luke too great care in the use of tenses; cf. 12.12, where ἐπικαλούμενον is used. In v. 25 the present tense appears in P⁷⁴ ℵ A 33 81 1175 2495 *al*; the aorist is in B D E Ψ 𝔐. Of course, both make sense; he had been given the name and now bore it. For John Mark see on 12.12. It is not necessary to conjecture that Barnabas and Saul had come to know him because they had stayed in the house of Mary his mother; but it may be correct that Luke deduced the statement of this verse from the data of 12.12 and 13.5 (Pesch 371). His role is looked at from the other side in *Acta Barnabae* 1 (L.-B. 2.2.292), συνακολουθῶν Βαρνάβᾳ καὶ Παύλῳ — not 'they took him' but 'he joined the party'.

The commentary of Ephrem on this verse (*Begs.* 3.416) runs (Conybeare's translation): Shavul autem et Barnabas qui tulerunt cibaria sanctorum in Ierusalem, reversi sunt cum Iohanne qui vocatus est Marcus, et Lucas Syrenaicus. Hi autem ambo evangelistae sunt, et ante discipulatum Pauli scripserunt, et idcirco iterabat ex evangelio eorum ubique. With this should be compared the reading with ἡμῶν at 11.28, and Bultmann's conjecture at 13.2. It is however doubtful whether any of these facts and conjectures means more than that in the tradition surrounding Acts there arose a desire to bring the supposed author into as close contact with his story as possible.

XI
ANTIOCH INITIATES THE WIDER MISSION
(13.1–14.28)

33. BARNABAS AND SAUL COMMISSIONED FROM ANTIOCH. 13.1–3.

(1) In Antioch, in the local church, there were prophets and teachers, Barnabas and Symeon (called Niger) and Lucius (of Cyrene), Manaen (an intimate friend of Herod the Tetrarch), and Saul. (2) While they were waiting upon the Lord and fasting, the Holy Spirit said, 'Set apart for me Barnabas and Saul for the work to which I have called them.' (3) Then they fasted and prayed and laid their hands on them, and sent them on their way.

Bibliography

E. Best, *JTS* 11 (1960), 344–8.

E. F. F. Bishop, *ExpT* 51 (1940), 148–53.

J. Coppens, as in (16).

S. Dockx, *NRTh* 98 (1976), 238–50.

J. Dupont, *Nouvelles Études*, 163–71.

H. Greeven, *ZNW* 44 (1953), 1–43.

T. Y. Mullins, *JBL* 95 (1976), 603–14.

J. Murphy-O'Connor, *RB* (1982), 71–91.

E. Peterson, *RechScR* 36 (1949), 557–79.

E. Peterson, *NuntSodalNeotUps* 2 (1949), 9f.

H. Schürmann, *FS* Erfurt, 107–47.

Commentary

This short paragraph marks a major departure in Luke's story. Up to this point, contacts with Gentiles (one might almost say, missionary activity in general) have been almost fortuitous. Philip was despatched along an unusual road not knowing that he would encounter an Ethiopian eunuch reading Scripture; Peter was surprised by the gift of the Holy Spirit to an uncircumcised and unbaptized Gentile; the missionaries to Antioch did not set out with the intention of evangelizing Gentiles. Here, however, though the initiative is still ascribed to the Holy Spirit (v. 2), an extensive evangelistic journey into territory in no sense properly Jewish (though there was a Jewish element in the population, as there was in most parts of the Empire) is deliberately planned, and two associates of the local church are commissioned to execute it.

The paragraph contains a description of the leadership of the church in Antioch (there are prophets and teachers); a list of names of some of the leaders (Barnabas, Symeon, Lucius, Manaen, and Saul); a reference to (hardly a description of) a church gathering (ministering and fasting; a communication from the Holy Spirit, made presumably by one of the prophets); and a form of commissioning and blessing (fasting, prayer, and the imposition of hands). Part of this could have been simply read back by the author of Acts from the practices of his own time, but there is good reason for thinking that he is at least in part dependent on earlier tradition. It seems to have been his own view (11.30; 14.23; 15.2, 4, 6, 22, 23; 16.4; 20.17; 21.18) that church officials included presbyters (also perhaps called bishops, ἐπίσκοποι, 20.28); he has not introduced these words here, probably because his source told him that the church at Antioch had prophets and teachers and mentioned no other ministers. It is improbable that he introduced the personal names he cites with no traditional basis; apart from Barnabas and Saul they are quite unessential to the narrative. Bultmann (*Exegetica* 418f.) may well be right in thinking that the list points to written rather than oral tradition, but the point cannot be proved. λειτουργεῖν is not a word that Luke uses elsewhere to describe what Christians do when they meet (elsewhere he uses the word-group only at Lk. 1.23, of the activity of priests in the Temple), nor has he spoken of fasting as a Christian practice; on the contrary, he associates Christian gatherings with eating (2.42, 46; 9.19; 10.10; etc.). On the other hand, 'the Holy Spirit said' is a Lucan expression (cf. 10.19, and see the note), and the imposition of hands recalls 6.6. There is a high measure of probability in the view that Luke is here dependent on Antiochian material which he edited. This will stand in relation with what precedes (11.27–30) and what follows (13.4–14.28), and it seems likely that Luke was able to draw at Antioch on a story that recounted the founding and establishing there of a mixed Jewish and Gentile church which traced its spiritual ancestry back to the work of Stephen and his associates in Jerusalem, and continued with missionary work based on that church. This is not to claim that the story was told as a continuous whole, still less that it existed on paper (though some of it may have been written down). It appears that 13.1–3 stands in the midst of a considerable sequence in which the church of Antioch looks back to its origins and also

relates its own contribution to Christian missionary expansion.
Bultmann (see on v. 2) thinks that in 11.27–30; 13.1–3 we have the
beginning of the 'We' source, and that the missionary tour of chs. 13,
14 must be placed after rather than before the Council of ch. 15. In
any case this narrative, in which Barnabas and Saul leave Antioch at
13.3f. and return there in 14.26–28, must all be considered as written
from an Antiochene point of view on the basis of information
supplied at least in part by Antioch. The question what, in this
sentence, 'in part' may mean must be considered from point to point
as chs. 13 and 14 are dealt with. Here it may be said in advance that
the most probable view is that Luke found in Antioch some account
of churches having some connection with Antioch as centre, and
collected stories that referred to them. The speeches, including the
synagogue sermon at Pisidian Antioch, are probably his own
composition, though, as with the Petrine speeches, which this speech
resembles, it would accord with his method and intention if in the
process he used material as old as he could get. For the most part
there is no inherent connection between the places visited and the
events said to happen in them; the place-names could be redistributed
and no problems would result. This is not to say that Paul did not
travel in the cities mentioned; and if the author of Acts (or of a source
of Acts) was a companion of Paul's there is no reason why he should
not have obtained from Paul himself (as well as from other sources)
information about journeys that took place before he joined the
travelling party. He may also have collected information on the spot,
as well as in Antioch. It is true that there was trouble between Paul
and one element in the church at Antioch (Gal. 2.13), but (according
to Acts) Paul returned and spent some time there (18.22f.). It must
however be added that most of the incidents in chs. 13 and 14 (all
perhaps except the story of Elymas and the events at Lystra) seem
formal and stylized, and show less local detail and less close
connection with the events than do the stories of the later Pauline
missions.

Thus we have (as might be expected) in this paragraph a combination
of Antiochene tradition, which may run back to a fairly early date,
with Lucan editing, which belongs to the date of composition of
Acts. The resultant picture of the early church and its ministry is
accordingly complex, though features that strongly suggest a late
date are neither numerous nor important. E. Best (*JTS* 11 (1960),
344–8) emphasizes the parallel in language with Num. 8 and the
narrative in which 'the Levites are set apart to a professional ministry
to God' (347), with the laying on of hands. He concludes, 'Likewise
Paul and Barnabas are set apart to a professional ministry to do for
the Church what it can no longer do for itself' (348). The appointment
does not 'inaugurate the lay/clerical distinction within the Christian
community; it is prophets and teachers who at the command of the

Holy Spirit separate Paul and Barnabas from among themselves; if the distinction already existed Paul and Barnabas were, even prior to this ceremony, members of the 'clergy'; if the distinction did not exist this did not create it' (348). Best is here recognizing the fluid state of the early development of the ministry, but not recognizing it adequately. We can hardly describe this step as the inauguration of a full-time ministry, for Paul seems to have been a full-time Christian worker before it (11.26, 30), and there is evidence both in Acts (18.3; 20.34) and in the epistles that he was a part-time worker after it. It may be nearer to the truth to say that Barnabas and Saul became apostles *of the church of Antioch* (see 14.4, 14, and the notes, and cf. 2 Cor. 8.23), provided that it is recognized that, in Paul's own conviction, he became an apostle at the time of his conversion (though he may not have understood at once the full meaning of his vocation). How formal the manner of appointment was, it is difficult to say. It says much for Luke's understanding of his source, and for his accuracy, that he does not introduce the word πρεσβύτερος, or any of the words that were coming into use at the time when he and the author of the Pastorals were writing. It is however right to note the parallel between Luke's narrative (with fasting, prayer, and the imposition of hands for those who had already been singled out by the Spirit — that is, probably, by the words of the prophets) and the account of ordination in the Pastorals. For prophecy, cf. 1 Tim. 1.18; 4.14; for the laying on of hands, cf. 1 Tim. 4.14; 2 Tim. 1.6; and see Wilson (*Pastorals* 58f.). See also G. Strecker (*ZNW* 53 (1962), 67–77), and the criticism of that part of Strecker's article that relates to the present point by Wilson (*Gentiles*, 181f.): 'The rather tortuous attempt to show that the mission in 13.1f. is, by a series of connections, legitimised by Jerusalem is highly improbable. Nothing in 11.27–13.4 suggests that this is the case; the only legitimiser is the Spirit, not the Jerusalem Church' (182).

1. The new paragraph begins in connection with rather than disjunction from that which precedes; the μὲν οὖν with which Luke often turns to a new subject is missing. Whatever is made of the textual question in 12.25 it is assumed that the scene has changed from Jerusalem to Antioch (on which town see the note on 11.19). For the interconnection of the paragraphs from 11.27–30 onwards see the introductions to this and to the preceding paragraph.

κατὰ τὴν οὖσαν ἐκκλησίαν. For the use of the participle see 5.17 (and the note); and 14.13 (D). This may be a case of the separation of a participle from its adjunct (here, ἐν ᾿Αντιοχείᾳ): the church that was in Antioch. But BDR § 474. 5(c), n. 9 rightly prefer 'In Antioch, in the local church'; so also M. 1.228 (quoting BM iii. p. 136 (AD 18), ἐπὶ ταῖς οὖσαις γειτνίαις, and other papyri); 3.152.

In the local church at Antioch were προφῆται καὶ διδάσκαλοι. At 2.17f. the words of Joel are used to foretell the rise of Christian prophecy; at 11.27, prophets come down from Jerusalem to Antioch. E. Peterson (*Nuntius* 2 (1949) 9f.) thinks that these are the prophets referred to here; E. Schweizer (*CONT* 22c) rightly disagrees. See also 15.32; 19.6; 21.9, 10. It is quite possible (so e.g. Roloff 193) that these were travelling prophets (cf. *Didache* 11–13) who had settled in Antioch; whatever they may have been previously they do now appear to have settled. Teachers are mentioned in Acts here only, but cf. διδάσκειν (1.1; 4.2, 18; 5.21, 25, 28, 42; 11.26; 15.1, 35; 18.11, 25; 20.20; 21.21, 28; 28.3) and διδαχή (2.42; 5.28; 13.12; 17.19). Luke's own preferred word for ministers is πρεσβύτεροι (11.30; 14.23; 15.2, 4, 6, 22, 23; 16.4; 20.17, 18), who were also sometimes known as ἐπίσκοποι (20.28). He is probably dependent here on information derived directly or indirectly from Antioch, and it may be inferred that the words indicate the organization of the church at Antioch. Cf. 1 Cor. 12.28 (also Rom. 12.6f.; Eph. 4.11), where apostles stand before prophets and teachers. It is disputed whether in this passage *apostles* are to be understood in the sense in which Paul understood his own ministry or are, like prophets and teachers, local ministers (see *Signs* 46f.). It is certain that usage of the word ἀπόστολος was not uniform in the early church, and it may be correct that when prophets were sent out from Antioch on mission they were (as perhaps Barnabas and Paul in 14.4, 14) known as apostles. Prophecy was undoubtedly thought of as a spiritual gift (cf. especially 2.17f.; 19.6); so probably was teaching. The distinction between the two may have been a matter of manner rather than of content. Cf. the association of prophets and teachers in *Didache* 15.1; and see Schneider (2.113). It seems clear from what follows that the prophets and teachers, in addition to giving inspired exhortation and instruction, took the lead in planning and administering the church's work. The suggestion (Barth, *CD* 4.2.201) that διδάσκαλοι are found only in Gentile churches where there was no possibility of confusion with the one Teacher will hardly stand against 2.42.

The two general terms, *prophets and teachers*, are followed by five names, whose bearers should probably be thought of as either prophets or teachers — or both, since there is no reason why the same person should not sometimes prophesy and sometimes teach. This is made explicit by D* vg (ἐν οἷς for ὅ τε); in any case, the list is most naturally taken as in apposition with the designations. Bauernfeind 168 observes that when Barnabas and Saul became ἀπόστολοι (14.4, 14) the church possessed the three categories of 1 Cor. 12.28 — apostles, prophets, and teachers. The Western reading quoted above probably reflects that five was a small number of officers for a church such as Antioch; Schmithals 119 seems to hold a similar view, since he suggests that the list may originally have included

Judas and Silas (15.27, 32). Why their names should have been removed does not appear. Schmithals also notes the position of Saul at the end of the list; he is down-graded in this way as part of Luke's attack on the false teachers who appealed to him. This is not more convincing than the conclusion (121; cf. Strecker above), 'Die Legitimität des Paulus beruht auf der Legitimierung durch die Zwölf Apostel'. Haenchen's observation (378) that no names are repeated from the list in 6.5 is more important, and the conclusion, 'Der Stephanuskreis verfügte über eine grössere Anzahl hervorragender Persönlichkeiten' is probably correct. The names are listed by means of the following particles: ὅ τε Β. καὶ Σ. . . . καὶ Λ. . . ., Μ. τε . . . καὶ Σ. Luke is probably importing variety into his list, and not setting out pairs or groups (e.g. three prophets and two teachers). If any pair had been singled out it would have been Barnabas and Saul, and we should have had ὅ τε Β. καὶ Σ., κτλ. For Barnabas see 4.36, and the note; he was not the founder of the church in Antioch, but was involved very nearly from the beginning (11.22). It was he who brought Saul to Antioch (11.25f.). He accompanies Saul in the missionary journey of chs. 13 and 14, but separates from him at 15.39f. (cf. Gal. 2.13). Symeon is distinguished from Simon Peter (Symeon at 15.14; cf. 2 Peter 1.1) by the addition of ὁ καλούμενος (ἐπικαλούμενος, D 424 pc) Νίγερ. The construction is correct: the appositive has the article because this Symeon is being distinguished from another. Niger (a Latinism, *black*) occurs nowhere else in the NT; occasionally elsewhere, e.g. of a Peraean distinguished for his bravery (Josephus, *War*, 2.520; this means that nothing can be inferred from the name of Symeon Niger's race). The appositive with Lucius also has the article, incorrectly, unless we are intended to distinguish him from another Lucius (perhaps him of Rom. 16.21). This seems improbable, since this Lucius is not mentioned in Acts. It is equally improbable that Luke was distinguishing Lucius from himself (see the note on 12.25). This Lucius came from Cyrene; it will be recalled that they were men of Cyprus and Cyrene who first in Antioch spoke the word of God to non-Jews. It could conceivably be marginally important that doctors from Cyrene were of some repute (so Herodotus 3.131.3 as quoted by Wettstein (532), but the text is doubtful). Μαναὴν Ἡρῴδου τοῦ τετράρχου σύντροφος again is correctly described, without use of the article, since there is no other Manaen in the NT from whom he must be distinguished (though M. 3.206, stating the rule differently, regards this phrase as an exception). In the form Μαναήμ (A has Μαναήν) the name occurs at 4 Kdms 15.14, translating מנחם, *Comforter*, and occasionally elsewhere. It is 'ein nicht gerade seltener Name' (StrB 2.710; see Hemer 227)). Herod the Tetrarch (his title has the article in view of Herod (Agrippa I) in ch. 12) is the ruler of Lk 3.1, and other passages. On σύντροφος see not only the passages cited in BA 1582 but also an extended note in Deissmann, *BS* 310–12 (also Jeremias, *Jerusalem* 88; *ND* 3.37); 'it appears to have been in general use throughout the Hellenistic kingdoms' (Deissmann, 312, citing M. Fränkel, *Altertümer von Pergamon* viii. 1 (Berlin 1890), 111f.). Cf. 2 Macc. 9.29; also 1 Macc. 1.6 (συνέκτροφος). It was a court title (often as σύντροφος τοῦ βασιλέως) and means *intimate friend*. For Luke's interest in and possibly indirect contact with the Herods cf. Lk. 8.3. D has the surprising variant, (Μαναήν τε Ἡρῴδου καὶ τετραάρχου σύντροφος, which (though it is probably an accidental error) must be translated, Manean, son of Herod (the Great, presumably) and companion of (Herod, presumably) the tetrarch. At the end of the list stands Saul — whose activities fill almost the whole of the rest of Acts.

2. Bultmann (*Exegetica* 421) who accepts at 11.28 the reading with ἡμῶν, thinks that here Luke's (Antiochian) source, from which the 'We-passages' were derived, read λειτουργούντων δὲ ἡμῶν: an improbable view. λειτουργεῖν occurs nowhere else in the Lucan writings; the cognate noun is used at Lk. 1.23, of Zechariah's priestly ministry in the Temple. The general sense of the word-group is public service of any kind; it has no specifically religious connotation. This wide use is reflected in the NT; see Rom. 15.27 (ἐν τοῖς σαρκικοῖς λειτουργῆσαι); 2 Cor. 9.12; Phil. 2.30 (λειτουργία); Rom. 136; Phil. 2.25 (λειτουργός). A number of passages, however, especially in Hebrews, use the words in a religious context, and this is evidently intended here. This corresponds with the use of the group in the LXX, and in later Christian literature. On the whole group, see H. Strathmann and R. Meyer in *TWNT* 4.221–38. *Didache* 15.1 envisages circumstances in which bishops and deacons are taking over the service of prophets and teachers: ὑμῖν γὰρ λειτουργοῦσι καὶ αὐτοὶ τὴν λειτουργίαν τῶν προφητῶν καὶ διδασκάλων.

The leaders of the church in Antioch (it would be very difficult to give αὐτῶν a wider application than to the prophets and teachers of v. 1, though most commentators do this; Haenchen (380), for example, says that the presence of the community is not mentioned but is presupposed) are described as holding a service of worship. Luke gives no indication of the form taken by the service; there is no ground in the context for answering Richardson's question (*Theology* 297), 'Does this mean "While they celebrated the eucharistic liturgy"?' in the affirmative. There is more to be said for the suggestion that they were prophesying (see below) and teaching; and praying (v. 3). But the matter is one on which Luke gives us no information, and it is wise to recognize the fact. He does however add that a fast was in progress — this evidently is not a matter that relates simply to the period during which the leaders were assembled for worship. Fasting is not frequently enjoined in the OT. It accompanied mourning for the dead (e.g. 2 Sam. 1.12; 3.35); it might be prescribed in the Holy War (1 Sam. 14.24); it was part of the observance of the Day of Atonement (e.g. Lev. 16.29). According to post-biblical evidence (as late as the ninth century) Purim was preceded by a day of fasting on Adar 13. Fasting on other occasions might be privately undertaken (see I. Abrahams, *Studies* 1.121–8). Mk 2.18–20 suggests that Jesus and his disciples did not fast but that after the resurrection and ascension fasting became a Christian practice. It did not form a regular part of 'official' Greek and Roman religions, but was practised in some mystery cults (e.g. Sallustius, *De Dis et Mundo* 4 (Nock, p. 8, lines 20–22,ἐν κατηφείᾳ ἐσμὲν σίτου τε καὶ τῆς ἄλλης παχείας καὶ ῥυπαρᾶς τροφῆς ἀπεχόμεθα (ἑκάτερα γὰρ ἐναντία ψυχῇ)· εἶτα δένδρου τομαὶ καὶ νηστεία . . .; see Nock's note on p. lv). Paul twice uses the word νηστεία, but apparently with reference to occasions when he had been obliged to go without food than to religious observance (2 Cor. 6.5; 11.27). In Acts (apart from a reference in 27.9 to 'The Fast', that is, the Day of Atonement) fasting is mentioned again only at v. 3 and at 14.23, perhaps (see the note) in connection with the appointment of presbyters. In Mt. 6.16–18 it is assumed that Christians will fast; they must not do so ostentatiously. It seems clear that some Christians took up the practice of fasting from pious Judaism, partly as self-discipline, partly as a reinforcement to prayer (see E. Lohse, *Ordination* 73, n. 1). It may be significant that the three references to fasting in Acts (13.2, 3; 14.23) all stand in connection with Antioch. Fasting might be undertaken with a special intention; Bauernfeind (169) speaks of 'ein innerliches Ringen um die kommende Missionstat'.

In the course of the meeting, εἶπεν τὸ πνεῦμα τὸ ἅγιον: presumably through one of the prophets, but cf. 8.29; 10.19; 11.2; 19.1 (D *al*). The Spirit sometimes speaks directly. The Spirit's command leads to a special commission for Barnabas and Saul. δή indicates 'vigorous emphasis' (Page 161): Come set apart for me . . . The two are to be set apart for a special work (cf. Num. 16.9; 1 Chron. 23.13). It is interesting and important that Paul uses ἀφορίζειν of himself and of his call (Rom. 1.1, ἀφωρισμένος εἰς εὐαγγέλιον θεοῦ; Gal. 1.15, ὁ θεὸς ὁ ἀφορίσας με). The *work* (ἔργον) to which the two men are called will become clear in the following chapters. On the Spirit's words Blass (145) comments, 'Loquitur Iesus'; this is indeed suggested by μοι, and might lead to interesting trinitarian speculation; this however was certainly not in Luke's mind.

Zerwick § 21 and BDR § 293. 3 (e), n. 14 remark that it is classical not to repeat a preposition with a relative (εἰς τὸ ἔργον ὅ προσκέκλημαι), and compare 1.21; 13.38. It should be noted that the present case is not quite parallel in that εἰς follows upon ἀφορίσατε, and προσκέκλημαι would more naturally be followed by πρός (cf. Demosthenes 43.7 (1052), προσεκαλέσαντο τὴν γυναῖκα πρὸς τὸν ἄρχοντα—but also 43.15 (1054), προσεκαλέσατο Μακάρτατον . . . εἰς διαδικασίαν. Luke's meaning is clear.

Like the disciples in the gospels, Barnabas and Saul are sent as a pair. The partnership, however, is soon to break up; the Pauline circle will become larger.

Bauernfeind (169) remarks that what is instituted in this incident is 'nicht ein neues Amt . . . aber eine neue einschneidende Amtshandlung'. He also points out that the church of Antioch would be glad to use the account of the Spirit's direct intervention in response to a charge that they had taken unauthorized action.

3. Three steps are taken before the missionaries are sent on their way: fasting, prayer, imposition of hands. For fasting in general see v. 2. It seems to be associated with the appointment of presbyters at 14.23. It is best thought of as an additional circumstance of prayer. It is not mentioned in the appointment of the Seven (6.6), or of Matthias (1.21–26), nor does there seem to be evidence of it in early accounts of and rules for ordinations. It was not until quite late that ordinations were specifically connected with the so-called Ember Days (quattuor tempora) of fasting. Prayer scarcely calls for comment: religious men could hardly fail to ask for those whom the Holy Spirit had designated as his agents divine guidance and strength for the mission to which they were called. For the laying on of hands see on 6.6. This too must be regarded as an additional circumstance of prayer. 'Quid aliud est manuum impositio quam oratio super hominem?' (Augustine, as quoted by L. Duchesne, *Christian Worship*, 1910, 377, n. 1). The prayer is specifically related to the person on whom hands are laid. There is no means of detecting whether by ἐπιτιθέναι Luke meant what a Jew would have expressed by סמך or by שׂית (Delitzsch translates ויסמכו), but the incident undoubtedly calls to mind rabbinic ordination, though Lohse (*Ordination* 71–4) rightly observes that it cannot be identified with rabbinic ordination since Paul is already regarded as a teacher (rabbi). He adds (73), 'Weit näher liegt die Parallele zum jüdischen Apostolat, obgleich wir nicht sicher wissen, ob bei der Beauftragung und aussendung des *schaliach* die Handauflegung geübt wurde.' It is better to think in general terms, recalling the widespread use of hands in blessing. 'It is therefore an "installation", i.e., a placing in a particular sphere of service which differs in some respects from that previously occupied' (E. Schweizer, *CONT* 25c). Paul had known himself to be an apostle from the time of his conversion (Gal. 1.15–17), and we must therefore with Weiser (307f.), distinguish between the situation in Antioch and that within which Luke himself was writing. The former cannot be precisely defined. It was not rabbinic ordination, and we do not know that it corresponds in form with the authorization of

שליחים. The Christians in Antioch (and since Paul and Barnabas returned and reported to the church in 14.26f. we may think of the whole church as sending and commissioning them) were acting in a new situation, without precedents, and simply committed their brothers to the grace of God for the task ahead. As for Luke's situation, Weiser says that there was recognition of divine action but not ordination. Some would say that such recognition, together with the church's intercession, is ordination. Again, historian and theologian alike must beware of defining too narrowly the indefinable.

Luke uses ἀπολύειν in a variety of senses; here, 'sent them on their way'. Most often, in Greek generally, it means *to dismiss* (in various senses); for the present meaning cf. Tobit 10.12 (א); Josephus, *Ant.* 5.97 (χαίροντας . . . ὑμᾶς . . . ἀπολύομεν).

34. BARNABAS AND SAUL IN CYPRUS. 13.4–12.

(4) So they, having been sent out by the Holy Spirit, came down to Seleucia, and thence they sailed away to Cyprus. (5) Having arrived in Salamis they proclaimed the word of God in the synagogues of the Jews. They had John, too, as assistant. (6) When they had passed through the whole island as far as Paphos they found a man who was a magus, a Jewish false prophet whose name was Bar-Jesus. (7) He was with the Proconsul, Sergius Paulus, an intelligent man. He summoned Barnabas and Saul, and sought to hear the word of God. (8) But Elymas the Magus (for that is how his name is translated) resisted them, seeking to turn away the Proconsul from the faith. (9) But Saul, who bore also the name Paul, filled with the Holy Spirit, fixed his gaze upon him, (10) and said, 'You son of the devil, full of every kind of deceit and every kind of fraud, enemy of all uprightness, will you not stop perverting the ways, the right ways, of the Lord? (11) See now, the Lord's hand is upon you, and for a time you will be blind and will not look upon the sun.' And suddenly mist and darkness fell upon him, and he went about seeking someone to lead him by the hand. (12) Then, when the Proconsul saw what had happened, he became a believer, surprised by the teaching about the Lord.[1]

Bibliography

F. C. Burkitt, *JTS* 4 (1903), 127–9.

B. van Elderen, *FS* Bruce (1970), 151–61.

G. A. Harrer, *HThR* 33 (1940), 19–33.

W. C. van Unnik, *ZNW* 58 (1967), 240–6.

Commentary

The account of the 'first missionary journey' begins with a paragraph that is characteristically patchy. Information gathered by Luke in Antioch may have been almost confined to the list of names: Antioch, Seleucia, Salamis, Paphos. This Luke filled out with inference and added information, and wrote the account in his own style, of which signs appear frequently. He has nothing to say about Seleucia; if the next place named was Salamis there was no alternative to a sea voyage; Luke knew probably both the Pauline theological

---

[1] *Begs.*, he believed, in astonishment, on the teaching of the Lord.

principle 'To the Jew first and also to the Greek' and the Pauline missionary practice of starting work in the Synagogue, and he described a mission based on the synagogue at Salamis. He knew a tradition that associated John Mark with Barnabas, and associated him with and then dissociated him from Saul. In addition he had a Pauline story — Roloff (196) speaks of it as the first of a set of *Paulus-Legenden* (cf. 14.19f.; 19.14-17; 20.7–12) — located at Paphos and introducing the provincial governor, the proconsul Sergius Paulus, who resided there, and his court astrologer, Bar-Jesus (Elymas). It is not impossible that Luke has combined two or more stories here. This is suggested by the two characters involved (Barnabas and Saul *found* the magus; the proconsul *summoned* Barnabas and Saul) and two (despite μεθερμηνεύεται in v. 8) unconnected names given to the magus. See e.g. Dibelius (16); Bauernfeind (170); Conzelmann (73); against this, Pesch (2.21); Weiser (313).

This account of the present paragraph (in which Wilcox 175f., unconvincingly, finds traces of Aramaic origin) will be repeated, with some inevitable modification, in the introductions to the next three; see pp. 623, 625, 664-6, 690. Throughout chs. 13 and 14 Luke combines Antiochene tradition with extraneous information, presenting these with a good deal of editorial activity. The combination will probably help to solve one of the outstanding minor puzzles in Acts. Up to 13.8 the name Saul has been used; from 13.9 onwards the missionary theologian is always called Paul. In explanation of this Schmithals (123) is on the right lines with the observation that Paul was the generally known and used name (as the epistles show); earlier Luke used the name Saul in order to stress the bearer's roots in Judaism. To this we may add the probability that Saul was the name used in the old Antiochene tradition. The non-Antiochene story that Luke inserted in vv. 6–12 used the name Paul, and Luke made this the occasion for clearly identifying the man whose conversion he had narrated with the subsequently well-known Christian leader. Luke thus took the earliest opportunity of introducing the name he intended to use throughout the rest of his book.

If this was Luke's intention he shows at the outset the skill that he will manifest throughout his narrative of Paul's journeys — which Beyer (79) says should be thought of not as three separate journeys but as one missionary undertaking leading without significant intervals to Rome. It might be better to speak of a three act play, in which Luke combines two different kinds of tradition, one of which consists of a sequence of places visited, the other of incidents, usually more or less closely connected with particular places, and bringing out features of Paul's work or teaching that Luke thought should be communicated to his readers. Haenchen (389) thinks the Lucan interests brought out in the present passage to be: (1) apologetic —

at the outset of his career Paul is shown to be on the best of terms with a Roman proconsul, whose example other Roman officials might do well to follow; (2) Paul's precedence over all colleagues (at this point Barnabas); (3) a rooted objection to magic. To these points some would add a desire to show that Paul was the equal of Peter: Peter had rebuked and threatened Simon (8.20–22); Paul now pronounces sentence of blindness on Bar-Jesus. This is not convincing. It does not seem to have been Luke's intention to bring out the equality of Peter and Paul in this crude way. The effect rather is additive: both men condemn magical practices. We may add that both set themselves against any claim to be a 'divine man'; cf. 3.12; 10.26; 14.15.

Cyprus was a natural place for Antiochene missionaries, of whom Paul was at this time one, to start their work (cf. 4.36; 11.19). There is no confirmatory evidence for a mission there by Paul, but no reason to doubt it. The story linked him with a proconsul; there was no likelier place than Paphos for such an encounter. That he worked with Barnabas as a colleague is proved by Gal. 2.1, 9, 13 (even Barnabas); cf. 1 Cor. 9.6; and Barnabas is connected with Cyprus.

4. αὐτοί (οὗτοι is read by E Ψ 𝔐, οἱ by D p) changes the subject emphatically from that of 13.3. On μὲν οὖν, Luke's way of noting a new development in his story and at the same time asserting its connection with what precedes, see on 1.6. Barnabas and Saul had been sent on their way (ἀπέλυσαν, 13.3) by the church at Antioch, or its representatives, but in truth they were being sent out (Luke does not use the verb ἀποστέλλειν, which would unmistakably have called to mind the noun ἀπόστολος) by the Holy Spirit (cf. 13.2). Luke emphasizes that the new development, which must, at least as he understood it, have contemplated from the beginning a mission to the Gentiles, was undertaken under the direct instruction of the Holy Spirit. Instead of ὑπὸ τοῦ ἁγίου πνεύματος perp sa have ὑπὸ τῶν ἁγίων (a sanctis). This is an unusual Western reading; it accommodates this verse to the preceding one.

κατῆλθον (ἀπῆλθον, P⁷⁴ A; καταβάντες δέ, D (gig Lcf)), down from Antioch to the coast, where Seleucia was situated, near the mouth of the Orontes. The city (see 1 Macc. 11.8, Σελευκείας τῆς παραθαλασσίας) was founded in c. 300 BC by Seleucus I as his capital (replacing Seleucia on the Tigris, which he had founded in 312), but it soon gave place to Antioch (about fifteen miles higher up the Orontes; see 11.19), whose port it remained. It was a station of the Roman fleet (see *CAH* 10.236), though the harbour was inconveniently small. ἀπέπλευσαν: the verb occurs here for the first time in Acts, but the narrative henceforth requires it (14.26; 20.15; 27.1; it is not uncommon; see e.g. Thucydides 3.88.2). According to 11.19 Cyprus had already been reached by Christian missionaries, and the journey of Saul and Barnabas could be regarded as in the first instance a revisiting of converts already made and churches already established; no mention however is made of such converts and churches, and for this reason the notice in 11.19 is often discounted. There was a large Jewish population on Cyprus (1 Macc. 15.23; Philo, *Legatio ad Gaium* 282; Josephus, *Ant.* 13.284); according to Dio Cassius, in the rebellion of AD 116, the Jews of Cyprus killed 240,000 Gentiles. They also destroyed Salamis.

5. Salamis had at one time been capital of Cyprus but under the Romans (for whom Cyprus had since 22 BC been a senatorial province) it had been superseded by Paphos (see v. 6), possibly because the harbour at Salamis had become silted up. Under Constantius II (AD 324–361) it was refounded as Constantia. The correct reading here appears to be Σαλαμῖνι, but ℵ A E L have Σαλαμίνη (identical in pronunciation). On the orthography see M. 2.128; WS 94; BDR § 57. 3. The *Acts of Barnabas* 22; 23 (L.-B. 2.2.300) use the first declension form; so in Latin does the historian Justin (third century AD) of the more famous Salamis near Athens.

καταγγέλλειν and ὁ λόγος τοῦ θεοῦ (so apparently here, but D gig syᵖ saᵐˢ have κυρίου, which is correct in some passages) are stock terms used by Luke for the proclamation of the Gospel. Barnabas and Saul proclaimed it *in the synagogues of the Jews*. For the synagogue see on 6.9; for the proclamation of the Gospel in synagogues cf. 9.20; according to Acts it became for Paul a regular practice (13.14; 14.1; 17.1, 10, 17; 18.4, 19; 19.8), and that he continued to use the synagogue even after he had become offensive to it is proved by 2 Cor. 11.24. The constant repetition of this practice is Luke's version of Paul's 'to the Jew first but also to the Greek' (Rom. 1.16), but what was to Luke little more than a missionary technique (Jewish Christian preachers were sure to find an audience in the synagogue) is to Paul a theological principle — though there is no reason why he should not have made a practical application of the principle. If reference to the synagogues did not stand in the basic tradition used by Luke, Luke may have introduced it because he believed it to be Paul's custom, or possibly (or in addition) because the principle could be observed only if Paul preached to Jews before his encounter with Sergius Paulus. Schmithals (121) thinks that Luke had in mind, and wished to rebut, the Pauline false teachers.

John is presumably the man mentioned in 12.12, 25; see on those verses. ὑπηρέτης is used at Lk. 4.20 of a synagogue attendant; this meaning is not relevant. Lk. 1.2 refers to ὑπηρέται τοῦ λόγου on whom the evangelist is to some extent dependent. He does not say that they had written gospels, and the traditional ascription of the second gospel to John Mark cannot be treated as ascertained, or ascertainable, truth; the connection may however throw some light on what is meant here. At Acts 26.16 Paul himself is described as a ὑπηρέτης and μάρτυς of what he has seen and will see. The word is used of any subordinate assistant, also of a variety of special servants and helpers in social, political, and military contexts which do not seem relevant here; it is on the whole likely, in view of the fact that (according to Acts) John Mark's family was of some importance in the church of Jerusalem, that his functions in the missionary party were not confined to care of their material needs; he should be thought of as contributing to the work of preaching and teaching. What is said about the Holy Spirit in v. 4 is not directly applied to him, and it is sometimes held (e.g. by Haenchen 387, Schneider 2.120, and Weiser 315) that Luke expresses himself in this way so that Mark's defection in 13.13 may not appear as a sin against the Spirit. This may be so, but it is more probable that the reason why Mark is not mentioned at v. 4a is simply that Barnabas and Saul are the principal actors in the story and that Mark, as an assistant, appears only in an addendum. Paul could scarcely have taken a harder line than he does in 15.38f. if he had believed that Mark had had a direct commission from the Holy Spirit. These verses imply that, in Paul's view, Mark had been or had appeared to be as firmly committed to the mission as himself and Barnabas.

For ὑπηρέτην, D 614 p sy^hmg sa mae have ὑπηρετοῦντα αὐτοῖς, E (vg) have εἰς διακονίαν. The former variant goes further in suggesting that Mark was a personal assistant rather than a colleague; the latter no doubt reflects 2 Tim. 4.11.

6. διελθόντες may imply not only a journey but a preaching tour (see on 8.4); if it was the latter no account of it has survived. This may but need not mean that it was totally unsuccessful. Antiochene tradition may have supplied not more than the names of Salamis and Paphos; in any case Luke gives that which attracts his attention and will, he believes, interest his readers. D* has περιελθόντων δὲ αὐτῶν, they went round, that is, presumably, they sailed round; this may be D's explanation of the failure to give any account of a mission in the intervening towns. Salamis lay to the eastern end of the island, and looked east; Paphos, at the other end of island, beyond Citium, Amathus, and Corium, looked west. Both were on the southern coast along which stretched a road which Barnabas and Saul could have traversed. If they did so they hardly covered ὅλην τὴν νῆσον in any strict sense, though the use of these words in what is not a textbook of geography is understandable enough. Salamis and Paphos are taken to represent the whole island at *Orac. Sib.* 4.128f. (καὶ τότε δὴ Σαλαμῖνα, Πάφον θ' ἅμα σεισμὸς ὀλέσσει, Κύπρον ὅταν πολύκλυστον ὑπερκλεονέῃ μέλαν ὕδωρ); 5.450–452. Paphos had now (see on v. 5) surpassed Salamis in importance; there is no need to doubt that the proconsul (v. 7) had his residence there. There was an Old Paphos, Παλαίπαφος, very old indeed, for it went back to Mycenaean times, but already before the Ptolemies took over Cyprus a new town, ten miles further north, closer to the sea, and with a better harbour, had supplanted it. The man whom the missionaries encountered (εὗρον does not imply that they looked for him) was everything that Luke did not like — μάγος, ψευδοπροφήτης, Ἰουδαῖος. The Jews (he thought) were always making trouble for the Christians; for μάγοι see on 8.9; a *false* prophet negates an institution of which Luke thought highly (and of which the missionaries were representatives). The double name (Bar-Jesus and Elymas) and the double description of him suggest that he stood on the boundary between Judaism and heathenism (Stählin 176). Men of his kind would find it convenient to have a powerful protector; see on v. 7, and cf. Betz (110). His name is given in this verse as Bar-Jesus, which appears to be a transcription of Aramaic and to mean Son of (=bar) Jesus (Joshua). It is not clear how this can be translated in the way given in v. 8; see on that verse, and note also v. 10, υἱὲ διαβόλου, which may be regarded as an aggressive play upon Son of Jesus. The text here is uncertain. The addition of interpretations borrowed from v. 8 (e.g. ὃ μεθερμηνεύεται Ἐλύμας, E) may be dismissed as due to assimilation, and the substitution of ὀνόματι for ᾧ ὄνομα is an attempt to improve the grammar. None of the following forms of the name itself can however be immediately eliminated: Βαριησοῦς; Βαριησοῦ; Βαριησοῦμ; Βαριησοῦαν; perhaps also the Syriac Barshuma. Βαριησοῦς and Βαριησοῦν (accusative agreeing with μάγον κτλ.) may be taken as attempts to improve the grammar. Βαριησοῦ and Βαριησοῦαν (accusative) may be regarded as alternative transliterations of בר־יׁשוע. It does not seem possible to account for all the variations as attempts to avoid Jesus as a nomen sacrum (Dinkler, *Signum Crucis* 30); but the Syriac *bar šuma'*, son of the name, may be one. In rabbinic use, שם (name) may stand for God; a Syriac translator who could not bring himself to say *bar yesu* might make the corresponding substitution (StrB 2.711).

7. Bar-Jesus was with, that is, was at the court of, the proconsul (ἀνθύπατος is the usual Greek equivalent of the Latin title; as a senatorial province Cyprus had a proconsul at its head) Sergius Paulus. The identity of this man is admirably discussed by Lake in *Begs.* 5.455–459; see more recently, and much more briefly, Schneider (2.121); also B. van Elderen in FS Bruce (1970) 151–6. Lake shows that some inscriptions which appear to refer to Sergius Paulus and to connect him with Cyprus have been misunderstood and are inapplicable. One inscription (*CIL* vi. 4, ii. p. 3116, no. 31545) does refer to one L. Sergius Paulus. It names five men, of whom he is one, as curatores riparum et alvei [Tiberis]. Three are unknown; one, Paullus Fabius Persicus, was one of the Fratres Arvales, and probably

Magister in AD 35. The inscription is dated by a reference to the Emperor Claudius; it must therefore fall between AD 41 and 54. 'The name of L. Sergius Paullus suggests that he may be the Sergius Paulus of Acts. The date would fit admirably if he went to Cyprus soon after being one of the Curators of the Tiber' (Lake 458). It would of course be necessary to suppose that his curatorship fell fairly early in Claudius' principate. van Elderen refers to another inscription which he thinks to be of greater value than that in *CIL*. This is to be found in *Inscriptiones Graecae ad Res Romanas pertinentes*, ed. R. Cagnat, III 935. The date lines are given by van Elderen (following J. L. Myers) thus

  9 Κλαυδ]ίου Καίσαρος Σεβαστοῦ καὶ
 10 ἐπὶ Κ]οίντου Σεργ-
 11 [ίου Παύλου ἀνθυπάτου]

'Palaeographically, the inscription belongs to the first century' (van Elderen 155). It will be seen that whereas the Latin inscription gives the praenomen L(ucius) the other (found at Cytheria on Cyprus) gives, by a very probable reconstruction and retranscription into Latin, (Qu)intus. The two inscriptions do not refer to the same man, and we must choose. It seems clear (pace van Elderen) that one should prefer the inscription that contains Sergius Paullus in full to that which, as it now stands, contains no more than the letters σεργ. Moreover, Hemer (109) draws attention to a new reading of line 9, which restores not Κλαυδ]ίου but Γ]αίου, a fragmentary letter being read not as Δ but as A. Dating in the time of the emperor Gaius (Caligula) would make the proposed identification impossible. Thus no inscription contains decisive confirmation of a proconsul Sergius Paulus or helps us to date the mission to Cyprus. See however *ND* 1.45 for another first century inscription referring to a different proconsul in Cyprus, and 4.138 for the connection of the Sergii Pauli with Pisidian Antioch; could this be why Paul made Pisidian Antioch his next goal?

According to Luke, Sergius Paulus was ἀνὴρ συνετός, an intelligent man; the outcome of the incident (v. 12) may have to some extent prejudiced Luke's judgment. He took the initiative in summoning Barnabas and Saul; Luke does not say that they sought out this influential Gentile, or any Gentile. He sought to hear the word of God (see v. 5).

D(c) has συγκαλεσάμενος . . . καὶ ἐζήτησεν, a participle being linked with a finite verb by καί. For the view that this may indicate Semitic influence see Black (*AA* 69).

8. At this point the magus, who may perhaps be thought of as court astrologer, intervenes. ἀνθίστατο, middle; cf. 6.10, where in a similar context the active is used. If Luke intends any difference, which is doubtful — he may be following sources — the present verse will suggest that the magus spoke up on his own account; he was not representing the proconsul, who in fact turned out to be of a different mind.

The magus is now called Ἐλύμας, and it is affirmed that so his name μεθερμηνεύεται. After an ὄνομα which is undoubtedly Semitic in form (v. 6) this word can mean only, *is translated*. It is however impossible to translate Bar-Jesus as Elymas, since Elymas (Ἐλύμας) is not a Greek word (at least, it is not listed in LS; ἔλυμος has several meanings: *case, quiver*, a kind of *pipe, millet*). It might be wise to cut short discussion of the problem that results by saying with Bengel, '*Barjehu* et *Elymas*, nescio quomodo, synonyma sunt.' Failing this, the simplest and probably correct solution is that both names were, in the tradition (or traditions) that Luke used, applied to the man in question, and that Luke assumed that the form that appeared to be Greek must be a translation of the Semitic; cf. 4.36. The assumption is a natural one, though Luke might have reflected that the Latin *Paul* is not a translation of the Semitic *Saul* (v. 9). There are however other possibilities; for much detail see P. W. Schmiedel in EBib, s.v. Barjesus; Clark (350–4); Metzger (402f.); Hemer (227f.); and all the commentaries. One line of attack is to reconsider the meaning of Βαριησοῦς (with the textual variants) in the light of Ἐλύμας, or rather of the variant Ετοιμας which appears in D, supported, with not a little variation, by a number of Old Latin MSS and Lucifer. This form of the name, which suggests the adjective ἑτοῖμος, *ready*, has given rise to the suggestion that behind Βαριησοῦς should be seen the Aramaic and Syriac root *š-w-*' which, among other things, signifies (according to Driver, quoted by Clark; the Aramaic שוא does not appear in Jastrow, though the corresponding Syriac word is in Payne Smith) *to be equal, sufficient, worth, deemed worthy*, hence perhaps *ready* for some purpose. Another suggestion rests upon a variant in Josephus, *Ant.* 20.142, which is often read Σίμωνα ὀνόματι . . . Ἰουδαῖον, Κύπριον δὲ τὸ γένος, μάγον εἶναι σκηπτόμενον. In this passage there is substantial evidence for reading, instead of Σίμωνα, Ἄτομον (printed in the text e.g. of L. H. Feldman) and this form of the name is not unlike Ἐτοιμᾶς; either could be a corruption of the other, and J. R. Harris (*Expositor*, fifth series, 5 (1902), 189–95) thought that Ἔτοιμος should be accepted as the original text of Acts. F. C. Burkitt (*JTS* 4 (1903), 127–9) conjectured that the text had suffered corruption and that Bar-Jesus was originally glossed by Luke ὁ λοιμός, *the pest, the pestilent fellow*. On the assumption that Elymas represents not the name Bar-Jesus but the occupation of the magus it has been suggested that we should think of the Aramaic חלמא, *an interpreter of dreams*, or of אלימא, *strong, powerful*; alternatively, there is the Arabic '*alim, wise, learned*. See L. Yaure (*JBL* 79 (1960), 297–314). But 'Why should a Jew in Cyprus at the court of a Roman consular governor be called by an obscure Arabic nickname?' (*Begs.* 4.144). A simple error seems the best explanation.

Apparently the proconsul was inclined to look with favour on the message of Barnabas and Saul: ἥδιστα ἤκουεν αὐτῶν (D*(E)sy^h** mae). This the magus intended to discourage; acceptance of the Christian message would no doubt have meant the end of his employment (whether because the proconsul no longer believed in sorcery or because he thought the missionaries more powerful sorcerers). ἡ πίστις can here be hardly other than *the faith*, though it is noted in v. 12 that Sergius Paulus *believed*, that is, became a believer, that is, exercised faith.

9. Σαῦλος δέ, ὁ καὶ Παῦλος. For the first time the name Paul is used; henceforth Σαῦλος is not used, but the transliterated Hebrew Σαούλ recurs in the repeated accounts of the conversion in chs. 22 and 26. That the same man should have borne both names, and used them from his youth, is in no way surprising; this does not explain why Luke suddenly takes up the one and drops the other. The formula ὁ καί has 'innumerable papyrus parallels' (M. 1.83); it is equivalent to ὁ καλούμενος (BDR § 268. 1, n. 4), that is, it does not describe a change of name but introduces an alternative name; Paul therefore did not borrow the name of the proconsul. Luke may however have thought this an appropriate occasion to introduce Saul's Roman name (Deissmann *BS* 313–17; Ramsay, *Paul The Traveller* 81–8). That Paul from this time seems regularly to have taken the lead, whatever colleagues accompanied him, does not account for Luke's dropping of the Hebrew and adopting of the Latin name at this point in his narrative. There may be more to be gained by asking why Luke had hitherto used the name Saul; the answer may be that he wished to show that the well-known Christian Paul had deep roots in Judaism. This, he may have considered, was now sufficiently demonstrated. See p. 609. Since the name Paul probably originated in Paul's pre-Christian youth there is little point in considering the meaning of the name. Augustine, *de Spiritu et Littera* 7 (12) is worth quoting less for Paul's own sake than for Augustine's as an interpreter and follower of Paul: Paulus Apostolus, qui cum Saulus prius vocaretur, non ob aliud, quantum mihi videtur, hoc nomen elegit, nisi ut se ostenderet parvum, tanquam minimum Apostolorum. For the views of Origen, Jerome, Chrysostom, and others, see *Begs.* 4.145f. StrB 2.712 quote Gittin 4.2 as an example of a Jew using two names.

πλησθεὶς πνεύματος ἁγίου emphasises that this was a notable occasion (cf. 2.4; 4.8). ἀτενίζειν is a Lucan word (see on 1.10). See however a baraita quoted by StrB 2.714 from Moed Qatan 17b (also Hagigah 5b; Sotah 46b; Nedarim 7b): Wherever the wise direct their eyes there is either death or misery.

10. Luke has no love for those who have illicit, and probably profitable, dealings with the supernatural. The magus is roundly cursed; cf. 8.20–23. For πλήρης with characteristics (such as δόλος, *deceitfulness*), see 6.3. παντός and πάσης (the latter omitted by D* *pc* gig — the variant may have originated in Latin where it was not necessary, as it was in Greek, to repeat *all* in a different gender) here mean *every kind of*. For ῥᾳδιουργία see Kremer (*Actes*, 289). It may be a simple synonym of δόλος but probably adds the sense of *fraud*, of making money by deception and trading on credulity. *Son of the devil* was probably understood at some stage in the tradition as the opposite of Bar-Jesus. 'Son of Jesus, do you call yourself? I say you are a son of the devil.' δικαιοσύνη (used in Acts only here and at 10.35; 17.1; 24.25) has an ethical, not Paul's theological sense. To practise deceit and fraud is to be an enemy of uprightness.

Luke now uses διαστρέφειν is a different sense from that of v. 8; it now means *to pervert*: Bar-Jesus is making straight roads crooked. The construction of παύεσθαι with participle is classical: BDR § 414, n. 9. The appended τὰς εὐθείας at the end of the clause recalls Hos. 14.10 (εὐθεῖαι αἱ ὁδοὶ τοῦ κυρίου, יהוה דרכי ישרים; it is unlikely that the passage is specifically referred to, since Hosea goes on to say that the transgressors shall stumble (יכשלו, ἀσθενήσουσι) in them, not that they will pervert them, but it provides a good example of Luke's 'biblical' (i.e. Septuagintal) speech. For διαστρέφειν with ὁδός cf. Prov. 10.9.

11. According to BDR § 442. 8d, n. 26, καὶ νῦν ἰδού (also at 20.22, 25) imitates the LXX; Gen. 12.9 is cited (ועתה הנה). χεὶρ κυρίου, as representing God's activity in the world, is also a biblical term; cf. e.g. Judges 2.15 (χεὶρ κυρίου ἦν ἐπ' αὐτοὺς εἰς κακά); cf. also Job 19.21. μὴ βλέπων τὸν ἥλιον is clearly a poetical expansion of τυφλός. Cf. Ps. 59(58).9. Wilcox (24) points out that the Hebrew and Greek of this verse lack the word *blind*, which occurs in the Targum. This is not enough to prove a connection; the imagery is too natural for that; cf. Aristophanes, *Plutus* 494, and Sophocles quoted in Plutarch, *De audiendis poetis* 23c. As Plümacher (47) remarks, 'Auch die Flüche der Apostel sind im biblischen Ton gehalten.'

The punishment of Bar-Jesus is to be limited in time: ἄχρι καιροῦ. The same expression is used at Lk 4.13 (cf. Heb. 9.10, with μέχρι). Omission of the article with a designation of time is classical; so BDR § 255. 3, n. 5; M. 3.179; cf. 5.19; 20.7; 28.23; but not 16.25. Presumably Paul hoped that a limited period of blindness would suffice to lead the magus to repentance. Whether or not it had this effect Luke does not say; contrast 8.24, where Simon appears to be penitent.

The punishment takes effect immediately, παραχρῆμα, a favourite word of Luke's; see on 3.7. For ἔπεσεν, P⁴⁵ᵛⁱᵈ P⁷⁴ C E 𝔐 have ἐπέπεσεν without difference of meaning. ἀχλύς occurs here only in the NT; it is for the most part a poetical word, used fairly frequently by Homer. It is used of the failure of sight in death (e.g. *Odyssey* 22.88, κατ' ὀφθαλμῶν δ'ἔχυτο ἀχλύς; cf. *Iliad* 5.696), also 'of one whom a god deprives of the power of seeing and knowing others' (LS 297, s.v.; e.g. *Iliad* 20.321, κατ' ὀφθαλμῶν χέεν ἀχλύν; cf. Josephus, *Ant.* 9.56, ἀχλὺν αὐταῖς (the eyes) ἐπιβαλόντα). For Luke's language here cf. also Philo, *Quod Deus Immut. sit* 130, ὥσπερ οἱ ἐν ἀχλύι καὶ σκότει βαθεῖ μηδὲν ὁρᾷ ... The word is also used by medical writers of blindness due to ulceration (so LS, referring to Hippocrates, *Prorrhetikon* 2.20; Theophrastus, *Historia Plantarum* 7.6.2; Dioscorides 2.78; Aetius 7.27). The use is too general to permit the inference that Luke was using medical language. It was pointed out in *Begs.* 4.146 (cf. Haenchen 385) that ἀχλύς is used by doctors in a way different from that in which it is used in Acts. ἀχλύς is used by Aquila at Ezek. 12.7, by Symmachus at Job 3.5. Bar-Jesus' loss of sight is confirmed by his search for someone to lead him by the hand (χειραγωγός; cf. the use of the cognate χειραγωγεῖν at 9.8; 22.11; also Plutarch, *Adv. Stoicos de communibus Notitiis* 10.6 (1063B), ... ἐχρῶντο ... ὥσπερ τυφλοὶ χειραγωγοῖς; Artemidorus, *Oneirocriticus* 1.48).

12. The subject of the sentence is certainly the proconsul (ὁ ἀνθύπατος, as at v. 7); there is one direct object (τὸ γεγονός) and one indirect object introduced by a preposition (ἐπὶ τῇ διδαχῇ τοῦ κυρίου) with three verbs, the indicative ἐπίστευσεν and the participles ἰδών and ἐκπλησσόμενος. It is not clear how these are to be arranged. Each of the verbs can be used absolutely: when he saw; he believed (i.e., became a believer); being astonished. The indirect object can be taken either with ἐπίστευσεν (he believed in the teaching of the Lord) or with ἐκπλησσόμενος (he was astonished at the teaching of the Lord). Sense but not the order of words may suggest that ἐκπλησσόμενος should be related to τὸ γεγονός, the event that Sergius Paulus had seen (ἰδών). If this way of taking the verse is accepted we should render: When the proconsul saw with astonishment what had happened (the blinding of Bar-Jesus) he believed in the teaching of the Lord (cf. the use of πιστεύειν ἐπί at Lk. 24.25). It must however be acknowledged that if this is what Luke meant he expressed himself very clumsily, and it is probably safer to give due weight to the order of the words, taking τὸ γεγονός as the object of ἰδών, ἐπίστευσεν absolutely (for this cf. 2.44 and elsewhere), and ἐκπλησσόμενος with ἐπὶ τῇ διδαχῇ τοῦ κυρίου: The proconsul, when he saw what had happened, became a believer (inceptive aorist; see Zerwick § 250; Schneider 2.124), being astonished at the teaching of the Lord. The construction is greatly simplified by two Western additions (which are thus almost certainly to be regarded as secondary). After τὸ γεγονός, D E (gig) syᵖ add ἐθαύμασεν καί, and after ἐπίστευσεν, D adds τῷ θεῷ. All is now clear: When the proconsul saw what had happened he marvelled and believed in God, being deeply impressed (for this meaning of ἐκπλήσσεσθαι cf. Herodotus 3.148.1, ὅκως δὲ ἴδοιτο ὁ Κλεομένης τὰ ποτήρια, ἀπεθαύμαζέ τε καὶ ἐξεπλήσσετο) by the teaching of the Lord.

Notwithstanding 2.42, where the genitive is subjective, τοῦ κυρίου will be an objective genitive: the teaching about the Lord given by Barnabas and Saul.

It has been maintained that Sergius Paulus was not truly converted (courtesy being perhaps mistaken for conviction) because he was not baptized. This argument would mean that there were no conversions on this missionary journey: there is no reference to baptism.

35. THROUGH PAMPHYLIA TO PISIDIAN ANTIOCH: PAUL'S SPEECH 13.13–52

(13) Paul and his party put out from Paphos and came to Perge in Pamphylia, but John separated from them and returned to Jerusalem. (14) But they went on from Perge and arrived at Pisidian Antioch. On the Sabbath day they went into the synagogue and sat down. (15) After the reading of the Law and the prophets the presidents of the synagogue sent to them, saying, 'Brothers, if you have any word of exhortation for the people, say it.' (16) Paul rose up, and having gestured with his hand said, 'My fellow Israelites, and you who fear God, listen. (17) The God of this people Israel chose our fathers and exalted the people during their sojourn in the land of Egypt. With uplifted arm he brought them out of it, (18) and for about forty years he nourished them[1] in the wilderness, (19) and he overthrew seven nations in the land of Canaan, and gave them (the Israelites[2]) their land as an inheritance, (20) for about 450 years. After this he gave them judges up to the time of Samuel the prophet. (21) After that they asked for a king, and God gave them Saul, the son of Kish, a man of the tribe of Benjamin, for forty years. (22) He removed him, and to be king raised up for them David, of whom he said by way of testimony, 'I have found David, the son of Jesse, a man after my heart; he will do all my will.' (23) Of this man's seed, God, in fulfilment of his promise, has brought to Israel a saviour, Jesus, (24) after John, before his coming, had proclaimed to all the people of Israel a baptism of repentance. (25) As John was completing his course, he said, 'What do you suppose me to be? I am not[3] what you think;[4] but see! there is coming after me one of whom I am not worthy to loose the shoes of his feet.' (26) Brothers, you who belong to the family of Abraham, and those among you who fear God, to us has the message of this salvation been sent. (27) For the inhabitants of Jerusalem and their rulers, though they did not recognize him or the words of the prophets, which are read every Sabbath, sat in judgment upon him and so fulfilled the prophetic message. (28) Though they found no valid[5] capital charge against him they asked Pilate that he should be killed. (29) When they had completed all the things that had been written about him, they took him down from the tree and laid him in a tomb. (30) But God raised him for the dead. (31) In the course of many days he appeared to those who had come up with him from Galilee to Jerusalem; these are now his witnesses to the

[1]*Begs.*, endured their behaviour; RSV, bore with them; NEB, bore with their conduct.
[2]The Israelites is not in the Greek.
[3]*Begs.*, As for what you suspect that I am, no! I am not he; RSV, What do you suppose that I am? I am not he; NEB, I am not what you think I am; NJB, I am not the one you imagine me to be.
[4]What you think is not in the Greek.
[5]Valid is not in the Greek.

People. (32) And we are bringing you the good news of the promise made to the fathers — (33) the good news that God has fulfilled it for us their children,[6] by raising up Jesus. This is as it stands written in the second[7] Psalm: Thou art my son; today have I begotten thee. (34) But that he raised him from the dead, no more to return to corruption, he has affirmed in this way:[8] I will give you the holy and sure promises[9] of David. (35) Therefore he says also in another Psalm:[10] Thou wilt not allow thy Holy One to see corruption. (36) For David, having served his own generation by the will of God,[11] fell asleep and was added to his fathers and saw corruption. (37) But he whom God raised up did not see corruption. (38) So let it be known to you, brothers, that through this man forgiveness of sins is proclaimed to you, and from all those things from which you could not be justified by the Law of Moses, (39) in this man everyone who believes is justified. (40) Beware therefore lest there come upon you that which was spoken in the prophets: (41) See, you despisers, and marvel and fade away; for I am working a work in your days, a work which you will not believe, even though someone explain it to you.'

(42) As Paul and Barnabas[12] were going out people begged them that these things might be spoken to them on the next Sabbath. (43) When the synagogue broke up, many of the Jews and devout proselytes followed Paul and Barnabas, who conversed with them and urged them to continue in the grace of God. (44) On the next Sabbath almost the whole city was gathered together to hear the word of the Lord. (45) When the Jews saw the crowds they were filled with envy and contradicted the things that Paul was saying, blaspheming.[13] (46) But Paul and Barnabas grew bold and said, 'It was necessary that the word of God should be spoken first of all to you, but since you thrust it aside and judge yourselves unworthy of eternal life, see! we are turning to the Gentiles. (47) For thus has the Lord given us charge: I have appointed thee as a light for the Gentiles, to be a means of salvation up to the end of the earth.'

(48) When the Gentiles heard this they rejoiced and glorified the word of the Lord, and those who were appointed to eternal life became believers. (49) And the word of the Lord was spread abroad through the whole region. (50) But the Jews incited the devout women of high standing and the leading men of the city; they raised a persecution against Paul and Barnabas and drove them out of their borders. (51) But they shook off the dust of their feet against them and came to Iconium. (52) And the disciples were filled with joy and with the Holy Spirit.

---

[6]*Begs.*, to our children; NEB, the children.

[7]*Begs.*, first.

[8]Greek, said thus.

[9]Promises is not in the Greek. *Begs.*, things; RSV, NEB, blessings.

[10]Psalm is not in the Greek. *Begs.*, another place; NEB, another passage; NJB, another text.

[11]RSV, . . . he had served the counsel of God in his own generation; NJB, When David in his own time had served God's purpose; similarly *Begs.*

[12]Greek, they.

[13]RSV, and reviled him; NEB, with violent abuse.

Bibliography

C. K. Barrett, as in (18).

W. H. Bates, *StEv* 6 (=*TU* 112, 1973), 8–10.

O. Bauernfeind, *FS* Heine, 64–78.

P. Billerbeck, *ZNW* 55 (1964), 143–61.

J. W. Bowker, as in (4).

T. R. S. Broughton, *FS* Lake, 131–8.

F. F. Bruce, *FS* Ellis, 71–9.

G. Delling, as in (4).

G. Delling, *FS* Cullmann (1972), 187–97.

F. G. Downing, as in (18).

J. Dupont, *Études*, 133–55, 283–307, 337–59.

J. Dupont, *Nouvelles Études*, 343–9.

E. E. Ellis, as in (4).

J. A. Emerton, as in (1).

C. F. Evans, as in (4) (*JTS* 7).

O. Glombitza, *NTS* 5 (1959), 306–17.

D. Goldsmith, *JBL* 87 (1968), 321–4.

R. P. Gordon, *NovT* 16 (1974), 285–9.

H. B. Green, *JTS* 40 (1989), 1–25.

P. Grelot, *RB* 88 (1981), 368–72.

M. Hengel, as in (7).

G. D. Kilpatrick, *JTS* 11 (1960), 53.

R. S. Mackenzie, *JBL* 104 (1985), 637–50.

P. H. Menoud, *Jésus Christ et la Foi* (1975), 130–49.

R. F. O'Toole, *Bib* 60 (1979), 361–72.

J. Schmitt, Kremer *Actes*, 155–67.

E. Schweizer, *FS* Schubert, 186–93.

U. Wilckens, *Missionsreden*, 50–55, 70f.

Commentary

The missionary journey continues by sea as the Pauline party (Luke's phrase shows that Paul, not Barnabas, is now the central figure) sails across from Paphos to Perge (in Pampylia), striking inland to Antioch (on the borders of Pisidia). At this point Luke incorporates a long synagogue sermon. If the framework of chapters 13 and 14 is supplied by Antiochene (*Syrian* Antioch) tradition, based perhaps on a list of churches known to be related to the

Antiochene mission (see above, p. 600), we must conclude that Luke supplied the speech from a different source; the Antiochene material will hardly have included a record of a particular address delivered by Paul in the 'other' Antioch. This seems in any case probable; the speech is similar to those ascribed to Peter in chs. 2, 3, and 10, and differs markedly from those attributed to Paul in chs. 17 and 20. Speeches in Acts are differentiated less with reference to the speakers than with reference to the audience. Here, like Peter, Paul in the synagogue is addressing Jews and proselytes; his audiences in chs. 17 and 20 are different. It will be important to note the points of resemblance between this synagogue sermon and the general pattern of speeches (see above, p. 130); and the differences.

The speech may be thought of as falling into three parts (so e.g. Pesch 2.30), punctuated by addresses to the audience in vv. 16b, 26a, 38a, or into four (so Weiser 322f.: vv. 16b–25; 26–31; 32–37; 38–41). It makes little difference if the middle section is split up or left as a unit. The theme of fulfilment is made specially prominent by the extensive survey of OT history; see vv. 23, 27, 29, 32, 33, 47. I have discussed this material in *FS* Greeven, 57–69; see also below. Inevitably the fulfilment focuses on Jesus, to whose life, death, and resurrection there are numerous references: vv. 23, 25, 29, 30, 31. Jesus is represented as David's heir, in whom David's prophecies are fulfilled, hence the Messiah; he is also Saviour (v. 23), and references to his resurrection imply his exaltation (v. 34; perhaps v. 33); also to be noted is the comparison with John the Baptist in v. 25. There is no reference to the Holy Spirit in this speech (but cf. παρρησιασάμενοι in v. 46), or to the return of Christ. The offer of salvation is made in vv. 38, 39, 47.

The most evident difference between this speech and those ascribed to Peter is the long review of the OT, which leads to an extended reference to John the Baptist, in vv. 17–25. This leads Conzelmann (75) to describe the speech as a *Mischtyp*, midway between those of Peter and that of Stephen (ch. 7). This exaggerates; the speech is much nearer to Peter's, and the suggestion that Paul is made to begin with the Exodus because Stephen had covered the period of the Patriarchs is also unconvincing — Stephen covered Moses and the Exodus too. There is a difference between the two treatments of the OT, but it is not this; see below. The speech probably reflects the extensive exegetical debate that must have gone on as soon as Jewish Christians began to make their voices heard in the synagogue, and does so in a way that reflects some credit on the debaters. There is a good deal of use of proof-texts, which would involve straight assertion and counter-assertion — Jesus did, or did not, fulfil such-and-such a prophecy — but there is also an attempt to look at the history of Israel as a whole and to see in it a pattern of God's action.

Luke can hardly have been unfamiliar with this kind of debate, which must have continued at least up to the time of Justin — an observation that rests on the fact, which may certainly be accepted as such, that the book was written with practical rather than merely antiquarian intent. Luke could assume (if he did not have more positive knowledge) that Paul would engage in this kind of disputation.

We may go further than this if the suggestion of J. W. Bowker ('Speeches in Acts: A study in Proem and Yelammedenu form', *NTS* 14 (1967), 96–111) is accepted. Synagogue homilies that have survived fall into two groups, those which start from a Proem text, and those which start with a problem and the request Yelammedenu rabbenu, Let our rabbi instruct us. The proem was not taken from either the seder or the haftarah of the day, but it had to contain at least one word that tallied with a word in the haftarah. The proem was interpreted by a further series of texts, which led eventually to a text taken from the seder. In regard to Paul's sermon, Dr Bowker suggests that the seder was Deut. 4.25–46, the haftarah 2 Sam. 7.6–16, and the proem text 1 Sam. 13.14. 'Acts 13.17–21 is an introduction, linking the seder reading with the proem text, and 13.22–41 is a typical proem homily' (op. cit., 104; see also my note in *FS* Lindars 241). It will be apparent here that much is hypothetical and that the correspondences are not exact. But exact correspondence could hardly be expected, and it is a matter of no small interest that there should be any degree of correspondence between Paul's sermon and a recognized form of synagogue homily. This is of course a very long way from the claim that what we read in Acts is an accurate account of what Paul said one Sabbath in the synagogue service in Pisidian Antioch.

Some unusual points in the account of Jesus (vv. 26–37) will be better dealt with in the notes below. In the final offer of salvation however occurs the only reference in Acts to justification by faith in Jesus (vv. 38, 39). This, though the wording is not truly Pauline (see below), occurs appropriately on Paul's lips; it was presumably placed there by Luke. It is backed up by a scriptural warning of the danger of rejecting the offer (vv. 40, 41). This leads to a final distinguishing feature of Paul's ministry in Pisidian Antioch. The speech is given, as it were, in two instalments. After the sermon, the congregation, deeply interested, breaks up. Next Sabbath not only Jews and others accustomed to attend synagogue but almost the whole city is gathered to hear the word of the Lord. This leads to division and especially to opposition on the part of 'the Jews' (does Luke imply that those who at first were favourably impressed changed their minds?), and Paul announces that henceforth he is turning to the Gentiles. The problems raised by this proposal are discussed in the notes (pp. 656f.). Here one more general issue may be mentioned. Gal. 2.9 appears, superficially at least, to mean that whereas Peter, James, and John would retain responsibility for evangelizing Jews, Paul would confine himself to Gentiles. This agrees neither with what is described in Acts nor with what may be inferred from other epistles (e.g. 1 Cor. 9.20). This matter, however, is one that concerns primarily the student of Galatians; so far as it arises in Acts it is better discussed in relation to ch. 15. For the present it may suffice to quote *Begs.* 4.159: 'The suggestion can scarcely be that Paul had not preached to Gentiles already, but rather that he would continue to do so, without troubling about the Synagogue. Far too much attention is paid to Gal. 2.7–9 as though it means that Paul and Barnabas were never to preach to the Jews.' Notwithstanding the present passage and the parallels in 18.6 and 28.28, Paul, apostle of the Gentiles, never ceased to be concerned for the salvation of Israel. On the whole it seems that Luke, though by no means out of touch with Paul, has compiled a programmatic conclusion for the paragraph. Weiser (339f.) draws a parallel between Paul's synagogue sermon and that ascribed to Jesus in Lk. 4.16–30; each foreshadows the story of the preacher as a whole, and each includes an interest in the non-Jewish world. In Acts we have a characteristically Lucan way of expressing the Pauline proposition 'to the Jew first, and also to the Greek', (e.g. Rom. 1.16). What in Paul is essentially a theological principle becomes a piece of missionary tactics — as it may well have done on occasion with Paul himself; see *ZThK* 86 (1989), 25.

The paragraph as a whole, then, is mostly Luke's work. On this most commentators agree; e.g. Roloff (203), 'Der Abschnitt enthält nur wenig vorlukanisches Material'. When Paul appears in a synagogue the debates already mentioned (9.22, 29; 13.5) and frequently to be mentioned (14.1–5, 19; etc.) must be exemplified, and inevitably it is the OT that is to be debated — at least, Paul's side of the debate is given. The sermon follows the common pattern (not unrelated to contemporary synagogue homilies) but is made to lead up to the theme, or at least the language, of justification. The upshot is a situation that leads Paul to announce his intention of leaving the Jews in their unbelief and turning to the Gentiles. This is to be taken not as a once-for-all, irrevocable decision, but rather as a recurring pattern in his ministry. Finally the thread of the (Syrian) Antioch narrative is picked up as the missionaries move on to Iconium. '13.42 is the final observation on the speech. In 13.43 the itinerary obviously continues, its thread being broken off, perhaps, in 13.14; ἐκάθισαν is quite pointless and was introduced, no doubt, in order to lead on to the speech. The itinerary could thus be reconstructed something like this: "They went on the sabbath day into the synagogue and preached. When the synagogue broke up there followed . . . etc."' (Dibelius 6).

One further point remains to be mentioned here and taken up later.

Verses 31, 32 appear to distinguish between the original eye-witnesses of the resurrection and those who like Paul preach the resurrection but cannot claim to be eye-witnesses. The question of the relation between Paul and the Twelve, and the question of his own status, are thus raised. They will be considered below in the commentary on the verses, again on ch. 14, and in Vol. II. It is doubtful whether Luke ever cleared his mind on the issue; it is hardly adequate to say that he thought of Paul as a Musterschüler of the Twelve (Schmithals 127).

13. ἀναχθέντες: Luke frequently uses ἀνάγεσθαι for embarking and putting to sea (13.13; 16.11; 18.21; 20.3, 13; 21.1, 2; 27.2, 4, 12, 21; 28.10, 11); this use of the word is classical (from Homer) and Hellenistic. For Paphos see v. 6.

οἱ περὶ Παῦλον clearly includes Paul (Paul and his party); so also 21.8 (𝔐). This is the classical use (e.g. Plato, *Cratylus* 440c, οἱ περὶ Ἡράκλειτον); in later Greek the person named is often excluded (cf. Mk 4.10; Lk. 22.49), or is intended alone. See M. 3.16, 270; BDR § 228. 1. That Paul is named as the centre of the group shows that now he, not Barnabas, is thought of as leader.

Perge (in the neighbourhood of the modern Murtana) lies near but not on the south coast of Asia Minor; it could however be reached by ship, since the Kestros was navigable for 11 km, far enough to reach the river port, though the main part of the town lay about 5 km further off. Perge was an important centre for the worship of Artemis (Cicero, *In Verrem* 1.20 (54): Pergae fanum antiquissimum et sanctissimum Dianae scimus esse). It was a large town; it is said that the theatre and stadium had each a capacity of c. 20,000 (Stählin 180). There seems to be no direct evidence of the presence of Jews in Perge (if in fact there were none this might account for the fact that there is no record of preaching there) but there were not a few in the province of *Pamphylia* (see 1 Macc. 15.23; Philo, *Leg. ad Gaium* 281; inscriptions given in *NS* 3.33). Pamphylia (there is a good short note in *Begs.* 4.147) was a small province occupying the coastal area south of Pisidia and between Lycia (to the west) and Cilicia (to the east). Greek colonization was said to have begun as early as the period of the Trojan War. Pamphylia was subject to the Seleucids till 189 BC when it became Roman. It was at first included in Cilicia but became a separate unit in 25 BC. In AD 43 Claudius united Lycia with Pamphylia as a senatorial province. There were further changes, under Nero or Galba, and Pamphylia was attached to Galatia (W. T. Arnold, *Roman Provincial Administration*, Oxford 1914, 274). Ramsay (*Paul the Traveller* 181) infers from the fact that Pamphylia is not mentioned in 1 Peter 1.1 that no church was established there; a very insecure inference, not confirmed by 14.25.

ἀποχωρήσας, John *withdrew, separated* from them, presumably after their arrival in Perge, not impossibly before they set sail from Paphos. On John (Mark) see 12.12, 25; 13.5. For the outcome of his departure see 15.38, which shows that John's return to Jerusalem was regarded, at least by Paul (as represented by Luke), as blameworthy desertion; in themselves the words of the present verse are neutral. See further Col. 4.10; Phm. 24; 2 Tim. 4.11. If these verses, or any of them, were written by Paul himself (and perhaps even if not) we must conclude that John Mark was forgiven and restored to service with Paul. Luke does not tell us and we therefore do not know why John deserted Paul and Barnabas. He may simply have lost enthusiasm for the work on which the party was engaged; he may have found conditions harder than he expected; he may have been frightened by the prospect of work in a strange place (he was a nephew of Barnabas, a Cypriote, so that work on the island may not have seemed so forbidding); Ramsay (*Paul the Traveller* 90–4) thinks that the cause was Paul's change of plan arising out of his illness (he determined to strike up into the hills as a relief from fever), and many subsequent writers have taken up the suggestion; he may not have approved of a mission that was showing signs of turning more and more to the Gentiles. The *Acts of Barnabas* (purporting to have been written by John) represent him as acting (though not precisely at this point) under the direction of the Spirit: 5 (L.-B. 2.2.293), . . . βουλόμενος ἐπὶ τὰ δυτικὰ μέρη ἀποπλεῦσαι· καὶ οὐκ εἴασέν με τὸ πνεῦμα τὸ ἅγιον. According to 15.37–39 John Mark was later to be found in Antioch; Schmithals 125 thinks that he returned to Antioch, not Jerusalem, and that Luke for reasons of his own introduced Jerusalem.

14. αὐτοὶ δέ, Paul and Barnabas, undeterred, continued their journey. διελθόντες does not here (as e.g. at 13.6) seem to indicate a preaching tour. For Ramsay's suggestion that Paul travelled inland in order to cure an attack of malaria see on v. 13; it seems improbable that a man suffering from malaria would be able to make such an ascent. They reached *Pisidian Antioch*. There were many towns called Antioch, related to, in many cases founded by, members of the family of Antiochus (one of the successors of Alexander); see on 11.19. This Antioch was properly in Phrygia and its most correct designation is Ἀντιόχεια πρὸς Πισιδίαν (or Πισιδίᾳ), *towards* Pisidia, near the Pisidian frontier (and thus distinguished from another Phrygian Antioch, on the Maeander). It had been made a colony by Augustus and was a Roman city. Many inscriptions are in Latin. It may have been the place of origin of Deborah, presumably a Jewess, mentioned (as [Ἀ]ντιόχισσα) in *MAMA* 4.202. There is no reason to doubt the evidence of this passage in Acts that there was a substantial Jewish population; for this see also Josephus, *Ant.* 12.147–153. For τὴν Πισιδίαν (P⁴⁵ P⁷⁴ ℵ A B C 453 1175 *pc*), τῆς

Πισιδίας is read by D E Ψ 𝔐 lat sy. This reading is further from the usual designation than the accusative adjective; it is not for that reason to be dismissed as incorrect, but it probably reflects the reorganization of the provinces under Diocletian, perhaps also the fact that the adjective Πισίδιος is otherwise unattested; *Pisidian* is Πισιδικός; see however Hemer 109f., 228.

For the synagogue as a Jewish institution see on 6.9. Paul and Barnabas went to the Sabbath service. The Aramaic שבתא sounded so much like a Greek neuter plural that it gave a great deal of trouble to writers (and no doubt speakers) of Greek. In Acts, when Sabbath is referred to without any accompanying word (such as ἡμέρα) the singular form σάββατον is used (so 1.12; 13.27, 42, 44; 15.21; 18.4) except at 17.2 where several Sabbaths (or weeks) are referred to (σάββατα τρία). Here and at 16.13 we have τῇ ἡμέρᾳ τῶν σαββάτων; at 20.7, τῇ μιᾷ (=τῇ πρώτῃ ἡμέρᾳ) τῶν σαββάτων. Having entered the synagogue ἐκάθισαν. Early synagogues often appear to have had stone benches 'built against two or three of the walls' (*NS* 2.442). Of wooden benches placed in the body of the buildings nothing of course remains, but it seems that Essenes and members of the Qumran sect sat (Philo, *Quod omnis probus* 81, καθ' ἡλικίας ἐν τάξεσιν ὑπὸ πρεσβυτέροις νέοι καθέζονται; 1 QS 6.8, 9, The priests sat (ישבו) in the first place and the elders in the second and the rest of all the people sat (ישבו) each in his own place), though all stood for prayer.

There is no reason to think that Paul (and Barnabas), even after the agreement of Gal. 2.9, would have refused to enter a synagogue. Apart from the fact that Paul evidently retained a sense of responsibility for Israel (Rom. 9.1–3; 10.1), was prepared to be a Jew to Jews (1 Cor. 9.20), and experienced severe synagogue discipline (2 Cor. 11.24), the synagogue provided him with access to some Gentiles sufficiently familiar with Judaism to understand what he was talking about.

15. For the order of worship in the Synagogue see *NS* 2.447–54 ('As principal parts of the service, the Mishnah mentions the recitation of the *Shema* ', the Prayer, the reading of the Torah, the reading of the prophets, the priestly blessing. To this was added the translation of the portion of Scripture read aloud, . . . and its exposition by means of an elevating discourse' — p. 448); also P. Billerbeck, 'Ein Synagogengottesdienst in Jesu Tagen' (*ZNW* 55 (1964), 143–61); StrB 4.153–88; Bousset, *RJ* 172ff. The present verse refers only to the Torah and Haftarah lections, the other parts of the service being taken for granted. The ἀρχισυνάγωγοι address the visitors. For this word see 18.8, 17, and see *NS* 2.433–6. Persons bearing this title are frequently mentioned in inscriptions. It corresponds to the Hebrew ראש הכנסת of the Mishnah (see Sotah 7.7, 8). It seems that the ἀρχισυνάγωγος (see *ND* 4.213–220) was responsible for the worship of the synagogue, that is, for arranging for suitable persons to read the prayers and the lections, and, if it seemed good, to preach. Normally there was one such officer; if Luke is right in using the plural it may be deduced that the community in Pisidian Antioch was a large one. They address Paul and Barnabas as fellow Jews; for ἄνδρες ἀδελφοί see on 1.16. παράκλησις is used also at 4.36; 9.31; 15.31. The cognate παρακαλεῖν is more frequent, and refers to exhortation or preaching (e.g. 2.40). λόγος παρακλήσεως is *word of exhortation*, hortatory discourse, sermon. The words of the synagogue presidents are usually taken to mean, 'If you have anything to say, say it.' Thus εἰ introduces the protasis of a simple conditional sentence, λέγετε (imperative) being the apodosis. This has been questioned by C. Burchard (*ZNW* 61 (1970), 166f.), who, adducing 4.19, argues that εἴ τίς ἐστιν . . . introduces an indirect question, 'Tell us whether you have . . .'. On this view, what is contained in vv. 16–41 is not Paul's λόγος παρακλήσεως but 'eine programmatische Erklärung über seine und Barnabas' Tätigkeit' (167). Then (v. 44) next Sabbath the whole city is gathered together to hear the word of the Lord. This suggestion is grammatically possible, but it is excluded by the fact that vv. 16–41 do constitute a sermon of the kind occurring elsewhere in Acts. Moreover, v. 43 (προσμένειν) implies that some have already been converted, and v. 46 that the 'word of God' has already been spoken. It may or may not seem probable that responsible presidents would invite strangers to preach (though Paul at least was presumably a trained and qualified rabbi); it seems that this is what Luke thought they did. For the scene cf. Philo, *de Spec. Leg.* 2.62 (. . . the scholars sit . . . while one of special experience rises and sets forth . . .).

For λαός see on 4.25; here the word may refer to the people in the synagogue, but these were, or represented, also the elect (Jewish) people of God.

16. Paul rose up; normally the synagogue preacher sat (see StrB 1.997 and cf. Lk. 4.20; see also however Philo, *de Spec. Leg.* 62, quoted on v. 15 — Diaspora synagogues may well have picked up Greek customs). In any case Paul would not have been sitting on the βῆμα, and standing may have been necessary if he was to be seen and heard. κατασείειν occurs in the NT only here, and at 12.17 (see the note); 19.33; 21.40. It suggests a Greek rhetor rather than a synagogue preacher, but any lively orator is likely to have moved hand and arm. For ἄνδρες Ἰσραηλῖται cf. 2.22. These words would presumably take in all Jews assembled in the synagogue. οἱ φοβούμενοι τὸν θεόν, connected with the preceding words by καί, might be supposed to refer to a different group; this raises acutely the question (see on 10.2) whether there was a distinct group of 'God-fearers' who were neither born Jews nor circumcised and baptized proselytes but were attracted by the theology and ethics of Judaism and practised some elements of the Law. The question is complicated by the fact that expressions such as this (and we must bear in mind also the similar phrase σεβόμενος τὸν θεόν — 16.14; 18.7; cf. 17.17) may well have been used in different ways in different sources of Acts (it is most unlikely that ch. 10 and ch. 13 were derived from the same source), and by the occurrence in this chapter of οἱ ἐν ὑμῖν φοβούμενοι τὸν θεόν (v. 26), τῶν σεβομένων προσηλύτων (v. 43), and τὰς σεβομένας γυναῖκας (v. 50). At this point the following observations may be made. (a) There was a great gulf between Jews and proselytes on the one hand and, on the other, the rest of mankind. The former group stood within God's covenant, the latter were outside it; and to enter it was no easy matter. (b) It would be strange if, in v. 16, Paul addressed the Jews present and a group of, doubtless well-disposed, outsiders, but ignored the proselytes completely. In fact we know that he did not ignore the proselytes for they are mentioned in v. 43. (c) In v. 26 (see the note) it is natural to think that Paul is addressing Jews and proselytes, for he continues with ἡμῖν; even if ὑμῖν is read, the descendants of Abraham and οἱ φοβούμενοι are put together as only Jews and proselytes would be. (d) In v. 43 the proselytes are described by the participle σεβόμενοι. (e) In v. 50 the same participle is used of leading women to whom the Jews have ready access. (f) Outside the NT there is some, but only a little, evidence for the existence of a class of persons known as θεοσεβεῖς, God-worshippers; see the inscriptions referred to in the note on 10.2. These were, it seems, Gentile adherents of the synagogue; not proselytes, but sympathetic to Judaism. There is no doubt that such a group existed, or that a family sometimes moved into Judaism over more than one generation (Juvenal, *Satire* 14.96–106): the father was a sympathizer before the son was a proselyte. The question that remains, and still remains unanswered, is how widely a term such as θεοσεβής was used and recognized in a technical, or semi-technical, sense. More descriptive expressions such as Luke uses (φοβούμενοι or σεβόμενοι τὸν θεόν) are somewhat less likely to be technical. StrB 2.716–21 note the occurrence at 2 Chron. 5.6 of the expression οἱ φοβούμενοι; they also observe that there is no corresponding Hebrew. It should also be noted that these φοβούμενοι are mentioned between πᾶσα συναγωγὴ Ἰσραήλ and οἱ ἐπισυνηγμένοι αὐτῶν (whom StrB take to be proselytes) and that all are engaged in offering sacrifices. It is doubtful whether sympathizers would be allowed to do this. Of passages adduced from Josephus, *Apion* 2.123 could refer to proselytes (many Greeks εἰς τοὺς ἡμετέρους νόμους συνέβησαν εἰσελθεῖν); 2.282–4 speaks of the spread of Jewish customs, but adds that the Gentiles in question try to imitate our harmony (ὁμόνοια) and charity, whereas adherents of the synagogue would be at least on the fringe of (not imitating) 'our harmony' and (to judge from the Aphrodisias inscription) participated in 'our charity'; *Ant.* 14.110 speaks of τῶν κατὰ τὴν οἰκουμένην 'Ιουδαίων καὶ σεβομένων τὸν θεόν who contributed to the wealth of the Temple, and these σεβόμενοι could be sympathizers, not proselytes, but the interpretation is not certain. StrB 2.716 notes that the Hebrew equivalent, שמים יראי occurs 'nur sehr selten'. It cannot be regarded as certain that any ancient reader of Acts would have quickly recognized οἱ φοβούμενοι, or οἱ σεβόμενοι, τὸν θεόν as the title of an order, even an informal order, of synagogue adherents. In the present verse, Paul (as represented by Luke) is probably addressing Jews and proselytes; or, just possibly, he is defining Jews: 'My fellow Jews, yes, you who fear God as no other nation does.'

For ἀκούσατε, cf. 2.22; 7.2; 15.13; 22.1.

17. Paul embarks upon a sketch of the history of his people. If this speech was ever delivered in a synagogue the story was no doubt told in greater detail and at greater length. Abraham and the patriarchs are not mentioned by name and the whole of the period before the Exodus is compressed into this verse. According to Haenchen (392) Luke omits this material because it is already dealt with in ch. 7. The opening clause has the effect of defining what is meant by speaking of God as the God of Israel (the λαός, the word being used as it usually is in Acts; see on 4.25). He is the God of Israel not in the sense that Israel have picked him out of a number of eligible deities (τοῦ λαοῦ τούτου 'Ισραήλ is not a possessive genitive) but because he has chosen, ἐξελέξατο, Israel. The relation between God and people results from an act of election on God's part. This is put into effect in an act of salvation. God exalted (ὕψωσεν; elsewhere the verb is used only of Christ, whom God exalted: 2.33; 5.31) the people in Egypt; they were slaves but he gave them victory over their Egyptian overlords and brought them out μετὰ βραχίονος ὑψηλοῦ. The expression is septuagintal; see especially Exod 6.1, 6; 32.11 (the phrase seems to translate sometimes literally נטויה זרע sometimes חזקה יד. Paul makes it clear that he was preaching none other than 'the One who had long ago made Himself known to their fathers' (Calvin 365).

18. ὡς (taken in the sense of *about*; see also on v. 19) is omitted by D E gig vg syᵖ, probably because it seemed unnecessary; the traditional period was forty years (Exod. 16.35; Num. 14.33, 34) and there was no need to qualify it. It is however characteristic of Luke to qualify numbers with ὡς or ὡσεί, and he probably wrote the word. τεσσερακονταετὴς χρόνος seems to be Luke's own expression; it is not used in the LXX.

The verb in the sentence is textually uncertain. ἐτροποφόρησεν, *he put up with their ways*, is read by ℵ A*vid B C² D 𝔐 vg, ἐτροφοφόρησεν, *he nourished, fed, them* (provided them with food, but perhaps more generally, *cared for*, as a nurse), P74 Ac C* E Ψ 33vid 1175 *pc* d gig sy co. The note in *Begs.* 4.149 suggests that there is little or no difference in meaning between the two words; that ἐτροπ. is the right spelling, but that π may represent φ, changed (because of the following φ) for the sake of euphony. On the other hand, M. 2.109 affirms that 'there is no probability that the former [ἐτροπ.] could arise from the latter [ἐτροφ.] phonetically'. Luke's sentence recalls Deut. 1.31, where unfortunately there is a similar variant: ἐν τῇ ἐρήμῳ . . . ἐτροφοφόρησέν (B and 28 others; ἐτροπ. in 10 MSS) σε κύριος ὁ θεός σου, ὡς εἴ τις τροφοφορήσει (Bc *al*; τροπ. B* N 75 Origen 3/6) ἄνθρωπος τὸν υἱὸν αὐτοῦ. In each case the Hebrew root is נשא. The variations here support the view of *Begs.* 4, that writers were prone to confuse the two forms and to regard them as equivalent. There is something to be said for the argument that there would be a tendency to conform Paul's words to the majority text of the LXX passage to which they appear to refer, so that ἐτροπ. would be the likely reading in Acts; the agreement of ℵ B D supports this conclusion. The difficulty however is well illustrated by comparison of Schneider (2.132) who chooses ἐτροπ. as the lectio difficilior, and Ropes (*Begs.* 3.120), who writes that ἐτροφ. 'suits the context better, and may be preferred on that ground'. Neither word is common. τροφ. occurs in 2 Macc. 7.27; the existence of τροπ. (and probably its existence in a current Greek phrase) is proved by Cicero, *ad Atticum* 13.29.2 (. . . nihil est quod ego malim. in hoc τὸν τύφον μου πρὸς θεῶν τροποφόρησον). Blass (149) questions the existence of τροφ.: 'Non video quomodo formari potuerit τροφοφ., at est formatum τροποφ. (Cic. *ad Att.* 13, 29, 2) = φέρειν τὸν τρόπον τινός, patienter ferre aliquem.' But he does not adequately dispose of the LXX occurrence of this word when he adds, 'Etiam 2 Macc. 7.27 minime de τροφῇ agitur.' The decisive argument seems to be that, in the context, Paul is dealing not with Israel's wayward conduct (in this his speech may be contrasted with Stephen's), but with the benefits bestowed on them by God; hence ἐτροφ. may (with anything but complete confidence) be preferred. R. P. Gordon (*NovT* 16 (1974), 285–7) draws attention to the Targumic expression סופק צורכא, which occurs at Deut. 2.7; 32.10; Hos. 13.5; Zech. 9.11 and describes God's care for Israel in the wilderness. He regards this as a confirmation of Targumic influence in this speech. See on v. 22.

19. Pesch (2.35) explains the absence at this point of any reference to the law by the observation that for Luke it was irrelevant to the story of salvation; this is difficult to support in view of the references to Moses and the law in ch. 7.

As printed and punctuated in NA²⁶ v. 19 is linked with both v. 18 and v. 20: God dealt with the people in the wilderness and (καί) having destroyed . . . he assigned . . . their land for about 450 years. And afterwards . . . This probably represents Luke's intention, but the construction is disturbed by variant readings. καί is omitted by B 6 81 *pc*. If this reading is accepted ὡς in v. 18 must be translated not *about* but *when*: and when he had . . . in the wilderness, having destroyed . . . he assigned . . . This is less likely as a translation of ὡς and overestimates the importance of B; the omission of καί may have been accidental, due, perhaps, to a partial haplography (ΚΑΙΚΑΘ . . .). The connection with v. 20 is affected by a complicated set of variants. The simplest variation (that of D² E Ψ 𝔐) changes the order of the opening words of v. 20: καὶ μετὰ ταῦτα, ὡς ἔτεσιν τετρακοσίοις καὶ πεντήκοντα . . . (and afterwards, for about 450 years . . .). This clearly starts a new sentence. D* gig have καὶ ἕως (sic) ἔτεσι υ' καὶ ν'. . . (and for (literally, up to, as far as) 450 years . . .). This too begins a new sentence. The printed text (. . . ὡς ἔτεσιν τετρακοσίοις καὶ πεντήκοντα. καὶ μετὰ ταῦτα . . .) is read by P⁷⁴ ℵ A B C 33 36 81 453 1175 *pc* vg. Ropes (*Begs.* 3.121) thinks that the Western text is to be preferred, but the variations were probably intended to prevent the reader from interpreting the text to mean that the dispossessing of the seven nations and the settling of the Hebrews in Canaan occupied 450 years and was followed by a further period during which the people were ruled by judges. This cannot have been Luke's intention, though his meaning is not expressed as clearly as possible. For the reckoning of time see below on v. 20.

καθαιρεῖν is not infrequently used of the overthrow of peoples; e.g. Herodotus 1.71.1, Croesus ἐλπίσας καταιρήσειν Κῦρόν τε καὶ τὴν Περσέων δύναμιν. For the seven nations see Deut. 7.1 (ἐξαρεῖ ἔθνη μεγάλα ἀπὸ προσώπου σου . . .); similarly Josh. 3.10; 24.11; at Deut. 20.17 there are six. At 1 QM 11.8f. they have become the eschatological foes of Israel; see Braun 169. Χανάαν, as at 7.11. κατακληρονομεῖν is predominantly a septuagintal word, rendering for the most part various forms of שׁרי and נחל, and thus varying in meaning between *give as an inheritance* (so evidently here) and *receive as an inheritance*.

τὴν γῆν αὐτῶν (P⁷⁴ ℵ B Ψ 33 81 1175 *pc*), though certainly original, is awkward because the reference of the pronoun is not made clear by the structure of the sentence. αὐτοῖς τὴν γῆν αὐτῶν (A C D² E 𝔐 lat syᵖ) is a clumsy improvement, τὴν γῆν τῶν ἀλλοφύλων (D* syʰ**mae) makes everything clear.

20. For the textual variants at the beginning of this verse see the note on v. 19. The dative ἔτεσιν τετρακοσίοις καὶ πεντήκοντα for duration of time is surprising (but cf. 8.11; also 28.12 B, ἐπεμείναμεν ἡμέραις τρισίν). BDR § 201 suggest that the customary accusative may have been avoided because of the proximity of the object accusative, and that the Latin ablative of time (vixit annis n.) may have contributed. The period stated, 450 years, may well have been simply an approximation, though *Begs.* 4.150 points out, 'This seems to represent a mechanical addition of all the notes of time in the Judges, without considering synchronisms, which makes 410 years, to which the addition of the forty years of Eli makes 450 (Judges 3.8, 11, 14, 30; 4.3; 5.31; 6.1; 8.28; 9.22; 10.2, 3, 8; 12.7, 9, 11, 14; 13.1; 15.20; 1 Sam. 4.18). But it is to be noted that this applies only to the Hebrew text. The LXX, which agrees with the Hebrew throughout the list of dates in Judges, gives Eli only twenty years instead of forty, in 1 Sam. 4.18.' This calculation explains the period of 450 years only if it applies to the time of the judges (see on v. 19). If the period is taken (following the most obvious sense of the Old Uncial reading) to refer to the time between the exodus and the settlement in Canaan it is manifestly absurd; if it relates to the time between the call of Abraham (v. 17, ἐξελέξατο τοὺς πατέρας ἡμῶν) and the settlement it is difficult to support precisely. According to 1 Kings 6.1 the interval between the exodus and Solomon's commencing the building of the Temple was 480 years (MT; LXX, 440). From this the reigns of Saul and David, together with the first four years of Solomon's reign would have to be subtracted, and a number substantially lower than 450 would be reached. The official rabbinic reckoning (see StrB 2.724ff.) was 383 years for the period of the judges, 440¹/₃ between the entry and the building of the Temple. Blass (150), noting that 450 does not agree with 1 Kings 6.1, adds 'sed cum Iudaeorum traditione conveniebat, ex qua (Ioseph. Ant. 8, 3, 1.10, 8, 5 [=8.61; 10.147]) ab exodo usque ad exstructum templum fuerunt anni DXCII, de quibus subtrahendi ter quadrageni (peregrinationis, Sauli, Davidis) decemque Salomonis, ut relinquantur CCCCLXII.' The answer is not quite right, and it is interesting to compare Wettstein (536f.): 'quibus 592 annis si demas annos 40 quos in deserto degerunt, 17 Josuae, 40 Samuelis et Saulis, 40 Davidis, 4 Salomonis, residui erunt CCCCL.' Unfortunately, Josephus is not consistent (*Begs.* 4.150).

κριτάς borrows the word from the Greek translation of the Book of Judges; the שֹׁפְטִים were of course much more than judicial functionaries. Samuel (cf. 3.24) was one of them, but is here designated a prophet. It was recognized that he filled both roles. For the article before προφήτου (read by C D E Ψ 𝔐; omitted by P⁷⁴ ℵ A B 81 *pc*) cf. the notes on 10.6; 12.1; 13.1; there is no question here of distinguishing a Samuel who was a prophet from another Samuel who was not, and the style is better if the article is omitted; this probably means that Luke wrote it.

21. ἐκεῖθεν is most often *from that place*, here (as occasionally elsewhere) *from that time, after that*. ἠτήσαντο: the subject is evidently the Hebrew people, Israel. The active is common in petitions to God; the middle suggests that the request was made to Samuel (BDR § 316. 2, n. 3). See 1 Kdms 8.5 and especially 10 (τοὺς αἰτοῦντας παρ' αὐτοῦ βασιλέα). The request was made to Samuel, and although both he and God were unwilling in this way to assimilate Israel to the surrounding nations (1 Kdms 8.5), in the end God granted their desire: ἔδωκεν αὐτοῖς τὸν Σαούλ. See 1 Kdms 10.21–26. For the OT king the uninflected form is used.

King Saul was a man ἐκ φυλῆς Βενιαμίν; so was Saul of Tarsus (Rom. 11.1; Phil. 3.5). It has been suggested that the preacher mentioned this as a matter of pride. 'The allusion to Saul might be a genuine reminiscence: was it a synagogue practice to glorify your eponymous hero in the OT? Cf. the glorification of Eliezer, Abraham's servant, by R. Eliezer in Talmud Yoma 28b' (Knox, *Hellenistic Elements* 17). This does not seem probable; see the next verse.

The period of forty years for Saul's reign is not given in the OT, but see Josephus, *Ant.* 6.378 (eighteen years during Samuel's life, twenty-two after his death), also however *Ant.* 10.143 (twenty years). According to the Hebrew of 1 Sam. 13.1 Saul reigned two years; the text of this verse is undoubtedly corrupt.

22. μεταστήσας αὐτόν must cast considerable doubt on the suggestion (see on v. 21) that Saul of Tarsus was mentioning with pride the distinction of his fellow tribesman, Saul the son of Kish. King Saul served for a time, but in the end God set him aside in favour of David (1 Sam. 15.23; 16.1, 12, 13). For μεθιστάναι meaning *to remove from office*, cf. Euripides, *Iphigeneia in Tauris* 775 (but the analogy is not close). God *raised up* (ἤγειρεν) David, not in the sense of raising him from death but in that he brought him forward (see the note on 5.30) *as king*, εἰς βασιλέα. The use of εἰς to denote a predicate 'cannot fairly be described as a Hebraism, for the vernacular shows a similar extension of the old use of εἰς expressing destination: so for example KP 46 (ii/AD), ἔσχον παρ' ὑμῶν εἰς δά(νειον) σπέρματα, a recurrent formula' (M. 1.71f.; on p. 76 Moulton adds a reference to Marcus Aurelius 6.42, which however is only doubtfully relevant). Radermacher (100) writes similarly that 'das Auftreten der Präposition durchaus im Geiste zusammenhängender, griechischer Sprachentwicklung liegt,' and on pp. 16f. he quotes not only papyri but Heliodorus, *Aethiopica* 6.14; Vettius Valens 59.7K; and Aeneas Tacticus 114.5H (40.7). The relative frequency of the construction in the NT (cf. Acts 7.21) however justifies the judgment of BDR § 157. 5, 'semitischer Einfluss ist unverkennbar, wenn auch das Griechische Ansätze zu diesem Gebrauch gehabt hat.' Predicative ל is very common in Hebrew.

In εἶπεν ματυρήσας the aorist participle denotes time coincident with that of the finite verb; it has the same punctiliar force as εἶπεν, and the sense shows that the two points of time were identical: it was when he spoke that he bore witness. The testimony in question is based on the OT, though it is not an exact quotation. Ps. 88 (89).21a: εὗρον Δαυὶδ τὸν δοῦλόν μου (מצאתי דוד עבדי); 1 Kdms 13.14: ζητήσει κύριος ἑαυτῷ ἄνθρωπον κατὰ τὴν καρδίαν αὐτοῦ (בקש יהוה לו איש כלבבו). The two passages are conflated (perhaps from memory). David is described as the son of Jesse (the article τοῦ before Ἰεσσαί is not classical, and in D is replaced by υἱόν; see BDR § 162. 2, n. 3 and contrast 20.4); ἄνδρα (omitted by B) replaces ἄνθρωπον; it is added that David ποιήσει πάντα τὰ θελήματα μου. Elsewhere in the NT only at Eph. 2.3 is θέλημα used in the plural. The meaning is clear: David will do all the several things willed by God; *everything I will*. This expression however reflects the form taken by 1 Sam. 13.14 in the Targum, which in place of the Hebrew איש כלבבו has גבר עביד רעותיה (Wilcox 21–4). The word רעותה may be pointed as either a singular (*r‘utheh*) or a plural (*ra‘watheh*), that is, in Greek as θέλημα or θελήματα; of the clause as a whole ἀνὴρ ὃς ποιήσει τὰ θελήματα αὐτοῦ would be a good translation. Thus the form of words in Acts contains both the MT and LXX words *after my heart* and the Targum words, *who shall do (my) will*. Wilcox, following Bruce, also points out that the Psalm and the passage from 1 Kdms 13 are similarly combined in 1 Clement 18.1 ((εὗρον) ἄνδρα κατὰ τὴν καρδίαν μου, Δαυεὶδ τὸν τοῦ Ἰεσσαί, ἐν ἐλέει αἰωνίῳ ἔχρισα αὐτόν. These are important observations but it will be well to be cautious in drawing inferences from them. See J. A. Emerton *JSS* 13 (1960), 287f. That *after my heart* was interpreted to mean *who will do my will* seems clear, but how this interpretative phrase came to be united with the phrase that it interprets, and how this combination found its way into the present passage in Acts, is anything but clear. The combination does however add some weight to the view that the sermon traditions used in Acts are old enough to go back to Jewish Christian material. For the question whether Clement knew Acts see p. 35.

23. From David, Paul leaps over the centuries to Jesus. τούτου ὁ θεὸς ἀπὸ τοῦ σπέρματος lays unusual emphasis on David: It was of this man's seed that God . . . D rewrites in more conventional style: ὁ θεὸς οὖν ἀπὸ τοῦ σπέρματος αὐτοῦ: So God, of his [David's] seed, . . . The promise made to David has not been mentioned or alluded to in the text; 2 Kdms 7.12 is no doubt in mind. ἤγαγεν is a simple but (in this sense) unusual word; ἤγειρε (C D 33 36 323 453 614 945 1241 *al* gig sy sa mae Theodoret) conforms to v. 22, and to many other biblical passages. God fulfilled his promise *to Israel*, especially as represented by the house of David, bringing to his people a Saviour; cf. 5.31. Luke makes no attempt to define here what he means by salvation, or a Saviour; see on vv. 38f. For σωτῆρα Ἰησοῦν, P⁷⁴ E 𝔐 have (εἰς in some MSS) σωτηρίαν. This variant is well explained as due to the misreading of σωτῆρα ιν̄ (the name Jesus contracted).

24. This verse is added almost in the form of an afterthought: we must not forget to mention the forerunner, John the Baptist. His importance in the early Christian understanding of the eschatological significance of the work of Jesus is amply attested in Acts; see 1.5 and the note. προκηρύσσειν occurs here only in the NT, but the meaning of the prefix is clear (for κηρύσσειν itself, used of John, see 10.37), and hardly necessary in view of πρὸ προσώπου τῆς εἰσόδου αὐτοῦ. πρὸ προσώπου recalls the Hebrew לִפְנֵי; M. 2.466 says rightly, 'the influence of the Greek of the LXX is unmistakable', but BDR § 4.3 , n. 8, also rightly, that such expressions may come 'aus dem gesprochenen Judengriechisch'. The two opinions are fully compatible; the LXX is the chief source of our knowledge of colloquial Jewish Greek. See also BDR § 217. 1, n. 2, with the note that the temporal use of πρὸ προσώπου is an 'ungenaue Anwendung des Septuagintismus'. πρὸ προσώπου κυρίου (Lk. 1.76, A C D al) is natural enough, but πρὸ προσώπου with εἴσοδος is surprising. Wilcox 162 compares Lk. 9.31 (ἔξοδος). Cf. also Mal. 3.1. Schille 294 thinks of 'das Ritual des festlichen Empfanges eines Herrschers'. The noun clearly refers to the entry of Jesus upon his public ministry (as at 1 Thess. 1.9; 2.1 it refers to Paul's entry upon his ministry in Thessalonica), and the phrase as a whole simply states that the work of John the Baptist preceded that of Jesus. It consisted in the proclamation of a baptism (cf. 10.37), here, though not earlier in Acts (cf. 19.4), described as a baptism of repentance, that is, a baptism whose distinguishing feature was that it was accompanied by, and was an outward sign of, repentance. Thus John summoned the whole of the people (παντὶ τῷ λαῷ) of Israel to repent and manifest their penitence in the act of baptism. παντί is emphatic; the whole people must return to God (for μετάνοια see on 2.38). Wilckens (102) notes the emphatic προ. . . . πρό: John is separated from Jesus.

Weiser, who (325) argues that vv. 24f. is a Lucan contribution to the speech, gives (332f.) an excellent discussion of the question whether John was thought by Luke to belong to the 'law and the prophets' or to the time of Jesus. Although Jesus has been mentioned in v. 23 it seems clear that in this passage John's preaching is thought of as preliminary to the work of Jesus. See however on the next verse.

25. The beginning of the ministry of Jesus is now placed towards the close of John's; the imperfect ἐπλήρου means *was completing*, not *had completed*. Some overlap is suggested. The gospel, by anticipating (Lk. 3.20) Herod's arrest of John, leaves the temporal relation between the two obscure; the Fourth Gospel describes an overlap (Jn 3.23, 24; 4.1). For the metaphorical use of δρόμος cf. 20.24 (and 2 Tim. 4.7); it seems to be unusual in Greek, and when the word is used metaphorically it is mostly in the sense of 'being on' or 'getting off course'. The notion of competition is often included, at least in the background; cf. 1 Clement 6.2. δρόμος δημόσιος is used for the Latin *cursus publicus*; allowing for the very different setting this is probably as close a parallel to the present use as can be found.

John's words are in NA²⁶ printed and punctuated τί ἐμὲ ὑπονοεῖτε εἶναι; οὐκ εἰμὶ ἐγώ. Instead of τί ἐμέ (P⁷⁴ ℵ A B E 33 81 1175 *pc*), τινά με is read by P⁴⁵ C D Ψ 𝔐 latt syᵖ. Both readings are ancient; since a masculine pronoun is unlikely to have been changed into a neuter we may prefer τί ἐμέ and translate the text as punctuated, *What* (rather than *Whom*) *do you suppose me to be? I am not that* (that is, I do not hold the office you have in mind). This punctuation and this rendering are approved by Moule (*IB* 124: Moule translates, I am not (the one)). Others however take τί (interrogative) to have been used as if it were the relative ὅ. The question mark is then dropped and we have the single sentence, *I am not what you suppose me to be*. This use of the interrogative pronoun is Hellenistic (BDR §§ 298. 5, n. 8; 299. 2, n. 2), and M. 1.93 cites some partial anticipations of it in classical authors (Sophocles, *Oedipus Tyrannus* 1068, εἴθε μήποτε γνοίης ὃς εἶ, and Plato, *Euthyphro* 14e, ἃ μὲν γὰρ διδόασι, παντὶ δῆλον — it will be noted that in each of these the relative is used where the interrogative would be expected). Neither of these possibilities can be excluded; the former perhaps deserves preference because the question accords well with the deliberative, questioning tone of Lk. 3.15 (. . . μήποτε αὐτὸς εἴη ὁ χριστός). It is, of course, clear on any reading of the text, that John is making a disavowal (cf. Jn 1.19–23; Justin, *Trypho* 88.7), and as good as certain what the disavowal was. Though some might believe him to be the Messiah, John knew that he was not, and said so plainly. His coming, however, was related to the coming of the Saviour, Jesus (v. 23). For the use of ὑπονοεῖν cf. Aristophanes, *Plutus* 361. The wording of the remainder of the verse is similar to but not identical with that of Lk. 3.16 (ἔρχεται δὲ ὁ ἰσχυρότερός μου, οὗ οὐκ εἰμὶ ἱκανὸς λῦσαι τὸν ἱμάντα τῶν ὑποδημάτων αὐτοῦ). It is interesting to observe that the superfluous (and Semitic) pronoun αὐτοῦ does not appear in Acts (see Knox, *Hellenistic Elements* 8); there is a general compression (ἰσχυρότερος and τὸν ἱμάντα are omitted; ποδῶν however is added). The substance remains the same, also the image by means of which it is expressed.

John is not worthy to untie Jesus' shoes. On this menial task see Daube (*NTRJ* 266f.). According to Ketuboth 96a, R. Joshua ben Levi 'held that a disciple should do for his teacher anything a slave would do — except take off his shoes.' John, however, did not consider himself worthy to perform even this task — the infinite superiority of Jesus is underlined. This emphasis may have been due to the presence in Asia Minor of groups of disciples of John the Baptist, of whom Luke was aware (cf. 18.25; 19.3). So Stählin (182); Roloff (205) finds this only a Nebenmotiv, but it is probably to be recognized as a not unimportant contact between Acts and John.

26. The preliminary sketch of the *praeparatio evangelica* in the OT ended, Paul comes to the core of his message and addresses his hearers afresh. For ἄνδρες ἀδελφοί see 1.16 and the note; it addresses the whole group which is defined in the next words. υἱοὶ γένους Ἀβραάμ corresponds to the ἄνδρες Ἰσραηλῖται of v. 16. As in that verse so here there is added (by the copula καί) an address to οἱ φοβούμενοι τὸν θεόν, with the difference that here ἐν ὑμῖν stands between the article and the participle. In addition there is doubt about the word καί, which is omitted by P⁴⁵ B, a small but important combination, especially since the memory of v. 16 might lead a copyist to add the word. A further textual complication arises in the next clause, but, as was pointed out in the note on v. 16, it seems best to take οἱ φοβούμενοι to be not uncircumcised 'God-fearers' but proselytes. They are ἐν ὑμῖν, *among you*. This may mean no more than that they are at the time of speaking in the same building; it is better understood to mean that they have joined your ranks. Paul addresses as *brothers* all fellow members of the ancient people of God, born Jews, defined as descendants of Abraham, and proselytes, who have attached themselves to the people by the appointed means. ἡμῖν further associates both groups with Paul; this word is read by P⁷⁴ ℵ A B D Ψ 33 81 614 *pc* sin w sy^hmg sa mae, and is probably correct; ὑμῖν, read by P⁴⁵ C E 𝔐 lat sy bo, however, also puts the descendants of Abraham and the φοβούμενοι together, implying that the latter are proselytes. If the καί before οἱ φοβούμενοι is omitted the phrase must presumably be understood to be restrictive; Descendants of Abraham — those at least among the whole audience who truly fear God — to you . . .

To the congregation thus defined Paul brings a message of salvation, ὁ λόγος τῆς σωτηρίας ταύτης. *This* salvation looks back to v. 23, either because σωτηρία is mentioned here or more probably because it is implied (in the reading σωτῆρα). The message has been sent to us — Jews; cf. v. 46 (and contrast 28.28). It was necessary that the word of God should be spoken first to those to whom the promise had been made. As at v. 23, no attempt is made at this point to define the meaning of salvation; at vv. 38, 39 it appears that it consists in the forgiveness of sins, or justification. Paul proceeds, in the manner of the Petrine speeches in earlier chapters to show how prophecy and the promise have been fulfilled in the life, death, and resurrection of Jesus. Weiser 326 argues that the reference to the Passion is Lucan, that to the resurrection (v. 30) traditional.

27. On the text of vv. 27–29 see below; also Ropes's detached note (*Begs.* 3.261–3).

Conzelmann (76) describes γάρ as merely an Übergangspartikel, and then surprisingly (but correctly) goes on to say that it provides the ground on which the proclamation of salvation can now be made (v. 26). The agents of the fulfilment (ἐπλήρωσαν) were those who condemned Jesus, the inhabitants of Jerusalem (οἱ κατοικοῦντες ἐν 'Ιερουσαλήμ — contrast 1.19, where there is no ἐν) and their rulers (οἱ ἄρχοντες αὐτῶν; cf. 3.17). They unconsciously fulfilled prophecy because they did not know, recognize, Jesus (τοῦτον: it is surprising that the name is not used; Luke may have taken up a fresh source — which would mean that he was compiling the speech) or the *voices*, φωνάς, *utterances, messages* (an unusual meaning for φωνή, but cf. 12.22) of the prophets. For not understanding the prophets there was no excuse, since these were *read every Sabbath*, in the Synagogue, as the Haftaroth corresponding to the Torah lections. They were read (ἀναγινώσκειν) but not understood (ἀγνοεῖν); for the contrast cf. 8.30 and see Daube (*NTRJ* 434ff.). Luke does not raise the question whether the prophecies could have been fulfilled if they had been understood. For φωνάς, E has, more naturally but wrongly, γραφάς; D* omits all reference to Jesus (τοῦτον) and writes μὴ συνίεντες τὰς γραφὰς τῶν προφητῶν.

A further participle, κρίναντες, stands between ἀγνοήσαντες and ἐπλήρωσαν. This presumably refers to the Jewish 'trial' of Jesus and looks forward to the μηδεμίαν . . . εὑρόντες of the next verse: *having sat in judgment* . . . The sentence is much easier if, with Pallis (66), we omit the καί after ἀγνοήσαντες. τοῦτον is then to be taken as the object of the (rather distant) κρίναντες: Because they did not understand . . . they judged him. But after this ἐπλήρωσαν follows awkwardly (and evokes a further emendation). Dibelius (91f.) also suspects corruption in the text and wishes to take only τὰς φωνάς as the object of ἀγνοήσαντες.

28. εὑρόντες: concessive use of the participle, *although they found* . . . αἰτία is frequently found in forensic speech; αἰτία θανάτου is *causa capitalis* (BA50), a capital charge. The phrase however is not quite rightly used; there was a capital charge; what could not be found was the evidence to prove it. D 614 lat sy^{h**} co add ἐν αὐτῷ. Pallis 66 wishes to read εὑρόντος (that is, Pilate). For the substance cf. Lk. 23.22; now it is affirmed that not only Pilate but the Jews also were unable to find evidence against Jesus (Schille 295).

Notwithstanding this lack of proof they asked (ἠτήσαντο; on the voice see on v. 21; ἤτησαν τὸν Π. in א* is a slip) Pilate to do away with him. In the reading of D* (κρίναντες αὐτὸν παρέδωκαν τῷ Πιλάτῳ ἵνα εἰς ἀναίρεσιν), κρίναντες may be in the right place, παρέδωκαν recalls Mk 15.1 (not Lk. 23.1), and the last three words are a confusion of two constructions (ἵνα and a subjunctive, εἰς with the cognate noun) after ἠτήσαντο. This seems more probable than the suggestions of Wilcox (120: דִּלְקַטְלָא, *in order to put to death*, or *that he [Pilate?] might put him to death*, was misread as דִּלְקַטְלָא, *for [his] killing, execution*) or Black (*AA* 74f.: the original Aramaic was בְּדִיל לְקַטְלֵיהּ). In the Old Uncial text the two accusatives will be observed (Πιλᾶτον, αὐτόν); 'Bei ἐρωτᾶν, παρακαλεῖν usw ist der Inf. noch selbständiger als beim eigentlichen AcI [= Akkusativum cum Infinitivo], und kann somit trotz des Objektsakkusativs einen weitern Akk. als Subjekt zu sich nehmen, namentlich bei Passivkonstruktionen' (BDR § 409. 5, n. 7). Cf. v. 29 D and 21.12; and see also Radermacher (148). Vv. 27f. are a Lucan formulation according to Wilckens (134–7).

29. This verse completes the account of the execution of Jesus. The thought of v. 27 is repeated: it was the enemies of Jesus who, unwittingly, fulfilled the prophecies concerning him, *all the things that had been written concerning him*. It was foretold that he should suffer (cf. 3.18), and they saw to it that he did. This meant his crucifixion (mentioned explicitly not in the Old Uncial text but in the Western text; see below); accordingly the next step was his deposition from the cross. καθαιρεῖν is a Lucan word (Lk., 3; Acts, 3; rest of the NT, 3), used already in v. 19 but in a different sense. Here the participle καθελόντες applies to the subject of ἐτέλεσαν and, as pointed out above, this must refer to the enemies of Jesus, unless we take the unlikely view that we have here an example of the impersonal use of the third person plural, which is unusual in the Lucan writings (but see 3.2). At Lk. 23.53 καθελών is applied to Joseph of Arimathaea; Luke himself knew that they were friendly hands that took down the body of Jesus from the cross. It is difficult to believe that the man who wrote this in the gospel seriously wished to attribute to Paul the view that it was Jesus' Jewish opponents who buried him, though Stählin (183) makes the point that the story as told here helps to prove that Jesus was truly dead and buried and that his grave was subsequently found empty as the result of supernatural action. 'It may be that Luke took the word for burying in an indefinite way. Even if you wish to apply it to those same men, it will be synecdoche. For He was buried by Pilate's permission, but on the other hand guards were placed at the sepulchre by the decision of the priests. Therefore even if Joseph and Nicodemus committed Christ to the sepulchre, it is incorrect, but yet not absurd, to attribute that to the

Jews' (Calvin 374). It may be that Haenchen (394) says all that is necessary: 'In Wirklichkeit hat Lukas nur den Bericht äusserst verkürzt.' The cross here is τὸ ξύλον; cf. 5.30; 10.39. See Deut. 21.22 and Gal. 3.13 as well as the notes on the passages mentioned. The early Christians, or some of them, found importance in the reference to Deuteronomy; there is no attempt here to bring out any theological significance in the choice of the word. Finally 'they' placed the body of Jesus in a tomb. Cf. Lk. 23.53, ἔθηκεν αὐτὸν ἐν μνήματι. The word τιθέναι is not used elsewhere in Acts of the burial of Jesus, but cf. 7.16.

27-29. The MSS which bear witness to the Western text diverge in these verses not only from the Old Uncial text but also from one another. Clark (81) reconstructs the original Western text as follows (using the στίχοι of D):

```
      οἱ γὰρ κατοικοῦντες ἐν Ἰερουσαλὴμ
      καὶ οἱ ἄρχοντες αὐτῆς
      μὴ συνιέντες τὰς γραφὰς τῶν προφητῶν
      τὰς κατὰ πᾶν σάββατον ἀναγινωσκομένας
  5   κρίναντες ἐπλήρωσαν
      καὶ μηδεμίαν αἰτίαν θανάτου
      εὑρόντες ἐν αὐτῷ
      κρίναντες αὐτὸν παρέδωκαν Πιλάτῳ
      εἰς ἀναίρεσιν· ὡς δὲ ἐτέλουν
 10   πάντα τὰ περὶ αὐτοῦ γεγραμμένα
      ἠτοῦντο τὸν Πιλᾶτον τοῦτον μὲν σταυρῶσαι
      [τὸν δὲ Βαραββᾶν ἀπολῦσαι]
      σταυρωθέντος δὲ ἠτοῦντο τὸν Πιλᾶτον
      ἀπὸ τοῦ ξύλου καθελεῖν αὐτόν·
 15   καὶ ἐπιτυχόντες πάλιν
      καὶ καθελόντες ἀπὸ τοῦ ξύλου
      ἔθηκαν εἰς μνημεῖον
```

Clark (356) is inclined to follow a suggestion of Bornemann's that what is given here as line 12 should be added to the text of D; μέν in line 11 requires a δέ clause, and a reference to Barabbas neatly supplies one.

Ropes (*Begs.* 3.261) gives a similar reconstruction. His differs from Clark's as follows (ignoring orthographical variations): In line 5 he omits κρίναντες; for lines 11-14 he reads ἠτοῦντο τὸν Πιλᾶτον μετὰ τὸ σταυρωθῆναι αὐτὸν ἀπὸ τοῦ ξύλου καθαιρεθῆναι; in line 15 he omits πάλιν; for line 16 he reads καθεῖλον καί. Clark and Ropes both discuss the variants at much greater length than is possible here. It will be observed that each proceeds on the assumption that there was one original Western text to which the various authorities (see Introduction, pp. 21–9) bear witness with greater or less accuracy. It is doubtful whether this assumption is valid; probable that the Old Uncial text (which is too awkward to be easily accepted as a secondary, edited, product) was found obscure and unusual and was rewritten in various ways but always with reference to familiar and smoother accounts of the passion. The main exception to this is the verb ἐπιτυγχάνειν (v. 29, D (sy^hmg)), which is in no Passion Narrative and may be a genuinely old reading.

30. This verse states the core of the Gospel as understood by Luke in words almost identical with those of 3.15; 4.10; 10.40; see the notes on those verses, also v. 37. D is more closely conformed to 3.15; 4.10, with ὃν ὁ θεὸς ἤγειρεν, but omits ἐκ νεκρῶν; this may be original.

31. ὃς ὤφθη ἐπὶ ἡμέρας πλείους. Cf. 1.3, δι' ἡμερῶν, referring to the same events. Moule (*IB* 56) suggests the explanation that διά is really (in this use) adverbial and simply *takes the mind through the period*, so that it depends on the *Aktionsart* of the verb whether the event is thought of as taking place in the course of or at the end of the period described. Here, after an aorist (the present participle ὀπτανόμενος is used at 1.3), διά would suggest *at the end of*; hence 'another and less ambiguous preposition is used'. There is no doubt of the meaning here; ὤφθη sums up a number of appearances as one event of manifestation. The appearances took place over a considerable period; Luke would have seen no contradiction between πλείους and the forty of 1.3. The appearances were granted to those who had accompanied Jesus from Galilee to Jerusalem, that is, to those defined in 1.21, 22 as possible candidates for appointment to the place among the apostles left vacant by Judas. In the NT συναναβαίνειν is used only at Mk 15.41, of women who had accompanied Jesus to Jerusalem; ἀναβαίνειν is regularly used of journeys to the capital — see on 11.2. It is to be noted that in this speech Paul does not claim that the risen Jesus ὤφθη, *appeared*, to him, as he does at 1 Cor. 15.8. The way in which Paul expresses himself in the letter suggests that his claim did not go unchallenged; the challenge no doubt increased the vehemence of his assertion. It therefore seems unlikely that he would have spoken as he is represented as doing here (see further below), unless, as is possible, the controversy reflected in 1 Cor. 15 did not arise till a later date. An alternative explanation is suggested by Bengel: Paul did not wish to separate himself from Barnabas. More probably we should recognize that the speech before us is not of Paul's own composition but was written by Luke from his own point of view, from which Paul was seen as an outstanding evangelist but not as an apostle in the same sense as the Twelve. See on 14.4, 14, and the general discussion in Vol. II.

The text of D differs in this half of the verse, though the sense is substantially unaltered: οὗτος ὤφθη τοῖς συναναβαίνουσιν αὐτῷ ἀπὸ τῆς Γαλιλαίας εἰς Ἰερουσαλὴμ ἐφ᾽ ἡμέρας πλείονας. The choice of the present instead of the aorist participle is curious.

It was those who had accompanied Jesus during his ministry and had seen him after his resurrection who were his witnesses (cf. Haenchen 395). This agrees with 1.22; and, as there, the definition seems to exclude Paul. The use of it probably lies behind the controversy that evidently attended his claim to apostleship (e.g. 1 Cor. 9.2). Those appointed were appointed witnesses πρὸς τὸν λαόν. For Luke's use of λαός see on 2.47; 3.9. The Twelve had a special mission to Israel; see on pp. 93f. It may be that Luke, thinking of Paul as the great Gentile missionary, considered him to be a witness not to the (Jewish) people but to the Gentiles (cf. Gal. 2.8f.); he does not however say this, and here and elsewhere in Acts Paul evangelizes Jews.

The original text probably ran οἵτινες νῦν εἰσιν μάρτυρες, but there is doubt about νῦν, which is omitted by B E 𝔐 and placed after εἰσιν by ℵ 36. D 614 lat syʰ have ἄχρι νῦν (perhaps implying that whereas up to the present the Twelve had been the appointed witnesses they have now been joined by Paul). Ψ has, instead of νῦν, συν, which presumably must be joined to the following letters so as to make the word σύνεισιν. Similar statements occur at 2.32; 3.15; 5.32; 10.39 without νῦν, and the word should probably be retained here. On οἵτινες for οἵ, see on 7.53.

32. The emphatic pronoun ἡμεῖς suggests a contrast with the witnesses just mentioned. This is not necessarily to be read out of the text, which could be taken to mean: the eye-witnesses affirm the truth of the resurrection of Jesus, and we (who happen on this occasion to be present in Antioch) bring you the good news of this event and of the consequences that flow from it (and will be drawn out in the following verses). Blass (152) puts it neatly: 'ut illi illis, sic nos vobis'. This however would be better expressed without ἡμεῖς, and this word strongly suggests if it does not require the contrast. If the contrast is accepted it leads to the comment (of e.g. Bauernfeind 175f.) that this is not how the historical Paul would speak — or did speak. But 'Von da her ist es konsequent, dass der lukanische Paulus sich nicht selbst in die Zeugenreihe einschliessen kann; seine Christophanie vor Damaskus gilt nicht als Ostererscheinung' (Roloff 206). It goes too far, however, to say (with Schille 295) that Luke is here dealing with the authority of the next, post-apostolic, generation; for Luke, Paul is a unique figure. See above, on 14.4, 14, and in Vol. II.

Only here does εὐαγγελίζεσθαι take a double accusative of the persons evangelized and the good news brought to them, though here τὴν ἐπαγγελίαν is really preliminary to the good news itself ('aus dem folgenden ὅτι-Satz vorausgenommen', BDR § 152. 2, n. 2), which is that God has now fulfilled the promise (v. 33). The promise was made to *the fathers* (D E *pc* lat syᵖ add ἡμῶν without altering the sense, though emphasising that Paul is speaking as a Jew to Jews). τοὺς πατέρας will include more than the patriarchs in view of the references to David that follow. The Gospel (it is implied) fulfils the forward-looking meaning of the OT as a whole. Paul 'points out that he is introducing nothing new, or different from the Law and the Prophets, but that he is revealing the fulfilment of that teaching, which . . . was delivered to them by God' (Calvin 375). There is however a difference between a promise and its fulfilment.

33. ὅτι introduces the content of the good news (εὐαγγελιζόμεθα, v. 32). God fulfilled (the compound ἐκπεπλήρωκεν, used here only in the NT, may suggest complete fulfilment, or be a mere variant on the simple form πληροῦν, 1.16; 3.18; 13.27, and frequently elsewhere in the NT) the promise made to the fathers for us their children, τοῖς τέκνοις αὐτῶν ἡμῖν; but the reading is far from certain. The words quoted (from NA²⁶) are contained in C³ E 𝔐 sy; not a powerful combination. The best attested variant is τοῖς τέκνοις ἡμῶν; this is read by P⁷⁴ A B C* D (ψ *pc* p) lat, but hardly makes sense. Paul cannot have meant that the fulfilment (which, as he is about to say, took place through Jesus) failed to benefit the generation in which it took place. τοῖς τέκνοις αὐτῶν (1175 *pc* gig) and τοῖς τέκνοις ἡμῖν (*pc*) make sense but are very scantily attested. ἐφ' ἡμῶν and ἡμῖν καὶ τοῖς τέκνοις ἡμῶν have been conjectured; ἡμῶν has been regarded as a primitive corruption, or as possibly an accidental error made by Luke himself (so Kilpatrick, *FS* Casey 74). The best suggestion seems to be that Luke wrote (or intended but failed to write) τοῖς τέκνοις ἡμῖν; that this speedily became, if it was not from the beginning, τοῖς τέκνοις ἡμῶν (so Ropes, *Begs*. 3.124); this was seen to be impossible and was changed to τοῖς τέκνοις αὐτῶν ἡμῖν. Cf. Ps. Sol. 8.39. It is well to note also the suggestion that ἡμῖν should be taken not with ἐκπεπλήρωκεν but with ἀναστήσας.

If the suggestion just mentioned is adopted (and quite possibly if it is not), ἀναστήσας will mean that God raised up Jesus, not in the sense of raising him from death but as bringing him on the stage of history (cf. Lk. 1.69, ἤγειρεν κέρας σωτηρίας ἡμῖν; Acts 3.22, προφήτην ὑμῖν ἀναστήσει κύριος; see on 3.26). Here the latter meaning is probable, (a) because the resurrection is dealt with in v. 34, and (b) because the quotation from Ps. 2 which follows is to be associated with Jesus' entrance upon his ministry at his baptism; see below. Conzelmann (77), following Lövestam, takes the opposite view; so e.g. does Schmithals (128). Roloff (207) thinks that the reference is to the exaltation of Jesus. Reference to the resurrection is affirmed by the reading of A² gig, in which *Jesus* is replaced by αὐτὸν ἐκ νεκρῶν. D, with some support from 614 and sy^{h**}, characteristically has τὸν κύριον 'Ιησοῦν Χριστόν.

The appearance of Jesus (however this is to be understood) was in accordance with OT prophecy, claimed by the common word γέγραπται. The rest of the reference creates difficulties. The reading of P⁷⁴ ℵ A B C Ψ 33 81 945 1739 *al*, τῷ ψαλμῷ γέγραπται τῷ δευτέρῳ makes good sense and is supported by E 𝔐 with only a variation in order. But D (1175) gig have ἐν τῷ πρώτῳ ψαλμῷ γέγραπται, a reading so difficult (since the quotation is from Ps. 2.7) that it must be considered seriously. P⁴⁵ᵛⁱᵈ t also may seem to be dealing with a difficulty when they write ἐν τοῖς ψαλμοῖς γέγραπται. On this reading see Ropes's detached note in *Begs*. 3.263–265; for the evidence of Tertullian see Kilpatrick in *JTS* 11 (1960), 53. There is evidence both in rabbinic (Berakoth 9b) and in patristic (see Ropes, loc. cit.; Metzger 412–14; and their references to Justin, 1 *Apology* 40; Tertullian, *adv. Marcionem* 4.22; Cyprian, *Testimonia* 1.13) sources that the first two Psalms (as we reckon them) were combined as one. This adds probability to the view that Luke wrote *first* and that this was corrected to *second* by those who in their Psalter divided the Psalm. But Haenchen (395) may well be right with the dry comment that in his reading the writer of D 'beweist damit sein gelehrtes Wissen'.

Schweizer (*Beiträge* 99) claims that the way the quotation is used here associates the sonship of Jesus with his resurrection; if that is correct we may compare Rom. 1.4. But as is pointed out above ἀναστήσας can bear, and probably does bear, a different meaning, and, as is often pointed out (Justin, *Trypho* 88; 103; Clement of Alexandria, *Paidagogos* 1.6.25; Epiphanius, *Haer*. 30.13), the Psalm recalls the baptism of Jesus (according to the Western text of Lk. 3.22, the voice from heaven uses exactly the same words that are quoted here). Acts makes little use of 'Son of God' as a designation of Jesus (see on 9.20), and the term is never developed in a metaphysical sense. Stauffer (*Theologie* 94) is probably right in the view that here it means *Messiah*; Jesus is the Messianic Son of God (cf. Ps. Sol. 17.23f.). γεγέννηκα corresponds to ἀναστήσας. Ps. 2 is a royal, and hence a messianic Psalm; when the king accedes to the throne he is adopted into the divine family. Jesus is both Son of David (cf. Rom. 1.3) and Son of God; these are complementary, not contradictory propositions. Ps. 2.7 is quoted in precise agreement with the LXX; the Western text continues the quotation, adding 2.8, αἴτησαι παρ' ἐμοῦ, καὶ δώσω σοι ἔθνη τὴν κληρονομίαν (see on 7.5) σου καὶ τὴν κατάσχεσίν σου τὰ πέρατα τῆς γῆς (cf. 1.8). The point of the addition (which cannot be regarded as original) lies in the word ἔθνη; the editor saw the opportunity of bringing in a reference to the mission to the Gentiles.

Roloff (206f.) makes the point that the quotation in this verse, and those in vv. 34 and 35, interpret one another. This must be borne in mind.

34. For ὅτι at the beginning of the verse D 614 1175 *pc* gig read ὅτε. This has the effect of applying the quotation from Isa. 55.3 more closely to the resurrection.

ἀνέστησεν is now used with reference to the resurrection, as is made clear by the addition of ἐκ νεκρῶν, and the reference to διαφθορά. The plain affirmation — God raised Jesus from the dead, never again to return to the corruption of the grave — is made first, and then supported by two quotations, from Isa. 55.3 and (in v. 35) Ps. 16.10. Of these the former raises considerable difficulty; the common word (ὅσιος) shows that they must be understood together.

The quotation is introduced by εἴρηκεν (cf. 17.28; also 2.16; 13.40, τὸ εἰρημένον); the prophet is thought of as speaking his message, or rather, God speaks through the prophet. δώσω ὑμῖν τὰ ὅσια Δαυὶδ τὰ πιστά agrees with the LXX of Isa. 55.3 except that δώσω replaces διαθήσομαι ὑμῖν διαθήκην αἰώνιον. The Greek agrees closely with the Hebrew, ואכרתה לכם ברית עולם חסדי דוד הנאמנים, except that for חסדי it has τὰ ὅσια. This is no doubt related to the fact that the related word חסיד sometimes means ὅσιος, though in Isa. 55.3 חסד must have a different meaning, *faithful love*, or *mercy*. At this point the quotation of Ps. 16.10 in v. 35 must be borne in mind (it was no doubt already in Luke's mind). It supplies an example of the meaning of ὅσιος (the Hebrew is חסיד), and uses the verb διδόναι. It is tempting to say that when God did not *give* (allow) his Holy One, Jesus, to see corruption he did *give* to him the *holy* and firm promises made to David (see v. 23). This interpretation would serve were it not for ὑμῖν in the present verse; this is part of the quotation from Isa. 55.3 but can hardly for that reason be dismissed as meaningless. It is again tempting to say that τὰ ὅσια is to be interpreted by τὸν ὅσιον in v. 35, that is, as Christ: I will give to you David's great descendant, Jesus, risen from the dead. But, again, it is impossible to interpret the neuter plural τὰ ὅσια as equivalent to an individual person. We must note that Luke has omitted the reference (found in both Greek and Hebrew of Isa. 55.3) to *covenant*. The word διαθήκη occurs in Acts only at 3.25; 7.8 and was certainly not an important element in Luke's theological vocabulary (notwithstanding Lk. 22.20, 29, where it is traditional). If he decided that this part of the thought of Isa. 55.3 was not needed he may (perhaps influenced by his next quotation) have used δώσω as the simplest substitute. We may paraphrase: I will fulfil for you (that is, for the Christian generation) the holy and sure (promises made to)

David, by raising up, by not allowing to see corruption, (not David himself but) his greater descendant, who was himself holy. Instead of *promises made to* David it would be possible to take the words to mean *promises, prophetic words, spoken by* David, or God's holy and faithful *dealings with* David, now reproduced in his dealings with the people of David's messianic descendant. It is possible that, in addition to Isa. 55.3, 2 Chron. 6.42 (μνήσθητι τὰ ἐλέη (יסח) Δαυίδ) is in mind. Schneider, referring (2.137) to the use of ὅσια to denote 'göttliche Verfügungen' over against 'menschliche Satzungen' (Plato, *Politicus* 301d; Xenophon, *Hellenica* 4.1.33; cf. Wisdom 6.10; Josephus, *Ant.* 8.115), translates (2.127) 'die zuverlässigen Heilsverfügungen gegenüber David'. On the whole matter see Dupont 337–359.

35. διότι: the variant διό (C E Ψ 𝔐) makes little difference to the sense, but D by omitting the word altogether removes the connection between the two verses.

Luke, who in v. 33 had referred to the second Psalm, now gives another but less exact reference: ἐν ἑτέρῳ. Presumably we should supply ψαλμῷ, though this is not so clear as it would be if the quotation from Isaiah had not intervened. Luke may mean simply, In another place. D lat have ἑτέρως; perhaps, *He puts it differently.* This would fit D's omission of διότι (above). Luke has already used this quotation of Ps. 15 (16).10 at 2.27; as there so here he agrees exactly with the LXX (except that here for οὐδέ, with which the LXX link this statement with that which precedes, he has οὐ). Someone described as God's Holy One will not be allowed (for this use of διδόναι see on 2.27) to see, that is, to experience, corruption, in the grave. It would be natural to suppose that the person in question was David, the author (as was supposed) of the Psalm. That this was incorrect is shown in the next verse (as it is in 2.29). David was undoubtedly dead and buried, and his body was experiencing corruption. For ὅσιος as a Christological term, see on 2.27; for ἅγιος, on 3.14.

36. David died and was buried; that is clear, but the precise meaning of Luke's sentence is not. (a) The dative τῇ βουλῇ may be taken with ὑπηρετήσας, the dative γενεᾷ with ἐκοιμήθη: David, having served the will of God, fell asleep in his own generation (that is, David was a good man, but he died and is dead). (b1) Both datives may be taken with ὑπηρετήσας: David, having in his own generation served the will of God, fell asleep (his service fell in his own time; he now sleeps in death). (b2) Both datives may be taken with ὑπηρετήσας: David having served his own generation by the will of God, fell asleep. (c) γενεᾷ may be taken with ὑπηρετήσας, τῇ βουλῇ, with ἐκοιμήθη: David, having served his own generation, by the will of God fell asleep (that is, God himself appointed death for David, intentionally leaving the promise open for another). (d) A completely different line of interpretation takes γενεᾷ to refer to David's own, natural, human, generation, in contrast with the Messiah, who was begotten by God as his own Son (see Rengstorf, *TWNT* 8.541, n. 87). None of these ways of taking the Greek is impossible (though (d) seems improbable). *Begs.* 4.156 takes the view that (b2) is 'the most natural way of reading with the Greek'. One may agree, though without strong conviction.

For ἐκοιμήθη meaning *died* see on 7.60. It may be significant that in Acts the word is used only of 'good' men. A further synonym follows; cf. Judges 2.10 (πᾶσα ἡ γενεὰ ἐκείνη προσετέθησαν πρὸς τοὺς πατέρας αὐτῶν; אל־אבותיו ויאספו and the frequent (e.g. 3 Kdms 2.10) ἐκοιμήθη μετὰ τῶν πατέρων (וישכב עם־אבותיו). In these OT passages the thought is probably either that the dead man joined his ancestors in the grave, or that he joined them in Sheol. How far Luke would have shared, how far modified, this view is not clear. He simply chooses to use a biblical expression for death. At least it is clear that David's body experienced (εἶδεν) corruption.

37. Not so the body of Jesus. ὅν stands for οὗτος (or αὐτὸς) ὅν . . . The use of the relative as subject for the main verb is classical. ὁ θεὸς ἤγειρεν repeats a number of passages (3.15; 4.10; 5.30; 10.40; 13.30); οὐκ εἶδεν διαφθοράν expresses the fundamental proposition in the terms of the Psalm quoted. Luke has in mind the fact that a body raised so quickly out of the tomb would have had no time for putrefaction. For him the resurrection means the reanimation of a dead body, and its emergence from the grave as a reanimated body.

The OT argument which began in v. 33 is now closed (Roloff 207), and the way is open for the concluding part of the discourse.

38. Up to this point, Paul, as reported by Luke, has been giving a factual account of the history of Israel and its fulfilment in the life, death, and resurrection of Jesus. He now draws the appropriate conclusions and sets before his hearers that which is offered to them in the Gospel and the basis on which it may be received. γνωστός is a Lucan word (Lk., 2; Acts, 10; rest of the NT, 3), and γνωστὸν ἔστω is a Lucan idiom (cf. 2.14; 4.10; 28.28; nowhere else in the NT). On this phrase see Wilcox 90f., referred to on 2.14. For ἄνδρες ἀδελφοί see on 1.16.

ὅτι introduces the content of the message proclaimed. διὰ τούτου is emphatic, picking up what has been said about Jesus: it is through this man, Jesus, that . . . δι' αὐτοῦ (E 2495 *pc*) does not change the sense, but διὰ τοῦτο (P⁷⁴ B* 36 (1175) *al*) introduces a logical connection which is out of place. It may be that the υ 'slipped out by haplography' (Ropes, *Begs.* 3.125). καταγγέλλειν is one of

Luke's regular 'preaching' words; see on 4.2 (cf. 3.24 for the proclamation of the OT prophets). What is proclaimed is ἄφεσις ἁμαρτιῶν; see on 2.38. So far Paul's sermon agrees with Peter's, and Luke is probably following a preaching source, though as Bauernfeind says, 'Die gemeinsame Basis aller urchristlichen Missionspredigt ist nicht zu unterschätzen' (177). Since however this is Luke's first (and indeed his only) account of an evangelistic sermon by Paul (the Areopagus speech in ch. 17 is of a special kind), he elaborates the theme of forgiveness by incorporating the Pauline terminology of justification.

According to B C² E Ψ 𝔐 gig vgᶜˡ sy the new clause is connected with the preceding by καί; this is omitted by P⁷⁴ ℵ A C* D pc t w vgˢᵗ. This variant is probably connected with the addition after καταγγέλλεται of καὶ μετάνοια, which can be connected with what follows: . . . and repentance from all those things. But by no means all those MSS that omit καί have καὶ μετάνοια.

Neither in this verse nor in the next does Luke attempt to explain what is meant by the verb δικαιοῦν. If the logic of his words is pressed they could be taken to imply that there are some things from which you might be justified by the law of Moses but others for which different treatment is necessary. It is doubtful whether Luke intended to say this. More probably he means, but does not quite say, There are many things from which you need to be justified; the law of Moses is inadequate to achieve this; the only way is the way of faith. The use of ἀπό suggests that δικαιωθῆναι does not have its usual Pauline forensic sense, but means something more like *release from*. Forgiven, the believer is actually set free from sin, sins no more. Some see this meaning in Rom. 6.7 (δεδικαίωται ἀπὸ τῆς ἁμαρτίας), but it is not to be found elsewhere in Paul, though Paul insists that the justified man is set free for the service of righteousness. ἐν (in ἐν νόμῳ) is partly instrumental, but has some locative force: there is no justification for those who choose to live simply in the area marked out by the law of Moses. Again, one may question whether this is truly the Pauline position. For the relation between the law of Moses and salvation see further on 15.1, 5, and the discussion in the rest of ch. 15.

The words of v. 38, taken with those of v. 39, support Wilson's judgment (*Pastorals* 27): 'Luke reproduces a somewhat garbled version of Paul's teaching which he received from tradition and believed to be accurate.' With this should be put Bauernfeind's (177), '"Paulus predigte von der Rechtfertigung aus Glauben," mehr will Lk nicht sagen.' And what Luke says about the law is to be interpreted in terms of 15.8ff. — though we should add to this remark of Bauernfeind's, of 15.8ff. understood in the context of ch. 15 as a whole. Vielhauer in his essay on the Paulinism of Acts not only claims that Paul did not formulate vv. 38f., with which we may agree, but adds (*FS* Schubert 41), 'Justification is equated with the forgiveness of sins and thus is conceived entirely negatively, which Paul never does.' It is true, as Vielhauer goes on to say, that forgiveness of sins is not a Pauline theme, but the rest of his statement is questionable. (1) These verses do not equate justification with forgiveness; they associate the two, but they are joined in the text by καί, which it is more natural to take additively than explicatively. (2) There is no reason why forgiveness should be regarded as a purely negative concept. That it may be understood negatively is true; that it must be so understood is not. (3) There is a close relation between Paul's understanding of justification and forgiveness. 'Justification then means no legal fiction but an act of forgiveness on God's part, described in terms of the proceedings of a law court' (*Romans* 72). Of particular importance is Rom. 4.7, where Paul explains the justification of the ungodly by quoting Ps. 32.1, Blessed are those whose iniquities have been forgiven. Vielhauer then is not wholly right; but he is on the whole right. We cannot ascribe these verses to Paul. On a central question of faith Luke shows his devotion to Paul but less than full understanding of his theology.

39. ἐν τούτῳ is parallel to διὰ τούτου in v. 38, and bears the same emphasis. It is not clear whether ἐν τούτῳ is to be taken with πιστεύειν (everyone who believes in him is justified) or with δικαιοῦται (everyone who believes is justified in him). Luke would probably have rejected neither way of interpreting his words, but 'believing in him' is a simpler concept, more in harmony with Luke's style, than 'being justified in him'. After τούτῳ, D 614 sy[hmg] add οὖν; this is to be connected with the variant in v. 38. At the end of the verse, D (614 t sy[hmg]) add παρὰ θεῷ. This gives to δικαιοῦται a more Pauline sense: believers are brought into a right relation with God.

Bengel comments on the relation between law and Christ in these verses. It is mistaken to distinguish between the moral and the ceremonial law. 'Judaeis non tam familiarem debemus putare fuisse legis divisionem in moralem et ceremonialem, quum utraque simul vigeret, quam nobis est hodie. quare hic locus de universa lege agit. Moses est Moses, sive de ritibus, sive de moribus praecipiat: et e diverso Christus est Christus. — ἐν τούτῳ, *in Hoc*) Antitheton ad *legem Mosis*.' So far as this observation is valid it has the effect of bringing Luke closer to Paul.

Roloff (208) writes, 'Dass es [the offer of forgiveness and justification] an den Empfang der Taufe und an den Vollzug der Umkehr gebunden ist, wird als dem Leser bekannt vorausgesetzt'. It would be better to observe simply that there is no reference to baptism; there is no such reference in the whole of chs. 13 and 14, though converts are made and churches established and provided with elders (14.23). It is certainly possible that this is due to the fact that baptism was so universal a practice that it seemed unnecessary to mention it; this consideration however did not prevent the mention of baptism at e.g. 16.15, 33; 18.8. The sporadic references to baptism in Acts may mean that baptism was differently evaluated in different strands of tradition, and that the rite was not universal in the NT period.

40. Forgiveness, Justification, are available freely on the basis of faith alone. But the consequence of refusal is disaster, and this has already been made known by the OT prophets. The hearers must *beware* (this use of βλέπειν, with following μή, elsewhere in the Lucan writings only at Lk. 21.8, where it is drawn from Mk 13.5; it is mainly biblical, but see *BGU* 1079.24) lest there come upon them (the last two words are implied in ἐπέλθῃ; ἐφ᾽ ὑμᾶς is unnecessarily added by A C E Ψ 097 𝔐 gig vg sy co Basil) that which was spoken (τὸ εἰρημένον; cf. the use of εἴρηκεν in v. 34) in (or by) the prophets (ἐν τοῖς προφήταις; the prophets (plural) will refer to the book of the Twelve (minor) Prophets). The reference is to Hab. 1.5.

41. Luke proceeds to write out the quotation, in substantial but not complete agreement with the LXX. Where Luke has θαυμάσατε καὶ ἀφανίσθητε, LXX has ἐπιβλέψατε (possibly omitted because Luke has just used βλέπειν in a different sense) καὶ θαυμάσατε θαυμάσια (Luke avoids a Semitism) καὶ ἀφανίσθητε; for ὅτι, LXX has διότι; LXX reverses the order of ἐγώ and ἐργάζομαι; LXX does not have the second ἔργον (but in Acts it is omitted by D E 𝔐 gig p). There is no strong motivation behind any of these differences; Luke may have had a somewhat different LXX text. ἔργον ἐργάζεσθαι looks like a Semitism but is not unGreek; see Euripides, *Hecuba* 122, σὺ τοὖργον εἴργασαι τόδ᾽, ὡς λέγει;; Aristophanes, *Plutus* 445f., δεινότατον ἔργον παρὰ πολὺ ἔργων ἁπάντων ἐργασόμεθ᾽...

Habakkuk's words, whatever their original intention, lent themselves well to Luke's (Paul's) purpose. A couple of wandering Christian preachers could well be despised by a large and influential synagogue. ἀφανίζειν is *to destroy*, in various senses; Josephus, *Ant.* 1.76, of the sinners at the flood, οἱ μὲν οὕτως ἀφανίζονται πάντες — they were wiped off the face of the earth; in a different sense, Thucydides 3.83.1, τὸ εὔηθες ... τὸ γενναῖον ... καταγελασθὲν ἠφανίσθη, laughed out of existence. It is interesting to note at the end of this paragraph (83.2), οἱ δὲ καταφρονοῦντες ...διεφθείροντο. For Luke, the ἔργον that God has worked is that which he has done in Christ, and the unbelief of Israel, their rejection of God's work, had been foretold. This theme will be worked out further, in narrative terms, in the remainder of this paragraph. It is one that constantly recurs in Acts; see v. 46; 18.6; 28.28. Others see the Gentile mission as itself the work that God is now performing; so e.g. Roloff (208), making the interesting connection between the ἔργον here and the ἔργον of 13.2. Stählin (185) thinks that the ἔργον refers either to the world mission or to the last things. 1 QpHab 2.1–10 also sees the passage in Habakkuk as referring to the renegades (the בוגדים) of the last days, but there is no reference to the Gentiles.

At the end of the verse D (614 sy^h**) mae have καὶ ἐσίγησαν; it is not clear who should be understood as the subject of this verb. Does it mark the point at which Paul (and Barnabas) stopped speaking or describe the stunned silence of the synagogue congregation after the warning of this verse?

42. The remainder of the narrative is probably Luke's own construction (Weiser 328f.). ἔξειμι is used only in Acts in the NT (13.42; 17.15; 20.7; 27.43): *As they were going out.* Many MSS add ἐκ τῆς συναγωγῆς τῶν Ἰουδαίων — a fact Luke probably thought too obvious to be worth recalling. *They* will refer to Paul and Barnabas.

παρεκάλουν is the reading of P^74 ℵ A C Ψ 097 33 (36) 81 614 945 1175 1739 *al.* If it is accepted the verb has no expressed subject. It is most natural to take the subject to be those who had been present in the synagogue and wished to hear Paul speak again; some think that the reference must be to the rulers of the synagogue, since they had the right to invite preachers (see v. 15). The majority of MSS (𝔐) supply τὰ ἔθνη as subject, presumably assuming that the Jewish congregation remained inside till v. 43. This is accepted by Bauernfeind (178), but it anticipates a later stage in Luke's story. B strangely changes the verb, reading εἰς τὸ μεταξὺ σάββατον ἠξίουν.

μεταξύ usually means *between*, 'but in late writers, like μετά (Adv.), *after, afterwards*' (LS 1115). BDR § 206. 1 write 'klass. auch Apg 13.42 εἰς τὸ μεταξὺ σάββατον,' but this judgment apparently refers only to the use of εἰς where ἐν might have been expected. It is assumed that there will be no further opportunity for hearing a sermon until the next Sabbath. It is true (and is emphasized by Schille 290, 297) that there were mid-week meetings in the synagogue; these took place on Monday and Thursday (Megillah 3.6; 4.1; cf. 1.3). But the great majority of Jews, being occupied at work during the week, would not be able to attend them, and would naturally think of the next Sabbath.

D corrects μεταξύ to the (classical) ἐξῆς.

43. One fundamental meaning of λύειν is 'to resolve a whole into its parts, dissolve, break up' (LS 1068); it is therefore naturally used (and had been similarly used from the time of Homer, e.g. *Iliad* 1.305, λῦσαν δ' ἀγορήν) for the breaking up of the synagogue gathering. συναγωγή here has a different meaning from that which it has in v. 14; it was the gathering, not the building, that was resolved into its parts.

Many of the Jews followed Paul and Barnabas, many also τῶν σεβομένων προσηλύτων. Luke here uses a noun that had come to have a precise meaning; proselytes were converts to Judaism who had fulfilled all the requirements of their new religion: they had been both circumcised and baptized and had offered (or caused to be offered) a sacrifice. There is no reason to dismiss this word as a copyist's gloss (Roloff 209); if it causes difficulty there must first be an attempt to solve the difficulty without altering its constituents. The persons in question are further described by a participle, σεβομένων. σέβεσθαι occurs in Acts here and at 13.50; 16.14; 17.4, 17; 18.7, 13; 19.27 (elsewhere in the NT only Mt. 15.9; Mk 7.7, both quotations of Isa. 29.13). σεβόμενος is clearly related in Luke's use to φοβούμενος; see on v. 16. Again, there is no need to conjecture that καί has fallen out between σεβομένων and προσηλύτων; the participle describes the noun. This means that there is only one group before us, consisting of proselytes, *devout proselytes*, perhaps *worshipping proselytes*, that is, proselytes who had duly attended the Sabbath service in the synagogue. *Jews* will mean Jews by birth, proselytes, Jews by conversion and adoption. There is no problem, and there is no evidence here that should lead us to think of synagogue adherents, even if σεβόμενος τὸν θεόν, θεοσεβής, or θεοσέβιος, were current as technical terms describing such adherents. See Wilcox (*JSNT* 13 (1981), 108f.). These born Jews and proselytes followed (ἠκολούθησαν) Paul and Barnabas. In Acts (12.8, 9; 21.36) this verb always refers to literal *following, accompanying*, and has this meaning here. After Βαρναβᾷ, 614 sy[h**] add ἀξιοῦντες βαπτισθῆναι. This was probably added because it was recognized that the next clauses implied (see below) that some of them had been converted; how could they continue in the grace of God if they had not been admitted to it? Copyists assumed that this implied baptism; Luke (or the tradition he is writing up) did not make this assumption; see on v. 39. The aorist ἠκολούθησαν sums up a movement of a crowd from the synagogue; the present participle προσλαλοῦντες and the imperfect ἔπειθον describe the continuing process of oral persuasion. Contrast 27.43; 28.14; and see Zerwick § 252. For προσμένειν cf. 11.23, and the note. It implies arrival at a point at which the hearers are urged to continue: they have become Christians and must not give up their new faith. For ἡ χάρις τοῦ θεοῦ we may refer again to 11.23. Luke uses the word χάρις in various ways and with no precise definition. Here he presumably means that by sending preachers God has made his grace available to the Jews and proselytes of Antioch; they have been shown both the blessings that flow from the message of grace (vv. 38, 39) and the dangerous consequences of rejecting it (vv. 40, 41). Now, having received it, they must continue in it.

The Western editors evidently thought that the success of the mission in Pisidian Antioch needed greater emphasis. D (sy^hmg) add ἐγένετο δὲ καθ᾽ ὅλης τῆς πόλεως διελθεῖν τὸν λόγον τοῦ θεοῦ; E vg^mss (mae) add ἐγένετο δὲ κατὰ πᾶσαν πόλιν φημισθῆναι τὸν λόγον. For *the word of God* see v. 46.

44. τῷ δὲ ἐρχομένῳ σαββάτῳ. This must be τὸ μεταξὺ σάββατον of v. 42; the expression is clear enough — *the coming Sabbath* — but τῷ ἐχομένῳ would have been more usual, and is read by P^74 A E* 33 *pc*. There is a good note in *Begs*. 4.158, but in it it is claimed that ἐρχόμενος is used in this way in Josephus, *Ant*. 6.174, 235. In fact modern editions of Josephus read ἐχομένῃ in both places, apparently without variant. Had Lake and Cadbury been using Wettstein (who quotes the two Josephus passages with ἐρχομένῃ) and failed to check the reference? It seems scarcely credible. For failure to refer to the mid-week services in the synagogue see on v. 42.

Almost (σχεδόν, only here and at 19.26; Heb. 9.22 in the NT) *the whole* (πᾶσα, but D has ὅλη) *city was gathered together* (one must suppose, in and around the synagogue) *to hear the word of the Lord*. This is the text of P^74 ℵ A B² 33 81 323 945 1175 1739 *al* gig vg^st sa; B* C E Ψ 𝔐 vg^cl sy bo have τὸν λόγον τοῦ θεοῦ (which agrees with v. 46 and the majority of similar passages in Acts, but may well have been conformed to them); D (mae) differ much more widely: Παύλου πολύν τε λόγον ποιησαμένου περὶ τοῦ κυρίου. There is no added substance in this variant, which illustrates the Western custom of brightening the text. It may add to the weight of the evidence for κυρίου.

45. οἱ ᾽Ιουδαῖοι can hardly refer to all the Jews, since some of them seem to have been favourably impressed by what Paul had said. Those who were not were filled with envy; for ἐπλήσθησαν with a moral quality cf. 3.10; for ἐπλήσθησαν ζήλου cf. 5.17. This implies that they would have been glad to make an equal impression on their Gentile neighbours and thus indicates some enthusiasm for proselytisation. There is no doubt that enthusiasm varied greatly; it would be only human if in Antioch it was fomented by Christian successes. Luke however is probably giving his standard picture of Jewish opposition. This was naturally expressed in contradiction (ἀντέλεγον) of what Paul was saying: his message may be attractive but it is not true. This led them into blasphemy, since what Paul was saying was (for Luke) the word of God.

The Western text shows in this verse a number of apparently pointless variations — worth noting, because they show the Western editors simply engaged in a measure of free rewriting, with no special historical or theological case to support. For τοὺς ὄχλους,

D has τὸ πλῆθος. After τοῖς, λόγοις is added by D, λόγοις τοῖς by E gig (syᵖ). After ὑπό, τοῦ is added by C D E 097 𝔐. For λαλουμένοις, P⁷⁴ C D 097 𝔐 have λεγομένοις. After λεγόμενοις, D 097 𝔐 p* syʰ add ἀντιλέγοντες καί (an unfortunate repetition of ἀντέλεγον). E gig add ἐναντιούμενοι καί (which is little better).

In these variants Wilcox (135f.) tentatively suggests that we may see traces of divergent (ἀντιλέγοντες, βλασφημοῦντες) renderings of a Semitic original. 'Such a fact would weigh in favour of the authenticity and antiquity of the story concerned, suggesting for it a Semitic origin' (136). This is not convincing.

46. Contradiction did not silence Paul and Barnabas. παρρησιάζεσθαι is characteristic of Acts (9.27, 28; 13.46; 14.3; 18.26; 19.8; 26.26; elsewhere in the NT only twice). παρρησιασάμενοι εἶπαν, *they boldly said*, participle and finite verb describe coincident action. It is not suggested here that what they said was in any particular sense inspired, though in analogous circumstances Luke describes Christian speakers as filled with Holy Spirit (e.g. 4.8). What follows is a theological evaluation (cf. vv. 40, 41) of the rejection of the message by Jews.

ἦν ἀναγκαῖον followed by an accusative and infinitive occurs also at Philo, *de Migr. Abr.* 82; Josephus, *Life* 413. The word of God had to be spoken first to you, Jews. Luke does not say why, but the reason is apparent in the first part of Paul's sermon. The Christian message was the fulfilment of Israelite history and especially of Israelite prophecy. No other people had so clear a right to hear what God now had to say, and (one would *a priori* suppose) no other nation would be so likely to understand and accept what was said. But failure to accept it on the part of the Jews would not be the end of God's action. ἐπειδὴ (א* B D* 36 *pc*; P⁴⁵ P⁷⁴ C Eᶜ 81 326 *pc* have ἐπεὶ δέ, אᶜ A Dᶜ E* Ψ 𝔐 Cyril have ἐπειδὴ δέ) ἀπωθεῖσθε (cf. 7.27, 39) αὐτόν, *since you reject it, thrust it aside, and* thereby *judge yourselves unworthy of* the *eternal life* which is now in the Gospel being offered. It is seldom that Luke uses irony in this way. They did not judge themselves unworthy of eternal life, but their action had the effect of turning away the offer of eternal life. This verse, and v. 48, are the only places in Acts where the term ζωὴ αἰώνιος occurs; ζωή without the adjective but with the same meaning occurs at 11.18 and perhaps 5.20. It may occur here (like δικαιοῦν in vv. 38f.) as a mark of Pauline theology (though outside Romans ζωὴ αἰώνιος occurs only at Gal. 6.8).

ἰδοὺ (another example of Luke's 'biblical' style) στρεφόμεθα εἰς τὰ ἔθνη. It would be natural to understand these words as a decisive and radical turning-point in Paul's mission: henceforth the Jews would be left to their fate and he would confine his attention to the Gentiles. This is not what Luke means. Already before this point Paul had evangelized Gentiles (11.25f.): indeed, in his call he had been commissioned to act as missionary to the Gentiles (9.16; 22.21; 26.17). 'The suggestion can scarcely be that Paul had not preached to Gentiles already, but rather that he would continue to do so, without troubling about the Synagogue. Far too much attention is paid to Gal. 2.7–9 as though it means that Paul and Barnabas were never to preach to the Jews' (*Begs.* 4.159). Nor did he after this point cease to preach to Jews. This was 'keine Absage an die Judenmission' (Pesch 2.47). He left Pisidian Antioch for Iconium, and there his first step was to enter the synagogue of the Jews (14.1). Moreover, we meet the same 'decisive' turning-point on two further occasions, at 18.6 and 28.28. The Jews were never abandoned, but their rejection of the Gospel provided the occasion for including the Gentiles — the occasion, but not the cause, for the mission to the Gentiles was already commanded in the OT (v. 47). Paul's own 'To the Jew first, but also to the Greek' (e.g. Rom. 1.16) is recalled, though it is broadly (but not exclusively) true that to Paul this was a theological proposition whereas Luke thinks in terms of practical missionary strategy. 'Die Juden können nicht die Einholung der Heiden in das Gottesvolk verhindern; sie können nur eines: sich selbst von diesem Gottesvolk und damit vom Heil ausschliessen' (Roloff 209). On this important passage see further Wilson (*Gentiles* 222–4).

47. The Lord's command (ἐντέταλται) is found in Isa. 49.6. Luke's words agree with the LXX, except that he omits ἰδού before τέθεικα, and εἰς διαθήκην γένους after σε. The former omission (possibly due to the use of ἰδού in v. 46) is insignificant, the latter throws the verse out of balance, concentrating on the Gentiles and excluding the reference to God's covenant with the (Jewish) people. εἰς διαθήκην γένους has in fact no equivalent in the Hebrew; it may be that Luke used a more faithful LXX version than that which we have. Dodd (*AS* 91) suggests that Isa. 49.8 also is in mind here, but it is difficult to see how this can be supported when all the words used are to be found in 49.6. In φῶς ἐθνῶν, ἐθνῶν will be a kind of objective genitive; the light, which is evidently related to if not synonymous with salvation, will shine upon the Gentiles. The dative ἔθνεσι would have been preferable; cf. Homer, *Iliad* 6.6, Τρώων ῥῆξε φάλαγγα, φόως δ' ἑτάροισιν ἔθηκεν; and note the reading of d, ecce lumen posui te super gentibus. τοῦ with the infinitive is here epexegetic (Hebrew, להיות): Your being a light to the Gentiles means that you will be . . . εἰς σωτηρίαν is often described as a Semitism (though derived of course from the LXX), since it is equivalent to the predicative use of ל; it is not always observed that the Hebrew text of Isa. 49.6 does not contain predicative ל. It reads simply להיות ישועתי, that you should be my salvation. Your presence will result in my salvation (see on 4.12) for the Gentiles. ἕως ἐσχάτου τῆς γῆς recalls 1.8. A long step has now been taken towards the completion of the programme of that verse.

In Lk. 2.32 Jesus is spoken of as φῶς εἰς ἀποκάλυψιν ἐθνῶν; here the same language is used of the preacher. The double use of the imagery is important (whether or not Luke formulated its importance in his own mind). Paul is a light of the Gentiles only in virtue of the Christ whom he preaches; Christ is a light to the Gentiles as he is preached to them by his servants.

48. The Gentiles hearing this rejoiced; a way of salvation had been opened to them, and it was not fenced with the unwelcome rite of circumcision. ἐδόξαζον is an unexpected word (it is not surprising that D gig mae substitute ἐδέξαντο); it can hardly mean anything other than that they gave glory to the Lord for the word that they had heard. For τὸν λόγον τοῦ κυρίου, τὸν θεόν (614 pc sy) is, in view of ἐδόξαζον, a natural 'improvement', and τὸν λόγον τοῦ θεοῦ (B D E 049 323 453 pc sa^ms bo) is due to assimilation to v. 46 (and other passages).

ἐπίστευσαν, they became believers, thus giving glory to the word. For this characteristic use of the verb see on 2.44. The subject of the verb is provided by the relative clause ὅσοι ἦσαν τεταγμένοι εἰς ζωὴν αἰώνιον. As in v. 46, ζωὴ αἰώνιος is a comprehensive term for Christian salvation. Some had been appointed (periphrastic pluperfect) thus to believe and thereby to receive eternal life. τάσσειν is a fairly common word in Acts (five) four times; five (four) times in the rest of the NT), but only at 22.10 does it have, as here, theological significance. The present verse is as unqualified a statement of absolute predestination — 'the eternal purpose of God' (Calvin 393) — as is found anywhere in the NT. Those believed who were appointed (the passive implies, by God) to do so. The rest, one infers, did not believe, did not receive eternal life, and were thus appointed to death. The positive statement implies the negative. This can hardly be avoided by saying, with Schmithals (127), that what we have here is not *Prädestinationslehre* but *Erbauungssprache*; for Schmithals goes on to say that faith is not human but divine work, which leads to the question whether, when faith is absent, God has omitted to work. Pesch 2.48f. argues that v. 46 shows that only positive predestination, not negative, is in mind; if men are not saved it is because they thrust aside the word of God. Earlier Bengel had made the same point: 'sic enim solet a Scriptura homini adscribi pernicies ipsius; sed salus ejus, DEO'. We may compare 10.35 where the matter of salvation is looked at from another angle but is expressed in equally unqualified terms: Anyone who fears God and practises righteousness is acceptable to him. In neither place does Luke say anything about the work of the Holy Spirit. It must be recognized that Luke, who was a narrator rather than a theologian, was apt to put down on its own the aspect of any question that concerned him at the time of writing, and did not, as Paul did, insist upon a rounded view obtained by viewing theological issues from all sides. Luke's language is Jewish. For the notion of enrolment in God's book of the saved cf. Exod. 33.32f.; Ps. 69.28; Dan. 12.1; 1 Enoch 47.3; 104.1; 108.3; Jubilees 30.20, 22; Rosh ha-Shanah 57a. For appointment to life cf. Berakoth 61b, Blessed art thou, Akiba, for thou hast been appointed to the life of the age to come (שאתה מזמן לחיי העולם הבא); similarly Moed Qatan 9a, and other passages. See also CD 3.20, without the root זמן: לחיי נצה.

49. διαφέρειν has a very wide variety of meanings; here one could translate quite literally, *the word was carried through the whole region.* Cf. Lucian, *Dialogi Deorum* 24.1, διαφέρειν τὰς ἀγγελίας τὰς παρ' αὐτοῦ (Zeus). In the subject, τοῦ κυρίου is omitted by P⁴⁵ *pc.* This is slender evidence, but the genitive could have been introduced under the influence of v. 48. If it is retained, the meaning is *the word of the Lord,* that is, the Christian message, carried through the whole area by, one must suppose, other assistants who did not share the official commissioning of Paul and Barnabas (13.1–3). If it is omitted λόγος will probably be *the report* — of what had happened. Cf. 19.10. δι' ὅλης follows naturally upon διεφέρετο, but καθ' (P⁷⁴ א A 33 226 945 1739) for δι' makes no difference to the meaning. χώρα is not as a rule a political term (though Ramsay takes it to be the *regio* Phrygia Galatica; see on 16.6) with a precise meaning: *the whole district,* the neighbourhood of Antioch.

50. The Jews now went beyond the verbal opposition of v. 45. παροτρύνειν, like the simple verb, means *to incite* (cf. Pindar, *Olympic* 3.38 (though with 'poor and late MSS' — Gildersleeve); Lucian, *Deorum Concilium* 4; *Toxaris* 35; Josephus, *Ant.* 7.118). The object of the verb is threefold or twofold, depending on whether or not καί is read after γυναῖκας. The word is read by א* E 𝔐 vg syʰ; this is hardly sufficient to justify it, and we should therefore take γυναῖκας to be qualified by both σεβομένας and εὐσχήμονας. For σεβόμενοι see on v. 43. It probably means simply, *pious, devout;* but the women can hardly be Jewish, since it is 'the Jews' who incite them. The Jews however have access to them, so that here if anywhere we may recognize adherents of the synagogue, though Wilcox (op. cit. 110) is right in saying that the matter is not certain. εὐσχήμων refers primarily to the outward form (σχῆμα) of the body, but came to mean *noble, honourable,* though this use was disapproved by Phrynichus (309: τοῦτο μὲν οἱ ἀμαθεῖς ἐπὶ τοῦ πλουσίου καὶ ἐν ἀξιώματι ὄντος τάττουσιν· οἱ δ' ἀρχαῖοι ἐπὶ τοῦ καλοῦ καὶ συμμέτρου), though it is no longer correct to add, with Rutherford (417), that 'the rejected signification seems confined to Christian writers'; see BA 661, citing Plutarch, Vettius Valens, and papyri. On the attraction that Judaism had for women see Bousset (*RJ* 81); cf. Josephus, *War* 2.560; and in Acts, 16.14; 17.4, 12, 34; other references in Reicke (*DFZ* 310f.). The Jews incited the pious women of high standing and the leading men (πρώτους, an old and common use of the adjective; e.g., Homer, *Odyssey* 6.60, μετὰ πρώτοισιν). It is to be noted that Luke here has no technical term for the chief men of the city, as he has in some later narratives (e.g. 16.20). It is suggested in *ND* 3.30f. that the πρῶτοι were probably Roman magistrates; some of the leading families are known to have been associated with the cult of the god Men and may have attacked Paul and Barnabas because they were a threat to the cult.

The subject of ἐπήγειραν may be the Jews, or those whom they had incited, or both. The result was persecution; cf. 8.1. According to the Western text they caused θλῖψιν μεγάλην καὶ (so D (mae); also E, with the omission of μεγάλην) διωγμόν. Paul and Barnabas were expelled; the word ἐκβάλλειν does not necessarily mean *to expel with violence*. ὅρια is no more precise in meaning than χῶρα (v. 49). For the persecution cf. 2 Tim. 3.11, which, though not written by Paul, is in contact with some kind of tradition about Paul — conceivably Acts itself.

51. At this point, or perhaps with the mention of Iconium, Luke seems to resume his use of the itinerary that outlined the missionary work of Paul and Barnabas. His insertion describing the sermon at Antioch and its consequences is at an end. In leaving the city that had rejected them the missionaries followed the injunction given to disciples in the Mission Charge, though surprisingly Luke's wording here is nearer to Mt. 10.14 than to Lk. 10.11; see *FS* Dupont 693. Only in Matthew is the verb ἐκτινάσσειν used. It is clear that the new circumstances give a different force to the observation made by StrB with reference to the gospel saying. 'Schüttelte man daher den Staub einer Stadt von den Füssen ab, so drückte man damit aus, dass man den Ort dem Gebiet der Heiden gleichstelle und mit seinen Bewohnern keine Gemeinschaft habe' (1.571). Here the town in question is in Gentile territory; and it is the Jews in it (v. 50) who are responsible for the ejection of the missionaries. That is to say, the action presupposes a new identification of the people of God, who are no longer simply identified with Jews by race. 14.21, 22 as well as v. 52 imply the existence of Christians in Antioch, so that the 'people of God' is in truth represented there. Paul and Barnabas' action in wiping off the dust of their feet must be directed simply against the recalcitrant and unbelieving Jews and expresses in action the warning of v. 41.

ἦλθον (D has κατήντησαν) εἰς Ἰκόνιον. See Xenophon, *Anabasis* 1.2.19, . . . εἰς Ἰκόνιον, τῆς Φρυγίας πόλιν ἐσχάτην. It lay within the area added in 25 BC to the old Kingdom of Galatia (and thus formed part of what is sometimes known as 'South Galatia'; see on 16.6); to Pliny (*Natural History* 5.95) it was urbs celeberrima. Under Claudius it was allowed the name Claudiconium (*CAH* 10.679). It evidently (14.1) possessed a synagogue.

52. Luke, as usual, makes it clear to his reader that persecution cannot halt the Gospel. There were disciples (for μαθηταί as a term for Christians see 6.1) and they were filled with joy (cf. 8.8; 15.3; for filling with moral or spiritual characteristics see 6.3) and with the Holy Spirit (cf. 2.4). According to Stählin (188) this description presupposes baptism; it would be equally reasonable to say that it presupposes a source with only small interest in baptism; see on v. 43. For the wording of the verse cf. *P.Oxy.* 46 (1978).3313, 3f. (quoted in *ND* 3.10–15): χαρ[ᾶς ἡμ]ᾶς ἐπλήρωσας εὐαγγελισαμένη τὸν γ[άμον] τοῦ κρατίστου Σαραπίωνος . . .

36. IN AND AROUND LYSTRA 14.1–23

(1) In Iconium they followed their custom and entered[1] the synagogue of the Jews, and so spoke that a great company of both Jews and Greeks became believers. (2) But the unbelieving Jews incited the Gentiles and poisoned their minds against the brothers. (3) So[2] they stayed a considerable time, speaking boldly in the Lord, who bore witness to the word of his grace by causing signs and portents to be done at their hands. (4) The population of the city was divided, and some were on the side of the Jews, others on the side of the apostles. (5) But when there was a move on the part of both Gentiles and Jews, along with their rulers, to outrage and to stone them, (6) they perceived this and fled for refuge to the cities of Lycaonia, Lystra and Derbe, and the surrounding region, (7) and there they were occupied in evangelism.

(8) In Lystra there used to sit a man, powerless in his feet, lame from his mother's womb, who had never walked. (9) This man heard Paul speaking. Paul fixed his eyes on him, and when he saw that he had the faith for healing, (10) he said with a loud voice, 'Get up, and stand erect on your feet.' He jumped up and began to walk. (11) The crowds, when they saw what Paul had done, lifted up their voice in Lycaonian and said, 'The gods have come down to us, made like men.' (12) They called Barnabas Zeus and Paul Hermes, because he took the lead in speaking. (13) The priest of the Zeus whose holy place was outside the city, with the crowds, brought out to the gates bulls and garlands, and wished to offer sacrifice. (14) But when the apostles Barnabas and Paul heard this, they tore their clothes and sprang into the crowd, shouting, (15) 'Men, why are you doing these things? We too are men, of like passions[3] with yourselves, who bring you the good news that you should turn away from these vain things to the[4] living God, who made heaven and earth and sea and all the things that are in them. (16) In generations gone by he permitted all the Gentiles to go their own ways; (17) yet he never left himself without witness in that he did good and sent you from heaven rain and fruitful seasons, filling your hearts with food and gladness.' (18) It was with difficulty that, by saying these things, they prevented the crowds from sacrificing to them.

(19) But there came Jews from Antioch and Iconium; they got the crowds on their side, stoned Paul, and dragged him outside the city, supposing that he was dead; (20) but when the disciples surrounded him he got up and went into the city. On the next day he left with Barnabas for Derbe. (21) When they had evangelized that city and made a considerable number of disciples

---

[1]*Begs.*, they went in together; RSV, they entered together.
[2]NEB omits.
[3]NEB, NJB, mortal.
[4]*Begs.*, RSV, a.

they returned to Lystra, Iconium, and Antioch, (22) strengthening the souls of the disciples, exhorting them to abide in the faith, and explaining to them[5] that it is through many afflictions that we must enter the kingdom of God. (23) When they had appointed for them elders in each church they prayed, held fasts, and committed them to the Lord in whom they had put their faith.

Bibliography

M. Ballance, *AnSt* 7 (1957), 145–51.

J. Beutler, *ThPh* 43 (1968), 360–83.

F. F. Bruce, as in (35).

C. Burchard, as in (29).

F. G. Downing, as in (9).

J. Dupont, *Nouvelles Études*, 112–32, 171–85, 350–7.

B. van Elderen, as in (34).

J. C. Fenton, *ExpT* 77 (1966), 381–3.

B. Gärtner, *SEÅ* 27 (1962), 83–8.

K. Haacker, as in (1).

O. Lagercranz, *ZNW* 31 (1932), 86f.

E. Lerle, *NTS* 7 (1961), 46–55.

E. Nellessen, Kremer *Actes*, 493–8.

G. Ogg, *NTS* 9 (1963), 367–70.

M. Pohlenz, *ZNW* 42 (1949), 69–104.

M. Silva, as in (8).

A. Vögtle, *FS* Schürmann, 529–82.

Commentary

The paragraph presents a lively account of events in Pisidia and Lycaonia. Whatever 13.46 (στρεφόμεθα εἰς τὰ ἔθνη) may mean, Paul and Barnabas have not finished with the Jews but begin the new mission to Iconium in the synagogue. It spreads to the Gentile population of the city; the result is division, but the opposition is strong enough to force a retreat to Lystra, Derbe, and the surrounding countryside. At Lystra a miraculous healing profoundly impresses the local residents; they have to be restrained from offering sacrifice to Barnabas and Paul, who have no mind to be regarded as divine but take the opportunity of presenting the Gospel in the form it must take for the heathen. Their first step must be to abandon polytheism and

---

[5]Explaining to them is not in the Greek.

recognize the existence of one true God only. Hitherto this one true God has not pressed his claim, but his providential care for mankind is evident in the cycle of nature. The welcome at Lystra is warm though theologically uninstructed; but the Jews of (Pisidian) Antioch and Iconium follow Barnabas and Paul, stone Paul, and leave him for dead. He recovers, and with Barnabas leaves for Derbe. They return to Lystra, Iconium, and Antioch, strengthening the disciples and appointing elders as they go.

It is probable that the Christians at (Syrian) Antioch preserved the memory of and perhaps links with, the churches of Cyprus, Perge, (Pisidian) Antioch, Lystra, and Derbe. To what may have been little more than a list of names Luke has been able to attach both narrative and preaching material. Traces of Luke's style and of his interests are spread fairly evenly through the whole section and as it stands it must be regarded as Luke's own composition (cf. Lüdemann 165–71). This is not to say that it is fictitious; Luke had information of various kinds.

He probably had least specific information about the mission in Iconium. The theme of Jewish persecution runs throughout his book, and vv. 1–6 contain little more than a statement of the theme which seems to be based on the much more circumstantial account of events in Pisidian Antioch (note κατὰ τὰ αὐτά in v. 1). There was a successful mission; disaffected Jews stirred up opposition; the population was divided; violence was threatened; the evangelists escaped. Haenchen 406 speaks of this section as a bridge between the more striking events at Pisidian Antioch (13.14–51) and at Lystra (vv. 8–20). This is correct as far as the tempo of the three scenes is concerned; vv. 1–6 are important in the structure of the book precisely as the earlier summary passages (2.42–47; 4.32–35; etc.) are; they show how Luke understood the whole early Christian movement. In this paragraph the order of vv. 2 and 3 is surprising; see the notes. Some would reverse them, some regard one as an insertion. It is probable that in v. 6 Luke returns to the itinerary. This would explain the reference to Derbe, a place which is not reached till v. 20, after a long account of events at Lystra.

This observation confirms the view that vv. 8–18 constitute a self-contained episode (Plümacher 92f.). The passage could be lifted out and it would hardly be possible to detect its absence (Schmithals 130). Paul preaches, but this is mentioned only incidentally (v. 9); the first main event is the cure of a lame man, told in straight-forward manner. Those who think that Luke was concerned to draw up a neat balance between Peter and Paul may suppose that the healing of the lame man at Lystra (vv. 8–10) corresponds to the cure of the lame man at the Temple gate (3.1–10); there are parallels, but both are stylized miracle stories told in simple and conventional terms. It is more significant that whereas in 3.12 Peter finds it necessary to deny that he and John have cured the lame man by their power and piety, so here Paul and Barnabas are put in the position of having to refuse sacrifice and to affirm that they are not divine but human. This denial that apostles and evangelists are anything other than human is another Lucan theme. There is no good reason for thinking that the narrative originally concerned only Barnabas.

Paul's brief discourse (vv. 15–17) anticipates some of the themes of the Areopagus speech (17.22–31). It will be better to discuss the subject-matter at that point, but the question of source cannot be avoided here. It is unlikely that the traditional material available at Antioch contained accounts of impromptu speeches. Luke probably inserted this one. It reflects in some respects the attitude and message of 1 Thess. 1.9, 10, but is probably based upon, or drawn from the same source as, the Areopagus speech, and though we know little about Paul's manner of mission preaching it must be considered doubtful whether the Paul who is known to us from the epistles was accustomed to make, even to Gentiles, an approach that owed so much to natural theology. The little speech probably reflects use made by some Christians of Hellenistic Jewish material (Hengel 89), but the pragmatic appeal to Gentiles, which takes the line that 'Gentiles are, in their own way, as devout and as likeable as the Jews' (Wilson, *Gentiles* 245) is not Paul's, who seems to have had his own method (*ZThK* 86 (1989), 25–30). To a possible Antiochene reference to Lystra Luke appears to have added a conventional miracle story and a Hellenistic-Jewish speech.

After the exaggerated acclamation of Paul and Barnabas in vv. 11–18 reaction follows in vv. 19, 20. Behind these verses there probably lies Antiochene tradition, which finds some confirmation in Paul's own reference to a stoning (2 Cor. 11.25; cf. 2 Tim. 3.11). In the verses as they stand however there are notorious difficulties. Is it likely that disaffected Jews travelled over 100 miles from Antioch, as well as the shorter distance from Iconium, to attack Paul? They may have done so; for a contact between Antioch and Lystra see on v. 19. But if they did, why should they attack Paul alone and spare Barnabas? If Paul was so gravely injured as to be supposed dead, how could he on the next day travel the better part of a further 100 miles to Derbe? Luke has not fully thought through the tradition he found, but this does not rob it of all historical value.

Further suffering, heightened by escape from death, is a suitable introduction to v. 22, where Luke states his own kind of *theologia crucis* (*FS* Dinkler 73–84). It is not Paul's, it is not as profound as Paul's; but it exists. There is no way into the kingdom of God but by suffering. But suffering can be borne; the Lord will often deliver his people from it; and if (as in the case of James) suffering ends in death this is not to be feared.

The concluding verses are again marked by generalization and are probably Luke's own work. This is almost certainly true of v. 23, not only because the genuine Pauline epistles never speak of elders (presbyters), but because none are mentioned in 13.1–3. It is hardly likely that the representatives of the church of Antioch would institute in the daughter churches a kind of ministry that the mother itself did not have. This is not to say that Paul and Barnabas did not ask some of their first and most trustworthy converts to keep an eye on the rest. Paul evidently made such an arrangement in, for example, Thessalonica (1 Thess. 5.12, 13). Luke would supply a term that had become current in the church of his own day, and indeed probably inferred the appointments from general acquaintance with church practices.

The paragraph raises also the question of the status and description of Paul and Barnabas themselves. Only in this chapter is Paul described as an ἀπόστολος, as also is Barnabas; elsewhere this term is reserved for the Twelve (excluding Judas Iscariot and including Matthias), that is, for men who were not only witnesses of the risen Christ but had accompanied him during his ministry (see especially 1.21, 22). At v. 14 there is a textual problem (for which see the notes), but at least the possibility cannot be excluded that in this verse both Paul and Barnabas are spoken of as apostles. It is more difficult to avoid this conclusion at v. 4, where (see the notes) the alternative explanations are weak. Opinions differ on the question whether these verses are to be regarded as pieces of traditional material (so e.g. Roloff 211) or as Lucan redaction (so e.g. Schneider 2.152). According to Maddox (71f.; 85, n. 18), in these places 'the old tradition is shining through', but it is at least arguable that we see here the apostles of the *Didache* (11.3–6), wandering preachers who were certainly not among the Twelve. From the literary point of view it may be best to conclude that the word ἀπόστολος occurred in the Antiochene material on which Luke drew but that it was used not in the sense of 'one belonging to the Twelve, appointed by Jesus himself' (it would be even harder to bring in Barnabas on this level than Paul) but to mean 'one sent out as a missionary by the church (of Antioch)'. That is, in this chapter, Paul and Barnabas are ἀπόστολοι ἐκκλησιῶν (2 Cor. 8.23), envoys of churches, in this case, of the church of (Syrian) Antioch. Luke never uses the word again of Paul because it would not have been a valid description of him; from ch. 16 onwards Paul was an independent missionary (cf. Gal. 1.1), no longer reporting back to Antioch (and possibly to some extent separated from and in disagreement with it — Gal. 2.11–14). If this is correct the word ἀπόστολος would belong to the Antioch source (this word being understood in a broad sense); if it does so belong, vv. 4 and 14 would probably carry with them into the source some of their immediate context — the division of the people of Iconium, and the resistance of Barnabas and Paul to the divine honours offered them at Lystra. This however does not go far enough. The problem is handled by Wilson (*Gentiles* 115–18) with brusque common sense: Luke was content to allow two logically contradictory ways of using the word ἀπόστολος to stand side by side in his book. Both were valid ways of using it. It was correct to say that an apostle was one who had known Jesus during his ministry, could bear witness to his resurrection, and had been specifically appointed by Jesus. But it was also correct to describe Paul as an apostle; where could you find a more truly apostolic figure? This is well as far as it goes: Luke was writing neither a textbook of systematic theology nor a corpus of canon law. But one thing is to be said. There are more kinds than one of 'apostles of churches'. Some may be delegates appointed to discharge a particular function, such as handling and conveying sums of money (2 Cor. 8.23). But Paul and Barnabas were appointed by the Holy Spirit (13.2) before they were appointed by the church of Antioch (13.3). They were sent not by men but by God, as truly as were the prophets (see e.g. Gal. 1.15 and cf. Jer. 1.5; Isa. 49.1). Luke therefore was prepared to call them apostles, and did so; but he did so seldom, perhaps because he knew that there were those who would not so describe them (1 Cor. 9.2; see *Signs* 35–47). Cf. Lüdemann (165).

1. For Luke's use of (καὶ) ἐγένετο (δέ), here followed by an accusative and infinitive, see on e.g. 5.7; 9.32, 37. He uses his 'biblical' style. For Iconium see on 13.51. It lay on the Via Sebaste, by which it was connected westwards with Pisidian Antioch, eastwards with Lystra and Derbe. Many (fictitious) incidents in Iconium are recorded in the *Acts of Paul and Thecla*.

κατὰ τὸ αὐτό is often taken to have the same meaning as ἐπὶ τὸ αὐτό (see on 2.47), *together*. The Vulgate translates *simul*, and at 3 Kdms 3.18 the phrase translates יחדו. Blass (156) however writes, 'recte Gigas [one can add d] *similiter . . .* pessime vulg. *simul*'. There seems to be no good reason why Luke should stress the fact that the two missionaries entered the synagogue together; why should they have done otherwise? Calvin (2.1) takes the phrase to apply to the Jews: Paul and Barnabas went in with the crowd. Again this hardly seems worth saying. It is better to understand Luke's point to be that they followed their custom (cf. 17.2). Their experience in the synagogue at Pisidian Antioch had been a lively one, but it did not lead to a change of policy or tactics. Luke is presumably thinking of the Sabbath service, when anyone allowed to speak would be assured of a number of hearers. For the synagogue as an institution see on 6.9.

Elsewhere in the NT οὕτως is taken up by ὥστε only at Jn 3.16, but the construction is classical; e.g. Herodotus 7.174, Θεσσαλοὶ . . . οὕτω δὴ ἐμήδισαν . . . ὥστε . . . ἐφαίνοντο . . . Luke no doubt intends his reader to think that, between them, Paul and Barnabas spoke on lines similar to those he ascribed to Paul in the synagogue at Pisidian Antioch (13.16–41), and with a similar result (13.42f.). πλῆθος is a Lucan word (Lk., eight; Acts, seventeen (sixteen); rest of the NT, seven times); πλῆθος πολύ occurs at 17.4 (note also the reading of E in v. 7 below). It seems probable that Luke is here expanding what may have been little more than a bare reference to Iconium. He may not have asked himself how Greeks ("Ελληνες) as well as Jews can have heard what Paul and Barnabas said in the synagogue. The Greeks can hardly be proselytes, and, though Stählin 188 for example thinks that they must be 'God-fearers', they are not described by Luke's usual word σεβόμενοι (or φοβούμενοι). Luke is moving rapidly towards the point at which he can blame Jewish trouble-makers for division in the city and a move against the missionaries.

A large crowd of Jews and Greeks became believers (for the meaning of the aorist infinitive πιστεῦσαι see on 2.44); but v. 5 suggests that a majority of both groups remained unconvinced.

2. Among opponents we hear first of disobedient, that is unbelieving (for this use of ἀπειθεῖν cf. 19.9; Jn 3.36; Rom. 2.8; 1 Peter 3.1; 4.17; *al.*; ἀπιστεῖν is used at 28.24) Jews. ἐπήγειραν can hardly be intransitive and will therefore share with ἐκάκωσαν the object τὰς ψυχάς. Herodotus 7.139.5 (οὗτοι — the Athenians — ἦσαν οἱ ἐπεγείραντες [τὸ Ἑλληνικόν] — the rest of Greece, against Xerxes) is an interesting but not very important parallel. κακοῦν is more often *to injure, distress, ill-use*. In *Begs.* 4.161 it is rendered *irritate*, with references to Josephus, *Ant.* 16.10, 205, 262 (all of which seem to permit if not to require a different meaning) and *P.Tebt.* 2(1907).407, 9 (which is taken somewhat differently by BA 808). In the present context the word must mean that the Jews caused the Gentiles (ἔθνη) to be disaffected towards the brothers. It is not clear whether these ἔθνη are to be identified with the "Ελληνες of v. 1 or distinguished from them; if distinguished, the Greeks are more likely to be non-Jews having some association with the synagogue, whereas the ἔθνη will be untouched by Judaism. This is perhaps the better way of taking the two words, but it is (see above) idle to look for absolute precision in v. 1. The Jews excited the Gentiles, and incited them to opposition, κατὰ τῶν ἀδελφῶν. ἀδελφοί, from 1.15, normally refers to Christians, except when it refers to fellow Jews (e.g. at 2.29). At this stage, however, though a large company had become believers (v. 1) there seems scarcely to have been time for a recognized company of 'brothers' to have come into being; the alternative reference would be to the two brother evangelists, Paul and Barnabas. Paul himself uses the word in a similar sense (e.g. 1 Cor. 1.1, Σωσθένης ὁ ἀδελφός). On the whole, however, it seems best to suppose that if Luke was writing up a short account of the mission to Iconium on the basis of little precise knowledge he had not considered the difficulty involved in a reference to a group of *brothers*. And the difficulty may not have been very great; 1 Thessalonians contains good evidence that the new congregation in Thessalonica very speedily attracted unpopularity.

The Western text appears to have been concerned to 'improve' the somewhat sketchy report of this verse. E 614 *pc* gig sy[h] provide an object for ἐπήγειραν (see above): οἱ δὲ ἀπειθοῦντες (present instead of aorist) 'Ιουδαῖοι ἐπήγειραν διωγμόν. D (sy[hmg]) have a fuller and more circumstantial beginning: οἱ δὲ ἀρχισυνάγωγοι τῶν 'Ιουδαίων καὶ οἱ ἄρχοντες τῆς συναγωγῆς (this duplicates ἀρχισυνάγωγοι, for which see 13.15) ἐπήγειραν αὐτοῖς (noted by Black, *AA* 104, cf. Wilcox 131, as an ethic dative suggestive of Aramaic) διωγμὸν κατὰ τῶν δικαίων. This substitute for *brothers* shows an editor borrowing another Christological term for the description of Christians, and perhaps also losing no opportunity of asserting the innocence of Christians; Ramsay (*Church* 46) thinks that διωγμὸς κατὰ τῶν δικαίων 'looks like a stock phrase, which had established itself in Christian usage', but he gives no evidence for this. 'On prend τῶν δικαίων, comme souvent en bon grec, comme un neutre, "le droit", et non comme un masculin, "les justes" (Delebecque 70). This seems less probable in biblical Greek than in 'good Greek'. At the end of this verse, and no doubt to explain the beginning of the next, additions are made. D gig p w sy[hmg] mae have ὁ δὲ κύριος ἔδωκεν ταχὺ εἰρήνην; E has ὁ δὲ κύριος εἰρήνην ἐποίησεν.

3. If the Western readings just mentioned are rejected, as they should be, there is a difficult connection between vv. 2 and 3: The Jews incited the Gentiles against the brothers, so (μὲν οὖν) Paul and Barnabas stayed a considerable time, speaking boldly . . . This is not impossible: Paul and Barnabas stayed because the brothers needed their support, and the greater the opposition the bolder they became. It is however true that to reverse the two verses, as is suggested in *Begs.* 4.161f. (but also rejected, since it is clear that the difficulty was already there when the Western editors were at work), would make an easier connection, and would make it quite unnecessary to give a very unusual adversative sense to μὲν οὖν, which could have its usual resumptive sense after v. 1. The suggestion is mentioned, but without conclusive comment, by M. 3.337f. and by Moule (*IB* 163), but Moule notes similar use of μὲν οὖν at 17.17 (possibly); 25.4; 28.5; and perhaps Heb. 9.1, which has the effect of supporting the text as it stands. It may be best (cf. vv. 1, 2) to think that Luke was putting together, in not too well connected a way, an account of work at Iconium, which he supposed must have followed a pattern similar to that at Pisidian Antioch. Notwithstanding the difficulties Paul and Barnabas stayed a considerable time (ἱκανὸν χρόνον, a Lucan expression; see 9.43). διατρίβειν also is a Lucan word (Acts 12.19; 14.3, 28; 15.35; 16.12; 20.6; 25.6, 14; Jn twice). διέτριψαν is a constative aorist: M. 3.72; also BDR § 332. 1, n. 2, where the imperfect of 14.28 is noted; that is open-ended; here a time limit is given by vv. 5, 6. D has διατρίψαντες, which has been thought Semitic; see Wilcox 122f.

παρρησιάζεσθαι again is a Lucan word (see on 9.27), confirming the view that Luke is here composing a narrative. It may on occasion mean inspired speech, and it is unlikely that Luke would have questioned that Paul and Barnabas were on this occasion filled with the Holy Spirit, but the context speaks of the threat to the missionaries and it is their boldness rather than their inspiration that Luke intends to emphasise here. ἐπί with the dative τῷ κυρίῳ can hardly indicate the content of what Paul and Barnabas said ('bearing bold witness to . . .'); it will rather point to the ground of their confident boldness ('speaking boldly in the Lord . . .'). The Lord encouraged them by joining his witness to theirs, as he allowed, or caused (for this use of διδόναι see on 2.27; it recalls the Hebrew נתן; see BDR § 392. 1, n. 6) σημεῖα καὶ τέρατα (for this common expression in Acts see on 2.22) to happen at (though) their hands (another Hebraism, copied from the LXX: בידם).

For διδόντι, ℵ 81 2495 have διδόντος; 104 323 945 1175 1739 pc have καὶ διδόντι. It is very probable that Luke wrote διδόντι, the reading of nearly all MSS, but he must have found it difficult to know whether to make his participle agree with κυρίῳ and μαρτυροῦντι or with αὐτοῦ. For *signs and portents* as testimony cf. 15.12 (also e.g. Mk 16.17, 20 — the 'longer ending' of Mark, which may show acquaintance with Acts); but here the testimony is to *the word of his* (the Lord's) *grace*; that is, the central thought, even if Luke is using an established phrase, almost a cliché (cf. 20.32), is not of wonder-working power, but of the loving favour of God (in this context, cf. 11.23; 13.43; 14.26) made apparent in the Gospel preached by Paul and Barnabas.

4. The πλῆθος is now not the large company of those who became believers (v. 1), but the whole population of the city, or at least the greater part of it. This was divided, ἐσχίσθη. D has ἦν δὲ ἐσχισμένον; this reflects the fact that D already has ἐσχίσθη in v. 2; the periphrastic perfect indicates that the division continued unhealed. The lines of the division are stated in balanced clauses introduced by οἱ μέν and οἱ δέ. Cf. Xenophon, *Symposium* 4.59, . . . ἐσχίσθησαν, καὶ οἱ μὲν εἶπον . . . οἱ δὲ . . . The operative word in each clause is σύν, which, according to M. 3.265 'has something of the inclusive meaning of *on the side of*'. This seems sufficiently obvious, and is a normal meaning of the word; see LS 1690 s.v. A 2, and cf. Xenophon, *Hellenica* 3.1, . . . βούλοιντο σὺν τοῖς ῞Ελλησι μᾶλλον ἢ σὺν τῷ βαρβάρῳ εἶναι.

Some sided with the Jews; that is, they disbelieved what had been said by Paul and Barnabas, taking them to be deluded, or perhaps as intentionally deceiving their hearers, perverting Judaism and leading Gentiles astray.

Others sided with the apostles. It is most natural to take the apostles to be Paul and Barnabas, to whom the Jews were opposed. The same two men appear to be described by the same title at v. 14 (but see the textual note on that verse); nowhere else in Acts, however, are they so described, and the word apostle (1.2, 26; 2.37, 42, 43; 4.33, 35, 36, 37; 5.2, 12, 18, 29, 40; 6.6; 8.1, 14, 18; 9.27; 11.1; 15.2, 4, 6, 22, 23; 16.4) is elsewhere confined to the eleven named in 1.13 who had accompanied Jesus during his ministry, together with Matthias, who was appointed to join them (1.26). In terms of the definition applied in 1.21f. Paul certainly and Barnabas probably cannot have been an apostle (Bruce 1.278 thinks that Barnabas may have been one of the 120 (1.15)). It is true that Paul describes himself as an apostle (e.g. Rom. 1.1) and insists very strongly on his apostolic status (e.g. 1 Cor. 9.1f.), and 1 Cor. 9.6; Gal. 2.1, 9 suggest though they do not prove that he thought of Barnabas also as an apostle, as he seems also to have thought of Andronicus and Junias (Rom. 16.7). There is thus a matter here that calls for explanation. The following suggestions have been made. (1) Luke was simply careless; he did not notice that his definition excluded Paul from apostleship. Most unlikely; it cannot be pure coincidence that from 14.15 to 28.31 Paul is never called an apostle; this silence (like the fact that the word is not used in the accounts of Paul's conversion and call) is part of what has to be explained. (2) Luke knew that he must not call Paul an apostle (in addition to his definition he may have known that to do so would evoke controversy); but his admiration for Paul (of which there can be no question) was so great that here, and at v. 14, the word slipped through. Luke's heart overcame his head. (3) *The apostles* does not refer to Paul and Barnabas but to those properly so described. It was the message of the apostles (proper) that Paul and Barnabas proclaimed (cf. 13.31, 32), so that those who agreed with Paul and Barnabas were effectively on the side of the apostles (Peter, John, and the rest). If Luke meant that it is unfortunate that he did not express himself more clearly. (4) Paul and Barnabas were apostles but in a sense different from that in which Peter and John were apostles. They had been sent out (13.1–3) by the church of Antioch, to which in due course they reported back (14.26, 27); that is, they were apostles of a church (cf. 2 Cor. 8.23, ἀπόστολοι ἐκκλησιῶν). If after this chapter Paul is no longer described as an ἀπόστολος this might be because he no longer was an apostle of the church of Antioch, or of any other; he was working on the lines described in Gal. 1.1.

Of these explanations the first three, especially the first and third, are exposed to very considerable objection. If (4) is accepted the use must presumably be taken to be part, even if a modified part, of the old Antiochene source; cf. Conzelmann (*Geschichte* 138); Hahn (*Mission* 134). See the introduction to this section, pp. 666f. Luke is not simply juxtaposing inconsistent opinions and usages.

5. Both Gentiles and Jews now shared in a move (ὁρμή suggests something rather stronger, rather more violent, than *move*, but alternatives, such as *a rush*, go too far; cf. Thucydides 4.1; Plato, *Philebus* 35d) against *them*, who (whatever we make of *apostles* in v. 4) must now be understood as Paul and Barnabas, since αὐτούς at the end of v. 5 supplies the subject of the verbs in vv. 6, 7. Those who were on the side of the Jews (v. 4) evidently prevailed, at least to the extent of constituting a united movement and winning over the rulers (ἄρχοντες) of the city (for αὐτῶν will refer to both ἔθνη and 'Ιουδαῖοι, so that these will not be rulers of the synagogue — v. 2 D).

At this point καὶ πάλιν ἐπήγειραν διωγμόν is added by Codex Thomae, a Greek MS regarded by Clark (226–33) as the source of the Harclean marginal readings; see Clark (357). The addition is rather part of the Western smoothing out of a paragraph not marked by continuity.

The content of the move against the missionaries is expressed in two infinitives (BDR § 393. 5, n. 7), ὑβρίσαι (a general term, *to insult* or *to injure*, or both) and λιθοβολῆσαι. It does not seem probable that Luke distinguished between this word (used here and at 7.58, 59 — see the notes) and λιθάζειν (used in this section at v. 19, and at 5.26); see Knox (*Hellenistic Elements* 18). In concerted action of this kind one would not expect Jewish legal procedures to be observed.

6. For συνιδόντες see on 12.12. There is no need to conjecture σπεύδοντες, *they made haste*. Chrysostom's οὐ περιέμειναν τοίνυν, ἀλλ' εἶδον τὴν ὁρμήν, καὶ ἔφυγον suggests that the *move* (v. 5) had reached the stage of visible action. As soon as Paul and Barnabas perceived what was intended they took flight. καταφεύγειν usually suggests a destination, as here: they fled and took refuge in . . . 'The text implies that Iconium was not in Lycaonia' (Hemer 110; cf. 178, 228–230).

τὰς πόλεις τῆς Λυκαονίας Λύστραν καὶ Δερβήν suggests 'the cities of Lycaonia, namely, Lystra and Derbe', implying that these were the only, or at least the principal, cities in the region. This was not so, though Lycaonia was not a thickly populated or developed area. Cilicia lay to the south, Cappadocia to the east, Phrygia to the

north, Pisidia (see on 13.14) and Isauria to the west, though there
were few firmly drawn and established boundary lines. In addition
to the towns mentioned, Laranda was of some importance, and a
military colony Parlais was established by Augustus, partly in
order to protect the bare countryside from the attacks of robbers.
In 25 BC part of Lycaonia, together with parts of Phrygia, Pisidia,
and Pamphylia were united with the old kingdom of Galatia (see on
16.6) to form a province, to which later other territories were
joined. Lycaonia remained on the whole unhellenized (cf. v. 11);
sheep-grazing was a profitable pursuit. For Lystra see Ramsay
(*Church* 47–54; *Cities* 407–19). It lay SSW of Iconium, about six
hours distant. It is the modern Khatyn Serai. It had been made a
colony by Augustus and lay on the 'Imperial Road' (τὴν βασιλικὴν
ὁδὸν τὴν ἐπὶ Λύστραν, *Acts of Paul and Thecla* 3 (L.-B. 1.237.4)
which connected Antioch and Laranda. According to 16.1 it was
the home of Timothy. In the present verse Lystra is treated as a first
declension feminine singular noun (accusative Λύστραν; so also v.
21; 16.1), but elsewhere it is second declension neuter plural
(dative Λύστροις, 14.7 D E, 8; 16.2; 2 Tim. 3.11). See M. 1.48;
2.147; BDR § 57. 2. The site of Derbe has fairly recently been
established; see B. van Elderen, *FS* Bruce (1970) 156–61 (with
references to earlier work by M. Ballance). It is proved by
archaeological evidence to have been in the neighbourhood of
Kerti Huyuk, 'a sizeable, although not prominent, mound located
about fifteen miles north-northeast of Karaman (ancient Laranda).
Karaman is about sixty-five miles southeast of Konya (ancient
Iconium)' (van Elderen 157). Derbe was honoured by Claudius as
Claudioderbe (cf. Iconium, on 13.51). περίχωρος occurs here only
in Acts, but five times in Luke; in the rest of the NT only three
times. It may be seen as another probable pointer to Luke's own
hand and a mark of imprecise knowledge. Luke does not wish to
imply that Paul and Barnabas confined themselves to the two cities.

At the beginning of the verse D reads συνιδόντες καὶ κατέφυγον;
see Black (*AA* 69) for the possible Aramaism. After Λυκαονίας, C*
D* add εἰς; a more interesting addition is sicut ihs dixerat eis
LX[XII], for which h is cited (cf. Lk. 10.10). See however the
warning in Metzger (421); the reading follows a decipherment by E.
S. Buchanan, but not all palaeographers have been able to see it in
the MS. The surrounding area is magnified by ὅλην in D E lat (mae).
This has the effect of underlining what is said in v. 7.

7. κἀκεῖ, there, in the cities and the surrounding country.
εὐαγγελιζόμενοι ἦσαν, they were evangelizing, or, to bring out
the emphasis on continuous action which no doubt is intended, they
pursued the work of evangelism.

Western editors evidently felt that further description was called for, and that v. 8 required that Paul and Barnabas should settle in Lystra. Hence additions:

καὶ ἐκινήθη ὅλον τὸ πλῆθος ἐπὶ τῇ διδαχῇ· ὁ δὲ Παῦλος καὶ Βαρναβᾶς διέτριβον ἐν Λύστροις, D h w vgˢ (mae).

τὸν λόγον τοῦ θεοῦ. καὶ ἐξεπλήσσοντο πᾶσα ἡ πολυπλήθεια ἐπὶ τῇ διδαχῇ αὐτῶν. ὁ δὲ Παῦλος καὶ Βαρναβᾶς διέτριβον ἐν Λύστροις, E.

8. The generalities of vv. 1–7 are left behind and Luke embarks upon the story of a particular event, or rather sequence of events. They may have been reported in Syrian Antioch; Luke may have heard them told in Lystra, or by companions of Paul. The order of words is unusual. τις precedes the substantive to which it relates; it does so also at 9.10, but the opposite order in 8.9; 10.1 is more usual. τοῖς ποσίν, defining the area in which the man is ἀδύνατος, is separated from the adjunct by ἐν Λύστροις (for the declension see on v. 6); the dative τοῖς ποσίν also is unexpected. See BDR § 197. 1, and especially Radermacher (99): 'Es handelt sich in diesem Falle schwerlich um eine ganz andere Auffassung, nämlich die instrumentale, die im Griechischen uralt war, in klassischer Zeit hinter dem modern gewordenen Akkusativus relationis verschwand, und nun in der Volkssprache wieder hervortritt. ἀδύνατος τοῖς ποσίν (Act 14.8) ist einer, der mit den Füssen nichts zu leisten vermag.' ἀδύνατος is not often used of specific sicknesses, but the general meaning is clear. In Lystra there used to sit (frequentative imperfect; presumably to beg; cf. 3.2) a man who was powerless, had no strength, in his feet. He sat because he could not stand. This is made more explicit, and the gravity of the situation is underlined, in the following words. The man had been lame from his mother's womb (χωλὸς ἐκ κοιλίας μητρὸς αὐτοῦ), lame, that is, from the moment of birth; consequently he had never walked. The language recalls that of 3.2, whence Preuschen (88), following Blass, thinks it was interpolated. More probably we should recognize one of Luke's characteristic Septuagintalizing phrases (cf. especially Ps. 22 (21).11; Isa. 49.1).

The unusual word order (given by ℵ* B 1175; see above) is improved by D E h mae, which omit ἐν Λύστροις, and by P⁷⁴ ℵᶜ A C Ψ 𝔐, which have . . . ἀνὴρ ἐν Λύστροις ἀδύνατος τοῖς ποσίν . . . χωλός is omitted by D gig, presumably as unnecessary.

9. Luke connects the miracle story with the context by noting that the lame man had on some occasion heard Paul speaking. This translates the aorist ἤκουσεν, read by P⁷⁴ ℵ A D E L Ψ 33 81 614 945 1175 1739 2495 *pm*, probably rightly. B C P 6 323 1241 *pm* have the imperfect, he used to listen to Paul as he spoke. D adds that he was ὑπάρχων ἐν φόβῳ; h that he listened libenter. No mention has been made of a synagogue in Lystra; we do not know where Paul may have spoken.

Paul fixed his eye on the man (ἀτενίζειν is a Lucan word; see on 1.10 and cf. 3.4) and saw that he had πίστιν τοῦ σωθῆναι. For this consecutive use of τοῦ and the infinitive see Zerwick § 384 ("fidem ita ut salvari posset'); BDR § 400. 2, n. 4 ('den zur Errettung nötigen Glauben'). σωθῆναι here means in the first instance *to be cured* (of lameness); the result of it is expressed in ἥλατο καὶ περιεπάτει (v. 10). But in a Christian writer the word is seldom without an overtone; see on 4.12.

10. μεγάλῃ φωνῇ is read by ℵ B C D* 81 1175 *pc* co, *with a loud voice*; P⁷⁴ A Dᶜ E Ψ 𝔐 have μεγάλῃ τῇ φωνῇ. If this is read the adjective will be predicative (BDR § 270. 3, n. 4), *with a voice which was loud*. There is of course no noticeable difference in meaning. The word of command differs somewhat from that of 3.6; there is no reference to *the name of Jesus Christ* (the reference is added in the Western text). According to Schille (305) the longer Western text makes the people's error (v. 11) less probable; in view of the analogous error guarded against in 3.12 this seems doubtful. In essence the healing word is the same as that in the earlier miracle. ἀνάστηθι is used at 9.34. ἐπὶ τοὺς πόδας σου (thought by Wilcox 133f. to be a possible Semitism) is added because the man has been said to be ἀδύνατος τοῖς ποσίν (v. 8). The words are similar to those of Ezek. 2.1 (στῆθι ἐπὶ τοὺς πόδας σου); this however scarcely justifies Stählin (191) in taking the loud voice to be the voice of God. ὀρθός also is added; it implies a man who has never been able to stand erect.

Complete healing results. ἥλατο (cf. 3.8, ἐξαλλόμενος . . . ἀλλόμενος), aorist, *he jumped up*, καὶ περιεπάτει (cf. 3.8, περιεπάτει . . . περιπατῶν), imperfect, *he began to walk and continued to do so*.

After ὀρθός, D syʰᵐᵍ mae add καὶ περιπάτει, making the command fit its consequence, and the man's disability (v. 8). Black (*AA* 65) notes the paratactic connection of the imperatives in the Western text, but it would be wrong to infer a Semitic original. For ἥλατο, D⁽ᶜ⁾ syʰᵐᵍ mae have εὐθέως παραχρῆμα ἀνήλατο, and E has παραχρῆμα ἐξήλλετο. Both variants reinforce the wonder of the cure by stressing its immediacy. εὐθέως and εὐθύς sometimes appear in combination with παραχρῆμα (e.g. Demosthenes 48.40; 52.6), but such cases are perhaps rightly treated as glosses. For παραχρῆμα Hesychius has παραυτίκα, ἀθρόως, εὐθέως, and for εὐθύ he has (i.a.) παραχρῆμα.

11. Luke more often uses ὄχλος in the singular than the plural; of seven occurrences of the plural, five occur in chs. 13 and 14 — possibly a characteristic of the Antiochian source, or tradition. The plural is of course simply an intensive. For ἐπαίρειν τὴν φωνήν cf. 2.14; 22.22 — three out of five uses of ἐπαίρειν in Acts. This is another of Luke's Septuagintalisms; cf. e.g. Judges 21.2 (קולם וישאו). They spoke Λυκαονιστί. For ¬ιστί as a suffix denoting *in what language* see M. 2.163. The Lycaonian language (see *Begs.* 5.237; Hemer 110f.) is not known, but its persistence is attested by the local use of Latin for official purposes (in inscriptions) which suggests that the population was not strongly hellenized — though presumably they knew enough Greek to understand what Paul and Barnabas said to them, though it has been suggested that had they understood them better they would not have made the mistake of identifying the evangelists with gods. Chrysostom thought that the use of the local language, which Paul and Barnabas would not understand, explained the fact that the missionaries allowed the preparations for sacrifice to go so far (v. 13) before putting a stop to them.

Paul and Barnabas were taken to be gods; the article with θεοί may point forward to the gods to be mentioned in v. 14 (on which see the note). It is unlikely that the Lycaonians believed that there were only two gods; hence, 'The gods whom we particularly associate with our region have come down'. κατέβησαν, that is, from heaven, where gods normally live. The idea of divine visitants is old; see e.g. Homer, *Odyssey* 17.485–487: καί τε θεοὶ ξείνοισιν ἐοικότες ἀλλοδαποῖσι, παντοῖοι τελέθοντες, ἐπιστρωφῶσι πόληας, ἀνθρώπων ὕβριν τε καὶ εὐνομίην ἐφορῶντες. ὁμοιωθέντες, *made* (presumably by their own choice and act) *like* .. BA 1150 cite Diodorus Siculus 1.86.3 (ὁμοιωθῆναί τισιν ζώοις) and Aesop, *Fabulae* 89P = 140H ('Ερμῆς ὁμοιωθεὶς ἀνθρώπῳ).

12. Gods ought to be addressed by the right names, so that ἐκάλουν (the imperfect may suggest, 'they were for calling . . .') will mean that Barnabas was identified with Zeus, Paul with Hermes, though, speaking in Lycaonian, the crowds no doubt used different names (Pappas and Men, perhaps). Cf. Lucian, *de Syria Dea* 31, where, in an analogous linguistic context, the writer speaks of images of Hera and Zeus, whom the local inhabitants ἐτέρῳ οὐνόματι κληΐζουσι. Luke means that they regarded Barnabas as the supreme god, 'father of gods and men', and Paul as one who served as a messenger of other gods and especially of Zeus. Chrysostom (Cramer, *Catena* 235) thought that Barnabas was so identified because of his impressive appearance: ἐμοὶ δοκεῖ ἀπὸ τῆς ὄψεως ἀξιοπρεπὴς εἶναι ὁ Βαρναβᾶς. Paul was identified with Hermes ἐπειδὴ αὐτὸς ἦν ὁ ἡγούμενος τοῦ λόγου. Hermes as a messenger would not necessarily speak for Zeus in Zeus' presence. Horace speaks of him (under the Latin name) as the messenger (*Odes* 1.10.1–6, Mercuri . . . te canam, magni Iovis et deorum nuntium) and uses the derived adjective to describe literary men (*Odes* 2.17.29f., (Faunus is) Mercurialium custos virorum). Cf. Iamblichus, *de Myst.Aeg.* 1.1, Hermes is θεὸς ὁ τῶν λόγων ἡγεμών.

ἡγεῖσθαι with a genitive means *to rule, to have dominion, over*; e.g. Herodotus 1.95.1, ἡγήσαντο τῆς Ἀσίας. With the genitive τοῦ λόγου this may mean that Paul had command of speech, of the art of speaking, was a very good speaker, or that he was in charge of the speaking done by the pair. In either case (unless the latter means simply that he, not Barnabas, addressed the lame man), Paul is being highly praised as a speaker. This is not how Paul describes himself in 1 Cor. 2.1–5 or how his opponent describes him in 2 Cor. 10.10; cf. 11.6. It is true that Paul may be animated by modesty, his opponent by spite; and his epistles are undoubtedly marked by a splendid if sometimes unconventional eloquence. Clarke (*NTP* 138f.) argues that Paul was the kind of stammerer who sometimes, with a sympathetic audience, as here, 'pulls off a brilliant success'. A simpler explanation is that Luke, who greatly admired Paul, did not know him personally.

The identification of Barnabas and Paul with Zeus and Hermes may owe nothing either to Paul's eloquence or to Barnabas' good looks. The two gods (or their Lycaonian equivalents) might already have been familiar as a pair of deities associated with the area. It was Zeus and Hermes who were entertained by the aged couple Philemon and Baucis; the geographical notes in Ovid's version of the story (*Metamorphoses* 8.618–724) are not as definite as is sometimes suggested, but they are not inconsistent with the neighbourhood of Lystra; and in this area there are inscriptions which put the two gods together; see details in Conzelman (79f.). Haenchen is hardly just in denying their importance altogether on the ground that they are no earlier than the third century, but the support they give to the legend retold by Ovid is slight.

For Δία, the usual accusative of Ζεύς, P⁷⁴ D E H L 81 1175 1739 *al* have Δίαν, which does not appear to be used elsewhere as the accusative. It may have originated in a slip, but should probably be accepted as a variant form, used in some quarters.

13. The subject of the next clause appears in the great majority of MSS as ὁ ἱερεὺς τοῦ Διὸς τοῦ ὄντος πρὸ τῆς πόλεως. This is (Ropes in *Begs.* 3.132) 'unhellenic'; Ropes thinks that it may reflect a Semitic original. It is however reasonably clear: The priest of (a statue or shrine of) Zeus who (which) was before the city. Such a shrine or statue is easy to credit; even if it did not exist Luke could well have believed that it did. Many however prefer the reading of D (gig); 'it is either original or represents a correction based on exact knowledge of the probable situation' (*Begs.* 4.165). The variant runs: οἱ δὲ ἱερεῖς τοῦ ὄντος Διὸς πρὸ πόλεως), with corresponding plural participle and finite verb, ἐνέγκαντες and ἤθελον. This is preferred (a) because it was customary for shrines to have not a single priest but a college of priests (*CIG* 2963, τῆς μεγάλης θεᾶς [Ἀρτεμί]δος προπόλ[εω]ς ἱερεῖς; Aeschylus,

Seven against Thebes 164); (b) because the idiom appears to be that of 5.17; 13.1; (c) because πρὸ πόλεως (or as a single word, προπόλεως), without τῆς, was a recognized quasi-adjectival form (cf. *Bull. corr. Hell.* 1.136, ἡ γερεῖα τοῦ προπόλεως καὶ ἐπιφανεστάτου θεῶν Διονύσου). For the construction of the Western variant see M. 1.228; 3.152; but see also BDR § 474. 5 (a), n. 7; 5 (c), n. 9, where it is treated as a case of the separation between a participle and its complement which occurs in Classical Greek. BDR quote Thucydides 7.14.2, αἱ γὰρ νῦν οὖσαι πόλεις ξύμμαχοι, the cities now allied; also Herodotus 9.22.1, and other passages. If BDR are right there is no difference in meaning between the two texts (apart from the number of priests concerned). The omission of τῆς, and the possible conjunction of two words in one (προπόλεως) is however attractive; for this see the evidence cited above, and BA 1405f. s.v. πρό, overtaking now the early observation of Ramsay (*Church* 51). But 'the plausible details might as easily be the work of a reviser' (Hemer 196).

The priest (or priests) of Zeus brought (ἐνέγκας (-αντες); φέρειν used in the sense of ἄγειν) oxen and garlands (στέμματα, with which sacrificial victims were often adorned; e.g. Herodotus 7.197.2, θύεταί τε ἐξηγέοντο στέμμασι πᾶς πυκασθείς), with the intention of offering sacrifice to the supposed gods. He was accompanied by the crowds (cf. v. 11). For θύειν, D has ἐπιθύειν; for the significance of this variant see G. D. Kilpatrick in *ZNW* 74 (1983), 151f. There is evidence for the view that the compound verb refers to unlawful sacrifice, such as sacrifice to pagan gods. The oxen and garlands were brought ἐπὶ τοὺς πυλῶνας; the gates will be either the gates of the Temple of Zeus (so e.g. Page 172; cf. Plutarch, *Timoleon* 12 (241): οἱ μὲν ἱεροὶ τοῦ νεὼ πυλῶνες), or the gates of the city — this would correspond with the fact that 'Zeus' was πρὸ [τῆς] πόλεως.

14. The commonly accepted text here describes both Paul and Barnabas as apostles; for the questions raised by this see on v. 4, and the introduction to the section. Here there is textual uncertainty in that for ἀκούσαντες δὲ οἱ ἀπόστολοι, D (gig h sy^p) have ἀκούσας δέ. This reading contains a false concord, since the plural subject (Barnabas and Paul) requires a corresponding plural participle; grammatically at least D contains the more difficult reading; if this is accepted the word ἀπόστολοι drops out. An alternative view is that the Western editor objected to the description of Barnabas as an apostle, and, as the quickest way out, simply omitted the word ἀπόστολοι. This however does not explain why he also changed the plural participle into the singular, and there must therefore remain a possibility (no stronger word can be used) that the short text (and the Western text usually expands) is correct. It is preferred by G. D.

Kilpatrick (*FS* Casey 69f.). Preuschen (89) omits ἀπόστολοι, reads the singular ἀκούσας, and drops Παῦλος; the incident originally concerned Barnabas alone; cf. Bauernfeind (182). If both names are included Barnabas may be mentioned first because he had been identified with Zeus; but it is unlikely that Luke would allow his order to be determined by the heathen hierarchy.

When Barnabas and Paul understood what was afoot (delayed perhaps by their failure to understand the Lycaonian language), they took immediate and energetic action. They tore their own clothes (whether ἑαυτῶν (ℵ ᶜ A B 33 36 453 *pc*) or αὐτῶν (P⁷⁴ ℵ* C D E Ψ 𝔐) is read this must be the meaning), as the High Priest had done at the trial of Jesus (Mt. 26.65; Mk 14.63; not Lk.), and for the same reason. Each intended to indicate that he had heard blasphemy (cf. Sanhedrin 7.5: when explicit evidence of blasphemy is given 'the judges stand up on their feet and rend their garments, and they may not mend them again'). According to M. 1.157, διαρρηξάμενοι (middle) τὰ ἱμάτια (without ἑαυτῶν) would be more idiomatic; contrast 16.27. But see BDR § 310. 1, n. 1; the active voice is also classical, e.g. Aeschylus, *Persians* 198f., τὸν δ' ὅπως ὁρᾷ Ξέρξης, πέπλους ῥήγνυσιν; 1030, πέπλον δ'ἐπέρρηξ' ἐπὶ συμφορᾷ κακοῦ. From διέρρηξα it is impossible to tell whether Luke starts from a present διαρρηγνύναι or διαρρήσσειν; see BDR § 101, n. 72; M. 2.403. For the action cf. 22.23; the parallels noted by Betz (72, 78, 140) are interesting but not so important as the Jewish reaction to blasphemy. In addition to tearing their clothes, Barnabas and Paul sprang (ἐξεπήδησαν) among the crowds, shouting (κράζοντες). The former verb may mean that they rushed *out* of the city to the temple, but it is unwise to build on the compounding ἐκ (*Begs.* 4.165). The two act and shout so as to make it clear that they are no more than human. There is an interesting verbal parallel in Judith 14.16f. διέρρηξεν τὰ ἱμάτια αὐτοῦ ... καὶ ἐξεπήδησεν εἰς τὸν λαόν, καὶ ἐβόησεν (v. l., κράζων) ..., but the motives of Bagoas, when he discovered the headless body of Holofernes, were different from those of the two missionaries.

Black (*AA* 69) points out in D another example of the connection of a participle with a finite verb by καί, and suspects Semitism.

15. ἄνδρες: there is no ἀδελφοί in the address here; this seems to be reserved for fellow Jews or fellow Christians. τί asks Why? cf. Demosthenes 55.5 (1273), Τεισία, τί ταῦτα ποιεῖς; Why are you making preparations for sacrifice? καὶ ἡμεῖς is emphatic: We too, ourselves. So, at the end of the sentence, are ὑμῖν and ἄνθρωποι: men, human not divine, on the same level with yourselves. ὁμοιοπαθής (Wisdom 7.3; 4 Macc. 12.13) occurs in the NT elsewhere only at James 5.17: Elijah was a human being, like ourselves; he shared the same experiences and the same feelings (πάθη).

Negatively they are not θεοί but ἄνθρωποι; positively they are bringers of good news, εὐαγγελιζόμενοι. Here only in the NT is εὐαγγελίζεσθαι followed by an infinitive. See BDR § 392, n. 10; instead of ἐπιστρέφειν, D has ὅπως . . . ἐπιστρέψητε, perhaps affected by d, ut . . . convertamini. The verb has so fully taken on the sense of proclamation that it means almost *to command: telling you to turn* . . . It retains however enough of its fundamental sense to suggest that God has patiently waited for the present moment in which he makes turning possible. ἐπιστρέφειν (see on 3.19) has the double sense of turning from (idolatry) and turning to (the true God).

Idols are μάταια, vain, empty things; cf. Rom. 1.21; 8.20 (Knox, *Acts* 70). The word is used in this sense in the OT, e.g. Lev. 17.7 (= שְׂעִיר); 3 Kdms 16.2 (חטא), 13 (הבל). In non-biblical Greek it does not have this sense of *false god*, but it is used of empty talk, and of vain and foolish persons, so that it would be sufficiently meaningful to a Gentile audience. The true God, to whom men should turn, is the living God. The absence of an article does not imply the existence of one among a number of living gods; cf. 1 Thess. 1.9, θεῷ ζῶντι καὶ ἀληθινῷ; θεὸς ζῶν is almost a proper name. His being is further defined as Creator in language based on the OT; see Exod. 20.11; Ps. 145 (146).6; and cf. 4.24. The same thought, expressed in similar words, occurs frequently in the OT. Paul and Barnabas do not profess to be quoting the OT, nor do they appeal to its authority; as in the Areopagus speech (especially 17.24–26) they use the OT to express thoughts which some at least among the more thoughtful of their Gentile hearers would recognize as accepted by Greek philosophical monotheists. The first step required in non-Jewish hearers of the Gospel is that they should recognize that there is but one God, and take him and his requirements seriously. This, from the point of view of the speaker, is an axiom of biblical revelation, but though he uses the language of Scripture (see Stählin 193f. for a very important list of biblical allusions) he does not appeal to an authority which, by definition, his hearers would not accept. Unlike the Areopagus speech (and the allusion to Paul's preaching at Thessalonica in 1 Thess. 1.9, 10) the speech at Lystra contains no reference or even allusion to Jesus. Weiser (353) notes the absence of Christusverkündigung, and explains it on two grounds. (1) The immediate necessity was to clear up pagan misunderstanding, and (2) the Christusverkündigung is to be given in ch. 17 (see 17.31). This is not a satisfactory explanation. The brief reference to judgment in 17.31 hardly amounts to Christusverkündigung; and it would have been possible, and more Pauline, and more in line with εὐαγγελιζόμενοι, to deal with the error of the crowd in a more positive, Christian way. Pesch (2.60) rightly draws attention to the educational task of Christianity, implied by this incident, but if in this process (to use Pesch's words) Schöpfungstheologie and Geschichtstheologie are to be combined, it would be more in the Pauline manner to include in the Geschichte the most important event in all history (cf. 1 Cor. 1.17, 18; 2.2). Luke would probably have agreed with Calvin's comment (2.11: 'It would have been useless for them to attempt to bring them to Christ at once'); whether Paul would have agreed is not so clear. Monotheism was doubtless a necessary theme in early Christian preaching; for a list and discussion of monotheistic formulas see Stauffer (*Theologie* 220f.); in Acts, 17.24; 22.14; 24.14. No doubt some preachers approached the question by way of natural theology. For Paul's way, see *ZThK* 86 (1989), 25–30.

16. God had created the universe; yet the Gentile inhabitants of Lystra now had to be told about him and drawn away from misleading substitutes. How was it that they had not known him? Because, with the exception of his own people, Israel, who are not mentioned here, he had himself withdrawn from human affairs to the extent of leaving all the Gentiles to manage on their own. To this extent they may be excused; cf. 17.30, and contrast Rom. 1.20.

παροίχεσθαι, *to pass by*, is used of *by-gone* time from Homer onwards, but nowhere else in the Greek Bible. It fits well in a speech directed to Gentiles. Cf. *Syll.*³ 885.5, διὰ τῶν παρῳχημένων χρόνων. γενεά here clearly has the meaning generation; 'in by-gone generations'. ἔθνη here may be translated *nations* or *Gentiles*; the effect is in either case the same. All except the Jews were permitted πορεύεσθαι ταῖς ὁδοῖς αὐτῶν; contrast 8.39, where with πορεύεσθαι the accusative of ὁδός is used; but cf. 21.21; 9.31, and see BDR § 198. 5, n. 6. Knox (*Acts* 70) compares Rom. 1.28, παρέδωκεν ... Cullmann (*Heil* 144) raises the interesting question of the relation of the neglect of the Gentiles to the mainstream of Heilsgeschichte, and suggests that one may think of a Religionsgeschichte, 'die wirklich vom Zentrum der ganzen biblischen Offenbarung aus zu schreiben wäre.' Luke does not however show any awareness of such contacts. With the exception to be noted in the next verse, the Gentiles had been left to themselves. This suggests that, as far as Luke's own understanding of the matter is concerned, we should not lightly draw into the discussion of the Apostolic Decree (15.29) the so-called Noachian ordinances.

17. God did not intervene in the affairs of the Gentiles, as he did intervene in the affairs of Israel; but this did not mean that his hand could not be discerned by anyone who was minded to look for it; nor did it mean that the Gentiles were uncared for. Had this been so they would have starved to death. Cf. 17.25.

In the NT καίτοι occurs here only and at Heb. 4.3, where it takes a participle. Cf. Jn 4.2, καίτοιγε; Acts 17.27, καί γε, with a number of variants, including καίτοι. Here it means *and yet* (Heb. 4.3, *although* — the usual concessive use). It is difficult to know how to translate αὐτόν (NA²⁶; P⁴⁵ ℵ* A B E 6 *pc*); if ἑαυτόν (P⁷⁴ ℵᶜ C D Ψ 𝔐) is not read it is surely proper to write αὐτόν, even though this form became very rare in the Hellenistic period (BDR § 64. 1, n. 2; M. 3.41; Zerwick § 210). It was *himself* that God did not leave without witness. ἀμάρτυρος occurs here only in the NT; cf. Thucydides 2.41.4, οὐ δή τοι ἀμάρτυρόν γε τὴν δύναμιν παρασχόμενοι. There is much in this short speech to suggest that Luke was drawing on a source rather than composing freely; Blass (161) speaks of the language of this verse as 'lectis vocabulis repleta'. In the bounty of nature there was testimony to both the being and the nature of God, though (as v. 16 indicates) the testimony was not forced upon the Gentiles. ἀγαθουργεῖν occurs here only in the NT, though the uncontracted ἀγαθοεργεῖν occurs at 1 Tim. 6.18. The verbs hardly occur in pre-Christian Greek though the cognate nouns are fairly common. The participle here must be rendered *in that he did good*. The good that God did is specified in his provision through the processes of nature for the material needs of men.

οὐρανόθεν: also at 26.13 (nowhere else in the NT). ὑετός: also at 28.2; a better word than βροχή, βρέχειν (Phrynichus 268, Rutherford 352). διδούς governs ὑετούς and also καιρούς καρποφόρους. καιρός is here rightly used of an appropriate season of the year; καρπόφορος (here only in the NT and used more frequently of trees and lands) points to harvest time. The result of God's gift of rain and fruitful seasons is that he fills (ἐμπιπλῶν, from ἐμπιπλᾶν, a hellenistic form of ἐμπιμπλάναι; see BDR §§ 94. 2, n. 4; 101, n. 69) your hearts with food and rejoicing. The heart is more likely to be filled with rejoicing than with food; it may be this that suggests to Zerwick (§ 460) and to BDR (§ 442. 9(b), n. 28) that we have here an example of hendiadyoin: implens laetitia de cibo. Both add another example from the preceding clause: dans tempora pluviis fructifera. The latter is somewhat less convincing. Page (173) notes the sequence of participles: ἀγαθουργῶν . . . διδούς . . . ἐμπιπλῶν, each subordinate to the preceding one: God bears witness by doing good, that is, by giving rain, and so filling . . . The goodness of God in the natural order is a widespread theme. So e.g. Cicero, *de Natura Deorum* 2.53, Sed illa quanta benignitas naturae, quod tam multa ad vescendum . . .; Berakoth 9.2, [If a man saw] shooting stars, earthquakes, lightnings, thunders and storms he should say, 'Blessed is he whose power and might fill the world'. [If he saw] mountains, hills, seas, rivers and deserts he should say, 'Blessed is the author of creation' . . . For rain and good tidings he should say, 'Blessed is he, the good and the doer of good'.

Bultmann (*E. and F.* 146f.) observes that 'Under the influence of the Greek enlightenment, there had taken place in Hellenistic Judaism a new conceptual formulation of monotheistic faith, together with a total interpretation of the world in the manner of the philosophy of religion and a critique of polytheism and its cult as well as the moral life of the Gentiles', and adds 'In all probability such ideas played an even larger role in [Paul's] actual missionary preaching; thus they are presented also in Acts 14.17; 17.23ff.'. There is no doubt that some early Christian writers made use of this approach; see e.g. 1 Clement 19, 20; Justin, 2 *Apology* 5.2; how far Paul did so is another question which cannot be further discussed here. See above, pp. 665, 680f., and in Vol. II.

18. ταῦτα λέγοντες, by saying these things. μόλις and μόγις (D 1175 *pc*) both mean *hardly, scarcely, with difficulty*. So far the variant is insignificant; both words emphasise the awestruck wonder of the people, and thus emphasise the greatness of the miracle. But 'unaufgeklärt ist das Verhältnis von μόλις zu μόγις, die beide im NT und bei att[ischen] Autoren und in Pap[yri] belegt sind' (BDR § 33.3). In a note (3) however the same authors make the scarcely consistent observation, 'μόλις scheint vulgär zu scin, μόγις galt als attisch'. μόγις is the form used by Homer and is 'rare in Attic prose, except in Plato, where it is commoner than μόλις' (LS 1140, s.v. μόγις). Correspondingly, on μόλις LS 1142 say that it is a 'post-Homeric synonym of μόγις, prevailing in Tragedy, Comedy, and Attic prose, though in Plato and later prose μόγις was preferred.' In fact both forms appear to be used in papyri and later Hellenistic Greek. One can think only of a personal, perhaps of a local, preference of the Western editor.

καταπαύειν, to put an end to, to stop a person doing something. Here the verb is constructed with τοῦ μή and the infinitive. See BDR § 400. 4, n. 6. An awkward addition is made by C 6 33 36 81 104 453 614 1175 *al* (h) sy^hmg: ἀλλὰ πορεύεσθαι ἕκαστον εἰς τὰ ἴδια. This clause cannot properly depend on κατέπαυσαν; another verb, such as παρήγγειλαν, must be supplied. They prevented the crowds from sacrificing and told them to go home.

19. So far the reaction of the people of Lystra to Paul and Barnabas has been favourable, though badly misdirected. It was disturbed from without. ἐπέρχεσθαι is a Lucan word (Lk., three; Acts, four; rest of the NT, twice), often suggesting the arrival of something unpleasant (Lk. 11.22; 21.26; Acts 8.24; 13.40), though the suggestion is not inherent in the word itself. Jewish opponents from the neighbouring towns which the missionaries had recently visited (for (Pisidian) Antioch, see on 13.14, for Iconium, on 13.51) pursued their opposition and followed them to Lystra. It is surprising that animosity should drive opponents 100 miles; but Colonia Lystra had put up a statue in Pisidian Antioch (*Begs.* 4.162), and there may have been some contact otherwise unknown between the two towns. πείθειν has several times (5.36, 37, 40; 12.20) been used in the sense of *to get someone on one's side* and has this meaning here. The Jews persuaded the people of Lystra to accept their position with regard to Paul and Barnabas. Persuasion quickly led to action. It does not seem possible to distinguish between λιθάζειν and λιθοβολεῖν (see on v. 5).

The fact that of the two missionaries only Paul was stoned has been felt as a problem. This is a false impression. If Luke was constructing a story on the basis of tradition he probably had if not the text of 2 Cor. 11.25 at least related memory to draw on: Paul had been stoned. There was no such tradition about Barnabas and the prudent historian did not create one. If we are to think not of a reconstructed narrative but of a historical event, again there is no problem. Paul's was the face the crowd knew for he had performed a public and well publicized act in healing a lame man; he would be the natural target. Luke's account may or may not be historically accurate; at least it makes reasonable sense. Weiser of course is right when he says (353) that Luke's intention was to show (1) that there was increasing opposition from Jews, and (2) that God overcomes opposition.

ἔσυρον: the imperfect is surprising, but (unless Luke is simply being careless about tenses) it will point to an attempt to get rid of the (supposed) corpse terminated by the punctiliar action of the disciples (κυκλωσάντων) and of Paul (ἀναστὰς εἰσῆλθεν — the intention of getting rid of him, dead or alive, was frustrated; v. 20). See BDR § 327. 1, n. 1. They supposed that Paul had died, that is, was dead, τεθνηκέναι. D has the alternative form of the infinitive, τεθνάναι; see M. 2.240.

For the text of vv. 19, 20, see on v. 20.

20. As usual in Acts, μαθηταί will be Christian disciples, Christians (see on 6.1). The narrative so far hardly suggests that the missionaries had had the time to make converts, but Luke was no doubt setting out to write an interesting and attractive story and thought the proposed sacrifice and attempted murder better than the instruction of converts. The desire to account for the presence of disciples may to some extent explain the variants in vv. 19, 20.

Surrounded by disciples Paul got up and went into the city. h sa mae add, when it was evening — so that he might escape observation? This is perhaps a better observation than 'in Angleichung an die Passion Jesu' (Schille 308). Luke has been careful not to say that Paul was dead, only that his attackers supposed that he was dead. He may have thought that Paul had been seriously injured, almost killed, and that he was describing a miraculous healing; or that Paul had escaped serious injury — which also would have been a miracle. In one way or another God protects his servants; this is Luke's narrative and biographical way of expressing the triumph of the word of God. 'Entering the city' is enough to show (cf. also v. 21) that Paul was not defeated by the opposition; but it was time to move. For Derbe see on v. 6. Paul must have been in good health if he set out on a journey of over sixty miles, though of course Luke does not say how long it took the two travellers to reach their destination. The Western text fills out the bald narrative of vv. 19, 20. Among the most important variants are the following; for further detail see Metzger 424. Instead of ἐπῆλθαν δέ, we have διατριβόντων δὲ (om.D*) αὐτῶν καὶ (om.C) διδασκόντων ἐπῆλθον (C D(*, E) 6 33 36 81 323 453 945 1175 1739 al h syʰᵐᵍ mae). For πείσαντες, D has ἐπισείσαντες, and for the whole clause καὶ . . .ὄχλους, καὶ διαλεγομένων αὐτῶν παρρησίᾳ (ἀν)έπεισαν τοὺς ὄχλους ἀποστῆναι ἀπ' αὐτῶν λέγοντες ὅτι οὐδὲν ἀληθὲς λέγουσιν ἀλλὰ πάντα ψεύδονται. In v. 20, for αὐτόν, (P⁴⁵) D (E) have αὐτοῦ; they were Paul's disciples who surrounded him; cf. 9.25.

21. εὐαγγελισάμενοι (ℵᶜ B C Ψ 𝔐), aorist, is the tense required by the grammar of the sentence: it was after they had evangelized Derbe that Paul and Barnabas returned to Lystra, Iconium, and Pisidian Antioch. 'The aorist alone yields a possible sense' (Ropes, *Begs.* 3.137). This means however that εὐαγγελιζόμενοι (P⁷⁴ A D E H P *pc*), present, is the harder reading; it may well be what Luke wrote. See H. G. Meecham, on 'The present participle of antecedent action' (*ExpT* 64 (1953), 285f.). For τὴν πόλιν ἐκείνην (Derbe), τοὺς ἐν τῇ πόλει (D (gig) h (syᵖ)) is a rather wooden 'improvement'. ἱκανός is a favourite Lucan word (see on 9.43); πολλούς (D) means nothing different. μαθητεύειν (here only in Acts; Mt. 13.52; 27.57; 28.19 — a word in use in the church of Syrian Antioch?) means *to make (a) disciple(s)* (not, as usually, *to be a disciple*; see Zerwick § 66). The work in Derbe was successful and no opposition was recorded. To Luke Derbe was probably no more than a name on an Antiochian list. There had been difficulties and opposition in Lystra, Iconium, and Pisidian Antioch, but this did not prevent the missionaries from returning and taking the necessary steps to establish the communities that had been founded. Rather, it made return desirable, and answers the question raised by some commentators: Why did the travellers not press on to Tarsus, and so return to Syrian Antioch by the overland route? There were good reasons for acting otherwise. M. 3.80 takes the participle ἐπιστηρίζοντες (v. 22) to express purpose: they returned . . . in order to strengthen. This (as is suggested here) is probably true, but the present participle is not normally used to express purpose and here it probably expresses the fact: they returned, strengthening as they went . . .

The three destinations of the return journey are all introduced by εἰς (the third εἰς is omitted by B D 𝔐); Black (*AA* 115) sees in the repetition of the preposition a possible mark of Semitism. For Lystra see on 14.6; for Iconium on 13.51; for (Pisidian) Antioch on 13.14.

22. In the NT ἐπιστηρίζειν occurs only here and at 15.32, 41, without substantial difference in meaning. New disciples need to be strengthened, confirmed, established in the faith; that the expressed object is τὰς ψυχὰς τῶν μαθητῶν means that the disciples are being considered under the aspect of religion. For the connection of ἐπιστηρίζοντες with ὑπέστρεψαν see on v. 21; the participle 'ergänzt einen komplexiven Aor. dadurch, dass es dieselbe Handlung schildert' (BDR § 339. 2, n. 6). The process of strengthening is described in the next lines; it includes exhortation, the warning that suffering must come but leads to the kingdom, the appointment of ministers, and committal to the Lord. Weiser (357) notes that they contain information about Lucan eschatology, the churches affected at this time by persecution, the situation of the church in Luke's own time, and the nature of Christian existence, understood as the daily carrying of the cross. See further below.

For παρακαλεῖν see on 2.40. For ἐμμένειν τῇ πίστει cf. 13.43, προσμένειν τῇ χάριτι τοῦ θεοῦ. It is doubtful whether Luke meant anything different by the two expressions. τῇ πίστει may mean *faith* (fides qua) or *the faith* (fides quae); in either case it implies confidence in the grace of God.

After καί there is an ellipsis: λέγοντες, or a synonym, must be supplied: the clause that follows is a statement of fact, not an exhortation — unless indeed it is dependent on παρακαλοῦντες, though if this were so we should have a mixed construction, first an infinitive, then ὅτι and a finite verb. See BDR § 397. 3, n. 7 and especially § 479. 2, n. 5. The inhabitants of the Lycaonian cities have witnessed the sufferings of Paul (cf. 9.16) and Barnabas; they must learn the general truth that the kingdom of God is entered only through many tribulations. The exact bearing of this proposition calls for discussion. What is the kingdom of God, and when is it entered? The expression is several times used in Acts (see on 1.3) as a general summary term for the body of proclaimed Christian truth. It is not so intended here but refers to the final state of blessedness into which believers may hope to enter if they continue in faith and in the grace of God. According to Maddox (136f., 153) it is thought of as belonging to the present; Conzelmann (81) thinks of it as entered at death; it thus represents such an individualizing of eschatology as is to be seen elsewhere in Acts (see on 7.55, 56). The tribulations through which Christians must pass recall the Jewish apocalyptic theme of the Messianic affliction, the travail pains of the Messiah, which must precede the good time to come, a theme which formed an important starting-point for the Christian understanding of the suffering and death of Jesus as well as of the sufferings of Christians themselves. Acts as a whole contains (as does this section) the record of wonderful escapes and deliverances, which prove to Luke the ultimate triumph of the Gospel and the unfailing care of God for his people. But he does not hesitate to tell stories of suffering (e.g. v. 19) and knows that these play an important part in Christian existence, though he never explains (as Paul does) why this should be so. It is not true to say that Luke has no theologia crucis, though it is true to say that his is not Paul's theologia crucis, nor is it so profound. See *FS* Dinkler (73–84). Stählin (196) rightly interprets '. . . dass der Weg der Christen auch eine Nachfolge im Leiden ist'. According to Schille (309), 'θλῖψις deutet die Verfolgung nicht mehr als apokalyptische Wehen, sondern als ein Kennzeichen christlicher Existenz.' This is right in what it affirms, wrong in what it denies. θλῖψις is both; its eschatological significance is not lost when its existential meaning is grasped. Paul was capable of holding together both aspects of Christian existence, and though Luke did not see them in their distinction from and in their relation to each other his words are capable of being taken in both senses and (to judge from what he writes elsewhere) he would not have disclaimed either.

Stauffer (*Theologie* 164f.) draws attention to the 'doxologische Form der Märtyrertheologie'. 'Ja, wir begegnen in unsern Texten vielfach der Überzeugung, dass der Blutzeuge, anders als die Mehrzahl der Frommen, ohne Zwischenstadium vom Hinrichtungsort aus unmittelbar in die Himmelswelt entrückt werde (Phil. 1.23; 3.10f.; Apok. 3.21; Ignatius *Rom.* 2.2; *Mart. Pol.* 18.3). Unter Martern sind sie ausgezogen aus der Erdenstadt, nun leben sie in der Himmelsstadt, ungekränkt, frohlockend (1 Clem. 5.4ff.; Hermas, *Similitude* 1.6; cf. Mt. 7.14; Acts 14.22; Hermas, *Vision* 2.2.7; 3.2.1; *Mart. Pol.* 19.2).' For the present passage this goes too far; the warning and the promise are addressed to all Christians, not only to martyrs.

Conzelmann (81) rightly distinguishes between the thought expressed here and the Greek notion of παιδεία through suffering.

23. χειροτονεῖν was originally *to stretch out the hand* and so *to vote* in a deliberative assembly (e.g. Plutarch, *Phocion* 34 (758), τὸν δῆμον ἔδει χειροτονεῖν περὶ τῶν ἀνδρῶν, that is, for their acquittal or condemnation), hence *to vote* in an election for the appointment of a person to an office (e.g. Xenophon, *Hellenica* 6.2.11, ἐψηφίσαντο δὲ καὶ ἑξήκοντα ναῦς πληροῦν, Τιμόθεον δ'αὐτῶν στράτηγον ἐχειροτόνησαν). From this kind of democratic appointment the word came to mean appointment by an authority (e.g. Lucian, *De Morte Peregrini* 41, τινας ἐπὶ τούτῳ πρεσβευτὰς τῶν ἑταίρων ἐχειροτόνησε); so here. Paul and Barnabas provided the elders for the disciples whom they were thereby helping to withstand the troubles they were sure to encounter (v. 22). This was, no doubt, a kind of ordination, in that it gave some Christians a special kind of responsibility and service; cf. 6.6; 13.1–3; 20.17, 28. The word χειροτονεῖν, however, implies nothing with regard to the imposition of hands. These appointments were made by Paul and

Barnabas for the churches. In *Didache* 15.1 churches are urged to make their own appointments (χειροτονήσατε οὖν ἐαυτοῖς); Ignatius, *Philadelphians* 10.1; *Smyrnaeans* 11.2; *Polycarp* 7.2 are similar, though they do not relate to ordinary appointments to the presbyterate. 1 Clement 44 reflects a transition. In the first instance appointments were made (the verb is καθιστάναι) by apostles; later (though the meaning of this important passage is not wholly clear) they were made by others, ἐλλόγιμοι ἄνδρες. On the development of the ministry in the period to which Acts is relevant see the discussion in Vol. II. For πρεσβύτεροι see on 11.30; Weiser (359) rightly points out that the use of the plural suggests that the presbyters worked as a collegium. The word is Luke's, and seems at this stage not to have been used at Antioch (13.1–3); Luke presumably thought, judging from the experience of the church of his own day, that each community (κατ᾽ ἐκκλησίαν) should be supplied with elders; see above. Evidently he also thought that their appointment should be accompanied by prayer and fasting; cf. 13.3.

It is not clear whom Paul and Barnabas committed to the Lord; the antecedent may be αὐτοῖς, the μαθηταῖ of v. 22; or the elders whom they appointed (cf. 20.32). It is unthinkable that they failed to pray for any of the disciples, but Luke may have had the elders specially in mind.

πεπιστεύκεισαν, pluperfect, without the augment, as is usual in the NT (though not in other examples of Hellenistic Greek: M. 2.190; otherwise BDR § 66. 1). D has the perfect, πεπιστεύκασιν.

37. BACK TO ANTIOCH 14.24-28

(24) They passed through Pisidia and came to Pamphylia. (25) Having spoken the word in Perge they went down to Attalia, (26) and thence they sailed away to Antioch, whence they had been committed to the grace of God for the work that they had now completed. (27) When they arrived and had assembled the church they reported the things that God had done with them, and that he had opened a door of faith for the Gentiles. (28) They stayed no short time with the disciples.

Bibliography

J. Dupont, as in (36) (*Nouvelles*, 350-7).

J. M. Ross, *ExpT* 63 (1952), 288f.

R. Schnackenburg, *BiLe* 12 (1971), 232-47.

A. Vögtle, as in (36).

Commentary

The importance of this paragraph, probably based upon the Antiochene record but rounded out by Luke with traces of his own style in v. 24 (διελθόντες), v. 25 (λαλεῖν τὸν λόγον), v. 26 (ἀποπλεῖν, παραδίδοσθαι τῇ χάριτι), and v. 28 (οὐκ ὀλίγος), is that it matches 13.1-3 and brings the missionaries back to the place whence they set out. The whole narrative of chs. 13 and 14 is set in an Antiochene framework and is told from an Antiochene point of view, though, as have seen, Luke seems to have inserted here and there material that he drew from other sources. Without them, indeed, the story would have been very much shorter. It is probably Luke himself who, with ch. 15 in mind, emphasises, not only by a note at the end but especially by the synagogue sermon in Pisidian Antioch and its outcome (13.46f.), the fact that the mission had seen a door of faith opened to the Gentiles (v. 27); this would not have surprised the Christians at Antioch (in Syria), some of whom had already passed though that door (11.20). But it did more than surprise some of the Christians of Judaea (15.1), and had, through their objection and its overcoming, the effect of laying the foundation for the rest of the book.

24. διελθόντες. For διέρχεσθαι see on 8.4; it could well bear here the meaning that Luke seems often to attach to it, of making a preaching tour; the travellers were prepared to interrupt their journey in order to speak the word in Perge (v. 25) and may have done so elsewhere. But Luke has now used up his narrative material and gives little more than a list of places.

The outward journey is now made in reverse; for Pisidia see 13.14, for Pamphylia, 13.13. For the question why Paul and Barnabas did not return overland through Tarsus see 14.21.

25. λαλεῖν τὸν λόγον is one of Luke's ways of describing the work of Christian preachers (e.g. 11.19; 16.6), though more often the word λόγος is qualified by a genitive, τοῦ θεοῦ (added here by P[74] E gig bo[ms]) or τοῦ κυρίου (added here by ℵ A C Ψ 33 81 326 614 *al* vg sy[p h**]). These additions are assimilations to other passages; B D 𝔐 co are right with the short text.

ἐν Πέργῃ is the reading of most Greek MSS (ℵ[c] B C D E Ψ 𝔐; P[74] has ἐν τῇ Πέργῃ), and is probably the original text. ℵ* 81 however have εἰς τὴν Πέργην; A has εἰς Πέργην. Luke, like other Hellenistic writers, not infrequently uses εἰς and the accusative where ἐν and the dative would be expected, and may possibly have done so here, with copyists 'correcting' his usage. The 'correctors', however, are very many, and unanimous, and may on this occasion give us the original and not a corrected text. It is scarcely possible to translate εἰς τὴν Πέργην, 'having spoken the word to Perge.'

κατέβησαν. Perge was some miles up stream (see 13.13), and Attalia (modern Antalya) on the coast. This seaport was of relatively recent foundation by Attalus II Philadelphus, c. 150 BC. It is hard to understand Conzelmann's comment (81) that this note of itinerary is redactional. The evangelists had entered Pamphylia through Perge, and only some kind of traditional itinerary, whether accurate or not, would have led Luke to introduce a further locality of which he has nothing to say except that the party came to it and then left it (unless we follow D (614 *pc*) sy[h**] mae, who add εὐαγγελιζόμενοι αὐτοὺς — no doubt because they wished to make it clear that Paul and Barnabas seized every opportunity of evangelism).

26. κἀκεῖθεν is characteristic of Luke (Mk, one; Lk., one; Acts, eight times). Paul and Barnabas sailed from Attalia to Syrian Antioch (see on 11.19), this time not calling in Cyprus, which thus missed the confirmation described in 14.22. ἀποπλεῖν is used at 13.4; 14.26; 20.15; 27.1, but this relatively frequent use may be little more than a function of the story Luke has to tell.

Luke recalls the commissioning of Paul and Barnabas at 13.1-3 and sums up the work they had now completed. At the beginning of the journey there was fasting, prayer, and the laying on of hands. The theological significance of these actions was a committing to the grace of God. BDR § 347. 1 rightly say that the pluperfect (ἦσαν παραδεδόμενοι) refers to 'einen in der Vergangenheit liegenden Zustand', but it is not clear why they should add, with reference to the present example, 'das hatte zur Wirkung, dass sie dorthin [to Antioch] auch zurückkehren mussten'. That it was both natural and proper that Paul and Barnabas should return to Antioch and report to the church there is clear; that they were obliged to do so is not, and is not required by the grammar of the sentence. The grace of God is hardly comparable with the centurion to whom Paul was committed (παρεδίδουν, 27.1) for the voyage to Rome, whose duty it was to see Paul duly delivered to the destination laid down for him. εἰς τὸ ἔργον (the expression used by the Holy Spirit, 13.2) cannot be taken in an exclusive sense, as though the church at Antioch would pray for Paul and Barnabas only so long as they remained under their control; in any case, the ultimately controlling authority was the Holy Spirit.

χάρις nowhere in Acts receives a precise theological definition. In the present section, dealing with the 'first missionary journey' it is used at 13.43; 14.3. It refers to the active love of God which enables men to do his will (4.33; 6.8) and several times has, as here, particular reference to the protective care of God who watches over his people and especially over his missionaries (15.40 (with παραδοθείς); 20.32 (with παρατίθεσθαι); cf. 13.43 (it is possible to renounce the grace of God, and thus to lose his protection)).

27. Paul and Barnabas arrived in Antioch and gathered together (συναγαγόντες; D has συνάξαντες — it was a tendency of the Koine to replace second aorists with first: BDR § 75) the church, τὴν ἐκκλησίαν, that is, the local community of Christians, the μαθηταί of v. 28; cf. 13.1. Here the word ἐκκλησία may have the special sense of the *assembled* body of Christians (cf. e.g. 1 Cor. 14.4; see *1 Corinthians* 316). The relation of Paul and Barnabas to the ἐκκλησία is complex; they were appointed by it, but they now exercise leadership within it by calling the members together (Stählin 197). To the assembled church, which, through its representatives, had sent them on their mission, they now reported not what they had done (as e.g. at 3.12 Luke insists that apostles and others do not act on the basis of their own power or piety) but what God had done through them. Conversions and healings were alike the work of God; cf. 15.4.

The words ἐποίησεν ὁ θεὸς μετ᾽ αὐτῶν appear in different orders in the MSS, and D has the surprising text ὁ θεὸς ἐποίησεν αὐτοῖς μετὰ τῶν ψυχῶν αὐτῶν; gig has the same text but without αὐτοῖς (cum animabus eorum). The text of the great majority of MSS has been held to show Semitism in its use of μετά; see Torrey (38; on 15.4) and M. 2.466. *Begs.* 4.169 argues that ποιεῖν μετά is equivalent to ποιεῖν with the dative, quoting Lk. 1.72; Tobit 12.6;

13.6; Judith 8.26; (1 Macc. 10.27), but note that the same use is to be found in *P. Amh.* 2(1901). 135, 15 (2nd Century AD); Hermas, *Mandate* 5.2.1; *Similitude* 5.1.1. They also point to Acts 15.4 and to 16.40, where D has ἐν αὐτοῖς, but d cum eis. Moule (*IB* 184) thinks Semitism doubtful, and says (61) that the clause 'may well mean *all that God had done in fellowship* or *cooperation with them* — in which case it is plain Greek.' Bauernfeind (185) thinks it possible that we should after αὐτῶν supply ὧν; it is not clear whether he thinks that the two letters were originally present and dropped out by haplography. It is difficult to avoid the conclusion that there is some Semitic influence behind the reading of D; see Wilcox (84f., 154f.). 'It is generally recognized that the reading μετὰ τῶν ψυχῶν αὐτῶν reflects Semitic influence and is linguistically equivalent to μετὰ αὐτῶν in the usual text. The preceding αὐτοῖς is less easy to account for, but it probably represents the Aramaic proleptic pronoun, which is superfluous in Greek' (Metzger 426). It is on the whole likely that the text of D is due to conflation (see Clark 185) and that αὐτοῖς and μετὰ τῶν ψυχῶν αὐτῶν are equivalents: what God did for them, what God did with their souls. Both readings could have arisen from failure to see that μετ' αὐτῶν referred to what God had done (for others) through their instrumentality. The phrase as it stands in texts other than D 'expresses the presence and implies the assistance of God' (Page 174). Cf. 15.4; also 11.21.

What God had done with Paul and Barnabas is stated in the last clause of the verse. This undoubtedly refers to the conversion of the Gentiles (cf. 15.3). If the words were taken on their own they might well suggest that now for the first time Gentiles had become Christians; this Luke cannot mean, since the church that had initiated the mission was itself partly Gentile (11.20) — not to mention the conversion of the eunuch in ch. 8 and of Cornelius in ch. 10. Nowhere else in Acts is θύρα used metaphorically; clearly it here means a 'way in', but in precisely what sense is not clear. M. 3.212 asks but does not answer the question whether the genitive πίστεως is objective (*leading to faith*) or subjective (*where faith enters*). There is a third possibility. πίστεως may be an appositional genitive, the meaning being *a door (into salvation) consisting of faith*. It would however be mistaken to attempt a very precise definition. Luke means here what he had already written in 11.18 (on which see the note), where he means that Gentiles may repent and so have life. Here he means that Gentiles may believe, and thereby receive all the blessings to which faith leads; that is, the way of faith is open for them, faith may come to them, and by their faith they become Christians. Cf. Roloff (220), faith is 'das Christsein, die Zugehörigkeit zum Volk der Glaubenden'; Pesch (2.65), the Gentiles receive 'Zugang zum eschatologischen Tempel des Gottesvolkes'. Paul uses θύρα metaphorically; 1 Cor. 16.9; 2 Cor. 2.12; cf. Col. 4.3; see also Lk.

13.24 (not in the Matthean parallel); Jn 10.7, 9; Rev. 3.8, 20; also the obscure words ascribed in Hegesippus (Eusebius, *HE* 2.23.8) to the Jews who questioned Jesus, τίς ἡ θύρα τοῦ Ἰησοῦ;

28. διέτριβον, imperfect, contrast 14.3, διέτριψαν, aorist. The point is that there (see the note) the length of the stay is determined (by 14.5, 6); here it is not. The stay is indefinite. So BDR § 332. 1, n. 2. The statement is repeated in 15.35, a probable indication that the story of the Council in ch. 15 has been inserted at this point (Stählin 197).

χρόνον οὐκ ὀλίγον, an example of the litotes characteristic of Acts; cf. 12.18; 15.2; 17.4, 12; 19.23, 24; 27.20. It is impossible to know whether Luke means a week or some months, or even more; and very probable that Luke himself did not know. He means that Paul and Barnabas settled back into the life of the church that had sent them on their mission (13.1-3), and that the Council of ch. 15 did not happen immediately (Roloff 221).

The μαθηταί are the ἐκκλησία of v. 27 resolved into its individual components. The equivalence must be borne in mind when other occurrences of the word μαθηταί (e.g. 18.23; 21.4) are considered.